RECORDS OF THE SALEM WITCH-HUNT

This book represents the first comprehensive record of all legal documents pertaining to the Salem witch trials, in chronological order. Numerous newly discovered manuscripts, as well as records published in earlier books that were overlooked in other editions, offer a narrative account of the much-written-about episode in 1692–93. The book may be used as a reference book or read as an unfolding narrative. All legal records are newly transcribed, and errors in previous editions have been corrected. Included in this edition is a historical introduction, a legal introduction, and a linguistic introduction. Manuscripts are accompanied by notes that, in many cases, identify the person who wrote the record. This has never been attempted, and much is revealed by seeing who wrote what, when.

Bernard Rosenthal has written widely on American literature and culture. His monographs include *City of Nature* and *Salem Story*, and he has also edited many published volumes, including *The Oregon Trail* by Francis Parkman, Jr. He is also the author of numerous articles and reviews. Rosenthal has received at different times four grants from the National Endowment for the Humanities as well as a grant from the National Historical Publications and Records Commission in support of this book. One of his NEH grants was in collaboration with Benjamin Ray, partially in support of this book; another was to support this book's completion. Rosenthal was also a Fulbright lecturer in 1996–97 at Tampere University in Finland. He is Professor Emeritus at the State University of New York at Binghamton.

RECORDS OF THE SALEM WITCH-HUNT

General Editor

Bernard Rosenthal

ASSOCIATE EDITORS

Gretchen A. Adams	Merja Kytö
Margo Burns	Matti Peikola
Peter Grund	Benjamin C. Ray
Risto Hiltunen	Matti Rissanen
Leena Kahlas-Tarkka	Marilynne K. Roach

Richard B. Trask

PROJECT MANAGER

Margo Burns

CAMBRIDGE
UNIVERSITY PRESS

CAMBRIDGE UNIVERSITY PRESS
Cambridge, New York, Melbourne, Madrid, Cape Town,
Singapore, São Paulo, Delhi, Mexico City

Cambridge University Press
32 Avenue of the Americas, New York, NY 10013-2473, USA

www.cambridge.org
Information on this title: www.cambridge.org/9780521661669

First published 2009
Reprinted 2012

A catalog record for this publication is available from the British Library.

Library of Congress Cataloging in Publication Data

Records of the Salem witch-hunt / Bernard Rosenthal . . . [et al.].
   p. cm.
Includes bibliographical references and index.
ISBN 978-0-521-66166-9 (hardback)
1. Trials (Witchcraft) – Massachusetts – Salem.   2. Witchcraft – Massachusetts – Salem –
History.   3. Massachusetts – History – Sources.   I. Rosenthal, Bernard, 1934–   II. Title.
KFM2478.8.W5R43 2009
133.4′3097445 – dc22   2007026402

ISBN 978-0-521-66166-9 Hardback

Images on pages 3–13 are by Margo Burns, with the kind permission of the Peabody Essex Museum.

I Petition to your honours not for my own life for I know I must die . . . I Question not but your honours does to the uttmost of your Powers in the discouery and detecting of witchcraft and witches and would not be gulty of Innocent blood for the world but by my own Innocencye I know you are in the wrong way . . . I being confident there is seuerall of them has belyed themselue.

– *Mary Esty, executed September 22, 1692*

CONTENTS

ASSOCIATE EDITORS

Gretchen A. Adams is an Associate Professor of History at Texas Tech University. Her specialty is in the political and print culture of early America and its colonial antecedents. She is the author of *The Specter of Salem: Remembering the Witch Trials in Nineteenth-Century America* (2008).

Margo Burns is the Director of The Language Center at St. Paul's School in Concord, New Hampshire. Her special interests include seventeenth-century colonial New England, historical linguistics, and the integration of technology in the humanities. She has chaired a panel at the Berkshire Conference of Women Historians, presented at the conference of the Omohundro Institute of Early American History and Culture, and published in the *William and Mary Quarterly* on the subject of the Salem witch trials.

Peter Grund is Assistant Professor of English Language Studies at the University of Kansas (Lawrence). He has published widely on linguistic and discoursal features of early scientific texts in English (especially alchemy) and on the language and manuscripts of the Salem documents. His research interests include historical sociolinguistics, historical discourse analysis, and editorial theory.

Risto Hiltunen is Professor of English at the University of Turku, Finland. His research interests include history of English, medieval and early modern English, the English language in legal settings, and discourse studies, especially from a historical point of view. His recent publications have appeared in *Inside Old English* (2006) and *Journal of Historical Pragmatics* (2007).

Leena Kahlas-Tarkka is Lecturer of English Philology at the University of Helsinki and a senior researcher in the Research Unit for Variation, Contacts and Change in English at the same university. Her main interest areas are diachronic syntax and, more widely, medieval English language and literature. She has published one monograph on Old and Early Middle English syntax and articles on various aspects of historical English, and she has edited several volumes.

Merja Kytö is Professor of English Language in the Department of English at Uppsala University, Sweden. Her fields of interest include corpus linguistics, the history of English, and the development of early American English, in particular. Among her recent publications are *Nineteenth-Century English: Stability* *and Change* (2006, edited with Mats Rydén and Erik Smitterberg) and articles included in collected volumes and international journals (e.g., *Journal of Historical Pragmatics, Journal of English Linguistics, American Speech*). She has participated in the compilation of historical corpora, among them the *Helsinki Corpus of English Texts, A Corpus of Nineteenth-Century English*, and, recently, *A Corpus of English Dialogues 1560–1760*.

Matti Peikola is Adjunct Professor of Philology in the Department of English, University of Turku, Finland. He specializes in manuscript and textual studies with a focus on Late Middle English writing, especially texts associated with the Wycliffite (Lollard) movement. He has recently published in *The Journal of the Early Book Society* and *The Journal of Historical Pragmatics* and is one of the contributors to *Medieval Texts in Context* (2008).

Benjamin C. Ray is Professor of Religious Studies at the University of Virginia and the Director of the Salem Witch Trials Documentary Archive (http://jefferson.village.virginia.edu/salem) which is an extensive digital resource of primary and secondary source materials on the Salem episode. He is the author of books and articles on the religions of sub-Saharan Africa, as well as of several articles on the subject of the Salem witch trials. His most recent work is *A Magic Still Dwells: Comparative Religion in the Postmodern Age* (2000), edited together with Kimberley C. Patton.

Matti Rissanen is Emeritus Professor of English Philology at the University of Helsinki and an active researcher and team leader at the Centre of Excellence for the Study of Variation, Contacts and Change in English at the same university. His scholarly publications include close to two hundred items: monographs, edited volumes, articles, and reviews. He is Honorary Doctor at Uppsala University and Honorary Member of many international scholarly societies.

Marilynne K. Roach, an independent scholar in Watertown, Massachusetts, found that the twenty-seven years spent researching her book *The Salem Witch Trials: A Day-by-Day Chronicle of a Community Under Siege* (2002) has by no means exhausted the subject. As a freelance writer she has contributed articles to historical and genealogical journals, and as a graduate of Massachusetts College of Art, she has illustrated several works of her own and other authors with an emphasis on history.

Richard B. Trask is Town Archivist for Danvers, Massachusetts (old Salem Village). His projects have included restoring his seventeenth-century home; excavating the 1681 Reverend Samuel Parris parsonage; serving as curator of the 1678 Rebecca Nurse Homestead; writing *The Devil Hath Been Raised* (1992); serving as historian to various films, including "Three Sovereigns for Sarah"; and co-designing the 1992 Salem Village Witchcraft Victims' Memorial. Trask has taught history and lectured extensively. He is a descendant of several witchcraft victims. An authority on studying historical photography, Trask has consulted for CBS News, the President Kennedy Assassination Records Review Board, and the National Archives. He has written eight books.

ACKNOWLEDGMENTS

There are many professional debts to acknowledge, and I know my colleagues join me in expressions of appreciation. I begin by thanking the National Endowment for the Humanities for funding a joint proposal from Benjamin Ray and myself that made possible the Virginia site for Ray, and money for me to hire a project manager, as well as travel money to bring people to manuscript sites in support of creating a new edition.

A key person, Joseph Flibbert, an old friend, a Professor at Salem State College, and a very knowledgeable and committed scholar, was already part of this team as the person responsible for coordinating manuscript holdings. Tragically, he died before he could see where his work would have led him. This book is dedicated to his memory with the hope that it appropriately honors him.

For many reasons this book took longer than anticipated, and I mention this here only because changes in the publishing industry during that long period made the book difficult for Cambridge University Press to publish without subvention support. To address this financial problem I took a summer off from working on the book, and with major assistance from Margo Burns requested financial support from the National Historical Publications and Records Commission. The proposal was successful, and I am deeply grateful for the award given to me in support of the book. I am similarly grateful to Timothy Connelly at NHPRC, who proved so helpful and patient in addressing my seemingly endless questions. Regarding awards, I received fellowships from the National Endowment for the Humanities in support of this book. Without that support from NEH the book would not have appeared, at least not in so ambitious a form. In expressing appreciation to the granting agencies, I emphasize that both the collaborative proposal with Professor Ray, the first NEH grant supporting the book, and the proposal to NHPRC made clear the names and records of my colleagues working on this edition, which surely influenced the favorable decisions. The grant I received from NEH to complete the book did not specifically include the names of my colleagues, but without their role in creating this edition I would not have had the proposal to make that I did. I also acknowledge my appreciation to the English Department at SUNY Binghamton; to its Chairs, David Bartine and Susan Strehle; to Peter Mileur, Dean of Arts and Sciences; and to Mary Ann Swain, Vice President for Academic Affairs.

Additionally, Peter Grund, Risto Hiltunen, Leena Kahlas-Tarkka, Merja Kytö, Matti Peikola, and Matti Rissanen wish to acknowledge the support of their university departments and respective research units, which made it possible for

them to use their facilities in their work. They are also indebted to their helping
hands as acknowledged below. However, as always, their greatest debts were
incurred when the time that would have been spent with their dearest and nearest
was spent on the transcriptions. The names of those involved are too numerous to
list, so their patience and understanding can only be collectively – and with heart-
felt thanks – acknowledged. For Risto Hiltunen and Matti Peikola: Academy of
Finland and University of Turku. For Matti Rissanen and Leena Kahlas-Tarkka:
Research Unit for Variation, Contacts and Change in English (VARIENG) at
the Department of English, University of Helsinki, and Academy of Finland.
Peter Grund and Merja Kytö wish to thank the English Department at Uppsala
University, and Peter Grund also extends his thanks to the English Department
at the University of Kansas.

Ann Sanow at Cambridge University Press as commissioning editor believed
in this book at the outset and strongly supported its publication. Subsequently
Cambridge's editors for it became first Ray Ryan and then Eric Crahan. Their
support, patience, and encouragement have been vital to the creation of the book.
Catherine Felgar at Cambridge University Press patiently guided the production
of the book. Alan Gold, formerly of Cambridge University Press, created the
book's design. Mary Cadette, at Aptara, Inc., generously assisted in addressing
difficult issues as the manuscript moved to completion as a book. All are deeply
appreciated.

There are many other acknowledgments, and given the number of people
involved in this project among those to be thanked are some never met by some of
us who have worked so long on this edition. But whoever has helped one of us has
helped all of us. To explain what each did would lead to too extensive an essay. In
some cases their institutional affiliation is noted; in others it is institutions that are
thanked; and in some cases individuals are acknowledged for help independent of
any institution. We thank all of those who have not already been thanked in notes
to the introductory material. Our deep appreciation goes to Irene Axelrod (Phillips
Library, Peabody Essex Museum), Robert Berkhofer (Western Michigan University), the Board of Trustees and Staff of the Peabody Institute Library in Danvers,
Elizabeth Bouvier (Massachusetts Archives), Ina Brownridge (SUNY Binghamton), Simina Calin (Cambridge University Press), Eric Carr (Karpeles Manuscript
Library), Tuula Chezek (VARIENG), Martha Clark (Massachusetts Archives),
Michael Comeau (Massachusetts Archives), Theodore Covey, John C. Dann
(William L. Clements Library), Danvers Archival Center, John Davidson (Colo-
nial Williamsburg Foundation), Dean DeFino, Barbara DeWolfe (William L.
Clements Library), Jedediah Drolet (Cornell University), Peter Drummey (Mas-
sachusetts Historical Society), Janis Duffy (Massachusetts Archives), Thomas
Dziuszko (William L. Clements Library), Judith Fichtenbaum (Chelmsford His-
torical Society, Massachusetts), Kathy Flynn (Phillips Library, Peabody Essex
Museum), Samuel K. Fore (Colonial Williamsburg Foundation), The Form of
1973 (St. Paul's School, New Hampshire), William M. Fowler, Jr. (Massachusetts
Historical Society), Bethany Fox (VARIENG), Wayne Furman (New York Public Library), Marla Gearhart (Phillips Library, Peabody Essex Museum), Leigh
Golden (Beinecke Library), Nicholas Graham (Massachusetts Historical Society), Gail Greve (Colonial Williamsburg Foundation), Jeffrey Hackney (Oxford
University), Michael Hall (Oxford University), John Hannigan (Massachusetts

Archives) Nacima Hasnat (New York Public Library), Helge Axelsson Johnsons Stiftelse, Frances Hill, Marianna Hintikka (VARIENG), Clive Holmes (Oxford University), Stephen Innis (University of Virginia), Jane Kamensky (Brandeis University), Richard Kaplan (Massachusetts Archives), Britta Karlberg (Phillips Library, Peabody Essex Museum), Carol F. Karlsen (University of Michigan), David and Marsha Karpeles (Karpeles Manuscript Library and Museum), Päivi Kilpinen (VARIENG), Bruce Kirby (Library of Congress), David Konig (Washington University, St. Louis), Thomas Knoles (American Antiquarian Society), Omar David Laiton (SUNY Binghamton), William La Moy (Phillips Library, Peabody Essex Museum), Kristin Landon (copy editor), Sara Lilja (Uppsala University), Richard Lindeman (Bowdoin College), Marilyn Lloyd, Carol Majahad (Director, North Andover Historical Society), William Marquis (Cornell University), Megan Milford (Massachusetts Historical Society), Gerald Mollen (Broome County District Attorney, New York), Marko Nenonen (University of Tampere), Nicholas Noyes (Maine Historical Society), Oskar Öflund Foundation, Mark Pendergrast, Ann Marie Plane (University of California, Santa Barbara), Paul Plante, Jean Marie Procious, Kate Elizabeth Queram (Cambridge University Press), Jody Randazzo, The Rebecca Nurse Homestead in Danvers, Elizabeth Reis (University of Oregon), Douglas Rendell (Peabody Institute Library, Danvers), Enders Robinson (Columbia University, Emeritus), Laura Rosenthal (University of Maryland), David Shadduck, Frank Smith (Cambridge University Press), Emily Spangler (Cambridge University Press), Ruth Stanek (SUNY Binghamton), Tara Stevens, John D. Stinson (New York Public Library), Sweden America Foundation, Paul Szarmach (Medieval Academy), Kathy Szyska (Archivist, North Andover Historical Society), Tuuli Tahko (VARIENG), Janice Thompson (Boston Athenaeum), Mellanie Tossell (Phillips Library, Peabody Essex Museum), Ethel Trask, Eva Veilleux, Joanna Vennala, Joe Walker (SUNY Binghamton), Jane Ward (Phillips Library, Peabody Essex Museum), Molly Warsh, William Reece Company, Caroline Williams (Cambridge University Press), Pamela Worden (John W. Rogers Middle School), Mary Jane Wormstead, George H. Yetter (Colonial Williamsburg Foundation), Molly Zahn, and Roberta Zhongi (Boston Library).

Through the generosity of Mary Beth Norton, we were provided with manuscripts she had discovered, as well as their locations. These include the Examination of Daniel Eames; the Deposition of Elizabeth Hubbard v. Abigail Row, Esther Elwell, and Rebecca Dike; the Deposition of Thomas Burnam, Jr. v. Rachel Clinton; the Indictment of Daniel Eames for afflicting Mary Warren; and the Account of William Dounton. For general courtesies and permissions we thank the American Antiquarian Society; the Beinecke Rare Book and Manuscript Library; Boston Public Library/Rare Books Department, courtesy of trustees; the British Library; the British National Archives; the Clements Library, University of Michigan; the Colonial Williamsburg Foundation; the Commonwealth of Massachusetts, Massachusetts Archives; the Danvers Archival Center; Division of Rare and Manuscript Collections, Cornell University; the James Duncan Phillips Library, Peabody Essex Museum Collections; the Karpeles Manuscript Library; the Massachusetts Historical Society; the National Archives in Washington, DC; the New York Public Library Astor, Lenox and Tilden Foundations; the Wellcome Library, London; and William Reece Company.

We also thank the kind and generous people associated with these institutions, and we apologize to those who have helped and by unintentional omission have not been named in these acknowledgments.

The introductory material was read carefully in the preliminary stages by individuals who have proved enormously helpful. Their insights have only added to the quality of this material, and errors or shortcomings are not due to them. For reading the language essay, we are grateful to Edward Finegan (University of Southern California) and William Kretzschmar (University of Georgia). For reading the introductory historical essays, we are grateful to John M. Murrin (Princeton University, Emeritus) and Mary Beth Norton (Cornell University). For reading the biographical material, we are grateful to David L. Greene. All have given generous and valuable help with their insightful criticism.

On a personal note, my family has been patient with me while I gave so many years to this project. My son Dan Rosenthal and his wife, Rosalind Rosenthal, live close to the Phillips Library, Peabody Essex Museum, and I have stayed in their home often while doing research there – not the best way to visit them and their children, James and Rachel. My wife, Evelyn, has been patient personally. Professionally she has photographed manuscripts for me at the British National Archives. I have missed visits with my daughters, Helen Robinson and Laura Rosenthal, and their husbands and children. All have been very patient with me.

My final professional debt is to Mary Beth Norton. A number of years ago, my good colleague at SUNY Binghamton, Kitty Sklar, who had earlier kindly read in manuscript my book *Salem Story*, introduced me to her longtime friend, Mary Beth Norton, who was then writing a book on the Salem witch trials. This led to long e-mails and personal conversations through the completion of that book, *In the Devil's Snare*, and conversations that have continued as I have worked on this one. She has been remarkably generous to me, and patient, as I have sometimes peppered her with queries, finding myself quite fortunate to be able to look to her for information, to test ideas, at times to disagree, but always to benefit from the discussions. Not everyone directing so complex a project as this has been fortunate enough to have the friendship and intellectual support of one of the great scholars of her generation. I am deeply grateful to her, and I know that my colleagues in this edition share that gratitude. She is of course innocent of any errors that may appear in the book.

– Bernard Rosenthal

I. LIST OF FACSIMILE PLATES

Salem May the 20th. 1692

There being Complaint this day made before mee
by John putnam Junr. and Benjamin Hutcheson
both of Salem Village, for themselfes and also for
their Neighbours, in behalfe of their Majesties
against Marah Easty the wife of Isaac Easty of Topsfield
for Sundry acts of witchcraft by her Committed
yesterday and this present day of the date hereof
upon the Bodys of Ann putnam Marcy Lewis
Mary Walcot and Abigail williams of Salem
Village to ye wrong and Injury of their bodys
therefore Craved Justice   John putnam Junr
                               Benjamin Hutchinson

To the Marshull of the County of Essex or depty
or Constable of Salem
You are in their Majesties names hereby required
to apprehend and forthwith bring before mee
at ye house of mr Thomas Beadle in Salem the
Bodys of Mary Easty the wife of Isaac Easty of
Topsfield to be Examined Relating to
Sundry acts of witchcraft by her Committed yesterday
and this present day according to Complaint abovesd
and hereof you are not to faile Dated Salem
May 20th 1692   John: Hathorne. Assist
                    ꝑ order of ye Governr

May 20th 1692
I have taken the body of the above named Mary Estw
and brought her att ye time and place above named
                    ꝑ me Geo: Herrick
                    Marshall of Essex

The Examination of Eliz: How. 31. May. 1692

Mary Lewis & Mary Walcot fell in a fit quickly after the examinant came in
Mary Walcot said that this woman the examinant had pinchd her & choaked th'
month.   Ann Putman said she had hurt her three times
what say you to this charge? Here are they that charge you with witchcraft
If it was the last moment I was to live, God knows I am innocent
of any thing in this nature

Did not you take notice that now when you looke upon Mary Lewis she was struck down
       I cannot help it.
You are charged here, what do you say?
I am innocent of any thing of this nature
Is this the first time that ever you were accused?
       Yes

Do not you know that one at Ipswich hath accused you?
This is the first time that ever I heard of it
You say that you never heard of these folks before

Mary Lewis at length speaks & charged this woman with hurting & pinching
her: And then Abigail Williams cryed she hath hurt me a great many
times, a great while & she hath brought me the book.
       Ann Putman had a pin stuck in her hand.
What do you say to this?
       I cannot help it.
What consent have you given?
       Mary Warren cryed out she was prickt
       Abig: Williams cryed out that she was pinched, & great prints were seen
in her arm
       Have not you seen some apparition?
No, never in all my life
They that have confessed, they tell us they used images & pins, now tell us
what you have used.
You would not have me confess that which I know not
She lookt upon Mary Warren, & said Warren violently fell down.
Look upon this maid viz: Mary Walcot, her breif being towards the examinant
Mary Warren & Ann Putman said they saw this woman upon her.
Susan: Sheldon saith this was the woman that carryed her yesterday to the Pond
Sus: Sheldon carried to the Examinant in a fit & was well upon grasping her arm.
You said you never heard before of these people
Not before the warrant was served upon me last sabbath day
John Indian cryed out Oh she bites, & fell into a grievous fit, & so carried to her
in his fit & was well upon her grasping him.
What do you say to these things, they cannot come to you?
Sr I am not able to give account of it
cannot you tell what keeps them off from your body?
I cannot tell, I know not what it is?
That is strange that you should do these things & not be able to tell how.

This a true account of the examination of Eliz: How taken from my
                 written
characters at the time thereof witness my hand Sam: Parris

May ye 9 1692.

Elisabeth hubord aged about 17 yers saith that ye last second day at
night: There apeared a little black heard man to me in blackish aparill
I asked him his name e he told me his name was borrous; Then he tooke
a booke out of his pocket: e opened it e bid me set my hand to it
I tould him I would not: ye lines in this book was read as blod then
he pincked me twise e went away: The next morning he apeared to me
a gaine and tould me he was above a wizard: for he was a conjuror So went away
but sins that he hath apeared to me every day e night very often
and urged me very much to set my hand to his book: and to run away
telling me if I would do so I should be well e that I should need
feare no body; e withall tormented me severall ways every time he
came exept that time he told me he was a conjuror: This
night he asked me very much to set my hand to his book or else
he sayed he would kill me; withall tortoring me very much
by biting and pinching squesing my body e runing pins into me
also on the 9th may 1692 being the time of his examination mr
George Burrough or his Appesarance did most greviously afflict
and torment the bodyes of mary walcot mercy lewes Ann
putnam and Abigail williams for if he did but look upon
them he would strick them down or almost chook them to
death also severall tims sence he has most dreadfully afflect
ed and tormented me with variety of torments and I beleve in my
heart yt mr George Burrough is a dreadfull wizzard and that he
has very often tormented me and also the above named parsons
by his acts of witchcraft
                                Jurat in Curia

Eliz Hubbard declared: ye above written evidence: to be ye truth: upon her oath: that
she had taken: this she owned before ye Jury of inquest Augst 3 1692

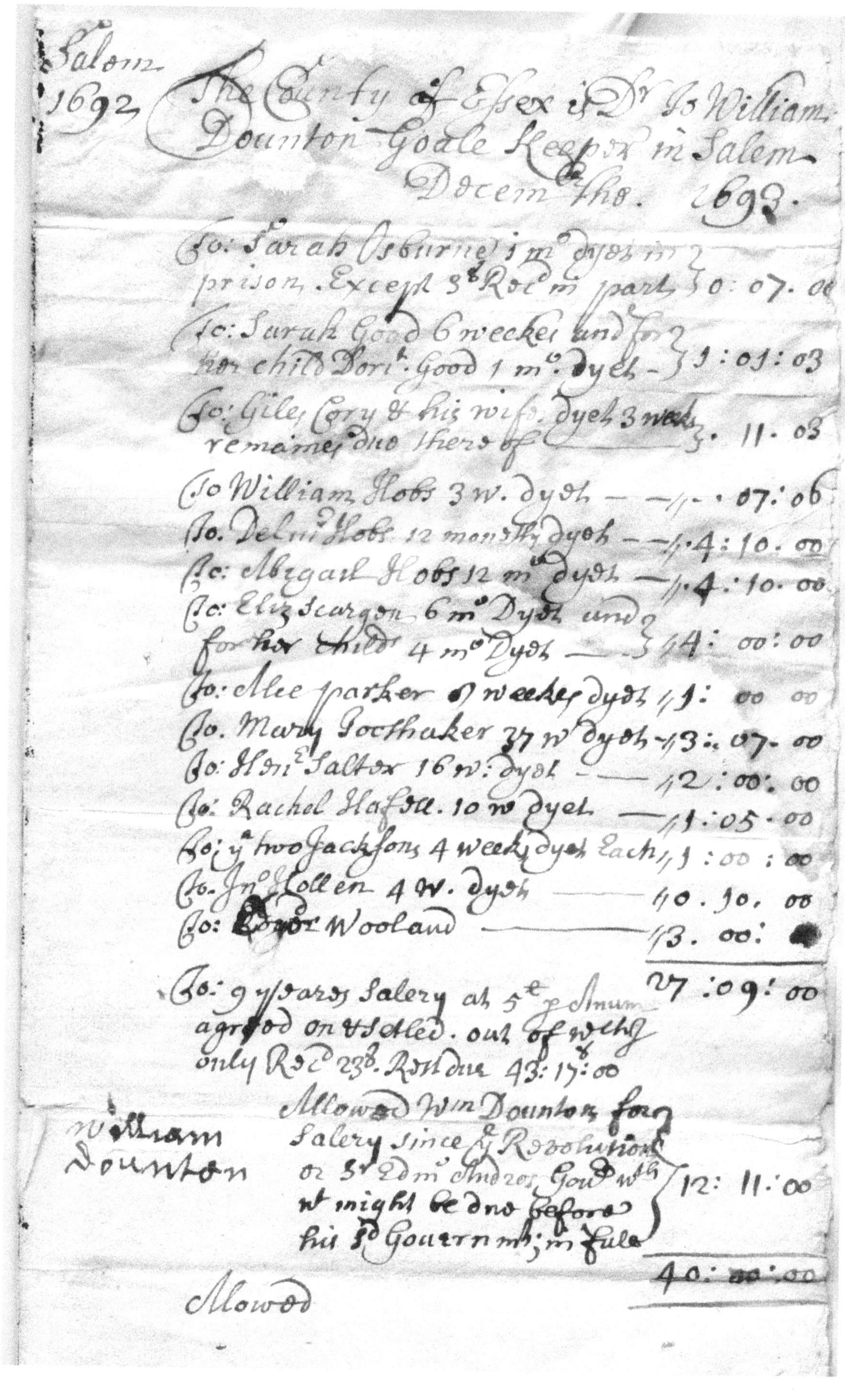

61

Anno Regni Regis et Reginæ et Mariæ
nunc Angliæ &c Quarto!

Essex ss The Juro: for our Soveraigne Lord & Lady the King &
Queen present That Rebeckah Nurse the wife of ffrancis Nurse of
Salem Village in the County of Essex husb —

the ffour & twenty th Day of March — in the ffourth
Year of the Reigne of our soveraigne Lord & Lady
William & Mary by the Grace of God of England
Scotland ffrance & Ireland. King & Queen —
Defend: of the ffaith &c. and divers other Dayes
& times as well before as after. certaine detestable
Arts called Witchcrafts & Sorceries wickedly and
ffelloniously hath vsed Practised & Exercised at and
within the Towneship of Salem in the County of —
Essex aforesd: in upon and agt: one Abigail Williams of
Salem Village aforesd: in the County aforesd Singlewoman —
by which said wicked Arts the said Abigail Williams —
the sd: ffour & twentieth Day of March — in the ffourth
Year abovesd and divers other dayes & times aswell
before as after was & is hurt tortured Afflicted &
consumed Pined wasted & tormented agt: the Peace
of our Soveraigne Lord & Lady the King & Queen
and agt: the forme of the Statute in that Case
made & Provided

Wittnesses
Abigail Williams
Mary Walcott
Elizabeth Hubbard
Ann putnam Jun e

110

We whose names are under-written haueinge seuerall
yeares knowne John ffrorton and his wife do
testofy that we neuer heard or understood
that ther weare euer suspected to be guilty of the
crime now charged vpon them and seuerall of vs
being their neare neighbours do testofy
that to our apprehension they lived
christian like in their family and weare
euer ready to helpe such as stood in
need of their helpe

Nathaniel ffelton sen: &
and mary his wife

Samuel Marsh
and Presilla his wife

James ffoullen and

Ruthy his wife

       John ffelton

Nathaniell ffelton iun

Samuell ffrayle
and an his wife
Zachriah marsh
and mary his wife
Samuel Endecott
and hanah his wife

Samuell Stone

George Locker

Samuell Gaskill
& prouided his wife

George Smith

Ed Edward: Gaskill

To the Keeper of theire Majes^ts Goale in Boston

You are in theire Majes^ts names hereby required
to take into your care and safe custody the Bodys of
Martha Cory the wife of Giles Cory of Salem Farmes Hus=
=bandman Rebecka Nurse the wife of Frans Nurse
of Salem village husbandman. Dorothy Good the daughter
of Wm Good afores^d husbandman. Sarah Cloyce the wife
of peter Cloyce of Salem village husbandman. John
Procter of Salem Farmes husbandman and Elizabeth
the wife of s^d John procter of Salem Farmes Husbandman
who all and every one of them, stand charged in behalfe
of theire Majes^ts for feloniously Committing sundry
acts of witchcrafts Latily, at Salem village, on the
Bodys of Ann putnam the daughter of Thomas putnam
Abigail Williams Eliz. Hubberd, & others of Salem
village afores^d whereby great hurt hath benn donne
to theire bodys Contrary to ye peace of our Sov^r. Lo^d & Lady
W^m & Mary of England &c King & Queen, whome You
are all well to secure. Untill thay shall be delivered
by due order of Law And hereof you are not to faile
Dated Boston May 25th 1692

John Hathorne
Jonathan Corwin } Assis^ts

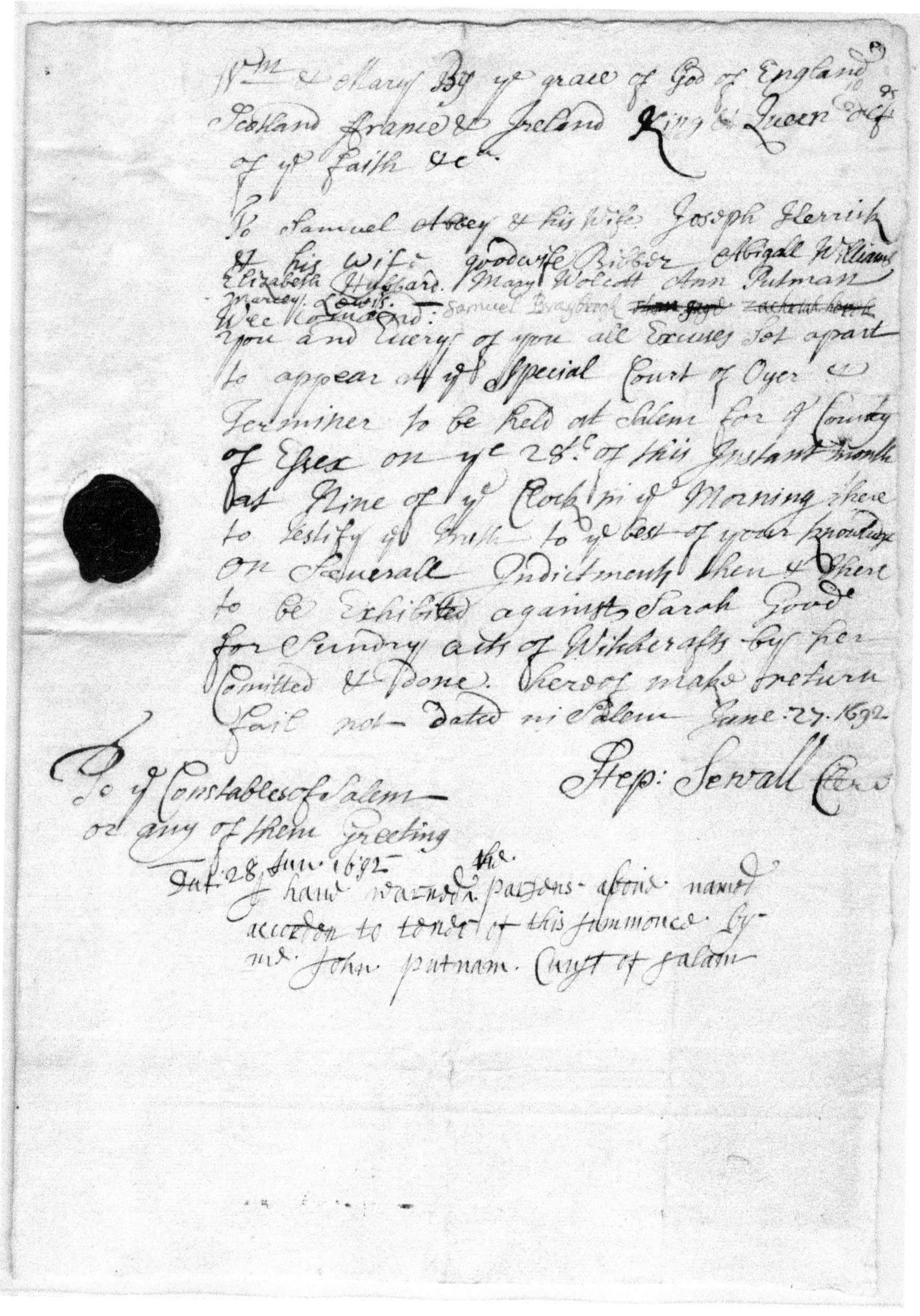

Page 10 — Facsimile Plates

Wᵐ & Mary By ye grace of God of England
Scotland France & Ireland King & Queen defenders
of ye faith &c.

To Samuel Abbey & his wife, Joseph Herrick
& his wife, goodwife Bibber, Abigall Williams
Elizabeth Hubbard, Mary Wolcott, Ann Putman
Marcey Lewis: Samuel Braybrook [struck out] Zachariah
Wee Command you and Every of you all Excuses set apart
to appear at ye Speciall Court of Oyer &
Terminer to be held at Salem for ye County
of Essex on ye 28ᵗʰ of this Instant month
at Nine of ye Clock in ye Morning there
to testify ye truth to ye best of your knowledge
On Severall Indictments then & there
to be Exhibited against Sarah Good
for Sundry acts of Witchcrafts by her
Comitted & Done. hereof make returne
faile not— Dated in Salem June 27 1692

Step: Sewall Clerk

To ye Constables of Salem—
or any of them Greeting

Jun 28 June 1692
I have warned the persons above named
according to tenor of this summonce by
me John putnam Cunst of Salem

To George Corwin Gent' high Sherriffe of y'e County
of Essex Greeting

Whereas Bridgett Bishop al's Oliver the wife of Edward Bishop of
Salem in the County of Essex Sawyer at a speciall Court of Oyer and Terminer held at
Salem the second Day of this instant month of June for the Countyes of Essex
Middlesex and Suffolk before William Stoughton Esq' and his Associates
Justices of the said Court was Indicted and arraigned upon five severall Indictments
for useing practiseing and exerciseing on the Nineteenth day of Aprill
last past and divers other dayes and times before and after certaine acts of
Witchcraft in and upon the bodyes of Abigail Williams, Ann putnam Jun'
Mercy Lewis, Mary Wallcott and Elizabeth Hubbard of Salem Village
singlewomen whereby their bodyes were hurt afflicted pined consumed
wasted and tormented contrary to the forme of the Statute in that Case made and
provided To which Indictm't the said Bridgett Bishop pleaded not guilty
and for her Tryall thereof put her selfe upon God and her Countrey whereupon
she was found guilty of the felonyes and Witchcraft whereof she stood
Indicted and Sentence of Death accordingly passed ag'st her as the Law
directs Execution whereof yet remaines to be done These are therefore
in the name of their Maj'ties William and Mary now King & Queen over
England &c'a to will and Command you That upon fryday next being the
Tenth day of this instant month of June between the houres of Eight and
Twelve in the afternoon of the same day You safely conduct the s'd Bridgett
Bishop al's Oliver from their Maj'ties Gaol in Salem aforesaid to the place of
Execution and there cause her to be hanged by the neck untill shee be dead
and of your doings herein make returne to the Clerk of the s'd Court and
precept And hereof you are not to faile at your perill and this shall be your
sufficient Warrant Given under my hand & Seal at Boston the Eighth day
of June in the fourth yeare of the Reigne of our Soveraigne Lord and Lady
William & Mary now King & Queen over England &c'a Anno'q Dom. 1692

Wm Stoughton

June 10th = 1692
According to the within written precept I have taken the body
of the within named Briget Bishop out of their Maj'ties
Goal in Salem and Safely Conveyed her to the place provided
for her Execution and caused y'e s'd Briget to be hanged
by the neck untill Shee was dead and buried in y'e place
all which was according to the time within Required and
So I make Returne by me — George Corwin Sheriffe

The humble petition of mary Eastick unto the honoured his Excellencye Sr Wm Phipps and to
Judge and Bench now siting In Judicatature in salem
and the Reuerend ministers humbly sheweth

That wheras your poor and humble Petition being con
demned to die Doe humbly begg of you to take it into your Ju
dicious and pious considerations that your poor and humble
petitioner knowing my own Innocencye Blised be the lord for
it and seeing plainly the wiles and subtility of my accusers by my
Selfe can not but Judg charitably of others that are goin
y Same way of my Selfe if the Lord steps not mightily in I was
confined a whole month upon the same ac
ccount that I am condemned now for and then cleared by the
afflicted persons as some of your honours know and in
two dayes time I was cryed out upon by them and
have been confined and now am condemned to die the lord a
boue knows my Innocencye then and likewise does now
as att the great day will be knoawn to men and Angells
I Petition to your honours not for my own life forI
know I must die and my appointed time is sett but the
Lord he knoawes it is that if it be possible no more Innc
blood may be shed which undoubtidly cannot be
Auoyded In the way and course you goe in I Question not
but your honours does to the uttmost of your powers
in the discouery and detecting of witchcraft and witches
and would not be gulty of Innocent blood for the
world but by my own Innocencye I know you are in
the wrong way the Lord in his infinite mercye direct
you in this great work if it be his blessed will that no more
Innocent blood be shed I would humbly begg of your that
your honours would be plesed to examine theis Aflicted
Persons strictly and keepe them apart some time and
likewise to try some of these confesing witchis I being
confident there is seuerall of them has belyed themselues
and others aswill appeare if not in this word I am sure
in the world to come whither I am now going and I questi
on not but youle see an alteration of thes things they say my
Selfe and others hauing made a league with the Diuel
we cannot confesse I know and the lord knoawes as
will thorly appeare they belye me and so I Question not
but they Doe others the lord aboue who is the searcher of
all hearts knoawes that as I shall answer it att the

Tribunall seat that I know not the Least thinge of witchcraft therfore I cannot I dare not belye my own soule I beg your honers not to deny this my humble petition from a poor dyinge Innocent person and I question not but the Lord will give a blesing to yor endeuers

To his Excellencey Sr
Wm Phipps Governer and
to the honoured Judge and
Magistrates now setting in
Judicature in Salem

Mary Esty petition

II. GENERAL INTRODUCTION

BERNARD ROSENTHAL

In popular and in academic culture, the Salem witch trials have been absorbed into American imagination as few other events have. If assumptions as to what actually happened during that episode vary wildly between rigorous academic scrutiny and a persistently evoked cultural memory of a magic past that never was where witches were persecuted for their beliefs, the most basic beginning point for understanding the event must be the records that survive. *Records of the Salem Witch-Hunt* includes or references all known extant manuscripts and all known published documents of manuscripts no longer extant. The manuscripts have been transcribed from the original documents using editorial principles described later in the introductory material of this book. The principle of organization has been to present these newly transcribed documents, and previously published ones, in an order reflecting as accurately as possible their chronological occurrence. The goal has been to create a narrative through the documents as to what actually happened, and to identify when possible the people who recorded those documents.

Of the Salem witch trials, much has been written, and disagreements have inevitably been many. This edition will not settle those differences, but if it succeeds it will give the reader the most comprehensive, most carefully and consistently transcribed record ever produced of the Salem witch trials, as well as a chronological ordering of the documents. With this material before them, people researching these records will be able to do so with greater confidence that they can draw their conclusions from reliable data. Those doing very extensive research will, of course, recheck selected manuscripts themselves, but the edition should significantly ease the task of getting accessible, reliable information. At least that is the hope that the editors bring to this edition. With that goal in mind, exploring some key issues of the Salem witch trials,

as well as a consideration of how this subject of witchcraft had been addressed previously in Massachusetts Bay and in England, may offer a useful beginning for visiting, or revisiting, some of the issues, historical and linguistic, that people may want to consider when examining the documents, their order, and the notes seeking to highlight pertinent matters.

On most outlines of the event there has been little disagreement. A consensus exists on the following: Sometime in the winter of 1692 Betty Parris, the nine-year-old daughter of Samuel Parris, minister of Salem Village, began behaving in very strange ways as did Parris's niece, eleven-year-old Abigail Williams, who lived with the family.[1] The ages of the two girls are approximate given the casualness with which ages are identified in the surviving records. But they are close enough to be used confidently.

The episode in the Parris household took place in a culture where complaints of witchcraft were not unknown, and where a major case had occurred in 1688, leading to the execution of a woman named Glover. She was accused of afflicting four children between the ages of five and thirteen from a Goodwin family living in Boston who appear to have exhibited behaviors similar to those that later occurred in the Parris household.[2] The story of the

---

[1] The word "niece," as Abigail was sometimes described, meant "kinswoman" and was not necessarily used as it is today. The exact relationship between Samuel Parris and Abigail Williams has not been established.

[2] "Glover" has often been referenced by many historians as "Mary Glover," the name of another woman connected to a witchcraft case and apparently conflated with the woman executed for witchcraft in connection with the Goodwin case. No evidence to support the name of "Mary" for her has been established. In Boston, at the church of Our Lady of Victories, there is a plaque commemorating the same woman as a Catholic martyr, and here she is named "Ann Glover." The source for "Ann" has not been reliably established. The word "martyr" on the plaque does not indicate that she was canonized. She was not.

Goodwin children is best known through Cotton Mather's *Memorable Providences* (1689). Mather was instrumental in containing the episode, which claimed no victims other than Glover, convicted of witchcraft and executed. Other precedents occurred throughout New England history, but with a total of executions fewer than the total that occurred in 1692.[3] In addition to these, the story of witch trials in Sweden that occurred in 1669–1670 was known in Massachusetts Bay, discussed by Mather in *The Wonders of the Invisible World* (1693) and referenced by Robert Calef in *More Wonders of the Invisible World* (1700).[4] Sir William Phips, in his account of first arriving in Massachusetts as the new Governor, described the witchcraft matters he encountered in a language closer to what was in the literature about Sweden, which he references, than to what was happening in Massachusetts Bay in May 1692.[5]

More immediately, two other incidents, not widely noted, if at all, may have offered part of the particular background for more recent witchcraft episodes in Massachusetts Bay. One concerned the case of a woman named Martha Sparks, from Chelmsford in Middlesex County, whose case may have more significance than has been realized. She was accused of witchcraft in 1691 and sent to prison in Boston by Thomas Danforth on October 28, 1691, where she remained till December 6, 1692, two days after a recognizance was granted.[6] So even before the first legal actions leading to the Salem witch trials occurred, this woman was in prison on witchcraft charges and remained there till after the last executions. Although she was never brought to trial, it seems likely that the presence of a "witch" in prison would have been broadly known in the region.

Another incident immediately preceding the claims coming out of the Parris household concerned a girl named Mary Knowlton. In March 1692, Thomas Knowlton of Ipswich, in testimony against Rachel Clinton, also of Ipswich, referred to the fits his daughter was having in late December 1691 or early January 1692, probably before the Salem Village behaviors, fits attributed to witchcraft committed by Rachel Clinton. The imprisonment of Martha Sparks in 1691 and the claims of Thomas Knowlton give good reason to suspect that the Salem Village behavior of Betty Parris and Abigail Williams in December 1691 or January 1692 had more recent, known antecedents than the Glover case.[7] One can only speculate as to what Betty and Abigail knew about Sparks and Clinton, but this recent "witchcraft" should not be overlooked in considering the origins of the 1692 claims.

In response to the behavior of Betty and Abigail, and the conclusion of a physician that the afflicted were bewitched, Parris was joined by other ministers in a day of prayer that did not stop the behavior of the children.[8]

[3] For varying perspectives on these other New England cases, see John Demos, *Entertaining Satan* (Oxford: Oxford University Press, 1982); Richard Godbeer, *The Devil's Dominion: Magic and Religion in Early New England* (Cambridge: Cambridge University Press, 1992); Carol F. Karlsen, *The Devil in the Shape of a Woman* (New York: W.W. Norton, 1987); Elizabeth Reis, *Damned Women: Sinners and Witches in Puritan New England* (Ithaca, NY: Cornell University Press, 1997); and Richard Weisman, *Witchcraft, Magic, and Religion in 17th-Century Massachusetts* (Amherst: University of Massachusetts Press, 1984). For a list of New England cases other than the Salem witch trials and their dispositions, see Demos, pp. 401–409.

[4] For a perceptive and informative essay that combines an overview of New England cases, historical background, and an examination of the Salem trials see John M. Murrin, "Coming to Terms with the Salem Witch Trials," *The Enduring Fascination with Salem Witchcraft* (Worcester, MA: American Antiquarian Society, 2003), pp. 309–347. *Wonders*, p. 48. Although the publication date of *Wonders* is 1693, the book appeared in 1692. The reference to the Swedish trials appears on p. 48, but p. 48 appears twice in the book in different sections with different content. *More Wonders*, p. 8.

[5] All documents in this edition have been given an identification number. No. 693. The letter is dated October 12, 1692, and contains a general account of his version of what happened. The edition uses what is probably the original in the British National Archives, Colonial Office (CO) 5/857, p. 88. Copies of the letter are there also. Page entries rather than folio entries are used here for convenience. Unfortunately, many of the folios (cited as pages here) have multiple page numbers created at different times by archivists. On the history of Phips, see Emerson W. Baker and John G. Reid, *The New England Knight: Sir William Phips, 1651–1695* (Toronto: University of Toronto Press, 1998).

[6] No. 841, No. 713. A petition for her release had come on November 1. See No. 703.

[7] See No. 38. I am grateful to Mary Beth Norton for valuable help in dating a key manuscript relating to Rachel Clinton and to John Demos for sharing his insights, which allowed me to rule out as the date of the document the "1687" that appears in a modern hand on the manuscript. Neither are responsible if the 1692 dating proves incorrect.

[8] Robert Calef, *More Wonders*, p. 91. John Hale says that Parris consulted a group of physicians, with one of them, unidentified, giving the diagnosis of witchcraft. Whether this diagnosis came on March 11, the date Calef gives, or even whether Calef is accurate in ascribing that date is uncertain, although there were almost certainly prayer meetings before then. People have generally assumed that the physician diagnosing witchcraft was Dr. William Griggs, but no primary source confirms this. Hale, *A Modest Enquiry into the Nature of Witchcraft*, published in 1702 but probably completed in 1697, p. 23. The opinions of the other physicians are not extant.

The diagnosis of witchcraft in the context of beliefs at that time was not unreasonable. Indeed, even in 1692, when the Salem trials occurred, in neighboring Connecticut witchcraft claims were also raised, although unlike Massachusetts Bay, the cases in Connecticut were treated in the normal, judicious, New England way, with no executions in this instance resulting from the charges and with very few people actually being accused.[9] People in New England generally believed in witchcraft, and those who may not have shared that belief had the sense to keep such views to themselves.[10] And even as Parris and the other ministers prayed, the legal process of bringing witches to justice had already begun, with the first arrest warrants issued on February 29 and the first examinations occurring on March 1.[11] On other occasions, as with Mather in the Goodwin case and Samuel Willard in the case of Elizabeth Knapp, Willard's sixteen-year-old servant claiming fits, ministers had persisted with prayer and had succeeded

in limiting the spread of accusations.[12] This time, however, continuing prayer notwithstanding, something different happened, and the heart of understanding the causes of the Salem witch trials rests in finding out why those in power chose to depart from the New England tradition of not encouraging such charges.[13]

At the same time many other lines of inquiry remain open, primarily those relating to Salem Village quarrels. The paradigm for this line of inquiry was set by Charles W. Upham in his two-volume *Salem Witchcraft*, published in 1867. No book has dominated the direction of future scholarship as has Upham's, whose attention to Salem Village issues generally set the course for future studies of the Salem witch trials. Scholars in the nineteenth century followed him, and the most influential scholarly study of the twentieth century relating to that episode, *Salem Possessed: The Social Origins of Witchcraft* by Paul Boyer and Stephen Nissenbaum, was keyed to Salem Village issues.[14] Unlike Upham, Boyer and Nissenbaum did not dwell on moral outrage, but sought instead to assess, analyze, and show the explanatory value of social conflict within the community. Although they touched upon broader issues in Massachusetts Bay, their emphasis remained firmly in the Upham tradition of seeing the event as primarily one of Salem Village quarrels. Among various matters basic to their study was the role of Samuel Parris, the man seen in nineteenth-century scholarship as the major villain. Also basic to their study was the role of Thomas Putnam's support for Parris in Salem Village quarrels.[15]

---

[9] For an overview of the Connecticut cases, see Richard Godbeer's *Escaping Salem: The Other Witch Hunt of 1692* (New York: Oxford University Press, 2005). In spite of the fictional elements in the book, it remains excellent as to the circumstances and dispositions of the cases. For overviews of New England cases generally, see footnote 3.

[10] Belief in witchcraft, uncontested in Massachusetts Bay, was, however, at the time very much contested in England under the same monarchy that ruled Massachusetts Bay. Examples of the controversy in England abound, but we see it most accessibly in two books, John Webster's *The Displaying of Supposed Witchcraft* (1677) and Joseph Glanvil's *Saducismus Triumphatus* (1681). Webster, as the title suggests, argued against the reality of witchcraft, while Glanvil supported the view. The debate was not secular versus religious. The argument was purely theological over whether witches existed with powers to do harm. Since Massachusetts was far less open to free inquiry than England, and since it had been settled by people whose leaders had left England in significant part because of their radical theological views – radical compared to England's relative acceptance of religious tolerance (excluding Catholics) – it comes as no surprise that the traditional belief in witchcraft was simply part of New England culture. For New England's religious views of the time, see David D. Hall, *Worlds of Wonder, Days of Judgment* (Cambridge, MA: Harvard University Press, 1989). For the debate between Webster and Glanvil, see Thomas Harmon Jobe, "The Devil in Restoration Science: The Glanvil-Webster Witchcraft Debate," *Isis*, Vol. 72 (1981), pp. 343–356.

[11] For Samuel Parris see Larry Gragg, *A Quest for Security: The Life of Samuel Parris, 1653–1720* (New York: Greenwood Press, 1990), *The Sermon Notebook of Samuel Parris 1689–1694*, ed. James F. Cooper, Jr., and Kenneth P. Minkema (Boston: The Colonial Society of Massachusetts, 1993), and Marilynne K. Roach, "Records of the Rev. Samuel Parris Salem Village, Massachusetts, 1688–1696," *New England Historical and Genealogical Register*, Vol. 157 (2003), pp. 6–30.

[12] For Samuel Willard and Elizabeth Knapp, see *Witch-Hunting in Seventeenth-Century New England: A Documentary History: 1638–1692*, ed. and intro. David D. Hall (Boston: Northeastern University Press, 1991), pp. 197–212.

[13] For viewing the episode this way, see Weisman, *Witchcraft, Magic, and Religion* and Bernard Rosenthal, *Salem Story: Reading the Witch Trials of 1692* (Cambridge: Cambridge University Press, 1993). It has so far reached its fullest expression with Mary Beth Norton's landmark book, *In the Devil's Snare: The Salem Witchcraft Crisis of 1692* (New York: Alfred A. Knopf, 2002).

[14] Cambridge: MA: Harvard University Press, 1974.

[15] Recent challenges to the case made by Boyer and Nissenbaum came in papers presented at the Twelfth Annual Conference of the Omohundro Institute of Early American History and Culture held in Quebec City in June 2006. Richard Latner argued that the analysis of social mobility used by Boyer and Nissenbaum was based on one data point, a statistically invalid methodology, and that the tax record of 1695 that they used was misleading when compared and analyzed by using earlier tax records to provide multiple data points. Benjamin Ray argued that Boyer and Nissenbaum's map of the accusations in Salem Village is significantly incomplete, highly interpretive, and contains many errors.

The first legal action that took the matter beyond Parris's reliance on prayer appears on arrest warrants dated February 29. Justice of the Peace John Hathorne recorded two complaints of witchcraft against two local women, Sarah Good and Sarah Osburn, as well as against Tituba, the "Indian servant" (slave) of Parris. Both were on behalf of four men, one of whom, Thomas Putnam, would play a major role in the events that unfolded well beyond Salem Village. Although at the time, Massachusetts Bay was without a Charter – it would arrive in May – legal proceedings had not come to a halt, and the absence of a Charter did not prevent capital prosecutions.[16] Consistent with traditional legal procedures, Hathorne ordered the arrest of the women for the purpose of examining them. Tituba confessed at this examination, thus giving credibility to witchcraft claims. According to Calef, Parris had beaten her into both confessing and accusing, but no independent confirmation of this survives.[17]

These arrests, however, came without the traditional requirement that bond be posted by the person lodging a complaint, a significant departure from English law. Other than this departure, the pattern of complaint, arrest warrant, examination, imprisonment, grand jury hearing, and trial that followed was consistent with English law.[18] A likely but not certain source of legal procedure would be Michael Dalton's *Countrey Justice*, 1618, which after various reprintings appeared again in 1690 in an edition that included changes made in 1689 with the ascension of William and Mary to the English throne.[19] Whether

Dalton was used directly or not, however, what followed legally in Massachusetts Bay usually remained consistent with the legal commentary with the major exception of the bond issue.[20]

However, the failure of John Hathorne and Jonathan Corwin, Justices of the Peace, to require bond in the first cases made charges of witchcraft easier to lodge, and by the time the law began to be followed, as it eventually did, matters may have spread too far. It is surely speculative to suggest that had the law been followed the matter might have been contained, but it remains a speculation worth considering. The first instance of the law being followed by the magistrates occurred on March 29 at an Ipswich court in connection with the case of Rachel Clinton.[21] However, this did not change the behavior of Hathorne and Corwin, and it was not until July 19, when they and Bartholomew Gedney were joined by Justice of the Peace John Higginson, that these justices joined Higginson in requiring bond before issuing arrest warrants.[22] Higginson was the new variable, and from that date on, the law on posting bonds was followed in every case. But prior to July 19, with rare exceptions, charges of witchcraft made no demands on the person bringing the charge. It was a long stretch of legal violation that began on February 29 with complaints and arrest following, and without bond posted until July 19.

After the examination of the accused women, they were imprisoned, with one, Sarah Good, eventually going to trial in June 1692 and being executed in July of that year; another, Sarah Osburn, dying in prison on May 10, 1692, before a grand jury could address her case; and Tituba not being sent to trial by the grand jury that met on her case on May 9, 1693.[23]

He concluded that Salem Village was not geographically divided between accusers and accused.

    These arguments have since appeared in print. See Richard Latner, "Salem Witchcraft Factionalism, and Social Change Reconsidered: Were Salem's Witch-Hunters Modernization's Failures?" *William and Mary Quarterly*, 3d ser., 65, no. 3 (July 2008): 423–48 and in the same issue, Benjamin C. Ray, "The Geography of Witchcraft accusations in 1692 Salem Village," 449–78. Also in this issue is a response to Latner and Ray by Boyer and Nissenbaum, "Salem Possessed in Retrospect," pp. 503–534.

[16] For example, see David Thomas Konig, *Law and Society in Puritan Massachusetts: Essex County, 1629–1692* (Chapel Hill: University of North Carolina Press, 1979), p. 165.

[17] *More Wonders*, p. 91.

[18] The posting of bond represented surety that the person making the complaint would pursue the prosecution. At some point, probably not in the early stages of arrests, Dudley Bradstreet communicated with Bartholomew Gedney and John Hathorne on legal procedures, including the subject of bonds. See note to No. 503.

[19] Norton, *In the Devil's Snare*, p. 200, points out that Joseph Keble's *An Assistance to Justices of the Peace* (London, 1683) used Dalton heavily and was available to the judges. For more

detailed discussion of the legal procedures used, see Trask's "Legal Procedures" in this volume. For Dalton on the posting of bond, see *The Countrey Justice* (1690 edition), p. 406. For English law regarding the posting of bond for prosecutions see the Marian committal statutes 2 & 3 Phil. & Mar., c.10 (1555). I am deeply grateful to David Konig for providing me with this Marian information.

[20] Another possible departure from Dalton was friendlier to the accused in that beginning in October 1692, bond was given for some people imprisoned and awaiting trial. Doing this was inconsistent with the law on felony cases where murder was involved. It may be, however, that cases were carefully screened to exclude people with such a charge against them. For bail and murder, see Dalton, p. 420.

[21] See No. 34.

[22] See No. 421.

[23] The documents in the edition vary in referencing grand jury hearings as juries of inquest and grand juries. The latter term is used editorially in this edition. Grand juries did not create

Broadly speaking, two sets of witch trials occurred during 1692 and 1693. The first occurred under the Court of Oyer and Terminer, in 1692, where all the trials were held in Salem, although the majority of people involved were not from Salem.[24] In 1692 a plurality of accusations and imprisonments came from cases in the Andover area, but many of these cases did not come to trial until 1693. The 1693 trials occurred under the Superior Court of Judicature at more than one location. The special court that heard the 1692 cases was established by the governor, William Phips, when he came to Massachusetts Bay with the new charter. The charter was published on May 16, and the Court of Oyer and Terminer was established on May 27.[25] The court may not have been set up specifically to deal with the witchcraft cases – the word "witchcraft" does not appear in the authorizing document – although the people in prison on witchcraft charges certainly constituted the significant segment, cited in a letter by Phips of those "thronging of the Goals at this hot season of the year; there being no Judicatories or Courts of Justice yet Established."[26]

The lack of courts did not mean that the initial examinations were considered illegal, since they were recognized by the Court of Oyer and Terminer as legitimate, and since much judicial business was conducted while the colony was without a Charter. Additionally, on June 15 Phips signed into law an act that kept all laws in force that had been made prior to the new Charter, as long as they did not violate English law.[27] Subsequent commentary on this period carries debates over the legality of the Court of Oyer and Terminer, but they are not relevant to how the court was seen at the time. Similarly, judicial procedures that occurred while the colony was without a Charter seem not to have been challenged at the time. For example, on April 28 "Sam̄ Passanauton an Indian" was imprisoned and held for eight and a half weeks, and it is unlikely, given his release, that he was in jail on witchcraft charges.[28] However, the arrival of Phips with a new Charter opened the way for reconstituting the entire judicial system so that it would be compatible with the new rule of law. Creating a Court of Oyer and Terminer represented an initial step, and none of the surviving records suggest that there was any controversy over its creation. Although the court functioned primarily in addressing "witchcraft" cases, it dealt with at least one other, as in the example Samuel Sewall gives in his Diary for the meeting of the Court of Oyer and Terminer in Boston on October 10, 1692, for a murder trial.[29] Other names appear in the jail lists that have no verifiable connection to the witchcraft cases. Whether this means there was none, or whether one existed and the documents related to that connection do not survive, is a matter for further research. Other times a name appears where the person is almost certainly one caught up in the witchcraft accusations, but where almost nothing about the individual's case appears. For example no arrest warrants or judicial procedures, except for jail accounts, survive in connection with Mary Cox, who was put in irons two days after the Court of Oyer and

---

indictments, but had indictments presented to them. Their role was to decide whether to drop the case or to recommend that it proceed. When nobody appeared against the person under indictment, the individual was "cleared by proclamation." Modern grand juries in America vary significantly on indictments between the states and the federal government, and among the states.

[24] The geography of Salem, Salem Village, and Salem Farms has led to various interpretations of who came from where. Based on the indictments, which identified the legal residences of individuals, two of the twenty executed were from Topsfield, one from Ipswich, three from Andover, one from Amesbury, one from Marblehead, one from Rowley, three from Salem Village, and seven from Salem. George Burroughs is identified as "late of falmouth" in No. 453, although he had in the past been the minister at Salem Village. Burroughs had been living in Maine.

[25] See No. 220. Appointed to the court were William Stoughton as the chief justice, and Jonathan Corwin, Bartholomew Gedney, John Hathorne, John Richards, Nathaniel Saltonstall, Peter Sergeant, Samuel Sewall, and Wait Winthrop. At some point, according to Thomas Brattle, Saltonstall left the court, dissatisfied with it. "Copy of a MS Letter ... Written by Thomas Brattle, F.R.S. and Communicated to the Society by Thomas Brattle, Esq. Of Cambridge," *Collections of the Massachusetts Historical Society* (Boston, 1798), p. 75. Just when Saltonstall left is unknown, and no record of a replacement for him has been found. A number of sources indicate that Corwin replaced him, but that is not correct, since Corwin was already on the court. The origin of this appears to be Upham, *Salem Witchcraft*, Vol. 2, p. 251. This is reinforced by a note in George Lincoln Burr, *Narratives of the Witchcraft Cases 1648–1706* (New York: Charles Scribner's Sons, 1914), p. 185 n1.

[26] No. 220. The implication that trials could not have been held in the absence of the new Charter, inconsistent with some trials

having been held during the period without a Charter, indicates the inconsistent response to the legal status of Massachusetts Bay. In a letter from Phips, dated October 12, 1692, he says that the Court of Oyer and Terminer was set up to try witches. Phips was justifying his role, and although his claim that the court was established to address the witchcraft cases may be valid, nothing in the authorizing document confirms this. For the latter, see No. 693.

[27] Mass. Archives Collections, Vol. 47, No. 109.

[28] No. 612.

[29] *The Diary of Samuel Sewall 1674–1729* ed. M. Halsey Thomas, 2 vols. (New York: Farrar, Straus and Giroux, 1973), I, p. 298. No evidence has been found to support the idea that this was a different Court of Oyer and Terminer.

Terminer was constituted.[30] She was in jail until November 22, 1692.[31] Such cases make it extremely difficult to get an accurate count of the people caught in the witchcraft accusations.

As charges spread, before and after the first trial, so also did the number of those claiming affliction. They were primarily, but not exclusively, females in their teens or younger with charges almost always leading to imprisonment. Prisoners were placed in chains even before Phips arrived and redundantly ordered people accused of witchcraft to be chained. A primary source reveals only one instance where the accusers withdrew their accusation.[32] Calef reports another where no primary source survives. In this case, a Boston man accused of witchcraft during the accusations at Andover sent "a Writ to Arrest those Accusers in a Thousand Pound Action for Defamation, with instructions to them, to inform themselves of the certainty of the proof...."[33] If Calef can be trusted, this episode is significant in supporting the link between young accusers and adult supporters. It certainly seems likely that a withdrawn accusation based on fear of financial punishment would have had its origin in the financial fears of adult supporters who had some money to lose. It is reasonable to speculate that one or more adult supporters told the accusers to back off in this instance. This event, however, was a departure from the basic pattern of accusation, complaint, arrest, and examination. Among other departures was an accusation against Reverend Samuel Willard by one of the accusers during a court proceeding. She "was sent out of the Court, and it was told about she was mistaken in the person."[34]

After the accused were imprisoned their fate varied. Those who did not confess usually had indictments presented against them to a grand jury. As the 1692 trials were close to ending, indictments were also drawn against confessors, a few of whom were eventually condemned, but none executed.[35] Confessors were indicted for covenanting with the Devil. Although all witchcraft implied such a covenant, those who did not confess were charged primarily for sending their spectres to harm the accusers on the day of the examination, and not specifically for the affliction that precipitated the accusation. There was a good reason for this, since such "tormenting" of the accusers

at the examinations could be seen by responsible adult witnesses, of which two were required to support the claim.[36] The spectres appeared visible only to the "afflicted." As accusations spread, more and more people confessed, perhaps to avoid execution, perhaps from family pressure on the same or other grounds. For a compelling description of the pressures to confess, see the declaration of Mary Osgood and others as they recanted their confessions.[37] The great majority of confessors such as Mary Osgood had their cases addressed by grand juries in 1693 by the Superior Court of Judicature after the Court of Oyer and Terminer that tried the 1692 cases had been dissolved. Under the 1693 Court evidence of spectral affliction remained embedded in various cases, but no longer remained as central to the outcome of those cases. It had returned to its traditional place as a "presumption," and the line to a "proof" was no longer crossed. Grand juries overwhelmingly rejected indictments presented to them. Only three cases in 1693 led to guilty verdicts and condemnation – all three, confessors. A semblance of normality had returned. These people, Elizabeth Johnson, Jr., Mary Post, and Sarah Wardwell, received reprieves, however, from Governor Phips. Overwhelmingly, in 1693 the majority were found not guilty and released subject to their paying jail fees.

Starting in October 1692, for the first time in the episode some of the imprisoned were released on bail, "Recognizances," while they awaited their trial. Many remained in prison. After the exonerations in January and February 1693, most prisoners were released, but some were not, since they did not have the money to pay their jail fees. They remained imprisoned under very harsh conditions, but it is impossible to tell how many of those imprisoned did not survive the winter of 1693 as a result of those conditions. One woman, Lydia Dustin, is known to have died that winter, but there is no way to establish the cause, nor can we be certain that others did not also die in those months. In May 1693 the last cases were heard, and there were no more convictions.

---

[30] No. 612.

[31] No. 841.

[32] No. 83.

[33] *More Wonders*, p. 110.

[34] *More Wonders*, p. 103.

[35] Samuel Wardwell was an executed confessor, but only after he retracted his confession.

[36] "The Body of Liberties" in 1641 required two witnesses in a capital case. Edwin Powers, *Crime and Punishment in Early Massachusetts 1620–1692* (Boston: Beacon Press, 1966), p. 91.

[37] No. 749. Trying to understand false confessions remains a subject under examination by research psychologists. For a modern experiment on this subject, see Saul M. Kassin and Katherine L. Kiechel, "The Social Psychology of False Confessions: Compliance, Internalization, and Confabulation," *Psychological Science*, Vol. 7, No. 3 (May 1996), pp. 125–128.

What actually happened during the various stages of the legal procedures is in some cases pretty clearly understood, and in others in need of best guesses. That is, the records of the examinations are numerous enough so that one can read them and get a very good picture of what these examinations were like. Matters get murkier when cases come before the grand jury or go to trial. At the grand jury hearings, it is probable that the attorney general, first Thomas Newton and later Anthony Checkley, continuing into 1693, argued the cases against the accused by presenting depositions to which people swore, or perhaps by testimony without a prior deposition. The grand jury could support the indictment by endorsing it as a "true bill," meaning it accepted the charge, or not endorsing it by returning an "ignoramus." When the charge was accepted and the accused stood trial, the person had no legal counsel, other than from the Court. The procedure was very short, the grand jury procedure and the trial sometimes both occurring on the same day, and sometimes with more than one person on the same day being brought before the grand jury and the trial jury. This was not a reflection of "witchcraft hysteria" but was instead consistent with English tradition in trial cases.[38]

Documents used at trials appear to have been more selective than those used at the grand jury considerations, with heavier reliance on the strongest supporting depositions or testimony. Although trials were not limited to repeating depositions or testimony about what happened at the day of the examination, heavy use was made of that. Also, both during the grand jury hearings and during the trials, the "afflicted" were present and behaving as at the examinations. Thus, grand jurors and trial jurors believing that the "afflictions" were not counterfeit – fraudulent – would have confirming evidence. The "afflictions," as at the examinations, centered heavily on charges that the spectres of the accused were assaulting the "afflicted," spectres visible only to them. Cotton Mather is ambiguous as to whether the "touch test," whereby the "afflicted" were brought out of a fit by the touch of an accused person, was used at trial or simply referenced there, but Brattle is unambiguous as to the presence of the "afflicted" at trial, and it is difficult to believe that their behavior there was different from what it was at the examinations. In the "touch test," the accused would be asked

to touch one of the "afflicted," and people could see that it worked when the touch brought the person out of the fit.[39] More confirming as to the behavior of the "afflicted" at the trials, Cotton Mather writes, in connection with the trial of Bridget Bishop, "There was little occasion to prove the *Witchcraft*, it being evident and notorious to all beholders." He also tells the story of how Susannah Shelden at the trial of Martha Carrier "in open Court had her hands Unaccountably ty'd together with a Wheel-band, so fast that without cutting, it could not be loosed; It was done by a *Spectre*."[40] Juries had to choose between witchcraft and counterfeiting. As at the grand jury, the defendant could not have legal counsel, nor could the person have anyone give sworn, supporting testimony. Unsworn supporting testimony was permitted and sometimes given. At the end of the trial, the jury probably received a charge from Stoughton as to how it should consider the case. An account of the charge of Matthew Hale in a 1662 witchcraft case in England may offer an example. According to the account, Hale informed the jury that witchcraft was a reality and gave what appear to be neutral instructions to the jurors. They were to decide whether the accusers were bewitched, and they were to decide whether the accused had bewitched them if they were.[41] There is little reason to doubt that the Salem jurors received comparable instructions.

After the accused was found guilty, normally a period of a few days elapsed before the court pronounced sentence.[42] The punishment for witchcraft was death, as

---

[38] J. H. Baker, *An Introduction to English Legal History* (London: Butterworths, 1990), pp. 581–582. See also Trask, "Legal Procedures," in this edition.

[39] Cotton Mather's reference to the touch test is in connection with the trial of Elizabeth How, *Wonders*, pp. 76–77. On p. 66 he describes a similar revival through touch in the case of Bridget Bishop. For the theory behind the "touch test" or a similar "sight test," see Brattle, p. 63.

[40] *Wonders*, p. 66 for witchcraft as evident; p. 42 for the Shelden episode (p. 42 coming after p. 66).

[41] *A Tryal of Witches, at the Assizes Held at Bury St. Edmunds for the County of Suffolk; on the Tenth Day of March, 1664. Before Sir Matthew Hale K^t Then Lord Chief Baron of His Majesties Court of Exchequer*. This was "Taken by a Person then Attending the Court" (London, 1682), p. 55.

[42] Calef offers an important clue on the lag between trial and sentencing when he writes that on September 9, 1692, "Six more were tried, and received Sentence of Death" and that on September 17, 1692, "Giles Cory was prest to Death," *More Wonders*, p. 106. When testable on legal proceedings, Calef's dating is close if not always precisely accurate. Yet Cory was pressed to death on September 19, and the other six were probably tried on September 6 and 7. So in the murkiness of his prose his dating here strongly suggests sentencing dates. Where a person refused to agree to a trial, as in the case of Giles Cory, the punishment was pressing to death (*peine fort & dure*) – revenge, according

indicated in Exodus 22:18 ("Thou shalt not suffer a witch to live"), and when the sentence came, that was the punishment ordered and carried out, except in the cases of the condemned confessors, or where the condemned was pregnant, as in the cases of Abigail Faulkner Sr. and Elizabeth Procter.[43] One woman, Dorcas Hoar, who had maintained her innocence and had not been a confessor, was given a reprieve the day before her scheduled execution after finally confessing, leading to a successful appeal by four ministers that her execution be delayed.[44] While it seems clear that the prosecutions in the Salem witch trials were pursued with rules of evidence that differed from the cautionary advice of the authorities most likely to have been consulted, such as Richard Bernard, John Gaule, and William Perkins, the reasons for that behavior bear continuing examination.

At the same time, the legal records show a scrupulous attention to following systematic, orderly procedures even though the general legal response to witchcraft charges was inconsistent with opinions of learned witchcraft authorities, as discussed below. Although popular images are those of a society in the grip of "hysteria," there is nothing in the judicial attention to order and detail to suggest the legal authorities behaved that way. Certainly there were disruptions in the court by the "afflicted," but these disturbances did not change the orderly, bureaucratic handling of cases. That the court partly failed to follow advice from the main authorities on discovery of witchcraft may indicate bad judgment or other motives but does not demonstrate a judicial system out of control, or a society submerged in a state of panic. Even the failure in the

early stages to require bond for prosecution was eventually remedied. Indeed, however much "witchcraft" at Salem has captured popular imagination, it is clear from reading the minutes of the Governor and Council that while the issue remained one of concern to the authorities, it was not in any way the primary one. Government officials were worrying about Indian wars, naval and trade issues, matters of taxation, the killing of wolves, and a variety of other matters that took up far more of their recorded time than the witchcraft issue. On June 8, two days before the first execution in 1692 for witchcraft, that of Bridget Bishop, nine acts were passed by the general court, none of which had any connection to witchcraft.[45] Reading the diary of Samuel Sewall is instructive as one notes how small a part the witch trials play in his record. Such a conclusion does not reject the idea of anxiety, or in some instances panic, within the regional community, especially among those not in power and those threatened. Surely such responses were inevitable. Yet the anxiety and panic were not so pervasive that people were afraid to sign their names to petitions in support of accused people, such as Mary Bradbury, Rebecca Nurse, and John and Elizabeth Procter, and it is well to keep in mind that there is not a single instance of a person signing a petition in behalf of these people who was subsequently arrested.[46]

Among those usually not seriously threatened were people in powerful positions. Such people found ways to escape, as did Mary Bradbury after she was condemned, and they were safe once they reached other jurisdictions. Thomas Brattle points clearly to the preferential treatment of the accused Hezekiah Usher and of the failure of

---

to Dalton, for that refusal, *Countrey Justice*, p. 519. "The Body of Liberties" disallowed executions before four days had passed after condemnation, although exceptions were allowed. *Crime and Punishment in Massachusetts*, p. 555.

[43] The requirement of death for witchcraft was a legal one found in *The General Lawes and Libertyes Concerning the Inhabitants of the Massachusets* (Cambridge, MA, 1648). The spelling of "Procter" here differs from more modern spellings of that name. This edition attempts to follow common, though certainly not consistent, name spellings. Brattle, p. 76, was incorrectly skeptical of Procter's pregnancy, since she gave birth to a son in March 1693. Enders A. Robinson, "Andover Witchcraft 1692," North Andover Historical Society, October 24, 2007, p. 13. The pregnancy of Abigail Faulkner Sr. notwithstanding, it seems unlikely that she would have been executed, since no confessor suffered the fate.

[44] No. 676. The appeal was to Phips, but he may not have seen it. The stay was granted by Bartholomew Gedney, and the four ministers were John Emerson Jr., Daniel Epps Jr., John Hale, and Nicholas Noyes. The execution never occurred.

[45] *Several Acts and Laws Passed by the Great and General Court or Assembly of Their Majesties Province of the Massachusetts-Bay, in New England Convened and Held at Boston, the Eighth Day of June 1692* (Boston, 1692). For a valuable essay on publications in 1692 on the witchcraft issues, see Mary Rhinelander McCarl, "Spreading the News of Satan's Malignity in Salem: Benjamin Harris, Printer and Publisher of the Witchcraft Narrative," *Perspectives on Witchcraft: Rethinking the Seventeenth-Century New England Experience* (Salem: *Essex Institute Historical Collections*, January 1993), pp. 39–61.

[46] Daniel Andrew, who signed a petition for Rebecca Nurse, was ordered arrested, but escaped. That signing the petition played a role in accusing him is possible, but more likely it was his connection to the Jacobs family, broadly accused, with George Jacobs Sr. executed. George Jacobs Jr., like Daniel Andrew, was accused and fled. Jacobs was not a signatory to the Nurse petition. Boyer and Nissenbaum make a case for Andrew's arrest on other grounds. See, for example, *Salem Possessed*, pp. 181–182. On petitions of support see No. 254, No. 431, No. 495, and No. 496.

the authorities to pursue high-status prisoners who had escaped.[47] Ann Dolliver, though arrested and examined on June 6, disappears from the surviving records after that. As the sister of John Higginson Jr., a magistrate heavily involved in witchcraft cases, and the daughter of Reverend John Higginson, she appears to have had protection from further judicial action. Philip English, although at one point hiding in dirty laundry, and eventually arrested, nevertheless managed to get out of the province of Massachusetts Bay.[48] High status did not guarantee protection from the judicial system in the witch trials, but it significantly improved one's chances, and nobody in this category was executed unless one considers George Burroughs to be a high-status person. Puritans were not very different from later Americans who would find judicial outcomes often having some relation to economic or social status. Even some influence peddling may have occurred, as in the use of Mary Gedney's tavern to put up witnesses and jurors, for which she was reimbursed. As she was Justice of the Peace Bartholomew Gedney's sister-in-law, it seems likely that some business came her way through the good offices of the man helping to generate the numbers of jurors and witnesses needing accommodation.[49] Nothing in this should be construed as meaning that the Salem witch trials were about making money, but rather that, then as now, having good contacts or being in a powerful position made it easier to profit and to achieve safety.[50]

As a result of the episode, nineteen people were hanged, one was pressed to death, and an indeterminate number, five known, died while in prison.[51] What happened to arrested people where further records about them do not survive often remains unknown. Estimates as to the number of people accused and arrested vary, with most scholars traditionally calculating about 150. These are not wild guesses, but estimates based on information from surviving documents. The problem is that various documents do not survive, so the actual number cannot be indicated with certainty as can be done with the number of people judicially executed. A contemporary document indicates a number of 200 accused people, but the accuracy of this remains unknown.[52]

Agreement exists that the handling of the charges by the judicial authorities strayed radically from traditional colonial ways of handling witchcraft cases and that this unusual behavior by the authorities explains the spreading of accusations, imprisonments, and executions. Similar agreement exists that the contentious issue of "spectral evidence" was allowed by the court until it was disbanded in October of that year, although the trials continued into 1693, not ending until May of that year, these continuing trials conducted without relying on "spectral evidence." While the subject of "spectral evidence" was controversial in 1692, there is almost no controversy, then or now, that this issue was central to what happened in the Salem witch trials. Spectral evidence was simply acceptance of the claim that a person's "spectre" – some spirit willingly sent out from the person – harmed people through the agency of the Devil. While convictions were not exclusively based on

---

[47] Brattle, p. 69. Brattle is generally, but not completely accurate on this point.

[48] For this episode in English's experience, see Margaret Casnoe's deposition, July 8, 1738, No. 976. For English getting to New York and for the special treatment he received while in prison, see *In the Devil's Snare*, p. 238.

[49] No. 835 and No. 866. Perhaps diminishing the case for such influence is the fact that accommodation space was needed, and Mary Gedney was not alone in getting paid for providing it. Nathaniel Ingersoll was also reimbursed for providing such service. See No. 866.

[50] Sheriff George Corwin regularly took possessions from people caught in the witchcraft episode. What he did with money and property he seized has never been established. For those seizures and issues of legality, see Larry Gragg, *The Salem Witch Crisis* (New York: Praeger, 1992), pp. 128–130. David C. Brown argues that most of the forfeitures by Corwin were legal, although he agrees that Corwin exceeded the law in three cases. Brown's basic reasoning for the other cases is that Phips, in establishing the Court of Oyer and Terminer, directed it to follow the laws and customs of England, which in the cases of forfeiture were different from the prohibition against it in the "Body of Liberties," 1641. Yet Brown cites a letter by Phips, February 21, 1693 (No. 836), in which he accuses Stoughton of seizing "estates, goods and chattels" without Phips's consent, implying that he saw it as

illegal. "The Forfeitures at Salem, 1692," *The William and Mary Quarterly*, 3rd ser., 50 (1991), pp. 85–111. The whole subject of where that money went bears further scrutiny. One insight into the complexity of the issue occurs when Gragg names as legal seizures ones that Brown sees as illegal seizures. On May 15, 1694 at a Superior Court of Judicature, Court of Assize, and General Jail Delivery in Ipswich a ruling came that money was still due to Corwin for his services, and that he was not liable for any goods or money seized by him. The court, presided over by William Stoughton, unambiguously saw his actions as legal. See Upham, Vol. 2, pp. 472–473. This, of course, does not close the debate.

[51] Those known to have died in prison are Lydia Dustin, Ann Foster, Sarah Good's infant, Sarah Osburn, and Roger Toothaker. On Sarah Good's infant, see Marilynne K. Roach, *Records of the Rev. Samuel Parris Salem Village, Massachusetts, 1688–1696*, pp. 9, 14.

[52] Evan Haefeli, "Dutch New York and the Salem Witch Trials: Some New Evidence," *Proceedings of the American Antiquarian Society*, Vol. 110 (2003), p. 303.

spectral evidence, no conviction in 1692 or 1693 occurred without it.[53]

The controversy on this issue in 1692 centered mainly on the question of whether God would allow the Devil to give a human the power to do harm in such a way, or whether it was in fact the Devil afflicting in someone else's appearance. That the Devil could do this was agreed upon, based upon the interpretation of the "Witch of Endor" story in 1 Samuel 28, where a woman raises the appearance of Samuel at Saul's request. No disagreement seemed to exist over the proposition that in fact Samuel was not raised, but that it was the Devil who came in the appearance of Samuel. Those defending the proceedings insisted that convictions were based on evidence other than spectral evidence. Those unhappy with the proceedings felt that too much weight was given to this kind of evidence. Accused people often cited in their defense, without success, this Biblical account, and when in 1693 spectral evidence had generally been discredited, the number of convictions dropped dramatically. When Increase Mather wrote his *Cases of Conscience*, which helped bring the 1692 cases to an end, his title began with "Cases of Conscience Concerning Evil Spirits Personating Men."[54]

The context of Mather's essay, however, spread well beyond the Salem witch trials in that his writing was part of the broader debate in England over the reality of witchcraft, which was vigorously argued by Richard Baxter in his *The Certainty of the Worlds of Spirits* (1691) in what was becoming more and more a losing fight against those doubting the reality of witchcraft.[55] Baxter's book is not useful for clarifying judicial procedures for discovering witches, but it importantly links New England to the debate in the motherland. Thus, in making his case, one filled with examples of witchcraft, at one point Baxter turns across the ocean to support his views: "They that will read Mr. Increase Mathers Book, and especially his Sons, Mr. Cotton Mathers Book of the Witchcrafts in New-England, may see enough to Silence any Incredulity that pretendeth to be Rational."[56] Although Increase Mather believed in witchcraft, this did not deter him from urging better methods for finding witches, and eventually, he and others objected on theological grounds to the use of spectral evidence, a view that gained in ascendancy. They did not argue against the existence of witches, but they urged better methods of proof and succeeded in diminishing the centrality of spectral evidence from the trials held after the Court of Oyer and Terminer ended. This centrality of spectral evidence to the trial cases of 1692 is implicitly made clear by the House of Representatives on July 20, 1703, where a Bill was ordered drawn up banning the use of spectral evidence for taking away a person's life or even a person's good name.[57]

After the trials ended, reactions to them soon developed, leading eventually to a broad consensus that something had gone terribly wrong. In the years that followed, specific legal steps were taken to address the injustice, including compensation for families of those executed or condemned but not executed, although no compensation came to those who had been imprisoned but not condemned or executed. Indeed, doubts about the correctness of what had been done were so great that even condemned confessors received compensation, as for example Abigail Hobbs. In September 1710, William Hobbs, her father, asked for 20 pounds compensation so "that our names may be Repayered."[58] In December 1711 she was awarded 10 pounds compensation.[59] Other condemned confessors also received compensation then. By 1711, if the government actions reflect the broader view in Massachusetts Bay, as they probably do, the confessions of 1692 had simply been discredited, as had most of the people whose testimony in part led to the death of others. It all had been a grand delusion, and nobody was legally guilty of anything – neither accusers nor accused, nor sheriffs, nor judges, nor anybody.[60]

[53] Wendel D. Craker correctly asserts that nobody was tried solely on spectral evidence. However, nobody came to the trial stage without spectral evidence as part of the case record, and in the five cases Cotton Mather describes in *Wonders* each has a component of spectral evidence. "Spectral Evidence, Non-Spectral Acts of Witchcraft, and Confession at Salem in 1692," *The Historical Journal*, Vol. 40, No. 2 (1997), pp. 331–358.

[54] Written in 1692, its full title is *Cases of Conscience Concerning Evil Spirits Personating Men; Witchcrafts, Infallible Proofs of Guilt in such as are Accused with that Crime*. While suggesting that something had gone wrong with the trials, Mather insisted on the reality of witchcraft.

[55] Richard Baxter, *The Certainty of the Worlds of Spirits*. London, 1691. On the connection to the debate in England, see also footnote 10.

[56] *Certainty*, p. 80. He apparently refers to Increase Mather, *An Essay for the Recording of Illustrious Providences* (Boston, 1684), and Cotton Mather, *Memorable Providences, Relating to Witchcrafts and Possessions* (Boston, 1689).

[57] No. 879.   [58] No. 912.

[59] No. 934.

[60] The reversal of attainders on October 17, 1711, specifically protected sheriffs, constables, and jailers from liability. No. 931.

SEEING SPECTRES

To this point, there is probably general agreement among historians about most of what has been narrated. But controversy exists among them once one looks a bit more closely into the outline. One issue of contention concerns the behavior of Betty and Abigail, as well as the similar behavior from others following them. What caused their strange behavior? In March, somewhat after the original behaviors, a former minister of Salem Village, Deodat Lawson, gives a vivid description of the behavior of Abigail Williams in his *A Brief and True Narrative of Some Remarkable Passages Relating to Sundry Persons Afflicted by Witchcraft . . .*(1692).[61] Lawson begins his account with events of March 19, 1692, as he describes Abigail Williams "stretching up her arms as high as she could, and crying Whish, Whish, Whish! several times; Presently after she said there was Goodw. N. [Rebecca Nurse] and said, Do you not see her? Why there she stands! And the said Goodw. N. offered her The Book, but she was resolved she would not take it, saying Often, I wont, I wont, I wont, take it, I do not know what Book it is: I am sure it is none of Gods Book, it is the Divels Book, for ought I know. After that, she run to the Fire, and begun to throw Fire Brands, about the house; and run against the Back, as if she would run up Chimney, and, as they said, she had attempted to go into the Fire in other Fits."[62]

Many repetitions of similar behavior and accusation by Abigail are recorded beginning in March and ending on June 30, 1692, when she disappears from the judicial records. By the time Lawson observed Abigail's behavior, Betty may have been living in the house of Stephen Sewall, who would become the clerk of the court of Oyer and Terminer.[63] Betty, after early accusations of witchcraft, disappears from the scene. Abigail continues, and others join her, young and mature women, as well as John Indian, one of Parris's slaves. Many others outside the initial group, male as well as female, would be added to the list of accusers. Those accusing at the earliest stages included, according to Calef,

Mrs. Pope, Mrs. Putman, Goodwife Bibber, and Goodwife Goodall, Mary Walcott, Mercy Lewes (at Thomas Putnam's) and Dr. Griggs Maid [Elizabeth Hubbard], and three Girls, Viz. Elizabeth Parris, Daughter to the Minister, Abigail Williams his Niece, and Ann Putman, which last three, were not only the beginners, but were also the chief in these Accusations. These Ten were most of them present at the Examination [of Martha Cory].[64]

Lawson's observation on Abigail's behavior opens a window into some of the most basic aspects of the witchcraft accusations and offers an opportunity to point to the different ways that behavior has been explained and the controversies that surround those views. Two critical motifs emerge in Abigail's claims. One is her ability to see the spectre of Rebecca Nurse, to claim surprise that nobody else could see it. The other motif concerns the signing of the "Book." As with other activity in the narratives concerning relations with the Devil, this signing was a parody of Christian ritual, in this case the signing of a church covenant. Time after time accusers and confessors tell narratives of a "witch" offering them the book to sign. That it was the Devil's book did not need to be said. Everybody understood it. The relationship with the Devil was contractual, legalistic. One needed to agree in writing, even if that writing was only a drop of one's blood, or a mark of some kind, to serve the Devil. In return the Devil made promises never kept and left some mark on the body of the person who had made the bargain, places where his "familiars" suckled. Most prominent among these promises was material gain. In such bargains the Devil was offering prosperity in return for assisting in overthrowing Christ's kingdom. Over and over the records reflect stories of this bargain as well as other bargains made less often. The contractual relation was not a Massachusetts Bay novelty, but was part of traditional English views on this bargain with the Devil.

The main controversy about Abigail's behavior, and the behavior of almost all the others making similar spectral accusations and claiming harm from the "witches" in the form of pinching, being stuck with pins, being made

---

[61] Parts of Lawson's account are carried in the edition even though his commentary does not qualify as a legal record. They are included in the chronological presentation because of the exceptionally valuable reporting of the examinations. The reliability of Lawson's account is probably neither better nor worse than that of most other recorders of examinations.

[62] *A Brief and True Narrative*, p. 3.

[63] The story of Betty residing in Sewall's house is often repeated, but difficult to confirm. George Lincoln Burr has a note on this, but is vague except for establishing that she was there on March 25. *Narratives of the Witchcraft Cases 1648–1706* (1914), p. 160, n1. His source is Lawson, p. 7, who gives that date to describe what Betty said on that day at Sewall's house. Lawson is silent as to whether Betty resided there or whether she happened to be there that day. No other source for Betty living in the Sewall household has been established.

[64] *More Wonders*, p. 92.

mute, having their hands tied, being pulled in chairs, and in general being seriously hurt, concerns the issue of how to account for the claims. As the community grew away from accepting those claims as valid, more and more people followed the lead of Thomas Brattle, a prominent merchant. Brattle was a friend of Samuel Sewall, who served as a judge on the Court of Oyer and Terminer, but his letter – the extent of its circulation remaining a matter for speculation – raised serious doubts about the credibility of the accusers and the wisdom of the court in believing them, noting among other things that those claiming grievous injury remained spry and healthy.[65] Reverend William Milborne, a Boston minister of the First Baptist Church, had protested against the court in June and had been ordered arrested in response.[66] Other contemporaries held similar views, as for example Robert Calef, who attacked the "witch hunters" in his *More Wonders of the Invisible World*, a direct response to Cotton Mather's *The Wonders of the Invisible World*, his defense of the court. The Reverend Samuel Willard, writing in 1692, reveals the existence of "the common vogue, that they [the 'afflicted'] are scandalous persons, liars, and loose in their Conversation [that is, behavior], and therefore not to be believed."[67] Indeed, at one point Willard went a step further and raised the possibility that the "afflicted" were not only liars, but witches themselves.[68] The surviving records also show that some less prominent people in the community, particularly those whose families were affected, saw the behavior of accusers as fraud. There is no reliable way to determine how many held this view, but the belief by some later commentators that people of that era were so blinded by their cultural assumptions that fraud was not considered in the community as a possibility simply does not hold up under scrutiny. This neither proves nor disproves fraud, but simply indicates that belief in it was a component in the collective response to the "witchcraft" episode.

When Thomas Hutchinson some years later wrote his *History of the Colony and Province of Massachusetts-Bay*, he assumed fraud on the part of the accusers as he continued the belief that began its strong development during and after the trials.[69] The view articulated by Hutchinson remained dominant well into the eighteenth century and strong in the nineteenth century, at least among historians. Among the general public a belief in witchcraft as the cause remained for some, as it sometimes does in popular culture today. Hutchinson's view remains the default view. That is, one can show with no difficulty evidence of fraud, or as earlier theological writers on the subject called it, "counterfeiting." But other assessments have emerged reflecting growing beliefs that something, independent of witchcraft and fraud, was needed to explain the behavior of the "afflicted." In 1870, William Frederick Poole discovered some documents from a draft by Hutchinson that did not appear in Hutchinson's published *History*. All of these have been collected and published by Richard Trask in his *"The Devil hath been raised": A Documentary History of the Salem Village Outbreak of March 1692* and included in this edition. In Poole's essay, "The Witchcraft Delusion of 1692. By Thomas Hutchinson," *The New-England Historical & Genealogical Register and Antiquarian Journal*,[70] he writes, Hutchinson's

theory on the subject – that it was wholly the result of fraud and deception on the part of the "afflicted children" – will not be generally accepted at the present day, and his reasoning on this point will not be deemed conclusive. That there were fraud and deception attending it, no one will doubt; but there is now a tendency to trace an analogy between the phenomena then exhibited, and modern spiritual manifestations.

Although one is not likely to find a modern historian today who sees "modern spiritual manifestations" as an alternative to fraud, and while one is not likely to find a modern historian who argues that zero fraud occurred, many are unsatisfied with such an explanation as a generalization among the accusers. Similarly, many accept it. The challenge for those rejecting fraud as an explanation is to offer an evidence-based alternative. The challenge for those accepting fraud as an explanation is to offer an explanation as to why such fraud occurred. However, the greater burden remains on those looking for the alternative

---

[65] Brattle, p. 77. For another valuable insight into skepticism about the procedures, see "Dutch New York and the Salem Witch Trials: Some New Evidence," pp. 277–308.

[66] Milborne was allowed to be free on bond. No. 320.

[67] *Some Miscellany Observations on Our Present Debates Respecting Witchcrafts, in a Dialogue Between S. & B.* (Philadelphia, 1692), p. 12.

[68] *Some Miscellany Observations*, p. 15. On Willard see Stephen L. Robbins, "Samuel Willard and the Spectres of God's Wrathful Lion," *The New England Quarterly*, Vol. 60 (March–December, 1987), pp. 596–603.

[69] (Vol. I, 1764; Vol. II, 1767; Vol. III, posthumously published, 1828). Ed. Lawrence Shaw Mayo (Cambridge, MA: Harvard University Press, 1936). For Hutchinson on fraud, see particularly II, p. 47.

[70] Trask (Yeoman Press; Revised Edition, 1997). Poole, Vol. 24 (1870), pp. 381–414. The quotation is from p. 382. For more detailed information on Poole, see Trask, "Legal Procedures."

to fraud, since those who support the centrality of fraud among the main accusers have some hard evidence, as for example, the explanation of Margaret Jacobs as to why she behaved as she did. She acknowledged her fraud and reported it as in response to threats from the magistrates.[71] Many other confirming pieces of evidence survive. Even as one explores the pros and cons of the fraud debate, it remains necessary to emphasize the certainty that the direction the episode took rests not in explaining the "fits" of the "afflicted" but in explaining the response to them. Nevertheless, interest in the causes of their behavior remains high. As to those other than the "afflicted" who made accusations, certainly many of them were based on accounts perceived by them as real, with explanations varying. One of the intriguing psychological possibilities in a limited number of cases concerns the phenomenon of "sleep paralysis," where people may awake, be unable to move, and perceive a person or object in the room or on top of them. The experience is real to them.[72] Sometimes, however, a narrative given as testimony appears to have been invented, as in the case of Samuel Gray, who in a death-bed confession repented the "groundless" testimony he had given against Bridget Bishop, the first to be tried.[73]

Alternative theories to Poole's vague support for "spiritual manifestations" among the "afflicted" have occurred in numerous medical, theological, or psychological expla-nations. The easiest of these to remove from serious consideration are the medical models, assuming one excludes psychological explanations from that category. Over the years many disease theories have been proposed to explain the behaviors, but only one has shown a capacity to endure in popular culture, although not in the scholarly community. This is the "ergot theory," the notion that somehow contaminated grain led to hallucinogenic responses from the accusers. The theory gained credibility as a result of its presentation in the highly respected journal *Science*, "Ergotism: The Satan Loosed in Salem?"[74] With publication in such a prestigious journal, the idea caught on with many in the general public as it spread to popular culture through books and television, although not likely with scholars of the witch trials, since the evidence, independent of the science, did not conform to the events as they happened. Later in December of that year, an article appeared in the same journal, *Science*, that conclusively refuted the theory. This was by Nicholas P. Spanos and Jack Gottlieb, "Ergotism and the Salem Village Witch Trials."[75] Spanos and Gottlieb presented an essay well informed about the basic events of 1692 as well as about the science of ergotism. The article should have ended the discussion, but it has stayed very much alive in popular culture and remains so today, although rarely among historians. Many have heard of ergotism; relatively few have heard of Spanos and Gottlieb. Other medical models have not caught the public imagination in the same way and have simply not caught on. No existing medical model explains the behavior of the accusers, and one will search with difficulty for any academic historian who supports any medical model. The issue is addressed here because so much of popular culture associates the Salem witch trials with some kind of medical, or chemical, or magical occurrence. Historians of the Salem witch trials can usually count on a call from the media at Halloween time.

But it was of course not a Halloween issue in 1692, and the search for explanations remains. The main alternative to seeing fraud as the central fact of the accusations is the psychological one. Here matters get more complex. Beginning with myth moving toward psychology, we have the long-standing view that the events that began in the Parris household grew from girls experimenting with magic and the consequences of that. In 1867 Charles W. Upham in his *Salem Witchcraft* introduced this myth of a circle

---

[71] No. 512.

[72] For a discussion of the syndrome, see David J. Hufford, *The Terror That Comes in the Night* (Philadelphia: University of Pennsylvania Press, 1982). For the syndrome as it might relate to cases involving Bridget Bishop and Susannah Martin, see pp. 221–222. Hufford is skeptical that the instances he describes were indeed episodes of "sleep paralysis," but he does not rule it out. The syndrome of experiencing an illusionary person present in the room or sitting astride someone is a recognized psychological phenomenon. I am grateful to Richard McNally, psychologist at Harvard University, and to Marc Sageman, psychiatrist at the University of Pennsylvania, for information on "sleep paralysis" and the Hufford book. McNally has suggested to me that Richard Coman's description of his encounter with Bridget Bishop was consistent with symptoms of sleep paralysis, although he made no diagnosis. For Coman, see No. 282. A further valuable discussion on "sleep paralysis" appears in Richard J. McNally and Susan A. Clancy, "Sleep Paralysis, Sexual Abuse, and Space Alien Abduction," *Transcultural Psychiatry*, Vol. 42 (March 2005), pp. 113–122. Cases such as this, of course, are in no way presented as explanatory for the Salem witch trials or for behaviors of others.

[73] *More Wonders*, p. 100 for the retraction. The word "groundless" is Calef's reporting. No confirmation or refutation of this claim by Calef has been found. On who was historically in New England most vulnerable to witchcraft charges, see *The Devil in the Shape of a Woman*.

[74] Linnda Caporeal, Vol. 192, No. 4234 (April 2, 1976), pp. 21–26.

[75] Vol. 194, No. 4272 (December 24, 1976), pp. 1390–1394.

of girls (with some older women also involved) engaging in fortune telling and other magic, heavily influenced by Parris's slaves Tituba and John Indian. He speculated that their reaction to this may have precipitated the behavior of the impressionable girls in the circle, to which Betty and Abigail belonged, even as he attributed some of the accusations from this group simply to fraud.[76] John Indian has been essentially omitted from the cultural myth that followed, with Tituba seen as the primary person presiding. John Indian has not fit in with our cultural narrative from *Gilgamesh* to Eve and beyond as "woman" being the progenitor of sin and death. Where Upham found his story of John and Tituba remains unknown and unverified. For whatever reasons, for about a century and half after Upham introduced this idea nobody bothered to check it. Once it was checked, however, no foundation was found.[77] That is, nothing to support the idea has so far ever been found in any written record prior to Upham's narrative. Nevertheless, here and there historians still write as if the event actually happened. Obviously, one cannot prove it did not happen, but it has no evidentiary status. The story is important in addressing psychological explanations, because historically it has been so central to them. However, even though the Tituba myth ought not to be taken seriously unless new evidence emerges, that does not do away with the underlying belief that girls dabbling in magic led to behaviors that could be given psychological explanations.[78] This is primarily because of a remaining belief in the fortune-telling story, based on a passage from John Hale's *Modest Enquiry into the Nature of Witchcraft*. According to Hale:

I fear some young persons through a vain curiosity to know their future condition, have tampered with the Devils tools, so far that hereby one door was opened to Satan to play those pranks; *Anno.* 1692. I knew one of the Afflicted persons, who (as I was credibly informed) did try with an egg and a glas to find her future Husbands Calling; till there came up a Coffin, that is, a Spectre in likeness of a Coffin. And she was afterward followed with diabolical molestation to her death; and so dyed a single person.[79]

As Mary Beth Norton has convincingly argued, the episode to which Hale refers happened independently of the events connected with the original claims of affliction.[80] At the same time, the Hale observation continues by many to be linked to those claims. Perhaps that view will in time recede as the Tituba myth recedes and also as Norton's analysis of interpreting Hale takes a wider hold; signs of that happening are appearing at least in the scholarly community. However, Hale's narrative and the Tituba myth have very much established the view, even if the underlying basis for it has crumbled, that an identifiable psychological incident triggered the original behaviors and the subsequent claims of the "afflicted." As one medical model after another has collapsed under scrutiny, the psychological argument has nevertheless remained powerfully embedded in assessments of the witch-hunt even among those who believe in the case for fraud. That is, one line of reasoning goes that, yes, they were pretending to be afflicted, and they were lying when they made their accusations, but that behavior can be explained psychologically or psycho-socially. Some scholars have argued that young, powerless females found themselves empowered and seized the opportunity for that empowerment.[81] Alternatively, those not believing in fraud as explanatory have taken the view that some psychological mechanism came into play leading the "afflicted" to believe that witches really were attacking them, really sticking pins

[76] *Salem Witchcraft*, Vol. II, pp. 2–6.
[77] See *Salem Story*, pp. 10–14. A mistake occurs in this book as to Tituba's court date based on an incorrect transcription in Paul Boyer and Stephen Nissenbaum, *The Salem Witchcraft Papers: Verbatim Transcripts of the Legal Documents of the Salem Witchcraft Outbreak of 1692*, 3 vols. (New York: Da Capo Press, 1977), subsequently cited as SWP. In Vol. 3, p. 755, Tituba's indictment is dated May 1692, when in fact a grand jury did not meet on her case until May 1693. Some erroneous conclusions were drawn from this incorrect transcription, and the current edition has its genesis in part in that error, as well as in errors not missed while *Salem Story* was being written. However, Boyer and Nissenbaum did not originate the transcription mistakes, since they used the transcriptions appearing in typescript by the Works Progress Administration in 1938 under the direction of Archie Frost. The errors notwithstanding, WPA did an impressive job of transcribing many of the documents. See Trask's "Legal Procedures" in this volume.
[78] For speculations on the historical Tituba, see Bernard Rosenthal, "Tituba's Story," *The New England Quarterly*, Vol. 71 (June, 1998), pp. 190–203; Bernard Rosenthal "Tituba," *OAH Magazine of History*, Vol. 17 (July 2003), pp. 48–50, ed. Elizabeth Reis; Elaine G. Breslaw, *Tituba, Reluctant Witch of Salem: Devilish Indians and Puritan Fantasies* (New York: New York University

Press, 1996); and Peter Charles Hoffer, *The Devil's Disciples: Makers of the Salem Witchcraft Trials* (Baltimore: Johns Hopkins University Press, 1996).
[79] *A Modest Enquiry*, pp. 132–133.
[80] *In the Devil's Snare*, pp. 23–24.
[81] For example, see Mary Ryan, *Womanhood in America: From Colonial Times to the Present* (New York: New Viewpoints, 1975), who sees the female accusers as engaging in "a disguised form of rebellion," p. 80.

in them, even though no historian doubts that they were doing it themselves or cooperating among each other to insert pins.

That some psychological mechanism was at work is surely true, just as some biological, anthropological, religious, cultural, sociological, evolutionary, and other mechanisms were at work. But to say that there must have been a psychological motive without providing a science-based theory to support it and not to show the evidentiary application of that theory to the event is not saying much. When Boyer and Nissenbaum in *Salem Possessed* made their powerful case for the discontent of the Putnam family, they provided their evidence to support that argument. When they tried to make a psychological connection between the distress of Ann Putnam Sr. and her accusation of Rebecca Nurse as some kind of psychological surrogate, they left the realm of evidence and entered into Freudian psychology.[82] This is a realm where evidence does not apply, since nothing in science supports the concept of Freud's that they used. One can neither prove it nor disprove it.

Sometimes, however, a psychological finding with scientific evidence behind it can be helpful, as in the case of "sleep paralysis" possibly explaining some behaviors as genuine experiences with perceived reality. However, even in this kind of association, the most that can be said is that the symptoms are consistent with known symptoms of people today who have experienced this kind of event. We cannot confirm on the basis of Richard Coman's testimony that he indeed suffered from sleep paralysis. Again, we can say that what he describes is consistent with that syndrome. The same caution should be used with all psychological attempts to explain the behaviors of those claiming affliction.

Reasonable psychological guesses, of course, remain appropriate. The Andover cases offer some useful examples. Although when thinking about the Salem witch trials we reasonably start with the events in Salem Village, it is easy to forget what historians know, that as Richard Latner writes, "more Andover inhabitants were charged with witchcraft than those of any other New England community."[83]

During this Andover phase, roughly from the end of July to the middle of September, 1692, something happened that changed the dynamics of the episode. People in large numbers began to confess, and parents at times found themselves accused by their own children. Some of these confessions were simply pragmatic, as we see in the words of Reverend Francis Dane on January 2, 1693, when the Superior Court of Judicature was preparing to continue trying the cases that had remained from 1692. Dane refers to the "speech that was frequently spread among us, of their liberty, if they would confess," and thus some did.[84] But this pragmatism notwithstanding, "psychological" workings are more easily found in this Andover phase. That is, in a number of cases families put intense pressures on women to confess to witchcraft, perhaps some of it along the lines that Dane describes. Many did confess, although all eventually retracted. The reasons for those pressures are speculative, but they plausibly fit into two main categories. One is that relatives of accused women pressured them to confess in order to save them, since by the summer of 1692 reasonable people could see that confessors were not being executed. But the other real possibility, and there is written commentary in the records by these women to support the idea, is that some of them under intense pressure and accusation came to believe that they were witches. So in such cases there is surely a psychological mechanism at work, whatever it is, that can be inferred from written evidence. When Richard Carrier denies he is a witch, is taken out of the room and tortured, and comes back and confesses and accuses, we can say with reasonable confidence that although he is clearly counterfeiting there is an understandable psychological motivation behind that. Similarly, when children accuse their parents, as they did in Andover, or as Sarah Good's child did in Salem Village, we can by analogy look at modern cases of children making what many would agree were false accusations and can find testable psychological or sociological causes. This is far easier to do with contemporary information and contemporary evidence.[85]

Whatever the psychological reasons were for the various claims made by accusers in the face of evidence highly consistent with fraud, as in sticking themselves with pins and saying that witches did it, any psychological explanation for this or other examples of events that appear

---

[82] *Salem Possessed*, p. 148.

[83] "'Here are No Newters': Witchcraft and Religious Discord in Salem Village and Andover," *The New England Quarterly*, Vol. XXIX, No. 1 (March 2006), p. 106.

[84] No. 745.

[85] For Sarah Good's child, see No. 33. One of the most illuminating examples of false accusations by children who came to believe those accusations may be found in the PBS Frontline production of *Innocence Lost* that was first aired May 27, 1997. See also Debbie Nathan and Michael Snedeker, *Satan's Silence: Ritual Abuse and the Making of a Modern Witch Hunt* (New York: Basic Books, 1995).

as fraud requires a scientifically verifiable psychological syndrome that can be shown as consistent with the facts of the historical event being described, and one that can offer a more satisfying explanation than "counterfeiting."[86]

What then is the evidence to support the claim of fraud or "counterfeiting" by the "afflicted," if not in every case, but in many cases, especially those involving the core accusers? One finds it in the inability at times of the accusers to identify the very people they claim were afflicting them, one of Willard's points.[87] One finds it in the futile attempt of Sarah Churchill to get somebody to believe that she is making it up.[88] One finds it in the instances where Susannah Shelden is discovered tied up so tightly – on four different occasions – that she needs to be cut loose. She accuses two different "witches" of doing this.[89] One finds it in the testimony of Margaret Jacobs as to how the "afflicted" threatened her if she would not confess, so to save her life she did and herself became an accuser, who subsequently retracted.[90] One finds it in the case of Richard Carrier, who held to his denial of witchcraft, but after being taken away for awhile, his hands and feet tied, threatened and tortured, returned and became an accuser claiming affliction.[91] One finds it in John Alden's account, where he writes that after "Captain Hill" had been accused of hurting the "afflicted" in court "a man standing at her back to hold her up; he stooped down to her Ear, then she cried out, Aldin." Alden's account of this incident is tantalizing in that he goes on to say that "one of the Magistrates asked her if she had ever seen Aldin, she answered no, he asked how she knew it was Aldin? She said, the Man told her so."[92] One finds it in the many cases of the accusers sticking pins in themselves and claiming that witches put them there, and in one case a person observed that happening, although even without such observation either the accusers put pins in themselves, associates did it, or witches did it.[93] One finds it in the capacity of the accusers to recover quickly and be active and healthy without periods of recuperation once they had their way.[94] The evidence of fraud is frequent in the records. The reasons for that fraud are the subject for separate studies, but the evidence that it happened is difficult to negate.

A more complex matter as to the question of fraud concerns the role of Thomas Putnam in preparing depositions for grand juries as well as his recording of other documents. By far, he wrote more depositions for presentation to grand juries than others did, and he adjusted them for grand jury or trial use. His success rate was high in getting grand juries to act against the accused. Although it is true that the same could be said for the others who prepared depositions, since he did so many of them, and since grand juries tended to show more independence than trial juries, his performance on behalf of the Court in getting cases to trial cannot be overlooked. He rarely presented a deposition that brought an ignoramus from a grand jury, and his record in getting true bills seems to have been close to perfect. Part of what he did was to add to depositions in one form or another the words "I verily believe in my heart that so and so is a witch," and the accusers faithfully swore to this. Most of these accusers were Salem Village ones, Elizabeth Hubbard, Mercy Lewis, Ann Putnam, Jr., Mary Walcott, and Abigail Williams. But Putnam handled depositions from Andover also, although the variety of recorders is greater there. Simon Willard, another recorder, used a form of the phrase "I verily believe," although the "heart" belonged to Putnam, a word not used by other recorders even when the same accusers were being recorded.[95] Putnam included the word in many cases that he recorded. In one sense, the frequent repetition of such phrasing can be seen as formulaic judicial language, which it may have been. At the same time, there was an alternative way to present a case without introducing words probably not spoken by those to whom they were attributed, and many depositions sworn before

---

[86] The best attempt to address broadly the witch trials in psychological terms is Chadwick Hansen, *Witchcraft at Salem* (New York: George Braziller, 1969). Those who do not believe in some general assumptions of Freud's will not find his overall argument convincing; those who do may. Hansen's book, written before the Tituba myth had been examined, offers very useful general information about the trials.

[87] *Dialogue Between S. & B*, p. 20.   [88] No. 261.

[89] No. 333.   [90] No. 753.

[91] No. 428.

[92] *More Wonders*, 98. If Alden's account is accurate, it suggests that one of the unidentified magistrates was possibly probing for counterfeiting, but even having found it the Court acted against Alden in any case and apparently took no action against the accuser. Who the magistrate was, and who the man was who made the identification, would be valuable to know, but no source supplies this information. No. 234.

[93] No. 366. This is an instance where a grown woman and not a child or teenager was doing it. Many other examples appear.

[94] Brattle, p. 77.

[95] In one document, No. 9, Putnam omits his signature phrase, of "I verily beleiue", but another recorder provides it, although he leaves out the "heart."

grand juries in 1692 against people accused of witchcraft carry no such formulaic language.

One sees this, for example, but elsewhere as well, in the depositions prepared by Samuel Parris for Abigail Williams, the one Salem Village accuser whose main recorder was not Putnam, but Parris. Abigail Williams was as virulent as others in making her claims, but it seems clear that Parris followed her language in a way that Putnam apperently did not follow the language of those whose depositions he prepared. One simply does not see the formulaic phrasing in the Parris depositions. He seems not to have fixed them for making a better case to the Court. Parris's handling of Williams's depositions offers the most useful contrast to Putnam, even though Williams was involved in fewer cases. It is not possible to guess what the outcomes would have been had Putnam not been so good at what he did. At the same time, this skill does not mean that there was anything fraudulent in his presentations. How people have and will assess his enthusiasm and competence will no doubt vary. As for other recorders, particularly those in the examination stage, they appear to have recorded what they saw, and they often saw different things, as easily noticed in comparing the two examinations of Bridget Bishop on April 12, 1692.[96] Putnam is more predictable.

Putnam, along with Samuel Parris, has historically been seen as one of the instigators of the Salem witch trials. It is hard to read an account of this episode without his identification in one way or another as deeply implicated in the episode. *Salem Possessed* builds its account heavily around the Putnam family fortunes, and Enders A. Robinson sees a conspiracy, with Thomas Putnam at the head of it.[97] Whatever the role of Thomas Putnam, there can be no doubt about his significance in writing depositions, adjusting them to fit legal needs, such as signing someone else's name to a document, or adding prose to strengthen a case. Perhaps more striking, however than Putnam's role in writing depositions is the fact that when Putnam lodged his last formal complaint, on July 1, his name had appeared on well over half of all felony complaints of witchcraft that had appeared earlier. On July 19, a complaint by Joseph Ballard of Andover came with bond for that complaint being posted. The names of Corwin, Gedney, and Hathorne appear on that document (No. 421), as well as the name of John Higginson Jr., although all these "signatures" were written by Hathorne. After July 19 all complaints came with bond, as they had normally not come before that date. Whether Putnam stopped making complaints because the free ride was over or whether he stopped making complaints because he had run out of people to accuse, or because activity had shifted to Andover, or for some combination of these reasons, remains open to consideration. Also open to further examination is the question as to why the key Justices of the Peace allowed complaints without the posting of bond until Higginson became active in receiving them (Corwin, Gedney, and Hathorne, though Judges on the Court of Oyer and Terminer starting May 27 continued to receive complaints as in their role of Justices of the Peace). The correlation between the ending of ignoring bond requirements for complaints and the ending of Putnam's complaints is stark. Whether there is a causal relationship may be debated. The cessation of Putnam's complaints, of course, did not mean the slowing down of witchcraft complaints. More people were complained against after July 19, beginning the Andover phase of the search for witches, than before that date.

Regardless of Putnam's motives, he had a formal role in the judicial proceedings, and the Superior Court of Judicature in 1693 compensated him five pounds for the work he had done.[98] That is, he was paid for his work on behalf of the court in a legitimate role as a court recorder. He was not the only person in this role, but he was a major figure in it. His handwriting, his spelling, and his prose are easily identifiable. One hundred and twenty known depositions or recorded testimonies were written by him, and his significance in initiating complaints is major. Whether accusers sought him out or whether he sought them out has never been definitely established. A circumstantial case for either can be made. Yet it is close to certain that a number of accusations made came against people unknown to the accusers, although the sources of such names varied. Whether Putnam was simply a conscientious citizen, or whether he was acting out of other motives or some combination of these two possibilities remains as a matter for consideration.

[96] For an excellent discussion of this issue, based on the Bridget Bishop examination recordings, but applicable more broadly, see Marion Gibson, *Witchcraft and Society in England and America, 1550–1750* (Ithaca, NY: Cornell University Press, 2003), pp. 208–209. Nos. 63 and 64.

[97] *The Devil Discovered: Salem Witchcraft 1692* (Prospect Heights, IL: Waveland Press, 1991), p. 110. Robinson follows *Salem Possessed* in the village quarrels approach. His genealogies are particularly valuable.

[98] No. 866.

How these names he used, as well as the names others used, were generated remains one of the most intriguing and unknown aspects of the events of 1692. On May 28, for example, Joseph Holton and John Walcott of Salem Village filed a complaint against Martha Carrier of Andover, Elizabeth Fosdick of Malden or Charleston, Wilmot Redd of Marblehead, Sarah Rice of Reading, Elizabeth How of Topsfield, John Alden of Boston, William Procter of Salem Farms, John Flood of Boston, Mary Toothaker of Salem and her daughter Margaret, and Arthur Abbott of Topsfield, all for afflicting Salem Village accusers, Mary Walcott, Abigail Williams, Mercy Lewis, Ann Putnam, and unnamed "Others." The name of Mary Toothaker appears on the complaint. No other first name of a female does, nor does the first name of Abbott.[99] The women are identified by their marital status, all married women, their husbands identified by first and last names. The spread of age is broad, from grown women to nine-year-old Margaret Toothaker. Males are in the group. So the most traditional characteristic of who is most likely to be named as a witch, an unprotected widow, does not apply. How did Holton and Walcott get these names, presumably a number of them being people whom they did not even know? Did those claiming to be afflicted by this group provide the names? It is highly unlikely that the accusers knew most of the people they claimed were afflicting them. Possibly they had heard the names in other contexts from adults who suspected these people. Possibly the names were randomly chosen from names they had simply heard. Possibly the accusers did not even choose the names that appeared on the complaint.[100] At first, Putnam seems unconnected to this list, since the complaint does not bear his name, and the document is recorded by John Hathorne. Yet on that same day, Putnam listed the accused, the accusers, and added a new name to the list, that of Elizabeth Paine.[101] Whether Putnam was responsible for this collection of accusations or had any hand in it we do not know. We only know that he was there and recording.

FINDING WITCHES

Judicial procedures took major shape when the first trial took place, that of Bridget Bishop on June 2, 1692. The court needed to take some position on issues historically contested among theologians as to how one finds sufficient evidence to convict a witch. Methods of extreme torture and deception as used on the continent, such as those described in the infamous *Malleus Maleficarum* by Heinrich Kramer and James Sprenger (c. 1486) and widely used especially in Germany and France, were not normally used in England, but at least two of the English theologians whose works were consulted, William Perkins and Richard Bernard, certainly recommended torture as a way of extracting confession.[102] Although the Province of Massachusetts Bay was a community that largely saw itself as English and understandably drew its legal traditions from the motherland, even that did not make things simple. Witch trials in England were coming to an end, and the concept of the reality of "witchcraft" was a contested concept there. Believing, as they apparently did, in the reality of witchcraft, the judiciary had a rich body of literature from which to choose regarding how one discovers a witch.

When Increase Mather, supported by other clergymen, made his argument for caution in *Cases of Conscience*, he cited the key English authorities on discovering witches and implicitly showed how the court had deviated from their advice as well, probably identifying some of the sources the judges consulted.[103] Our best clue as to the authorities for the clergy can probably be found in references Increase Mather makes, in *Cases of Conscience* (1692) to Perkins, Bernard, and *Select Cases of Conscience Touching Witches and Witchcrafts* by John Gaule (1646).[104] Increase Mather, when he finally did so, pointed to these

---

[99] That this was Arthur Abbott represents a best guess rather than certain knowledge.

[100] No. 221.   [101] No. 222.

[102] *A Discourse of the Damned Art of Witchcraft* by William Perkins (Cambridge, 1608), p. 45, and *A Guide to Grand Jury Men* by Richard Bernard (London, 1627), p. 253. Regarding the *Malleus Maleficarum*, the names of the authors are variously rendered in translation, and here the names follow the usage of Montague Summers's edition, originally published in London by John Rodker in 1928.

[103] That much of the clergy had serious doubts about the proceedings can be seen from the list of clergymen who endorsed Mather's book: William Hubbard, Samuel Phillips, Charles Morton, James Allen, Samuel Whiting, Samuel Willard, John Baily, Jabez Fox, Samuel Angier, John Wise, Joseph Capen, Nehemiah Walter, Michael Wigglesworth, and Joseph Gerrish, p. 15. Cotton Mather is noticeably absent from this list. He played a prominent role, however, in "The Return of Several Ministers," June 15, giving cautions to the Court consistent with traditional writings on discovering witches, including a caution about spectral evidence.

[104] Perkins, *A Discourse of the Damned Art of Witchcraft*, p. 32; Bernard, *A Guide to Grand Jury Men*, p. 33; Gaule, *Select Cases of Conscience Touching Witches and Witchcrafts*, p. 48.

well-known authorities on witchcraft to address controversies in the Province of Massachusetts Bay. Above all, he seems to have admired Perkins.

Early on Perkins makes clear, referencing Exodus 22:18, that a witch must not be permitted to live. The problem, and Perkins addresses it, is the difficulty of determining who is a witch, given the powers that God has allowed the Devil to use. The task before any judicial body must be to separate illusions by the Devil from realities of witchcraft. Superstitious attempts to discover witches need to be avoided, and the world is a tricky place for finding the truth in such matters. Dreams might be valuable for discovering your sins, but at the same time dreams may be creations of the Devil. How do you tell? That was the core problem Perkins addressed in asking the identical question about witchcraft, whether on the subject of dreams or other matters.

Perkins affirmed that the case for proving witchcraft must be a judicial one and must be treated like other crimes addressed by judicial magistrates, just as magistrates hear cases of plain murder. Rules and procedures must be followed in spite of the particularly difficult problems associated with witchcraft. He listed two requirements: examination and conviction, and under each he clarified what he meant by that. The examining magistrate is required to be free of personal motives against the accused and must have some "presumption" for believing that the accused person might be a witch. The first of these presumptions is simply that the person has been named as a witch by "common report."[105] However, this remains at the level of presumption, and Perkins observed that, although such charges indeed raise suspicions, magistrates must realize that sometimes innocent people are accused. On this point the court at Salem in 1692 seemed not to follow Perkins very closely, since it never found anybody innocent.

A further presumption was accusation by a known witch, but this alone could not be conclusive. Also in the category of presumption were deaths that followed curses, quarreling and threatening, and association with a witch. Another presumption rested with the Devil's mark. Magistrates needed to determine whether a mark on a person was from the Devil or not. Body searches for such marks were part of the Salem judicial procedures. The final presumption in an examination was behavior by the accused giving inconsistent or uncharacteristic responses to questions asked. Reading the examinations reveals how often the magistrates looked for inconsistencies or contradictions in responses from the accused.

All of these presumptions were reason for further judicial action, although not for conviction. As to the kind of examination, Perkins offered two. One consisted simply of interrogation by the magistrate. The other was torture, perfectly acceptable in cases where the presumptions were strong and the accused was stubborn and resisting confession. The court at Salem and the magistrates in examinations used all the presumptions at one time or another if not in every case. The records do not show torture as widespread, but they do confirm that it occurred.[106] How often it occurred independent of the verifiable cases can only be a matter of speculation.

After addressing the presumptions, Perkins turns to what is required for conviction to follow. Presumption alone must not lead to conviction. Solid proof is required. He sees as insufficient or worse some traditional approaches, such as having the accused hold something scalding and being found guilty if unable to endure it; scratching the accused with resulting relief from the witchcraft of the accused; burning something bewitched with the aim of exposing the person having done it; or the water test, where a person is thrown bound into a body of water and thought guilty if remaining afloat and innocent if sinking. Further presumptions inadequate for conviction are accusations by a wizard, claims that after being threatened or hurt by the accused that the person was indeed hurt, or death-bed claims against someone whose bewitchments were believed to be causing the impending death. But presumptions in general reflected step one for Perkins. They were not proof, but they offered the requirement of investigations toward true proof. If the person would not confess, then the only other alternative was the testimony "of two witnesses, of good and honest report" who could confirm that the defendant had made a league with the Devil or had been seen to practice witchcraft, which of course required such a league.[107] One may understand how the Court at Salem did not find this task easy, but on the issue of two reliable witnesses, it certainly sought to follow the advice of Perkins. When Thomas Putnam signed another name to a document, as in

---

[105] *A Discourse of the Damned Art of Witchcraft*, p. 44.

[106] Torture had been banned in 1672 except in certain circumstances among convicted people. See *Crime and Punishment in Early Massachusetts 1620–1692*, p. 88.

[107] *A Discourse of the Damned Art of Witchcraft*, p. 46.

nos. 137 and 157, it was to meet this requirement. He probably did so with the person's knowledge, but this can only be a matter of speculation.

However, on the issue central to what happened in the Salem witch trials, the Court did not follow Perkins. Perkins made clear that the Devil has the power to resemble an innocent person in form and in voice, and that such evidence could not go beyond presumption to proof, as it did in Salem where spectral evidence remained at the heart of the convictions, other evidence notwithstanding. The indictments make this clear. Overwhelmingly, those indicted were accused of afflicting somebody on the day of the examination, implicitly at the examination where all could see the spectral assaults. Such evidence for Perkins could not go beyond presumption, but in Salem it represented an essential component of proof. Adult witnesses confirmed the "afflictions" at the examinations. In addition to the indictments, Governor Phips was consistent with Brattle in confirming the specific use of spectral evidence at the trials – the accused in open court claiming, as they did in preliminary examinations, that the spectres of the accused were afflicting them.[108] Certainly all historians know about the issue of spectral evidence, but the fundamental departure from guidelines such as those by Perkins has not received widespread attention. The necessity for that attention, if we are to understand what happened, is that the behavior of the court departed radically not only from New England tradition but from William Perkins, one of the main authorities for those who believed in prosecuting people for witchcraft. Hovering in the background, however, may have been Joseph Glanvil, the main defender in England of belief in witchcraft. Although Glanvil did not argue for the use of spectral evidence in trials, he vigorously supported the reality of apparitions.[109] How this might have influenced the court's use of spectral evidence can only be conjectural. Glanvil, however, though the leading proponent in the late seventeenth century of the reality of witchcraft, gave scant attention in his book to legal procedures for detecting witches.

One sees more such attention in *A Tryal of Witches*, cited by John Hale and Cotton Mather as one of the sources used by the Salem judges and referenced primarily for its support of witchcraft as a reality, but it also gives some insights into legal procedures used, such

as the sequence of indictment, arraignment, plea, trial, verdict, acceptance of the verdict, sentencing, and execution.[110] *A Tryal of Witches* is useful in modeling the alternative choices to Perkins, Bernard, and Gaule made by the judiciary. This trial of two women, Amy Denny and Rose Cullender, at Bury St. Edmunds, England, involved accusations of bewitching seven children, three of whom appeared at the trial. Like the core Salem accusers, the three main ones in 1662 claimed severe affliction and had fits even more drastic than those expressed in Massachusetts Bay. These accusers were particularly skillful in their ability to vomit pins and other items, or at least to persuade people that they were vomiting them. Their later counterparts could do no better than sticking themselves with pins and claiming that spirits did it. But what makes the *Tryal* narrative especially revealing of the attitudes of the Salem judges is that Matthew Hale, aware of the continuous danger of counterfeiting, even if he was gullible on the vomiting of pins, ordered a touch test designed to check for counterfeiting. One of the girls, probably Elizabeth Pacy, was blindfolded and touched by someone designated by the court rather than by the accused, Rose Cullender, whom she was expecting. Her response was identical to the fits she went into when Cullender touched her on other occasions, and the immediate response by those conducting the test was that they "returned openly protesting, that they did believe the whole transaction of this business was a meer Imposture."[111] That an explanation was subsequently accepted that this test actually proved Cullender was a witch is another story. What matters here is that Hale cared enough about the issue of counterfeiting to conduct the test. Surviving evidence indicates that the Salem judges who looked to Matthew Hale as one of their authorities did not make testing for counterfeiting part of their regular procedures, although in isolated instances one might infer that they did. It is hard to avoid the conclusion that for whatever motives, the Salem judges wanted convictions. Cotton Mather, in giving a very thorough narrative of what is found in *A Tryal of Witches*, references this episode in *Wonders* and acknowledges the problem it created, but omits the conclusions reached by those conducting the test that the charges were based on counterfeiting.[112] Mather also in writing about the Swedish witch trials omits the fact that they came to an end when the accusing children

---

[108] No. 836.

[109] *Saducismus Triumphatus*, pp. 83–84.

[110] *Wonders*, p. 55; *A Modest Enquiry*, p. 28. Hale provides names of others he says were consulted by the judges.

[111] *A Tryal of Witches*, p. 44.   [112] *Wonders*, p. 59.

confessed that they had made up their stories.[113] Whether Mather knew this or not is uncertain.

Rose Cullender and Amy Denny were found guilty on thirteen indictments considered by the jury for half an hour. The trial began on March 10, 1662, and heard evidence till the afternoon of March 13. On March 14, "the Judge and all the Court were fully satisfied with the Verdict,"[114] and the women were executed on March 17. This particular case was lengthy by the standards of the time, with the Salem cases more typical in length of English felony cases. Often, grand jury hearings and trials were concluded in the same day.[115] Other similarities include the use of spectral evidence, although unlike at Salem, it was not central to the trial, and the extent of its influence in persuading the jurors is not clear. Other kinds of evidence dominated the trial. However, for those in Salem accepting spectral evidence as legitimate, this offered a precedent. But those authorities who addressed broad issues of how to discover witches, as the author of *Tryal* did not, came down with consistent cautions against spectral evidence as a proof.

Richard Bernard shared Perkins's view on this subject. There could be no doubt as to the Devil's ability to take the shape of an innocent person.[116] To convict a person of witchcraft one needed "to prove a league made with the Devil. In this only act standeth *the very reality of a Witch*; without which neither she nor he (howsoever suspected and great showes of probability concurring) are not to bee condemned for witches."[117] And highly germane to what happened at Salem: "If this be not proved, all the strange fits, apparitions, naming of the suspected in trances, suddaine falling downe at the sight of the suspected, the ease which some receive when the suspected are executed, bee no good grounds for to judge them guiltie of Witchcraft."[118] So the very acts that drove the Salem witch trials were rejected by Bernard as proof of witchcraft. This hardly meant that Bernard doubted witchcraft. On the contrary, for him it was there, dangerous, and required execution for those found guilty of making such a pact with the Devil. The problem was how to prove it. And the impediments were great.

High among these impediments was "counterfeiting," requiring the necessity to explore it as exemplified by Matthew Hale. Such behavior represents a basic strand in the English history of "witchcraft." A true believer in the reality of witchcraft, Bernard goes so far as to cite Reginald Scot, whose *Discoverie of Witchcraft* (1584) ridiculed various accounts of witchcraft, the book earning the ire of King James, who had the copies burned. So great was the problem of counterfeiting that in his passionate defense of the reality of witchcraft, Joseph Glanvil had to insist that in spite of so many impostures "a single relation for an Affirmative [evidence of witchcraft], sufficiently confirmed and attested, is worth a thousand tales of forgery and imposture."[119] Indeed, Bernard cites King James, whose initial enthusiasm for witch finding elided into skepticism. Both Scot and James catch Bernard's attention, because they address the issue of counterfeiting, that is, someone pretending to be bewitched. Among the examples Bernard uses is the story of William Perry, known as "the Boy of Bilson," whose deceptions were much more skillful than those of the Salem accusers in that he did what they never did, vomited rags, thread, and pins.[120] His fraud was exposed, but this of course does not prove fraud by the Salem "afflicted." What it does demonstrate clearly is that witch finders needed to investigate carefully the possibility of such counterfeiting. Bernard made an observation, stunningly appropriate to the Salem trials. True victims, Bernard writes, "*pineth* away in body" [Bernard's italics].[121] Indictment after indictment in the Salem trials invokes this image, concluding that the accused has caused the victim to be "consumed, pined, wasted, and tormented." But they did not pine away in the Massachusetts Bay cases, and Stoughton flatly rejected Bernard's position when he told the jury at the trial of Bridget Bishop that the

---

[113] For the retractions see Brian P. Levack, *The Witch-Hunt in Early Modern Europe* (Harlow, England; New York: Longman/Pearson; third edition, 2006), pp. 227–228. For a broader and more detailed discussion of the Swedish episode, see Bengt Ankarloo, "Sweden: The Mass Burnings (1668–1676)," *Early Modern European Witchcraft: Centres and Peripheries*, ed. Bengt Ankarloo and Gustav Henningsen (Oxford: Oxford University Press, 1993), pp. 285–317. For Mather's access and that of other English speakers to the Swedish witchcraft narrative, see E. William Monter, "Scandinavian Witchcraft in Anglo-American Perspective," in *Early Modern European Witchcraft*, pp. 425–434.

[114] *A Tryal of Witches*, p. 58.

[115] Baker, *An Introduction to English Legal History*, observes that English felony cases in the 1600's "rarely" took "more than half an hour," p. 582.

[116] *A Guide to Grand Jury Men*, p. 119.

[117] *A Guide to Grand Jury Men*, p. 212.

[118] *A Guide to Grand Jury Men*, p. 213.

[119] *Saducismus Triumphatus*, p. 84.

[120] Rossell Hope Robbins, *The Encyclopedia of Witchcraft & Demonology* (New York: Bonanza Books, 1981 Edition), pp. 48–49.

[121] *A Guide to Grand Jury Men*, p. 65.

afflicted only needed to show a tendency to pine away.[122] The issue here, of course, is not to demonstrate that the trials were unfair, but to point out that they did not follow the procedures of the authorities in dealing with witchcraft in spite of their efficient and orderly nature. For Bernard, the greatest of all ways to deal with witchcraft was to do what Cotton Mather tried with the Goodwin children a few years earlier, praying and refusing to name the people accused, and what Samuel Parris tried at the outset of the episode in Salem Village, prayer.[123] If Parris named anybody not previously accused, we have no record of it.

The most articulate appeal to search for counterfeiting came from the condemned Mary Esty. In a petition that she knew was hopeless for saving her own life, she appealed for the authorities to do in these cases what Bernard had said they should do in all cases, although she did not reference him:[124] check for counterfeiting. To avoid the shedding of innocent blood, a metaphor standard in Perkins and Bernard, and widespread elsewhere, Esty urged the court to examine the accusers strictly and to keep them apart.[125] They obviously could not conspire to make up the same stories if isolated from each other, and the injunction from the "witchcraft" authorities such as Bernard was so strong that the decision not to do so, and no evidence survives to demonstrate that it was done, reminds us again of the radical nature of the court, throwing authoritative guidelines to the wind. Rather than question people privately, out of public gaze, the magistrates conducted examinations in public and with the accusers together. They ignored, based on the evidence we have, what Esty had requested, identical to Bernard's advice to examine the accused in isolation, away from the accusers. And although Esty claimed that some of the accusers had lied, nothing survives to suggest that the court considered, as Bernard insisted upon, that the "Conversation" (behavior in general) of those claiming affliction, be inquired into carefully.[126] The Court's inclination seemed closer to Glanvil's view cited above that although there are "frequent impostures," discovering one witch "is worth a thousand tales of forgery and imposture."

On various other matters, Bernard's advice offered guidelines clearly followed, whether from reading him or otherwise. At the outset, as Samuel Parris records, his parishioner Mary Sibley had instructed Parris's slave John Indian to make a witch cake from meal and the urine of the afflicted children to reveal who was bewitching them.[127] Bernard had condemned such practices, and Parris condemned them too, even claiming that the witch cake episode was the event that let loose the Devil in Salem Village. Here, Parris and Bernard were in complete agreement as to the sinfulness and danger of such practice – going to the Devil for help. They may also have shared views on torture in that Bernard thought it appropriate.[128] Whether Parris's beating of Tituba, as claimed by Calef, fits this is probably unlikely but would depend on more information than we have.

But Parris offered little if anything on finding witches, as opposed to Bernard, who, like Perkins, divided the task of discovering witchcraft into presumptions and proofs. His presumptions included cursing, threatening, visiting the ill after cursing them, being named by people in fits, apparitions seen by people in fits, accusations by witches or wizards, and using the sieve and scissors with certain words, all to be found in the records in this edition. With these presumptions, however, Bernard warns of the need for caution, especially in the matter of apparitions, emphasizing to his readers the Biblical episode, invoked so often in futile defense at Salem, that the Devil could indeed take the shape of an innocent person.

As for proof, Bernard emphasized the need to show a league with the Devil as the only acceptable evidence for condemnation as a witch.[129] Signs of this included appearance of the Devil's mark, being seen with spirits, being heard calling for spirits, making accurate predictions, giving someone something that causes pain or death, being implicated by confessing witches, a token from God, and of course a confession. All scholars of the Salem trials know that through most of 1692 no confessing "witch" was condemned, and only in September, when this became an

[122] Brattle, p. 77.
[123] For Mather and the Goodwin children, see *Memorable Providences.*
[124] No. 654 (Plates 10 and 11).
[125] No. 654. Esty's appeal echoes language from Bernard and others to the point where it encourages the belief, although certainly not the proof, that she had strong assistance from a minister in writing it.
[126] *A Guide to Grand Jury Men*, pp. 244–245.
[127] Other accounts that include Tituba in making this cake are unreliable in light of Parris's explanation recorded in the Salem Village Church Record. See *Salem-Village Witchcraft: A Documentary Record of Local Conflict in Colonial New England*, ed. Paul Boyer and Stephen Nissenbaum (Belmont, CA: Wadsworth Publishing Company, 1972), Danvers Church Record, pp. 278–279. For its earliest published source, see *Salem Story*, p. 225 n36, and on the witch cake, pp. 25–27.
[128] *A Guide to Grand Jury Men*, p. 253.
[129] *A Guide to Grand Jury Men*, p. 299.

embarrassment, were such confessors sentenced to death. But none were executed except for Samuel Wardwell, who had retracted his confession. In turning this fundamental principle upside down, for non-confessors were indeed executed, the Salem trials failed to heed the advice of Bernard and of tradition in witchcraft cases. Why they did so has no universal agreement among historians, but the most probable reason is that the authorities found the need to justify their actions more compelling than issues of accurately finding witches, and by keeping confessors alive, they ensured a steady flow of confirmation. As more and more confessed, the Court had further confirming evidence to justify its actions. The Devil was attacking the Kingdom of Christ. Alternative explanations may be argued by others.

Traditional English approaches were not totally ignored, of course, as in the requirement of two adult, humane witnesses being needed for witchcraft cases. However, these depositions, when addressing accusations by the "afflicted," do not show witnessing of witchcraft by the witnesses. Instead, not really consistent with what Bernard was saying, they confirm that the deponents had seen the "afflicted" claim that the spectre of so and so was torturing them. Sometimes these spectres attacked in open court, but only the accusers maintained that they saw them. In assessing legal practices of the seventeenth century, one always needs to approach judging them with caution, keeping in mind that many assumptions of the time were different from now. However, if we judge them by the assumptions of their authorities, they failed to do justice, contrary to the views of those who argue that all we need to do is understand their assumptions for us to see that they were behaving within reasonable boundaries of their time. This was simply not the case if we assess their behavior by the rules of the advice from Perkins and Bernard. Indeed, what opposition to the trials existed came predominately from the clergy. They understood these violations, but tempered their knowledge with great caution so as not to criticize the judicial authorities publicly. Samuel Willard did so elliptically in his sermons, and anonymously in his publication on the *Dialogue Between S. and B*. More openly but much less severely, in "The Return of Several Ministers," a group of ministers cautioned the court. This was on June 15, shortly after the first execution, that of Bridget Bishop.[130]

The other book Mather cited, John Gaule's *Select Cases of Conscience Touching Witches and Witchcrafts* (1646), offers no significant deviation from the views expressed by Bernard and Perkins, except in some arcane differences, such as his belief that the use of the sieve and scissors is not a presumption.[131] On the key evidence needed for conviction he is in harmony, emphasizing confession as primary. At the same time, he cautions against simply accepting confessions without investigating whether the confessor "was forced to it, terrified, allured, or otherwise deluded."[132] This describes pretty well many of the confessions, especially, but not exclusively, during the Andover phase of the witch-hunt. He also emphasizes a view, not inconsistent with Perkins or Bernard, of the need for having informed jurors for witchcraft cases. He cautions against leaving the matter to the unlearned and is the most specific of the three in defining the kind of person who should serve on such juries: "the most Eminent Physitians, Lawyers and Divines, that a Country could afford," and not juries comprised "of ordinary Country People."[133] What little we know of the Salem jurors, and our clear knowledge of the wording of the call for jurors, suggests that Gaule's injunction on this point was not followed. And although both Perkins and Bernard point to the risk of condemning the innocent, and Gaule certainly believed in condemning the guilty, more than the others he emphasizes that "God forbid they should be thus punished for Witches; that indeed are no Witches. For so Innocent blood may be brought upon a Land."[134]

But by the time Increase Mather published his *Cases of Conscience*, "innocent blood" had been shed, and Mather implicitly makes clear that the Court is under censure for this from some sources. His response is that it deserves pity instead of criticism for its difficulties, and he winds up endorsing his son's defense of the Court in *The Wonders of the Invisible World*,[135] expressing surprise that anyone would think that the two differed on the subject. Yet Increase Mather implicitly gutted the reasoning of the Court on two major issues. One was the inappropriateness of spectral evidence, since the Devil could take the shape of an innocent person, and the other the inappropriateness of accepting the accusations of confessors, who were by definition in league with the Devil. Thus, the

---

[130] A modernized version of "The Return" appears in *Salem-Village Witchcraft*, pp. 117–118.

[131] *Select Cases of Conscience*, p. 76.
[132] *Select Cases of Conscience*, p. 192.
[133] *Select Cases of Conscience*, p. 195.
[134] *Select Cases of Conscience*, p. 177.
[135] *Wonders*, p. 58.

Court followed with reasonable consistency judicial practices in England for normal felony cases. It did not do the same for the witchcraft cases.[136] The legal records, among many other stories, tell that one.

A NEW EDITION

Of the many stories told in the new edition, the obvious question to ask is whether new insights come from them, and the answer is yes. Beyond the value of having correct transcriptions to use in assessing the legal records, the process of editing these manuscripts has revealed information on a variety of matters. Some are curiosities, as in discovering that Sarah Good's four-year-old daughter, arrested and imprisoned, and an accuser of her mother, described for a few hundred years by scholars as "Dorcas" Good, was in fact Dorothy Good.[137] The "Dorcas" came from a common problem of people not knowing the names of the accused, especially the first names of females. When the error was caught in 1692 it was corrected to "Dorothy." And even though almost every surviving document refers to her as Dorothy, the error of Dorcas came through the ages as her name. Cultural historians, folklorists, or others may find this matter of choosing a name a subject of interest, or it may remain simply as a curiosity.[138]

The mistake about Dorothy Good's name, emanating from John Hathorne not accurately knowing her name, a mistake he subsequently corrected, reoccurs with the identity of others, and the documents reveal the extent to which people did not know the names of people accused, especially the first names of females. Historians have understood this for a long time. What the edition reveals in this matter, however, is that often these first names that appear in other printed editions are names that were inserted at a later stage of a document's history. The extent to which the legal authorities wanted to produce accurate records becomes much clearer. The handling of indict-

ments, also involving the filling in of names, reveals a process of blank indictments produced with names and dates filled in, sometimes by the Attorney General. Names are also crossed out and replaced with others to conform to the charge. Letters are overwritten with other letters. Sometimes these matters simply represent a desire for clarity and accuracy, useful information for historians and languages scholars. Sometimes these changes tell what might have been expected when the document was first created, and how that expectation changed.

To identify those writing the documents and making insertions, a database of recorders was created for the edition and has made possible a number of identifications as to who wrote what, and at times when. Sometimes the recorder remains unidentified, although his hand is recognizable. So "Recorder X" might be the person who performs a particular function regularly, such as preparing a boilerplate indictment form, but when another recorder fills in blanks, the reader can see it, since the insertion is editorially indicated. This applies to all kinds of documents. The hand information also opens widely the opportunity for further study as to the various roles of people in the process, as in the case of Thomas Putnam signing someone else's name to a document, or others doing this, since Putnam was not alone in such activity. Whether one draws conspiratorial conclusions from such findings, or whether one draws bureaucratic, legal, or other conclusions, the edition presents the information that allows those conclusions in the contexts of arguments constructed.

The construction of this database began in 2000 originally by Margo Burns and Matti Peikola. Peikola did the first major compilation of scribal hand data, extracted from a quarter of the documents during the first round of the transcription process, establishing a basic format to describe about 100 unique "hands" according to four classes of distinctive features: letter formation, orthography, abbreviation, and punctuation. Margo Burns continued to build on this data and designed a database with a web-based interface to manage the information using visual samples and descriptions of each person's handwriting, with a list of which documents contain that handwriting, identifying which numbered hand it is in the transcription, an approximate size of the sample in that document, and whether the document includes a signature. Peter Grund joined the effort later, at first to extract the scribal data from additional transcriptions, and then to work closely with the other two as the project evolved.

---

[136] On legal practices in Massachusetts Bay, see David Konig, *Law and Society in Puritan Massachusetts*, and Edwin Powers, *Crime and Punishment in Early Massachusetts 1620–1692*. For general matters in English law, see particularly Baker, cited above, James Swanston Cockburn, *A History of English Assizes 1558–1714* (Cambridge: Cambridge University Press, 1972), and *The English Legal System*, ed. G. J. Hand and D. J. Bentley (London: Butterworths, 1977).

[137] No. 22. See note on this document.

[138] I am indebted to the onomastic and folklore scholar Wilhelm Nicolaissen for confirming that Dorcas is not a diminutive or variation of Dorothy.

The group identified more than 250 unique hands across all the documents.

The handwriting of a few of the recorders has been known for a long time among some of the historians who have examined the manuscripts, especially that of Jonathan Corwin, John Hathorne, Samuel Parris, and Thomas Putnam. They are easily identifiable, and their handwriting appears on many documents connected to their signatures – although the extent of their written contributions has never before been as fully accessible. The identities of most of the other recorders have been more difficult to establish with a degree of certainty, or even at all. The names of more than 60 percent of the recorders remain entirely unknown. Yet many names of recorders are now known as probable, but are not identified in the edition because those identifications fall short of certainty.

The database, nevertheless, has enabled us in the edition to name recorders in documents to an extent never before possible. By comparing a sample of the handwriting of a known person, such as Thomas Newton, the first Attorney General prosecuting the witchcraft cases, we have been able to name otherwise unsigned and sometimes very small contributions by him in other documents. His successor was Anthony Checkley. By consulting a contemporary deposition in an unrelated case, which Checkley had signed, we were able to match this known sample of his writing to one of our unnamed hands, and discern a similar pattern of participation in the creation of indictments. Just before the edition was ready for submission, the last unpublished manuscript in this edition was examined and transcribed. This was a petition by Anthony Checkley that further confirmed his handwriting as well as revealing his lack of financial rewards for his services.[139] The handwriting of Stephen Sewall, Clerk of the Court of Oyer and Terminer, has been clearly established, and he is revealed as a recorder on a full third of all the documents, although in a great many of these documents, his contribution was limited to a three-word notation at the bottom of depositions, "Jurat in Curia," importantly indicating that the deponents officially swore to their trial testimony and confirming such documents as part of the trial record.

It was not the editorial team's original intention to have the edition include the identity of recorders. The database was developed as a tool to support more accurate transcriptions and to provide additional evidence to date otherwise undated documents. It is rough around the edges, and it appeared that polishing it for complete publication would take too much time away from completing the edition in an already lengthy publishing endeavor. Numerous samples in documents are fairly small, making certain identification difficult. A handful of recorders whose important contributions show up in dozens of documents are yet to be named, although their handwriting is identifiable. As useful as the database has been, it is not a finished work. Burns, Grund, and Peikola are planning to continue work on this database and make it available online to other researchers. For the purposes of this edition names used in the document notes to identify recorders have been chosen very conservatively from the database with a high degree of confidence as to accuracy. They are Attorneys General Anthony Checkley and Thomas Newton; Magistrates Jonathan Corwin, Bartholomew Gedney, John Hathorne, John Richards, Samuel Sewall, and William Stoughton; Governor's Assistant Elisha Hutchinson; Justices of the Peace Dudley Bradstreet and John Higginson, Jr.; Clerks of the Court Jonathan Elatson and Stephen Sewall; Captain Thomas Bradbury; Deputy Sheriff George Herrick; ministers John Hale of Beverly and Samuel Parris of Salem Village; official scribes William Murray, Thomas Putnam, and Simon Willard; Salem Village residents Ezekiel Cheever and Edward Putnam; and Andrew Elliott of Beverly. We also assume authenticity of the signature in the document, No. 5, where Joseph Putnam of Salem Village is identified as the recorder.[140]

Also involved in the "hand" matter is the issue of signatures. Through a detailed study of the hands of the main judicial authorities it has been achievable to establish authenticity of many signatures. Unless otherwise indicated, the reader can assume a signature's authenticity in this group. However, to establish authenticity in the signatures of others where the hand cannot be verified, the signature is simply transcribed. At the same time instances of inauthentic "signatures" do occur, and when possible or practical these are identified in a note accompanying the document. Where appropriate, other observations are made on signatures. Marks, "signatures" from those who were presumably illiterate, are reproduced

---

[139] No. 852. This petition was located in the Massachusetts Archives by Molly Warsh, a Cornell University student of Mary Beth Norton, and generously called to my attention by Mary Beth Norton.

[140] For further discussion about the recorders, see the Linguistic Introduction.

as they appeared. They appear in SWP with varying degrees of accuracy, but in *Records of the Salem Witch-Hunt* marks made in 1692 appear as exact facsimiles from the manuscripts, except when the mark is simply an "X." Marks made after 1692 are also indicated simply with an "X." Conclusions as to whether marks were made by the person whose name is associated with them are not drawn. The marks of the core accusers from Salem Village vary in consistency, with Mary Walcott and Abigail Williams pretty consistent and Ann Putnam Jr. (with a very small sample) inconsistent, as is Elizabeth Hubbard with a larger sample.[141] Individual scholars will have to decide what, if anything, to make of this.

The analysis of hands also helps in dating events. For example, witnesses were summoned to testify at a grand jury hearing on September 6 on indictments against Sarah Cloyce. A grand jury definitely heard her case in January 1693 for indictments that had been drawn the previous September. If a grand jury began but did not conclude her case in September, she would not have been the only person with a case beginning in September and not concluded until January. Much speculation has appeared as to her fate in view of the execution of her two sisters, Mary Esty and Rebecca Nurse, with one common theme being that she must have escaped and been in hiding or else she would have been tried in September. However, others who came before the Court of Oyer and Terminer in September also came before the Superior Court of Judicature in January. In the case of William Procter, two indictments were returned ignoramus in September, but he faced a third indictment in January with the same result. Rebecca Jacobs, Margaret Jacobs, Sarah Buckley, Mary Whittridge, and Job Tookey were in that order the first five tried in January based on the September true bills. These cases do not specifically create new information about Sarah Cloyce, but they do put her case in a clearer context, and of course they tell us about the history of other cases carried from 1692 to 1693. Scholars have been able to tell from other evidence that a grand jury heard the case of Sarah Cloyce in 1693. What they could not tell was the fact that other cases addressed in 1693 had been part of cases that had begun in September 1692, as Sarah Cloyce's may have. It was through comparisons of handwriting on the indictments that we were able to determine whether documents in these cases were written, including docket information, in 1692 or 1693 or both, since we were able to identify the hands of the recorders who constructed and added to the documents in September 1692 and January 1693. That Sarah Cloyce might have escaped in September remains a possibility, but handwriting analysis on documents now makes it clear that the most likely explanation is that, as with others, her case was simply carried over from 1692 to 1693.[142] Still in the realm of "best guess" is why these cases started in September were held over to January. The most likely reason is that the Court, under attack, and flooded with accused, was simply overwhelmed, but others may have better guesses.

A puzzle of wider interest has been the matter of what happened to a summary of the trial records of 1692 that was probably prepared, as was one for 1693.[143] No answer to this has conclusively emerged. However, although some scholars have suspected it, now it is clear that trial documents are part of all of the editions that have been published. The difficulty has been to know that, and once knowing it, to be able to identify which documents were used at the trials. That problem has been solved except for a very few anomalies. Documents used at trials are identified as such in the edition. Indictments with true bills, by definition used at trials, are not identified specifically as trial documents, since this would be redundant. The identification of documents at the trials offers important insights into what constituted good trial evidence. Scholars will get different clues to this by examining the contents of documents not used at trials, even in cases where they were used by grand juries. The legal authorities were meticulous as to what they regarded as good trial evidence.

A central goal in creating this edition has been to give a reliable chronology of all the known documents, something never yet provided in print. This chronology is presented with varying degrees of confidence, the reader always alerted to the extent of that confidence.

---

[141] Mercy Lewis used signatures, and she may have been literate. There is not a large enough sample of her signatures to determine whether the extant ones that appear are authentically hers.

[142] For Sarah Cloyce in popular culture, perhaps the best known is the fictional PBS presentation, *Three Sovereigns for Sarah: A True Story*, first aired May 27, 1985. In 1867 Upham was probably the first to raise the question of the puzzle as to her fate, II, p. 326.

[143] On the requirement for keeping such records see Powers, p. 437. For more discussion on this issue, see Trask, "Legal Procedures." Peleg Whitman Chandler refers to a copy of the Record Book that has been "lost or misplaced." *American Criminal Trials.* 2 vols. (Boston and London, 1841), Vol. I, p. 426. For internal manuscript evidence of a Record Book, see note to Document 875.

Overwhelmingly, the dating selected is safe, sometimes to the day, sometimes within a day or two. The establishment of the chronology in this edition will of course be scrutinized by scholars, and inevitably there will be differences of opinion. However, key tools for that scrutiny are in the edition and will be valuable whether one agrees or disagrees with some of the decisions made about the chronology. Moreover, the records can be assessed with the documents having been restored. That is, over the years various documents have been cut by archivists and separated, and the task of putting them back all together has sometimes been complex. But they have been returned to their original forms, and assumptions made from the documents no longer depend on scrutiny of partial records. One example of this concerns what is called in the edition the *Andover Examinations Copy*. Probably in 1692 a copy of all the Andover examinations was made from the original documents. Some of these original documents have been lost, but through reconstructing the *Andover Examinations Copy* it has been possible to fill in missing documents. Because of the need to do this we have made an exception for this collection and have broken it up chronologically. However, the person who wants to see it as a whole can do so by simply copying and pasting together the records from it as they appear chronologically in the edition.

Another important goal has been to create a resource for language scholars to study early American English, as addressed in the linguistic introduction. An early concern had been whether in doing so we would make the record less accessible to a general public interested in the subject but not familiar with seventeenth-century language usage. We were even concerned that some historians, although certainly able to read the original language, might prefer some modernization, as Boyer and Nissenbaum did in SWP. In search of opinions on this matter, two groups were surveyed. One consisted exclusively of historians and the other of people who subscribed to an e-mail listserve moderated by Margo Burns, the Salem Witch List at rootsweb.com. This is a discussion list where descendants of people in the Salem episode give and receive information about the Salem witch trials and people involved in them. Some in this group may be professional historians, but it largely appears to be a group more representative of non-professional historians who have a serious interest in the subject. The survey was not scientific, but served to give some impression of what might be preferred. The people on the list were sharply divided, roughly half and half,

over whether to retain the original language or whether to modernize. The historians were almost unanimous in wanting the transcriptions to follow seventeenth-century language forms, the one exception being a response that either way was fine. No attempt was made to ask language scholars, since their preference for the original was assumed. On the basis of this information, and on the basis of what the editors wanted, the decision was made to follow as closely as possible the seventeenth-century forms.

The documents in the edition are all titled, and each comes with notation carrying varying degrees of information. Some carry historical matter, some language matter, some carry both, and some carry only archive information. The content of the notation depends on what the context requires. Where known, the recorder is identified in the note, referencing the bracketed insertion of the "Hand" in the manuscript. When the recorder is not identified, changes of handwriting are still shown as, [Hand 1], [Hand 2], and so forth. If the document was used at trial, or a seal appears on the manuscript, the information is noted. All documents carry an identification number to help the reader find a given document, all of which are listed in a separate section by number and title. Deciding when to put information into a note has been a challenge. That is, an obscure word might appear in one document and then be repeated in various other documents. Should it be glossed each time? Or, when, for example, Thomas Putnam adds his variation of "I believe in my heart," should this be noted each time? Such repetition in a note can become tedious for the person reading it from beginning to end – an ideal way to get a full sense of what happened. However, another person may approach the book specifically for one piece of reference information, and if, to stay with the Putnam example, the notation is not made every time, then it might be completely missed. Or seeing it only once, and not having read the General Introduction, the reader will be confused. The resolution of this issue, far from a perfect one, has been simply to use editorial judgment. Depending on the document, a decision has been reached each time whether to repeat information, to add new information, or to conclude that the document can stand on its own without a language or historical gloss. The hope is that this will generally work, but the reader puzzled by a document should check related documents to see whether a gloss is found in those, often in a document coming shortly before or after the one without a gloss.

The location of the manuscript, or the published source of the record, will be cited in the note. Together, these documents, whether from manuscripts or records from previously published sources, have been brought together in *Records of the Salem Witch-Hunt*, so that researchers will now have a central source for all of the known published ones, and some obscurely published ones that simply had not shown up in studies about the trials. Manuscripts never published before appear in the edition, and a few manuscripts published in SWP have been questioned as to whether they apply to the Salem witch trials and have been placed in an Appendix. As to the bulk of the records, those presented from the manuscripts, the examination of them has revealed some previously "original" documents to be copies – in addition to those already known as copies – and some published parts to be notations by later archivists. Where they add useful information some copies of manuscripts have been included, with other copies referenced as to their location. Above all, in regard to the manuscripts, the reader will have a collection of legal documents that has undergone a process of meticulous checking for accuracy. Every manuscript published here has been transcribed and checked by a minimum of four editors each, and some by six or more. Where differences of opinion or problems to be solved have occurred, the document at issue has been called to the attention of others involved in transcribing, and discussions have been held to resolve these matters. Such discussions have been of, to give a few examples, how to read a particular number, a letter formation that left immediately unclear how the word should be transcribed, and even whether a mark on a manuscript was punctuation or incidental.[144] The great majority of manuscripts were physically examined, with all the manuscripts being examined from images. In all cases where the image suggested a problem, one or more of the editors visited the archive to make a special inspection of the manuscript. If we have succeeded, what follows is a reliable record of legal documents of the Salem witch trials, arranged chronologically, accompanied by notes on history and language where appropriate, and as meticulously checked as we could. In a better world we could promise no errors.[145]

[144] Particularly valuable in general and for numbers specifically has been Samuel A. Tannenbaum, *The Handwriting of the Renaissance* (New York: Columbia University Press, 1930). Although Tannenbaum focuses on the Renaissance, his insights helped clarify a number of significant issues.

[145] See Editorial Principles.

THE EDITORS

The flow of information, and the collaboration among the editors, in creating this book has been varied and complex, so to identify the role of each one risks misunderstanding the various ways in which the editors contributed. With that caveat, some aspects of the roles of each may be described briefly.

Although Gretchen Adams, Margo Burns, and I made transcriptions of various documents, the primary transcribers were Peter Grund, Risto Hiltunen, Leena Kahlas-Tarkka, Merja Kytö, Matti Peikola, and Matti Rissanen. The six people under the coordination of Merja Kytö addressed most of the language issues. Historical notes are primarily mine although during the period when most of them were constructed Margo Burns provided key images and web resources, as well as her own insights, to help shape many of them. Also contributing to the construction of the notes, particularly those addressing the month from March through August 1692, was Richard Trask. Other contributions to the notes of various kinds came from Marilynne K. Roach and the other editors, with Gretchen Adams intensively reviewing them all. Marilynne K. Roach also contributed to the sorting out of identities for the Concordance of Names.

Benjamin Ray created the initial set of digital images of the legal records as part of the NEH supported websites "Salem Witch Trials Documentary Archive and Transcription Project" for the transcribers to work with. These were mostly digitized microfilm images but also many original color scans, in cases where no microfilm images existed. He has also had prime responsibility for providing accurate citations for the documents at the various archives where they are currently held. Subsequently, Margo Burns provided numerous additional color images of manuscripts that were circulated digitally to all the editors. She created a website through which all information relevant to the edition flowed and was responsible for reproducing previously published transcriptions. In creating key images from manuscripts and arranging them for analysis, she and the whole editorial team were able to reach conclusions that would otherwise have not been made. The editors made various trips to the archives, and inspected most of the manuscripts, as well as all of the images.

The creation of the chronology has been the primary responsibility of Richard Trask and me, with Margo Burns contributing significantly to it. Trask has also intensively examined manuscripts, and although not active in transcribing them for this edition, has engaged in issues related generally to transcription matters. His discoveries of several manuscripts and previously published transcriptions that generally remained unknown were published in his *The Devil Hath Been Raised* and are printed in this edition from the sources where he found them. Gretchen Adams has checked for the earliest publication of manuscripts material, and these sources have been used in the edition, except for Thomas Hutchinson's *History of the Colony and Province of Massachusetts-Bay*. Margo Burns has been responsible for creating the technological framework and for bringing the disparate parts of the book into orderly form. She also had a primary role in designing the organization of the book. The overall coordination of the edition and the making of final decisions have been my responsibility.

III. LEGAL PROCEDURES USED DURING THE SALEM WITCH TRIALS AND A BRIEF HISTORY OF THE PUBLISHED VERSIONS OF THE RECORDS

RICHARD B. TRASK

The story of the 1692 Salem Village witchcraft outbreak is a fairly minor, though well-recorded, topic in world history. Its popular fascination continues to be out of proportion to its relative historical importance and remains the subject of innumerable scholarly as well as popular books and articles.

Unlike most of the previous witchcraft cases in old and New England, a significant number of the legal papers of the 1692/93 Massachusetts proceedings have survived. Today, preserved within judicial archives and various manuscript repositories, are around 950 of these legal and court papers representing more than 140 individually named witchcraft cases. Included among these documents are complaints, warrants and returns, mittimuses, depositions, preliminary examinations, indictments, summonses, recognizances, petitions, letters, and confessions. The Salem witchcraft cases have always afforded researchers a fairly extensive accumulation of primary source documents representing a diversity of people, yet combined into a body of knowledge that is manageable enough to be examined by authors and historians in microcosm. In popular culture the topic also possesses both the mysterious quality of the occult and a "Who dunnit?" mystique, factors that have combined to keep Salem witchcraft an active subject of popular history and university presses.

Many of these researchers into the Salem witchcraft events have, however, relied heavily upon printed transcripts of the original documents replicated in seventeenth-century writings of Cotton Mather, Robert Calef, and John Hale, as well as later transcriptions of the documents produced during the eighteenth, nineteenth, and twentieth centuries. Unfortunately such a reliance upon gathered transcripts, with their various inherent transcription weaknesses, including misread words, deletion of words and lines of text and other similar mistakes creeping

into the transcripts, has resulted in minor and even major mistakes becoming accepted as part of the traditional body of facts. It was the realization of this imprecision of previous transcription projects and the complexity of creating a new, more accurate edition that led this new work's editor-in-chief Bernard Rosenthal to ask others to join him as Associate Editors to create a new, more accurate and comprehensive edition. The project has required retranscribing all extant manuscripts.

Concurrently, we have also searched for previously unidentified witchcraft legal records awaiting discovery in traditional library and archive sources or from within private collections. As a result of this new project and contributed searching by its editors, more than thirty documents or portions thereof previously unknown, or not previously published in full transcription projects, have come to light and been made part of this new edition. We also determined to include transcriptions of original documents, now lost save for their being reprinted in earlier published sources, and also to augment this body of legal documents with a finite number of 1692 contemporary descriptions reflecting specifically on the legal process of the cases. Included in this category of documentation are such sources as the 1692 published description of the examinations of Martha Cory and Rebecca Nurse as recorded by Rev. Deodat Lawson in his short but important tract, *A Brief and True Narrative of Some Remarkable Passages Relating to Sundry Persons Afflicted by Witchcraft, at Salem Village*.

LEGAL PROCEDURES – PRELIMINARY EXAMINATIONS

In order to understand the documents and their context best, one must be aware of the judicial procedures followed by the Puritans of late seventeenth-century Massachusetts. The Massachusetts legal system generally followed a procedural pattern used by its English counterparts in the mother country. If brought as far as to a jury trial, an accused person would of necessity go through three distinct legal processes. During any of these three legal steps new documents could be introduced into the case. Following arrest, the accused would go through the first step, being a preliminary hearing. If not released, but rather held for further legal action, the accused would at some point be brought before a grand jury that would determine whether the charge warranted a trial. If the grand jury thought it did, a "true bill" would be returned and the third process, arraignment and a jury trial, would ensue. During each one of these procedures evidence would be produced in written form, such evidence possibly incorporated with new evidence generated during the next step of legal action.

When there was suspicion of a crime, or when an adult wanted to report illegal activities to the authorities for potential legal action (in this case a suspicion of witchcraft being practiced), the informant would make a formal accusation before a local justice of the peace, more commonly referred to as a "magistrate." The informant could make the accusation on behalf of another, as for example in many Salem cases when an under-age child was an apparent victim of another's witchcraft. Upon a formal complaint being made to a magistrate, that official would issue a warrant requiring the county sheriff or a local constable to bring the accused before authority at a specific date and place and there to be examined relating to the accusation. Normally, bond would be posted by the person making the complaint as surety that he would follow through on it. For whatever reason, this procedure was not followed in the early stages of the 1692 witchcraft cases.

Upon serving the warrant, the officer would physically bring the accused before the magistrate. He would subsequently note in writing a "return" on the warrant indicating its successful (or unsuccessful) execution. An examination, the first of three potential legal steps, would be conducted by one or more magistrates. Their task was to determine whether the accusation had any true substance. If in the opinion of the magistrates there was enough information gathered from the accused and/or from others present as having witnessed illegal activity, the accused could be held for trial before the appropriate court. At the county level was the Quarterly Court with an internal grand jury system

of its own that could try both civil and criminal cases, except in those cases where punishment could be for life, limb, or banishment. The Court of Assistants would hear capital cases or cases referred on appeal from the county courts.

The typical witchcraft warrant issued by a magistrate in 1692 would state the name of one or more male adults who swore to the complaint, along with the names of the persons who claimed that the accused practiced witchcraft upon them. The first of the Salem witchcraft apprehension warrants were issued on leap-year day, February 29, 1692, under signatures of local Justices of the Peace John Hathorne and Jonathan Corwin. Three Salem Village residents, Sarah Osburn, Sarah Good, and Tituba, were seized and brought to Nathaniel Ingersoll's Ordinary for a March 1, 1692, examination by the two Salem magistrates. News of the examinations, as well as a previously scheduled earlier morning village meeting, ensured a large public presence for this very unusual and exciting local event. The crowd of spectators was so large that the place of examination was changed to the more spacious Salem Village Meeting House, located just a short distance down Meeting House Lane from Ingersoll's Ordinary.

The examination procedure followed with these and with subsequent suspected witches took on a similar form when conducted in public places. Though some examinations would eventually be conducted in jail, they were often follow-up examinations after earlier public questioning of a suspect. Eventually many towns in Essex, Middlesex, and Suffolk Counties produced witch suspects. The examinations, no matter the town of origin, usually were within the geographical boundaries of Salem, the shire town of Essex County. Several examinations, both early and late in the chronology of the witchcraft events, took place in Ipswich and elsewhere, but these non-Salem locations were the exceptions. Most of the examinations conducted during the first several months of the perceived witchcraft outbreak took place at Ingersoll's Ordinary or at the Salem Village Meeting House (both located on what is now Hobart Street in Danvers), within the Salem Village Parish of Salem town. Later both the Salem Meeting House (the site located on present-day Washington Street in Salem) and the Thomas Beadle Tavern (the site located on present-day Essex Street in Salem) were also scenes of witchcraft examinations. In the seventeenth century, ordinaries (public places where people could purchase food and drink), taverns (places where people could sleep over, as well as obtain nourishment), and meeting houses (places where religious and civic meetings were conducted) were public spaces used for all manner of local gatherings.

As to the physical setup of the preliminary hearings, it appears that the magistrates would position themselves in seats before a table and face the accused, witnesses, and spectators. Meeting houses generally had as part of their furnishings a long joined table used for church communion and civic meetings. Such a table could well serve the use of the magistrates. Several references indicate that the accusing persons sat in the front facing the magistrate's table. In a meeting house, the accused would stand within one of the front rectangular, waist-high, wooden-walled pews, the pew rail around the top serving as the bar before which the accused stood. Witnesses and curious spectators would sit in pews or on stairs, or stand in the alleys, with any overflow crowd viewing from outside through window openings.

Nathaniel Cary, husband of Elizabeth Cary, who was accused of witchcraft, gave a graphic account of the abuse his wife suffered. A portion of his account spoke of the physical layout during an examination he witnessed at the Salem Village Meeting House on May 24, 1692. "The Prisoners were called in one by one, and as they came in were cried out of, &c. The Prisoner was placed about 7 or 8 foot from the Justices, and the Accusers between the Justices and them; the Prisoner was ordered to stand right before the Justices, with an Officer appointed to hold each hand. . . ."[1] At most public examinations, the proceedings usually began with prayer by a minister, followed by a reading of the warrant and the accused being asked to answer the charge.

At least two magistrates were always present to question the accused. If it was believed that other adults had information pertinent to the accusations, a magistrate might have previously issued a summons instructing a constable to have such witnesses appear before them to give such testimony. Though testimony at these preliminary hearings could be given orally, there is much evidence that depositions would be drawn up prior to the examination. And if the accused went to trial, the majority of evidences heard at trial would be in written form. This preference for written evidence dates back in Massachusetts to 1650 when, because of the inconvenience of the court recording voluminous oral testimony, the quarterly courts declared that henceforth all testimony was to be given in writing and that it would be attested in court if the witness lived within ten miles of it, or before a magistrate if the witness lived at a greater distance. And though this procedure refers to Quarterly Court cases, there is evidence that it was also followed in preliminary hearings.[2]

DEPOSITIONS AND EXAMINATIONS

Depositions, also referred to as "testimonies" or "statements," were a familiar class of legal documentation in which one or more people gave personal evidence that reflected upon someone, usually an accused person.[3] The quality of depositions ran the gamut from valid, eyewitness testimony to second-hand rumors, hearsay testimony, and fits of fancy. In every settlement there were at least several men who could write clear, readable English, and as a favor or for a fee would write up for their neighbors such legal documents as wills, promissory notes, deeds, and depositions. Thomas Putnam (1652–1699) was a prominent yeoman in Salem Village who had served in King Philips's War. For many years as the parish clerk, he had written up the records of transactions of Salem Village, as well as performed other writing chores for his neighbors. Thomas Putnam was the eldest son of one of the most prominent patriarchs in the village and, along with his wife Ann (Carr), was an original 1689 covenant member of the Church of Christ at Salem Village. Among the earliest accusers in 1692 were Putnam's twelve-year-old daughter Ann Jr. and his wife, who both claimed to be afflicted by witches. They both also testified in numerous cases as accusations spread, although Ann Jr. accused far more frequently. Examination of the handwriting of the witchcraft legal documents reveals that Thomas Putnam wrote out a large number of depositions of numerous accusers and other supporting witnesses. These documents were used as evidence at examinations, at grand juries (often called juries of inquest), and during the trials themselves. Thomas Putnam's household was in the very thick of the events, not only as claimed victims of witchcraft, but with Thomas himself at the least being a complainant against thirty-five persons and giving testimony against seventeen accused. And at the same time he was recording, even fashioning, a good amount of the evidences presented.

---

[1] Robert Calef, *More Wonders of the Invisible World* (London, 1700), p. 96. No. 203.

[2] *Records and Files of the Quarterly Courts of Essex County* (Salem, MA, 1911), v. I, p. vi.

[3] For other discussion on depositions and examinations, see Linguistic Introduction.

By a close inspection of many of these depositions, one can notice changes in color of ink, the varying pressure and amount of the ink applied to the paper by quill pens, and obvious additions or deletions of words. Through such painstaking scrutiny it becomes clear that many of these depositions were not created at one sitting. Rather, the text was often added to at a later time with additional information written into a deposition as a continuation of the text following its initial creation. Sometimes a deposition is added to reflecting occurrences at the accused's preliminary examination, whereas at other times material is added prior to a grand jury hearing or trial.

Several very obvious examples should suffice. On May 9, 1692, a presently unidentified person wrote down the testimony of one of the accusers, Elizabeth Hubbard, concerning George Burroughs, whose spectre she claimed had appeared to her. This handwritten testimony was read that same day during Burroughs's examination. Rev. Samuel Parris (1653–1720), the minister at Salem Village who was requested to record the Burroughs examination, notes that Hubbard and other of the "afflicted" girls' ". . . Testimony going to be read & they all fell into fits." After the examination was concluded Thomas Putnam took this original deposition and beginning where the previous text left off, he added a description of what transpired at the hearing beginning: ". . . also on the: 9th may 1692 being the time of his Examination Mr. George Burroughs or his Apperance did most greviously afflect. . . ." Further notes on the bottom of the testimony show that this same document was introduced for use at the grand jury inquest of August 3, 1692, and was sworn to for use during Burroughs's trial on August 5, 1692.[4]

Another clear example of text being added is seen in the deposition of Mercy Lewis (a servant in the Thomas Putnam house) recorded in the handwriting of Thomas Putnam on May 10 or early May 11, 1692, relating to the apparition of George Jacobs Sr. hurting Lewis. At Jacobs's examination before magistrates on May 11, Rev. Parris, again being asked to take down testimony, records: "Mercy Lewes testimony read." This reference is undoubtedly to the deposition written by Putnam. Then following the Jacobs examination, during which Jacobs's spectre continued to hurt the girls, this same Lewis deposition used at the examination is expanded with new text added by Thomas Putnam. Putnam picks up exactly where the previous text left off, the ink color and thickness changing, while the chronology of events recorded continues into events during the examination itself. The new added text by Thomas Putnam begins at the tail end of the original last sentence at a semicolon to read ": also on the 11th may 1692 being the day of the Examination of George Jacobs then I saw that it was that very man. . . ." As is the case for many depositions, this same document was later also presented at Jacobs's grand jury inquest, as noted at the bottom of the deposition in someone else's hand. The names of two other accusers, Mary Walcott and Elizabeth Hubbard, present in the added-to deposition of May 11 are now scratched out in the text body, in an apparent cleaning up of the deposition to use it solely as a Mercy Lewis statement.[5]

Yet another example of clearly added text by Thomas Putnam is seen by examining the original deposition of Mary Walcott v. John Willard following his May 18 examination. In this case, however, Walcott's testimony is not mentioned in the examination record itself.[6] Thus depositions were not necessarily documents generated at one time, but rather could be drawn up before an examination, expanded upon after the examination, corrected or altered to be useful at other legal proceedings, and sometimes read for use at a grand jury session and/or at an eventual trial.

The surviving witchcraft legal papers, though extensive, are far from complete. Even the most cursory perusal of the approximately 950 extant records will quickly show significant gaps in which now missing documents can be presumed to have been originally produced and used. It appears, for example, that every accused person when brought before local magistrates for examination should have had his or her examination recorded on paper in some form. Though many of these examinations do survive, there are significant gaps. At least fifty-eight named cases remain where no examination is extant, though other documentation indicates examinations were, in fact, held. Documents in other categories, including complaints, warrants, depositions, and indictments, are also known to be missing, as references to them in other documentation point to their original existence.

Some of these documents may still be awaiting discovery, either in private, unknowing hands or buried away in institutions and not yet uncovered. While this edition was in its research phase, three of the editors, as well as several colleagues, uncovered a number of documents in various locations. Also, the first witchcraft documents offered on

---

[4] No. 120; No. 122.   [5] No. 133; No. 134.   [6] No. 180.

the open market in many years became available, being a deposition and an indictment concerning Margaret Scott. The documents were offered for well over $100,000, indicating the high monetary value of these and other yet undiscovered documents.[7]

Though a good portion of the extant witchcraft legal records are made up of repetitive, formulaic warrants and indictments, the most revealing are those represented by depositions and examinations. Depositions make up about 400 of the documents, close to half of the surviving 1692 legal papers. They are rich in folk detail and give us a sampling of speech patterns and pronunciations, together with the concerns, mentionings of everyday objects, and the lifestyle of the seventeenth-century common person.[8] The preliminary examinations are also rich for historical and linguistic study. These hearings include about 100 surviving manuscripts. The editors of this new transcription edition are fortunate to be able to add to this group of examinations, in addition to other new finds, five more that we located in recent years. These examinations are of Giles Cory held on April 18, 1692 (this examination only surviving as an 1823 transcription of the original written by Rev. Samuel Parris); Ann Dolliver held on June 6, 1692 (the original document written by Simon Willard); Mary Ireson held on June 6, 1692 (the original document written by Simon Willard); Daniel Eames held on August 13, 1692 (the original document written by John Higginson Jr.); and Margaret Prince held on September 5, 1692 (a 1936 published facsimile copy of the original document written by Simon Willard).[9]

Examinations are particularly interesting and worthy of careful comparison when two or more versions of the same hearing were recorded. At the March 1, 1692, examinations of Tituba, Sarah Good, and Sarah Osburn, no fewer than four men took down testimony – Ezekiel Cheever, Jonathan Corwin, John Hathorne, and Joseph Putnam. The event was so unusual and important that several records were made of it. The Bridget Bishop examination of April 19, 1692, likewise comes down to us in versions taken down by both Rev. Samuel Parris and Ezekiel Cheever. Such transcripts give us an opportunity

to compare what recorders believed to be important to note and how close direct testimony quotations compare to one another when recorded by more than one person.

Rev. Samuel Parris took down a large portion of the earliest hearing examinations. Parris's choice by the magistrates to serve as recorder was probably obvious to them. He was the titular spiritual leader in the village where the earliest examinations took place, one familiar with the local people involved, and wrote with a very clear, readable hand. It apparently was not problematic to the magistrates or others that members of Parris's family were sufferers of the invisible world, that he himself gave depositions against some of the accused, or that his own slave was one of the suspected witches.

Besides Rev. Parris, several other men were requested to take down testimony at witchcraft examinations during the ensuing months. Hearings continued from March 1 until the end of September 1692. Captain Simon Willard (1649–1731), a Salem weaver and clothier who in the early 1690s had served as a Salem constable, recorded a number of examinations. He was brother of Rev. Samuel Willard, who had experienced a witchcraft case firsthand as a young minister at Groton, Massachusetts, and who by 1692 was minister at the South Meeting House in Boston and sympathetic to many of the accused. Salem merchants William Murray (b. 1656) and John Higginson Jr. (1646–1720) were also called upon to write down examinations. Higginson was son of the pioneer Salem minister Rev. John Higginson and was also a justice of the peace, and as such also participated in the questioning of accused during a number of examinations.

A researcher utilizing any of these seventeenth-century primary source examinations must understand that in reading them we see events through the eyes, writing style, and prejudice of the original recorder, whose perception of the reality of that time may not be reality itself. Typically the men who wrote these examinations were not neutral court officers, but rather persons deeply concerned with and involved in the Puritan community. They jotted down what they believed to be significant, and given the slowness of writing with pen and ink, the best of them could not capture all the words and actions taking place around them. Rev. Samuel Parris was a fervent believer in the reality of a witch attack on Salem Village, although even with his built-in biases, he felt an obligation as a recorder and undoubtedly attempted to do this duty well. At the end of a May 2, 1692, transcript made

---

[7] Through the courtesy of the current owner, transcripts were made from facsimiles provided to us of these two Scott-related documents and included within this volume: No. 471 and No. 641.

[8] For additional material on speech paterns and pronunciation, see the Linguistic Introduction.

[9] No. 65, No. 309, No. 310, No. 509, No. 545.

during the examination of an accused person, Parris notes, "This is a true account of the Examination of Dorcas Hoar without wrong to any party according to my original from Characters at the moments thereof."[10]

As a recorder Parris appears to have made quick, real-time notations during the examinations, later recopied to present a more accurate and physically tidy record. His reference to "my original, from characters at the moments thereof" appears to refer to his original draft. Some have speculated that Parris took examination notes using a form of shorthand.[11] Indeed a sampling of his shorthand survives on the reverse of the May 9, 1692, examination of George Burroughs, these shorthand notations referring to a Bible text and apparently having no relationship to the examination. No extant example exists, however, of his using shorthand relative to the witchcraft legal records, and it could be that his reference to "characters" simply means draft handwritten material. This indication is somewhat strengthened when one notes that two surviving examinations, those of Susannah Martin on May 2, 1692, and of John Willard on May 18, 1692, include two copies each, both written by Parris. In each case one copy appears to be an early version and the second copy a later, revised version. Though the content is essentially the same, in the revised version Parris's handwriting appears more carefully transcribed, and occasionally a few words are added to explain better the meaning from that of the earlier draft. In both surviving cases the second text appears to be a slight revision, rather than simply an additional copy. Of the two copies of the Willard examination, the one that appears as a revised draft, No. 174, includes Parris' notation about his attempting to be accurate, whereas what seems to be the first draft, No. 173, has no such note.[12]

THE COURT OF OYER AND TERMINER

Because of the severe, secret, and potentially decimating crime of witchcraft being apparently perpetrated in 1692 Massachusetts, many of the accused people were transferred from local lock-ups to more substantial jails in Charlestown and Boston. Various mittimuses were issued for these transfers, they being a formal writ transferring a prisoner from one court or legal jurisdiction to another.

In May 1692, a new royal governor appointed by King William and Queen Mary arrived in Massachusetts with a new governmental charter. What Sir William Phips found was a judicial and public order crisis in which scores of people accused as witches were languishing in overcrowded jails. The new governor was advised by several influential persons to speedily establish a special court to handle the judicial backlog, even before the accession of a new General Court. On May 27 a Special Commission of Oyer and Terminer was promulgated "in council" by Phips with authority to "hear and determine" the ever-growing number of cases of persons held under suspicion of practicing witchcraft.[13] The court was to act "according to the Law, & Custom of England, and of this their Maj[ties] Province."[14] The judge-commissioners appointed by Phips were headed by newly appointed Lieutenant-Governor William Stoughton and included eight other prominent men in government and commerce. Five justices would constitute a quorum to hear cases. As was typical throughout the English colonies and in the mother country itself, trial judges were seldom lawyers or students of the law, though from experience within multiple offices of government all the newly appointed judges possessed political and practical experience. Most of the appointed commissioners who were local magistrates or served on the Court of Assistants had experience in hearing and judging all manner of civil and criminal cases. It would be their duty to see to it that all sides of a case were given an appropriate and fair hearing.[15]

The only lawyer generally present at a colonial trial was the Crown's attorney general. His job was to bring accused persons through the grand jury process, and if bills of indictments were approved, to prosecute those persons at the resulting trial. Thomas Newton (1660–1721) was appointed attorney general and began serving on May 27. Newton prosecuted all Oyer and Terminer cases, beginning June 2, and served in this capacity from June 2 until after the July 1692 trials, with Anthony Checkley approved by the Governor's Council on July 26 as Newton's replacement. Captain Stephen Sewall (1657–1725), a merchant of Salem and younger brother of Commissioner Samuel

---

[10] No. 102. Parris repeats this statement at the end of the May 18 examination of John Willard, No. 174.

[11] For a different view on the issue of "characters" and "shorthand," see the Linguistic Introduction. No. 174.

[12] No. 120; No. 104; No. 105; No. 173; No. 174.

[13] For the court having a broader mandate, see General Introduction.

[14] No. 220.

[15] Chadwick Hansen, *Witchcraft at Salem* (New York: George Braziller, 1969), pp. 120–122; Peter Charles Hoffer, *The Devil's Disciples* (Baltimore: The Johns Hopkins University Press, 1996), pp. 135–139.

Sewall, was appointed "to officiate as Clerk of the Special Court," and as such he gathered all pre-trial records and would take in newly written evidence both for and against an accused, prove documents that were sworn in court for trial use, and docket and preserve the case records.[16] Sewall continued to keep custody of the previous examination and deposition papers, as well as those generated by the Court of Oyer and Terminer. A man of much practical, clerical experience, prior to 1692 Sewall had served as Clerk of Courts and Register of Deeds for Essex County. On July 21, 1692, he was additionally appointed Register of Probate for Essex County by Governor Phips.

The establishment of the special Court of Oyer and Terminer, with its associative grand jury considering indictments, did not preclude continued activity on the local level regarding witch accusations. During the entire grand and petty jury activity of the Court of Oyer and Terminer, various justices of the peace in their local places of jurisdiction continued to hear accusations, issue warrants, conduct examinations, and write and hear depositions relating to new cases brought before them. If evidence seemed significant enough, the jailed witch suspect was then a potential subject for the attorney general and proceedings at the Court of Oyer and Terminer.

INDICTMENTS

Prior to a jury trial before the Court of Oyer and Terminer, the proscribed procedures of a capital court case had to be followed. An indictment was drawn up by the government, written in a clerical/court hand with abbreviations and some formulative Latin legal phrases included. Many of the handwritten indictments used during the 1692 cases had boilerplate legalese previously written out, with blank spaces provided that would be filled in for a specific new case. Indictments naming specific persons and events were drawn up by the attorney general and then presented for the grand jury to consider. Unfortunately indictments relating to the 1692/93 witchcraft cases were not dated when drawn up, so that in determining when an indictment was actually acted upon by the grand jury, one must look to other evidence. A separate indictment was issued against an accused for each victim of his or her witchcraft. The language in the indictment often described the alleged victim as being "Tortured Afflicted Tormented Consumed Pined and wasted...."

Or the indictment might describe a class of crime, such as the accused making a "Diabolicall Covenant with the Devill."[17]

In many cases the attorney general included in the indictment a specific dated event, usually the accused's earlier preliminary hearing before local magistrates. By naming this event, one or more witnesses who had been present could testify to the accused's public use of witchcraft upon some of the "afflicted" during the examination itself. This testimony would seem to satisfy the "two witness" rule needed for proving witchcraft, often described as a secret crime. In the case of John Willard, in early June 1692 he had seven individual indictments drawn up against him, each naming a specific victim. These accusations all harkened back to his supposed display of witchcraft upon these women and girls during his May 18, 1692, examination.

THE GRAND JURY

On May 30, 1692, a precept went out under the signatures of William Stoughton and Samuel Sewall for calling men to serve on juries. An impaneled grand jury composed of eighteen men from various Essex County towns would be presented with evidence against those cases chosen by the attorney general. The evidence presented would be drawn from the body of previously written examinations and depositions, and also by means of oral testimony. This grand jury evidence was read with the deponent present to take an oath that the document presented was the truth. The oath was then noted at the bottom of each document as "Owned before the Grand Jury" or "the Jury (or Jurors) of Inquest," or "the Grand Inquest."

If the grand jury found the evidence presented to it to be tending to prove the crime, the jury foreman would so sign the indictment with a notation that read "Billa Vera," meaning a true bill of indictment had been issued. In some cases, while one indictment would be found compelling enough to go to trial, another indictment against the same person might be found wanting of enough proof for trial. Indictments rejected by the grand jury were typically marked at the bottom or on the reverse with the word "Ignoramus" (Latin for "we don't know"), meaning the jury was ignorant of the crime, and thus it was groundless to go to trial on this charge.

[16] *Witchcraft at Salem*, pp. 135–139.

[17] As per example, two indictments against Susannah Post: No. 774 and No. 775.

Members of the grand jury, meeting without the presence of judges, were more independent in weighing evidence than was the later trial jury. At these petty jury trials the judges exerted a strong influence. It also seems to be the sense of the surviving documents that those "afflicted" persons brought before the grand jury were more restrained in exhibiting their torments than at the trials themselves. A noted exception is found in the added testimony of Susannah Shelden, who was "seized with Sundry fits" while giving testimony before the grand jury against Sarah Good.[18] No indictment was issued naming Shelden, however, nor does her name appear among the list of witnesses to be heard at Good's trial. Throughout the Salem witch trials only two indictments named Shelden, and both were returned with an ignoramus. Grand juries were more discriminating than trial juries.

Some true bills of indictment were almost immediately acted upon, with a trial convened the same day that the indictment was handed down. In other instances, indictments could be withheld so that a trial was not scheduled for weeks or months, depending upon the timing of sessions of the Court of Oyer and Terminer or the strategy decided upon by the attorney general.

THE TRIALS

The Court of Oyer and Terminer met for its first session at the Salem Court House from June 2 to June 3, 1692. Session two lasted from June 28 to July 2, and session three took place from August 2 through August 5. The fourth session was the longest, dating between September 6 and 17 with a two-day break in the proceedings. The grand jury typically met concurrently at the beginning of each session, considering and acting on indictments that had been presented to it. Though scheduled for an October session, the Court of Oyer and Terminer fell that month under political pressure, with Governor Phips retracting the commission.[19]

When the attorney general had a true bill on an indictment and was ready to bring a case to trial, the accused would be "brought before the bar," arraigned, and as to the indictment would be asked to plead guilty or not guilty. If the plea was "not guilty," the person was then expected to agree to the formulaic declaration of being put upon

trial "by God and the Country." This declaration of innocence and willingness to be tried would then allow for the trial to commence. A notable exception to this standard practice was the action of Giles Cory of Salem Farmes. He had been arrested, examined, and jailed in April 1692. Subsequently the grand jury returned a true bill against him on September 9. At his arraignment, he is believed to have pled "not guilty" to the indictment, but would not declare a willingness to be tried before the special court. Cory's obstinate behavior led to his being subjected to *peine forte et dure*, the torture of stones placed upon his body in an attempt to get him to acquiesce to being tried by the authority of the court. Whether the torture was meant to get Cory to agree to trial or a de facto execution, the old man died under this torture, giving a silent though profound statement of his contempt for the justice of this "hanging" court. Many in authority saw this belligerence as a case of "self-murder" and ignored his point of protest.[20]

For the formal trial before the Court of Oyer and Terminer, a petty jury, also referred to as a trial jury or "jury of tryalls," was gathered from among a pool of men from area towns. Jurors could be questioned and challenged by the accused, with some jurors rejected for cause. An impaneled jury was composed of twelve men taken from an initial pool of forty-eight "honest and lawfull men" who had met the requirements of an estate worth 40 shillings per annum or a purchased estate worth at least £50. Rev. Deodat Lawson, a former Salem Village minister and witness to many of the events of 1692, wrote about this process of jury selection in a printed tract published in 1704. Concerning the trial of George Burroughs, Lawson noted that Burroughs "had the Liberty of Challenging his *Jurors*, before empannelling, according to the *Statute* in that case, and used his Liberty in Challenging many. . . ."[21]

Once the jury had been sworn in, the trial would commence. According to a September 1691 murder trial before the Court of Assistants held in Boston in

---

[18] No. 338.

[19] Mary Beth Norton, *In the Devil's Snare* (New York: Alfred A. Knopf, 2002), p. 289; Samuel Sewall, *Diary*, October 26 and 29, 1692.

[20] *Witchcraft at Salem*, pp. 153–154; *More Wonders*, p. 106; Richard B. Trask, *The Devil Hath Been Raised* (Danvers, MA: Yeoman Press; Revised Edition, 1997), p. 154; *Diary*, September 19, 1692.

[21] Bradley Chapin, *Criminal Justice in Colonial America, 1606–1660* (Athens, GA: The University of Georgia Press, 1983), p. 40; *The Devil's Disciples*, p. 156; Deodat Lawson, *Christ's Fidelity the Only Shield Against Satan's Malignity*. Second Edition. (London, 1704), p. 115. See also No. 232 and warrants for jurors in December 1692 for the 1693 trials, Nos. 532 and 730–740.

which ten Assistants, including Stoughton and several soon-to-be serving witchcraft judges, sat, the chronological procedures of the trial were succinctly described in the record book as, "The Indictment Examination & evidences were read & the prisoner made her defense, The Jury return their Verdict." The witchcraft cases were probably conducted similarly, with read testimony being the major quantity of the presentation.[22]

In a transcription of a letter historically ascribed as written in October 1692 by Boston merchant and scholar Thomas Brattle (1658–1713), Brattle wrote of the procedures used at the witchcraft trials. His letter was highly critical of the proofs and procedures used in the trials. Brattle writes,

1. The afflicted persons are brought into court; and after much patience and pains taken with them, do take their oaths, that the prisoner at the bar did afflict them: And here I think it very observable, that often, when the afflicted do mean and intend only the appearance and shape of such an one, (say G. Proctor), yet they positively swear that G. Proctor did afflict them; and they have been allowed so to do; as tho' there was no real difference between G. Proctor and the shape of G. Proctor....

2. The confessors do declare what they know of the said prisoner; and some of the confessors are allowed to give their oaths; a thing which I believe was never heard of in this world; that such as confess themselves to be witches, to have renounced God and Christ, and all that is sacred, should yet be allowed and ordered to swear by the name of the great God!...

3. Whoever can be an evidence against the prisoner at the bar is ordered to come into court; and here it scarce ever fails but that evidences, of one nature and another, are brought in, though, I think, all of them altogether alien to the matter of inditement; for they none of them do respect witchcraft upon the bodies of the afflicted, which is the alone matter of charge in the indictment.

4. They are searched by a Jury; and as to some of them, the Jury brought in, that [on] such or such a place there was a preternatural excrescence.[23]

One can possibly obtain a glimpse into the strategy used by the Crown's prosecutor in putting together his case

for trial by examining an undated document from among the Sarah Good case records. One of the first three women to be accused, Good was examined on March 1, 1692. True bills of indictment were handed down against her on June 28 and her trial apparently commenced the same day, continuing to June 29. An undated paper survives from among the Good court documents that includes on one side a listing of indictments against Good and witnesses for each indictment. On the opposite side are notes written in the handwriting identified as that of Attorney General Thomas Newton. Newton outlines abstract testimony by several confessed witches, as well as by afflicted persons, and other witnesses against Good. This document looks to be a summary of the case against Good written quite possibly prior to her trial.[24]

TYPES OF TRIAL EVIDENCE

Seventeenth-century English trials were not necessarily long, drawn-out events. In many instances a jury trial could be completed within an hour or so, depending upon the number of documents presented and whether the defendant had evidences as well. Those claiming to having been afflicted and other witnesses would give their oath that their written testimony was the truth. Some of their depositions had been drawn up months earlier, others written out or added to at the direction of the prosecutor to make them appropriate and specific to the case at hand. The oath was probably made after the document was read in court. Court Clerk Sewall would write on the deposition the words "Jurat in Curia," or in a few cases some variation of those words, usually at the bottom of the document. This notation indicated that the document was used in the trial. In the 1693 cases Jonathan Elatson, Clerk of the Superior Court of Judicature, made the same notation indicating trial usage.

One class of important evidence used in court for which there was not necessarily a previously drawn-up written record was the testimony of confessors who gave evidence specifically against the accused "viva voce," meaning by voice or in person. Another class of evidence within the legal records that survive is evidence not sworn to, but undoubtedly presented during the trial as being favorable to the accused. It appears that during most trials the accused did not present any formal defense. Though each

[22] *Records of the Court of Assistants of the Colony of Massachusetts Bay, 1630–1692* (Boston: Rockwell & Churchill Press, 1901), p. 357.

[23] "Copy of a MS. Letter...Written by Thomas Brattle, F.R.S. and communicated to the Society by Thomas Brattle, Esq. Of Cambridge." *Collections of the Massachusetts Historical Society* (Boston, 1798), pp. 66–67.

[24] No. 345. For another view on dating this document see note to No. 345.

defendant had the right to do so, the circumstances of the trial and the lack of legal advisors hindered any effective defense. Legal tradition also disallowed a defendant from swearing an oath of innocence or in other testimony for fear that a false oath would endanger one's soul. Those witnesses who presented exculpatory evidence and those who submitted petitions signed by family and neighbors speaking well of the defendant were also not allowed to swear to their testimony.[25]

At the pre-trial jury selection on August 5, 1692, defendant George Burroughs, a sometime minister, had challenged some of the jurors. Then at the trial itself Burroughs put up a defense. Rev. Cotton Mather (1663–1728) was author of the book *The Wonders of the Invisible World*, which was written in 1692 and had a publication date of 1693 for both the Boston and the later London edition. In this volume Mather synopsized five of the trials, including Burroughs's. According to Mather, Burroughs asked questions throughout the proceedings and presented a paper to the jury for its consideration. Apparently Burroughs obtained material from a supporter replicating some of the reasoning found in an anti-witchcraft volume by Thomas Ady, originally printed in London in 1656. Burroughs wrote out some of this information and presented it to the jury. Mather, whose loathing for Burroughs is apparent even at a distance of more than 300 years, reported of his defense: "This paper was Transcribed out of Ady; which the Court presently knew, as soon as they heard it. But he [Burroughs] said, he had taken none of it out of any Book; for which, his Evasion afterwards, was, That a Gentleman gave him the Discourse in a Manuscript, from whence he Transcribed it. The Jury brought him in *Guilty*: But when he came to Die, he utterly deni'd the Fact, whereof he had been thus convicted."[26]

The last in the line of legal documents generated during a witchcraft case that reached trial was the death warrant. Only two survive.[27] Once the verdict was given at trial and after the death sentence was pronounced, at least three days had to pass prior to execution. This brief time was built into the process to give an opportunity to the

condemned for a possible appeal. Though the governor gave Rebecca Nurse a reprieve, he subsequently withdrew it, and any attempts by others failed.[28] The Bridget Bishop death warrant issued on June 8, 1692, is perhaps the most famous and most reproduced of all the witchcraft documents. It was first published as a facsimile plate in Charles Upham's 1867 work *Salem Witchcraft*.[29] The Bishop death warrant and its return dated June 10, 1692, indicating that the punishment had been carried out by Sheriff George Corwin, was photographed by Salemite E. R. Perkins, an early photographic printing of a facsimile of a Salem witchcraft document. The other death warrant came to light in 1939 when it was purchased by the Boston Public Library along with other witchcraft documents. This warrant was issued against five people convicted of witchcraft including Rebecca Nurse, all "to be hanged by yᵉ Necks vntill they be dead," which sentence was carried out on July 19.[30] Both surviving warrants were ordered under the signature of William Stoughton.

Given the fact that a number of the legal records are obviously now missing, it is difficult to gauge the number of documents generated in a typical case. One clue to this, however, is found on the reverse of indictment "No. 1" against Rebecca Nurse. Court Clerk Stephen Sewall wrote on this indictment a copy of a memorandum he had given to a member of the Nurse family. The family member apparently inquired as to the trial records in Rebecca's case. Sewall attested:

In this Tryall are Twenty papers besides this Judgment & these were in this Tryall as well as other Tryalls of yᵉ Same Nature Seuerall Euidences viva voce which were not written & so I can giue no Copies of them Some ffor & Some against yᵉ parties Some of yᵉ Confessors did alsoe Mention this & other persons in their Seuerall declaracõns which being promised. & Considered yᵉ sd 20 papers herewith fild is yᵉ whole Tryall.[31]

[28] On Rebecca Nurse's reprieve, Calef, *More Wonders*, p. 103.
[29] Charles W. Upham, *Salem Witchcraft; With an Account of Salem Village, and a History of Opinions on Witchcraft and Kindred Subjects* (Boston: Wiggens and Lunt, 1867), v. II, opposite p. 266. Perhaps the earliest engraved facsimile of a witchcraft document is that reproduced in Peleg W. Chandler, *American Criminal Trials* (Boston, 1841), v. I, opposite p. 120.
[30] No. 418.
[31] No. 285. This number of documents as given by Sewall does not conform to the number of documents now extant. Of the body of Nurse legal papers there are fifteen indictments, summonses, and depositions used by the grand jury or at the trial, an additional six of which are petitions or depositions supporting Nurse, at least three depositions naming Nurse and another accused person

[25] *The Devil's Disciples*, p. 156.
[26] Quoted from the easier to obtain London edition. Cotton Mather, *The Wonders of the Invisible World: Being an Account of the Tryals of Several Witches, Lately Executed in New-England* (London, 1693) p. 65; Thomas Ady, *A Candle in the Dark* (London, 1656).
[27] No. 313; No. 418.

A MISSING RECORD BOOK?

The witchcraft case files include almost 950 legal documents, including those specifically noted by Clerk Stephen Sewall as having been sworn to in court. But what of a record of the trial proceedings themselves gathered into a single record book? There has always been speculation that such a journal or record existed. The Puritans were nothing if not careful record keepers. In the 1640s the General Court of Massachusetts ordered that "every judgement, with all evidence, bee recorded in a booke, to be kept to posterity."[32] Record books of the Court of Assistants and of the Quarterly Courts survive, while the more than thirty witchcraft trials held from January through May 1693 heard by the newly established Superior Court of Judicature are also extant in a record book. The first two courts mentioned include in their record books a synopsis of each trial and copies of pertinent trial documents.

The 1693 witchcraft trial record book is less inclusive and more formulaic than the other two. Each case records the names of the foreman and eleven other men consisting of the Jury of Tryalls and states that the accused was arraigned after having been indicted. Quotations are included of the salient indictment charge and the plea that was entered. It is often also recorded that the evidence and examination (earlier preliminary hearing) were heard, as well as any defense by the accused, though never giving any detail or actual testimony. Finally there is a record of the verdict and the disposition of the case. It is quite possible, even probable, that if a trial record book did exist for the Court of Oyer and Terminer, the information gleaned from it would not substantially add to the surviving records themselves, unless some testimony was also transcribed into the record book. It would certainly be interesting to view the write-up regarding Giles Cory's case. Cory stood mute to going to trial and was ordered tortured. It would also be instructive to read of the treatment of the Rebecca Nurse trial. When she was found not guilty by the jury, pandemonium broke out in the court and the bench then directed the jury that they perhaps should reconsider some testimony. The jury came back later with a guilty verdict.[33]

Nineteenth-century author Charles W. Upham, whose 1867 book *Salem Witchcraft* is today still an influential source of local Salem and witchcraft history, saw in a missing Salem witchcraft trials record book an attempt by contemporaries of the trials to obliterate memory of this shameful time. Upham wrote:

The effect produced upon the public mind, when it became convinced that the proceedings had been wrong, and innocent blood shed, was the universal disposition to bury the recollection of the whole transaction in silence, and if possible, oblivion. This led to a suppression and destruction of the ordinary materials of history. Papers were abstracted from the files, documents in private hands were committed to the flames, and a chasm left in the records of churches and public bodies. The journal of the Special Court of Oyer and Terminer is nowhere to be found.[34]

CONTEMPORARY PUBLISHED ACCOUNTS OF THE TRIALS

Besides the legal papers that do survive, we can glimpse a few tantalizing images of the trials themselves as recorded by contemporaries. Thomas Brattle in his October 1692 letter comments on Judge Stoughton's instructions to jurors: "I remember that when the chief Judge gave the first jury their charge, he told them, that they were not to mind whether the bodies of the said afflicted were really pined and consumed, as was expressed in the indictment; but whether the said afflicted did not suffer from the accused such afflictions as naturally *tended* to their being pined and consumed, wasted, etc. This, said he is a pining and consuming in the sense of the law."[35] Other peeks into the trial procedures are given by Deodat Lawson, as reproduced in a 1704 reprinting of a witchcraft sermon given by him in 1692 at Salem Village, and expanded with notes. Lawson mentions testimony at several trials including that of Burroughs, writing, "I was present when these things were Testified against him."[36]

Robert Calef, a vociferous critic of the proceedings and also of the Mathers, wrote *More Wonders of the Invisible World*, which was published in 1700. Although Calef has been accused of being a partisan and at times slanderous

---

in the same document, together with the March warrant and examination not included in this count as trial records.

[32] Edwin Powers, *Crime and Punishment in Early Massachusetts, 1620–1692: A Documentary History* (Boston: Beacon Press, 1966), p. 437.

[33] *More Wonders*, pp. 106, 102–103.

[34] *Salem Witchcraft*, II, p. 462. Upham seldom mentioned specific sources for his information, though it is known he locally gathered facts and oral traditions not now extant in any other form. For a further discussion of the Record Book issue see the General Introduction, p. 40.

[35] Brattle, p. 77.   [36] *Christ's Fidelity*, p. 115.

writer, and although he did not attend any of the witchcraft trials, he did provide valuable information, including several eyewitness accounts of the events. He also included in his volume several documents reflecting upon the legal proceedings not preserved elsewhere, as well as copies of indictments and mittimuses of several of the accused people.[37] Also preserved by Calef is a case of an apparent attempt at trickery perpetrated in the court during the trial of Sarah Good. One of the afflicted persons cried out in court that Good's "spectre" had stabbed her in the breast, and produced a piece of knife blade that she said had been broken in the stabbing attempt. A young man came forward from among the spectators to say that he had broken his knife the day before and had cast away the broken part, whereupon the broken piece produced in court by the afflicted person was compared with his broken knife blade and the court "saw it to be the same." According to Calef, the afflicted person's subterfuge was let to pass: "the young Man was dismissed, and she bidden by the Court not to tell lyes; and was improved after (as she had been before) to give Evidence against the Prisoner."[38]

Yet another legal document is preserved only in the writings of a contemporary observer. Rev. John Hale (1636–1700), as minister at Beverly, was intimately involved in the witchcraft proceedings. In 1697 he wrote a manuscript attempting to shed light upon the events of 1692. His book was published in 1702. Among the text in Hale's volume is a transcription of a confession written in prison by William Barker Sr. of Andover.[39]

Cotton Mather's Wonders

The first author who put to print what was purported to be an account of the Salem witchcraft trials, and to use the trial records in the telling, was Rev. Cotton Mather. By the fall of 1692 Mather had been strongly requested by Governor Phips and other officials to gather a history of the trials that would show favorably the intentions of the court and the true and dangerous presence of witchcraft in the country. Needing documentation for his text, Mather wrote to Clerk Stephen Sewall on September 20, 1692, just a few days before a group of eight convicted witches were to be executed. Apparently renewing an even earlier request, Mather asked that the clerk "would please

quickly perform what you kindly promised, of giving me a narrative of the evidences given in at the trials of half a dozen, or if you please a dozen, of the principal witches that have been condemned." Saying that, though he understood it would take Sewall time to comply, Mather offered that he was exposing himself in the defense of his friends and also mentioned how the governor desired this favor from Sewall. Mather requested that Sewall include a letter reiterating what he had verbally told Mather about "the awe which is upon the hearts of your juries," and some "observations about the confessors." The hangman's ropes hadn't as yet been retired and the interpretation of Salem witchcraft was beginning.[40]

As published, the London edition of *The Wonders of the Invisible World* contained a section of twenty-three pages reporting on the trials of five of the more notorious of the condemned – George Burroughs, Bridget Bishop, Susanna Martin, Elizabeth How, and Martha Carrier. Mather, never present at a Salem trial, undoubtedly relied upon a narration put together by Stephen Sewall and possibly also legal papers lent by Sewall to Mather. Mather's descriptions of the five witchcraft trials were not in the format of a focused account of each trial, but rather as a selection and paraphrasing of evidences. Some of the material published as part of the trial history was probably never used at the trial itself, but rather at the earlier examinations or during the grand jury inquests. In his recounting of the Susannah Martin trial of June 29, Mather includes eight questions by a magistrate and Martin's answer to them from her May 2, 1692, examination. The Mather transcription is not a verbatim transcript when compared to either of the two draft texts recorded by Rev. Parris, the original examination recorder. Rather, they are a "cleaned," easier to understand version.[41]

In describing the trial of Elizabeth How, Mather begins, "Elizabeth How pleading *Not Guilty* to the Indictment of Witchcrafts, then charged upon her; the Court, according to the usual Proceedings of the Courts in *England*, in such Cases, began with hearing the Depositions of several afflicted People." A comparison of Mather's four pages of text recounting the trial of How with the surviving How legal documents shows that Mather described depositions of seven people against

[37] *More Wonders*, pp. 95–100, 113–114 etc., 94.
[38] *More Wonders*, pp. 161–162.
[39] John Hale, *A Modest Enquiry Into the Nature of Witchcraft* (Boston, 1702), pp. 33–34. No. 527.

[40] Kenneth Silverman, comp., *Selected Letters of Cotton Mather* (Baton Rouge: Louisiana State University Press, 1971), pp. 43–45.
[41] *Wonders*, p. 71.

How, including one Martha Wood whose deposition is not now extant.[42] Contrary to the implication of Mather's text, not all these depositions were necessarily used during the How trial itself. Mather also mentioned testimony being given by persons claiming to have been afflicted, though the only specific deposition that comes down to us is one by Sarah Bibber. Possibly as many as four other accusers claiming affliction may have given written depositions, as they are listed as witnesses in the How case, though none of their depositions survive in the gathered records. Mather also recounted the "Confessions of several other (penitent) witches" given as testimony against How in this case.[43] The author completely ignores (given that he was aware of their existence) seven depositions by people who spoke in favor of How and her good character. This, the first published description of the Salem trials, actually was a melding of various documents used during all phases of the legal proceedings. It was an oversimplified and not totally accurate account of various trials without the nuances of describing the three-part legal procedures followed in capital cases.

Hutchinson's History

The next major use of original documents in describing the events of the 1692 witchcraft episode occurred during the third quarter of the eighteenth century. Thomas Hutchinson (1711–1780) was a Boston-born Harvard College graduate. Beginning his professional life as a merchant, Hutchinson turned to a political career that led to his becoming speaker of the Massachusetts House of Representatives, member of the governor's council, a judge of probate, and justice of common pleas in Suffolk County. In 1758 he was appointed lieutenant governor and in 1760 was made chief justice of the Superior Court, the major colonial judicial position, which he held concurrently with that of lieutenant governor. Possessing a large library and collecting papers about his native province, Hutchinson began a writing project in 1763 of a multi-volume history of the Colony and Province of Massachusetts. The first volume of his history was published in 1764, and by the summer of 1765 Hutchinson was about two-thirds into writing his second volume, beginning his text with the arrival of Governor Phips and the new provincial charter of 1692.

The early section of this second volume would include an account of the witchcraft events of 1692. Hutchinson with his unique combined office had, as one later observer would write, "opportunities of access to original papers such as no person now possesses."[44] Much of his research material, including original witchcraft documents, was kept by Hutchinson at his mansion house in Boston. Hutchinson's politics were decidedly pro-Crown, and during the Stamp Act Crisis of 1765 his fellow citizens were vehemently against the Crown's policies and its representatives. On August 26, 1765, a violent mob attacked Hutchinson's home, breaking in with axes and tearing up the mansion and its contents. His library, his in-progress manuscript history of Massachusetts, and his numerous historical papers, including the witchcraft documents, were thrown into the street and otherwise looted or destroyed. The next day a neighbor, Rev. John Eliot, retrieved a number of books and papers that had been strewn in the street by the mob, including most of Hutchinson's manuscript history. Amidst all his political tribulations and personal problems, Hutchinson was able to complete the second volume on the history of Massachusetts and had it printed in Boston in 1767.[45]

Among the material in this second volume dealing with the 1692 witchcraft episode were transcriptions of at least eleven legal documents, including the examinations on April 11, 1692, of Sarah Cloyce and Elizabeth Procter; Margaret Jacobs's recantation of her confession; and Sarah Carrier's confession of August 11, 1692. Of these documents, none survive as an original 1692 manuscript, save for an indictment against George Burroughs for afflicting Mary Walcott, which found its way eventually to the collections of the Massachusetts Historical Society. The others were probably destroyed or carried off the night of August 26, 1765. Yet even Hutchinson's 1767 printed history excludes some primary source text that can be found within his surviving manuscript draft of the book. In 1870 William Frederick Poole consulted the original manuscript kept at the Massachusetts State Archives.

---

[42] *Wonders*, pp. 76–79. Wood deposition: No. 394.
[43] *Wonders*, pp. 76–79.

[44] William Frederick Poole, "The Witchcraft Delusion of 1692. By Gov. Thomas Hutchinson. From an Unpublished Manuscript (An Early Draft of this History of Massachusetts) in the Massachusetts Archives," *New England Historical and Genealogical Register and Antiquarian Journal*, Vol. 24, No. 4 (October 1870), pp. 381–382.
[45] Lawrence Shaw Mayo, ed., *The History of the Colony and Province of Massachusetts Bay by Thomas Hutchinson* (Cambridge, MA: Harvard University Press, 1936), Vol. I, pp. xi–xv.

According to Poole, "I saw, on closer examination, that this was an earlier draft, and the identical manuscript which had passed the ordeal of the riot of 1765; for portions of it were much defaced, and bore the marks of being trampled in the mud." Poole discovered that much of the text had been "changed, abridged and sometimes omitted" in the published version, and that the earlier draft was most likely more accurate in the transcribing of original documents. Hutchinson "doubtless prepared it with the original authorities before him."[46]

Poole had this manuscript section of Hutchinson's history of the witchcraft delusion of 1692, including helpful notes inserted by Poole himself, printed within the *New England Historical and Genealogical Register* in October 1870. From a careful comparison of the 1767 printed text with the surviving manuscript draft by Hutchinson, fragments of original documents, some cut out for brevity and some just fragments of now unknown documents, survive in a more complete form in his draft manuscript. These additional texts relate to the examination of Mary Lacy Jr. and of Richard Carrier; testimony of Lacy Jr. and Sr. and Richard Carrier to the jury at the trial of George Burroughs; testimony of Deliverance Dane; and a fragment of the examination of Joan Penny. Unfortunately for history, even these documents reproduced in the draft manuscript were not complete. At a point in Hutchinson's transcribing the examination of Mary Lacey Jr., Hutchinson inserted the comment in his draft, "The examination contains many pages more of the same sort of proceedings which I am tired of transcribing."[47]

One other clump of witchcraft legal records preserved now only in print is one of the first groups of witchcraft documents reproduced in a local history volume. In 1840 Thomas Gage wrote *The History of Rowley*. In the volume he reproduced in transcript form what appeared to divide into six separate documents, all relating to the trial of Rowley resident Margaret Scott. Scott was arrested in early August 1692, convicted at trial in September and executed on September 22. The documents include two indictments against her and several depositions used at the grand jury and trial. Of original documents kept in various repositories, only two extant Scott documents had been preserved. As mentioned earlier, two of these original six Scott documents for which we only previously had the

printed version from the Rowley book surfaced in 1998 and were offered for sale.[48]

ARCHIVAL ESTRAYS

Undoubtedly most of the original accumulation of witchcraft-related legal documents gathered by Stephen Sewall were deposited by him as part of the Essex County court records. Sewall also served as Register of Probate for Essex County and Clerk of the Court of Pleas, of the Peace, and of the General Quarter Sessions until his death in 1725. The witchcraft papers were stored among the other county records that included trial papers, probate records, and land deeds kept at the court house in Salem. Over the years others besides Mather and Hutchinson gained access to the witchcraft files, and many papers apparently disappeared. Most likely some of the witchcraft legal documents were retained by officials in 1692/93, following their official use. With the passage of time these papers were often forgotten and simply became part of a person's personal estate. Other of these documents could have been pilfered as curiosities or souvenirs, or as Charles Upham suggested, some could have been purposefully destroyed.

A good number of survivor documents eventually found their way to history collections within libraries or historical organizations. In the early 1800s Hon. John Pickering (1777–1845), lawyer, philologist, and statesman, was given a group of witchcraft legal papers, probably because of his interest in the law and in language. According to Nathaniel Ingersoll Bowditch, as Pickering was an officer of the court, he "had some scruples of conscience about retaining them himself; and therefore, after examining them, gave them to my late father," Dr. Nathaniel Bowditch, the noted Salem mathematician and astronomer.[49] This collection was bound in a presentation volume and given in 1860 by N. I. Bowditch to the Massachusetts Historical Society. Over the years, this, the oldest historical society in the nation founded in 1791, has accumulated other such "archival estrays" and now includes a significant collection of over 50 Salem witchcraft documents. The examination of

---

[46] Poole, p. 381.

[47] Reprinted, *The Devil Hath Been Raised*, pp. 156–157, 159, 164; *NEHGR*, p. 401.

[48] Thomas Gage, *The History of Rowley* (Boston: Ferdinand Andrews, 1840), pp. 169–175. In 1841 Peleg Chandler included more than a dozen transcriptions of witchcraft documents, including a Mercy Lewis deposition not now extant. *American Criminal Trials*, v. 1, pp. 426–434. See No. 227, note.

[49] *NEHGR*, p. 397.

George Burroughs, for example, was found among John Hathorne's papers and from 1843 was in the possession of I. F. Andrews, Esq., until its deposit within the Massachusetts Historical Society.[50]

Other significant collections of Salem witchcraft legal records are at the Massachusetts State Archives or have found their way to manuscript repositories including those of the Essex Institute, now the Peabody Essex Museum in Salem; the Boston Public Library; and the New York Public Library. Occasionally documents have also found homes in a handful of other institutions and with several private collectors. Among those institutions that have one or two such documents are the William L. Clements Library in Michigan, the Karpeles Manuscript Library in California, and the Beinecke Rare Book and Manuscript Library at Yale.

The Essex Institute became a repository for some twenty-four witchcraft papers donated during the nineteenth century, including gifts in the 1850s from Daniel A. White and in 1865 from W. D. Pickering. Several witchcraft documents acquired by Danvers antiquarian and witchcraft scholar Samuel P. Fowler were donated through his daughter Harriet among numerous local history manuscripts collected into large scrapbooks. One item in the Institute's collection that had been separated into individual leaves and scattered among the other witchcraft documents was what was originally a twenty-page string-bound manuscript booklet. At the head of the booklet are the words, "Several Examinations." The ten double pages contained twenty witchcraft preliminary examinations of nineteen separate accused persons conducted by several magistrates during the period of July 21 through September 1, 1692. Notes are appended to the bottom of some of the examinations of a later date indicating that the accused person later acknowledged the confession before a magistrate.[51]

TRANSCRIPTION PROJECTS

During the decade of the 1850s, Massachusetts state, county and local government agencies began to realize the need for ordering and preserving the vast accumulation of historic records in their custody. In May 1851 the Massachusetts General Court passed "An Act for the Better

Preservation of Municipal and Other Records." Chapter 161 noted the duty of those with custody of public records to arrange them "in a careful and orderly manner convenient for examination and reference." In cases where the documents have been worn, etc., "it shall be their duty to have a fair copy of such records seasonably taken by competent and skilful transcribers . . . the same to be certified to be true copies of the originals by the clerk of such county, city or town."[52]

This present volume before you is in the tradition of several earlier, useful books that gathered together the witchcraft documents and attempted to make them available in printed form. The Essex Institute in Salem was established in 1848 by the merger of two older societies. Its objective was "the collection and preservation of all authentic memorials relating to the civil history of the County of Essex."[53] This organization went on to become one of the premier county historical societies in the country. In 1992 it merged with the Peabody Museum of Salem to become the Peabody Essex Museum. Though this new morphing of two spectacular organizations has in recent years brought about a diminishing of the collection of Essex County historical materials, its Phillips Library is still one of the richest historical libraries in the country.

In April 1859, the Institute published its premier issue of the *Historical Collections of the Essex Institute*, which periodical would continue publishing until the last decade of the twentieth century. It was a rich source of historical documentation and research papers reflecting upon Essex County. In the first two issues of the *Historical Collections*, the Institute published the first large-scale reproduction of witchcraft transcripts. Beginning in the February 1860 issue and continuing into the 1861 volume, George F. Chever published a lengthy article about Salem merchant Philip English, who was accused of being a witch. The article included much about the history of the Salem witchcraft throughout Chever's 109 pages of small, double-column typeface. Included were several dozen witchcraft related transcriptions taken from records at the Essex County clerk's office. Chever mentions that "some of the witchcraft trials are missing" from the files, though the surviving documents had been mounted in what was described as "Vol. Salem Witchcraft"

---

[50] No. 120.

[51] These are referenced in this edition as "Andover Examinations Copy."

[52] *Massachusetts Acts of 1851*, Chapter 161, pp. 655–656.

[53] *Historical Collection of the Essex Institute* (Salem, April 1859), Vol. 1, p. 1.

and included about 500 pages.[54] This appears to be the earliest large-scale attempt to publish witchcraft documents from within the county files. The transcriptions are fairly true to the words of the original documents, though proper names are capitalized and punctuation is modernized. Spelling is attempted to be consistent with a reading of the original handwriting.

Concurrent with the Chever article, the April 1860 issue of the *Historical Collections* included an article by Lincoln R. Stone on 1692 witchcraft victim George Jacobs, wherein the author reproduced sixteen documents comprising all the surviving records of the Jacobs case from within the Essex County court files. The documents had been copied out in transcription by Ira J. Patch, a clerk at the county court house who devoted much time transcribing witchcraft cases and other early public records.[55]

The Woodward Edition

The first major transcription project involving the Salem witchcraft records was underwritten by Roxbury, Massachusetts, resident William Elliot Woodward (1825–1892). Between 1864 and 1865, at his own expense, W. Elliot Woodward had printed a two-volume set titled *Records of Salem Witchcraft, Copied From the Original Documents*. His Salem witchcraft records project was the first major publishing enterprise in what turned into an extensive list of other such projects undertaken by Woodward. In 1865 and 1866 he underwrote two additional witchcraft works compiled by historian Samuel Gardner Drake.

Woodward's initial witchcraft project put into print the slightly more than 500 transcriptions of the 1692 legal records preserved at the Essex County Court House in Salem. In his 1864 "Preface" to this document publication, Woodward explained that of the original manuscripts: "only detached portions had ever been printed and thus made accessible to the public." This new work would thus make this rich body of historic papers available to a much larger audience. He also noted, "I placed the sheets in the hands of the printer as they came from the transcriber, and they are now presented without addition or diminution, *verbatim et literatim*. . . ." Woodward's publication was not the result of a massive, independent transcribing project,

but rather the result of putting into print "a manuscript volume consisting of copies of the original Witchcraft papers in the Clerk's Office, written by Ira J. Patch, Esq." The original transcription, which was apparently accomplished by Patch prior to 1859, as an attested statement by Clerk of Courts Asahel Huntington dated October 22, 1859, is included on the final page of text in the Woodward volume. Huntington attests that the foregoing are "true copies made at the direction of said County Commissioners, under the authority of a law of the Commonwealth, passed May 15, 1851." Thus Patch was the actual source for the transcribing of the witchcraft papers in the Court House, and most likely also the source of both of the earlier Essex Institute *Historical Collections* transcriptions.[56]

Though the Woodward edition has been used by numerous writers since the 1860s and reprinted several times in the twentieth century, it did not attempt to gather the significant number of 1692 witchcraft documents housed elsewhere. It only reproduced those documents housed within the Salem Court House. The print run of the two-volume set was a modest 215 copies, including fifteen on large paper. A subscription list for the set was circulated prior to publication and all sets were numbered and many signed by Woodward. The transcription format included the use of the old-style long letter "s," "J" used for "I," and superscript letters found in the documents themselves were so set in type. The printed layout of the body of the document attempted to keep true to the shape of the original. Each independent document was given a simple title printed in italics and centered just above the transcription.

Famed Albany, New York, printer and antiquarian Joel Munsell (1808–1880) performed the presswork. Woodward commented of the printer's typography: "How well Mr. Munsell has done his work is plainly to be seen, so far as general appearance is concerned; but the painstaking care with which the ancient orthography and punctuation, or rather the lack of this last have been followed, can only be appreciated by those who have compared the volumes with the original records."[57] One document from the Salem Court collection was inadvertently left out, being a

[54] George F. Chever, "Philip English," *HCEI* (Salem, 1860), Vol. II, pp. 29–30.

[55] Lincoln R. Stone, "An Account of the Trial of George Jacobs for Witchcraft," *HCEI* (Salem, 1860), Vol. II, pp. [49]–57.

[56] W. Elliot Woodward, *Records of Salem Witchcraft, Copied From the Original Documents* (Roxbury, MA, 1864 & 1865), Vol. I, pp. [v]–vi; Vol. II, p. 268; tipped-in note in a copy of the book owned by Danvers Archival Center, Danvers, MA.

[57] Woodward, I, pp. v–vii.

statement by John and Mary Arnold for Mary Esty and Sarah Cloyce.[58]

The two-volume set included 546 pages divided into forty-three named cases, followed by a grouping of miscellaneous other witchcraft cases and post-1692 documents. The last seventeen pages of text included documents of earlier seventeenth-century New England witchcraft cases. The forty-three individual Salem cases are ordered by the initial date of the accused's warrant or examination. Within the individual case groups, however, there is no logical chronological ordering. If present, warrants come first, followed by indictments and then by examinations.

Unfortunately, the transcriptions themselves are replete with errors. A copy of the work within the collections of the Danvers Archival Center includes a tipped-in 1868 letter from Essex County Court Clerk Asahel Huntington (who served as clerk from 1852 to 1872), presenting the book set to Charles W. Upham. Throughout the volume are penciled marginal notes, possibly by Upham's son William P., correcting the numerous transcription errors and occasionally identifying the person in whose handwriting the original document was written. The Woodward publication was a significant though flawed work used by several generations of historians.

Charles Upham's Work

Upon the heels of the Woodward edition came what has long been regarded as the most influential history of the Salem witchcraft trials. Charles Wentworth Upham (1802–1872) was a prominent Salem minister, mayor of the community, and one-term Congressman. In 1831 he had published *Lectures on Witchcraft*, taken from a series of talks he had presented around the Salem area. His new work was published in Boston in 1867 and titled *Salem Witchcraft; With an Account of Salem Village and a History of Opinions on Witchcraft and Kindred Subjects*. His highly influential two-volume tome outlined in Volume One the history of Salem and Salem Village, and in Volume Two concentrated on the events of 1692. Assisting Upham at every turn was his son William Phineas Upham (1836–1905). The son was a probate court lawyer whose love of local history led him to serve as curator of manuscripts at the Essex Institute from 1863 until his death, and to serve nineteen years as its librarian. He also indexed records, edited many history transcription publications, and in a

multi-year project compiled and mounted thousands of early Essex County Court file documents into nineteen folio volumes as a preservation project for the county commissioners. In 1870 William Poole noted that the surviving witchcraft court records in Salem "have been very carefully arranged and mounted by Mr. William P. Upham." The documents were mounted into two large scrapbook volumes, one of which was kept in a case for public viewing at the Salem Court House.[59]

Concerning the original documents, Upham described in the preface to his 1867 work that:

a very large portion have been abstracted from time to time by unauthorized hands, and many, it is feared, destroyed or otherwise lost. Two very valuable parcels have found their way into the libraries of the Massachusetts Historical Society and the Essex Institute, where they are faithfully secured. A few others have come to light among papers in the possession of individuals. It is to be hoped, that, if any more should be found, they will be lodged in some public institution; so that, if thought best, they may all be collected, arranged, and placed beyond wear, tear, and loss, in the perpetual custody of type.

The papers remaining in the office of the clerk of this county were transcribed into a volume a few years since; the copyist supplying, conjecturally, headings to the several documents. Although he executed his work in an elegant manner, and succeeded in giving correctly many documents hard to be deciphered, such errors, owing to the condition of the papers, occurred in arranging them, transcribing their contents, and framing their headings, that I have had to resort to the originals throughout.[60]

Except in a few instances of replicating a document in the original spelling and punctuation as a curiosity for the reader, Upham stated that the transcriptions used in his book did not attempt to preserve the original orthography. Rather, he used current spelling and punctuation, though not changing words or altering structure. Upham made frequent use of the original documents, including all or most of some seventy-five documents, with examinations and depositions most frequently used. He also made use of documents in other collections such as several Nurse documents at the Massachusetts Historical Society, the entire examination of Martha Cory from the Essex Institute, and quotes of documents including a now-lost

[58] No. 602.

[59] Robert S. Rantoul, *William Phineas Upham: A Memorial* (Boston, 1910), p. 14; *NEHGR*, p. 397.

[60] *Salem Witchcraft*, v. I, pp. x–xi.

Giles Cory examination manuscript, and material quoted by Calef and by Hutchinson.[61]

The WPA Project

In the 1930s, a Depression era "New Deal" work project under the federal Works Progress Administration (WPA) was initiated to put local researchers and clerical staff to work to bring together a new transcription of the Salem witchcraft papers. Many history-related projects were undertaken by the WPA, including the creation of historic murals in public buildings, writers' history projects, and the sorting and indexing of municipal historic records. This Salem project was under the supervision of Essex County Clerk of Courts Archie N. Frost. A group of researchers and typists meticulously gathered and transcribed not just the witchcraft material in the Court House, but also from the Essex Institute, the Massachusetts Archives, Suffolk County and Middlesex County files, the New York and Boston Public Libraries, the Massachusetts Historical Society, and other sources. Also included in this project were the 1693 witchcraft cases heard by the Massachusetts Superior Court of Judicature, post-1692 bills submitted by jailers, etc., and papers relating to the victims' families receiving recompense in the early 1700s.

The WPA project researchers meticulously re-transcribed all the papers using the original documents themselves. Their work greatly improved the accuracy of the transcripts produced from the Patch/Woodward nineteenth-century version, although many errors remained and some new ones were created. The WPA project retained the "archaic usage" of the letters "J" for "I"; "f" for "s"; "y" for "th"; and "v" for "u." The transcripts themselves were divided up in alphabetical order by the last name of the accused. Thus "John Alden" became the first of the individual case records reproduced. At the bottom left of each completed transcription a note was included to indicate where the original was held. In the case of the Essex County Court House records, they were identified as "Essex County Archives, Salem," the original

documents retaining their same location volume and page number from the nineteenth-century ordering of them in the two large scrapbooks. Unfortunately this fine WPA transcription project, completed in 1938 and including about 1,300 typescript pages gathered into three bound volumes, was underutilized. The typescript volumes and a carbon copy were available only at the court house itself, at the Essex Institute, and later in the 1970s as an electrostatic copy at the Danvers Archival Center.

The SWP Edition

Then in 1977 DaCapo Press printed a three-volume set of books titled *The Salem Witchcraft Papers* based on the WPA typescript transcripts. This collection generally remained true to the layout and transcription of the WPA work and was edited by Paul Boyer and Stephen Nissenbaum, authors of the influential 1974 book, *Salem Possessed: The Social Origins of Witchcraft*. Their edition of *The Salem Witchcraft Papers* is referred to in *Records of the Salem Witch-Hunt* as *SWP*. Boyer and Nissenbaum obtained the permission from the Essex County Commissioners to use all the transcriptions from the earlier WPA project, and *SWP* became the first publication that attempted to print all the known legal papers connected to the Salem witchcraft trials. As with the WPA typescript edition, the transcripts were grouped alphabetically, according to the individual cases, with Volume Three including post-1692, "Additional Documents." The editors acknowledged the problem with placement of documents that named multiple accused persons. They modernized the archaic usages retained in the WPA work and did not superscript letters. This edition included titles to each document at the beginning and a location statement at the bottom left side, which generally conformed to the WPA usage. A highly readable and useful narrative of the Salem witchcraft episode and notes on how best to use the seventeenth-century gathered documents introduced the transcriptions themselves.

As for the documents themselves, they were not re-examined to produce new transcriptions, and the same errors, misreadings, inaccurate conflation of the Alice and Mary Parker cases, missing words or phrases, and other transcription problems evident in the 1938 work were replicated in this 1977 work. The editors did expand upon the documents included, however, by adding some documents only available in print found in books by Mather, Calef, Hale, Hutchinson and Upham. Also made part of *SWP* were sixteen witchcraft documents from the Boston

---

[61] No. 65 of April 19, 1692, was printed as an addendum on pp. 310–312 of an 1823 Salem reprint by J. D. and T. C. Cushing Jr. of Robert Calef's work, *More Wonders of the Invisible World*. The introductory sentence included that "The files of office contain numerous documents . . . of which the following will serve as a specimen." If the Cory examination was previously within the Essex Court files, it hasn't been there since at least the mid-nineteenth century.

Public Library. These documents included seven important papers relating to the John Willard case.[62]

In copying WPA transcriptions, the *SWP* edition carried over in certain instances words or letters that could not be verified by manuscript inspection. In some cases transcriptions came from portions of manuscripts that were lost or degraded. However, it is impossible to confirm this conclusion. In *Records*, when something is lost in the manuscript, but carried in Woodward, or *SWP*, the words are included and referenced to the edition used. Many of these, however, are probably intelligent guesses rather than transcriptions based on better manuscripts. The current editors felt it best to include these in spite of uncertainty as to authenticity, or in some cases skepticism. Such inclusions appear as, for example, [*SWP* = Village] or [*Woodward* = Village].[63]

For generations the Essex County Archives Collection of more than 500 witchcraft documents had been stored in the environmentally fluctuating conditions and relatively lax security of the Essex County Court House. In December 1980 the Superior Court agreed to deposit these documents to the safety and security of the fireproof annex of the Essex Institute on Essex Street, just several blocks away from the County Court House complex on Federal Street. For its part the Institute promised to make available for viewing within a secure display several witchcraft documents that the general public could see without needing to pay admission to the Institute. In 1981 the documents were dismounted from the two nineteenth-century scrapbooks and conserved and repaired as necessary. Donald Gleason processed and indexed the papers, assigning each item an individual number. Though the papers remained in the same general arrangement as when mounted in the scrapbooks, the numbers themselves were not the same as replicated in WPA or *SWP*. By the early years of the twenty-first century, the documents were being stored in acid-free folders, with only one document per folder. These folders are stored in Hollinger acid-free legal-size boxes on secure shelves within the fireproof manuscript storage area. The documents have also been microfilmed.[64]

---

[62] *SWP*, pp. 3–4, 31–40. The new witchcraft documents had been purchased by the Library in 1938 from Goodspeed's Book Shop. Goodspeed's had obtained them from the New York auction house Parke Bernet, which represented a private client.

[63] See Editorial Principles.

[64] *Salem Witchcraft Papers from the Essex County Archives and the Essex Institute: 1692–1713* (35-mm microfilm), Introduction, p. 12. As of 2007, Associate Editor Benjamin C. Ray maintains

A Chronological Edition

The previous major witchcraft transcription projects (Woodward, WPA, and *SWP*) each share in common an alphabetical, case-by-case compilation, whereby documents related to specific individuals were grouped together. This clustering by named case creates problems, however, whenever more than one accused person is named in a document. With which person should a multi-named document be ordered in the book? Should the document be repeated in each case? Or should they go in alphabetical order, putting the warrant with the person who comes first in the alphabet? Or with the person first examined? This ordering also makes the events of 1692 appear as segmented, independent cases with little connection to one another.

This writer first attempted a chronological ordering of witchcraft documents in a 1992 book titled *The Devil Hath Been Raised*. The volume was limited to documents concerning events from February 29 through March 31, 1692, when the claims of witchcraft affliction first took hold primarily within Salem Village, and when the significant precedents that would dominate the judicial response to the events became established. This chronological approach included civil and church records, as well as two sermons preached on witchcraft in Salem Village, together with the witchcraft legal documents. The objective was to be as all-inclusive for this critical first month of the witchcraft outbreak as surviving records would allow. A re-transcription of all the March witchcraft documents was also performed, resulting in a number of previous transcribing mistakes being corrected.

The editors of *Records*, in looking to create an accurate and comprehensive edition, agreed that a chronological record of the legal documents, as modeled by *The Devil Hath Been Raised*, could offer a fresh and exciting format. Such an ordering should display the actual flow of events of 1692 as they happened in real, linear time, rather than grouping them as cases where key parts of one person's case may actually show up under another's case and where the record of concurrent cases is not displayed. It was realized, however, that creating the day-by-day format beyond March 1692 would grow increasingly difficult.

a website at the University of Virginia, "Salem Witch Trials Documentary Archive" (http://etext.virginia.edu/salem/witchcraft), where most of the manuscript images can be seen, although the color images, which are the next best thing to actual manuscript inspection, remain a pending project.

The seemingly straightforward chronological principle would become complicated, not only by the absence of explicit dates on a large number of documents, but also by the fact that many of the documents were later added to by the original recorder, or with other written materials appended to it at various points during the legal process. For an explanation of how documents in the edition are ordered, see "Chronological Arrangement."

One's approach to this rich and varied body of existing witchcraft legal papers must be with the knowledge that it does include meaningful gaps in information and that all the judicial documents give us only a part of the reality of the events. Yet with such cautions in mind, these records are for us a valuable means of better understanding the 1692 witchcraft cases as seen and perceived over real time by the participants themselves. In spite of the difficulties outlined, such a chronological approach should allow the documents themselves to unravel the story day by day, incident by incident, and legal procedure by legal procedure. This is the "best evidence" we possess in that it survives in its original form. Though it can at times be difficult to decipher the handwriting and spelling, understand the antiquated, arcane language, and plod through the absence of consistent punctuation within the original documents, these artifacts and their accurate transcriptions can speak to the careful reader with extraordinary authority.

IV. LINGUISTIC INTRODUCTION

PETER GRUND, RISTO HILTUNEN, LEENA KAHLAS-TARKKA,
MERJA KYTÖ, MATTI PEIKOLA, AND MATTI RISSANEN[1]

1. INTRODUCTION

The rise of a new linguistic variety is always an exciting phenomenon, as regards both the early stages of the variety and its subsequent life cycle. Among the transported extraterritorial varieties of English, American English is of particular interest, having been the first to emerge and having developed into a language variety of worldwide significance.[2] The roots of this variety lie in the British English local varieties of the early seventeenth century, but once in the colonies, the new variety and its local forms followed their own paths of development. The records of the Salem witch-hunt provide firsthand evidence of language use of the period in both specialized, formal writing and in less formal, speech-related contexts.

It is important to place the Salem records in their socio-historical setting as regards the development of early American English in general. The writings, both printed works and manuscript records, that have survived from early New England are of a primarily utilitarian nature, produced by first-generation settlers and their descendants. Among these writings are not only legal documents such as those included among the Salem records but also town records, diaries, travel journals, and accounts of "memorable providences" (i.e., natural phenomena allegedly indicative of God's works). They exhibit a wide range of linguistic variation, reflecting both features characteristic of the local dialects transported from the mother country and the results of dialect mixture and various leveling phenomena inherent in early settler communities. Most early immigrants to New England came from all over England, but the East Anglian counties were best represented.[3]

In discussions of extraterritorial linguistic varieties, attention has been paid to factors promoting and/or retarding change. Even though these factors pertain to language change in general, the new regional and socio-demographic environment of an emerging variety, and constant changes in it, may further increase the tension between linguistic innovation and conservatism. In terms of regional and/or social variation, two main directions of development have been distinguished: unification and diversification. At the same time as the new variety develops toward uniformity (various types of settler inputs start merging), it begins to diverge from the usage of the mother country.[4] Continuous waves of migration and other extralinguistic factors tend to intensify the influence of these forces. For instance, isolation of speech communities in the new environment tends to encourage conservative features in a language variety[5] and even leads to phenomena referred to as "arrest of development" or the

---

[1] The different sections of the linguistic introduction were written by the following people: Section 1, Merja Kytö; Section 2, Peter Grund; Section 3, Matti Peikola; Section 4, Peter Grund and Merja Kytö; Section 5, Leena Kahlas-Tarkka and Matti Rissanen, with contributions from all the authors to the discussion on vocabulary; Section 6, Risto Hiltunen; Section 7, Risto Hiltunen in collaboration with Matti Peikola; and Section 8, Matti Peikola in collaboration with Peter Grund. Naturally, the authors have worked in close collaboration, exchanging comments on their drafts. The work was coordinated by Merja Kytö.

[2] Raymond Hickey, ed., *Legacies of Colonial English. Studies in Transported Dialects* (Cambridge: Cambridge University Press, 2004).

[3] John Algeo, "External History," in *The Cambridge History of the English Language*, Vol. 6, *English in North America*, ed. John Algeo (Cambridge: Cambridge University Press, 2001), p. 8.

[4] See, e.g., Eric Partridge and John W. Clark, *British and American English since 1900* (London: Andrew Dakers, 1951), pp. 206–207; Raven I. McDavid, Jr., *Varieties of American English. Essays by Raven I. McDavid, Jr., Selected and Introduced by Anwar S. Dil* (Stanford, CA: Stanford University Press, 1980), pp. 117–125.

[5] Peter Trudgill, *On Dialect. Social and Geographical Perspectives* (Oxford: Basil Blackwell, 1983), p. 103.

"colonial lag."[6] In other words, despite the language developing in new directions in the mother country, the planters may continue using the form of the language that they brought along with them and adopt the new developments only later on, or never.

Considering the dynamic interplay of the factors that must have influenced the settlers' speech habits, and the changing language of their descendants, sources such as the Salem witchcraft records are of prime interest to those studying language change. At the same time, they provide a valuable opportunity for observing how language is used in this specific legal setting. In the course of the seventeenth century, the English language had started to develop toward what later became a standard variety, but variation still characterized usage in the 1690s, both in England and in the early colonies. Moreover, many of the Salem recorders lacked formal education, and their spelling and other linguistic habits provide interesting insights into the language of the period. Particular attention can also be paid to the recordings of the utterances of slaves such as Tituba and Candy.[7] Some of the recorders seem to have made a conscious effort to reproduce faithfully even the "broken" English features in their utterances.

The aim of this Linguistic Introduction is to describe the language of the Salem records in empirical terms, ranging from spelling practices of the recorders to issues of interest on the more general discourse level. Our primary purpose is to draw attention to the fact that there is a great deal of material of linguistic interest in the documents. Some of the issues discussed can be pursued further in the more specific studies cited as references. It is hoped that the overview presented here will be helpful for the reader and that it will stimulate further research into the properties and uses of the language in this unique material. The following sections will describe the text categories found in the Salem collection (Section 2), the recorders and their practices (Section 3), the evidence provided by the documents on the spelling, pronunciation, and punc-

tuation habits of the period (Section 4), the morphology, syntax, and vocabulary of the language (Section 5), the discourse level and processes characteristic of the various language use situations (Section 6), common legal terms and Latin vocabulary (Section 7), and the abbreviation strategies employed by the recorders (Section 8). Although the discussion is structured with reference to these levels of language, the levels are of course interrelated. For this reason, one and the same linguistic phenomenon may be relevant to several levels and hence to more than one section.

2. TEXT CATEGORIES

The Salem documents are often referred to as a body of texts. However, it is important to recognize that they constitute a heterogeneous collection that comprises a number of different text categories, and that these categories differ substantially from one another in linguistic and structural makeup.[8] The major text categories are depositions (ca. 400), indictments (ca. 120), examinations (ca. 100), warrants and mittimuses (ca. 80), petitions (ca. 60), accounts, bills, receipts, orders of payment, etc. (ca. 60), recognizances (ca. 20), complaints (ca. 20), summonses (ca. 20), letters (ca. 20), and other (ca. 100).[9] On the basis of features such as origin, use, and structural and linguistic characteristics, the text categories can be divided into two types: speech-related texts, including examination records and depositions; and formulaic legal documents, including (among others) indictments, warrants, summonses, and complaints (see also Section 6).[10]

---

[6] Ernest Weekley, *The English Language, with a Chapter on the History of American English by Professor John W. Clark* (London: André Deutsch, 1952 [1928]), p. 112; Albert H. Marckwardt, *American English* (New York: Oxford University Press, 1958), Chapter 4.

[7] Matti Rissanen, "'Candy No Witch, Barbados': Salem Witchcraft Trials as Evidence of Early American English," in *Language in Time and Space. Studies in Honour of Wolfgang Viereck on the Occasion of his 60th Birthday*, ed. Heinrich Ramisch and Kenneth Wynne (Stuttgart: Franz Steiner Verlag, 1997), pp. 183–193.

[8] The term *text category* is used here to denote a group of texts that have one or more extra-linguistic features in common, such as a shared name, shared function, or other shared contextual characteristics.

[9] This approximate count is primarily based on the number of documents. A few documents contain more than one example of a text category, but they have been counted only once here. An exception is the *Andover Examinations Copy*, where the different examinations have been counted as separate items. The point of the count is simply to give an overview of the relative frequency of the categories. The category *other* comprises a mix of categories including oaths of office, physical examinations, witness lists, summaries of evidence, legislation, etc.

[10] Some of the minor text categories such as receipts, accounts, and records of physical examinations may be valuable sources for certain types of linguistic research (especially lexical studies). However, since these texts are infrequent and/or were produced (considerably) after 1692, they will not be included in the discussion.

The examination records and depositions provide particularly fascinating material since they purport to represent the spoken language of the period. The examinations are records of the pre-trial hearings of suspected witches, which were held to establish whether an alleged witch should be formally charged.[11] These records derive from no longer extant notes or shorthand notation made by one or more recorders attending the hearing. Samuel Parris and Simon Willard, in particular, make clear in notes at the end of some of their examinations that the records are based on "characters ^{written} at the time" of the examination.[12] In the sixteenth and seventeenth centuries, "characters" was a technical term for shorthand.[13] A large number of manuals advocating different systems of English shorthand were in circulation in the seventeenth century, two of the most popular being John Willis's *The Arte of Stenographie* (1602) and Thomas Shelton's *Tachygraphy* (c. 1626).[14] Since manuals of all kinds printed in England circulated in New England, Parris and Willard (and perhaps others) would undoubtedly have had access to most of the manuals current in late seventeenth-century England.[15] Although no shorthand records of examinations have survived, shorthand does appear in a few documents in other contexts. The most significant example is found on the manuscript of No. 120, where some comments in an unidentified type of shorthand have been added, most probably by Parris.[16] If Parris and Willard were proficient users of shorthand, they were more likely to be able to record more and perhaps more accurately than writers who used other types of systems, such as simple note-taking.[17]

The recorders have three main modes of presenting what was said or what took place during the courtroom proceedings: direct speech, indirect speech, and metatextual comments. Most of the examination records contain passages of all three types of discourse, but the proportions vary. Samuel Parris, for example, primarily writes examinations in direct speech, whereas the Salem merchant William Murray prefers to record examinations in indirect speech.[18] Examinations given predominantly in direct speech present the courtroom proceedings as a dialogue between the accused and the interrogator (sometimes marked in the text by *Q* for *Question* and *A* for *Answer*).[19] These records are characterized by the use of discourse markers and interjections (e.g., *well, why, oh*), first- and second-person pronouns, interrogative pronouns, and present-tense verb forms: that is, features that are also common in Present-Day spoken language.[20] Records in indirect speech, on the other hand, rarely include the interrogator's questions and introduce the accused person's answers with *he/she said/answered*. They are characterized by third-person pronouns, past-tense verbs, more complex syntactic constructions (e.g., subordination and use of participles), and more polysyllabic words than in direct speech recordings.[21] The recorder may also occasionally summarize the interrogation in his own words, describe events outside the dialogue between the interrogator and the accused (such as the alleged afflictions of the victims of witchcraft), or add evaluative comments on a statement or behavior of the accused.[22] These metatextual passages are usually brief.

Although the examination records purport to represent the speech of the accused, interrogator, and possible

[11] The examinations also include records of confessions.

[12] E.g., No. 241 and No. 507. See also Peter Grund, "From Tongue to Text: The Transmission of the Salem Witchcraft Examination Records," *American Speech*, Vol. 82 (2007), pp. 124–126.

[13] *OED* s.v. *character* 3b.

[14] Adele Davidson, "'Some by Stenography?' Stationers, Shorthand, and the Early Shakespearean Quartos," *Papers of the Bibliographical Society of America*, Vol. 90 (1996), pp. 422–423.

[15] Peter Charles Hoffer, *Law and People in Colonial America* (Baltimore, MD: The Johns Hopkins University Press, 1992), p. 7; Tamara Plakins Thornton, *Handwriting in America: A Cultural History* (New Haven, CT: Yale University Press, 1996), pp. 9, 12.

[16] The nineteenth-century antiquarian William P. Upham made an attempt to transcribe the shorthand passage. If the transcription is correct, it seems to cite biblical passages. The transcription is now found in Rev. Samuel Parris Witchcraft Ephemera File, Danvers Archival Center, Danvers, MA.

[17] For the use of shorthand in the 1688 witchcraft trial against Goody Glover, see Robert Calef, *More Wonders of the Invisible*

World, or, the Wonders of the Invisible World Display'd in Five Parts (London, 1700; Wing/C288), p. 151.

[18] See, e.g., No. 174, No. 104, No. 540, No. 533. Risto Hiltunen shows that indirect speech recording became increasingly common as the trials progressed. He suggests that this may have been due to the fact that indirect recording seems to have been less time-consuming than direct-speech recording, a factor that became important because of the growing number of examinations in August and September; Risto Hiltunen, "Salem 1692: A Case of Courtroom Discourse in a Historical Perspective," in *Approaches to Style and Discourse in English*, ed. Risto Hiltunen and Shinichiro Watanabe (Osaka: Osaka University Press, 2004), p. 8; see also Section 6.

[19] E.g., No. 429.

[20] See Peter Grund, Merja Kytö, and Matti Rissanen, "Editing the Salem Witchcraft Records: An Exploration of a Linguistic Treasury," *American Speech*, Vol. 79 (2004), pp. 151–152.

[21] See Grund, Kytö, and Rissanen, "Editing," pp. 151–152.

[22] See the beginning of No. 440 and No. 150.

other witnesses, they cannot be used uncritically as evidence of the spoken language of the courtroom participants. It is crucial to acknowledge the role of the recorder in shaping the now extant texts. Besides the metatextual comments, scribal interference is obvious in passages of indirect speech, since the recorder must have changed at least some features to produce the indirect reporting. However, even in the records written primarily in direct speech, the influence of the recorder should not be underestimated. This is shown, for example, by the fact that multiple records of some examinations, written down by different people, have been preserved. Although these records claim to depict the same courtroom proceedings, they frequently vary widely in content and in particular in linguistic form.[23]

The second speech-related text category is depositions, which are written records of the oral testimony of witnesses who report on their experiences or actions in a particular context.[24] The Salem depositions were mostly taken down outside the court, either by the witnesses themselves or by someone who was familiar with deposition recording (see Section 3). They were subsequently filed with the court, and, if they were admitted into evidence, they were read aloud and sworn to by the witnesses in court. Since more than fifty recorders were involved in writing the Salem depositions, a great deal of variation exists among the depositions in structure and linguistic form. However, certain features tend to be present in a majority of the depositions and were probably part of the standard conventions of deposition writing.[25] Almost all depositions begin with the formulation *the deposition/testimony of* and then state the name and usually age of the witness; in rare instances, the place of residence or profession is added. The personal data are usually followed by the phrase *testifieth and saith* (or a

similar formulation).[26] Other formulaic features found in many depositions include the legal formula *the said* + name or *deponent*, and the closing formula *and further saith not*, though the employment of these features varies greatly.[27]

The main body of the depositions is given as a narrative in the first person (e.g., *I/we saw...*) or in the third person (*he/she/the said deponent(s)/they saw...*) where the witnesses relate their experience; some recorders employ the two strategies interchangeably.[28] It is conspicuous that first-person depositions are more common in the Salem material than third-person records. This is in stark contrast to contemporaneous depositions in England, which are predominantly recorded in the third person.[29] This difference may perhaps be attributed to the scribal situation: unlike most English scribes, many of the Salem recorders do not seem to have been court clerks or people educated in legal writing and may thus have been less aware of deposition conventions. Although the majority of the depositions are given as first-person narratives, they are mostly recorded in indirect speech; that is to say, when the witness reports on what he/she or an additional person said, the statements are frequently in indirect speech (i.e., *I said to him that he should come* instead of *I said to him: You should come*). Only occasionally are passages given in direct speech, and these are as a rule brief.[30]

Since witnesses commonly report on what other people have said and since the witnesses' statements have been filtered through the recorder, it is in most cases impossible to determine whose language the deposition reflects (see also Section 4). This situation is made even more complex if there are several layers of reporting, as in Joseph Ballard's deposition in No. 630: "Joseph Ballard... saith that my brother John ballard told me that Samuel Wardel told him that I had reported that he had bewich{ed} my wife..." (see also Section 6). Some depositions also appear to be copies of earlier documents, and others may have been produced from model documents. In the former, the language is even further removed from the original language reported or used by the witness, whereas in the latter it does not reflect the language used by

23 For a more detailed discussion, see Grund, "From Tongue to Text." For examination records existing in more than one copy, see No. 523 and No. 524, No. 173 and No. 174, and No. 5 and No. 6.
24 Bridget Cusack, ed., *Everyday English 1500–1700: A Reader* (Edinburgh: Edinburgh University Press, 1998), p. 92. In the category of depositions are included all kinds of witness statements in the Salem corpus, even if they were not sworn to in court and used as evidence in the trials.
25 Similar features are found in some contemporaneous manuals for justices of the peace from England. See, e.g., William Brown, *The Clerk's Tutor in Chancery* (London, 1688; Wing/B5079), p. 93. For the circulation of such manuals in New England, see Hoffer, *Law and People*, p. 7.

26 E.g., No. 605, No. 374.
27 E.g., No. 321, No. 687.
28 E.g., No. 278, No. 18, No. 617.
29 Cusack, *Everyday English*, p. 93; Terry Walker, Thou *and* You *in Early Modern English Dialogues: Trials, Depositions, and Drama Comedy*, Pragmatics and Beyond New Series, Vol. 158 (Amsterdam: John Benjamins, 2007), p. 13.
30 E.g., No. 85, No. 575.

the witness at all but rather repeats a fixed or formulaic statement.[31]

The more formulaic legal documents exhibit less linguistic and structural variation than the examinations and depositions. The writing of these documents was obviously constrained by strict conventions that probably had to be followed in order for each document to have the appropriate legal force. The similarity between the Salem documents and model documents found in manuals for justices of the peace that circulated in New England at the time shows that the recorders followed well-established legal conventions.[32] The recorders of these formulaic documents are also less diverse than those of the examinations and depositions: they primarily include clerks, justices of the peace, and other people trained in or familiar with legal writing (see Section 3). Among these legal documents, indictments are the most numerous. These documents, which outline formal charges against an alleged witch, are very formulaic and more uniform than other text categories. The reason for this is that the indictments appear to have been "mass-produced" by two or three recorders in particular, who left empty spaces for the name of the accused and accuser and other personal information to be supplied. These details were later filled in as necessary by the same recorders that made the template or by other recorders employed by the court (see Facsimile No. 5). Structurally, the indictments contain a number of components: (1) place where the indictment was issued (commonly in the left margin); (2) year of the indictment (frequently in Latin); (3) opening formula; (4) name and personal details of the accused; (5) charge; (6) name and personal details of the accuser or victim of alleged witchcraft, and time and place where the crime was committed; and (7) the nature of the crime. The indictments also exhibit very little variation in their linguistic characteristics: they primarily consist of one long syntactically complex sentence, and they rely heavily on the use of near-synonyms, the repetition of the same stock phrases, and the employment of a highly technical vocabulary (see Section 5).[33] Indictments thus illustrate English used in a very specialized legal context.

Like indictments, summonses for witnesses, arrest warrants, mittimuses, complaints, recognizances, and petitions provide examples of English used for very specific purposes, and in comparison with examination records and depositions they exhibit a more static structure and homogeneous linguistic characteristics. Summonses, for example, consist of a number of clearly distinguishable components, including an invocation of the king and queen of England, an address to a constable and/or to the summonsed witnesses, a request for the presence of the witnesses at the court, the time and place of the court session, and the case in question.[34] Complaint documents, which record an accuser's initial allegation of witchcraft against a suspected witch, similarly have a fairly invariable structure. They also employ a set of stock formulations, such as *on behalf of their Majesties* and *for sundry acts of witchcraft by her/him committed upon the bodies of. . . .*[35] The lack of variation between individual examples of the same text category may be attributed to scribal preferences as well as to fixed conventions: the summonses and the bulk of the orders of payment (written mainly in 1712), for instance, appear chiefly to have been produced by a single recorder.[36] Arrest warrants, on the other hand, show more variation in their characteristics than some of the other formulaic documents. Some warrants include a passage stating that a complaint has been made (which is similar in formulation to the complaint documents). Others only state the requirement that a constable or marshal arrest an accused person.[37] Again, scribal preferences may be a factor here, since dissimilarities occur among warrants written by different justices of the peace (e.g., John Hathorne, Jonathan Corwin, John Higginson Jr., and Dudley Bradstreet).[38] Most of the warrants also incorporate a short return from the officer who carried out the arrest. These returns tend to be brief and formulaic in nature. Finally, petitions (for the release of a prisoner or for restitution) are unlike the other text categories discussed here in that they

---

[31] E.g., No. 552 and No. 602, No. 666. See also Risto Hiltunen and Matti Peikola, "Trial Discourse and Manuscript Context: Scribal Profiles in the Salem Witchcraft Records," *Journal of Historical Pragmatics*, Vol. 8 (2007), pp. 43–68; Peter Grund, "The Anatomy of Correction: Additions, Cancellations, and Changes in the Documents of the Salem Witchcraft Trials," *Studia Neophilologica*, Vol. 79 (2007), pp. 3–24.

[32] See, e.g., Michael Dalton, *The Covntrey Ivstice* (London, 1619; STC [2nd ed.]/6206), pp. 364–365; Thomas Fidell, *A Perfect Guide for a Studious Young Lawyer* (London, 1658; Wing [2nd ed.]/F850), pp. 225–236; *The Practick Part of the Office of a Justice of the Peace* (London, 1681; Wing/P3147), p. 260. See also Grund, "Anatomy of Correction," pp. 12–14.

[33] E.g., No. 401, No. 664. See also Hiltunen and Peikola, "Trial Discourse."

[34] E.g., No. 323, No. 554.   [35] E.g., No. 224.

[36] E.g., No. 953, No. 550 (Stephen Sewall).

[37] E.g., No. 196, No. 308.

[38] E.g., No. 438, No. 118, No. 682, No. 451.

originated outside court and were then filed with the court, thus resembling depositions in this respect. However, like the documents originating in court, they tend to be fairly formulaic, written primarily by recorders who appear to have been familiar with a set of conventions appropriate for petitions.[39]

3. RECORDERS

The official legal nature of the Salem documents may create the impression that they were recorded routinely by just a few court clerks and presiding magistrates. Boyer and Nissenbaum's almost complete silence about this aspect of the documents easily leads to a similar conclusion, as if the role played by the recorders were too trivial to warrant discussion.[40] Nothing could be further from the truth. One of the key findings of the present project has been the recognition of the recorders and their writing practices as an important shaping force behind the documents. What previously may have appeared to be random or erratic linguistic variation between the documents can now in many cases be attributed to choices made by different recorders. Such constrained variation occurs on all levels of language, from orthographic minutiae to patterns of discourse and text structuring (see further Sections 2, 4–6). The role of the recorders as intermediaries between the original utterances of the Salem participants and the forms in which these utterances were written down in the documents means that no generalizing assumptions can be made about the language of, say, individual deponents or confessors without first paying attention to the context of recording: it always needs to be considered whether the linguistic phenomenon under scrutiny is more likely to reflect the choices made by the recorder than by the accuser, defendant, or witness to whom it is attributed in the documents (see also Section 2).[41]

A conspicuously large number of people (more than 250) took part in the writing down of the records. This figure is based on the editors' preliminary observations on features of the handwriting in the documents, built into a relational database by Margo Burns.[42] What is said here about the recorders is necessarily tentative in many

ways; this particularly applies to the quantification of the recorders' output. It is likely, nonetheless, that the total number of recorders will remain an estimate even when the work on them has been brought to a conclusion with the completion of the database. In some cases the brevity of an entry makes it very difficult to compare meaningfully with other ostensibly similar samples of handwriting, to determine whether they were penned by the same or different recorders. The short entries regularly found on the reverse of indictments are a case in point. Another source of difficulty lies in the capability of some professional penmen to master more than one script (a model for handwriting). The same recorder could apply different scripts to different types of document or even to different parts of one and the same document.[43] In the Salem records this phenomenon may, for instance, account for some of the variation in the handwriting in indictments between the "boilerplate" sections that were prepared in advance and the sections that were filled in individually for each case (see also Section 2).[44]

At the moment approximately 40 percent of the recorders have been tentatively identified by name. In the majority of the cases, the identification is based on a positive match between a person's signature and a piece of text written in the same hand within a single document. Once the link is established, it is possible to attribute unsigned specimens of the same handwriting in other documents to the recorder in question. The method works well on most occasions, but it may run the risk of a false attribution when a person other than the one named in the signature has written both the signature and the specimen of text to which it is compared. Constables' returns on summonses and warrants are a typical location for this to happen. On Susannah Martin's arrest warrant, for example, Thomas Putnam wrote a return on behalf of Orlando Bagly, constable of Amesbury, and signed it with Bagly's name.[45] Similar cases occur in other text categories, too, as in the deposition of Elizabeth Booth against Elizabeth Procter where Thomas Putnam both recorded the deposition and signed it as Booth.[46] The practice is also found in some petitions, such as the 1702/3 document to clear the records of Rebecca Nurse and several other persons

---

[39] E.g., No. 596.   [40] Cf. *SWP*, p. 39.

[41] Cf. Cusack, *Everyday English*, p. 93. See also Grund, "From Tongue to Text."

[42] Hiltunen and Peikola, "Trial Discourse," discuss the paleographic and linguistic criteria used in the profiling of the handwriting of the Salem recorders.

[43] See, for example, Thornton, *Handwriting*, p. 22. For a definition of the term *script*, see M. B. Parkes, *English Cursive Book Hands 1250–1500*, 2nd ed. (London: Scolar Press, 1979), p. xxvi.

[44] E.g., No. 809.   [45] No. 100.

[46] No. 383.

condemned for witchcraft.[47] It appears that in this document the recorder wrote the signatures of seventeen of the twenty-one petitioners. On some occasions text-internal personal details such as the age of the recorder may give rise to suspicions. This is the case, for example, in the statement evidently written and signed by the 94-year-old James How Sr. in defense of his daughter-in-law Elizabeth.[48]

As several researchers have pointed out, in the early colonial period writing literacy (as opposed to reading literacy) was still predominantly a career skill that was acquired by men who needed this ability in their profession.[49] It therefore comes as no surprise that all currently identified Salem recorders are male and for most of them writing seems to have been, if not strictly required by their occupation, at least strongly recommended.[50] In addition to clerks and secretaries (e.g., Isaac Addington, Stephen Sewall), the most obvious category comprises men holding various legal occupations and offices: magistrates (e.g., John Hathorne, Robert Pike); marshals and sheriffs (e.g., Samuel Gookin, George Herrick); and constables (e.g., John Ballard of Andover, Ephraim Wilds of

Topsfield).[51] Another almost equally prominent group includes members of the clergy (e.g., John Hale, Samuel Parris, Edward Payson).[52] It is worth noting that some of these legal and clerical recorders were merchants by profession or had worked as such at some point in their lives – a career that likewise involved writing as an essential skill.[53] The named recorders also include men who are identified in the documents with the status of a yeoman (freeholder). Some of them were holding a legal or clerical office at the time of the witch-hunt (e.g., Jonathan Putnam as constable, Edward Putnam as deacon), or prior to it (Thomas Putnam as parish clerk), but this does not seem to apply to all representatives of the group (e.g., Ezekiel Cheever).[54] It is possible that yeomen were likely to be chosen as recorders because of their social status.[55]

A greater part of the recorders still remain anonymous. Some of them are found in text categories or types of entries where signatures were not even expected (indictments, notes about deponents swearing their testimonies,

---

[47] No. 876.   [48] No. 341.

[49] See, for example, E. Jennifer Monaghan and E. Wendy Saul, "The Reader, the Scribe, the Thinker: A Critical Look at the History of American Reading and Writing Instruction," in *The Formation of School Subjects: The Struggle for Creating an American Institution*, ed. Thomas S. Popkewitz (New York: The Falmer Press, 1987), pp. 85–122; E. Jennifer Monaghan, "Literacy Instruction and Gender in Colonial New England," in *Reading in America: Literature & Social History*, ed. Cathy N. Davidson (Baltimore, MD: The Johns Hopkins University Press, 1989), pp. 53–80; Thornton, *Handwriting*, pp. 5–6.

[50] The witchcraft records written concurrently with the 1692 episode contain some probably authentic signatures by women, but in these cases the body of the document that precedes them appears to have been written in a different hand. See, for example, the testimonies of Mary English Regarding Mary Warren (No. 263) and Mary Webber v. George Burroughs (No. 446). However, as demonstrated by the comment of John Hale (in No. 189) concerning a note written by John Trask's wife Christian, there seems to have been some degree of female writing literacy in the local community that extended beyond the ability to sign one's name. In the early eighteenth-century material there are some documents possibly recorded by women, such as the letter of Mary Burroughs (No. 962). The findings reported by Mary Beth Norton, "Communications," *The William and Mary Quarterly*, 3rd ser., Vol. 48 (1991), pp. 639–645, and Joel Perlmann and Dennis Shirley, "When Did New England Women Acquire Literacy?" *The William and Mary Quarterly*, 3rd ser., Vol. 48 (1991), pp. 50–67, suggest that by the end of the eighteenth century the writing literacy rate of New England women had significantly improved.

[51] Isaac Addington (e.g., No. 873), Stephen Sewall (e.g., No. 324), John Hathorne (e.g., No. 79), Robert Pike (e.g., No. 140), Samuel Gookin (e.g., No. 265), John Ballard (e.g., No. 443), Ephraim Wilds (e.g., No. 579). Not all these recorders have been identified by name in the notes to individual documents, because their role in the writing of the documents has not been globally analyzed. For a list of the recorders identified in the notes, see "General Introduction."

[52] John Hale (e.g., No. 410), Samuel Parris (e.g., No. 120), Edward Payson (e.g., No. 471).

[53] The role of commerce in promoting colonial writing literacy has been discussed by Thornton, *Handwriting*, pp. 5–6. Of the identified Salem recorders, Jonathan Corwin, John Hathorne, Samuel Parris, and Stephen Sewall, for example, were or had been merchants; see Richard B. Trask, *The Devil Hath Been Raised: A Documentary History of the Salem Village Witchcraft Outbreak of March 1692; Together with a Collection of Newly Located and Gathered Witchcraft Documents* (Danvers, MA: Yeoman Press, 1997), pp. 124–130.

[54] Jonathan Putnam (e.g., No. 260), Edward Putnam (e.g., No. 21), Thomas Putnam (e.g., No. 251), Ezekiel Cheever (e.g., No. 3). Cheever was a tailor by profession (Trask, *The Devil*, p. 124); that he was son of a Boston schoolteacher may in part account for his writing skills.

[55] The data are few and no statistical significance can be attached to them, but the apparent absence of people identified with the lower status of a husbandman among the named recorders might also imply a social stratification in writing literacy similar to what has been observed in Early Modern England between yeomen and husbandmen; see David Cressy, *Literacy and the Social Order: Reading and Writing in Tudor and Stuart England* (Cambridge: Cambridge University Press, 1980), pp. 125–127. For yeomen as a class in colonial America, see, e.g., Allan Kulikoff, "The Transition to Capitalism in Rural America," *The William and Mary Quarterly*, 3rd ser., Vol. 46 (1989), pp. 120–144.

dockets, etc.); the majority occur, however, in depositions that are either left unsigned or which have been signed by a person other than the recorder. It is not uncommon to find that an anonymous recorder wrote down more than one deposition for a single individual or for members of a household.[56] The evidence provided by the depositions with named recorders suggests that it may be worthwhile to start the search for the identity of such anonymous recorders from the family or household members themselves. Samuel Parris, for example, recorded most of the depositions made by his niece Abigail Williams; the same applies to Thomas Putnam as the usual recorder of the depositions of not only his wife (Ann Putnam Sr.) and daughter (Ann Putnam Jr.), but also her maidservant (Mercy Lewis) and the step-daughter of his sister Deliverance (Mary Walcott).[57] In addition to the male members of the extended household as plausible recorder candidates, the data from the named recorders pinpoint local ministers, magistrates, and town clerks as other such individuals whose services were likely to have been sought by people whose writing skills were not adequate for the purpose of writing down depositions.[58]

Whether named or anonymous, the recorders are not evenly distributed across the text categories in terms of numbers. The main difference lies between the categories that were produced centrally at the court or otherwise written on the initiative of the magistrates (confessions, examination records, indictments, mittimuses, recognizances, summonses, warrants) and the categories that are more likely to have been written locally on the initiative of the accusers, defendants, and witnesses (depositions, petitions). As one would expect, it is in the latter group where the majority of the recorders are to be found. Of the text categories in the former group, most were written by just a few recorders each. The court clerk Stephen Sewall, for example, wrote practically all of the summonses for witnesses, and the magistrates John Hathorne and Jonathan

Corwin composed the bulk of the arrest warrants. In both types of document, however, the returns made on their reverse contain handwriting by a large number of constables.

The output of the Salem recorders provides a cross section of the models, styles, and registers prevalent in colonial handwriting around the turn of the eighteenth century – from formal legal hands (see Facsimile No. 5) and trendy mercantile roundhands (see Facsimile No. 8) to more old-fashioned hands that still show strong influence of the secretary script.[59] Such variation largely reflects the personal history of the recorders in terms of their age, education, and professional background. The main hand of No. 439, for example, belongs to the Salisbury captain Thomas Bradbury – an experienced penman who was over 80 at the time of the witchcraft episode.[60] He is one of the few recorders in the whole material using the archaic secretary form of the letter 'h,' although even here the modern form is found in the majority of the instances.[61] As suggested by the formality of the main hands in many indictments, for example, the conventions of the text category may also help to explain some of the variation observed in the handwriting of the Salem recorders.

[56] One anonymous recorder, for instance, wrote down three depositions that all involve Captain Jonathan Walcott's children as deponents (No. 205, No. 210, No. 213). He teamed with Thomas Putnam in recording a fourth deposition relating to the same family (No. 171). The reverse of No. 205 also contains a contribution by Putnam.

[57] See Trask, *The Devil*, pp. 124–131, for biographical information on these deponents.

[58] Cusack, *Everyday English*, p. 92, discusses the taking of depositions locally in Early Modern England. See Cressy, *Literacy*, p. 15, for the practice of people hiring writing services from their neighbors.

[59] "Secretary" may be regarded as the everyday script of sixteenth- and early seventeenth-century England. For general trends in the development of handwriting in Early Modern England and early colonial America, see Giles E. Dawson and Laetitia Kennedy-Skipton, *Elizabethan Handwriting 1500–1650: A Guide to the Reading of Documents and Manuscripts* (London: Faber and Faber, 1968), pp. 7–10; Anthony G. Petti, *English Literary Hands from Chaucer to Dryden* (London: Edward Arnold, 1977), pp. 15–21; L. C. Hector, *The Handwriting of English Documents*, 2nd ed. (Dorking: Kohler and Coombes, 1980 [1966]), pp. 60–64; Laetitia Yeandle, "The Evolution of Handwriting in the English-Speaking Colonies of America," *The American Archivist*, Vol. 43 (1980), pp. 294–311; Jean F. Preston and Laetitia Yeandle, *English Handwriting 1400–1650: An Introductory Manual* (Binghamton, NY: Medieval & Renaissance Texts & Studies, 1992), pp. vii–viii.

[60] For further examples, see Hiltunen and Peikola, "Trial Discourse." For Thomas Bradbury, see Mary Beth Norton, *In the Devil's Snare: The Salem Witchcraft Crisis of 1692* (New York: Alfred A. Knopf, 2002), pp. 181, 228. That the hand of No. 439 belongs to Bradbury can be verified by comparing it against earlier specimens of handwriting that bear his signature, such as the deposition of Richard Ormsby, from 1656, in the case of Eunice Cole of Hampton (Massachusetts Archives Collections, Vol. 135, No. 3).

[61] For the letter 'h' in the secretary script, see Hector, *The Handwriting*, p. 61; Samuel A. Tannenbaum, *The Handwriting of the Renaissance* (New York: Columbia University Press, 1930), pp. 46–47.

4. SPELLING, PRONUNCIATION, WORD BOUNDARIES, CAPITALIZATION, AND PUNCTUATION

Spelling and Pronunciation

The Salem documents supply rich material for the study of features of spelling and to some extent pronunciation in late seventeenth-century New England. At the time of the Salem trials, there was no standard orthographical system of English.[62] However, in formal court documents such as indictments, warrants, and summonses, which were primarily written by court clerks and justices of the peace, the spelling is highly regular and fairly close to modern standard conventions, anticipating what was later to become the standard spelling system.

Even more fascinating is the orthography found in documents such as depositions, constables' returns on summonses and warrants, and some examinations, many of which seem to have been written by recorders with less formal training in writing (see Section 3). These documents frequently contain spellings that appear to have been guided by the recorders' pronunciation.[63] The orthographical patterns in these documents can thus make features of late seventeenth-century pronunciation accessible to us, which we would not otherwise have access to in the absence of audio recordings.

Below, we outline some of the major spelling patterns in the Salem material, focusing on depositions, and relate the patterns to contemporaneous as well as Present-Day pronunciation. Ideally, when the phonetic status of a spelling is evaluated, it should be evaluated within the whole spelling system of a particular recorder. However, such an approach will have to await the conclusion of the work on the identification of recorders. We will concentrate on patterns in the Salem corpus as a whole, but we will also mention some individual patterns.[64] The discussion below is structured around the spellings found in the

Salem records: each entry heading lists the graphemes in the documents that are discussed in the entry. In the case of vowels in particular, the same grapheme may appear in more than one entry since the grapheme may be involved in different patterns of variation in different contexts.[65]

Vowels (in Stressed Syllables)

'a,' 'ai,' 'e,' 'ee,' and 'o': Words that are normally spelled with 'a' (or 'ea') in Present-Day English are found with 'a,' 'ai,' 'e,' 'ee,' or 'o' spellings in the Salem material (see also *vowel + 'r'* and *Vowels in Unstressed Syllables*). In a few words that are commonly pronounced [eɪ] in Present-Day English, 'ai' is used instead of 'a' by some recorders, as in "Aiged" and "straing" for *strange*.[66] On the other hand, 'a' is sometimes found instead of Present-Day 'ai' or 'ei,' as "agane" and "naghbours."[67] Other recorders prefer 'e,' as in "eged," "Rechell," "teke," or even 'ee' as in "greet" (for *great*).[68] This variable spelling probably indicates that several originally distinct vowel sounds had fallen together as one sound for some recorders (probably as a long vowel which in time developed into Present-Day [eɪ]).[69] This mirrors the development in contemporaneous England. In some words that are usually pronounced [æ] today, 'e' is used by some recorders instead of 'a,' as in "heth," "heve," and "Jennywary" for *January*, which may indicate a raising of the vowel.[70] Spellings with 'o' instead of 'a' are used by some recorders after 'w(h)' and 'qu' in, for example, "whot," "quolity," and "wose," which probably signals a pronunciation similar to the one found in these words in standard Present-Day British English ([ɒ]).[71]

'e' and 'i' (or 'ee'): The effects of two long-term sound changes, the development of [e] into [ɪ], on the one hand, and that of [ɪ] into [e], on the other, cause fluctuation

---

[62] Richard L. Venezky, "Spelling," in *The Cambridge History of the English Language*, Vol. 6, *English in North America*, ed. John Algeo (Cambridge: Cambridge University Press, 2001), pp. 342–343.

[63] Some phonetic spellings in depositions and examinations may represent the witness's pronunciation or the recorder's comprehension of what the witness said. Since this connection is difficult to prove, however, we attribute phonetic spellings primarily to the recorder. See Grund, Kytö, and Rissanen, "Editing," p. 159.

[64] For using spelling as an indication of pronunciation, see Roger Lass, "Phonology and Morphology," in *The Cambridge History*

of the English Language, Vol. 3, *1476–1776*, ed. Roger Lass (Cambridge: Cambridge University Press, 1999), pp. 65–66.

[65] For the key to the phonetic symbols used in this section, see J. C. Wells, *Longman Pronunciation Dictionary* (London: Longman, 1990).

[66] E.g., No. 262, No. 140.

[67] E.g., No. 160, No. 322.

[68] E.g., No. 413, No. 37, No. 243, No. 85.

[69] Lass, "Phonology," pp. 91–93, 95–98.

[70] E.g., No. 543, No. 681, No. 42. Lass, "Phonology," p. 85; Henry Cecil Wyld, *A History of Modern Colloquial English*, 3rd ed. (Oxford: Basil Blackwell, 1936), p. 198. The 'e' in "heth" and "heve" may also represent a reduced vowel sound. See *Vowels in Unstressed Syllables*.

[71] E.g., No. 681, No. 40, and No. 602. See Lass, "Phonology," p. 86; Wyld, *A History*, p. 202.

in the spellings of the Salem documents. Evidence of the former development includes spellings with 'i' where Present-Day English has 'e,' e.g., "tistimony," "nick(e)," "diuill," "cliver," "prity," and "hin" for *hen*.[72] However, these 'i' spellings are in the minority in the Salem material. Conversely, instances of the opposite development include spellings with 'e' or 'ee' where Present-Day English has 'i,' e.g., "penching," "tell," "reuer," and "ell."[73] Thomas Putnam, for example, uses exclusively "afflect" or "afflet" (in different forms) for *afflict*, and "sence" for *since*. Evidence of possible lengthening of the vowel is found in spellings such as "heet" for *hit*, "teel(l)" for *tell*.[74]

'o,' 'oa,' 'oo,' 'ou,' 'ow,' and 'u': The Salem documents exhibit great variation in the use of spellings with 'o,' 'oa,' 'oo,' 'ou,' 'ow,' and 'u.' An illustrative example is found in the spelling of the modals *could*, *should*, and *would*. *Could* is spelled "Cold," "coold," "could," or "cowld" in the documents, whereas *should* appears in the spellings "shold," "shoold," "should," and "shuld," and *would* in the spellings "wold," "woold," and "would."[75] Words that are spelled with 'o' in Present-Day English (and normally pronounced [əʊ] or [oʊ]) are often found with 'oo,' 'ow,' and sometimes even 'oa' spelling, as in "Gooe," "agow," "boane" for *bone*, and "choak," which is consistently preferred by Thomas Putnam.[76] Words that are spelled with 'o' or 'u' in Present-Day English (and are usually pronounced [ʌ]) vary between the two spellings in the Salem documents, such as in "sum" and "some," "Cum" and "come," and "somonses" and "sumonsed."[77] These spelling patterns are perhaps indicative of the falling together of several previously distinct sounds, at least for some recorders.[78]

vowel + 'r': There is a great deal of variation in the spelling of *vowel* + 'r' combinations in the Salem documents. A case in point is Present-Day *her*, which is found as "har," "her," "hir," "hor," or "hur."[79] Other examples of this phenomenon include (among others) "Gerle," "Cartify," "consarning" for *concerning*, "parsons" for *persons*, "burd," and "thirsday."[80] This variation reflects a number of very complex phonological developments that were taking place during the Early Modern period.[81] The variable spelling suggests that vowels that were originally pronounced in distinct ways (as [ɑr], [er], [ir], [ur]) had fallen together. The choice of *vowel* + 'r' combination seems to vary both according to lexical item and according to recorder: Thomas Putnam, for example, almost exclusively uses "parson" for *person*, but almost always prefers "hir" for *her*.[82] There are also many examples of the spelling 'er' for Present-Day English 'r' or 're,' such as "fier," "Desier," "atier" for *attire*, "tyerd" for *tired*, and "suer" for *sure*.[83] These spellings indicate the [ə] sound that developed in this position from the fifteenth century onwards and is pronounced even today in some varieties of English.[84] In a few cases, this vowel seems also to have developed between a medial consonant and 'r,' as in "Henery" and "Angery," found in the Salem records.[85]

Vowels in Unstressed Syllables

Variable spellings of vowels in syllables that are unstressed (or that do not take primary stress) suggest that originally distinct vowel sounds had fallen together under a reduced vowel sound, such as [ə], for some recorders. This is the pronunciation commonly found in this position in Present-Day English.[86] Illustrative examples of this phenomenon are found in, for instance, "pashan" for *passion*, "coler" for *color*, and "Diponant."[87]

[72] E.g., No. 465, No. 419, No. 524, No. 160, No. 558.
[73] E.g., No. 391, No. 365, No. 552.
[74] E.g., No. 354, No. 499, No. 633. Cf. William Matthews, "The Vulgar Speech of London in the XV–XVII Centuries," *Notes and Queries*, Vol. 173 (1937), pp. 56, 77; Henry Alexander, "The Language of the Salem Witchcraft Trials," *American Speech*, Vol. 3 (1928), p. 393.
[75] For *could*, see No. 385, No. 148, No. 684, No. 243; for *should*, see No. 256, No. 142, No. 336, No. 560; for *would*, see No. 384, No. 140, No. 784.
[76] E.g., No. 179, No. 87, No. 575, No. 112.
[77] E.g., No. 42, No. 174, No. 38, No. 441, No. 140, No. 614.
[78] See Lass, "Phonology," pp. 87–94.
[79] E.g., No. 497, No. 574, No. 112, No. 365, No. 317.
[80] E.g., No. 43, No. 602, No. 322, No. 60, No. 21, No. 707.
[81] Lass, "Phonology," pp. 108–113. See also Grund, Kytö, and Rissanen, "Editing," pp. 160–164.
[82] E.g., No. 54 and No. 668. See also Grund, Kytö, and Rissanen, "Editing," pp. 158–159.
[83] E.g., No. 279, No. 126, No. 36, No. 311, No. 322.
[84] Lass, "Phonology," p. 109; Wyld, *A History*, p. 300.
[85] E.g., No. 353, No. 279, No. 487, No. 463, No. 125. See Matthews, "The Vulgar Speech," p. 219.
[86] Wyld, *A History*, pp. 258–259. However, since Early Modern writers on pronunciation do not mention the pronunciation of unstressed vowels explicitly, Lass surmises that the variable spellings may be an indication that there was "a set of centralised vowels . . . whose qualities were reminiscent of certain stressed vowels"; Lass, "Phonology," p. 133.
[87] No. 561, No. 160, No. 38.

Consonants

'gh,' 'ght,' 't,' and 'f': The vacillation between these spellings reflects several developments recorded in Early Modern English. Spellings with 't' are sometimes found in words commonly spelled with 'ght' and vice versa, such as "brot" for *brought*, "poght" for *pot*, "ought" for *out*, and "abought."[88] These spellings signal that 'ght' and 't' represented the same sounds ([t]), as in Present-Day English. Originally, 'gh' was pronounced [χ] (as in Modern German *ach*) in this context, but this sound gradually disappeared during the Early Modern English period. In some words, the sound developed into [f], which is reflected in Salem spellings such as "enuf(e)" and "lafed," for Present-Day *enough* and *laughed*.[89] Among other interesting spellings in this category are instances such as "thof" for *though*, and "dafter" (for *daughter*, frequently in the documents by Edward Putnam and John Hathorne).[90] Oscillation is also attested in the spelling of words with front vowels preceding the former [ç] sound (as in Modern German *ich*), e.g., "righting"/"right" for *writing/write*, "brite" for *bright*, "frited," "frittng" for *frighted, frighting*, and "lite" for *light*.[91]

'ng' and 'n': The dropping of [g] in words such as *walking* is a common feature in Present-Day spoken (informal) English, and is recorded as early as the fifteenth century. This phenomenon also existed in late seventeenth-century Salem, which is evidenced by spellings such as "Raisen," "meten-house," "gowen" for *going*, "pudens" for *puddings*, "stockin," and "riggin."[92] There are also inverted spellings ('ng' for 'n') that underscore that 'n' and 'ng' spellings probably represented the same pronunciation for at least some recorders: "suding" for *sudden*, "Lening" for *linen*, "Childringe," "forting" for *fortune*.[93]

'h'-dropping: There are very few spellings in the Salem documents that imply that initial aspirated [h] was not always sounded, e.g., "oure," "ouer," both for *hour*, and "as"

for *has*.[94] However, there are several instances of the indefinite article *an* preceding words starting with 'h,' which could be taken as an indication of non-pronunciation of the [h] sound, e.g., "an honest woman," "an hood," "an halfe," "an heart," "an high-crown'd hat," "an hour."[95]

'r'-dropping and 'r'-insertion: The Salem documents contain evidence of the fluctuation in the pronunciation of the [r] sound, which is documented in English records at least as early as the fifteenth century.[96] On the one hand, 'r' has been dropped in medial position in spellings such as "Geale" for *girl*, "nuss" for *Nurse*, and "Googe" for *George*.[97] Several 'r'-less spellings are found in documents by Thomas Putnam, such as "pasons," "Chalstown," "toment," "uging" for *urging*, and "magarit" (though spellings with 'r' predominate).[98] There are also instances of 'r'-dropping in final position in spellings such as "doe" for *door*, "mothe" for *mother*, and "he" for *her*.[99] On the other hand, we find instances of 'r'-insertion in spellings such as "parth" for *path*, "worter" for *water*, "Dearth" for *death*, "surspected," "depersision" for *deposition*, "f(f)orknor" for *Faulkner*, "confarsed" for *confessed*, and "murst."[100] Although the insertion of 'r' in these words may mark vowel length, it seems more likely that it is, in fact, a sign of [r] dropping: since [r] was no longer pronounced in medial position, the letter could be inserted in words where it did not historically occur. The majority of those settling in eastern New England came from [r]-less areas in southeastern England and were users of the by then already prestigious [r]-less forms.[101]

's,' 't,' and 'sh': The [s] sound is sometimes represented by the spelling 'sh,' again as a reflection of a long-term

[88] E.g., No. 551, No. 385, No. 327.
[89] E.g., No. 185, No. 21, No. 378.
[90] E.g., No. 317, No. 72, No. 413. For background, see, e.g., Lass, "Phonology," pp. 116–118; Matthews, "The Vulgar Speech," pp. 169–170.
[91] E.g., No. 76, No. 391, No. 141, No. 160, No. 321.
[92] E.g., No. 37 and No. 40 (written by the same recorder), No. 551, No. 42, and No. 268 and No. 600 (written by the same recorder). See Lass, "Phonology," p. 120; Wyld, *A History*, pp. 289–290.
[93] E.g., No. 378, No. 560, No. 384.
[94] E.g., No. 551, No. 32, No. 376; No. 54, No. 137.
[95] E.g., No. 598, No. 77, No. 336, No. 63, No. 89, No. 464. Cf. Anders Orbeck, *Early New England Pronunciation as Reflected in Some Seventeenth Century Town Records of Eastern Massachusetts* (Ann Arbor, MI: Gi Wahr, 1927), pp. 81–82.
[96] See, e.g., Lass, "Phonology," pp. 114–116; Matthews, "The Vulgar Speech," pp. 218–219.
[97] E.g., No. 37, No. 289, No. 163.
[98] E.g., No. 136, No. 267, No. 671, No. 598, No. 644.
[99] E.g., No. 509, No. 412, No. 80. Note that some of these spellings may be incidental mistakes.
[100] E.g., No. 40, No. 41, No. 38 all by one and the same recorder; No. 558, No. 561, No. 559 all by one and the same recorder; No. 657, No. 5.
[101] For discussion and references, see Merja Kytö, "The Emergence of American English: Evidence from Seventeenth-Century Records in New England," in *Legacies of Colonial English. Studies in Transported Dialects*, ed. Raymond Hickey (Cambridge: Cambridge University Press, 2004), pp. 136–137.

sound change already at work in England.[102] This tendency was characteristic of several dialects (chiefly East Midland and Northern) and affected final [s] sounds (e.g., "kish" for *kiss*) but could be attested even in the middle and at the beginning of words.[103] Among characteristic examples in the Salem records can be given "shuch" for *such*.[104] Conversely, the [ʃ] sound could also be spelled as 's,' e.g., "soulder" for *shoulder*, "serins" for *Sherins*.[105] In unstressed syllables, such as in *-tion*, *-sion*, and similar spellings in Present-Day English, the development of the original [s] sound into [ʃ] is reflected in spellings such as "pashon," "ocashons," and "deposishtion."[106] Thomas Putnam uses predominantly "apperishtion" for *apparition*.

'wh,' 'w,' 'h,' and 'wr': The Salem records provide evidence of the loss of distinction between the previous [w] and [hw] sounds, which was taking place simultaneously in England.[107] Thus we find 'w' and 'wh' spellings used interchangeably to convey the initial sound in words such as "wen" for *when*, "hom" for *whom*, "wheal" for *well*, and "Whings" for *wings*. That words such as *written* and *wright* were pronounced by some recorders as in Present-Day English (instead of earlier [wr]) is indicated by spellings such as "reten" and "wheleright."[108]

'l,' 'n,' and 'r' representing syllabic segments: Spellings with 'l,' 'n,' and 'r' without a preceding vowel suggest that these three letters represent syllabic segments (i.e., the consonant on its own represents a syllable, as [n] in Present-Day English *button* [bʌtn]) or that a syllable has been lost. Examples of this phenomenon, which is also recorded in England in the same period, include "constabll," "rekninge," "wondred," and in particular forms of *threaten* as in "threatning."[109] However, spellings such as "midel," "bridil," and "Gerill" for *girl* signal that an [el] or [ɪl] pronunciation also occurred.[110]

Voicing and unvoicing of consonants: Examples exist throughout the Salem documents that suggest voicing of originally unvoiced consonants, a phenomenon that has also been recorded in studies of Early Modern texts from England.[111] 'B' instead of 'p' is especially common, as in "babtized," "debonant," "Debety" for *deputy*, "distember," "subtember" for *September*, and "bosit" for *possit* ('a medicinal drink'), but instances of other types of voicing also occur, as in "Bridged," "Gory" for *Corey*, and "visek" for *physic*.[112] Unvoicing is not as common but is suggested by, for instance, "desarfid" for *deserved* and "refil" for *revile*.[113]

Loss or addition of consonants: As in contemporaneous records from England, numerous spellings in the Salem records probably reflect the loss of consonants in speech, in either medial or final position. Absence of [d] may be reflected in instances such as "granmothers," "threshall" for *threshold*, "an" for *and*, and "chill" for *child*.[114] Similarly, absence of [t] may be signaled in, e.g., "gretes" for *greatest*, "nex," "tempen" for *tempting*, and "oges" for *August*.[115] Other examples, such as "solem" or "sollom" for *solemn*, "nume" for *numb*, and "Lime" for *limb*, indicate that letters that were never pronounced but only present in spelling ('n,' 'b') may have been dropped in writing, probably in approximation of speech.[116] We also find instances of unhistoric spellings with added consonants, e.g., "knotes" for *notes* and "knight" for *night*.[117]

Word Boundaries

The Salem records contain a number of spellings indicating that some recorders followed pronunciation closely and/or perhaps were not always sure about the boundaries between words. Among these spellings are instances such as "ofland" (for *of land*) and "astrang" (for *a strange*), "apoole" (for *a pole*), "awoman," "amoment," and "aman," where a preposition or the indefinite article has been written together as one item with its headword.[118] Conversely, some recorders use forms such as "a boue," "a bout," "a pon," and "a broad," where an initial "a" has been detached from the original form. Spellings also occur where verbal

---

[102] See, e.g., Matthews, "The Vulgar Speech," p. 186.
[103] See E. J. Dobson, *English Pronunciation 1500–1700*, 2 vols. (Oxford: Clarendon Press, 1957), Vol. 2, §373.
[104] E.g., No. 66, No. 601.
[105] E.g., No. 605, No. 322.
[106] E.g., No. 208, No. 378, No. 243.
[107] Lass, "Phonology," p. 122.
[108] E.g., No. 365, No. 598, No. 384, No. 5, No. 551. See Matthews, "The Vulgar Speech," pp. 204–205.
[109] No. 412, No. 384, No. 72, No. 142. See Lass, "Phonology," pp. 135–136; Wyld, *A History*, pp. 406–408.
[110] No. 21, No. 322, No. 38. See Matthews, "The Vulgar Speech," p. 132.

[111] Wyld, *A History*, pp. 312–313; Matthews, "The Vulgar Speech," pp. 149–151.
[112] E.g., No. 521, No. 559, No. 201, No. 358, No. 657, No. 598, No. 279, No. 48.
[113] No. 317.
[114] E.g., No. 35, No. 139, No. 374, No. 365.
[115] E.g., No. 202, No. 327, No. 543, No. 551.
[116] E.g., No. 708, No. 87, No. 378, No. 38.
[117] E.g., No. 632, No. 684.
[118] See No. 463, No. 370, No. 570.

endings have been separated from the verb, as in "be ing," "deny ing," and "say ing."[119] Spellings such as "of ten" and "nay bor hud"[120] also occur, which may reflect word-internal stress patterns.[121]

Capitalization

The use of capital letters in the Salem records differs significantly from Present-Day usage, but shows the same tendencies as contemporaneous English records. As for spelling in general, no standard system of capitalization existed at the time of the Salem trials.[122] Names of people, places, and months are far from always capitalized in the Salem documents. New sentences (where clear sentence boundaries can be established) rarely begin with a capital, and if they do, it is doubtful whether the capitals should be seen as connected with the beginning of a new sentence. By contrast, many words that would not be capitalized today frequently begin with capital letters.

Significantly, capitalization varies with each recorder. Some recorders use capital letters sparingly, whereas others use them liberally. The unidentified recorder of No. 365 (Hand 1), for example, only uses capitals for the first word of the deposition ("The") and in the names "Thomas Jacob" and "John," but not in "mery" (*Mary*) or in "bib-bor" (*Bibber*) or in any other word. Two of the unidentified recorders of the indictments, on the other hand, often employ capital letters, in particular in nouns, verbs, and adjectives, but also sometimes in prepositions and conjunctions.[123] This usage may perhaps be connected with the official nature of the indictments, the capitals being used for emphasis or for aesthetic reasons.[124] Some

recorders also show a preference for capitals of certain letters. For example, the recorder of a number of depositions against Rachel Clinton almost exclusively prefers capital 'C,' 'L,' and 'R' at the beginning of words instead of 'c,' 'l,' and 'r'; capital 'L' even appears word-medially.[125]

In a few cases, enlarged small letters (or minuscules) seem to function as capitals. A large minuscule 'a' is adopted by some recorders (especially in indictments), and large minuscule 'm' and 'n' also occur. A special case of minuscules used for capitals is 'ff' instead of 'F.' This usage, which is commonplace in Early Modern texts, is found throughout the Salem documents.[126] In fact, 'ff' far outnumbers 'F,' which is only employed by a limited number of recorders.[127]

Determining whether a letter form is capital or minuscule in the Salem documents is often difficult. This is particularly the case if the recorder uses the same form of letter for capitals and minuscules and only varies the size of the letters. The letters 'c/C,' 'p/P,' 's/S,' and 'w/W' are especially problematic to distinguish.

Punctuation

At the time of the Salem witchcraft trials, the use of punctuation marks had not yet been fully standardized. Consequently, compared with Present-Day English, the punctuation practices of the Salem recorders may often seem quite inconsistent if not arbitrary. However, the type of punctuation mark used, its function, and the extent to which it is used vary greatly with different recorders.[128]

The Salem recorders had most of the punctuation marks available today at their disposal. However, only a few of these occur in the records, and there are also marks that do not appear in Present-Day English. The period ('.'), the comma (','), the colon (':'), and the semicolon (';') are particularly common. The virgule ('/'), the question mark ('?'), the apostrophe ('''), double periods ('..'),[129] and

---

[119] See No. 377, No. 605, No. 368 (this document also has an instance of "me ting" for *meeting*).

[120] See No. 365 (Hand 1).

[121] In many documents it has not always been easy to determine whether a word was intended to be one or two items: there can be a good deal of variation in the length of the spaces separating items on a line. In these indeterminate uses, and in the cases discussed above, modernized forms have been opted for in the transcriptions.

[122] See, e.g., D. G. Scragg, *A History of English Spelling* (Manchester: Manchester University Press, 1974); N. E. Osselton, "Spelling-Book Rules and the Capitalization of Nouns in the Seventeenth and Eighteenth Centuries," in *Historical and Editorial Studies in Medieval and Early Modern English*, ed. Mary-Jo Arn and Hanneke Wirtjes (Groningen: Wolters-Noordhoff, 1985), pp. 49–61.

[123] See, e.g., No. 641, No. 804.

[124] Vivian Salmon, "Orthography and Punctuation," in *The Cambridge History of the English Language*, Vol. 3, *1476–1776*, ed.

Roger Lass (Cambridge: Cambridge University Press, 1999), pp. 50–51.

[125] See, e.g., No. 40, No. 37, No. 41.

[126] Tannenbaum, *The Handwriting*, p. 92.

[127] For 'F,' see No. 210 and No. 190.

[128] In addition to obviously intended punctuation marks, the Salem records also contain inadvertent marks probably left by the writers resting their writing implements on the paper or testing the ink. It is sometimes difficult to tell these incidental marks apart from actual punctuation marks.

[129] See, e.g., No. 519.

parentheses ('(. . .)') also occur, but more infrequently. Some recorders use several of these punctuation marks, whereas others prefer one particular mark or use no marks at all.[130] Simon Willard, for example, uses almost exclusively colons, and Edward Putnam prefers periods, which often appear above the line. Edward Putnam also uses an idiosyncratic marker that appears to signal a new paragraph.[131] Samuel Parris is among the rare recorders who use question marks.[132]

Scholars have proposed two main theories to account for Early Modern punctuation practices. On the one hand, punctuation in early texts has been taken to mark off grammatical units and thus help the reader to follow the text; on the other hand, punctuation has been seen to serve rhetorical purposes and mark the length of pauses and rhythmical units.[133] However, these functions tend to merge, as phrasal and syntactic units are often followed by pauses in speech.[134] How grammatical units can be marked off in some Salem records is shown by the following two examples by Simon Willard, who uses colons to indicate clausal units (1) and verb and adverbial phrases as well (2):

(1) S^d Tayler was bid to look on Mrs Mary Marshall: & did & s^d Marshall was struck down by it & s^d when she could speak it was s^d Tayler y^t struck her down: Mary lascy s^d also y^t s^d Tayler was upon s^d Marshall Tayler was told she had a dangerous eye: that struck

folk down: which gives ground to think she was a witch: but she s^d she was not sencible she was one (No. 546)

(2) Wardwell also s^d that s^d Lilly: did triumph: when she went away from ye firing of Hoopers hous but she s^d she was in her own hous all that time & that she never went: in body nor spirit nor ~~ever~~ ever had any inclynation to witchcraft: Maj^r Sway told her she had bin a frequenter of Dostins hous: but she s^d if she confessed any thing of this she shou{d} deny ye truth & wrong her own soul. (No. 544)

But Willard can also use colons (and other punctuation marks) for other purposes, e.g., to mark off single words (3):

(3) Sarah Vibber: owned to ye Jury of inquest that ye abowe written evidence: is truth: upon ye oath she hath taken: ~~Jly.~~ July 2: 92

Mary Warin: testifieth ["th" written over "d"] before ye Jury of inquest: that: she saw. Dorcas Hoare: of Beaverly: hurt and afflict: Susanah: Sheldon: then in ye presence of ye s^d Jury July: 2: 1692 (No. 402)

5. MORPHOLOGY, SYNTAX, AND VOCABULARY

The Early Modern English period, the sixteenth and seventeenth centuries, played an important role in the shaping of the English language. In this period the structural and dialectal variability and complexity of medieval English gave way to more standardized forms of the language. Shakespeare's or Queen Elizabeth's English is still rather difficult to read, and many words and expressions are easily misunderstood, whereas the language of the writings of Joseph Addison or Benjamin Franklin is fairly close to Present-Day English. In Early Modern English, for instance, some of the verbal endings disappeared, the personal and relative pronouns came to be used roughly in the way they are used today, the system of the auxiliary verbs *shall* and *will* was gradually established, and *do* came to be used in questions and negations. Other important morphological and syntactic changes referred to in this section are the loss of the so-called *his*-genitive (*the man his wife* 'the man's wife'), the final establishment of the past tense and participle forms of a number of strong verbs (*spoke* instead of *spake*; *have spoken* instead of *have spoke*),

---

[130] See, e.g., No. 128 (no punctuation marks).

[131] This mark has been represented in the transcriptions by starting a new paragraph; see No. 375, No. 601.

[132] See, e.g., No. 64, No. 86.

[133] For a standard work on the history of punctuation, see M. B. Parkes, *Pause and Effect. An Introduction to the History of Punctuation in the West* (Aldershot, Hants: Scolar Press, 1992); for discussion, see also Charles C. Fries, "Shakespearian Punctuation," in *Studies in Shakespeare, Milton and Donne, by Members of the English Department of the University of Michigan* (New York: Haskell House, 1964), pp. 67–86; Walter J. Ong, "Historical Backgrounds of Elizabethan and Jacobean Punctuation Theory," *Publications of the Modern Language Association of America*, Vol. 59 (1944), pp. 349–360; Vivian Salmon, "Early Seventeenth-Century Punctuation as a Guide to Sentence Structure," *Review of English Studies N. S.*, Vol. 13 (1962), pp. 347–360; Salmon, "Orthography and Punctuation," pp. 13–55; Merja Kytö, "'Therfor Speke Playnly to the Poynt': Punctuation in Robert Keayne's Notes of Church Meetings from Early Boston, New England," in *Language History and Linguistic Modelling. A Festschrift for Jacek Fisiak on his 60th Birthday*, ed. Raymond Hickey and Stanisław Puppel (Berlin: Mouton de Gruyter, 1997), pp. 323–342.

[134] See, e.g., Petti, *English Literary Hands*, p. 25.

the development of the *be* + *-ing* form, and the avoidance of double or multiple negation.[135]

The Salem documents give us valuable evidence of the character and development of English grammar and vocabulary in late seventeenth-century colonial circumstances (see Section 1). These documents still show a great deal of variation between the old and new forms, as, for instance, in the use of *-s* or *-th* as the third-person present singular ending of verbs, the formation of questions and negations with or without *do*, the use of *who* or *which* with personal reference, or the use of *thou* or *you* addressing one person. The richness of vocabulary, particularly of the words and phrases referring to late seventeenth-century American culture and rural society ("hiptshott," "3 graned" 'three-forked') and to beliefs in witchcraft ("apparition," "afflicted") is also of great interest.

The documents also make it possible to observe the variation of forms and usages in different types of text, from highly formal and stereotyped documents to the recordings of the utterances of men and women in varying social positions, educated and uneducated, in narrative contexts (depositions) and in dialogue (examinations); see Section 2. By comparing the occurrences of the variant forms in different text categories we can make observations about the paths of linguistic change in the colonial environment; about whether the changes first appear in everyday spoken language, or whether they come "from above," from formal or literary language.

Morphology and Syntax

As mentioned above, important changes in the system of verbal and nominal endings took place in the Early Modern English period. One was the replacement of the older *-th* ending by *-s* in the third-person present singular of verbs.[136] In the Salem documents *-th* is still common; in this respect their language can be regarded as conservative. This is particularly the case in the indictments and other texts representing formal language. The older ending is regularly used in frequently occurring formulaic phrases of the type "hath vsed Practised, & Exersised."[137] In depositions and examinations it is common in set expressions such as "testifieth & saith,"[138] and with some frequently used verbs such as *have* and *do*, although the form with *-s* also occurs. With most verbs the *-s* form is, however, more frequent than the *-th* form; note the form "saith" as against "sends," "brings," and "bids" in the following passage:

(4) she **saith** she **sends** the catt to bid hur pinch them: and the man **brings** the maid and **bids** hur pinch hur: (No. 5)

This kind of variation indicates that we are dealing with a change in progress; it is worth noting that with "saith" the recorder introduces what was said, while the subsequent verbs are included in the record of the witness's words.

The so-called *his*-genitive (*the man his wife* 'the man's wife') practically disappears from English by the end of the seventeenth century.[139] In the Salem documents there are a few examples of this type of genitive, mainly after proper names ending in *-s*; this may be just a spelling device to represent the pronunciation [ɪz]:

(5) abigail William, one of m^r parris **his** famyly and Elizabeth Hubert Docter Grigs **his** maid (No. 15)

---

[135] For an exhaustive general description of the English language and its development from the end of the fifteenth to the end of the eighteenth century, including all the features discussed in this section, see Roger Lass, ed., *The Cambridge History of the English Language*, Vol. 3, 1476–1776 (Cambridge: Cambridge University Press, 1999), especially Chapters 4 on syntax (Rissanen) and 5 on lexis and semantics (Nevalainen). See also, e.g., Charles Barber, *Early Modern English* (Edinburgh: Edinburgh University Press, 1997 [1976]); Terttu Nevalainen and Helena Raumolin-Brunberg, *Historical Sociolinguistics: Language Change in Tudor and Stuart England* (London: Longman, 2003); Terttu Nevalainen, *An Introduction to Early Modern English* (Edinburgh: Edinburgh University Press, 2006). Early American English is described in Algeo, "External History," with a very extensive bibliography. See also, e.g., Marckwardt, *American English*; Wolfgang Viereck, "On the Origins and Development of American English," in *Papers from the 6th International Conference on Historical Linguistics*, ed. Jacek Fisiak (Amsterdam and Poznań: Benjamins and Adam Mickiewicz University Press, 1985), pp. 561–569; Merja Kytö, *Variation and Diachrony, with Early American English in Focus. Studies on CAN/MAY and SHALL/WILL*, University of Bamberg Studies in English Linguistics, Vol. 28 (Frankfurt am Main: Peter Lang, 1991), and Kytö, "The Emergence."

[136] See, e.g., Orville Lawrence Abbott, "Verbal Endings in Seventeenth-Century American English," *American Speech*, Vol. 33 (1958), pp. 185–194; Merja Kytö, "Third-Person Present Singular Verb Inflection in Early British and American English," *Language Variation and Change*, Vol. 5 (1993), pp. 113–139.
[137] No. 330: see also No. 332, No. 331, etc.
[138] No. 336; see also No. 353, No. 24, etc.
[139] See, e.g., Barber, *Early Modern English*, pp. 200–201.

Old and/or dialectal past-tense and past-participle forms can be occasionally found in the Salem documents[140]:

(6) Mercy Lewes at length **spake**, & charged this woman with hurting & pinching her: (No. 241)

Other non-standard forms occurring in these documents are, e.g., "holden" for *held*, "rid" for *rode*.[141] The final *-n* does not always appear in the past participle in the same way as in Present-Day English:

(7) Sam^ll Wardwell Owned to this deponent that he **had Spoke** it to my Brother (No. 630)

An analogical weak past tense form can be used instead of the original strong form:

(8) shee allsoe said that shee **seed** a yalow ~~catt~~ burd that said unto hur sarue me and shee **seed** 2 catts (No. 5)

But it is to be noted that this passage represents the recorder's version of the speech of Tituba, who, judging by the recordings of her utterances, was not a native speaker of English.

The plural form *ye/you* of the second person pronoun replaced the singular form *thou* in the seventeenth century in most contexts; the older form was mainly used (1) to indicate affection or close relationship; (2) to indicate familiarity; (3) to indicate social difference, e.g., the master addressing his servant, or a parent addressing his/her child; or (4) as an insulting form of address.[142] *Thou* is not frequent in the Salem records, although isolated instances of types (2) and (4) can be found:

The accused to a witness:

(9) (Cloyce) when did I hurt **thee**? A. A great many times (No. 49)

From the stories of witnesses:

(10) I had had ben as good I had (for my oxn shoold never do me much more servis) vpon wch this deponent sayd d⟨o⟩st thretn me **thou** old wich or words to that efect resoluing to throw her into a brook that was fast by: (No. 311)

(11) she then cryed out it shall be known: **thou** wrech: hast **thou** vndone me body and soul. (No. 80)

The use of *who* (*whom*, *whose*) instead of the earlier *which*, referring to a person, was fairly well established in English in the seventeenth century.[143] This is also the case in the Salem documents. *Which* is, however, often used when apparitions are referred to:

(12) I saw the apperishtion of Sarah Good **which** did tortor me most greviously (No. 9)

There is also scribal variation showing that the usage was not yet quite established. Thomas Putnam, for instance, favors *which* when recording depositions, although he regularly uses *who* in the phrase "who testifieth and saith"[144]:

(13) The deposistion of mary walcott **who** testifieth and saith that I was for a considerable time afflectid by a woman **which** tould me hir name was Redd (No. 250)

The establishment of the auxiliary *do* in questions and negations is one of the most significant syntactic developments in Early Modern English.[145] The use of *do* in these contexts is well established in the Salem documents,[146] although there are some frequently used verbs, such as *know*, which are often negated without *do*:

(14) I know nothing of it. I am innocent to a Witch. I **know not** what a Witch is. (No. 64)

---

[140] See Kytö, "The Emergence," pp. 140–143. The variation in the strong and weak past tense and past participle forms occurring in seventeenth- and eighteenth-century English is discussed by Larisa Oldireva Gustafsson, *Preterite and Past Participle Forms in English 1680–1790: Standardisation Processes in Public and Private Writing*, Studia Anglistica Upsaliensia 120 (Uppsala: Acta Universitatis Upsaliensis, 2002).

[141] No. 259, No. 487, No. 426.

[142] See, e.g., Minna Nevala, *Address in Early English Correspondence. Its Forms and Socio-Pragmatic Functions*, Mémoires de la Société Néophilologique de Helsinki, Vol. 64 (Helsinki: Société Néophilologique, 2004), pp. 92–95; Terry Walker, Thou *and* You *in Early Modern English Dialogues: Trials, Depositions, and Drama Comedy*, pp. 42–43, 287–292.

[143] See, e.g., Xavier Dekeyser, "Relativizers in Early Modern English: A Dynamic Quantitative Study," in *Historical Syntax*, ed. Jacek Fisiak (Berlin: Mouton de Gruyter, 1984), pp. 61–87; Matti Rissanen, "The Choice of Relative Pronouns in Seventeenth-Century American English," in *Historical Syntax*, ed. Jacek Fisiak (Berlin: Mouton de Gruyter, 1984), pp. 417–435.

[144] No. 580.

[145] See, e.g., Alvar Ellegård, *The Auxiliary 'Do': The Establishment and Regulation of Its Use in English* (Stockholm: Almqvist and Wiksell, 1953); Arja Nurmi, *A Social History of Periphrastic DO*, Mémoires de la Société Néophilologique de Helsinki, Vol. 56 (Helsinki: Société Néophilologique, 1999).

[146] See Matti Rissanen, "Salem Witchcraft Papers as Evidence of Early American English," *English Linguistics*, Vol. 20 (2003), pp. 84–114.

(15) This Examinant w⟨a⟩s strucke bl⟨in⟩d, so that she **saw not** with whome Abigail spake. (No. 95)

The establishment of *do*-negation is also proved by the spelling *don't* (either with or without an apostrophe), which indicates the short pronunciation [dɔʊnt/doʊnt]:

(16) You did not answere to that question, **dont** you over-look them?
No I **don't** over-look them. (No. 90)

In questions, *do* is sometimes not used, e.g., with *say*, and with *come* in such idiomatic expressions as *come...about* and *come...to pass*:

(17) What **say you** to this are you guilty or not? (No. 90)
(18) It is said you were afflicted, how **came that** about? (No. 89)

The popularity of the auxiliary *do* in affirmative statements of the type *I did go home* as against *I went home* is one of the characteristics of Early Modern English.[147] This use of *do* is also common in the Salem documents. Many of the instances occur in frequently repeated phrases, such as "did...tortor," "did...aflict," and "did...owne,"[148] or, in the indictments, in the phrase "King William and Queen Mary doe present that...."[149] A clustering, repet-itive use of the auxiliary *do* in narrative contexts in deposi-tions is also typical of the documents. It seems that the speaker wishes to give his/her story special weight by using *do* in successive sentences, particularly with short and lightweight verbs; this use is of course related to the emphatic use of *do* in Present-Day English:

(19) when I came in sight of the house where John procter **did** liue, there was a uery hard blow strook on my brest which caused great pain in my stumoc & amasement in my head but **did** see no person near me only my wife behind me on the same hors, and when I came agains sd procters house according to my understanding I **did** se John procter & his wife att sd house procter himself loocked out of the windo & his wife **did** stand Just without the dore, I tould my wife of it, {&} shee

did loock that way & could see nothing but a littell maid att the dore. (No. 494)

In expressing pure future, Present-Day American English favors the auxiliary *will* even in the first-person singular, unlike formal southern British English. In spo-ken English the abbreviated form *'ll* is of course the most common form. The Salem documents indicate that at the earlier stages of American English both *shall* and *will* were used to indicate future roughly in the same way as in sixteenth- and seventeenth-century British English.[150] In the Salem documents *shall* can be used in all persons in examinations and depositions, although *will* is deci-sively more common.[151] The predominance of *will* may suggest the speech-related origin of the examinations and depositions.

In the first person, *will* often indicates intention and *shall* pure future:

(20) ∧{she} teleth me that i **shal** be wel if i **will** set my hand to the boob [= book] (No. 543)

When *shall* is used in the third person, it may indicate prediction, threat, etc., as in Present-Day English:

(21) when hir master hath asked hir about these thing[Lost] [= things] she Sayth thay **will** nott lett hir Tell, butt Tell hir if she Tells hir head **sh⟨a⟩ll** be Cutt off. (No. 6)

In such documents as indictments, warrants, and mit-timuses (for these text categories, see Section 2), third-person *shall* often occurs in formulaic phrases of the type "this shall be your Sufficient warrant":

(22) Bringe them before their Majesties ∧{Justices} of the peace in Salem in order to their Examination for wch this **shall** be your Sufficient warrant (No. 603)

The so-called progressive form, *be + -ing*, had not quite reached its present stage of usage in seventeenth-century English.[152] This construction is remarkably well established in the Salem documents. The most typical use is with the verb *go*, indicating both intention and

[147] See Matti Rissanen, "Periphrastic 'Do' in Affirmative State-ments in Early American English," *Journal of English Linguistics*, Vol. 18 (1985), pp. 163–183, and Matti Rissanen, "Spoken Lan-guage and the History of *Do*-Periphrasis," in *Historical English Syntax*, ed. Dieter Kastovsky (Berlin: Mouton de Gruyter, 1991), pp. 321–342.
[148] No. 9, No. 11, No. 148, No. 163, No. 185.
[149] No. 332; see also No. 581, No. 582, etc.

[150] See Kytö, *Variation and Diachrony*, pp. 277–336.
[151] See Rissanen, "Salem Witchcraft Papers," pp. 110–111.
[152] See Barbara Strang, "Some Aspects of the History of the *Be + ing* Construction," in *Language Form and Linguistic Variation. Papers Dedicated to Angus McIntosh*, ed. John Anderson (Amster-dam: John Benjamins, 1982), pp. 427–474; Johan Elsness, "On the Progression of the Progressive in Early Modern English," *ICAME Journal*, Vol. 18 (1994), pp. 5–25.

movement (23), although it can be used in a great variety of verbal constructions (24):

(23) wᵗ was itt like yᵗ Got⟨?⟩ you to doe itt A. one like a man Just as I **was goeing** to sleep Came to me (No. 6)

(24) Bridget Bishop **being now comeing** in to be examined relating to her accusation of suspicon of sundry acts of witchcrafts the afflicted persons are now dreadfully aff⟨l⟩icted by her (No. 63)

Be + *-ing* is common in examinations and depositions, and rare in indictments. This may be due to the fact that at its early stages of development this construction was more common in spoken expression than in more formal written contexts.

The construction *a* + *-ing* ("in such a posture as it seemed to be agoeing to fly at mee"[153]) is rapidly giving way to the construction without *a-* in the course of the seventeenth century. In the Salem documents it is much less common than the simple *-ing* form and mainly occurs in depositions.

There are some instances of the active *be* + *-ing* construction used in a passive meaning:

(25) about a fourthnight before Martha Carrier, was sent for to Salem to be examined, upon yᵉ Sabbath day when yᵉ ~~psl~~ psalm **was singing**, sᵈ Martha Carrier took me sᵈ deponent by yᵉ shoulder & shaked me, (No. 464)

In fact, the syntactic type *was being sung* only becomes popular in the course of the eighteenth century even in British English.[154]

In sixteenth-century English, double or multiple negation (the type *I didn't see no people nowhere*) was common, but in the seventeenth century there arose a tendency to avoid this kind of duplicating of the negative elements.[155] It does not occur very often in the Salem documents, not even in the recordings of the utterances of uneducated speakers. Even though scribal correction is possible, the rare occurrence of double negation implies that its disappearance is early and cannot be attributed solely to stigmatization by eighteenth-century grammarians. When the negative particle is followed by an indefinite pronoun, double negative is in most cases avoided by using a pronoun with *any(thing/body)* instead of *no(thing/body)*:

(26) Q. what, doth yᵉ Devill Tell you that he hurts yᵐ? A. noe he Tells me nothing. Q. doe you never See Something appear in Some shape? A. noe **never** See **anything**. (No. 6)

The instances of multiple negation mainly occur in combinations of *not*, *no(thing)* or *never* with *nor* as in "I never did, nor never saw you before."[156]

Vocabulary

The Salem documents give us interesting information on the development of the vocabulary and phraseology of English. Generally speaking, the words and expressions of the documents can be fairly easily understood on the basis of Present-Day English, the most obvious problems being caused by old-fashioned or irregular spellings that may reflect dialectal and societal pronunciations (see Section 4). Some words have of course become archaic or obsolete; most of them can be found in the depositions, and many are connected with rural or everyday life. These items include "tiang" ('tine, prong'), "3 graned" ('three-forked'), "hhᵈ" ('hogshead, a large cask for liquids'), "hipt-shott" ('having the hip out of joint'), "bosit" for *posset* ('a medicinal drink consisting of hot milk curdled with ale or wine, and spices'), and "paragon" ('a silk or wool fabric').[157] Even less specialized obsolete or archaic terms occur in the documents, such as "hunching" ('pushing, shoving'), "bilived" ('lived'), and "whoremasterle" ('characteristic of a lecher').[158] A few words have changed their meaning from the period of the Salem trials to present times. A prime example is "silly," which means 'ignorant' in George Jacobs Sr.'s protestation of innocence: "I am as silly about these things, as the child born last night."[159] Words not previously recorded by the *OED* include "Simplish" ('simple-minded'), "behaged" ('bewitched'), and "old cratten" ('the

---

153 No. 278. In this construction *a* goes back to the preposition *on*.
154 See, e.g., David Denison, "Some Recent Changes in the English Verb," in *English Diachronic Syntax: Proceedings of the Vth National Congress of the History of the English Language*, ed. Maurizio Gotti (Milan: Guerini, 1993), pp. 15–33; Marianne Hundt, "The Passival and the Progressive Passive: A Case Study of Layering in the English Aspect and Voice Systems," in *Corpus Approaches to Grammaticalization in English*, ed. Hans Lindquist and Christian Mair (Amsterdam: Benjamins, 2004), pp. 79–120.
155 See, e.g., Terttu Nevalainen, "Social Mobility and the Decline of Multiple Negation in Early Modern English," in *Advances in*

English Historical Linguistics (1996), ed. Jacek Fisiak and Marcin Krygier (Berlin: Mouton de Gruyter, 1998), pp. 263–291.
156 No. 102.
157 No. 179, No. 85, No. 279, No. 24, No. 598, No. 282.
158 No. 40, No. 149, No. 38.   159 No. 133.

Devil').[160] Furthermore, in at least one instance, the Salem records antedate the *OED* citation of a word: "burlling" ('whirling, twisting').[161]

There are also phrases that may cause difficulties of interpretation. George Jacobs Sr. says to his accusers, "If you can prove that I am guilty, I will lye under it" meaning 'I will carry the responsibility,' or, 'so much the worse for me.'[162] In the following quotation, "caried it" means, roughly, 'behaved.'

(27) Jams How sen[r] aged about 94 sayth that he liueing by her for about thirty years hath taken notes that she hath **caried it** well becoming her place as a daughter (No. 341)

Witchcraft was naturally connected with the Devil, and people believed that they could only be protected and saved from its ill effects by the help of God. Furthermore, late seventeenth-century New England society was deeply influenced by religious thinking and practices. It is therefore not surprising that the Salem documents contain a large number of words and expressions dealing with the Christian religion and supernatural evil forces.

The activities of the witches, or the male *wizards* and *conjurors*, are expressed by the verbs *bewitch, afflict, torture,* or *torment.*[163] The combination "Witchcrafts and sorceries"[164] is very common in these contexts, and the shapes of the witches seen by their victims are referred to by the nouns *apparition, appearance,* or *spectre.*[165] People confessed that they had been persuaded to sign the "Devils book" and make a "Couenant with the Devill" or "Diabollicall Couenant."[166] The Devil is referred to as "the Enemy," "Satan," "evil spirit," "prince of the aire," "the old serpent," "y[e] old boy," "old nick" and "old cratten."[167] Fortune telling, or owning and using a "book of Palmstry,"[168] was also connected with witchcraft.

The terms *pastor, minister,* or *preacher*[169] are used for the spiritual leader of the congregation. The term "the Crosse & Gall" refers to the Crucifixion,[170] and the instruction of the Bible is referred to by "y[e] prophecys of

scripture" and "the rules of the gospel" or "the ordinances of the gospell."[171] The noun *lecture* is used for occasions of preaching and religious instruction less formal than ordinary church services.[172]

As all Salem documents are in one way or another connected with law court trials, they also contain a number of recurrent lexical patterns characteristic of legal language. One notable feature still current in today's legal language is the frequent use of word pairs often comprising synonyms or near-synonyms.[173] Both grammatical function words and lexical content words are involved in this phenomenon. Examples of grammatical function words include "at and within"; "in & upon"; and "On or about"[174]; examples of lexical content words are found, for example, in "Wicked & diabollicall"[175]; "maner & forme"[176]; and "made and Prouided."[177] As some of these examples indicate, the elements of such pairs of words may go back to different source languages. For example, *made* is a native English word, whereas *provide* has been borrowed from Latin.

The pattern of using multiple near-synonyms is extended beyond word pairs into expressions that contain three or more constituent elements, for example "in upon and against"; "Wickedly Mallitiously and felloniously."[178] At its longest, this device contains as many as six different lexical items, as illustrated by "Tortured Aflicted Consumed Pined Wasted and Tormented."[179] Some of these expressions, such as "used practised and Exercised,"[180] echo the wording of earlier statutes against witchcraft, especially the King James Act of 1604.[181]

Because of its legal and official nature, the language of the Salem material contains a fair amount of Latinate technical vocabulary. This will be exemplified in Section 7 of this Linguistic Introduction.

---

[160] No. 745, No. 598, No. 72.   [161] No. 511.

[162] No. 133.

[163] E.g., No. 335, No. 338, No. 4, No. 60.

[164] E.g., No. 330.

[165] E.g., No. 375, No. 403, No. 309.

[166] E.g., No. 75, No. 845.

[167] E.g., No. 150, No. 75, No. 3, No. 538, No. 426, No. 72.

[168] No. 557.

[169] E.g., No. 571, No. 457, No. 95.

[170] No. 133.

[171] No. 189, No. 571.

[172] E.g., No. 243., No. 377. Cf. *OED* s.v. *lecture* n. 4b.

[173] David Mellinkoff, *The Language of the Law* (Boston: Little, Brown, and Company, 1963), pp. 345–366, and *passim*; Risto Hiltunen, *Chapters on Legal English*, Annales Academiæ Scientiarum Fennicæ, Ser. B, Vol. 251 (Helsinki: Suomalainen Tiedeakatemia, 1990), pp. 54–55.

[174] All three examples quoted from No. 802.

[175] No. 805.   [176] No. 812.

[177] No. 811.

[178] Both examples quoted from No. 809.

[179] No. 641.   [180] No. 789.

[181] See Marion Gibson, ed., *Witchcraft and Society in England and America, 1550–1750* (Ithaca, NY: Cornell University Press, 2003), pp. 5–7.

6. DISCOURSE

The levels of language discussed above, from sounds to sentences, are all equally indispensable for successful communication; in order to find out how the linguistic system works in various interactive contexts, however, we also need to consider the level beyond the basic grammatical elements, including sentences, and look at discourse. The term *discourse* has numerous definitions, but for the present purposes it may be understood to refer to continuous stretches of language, whether spoken or written, as manifested in texts. More specifically, discourse analysis, the branch of linguistics concerned with discovering regularities in discourse, focuses on the interface between the linguistic system, the participants, and the context in which the communicative event takes place.[182] Thus, in addition to studying the devices that hold texts together, discourse linguists are interested in how people communicate their ideas and beliefs in given social situations.[183] As records of discourse, texts are not randomly constructed but are shaped by the contexts in which they appear. Conversely, understanding texts presupposes contextualization. The Salem records, as we have them, are written texts, but – as pointed out in Section 2 – many of them have an obvious oral background. Examination records, for example, typically reflect the spoken discourse in the courtroom, at least to some extent. The interface between speech and writing is therefore one of the contextual features of the material to be taken into consideration.

For texts from earlier periods, however, recovering the embedded contextual information may be problematic in that contexts comprise both language-external and language-internal factors. For the Salem records, for instance, the external context involves a whole range of elements of the history and culture of seventeenth-century colonial New England, whereas the internal context has to do with the linguistic practices relevant to the communicative needs, purposes, and situations in that setting. As seen in this light, a discourse-oriented approach to the Salem material will aim at examining the documents in the con-text of their occurrence as interactive and communicative events between the participants involved. The interactive relationship highlighted by the Salem material is the relationship between the authorities of the community and those accused of witchcraft.

Although the predominant element in "Salem discourse" is the institutional legal discourse related to witchcraft, the texts also contain other layers: for instance, that of religious discourse. Religious and biblical references appear frequently in the argumentation of both prosecutors and defendants in the examination records, as in the following examples:

(28) I know nothing of appearance, & the God of Heaven will clear me

> Well they charge you not only with this but with dreadfull murthers, & I doubt not if you be guilty, God will not suffer evidences to be wanting.

> . . . .

> If you desire mercy from God, then confesse & give glory to God.

> Sʳ as for sins I am guilty of if the Minister askt me I am ready to confess.

> If you have ∧{thus} revolted from God you are a dreadfull sinner (No. 173)

The presence of religious discourse in the documents is not surprising, since religious beliefs underlie the entire incident. But in everyday social encounters there must also have been less formal ways of talking about the puzzling events behind the witchcraft incident and the religious and philosophical issues raised by it in the minds of ordinary New Englanders.[184] Unfortunately, such private "witchcraft talk" is almost completely overshadowed in the documents by institutional discourse. That such a discourse did exist, however, can occasionally be inferred even from the official records. The following example from a deposition reporting a complex exchange involving the Ballard brothers and Samuel Wardwell is a case in point:

(29) The testimony of Joseph Ballard of andouer eaged about 41 yeares saith that my brother John ballard told me that Samuel Wardel told him that I had reported that he had bewich{ed} my wife these

[182] For a survey of current issues in discourse studies, see Teun A. van Dijk, ed., *Discourse Studies: A Multidisciplinary Introduction*, 2 vols. (London: Sage Publications, 1995).

[183] In such a framework, discourse is "language use relative to social, political and cultural formations – it is language reflecting social order but also shaping social order, and shaping individuals' interaction with society," according to Adam Jaworski and Nikolas Coupland, eds., *The Discourse Reader* (London: Routledge, 1999), p. 3.

[184] There can be no doubt, for instance, as to the role of gossip as an important channel for spreading information about the process in the community; see Norton, *In the Devil's Snare*, pp. 154–155, and *passim*.

wordes weare spoken before I had ⟨£⟩ any knolidg
of my wife being aflicted by wichcraft after I meting
with said Samuel Wardel prisnor at the bar I told him
that I douteed that he was gilty of hurting my wife
for I had no sutch thoughts nor had spoken any sutch
wordes of him or any other parson and thearefore I
~~was~~ doe not know but you are gilty (No. 630)

Rather than merely summarizing the outcome, the
recorder provides a detailed account of the sequence of
interactive events, as supposedly narrated by the deponent.

That instances of more colloquial talk are relatively
scarce is explained by the predominance in the records of
the perspective of the court of law. During the transforma-
tion from spoken into written word, many of the features
distinctive of spoken discourse would have been removed
from the writing to make it conform to the standards of a
legal document.[185] The written records were usually prepared for the court and its officials, who also function,
directly or indirectly, as the addressees of the documents.
The general nature of the legal process is reflected in the
all-pervasive asymmetric power relationship between the
authorities and the suspected/accused persons, so salient
in the Salem material.

Since the witchcraft incident affected the entire community, it is to be expected that a great number of individuals feature in the documents either as active participants or among those mentioned or referred to. The
impact of the social stratification of the population on
the discourse of the documents needs to be assessed separately with reference to age, gender, ethnic background,
and social standing. In more general terms, the materials indicate a bipolar division of the participants into the
legal and religious authorities, on the one hand, and the
rest of the community, on the other. The voices of those
involved are variously present in different text categories.
Legal and religious voices are predominant throughout.
In documents framed as legal notices, such as indictments
and warrants, the authoritativeness of the text is further
underscored through the introduction into the discourse
of the supreme legal authority, the English Crown. Indictments typically open with a reference to *the jurors of our
sovereign lord and lady the king and queen*, while warrants
are issued *in their majesties' names*. The involvement of the
local magistrates is most concretely seen in the examina-

tion records, where their superior status authorizes them
to open and close the proceedings as well as to initiate
questions and more generally to allocate turns for permission to speak.[186] The authorities are thus responsible for
the major speech acts in the courtroom, including those
of accusing, questioning, commanding, and requesting, as
well as delivering the verdict. Such acts may be expressed
directly or indirectly.[187] A death sentence is an act of delivering a verdict at its starkest.[188] Indirectness, an essential
strategy of courtroom interaction more generally, is most
typically exploited in the examinations, where questions
put to the defendant may be framed in such a way as to
imply guilt.[189]

Regarding the roles of individual members of the
community, we find both accusers and accused. With the
exception of the group of the most active accusers performing in the courtroom, the primary scene for most people
voicing accusations against their fellow community members is that of filing a deposition. The legal framing of
depositional statements is primarily implemented by the
use of special phrases and formulae for openings and clos-
ings.[190] The most essential content of the depositions consists of a narrative, often related in the first person singular,
detailing the misdeeds of the accused. The narrative sections tend to contain few legal terms and phrases, but their
syntactic and textual structure may be complex, especially
if several participants and voices are involved, as is the case
in the deposition of Joseph Ballard v. Samuel Wardwell,
quoted above in example 29.

The picture of the Salem documents as involving multiple participants is further highlighted by the fact that in
addition to human beings supernatural creatures, ghosts,
animal apparitions, and familiars may also feature in the
discourse. In such instances, it is not always clear from the
context whether the creatures appearing to the afflicted

---

[185] For examples of records with traits of speech and references to
paralinguistic features, such as gestures and laughter, see No. 16,
No. 84, and No. 86.

[186] For further discussion, see Risto Hiltunen, "Tell Me, Be You
a Witch? Questions in the Salem Witchcraft Trials of 1692,"
International Journal for the Semiotics of Law, Vol. 9 (1996),
pp. 17–37; Dawn Archer, "Can Innocent People Be Guilty?
A Sociopragmatic Analysis of Examination Transcripts from
the Salem Witchcraft Trials," *Journal of Historical Pragmatics*,
Vol. 3 (2002), pp. 1–30.

[187] For an account of speech acts, including their direct and indirect
uses, see Stephen C. Levinson, *Pragmatics* (Cambridge: Cambridge University Press, 1983), pp. 226–283.

[188] Cf. No. 313, No. 418.

[189] An indirect reference to guilt is typically conveyed in the form
of a leading question, e.g., "what evil spirit have you familiarity
with" (No. 3).

[190] See also the discussion in Section 2.

were thought of as witches in animal shape, or as separate entities acting under the Devil, or as the Devil himself. The most common guise of the Devil is "the black man," but it is impossible to separate the Devil completely from the other apparitions. Almost all the creatures appearing to the afflicted are described as capable of communicating by speech. The following examples come from the examination records:

(30) she further sayth that she hes seen no appearance since but a ffly which did speake to her, and bid her afflict these poor creatur$^\varepsilon$s. (No. 523)

(31) y^e first time she saw him he was like a {gray} catt: he told her he was a prince: & I was to serve him (No. 519)

(32) about 2 Months agoe (but was Stopt) he Saith Somthing Speak to her & S^d y^t She Should not Confes She S^d Good$^\varepsilon$ falkner p$^\varepsilon$swaded her first & y^e black Man wth her & he asked me if I would Sett my hand to his book he would lett me haue fine Cloaths (No. 658)

The talking creatures, including the Devil and "the black man," typically speak to confessing witches, urging them to sign the book and thereby commit themselves to serving the Devil.

Interaction between the court magistrates and the accused is highlighted in the examination records consisting of question-answer sequences. The documents reveal the different strategies utilized by the parties in their argumentation. The two major question types that predominate in the Salem hearings are *yes/no* and *wh-* questions.[191] Both have an information-seeking purpose, but at the same time they function differently depending on the focus of the question. *Yes/no* questions are typically disjunctive: e.g., "are you guilty, or not?"[192] *Wh-*questions, on the other hand, may have a broader or more narrow focus, as in "Why do you hurt these persons?"[193]; "How long have you been a Witch?"[194] Such *wh*-questions often not only convey the presupposition that the accused is indeed guilty, but also function as coercive statements.

As such they serve the ultimate purpose of the examination by pressing defendants to confess – if need be, against their will. The examiners' view of the defendants as "guilty but unwilling to confess"[195] structures the interchange between the parties to a considerable extent, while at the same time highlighting the power of the magistrates in the examination process. We see a recurrent pattern in the records, in which the examiner first tries to establish the guilt of the accused. Depending on the defendant's answer to the opening question, two alternative paths open up for the examiner. If the answer is positive and the person confesses, the examiner will move to close the proceedings; if the answer is negative and the person denies the charge, the examiner will try to adduce further evidence against the defendant. In many cases the additional "evidence" is provided by the afflictions shown by the accusers present.

For the accused, the options are also twofold: either confess or deny the charge.[196] Complete and consistent denials, such as that of Sarah Good, were taken by the examiners as evidence of guilt.[197] An intermediate strategy, whereby guilt was admitted only after an initial stage of denial, was opted for by many, especially in the early examinations in April and May. In the later ones, from July through September, accounts of plain confessions predominate in the records. A decisive factor behind the choice of strategy was the growing awareness of the "confess and avoid the gallows" formula.[198] The pattern whereby those who denied were executed but those who confessed were saved is also reflected in the way the proceedings are recorded in the documents in direct or reported discourse.

The variation between direct and reported discourse is observable in both depositions and examination records.[199] In both cases it is closely connected to the process of rendering spoken discourse into writing by the recorders. The variation between direct and reported

[191] For further discussion of question types and functions in the Salem records, see Hiltunen, "Tell Me"; Archer, "Can Innocent People." For a comprehensive analysis of the subject in contemporaneous British trial proceedings, see Dawn Archer, *Questions and Answers in the English Courtroom (1640–1760): A Sociopragmatic Analysis* (Amsterdam: John Benjamins, 2005).

[192] No. 75.   [193] No. 89.

[194] No. 84.

[195] Archer, "Can Innocent People," p. 25.

[196] For a discussion of the examinations with special reference to confessions, see Kathleen Doty and Risto Hiltunen, "I Will Tell. I Will Tell: Confessional Patterns in the Salem Witchcraft Trials, 1692," *Journal of Historical Pragmatics*, Vol. 3 (2002), pp. 299–335.

[197] Cf. No. 3, No. 4, No. 5.

[198] Rosenthal, *Salem Story*, p. 42. See also Leena Kahlas-Tarkka and Matti Rissanen, "The Sullen and the Talkative: Discourse Strategies in the Salem Examinations," *Journal of Historical Pragmatics*, Vol. 8, No. 1 (2007); pp. [1–24].

[199] See also the discussion in Section 2.

discourse serves different purposes in different contexts. For example, direct discourse, reproducing the language as actually spoken, generally has a higher representational value in a legal context than reported discourse, where interference by the recorder may be more substantial. Reported discourse, on the other hand, has the advantage for the recorder of allowing for a way of summarizing longer passages of interaction in condensed form. The choice between the methods of reporting may sometimes have been deliberate, based on constraints of accuracy and completeness, but often it was no doubt dictated by considerations of the recording situation. In some cases, the preferences of individual recorders may even have played a role here.

It will be an important objective for further research to examine how the linguistic resources of seventeenth-century American English are utilized for the purposes of different types of interaction in the Salem documents. A closer look at the manifold manifestations of witchcraft in the discourse, with reference to the authorities with their power and the accused with their lives at stake, may help us to better understand not only the complexities of individual Salem documents, but also the involvement of individual participants and the process as a whole.

7. LEGAL TERMINOLOGY AND LATIN VOCABULARY

The following list exemplifies and comments on the most important Latinate technical terms in the Salem documents. Sometimes recorders who were apparently unfamiliar with Latin spelling and grammar came up with idiosyncratic forms of these words and phrases, such as "bill Avaro"[200] for *billa vera* and "Igno Rama"[201] for *igno-ramus*. Latin words may also crop up in depositions in a euphemistic function, when the recorder has wanted to avoid the "vulgar" English equivalents. An illustrative example is provided by the deposition of Charity Pitman v. Wilmott Redd, where the relevant Latin words are "mingere" ('urinate') and "cacare" ('defecate').[202]

alias ('also known as')
Found mainly in indictments, depositions, and receipts, as a further specification of the person's identity. In the

Salem records it is used of women to indicate an earlier or new family name. It is most frequently found with the names of "Martha Sprague alias Tyler"[203] and "Bridgett Bishop alias Olliver."[204] The name "Tyler" is a reference to the remarriage of Martha's mother to Moses Tyler,[205] while the name "Olliver" reflects Bridget's earlier marriage to Thomas Oliver.[206] Further examples include "widow alias Richards" (reference to Elizabeth Procter), "Hanah Fox alias Burroughs," and "Margret Jacobs alias Foster."[207] *Alias* is also sometimes used in place names such as "Salem Village Alias Salem."[208]

anno ('in the year')
A standard use in the opening formula of indictments, both to indicate the regnal year of the English sovereign and the Christian year as follows:

(33) Anno $\overline{RR}^s$ [= Regni Regis] & Reginæ Gulielmi & Mariæ Angliæ &c^a Quarto Annoqʒ Domini 1692

('In the fourth year of the reign of the king and queen William and Mary of England etc. and in the year of the Lord 1692') (No. 621)

In the earliest Salem indictments only the regnal year has been indicated with the quasi-Latinized form of the name of King William:

(34) Anno: Regis et Reginæ $\overline{Willm}$ et Mariæ: nunc Angliæ &c^c Quarto

('In the fourth year of the king and queen William and Mary now of England etc.') (No. 330)

Datings using *anno (Domini)* also occur in complaints, recognizances, and warrants.

billa vera ('true bill')
Endorsement in indictments by the grand jury indicating that the charge, as specified in the indictment, should "go before a petty jury for trial."[209] Often it is accompanied by the signature of the foreman of the jury.

---

[200] E.g., No. 296.   [201] No. 608.
[202] No. 629.

[203] E.g., No. 788.
[204] E.g., No. 273, abbreviated there as "a̅l̅s."
[205] Norton, *In the Devil's Snare*, p. 257.
[206] Rosenthal, *Salem Story*, pp. 82–83.
[207] All three examples quoted from No. 958.
[208] No. 652.
[209] Bryan A. Garner, ed. *Black's Law Dictionary* (= *BLD*). 7th ed. (St. Paul, MN: West Group, 1999), s.v. *true bill*.

capᵗ & recognit die ꝑdict ('taken and recognized on the day foresaid')

A phrase used in bonds and recognizances, sometimes without "capᵗ" or "capᵗ & recognit."[210] Cf. the English expression "this Recognizance taken before me."[211]

cogn̄ ('has acknowledged')

An abbreviation of Latin *cognovit*. In the legal context, the word meant that a prisoner had pleaded guilty and was awaiting sentence.[212]

copia vera, vera copia ('true copy')

A phrase used to indicate that a document is a legally admissible reproduction of the original.[213]

coram (prep. 'in the presence of, before')

Typically used before personal names in headings or signatures, for example "Coram Ja: Russell Samuell Hayman."[214] Cf. "Cor. me" (= *coram me*, 'in my presence').[215]

habeas corpus ('that you have the body')

A writ requiring a person to be brought before a court.[216]

ignoramus ('we do not know')

Endorsement in indictments by the grand jury indicating that the charge, as specified in the indictment, is without foundation and is rejected.[217] Like *billa vera*, it is often accompanied by the signature of the foreman of the jury.

imprimis ('in the first place, first')

Used to introduce the first item on a list or an inventory.[218] Cf. *item*.

item ('likewise, also')

Used to introduce a new item on a list or an inventory.[219] It is often abbreviated "īt."[220] Cf. *imprimis*.

jurat (lit. 'swears')

Typically found in indictments after names of witnesses, indicating that they have sworn to the truth of their testimony.[221] The expression *jurat in curia* (lit. 'swears in court') in the Salem cases almost always means it is a document used at trial.

non cull ('not guilty')

An abbreviation of *non culpabilis*.[222] A rare phrase found in indictments, apparently used as an equivalent of the more frequently used English expression *not guilty*.[223] In the Salem records, it records the verdict of the jury acquitting the defendant.[224]

ꝑ curiam ('by the court')

A phrase used to indicate that a written statement is an opinion of the whole court, without identifying the individual judge who wrote it.[225]

ponet se (lit. 'he/she will put himself/herself')

Abbreviation of *ponit se super patriam* ('he/she puts himself/herself upon the country,' possibly used in future tense). A defendant's plea of not guilty.[226] An expression found in indictments; sometimes further abbreviated as "Po: se."[227] or "Pontᵗ se."[228]

pro hac vice ('for this occasion/particular purpose')

An authorization for justices to hold a court temporarily outside their normal jurisdiction.[229]

pro tempore ('for the time being')

Indicates a temporary appointment to occupy a position.[230]

ss

An abbreviation that occurs in the opening formula of indictments, typically after the word *Essex*. Its etymology and precise meaning are disputed. For example, the following interpretations have been suggested: (1) an

---

[210] E.g., No. 720, No. 744, No. 880.

[211] No. 514.

[212] James Swanston Cockburn, *A History of English Assizes 1558–1714* (Cambridge: Cambridge University Press, 1972), p. 117. Cf. No. 616, No. 638.

[213] *BLD*, s.v. *copy*. E.g., No. 666, No. 865.

[214] No. 720.   [215] No. 744.

[216] *BLD*, s.v. *habeas corpus*. E.g., No. 253.

[217] *BLD*, s.v. *ignoramus*.

[218] *OED*, s.v. *imprimis*. E.g., No. 857, spelled "Impr{e}ms."

[219] *OED*, s.v. *item*, adv.   [220] E.g., No. 916, No. 919.

[221] *BLD*, s.v. *jurat*.   [222] *BLD*, s.v. *non culpabilis*.

[223] E.g., No. 828.

[224] See *BLD*, s.v. *not guilty* 2., but cf. *SWP*, p. 41, where the expression is, we believe, mistakenly viewed as a plea of the defendant denying the crime charged, i.e., as a synonym of *ponet se* (used in the sense of *BLD*, s.v. *not guilty* 1).

[225] *BLD*, s.vv. *opinion, per curiam*.

[226] *BLD*, s.v. *ponit se super patriam*.

[227] No. 828.   [228] No. 826.

[229] *BLD*, s.v. *pro hac vice*. No. 724.

[230] *BLD*, s.v. *pro tempore*. No. 977.

abbreviation of Latin *scilicet* ('namely'); (2) an equivalent of the paragraph mark (¶); (3) an abbreviation that indicates the place of sitting of the court; (4) an abbreviation of *sessions*.[231]

videlicet ('to wit, that is to say, namely')

Used to render a previous statement more specific.[232] Spelled in the documents for example as "Videllisett"[233] and "Videlisitt."[234] Often abbreviated as "viz."[235]

8. ABBREVIATIONS

The use of abbreviations is a recurring feature almost throughout the Salem records. Abbreviations are especially frequent in formal documents such as indictments and arrest warrants, but they also occur in less formulaic, speech-related texts such as depositions and examinations. Some abbreviations represent standard seventeenth-century English usage, while others may have had a more limited circulation mainly in legal and administrative texts; it is possible that some of the more infrequent abbreviations are *ad hoc* creations of the recorders.

Space does not permit a full listing of the hundreds of different abbreviations found in the material. The purpose of this section is to comment briefly on the various *types* of abbreviation that readers will come across in the edition and provide examples of them. It is hoped that the examples given will help readers to interpret other similarly formed abbreviations. In the edition, some potentially opaque abbreviations have been glossed by means of square brackets (see further "Editorial Principles," Section III).

In the examples below, the abbreviated words appear in the original spelling, with the exception that only proper names have been capitalized. The unabbreviated forms within brackets are given in Present-Day American English spelling.

I. Superscript letters

This is the most frequent type of abbreviation in the documents. A superscript letter at the end or middle of a word usually indicates that one or more letters have been omitted from it. In most cases, the superscript is the final letter of the unabbreviated word.

[231] See *BLD*, s.v. *ss*; *SWP*, p. 42; Gibson, ed., *Witchcraft*, p. 13n. The abbreviation "Sc." in No. 635 is probably a variant of *ss* (see also No. 744).

[232] *BLD*, s.v. *videlicet*.   [233] No. 723.

[234] No. 722.   [235] E.g., No. 916.

ag^t (*against*)	gent^n (*gentleman*)	rec^d (*received*)
Aug^t (*August*)	ind^t (*indictment*)	Saml (*Samuel*)
Box^d (*Boxford*)	jun^r (*junior*)	sarg^t (*sergeant*)
bro^r (*brother*)	lef^t (*lieutenant*)	s^d (*said*)
cap^n (*captain*)	l^d (*lord*)	Tops^d (*Topsfield*)
couen^t (*covenant*)	Med^x (*Middlesex*)	W^m (*William*)
defend^t (*defendant*)	n^t (*not*)	w^n (*when*)
depo^t (*deponent*)	o^r (*our*)	w^o (*who*)
d^r (*debtor*)	R^d (*Richard*)	w^t (*what*)

Two or more superscript letters similarly often correspond to the final letters of the unabbreviated word.

ab^{ts} (*abouts*)	Ipsw^{ch} (*Ipswich*)	rnd (*reverend*)
agst (*against*)	left^{nt} (*lieutenant*)	Will^{ms} (*Williams*)
assis^{ts} (*assistants*)	maj^{ties} (*majesties'*)	w^{ld} (*would*)
barr^{ll} (*barrel*)	Pickwth (*Pickworth*)	wth (*with*)

Superscript letter(s) do not always correspond to the end of a word, but may also come from its middle (or from both its middle and end); this feature particularly applies to conventional abbreviations of personal names.

acc^o (*account*)	Eliz^a (*Elizabeth*)	Now^{br} (*November*)
Ames^{br} (*Amesbury*)	good^m (*goodman*)	pl^t (*plaintiff*)
Benj^a (*Benjamin*)	good^w (*goodwife*)	Sep^t (*September*)
comp^a (*company*)	Jno (*John*)	sov^r (*sovereign*)
comp^{lt} (*complaint*)	Jona^t (*Jonathan*)	Th^o (*Thomas*)
cons^t (*constable*)	jus^{ts} (*justices*)	Tim^o (*Timothy*)
dep^o (*deposition*)	k^{nt} (*knight*)	w^c (*which*)
dep^t (*deputy*)	Nich^o (*Nicholas*)	w^t (*with*)

Although the medieval letter 'thorn' ('þ') was largely replaced by 'th' in English handwriting by the early sixteenth century or so, it survived until the eighteenth century in a few mostly conventionalized abbreviations. In such abbreviations, its form is indistinguishable from 'y.'

y^e (*the*)	y^n (*then*)	y^{rs} (*theirs*)
y^m (*them*)	y^r (*their, there*)	y^t (*that*)

Superscript abbreviations based on 'y' may resemble abbreviations using 'thorn.' The immediate context will usually provide the clue to the correct interpretation.

y^r (*your*) y$^\varepsilon$ (*your*)	y^u (*you*)

Superscripts also often appear in abbreviated ordinal numbers. The superscript letters found in these abbreviations may not match the endings of the corresponding unabbreviated ordinals. Sometimes the abbreviations are based on Latin forms.

1th (*first*)   3mo (*tertio*, i.e., 'third')   11mo (*undecimo*, i.e., 'eleventh')

1° (*primo*, i.e., 'first')   10^{d} (*tenth*)   25^{t} (*twenty-fifth*)

Numbers with superscripts may also occur in abbreviations of words other than numerals.

7^{br} (*September*)
9$^{b\varepsilon}$ (*November*)
x^{br} (*December*)
4^{t}night (*fortnight*)

II. Macron (¯)

A macron placed over one or more letters usually stands for an omitted 'm' or 'n,' although sometimes also for 'i' (especially in words ending with -tion).

apperishtiō (*apparition*)   examinācon (*examination*)
comĩtted (*committed*)   run̄ing (*running*)

Some recorders also employ a macron as a more general mark of abbreviation signaling any combination of omitted letters.

Abrā (*Abraham*)   R̅R̅s (*Regni Regis*)
Dom̄ (*Domini*)   s̄d (*said*)
rec̄ed (*received*)   sec̄ry (*secretary*)

III. $^{\varepsilon}$

Abbreviation is often signaled by a flourished stroke that vaguely resembles the modern capital 'E'; it has been reproduced in the edition as $^{\varepsilon}$. This mark of abbreviation often stands for the letter 'r' or a combination of one or more vowels followed by 'r' (sometimes also 'r' followed by a vowel).

aft$^{\varepsilon}$ (*after*)   hon$^{\varepsilon s}$ (*honors*)   o$^{\varepsilon}$ (*our*)
Andou$^{\varepsilon}$ (*Andover*)   m$^{\varepsilon}$ (*master, Mr.*)   s$^{\varepsilon}$ (*sir*)
attaind$^{\varepsilon}$ (*attainder*)   m$^{\varepsilon s}$ (*mistress, Mrs.*)   sen$^{\varepsilon}$ (*senior*)
esq$^{\varepsilon}$ (*esquire*)   maj$^{\varepsilon}$ (*major*)   yo$^{\varepsilon}$ (*your*)

As in the case of the macron, some recorders also use $^{\varepsilon}$ as a more general mark of abbreviation.

aflic$^{\varepsilon}$ (*afflicting*)   compl$^{\varepsilon t}$ cur$^{\varepsilon}$ (*curiam*,
chyrurg$^{\varepsilon}$ (*chirurgeon*,   (*complaint*)   i.e., 'court')
    i.e., 'surgeon')

Febr$^{\varepsilon}$ (*February*)   maj$^{\varepsilon}$ (*majesties'*)
impa$^{\varepsilon}$ (*empaneling*)   Oct$^{\varepsilon}$ (*October*)
Jos$^{\varepsilon}$ (*Joseph*)   Reb$^{\varepsilon}$ (*Rebecca*)
just$^{\varepsilon}$ (*justice*)   sov$^{\varepsilon}$ (*sovereign*)

Unlike other superscript marks used to indicate abbreviation, $^{\varepsilon}$ also tends to occur in the middle of a word instead of the final position.

hon$^{\varepsilon}$d (*honored*)   m$^{\varepsilon}$chant (*merchant*)   p$^{\varepsilon}$sons (*persons*)
Jan$^{\varepsilon}$y (*January*)   p$^{\varepsilon}$cept (*precept*)   v$^{\varepsilon}$s (*versus*)

IV. Colon, period

Some recorders use a colon (:) or a period (.) to indicate that the end of a word has been omitted. These abbreviations are most frequently used for personal names; the interpretation of the abbreviations using a single letter is highly context-specific.

Abig: (*Abigail*)   J. (*John*)   Nath: (*Nathaniel*)
childr: (*children*)   Mar. (*March*)   Sam: (*Samuel*)
Eliza. (*Elizabeth*)   N. (*Nurse*)   Tho. (*Thomas*)

V. Apostrophe

A few recorders employ an apostrophe (') to signal an omitted letter or a sequence of letters. Some abbreviations of this type undoubtedly reflect pronunciation (cf. example 16).

confirm'd (*confirmed*)   don't (*do not*)   'thō (*although*)

VI. Special signs

(A) ℗

There are several variant forms of abbreviations involving the letter 'p,' which for the sake of simplicity have been rendered with one symbol in the edition. One form often precedes a signature, where it stands for the Latin preposition *per* ('by'). When found as part of an English word it usually corresponds to the syllables "pre" or "per," but may also sometimes stand for "pro."

coo℗ (*cooper*)   ℗sent (*present*)
℗clamacon (*proclamation*)   ℗sons (*persons*)

(B) q̃

This sign stands for the Latin enclitic conjunction *-que* ('and'). In the Salem documents its use is restricted to "annoq̃" (*annoque* 'and in the year'), found especially in the headings of indictments.

(C) @

Depending on the context, this rare sign may stand for the prepositions *at* or *about*.

(D) 9

A sign of abbreviation for the prefix con-.

9fessed (*confessed*)

(E) &

A common sign of abbreviation for the word *and*. It also regularly stands for Latin *et* ('and'), especially in the abbreviations "&^{c}," "&c^a," and "&c^t" for *et cetera*. In the edition, this sign is used both for the modern ampersand form and the more archaic shorthand symbol known as Tironian *et*, both of which are found in the Salem records.

VII. No overt marker

It may also happen that a recorder uses no mark whatsoever to signal abbreviation. In such cases it is sometimes difficult to know whether a word has been intentionally abbreviated or whether its form simply reflects pronunciation (as in the third example below).

p (*per*)   sd (*said*)   condemnd (*condemned*)

V. EDITORIAL PRINCIPLES

I. TEXT

In editing the records of the Salem witch-hunt that survive in manuscripts, the leading principle has been to reproduce the text as it appears in the original documents as faithfully as possible, given the limitations of modern typography.[1] Accordingly, the spelling and punctuation used by the original recorders have been retained, including their use of capital letters and abbreviations. The following exceptions apply to this general rule:

(A) Spelling

Prefixes and other elements that are separated from the rest of the word in the original documents have not been kept separate in the edition (e.g., "in structed" > "instructed," "re ward" > "reward," "likly hode" > "likly-hode," "a cording ly" > "acordingly"). Correspondingly, articles and prepositions that are attached to their headword in the original documents have been separated (e.g., "ablack" > "a black," "ofland" > "of land"). These spellings have not been kept since they have been considered idiosyncratic. Moreover, it is often difficult to determine whether or not the recorder intended the elements to be written together. (See also the Linguistic Introduction, Section 4.)

(B) Punctuation

In the following three cases, punctuation marks found in the documents have not been retained in the edited text (see also the Linguistic Introduction, Section 4):

(1) dots and colons placed below superscript letters in abbreviations;
(2) single or double hyphens in word divisions at line breaks;
(3) dashes used as line-fillers.

(C) Capitalization

(1) Where there is ambiguity in interpreting whether a letter is a capital or a minuscule, capitals have been used in proper names and at the beginning of paragraphs; on all other occasions (including sentence boundaries), minuscules have been used (see also the Linguistic Introduction, Section 4). As regards letters that have the same shape and that seem to vary in size arbitrarily in the handwriting of a given recorder, each problematic instance has not been weighed separately, but all occurrences of the letters have been regularized according to the principles set out above (typically 'C,' 'P,' 'S,' 'W').

(2) Since capital 'I' and 'J' were frequently written the same way in the period, their rendering in the edition follows Present-Day English spelling conventions (e.g., "Iustice" > "Justice," "J" > "I").[2]

---

[1] This general principle is in keeping with the guidelines advocated by G. Thomas Tanselle for editing historical documents that were not originally intended for publication; see "The Editing of Historical Documents," *Studies in Bibliography*, Vol. 31 (1978), pp. 1–56; "Literary Editing," in *Literary and Historical Editing*, ed. George L. Vogt and John Bush Jones (Lawrence: University of Kansas Libraries, 1981), pp. 35–56. Cusack, *Everyday English*, has also influenced editorial principles used in the edition.

[2] See Tannenbaum, *The Handwriting*, pp. 104–105.

(D) Abbreviations

Macrons that do not signal an abbreviation have not been retained in the edited text. Similarly, superscript letters that do not seem to indicate an abbreviation have been written as if they were not superscript (e.g., "las^t" > "last").

(E) Modern or Unrelated Text

All identifiable modern (nineteenth- and twentieth-century) annotations have been left out of the edited text. These are typically shelfmarks or descriptions of the contents of the documents. The same applies to all scribblings and doodlings that the editors have considered to be meaningless in the context – whether made by the original hand or a later hand. A few documents contain material that is coeval with the witchcraft proceedings, but unrelated to them in content. Such texts have not been included in the edition.[3]

II. LAYOUT

In the treatment of the layout and other physical features of the original documents, the aim has been to reproduce these elements in the edition as far as it has been technically feasible and not detrimental to the readability of the text. Owing to these restrictions, the following features of the original layout have not been preserved in the edited text:

(A) lineation and exact line-spacing (as an exception, the original lineation has been retained in some documents, such as accounts, for the sake of readability, or when beginnings or endings of many consecutive lines have been lost due to physical damage);

(B) vertical or upside-down position of text;

(C) column division (with the exception of some accounts and lists of signatures);

(D) location of headings and other such material drawn over the left-hand margin;

(E) relative location of and spacing between the entries on the reverse; as a rule, the docket (document summary) is given first unless the main text continues from the front of the document;

(F) non-initial blank spaces in the line that have been interpreted as indicating a new paragraph (for the annotation of *unfilled* empty spaces in the line, see SQUARE BRACKETS below);

(G) curly brackets that keep multiple lines together in the original documents, in cases when the corresponding text in the edition takes up a single line only.

III. ANNOTATION

This section summarizes the conventions and symbols that have been used in the editorial annotation of the text.

ANGLED BRACKETS, ⟨ ⟩, surround letters or words that are difficult to interpret – either because the text is obscured by a crease, blot of ink, smudge, etc., or because the letter-forms themselves are ambiguous. The use of angled brackets indicates that the letters or words so marked have not been completely lost as a result of physical damage, but traces of them are visible (complete loss of text due to holes, tears etc. has been indicated with square brackets; see below). A QUESTION MARK within angled brackets stands for one or more consecutive letters in the document, judged by the editors to be illegible beyond reasonable inference. One or more consecutive illegible words have been marked by means of square brackets (see below).

CURLY BRACKETS, { }, surround letters or words written above or below the line or in the margin as a correction or afterthought by the recorders themselves or by other correctors. Carets (ˆ), which are used by many recorders to indicate the precise location of such additions, have been reproduced. The large curly brackets that occasionally appear in the edition, for example in the headings of indictments and next to the magistrates' signatures, are not editorial annotations, but reproductions of brackets found in the original documents at these places.

OVERSTRUCK letters or words indicate that they are canceled either by the recorder or by a later corrector. An overstruck question mark within angled brackets stands for one or more consecutive illegible letters that have been canceled.

SQUARE BRACKETS, [ ], have been used for editorial comments in Present-Day English that have been added into the text for information. They have two major functions.

---

[3] These texts include, for example, the ship-building order issued to Daniel Bacon Jr. in No. 231.

(a) To provide glosses or translations for words (and sometimes phrases) that may be difficult for readers to interpret. Extended linguistic comments on individual words or expressions have been placed in notes accompanying the document. The items annotated with square brackets are typically obsolete, idiosyncratically spelled, or in Latin. When used in the glossing/translating function, a square-bracketed annotation begins with an equal sign and immediately follows the word or phrase to which it applies. A question mark at the end of a gloss indicates that the gloss is uncertain. Some examples:

> brought books iwith [= in with] them
> this malloncely [= melancholy] subiect
> in that bhaffe [= behalf]
> Shee the [= the said] Hannah Post
> non Cull [= not guilty]
> maneft [= manifest?]

(b) To indicate such features of text and layout in the original documents whose typographic reproduction in the edition has not been feasible. The list below summarizes and explains the annotations used in this function.

[Reverse]

This annotation marks the point at which the writing found on the back of the document begins. In documents that comprise more than one leaf, [Reverse] marks the beginning of the final page, on which the docket appears; other pagination is only shown when it helps to clarify the text of the document (e.g., in accounts), indicated as [Page #]. The annotation [Column #] is similarly used when the column division of the document needs to be shown to clarify the meaning of the text.

[ ]

Square brackets surrounding an empty space indicate an empty space in the document. The use of this annotation usually implies that the recorder left a slot to be filled in later, but it was never filled in. It characteristically occurs with first names of female defendants and witnesses in indictments, summonses, and warrants.

[Lost]

This annotation is used to mark text that is completely lost in the document due to physical damage (hole, tear, crease, etc.) and of which no visible trace remains to allow its restoration by means of angled brackets. Depending on the extent of the damage, the annotation may correspond to any amount of lost text – from a single letter to several sentences. A gloss in square brackets follows the [Lost] annotation when it has been possible to conjecture the reading (or part of it) with reasonable certainty on the basis of the immediate context. If a conjectured reading has been obtained from *SWP* or Woodward, this has been specified in the gloss. Some examples:

> Suspit[Lost] [= suspicion]
> [Lost]nce [= allowance]
> wh[Lost]ever [= whatsoever?]
> made and [Lost] [*SWP* = declared] to be

[# word(s) illegible]

This annotation marks the presence in the document of one or more consecutive words that are illegible, but not canceled. For example, [2 words illegible], [3–4 words illegible].

[Period or Caret overstruck]

This annotation marks rare instances where either a period or a caret has been overstruck.

[# word(s) overstruck]

This annotation marks the presence in the document of one or more consecutive words that are canceled and illegible. For example, [2 words overstruck], [3–4 words overstruck].

["X" written over "Y"]

This annotation indicates a correction where a word or a sequence of letters/numbers has been written over another word or a sequence of letters/numbers. It immediately follows the word in which the correction occurs. If the original reading underneath the correction is illegible beyond reasonable certainty, the annotation has not been used. Some examples:

> Elzibeth buxtston ["s" written over "o"]
> hur ["ur" written over "er"]
> 1692 ["6" written over "7"]
> his ["his" written over "my"]
> this ["this" written over "an"?]

[Hand #]

This annotation marks a distinctive change in the handwriting of a document that the editors have interpreted to signal a change of recorder. In each manuscript document, the annotation begins from [Hand 1] and runs from the beginning of the document to its end. Since the numbers indicate the respective order of the hands in the document, they are document-specific and do not serve to identify a recorder beyond a particular document. Within a document, however, only one hand number is used for the output of any individual recorder. The annotation [Hand 1], for example, would therefore reoccur in a document on each subsequent occasion when the handwriting of the first recorder reappears after the stint of another recorder. If a hand number is followed by a question mark, the editors are uncertain about the change of recorder.

Changes of hand have not been indicated in signatures and, as a rule, in short strings of text that belong together with a signature. Such strings typically spell out the office of the person signing his name or present other information concerning this person. They may or may not be written in the same hand as the signature that accompanies them.

Text in **BOLD**, which is used in indictments only, serves to indicate names, dates, and similar information that have been inserted into a pre-prepared boilerplate form. Since hand changes are frequent in these documents, the insertions appear in bold to make them more visually apparent. Note, however, that hand changes after the main body of text, in, e.g., witness lists, on the reverse etc., have not been marked in bold since they are not part of the boilerplate form. Occasionally the hand that filled in the blanks made changes to the boilerplate document. These changes are not in bold.

IV. SIGNATURES AND MARKS

Authenticity of signatures has not been indicated in the transcriptions, but may be discussed in the notes when it appears to be an issue. Sixty-three personal marks (used in lieu of signatures) in the documents have been photographed and reproduced as facsimiles.

VI. CHRONOLOGICAL ARRANGEMENT

BERNARD ROSENTHAL AND MARGO BURNS

The principles used to organize the records in this edition differ from those used in previous major witchcraft transcription collections, although three basic features of each document have been important factors in the arrangement of the entries in all editions: who is named in the document, what type of legal document it is, and when it was used. The main challenges for organizing such a collection concern what to do when a record names more than one accused person, when the type of document has been used in more than one hearing or its use is not immediately apparent, when it has no dating whatsoever, and when combinations of these occur. *Records of the Salem Witch-Hunt* attempts an arrangement that deals with all of these challenges not only in a consistent, logical way, but in such a manner that the volume can be used as both a reference book of transcriptions of the manuscripts in their entirety, and a chronological presentation of the entire episode as it unfolded over time, for the first time prioritizing dating over case in the arrangement.

DATING THE RECORDS

Each record has been tagged with one to five dates, based on when it was first prepared, had material added to it, or is known to have been used in an official proceeding. The full transcription of each record is placed at the earliest date that can be established for it. Any subsequent dates are listed directly below the title of the full transcription. When a record has multiple dates, the subsequent entry titles appear in italics on the appropriate date, followed by a reference back to the original entry. In the example of a warrant, the subsequent entry indicates when the officer reported back to the court, but does not include the text of the return. Approximately 28 percent of the records have two dates associated with them, another 4 percent

have three dates, and a rare handful have four or five dates. Examinations often have additional dates because the examinations sometimes took place over several days, and additional dates on arrest warrants are found in the officers' returns on the following day. Most of the additional dates on depositions, testimonies, and statements are indications that the record was sworn to during a grand jury proceeding or at trial, after its initial creation or use. These additions are typically very short, some a mere three words long.

Depositions, testimonies, and statements were submitted, used, and sworn to at various stages of prosecution – before local authorities in inferior courts at the time of arrest, examination, and other hearings, and before a grand jury and at trial in the Court of Oyer and Terminer or the Superior Court of Judicature. Our titles use the words found in the documents themselves to describe their content. "Deposition" is used if the document specifically states that it is a "deposition," or refers internally to a "deponent," and "Testimony" is used if the document uses the word "testifieth." "Statement" is used in all other cases, but all three had a similar evidentiary use. Any of these that appear to have been partially written prior to an examination and were apparently used at the examination are placed on the date of that first examination. These documents and the accounts of the examinations were often used again when the accused person appeared before the grand jury and then again at trial, beginning in June 1692, after the Court of Oyer and Terminer was established to hear the cases. In some, the only date appearing on a deposition, testimony, or statement is the date the witness swore to it before the grand jury. If a date prior to the grand jury or trial cannot be gleaned by the use of other sources or is precluded by evidence in the text, then the earliest date that can be established for it, at the grand jury or trial, is used for the initial chronological placement.

Many of these documents have no date on them other than a reference to the day of an examination of someone accused of witchcraft. Dating such documents varies in complexity. As necessary, the reasoning behind the dating is included in the notes, but sometimes it is too long and complex to be explained in a clarifying note. However, a basic approach to dating depositions, statements, and testimony requires some detailed discussion at the outset. Take for example No. 11, a deposition in which Ann Putnam Jr. claims that Sarah Osburn began afflicting her on February 25, 1692. Osburn died in prison on May 10 before the Court of Oyer and Terminer had been established. Thus, one cannot expect a date on the document showing a grand jury addressing her case. For Thomas Putnam, the person who recorded it, to have created the deposition after May 10 would have made no sense. The range of dates for the deposition can reasonably be considered as anywhere from February 25 to May 10. Three plausible possibilities emerge. The document was prepared on February 25, in support of the complaint that would be lodged against her on February 29 and prior to her arrest on March 1, the day of Osburn's examination before the local magistrates. Or, it was prepared on March 1 for use at her examination. A third possibility is that it was prepared sometime after March 1 but prior to May 10, once the magistrates decided to hold Osburn over, with the idea that it would be used at a future proceeding against her.

On the deposition Ann is recorded as claiming that after the original affliction by Osburn "she conteinewed most dreadfully to afflect me tell the first day of march being the day of hir Examination and then also she did tortor me most dreadfully in the time of hir Examination: and also seuerall times sence ~~good~~ Sarah osburn has afflected me and urged me to writ in her book." Ann's citing of March 1 seems to rule out a date in February, unless one believes that the March 1 reference is a later addition, despite no apparent indication that the reference was added to the document. Possibilities for speculation grow. The most plausible choice for dating the text would be either March 1, or some date after that, but prior to May 10, thus narrowing probabilities from three to two choices. At first glance, it appears that the document was written after March 1, since it references that date in the past tense, but a broader look at an array of depositions throughout the episode of the Salem witch trials reveals repeated accurate references to the date of the examination. If written

months after the fact, the dates could have been taken from records or the deponents may have simply had remarkable memories, but the consistency of the accuracy of these dates makes it seems more likely that they were written on or soon after the day of the examination, when the events were fresh in everyone's mind. If we return to Ann Putnam Jr.'s deposition against Sarah Osburn and hypothesize its construction after March 1, we would have to explain what the circumstances would have been for its creation. If the authorities were preparing their case against Sarah Osburn to bring her before a grand jury, that would make sense, but that didn't happen. She died before any grand jury was even convened.

We know from the accounts of the examinations that written accusations were presented to the magistrates and were an integral feature of the proceedings. If this deposition against Osburn had been created weeks or months after her examination, we would still be missing the record of Ann's original claims against her. One missing document in a pool of many missing documents would not be surprising, but if the many depositions referencing the day of an examination were not prepared for or in response to the examination, we would have no record at all of what claims were made at the examinations, other than those specifically mentioned in the accounts of the examinations referencing the reading of evidence against the accused. It would be very puzzling if in this category of documentation, claims made on examination days were mostly missing. The assumption in this edition is that most such documents referencing the day of an examination were used or prepared that day or very soon thereafter, as in the example of Ann Putnam Jr.'s deposition against Sarah Osburn. One document that may add confirmation to this line of reasoning is No. 58, where the date of April 11 appears on the manuscript and where the events of that day are described in the past tense.

Many of the depositions in Thomas Putnam's handwriting have an additional distinctive feature: in the middle of them, there is a change in the color of the ink he used, almost always starting with a colon and followed by a description of additional afflictions by the accused on the day of examination. See, for example No. 9, a deposition of Ann Putnam Jr. against Sarah Good, a very similar document to her deposition against Sarah Osburn described above, but one that did go to a grand jury hearing. In the deposition against Osburn, there is no change in the ink used, and apparently no text was appended, but in the deposition against Good, there appears to be an addition to what Putnam had originally written. The problem then expands. On what date was the document first used against Good, and if portions were added later, on what date did that happen? In some of the documents, dates of accretion to documents can be identified with confidence, in others not, but reasonable speculations can often be made. In most of the cases, the added information in Putnam's hand specifies that the date of the afflictions occurred during the examination of the accused, and a specific line from the "afflicted" is given, starting with "I verily beleiue . . ." or a variation of this, that the accused afflicted her by using witchcraft. This formulaic addition coincides with the specifics of the charge as written in the indictments, raising the possibility that the additions were made to support the bill of indictment when it went before the grand jury.

A key problem in dating these documents relating to the examinations centers on Putnam's frequent additions of the affliction as having occurred "seuerall times sence." At times, Putnam's phrasing clearly appears in a different ink and was added later, but one simply cannot be certain how much later that addition occurred. It could have been days or weeks later, or it could have been the next day, or even later in the same day. The issue gets more difficult when the phrase appears with no ink change. This might at first glance appear to argue against dating the document on the day of the examination with the suggestion that it was prepared for presentation to a grand jury or trial court. However, such phrasing, appearing in the document used against Sarah Osburn, could not have been used for the grand jury or trial court, since she died on May 10 before there was even a court in session to receive the case. It is not testable as to whether documents that appear to have no ink change when the phrasing of "seuerall times sence" were written on a different day, but the assumption in the edition to date these is that such phrasing in the same ink does not argue sufficiently against the use of the document on the day of the examination, possibly later the same day in some cases, as seems likely in the Osburn document.

There can be no guarantee that the line of reasoning in dating many depositions and similar documents to the day of an examination is accurate, and other scholars may reasonably disagree with it and suggest alternative datings for such documents. At the same time, the logic of the dating used in the edition fortuitously places the docu-ments in clusters of cases. That is, undated depositions regarding Sarah Osburn, to stay with that example, are placed close to documents regarding her arrest and examination. The decision to date these depositions close to the examination dates has not been made because of the convenience factor, but they will nevertheless be convenient for the reader. We believe that they are placed where they most probably belong, even with the awareness that some might have been written a day or two later. When a later date, such as a grand jury hearing, appears on a document, the question then becomes whether the first use of the document is for the grand jury, or whether the document was first used at the time of the examination. Conclusions on these vary, based on a variety of factors. Placing undated documents by the "afflicted" accusers to the date of the examination is generally done in the edition with a higher confidence level than undated documents by adult supporters. In some cases dated documents, such as grand jury testimony, believed to have been used earlier on the day of the examination are simply dated on conservative grounds to the recorded date because the evidence for use at the examination is not sufficient.

Bills of indictment for the Court of Oyer and Terminer do not carry a recorded date, but were always presented on the first day the grand jury met. Other documents sworn before the grand jury typically include a recorded date of those hearings. Therefore indictments are dated based on these other documents. An indictment marked "Ignoramus" went no further, but those marked "Billa Vera" were presented at trial.

The notation "Jurat in Curia" on a document (in the handwriting of Stephen Sewall, Clerk of the Court of Oyer and Terminer in 1692, or Jonathan Elatson, Clerk of the Superior Court of Judicature in 1693) indicates that it was used at the trial of the person named in the document. Because there is usually no date given with the "Jurat in Curia" notation, the document is placed on the day of the trial of the accused. In a few instances other trial markers are used, and the note with the transcription indicates that it was used at trial.

In some instances, no specific legal proceeding is apparent for a date given on a document. Before the Court of Oyer and Terminer was established, some documents are noted to have been "Sworn before the Court" before local magistrates, even though there were no examinations held that day. In mid-September, after Samuel Wardwell had recanted his previous confession before the grand jury, at least eight confessors affirmed their confessions before John Higginson Jr., a justice of the peace, although most of these cases did not go before a grand jury until January.

MANUSCRIPTS AND RECORDS

In preparing *Records of the Salem Witch-Hunt*, transcriptions of all manuscripts have been kept whole, each considered as an individual record in the legal proceedings. An exception to this rule, however, is a manuscript copy, probably made in 1692, of eighteen examinations in a single twenty-page document (*Andover Examinations Copy*, see No. 425). Four of the original manuscripts of these examinations are extant (No. 441, No. 523, No. 525, and No. 528), supporting the conclusion that this manuscript is a collection of copies of individual manuscripts, so the transcription of this manuscript has been divided and dated as eighteen individual records.

In a few other instances, we have concluded that two or three manuscripts that have been archived separately for years are actually multiple pages of single documents. Based on handwriting, matching torn edges, and textual clues, these have been reunited to re-form the original, single records. The primary benefit of restoring the integrity of each original record is the revelation of otherwise lost characteristics of the record. One specific example of how this affects the interpretation of a text can be found in No. 384, a deposition from Elizabeth Booth. This document comprises two sheets, archived in two different locations in the Essex County Court Archives. The first sheet contains Booth's statements against Elizabeth and John Procter. The second sheet contains statements against Martha Cory, with a dated oath that it was used at a grand jury on June 30, 1692. If taken as two separate documents, it would be possible to conclude that the first was not used at a legal hearing, and that the second was sworn before a grand jury in the case of Martha Cory on June 30, 1692. However, on June 30, grand juries heard cases against Elizabeth How, Elizabeth Procter, John Procter, and Sarah Wilds, and other evidence indicates that Martha Cory's grand jury was not held until August 4, 1692 (see No. 19). There are other depositions from Elizabeth Booth against the Procters that were sworn to on June 30, including No. 385, against Elizabeth Procter, in which the handwriting in the oath matches that in the oath with Booth's statement against Martha Cory. We have concluded that this is a single record, the second sheet a continuation of the first.

The oath on the second sheet was given at the grand jury hearing against Elizabeth Procter about the statements Booth made against her, and not, as it might seem if the two papers were taken as separate records, used against Martha Cory on the thirtieth.

Other examples include the restoration of the record of a deposition by Jarvis Ring, No. 149, the second manuscript sheet of which has been long archived with another deposition by the same man, and No. 164, in which three manuscripts that have been separated archivally form a single, continuous narrative of the spectral afflictions Susannah Shelden claimed to have experienced daily over the course of the last week of April. With texts that have only come down in transcriptions published by others, for which no original manuscript is known to exist, each has been kept intact as a single record, including typographical features such as italics. In one case, however, a copy of the mittimus to send John Alden and Sarah Rice to prison (see No. 252) is included within John Alden's account of his examination, imprisonment, and escape (see No. 234). The text of the mittimus has been extracted as a separate record and presented on the date when the mittimus was written.

ASSIGNING DATES TO THE ENTRIES
FOR THE RECORDS

An entry in the edition appears for each of the dates on which a record was used or added to. Each entry includes an indication of the degree of confidence the editors have in that date:

No symbol after the title of an entry indicates that the assigned date is certain. This is typically based on the inclusion of the date in the text of the document itself.

† after the title of an entry indicates that although there is no date present on the document itself, internal references or other evidence make the dating probable for the date given.

‡ after the title of an entry indicates also that there is no original date present in the record itself, and there is a lack of sufficient circumstantial evidence, so the date given is the best approximation, taking into consideration the document type, recorder, chronology of events, and dating of similar records within the same case.

[?] In a few entries, a date cannot be established with any level of confidence and is indicated by a question mark following the entry title. Such entries may be assigned a speculative date or may appear at the end of the most likely month.

ENTRY ARRANGEMENT WITHIN A SINGLE DATE

Entries dated on the same day are organized based on the probable order of use in the proceedings, according to the type of document, and also depending on the type of hearing when it was used. Within a group of a specific type, the entries are arranged alphabetically by the name of the person in whose case the record was used or, if that is not immediately apparent, by the name of the first accused person in the record, unless there is clear evidence that accurate chronology is inconsistent with alphabetical arrangement. If there are two of the same type of document against the same accused person, these are further arranged alphabetically by the name of the first accuser in the record. There are a few exceptions to this. Although the sets of the bills of indictment against most individuals are arranged alphabetically by the name of the person they allegedly afflicted, sets of indictments in the earliest cases prosecuted were numbered, so those sets are arranged numerically instead, based on the numbers on the manuscripts. Cases heard on a single day by the Superior Court of Judicature in 1693 are listed in the order in which they appear in the record book, not alphabetically.

The general principle for the arrangement of types of entries on a given day is this:

- If any officers of the Court were sworn in on that day, the **Oath of Office** starts the day. On some days, references to the completion of a previous day's business will be listed first, such as an **Officer's Return** on a warrant or summons issued on another day.
- **Complaints,** with or without **Bonds for Prosecution,** were the first new business of the day for local magistrates. **Warrants for the Apprehension** of an accused person follow the complaint, with the **Officer's Return** if the person has been brought in on the same day. Where there is a matching complaint and warrant against the same person on the same day, the two are kept together before listing the next complaint.
- Accounts of the **Examinations** of an arrested person before the local magistrates come next. Each person's examination is followed by a group of any **Depositions, Testimony,** and/or **Statements** against that person submitted on the day of the examination before listing the examination of the next individual.
- **Mittimuses** authorizing the transfer of prisoners from court to prison and recalling them from prison to appear in court come next.
- **Sworn documents** that are not grand jury or trial documents, before local magistrates at an inferior court and not from either of the superior courts, come next.
- Documents concerning the preparation for a grand jury before a superior court are grouped next – including **Summonses for Jurors** and **Witnesses,** followed by the result of any **Physical Examinations** of the bodies of the accused. Note that all 1692 grand jury and trial documents are under the Court of Oyer and Terminer. All 1693 grand jury and trial documents are under the Superior Court of Judicature.
- **Bills of Indictment** against each individual presented to a grand jury are next. Each set of indictments is followed by any **Sworn Depositions, Sworn Testimony,** and/or **Sworn Statements** against that person submitted and/or sworn to the grand jury. Any other documents presented to the grand jury are also included here. Often, these same documents are also used at the trial. If these documents were used at a trial on a different day, that subsequent date is referenced. If they were used at a trial on the same day, however, they are not listed a second time on the same day. Because bills of indictment came to grand juries before depositions, statements, or testimony were heard, the entries for them are presented in that order. The results from the grand jury, true bills or ignoramuses, appear on the bills of indictment, having been added, we assume, on the same day of the hearing.
- After this come any documents concerning the trial itself, beginning with any written **Pleas** submitted at arraignment, and **Case Records** from judicial record books. Each individual case is followed by a group of the **Depositions, Testimony,** and/or **Statements** used against the accused at trial before listing the documents in the case against the next individual. These are often documents already used at the grand jury and again at trial. Any other documents presented at trial, including **Statements** and/or **Petitions** in support of the accused and **Rebuttal Statements** against accusers, are also included here.
- Any remaining documents dated that day – including **Warrants for Executions,** official **Letters, Records of the Governor's Council, Legislative Bills** or **Acts,**

Accounts, and any other documents – are listed at the end of the date's entry.

- Documents listed after the last cases tried by the Superior Court of Judicature are listed in chronological order. When multiple documents appear on the same day, they are listed alphabetically when of the same type and when the correct chronology is not known. If there is an assortment of document types on a given day, documents are listed in the order that seems most appropriate to their use.

GRAND JURY, TRIAL, SENTENCING, EXECUTION, AND PROCLAMATION DATES

Headings appear with the dates of grand jury hearings, trials, sentencing dates, executions, and proclamations clearing a person of charges, but should be read with the following qualifications. These dates are included as available and based on the evidence of the documents. This does not preclude the possibility that a grand jury hearing or trial known to have occurred on a given date did not continue to the following day. For example, a heading for trials on August 5 definitely means that trials listed there occurred that day, but it is impossible in most cases to determine whether any of those trials continued to the next day. Such listings must always be seen as known dates that do not rule out a continuation to the next day. In a handful of cases that went to trial, there is simply no evidence to determine the specific date of a grand jury hearing, and so they are not included, although it is clear that they occurred. In cases when the bills of indictment were returned ignoramus by a grand jury, "Cleared by Proclamation" was sometimes noted. The phrase also occasionally appears on recognizances, when an accused person appeared back in court after having been released on bond.

A related issue concerns the heading of "Sentenced," which the edition carries only on September 17, to list a number of people identified by Robert Calef as being sentenced to death that day. There is inconsistent evidence as to when sentencing occured after a guilty verdict was rendered. The two extant warrants for execution indicate that the date these sentences were passed occured days after trial, but in the case of Abigail Faulkner Sr., conviction and sentencing clearly occured on the same day. Calef's dating may mean a trial date, or it may mean a separate sentencing date. However, in the cases of four confessors – Abigail Hobbs, Rebecca Eames, Mary Lacey Sr., and Ann Foster – we know by the "Cogn$^\varepsilon$" notation on their indictments (acknowledging the charge), that they pled guilty to the charges at arraignment. Thus, they did not have trials and went directly to sentencing, and they are accordingly placed without a trial date under the "Sentenced" heading.

We have undoubtedly placed some entries on dates that others may dispute, or that will be proven incorrect as more of the original records of events chronicled in this edition surface. Every document has required close scrutiny and consideration as to dating, even when a date appears on it. Such scrutiny does not guarantee accuracy, but the chronology that follows reflects a determined effort to come as close as we can to present a chronology that we believe reflects the events of 1692 and 1693 as well as dates following those years.

VII. RECORDS OF THE SALEM WITCH-HUNT

June 1692

October–December 1692

Appendix: Documents Carried in *SWP* Not Considered Related to 1692/93 Witchcraft Cases

Monday, February 29, 1692

1. Warrant for the Apprehension of Sarah Good, and Officer's Return

See also: March 1, 1692.

[Hand 1] Salem ffeb$^\varepsilon$ the 29th 1691/2

Whereas M^{rs} [= masters] Joseph Hutcheson Thomas Putnam Edward Putnam and Thomas Preston Yeomen of Salem Village in y^e County of Essex personally appeared before vs, and made Complaint on Behalfe of theire Majes^{ts} against Sarah Good the wife of William Good of Salem Village aboues^d, for Suspition of Witchcraft by her Committed, and thereby much Injury donne. to Eliz Parris, Abigail Williams Anna Putnam and Elizabeth Hubert all of Salem village afores^d Sundry times within this two moneths and Lately. also doñ, at Salem village Contrary to y^e peace of our Souer$^\varepsilon$ L^d and Lady W^m & mary King & Queen of Engld &c – You are therefore in theire Majesties names hereby required to apprehend & bring before vs the Said Sarah Good, to Morrow aboute ten of y^e Clock in y^e forenoon at y^e house of ∧{L^t} Nathaniell Ingersalls in Salem Village. or as soon as may be then & there to be Examined Relateing to y^e aboues^d premises and hereof you are not to faile at your perile Dated Salem. feb$^\varepsilon$ 29th 1691/2

John Hathorne

Jonathan. Corwin

} Assis^{ts}

To Constable George Locker.

[Reverse] [Hand 2] I brought the person of Saragh Good the wife of william Good according to the tenor of the within warrant as is Atest by me

George Locker Constable

[Hand 3] 1. March. 1691/2.

Notes: Although the witchcraft crisis of 1692 has generally been seen as centering at the outset on suspected witchcraft against the daughter and niece of the Reverend Samuel Parris, Betty Parris, 9, and Abigail Williams, 11 or 12, the first extant legal documents, this and the following one, include charges for also afflicting Ann Putnam Jr., 12, and Elizabeth Hubbard, 17. ◊ Hand 1 = John Hathorne; Hand 3 = Samuel Parris

Essex County Court Archives, vol. 1, no. 4, Massachusetts Supreme Judicial Court, Judicial Archives, on deposit James Duncan Phillips Library, Peabody Essex Museum, Salem, MA.

2. Warrant for the Apprehension of Sarah Osburn & Tituba, and Officer's Return

See also: March 1, 1692.

[Hand 1] Salem ffeb$^\varepsilon$ the 29th day. 1691/2

March 1, 1692

Whereas m^{rs} [= masters] Joseph Hutcheson Thomas Putnam Edward Putnam and Thomas Preston Yeomen of Salem Village, in y^e County of Essex. personally appeared before Vs, And made Complaint on behalfe of Theire Majesties against. Sarah Osburne the wife of Alex^a Osburne of Salem Village afores^d, and titibe an Indian Woman servant, of m^r Saml Parris of s^d place also; for suspition of witchcraft, by them Committe^d and thereby much injury don̄ to Elizabeth Parris Abigail Williams Anna Putnam and Elizabeth Hubert all of Salem Village afores^d sundry times with in this two moneths and Lately also done, at s^d Salem Village. Contrary to ye peace and Laws of our Sov^ε Lord & Lady W^m and Mary of England &c King & Queene

You are there fore in theire Maj^ε names hereby required to apprehend and forthwith or as soon as may be bring before Vs ye aboues^d Sarah Osburne, and titibe Indian, at ye house of Lt Nathl Ingersalls in s^d place and if it may be by to Morrow aboute ten of ye Clock ^{in ye mo⟨rn⟩ing} then and there to be Examined Relateing to ye aboues^d premises. You are likewise required to bring at ye same tyme Eliz. parris Abig^l Williams Anna putnam and Eliz Hubert. or any other person or persons y^t can giue Euedence in ye aboues^d Case. and here of you are not to faile Dated Salem ffeb^ε 29th 1691/2

John Hathorne

To Constable Joseph }   } Assis^{ts}
Herrick Cons^t in Salem

Jonathan. Corwin

[Reverse] [Hand 2] according to this warrant I haue apprehended the parsons with in mentioned and haue brought them accordingly and haue mad diligent sarch for Images and such like but can find non

Salem village this 1th march 1691/92

℈ me Joseph Herrick Constable

Notes: Thomas Putnam wrote the return on the warrant and signed Herrick's name. ◊ Hand 1 = John Hathorne; Hand 2 = Thomas Putnam

Essex County Court Archives, vol. 1, no. 33, Massachusetts Supreme Judicial Court, Judicial Archives, on deposit James Duncan Phillips Library, Peabody Essex Museum, Salem, MA.

Tuesday, March 1, 1692

Officer's Return: Warrant for the Apprehension of Sarah Good
2nd of 2 dates. See No. 1 on Feb. 29, 1692

Officer's Return: Warrant for the Apprehension of Sarah Osburn & Tituba
2nd of 2 dates. See No. 2 on Feb. 29, 1692

3. Examinations of Sarah Good, Sarah Osburn, & Tituba, as Recorded by Ezekiel Cheever

[Hand 1] The examination of Sarah Good before the Worshipfull ass^{ts} John Harthon Jonathan Curren

(H) Sarah Good what evil spirit have you familiarity with (SG) none (H) have you made no contract withe the devil, (g) good answerd no (H) why doe you hurt these children (g) I doe not hurt them I scorn it. (H) who doe you imploy then to doe it (g) I imploy no body, (H) what creature doe you imploy then, (g) no creature but I am falsely accused (H) why did you go away muttering from mr Paris his house (g) I did not mutter but I thanked him for what he gave my child (H) have you made no contract with the devil (g) no (H) desired the children all of them to looke upon her, and see, if this were the person that hurt them and so they all did looke upon her and said this was one of the persons that did torment them. presently they were all tormented. (H) Sarah good doe you not see now what you have done why doe you not tell us the truth. why doe you thus torment these poor children. (g) I doe not torment them, H⟨?⟩who doe you imploy then (g) I imploy no body I scorn it (H) how came they thus tormented, (g) what doe I know you bring others here and now you charge me with it (H) why who was it (g) I doe not know but it was some you brought into the meeting house with you (H) wee brought you into to the meeting house (g) but you brought in two more (H) who was it then that tormented the children (g) it was osburn (H) what is it that you say when you goe muttering away from persons houses ^{(g)} if I must tell I will tell (H) doe tell us then (g) if I must tell I will tell it is the commandments I may say my commandments I hope (H) what commandment is it (g) if I must tell you I will tell it is a psalm (H) what psalm (g) after a long time shee muttered over some part of a psalm (H) who doe you serve (G) I serve God (H) what God doe you serve (g) the god that made heaven and earth though shee was not willing to mention the word God her answers were in {a} very wicked, spitfull manner reflecting and retorting aganst the authority with base and abuseive words and many lies she was taken in. it was here said that her housband had said that he was afraid that shee either was a witch or would be one very quickly the worsh m^r Harthon asked him his ~~Re~~ reason why he said so of her whether he had ever seen any thing by her he answered no not in this nature but it was her bad carriage to him and indeed said he I may say with tears that shee is an enimy to all good

Sarah Osburn her examination
(H) what evil spirit have you familiarity with (O) none. (H) have you made no contract with the devill (O) I no I never saw the devill in my life (H) why doe you hurt these children (O) I doe not hurt them (H) who doe you imploy then to hurt them (O) I imploy no body.
(H) what familiarity have you with Sarah good (O) none I have not seen her these 2 years. (H) where did you see her then (O) one day agoing to Town, (H) what communications had y⟨ou⟩ with her, (O) I had none, only how do you doe or so I d⟨i⟩d not know her by name (H) what did you call her then, Osburn made a ~~pa~~ stand at that at last said shee called her Sarah (H) Sarah good saith that it was you that hurt the children, (O) I doe not know that the devil goes about in my likenes to doe any hurt m^r Harthon desired all thes chidren to stand up and looke upon her and see if they did know her. which they all did and every one of them said that ~~she~~ this was ^{one of} the woman that did afflict ^{them} and that they had constantly seen her in {the} very habit that shee was now in three evidence do stand that shee said this morning that shee was more like to be bewitched then that shee was a witch. m^r Harthon asked her what made her say so; shee answered that shee was frighted one time in her sleep and either saw or dreamed that shee saw a thing like an indian all black which did pinch her in her neck and pulled her by the back part of her ^{head} to the dore of the house (H) did you never see anything else (O) no. it was said by some in the meeting house that shee had said that shee would never beleive that lying spirit any more. (H) what lying spirit is this hath the devil ever deceived you and been false

March 1, 1692

to you (O) I doe not know the devill I never did see him. (H) what lying spirit was it then

(O) it was a voice that I thought I heard, (H) what did it propound to you. (O) that I should go no more to meeting but ~~shee~~ I said I would and did goe the next sabboth day (H) were you never tempted furder, (O) no (H) why did you yeild thus far to the devil as never to goe to meeting since. (O) alas I have been sike and not able to goe her housband and others said that shee had not been at meeting thes yeare and two months.

The ⟨?⟩ examination of Titibe
(H) Titibe what ~~sp~~ evil spirit have you familiarity with (T) none (H) why doe you hurt these children, (T) I doe not hurt them (H) who is it then ~~the de~~ (T) the devil for ought I ~~ken~~ know (H) did you never see the ⟨?⟩ devil,, (T) the devil came to me and bid me serve him (H) who have you seen) (T) 4 women ~~and~~ sometimes hurt the children, (H) who were they? (T) goode Osburn and Sarah good and I doe not know who the other were Sarah good and osburn would have me hurt the children but I would not shee furder saith there was a tale man of Boston that ["t" written over "w"] shee did see (H) when did you see them) (T) Last night at Boston (H) what did they say to you they said hurt the children, (H) and did you hurt them ~~no~~ (T) no there is 4 women and one man they hurt the ~~s~~ children and then lay all upon hure and they tell me if I will not hurt the children they will hurt me (H) but did you not hurt them (T) yes but I will hurt them no more (H) are you not sorry that you did hurt them. (T) yes. (H) and why then doe you hurt them) (T) they say hurt children or we will doe worse to you H) what have you seen an man come to me and say serve me (H) what service (T) hurt the children and last night there was an appearnce that said ~~K~~ Kill the children and if ⟨I⟩ I would no go on hurtang the children they woud doe worse to me (H) what is this appearance you see (T) sometimes it is like a hog and some times like a great dog this appearnce shee saith shee did see 4 times (H) what {did} it say to you (T) ~~it s~~ the black dog said serve me but I said I am afraid he ^{said} if I did not he would doe worse to me (H) what did you say to it (T) I will serve you no longer then he said he would hurt me and then he lookes like a man and threatens to hurt me. shee said that this man had a yellow bird that keept with him and he told me he had more pretty things that he would give me if I would sere him. (H) what were these pretty things (T) he did not show me them. (H) what else have you seen (T) two cats a red cat and a black cat (H) what did they say to you (T) they said serve me (H) when did you see them ~~last~~ (T) Last night and they said serve me but I ~~shee~~ said I would not (H) what service (T) shee said hurt the children (H) did you not pinch elisabeth Hubbard this morning (T) the man brought her to me and made ~~hur~~ pinch her (H) why did you goe to Thomas putnums Last night and hurt his child (T) they pull and hall me and make goe (H) and what would have you doe Kill her with a knif Left [= lieutenant] fuller and others said at this {time} when the child saw these persons and was tormented by them that she did complain of a knif that they wold have her cut her head off with a knife (H) how did you goe (T) we ride upon stickes and are there presently (H) doe you goe through the trees or over them (T) we see no thing but are there presently (H) why did you not tell your master (T) I was afraid they said they would cut off my head if I told (H) would you not have hurt others if you cold (T) they said they wo⟨u⟩ld hurt others but they could not ~~s⟨h⟩~~ (H) what attendants hath Sarah good (T) a yellow bird and shee would have given me one (H) what ^{meate} did she give it (T) it did ^{suck} her betwen her fingers (H) Did not you hurt mʳ Currins child (T) goode good and goode osburn told that they did hurt mʳ Currens child and would have had me hurt him two but I did not (H)

what hath Sarah Osburn (T) yesterday shee ^{had} a thing with a head like a woman with 2 leggs and wings Abigill williams that lives with her uncle {mr} Parris said that shee did see this same creature ~~with goode osburn & yesterday being~~⟨?⟩ and it turned into the shape of goode osburn (H) what else have you seen with g osburn (T) an othere thing hairy it goes upright like a man it hath only 2 le⟨e⟩ggs. (H) did you not see Sarah good upon elisebeth ~~williams~~ {Hubbard} last Saterday (T) I {did} see her set a wolfe upon her to afflict her the persons with this maid did say that shee did complain of a wolf T shee furder said that shee saw a cat with good at another time (H) what cloathes doth the man ~~we~~ go in (T) he goes in black cloathes a tal man. with white hair I thinke (H) how doth the woman goe) (T) in a white whood and a black whood with a top knot (H) doe you see who it is that torments these children now (T) yes it is goode good shee hurts them in her own shape (H) ⟨&⟩ who is it that hurts them now (T) I am blind now I cannot see.
[Hand 2] Salem Village
March the 1ᵗ 1691/2

Written by. Ezekiell Chevers
Salem Village
March the. 1ᵗ 1691/2

[Hand 3] Sarah Goods Examination

Notes: Osburn's examination follows immediately after Sarah Good's accusation against her. Osburn makes no accusation against Tituba, who is examined next. With seventeen-year-old Elizabeth Hubbard being included with the children, the narrative of presenting young adults, or at times older ones, as included with the "children" takes shape. Osburn's defense addresses what would be the central issue of the unfolding events–that the Devil could take the shape of an innocent person. Attorney General Newton's notation [Hand 3] comes at a later stage, after the establishment of the Court of Oyer and Terminer, when he notes this document as part of the collection of evidence against Sarah Good. ◊ Hand 1 = Ezekiel Cheever; Hand 2 = John Hathorne; Hand 3 = Thomas Newton

Essex County Court Archives, vol. 1, nos. 11 & 12, Massachusetts Supreme Judicial Court, Judicial Archives, on deposit James Duncan Phillips Library, Peabody Essex Museum, Salem, MA.

4.   Examinations & Mittimus of Sarah Good, Sarah Osburn, & Tituba, as Recorded by John Hathorne

See also: March 2, 1692, March 3, 1692, March 5, 1692 & March 7, 1692.

[Hand 1] Salem Village
March the 1ᵗ 1691/2
Sarah Good the wife of Wᵐ Good of Salem Village Labourer, Brought before vs; by George Locker Constable in Salem. to Answer ~~mͬ~~ Joseph Hutcheson Thomas Putnam &c of Salem Village Yeomen (Complainants on behalfe of theire Majesties) against sᵈ Sarah Good for suspition of Witchcraft by her Committed and thereby much Injury doñe to the Body of Elizabeth parris. Abigaile Williams Anna Putnam & Elizabeth Hubert all of Salem Village aforesᵈ according to theire Complaints as pͬ warrants Dated Salem March 29ᵗʰ 1691/2

Sarah Good vpon Examination denyed yᵉ matter of fact (viz) yᵗ she ever vsed any witchcraft; or hurt yᵉ abouesaid Children or any of them,
The aboue named Children being all present positiuely accused her of hurting of them Sundry times within this Two moneths and also yᵗ morneing

March 1, 1692   Sarah Good denyed y^t she had benne at theire houses in s^d tyme, or neere them, or had don̄
                       them any hurt

all The abouesaid children then presente accused her face to face., vpon which thay Ware all
dredfully tortered & tormented for a short space of tyme, and ye affliction and torters being
ouer thay charged s^d Sarah Good againe. y^t she had then soe tortered them, and came to
them and. did itt. althow she was personally then Keept at a Considerable distance from them
Sarah Good being. Asked if y^t she did not then hurt them; who did it, And the children
being againe tortered, she looked vpon them, And Said y^t it was one of them Wee brought
into ye house with vs, Wee ~~Answerd~~ Asked her who it was, she then Answered and Sayd itt
was Sarah Osburne, and Sarah Osburne was then vnder Custody & not in the house; – And
the children being quickly after recouered out of there fitt sayd. y^t itt was Sarah Good and
also Sarah Osburne y^t then did hurt & torment or aflict them. althow both of them at y^e
same time at a distance or Remote from them personally; – there ware also sundry other
Questions put to her & Answers giuen therevnto by her. according as is also giuen in.

Salem Village March the 1^t 1691/2
Sarah Osburne the wife of Alexander Osburne of Salem Village. brought; before vs by
Joseph Herrick Constable in Salem; to Answer Joseph Hutcheson & Thomas Putnam &c
yeomen in s^d Salem Village Complainants on behalfe of theire Majes^{ts}, against s^d Sarah
Osburne, for Suspition of Witchcraft by her Committed, and thereby much Injury don̄e to
the bodys of Elizabeth parris Abigail Williams Anna putnam and Elizabeth Hubert all of
Salem Village aforesaid, according to theire Complaint, according to a Warrant, Dated
Salem ffebu^E 29th 1691/2

Sarah ~~Good~~ Osburne vpon Examination denyed ye matter of fact (viz) y^t she ever vnderstood
or vsed any Witchcraft or vsed any Witchcraft, or hurt any of ye aboues^d children

The children abouenamed being all personally present accused her face to face which being
don̄, thay ware all hurt aflicted and tortured very much: which being ouer and thay out of
theire fitts thay sayd y^t said Sarah Osburne did then Come to them and hurt them, Sarah
Osburn being then Keept at a distance personally from them. S Osburne was asked why she
then hurt them. she denyed. it: it being Asked of her how she could soe pinch & hurt them
and yet she be⟨?⟩ at that distance personally from y^m she Answered she did not then hurt
them. nor never did. she was Asked who then did it or who she Imployed to doe it, she
Answered she did not know y^t ye diuell goes aboute in her likeness to doe any hurt. Sarah
Osbur⟨n⟩ being told y^t Sarah Good one of her Companions had vpon Examination accused
her. she nottwithstanding denyed ye same, according to her Examination. wch is more at
Large giuen in. as therein will appeare

Salem Village
March 1st 1691
Titiba an Indian Woman brought before vs by Cons^t Jos Herick of Salem vpon Suspition of
Witchcraft by her Commited according to ye Comp^{lt} of Jos. Hutcheson & Thomas putnam
etc of Salem Village as appeares ⅌ Warrant granted Salem 29 febr^E 1691/2

Titiba vpon Examination, and after some denyall acknowledged ye matter of fact. according
to her Examination giuen in more fully will appeare. and who also charged Sarah Good and
Sarah Osburne with ⟨y⟩^e same,

[Reverse] Salem Village
March ye 1th 1691/2
Sarah Good Sarah Osburne and Titiba an Indian Woman all of Salem Villag Being this day
brought before vs vpon Suspition of Witchcraft &c by them and Euery one of them
Committed. titiba an Indian Woman acknowledging ye matter of fact. and Sarah Osburne
and Sarah Good denying ye same before ^[caret overstruck] vs ^{but}: there appeareing. in
all theire Examinations sufficient Ground to. secure them all. {And} in order to ffurther
Examination thay Ware all ꝑ mittimus sent to ye Goales in ye County of Essex.

Salem March 2^d Sarah Osburne againe Examined and also titiba as will appear in their
Examinations giuen in
{titiba againe acknowledged ye fa⟨ct⟩ & also accused ye other two.}

Salem March 3^d Sarah Osburn and titiba Indian againe Examined.
ye Examination now Giuen in
{titiba againe s^d ye same}

Salem March 5th Sarah Good and titiba againe Examined. & ^{in} theire Examination
titiba acknowledg ye same she did formerly and accused ye other two aboues^d
{titiba againe said ye same}

John Hathorne

ꝑ vs   } Assis^ts

Jonathan. Corwin

Salem
March the 7th 1691/2
Sarah Good Sarah Osburne and Titiba an Indian Woman all sent to the Goale in Boston
according to. theire Mittimuses then sent: to Theire Majes^ts Goale Keeper

Notes: Sarah Good's infant child, close to three months at the time, also went to prison and died there, probably before
June, 1692. Seventeen-year-old Elizabeth Hubbard continues to be included among "the children." Betty Parris was
present and accusing, but evidence of her subsequently continuing to do so is not apparent. The dating of the warrant as
March 29 appears to be a recording lapse for February 29. ◊ Hand 1 = John Hathorne

*Essex County Court Archives, vol. 1, no. 14, Massachusetts Supreme Judicial Court, Judicial Archives, on deposit James Duncan
Phillips Library, Peabody Essex Museum, Salem, MA.*

5. Examinations of Sarah Good, Sarah Osburn, & Tituba, as Recorded by Joseph Putnam

[Hand 1] ⟨1.⟩ whatt Sarah Good saith

1 with non 2 shee saith that shee did doe them noe harme 3 shee implyd noebvdey
[= nobody] to doe the children

4 shee ~~sha~~ saith that shee hath made. no contract nor couenant
5 shee saith that shee neuer did hurt the children 6 shee saith that she neuer had familyarity
att the deuell 7 shee saith that shee neuer saw the children in such a condition
shee saith that shee came nott to meting for want of cloase [= clothes]
who is itt shee usially discorceseth with nobodey: butt itt is a psalme or a comandement: hur
God is the god that made heauen and earth she hops: shee saith that shee neuer did nid
["i" written over "d"] noe harme to mr parr
she saith itt was nott she itt is Gamer Osborne that doth pinch and aflickt the children
william good saith thatt shee ~~saith that shee~~ is an enemy to all good
shee saith shee is cleare ["c" written over "a"] of being a wich

what Gamer Osborn saith

1 shee saith she had noe hand in hurting the children nether by hur self by instrements
⟨1 itt⟩ shee saith that shee saith that ~~shee~~ was more lickley beewicht then a wich
shee said shee would neuer beeleaue the deuell 1 the deuell did propound to hur that shee
should neuer goe to meting noe more
and att that time nothing was ⟨?⟩ sugested to hur elces
why did she pinch the young wo⟨o⟩eman, shee neuer did nor dont kno⟨w⟩ who did

what the Indyen woman saith

they haue don noe harme to ~~the⟨m⟩~~ {hur} shee saith shee doth nott know how the deuell
works – Who is it that hurts them the deuell frot [= for ought] I know. there is fowre ~~frott~~
that hurts the children – 2 of the women are Gamer Osburn and gamer Good and they say
itt is shee one of the ~~child~~ women is a tall and short women and they would haue hur goe ~~to~~
with them to boston and shee oned that shee did itt att furst butt butt she was sorry for itt: itt
was the apearance⟨s⟩ of a man that came to hur and told hur that she murst hurt the Children
and she said that 4 times shaps of a hodg or a dodge and bid hur sarue him she said that shee
could nott [2nd "t" written over "h"] then she said he would hurt hur – she allsoe said that
shee seed a yalow ~~catt~~ burd that said unto hur sarue me

and shee seed 2 catts and they said sarue me she murst more pinch the children
she saith she sends the catt to bid hur pinch them: and the man brings the maid and bids hur
pinch hur: and they doe pull hur and make hur goe with them to mr putmans to perplex
them: and they make hur ride upone a poall and they hould the poll
and osband [= Osburn] and good allsoe rids upone poalls
and they the 2 women would haue hur cill thomas putmans child
the 2 women and the man told hur that if she told ⟨to⟩ hur master they would cutt ["u"
written over "a"] of h[Lost] [= her] heed
and yesterday tetaby abigall sayd that she say [= saw] a thing with wings and 2 leedgs [=
legs] and uanished into the shape of Osborn and the indgen oneth the same: and allsoe
atends Osborn a short and hary thing with 2 ledgs and to Whings
allsoe tetaby oneth that sary good sent a wolfe to scare the dr maid

[Hand 2] Written by Jos Putnam
Salem Village
March the 1t 1691/2

[Reverse] [Hand 3] The papers Relateing to Sarah Good Sarah Osburne and Titiba Indian   March 1, 1692
Salem March: 1691/2
[Hand 4] ag^t Sarah Good

Notes: In Putnam's account all three women give confirming support for witchcraft, or at least the active presence of the Devil. Good is first in accusing Osburn, who in turn confirms her conversation with the Devil, while Tituba, third, accuses both Good and Osburn as well as two unnamed women. Good and Osburn deflect blame from themselves. Osburn seeks to diminish her role while not accusing the others. However, if Cheever's account is to be trusted, Putnam has distorted what Osburn said. The doctor referenced is William Griggs, and the maid is Elizabeth Hubbard. ◊ "nid": possibly an error where the recorder has blended elements of the words that immediately precede and follow this item in the text (i.e. "did" and "noe"). "Gamer": 'gammer, a (rustic) title for an old woman' (*OED* s.v. *gammer*, cf. *gaffer*). ◊ Hand 1 = Joseph Putnam; Hand 2 = John Hathorne; Hand 3 = Thomas Newton

Essex County Court Archives, vol. 1, no. 9, Massachusetts Supreme Judicial Court, Judicial Archives, on deposit James Duncan Phillips Library, Peabody Essex Museum, Salem, MA.

6. Two Examinations of Tituba, as Recorded by Jonathan Corwin

See also: March 2, 1692.

[Hand 1] Tittuba ye Ind^ε Woem^{εs} Exam^ε March. 1. 1691/2
Q. Why doe you hurt these poor Children? Whatt harme have thay done unto you? A. they doe noe harme to me⟨e⟩ I noe hurt y^m att all. Q. Why have you done itt? A. I have done nothing; I Can̄'t Tell when ye Devill works Q. what, doth ye Devill Tell you that he hurts y^m? A. noe he Tells me nothing. Q. doe you never See Something appeare in Some shape? A. noe never See anything. Q. Whatt ffamilliarity have you wth ye devill, or w^t is itt y^t you Converse wthall? Tell ye Truth, Whoe itt is y^t hurts y^m? A. the Devill for ought I know. Q. w^t appearanc or how doth he appeare when he hurts y^m, wth w^t shape or what is he like that hurts y^m? A. like a man, I think yesterday I being in ye Lentoe Chamber I saw a thing like a man, that Tould me Searve him & I Tould him noe I would nott doe Such thing. she Charges Goody Osburne & Sarah Good as those y^t hurt ye Children, and would have had hir done itt, she Sayth she hath Seen foure two of wch she Knew nott, she Saw y^m last night as she was Washing y^e Roome, thay Tould me hurt the Children & would have had me gone to Boston, ther was .5. of y^m wth y^e man, they Tould me if I would nott goe & hurt y^m they would doe Soe to me att first I did agree wth y^m butt afterward I Tould y^m I doe Soe noe more Q. would y^a [= they] have had you hurt y^e Children y^e Last Night A. yes, butt I was Sorry & I sayd, I would doe Soe noe more, but Tould I would ffeare God. Q. butt why d̶⟨?⟩d̶ did nott you doe Soe before? A. why they Tell me I had done Soe before & therefore I must goe on, these were the .4. Woemen & y^e man, butt she Knew none but Osburne & Good only, y^e other were of Boston. Q. att first beyning [= being] wth y^m, w^t then appeared to you w^t was itt like y^t Got⟨?⟩ you to doe itt A. one like a man Just as I was goeing to sleep Came to me, this was when y^e Children was first hurt, he sayd he would kill y^e Children & she would never, be well, and he Sayd if I would nott Serve him he would doe Soe to mee. Q. is y$^{⟨t⟩}$ y^e Same man y^t appeared before to you?, y^t, appeared y^e last night & Tould you this?, A. yes. Q. w^t Other likenesses besides a man hath appeared to you? A. Sometimes like a hogge ⟨S⟩ometimes like a great black dogge; foure Tymes. Q. but w$^{⟨t⟩}$ d[Lost] [= did] ⟨t⟩hey Say unto you? A. they Tould me Serve him & y^t was a good way; y^t was y^e black dog⟨ge⟩ I tould him I was afrayd, he Tould me he would be worse then to me. Q. w^t did you Say to him then ⟨aft⟩er that? A. I answer I will Serve you noe Longer: he Tould me he would doe me hurt

March 1, 1692

then. Q. w^t other Creatures have you seen? A. a bird. Q. w^t bird? A. a little yellow Bird. Q. where doth itt Keep? A. wth ye man whoe hath pretty things ⟨h⟩ere besides. Q. what other pretty things? ⟨A.⟩ he hath nott showed y^m ⟨yet⟩ unto me, but he S^d he would showe y^m me tomorrow, and ⟨he⟩ tould me if I would Serve him, I should have ye Bird. Q. w^t other Creatures did you See? A. I saw 2 Catts, one Red, another blac⟨k⟩ as bigge as a little dogge. Q. w^t did these Catts doe? A. I do⟨n⟩t Know, I have Seen y^m Two Tymes. Q. w^t did they Say? A. they Say Serve them. Q. when did you See y^m? A. I saw y^m last night. Q. did they doe any hurt to you or threaten you? A. they did Scratch me. Q. When? A. after prayer: and scratched mee, because I would not ⟨serve them⟩ and when y^a Went away. I could nott See. but thay stood before ye ffire. Q. what Service doe thay Expect fr̄o you? A. they Say more hurt to ye Children. Q. how did you pinch y^m when you hurt y^m? A. the Other pull mee & hall me to ye pinch ye Child^ε, & I am very Sorry ffor itt; whatt made you hould yo^ε arme when you were Searched? W^t had you there? A. I had nothing Q. doe nott those Catts Suck you? A. noe never yett I Would nott lett y^m, but y^a had almost Thrust me into ye ffire. Q. how doe you hurt those y^t you pinch? doe you gett those Catts? or other things to doe itt for you? tell us, how is itt done? A. ye man Sends ye Catts to me & bids me pinch y^m, & I think I went ouer to m^ε Griggs's & have pinched hir this day in ye morneing. The man broug⟨ht⟩ m^ε Griggs's mayd to me & made me pinch hir. Q. did you ever goe wth these Woemen? A. they are very strong & pull me & make me goe wth y^m. Q. where did you goe? A. up to m^ε Putnams & make me hurt the Child. Q. whoe did make you goe? A. a man y^t is very strong & these Two Woemen, Good & Osburne but I am Sorry. Q. how did you goe? whatt doe you Ride upon? A. I Rid upon a stick or poale & Good & Osburne behind me, we Ride Takeing hold of one another & don't know how we goe for I Saw noe Trees, nor path, but was presently there, when wee were up. Q. how long Since you began to pinch m^ε Parris's Children? A. I did nott pinch y^m att ye ffirst, butt he make me afterward. Q. have you Seen Good and Osburne Ride upon a poale? A. yes & have held ffast by mee: I was nott att m^ε Griggs's but once, butt it may be Send Something like mee, neither would I have gone, butt y^t y^a Tell me, they will hurt me; last night they Tell me I must Kill Some body wth ye Knife. Q. who were they y^t Told you Soe? A. Sarah Good & Osburne & y^a would have had me Killed Thomas Putnam's Child last night. the Child alsoe affirmed y^t att y^e Same Tyme thay would have had hir Cutt ~~hir own throat~~ of hir own head for if she would nott y^a Tould hir Tittubee would Cutt itt off & y^n she Complayned att y^e ⟨Sa⟩me Time of a knife Cutting of hir when hir master hath asked hir about these thing[Lost] [= things] she Sayth thay will nott lett hir Tell, butt Tell hir if she Tells hir head sh⟨a⟩ll be Cutt off. Q. whoe [Lost] [SWP = Tells] you Soe? A. y^e man, Good & Osburnes wife. Goody Good Came to hir last night w^n hir master was att prayr & would nott lett hir hear & she Could nott hear a good whyle. Good hath one of these birds y^e yellow bird & would have given mee itt, but I would not have itt & in prayer Tyme she Stoped my Eares & would nott lett me hear. Q. w^t should you have done with itt A. give itt to ye Children. wch yellow bird hath bin Severall Tymes Seen by ye Children. I Saw Sarah Good have itt on hir hand when she Came to hir when m^ε Parris Was att prayr: I Saw ye bird Suck Good betwene ye fore ffinger & Long ffinger upon the Right hand. Q. did you never practi⟨c⟩e witchcraft in your owne Countr⟨y⟩? A. noe Never before now. Q. did you [Lost] See y^m doe itt ⟨n⟩ow? A. yes. today, butt y^t was in ye morneing. Q. butt did you See y^m doe itt now while you are Examining. A. noe I did nott See y^m but I Saw y^m hurt att other Tymes. I saw Good have a Catt beside ye yellow bird wch was with hir Q. what hath Osburne gott to goe wth hir? A. Something I don't know what itt is. I can't name itt, I don't know how itt looks she hath two of y^m one of y^m hath Wings &

Two Leggs & a head like a woeman. the Children Saw ye Same butt yesterday wch afterward Turned into a Woeman. Q. what is ye other thing y^t Goody Osburne hath? A. a thing all over hairy, all ye fface hayry & a long nose & I don't Know how to tell how ye fface looks, wth Two Leggs, itt goeth upright & is about Two or three foot high & goeth upright like a man & last night itt stood before ye fire In m^ε Parris's hall. Q. Whoe was y^t appeared like a Wolfe to Hubbard as she was goeing frō Proctures? A. itt was Sarah Good & I Saw hir send ye Wolfe to hir. Q. what Cloathes doth ye man appeare unto you in? A. black Cloaths Some times, Some times Searge Coat of other Couler, a Tall man wth White hayr, I think. Q. what aparre⟨l⟩ doe ye woemen ware? A. I don't Know w^t Couller. Q. what Kind of Cloathes hath she? A. a black Silk hood wth a White Silk hood under itt, wth Topknotts, wch woeman I know no⟨t⟩ but have Seen hir in boston when I lived there. Q. wha⟨t⟩ Cloathes ye little Woeman? A. a Searge Coat wth a White Cap as I think. the Children haveing ffitts att this Very time she was asked whoe hurt y^m, she Ans^d Goody Good & ye Children affirmed ye Same, butt Hubbard being Taken in an Extreame ffitt after she was asked whoe hurt hir & she Sayd she Could nott tell, butt Sayd they blinded hir, & would nott lett hir see & after y^t was once or Twice taken dumb hir Self

Second Examination. March. 2. 1691/2

Q. What Covenant did you make wth y^t man y^t Came to you? what did he tell you. A. he Tell me he god, & I must beleive him & Serve him Six yeares & he would give me many fine things. Q. how long agone was this? A. about Six Weeks & a little more, ffryday night before Abigall was Ill. Q. w^t did he Say you must doe more? did he Say you must Write any thing? did he offer you any paper? A: yes, the Next time he Come to me & showed me⟨e⟩ some fine things, Something like Creatures, a little bird Something like green & white. Q. did you promiss him the⟨n⟩ when he Spake to you then what did you answer him. A. I then Sayd this I tould him I Could nott beleive him God, I toul⟨d⟩ him I ask my maister & would have gone up but he stopt mee & would nott lett me. Q. whatt did you promiss him? A. the first Tyme I beleive him God & then he was Glad. Q. what did he Say to you then? what did he Say you must doe? A. th⟨is⟩ he tell me they must meet together: Q. W^n did he Say you m⟨ay⟩ meet together? A. he tell me Wednesday Next att my m^{εs} house, & then they all meet together & thatt night I Saw y^m all stand in ye Corner, all four of y^m, & ye man stand behind mee & Take hold of mee to make mee stand still in ye hall. Q. time of Night? A. a little before prayr Time. Q. what did thi⟨s⟩ man Say to you when he Took hold of you? A. he Say go⟨e⟩ into y^e other Room & See y^e Children & doe hurt to them. and pinch y^m & then I went in, & would nott hurt y^m a good while, I would nott hurt Betty, I loved Betty, but y^a hall me & make me pinch Betty & y$^{⟨e⟩}$ next Abigall & then quickly went away altogether a [= after?] I had pinched y^m. Q. did thay pinch A. Noe. but they all lookt on & See mee pinch y^m. Q. did you goe into y^t Room in your own person & all y^e rest? A. yes, and my master did nott See us, for y^a Would nott lett my Master See. Q. did you goe wth y^e Company? A. Noe I stayd & y^e man stayd wth me. Q. whatt did he then to you? A. he tell me my master goe to prayer & he read in book & he ask me what I remember, but don't you remember anything. Q. did he ask you noe more but ye ffirst Time to Serve him or ye Second time? A. yes, he ask me againe, & y^t I Serve him, Six yeares & he Com⟨?⟩ ye Next Time & show me a book. Q. and when would he Come then? A. ye next fryday & showe⟨?⟩ me a book in ye day Time betimes in ye morneing. Q. and what Booke did he bring a great or litle booke? A. he did nott show itt me, nor would nott; but had itt in his pockett⟨?⟩. Q. did nott he make you write yo^ε Name? A. noe nott yett for my ["my" written over "his"] mistris

March 1, 1692

Called me into ye other roome. Q. whatt did he Say you must doe in that book? A. he Sayd write & Sett my name to itt. Q. did you Write? A. yes once I made a marke in ye Book & made itt wth red like Bloud. Q. did he gett itt out of your body? A. he Said he must gett itt out ye Next Time he Come againe, he give me a pin Tyed in a stick to doe itt w^{th}, butt he noe Lett me bloud wth itt as yett butt Intended another Time when he Come againe. Q. did you See any other marks in his book? A. yes a great many some marks red, Some yellow, he opened his book a great many marks in itt. Q. did he tell you ye Names of y^m? A. yes of Two no⟨e⟩ ⟨m⟩ore Good & Osburne & he Say thay make y^m mar⟨k⟩s in that book & he showed them mee. Q. how many marks doe you think there was? A. Nine. Q. did thay Write there Names? A. thay Made marks, Goody Good Sayd she made hir mark, butt Goody Osburne Would nott Tell she was Cross to mee. Q. when did Good tell you she Sett hir hand to y^e Book? A. the same day I Came hither to prison. Q. did you See y^e man thatt morneing? A. yes a litle in y^e morneing & he tell me y^e Magistrates Come up to Examin⟨?⟩ me. Q. w^t did he Say you must Say? A. he tell me, tell nothing, if I did he would Cutt my head off. Q. tell us Tr⟨u⟩[Lost] [= true] how many Woemen doe use to Come when you Rid abroad? A foure of y^m these Two Osburne & Good & those Two strangers Q. you say y^t there was Nine did he tell you whoe y^a were? A. noe he noe lett me See but he tell me I should See y^m y^e Next Tyme. Q. What Sights did you see? A. I see a man, a dogge, a hogge & Two Catts, a black and Red & ye strange monster was Osburnes y^t I mentioned before. this was ye hayry Imp ye man would give itt to mee, but I would nott have itt. Q. did he show you in ye Book wch was Osburnes & wch was Goods mark? A. yes I see there marks. Q. butt did he Tell ye Names of ye other? A. noe S^ε. Q. & what did he Say to you when you made your Mark? A. he Sayd Serve mee & always Serve mee. the man wth ye Two woemen Came frō Boston. Q. how many ["n" written over "y"] Times did you goe to Boston? A. I was goeing & ⟨th⟩en Came back againe I was never att Boston. Q. whoe Came back wth you againe? A. ye man Came back wth mee & ye woemen goe away, I was Nott willing to goe? Q. how farr did you goe, to what Towne? A. I never went to any Towne I see noe Trees, noe Towne. Q. did he tell you where ye Nine Lived? A. yes, Some in Boston & Some here in this Towne, but he would nott tell mee whoe thay were,

Notes: The person pinched at Griggs's is presumably Elizabeth Hubbard. In Tituba's second examination a contract with the Devil is described. This contract, including signing of the Devil's book, reflects an historical feature of witchcraft in the Christian tradition. ◊ "Lentoe": lean-to, 'belonging to or of the nature of a building whose rafters pitch against or lean on to another building or against a wall' (*OED s.v. lean-to*). ◊ Hand 1 = Jonathan Corwin

Salem Selections, Massachusetts Box, Essex Co., Manuscripts & Archives, New York Public Library. New York, NY.

7. Deposition of Elizabeth Hubbard v. Sarah Good†
See also: March 2, 1692.

[Hand 1] The Deposistion of Elizabeth Hubburd agged about 17 years who testifieth and saith that on the 26 february 1691/92 I saw the Apperishtion of Sarah good who did most greviously afflect me by pinching and pricking ^{me} and so she continewed hurting of me tell the first day of march being the day of hir Examination and then she did also most greviouly afflect and tortor me also dureing the time of hir Examynation and also seuerall times sence she hath afflected me and urged me to writ in hir book: also on the day of hir

Examination I saw the Apperishtion of Sarah good goe and hurt and afflect the
bodyes ^{of} Elizabeth parish Abigail williams and Ann putnam jur.
and also I haue seen the the Apperishtion of Sarah Good afflecting: the body of Sarah vibber

March 1, 1692

mark
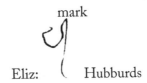

Eliz: Hubburds

[Reverse] also in the Night affter Sarah goods Examination: Sarah Good came to me
~~and did~~ barefoot and bareledged and did most greuiously torment me by pricking and
pinching me and I veryly beleue that Sarah good hath bewicked me also that night Samuell
Sibly that was then attending me strock Sarah good on hir Arme.
[Hand 2] Elizabeth Hubbard ag^t Sarah Good.

Notes: The docket was written by Thomas Newton, strongly suggesting that this was considered for grand jury and/or
trial use on June 28. However, for whatever reason, it appears not to have been used at either. Beginning with "also on
the day…." the ink changes with Thomas Putnam adding material either on the day or later. In this case the addition
was probably made on March 2. Note that Putnam recorded all the depositions in these three early cases. ◊ Hand 1 =
Thomas Putnam; Hand 2 = Thomas Newton

*Essex County Court Archives, vol. 1, no. 20, Massachusetts Supreme Judicial Court, Judicial Archives, on deposit James Duncan
Phillips Library, Peabody Essex Museum, Salem, MA.*

8. Deposition of Samuel Parris, Thomas Putnam, & Ezekiel Cheever v. Sarah Good, Sarah Osburn, & Tituba†

See also: May 23, 1692 & June 28, 1692.

[Hand 1] The Deposition of Sam: Parris aged about thirty & nine years testifyeth ⟨&⟩ saith
that Eliz: Parris jun^ε & Abigail Williams & Ann Putman jun^ε & Eliz: Hubbard were most
grievously & severall times tortured during the Examination of Sarah Good, Sarah Osburne,
& Tituba Indian before the Magistrates at Salem village 1. March. 1691/2 And the said
Tituba being the last of the abovesaid that was examined they the abovesd afflicted persons
were greivously distressed untill the said Indian began to confess & then they were
immediately all quiet the rest of the said Indian womans examination. Also Tho: Putman
aged about fourty years & Ezek: Cheevers aged about thirty & six years testify to the whole
of the abovesd & all the three deponents aforesaid farther testify that ~~when~~ ^{after} the said
Indian began to confess ^{she} was her self very much afflicted & in the face of authority at
the same time ^{&} openly charged the abovesaid Good & Osburne as the persons that
afflicted her the aforesaid Indian
{[Hand 2] m^r Paris on his oath owned this to be the truth before the Juryars for inquest this
28. of Jun: 1692}

[Hand 3] Sworne Salem May the 23^d 1692
Before vs John Hathorne
[Hand 4] Jonathan. Corwin
℘ ord^ε of ye Govern^ε & Councill
[Hand 5] Jurat in Curia

March 1, 1692   [Reverse] [Hand 1] The depo⟨s̄⟩ion of S. Parris. Tho: Putman & Ezek: Cheevers

ags^t { Sarah Good
       Sarah Osburne
       Tituba Indian

[Hand 6] Mr Sam^ll parris

Notes: It seems likely that on May 23 Hathorne and Corwin were reviewing cases for further judicial action. The grand jury and trial dates for this document are for the case of Sarah Good only. Sarah Osburn had died in prison on May 10, 1692, and Tituba was not brought before a grand jury until May 9, 1693, when an ignoramus was returned, never coming to trial. ◊ Used at trial. ◊ Hand 1 = Samuel Parris; Hand 3 = John Hathorne; Hand 4 = Jonathan Corwin

Essex County Court Archives, vol. 1, no. 34, Massachusetts Supreme Judicial Court, Judicial Archives, on deposit James Duncan Phillips Library, Peabody Essex Museum, Salem, MA.

9. Deposition of Ann Putnam Jr. v. Sarah Good†

See also: June 28, 1692.

[Hand 1] The Deposistion of Ann putnam {jur} who testifieth and saith that on the 25th of february. 1691/92 I saw the apperishtion of Sarah good which did tortor me most greviously but I did not know hir name tell the 27th of february and then she tould me hir name was Sarah good and then she did prick me and pinch me most greviously: and also sence seuerall times urging me vehemently to writ in hir book and also on the frist day of march being the day of hir Examination Sarah good did most greviously tortor me and also seuerall times sence: and also on the the first day of march 1692 I saw the Apperishtion of Sarah good goe and afflect and tortor the bodys of Elizabeth parish Abigail williams and Elizabeth Hubburd also I haue seen the Apperishtion of Sarah good afflecting the body:: of Sarah Vibber.

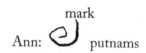

mark
Ann: putnams

[Hand 2] ann putnam ownid this har testimony to be the truth. one har oath. before the Juriars of Inquest this 28: of June. 1692
[Hand 3] And further say^s that shee verily beleiues that Sarah Good doth bewitch & afflicte her

sworn before the Court.

[Reverse] [Hand 4] Ann puttnam ag^t Sarah Good

Notes: The ink change after "and also on the . . ." reflects Thomas Putnam's later addition. ◊ Hand 1 = Thomas Putnam; Hand 4 = Thomas Newton

Essex County Court Archives, vol. 1, no. 19, Massachusetts Supreme Judicial Court, Judicial Archives, on deposit James Duncan Phillips Library, Peabody Essex Museum, Salem, MA.

10. Deposition of Elizabeth Hubbard v. Sarah Osburn†

[Hand 1] The Deposistion of Elizabeth Hubburd aged about 17 years who testifieth and saith that on the 27th of february 1691/92 I saw the Apperishtion of Sarah osborn the wife of

March 1, 1692

E̶x̶ Allexander osborn who did most greviously tortor me by pricking and pinching me most dreadfully and so she continewed hurting me most greviously tell the first of march 1691/92: being the day of hir Examination ^{being first of march} and then also Sarah osborn did tortor me most greviously by pinching and pricking me most dre⟨ad⟩fully and also seuerall times sence Sarah osborn has afflected me and urged me to writ⟨e⟩ in hir book

[Reverse] first 3

Notes: The "first 3" on the reverse may be Thomas Putnam's notation referencing the first three accused, or the first three afflicted. Alternatively, it may simply reference the March 1 date. ◊ Hand 1 = Thomas Putnam

Essex County Court Archives, vol. 1, no. 28, Massachusetts Supreme Judicial Court, Judicial Archives, on deposit James Duncan Phillips Library, Peabody Essex Museum, Salem, MA.

11. Deposition of Ann Putnam Jr. v. Sarah Osburn†

[Hand 1] The Deposistion of Ann putnam who testifieth and saith that on the 25th of ffebruary 1691/92 I saw the Apperishtion of Sarah osborn the wife of E̶ Allexandar osborn who did Immediatly tortor me most greviously by pinching and pricking me dreadfully and so she continewed most dreadfully to afflect me tell the first day of march being the day of hir Examination and then also she did tortor me most dreadfully in the time of hir Examination: and also seuerall times sence g̶o̶o̶d̶ Sarah osburn has afflected me and urged me to writ in hir book

[Reverse] [Hand 2] Ann putnam ag^t Sarah Osborne

Notes: Hand 1 = Thomas Putnam

Essex County Court Archives, vol. 1, no. 27, Massachusetts Supreme Judicial Court, Judicial Archives, on deposit James Duncan Phillips Library, Peabody Essex Museum, Salem, MA.

12. Deposition of Elizabeth Hubbard v. Tituba†

[Hand 1] The Deposistion of Elizabeth Hubbard agged about 17 years who testifieth that on the 25th february 1691/92 I saw the Apperishtion of Tituba Indian which did Immediatly most greviously torment me by pricking pinching and almost choaking me: and so continewed hurting me most greviously by times h̶u̶r̶t̶i̶n̶g̶: tell the day of hir Examination being the first of march and then also at the begining of hir Examination: but as soon as she began to confess she left ofe hurting me and has hurt {⟨m⟩e} but litle sence

[Reverse] [Hand 2] [Lost]ert [= Eliz Hubbert] Contra Titiba

Notes: The release from affliction upon confession of the accused would become part of a standard pattern. ◊ Hand 1 = Thomas Putnam

Essex County Court Archives, vol. 1, no. 32, Massachusetts Supreme Judicial Court, Judicial Archives, on deposit James Duncan Phillips Library, Peabody Essex Museum, Salem, MA.

13. Deposition of Ann Putnam Jr. v. Tituba†

[Hand 1] The deposistion of Ann putnam who testifieth and saith that on the 25th of ffebruary 1691/92 I saw the Apperishtion of Tituba Mr parishes Indian woman which did tortor me most greviously by pricking and pinching me most dread‑{fully} tell the first day of march being the day of hir Examination and then also most greviously allso at the begining of hir Examination: but sene [= since] she confesed she has hurt {me} be but little

[Reverse] [Hand 2] [Lost]n. [= Ann] putnam agst Tittuba I[Lost] [= Indian]

Notes: Hand 1 = Thomas Putnam; Hand 2 = Jonathan Corwin

Essex County Court Archives, vol. 1, no. 35, Massachusetts Supreme Judicial Court, Judicial Archives, on deposit James Duncan Phillips Library, Peabody Essex Museum, Salem, MA.

Wednesday, March 2, 1692

Continued from March 1, 1692: Examinations & Mittimus of Sarah Good, Sarah Osburn, & Tituba, as Recorded by John Hathorne
2nd of 5 dates. See No. 4 on March 1, 1692

Continued from March 1, 1692: Deposition of Elizabeth Hubbard v. Sarah Good†
2nd of 2 dates. See No. 7 on March 1, 1692

Continued from March 1, 1692: Two Examinations of Tituba, as Recorded by Jonathan Corwin
2nd of 2 dates. See No. 6 on March 1, 1692

Thursday, March 3, 1692

Continued from March 2, 1692: Examinations & Mittimus of Sarah Good, Sarah Osburn, & Tituba, as Recorded by John Hathorne
3rd of 5 dates. See No. 4 on March 1, 1692

Saturday, March 5, 1692

Continued from March 3, 1692: Examinations & Mittimus of Sarah Good, Sarah Osburn, & Tituba, as Recorded by John Hathorne
4th of 5 dates. See No. 4 on March 1, 1692

14. Statement of William Allen, John Hughes, William Good, & Samuel Braybrook v. Sarah Good, Sarah Osburn, & Tituba

March 5, 1692

[Hand 1] March 5th 1691/2

Wm Allin Saith yt on ye 1st of March att night he heard a strange noyse not useually heard and so Continued for many times so yt hee was afrighted and Comeing nearer to it he there saw a strange and unuseall beast lyeing on the Grownd so yt goeing up to it ye sd Beast vanished away and in ye sd place starte up 2 or 3 weemen and flew from mee not after ye manner of other weemen but swiftly uanished away out of our sight which weemen wee took to bee Sarah Good Sarah Osburne and Tittabe ye time was about an hour within night and I John Hughes saith ye same beeing in Company then wth sd allin as wittness our hands

William Allen
iohn hughes

William Allen further saith yt on ye 2d day of march ye sd sarah Good uissabley [= visibly] appeared to him in his chamber sd allen beeing in bed and brought an unuseuall light in wth her ye sd sarah came and sate upon his foot ye sd allen went to kick att her upon which shee uanished and ye light with her

William Good saith yt ye night before his sd wife was Examined he saw a wart or tett a little beloue her Right shoulder which he never saw before and asked Goodwife Engersol; whether she⟨e⟩ did not see it when shee searched her

~~William allen~~ {John Hughes} further saith yt on ye 2d day of march yt Comeing from Goodman Sibley aboute Eight of ye clock in ye night hee saw a Great white dogg whome H{e} ["H{e}" written over "I"] came up to but he would not stire but when He ["He" written over "I"] was past hee ye sd dogg fowllowed ~~mee~~ {him} about 4 or 5 pole and so disapeared ye same night ye sd John Hughes beeing in Bed in a closte Roome and ye dore beeing fast so yt no Catt nor dogg could Come in ye sd John saw a Great light appeare in ye sd chamber and Risseing up in his bed he saw a large Grey Catt att his beds foot

March ye 2d Samll Brabrook Saith yt Carrieng Sarah Good to ippswhich ye sd Sarah leapt of her horse 3 times which was Between 12 and 3 of ye clock of ye same day wch ye daughter of Thomas Puttman declared ye Same att her fathers house ye sd Brabrook futher saith yt sd sarah Good tould him that shee would not owne her selfe to bee a wicth unless she is proud [= proved] one shee sath yt there is but one Euidence and yt an Indian and therefore she fears not and so Continu⟨ed⟩ Rayling against ye majestrate and she Endevered to kill hers⟨elfe⟩

[Reverse] [Hand 2] Allin &c agt Sarah Good

Notes: Aside from the original complaints, the first adult statements against the accused appear here, and are from male accusers. ◊ Hand 1 = George Herrick; Hand 2 = Thomas Newton

Essex County Court Archives, vol. 1, no. 29, Massachusetts Supreme Judicial Court, Judicial Archives, on deposit James Duncan Phillips Library, Peabody Essex Museum, Salem, MA.

Monday, March 7, 1692

Continued from March 5, 1692: Examinations & Mittimus of Sarah Good, Sarah Osburn, &
Tituba, as Recorded by John Hathorne
5th of 5 dates. See No. 4 on March 1, 1692

Saturday, March 19, 1692

15. Warrant for the Apprehension of Martha Cory, and Officer's Return
See also: March 21, 1692.

[Hand 1] Salem March the 19th 1691/2
There being Complaint this day made, before vs, By Edward putnam and Henery Keney
Yeomā both of Salem Village, Against Martha Cory the wife of Giles Cory of Salem ffarmes
for suspition of haueing Committed sundry acts of Witchcraft and thereby donne Much hurt
and injury vnto the Bodys of Ann putnam the wife of Thomas putnam of Salem Village
Yeoman And Anna putnam ye daufter of s^d Thomas putnam and Marcy Lewis single
woman Liueing in s^d putnams famyly; also abigail William, one of m^r parris his famyly and
Elizabeth Hubert Docter Grigs his maid
You are therefore in theire Majes^{ts} names hereby required to apprehend and bring; before vs.
Martha Cory the wife of Giles Cory abouesaid on Munday next being the. 21^t day of this
Instant moneth, at the house of ^{L^t} Nathaniell Ingersalls of Salem Village ^{aboute twelfe
of the Clock in y^e Day.} in order to her Examination Relateing to the premises and hereof
you [Lost] [= are] not to faile Dated Salem March the 19th 16[Lost] [= 1691/2]

		John Hathorne	
ꝑ vs			} Assis^{ts}
		Jonathan. Corwin	

To. Geo Herrick Marshall
of the County of Essex
or any Constable in Salem

_____

[Hand 2] March 21st ^{I haue taken} Martha Cory and brought to y^e housse of Leu^t Nath:
Engersoll where shee is in y^e Costody of some persons by mee Required and is forth
Comeing att demand per m⟨e?⟩ Joseph Herrick Constable for Salem

[Reverse] [Hand 3]
Goody. Wild
Goody Oliuer

Notes: Ann Putnam Sr. and Mercy Lewis appear for the first time as accusers. Henry Kenney subsequently complained
against Rebecca Nurse at her examination on March 24. The reason for the names of Goody Wilds and Goody Oliver

on the reverse is unclear. Both women, Sarah Wilds and Bridget Bishop (often called Oliver based on her name from her previous marriage that ended when her husband died) were subsequently accused, tried, and executed. The possibility exists that Wilds and Bishop were named in the course of the March proceedings against Cory. ◊ Hand 1 = John Hathorne; Hand 2 = George Herrick

Essex County Court Archives, vol. 1, no. 38, Massachusetts Supreme Judicial Court, Judicial Archives, on deposit James Duncan Phillips Library, Peabody Essex Museum, Salem, MA.

Monday, March 21, 1692

Officer's Return: Warrant for the Apprehension of Martha Cory
2nd of 2 dates. See No. 15 on March 19, 1692

16. Examination of Martha Cory

[Hand 1] 21. March. 1691/2
Mr Hathorne. You are now in the hands of Authority tell me now why you hurt these persons
Martha Kory. I do not.
Who doth?
Pray give me leave to goe ["goe" written over "give"] to prayer
This request was made sundry times
We do not send for you to go to prayer
But tell me why you hurt these?
I am an innocent person: I never had to do with Witchcraft since I was born. I am a Gosple Woman
Do not you see these complain of you
The Lord open the eyes of the Magistrates & Ministers: the Lord show his power to discover the guilty.
Tell us who hurts these children.
I do not know.
If you be guilty of this fact do you think you can hide it.
The Lord knows
Well tell us w^t you know of this matter
Why I am a Gosple-woman, & do you think I can have to do with witchcraft too
How could you tell then that the child was bid to observe what cloths you wore when some came to speak wth yo⟨u⟩
Cheevers. Interrupted her & bid her not begin with a lye & so Edwd Putman declared the matter
Mr Hath: Who told you that
K He said the child said
Cheev: you speak falsly
Then Edw: Putman read again
Mr H. Why did you ask if the child told w^t cloths you wore
My husband told me the others told
Who told you about the cloaths? Why did you ask that question.
Because I heard the children told w^t cloaths the other wore

Goodm: Kory did you tell her
The old man denyed that he told her so.
Did you not say your husband told you so
K. –
H. Who hurtes these children now look upon them.
K. I cannot help it
H Did you not say you would tell the truth why you askt y^t question: how come you to the knowledge
I did but ask
You dare thus to lye in all this assembly
You are now before Authority, I expect the truth, you promised it, Speak now & tell ~~what cloths~~ who told you what cloths
K No body
H How came you to know y^t ye children would be examined what cloth y^u wore
Because I thought ye child was wiser than any body if she knew
Give an answer you said your husband told you
He told me the children said I afflicted them
H⟨ow⟩ do you know w^t they came for, answer me this truly, will you say how you came to know what they came for
I had heard speech that the children said I ~~afflicted them~~ troubled them & I thought that they might come to examine
But how did you know it
I thought they did
Did not you say you would tell the truth, who told you w^t they came for
No body
How did you know
I did think so
But you said you knew so
Childr: There is a man whispering in her ear.
H Q What did he say to you.
We must not beleive all that these distracted children say
Cannot ~~he tell~~ you tell what that man whispered
I saw no body
But did not you hear.
No, here was
Extream agony of all the afflicted
If you expect mercy of God, you must look for it in Gods way by confession
Do you think to find mercy by aggravating your sins
A true thing
Look for it then in Gods way
So I do
Give glory to God & confess then
But I cannot confess
Do not you see how these afflicted do charge you
We must not beleive distracted persons
Who do you improve to hurt them.
I improved none

Did not you say our eyes were blinded you would open them

Yes to accuse the innocent

Then Crossly gave in evidence

Why cannot the girl stand before you

I do not know.

What did you mean by that

I saw them fall down

It seems to be an insulting speech as if thy [= they] could not stand before you.

They cannot stand before others.

But you said they cannot stand before y^u

Tell me what was that turning upon the spit by you

You beleive the children that are distracted I saw no spit

Here are more than two that accuse you for witchcraft what do y^u say

I am innocent

Then Mr Hathorn read farther of Croslys evidence

What did you mean by that the Devil could not stand before you

She denyed it

3. or .4. Sober witnesses confirm'd it.

What can I do many rise up against me

Why confess

So I would if I were guilty

Here are sober persons what do you say to them

You are a Gosple woman, will you lye

Abigail cryed out next Sab: is sacrament day, but she shall not come there

Kory I do not care

You charge these children with distraction: it is a note of distraction when persons vary in a minute, but these fix upon you, this is not ye manner of distraction –

When all are against me w^t can I help it

Now tell me ye truth will you, why did you say that the Magistrates & Ministers eyes were blinded you would open them

She laught & denyed it.

Now tell us how we shall know

Who doth hurt these if you do not

Can an innocent person be guilty

Do you deny these words

Yes

Tell us who hurts these: We came to be a Terror to evil doers

You say you would open our eyes we are blind

If you say I am a Witch

You said you would show us

She denyed it.

Why do you not now show us

I cannot tell: I do not know

What did you strike the maid at Mr Tho: Putmans with.

March 21, 1692   I never struck her in my life

Here are two that see you strike her with an iron r⟨o⟩d.

I had no hand in it

Who had

Do you beleive these children are bewitcht

Thy [= they] may for ought I know I have no hand in it.

You say you are no Witch, may be you mean you never covenanted with the Devil. Did you never deal wth any familiar

No never

What bird was that the children spoke of

Th⟨en⟩ ⟨w⟩itnesses spoke

Wh⟨at⟩ b⟨ir⟩d was it.

I know no bird.

It may be: you have engaged you will n⟨o⟩t confess, but God knows

So he doth

Do you beleive you shall go unpunished

I have nothing to do wth withcraft

Why was you not willing your husband should come to ye former session here

But he came for all

Did not you take the saddle off

I did not know what it was for

Did you not know w^t it was for

I did not know ⟨t⟩hat it would be to any benefit

Some body said that she would not have them help to find out witches.

Did you not say you would open our eyes why do you not

I never thought of a Witch

Is it a laughing matter to see these afflicted persons

She denyed it

Severall prove it

Ye are all against me & I cannot help it

Do not you beleive there are Witches in the countrey

I do not know that there is any

Do not you know that Tituba confessed it

I did not hear her speak

I find you will own nothing without severall witnesses & yet you will deny for all

It was noted w^n she bit her lip severall of the afflicted were bitten

When she was urged upon it that she bit her lip saith she what harm is there in it.

Mr Noyes. I beleive it is apparent she practiseth Witchcraft in the congregation there is no need of images

What do you say to all these thing⟨s⟩ that are apparent

If you will all go hang me how can I help it.

Were you to serve the Devil ten years tell how many

She laught

The Children cryed there was a yellow bird with her

When Mr Hathorn askt her about it she laught

When her hands were at liberty the afflicted persons were pincht

Why do not you tell how the Devil comes in your shapes & hurts these, you said you would

How can I know how

Why did you say you would show us

She laught again

What book is that you would have these children write in

What book: where should I have a book I showed them none, nor have none nor brought none.

The afflicted cryed out there was a man whispering in her ears.

What book did you carry to Mary Walcott

I carryed none: if the Devil appears in my shape

Then Needham Said that Parker ^{some time agoe} thought this woman was a Witch

Who is your God

The God that made me

Who is that God

The God that made me

What is his name

Jehovah

Do you know any other name

God Almighty

Doth he tell you that you pray to that he is God Almighty

Who do I worship but y^e God y^t made

How many Gods are there

One

How many persons

Theree

Cannot you say so there is one God in three blessed persons

[Lost] [*SWP* = (then she was troubled)]

Do not you see these children & women are rational & sober as their neighbours When your hands are fastened

Immediately they were seized with fitts & the standers by said she was squeezing her fingers her hands being eased by them that held them on purpose for triall

Quickly after the Marshall said she hath bit her lip & immediately the afflicted were in an uproar

[Lost]⟨hy⟩ [= why] you hurt these, or who doth

She denyeth any hand in it

Why did you say if you were a Witch you should have no pardon.

Because I am a [   ] Woman

[Hand 2] Salem Village March the 21^t 1691/2

The Reuer^t m^r Sam^ll Parris being desired to take in wrighting the Examination of Martha Cory, hath returned it as afores^d

March 21, 1692

Vpon heareing the afores^d and seing what wee did then see, togather with ye charges of the persons then present Wee Committed Martha Cory the wife of Giles Cory of Salem ffarmes, vnto the Goale in Salem as ꝑ mittimus then Giuen out

John Hathorne

Jonathan. Corwin   } Assis^{ts}

[Reverse]
[Hand 3] Martha Kory Examaion

Notes: Martha Cory was a church member of Salem Village. Nicholas Noyes was a minister at Salem. A Daniel Needham was a trial juror in the 1693 case of Susannah Post. Whether the Needham in this document is the same person is not known. Crosly may be Henry Crosby, married to Deliverance Cory, daughter of Giles Cory and his first wife, Margaret. His name does not appear again. Parker may be John Parker, married to Mary, daughter of Giles Cory and his former wife, Mary Brite/Britz. Like Crosly, he seems not to have been involved in further cases. The bird referenced in the examination was implicitly a "familiar" of the Devil. The image of the bird as the Devil's familiar appears frequently. Parris's recording of this examination is his first in the judicial procedures of 1692. For the issue of clothing see No. 18. ◇ "improve": 'use, improve' (*OED* s.v. *improve* v^2). ◇ Hand 1 = Samuel Parris; Hand 2 = John Hathorne

Essex Institute Collection, no. 1, James Duncan Phillips Library, Peabody Essex Museum, Salem, MA.

17. Examination of Martha Cory, as Told by Deodat Lawson

On Monday the 21st of March, The Magistrates of Salem appointed to come to Examination of Goodw C. And about twelve of the Clock, they went into the Meeting-House, which was Thronged with Spectators: Mr. Noyes began with a very pertinent and pathetic⟨?⟩l Prayer; and Goodwife C. being called to answer to what was Alledged against her, she desired to go to Prayer, which was much wondred at, in the presence of so many hundred people: The Magistrates told her, they would not admit it; they came not there to hear her Pray, but to Examine her, in what was Alledged against her. The Worshipful Mr. Hathorne, asked her, Why she Afflicted those Children! she said, she did not Afflict them. He asked her, who did then? she said, I do not know; How should I know? The Number of the Afflicted Persons were about that time Ten, viz. Four Married Women, Mrs Pope, Mrs. Putman, Goodw. Bibber, and an Ancient Woman, named Goodall, three Maids, Mary Walcut, Mercy Lewes, at Thomas Putman's, and a Maid at Dr. Griggs's, there were three Girls from 9 to 12 Years of Age, each of them, or thereabouts, viz. Elizabeth Parris, Abigail Williams and Ann Putman; these were most of them at G. C's Examination, and did vehemently accuse her in the Assembly of afflicting them, by Biting, Pinching, Strangling, &c. And that they did in their Fit, see her Likeness coming to them, and bringing a Book to them, she said, she had no Book; they affirmed, she had a Yellow-Bird, that used to suck betwixt her Fingers, and being asked about it, if she had any Familiar Spirit, that attended her, she said, She had no Familiarity with any such thing- She was a Gospel Woman: which Title she called her self by; and the Afflicted Persons told her, ah! She was, A Gospel Witch. Ann Putman did there affirm, that one day when Lieutenant Fuller was at Prayer at her Fathers House, she saw the shape of Goodw. C. and she thought Goodw. N. Praying at the same time to the Devil, she was not sure it was Goodw. N. she thought it was; but very sure she saw the Shape of G. C. The said C. said, they were poor,

distracted Children, and no heed to be given to what they said. Mr. Hathorne and Mr.   March 21, 1692
Noyes replyed, it was the judgment of all that were present, they were Bewitched, and only
she the Accused Person said, they were Distracted. It was observed several times, that if she
did but bite her Under lip in time of Examination the persons afflicted were bitten on their
armes and wrists and produced the Marks before the Magistrates, Ministers and others. And
being watched for that, if she did but Pinch her Fingers, or Graspe one Hand, hard in
another, they were Pinched and produced the Marks before the Magistrates, and Spectators.
After that, it was observed, that if she did but lean her Breast, against the Seat, in the
Meeting House, (being the Barr at which she stood,) they were afflicted. Particularly Mrs.
Pope complained of grievous torment in her Bowels as if they were torn out. She vehemently
accused said C. as the instrument, and first threw her Muff at her; but that flying not home,
she got off her Shoe, and hit Goodwife C. on the head with it. After these postures were
watched, if said C. did but stir her feet, they were afflicted in their Feet, and stamped
fearfully. The afflicted persons asked her why she did not go to the company of Witches
which were before the Meeting house mustering? Did she not hear the Drum beat? They
accused her of having Familiarity with the Devil, in the time of Examination, in the shape of
a Black man whispering in her ear; they affirmed, that her Yellow-Bird, sucked betwixt her
Fingers in the Assembly; and order being given to see if there were any sign, the Girl that
saw it, said, it was too late now; she had removed a Pin, and put it on her head; which was
found there sticking upright.

They told her, she had Covenanted with the *Devil* for ten years, six of them were gone,
and four more to come. She was required by the Magistrates to answer that Question in the
Catechism, *How many persons be there in the God-Head?* she answered it but oddly, yet was
there no great thing to be gathered from it; she denied all that was charged upon her, and
said, *They could not prove a Witch*; she was that Afternoon Committed to *Salem*-Prison; and
after she was in Custody, she did not so appear to them, and afflict them as before.

Notes: Lawson had previously been a minister at Salem Village. "Goodw C." is Martha Cory. "Goodw. N" is Rebecca
Nurse. The pin episode described was a common one, where accusers claimed that a spectre had put the pin in them,
when they or their fellow "afflicted" had done it. The one narrated here is the first recorded example of this practice.

*Deodat Lawson. A Brief and True Narrative of Some Remarkable Passages Relating to Sundry Persons Afflicted by Witchcraft,
at Salem Village Which happened from the Nineteenth of March to the Fifth of April 1692 (Boston: Benjamin Harris, 1692),
pp. 4–5.*

18. Deposition of Ezekiel Cheever & Edward Putnam v. Martha Cory†

See also: Aug. 4, 1692 & Sept. 8, 1692.

[Hand 1] The deposition of Edward Putnum aged about 36 years and Ezekiel Cheever aged
about ["u" written over "t"] 37 years testifieth and sayeth that wee being often complained
unto. by An Putnum that goode Corie did often appear to her and tort⟨e⟩r her by pinching
and other wayes thought it our duty to goe to her and see what shee would say to this
complaint shee being in church covenant with us.
and accordingly upon the 12ᵗʰ day of march about ten of the clock we appiointed to goe
about the midle afternoon, and wee desired An Putnum to take good notice of what cloathes
goode Corie came in that so we might see whither shee was not mistaken in the person. and
accordingly wee went to the house of Thomas Putnam before we went to good [= goody]

Corie to see what An could say about her cloathes. and shee told us that presently after we had ~~spoken~~ told her that we would goe and talke with goode Corie ⟨?⟩shee came and blinded her but told her that her name was Corie and that shee should see her no more before it was night because shee should not tell us what cloathes shee had on and then shee would come again and pay her off.

then wee went both of us away from the house of Thomas Putnum. to the house of Giles Corie where we found ~~go~~ the abovesaid Corie all alone in her house. and as soone as we came in. in a smiling ^{manner} shee sayeth I know what you are come for you are come to talke with me about being a witch but I am none I cannot helpe peoples talking of me Edward Putnum answered her that it was the afflicted person that did complain of her that was the occasion of our coming to her. shee presently replied but does shee tell you what cloathes I have on we made her no answer ⟨?⟩ to this at her first asking where upon shee asked us again [2nd "a" written over "i"] with very great eagernes but does shee tell you what cloathes I have on.

at which questions with that eagernes of mind. with ["i" written over "e"] which shee did ~~askes~~ made us to thinke of what An Putnum had told us before we went to her. ~~to which~~ and wee told her no shee did not for shee told us that you came and blinded her and told her that shee should see you no more before it was night that so shee might not tell us what cloathes you had on. ⟨?⟩ shee made but litle answer to this but seemed to smile at it as if shee had showed us a pretty trick

wee had a ~~greatly~~ ^{deal} of talke with her about the complaint that was of her and ^{how} greatly the name of God and religion and thee church was dihonured by this meanes but shee seemed to be no way conserned for any thing about it but only to stop the mouthes of people that they might not say thus of her shee told us that shee did not thinke that there were any witches we told her wee were fully satisfied about ["ou" written over "ut"] the first three that they ^{were} such persons as they were accused for. shee said if they were we could not blame the devill for making witches of them for they were idle sloathfull persons and minded nothing that was good. but we had no reason to thinke so of her for shee had made a profession of christ and rejoyced to go and hear the word of god and the li⟨ke⟩ but ^{we} told her it was not her making an⟨?⟩ outward profession that would clear her from being a witch for it had often been so in the wourld that witches had crept into the churches. much more discourse we had with her but shee made her profession a cloake to cover all shee ~~fuder~~ furder told us that the devill was come down amongst us in great rage. and that God had forsaken the earth. and after much discourse with her being to much here to be related we returned to the house of the above said Thomas Putnum and we found that shee had done as shee said shee ~~wol~~ would for shee c⟨a⟩me not to hurt thee above said putnum as ~~shee~~ ^{An Putnum} told us all this time but after we were gone we understand that shee came again as shee did use to doe before ~~we~~ {greatly afflicting of her}

we doe furder testifie that upon her examination shee according to what was said of her that shee would open thee eyes of the magistrates and ministers. so shee did for shee made a most clear discovery witchcraft for by biting her lip it was observed that the ~~children~~ {afflicted persons} were bit when that was discovered then we observed that shee would ~~pinch~~ pinch them by niping her fingers togeather and when that was discovered and her hands held then shee afflict them by working with her feet and when that was discovered then shee pressed upon the seat with {with} her breast and mistres Pope was greatly afflicted by great pressure upon her stomack

[Hand 2] Jurat in Curia Sepr 8. 92

[Reverse] [Hand 3] M^ε Ezekell Cheevers: affirmd: to ye Jury of Inquest: that he saw: Martha wife to Giles Cory examined before ye Majestrates: at which time ⟨h⟩e observed that ye s^d Cory: some times did: bite her lip: and when she bit her lip: mercy Lewis and Eliza^th Hubbard and others of ye afflicted persons: were bitten: also when s^d Cory: pinched her fingers together: then mercy lewis & Elizabeth Hubbard and others were pinched: and ~~when~~ acording to: ye motions of s^d martha Coryes body; so was ye afflicted persons: afflicted: this he affirmd to be true acording to ye best of his observation: Mr Edward Putnam: {affirmd} ye same: to ye Jury of inquest that: Mr Cheevers doth. Mr Thomas Putnam affirmed ye same: all: upon oathe all of them

March 21, 1692

[Hand 4?] Edwd Putnam & Eliza. Cheever Depositi⟨o⟩n
[Hand 2] Ed Putman Elz Cheeuer

Notes: This document was probably next used on August 4 when a grand jury heard Cory's case. Her trial was September 8, and based on Parris's records of the Salem Village Church, it appears as if her condemnation to the gallows occurred on September 10. ◊ Used at trial. ◊ Hand 1 = Ezekiel Cheever; Hand 2 = Stephen Sewall; Hand 3 = Simon Willard

Essex County Court Archives, vol. 1, no. 39, Massachusetts Supreme Judicial Court, Judicial Archives, on deposit James Duncan Phillips Library, Peabody Essex Museum, Salem, MA.

19. Deposition of Elizabeth Hubbard v. Martha Cory†

See also: Aug. 4, 1692 & Sept. 8, 1692.

[Hand 1] The Deposistion of Elizabeth Hubburd agged about 17 years who testifieth and saith that about the 15th march ∧{1691/92} I saw the Apperishtion of martha Cory who did Immediatly hurt me and urged me to writ in hir book and so she continewed hurting of me by times tell the 21 march being the day of hir Examination: and then in the time of hir Examination she did torment me most dreadfully by biting pinching and almost choaking me the marks of which I shewed to seuerall and at the same time also I saw the Apperishtion of Martha Cory greviously afflect mircy lewes: and also seuerall times sence the Apperishtion of Martha Cory has most greviously afflected me and urged me vehemently to writ in hir book also on the day of hir Examination I saw martha Cory or hir Apperanc most greviously tormet mary walcott mercy lewes Abigail william and ann putnam and I beleue in my heart that martha Cory is a dreadfull wicth and that she hath uery often affleted and tormented me and the affermentioned parsons by acts of wicthcraft

[Hand 2] Jurat in Curia

[Hand 3] Eliz: Hubbard: declared ye above. written Evidence: to be ye truth: before ye Jury of inquest upon oath: Augst 4: 1692

[Reverse] [Hand 2] Eliz Hubbert against Martha Cory

Notes: The ink change with the phrase beginning with "also on the day of her examination," is a later addition by Thomas Putnam, in preparation for the grand jury or the trial. Of particular significance is the addition of "and I beleue in my heart that martha Cory is a dreadfull wicth. . . ." This is the first document in this edition showing Putnam's adding this phrase or a variation of it. However, exactly when he made the addition remains conjectural. ◊ Used at trial. ◊ Hand 1 = Thomas Putnam; Hand 2 = Stephen Sewall; Hand 3 = Simon Willard

Witchcraft Papers, no. 19, Massachusetts Historical Society. Boston, MA.

20. Deposition of Samuel Parris, Nathaniel Ingersoll, & Thomas Putnam v. Martha Cory†

[Hand 1] The Deposition of Sam: Parris aged about .39. years, & Nathanael Ingersol aged about fifty & eight yeares & Thomas Putman aged about fourty yeares all of Salem testifyeth & saith that severall of the bewitched persons were much afflicted at the Examination of Martha Kory, wife to Giles Kory of Salem, ~~& particu~~ before the honoured Magistrates .21. March. 1691/2 & particularly that ~~when~~ before her hands were held severall of the afflicted were pincht, & when said Martha bit her lip severall of them were bitten: & that some of the afflicted said there was a black man whispering in her ear, namely Mary Walcot and Abigail Williams both of which also were bit & pincht by her [Hand 2] as they said

[Reverse] [Hand 1] The Depo͞on of Sam: Parris ⟨&c⟩ ag^st Martha Kory

Notes: The inclusion of Thomas Putnam as a deponent was likely a later insertion by Parris in a blank space he had left in the document. ◊ Hand 1 = Samuel Parris; Hand 2 = Thomas Putnam

Essex County Court Archives, vol. 1, no. 42, Massachusetts Supreme Judicial Court, Judicial Archives, on deposit James Duncan Phillips Library, Peabody Essex Museum, Salem, MA.

21. Deposition of Edward Putnam v. Martha Cory†

See also: Sept. 8, 1692.

[Hand 1] The diposistion. of Edward Putnam aged about 38 ycarcs ho tcstifieths and saith one the. 14 day of march 1692 martha Cory. the wife of giles Cory. Came to the. house of Thomas Putnam: she being desired to Come and see his dafter ann Putnam: ho had Charged martha Cory to her face that she had hurt her by witchcraft but no sonner did martha Cory Come in to the hous of thomas Putnam but ~~the~~ ann. putnam fell in to greuious. feets. of Choking blinding feat and hands twisted in a most greuious maner and told martha Cory to her face that she ded it

and ~~e~~ emediately hur tonge was dran out of her: mouth and her teeth fasned apon it in a most greuious maner after ann putnam had ~~l⟨i⟩b~~ libberty. to spake ⟨a⟩ she said to martha Cory. ther is a yellow burd asucking. betwen your fore finger and midel finger I see it said ann putnam. I will Come and see it said she: so you may said martha Cory: but before an Came to her: I saw martha Cory put one of her fingers in the place whear ann had said she saw the burd and semed to giue a hard rub ann putnam Came. and said she see nothing. but emediately she was blinded after this ann putnam tryed to go to her and when she Came allmost to her still fell down blinded and Cold not Come at her any more: ann putnam allso told her she put her hands apon the face of Joseph poops ["s" written over "e"] wife one the Sabath day at meeting and shuing her how she did it emediately. her hands ware. fasned to her eyes [2nd "e" written over "s"] that they Cold not be pulled from them except they shuld haue ben broaken. off

after this. ann putnam said hear is a speet at the fier with a man apon it and goodey Cory you be aturnning. of it then marcy lues. toock a stick and struck at it and then it went away. but emediately it apered again and marcy lues ofred to strike it again but ann: putnam said do not if you loue your self ~~b~~ but presently. marcy lues. Cryed out with a greuious pane in her arme

as if one had struck her with ~~a~~ a stick apon her arme and ann putnam told goodey Cory she
see her strike marcy lues with a Iron rood apon her arme: and marcy lues and ann putnam
gru so bad with panes we desired goodey Cory to be gon.
[Reverse] and marcy. lues. said she saw shadows like women but Cold not disarn ho they.
ware but presently Cryed out in a uery. loud maner I onte [= won't] I onte and being asked
what they. wold haue her do she said they wold haue her neck twicted her teeth and mouth
~~shet~~ shut. and gru to shuch feets as wold put two or three men to it to hold her and was this
~~m~~ euening drawn toward the fier by unseen hands as she sat in a Chare and two men hold of
it yet she and Chare moueed toward the fier tho they labored to the Contrary her feat going.
formost. and I seeing. it steped to her feat and lifted with my stringht together with the other
two and all littel enuf to preuent her from going. in to the fier with her feat formost and this
destres [= distress] held tell about ~~au~~leuen [= eleven] of the Cloack in the night
I haue allso seen ~~se~~ maney bites before and sence apon ouer aflicted parsons. that haue told
me martha Cory did it the prisner now at the bar

Edward Putnam
[Hand 2] Jurat in Curia
S Sewall Cl[Lost] [= Cler]

[Hand 3] Edward Putman

Notes: The last sentence of the document is set off by marks, perhaps suggesting that it was written later. The ink,
however, is the same. ◊ Used at trial. ◊ Hand 1 = Edward Putnam; Hand 2 = Stephen Sewall

Witchcraft Papers, no. 20, Massachusetts Historical Society. Boston, MA.

Wednesday, March 23, 1692

22. Warrant for the Apprehension of Dorothy Good, and Officer's Return

See also: March 24, 1692.

[Hand 1] To The Marshall of Essex or his Dep^t
You are in theire Majest^ts names hereby requi[Lost] [= required] to bring before vs Dorcas
Good the Daufter [Lost] [= of?] Wm Good of Salem Village ^{to morrow Morneing} vpon
Suspition of acts of Witchcraft by her Committed according to Complaints made against her
by Edwd Putnam & Jona^t Putnam of Salem Village. and hereof faile not Dated Salem.
March 23^d 1691/2

John. Hathorne
𝆎 vs   } Assis[Lost] [= assistants]
Jonathan. Corwin

[Hand 2] March 23^d:1691/2
I doe apoint m^r Sam^ll Brabrook to be my lawffull Deputy to serve this Sumons and to make
A true Returne 𝆎 George Herrick Marshall of Essex

March 23, 1692

[Reverse] [Hand 1] March 24⟨th⟩ 1691/2 I haue taken yᵉ body of Dorcas Good and [Lost]ght [= brought] her to yᵉ house of leuᵗ Nath: Ingersol and is in Costody [Lost] mee

Sammuall brabrook [Hand 1] Marshalls Deputy

Notes: Dorothy Good is erroneously called "Dorcas" in this warrant, a name that has become standard usage in histories of the Salem witch trials. Hathorne made the original error but recorded it accurately in subsequent documents. For Hathorne's corrections, see No. 216 and No. 217. Dorothy was four or five years old and according to a jail bill of John Arnold was in prison from April 12 to December 10. On a number of occasions the first name of an accused female was not known by the accuser or the authorities. ◊ Hand 1 = John Hathorne; Hand 2 = George Herrick

Essex County Court Archives, vol. 1, no. 61, Massachusetts Supreme Judicial Court, Judicial Archives, on deposit James Duncan Phillips Library, Peabody Essex Museum, Salem, MA.

23. **Warrant for the Apprehension of Rebecca Nurse, and Officer's Return**
See also: March 24, 1692.

[Hand 1] To the Marshall of Essex or his deputie

There Being Complaint this day made (before V[Lost] [= us] by Edward Putnam and Jonathan Putnam Yeom[Lost] [= Yeomen] both of Salem Village, Against Rebeca Nurce the wife of franᶜˢ Nurce of Salem Village for vehement Suspition, of haueing Committed Sund⟨ry⟩ acts of Witchcraft and thereby haueing donne Muc⟨h⟩ hurt and Injury to the Bodys of Anā Puttnam the wife of Thomas Putnam of Salem Village Anna Puttnam yᵉ daufter of Said Thomas Putnam {&} Abigail Williams ~~And~~ &c

You are therefore in theire Majesties nam[Lost] [= names] hereby required to apprehend and bring before [Lost] [= us] Rebeca Nurce the wife of ffranᶜˢ Nurce of Sal[Lost] [= Salem] Village, to Morrow aboute Eight of yᵉ Clock in the forenoon at the house of Lᵗ Nathaniell Inge[Lost] [= Ingersoll] in Salem Village, in order to her Examination Relateing to the abouesᵈ premises and hereof you are not to faile Salem March the 23ᵈ 1691/2.

John. Hathorne ⎱
℀ vs   ⎰ Assisᵗˢ
Jonathan. Corwin ⎰

[Hand 2] March 24ᵗʰ ["4ᵗʰ" written over "3ʳᵈ"]. 1691/2 I haue apprehended yᵉ body of Rebeca Nurse and brought her to yᵉ house of Leuᵗ Nath: Ingers[Lost] [= Ingersoll] where shee is in Costody ℀ᵋ George Herrick Marshall of Essex

[Reverse] [Hand 1] in yᵉ Meeting house
Mary Walkott
Marcy Lewis
Eliz. Hubert
all these accused goody Nurce then to her face yᵗ she then hurt theme &c and thay saw besides yᵉ other on Contra Side

Notes: Rebecca Nurse became the second church member to be arrested. Unlike Martha Cory, a covenanted member of the church in Salem Village, Rebecca Nurse was a covenanted member of the church in Salem, even though she attended the closer church in Salem Village. "Contra Side" simply references those accusers on the front of the document not listed on the reverse. ◊ Hand 1 = John Hathorne; Hand 2 = George Herrick

Essex County Court Archives, vol. 1, no. 70, Massachusetts Supreme Judicial Court, Judicial Archives, on deposit James Duncan Phillips Library, Peabody Essex Museum, Salem, MA.   March 24, 1692

Thursday, March 24, 1692

Officer's Return: Warrant for the Apprehension of Dorothy Good, and Officer's Return
2nd of 2 dates. See No. 22 on March 23, 1692

Officer's Return: Warrant for the Apprehension of Rebecca Nurse
2nd of 2 dates. See No. 23 on March 23, 1692

24. Statement of Giles Cory Regarding Martha Cory

[Hand 1] The Evidence of Giles Choree testifieth & Saith y^tt Last satturday in the Evening. Sitting by the fire my wife asked me to go to bed. I told I would go to praye. & w^n I went to prayer I could nott utter my desires wth any sense, not open my mouth to speake
{2} My wife did perceive itt & came towards me. & said she was coming to me. After this in a litle space I did ac{c}ording to my measure. attend the duty
Sometime last weake I fetcht an ox well out of the woods. about noone, & he laiing down in the yard I went to raise him to yoake him butt he could nott rise butt dragd his hinder parts as if he had ben hiptshott. butt after did ris{e}
I had a Catt somtimes last weeke strangly taken on the Suddain. & did make me think she would have died presently. ~~butt~~ my wife bid me knock her in the head. butt I did not. & since she is well.
Another time going to duties I was interrupted for a space. butt affterward I was helpt according to my poore measure
My wife hath ben wont to Sitt up after I went to bed, & I have perceivd her to kneel down on the harth. as if she were at prayr, but heard nothing
~~At the Examenatio of Sarah~~ Good & others my wife was willing
March: 24^tt 1691/2

[Reverse] [Hand 2] Joh⟨n⟩

Notes: The meaning of the last sentence, referencing Sarah Good, is unclear, and it may be that the recorder intended to cross out the whole line. ◊ "hiptshott": 'having the hip out of joint' (*OED* s.v. *hipshot*).

Essex County Court Archives, vol. 1, no. 43, Massachusetts Supreme Judicial Court, Judicial Archives, on deposit James Duncan Phillips Library, Peabody Essex Museum, Salem, MA.

25. Examination of Dorothy Good, as Told by Deodat Lawson

The Magistrates and Ministers also did informe me, that they apprehended a child of *Sarah G.* and Examined it, being between 4 and 5 years of Age And as to matter of Fact, they did Unanimously affirm, that when this Child, did but cast its eye upon the afflicted persons, they were tormented, and they held her *Head*, and yet so many as her *eye* could fix upon were afflicted. Which they did several times make careful observation of: the afflicted complained, they had often been *Bitten* by this child, and produced the marks of *a small set of teeth*, accordingly, this was also committed to *Salem* Prison; the child looked *hail, and well* as other Children. I saw it at Lievt. *Ingersols* After the commitment of Goodw. *N. Tho: Putmans* wife was much better, and had no violent fits at all from that 24*th* of March to the 5*th* of *April*. Some others also said they had not seen her so frequently appear to them, to hurt them.

Notes: Goodw. N. is Rebecca Nurse. The examined child is Dorothy Good.

Deodat Lawson. A Brief and True Narrative of Some Remarkable Passages Relating to Sundry Persons Afflicted by Witchcraft, at Salem Village Which happened from the Nineteenth of March to the Fifth of April 1692 (Boston: Benjamin Harris, 1692), p. 9.

26. Deposition of Ann Putnam Jr. v. Dorothy Good†

[Hand 1] The Deposistion of Ann putnam who testifieth and saith that on the 3ᵗʰ march 1691/92 I saw the Apperishtion of Dorythy good: Sarah goods daughter who did Immediatly almost choak ^{me} and tortored me most greviously: and so she hath seuerall times sence tortored me by biting and pinching and almost choaking me t⟨e⟩mp⟨t⟩{ing} me also to writ in hir book and also on the day of hir Examination. being the 24 march 1691/92 the Apperishtion of Dorithy good did most greviously tortor me dureing the time of hir Examination and seuer⟨a⟩ll times sence

[Reverse] [Hand 2] Ann. puttnam a[Lost][= against] Dor⟨ot⟩hy Good

Notes: Beginning with "and also on the day . . ." the ink changes, reflecting a later addition by Thomas Putnam. ◊ Hand 1 = Thomas Putnam; Hand 2 = Jonathan Corwin

Essex County Court Archives, vol. 1, no. 63, Massachusetts Supreme Judicial Court, Judicial Archives, on deposit James Duncan Phillips Library, Peabody Essex Museum, Salem, MA.

27. Deposition of Mary Walcott v. Dorothy Good†

[Hand 1] The deposistion of mary walcott agged [2nd "g" written over "e"] about 17 years who testifieth that about the 21: march 1691/92 I saw the Apperishtion of Dorothy good Sarah goods daughter com to me and bit me and pinch me and so she continewed afflecting me by times tell 24 march being the day of hir Examination and then she did torment and afflect me most greviously dureing the time of hir Examination and also seuer⟨a⟩l times sence the ⟨D⟩ Apperishtion of Dorothy good has afflected me by biting pinching and almost choaking me urging me to writ in hir book

[Reverse] [Hand 2] Mary Walcott agˢᵗ Dorothy. Good
[Hand 1] Dorothy good

Notes: The similar language used by Thomas Putnam in writing this suggests an identical dating to No. 26, the deposition of Ann Putnam Jr. against Dorothy Good. ◊ Hand 1 = Thomas Putnam; Hand 2 = Jonathan Corwin

Essex County Court Archives, vol. 1, no. 64, Massachusetts Supreme Judicial Court, Judicial Archives, on deposit James Duncan Phillips Library, Peabody Essex Museum, Salem, MA.

28. Examination of Rebecca Nurse

March 24, 1692

[Hand 1] The Examination
of Rebekah Nurse at Salem Village
24. Mar. 1691/2

Mʳ Hathorn. What do you say (speaking to one afflicted) have you seen this Woman hurt you?

Yes, she beat me this morning

Abigail. Have you been hurt by this woman?

Yes

Ann Putman in a grievous fit cryed out that she hurt her.

Goody Nurse, here are two An: Putman the child & Abigail Williams complains of your hurting them What do you say to it

N. I can say before my Eternal father I am innocent, & God will clear my innocency

Here is never a one in the Assembly but desiers it, but if you be guilty Pray God discover you.

Then Hen: Kenny rose up to speak

Goodm: Kenny what do you say

Then he entered his complaint & farther said that since this Nurse came into the house we was seiz'd ^{twise} with an amaz'd condition

Here are not only these but, here is yᵉ wife of Mʳ Tho: Putman who accuseth you by credible information & that both of tempting her to iniquity, & of greatly hurting her.

N. I ha̶ am innocent & clear & have not been able to get out of doors these 8. or.9. dayes.

Mʳ Putman, give in what you have to say

Then Mʳ Edward Putman gave in his relate

Is this true Goody Nurse

I never afflicted no child never in my life

You see these accuse you, is it true

No.

Are you an innocent person relating to this Witchcraft.

Here Tho. Putmans wife cryed out. Did you not bring the Black man with you, did you not bid me tempt God & dye How oft have you eat & drunk yʳ own dam̄aon.

What do you say to them

Oh Lord help me, & spread out her hands, & the afflicted were greivously vexed

Do you not see what a Solemn condition these are in? when your hands are loose the pesons [= persons] are afflicted

   Then Mary Walcot (who often heretofore said she had seen her, but never could say or did say that she either bit or pincht her or hurt her) & also Eliz: Hubbard under the like circumstances both openly accused her of hurting them

Here are these 2. grown persons now accuse you, wᵗ say you? Do not you see these afflicted persons, & hear them accuse you.

The Lord knows I have not hurt them: I am an innocent person.

It is very awfull to all to see these agonies & you an old Professor thus charged with contracting with the Devil by the effects of it & yet to see you stand with dry eyes when these are so many what

You do not know my heart

You would do well if you are guilty to confess & give Glory to God

I am as clear as the child unborn

What uncertainty there may be in apparitions I know not, yet this with me strikes hard upon you that you are at this very present charged with familiar spirits: this is your bodily person they speak to: they say now they see these familiar spirits com⟨e⟩ to your bodily person, now what do you say to that

I have none Sir.

If you have confest & give glory to God. I pray God clear you if you be innocent, & if you are guilty discover you And therefore give me an upright answer: have you any familiarity with these spirits?

No, I have none but with God alone.

How came you sick for there is an odd discourse of that in the mouths of many

I am sick at my stomach

Have you no wounds

I have none but old age

You do know whither you are guilty, & have familiarity with the Devil, & now when you are here present to see such a thing as these testify a black man Whispering in your ear, & birds about you what do you say to it

It is all false I am clear

Possibly you may apprehend you are no witch, but have you not been led aside by temptations that way

I have not

What a sad thing is it that a Church member here & now an [= and] othe⟨rs⟩ of Salem, should be thus accused and charged

⟨Mrs.⟩ Pope fell into a greivous fit, & cryed out a sad thing sure enough: And then many more fell into lamentable fits.

Tell us have not you had visible appearances more than what is common in nature?

I have none nor never had in my life

Do you think these suffer voluntary or involuntary

I cannot tell

That is strange every one can judge

I must be silent

They accuse you of hurting them, & if you think it is [Lost] [*SWP* = unwillingly] but by designe ⟨you⟩ must look upon them as murderer⟨s⟩

I cannot tell what to think of it

Afterwards when she was somwhat insisted on she said I do not think so: She did not understand aright what was said

Well then give an answer now, do you think these suffer against their wills or not

I do not think these suffer against their wills

Why did you never visit these afflicted persons

Because I was afraid I should have fitts too

Note Upon the motion of her ^{body} ~~had~~ fitts followed upon the complainants abundantly & very frequently

Is it not an unaccountable case that when ~~thes~~ you are examined these persons are afflicted?

I have got no body to look to but God

Again upon stirring her hands the afflicted persons were seized with violent fits of torture
Do you beleive these afflicted persons are bewitcht

I do think they are

When this Witchcraft came upon the stage there was no suspicion of Tituba (Mr Parris's Indian woman) She profest much love to that Child Betty Parris, but it was her apparition did the mischief, & why should not you also be guilty, for your apparition doth hurt also.

Would you have me bely [= belie] ^{my} ~~your~~ self

She held her Neck on one side, & accordingly so were the afflicted taken.

Then Authority requiring it Sam: Parris read what he had in characters taken from Mr Tho Putmans wife in her fitts

What do you think of this.

[Reverse] This is a true account of the su͞me of her Examination but by reason of great noyses by the afflicted & many speakers many things are pr⟨ae⟩termitted

Memorandum

Nurse held her neck on one sid & Eliz: Hubbard (one of the sufferers) had her neck set in that posture Whereupon another Patient Abigail Williams cryed out set up Goody Nurses head the maids neck will be broke & when some Set up Nurses head Aaron wey observed y^t Betty Hubbards was immediately righted

[Hand 2] Salem Village March 24th 1691/2

The Reuer^t Mr Samuell Parris being desired to take in wrighting ye Examination of Rebekah Nurse hath Returned itt as aforesaid.

Vpon heareing the afors^d, and seing what wee then did see together with ye Charges of the persons then present wee Committed Rebekah Nurse ye wife of ffran^cs Nurce of Salem Village vnto theire Majes^ts Goale in Salem as Gaole in Salem as ⅌ a Mittimus then Giuen out, ~~and~~ in order to farther Examination

> John Hathorne
>
> Jonathan. Corwin } Assis^s

[Hand 3] Rebecka Nurses Examination

Notes: Henry Kenney had complained against Martha Cory on March 19, but disappears from the record after this examination of Rebecca Nurse. The reference to Tituba's spectral assault on Betty Parris offers the first indication that the claims against her were for spectral affliction. ◊ "Professor": 'one who makes open profession of religion; a professing Christian' (*OED* s.v. *professor* 2b). "praetermitted": 'left out; omitted' (*OED* s.v. *pretermit*, v.). "relate": 'evidence, story' (not in the *OED*). "Patient": 'sufferer' (*OED* s.v. *patient* B n.2.). ◊ Hand 1 = Samuel Parris; Hand 2 = John Hathorne; Hand 3 = Thomas Newton

Essex County Court Archives, vol. 1, no. 72, Massachusetts Supreme Judicial Court, Judicial Archives, on deposit James Duncan Phillips Library, Peabody Essex Museum, Salem, MA.

29. Examination of Rebecca Nurse, as Told by Deodat Lawson

On Thursday the Twenty fourth of march, (being in course the Lecture Day, at the Village,) Goodwife *N.* was brought before the Magistrates Mr *Hathorne* and Mr *Corwin*, about Ten of Clock, in the Fore Noon, to be Examined in the Meeting House; the Reverend Mr. *Hale*, begun with Prayer, and the Warrant being read, she was required to give answer, *Why she aflicted those persons?* she pleaded her owne innocency with earnestness. *Thomas Putman's* Wife, *Abigail Williams* and *Thomas Putmans* daughter accused her that she appeared to them, and afflicted them in their fitts: but some of the other said, that they had seen her, but knew not that ever she had hurt them; amongst which was *Mary Walcut*, who was presently after she had so declared bitten, and cryed out of her in the meeting-house; producing the *Marks of teeth* on her wrist. It was so disposed, that I had not leisure to attend the whole time of Examination, but both Magistrates and Ministers, told me, that the things alledged by the afflicted, and defences made by her, were much after the same manner, as the former was. And her motions did produce like effects as to *Biteing, Pinching, Bruising Tormenting*, at their *Breasts*, by her *Leaning*, and when, bended Back, were as if their Backs was broken. The afflicted persons said, the *Black Man*, whispered to her in the Assembly, and therefore she could not hear what the Magistrates said unto her. They said also that she did then ride by the *Mee*ting-house, behind the *Black Man. Thomas Putman's* wife, had a grievous Fit, in the time of Examination, to the very great Impairing of her strength, and wasting of her spirits, insomuch as she could hardly, move hand, or foot, when she was carryed out. Others also were there grievously afflicted, so that there was once such an hideous scrietch and noise, (which I heard as I walked, at a little distance from the Meeting house,) as did amaze me, and some that were within, told me the whole assembly was struck with consternation, and they were afraid, that those that sate next to them, were under the influence of *Witchcraft*. This woman also was that day committed to *Salem* Prison.

Deodat Lawson. A Brief and True Narrative of Some Remarkable Passages Relating to Sundry Persons Afflicted by Witchcraft, at Salem Village Which happened from the Nineteenth of March to the Fifth of April 1692 (Boston: Benjamin Harris, 1692), pp. 6–7.

30. Deposition of Ann Putnam Sr. v. Martha Cory & Rebecca Nurse, and Testimony of Ann Putnam Jr. v. Rebecca Nurse, Martha Cory, & Sarah Cloyce†

See also: May 31, 1692 & June 3, 1692.

[Hand 1] The Deposistion of Ann putnam the wife of Thomas putnam agged about 30 years who testifieth and saith that on the: 18th march 1691/92 I being wearied out in helping to tend my poor afflected child and Maid: about the middle of the affternoon I layd me down on the bed to take a little Rest: and Immediatly I was allmost prest and choaked to death: that had it not been for the mircy of a gratious God and the help of those that ware with me: I could not haue liued many moments: and presently I saw the Apperishtion of Martha Cory who did tortor me so as I cannot Express Redy to tare me all to peaces and y^n departed from ~~hir~~ me a litle while: but before I could recouer strenth or well take breath the Apperishtion of Martha Cory fell upon me agai[Lost] [= again] with dreadfull tortors and hellish temtations to goe along with hir and she also brought to me a litle Red book in hir hand and a black pen urging me vehemently to writ in hir book: and seuerall times that day she did most greviously tortor me allmost redy to kill me and on the 19th march: Martha Cory againe appeared to me and also Rebekah ^{nurs} the wife of ffrances nurs senr and they both did tortor: me a grate many times this day with such tortors as no toungu can Express because I would not yeald to their Hellish temtations that had I not been upheild by an Allmighty Arme I could not haue liued while night ye 20th march being Sabboth day I had a grat deal of Respitt. between my fitts: 21th march being the day of the Examinati of martha Cory: I had not many fitts tho I was ["was" written over "am"] very weak my strenth being as I thought almost gon: but on the: 22 march 1691/92 the Apperishtion of Rebekah nurs did againe sett upon in a most dreadfull maner very early in the morning as soon as it was well light and now she appeared to me only in hir shift and night cap and brougⱨ⟨h⟩[Lost] [= brought] a litle Red book in hir hand vrging me vehemently to writ in hir book and because I would not yeald to hir hellish temtations she threatened to tare my soule out of my body: blasphemously denying the blessed God and the power of the Lord Jesus Christ to saue my soule and denying seuerall places of scripture which ^{I} tould hir of: to Repell hir hellish temtations and for near Two hours together at this time the the Apperishtion of Rebekah nurs did tempt and tortor me before she left me as if Indeed she would haue kiled me: and allso the grates part of this day without very litle respitt: 23 march: I am againe afflete⟨d⟩ by the Apperishtions of Rebekah nurs: and martha cory: but cheafly by Rebekah nurs: 24th march being the day of the Examination of Rebekah nurs: I was seuerall times afflected in the morning by the Apperishtion of Rebekah nurs: but most dreadfully tortored by hir in the time of hir Examination: in so much that The Honoured Majestraits gaue my Husband leaue to cary me out of the meeting house: and as soon as I was caryed out of the meeting house dores it pleased Allmighty God. for his free grace and mircy sake to deliuer {me} out of the paws of thos Roaring lions: and jaws of those tareing bears that euer sence that time they haue not had power so to afflect me

[Reverse] [Hand 2] untill this .31. May. 1692 at the same moment that I was hearing my Evidence read by the honoured Magistrates to take my Oath I was again re-assaulted & tortured by my before mentioned Tormentor Rebekah Nurse

[Hand 3] Sworne Salem Village May the 31t
1692 Before vs John Hathorne
⎫
⎬ Assists
Jonathan. Corwin   ⎭

[Hand 4] ann putnom senear appearid before us the Juerris of Inquest: and oned this har euidens this 3. dy of June: 1692

[Hand 2] The testimony of Ann Putman junᵉ witnesseth & saith that being in the Room when her mother was afflicted she saw Martha Kory Sarah Cloyse & Rebekah Nurse or ["or" written over "in"] their apparition upon her mother

[Hand 3] Testified to ye truth thereof
by Ann putnam Salem
May. 31t 1692

March 24, 1692

Before vs John Hathorne

Jonathan. Corwin $\Big\}$ Assis^{ts}

[Hand 1] Ann Putnam sen^{r}
[Hand 5] Ann Putnam ag^{t} Kory. [Hand 6] and Nurce

Notes: On the reverse of the document Samuel Parris adds to the narrative of Ann Putnam Sr. as recorded by Thomas Putnam. The addition was most probably made on May 31, the date of the testimony. Ann Sr.'s portion of the document probably first appeared March 24. ◊ Hand 1 = Thomas Putnam; Hand 2 = Samuel Parris; Hand 3 = John Hathorne

Essex Institute Collection, no. 22, James Duncan Phillips Library, Peabody Essex Museum, Salem, MA.

31. Statement of Daniel Andrew, Peter Cloyce, Israel Porter & Elizabeth Porter for Rebecca Nurse‡

[Hand 1] We whos nams Are under writen being desiered to goe to goodman nurs his hous to speeke with his wife and to tell her that seuerel of the Aflicted persons mentioned her: and Acordingly we went and we found her in A weak and Lowe condition in body as shee told us and had been sicke allmost A weak and we asked howe it was otherwis with her and shee said shee blest god for it shee had more of his presents in this: sicknes then somtime shee haue had but not soe much as shee desiered: but shee would with the Apostle pres forward to the mark: and many other: places of scriptur to the Like purpos: and then of her owne Acord shee begane to speek of the Affliction that was Amongst them and in perticuler of mr parris his family and howe shee was greued for them though shee had not been to see them: by Reason of fits that shee formerly use to haue for people said it was Awfull to: behold: but shee pittied them with: all her harte: and went to god for them: but shee said shee heard that there was persons spoke of that wear as Innocent as shee was shee beliued and After much to this purpos: we told her we heard that shee was spoken of allsoe: well shee said if it be soe ye will of the Lord {be} done: shee sate still A whille being as it wear Amazed: and then shee said well [1 word overstruck] as to this thing I am as Innocent as the child unborne but seurly shee said what sine hath god found out in me unrepented of that he should Lay such an Affliction upon me In my old Age: and Acording to our best obseruation we could not decern that shee knewe what we came for before we tould her
Israel porter
Elizabeth porter

To the substance of what is Aboue we if coled there too: are Ready to testifie on: oath
Daniell Andrewe
Peter Clays

Notes: The statement here appears to have been written and probably used for the examination of Rebecca Nurse on March 24. It is based on events that probably happened on March 22. Daniel Andrew was complained against on May 14, 1692, and fled. The "signatures" are all written by Hand 1, probably Israel Porter.

Essex Institute Collection, no. 16, James Duncan Phillips Library, Peabody Essex Museum, Salem, MA.

Friday, March 25, 1692

32. Deposition of Edward Putnam v. Rebecca Nurse‡

See also: June 29, 1692.

[Hand 1] the depozition of Edward Putnam aged about 38 years ho testifieth. and saith. apon the 25 day of march. 1692. ann. Putnam Juner. was bitton ["itton" written over "eet"] by ₮ rebakah nurs. as she said and about 2 of the Clock the same day she was. strock. with her Chane the mark being in a kinde of a round ring. and 3. stroaks acros. the ring she had 6. blos. with a Chane in the space of half an ouer and she had one remarkabel. one with 6 stroaks acros her arme I saw the mark boath of bite and Chane.

[Hand 2] Jurat in Curia

[Reverse] [Hand 3] Edward Putman

Notes: Used at trial. ◊ Hand 1 = Edward Putnam; Hand 2 = Stephen Sewall

Essex County Court Archives, vol. 1, no. 75, Massachusetts Supreme Judicial Court, Judicial Archives, on deposit James Duncan Phillips Library, Peabody Essex Museum, Salem, MA.

Saturday, March 26, 1692

33. Examination of Dorothy Good, as Told by Deodat Lawson

On the 26*th* of *March*, Mr. *Hathorne*, Mr. *Corwin*, and Mr. *Higison* were at the Prison-Keepers House, to Examine the Child, and it told them there, it had a little *Snake* that used to Suck on the lowest Joynt of it Fore-Finger; and when they inquired where, pointing to other places, it told them, not there, but *there*, pointing on the Lowest point of the Fore-Finger; where they Observed a deep Red Spot, about the Bigness of a *Flea-bite*, they asked who gave it that *Snake*? whether the great Black man, it said no, its Mother gave it.

Notes: The child is Dorothy Good.

Deodat Lawson. A Brief and True Narrative of Some Remarkable Passages Relating to Sundry Persons Afflicted by Witchcraft, at Salem Village Which happened from the Nineteenth of March to the Fifth of April 1692 (Boston: Benjamin Harris, 1692), pp. 7–8.

March 29, 1692   **Tuesday, March 29, 1692**

34. Warrant for the Apprehension of Rachel Clinton, with Summons for Witnesses, and Officer's Return

[Hand 1] To The Constable of Ipswich
Whereas There is Complaint Exhibbitted to ye Honored Court now ~~Const(?)~~ holden at Ipswich In Behalfe of thair majesties. against Rachell formerly ye Wife of Laurence Clenton of Ipswich on ^{grounded} Suspistion of witchcraft; & whereas Recognizance is Entred, for prosecution
You are hereby Required in thair Majesties names forthwith or ~~s~~ as soon as may be to apprehend seize & bringe before The Honored Court to be holden at Ipswich {The Said Rachell Clenton.} on ye next morrow ~~morow~~ morning. at Eight a Clock In order to an orderly Examination, & conviction & hereof faile not at Your perrill & for so doeing this shall be Your warrant. of which You are to make a true returne as ye Law directs: Ipswich march. 29th 1692).
ℙ Curiam Thos Wade. Cle$^\varepsilon$

To ye Constable of Ipswich
You are hereby required In thair Majesties names to Sumons, warne & Require to appeare at ye Court to be holden at Ipswich on ye morrow morning. Vizt Mary fuller sen$^\varepsilon$ & mary ffullor Junior & Allexsander Thomson ju$^\varepsilon$, & Richard ffitts. & Doct$^\varepsilon$ John Bridgham & Thomas Maning & Nathaniel Burnam all of Ipswich & Thomas Knowlton ju$^\varepsilon$ & Mary Thorne To Giue in thair severall Evidences before ye Court to Cleare up. ye Grovnds of Suspition of Rachell Clentons Being a witch & hereof faile not at Your perrill but make a true returne vnder Your hand as ye Law directs
ℙ Curiam Thos Wade. Cle$^\varepsilon$

[Reverse] [Hand 2]
I have Serued this ~~Sp~~ warrant or Reed it {to} Rechell Clinton: this morning: and sesed hur Body: and Left hur in ye hands of Samuell ordeway: here in ye Court house Against you$^\varepsilon$s honoures shall Call for hur

and I haue Red the seuerieall worants one the other sid written this morning Saue only Richerd fitts and mary Thorne and Richerd fitts I could not find and mary Thorne is not well: as wittnas my hand Joseph ffull⟨er⟩ Constable of Ipwich: Dated this 29th march 1691/2

[Hand 1] Warrant against Rachell Clenton returned

Notes: Unlike the Salem Village arrest warrants, bond ("Recognizance") for prosecution is posted here. Such bonds were a normal part of the legal process in Massachusetts Bay, and why bond was not required in the original cases is a matter of speculation. However, it may be that if bond had been required at the outset there would have been fewer complaints and the spread of the episode might not have occurred. The warrant for Rachel Clinton is the first one not to have originated with the authorities who first looked into the Salem Village accusations.

Suffolk Court Files, vol. 31, docket 2660, p. 140, Massachusetts Supreme Judicial Court, Judicial Archives, Massachusetts State Archives. Boston, MA.

35. Statement of Samuel Nurse & John Tarbell for Rebecca Nurse‡

See also: June 29, 1692.

[Hand 1] John tarball being at the house of tohomas putnams upon the: 28 day of this instant march being the yeare 1692 upon descource of many things i asked them some questions and among others i asked this question wheter the garle that was afflicted did first speack of of goody nurs before others mentioned her to her they said she told them she saw the apperishton of a pale fast [= pale-faced] woman that sat in her granmothers seat but did not know har name: then ["n" written over "t"] i replyed and said but who was it that told har that it was good nurs: mercy lewes said it was goody putnam that said it was goody nurs: goody putnam said it {was} mercy lewes that told her: thus they turned it upone one another saying it w⟨a⟩s you & it was you that {to⟨l⟩d} her: this was before any was afflicte{d} at thomas putnams besids his daughter th⟨a⟩t they told his daughter it was goody nurs samuel nurs doth testifie two all aboue writen

[Reverse] [Hand 2] John Tarball

Notes: The statement was made no earlier than March 28, and no later than March 31. It may subsequently have been used in defense of Rebecca Nurse. ◊ Possibly used at trial.

Essex County Court Archives, vol. 1, no. 87, Massachusetts Supreme Judicial Court, Judicial Archives, on deposit James Duncan Phillips Library, Peabody Essex Museum, Salem, MA.

Wednesday, March 30, 1692

36. Deposition of Thomas Burnam Jr. v. Rachel Clinton†

[Hand 1] The Depsition of Thomas Burnam jun^r aged:48: years who testifieth & saith y^t som years sinc one sumer one of my Coues was uery often milked & som times tow of them in my yard by my house: & thinking to cach y^e milker: I took paines & watched & one with me & thos nights y^t I watched my Cowes ware not milked & I arose one night a litele before day & stood in my Indien Corn near whare my Cowes lay & sone I saw a female stand in y^e midele of y^e yeard. whar y^e cowes ware which by hear atier [= attire] I thought was Rachell ~~Hafell~~ {Clenton.} which as I thought uanished away: & another night I arose before day & walked in y^e street & Just one y^e breaking of day Came sudingly to my yeard wheare my Cowes lay & that Cow that was most comonly milked tood [= stood] & a parson amilking which presenly glanced from y^e Cow in y^e lickenesse of a gray Cat & run up y^e back side of my house scraching upon y^e shingells abought fourty foot: & so ouer y^e top of my house & further saith not=
[Hand 2] Except y^t y^e Spring following the same Cow was found dead on y^e Com̅on, not mired nor Cast. nor throw poverty, or any Disease y^t we know of.

March 30, 1692   Notes: The crossout of "Hafell" references Rachel Clinton's maiden name of "Haffield." "Clinton" is substituted in spite of Rachel's divorce from Lawrence Clinton in 1681.

Collection 77, Box 1, Folder 19, Maine Historical Society. Portland, ME.

37. Deposition of Mary Fuller Sr. v. Rachel Clinton†

[Hand 1] The Dep{o}sition of mary ffaller sener^ε Aged About 41 years saieth About y^e 23 or fouerth of Last march: 1691/2 About Tenn of the Clook ˄{Rechell Clenton} Cam to our house and Charged me with Raisen Lies of hur About my Daughter and mary Thorne and whille she s^d Rechell was Araueing [= raving]: my Brother Joseph ffullers Boy Cam in and said their Betty was fell Downe Ded And this was as shee s^d Rechell pased by: hur: Acomming to our house and further I Run up to my Brothers Joseph ffullers house ~~A~~ see the Geale [= girl] whot condition shee was in and shee continu⟨e⟩d for the space of Three hours with out any motision [= motion] of Life and before s^d Betty or Elizabeth: Huching: Could ["C" written over "sp"] ~~I speke Deponent testifieth~~ sp⟨a⟩ke I bed hur hold up hur hand If s^d Rachell was the Caus of it and shee Ded: and when shee Could speke shee s^d The wommon with A whit Cape pased by and struck me ["m" written over "hur"] on the forehead:

Suffolk Court Files, vol. 31, docket 2660, p. 140, Massachusetts Supreme Judicial Court, Judicial Archives, Massachusetts State Archives. Boston, MA.

38. Deposition of Thomas Knowlton Jr. v. Rachel Clinton†

[Hand 1] [Lost]he [= The] Deposition of thomas Knoulton aged: 50 years saith that About 3 wekes agoo th⟨a⟩t M^ε John ˄{Rogers} and his wife were Gon to Bosto[Lost] [= Boston] That Rechell y^e wife of Laron Clinton: y^t is now surspected to be A wich; went to M^ε Rogers house and told m^ε Rogers maid y^t she must haue sum meet and milk: & y^e s^d Rechell went into seue[Lost]iell [= several] Rumes of y^e s^d house: as m^ε Rogerses maid told me; and then sent for me this Diponant: to Geet hur away out of y^e hous[Lost] [= house] and when I Came into the house: ther was Rechell Clinton and when ˄{shee} sa⟨?⟩{w}e me Cum in shee y^e s^d Rachell went away: skoldi[Lost] [= scolding] and Railing. Calling of me y^e s^d Thomas: hell howne: and whoremasterle Roog: and s^d I was A Lime [= limb] of the Deuell: and shee sai[Lost] [= said] shee had Reither see the Deuill then ˄{see} me y^e said Thomas: and y^t samuel Aires: and Thomas smith Tailer Can testifie to the same Langues that Rachell used or Cald y^e said Knolten: and after this y^e said Rachell took up a stone and Thrue it Towards me and it fell short three or four yeards of from me s^d Knolten, a⟨n⟩[Lost] [= and] so Came Roling to me: and Gust [= just] Touched the Too of my sho[Lost] [= shoe] ⟨An⟩d presently my Grat Too was in at A Gret Reage as if y^e nail⟨e⟩ were hald up by a peir of pinchers: up by the Roots: a

and further y^e said Thomas Knolton Testifieth and saith: th⟨at⟩ About 3 months Agoo: that my D⟨a⟩ughter mary [1 word overstruck] Ded [Lost] ⟨?⟩e: and Cried out in a ⟨D⟩redfull mannor that shee was p[Lost] [= pricked?] of hur sid: with pins as shee thought: Being asked whoe pric⟨k⟩[Lost] [= pricked] hur: shee s^d shee Could not teell: and when shee was out of hur fitts I this Deponant asked hur; whether shee Gaue Rec⟨h⟩[Lost] [= Rachel] any

pines: and shee said shee Gaue Rachell: About seuen: & aftor this shee had one fitt mor of
Being prickt: and then Ther Came in to our house Curnilius [1st "i" written over "e"] Kent
and John Best, a⟨n⟩[Lost] [= and] saw mary Knolton in a solom Condition: Crying ["y"
written over "i"] as if shee would be prickt to Dearth: and then said Kent and Best and my
son Thomas went ouer and Threthen s^d Rachell: That if Euer shee prickt s^d mary Knolton
againe thay would Knock out hur Brains: and Euer sence: my Gerill hath bin well:

Notes: The manuscript carries the date of 1687, written by a later hand. However, this appears to be an error, since the 1692 Clinton documents are written by the same recorder. Also, Thomas Knowlton is on the witness list, March 29, 1692, to appear in court March 30, 1692. Thomas Knowlton's age is here transcribed as "50," even though to the modern eye it looks like "40." The decision to transcribe it as "50" is based on seventeenth-century number forms as described in Samuel A. Tannenbaum, *The Handwriting of the Renaissance*. Clinton is described in the document as married to "Laron Clinton" (Lawrence), although the two had divorced in 1681. For more on Knowlton and Clinton, see the General Introduction.

UNCAT MS, Witchcraft Collection, no. 4620, Division of Rare and Manuscript Collections, Cornell University Library.

April 1692

Monday, April 4, 1692

39. Complaint of Jonathan Walcott & Nathaniel Ingersoll v. Sarah Cloyce & Elizabeth Procter

[Hand 1] This. 4th ["4" written over "3"] Aprill. 1692. Capt Jonathan Walcott and Lev^t Nathaniell Ingerson personally Appeared before us & Exhibited there Comp^lt in behalfe of theyr Majestyes ffor y^m selves & Severall of theyr Neighbours against Sarah Cloyes wife of Peter Cloyes of Salem village & [   ] Proctur ∧{y^e wife of Jno Proctur} of Salem ffor high Suspition of Severall Acts of wichcraft donne or Comitted by y^m upon ye Bodyes of Abigall Williams & John. Indian of ye ffamily of m^ε Sam^ll Parris, & Mary Walcott daughter of one of ye Complaynants & Ann. Putnam and Mercy. Lewis of ye ffamily of Thomas Putnam whereby great hurt & damage hath bin donn to ye Bodyes of s^d persons & Therefore Craved Justice

[Reverse] [Hand 2] Walcut & Ingersol comp^ts

Notes: Corwin's failure to know the first name of Elizabeth Procter reflects the frequent occurrence of the accused, particularly women, not being known to the magistrates — or their first names not being known. ◊ Hand 1 = Jonathan Corwin

Essex County Court Archives, vol. 1, no. 96, Massachusetts Supreme Judicial Court, Judicial Archives, on deposit James Duncan Phillips Library, Peabody Essex Museum, Salem, MA.

40. Deposition of Thomas Boarman v. Rachel Clinton‡

[Hand 1] The Deposition of Thomas Boarman seno⟨u⟩ᵉ ^{aged: 47} This Deponant
testifieth and saith that som wimen of worth and quolity: Desired me To Aquaint the seuen
men yᵗ Rachell Clinton was a grat Disstūruen [= disturbance] ⟨?er⟩ unto them in yᵉ
meten-house in hunching them with hur Elboo: as thay went by hur sᵈ Clinton, and then yᵉ
same Day ther I yᵉ sᵈ Boarman: Desired yᵉ seuen men to take som Cear yᵗ Rachell Clenton:
might be foreworned: not to Com into Thoes wimens seets no more to Dissturbe them, and
as I the sᵈ Boarman was Riding whom: that night aftor I had bin with the select men: I saw
somthing appere at frenches Coue Before me: Like a Cat as I Apper^{r}prehended: and
then I Looked wishfully upon it; and it semed to be sumthing Like a Littell Doge: and then
I p⟨?⟩^{u}rsued it: and it Kept yᵉ same Distance in yᵉ parth before me: all though⟨?⟩ I Roud
["u" written over "a"] heard after it I could not ouer take it, then I Looked one my right hand:
and I saw a Grat surkle [= circle?] that moued as fast as I Roud along: and Then I thought
of Rachell Clinten then the Littell Creatur and yᵉ surkle uanished away: and further saith not

Notes: "hunching": 'pushing, thrusting' (*OED* s.v. *hunch*).

Suffolk Court Files, vol. 31, docket 2660, p. 140, Massachusetts Supreme Judicial Court, Judicial Archives, Massachusetts State Archives. Boston, MA.

41. Deposition of William Baker v. Rachel Clinton‡

[Hand 1] The Deposition of william Baker Aged: 36 years saith: About 10 years Agoo: I
Liuing with my master Rust: Ther was a Berrill of strong Bere Brued, & yᵗ Day it was
Broued Rachell clinton Came ther, & met with sum small Afrunt [= affront]: But whot it
was I can not tell: & yᵉ next Day morning the Bere was put in to yᵉ Berrill: & that Day said
Rachall went Bakwords and forrowords 6 or 7 tims: up & Dow the Lane yᵗ Leds to our house
& Ded not Com in to yᵉ house yᵗ Day: & that night following: hannah Rust: went Downe to
see whether the Bere worked or no: & puld out the tape & Could find no Bere in the Berril:
& shee Called us that is yᵉ four of yᵉ house besids me: or with me: and I saw that ther was no
Bere in the Berrill: nither was ther any Apperance of wet upon yᵉ flouer: and presently aftor
we fild the Berrill with worter [= water] and it was in A night and Day and Ded not Leke
any of it out as we Could see And aftor that ~~we~~ our folke Brued another Berril of Bere and
put it in yᵉ sam Berril & it Ded not ^{Leke} at all aftor that And further saieth not:

Suffolk Court Files, vol. 31, docket 2660, p. 140, Massachusetts Supreme Judicial Court, Judicial Archives, Massachusetts State Archives. Boston, MA.

42. Testimony of Mary Edwards & John Edwards v. Rachel Clinton

[Hand 1] Ipswich April yᵉ 4ᵗʰ 1692
The testimony of mary: edwards: ageed about 52: yeres: testyfieth & saith: yᵗ abought the
27ᵗʰ day: of: this Last{e} dissember <u>1691</u> that Rachell: ⟨dr⟩ Clenton came to: our: houes: &
was: uery: importenat [= importunate] with me yᵉ ["e" written over "t"] sᵈ mary: to: haue
Rome in our houes. to: kepe: thare: but I toulld: har yᵉ sᵈ Rachell yᵗ we ware no wayes:

April 4, 1692

prouided to acommedat har tharfore she must Rest har sellf contented:.) & at: this time: I y^e s^d mary: was mea⟨?⟩keing of blood pudens: and ∧{she} y^e aboue s^d Rachell siting by: y^e fier) by: har discorse had a great dissire to haue sum of thos: pudens: saying y^t it was: uery good food: & y^t I {she} Loueed it uery: well: so: I y^e s^d mary gaue: har: y^e s^d Rachell one of y^e pudens: y^e which she Reseaued uary: Cornfully: [= scornfully] & quickly. after rose up: out of. har seate & went away: muttering but ~~whot~~ whot she said I coulld not tell): but about y^e Latter end of Jennywary: ~~we~~ y^e s^d edwards: had nine pigges: y^t ware about eight weckes oulld that ware: tacken sudenly: &: ∧{fiue of them} died & about a fortnight after y^t y^e {s^d ewards}: had ~~edwards had~~ thre: yerelings ∧{tacken sudenly} y^t semid to: be uery: harty: & was: in good case: but sudenly was tacken with unusall fittes: Jumping & Roreing till thay tumbled doune within a Littell tim after one another) as: to: y^e ~~former~~ Latter part of this testymony Releating to y^e death of my pigges: ⟨?⟩ & yerlings I can attest two his

his

John s edwards, sen^r **ɯ** mark:.

& furthermore mary: edwards: heard ~~h~~ sum of har Chilldren aske y^e s^d Reachell how har hands ceame to: be scracht & swelld so & she: made: This answar & said y^t she: had two or thre: Roges: [= roguish] catts: y^t when she put doune har hand woulld e scrach it:

MS Ch K 1.40, vol. 2, p. 60, Rare Books and Manuscripts, Boston Public Library. Boston, MA.

43. Deposition of James Fuller Jr. v. Rachel Clinton‡

[Hand 1] The depotition of Jeams fuller Junier aged about eighteen years saith that on ye 18th Day of march Last: 1691/2 or there Abouts: as to the Day: About 9 or 10: of the Clock: I was talking with Good-man Perry & telling him how the s^d mary fuller my sister & mary Thorn wer taken Last night: & in ye mene while, whilst he and I was talking Rachell Clinton Cam in to our house & sat Downe by ye fier side I asked hur whot shee Came hether for at this time of night, & shee said shee Cam to see whot Lies the⟨m⟩ were y^t we Raisd of hur & I told hur I Ded not Know as I had Raisd Eny of hur: Presently my onkles Boy Cam in & told me that ther Betty was Ded, and as soon as Euer she s^d Rachall Herd them words: she Run out Adors: and I followed hur as herd as I could & when I Came to the Dore I Could see nothing of hur: & it was a uery Cler mone light night & I Run up to my onkls: Joseph ffullers House: to see whot y^e mattor was: & ther I found y^e Gerle Dede as y^e boye told me; & s^d olkl [= uncle] ffuller & I took hur up & Cerried hur in y^e house & so shee continued for y^e space of 3 or 4 hours: before ther was any Apperan{ce} of Life in hur; & y^e next Day I asked hur whot mad hur so Last night: & she told me: she see sumthing stand up at y^e Corner of y^e shope & shee went a littell way towords it & it Loced so Basly she turnd About to Run away from it & it follow{ed} hur & Knocked hur Down

Notes: "Basly": *Basely* could be interpreted as an adverb with the meaning 'in an evil way, with meanness' (*OED* s.v. *basely*). Alternatively, *basely* may here be used as the adjective *base* 'mean' (*OED* s.v. *base*). For adverbs used as adjectives, see Tauno F. Mustanoja, *A Middle English Syntax. Part I. Parts of Speech* (Helsinki: Société Néophilologique, 1960), pp. 649–650. Perhaps the former is the more likely.

MS Ch K 1.40, vol. 2, p. 68, Rare Books and Manuscripts, Boston Public Library. Boston, MA.

44. Deposition of Mercy Lewis v. Dorothy Good‡

[Hand 1] The Deposistion of Mircy lewes ^{aged about 19 years} who testifieth and saith that on the 3ᵈ April 1692 the Apperishtion of Dorrithy good Sarah goods daughter came to me and did afflect me urging me to writ in hir book and seuerall times sence Dorithy good hath afflected me by biting pinching and choaking me urging me to writ in hir book

[Reverse] [Hand 2] Mercy Lewis against Dorothy. Good.

Notes: The April 3 date in the manuscript is puzzling and may be a recording error for March 3, which is referenced by Ann Putnam Jr. in her deposition against Dorothy Good. See No. 26. If so, this document would most likely belong on March 24. Dorothy, four or five years old, was examined on March 24, 1692. However, the dating assignment here assumes an accurate recording. April 3 was a Sunday, and although judicial activity did at times occur on Sundays, it was not common, so the most likely date for the document is April 4 or after. ◊ Hand 1 = Thomas Putnam; Hand 2 = Jonathan Corwin

Essex County Court Archives, vol. 1, no. 62, Massachusetts Supreme Judicial Court, Judicial Archives, on deposit James Duncan Phillips Library, Peabody Essex Museum, Salem, MA.

45. Testimony of Mercy Lewis v. Sarah Osburn‡

[Hand 1] [Lost]ircy [= Mercy] lewes agged about 19 years who testifieth and [Lost]⟨d:⟩ of April 1692 the Apperishtion of Sarah Osborn [Lost]lected [= afflicted] me urging me to writ in hir book.

[Reverse] [Hand 2] Sarah Osborn

Notes: The torn part of the document carries a lost date. The content here is very similar to the preceding document with testimony by Mercy Lewis against Dorothy Good, and it is accordingly placed here on the speculation that the missing date referenced is April 3. This document represents the only extant one after March against Sarah Osburn, who died in prison on May 10. ◊ Hand 1 = Thomas Putnam

Essex County Court Archives, vol. 1, no. 30, Massachusetts Supreme Judicial Court, Judicial Archives, on deposit James Duncan Phillips Library, Peabody Essex Museum, Salem, MA.

Friday, April 8, 1692

46. Warrant for the Apprehension of Sarah Cloyce & Elizabeth Procter, and Officer's Return

See also: April 11, 1692.

[Hand 1] Salem Aprill 4ᵗʰ 1692

There Being Complaint this day made (Before vs) by Capᵗ Jonaᵗ Walcott, and Lᵗ Nathaniell Ingersall both of Salem Village, in Behalfe of theire Majesties for themselfes and also for seuerall of theire Neighbour(s) {~~Made Compl~~} Against Sarah Cloyce the wife of peter Cloyce of Salem Village; and Elizabeth Procter the wife of John Procter of Salem ffarmes for high Suspition of Sundry acts of Witchcraft donne or Committed by them vpon the bodys of Abigaile Williams and John Indian both of Mr Saml parris his famyly of Salem Village and Mary Walcott daufter of one of the abouesaid Complainants, And Ann Putnam and Marcy Lewis of the famyly of Thomas Putnam of Salem Village whereby great hurt and dammage hath benne donne to the Bodys of s^d persons abouenamed therefore Craued Justice.

April 8, 1692

You are therefore in theire Majes^{ts} names hereby required to apprehend and bring before vs Sarah Cloyce the wife of peter Cloyce of Salem Village and Elizabeth procter the wife of John Procter of Salem ffarmes; on Munday Morneing Next being the Eleuenth day of this Instant Aprill aboute Eleven of the Clock, at the publike Meeting house in the Towne, in order to theire Examination Relateing to the premises aboues^d and here of you are not to faile Dated Salem Aprill 8th 1692

To George Herrick Marshall }   John Hathorne }
of the County of Essex }   } Assis^{ts}
                                Jonathan. Corwin }

You are like wise to ^{warne & order.} ~~Summons~~ Eliz Hubert and Mary Warren not to faile of being present at y^e aboues^d tyme & place to giue in w^t Euedence thay know therein
[Hand 2] Aprill 11th 1692 I haue taken the persons of Sarah cloycie and Elizebeth Procter and brought them beefore this honorable Courte to answer as aboue
I haue allso warned y^e above named Elizebeth Hubbart to answer as above p$^\varepsilon$ Geo. Herrick Marshall of Essex

Notes: The warrant was not issued until April 8, although the complaint was made on April 4. ◊ Hand 1 = John Hathorne; Hand 2 = George Herrick

Essex County Court Archives, vol. 1, no. 91, Massachusetts Supreme Judicial Court, Judicial Archives, on deposit James Duncan Phillips Library, Peabody Essex Museum, Salem, MA.

47. Council Record Pertaining to Sarah Cloyce, Martha Cory, Dorothy Good, Rebecca Nurse, Elizabeth Procter, & John Procter

See also: April 11, 1692 & April 12, 1692.

[Hand 1] Salem Aprill 11 1692
At a Councill held at Salem and p$^\varepsilon$sent
Thomas Danforth Esqr Dep^t Gou$^\varepsilon$

James Russell –   Maj$^\varepsilon$ Sam$^\varepsilon$ Appleton
John Hathorne   Capt Samuell Sewall
Isaac Adington   Jona^t Corwin

Esq^{rs}

Whereas Complaint was Exhibited by Capt Jonathan Walcot and Leiu^t Nathaniell Ingersall both of Salem Village, on behalfe of theire Majes^{ts} not only for themselfes, but also for severall of theire Neighbours Against Sarah Cloyce the wife of Peter Cloyce of Salem village, and Elizabeth Procter the wife of John Procter of Salem ffarmes for high Suspition of Sundry acts of witchcraft donne or Committed by them vpon the Bodys of abigail Williams and John Indian both of m^r Saml Parris his famyly in Salem Village, Mary Walcot Ann Putnam and Marcy Lewis

&c – accord$^\varepsilon$ to s^d Compl$^{\varepsilon t}$ appears

Salem Aprill 8th

And Warrant being giuen forth for theire apprehention s^d Cloyce and Procter ware by George Herrick Marshall of Essex, brought before vs; and m^r Samuell Parris being desired and appointed to wright y^e Examination, did take the same & also read itt before y^e Councill in publike And John Procter of Salem ffarmes being then personally present was by Abigail Williams and Anna Putnam Charged with seuerall acts of Witchcraft by him Committed on ye person of ~~Goody~~ Mrs Pope ye wife of m^r Joseph Pope and Others, who ware at s^d tyme accordingly afflicted

apparent to all, likewise Marcy Lewis and [   ] Gold charged ^{s^d} John Procter at s^d tyme Also further Information being Giuen against s^d Jno Procter by m^r Samuell Parris. Aprill 12th as appeares. {vpon wch s^d Jno Procter & his wif⟨e⟩ and Sarah Cloyce ware all Committed to prison ꝑ aduise of ye Councill}

April 12th 1692

John Procter and Elizabeth Procter his wife and Sarah Cloyce, also: Rebecka Nurce, Martha Cory and Dorothy Good ware sent to Boston Goale ꝑ Marshall Geo: Herrick. – vpon high Suspition as aboves^d

[Reverse] [Hand 2] Councill at Salem Apr^{ll} 11th 1692

Notes: No evidence of a warrant for John Procter survives. It may be that an examination of him was expected on April 11, the day of his wife's examination, thus explaining the presence of these particular examiners – there for the examination of the first male accused. However, this is not certain, and the possibility remains that Procter was not formally charged until the accusations against him at his wife's examination were heard. This document is the closest to a warrant for the arrest of John Procter that is extant. "Gold" is probably a variant of "Gould," and the most likely accuser named "Gold" is Benjamin Gould, although Samuel Gould or Thomas Gould Jr. cannot be ruled out. The "further information" from Parris may be referencing Document 61. ◊ Hand 1 = John Hathorne

Essex County Court Archives, vol. 1, no. 92, Massachusetts Supreme Judicial Court, Judicial Archives, on deposit James Duncan Phillips Library, Peabody Essex Museum, Salem, MA.

Sunday, April 10, 1692

48. Deposition of Ephraim Shelden v. Sarah Cloyce

[Hand 1] The deposition of Ephram Shelden aged 20 years who testefieth and Sayth April 10th
92
I this deponent being at the house of Lewtent Ingersol when Mercy Lewes was in one of her fits I heard her cry out of Goodwife Cloyce and when she came to her selfe she was asked who she saw. she answered she Saw no body they demanded of her whether or noe ⟨s⟩he did

not see. Goodwife Nurse. or Goodwife Cloyce. or Goodwife Gory. she answered she saw. no
body./

[Reverse] [Hand 2] Eph: Shelden

Notes: Silence by accusers seems to have reflected uncertainty as to how to proceed.

Essex County Court Archives, vol. 1, no. 41, Massachusetts Supreme Judicial Court, Judicial Archives, on deposit James Duncan Phillips Library, Peabody Essex Museum, Salem, MA.

Monday, April 11, 1692

Officer's Return: Warrant for the Apprehension of Sarah Cloyce & Elizabeth Procter
2nd of 2 dates. See No. 46 on April 8, 1692

49. Examination of Sarah Cloyce & Elizabeth Procter

At a court held at Salem 11th April 1692, by the honoured Thomas Danforth, Deputy Governor. Q. John; who hurt you? A. Goody Procter first, and then Goody Cloyse. Q. What did she do to you? A. she brought the book to me. Q. John! tell the truth, who hurts you? have you been hurt? A. The first, was a gentlewoman I saw. Q. Who next? A. Goody Cloyse. Q. But who hurt you next? A. Goody Procter. Q. What did she do to you? A. She choaked me, and brought the book. Q. How oft did she come to torment you? A. A good many times, she and Goody Cloyse. Q. Do they come to you in the night as well as the day? A. They come most in the day. Q. Who? A. Goody Cloyse and Goody Procter. Q. Where did she take hold of you? A. Upon my throat, to stop my breath. Q. Do you know Goody Cloyse and Goody Proctor? A. Yes, here is Goody Cloyse. (Cloyse) when did I hurt thee? A. A great many times. (Cloyse) Oh! you are a grievous liar. Q. What did this Goody Cloyse do to you? A. She pinched and bit me till the blood came. Q. How long since this woman came and hurt you? A. Yesterday at meeting. Q. At any time before? A. Yes a great many times. Q. Mary Walcot! who hurts you? A. Goody Cloyse. Q. What did she do to you? A. She hurt me. Q. Did she bring the book? A. Yes. Q. What was you to do with it? A. To touch it, and be well. – Then she fell into a fit. Q. Doth she come alone? A. Sometimes alone, and sometimes in company with Goody Nurse and Goody Corey, and a great many I do not know. – Then she fell into a fit again. – Q. Abigail Williams! did you see a company at Mr. Parris's house eat and drink? A. Yes Sir, that was their sacrament. Q. How many were there? A. About forty, and Goody Cloyse and Goody Good were their deacons. Q. What was it? A. They said it was our blood, and they had it twice that day. Q. Mary Walcot! have you seen a white man? Yes, Sir, a great many times. Q. What sort of man was he? A. A fine grave man, and when he came, he made all the witches to tremble. Abigail Williams confirmed the same, and that they had such a sight at Deacon Ingersoll's. Q. Who was at Deacon Ingersoll's then? A. Goody Cloyse, Goody Nurse, Goody Corey, and Goody Good. Then Sarah Cloyse asked for water, and sat down as one seized with a dying fainting fit; and several of the afflicted fell into fits, and some of them cried out, Oh! her spirit is gone to prison to her sister Nurse. Q. Elizabeth Procter! you understand whereof you are charged, viz, to be guilty of sundry acts of witchcraft; what say you to it? Speak the truth, and so you that are afflicted, you must speak the truth, as you will answer it before God another day. Mary Walcot! doth this woman hurt you? A. I never saw her so as to be hurt by her. Q. Mary [= Mercy] Lewis! does she hurt you? Her mouth was stopped. – Q. Ann Putman, does she hurt you? – She could not speak. – Q. Abigail Williams! does she hurt you? – Her hand was thrust in her own mouth. – Q. John! does she hurt you? A. This is the woman that came in her shift and choaked me. Q. did she ever bring the book? A. Yes, Sir. Q. What to do? A. to write. Q. What, this woman? A. Yes, Sir. Q. Are you sure of it? A. Yes, Sir. Again, Abigail Williams and Ann Putman were spoke to by the court, but neither of them could make any answer, by reason of dumbness or other fits. Q. What do you say Goody Procter to these things? A. I take God in heaven to be my witness, that I know nothing of it, no more than the child unborn. Q. Ann Putman! doth this woman hurt you. A. Yes Sir, a great many times. – Then the accused looked upon them and they fell into fits. Q. She does not bring the book to you, does she? A. Yes, Sir, often, and saith she hath made her maid set her hand to it. Q. Abigail Williams! does this woman hurt you? A. Yes, Sir, often. Q. Does she bring the book to you? A. Yes. Q. What would she have you do with it? A. To write in it and I shall be well. Did not you, said Abigal, tell me, that your maid had written? (Procter) Dear Child, it is not so. There is another judgement, dear child. – Then Abigail and Ann had fits. – By and by they cried out, look you there is Goody Procter upon the beam. – By and by, both of them cried out of Goodman Proctor himself, and said he was a wizard. – Immediately, many, if not all of the bewitched, had grievous fits. – Q. Ann Putman! who hurt you? A. Goodman Procter and his wife too. – Afterwards some of the afflicted cried, there is Procter going to take up Mrs. Pope's feet. – And her feet were immediately taken up. – Q. What do you say Goodman Procter to these things? A. I know not, I am innocent. Abigail Williams cried out, there is Goodman Procter going to Mrs. Pope, and immediately, said Pope fell into a fit. You see the devil will deceive you; the children could see what you was going to do before the woman was hurt. I would advise you to repentance, for the devil is bringing you out. – Abigail Williams cried out again, there is Goodman Procter going to hurt Goody Bibber; and immediately Goody Bibber fell into a fit. There was the like of Mary Walcot, and divers others. Benjamin Gould gave in his testimony, that he had seen Goodman Corey and his wife, Procter and his wife, Goody Cloyse, Goody Nurse, and Goody Griggs in his chamber last thursday night. Elizabeth Hubbard was in a trance during the whole examination. – During the examination of Elizabeth Procter, Abigail Williams and Ann Putman, both made offer to strike at said Procter; but when Abigail's hand came near, it opened, whereas it was made up into a fist before, and came done exceeding lightly, as it drew near to said Procter, and at length with open and extended fingers, touched Procter's hood very lightly. Immediately Abigail cried out, her fingers, her fingers, her fingers burned, and Ann Putman took on most grievously, of her head, and sunk down.

Salem, April 11th, 1692. Mr. Samuel Parris was desired by the honourable Thomas Danforth, deputy-governor, and the council, to take in writing the aforesaid examinations, and accordingly took and delivered them in; and upon hearing the same, and seeing what was then seen, together with the charge of the afflicted persons, were by the advice of the council all committed by us,

John Hawthorne,

John [= Jonathan] Corwin,   Assistants.

Notes: The "white man" probably comes from stories of the Swedish witch trials. "John," questioned at the outset is John Indian, the first adult male to join the "afflicted." The adult female, Bathshua Pope, had done so earlier. Regarding Benjamin Gould, see note to No. 66.

Thomas Hutchinson, The History of the Province of Massachusetts-Bay, from the Charter of King William and Queen Mary, in 1691, Until the Year 1750, vol. 2, ed. Lawrence Shaw Mayo. (Cambridge, MA: Harvard University Press, 1936). pp. 21–23.

50. Deposition of Elizabeth Hubbard v. Elizabeth Procter†

See also: Aug. 5, 1692.

[Hand 1] The Deposistion of Elizabeth Hubburd agged about 17 years who testifieth and saith that about the begining of April 1692 I saw the Apperishtion of Elizabeth procktor the wife of John procktor sen[r] and she did Immediatly tortor me most greviously allmost redy to choak me to death: urging me to writ in hir book: and so she continewed afflecting of me by times tell the day of hir examination being the 11th of Aprill and then also I was tortored most greviously dureing the time of hir examination I could not spake a word and also seuerall times sence the Apperishtion of Elizabeth procktor has tortored me most greviously by biting pinching and allmost choaking me to death urging me dreadfully to writ in hir book

mark:

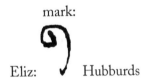

Eliz: Hubburds

[Hand 2] Jurat in Curia

[Reverse] [Hand 3] Elizabeth Hubbard ag[t] Eliz[a] procter.
[Hand 1] Elizabeth procktor

Notes: Although used at the trial of Elizabeth Procter, this document probably first appeared as a deposition at her examination on April 11. ◊ Used at trial. ◊ Hand 1 = Thomas Putnam; Hand 2 = Stephen Sewall; Hand 3 = Thomas Newton

Essex County Court Archives, vol. 1, no. 97, Massachusetts Supreme Judicial Court, Judicial Archives, on deposit James Duncan Phillips Library, Peabody Essex Museum, Salem, MA.

51. Deposition of Mercy Lewis v. Elizabeth Procter†

See also: June 30, 1692.

[Hand 1] The Deposistion of Mircy lewes aged about 19 years who testifieth and that on the 26th march ~~1691/2~~ 1692 I saw the Apperishtion of Elizabeth proctor the wife of Jn[o] proctor sen[r]: and she did most greviously tortor me by biting and pinching me most greviously urging me to writ in hir book and she continewed hurting me by temes tell the 11th April 1692 being the day of hir examination and then also dureing the time of hir examination she did ~~most greviously~~ tortor me most greviouly and also seuerall times sence: also on the day of

April 11, 1692

hir Examination I saw the Apperishtion of Elizabeth proctor. ~~afflect the bodys of mary walcott Abigaill williams and Ann putnam jur~~

Mercy Lewes

[Hand 2] Mercy Lewes [Hand 3] mircy lewes ownid this har testimony to be the truth one har oath: before the Juriars of Inquest this 30 of June 1692

[Reverse] [Hand 1] Mircy lewes against Elizabeth proctor.

Notes: The docket notation by Thomas Putnam indicates a clerical role in the Court that may be considered separate from his role as the recorder of accusations in cases he supported. The crossed out names strongly suggest that the document was used previously, probably at Elizabeth Procter's examination, with the names removed to limit the document to those who gave sworn testimony to the grand jury on June 30. ◊ Hand 1 = Thomas Putnam; Hand 2 = Andrew Elliot

Essex County Court Archives, vol. 1, no. 99, Massachusetts Supreme Judicial Court, Judicial Archives, on deposit James Duncan Phillips Library, Peabody Essex Museum, Salem, MA.

52. Deposition of Samuel Parris, Nathaniel Ingersoll, & Thomas Putnam v. Elizabeth Procter†

See also: June 30, 1692.

[Hand 1] The Deposition of Sam: Parris aged about .39. years & Nathanael Ingersol aged about fifty & eight years & Thomas Putman aged abou⟨t⟩ fourty yeares all of Salem testifyeth & saith that John Indian, Ann Putman, & Abigail Williams & others of the bewitched persons were severall times & greivously tortured at the Examination of Elizabeth Proctor wife to John Proctor of Salem Farmer before the Honoured Magistrates the .11ᵗʰ April .1692. & particularly that Eliz: Hubbard ⟨w⟩as in a Trance during the whole examination unable to speak a word th⟨ô⟩ [Lost] [SWP = often called upon] by sᵈ Magistrates, & also the said Abigail williams & Ann Putman then ⟨t⟩estifyed ⟨th⟩at [Lost]⟨e⟩y [= they] saw this Eliz: Proctor & [1 word illegible] ⟨?⟩band [SWP = her husband] ⟨J⟩ohn Pro[Lost] [= Procter] severall time⟨s⟩ afflicting of Bathshua Pope the wife of Joseph Pope of Salem yeoman, at which times the said Bathshua Pope was seized with violent fits; & ⟨fa⟩rther that the said Abigail Williams, & Ann Putman, both of them made offer to strike at ⟨sai⟩d Eliz: Proctor, but when said Abigails hand came near to said ⟨Eliz:⟩ Proctor, [Lost] [SWP = it] opened (whereas it was made up into a fist before) & came down exceeding lightly as it drew near to said Proctor, & at length with open & extended f⟨in⟩gers touche[Lost] [= touched] [SWP = said] Proctors hood very lightly, & immediately said Abigail cryed out, Oh! my fingers, my fingers, my fingers burne, & Ann Putman took on most greivously of her head, & sunk down, as far as she could being held up by such as tended her.

[Hand 2] Nath: Ingarson and thom. Putman did one their oaths owne this⟨e⟩ [Lost]eir [= their] testimonies to be the truth before the Juriars of Inques this 30 of June 1692

Notes: A tracing of this document is located in the collection of the Boston Public Library, Rare Books and Manuscripts, MS Ch. 2.500. ◊ Hand 1 = Samuel Parris

Essex Institute Collection, no. 18, James Duncan Phillips Library, Peabody Essex Museum, Salem, MA.

53. Deposition of Ann Putnam Jr. v. Elizabeth Procter†

See also: June 30, 1692 & Aug. 5, 1692.

April 11, 1692

[Hand 1] The Deposistion of Ann putnam {Jur} who testifieth and saith that on the 3th of march 1691/92 I saw the Apperishtion of gooddy procktor amongst the wicthes ~~which~~ {& she} did almost choake me Immediatly and bite and pinch me but I did not know who she was tell the: 6th of march ~~of march~~ that I saw hir att meeting and then I tould them that held me that yt woman was one that did afflect me: and seuerall times sence she hath greviously afflected me by biting pinching and almost choaking me urging me vehemently to writ in hir book: but on the 11th April 1692 the Apperishtion of Elizabeth proctor the wife of John pr(o)cktor: senr did most greviously torment me dureing the time of hir Examination and also seuerall times sence by biting pinching and allmost choaking me to death urging me vehemently to writ in hir book: also on the 11th April being the day of the Examination of Elizabeth proctor I. I saw the Apperishtion of Elizabeth proctor: goe and afflect the bodys of Mistris pope Mary walcott Mircy lewes Abigail williams and also all the time of hir examination she and hir: Husband and Sarah Cloys did most greviously afflect Elizabeth Hubbourd and would not let hir spake a word as I hard.

[Hand 2] ann Putnam owned this har testimony to be the truth one har oath before the Juriars of Inquest this: 30 dy of June: 1692

[Hand 3] Jurat in Curia

[Reverse] [Hand 4] Ann puttnam agt Eliza procter.

Notes: The ink changes beginning with "but on the 11th" indicate that what follows is a later addition. Since John Procter and Sarah Cloyce were also implicated, the possibility remains that this was also used against John Procter as well as against Elizabeth Procter. Sarah Cloyce was never tried, the grand jury in 1693 returning ignoramuses to the bills of indictment against her. ◊ Used at trial. ◊ Hand 1 = Thomas Putnam; Hand 3 = Stephen Sewall; Hand 4 = Thomas Newton

Essex County Court Archives, vol. 1, no. 101, Massachusetts Supreme Judicial Court, Judicial Archives, on deposit James Duncan Phillips Library, Peabody Essex Museum, Salem, MA.

54. Deposition of Thomas Putnam & Edward Putnam v. Elizabeth Procter†

See also: Aug. 5, 1692.

[Hand 1] The Deposistion of Thomas putnam agged 40 years and ~~Jno~~ {Edwar(d)} putna(m) agged 36 years who testifie and say that we haueing been ~~convers~~asant with diuers of the afflected parsons as mary walcott mercy lewes Eliz: Hubburt and ⟨?⟩ ann putnam and we haue seen them most dreadfully tomented and complaining of Elizabeth proctor for hurting them: but on the 11th April 1692 being the day of hir Examination the afforesaid parsons ware much affleted dureing the time of hir Examination also seuerall times sence we haue seen the afforesaid parsons most dreadfully tormented as if all their bones would haue been disjoyned complainig of gooddy proctor for hurting them: and we verily beleue in our hearts that Eliz: proctor the prizsoer at the barr as [= has] very often afflected the afforesaid parson by acts of wicthcraft

[Hand 2] & yt they haue seen many bites on ye aflicted psons wch they said was Elizabeth procter that did it. Jurat in Curia

attest Steph. Sewll C [= clerk]

April 11, 1692   [Reverse] Tho & Edw: Puttnam

Notes: No ink change occurs within Hand 1, but the document may nevertheless have been added to, beginning with "but on the 11th. . . ." ◊ Used at trial. ◊ Hand 1 = Thomas Putnam; Hand 2 = Stephen Sewall

Essex County Court Archives, vol. 1, no. 93, Massachusetts Supreme Judicial Court, Judicial Archives, on deposit James Duncan Phillips Library, Peabody Essex Museum, Salem, MA.

55. Deposition of Elizabeth Booth v. John Procter†
See also: Aug. 5, 1692.

[Hand 1] The deposistion of Eliz: Booth ^{aggd 18 years} who testifieth and saith that sence I haue ben afflected I haue been most greviously tormented by my neighbor John proctor sen^r or his apperance also I haue seen John proctor sen^r or his Apperance most greviously torment and afflect mary walcott mercy lewes and ann putnam jun^r by pinching twisting and almost choaking them
[Hand 2] Jurat in Curia

[Reverse] El. Booth

Notes: The April 11 date postulates that Procter's examination on April 11 had been planned. Some have argued that he was only denounced when he showed up to support his wife that day. If such is the case, the deposition might have been drawn on April 11, after the examination. Two accusers named Elizabeth Booth, one born 1674, the other 1676, appear in these records. Given the age recorded, this one is the one born in 1674. ◊ Used at trial. ◊ Hand 1 = Thomas Putnam; Hand 2 = Stephen Sewall

Essex County Court Archives, vol. 1, no. 51, Massachusetts Supreme Judicial Court, Judicial Archives, on deposit James Duncan Phillips Library, Peabody Essex Museum, Salem, MA.

56. Deposition of Elizabeth Hubbard v. John Procter†
See also: Aug. 5, 1692.

[Hand 1] The Deposistion of Elizabeth Hubburd agged about 17 years who testifieth and saith that I neuer saw the Apperishtion of Jno procktor sen^r before the day of his Examination which was the 11th Aprill 1692: but sence that the Apperishtion of Jno procktor sen^r has most greviously afflected me a grat many times by pinching pricking and beating me allmost choaking me to death urging me uehemently to writ in his book

mark
Eliz: ⌣ Hubburd⟨s⟩

[Hand 2] Jurat in Curia

[Reverse] [Hand 3] Elizabeth Hubbard ag^t John procter.

Notes: Used at trial. ◊ Hand 1 = Thomas Putnam; Hand 2 = Stephen Sewall

Essex County Court Archives, vol. 1, no. 49, Massachusetts Supreme Judicial Court, Judicial Archives, on deposit James Duncan   April 11, 1692
Phillips Library, Peabody Essex Museum, Salem, MA.

57. Deposition of Samuel Parris, Nathaniel Ingersoll, & Thomas Putnam v. John Procter, Elizabeth Procter, & Sarah Cloyce†

[Hand 1] The Deposition of Sam: Parris aged about .39. years, & Nathanael Ingersoll aged about fifty & eight yeares & also Thomas Putman aged about fourty yeares all of Salem testifyeth & saith that divers of the afflicted by Witchcraft were much tortured at the Examination of John Proctor of Salem Farmer before the honoured Magistrates the .11ᵗʰ April .1692. & particularly when Mʳ Joseph Popes wife was severall times afflicted, Ann Putman junᵉ & Abigail Williams testifyed that it was by John Proctor aforesaid & his wife Elizabeth, & also when Mercy Lewes was much afflicted at the same examination said Ann witnessed that it was by said Proctor & his ^{wife} & Goody Cloyse, also ~~Also~~ when Goody Bibber was much afflicted, Abig: Williams just before cryed out there is Goodman Proctor going to hurt Goody Bibber, & also said Abigail cryed out there is Goodman Proctor going to hurt Mary Walcot, & im̄ediately Mary Walcot was seized with a violent fit

[Reverse] The Depōtion of Sam: Parris &c. agsᵗ John Proctor

Notes: As Parris frequently did, the inclusion of Thomas Putnam as a deponent was likely a later insertion by Parris in a blank space he had left in the document, most likely, but not certainly, on the same day. ◊ Hand 1 = Samuel Parris

Essex County Court Archives, vol. 1, no. 47, Massachusetts Supreme Judicial Court, Judicial Archives, on deposit James Duncan
Phillips Library, Peabody Essex Museum, Salem, MA.

58. Testimony of Joseph Pope v. John Procter

See also: June 30, 1692.

[Hand 1] Aprill 11 = 1692
Joseph Pope {aged forty one years or thereabouts} testefyeth and saith yᵗ on yᵉ sd day this deponent heard John Procter {say} yᵗ if mᵉ Parish would lett him haue his Indian hee yᵉ sd Procter would soone Driue yᵉ Diuell out of him and further saith not

[Reverse] [Hand 2] Joseph Pope agᵗ Jnᵒ Procter Senᵉ

Notes: The prose in the document could suggest that it was written after April 11, but what may appear as past tense usage in this and other documents can at times be misleading. The April 11 date on the document can probably be trusted as the date of composition. *SWP*, II, p. 683, identifies this document as having been used on June 30 at a jury of inquest, but this indication does not appear on the surviving manuscript. It does survive in the WPA papers, but as a line separate from the document with a notation that it is a copy. Since WPA may have had access to evidence for a June 30 grand jury use, it is additionally dated there in this edition to reflect that possibility. No notation of it as a copy appears on the extant manuscript. ◊ Hand 1 = George Herrick; Hand 2 = Jonathan Corwin

Essex Institute Collection, no. 20, James Duncan Phillips Library, Peabody Essex Museum, Salem, MA.

April 11, 1692

59. Deposition of Ann Putnam Jr. v. John Procter†

See also: June 30, 1692.

[Hand 1] The Deposistion of Ann putnam ∧{Junr} who testifieth and saith I haue often seen the Apperishtion of Jnᵒ procktor⟨s⟩ senʳ amongst the wicthes but he did not doe me much hurt tell a little before his Examination which was on the 11ᵗʰ of April 1692: and then he sett upon me most grevivously and did tortor me most dreadfully also in the time of his Examination he afflected me very much: and seuerall times sence the Apperishtion of John procktor senʳ has most greviously tortored me by pinching and allmost choaking me urging me vehemently to writ in his book also on the day of his Examination I saw the Apperishtion of Jnᵒ proctor senʳ goe and affleet and most greviously tortor the bodyes of Mistris pope mary walcot⟨t⟩ Mircy lewes Abigail williams and Jno: Indian. and he and his wife and Sarah Cloys keept Elizabeth Hubburd speachless all the time of their Examination

                                            mark
                        Ann: ⟨⟩ putnams

[Hand 2] Ann Putman owned what is aboue written vpon Oath before & vnto yᵉ Grand inquest on yᵉ 30ᵗʰ Day of June 1692

[Reverse] [Hand 3] Ann puttnam agᵗ John procter.

Notes: An ink change beginning with "also on the day . . ." suggests that Putnam subsequently added this portion. However, the deposition was not used for trial purposes, perhaps because of multiple names of the accused. No indictment against Procter for afflicting Ann Putnam Jr. is extant, although her sworn testimony before the grand jury makes clear that one may have been drawn. ◊ Hand 1 = Thomas Putnam; Hand 2 = Andrew Elliot; Hand 3 = Thomas Newton

Essex County Court Archives, vol. 1, no. 53, Massachusetts Supreme Judicial Court, Judicial Archives, on deposit James Duncan Phillips Library, Peabody Essex Museum, Salem, MA.

60. Deposition of Thomas Putnam & John Putnam Jr. v. John Procter‡

See also: Aug. 5, 1692.

[Hand 1] The Deposistion of Thomas putnam agged 40 years and Jnᵒ putnam aged 36 years who testifieth and saith that we haueing ben conversant with diuers of the afflected parsons as mary walcott mercy lewes Abigail williams and Ann putnam and Elizabeth Hubburt and haue seen them most greviously tormented and often complaining of John proctor for hurting them also on the 11ᵗʰ of April 1692 being the day of John proctors Examination the affore named parsons ware much ~~af~~ afflected ⟨me⟩ dureing the time of his Examination: also seuerall times sence we haue seen the affore said parsons most dreadfully affle⟨ct⟩ed and complainig of John proctor for hurting them and we veryly ∧{beleue} that John proctor the prisoner att the barr has many times afflected and tormented the affore said parsons by acts of wicthcraft

                                    Thomas putnam
                                    Jon. Putnam
                        [Hand 2] Jurat in Curia

[Reverse] Thomas. Putman Jnᵒ Putman

Notes: Although in the same ink, the portion starting with the words "also on the 11th" is similar to additions Putnam made elsewhere in ink differing from what he used earlier in the manuscripts. ◊ Used at trial. ◊ Hand 1 = Thomas Putnam; Hand 2 = Stephen Sewall

Essex County Court Archives, vol. 1, no. 48, Massachusetts Supreme Judicial Court, Judicial Archives, on deposit James Duncan Phillips Library, Peabody Essex Museum, Salem, MA.

Continued from April 8, 1692: Council Record Pertaining to Sarah Cloyce, Martha Cory, Dorothy Good, Rebecca Nurse, Elizabeth Procter, & John Procter

2nd of 3 dates. See No. 47 on April 8, 1692

Tuesday, April 12, 1692

61. Statement of Samuel Parris Concerning Abigail Williams & Mary Walcott v. John Procter, Elizabeth Procter, Sarah Cloyce, Martha Cory, Rebecca Nurse, Sarah Good, & Dorothy Good†

[Hand 1] <u>1692</u> Apr. 4. <u>Abig: Williams</u> complained of Goodm: <u>Proctor</u> & cryed out w^t [1 word overstruck] are you come to, are you come to, you can pinch as well as your wife & more to that purpose

6. At night she complained of Goodm: Proctor again & beat upon her breast & cryed he pinc⟨ht⟩ her. [   ] The like I hear at Tho: Putmans house

12. Day. When the Marshall was sent up to enquire of John Proctor & the others & I was writing some what thereof as above I met with nothing but interruptions by reason of fits upon John Indian & Abigail, & Mary Walcot happening to come in just before, they one & another cryed out there is Goodm: Proctor very often. And Abigail said there is Goodm: Proctor in the Marshals lap, at the same time Mary Walcot was ~~sitt(i)ng~~ sitting by a knitting we askt her if she saw Goodm: ^{Proctor} (for Abigail was immediately seized with a fit) but she was ~~dea~~ deaf & dumb, yet still a knitting, then Mary recovered her self & confirmed what Abigail had said that Goodm: Proctor she saw in the Marshals lap Then John ⟨I⟩ cryed out to the Dog under the Table to come away for Goodm: Proctor was upon his back, then he cryed out of Goody Cloyse, O you old Witch & fell immediately into a violent fit that 3. men & the Marshall could not without exceeding difficulty hold him: In which fit Mary Walcot that was knitting & well composed said there was Goodm: Proctor & his wife & Goody Cloyse helping of him. But so great were the interruptions of John & Abigail by fits while we were observing these things to notify them, that we were fain to send them both away that I might have liberty to write {this}, without disturbance Mary Walcot abiding composed & knitting whilest I was writing & the two other sent away, yet by & by whilst I was writing Mary Walcot said there Goody Cloyse has pincht me now

<u>Note.</u> Mary Walcot never saw Proctor nor his wife till last night coming from the examination at Salem & then she saw Goody Proctor behind her brother Jonathan all the way from the widow Gidneys to Phillips where Jonathan made a little stay But this day & time I have been writing this she saw them many times.

April 18, 1692

Note. Just now as soon as I had made an ^{end} of reading this to the Marshall Mary W[Lost][= Walcott] immediately cryed O yonder is Good: Proctor & his wife & Goody Nurse & Goody Korey & G[Lost][= Goody] Cloyse & Goods Child & then said O Goodm: Proctor is going to choke me & immediately she: was choakt

[Hand 2] Munday 11ᵗʰ mᵒ [= month] ditto leuᵗ Nath: Ingersoll Declare⟨s⟩ yᵗ John Procter tould Joseph Pope yᵗ if hee hade John Indian in his Costody hee would soone beat yᵉ Diuell out of him: and so said to seuerall others

[Reverse] [Hand 3] Abigail Williams agᵗ John procter.
[Hand 4] Village papers concerning sundry persons vnder suspition of Witchcraft

Notes: Parris completed the document on April 12, but parts had been previously written, beginning with April 4. The date of April 11 at the end, written by George Herrick at a later date, signifies the day of the examination of the Procters. ◊ Hand 1 = Samuel Parris; Hand 2 = George Herrick; Hand 3 = Thomas Newton; Hand 4 = John Hathorne

Essex County Court Archives, vol. 1, no. 57, Massachusetts Supreme Judicial Court, Judicial Archives, on deposit James Duncan Phillips Library, Peabody Essex Museum, Salem, MA.

Continued from April 11, 1692: Council Record Pertaining to Sarah Cloyce, Martha Cory, Dorothy Good, Rebecca Nurse, Elizabeth Procter, & John Procter

3ʳᵈ of 3 dates. See No. 47 on April 8, 1692

Monday, April 18, 1692

62. Warrant for the Apprehension of Giles Cory, Mary Warren, Abigail Hobbs, & Bridget Bishop, with Summons for Witnesses, and Officer's Return

[Hand 1] Salem. Aprill the 18ᵗʰ 1692

There being Complaint this day made (Before vs) by Ezekiell Chevers and John Putnam Junᵉ, both of Salem Village Yeomen; in Behalfe of theire Majesties, for themselfes and also for theire Neighbours Against Giles Cory, and Mary Waren both of Salem ffarmes And Abigaile Hobs the daufter of Wᵐ Hobs of the Towne of Topsfeild ^{and Bridgett Bushop yᵉ wife of Edwᵈ Bishop of Salem Sawier} for high suspition of sundry acts of Witchcraft donne or Committed by them, vpon the Bodys of. Ann Putnam. Marcy lewis, and Abigˡ Williams and Mary Walcot & Eliz. Hubert of Salem Village
whereby great hurt and dammage hath benne donne to the Bodys of said persons aboue named. therefore craued Justice

You are therefore in theire Majesᵗˢ names hereby required to apprehend and bring before vs Giles Cory & Mary Waren of Salem ffarmes, and Abigail Hobs the daufter of Wᵐ Hobs of yᵉ Towne of Topsfeild ^{and Bridget Bushop yᵉ wife of Edwᵈ Bushop of Salem} To Morrow aboute Eight of the Clock in the forenoone, at yᵉ house of Lᵗ Nathaniell Ingersalls

in Salem Village in order to theire Examination Relateing to the premises aboues^d and here
of you are not to faile Dated Salem Aprill 18th 1692

<table>
<tr><td>To George Herrick Marshall
of the County of Essex }</td><td>John Hathorne

Jonathan. Corwin }</td><td>Assis^ts</td></tr>
</table>

You are likewise required to summons Margret Knight Lidya Nichols Elizabeth Nichols.
and Elizabeth Hubert Jonathan Putnam and Hephzibah ["i" written over "e"] Rea ^{& John
Hewe} all & everyone of them to appeare before vs at y^e aboues^d time & place to giue in w^t
evedence thay know Relateing {to} y^e aboues^d or like cases depending Salem Aprill 18th 1692

[Reverse] [Hand 2] Aprill 18th 1692
I haue taken y^e within named persons and brought them [Lost] [= to the] house of leu^t
Nath: Ingersoll according to y^e tenner of this warrant p^ɛ me Geo: Herrick Marshall of Essex

Aprill 18th = 1692
I haue sumoned the within named persons to apeare att y^e time and place within mentioned
to Give in whatt Euidence th⟨ey⟩ Know Relateing y^e premises p^ɛ me Geo: Herrick
                                                 Marshall of Essex

[Hand 3] Complaint Corey Hobs Warren &c^a

Notes: The name of Bridget Bishop, the first to be executed, was added to the warrant after its original composition. ◊
Hand 1 = John Hathorne; Hand 2 = George Herrick; Hand 3 = Stephen Sewall

*Essex County Court Archives, vol. 1, no. 112, Massachusetts Supreme Judicial Court, Judicial Archives, on deposit James Duncan
Phillips Library, Peabody Essex Museum, Salem, MA.*

Tuesday, April 19, 1692

63. Examination of Bridget Bishop, as Recorded by Ezekiel Cheever

[Hand 1] The examination of Bridget Bishop before the Worshipfull John Harthon and
Jonathan Curren esq^ɛs
Bridget Bishop being now comeing in to be examined relating to her accusation of suspicon
of sundry acts of witchcrafts the afflicted persons are now dreadfully aff⟨l⟩icted by her as they
doe say (m^r Harthon) Bishop what doe you say you here stand charged with sundry acts of
witchcraft by you done or commited upon the bodyes of mercy Lews and An Putnum and
others (B⟨u⟩shop) I am innocent I know nothing of it I have done no witchcraft (m^r Har)
Looke upon this woman and see if this be the woman that you have seen hurting {you}
mercy Lewes and An Putnum and others doe doe now charge her to her face with hurting of
them Mr Harthon) what doe you say now you see they charge you to your face (Bish) I never
did hurt them in my life I did never see these persons before I am as innocent as the child
unborn (m^r Harth) is not your coate cut (Bish) answers no but her garment being Looked
upon they find ⟨l⟩ it cut or toren two wayes Johnathan walcoa⟨t⟩te saith that the sword that

April 19, 1692

he strucke ^{at} gooode Bishop ^{with} was not naked but was within the ~~scab~~ scabberd so that ^{the} rent may very probablie be the very same that mary walcoate ~~tell~~ did tell that shee had in her coate by Jonathans stricking at her apperance

The afflicted persons charge her, with having ["i" written over "a"] hurt them many wayes and by tempting them to sine to the devils Booke at which charge shee seemed to be very angrie and shaking her head at them saying it was false they are all greatly tormented (as I conceive) by the shaking of her head (m^r Har) good Bishop what contract have you made with the devill (Bish). I have made no contract with the devill I never saw him in my ⟨li⟩fe.

An Putnum sayeth that shee calls the devill her God

[Lost] [= (M^r) Har) what say you to all this that you are ⟨?⟩ charged with can you not find in your [Lost]art [= heart] to tell the truth (Bish) I doe tell the truth I never hurt these persons in [Lost]⟨y⟩ [= my] life I never saw them before. (mercy Lewes) oh goode Bishop did you not come to our house the Last night and did you not tell me that your master made you tell more then you were willing to tell (m^r Har) tell us the truth in this matter how comes these persons to be thus tormented and to charge you with doing (Bish) I am not come here to say I am a witch to take away my life (m^r H) who is it that doth it if you doe not they say it is your likenes that comes and torments them and tempts them to write in the booke what Booke is that you tempt them with. (Bish) ⟨L⟩ I know nothing of it I am innocent. (m^r Harth) doe you not see how they are tormented you are acting witchcraft before us what doe you say to this why have you not an heart to confese the truth (Bs⟨h⟩) I am innocent I know nothing of it I am no witch I know not what a witch is. (m^r H) have you not given consent that some evill spirit should doe this in your likenes. (B) no I am innocent of being a witch I know no man woman or child here (Marshal⟨l⟩ Herrik) how came you into my bedchamber one morning then and asked me whither I had any curtains to sell shee is by some of the afflicted persons charged with murder (m^r Harth) what doe you say to these murders you are charged with (B) I am innocent I know nothing ~~about~~ of it now shee lifts up her eyes and they are greatly tormented ~~again~~ (m^r Har) what doe you say to these things here horrible acts of witch craft (Bish) ["(" written over ")"] I know nothing of it I doe not know whither be any witches or no (m^r Har) no have you not heard that some have confessed. (Bish) no I did not. two men told her to her face that they had told her here shee is taken in a plain lie now shee is going away they are dreadfully afflicted 5 afflicted persons doe charge this woman to be the very ~~w~~ ⟨wo⟩man that hurts them

[Lost] [*Woodward* = This] is a true account of what I have taken down at her examination according to best [Lost]derstanding [= understanding] and observation I have also in her examination taken notice that all her actions [Lost]e [= have] great influence upon the afflicted persons and that have ben tortered by her

Ezekie⟨l⟩ Cheev⟨er⟩

[Reverse] Examinac̄on ag^t B B[Lost] [= Bishop]
Bishop

Notes: Differences between Cheever's and Parris's version exemplify the subjectivity of examination recordings. Bridget Bishop was probably the fourth and last person examined that day. She immediately followed Mary Warren, who, like Abigail Hobbs, had confessed. Giles Cory did not. For consistency purposes, the examinations of April 19 are printed here alphabetically and not in the order in which they occurred. ◊ Hand 1 = Ezekiel Cheever

Essex County Court Archives, vol. 1, no. 137, Massachusetts Supreme Judicial Court, Judicial Archives, on deposit James Duncan Phillips Library, Peabody Essex Museum, Salem, MA.

64. Examination of Bridget Bishop, as Recorded by Samuel Parris   April 19, 1692

[Hand 1] 5   The Examination of Bridget
                              Byshop at Salem village
             19. ["9" written over "6"] Apr. 1692 ["2" written over "3"]
                     By John Hauthorn & Jonath: Corwin Esq⁵ˢ

As soon as she came near all fell into fits

Bridget Byshop, You are now brought before Authority to give acc° of what witchcrafts you are conversant in

I take all this people (turning her head & eyes about) to witness that I am clear.

Hath this woman hurt you speaking to yᵉ afflicted.

A(?)g Hubb(?)d ^{Eliz: Hubbard}, Ann Putman, Abigail Williams, & Mercy Lewes affirmed she had hurt them.

You are here accused by 4. or .5. for hurting them, what do you say to it?

I never saw these persons before; nor I never was in this place before.

Mary Walcot sais that her brother Jonathan stroke her appearance & she saw that ha he had tore her coat in striking, & she heard it tare.

Upon sea some search in the Court, a rent that seems to answere what was alledged was found.

They say you bewitcht your first husband to death.

If it please your worship I know nothing of it.

She shake her head & the afflicted were tortured.

The like again upon the motion of her head.

Sam: Braybrook affirmed that she told him to day that she had been accounted a Witch these .10. years, but she was no Witch, the Devil cannot hurt her.

I am no Witch.

Why if you have not wrote in the book, yet tell me how far you have gone? Have you not to do with familiar Spirits?

I have no familiarity with the Devil.

How is it then, that your appearance doth hurt these?

I am innocent.

Why you seem to act Witchcraft before us, by the motion of your body, which has in ^{seems to have influence} fluence upon the afflicted.

I know nothing of it. I am innocent to a Witch. I know not what a Witch is.

How do you know then that you are not a witch? & yet know not what a Witch is?

I do not understand know what you say.

How can you know, you are no Witch, & yet not know what a Witch is:

I am clear: if I were any such person you should know it.

You may threaten, but you can do no more than you are permitted.

I am innocent of a Witch.

What do you say of those murders you are charged with?

I hope, I am not guilty of Murder.

Then she turned up her eyes, & they the eyes of the afflicted were turned up

It may be you do not know, that any have confessed to day, who have been examined before you, that they are Witches.

No, I know nothing of it.

John Hutchinson & John Hewes in open Court affirmed that they had told her

April 19, 1692   Why look you, you are taken now in a flat lye.
                        I did not hear them.

                        Note Sam: Gold saith that after this Examination he askᵗ sᵈ Bridget Byshop if she were not
                        troubled to s⟨ee⟩ the afflicted persons so tormented, said Byshop answered no, she was not
                        troubled for them: Then he askᵗ her whither she thought they were bewitcht, she said she
                        could not tell what to think ab⟨ou⟩t them. Will Good, & John Buxton junᵉ was by, & he
                        supposeth they hear⟨d⟩ her also.

                        [Hand 2] Salem Village Aprill the .19ᵗʰ 1692 mʳ Samˡ Parris being desired to take into
                        Wrighting the Examination of Bridget Bishop, hath deliuered it as aforesaid And vpon
                        heareing yᵉ same, and seeing what wee did then see, togather wit[Lost] [= with] the Charge
                        of the afflicted persons th[Lost] [= then] present; Wee Committed sᵈ Bridg[Lost]
                        [= Bridget] Olliuer –
                             John Hathorne

                        [Reverse] [Hand 1] (4) The Examo̅c̅o̅n̅ of Bridget Byshop 19. Apr 1692

Notes: The note on Samuel Gold (Gould) may have been written after April 19. ◊ Hand 1 = Samuel Parris; Hand 2 =
John Hathorne

*Essex County Court Archives, vol. 1, no. 125, Massachusetts Supreme Judicial Court, Judicial Archives, on deposit James Duncan
Phillips Library, Peabody Essex Museum, Salem, MA.*

65. Examination of Giles Cory

The examination of Giles Cory, at a Court at Salem Village, held by John Hathorn and Jona.
Corwin, Esqrs. April 19, 1692.

Giles Cory, you are brought before authority upon high suspicion of sundry acts of
witchcraft; now tell us the truth in this matter.
I hope through the goodness of God I shall, for that matter I never had no hand in, in my life.
Which of you have seen this man hurt you?
Mary Wolcott, Mercy Lewis, Ann Putman, jr. and Abigail Williams affirmed he had hurt
them.
Hath he hurt you too? speaking to Elizabeth Hubbard.
She going to answer was prevented by a fit.
Benjamin Gold, hath he hurt you?
I have seen him several times, and been hurt after it, but cannot affirm that it was he.
Hath he brought the book to any of you?
Mary Wolcott and Abigail Williams and others affirmed that he brought the book to them.
Giles Cory, they accuse you, or your appearance, of hurting them, and bringing the book to
them.
What do you say? Why do you hurt them? Tell us the truth.
I never did hurt them.
It is your appearance hurts them, they charge you; tell us what you have done.

I have done nothing to damage them.

Have you never entered into contract with the devil?

I never did.

What temptations have you had?

I never had temptations in my life.

What, have you done it without temptations?

What was the reason (said goodwife Bibber) that you were frighted in the cow-house? and then the questionist was suddenly seized with a violent fit.

Samuel Braybrook, goodman Bibber, and his daughter, testified that he had told them this morning that he was frighted in the cow-house.

Cory denied it.

This was not your appearancce but your person, and you told them so this morning: why do you deny it?

What did you see in the cow-house?

I never saw nothing but my cattle.

Divers witnessed that he told them he was frighted.

Well, what do you say to these witnesses? What was it frighted you?

I do not know that ever I spoke the word in my life.

Tell the truth, what was it frighted you?

I do not know any thing that frighted me.

All the afflicted were seized now with fits, and troubled with pinches. Then the court ordered his hands to be tied.

What, is it not enough to act witchcraft at other times, but must you do it now in the face of authority?

I am a poor creature, and can not help it.

Upon the motion of his head again, they had their heads and necks afflicted.

Why do you tell such wicked lies against witnesses, that heard you speak after this manner, this very morning?

I never saw any thing but a black hog.

You said that you were stopt once in prayer; what stopt you?

I cannot tell; my wife came towards me and found fault with me for saying living to God and dying to sin.

What was it frighted you in the barn?

I know nothing frighted me there.

Why here are three witnesses that heard you say so to-day.

I do not remember it.

Thomas Gold testified that he heard him say, that he knew enough against his wife, that would do her business.

What was that you knew against your wife?

Why that of living to God, and dying to sin.

The Marshal and Bibber's daughter confirmed the same, that he said he could say that that would do his wife's business.

I have said what I can say to that.

What was that about your ox?

I thought he was hipt.

What ointment was that your wife had when she was seized? You said it was ointment she made by major Gidney's direction.

April 19, 1692

He denied it, and said she had it of goody Bibber, or from her direction.

Goody Bibber said it is not like that ointment.

You said you knew, upon your own knowledgment, that she had it of major Gidney.

He denied it.

Did not you say, when you went to the ferry with your wife, you would not go over to Boston now, for you should come yourself the next week?

I would not go over, because I had not money.

The Marshal testified he said as before.

One of his hands was let go, and several were afflicted.

He held his head on one side, and then the heads of several of the afflicted were held on one side. He drew in his cheeks, and the cheeks of some of the afflicted were suckt in.

John Bibber and his wife gave in testimony concerning some temptations he had to make away with himself.

How doth this agree with what you said, that you had no temptations?

I meant temptations to witchcraft.

If you can give way to self murther, that will make way to temptation to witchcraft.

Note. There was witness by several, that he said he would make away with himself, and charge his death upon his son.

Goddy Bibber testified that the said Cory called said Bibber's husband, damn'd, devilish rogue.

Other vile expressions testified in open court by several others.

Salem Village, April 19, 1692.

Mr. Samuel Parris being desired to take in writing the examination of Giles Cory, delivered it in; and upon hearing the same, and seeing what we did see at the time of his examination, together with the charge of the afflicted persons against him, we committed him to their majesties' goal.

John Hathorn

Notes: As indicated in the document, Samuel Parris recorded the examination. Giles Cory died on September 19 by being pressed to death after declining to stand trial. Although no other person in Massachusetts Bay met that fate, the procedure had been used in Europe. It is not clear whether Cory had the weights that killed him placed on him only on September 19, or whether he endured it for a few days before dying. It is also not clear as to whether he could have at any point saved himself by agreeing to stand trial once the procedure had begun, although in English law the punishment would clearly be an execution. ◊ "hipt": 'having the hip injured or dislocated' (*OED* s.v. *hipped, hipt* a[1], 3). "knowledgement": 'knowledge, cognizance' (*OED* s.v. *knowledgement* 2).

Robert Calef. Salem Witchcraft (Salem: Cushing and Appleton, 1823), pp. 310–12.

66. Deposition of Benjamin Gould v. Giles Cory, Martha Cory, & John Procter‡

See also: Sept. 9, 1692.

[Hand 1] ⟨₂⟩ the deposistion of baniamen gould aged about 25 yeares ho testifieth and saith one the 6 day of april 1692 giles Cory and his wife Came to my bead side and ~~when~~ locked apon me sum time and then went away. and emediately I had two penches. apon my side.

allso another time I saw. giles Cory and John proctir. and I had then shuch a paine in one of
my. feet that I Cold not ware my. shue for 2: or .3. days.

[Hand 2] & I doe beleiue in my:

April 19, 1692

[Hand 1] ~~Samuel.~~ [Hand 2] {Ben:} [Hand 1] gould
[Hand 2] Jurat

Notes: The "Jurat" appears to identify this as a deposition sworn to at the grand jury against Giles Cory on September 9, although it may have been prepared for the trial of Cory that never happened. Martha Cory's case had been heard on August 4, and Procter had been executed on August 19. The crossed out "Samuel" had been written by Edward Putnam with the incorrect partial "signature" of "Samuel" corrected to "Ben" by Stephen Sewall. Whose comment Sewall is recording when he writes "I doe beleiue in my:" is unclear. It evokes Thomas Putnam, but there is no indication of his presence. The possibility that this document is part of Gould's testimony on April 11 cannot be ruled out. ◊ Hand 1 = Edward Putnam; Hand 2 = Stephen Sewall

Essex County Court Archives, vol. 2, no. 88, Massachusetts Supreme Judicial Court, Judicial Archives, on deposit James Duncan Phillips Library, Peabody Essex Museum, Salem, MA.

67. Examination of Abigail Hobbs

See also: Sept. 9, 1692.

[Hand 1] The Examination of Abigail Hobbs
at Salem Village .19. Apr. <u>1692</u>
by John Hauthorn & Jonath: Corwin Esq^{Es} & Assistants

Abig: Hobbs, You are brought before Authority to answere to sundry acts of Witchcrafft committed by you against & upon the bodies of many, of which severall persons now accuse you. What say you? Are you guilty, or not? Speak the truth

I will speak the truth, I have seen sights, & been scared: I have been very wicked, I hope I shall be better: ⟨&⟩ God will keep me.

What sights did you see?

I have seen dogs & many creatures

What dogs do you mean, ordinary dogs?

I mean the Devil.

How often, many times?

But once.

Tell the truth.

I do tell no lye.

What appearance was he in then

Like a man.

Where was it.

It was at the Eastward at Casko-bay.

Where in the house, or in the woods?

In the woods.

In the night or in the day?

In the day.

How long agoe?

About 3. or .4. years agoe?

What did he say to you.

April 19, 1692

He said he would give me fine things if I did what he would have me.

What would he have you do?

Why he would have me be a Witch.

Would he have you make a Covenant wth him?

Yes.

And did you make a Covenant with him?

Yes, I did, but I hope God will forgive me.

The Lord give you Repentance

You say you saw dogs, & many sorts of creatures

I saw them at that time.

But have you not seen them at other times too?

Yes.

Where?

At our house.

What ~~who~~ were they like?

Like a Cat.

What would the Cat have you do?

She had a book, & would have me put my hand to it.

And did you?

No, I did not.

Well, tell the truth, did you at any other time?

Yes I did that time at the Eastward.

What other Creatures did you see?

I saw things like men.

What did they say to you?

Why they said I had better put my hand to the Book.

You did put your hand to the book you say.

Yes, one time.

What would they have you put your hand to their book too?

Yes.

And what would they have you do then, would they have you worship them?

They would have me make a bargain for so long, & do what they would have me do.

For how long?

Not for above 2. or .3. years.

How long did they agree with you for?

But for (2) two years.

And what would they then do for you?

They would give me fine cloths.

And did they?

No.

When you set your hand the last time to book, how long was that for?

It was for (4) four years.

How long is that agoe?

It is almost 4. yeares. The book was brought to me to set my hand to it for .4. years, but I never put my hand but that once at Eastward.

Are you not bid to hurt folks?

Yes.

Who are you bid to hurt?

Mercy Lewes, & Ann Putman.

What did you do to them, when you hurt them?

I pincht them.

How did you pinch them, do you goe in your own person to them.

No.

Doth the Devil go for you?

Yes.

And what doth he take your Spirit with him?

No: I am as well as at other times: but the Devil has my consent, & goes & hurts them.

Who hurt your mothe⟨r⟩ last Lords day, was it not you?

No.

Who was it?

I heard her say it was Goody Wilds at Topsfield.

Have you been in Company with Goody Wilds at any time?

No, I never saw her.

Well, who are your companions?

Why I have seen Sarah Good once.

How many did you see?

I saw but two.

Did you know Sarah Good was a Witch, when you saw her?

Yes.

How did you know it?

The Devil told me.

Who was the other you saw?

I do not remember her name.

Did you go & do hurt with Sarah Good?

No she would have me set my hand to her book also.

What mark did you make in the Devils book ⟨?⟩ when you set your hand to it?

I made a mark.

What mark?

Have you not been at other great meetings?

No.

Did you not hear of great hurt done here in the village?

Yes.

And were you never with them?

No I was never with them.

But you know your shape appeared and hurt the people here.

Yes.

How did you know?

The Devil told me, if I gave consent, he would do it in my shape.

How long agoe?

About a fortnight agoe.

What shape did the Devil appear in then?

Like a black man with an hat.
Do not some creatures suck your body?
No.
Where do they come, to what parts, when they come to your body?
They do not come to my body; they come only in sight.
Do they speak to you?
Yes.
How do they speak to you?
As other folks.
What do they speak to you, as other folks?
Yes, almost.

Then other questions were propounded to her but she was taken DEAF: And Mary Walcot, Mercy Lewes, Betty Hubbard, Abig: Williams, & Ann Putman jun$^\varepsilon$ said they saw Sarah Good, & Sarah Osburn run their fingers into the examinants ears: by & by she this examinant was blind with her eyes quite open.
A little after, she spake, & said, Sarah Good saith I shall not speak. And so the Court ordered. her being seized with dumbness to be taken away

Note. The afflicted. i.e. the bewitched persons were none of them tormented during the whole examination of this accused & confessing person Abigail Hobbs

Note. After this examination Mercy Lewes, Abigail Williams, & Ann Putman three of the sufferers said openly in Court, they were very sorry for the condition this poor Abig: Hobbs was in: which compassion they expressed over & over again.

[Hand 2] Salem Village Aprill the 19th 1692.

Mr Samuell Parris being desired to take in wrighting the Examination of Abigail hobs hath deliuered it as ~~followeth~~ {aforesaid}

Vpon heareing the afores^d and seing what wee then did see, togather with the Charge of the persons then present, Wee Committed said Abigail Hob⟨s⟩ to theire Majesties Goale.

John Hathorne ⎫
⎬ Assis^{ts}
Jonathan. Corwin ⎭

[Hand 3] this confesion & Examination is y^e ⎫
Truth as witnes my hand ⎬   The marke of
9 Sep^t 1692 ⎭   Abigall † Hobs.

Abigall Hobs Signed & owned this Confesion & Examination before me
9: Sep^t 1692   John Higginson Justice peace

[Hand 1] (1) The Examon of Abigail Hobbs 19. Apr. 1692

Notes: Abigail Hobbs "owned" this on September 9. As a confessed witch, she was not permitted to swear it. Clear evidence of her appearance before the grand jury on September 10 exists. In September, Higginson took a number of sworn statements from confessors, all of them apparently in preparation for grand jury presentation. Hobbs's confession along with Mary Warren's on April 19 are the first confessions since Tituba's. ◊ Hand 1 = Samuel Parris; Hand 2 = John Hathorne; Hand 3 = John Higginson Jr.

UNCAT MS, Miscellaneous Photostats (1692). Positive Photostat, Massachusetts Historical Society. Boston, MA.

68. Deposition of Priscilla Chub v. Abigail Hobbs†

The deposistion of prisceller chub aged about 31: years, this deponent testifieth and saith that sum time the last winter I was discourising with Abigaill Hobbs about her wicked cariges and disobedience to hir father and Mother and she tould me she did not care what any body said to hir for she had seen the divell and had made a covenant or bargain with him.

Notes: *SWP* has this in Essex County Court Archives, Vol. 1, 51, but it is not there and has not been located. The document printed here is from Woodward, which is identical with WPA. Except for very slight modernization, it is also identical with *SWP*. Although the manuscript could not be examined, internal evidence makes the recorder almost certainly Thomas Putnam, partly in view of his characteristic spelling of "deposistion." A corrected version of Woodward on this document was made, probably in the late 1860s, by William P. Upham, who also identified the recorder as Putnam. He saw a second hand of Jonathan Corwin. Upham also noted the spelling of "Hobbs" as "Hoobs." Upham's annotations are located at the Danvers Archival Center, Woodward, Vol. I, pp. 177–178.

W. Elliot Woodward, Records of Salem Witchcraft, Copied from ther Original Documents., 2 vols. (Privately printed, Roxbury, MA: 1864) Vol. 1, pp. 177–78.

69. Deposition of Elizabeth Hubbard v. Abigail Hobbs†

See also: Sept. 10, 1692.

[Hand 1] The deposistion of Eliz: Hubburd who testifieth and saith that I was afflected and tormented by Abigail Hoobs: se⟨ia⟩rall times before hir Examination allso on the day of hir Examination she did most greviously torment me also I saw Abigail Hoobs or hir Aperance most greviouly afflet and torment mercy lewes mary walcott and Ann putnam: on the: 19ᵗʰ April 1692 being the day of hir Examination but as soon as she began to confess she lefft ofe ~~confe~~ afflecting of us: and I beleue in my heart yᵗ Abigail Hoobs ⟨i⟩s [Hand 2] ^{was} [Hand 1] a wicth and that she has often afflted both me and the aboue said parsons by acts of wicthcra⟨ft⟩

[Hand 3] Eliz Hubbard ownd: the truth of yᵉ above writen evidence: to yᵉ Jury of Ingquesᵗ upon oath Septᵉ :10: 1692

[Reverse] [Hand 2] eliza: hubard

Notes: Hand 1 = Thomas Putnam; Hand 3 = Simon Willard

Essex County Court Archives, vol. 1, no. 161, Massachusetts Supreme Judicial Court, Judicial Archives, on deposit James Duncan Phillips Library, Peabody Essex Museum, Salem, MA.

April 19, 1692

70. Deposition of Margaret Knight v. Abigail Hobbs†

[Hand 1] the deposition of margaritt Knight aged about 18 years who testifieth and saith that about a year agoe Abigail Hoobs and hir mothor ware att my fathers house: and Abigail Hoobs said to me Mragaritt are you baptized: and I said yes: then said she my mother is not baptized but said I will ~~pa~~ baptizse ["se" written over "ed"] hir and Immediatly took watter and sprinckeled in hir Mothors face and said she did say baptized hir in the name of the ffather Son and Holy Ghost

[Reverse] [Hand 2] Ma. Knight

Notes: Hand 1 = Thomas Putnam

Essex County Court Archives, vol. 1, no. 158, Massachusetts Supreme Judicial Court, Judicial Archives, on deposit James Duncan Phillips Library, Peabody Essex Museum, Salem, MA.

71. Deposition of Mercy Lewis v. Abigail Hobbs†

[Hand 1] The deposistion of mircy lewes ^{agged about 19 years} who testifieth that about the 17th of April 1692 I saw the Apperishtion of Abigail Hoobs the daughter of william Hoobs com and afflect me by pinching and almost choaking me urging me to writ in hir book and so she continewed hurting of me by times tell the 19th of april: being the day of hir examination but as soon as she began to confess she left ofe hurting me

[Reverse] [Hand 2] Mercy. Lewis against Abigall. Hobbs.
[Hand 1] Abigail Hoobs

Notes: This deposition and those by Ann Putnam Jr. (see No. 73) and Mary Walcott (see No. 74) were not used at the grand jury, unlike the deposition of Elizabeth Hubbard (see No. 69). The reason why only one of the regular "afflicted" from this group was used is not clear. ◊ Hand 1 = Thomas Putnam; Hand 2 = Jonathan Corwin

Essex County Court Archives, vol. 1, no. 160, Massachusetts Supreme Judicial Court, Judicial Archives, on deposit James Duncan Phillips Library, Peabody Essex Museum, Salem, MA.

72. Testimony of Lydia Nichols & Elizabeth Nichols v. Abigail Hobbs†

[Hand 1] lidia Nickals aged about .17. years testifieth & saith that about a yeare & halfe agoe I asked ~~her~~ {abigaill hobs} how she darst lie out anights in yᵉ wods alone she told me she was not afraid of any thing for she told me she had sold her selfe ~~to yᵉ old boy~~ boddy & soull to yᵉ old boy

and sins this about a fortnight agoe yᵉ said abigaill hobs & her mother came to our hous my father & mother being not at home she begane to be rude & to behaue her selfe unseemly I told her I wondred she was not ashamed she bide me hold my tonge or else she would rays all the folks thereabouts & bid me look there was old nick or else old cratten sate ouer yᵉ bedshed [= bed-head] then her mother told her she little thought to a [= have] bin the

mother of such a dafter

Elisabeth nickals aged about .12: years testifieth y^e same she said at our hous about a fortnigh agoe

[Reverse] [Hand 2?] These may sertify whome it may concerne

[Hand 3] Lydia & Elizabeth Nickolls agst Abig^{ll} Hobbs

Notes: "old cratten": 'the Devil.' The word "cratten" is not attested in either *OED* or *MED*. However, both *OED* and *MED* record a word *crate* (mistake for *trate* or *trot*) meaning 'hag, old woman' or 'old man' (*MED* s.v. *crate* n.; *OED* s.v. *crate* and *trot* n^2). Henry Alexander, "The Language of the Salem Witchcraft Trials," *American Speech* 3 (1928): 398 relates the word to *craven* and *caitiff*, which seems less likely. "old nick": 'the Devil' (*OED* s.v. *Old Nick*). ◊ Hand 3 = Jonathan Corwin

Essex County Court Archives, vol. 1, no. 157, Massachusetts Supreme Judicial Court, Judicial Archives, on deposit James Duncan Phillips Library, Peabody Essex Museum, Salem, MA.

73. Deposition of Ann Putnam Jr. v. Abigail Hobbs†

[Hand 1] The Deposistion of Ann putnam who testifieth and saith that about the 13th of April 1692 I saw the Apperishtion of Abigail Hoobs the daughter of william Hoobs com and afflect me by biting pinching and almost choa⟨k⟩ing me urging me to writ in hir book and so she continewed by times hur⟨t⟩ing me tell the 19th of April being the day of hir examination but as soon as she began to confess she left ofe hurting me

[Reverse] [Hand 2] Ann. puttnam. agst Abigall. Hobbs.

Notes: Hand 1 = Thomas Putnam; Hand 2 = Jonathan Corwin

Essex County Court Archives, vol. 1, no. 162, Massachusetts Supreme Judicial Court, Judicial Archives, on deposit James Duncan Phillips Library, Peabody Essex Museum, Salem, MA.

74. Deposition of Mary Walcott v. Abigail Hobbs†

[Hand 1] The deposistion of Mary walcott aged about 17 years who testifieth and saith that about the 14th April 1692 I saw the Apperishtion of Abigail Hoobs the daughter of william Hoobs com and afflect me by pinching and allmost choaking me urging me to writ in hir book and so she continewed to afflect me by times tell the day of hir Examination being the 19th April but as soon as she began to confess she left ofe afflecting me

[Reverse] [Hand 2] Mary Walcott agst Abig[Lost] [= Abigail] Hobbs

Notes: Hand 1 = Thomas Putnam; Hand 2 = Jonathan Corwin

Essex County Court Archives, vol. 1, no. 159, Massachusetts Supreme Judicial Court, Judicial Archives, on deposit James Duncan Phillips Library, Peabody Essex Museum, Salem, MA.

75. Examination of Mary Warren

[Hand 1] The Examination of Mary Warren
At a Court held at Salem Village by
John Hauthorne
Jonath: Corwin
} Esq^{es}

{//} As soon as she was coming towards the Bar the afflicted fell into fits.

Mary Warren, You stand here charged with sundry acts of Witchcraft, what do you say for your self, are you guilty, or not?

    I am innocent.

Hath she hurt you (speaking to the sufferers) Some were Dumb. Betty Hubbard testifyed ags^t her, & then said Hubbard f⟨e⟩ll into a violent fit.

You were a little while agoe an Afflicted person, now you are an Afflicter: How comes this to pass?

I looke up to God, & take it to be a great Mercy of God.

What do you take it to be a great mercy to afflict others?

Betty Hubbard testifyed that a little after this Mary was well, she the said Mary, said that the afflicted persons did but dissemble.

{//} Now they were all but John Indian grievously afflicted, & Mrs Pope also, who was not afflicted before hitherto this day: & after a few moments John Indian fell into a violent fit also.

Well here was one just now that was a Tormentor in her apparition, & she owns that she had made a league with the Devil.

{//} Now Mary Warren fell into a fit, & some of the afflicted cryed out that she was going to confess, but Goody Korey, & Proctor, & his wife came in, in their apparition, & struck her down, & said she should tell nothing.

Mary Warren continued a good space in a fit, ~~the~~ ^{that} she did neither see, nor hear, nor speak.

Afterwards she started up, & said I will speak & cryed out, Oh! I am sorry for it, I am sorry for it, & wringed her hands, & fell a little while into a fit again: & then came to speak, but immediately her Teeth were set, & then she fell into a violent fit, & cryed out, Oh Lord help me, Oh good Lord save me!

And then afterwards cryed again, I will tell, I will tell, & then fell into a dead fit againe.

And afterwards cryed, I will tell, they did, they did, they did, & then fell into a violent fit again.

After a little recovery she cryed I will tell, I will tell, they brought me me to it; & then fell into a fit again: which fits continuing, she was ordered to be had out, & the next to be brought in, viz: Bridget Byshop

Some time afterwards she was called in again, but immediately taken with fits, for a while.

Have you signed the Devils book?

No.

Have you not toucht it?

No.

Then she fell into fits againe, & was sent forth for air.

After a considerable space of time she was brought in again, but could [Lost] [= not] give account of things, by reason of fits, & so sent forth.

Mary Warren called in, afterwards in private, before Magistrates & Ministers.   April 19, 1692
She said, I shall not speak a word: but I will, ~~speak~~ I will speak satan – she saith she will kill
me.
Oh! she saith, she owes me a spite, & will claw me off
Avoid Satan, for the name of God avoid.
And then fell into fits again: & cryed will ye; I will prevent ye, in the Name of God
Tell us, how far have you yeilded?
A fit interrupts her again.
What did they say you should do, & you should be well?
Then her lips were bit so that she could not speak. so she was sent away

Note That not one of the sufferers was afflicted during her examination after once she began
to confess, thô they were tormented before.

[Hand 2] Salem Village Aprill 19th 1692.

Mr Samuell Parris being desired to take in wrighting the Examination of Mary Warren hath
deliuered it as aforesaid And vpon heareing the same and seeing what wee did then see,
togather with ye Charge of the afflicted persons then present. Wee Committed said Mary
Warren

John Hathorne }
                      } Assists
Jonathan. Corwin }

[Reverse] [Hand 1] (3) The examcon of Mary Warren
19. Apr. 1692

Notes: Mary Warren would soon capitulate and join the accusers, eliminating the last major challenge to their credibility.
◊ Hand 1 = Samuel Parris; Hand 2 = John Hathorne

Essex County Court Archives, vol. 1, no. 111, Massachusetts Supreme Judicial Court, Judicial Archives, on deposit James Duncan Phillips Library, Peabody Essex Museum, Salem, MA.

76. Statement of Elizabeth Hubbard v. Mary Warren & Bridget Bishop‡

[Hand 1] mary waring brought the book to elisibath houbard and would haue hur sat hur
hand to the book which she brought unto hur and she said i wont i wont i wont {⟨?⟩}a{⟨?⟩} if
you sat your hand to the book you shall be well for i did so and i am well and i told hir i
would not then she told me i should neuer be well {then} ["n" written over "i"] told hur i
would not if i am neuer well o you wicked wich mary waring why will you du so

now whilest i was righting [= writing] thes lins thes lins thar came in mary waring and
anothr woman with hur whch woman mary waring shap {said} ws [= was] goodey oleuer
and that woman came in hur sheft

[Reverse] [Hand 2] Elizab. Hubbard agst Mary. Warren

April 20, 1692   Notes: At some point this document, originally on one piece of paper, was separated into two pieces, with the second piece continuing in the same hand after a space with "now whilest i was righting." The text is here restored as one record. ◊ Hand 2 = Jonathan Corwin

Essex County Court Archives, vol. 1, nos. 117 & 152, Massachusetts Supreme Judicial Court, Judicial Archives, on deposit James Duncan Phillips Library, Peabody Essex Museum, Salem, MA.

Wednesday, April 20, 1692

77. Examinations of Abigail Hobbs in Prison

See also: May 12, 1692.

[Hand 1] Abigail Hobbs's Examination 20. Apr. 1692 in Salem Prison.
This Examinant declares that Judah White, a Jersey maid that Lived with Joseph Ingᵉson at Cascoe, but now lives at Boston, with whome this Examinant was very wel formerly acquainted, came to her yesterday in apparition, ~~as she was g~~ together with Sarah Good, as this Examinant was goeing to Examination, and advised her to fly, and not to goe to be Examined, she told them that she would goe; They charged her if she did goe to Examination not to Confes anything. she said she would Confes all that she knew; They told her also Goody Osburn was a witch. This Judah White came to her in fine Cloaths, in a sad coloured silk⟨?⟩ Mantel, with a Top knot and an hood – she Confesseth further that the Devil in the shape of a Man came to her and would have her to afflict Ann Putnam, Mercy Lewis, and Abigail Williams, and brought their images with him in wood like them, and gave her thorns, and bid her prick them into those images, which she did accordingly into Each of them one. and then the Devil told her they were afflicted, which accordingly they were and Cryed out they were hurt by Abigail Hobbs. she Confesseth, she was at the great Meeting in Mᵉ Parris's Pasture when they administred the sacramᵗᵗ, and did Eat of the Red Bread and drink of the Red wine att the same Time.

Abigail Hobbs Examination att Salem Prison May. 12. 1692
Q. Did Mᵉ Burroughs bring you any of the poppets of his wives to stick pinns into? ⟨A⟩ An: I do not Remember that he did. Q. Did he of any of his Children, or of the Eastward souldrᵉˢ? A. No. Q. Have you known of any that have been kill'd by Witchcraft. A. No. No=Body. Q. How came you to speak of mᵉ Burrougs's Wifes yesterday? A. I dont know. Q. Is that true about Davis's son of Cascoe? and of those of yᵉ Village? A. yes it is true. Q. what service did he put you upon? and who are they you afflicted? A. I cannot tel who, neither do I know whether they dyed. Q. were they strangers to you, that Burrougs would have you afflict? A. Yes. {B} Q. and were they afflicted accordingly? A. Yes. Q. cant you name some of them? A. No I cannot Remember them. Q. where did they Live? A. att the Eastward. Q: Have any Vessells been cast away by you? A. I do not know. Q. Have you Conse⟨n⟩ted to the Afflicting any Other besides those of the Village? A. Yes. Q. who were they? A. I cannot tell, But it was of such who lived att the fort side of the River about half a mile from the fort, toward Capt. Bracketts. Q: what was the hurt you did to them by Consent? A. I dont know. Q. was the⟨re⟩ any thing brought to y⟨o⟩[Lost] [= you] ⟨li⟩ke them? A. yes. ~~Q⟨did⟩~~ Q wh⟨a⟩t did you stick into the⟨m⟩? A. ⟨Thorns. Q.⟩ [Lost]

[*Woodward* = did some] ⟨of th⟩em d⟨y⟩? A Yes. [Lost] [*Woodward* = one] of them was Mary [Lost] [*Woodward* = Laurence that dyed. Q. Wher Q. where] did you stick the thorns? A. I do not ⟨k⟩now Q. was i⟨t⟩ about ⟨the middle of her⟩ [Lost] [*Woodward* = body?] A. Yes and I stuck it right in. Q. what provoked you, had she displeased you? A. Yes by some words she spoke of mee. Q. who brought the image to you? A. It was M^ε Burroughs. Q. How did he bring it to you? A. In his own person Bodily. {B} Q. where did he bring it to you? A. Abroad a little way of from o^ε House. Q and what did he say to you then? A. He told mee He was angry with that ffamily. Q. How many years since was it? A. Before this Indian Warr. Q. How did you know m^ε Burroughs was a Witch? A. I dont know. she owned again she had made two Covenants with the Devil, first for two years, and after that for four years, and she Confesseth herself to have been a Witch these six Years. Q. did the Maid Complain of pain about the place you stuck the thorn in. A. yes, but How long she Lived I dont know? {B} Q. How do you know Burroughs was Angry wth Lawrences ffamily? A. Because he told mee so: Q. where did any other live that you afflicted? A. Just by ye Other toward James Andrews's, and they dyed also. Q. How many were they more then one? A. yes. Q. and who brought those Poppets to you? A. M^ε Burroughs. Q what did you stick into them? A Pinns, and he gave them to mee. Q. Did you keep those Poppets? A. no, he carryed them away with him. Q. was he there himself with you in Bodily perso⟨n⟩ A. yes, and so he was when he appeared to tempt mee to set my hand to the Book, he then appeared in person, and I felt his hand att the same time. Q. were they men, Women or Children you killed? A. They were both Boys and Girls. Q. was you angry wth them yourself? A. Yes, thō I dont know why now. Q. Did you know m^ε Burroughs'⟨s⟩ Wife? A. Yes. Q: Did you know of any poppets prickd to kill her? A. No, I dont Q. Have you seen several Witches att ye Eastward. A. Yes, But I dont know who they were

[Reverse] [Hand 2] Abigail. Hobs Examinations

Notes: The Abigail Hobbs examinations of April 20 and May 12 are recorded on the same document. Note that the accusation of George Burroughs on May 12, after his arrest, does not appear on the April 19 or 20 examinations of Hobbs. The significance of Burroughs to the recorder is highlighted by the inclusion of the letter "B" in the left margin as his name recurs. In the transcription these "B" marks appear as "{B}" although not in the margin as on the manuscript, as a result of lineation differences between the edition transcription and the manuscript. ◊ Hand 2 = John Hathorne

Essex County Court Archives, vol. 1, no. 155, Massachusetts Supreme Judicial Court, Judicial Archives, on deposit James Duncan Phillips Library, Peabody Essex Museum, Salem, MA.

78. Examination of Mary Warren in Prison†

[Hand 1] Mary Warrens Examination in Salem Prison

She Testifys that Her master Proctor was always very averse to the putting up Bills for publick prayer. Qu: Did you not know it was the Devils book when you signed? A. No, But I thought it was no good book. Q: after you had a Mark in the Book what did you think then? A. Then I thought it was the Devils Book. Q. How did you come to know your Master, and Mistris were Witches? A. The Sabbath Even after I had put up my note for thanks in publick, my Mistris appeared to mee, and puld mee out of the Bed, and told mee that she was a witch, and had put her hand to the Book, she told mee this in her Bodily person, and that This Examinant might have known she was a Witch, if she had but minded what Books she read in. Q. what did she say to you before you tormented the Children? A. The night after she told mee she was a Witch, she in ℘son told mee this Examinant, that my self and her son John would quickly be brought out for witches. This Examinant saith that Giles Cory in apparition told her, the night before that the Magistrates were goeing up to the farms, to bring down more witches to torment her. Moreover being in a dreadful fit in the prison she Charged it on Giles Cory, who was then in Close prison, affirming that he came into the Room where she was, and afflicting her, Charged her not to Come into the Other Room while he was Examining. But being sent for and he Commanded to Look upon her, He no sooner turned his face to her but shee fel into a dreadful fit again. and upon her Recovery Charged him to his face with being yᵉ procurer of it. Moreover the said Cory in prison formerly threatned her that he would fitt her for itt, because he told her she had Caused her Master to ask more for a peice of Meadow then he was willing to give she Likewise in her fitt in the Other Room before she had seen Giles Cory in person, Charging him with afflicting off her, described him in all his garments, both of hat, Coat, and the Colour of them with a Cord about his wast, and a white Cap on his head, and in Chains, as several then in Company Can affirm.

[Reverse] [Hand 2] [Lost]bs. and Examination

Notes: Mary Warren was probably examined in prison the same day as Abigail Hobbs. It is not known who was examined first that day. The meaning of "bs." on the reverse is unclear. ◊ "fitt": 'to visit (a person) with a fit penalty, to punish' (*OED* s.v. *fit* v¹, 12). ◊ Hand 2 = John Hathorne

Essex County Court Archives, vol. 1, no. 115, Massachusetts Supreme Judicial Court, Judicial Archives, on deposit James Duncan Phillips Library, Peabody Essex Museum, Salem, MA.

Thursday, April 21, 1692

79. Warrant for the Apprehension of William Hobbs, Deliverance Hobbs, Nehemiah Abbott Jr., Mary Esty, Sarah Wilds, Edward Bishop Jr., Sarah Bishop, Mary Black, & Mary English.

[Hand 1] Salem Aprill the 21ᵗʰ 1692

There Being Complaint this day made (before vs) by Thomas Putnam and John Buxton of Salem Village Yeomen, in behalfe of theire Majesᵗˢ, for them selfes and also for severall of theire Neighbours, Against Wᵐ Hobs ^{husbandman} and. Del[Lost] [= Deliverance] his wife, Nehemiah Abot Junʳ Weauer. Mary East⟨y⟩ the wife of Isaac Easty and Sarah Wilds the wife of John Wilds all of the Towne of Topsfeild ^{or Ipswitch}: And Edward Bushop husbandman & Sarah his wife of Salem Village, and Mary Black a Negro of Levtᵗ Nat⟨h⟩ [= Nathaniel] Putnams of Salem Village also And Mary English the wife of Phillep English Merchant in Salem for high Suspition of Sundry acts of Witchcraft donne or Committed by them Lately vpon the Bodys of Anna Putnam & Marcy Lewis belonging to the famyly of yᵉ abouesᵈ Thomas Putnam Complainᵗ and Mary Walcot yᵉ daufter of Capᵗ Jonaᵗ Walcot of sᵈ

Salem Village and others, whereby great hurt and dammage hath benne donne to ye bodys of   April 21, 1692
said persons aboue named therefore Craued Justice.

You are therefore in theire Majes^ts names hereby required to Apprehend and bring before vs
William Hobs {husbandman} and his wife Nehemiah Abot Jun^ʳ weauer Mary Easty the
wife of Isaac Easty and all the rest aboue named to Morrow aboute ten of the Clock in the
forenoon at the house of Leiu^t Nath^ll Ingersalls in Salem Village. in order to theire
Examination Relateing to the premises abouesayd and hereof you are not to faile Dated
Salem Aprill 21th 1692.

John: Hathorne ⎫
                              ⎬ Assis^ts
Jonathan. Corwin ⎭

To: Geo: Herrick Marshall of Essex and any or all ye Constables in Salem or Topsfeild or
any other Toune

[Reverse] [Hand 2] [2–3 words illegible]

Notes: Why this large group was targeted on April 21 requires further investigation. Perhaps the examinations of Abigail
Hobbs and Mary Warren generated new names in addition to any named in the examination record, but this is simply
speculation. Nehemiah Abbott Jr. would become the only arrested person to have an accusation against him withdrawn.
The returns in connection with this warrant have not been located. ◊ Hand 1 = John Hathorne

*Essex County Court Archives, vol. 1, no. 163, Massachusetts Supreme Judicial Court, Judicial Archives, on deposit James Duncan
Phillips Library, Peabody Essex Museum, Salem, MA.*

80. Examination of Mary Warren

[Hand 1] Mary Warins examination Aprill 21: 1692
Being Asked by: y^e Hon^ʳ Majestrates: whether ye bible that then was showed her: was y^e
book: y^t was brought: to her: to touch: & that she saw ye fflurrish in
          answered no: she see she was deceived
being asked whether ~~Mercy~~ she had not told Mercy Lewis that she had signed to a book:
Answerd no
She was Asked: whether her: Mistris had brought a book to her to sign Answerd. heir
Mistris brought none. but her Master brought one
being Asked whether she signed to it: answerd: not unles putting her finger to it was signing
being Asked whether she did not se a spot where she had put her finger
          Answerd there was a spot:
she was Asked what couller: ye spot was: Answered: black
she was Asked whether. her Mast^r did not thretten her to run ye hot tongs downe her throat
if she did not sign
          Answered that her M^r threttned her to burn her out of her fitt
being Asked whether she had made a mark in ye book
{+} Answered she made no mark but with her top of her finger {+}
she was asked what she dipt her finger in when it made ye mark:

Answered: in nothing: but her mouth

she was Asked whether her finger was wett when she touched ye book w^t it

Answered she knew not that it was wett: or whether it was wett w^t sweat or with sider: that she had bin drinking of she knew not: but her finger did make a mark and ye mark was black

she was asked whether any but her M^r and M^{rs} was with her: when she was threttoned with y^e hott tongss: answerd none but them

she s^d her Mast^r put her hand to y^e book: and her finger made a black spott which made her tremble: then she ~~she s^d was undone~~ s^d she was undon body and soul and cryed out greivously.

she was told ~~he was~~ y^t it was he [= her] own Vollantary act: she would have denyed it: but she was told y^e devil could have done nothing: if she had not yeilded and y^t she for eas to her body: not for any good for her soul: had done it with this she much greived: and cryed out:

she s^d her Mast^r & Mistris thretned to drown her: & to mak her run through ye hedges

she was Asked whether she had not seen her Mast^r & Mistris since she came to prison

answerd she thought she saw her Mast^r & dare say: it ~~was~~ was he: she was Asked whhat he sayd to her: answerd nothing

after a fitt she cryed out I will tell: I will tell: thou wicked creature it is you stopt my mouth: but I will confess ye little that I have to confess being asked: who she would: tell off whether goodwife Procter or no:

answered o Betty Procter it is she: it is she I lived with last

she then cryed out it shall be known: thou wrech: hast thou vndone me body and soul. she s^d also she wishes she had made me mak: a through league

she was again Asked what her finger was blacked with when she toucht ye book.

Answered she knew not that her finger was black: til she se it black: ye book and after she had put her finger to ye book: she eat: bread and butter and her finger blacked ye bred & butter also

being asked: what: her mistris now sayd to her: when she complaind of her mistris she s^d her mistris bid her not tell y^t that her mistris was a wich

Coming out of another fit s^d she would tell she would tell: she s^d her Mast^r {now} bid her not tell: that he: had some times gone: to make away with himselfe for her Master had told her that he had bin about some times to make away with him self becaus of his wives quarrilling with him

being Asked how she knew: goodwife Procter was a wich

she coming out of a fit s^d she would: tell she would tell: and she s^d her mistris Procter s^d she might know she was a wich if she herkend to what she used to read

she sayd her Mistris had many books, and her Mistris carried one book with her to Reddin when she went to se her sister

being Asked whether she knew her Mistris to be a wich before she touched ye book: and how she knew it: she s^d her Mistris: told her she had set her hand to ye devils book: that same night: that: I was thrown out of bed: s^d she: which was y^e same night after she had a note: of thanks giving: put up: at y^e meeting hous

she s^d her mistris came to her: her body: not her shape as ~~she~~ far as she kne⟨w⟩ she afirmd: her mistris was a wich

being Asked whether: se [= she] had seen any of y^e wiches: since she came to prison: s^d she had seen goodman Cory: & Sara Good: they brought y^e book to her to sign

but she would not own that she knew her master to be a wich or wizzard

being asked whether she did not know her finger would make a mark if she touched y^e book with it: she answerd no: but her master annd mistris asked her to read: and she s^d ye first

word she read was moses: ye next word she could not tell what it was but her m^r and mistris
bid her: if she could not pronownce ye word: she should touch ye book

being asked why she would not tell the wholle truth:

she s^d she had formerly not told all ye truth. becaus she was thretned to be torn in peices: if she did.[period overstruck] but now she would and had told ye truth

being Asked whether she did not suspect it was ye devils book that she touched answerd she did not suspect it before: she se: her finger blacked it

she was Asked why: she yeilded to do as she did: answered that her Master s^d if she would not: when she was in her fit she should run: into y^e fire or: water if she would and destroy. her selfe

being Asked whether she had not bin instrumentall to afflict y^e aflicted parsons Answer no but when she: heard: they were aflicted in her shape: she began to fear: it was y^e ⟨Devill⟩ [Lost] [*SWP* = that hurt in her shape]

being Asked: whether she had im[Lost] [= images] to st⟨?⟩k [= stick] pins or [Lost]rns [= thorns] into to hurt peple with: answerd no:

she was asked whether y^e devil never asked her consent: to: hurt in her shape answerd no: she had heard her master and mistris tell of immages and of sticking of thorns in them: to hurt peple with

she was asked: whether she knew of any Images in y^e hous: sayd no

being asked if she knew of any oyntment they had in ye hous: she s^d her M^{rs} oynted her once: for some ayll she had: but it was with oyntment y^t came from Mrs Bassits of Linn the coullour of it was greenish

she was asked how it smelt: sayd very ugly to her

she s^d when: she toucht ye book she went to put her finger to another line but still her finger went to ye same place: where her finger had blackt

Mr Noys told her she had then touched ye book twice: and asked her whether she did not not suspect it to be ye devils book before she toucht it ye second time: she s^d she feare it was no good book:

being asked what she ment by no good book: she s^d a book to deceiv

[Reverse] [Hand 2] Mary Warens Examination. [Hand 3] ve. Procter

Notes: The continuing examination of Mary Warren appears to reflect the desire of her questioners to build their case against John and Elizabeth Procter as well as to establish the credibility of the regular accusers. The "Bassits" reference is to Elizabeth Procter's family name, Bassett. "Noys" is presumably the Salem minister, Nicholas Noyes. ◊ "through": 'thoroughgoing, fully executed' (*OED* s.v. *thorough* a, 2a and s.v. *through* a 2). ◊ Hand 1 = Simon Willard; Hand 2 = John Hathorne; Hand 3 = Stephen Sewall

Essex County Court Archives, vol. 1, nos. 113 & 114, Massachusetts Supreme Judicial Court, Judicial Archives, on deposit James Duncan Phillips Library, Peabody Essex Museum, Salem, MA.

81. Summons for Witnesses v. Rachel Clinton, and Officer's Return

See also: April 22, 1692.

To Sarje't John Choate, sen'r. To Jonas Gregory, To James Burnam, all of Ipswich, Mary Andrews, Sarah Rogors, Marguriet Lord, Sary Halwell, you & each of you are hereby Required in thair majesties names To make Your personall apperance before ye Worshipfull Maj'r Sam'll Appleton Esq., & ye Clerk of ye Court to be at ye house of Mr. John Spark in

April 21, 1692

Ipswich on ye 22d Day of This Instant aprile, at two o'clock afternoon. Then and There to Give in Your severall respective Evidences in behalf of thair majesties concerning wch Clearing up of ye Grounds of Suspission of Rachell Clentons being a witch, who is Then and Thair to be upon further Examination. Therefore So make Your apperance according to this Sumons fail nott at your perril.

Ipswich, Dated aprill 21st, 1692

Curiam Tho's Wade, Clerk.

Yᵉ Constable of Ipswich is alike Required to Give notis to ye said persons, & to make returne as ye Law Directs. Curr T. W. Clk.

According to this within written I haue Sumonsed and warned them: to Apere According to Time & Place by me William Baker, Constable.

Date this 22d of april, 1692.

Notes: No record of an indictment for Clinton survives. However, she was in prison from April 11, 1692 to January 12, 1693, having apparently succeeded in her petition to be released on bail. In the petition her maiden name, "Rachel Hafield," is used. See No. 702.

Thomas Franklin Waters. Ipswich in the Massachusetts Bay Colony. (Ipswich: Ipswich Historical Society, 1905), p. 461.

82. Letter of Thomas Putnam to John Hathorne & Jonathan Corwin

These to the Honored John Hathorne and Jonathan Corwin, Esqrs., living at Salem, present.

Salem Village, this 21st of April, 1692.

Much Honored, – After most humble and hearty thanks presented to Your Honors for the great care and pains you have already taken for us, – for which you know we are never able to make you recompense, and we believe you do not expect it of us; therefore a full reward will be given you of the Lord God of Israel, whose cause and interest you have espoused (and we trust this shall add to your crown of glory in the day of the Lord Jesus): and we – beholding continually the tremendous works of Divine Providence, not only every day, but every hour – thought it our duty to inform Your Honors of what we conceive you have not heard, which are high and dreadful, – of a wheel within a wheel, at which our ears do tingle. Humbly craving continually your prayers and help in this distressed case, – so, praying Almighty God continually to prepare you, that you may be a terror to evil-doers and a praise to them that do well, we remain yours to serve in what we are able,

Thomas Putnam.

Notes: Scholars have agreed that the letter references an accusation against George Burroughs, former minister of Salem Village. It may bear further consideration, however. Putnam, along with Jonathan Walcott, did not enter a complaint against Burroughs until April 30. Upham, on whom we depend entirely for the letter and any other material that went with it, makes no specific reference to the complaint, but argues that secrecy was needed to keep Burroughs from hearing the news and escaping. Upham is simply speculating, and on whatever date an arrest warrant would have been issued, the word would have been out. Burroughs was not brought back until May 4, so if the issue was timing, he could have had time to escape whether the arrest warrant was on April 21 or April 30, its actual date. The circumstantial case for the letter referring to Burroughs remains strong but not conclusive. On March 24 Deodat Lawson in a sermon had referred to Jeremiah 19:3 for ears tingling. The "wheel within a wheel" seems to come from Ezekiel 1:16 heralding God's impending presence and voice.

Charles Wentworth Upham. Salem Witchcraft; with an account of Salem village, and a history of opinions on witchcraft and kindred subjects, Volume 2 (Boston: Wiggin & Lunt, 1867), pp. 139–40.

April 22, 1692

Friday, April 22, 1692

Officer's Return: Summons for Witnesses v. Rachel Clinton
2nd of 2 dates. See No. 81 on April 21, 1692

83. Examination of Nehemiah Abbott Jr.

The examination of Nehemiah Abbot, at a court at Salem village, by John Hawthorne and Jonathan Corwin Esqrs. 22d April 1692.

What say you, are you guilty of witchcraft, of which you are suspected, or not? No Sir, I say before God, before whom I stand, that I know nothing of witchcraft. Who is this man? Ann Putman named him. – Mary Walcot said she had seen his shape. What do you say to this? I never did hurt them. Who hurt you Ann Putman? That man. I never hurt her. Ann Putman said, he is upon the beam. Just such a discovery of the person carried out, and she confessed; and if you would find mercy of God, you must confess. – If I should confess this, I must confess what is false. Tell how far you have gone, who hurts you? I do not know, I am absolutely free. As you say, God knows. If you will confess the truth, we desire nothing else that you may not hide your guilt, if you are guilty, and therefore confess if so. I speak before God that I am clear from this accusation. What, in all respects? Yes in all respects. Doth this man hurt you? Their mouths were stopped. You hear several accuse you, though one cannot open her mouth. I am altogether free. Charge him not unless it be he. This is the man say some, and some say he is very like him. How did you know his name? He did not tell me himself, but other witches told me. Ann Putman said, it is the same man, and then she was taken with a fit. Mary Walcot, is this the man? He is like him, I cannot say it is he. Mercy Lewis said it is not the man. They all agreed, the man had a bunch on his eyes. Ann Putman, in a fit, said, be you the man? ay, do you say you be the man? did you put a mist before my eyes? Then he was sent forth till several others were examined. When he was brought in again, by reason of much people, and many in the windows so that the accusers could not have a clear view of him, he was ordered to be abroad, and the accusers to go forth to him and view him in the light, which they did, and in the presence of the magistrates and many others discoursed quietly with him, one and all acquitting him, but yet said he was like that man, but he had not the wen they saw in his apparition, Note, he was a hilly faced man and stood shaded by reason of his own hair, so that for a time he seemed to some by-standers and observers, to be considerably like the person the afflicted did describe.

Mr. Samuel Parris, being desired to take in writing the examination of Nehemiah Abbot, hath delivered it as aforesaid, and upon hearing the same did see cause to dismiss him,

John Hawthorne,

Jona. Corwin,

  } Assistants.

April 22, 1692   Notes: After some discussion and uncertainty among the accusers, Abbott was freed. Why the accusers changed their mind is unknown. ◊ "free": 'guiltless, innocent' (*OED* s.v. *free* a, 7). "bunch": 'protuberance, swelling' (*OED* s.v. *bunch* n[1], 1a). "wen": 'protuberance' (*OED* s.v. *wen* 1a).

Thomas Hutchinson, The History of the Province of Massachusetts-Bay, from the Charter of King William and Queen Mary, in 1691, Until the Year 1750, vol. 2, ed. Lawrence Shaw Mayo. (Cambridge, MA: Harvard University Press, 1936). p. 35.

84. Examination of Mary Black, and Clearing by Proclamation
See also: Jan. 11, 1693.

[Hand 1] The examination of Mary Black (a Negroe) at a Court held at Salem Village 22. Apr. <u>1692</u> By the Magistrates of Salem
Mary, you are accused of sundry acts of witchcraft: Tell mee be you a Witch?
– Silent.
How long have you been a Witch?
I cannot tell.
But have you been a Witch?
I cannot tell you?
Why do you hurt these folks
I hurt no body
Who doth?
I do not know.
{Benj[a] Putman} Her Master saith a man sat down upon the farm with her about a twelve month agoe.
What did the man say to you?
He said nothing.
Doth this Negroe hurt you?
Severall of them said yes.
Why do you hurt them?
I did not hurt them.
Do you prick sticks?
No I pin my Neckcloth
Well take out a pin, & pin it again.
She did so, & severall of the afflicted cryed out they were prick[t]. Mary Walcott was prick[t] in the arm till the blood came, Abigail Williams was prickt in the stomach & Mercy Lewes was prickt in the foot.

[Hand 2] m[r] Samuell Parris being desired to take in wrighting the Examination of Mary Black a Negro Woman deliuered itt as aforesaid
And vpon heareing the same and seeing what wee did then see togather with y[e] Charge of y[e] afflicted persons then present Wee Committed s[d] Mary black

                                                John Hathorne }
                          ⫯ vs   } Assis[ts]
                                                Jonathan. Corwin }

[Reverse] [Hand 1] (9) The ⟨E⟩xa⟨min⟩ation of Mary Black   April 22, 1692
22. Apr. <u>1692</u>

[Hand 3] Cleer'd by proclama$\overline{con}$
Jan$^\varepsilon$y .11. 1692
[Hand 4] M$^\varepsilon$ Nathaniell Putnam of Salem Village
his negro

Notes: As with the other slaves caught in the episode, Mary Black was not brought to trial in 1692. Nobody appearing against her, she was cleared in 1693. The January 11, 1692, date is from use of the old calendar and is for 1693. ◊ Hand 1 = Samuel Parris; Hand 2 = John Hathorne; Hand 4 = Jonathan Elatson.

Massachusetts Archives Collection, vol. 135, no. 20. Massachusetts State Archives. Boston, MA.

85. Statement of Benjamin Hutchinson v. George Burroughs‡

[Hand 1] Beniemin huchension. sd that one the 21 {of} aprell 92 abegeral Wiluams sd that there was a lettell black menester that Liued at Casko bay he told me so and sd that he had kild 3 wife{s} & t⟨?⟩ {two} for himself and one for m$^{⟨\varepsilon⟩}$ Losen: and that he had made nine Weches in this plase and sd that he Could hold out the heuest gun that Is in Casko bay, w^c ∧{w^t one hand} ⟨to⟩ no man Can Case hold out w^t both hands this Is about a 11 a clock and I ask her Where about this lette man stood sd she Just where the Cart wheell wer⟨e⟩ along I had a 3 graned [Hand 2] irne fork in my hand and I thru it [2–3 words overstruck] w⟨he⟩r she said. he stud and she presently feell in a letel feet and wh⟨e⟩n it twas ouer {said she} you haue toren his coot ⟨I⟩ for I hard it tare wher ebouts said I one won side said she

then we come into the house of left Ingersoll and I went {in} to the g{r}eat Roome and I abigle come in and said ther {he} stands I said wher wher and presently draed my rapyer but he emmedetly was gon as she said then said she ther is a gray catt {then} i said wher abouts doth she stand ther sd ~~shee~~ she ther then I struck wit[Lost] [= with] [1–2 words overstruck] with my rapyar th⟨e⟩n she fell in a fi⟨e⟩t and when it twas ouer she said you ~~ki~~ kild hur and immedetly Sary good coma [= came] and carrid ~~it~~ hur away ⟨&⟩ this was about 12 a clock

[Hand 3] The same day aftor lecttor in y^e said: Ingersolls chambor abigaill wiliams mary walcot said that goody hobs of topsell bitt ~~them~~ mary walcot by y^e foot thene both falling into a fit as soone as it was ouer y^e said william hobs and his wife goe both of theme along y^e table; y^e said hucheson tooke his rapier stabed ~~her~~ gooddy hobs one y^e side as abigaill williãs & mary walcot saide; y^e said abigaill & mar [= Mary] said y^e roome was full of y^m then {y^e} said hucheson {& Ely putnam} stabed with the⟨i⟩r raperres at a uentor [= venture] y^n said ~~y^e~~ mary & abigell you haue killed a greet black woman of Stonintown. and an Indian that come with her for y^e flore is all couered with blod. then {y^e} said mary and abigaill looked out of dors & said: y^e [= they] saw a greet company of the{m} one a hill & there was three of them lay dead y^e black woman & the⟨?⟩ indian & one more y^t y^e knew not This being about .4. a clock. in y^e aftornoone

[Reverse] [Hand 4] Ben Huchison

April 22, 1692   Notes: Benjamin Hutchinson's citing of April 21 as the day Abigail Williams identified Burroughs as "black," a designation that would occur frequently, may signify the earliest use of that association. No record survives of such usage during the period when Burroughs was minister of Salem Village, 1680–1683. No identification of the "greet black woman of Stonintown" has been established. The document also identifies Abigail Williams as the first person known specifically to have claimed affliction by Burroughs. ◊ "Case": The meaning is unclear. Perhaps it is a short form of *percase* 'as it chanced, perhaps' (*OED* s.v. *percase*), or a preposition such as *by* or *upon* may have been left out in the phrase *by/upon chance* 'perhaps' (*OED* s.v. *case* n[1] 2b). "graned": 'forked' (*OED* s.v. *grained* ppl. a.[3]).

Essex County Court Archives, vol. 2, no. 35, Massachusetts Supreme Judicial Court, Judicial Archives, on deposit James Duncan Phillips Library, Peabody Essex Museum, Salem, MA.

86. Examination of Mary Esty

[Hand 1] The Examination of
Mary Eastie
At a Court held at Salem village
22. Apr. 1692
By the Wo͞p [= worshipful]
John Hathorne
&
Jonathan Corwin.

At the bringing in of the the accused severall fell into fits.
Doth this woman hurt you?
Many mouths were stopt, & several other fits scizcd thcm
Abig: Williams said it was Goody Eastie, & she had hurt her, the like said Mary Walcot, & Ann Putman, John Indian said he saw her with Goody Hobbs.
What do you say, are you guilty?
I can say before Christ Jesus, I am free.
You see these accuse you.
There is a God —
Hath she brought the book to you?
Their mouths were stopt.
What have you done to these children?
I know nothing.
How can you say you know nothing, when you see these tormented, & accuse you that you know nothing?
Would you have me accuse my self?
Yes if you be guilty.
How far have you complyed wth Sa⟨ta⟩n, whereby he takes this advantage ag^t you?
Sir, I never complyed but prayed against him all my dayes. I have no complyance with Satan, in this. What would you have me do?
Confess if you be guilty.
I will say it, if it was my last time, I am clear of this sin.
Of what sin?
Of Witchcraft.
Are you certain this is the woman?

Never a one could speak for fits

By & by Ann Putman said that was the woman, it was like her, & she told me her name.

It is marvailous to me that ~~she~~ you should somtimes think they are bewitcht, & somtimes not, when severall confess that they have been guilty of bewitching them.

Well Sir would you have me confess that that I never knew?

Her hands were clincht together, & then the hands of Mercy Lewes was clincht

Look now your hands are open, her hands are open.

Is this the woman?

They made Signes but could not speak, but Ann Putman afterwards Betty Hubbard cryed out Oh.

Goody Easty, Goody Easty you are the woman, you are the woman

Put up her head, for while her head is bowed the necks of these are broken.

What do you say to this?

Why God will know.

Nay God knows now.

I know he dos.

What did you think of the actions of others before your sisters came out, did you think it was Witchcraft?

I cannot tell.

Why do you not think it is Witchcraft?

It is an evil Spirit, but whither it be Witchcraft I do not know

Severall said she brought them the Book & then they fell into fits.

[Hand 2] Salem Village March 24th 1691/2.

Mr Same Parris being desired to take in wrighting the Examination of Mary Eastie hath deliuered itt as aforesaid

Vpon heareing the aforesaid, and seeing what wee then did see, togather with the Charge of the persons then present Wee Committed sd Mary Easte to theire Majests Goale

John Hathorne ⎫
                           ⎬ Assists
Jonathan. Corwin ⎭

[Reverse] [Hand 1] (5) The Examination of Mary Eastie.
22. Apr. 1692

Notes: The March 24 date is an incorrect entry by Hathorne. Mary Esty was not ordered arrested until April 21 and was imprisoned April 22. She was released on May 18, but rearrested on May 20 after Mercy Lewis vigorously persisted in her claims of affliction by Mary Esty. Esty's sister, Rebecca Nurse, was examined on March 24. ◊ "free": 'guiltless, innocent' (OED s.v. free a, 7). ◊ Hand 1 = Samuel Parris; Hand 2 = John Hathorne

Essex County Court Archives, vol. 1, no. 281, Massachusetts Supreme Judicial Court, Judicial Archives, on deposit James Duncan Phillips Library, Peabody Essex Museum, Salem, MA.

April 22, 1692

87. Deposition of Margaret Reddington v. Mary Esty‡

[Hand 1] the depesiasian of margret Redengton eged abou{t} seuentiy yers testifieth and saith that about three yers agow I was at goodmon esties and tallking with his wife about an Infermety ~~an~~ I hade and presantly after I fell Into a most sollom condision and the thrssday before the thanksgiuing ["thanksgiuing" written over "thangs⟨k⟩giuen" by Hand 2] that wee hade ~~go~~ {last.} In the afternone I was exseding elle and that night godey estiey apered to mee and profered me a pece of fresh mete and I tolld hare twas not fete for the ~~doges~~ and I woulld haue non of ite and then she Vanished awaye

Notes: Margaret Reddington's name is on the witness list for Mary Esty's trial in September, but no evidence survives to indicate that she was at the trial. Margaret Reddington was most likely called because of this deposition. It probably came at the examination of Mary Esty on April 22 and is accordingly placed here on that date.

Essex County Court Archives, vol. 1, no. 293, Massachusetts Supreme Judicial Court, Judicial Archives, on deposit James Duncan Phillips Library, Peabody Essex Museum, Salem, MA.

88. Deposition of Samuel Smith v. Mary Esty‡

[Hand 1] The deposistion of Samuell Smith of Boxford aged about 25 yeas who testifieth and saith that about fiue {years} sence I was one night att the house of Isaac Estick senr of Topsfeild and I was as farr as I know to Rude in discorse and the aboue said Esticks wife tould {said to} me I had {would} not best {haue you} be so rude in discorse for I might Rue it hereafter and as I was agoeing whom that night about a quarter of a mille from the said Esticks house by a stone wall I Receiued a little blow on my shoulder. with I know not what and the stone wall rattleed uery much which affrighted me my horse also was affrighted uery much but I cannot giue the reson of it

[Reverse] [Hand 2] Saml Smith agt G Easty
[Hand 1] thri⟨c⟩e
[Hand 3] J⟨?⟩e⟨?⟩

Notes: Smith was on a witness list dated September 5, to appear before the court on September 6, but no record of trial testimony from him against Mary Esty survives. The deposition was probably from Mary Esty's examination on April 22 and is dated here on the same basis as Margaret Reddington's deposition preceding this entry, No. 87. ◊ Hand 1 = Thomas Putnam.

Essex County Court Archives, vol. 1, no. 292, Massachusetts Supreme Judicial Court, Judicial Archives, on deposit James Duncan Phillips Library, Peabody Essex Museum, Salem, MA.

89. Examination of Deliverance Hobbs

[Hand 1] (1) The Examination of Deliverance Hobbs .22. Apr. 1692
At a Court held at Salem village by

John Hauthorn
Jonath: Corwin } Esq^εs

Mercy Lewes do you know her that stands at the Bar (for the Magistrates had privately ordered who should be brought in, & not suffered her name to be mentioned) Do you know her? speaking to another; but both were struck dumb.

Ann Putman jun^ε said it was Goody Hobbs, & she hath hurt her much

John Indian said he had seen her, & she choakt him

Mary Walcot said, yesterday was the first time that she saw her. i.e. as a Tormentor.

Why do you hurt these persons?

It is unknown to me.

How come you to commit acts of Witchcraft?

I know nothing of it.

It is you, or your appearance, how comes this about? Tell us the truth.

I cannot tell.

Tell us what you know in this case. Who hurts them if you do not?

There are a great many Persons hurts us all.

But it is your appearance.

I do not know it.

Have not you consented to it, that they should be hurt?

No in the sight of God, & man, as I shall answere another day.

It is said you were afflicted, how came that about?

I have seen sundry sights.

What sights.

Last Lords day in ~~the~~ ^{this} meeting house & out of the door, I saw a great many ^{birds} cats & dogs, & heard a voice say come away.

What have you seen since?

The shapes of severall persons.

What did they say?

Nothing.

What neither the birds, nor persons?

No.

What persons did you see?

Goody Wilds & the shape of Mercy Lewes.

What is that? Did either of them hurt you?

None but Goody Wilds, who tore me almost to peices.

Where was you then?

In bed.

Was not the book brought to you to signe?

No.

Were not you threatened by any body, if you did not signe the book?

No, by no body.

What were you tempted to under your affliction?

I was not tempted at all.

Is it not a solemn thing, that last Lords day you were tormented, & now you are become a tormentor, so that you have changed sides, how comes this to pass?

Abig: Williams ~~cry out there~~ & Ann Putman jun^ε cry out there is Goody Hobbs upon the Beam, she is not at the Bar, they cannot see her⟨t⟩ there: thô there she stood.

April 22, 1692

What do you say to this, that thô you are at the bar in person, yet they see your appearance upon the beam, & whereas a few dayes past you were tormented, no⟨w⟩ you are become a Tormentor? Tell us how this change comes. Tell true.

I have done nothing.

What have you resolved you will not confess? Hath any body threatened you if you do confess? You can tell how this change comes.

She lookt upon John Indian, & then another, & then they fell into fits.

Tell us the reason of this change: Tell us the truth what have you done?

I cannot speak.

What do you say? What have you done?

I cannot tell.

Have you signed to any book?

It is very lately then.

When was it?

The night before the last.

Well the Lord open you heart to confesse the truth. Who brought the book to you?

It was Goody Wilds.

What did you make your mark with in the book?

Pen & Ink.

{Who brought the Pen & Ink?}

They that brought the book, Goody Wilds.

Did they threaten you if you did not signe?

Yes, to tear me in peices.

Was ther⟨e⟩ any else in company?

No Sir;

What did you afflict others by? Did they bring images?

Yes.

Who brought the images?

Goody Wild & Goody Osburn.

What did you put into those images.

Pins, Sir:

~~What do you~~ Well tell us who have you seen of this company?

None but those two.

Have you not seen many?

No, I heard last night a kind of Thundring.

How many images did you use?

~~But two. three.~~ But two.

Nay here is more afflicted by you. You said more. Well tell us the truth recollect your self

I am amazed.

can you remember how many were brought?

Not well, but severall were brought.

Did not they bring the image of John Nichols his child?

Yes.

Did not you hurt that child?

Yes.

Where be those images, at your house?
No they carryed them away again.
When?
They carryed some then, & some since.
Was it Goody Wild in body, or appearance?
In appearance.
Was there any man with them?
Yes a tall ^{black} man, with an high-crown'd hat.
Do you know no more of them?
No Sir:

Note All the sufferers free from affliction during her examination after once she began to confesse, thô at sundry times they were much afflicted till then.

Note Wheras yesterday at Deacon Ingersols Mary Walcot & Abigail ~~Will~~ Williams cryed there stands Goody Hobbs, showing also where, Benjᵃ Hutchinson struck at her with a Rapier, & the afflicted that is the said Mary & Abigail said, oh you have struck her on the right ^{side} ~~s⟨?⟩d~~: Whereupon the Magistrates asking her after the publick examination whither she had received any hurt yesterday, she said yes in her right side like a Prick, & that it was very sore, & done when she was in a Trance, telling ^{us} also in what house and room it was done. Whereupon the Magistrates ^{required} some women to search it, who found it so as she had confessed. Also a lit⟨t⟩le after the said prick in her side, she [Lost] [= had?] som what in her left eye like duste, wᶜʰ agrees with wᵗ the afflicted farther said that Benjᵃ Hutchinson afterwards toucht her eye wᵗʰ the same Rapier, & said pointing to the place there was a mark which the Marshall being by said so there was.

[Hand 2] Salem Village ~~May~~ ^{Aprile} the 22ᵗʰ 1692

mʳ Samˡ Parris being desired to take in wrighting yᵉ Examination of Deliuerance hobs hath deliuered itt as aforesaid
And vpon heareing the Same and seeing what wee did see togather with the Charg of the afflicted persons against them, Wee Committed her.
    John Hathorne

[Hand 1] (1) The Examicō̄n of Deliverance Hobbs 22. Apr. <u>1692</u>

Notes: The strategy of not speculating on the identity of the accused worked with Mercy Lewis, who maintained silence. The information, however, had almost certainly been given to Ann, possibly by her father. When Mercy Lewis was charged with appearing as a shape, nothing followed other than the query as to whether Lewis had hurt Deliverance Hobbs. The examiners were content not to pursue the issue, either because the shape of Mercy Lewis had done no harm or because, as is more likely, she was a "friend" of the judiciary in the proceedings. ◊ "som what": 'some thing of unspecified nature' (OED s.v. somewhat n, 1b). ◊ Hand 1 = Samuel Parris; Hand 2 = John Hathorne

Essex County Court Archives, vol. 2, no. 101, Massachusetts Supreme Judicial Court, Judicial Archives, on deposit James Duncan Phillips Library, Peabody Essex Museum, Salem, MA.

90. Examinations of Sarah Wilds & William Hobbs

[Hand 1] [Lost]ination [= examination] of
Sarah Wilds
At a Court held at Salem village [Lost]
<u>1692</u> by the wop̄ [= worshipful]:
John Hathorn
&
Jonathan Corwin.

The sufferers were siezed with son[Lost] [= sundry?] [Lost] the accused came into the Court
Hath this woman hurt you?
Oh she is upon the beam.
Goody Bibber that never saw her before say[Lost] [= said] she saw her now upon the beam,
& then said Bibber fell into a fit
What say you to this are you guilty or not?
I am not guilty Sir.
Is this the woman? speaking to yᵉ afflict[Lost] [= afflicted]
They all, or most, said yes, & then fell [Lost] [*SWP* = into fits]
What do you say, are you guil[Lost] [= guilty]
I thank God I am free.
Here is a clear evidence that [Lost] [*SWP* = you have] been not only a Tormentor ⟨b⟩[Lost]
[*SWP* = but that] You have caused one to sig[Lost] [= sign the] book, the night before last
[Lost] [*SWP* = What do] ⟨y⟩ou say to this?
[Lost] [= I] never saw the book in my life [Lost] [*SWP* = and I never] [Lost]sons [*SWP* =
saw these persons] before.
[Lost]e [*SWP* = Some of the] afflicted fell into fits.
[Lost] [*SWP* = Do] you deny this thing that is [Lost] [= apparent]
All fell into fits, & com[Lost] [= complained] that the accused hurt th[Lost] [= them]
Did you never consent that [Lost] [= these] be hurt?
Never in my life.
She was charged by some [Lost] with hurting John Herricks mo[Lost] [= mother]
The accused denyed it.
Capᵗ How gave in a relation [Lost] confirmation of the charge before made
She was ordered to be taken away, & they all cryed out she was upon the Beam, & fell into
fits.

The Examination of
William Hobbs
At the Same Court

[Lost]th [= Hath] this man hurt you?
[Lost]everal [= Several] answered Yes:
[Lost]dy [= Goody] Bibber said no.
[Lost]at [= What] say you, are you guilty or not?

[Lost] [= I] can speak in the presence of God safely, as ⟨I⟩ must look to give account another
day, ~I~ that I am as clear as a newborn babe.
Clear: of what?
Of Witchcraft.
Have you never hurt these?
No.
Have you not consented that they should be hurt?
Abigail Williams Said, he was going to Mercy Lewes, & quickly after said Lewes was seized
with a fit.
Then said Abigail cryed, he is coming to Mary Walcot, & said Mary presently fell into a fit
also.
[Lost]w [= How] can you be clear when the Children [Lost] [*SWP* = saw] somthing come
from you & afflict [Lost]ese [= these] persons?
Then they fell into fits & halloo'd [Lost] [Lost]cted [= afflicted] greatly.
[Lost]ur [= Your] wife before you God wa[Lost] open her mouth, & she ha[Lost]
[Lost]fession: [= confession] And you see⟨med⟩ [Lost] before us.
[Lost]m [= I am] clear of any Witch.
[Lost]at [= What] do you call it, an over-look[Lost] [*SWP* = over-looking of] [Lost]m
[= them]? you look upon them & they are [Lost] [*SWP* = hurt]
[Lost]urt [= I hurt] none of them.
Then they all fell into great fits again
When were you at any publick Religious meeting
Not a pretty while.
Why so?
Because I was not well: I had a distemper that none knows.
Can you act Witchcraft here, & by casting your eyes turn folks into fits?
You may judge your pleasure, my soul is clear.
Do you not see you hurt these by your look
No, I do not know it.
You did not answere to that question, dont you over-look them?
No, I don't over-look them.
What do you call that way of looking upon persons, & striking them downe?
You may judge your pleasure.
Well but what do you call it?
It was none of I.
Who was it then?
I cannot tell who they are.
Why they say, they see you going to hurt persons & imme [Reverse] immediately hurt
Persons.
Abig: Williams said he is going to hurt Mercy Lewes ⟨n?⟩[Lost]
& imediately s^d Mercy fell into a fit, & divers others [Lost]
Can you now deny it?
I can deny it to my dying day.
What is the reason you go away when [Lost] [*SWP* = there] is any reading of the Scripture
in your [Lost] [*SWP* = house]
He denyed it.

Nathanael Ingersol & Tho: Haines tes[Lost] [= testified] that this Ho⟨b⟩bs's daughter had told them [Lost] [*SWP* = so]

As soon as your daughter Abigail, & aft[Lost] [= after] to day your wife confessed they left torturing & so would you, if you would confess: Can you still deny that you are guilty?

I am not guilty.

If you put away Gods ordinances, no wond[Lost] [= wonder] that the Devil prevails with you to keep his Counsell. Have you never had any apparition.

No Sir.

Did you never pray to the Devil that your daughter might confess no more?

~~W~~ No Sir.

Who do you worship?

I hope I worship God only.

Where?

In my heart.

But God requires outward worship [Lost] not worship him in publick, n⟨or⟩ [Lost] [Lost]orship [= I worship] him in my heart.

[Lost] worship him in your family [Lost] [Lost]amily [= family], speak the truth: [Lost]

[Lost] not given the Devil advant[Lost] [= advantage] [Lost]gain⟨st⟩ [= against] you thereby?

He was Silent a considerable spa[Lost] [= space] [Lost] then said Yes.

Have you not known a good while that your daughter was a witch

No Sir.

Do you think she is a witch now

I do not know.

Well if you desire mercy from God, own the truth.

I do not know any thing of that nature.

What do you think these people aile?

More than ordinary?

But what more than ordinary

– Silent

Why do you not answere what do they aile?

I do not know what ⟨t⟩hey aile. I am sorry. It is none of I

What do you think they aile?

There is more than ordinary.

What is that?

I cannot tell.

Do you think they are bewitcht.

I cannot tell.

Not tell when your wife & daughter o[Lost]

Did not you give consent that these should be [Lost]

Never in my dayes.

What do you think cured your wife, she was [Lost]

[Lost] these the other day

[Lost] [Lost]eat [= great] God in Heaven knows.

[Lost] know that. We do not ask that: bu[Lost] [= but] [Lost]ther [= whether] you do not know what cured [Lost]

[Lost] tell. I know nothing

[Lost] ⟨?⟩tman [= Putman] said he told me that if his wife [Lost] [Lost]ot [= not] write in the book he would kill her, [Lost] was the same time that she did signe [Lost]ppears [= appears] by ^{the} time of her appearing as a [Lost]mentor [= tormentor] to Mr Parris family & others

Did not you say so?

I never said so.

[Hand 2] Salem Village Aprill 22th 1692

Mr Saml Parris being desired to take [Lost] [= in] wrighting ye Examination of [Lost]ah [= Sarah] Wilds ^{and Wm Hobs} deliuered it as aforesd [Lost]pon [= upon] heareing ye same and seeing [Lost]ee [= what we] did see at ye tyme of he[Lost] [= her] [Lost]ation [= examination] togather with ye Char[Lost] [= charge] [Lost]licted [= of the afflicted] persons against he[Lost] [= her] [Lost]mmitted [= we committed] her to their M[Lost] [= majesties gaol]

John Hathor[Lost] [= Hathorne]

[Hand 1] Examination of [Lost]rah [= Sarah] Wilds & William Hobbs
22. Apr. 1692

Notes: The manuscript begins with the examination of Sarah Wilds on the left portion of the manuscript. The record of the examination of William Hobbs begins on the right side and continues on the reverse, with much of it lost. ◊ "over-look": 'to cast the evil eye on, to bewitch' (*OED* s.v. *overlook* v, 7). ◊ Hand 1 = Samuel Parris; Hand 2 = John Hathorne

Essex County Court Archives, vol. 1, no. 164, Massachusetts Supreme Judicial Court, Judicial Archives, on deposit James Duncan Phillips Library, Peabody Essex Museum, Salem, MA.

91. Deposition of Nathaniel Ingersoll & Thomas Putnam v. Sarah Wilds‡

See also: July 2, 1692.

[Hand 1] The Deposistion of Nathaniell Ingrsoll agged about 58 years and Thomas putnam aged about 40 years. who testifieth and saith that wee haueing been conuersant with seuerall of the afflected parsons as namely Mary walcott mercy lewes Abigaill williams and Ann putnam jr we haue often seen them afflected and hard them say that one gooddy wilds of Topsfeild did tortor them: but on the 22 April 1692 being the day of the Examination of Sarah wilds of Topsfeild: the afforeme⟨n⟩tioned parsons ware most greviously tortored dureing the time of ~~his~~ hir Examination for if she did but look on them she would strick them down or allmost choak: them and if she did clinch hir hands or hold hir head asid the afflected parsons aboue mentioned ware i[Lost] [= in] like manr tortured: and seuerall times senec wee haue seen th[Lost] [= the] aforementioned parsons tortored and haue seen the marke in ther flesh which they said Sarah wilds did make by tortoring them and wee beleue that Sarah wilds the prisoner att the barr has seuerall times Afflected and tormented the affore named parsons by acts of wicthcraft:

[Hand 2] Jurat in Curia

April 22, 1692   [Reverse] Na: Ing$^\varepsilon$soll
                      Tho. Putman
                      [Hand 3] Tho⟨$^\varepsilon$s⟩ Boston
                      [3–4 words overstruck]

Notes: Used at trial. ◊ Hand 1 = Thomas Putnam; Hand 2 = Stephen Sewall

Essex Institute Collection, no. 9, James Duncan Phillips Library, Peabody Essex Museum, Salem, MA.

92. Deposition of Ann Putnam Jr. v. Sarah Wilds†

See also: June 30, 1692.

[Hand 1] The Deposistion of Ann putnam Junr who testifieth and saith I haue ben afflected euer sence the beginig of march with a woman that tould me hir name was willds and that she came from Topsfeild but on the 22 April 1692 Sarah willds did most greviously torment me dureing the time of hir Examination and then I saw that Sarah willds was that very woman that tould me hir name was willds and also on the day of hir Examination I saw Sarah willds or hir Appe⟨r⟩ance most greviously tortor and afflect mary walcott Mircy lewes and Abigail willia⟨m⟩ and seuerall times sence Sarah willds or hirs Apperance has most greviously tortored and afflected me with variety of tortureres as by pricking and pinching me and almost choaking me to death

[Hand 2] Anne Putnam Jun$^\varepsilon$ declared: y^e above written: evidence: to be truth: before y^e Jury of inquest: June: 30th :1692: upon oath

[Reverse] [Hand 3] Ann Putman

Notes: Hand 1 = Thomas Putnam; Hand 2 = Simon Willard; Hand 3 = Stephen Sewall

Essex Institute Collection, no. 10, James Duncan Phillips Library, Peabody Essex Museum, Salem, MA.

93. Deposition of Mary Walcott v. Sarah Wilds†

See also: June 30, 1692 & July 2, 1692.

[Hand 1] The Deposistion of Mary walcott ageed about 17 years who testifieth and saith that in the begining of Appril 1692 there came to me a woman which I did not know and ^{she} did most greviously torment me by pricking and pinching me and she tould me that hir [Hand 2] ^{name} [Hand 1] was wilds and that she liued at Topsfeil and she continewed hurting {me} most greviously by times tell the day of hir Examination which was the 22 day of Appril 1692: and then I saw hir {that} Sarah ⟨u⟩ wildes was that very same woman that tould me hir name was wildss and Sarah wilds did most greviously torment me dureing the time of hir Examination for when euer she did but look upon me w she would strick me down or almost choak me to death: also on the day of hir Examination I saw Sarah wilds or hir Apperance most greviously torment and afflect mercy lewes Abigaill williams and Ann putnam Junr by stricking them down and almst [= almost] choaking them to deatth. also seuerall times since Sarah willds has most greviously tormented me with variety of tortor and I verily beleue she is a most dreadfull wicth

[Hand 3] Jurat in Curia

[Hand 4] Mary Walcot declared to y^e Jury of inquest: that y^e above written evidence is y^e truth: upon oath: June 30th 1692

[Reverse] [Hand 3] Mary Wolcot

Notes: Used at trial. ◊ Hand 1 = Thomas Putnam; Hand 3 = Stephen Sewall; Hand 4 = Simon Willard

Essex Institute Collection, no. 11, James Duncan Phillips Library, Peabody Essex Museum, Salem, MA.

94. Mittimus for William Hobbs, Deliverance Hobbs, Mary Esty, Sarah Wilds, Edward Bishop Jr., Sarah Bishop, Mary Black, & Mary English

To Their Majesties Goal-keeper in *Salem.*

You are in Their Majesties Names hereby required to take into your care, and safe custody, the Bodies of William Hobs, *and* Deborah *his Wife*, Mary Easty, *the Wife of* Isaac Easty, *and* Sarah Wild, *the Wife of* John Wild, *all of* Topsfield; *and* Edward Bishop *of* Salem-Village, *Husbandman, and* Sarah *his Wife, and* Mary Black, *a Negro of Lieutenant* Nathaniel Putmans *of* Salem-Vilage; *also* Mary English *the Wife of* Philip English, *Merchant in* Salem; *who stand charged with High Suspicion of Sundry Acts of Witchcraft, done or committed by them lately upon the Bodies of* Ann Putman, Mary Lewis *and* Abigail Williams, *of* Salam-Village, *whereby great Hurt and Damage hath been done to the Bodies of the said Persons, according to the complaint of* Thomas Putman *and* John Buxton *of* Salem-Village, *Exhibited.* Salem Apr. 21. 1692. *appears, whom you are to secure in order to their further Examination. Fail not.*

John Hathorn,
Jona. Curwin,   } *Assistants.*

Dated Salem Ap. 22. 1692.

To Marshal George Herrick *of* Salem Essex. *You are in their Majesties Names hereby required to convey the above-named to the Goal at* Salem. *Fail not.*

John Hathorn,
Jona. Curwin,   } *Assistants.*

Dated Salem Apr. 22. 1692.

Notes: In the original publication in 1700 of *More Wonders of the Invisible World*, Mercy Lewis's first name is given as "Mary" and is accordingly carried that way in this edition. Subsequent printings of *More Wonders* revised her name to "Mercy" based on an errata sheet, a handwritten copy of which is contained in a copy of the 1700 edition in the collection of the Massachusetts Historical Society. The volume may have been owned by Cotton Mather, whose signature appears in it. The similar misnaming of Deliverance Hobbs as "Deborah" may reflect the not unusual occurrence of women's names being unknown to judicial authorities and to those accusing them or could have been an error that was not corrected in the errata sheet.

April 23, 1692   *Robert Calef. More Wonders of the Invisible World, Display'd in Five Parts. (London: Nath. Hillard, 1700), p. 94.*

Saturday, April 23, 1692

95. Examination of Deliverance Hobbs in Prison†

[Hand 1] The first Examination of Deliverance Hobbs in prison.
She continued in the free acknowledging herself to be a Covenant Witch, and further Confesseth she was warned to a meeting yesterday morning, and that there was present Procter and his Wife, Goody Nurse, Giles Cory, and his Wife, Goody Bishop alias Oliver, and m$^\varepsilon$ Burroughs was y^r Preacher, and prest them to bewitch all in the Village, telling them they should do it gradually and not all att once, assureing them they should preveil, He administred the sacrament unto them att the same time with Red Bread, and Red Wine like Blood, she affirms she saw Osburn, Sarah Good, Goody Wilds; Goody Nurse; and Goody Wilds distributed the bread and Wine, and a Man in a Long crownd white Hat sat next ye Minister and they sat seemingly att a Table, and They filled out the wine in Tankards, The Notice of this meeting was given her by Goody wilds. She her self affirms did not nor would not Eat nor drink, but All the Rest did who were there present, therfore they Threatned to Torment her. The meeting was in the Pasture by m$^\varepsilon$ Parris's House. and she saw when Abigail Williams ran out ~~and~~ to ["t" written over "s"] speak with them: But by that Ti⟨m⟩e Abigail was come a little distance from the House This Examinant w⟨a⟩s strucke bl⟨in⟩d, so that she saw not with whome Abigail spake. she furt[Lost] [= further] saith, that Goody Wilds to prevail with her to sign, told her that If she would put her hand to the book she w^{ld} give her some Cloaths, and would not afflict her any more – Her Daughter Abigail Hobbs being brought in att the same time while her Mother was present was immediatly taken with a dreadful fitt, and her Mother being asked who it was that hurt her daughter, answered it was Goodman Cory, and she saw him, and the Gentlewoman of Boston striving to break her Daughters Neck

[Reverse] [Hand 2] Deliueranc H[Lost] [= Hobbs] Mary Waren

Notes: Deliverance Hobbs was also examined in prison in a dated document, May 12. Since in April confessors were quickly examined in prison, it seems likely that this undated document records an examination probably held on April 23, the day after her court examination and confession. Thomas Putnam in a letter dated April 21 had made cryptic remarks almost universally interpreted by scholars as implicating George Burroughs (see No. 82), so the naming of Burroughs a couple of days later by a confessor seems consistent with the developing Burroughs connection. If the dating here is correct, Deliverance Hobbs was the first to relate the narrative of Burroughs conducting the Devil's sabbath. ◊ Hand 2 = John Hathorne

Essex County Court Archives, vol. 2, no. 102, Massachusetts Supreme Judicial Court, Judicial Archives, on deposit James Duncan Phillips Library, Peabody Essex Museum, Salem, MA.

Saturday, April 30, 1692

96. Complaint of Jonathan Walcott & Thomas Putnam v. George Burroughs, Lydia Dustin, Susannah Martin, Dorcas Hoar, Sarah Morey, & Philip English

[Hand 1] Salem Aprill the 30ᵗʰ 1692

There Being Complaint this day made (Before vs) by Capᵗ Jonathan Walcot and Serjᵉ Thomas Putnam of Salem Village, in behalfe of theire Majesties, for themselfes, and also for Seuerall of theire Neighbours Against George Burroughs Minester in Wells in the prouince of Maine Lydia Dasting in Reading Wido⟨w⟩ Susanah Martin of Amesbury widow. Dorcas Hoar of Beverly Widdow, and Sarah Murrell of Beverly And Phillip English of Salem Merchant ffor high Suspition of Sundry acts of Witchcraft do⟨ne⟩ or Committed by them vpon the Bodys of Mary Walcot Marcy Lewis Abigail Williams Ann Putnam and Eliz Hubert and Susanãh Shelden (Viz) vpo[Lost] [= upon] Som: or all of them, of Salem Village or ffarm[Lost] [= farms] whereby great hurt and dammage hath benne do⟨nne⟩ ⟨to⟩ yᵉ Bodys of sᵈ persons aboue named therefore Craued Justice

$$\left.\begin{array}{l}\text{Signed by Both}\\\text{the Complainers}\\\text{aboues}^{d}\end{array}\right\}\quad\begin{array}{l}\text{Jonathan Walcott}\\\text{Thomas putnam}\end{array}$$

The aboues ᵈ Complaint was Exhibited before vs this 30ᵗʰ aprill 1692

$$\left.\begin{array}{l}\text{John Hathorne}\\[1em]\text{Jonathan. Corwin}\end{array}\right\}\ \text{Assis}^{ts}$$

Notes: Burroughs, a clergyman, emerged in the subsequent narratives as the leader of the Devil's assault on the colony. He took a central place in Cotton Mather's defense of the trials as written in *Wonders of the Invisible World*. ◊ Hand 1 = John Hathorne.

Essex Institute Collection, no. 17, James Duncan Phillips Library, Peabody Essex Museum, Salem, MA.

97. Warrant for the Apprehension of George Burroughs, and Officer's Return

See also: May 4, 1692.

[Hand 1] To Jnᵒ Partredg ffield Marshal
You are Required in their Majˢᵗˢ names to aprehend the body of mʳ George Buroughs at present preacher at Wells in the provence of Maine, & Convay him with all speed to Salem before the Magestrates there, to be Examened, he being suspected for a Confederacy with the devil in opresing of sundry about Salem as they relate. I haveing Receved perticuler Order from the Governᵉ & Council of their Majˢᵗˢ Colony of the Masathusets, for the same, you may not faile here in. Dated in Portsmouth in the provenc of Hamshire, Aprel. 30ᵗʰ 1692.

Elisha Hutchinson Majᵉ

April 30, 1692

[Hand 2] By Virtue of this warrant I Apprehended s^d George Burroughs and haue Brought him to Salem and Deliuered him to the Authority there this fourth day of May 1692

John Partidge [Hand 3] feild
marshall of the Prouins
of new hansher and maine

[Reverse] [Hand 4] Warrant ag^t Burroughs
[Hand 5] ye Marchalls Returne

Notes: Both the warrant and return are unusual, reflecting the involvement of Burroughs in the case. The warrant was written by Elisha Hutchinson rather than as normally by the magistrates. The return is in Hathorne's hand, although the signature of Partridge appears authentic. The authorization from the Governor and Council probably reflects the importance of Burroughs, perhaps because he was a dissident minister. Burroughs also had a history of enmity among some in Salem Village, particularly Thomas Putnam, who participated in the complaint. It must be kept in mind, however, that at the end of May several other warrants for people less prominent than Burroughs were ordered by the Governor and Council. ◊ Hand 1 = Elisha Hutchinson; Hand 2 = John Hathorne; Hand 5 = Jonathan Corwin

Witchcraft Papers, no. 1, Massachusetts Historical Society. Boston, MA.

98. Warrant for the Apprehension of Lydia Dustin, and Officer's Return

See also: May 2, 1692.

[Hand 1] To y^e Constable of Reading

You are in theyr Majestyes Names Required to Apprehend and bring before vs [Hand 2] Lydah [Hand 1] Dasting of Reading Widdow in ye County of Midlesex on Munday Next being ye Second day of ye Month of May Next Ensueing ye date hereof, about Eleven of ye Clock in ye forenoone, att ye house of Lev^t Nath^ll Ingersolls in Salem Village, in Order to hir Examination, relateing to high Suspition of Severall acts of Witchcraft done or Comitted by hir upon ye Bodys of Mary Walcott, Ann. Putnam, Mercy. Lewis & Abigall. Williames all of Salem Village, whereby great hurt ⟨&⟩ damage hath bin done to ye Bodys of Said persons according to Complaint of Capt Jonathan. Walcott & Serg^t Thomas Putnam in behalfe of theyr Majestys for y^mselves & severall of theyr Neighbours, and hereof you are nott to fayle att your perrill. dat^d Salem Aprill. 30th 1692.

John Hathorne ⎱
⍴ vs   ⎰ Assis^ts
Jonathan. Corwin ⎰

[Reverse] [Hand 3] Pursewence to a warant from yo^ε honrs baring date the 30 of aprill last for the aprihending and bringing of ye person of Lidea Dasting in obedience ther to I haue brought the said Lidea Dasting of Redding to ye hous of Le^t Ingersons in Salem viledg dated in ~~may the: 2d~~ Salem viledg the 2^d day of may 1692

Atest. John Parker of Redding

[Hand 4] L. Dastin ~~S Dustin~~

Notes: The insertion of Dustin's first name by another hand indicates that a blank space was left for that insertion, her name not known at the time of the warrant. Although the accused were mainly from Essex County, they were not exclusively so, as in this case. ◊ Hand 1 = Jonathan Corwin

Essex County Court Archives, vol. 2, no. 98, Massachusetts Supreme Judicial Court, Judicial Archives, on deposit James Duncan Phillips Library, Peabody Essex Museum, Salem, MA.   April 30, 1692

99. Warrant for the Apprehension of Philip English, Sarah Morey, & Dorcas Hoar, and Officer's Return

See also: May 2, 1692.

[Hand 1] To the Marshall of the County of Essex
or his Lawfull Deputy

You are in theire Majes^ts names hereby required to Apprehend and bring before vs Phillip English of Salem Merchant, Sarah Murre⟨l⟩ of Beverly and [Hand 2] Darcas [Hand 1] Hoare of Beverly Widdow all in the County of Essex on Munday next being the second day of the Moneth of May next Ensueing ye date hereof, aboute Eleven of ye Clock in ye forenoon at the house of Lt Nathaniel Ingersalls in Salem Village in order to theire Examination Relateing to high Suspition of Sundry acts of Witchcraft donne or Committed by them vpon ye Bodys of Mary Walcot Marcy Lewis Abigail Williams Ann Putnam and Elizabeth Hubbert and Susanah Shelden (viz) vpon some or all of them, belonging to Salem village or farmes whereby great hurt & dammage hath benne donne to ye Bodys of s^d persons according to Complaint of Capt Jonathan Walcot and Serjent Thomas Putnam, in behalfe of their Majesties, for themselfes and also for severall of theire Neighbours And hereof you are not to faile at your perill Dated Salem Aprill 30th 1692.

John: Hathorne
₱ vs   } Assis^ts
Jonathan. Corwin

[Hand 3] May 2^d: 1692 I haue taken ye bodys of ye aboue named Sarah Murrell and Darcas Ho{a}re and brought them unto ye house of leu^t Nathane{i}ll Ingersoll att y^e time ~~aftersd~~ abouesd

p^ɛ mee Geo: Herrick
Marshall of Essex

m^ɛ Phillip English not beeing to bee found

p^ɛ GH

[Reverse] [Hand 4] P. English S. Murrell Dorcus Hoar

Notes: Philip English was eventually found and imprisoned, but he escaped to New York. ◊ Hand 1 = John Hathorne; Hand 3 = George Herrick

Essex County Court Archives, vol. 1, no. 169, Massachusetts Supreme Judicial Court, Judicial Archives, on deposit James Duncan Phillips Library, Peabody Essex Museum, Salem, MA.

100. Warrant for the Apprehension of Susannah Martin, and Officer's Return

See also: May 2, 1692.

[Hand 1] To The Marshall of the County of Essex or his Lawfull deputie or to the
Constable of Amesbury.

You are in theire Majes^{ts} names hereby required forthwith or as soon as may be to apprehend and bring (before vs) [Hand 2] Susanna [Hand 1] Martin of Amesbur⟨y⟩ ~~Widdow~~ in ye County of Essex Widdow at ye house of Lt Nathaniell Ingersalls in Salem Village, in order to her Examination Relateing to hi⟨gh⟩ Suspition of Sundry acts of Witchcraft donne or Committed by her vpon ye Bodys of Mary Walcot Abigail Williams Ann Putnam and Marcy Lewis of Salem Village or farmes

Whereby great hurt and dammage hath benne donne to ye bodys of Said persons according to Compl^t of Capt Jonathan Walcot & Serj^ɛ Thomas Putnam in behalfe of theire Majes^{ts} this day Exhibited before vs for themselfes and also for ~~ther~~ Seuerall of theire Neighbours and here of You are not to faile at your perills. Dated Salem Aprill 30th 1692

John: Hathorne
$\wp$ vs   ⎫ Assis^{ts}
Jonathan. Corwin   ⎬

[Reverse] [Hand 3] Susanna Martin
[Hand 4] according to this warrant I haue apprehended Susanna Mratin widdow: of Amsbery and haue brought or caused hir to be brought to the place appointed for hir examination $\wp$ me orlando Bagly Constable of Amsbery
Salem village this 2th may 1692

Notes: Constable Bagly's "signature" on the return was written by Thomas Putnam. ◊ Hand 1 = John Hathorne; Hand 4 = Thomas Putnam

Essex County Court Archives, vol. 1, no. 171, Massachusetts Supreme Judicial Court, Judicial Archives, on deposit James Duncan Phillips Library, Peabody Essex Museum, Salem, MA.

Unknown Date in April 1692

101. Statement of Mary Warren v. John Procter & Elizabeth Procter [?]

[Hand 1] Mary Warrens Confession ag^t Jo: Procter & vx$^{⟨ɛ⟩}$
Charges them personally to cause her to signe or ~~makeng~~ ["e" written over "i"] a mark in the book and both of them comitting acts of W⟨?⟩itc{h}raft & being soe. & per⟨s⟩[Lost] [= personally] threatned the Exaīt [= examinant] with tortures if she would not ~~do it~~ signe & since con⟨f⟩[Lost] [= confession] have oftimes afflicted & tormented her. large in her Confessions vide [= see].

Notes: This is most probably late April when Mary Warren, after much indecisiveness, decided to join the accusers. ◊ "vx$^{⟨ɛ⟩}$": abbreviation of Latin *uxor* 'wife.' "large": 'a great deal' (*OED* s.v. *large* B.1.). ◊ Hand 1 = Thomas Newton

Essex County Court Archives, vol. 1, no. 55, Massachusetts Supreme Judicial Court, Judicial Archives, on deposit James Duncan Phillips Library, Peabody Essex Museum, Salem, MA.

May 1692

Monday, May 2, 1692

Officer's Return: Warrant for the Apprehension of Lydia Dustin
2nd of 2 dates. See No. 98 on April 30, 1692

Officer's Return: Warrant for the Apprehension of Philip English, Sarah Morey & Dorcas Hoar
2nd of 2 dates. See No. 99 on April 30, 1692

Officer's Return: Warrant for the Apprehension of Susannah Martin
2nd of 2 dates. See No. 100 on April 30, 1692

102. Examination of Dorcas Hoar

[Hand 1] The Exanimation of Dorcas ~~Heor.~~ Hoar .2. May .1692.
Severall of the afflicted fell into fits as soon as she was brought in.
Eliz: Hubbard said this woman hath afflictd me ever since last sab: was seven night, & hurt
me ever since, & she choakt ~~her~~ her own husband.
Mary Walcot said she told me the same
Abig: Williams said this is the woman that she saw first before ever Tituba Indian or any else.
Ann Putman said this is the woman that hurts her, & the first time she was hurt by her was
the sab: was seven night.
Susan: Sheldon accused her of hurting. her last moonday night.
Abig: Williams & Ann Putman said she told them that she had choakt a woman lately at
Boston
   Eliz: Hubbard cryed why do you pinch me the mark was visible to the standers by. The
Marshall said she pincht her fingers at that time.
   Dorcas Hoar why do you hurt these?
I never hurt any child in my life.
It is you, or your appearance.
   How can I help it?
What is it from you that hurts these?
I never saw worse than my self.
   You need not see worse. They charge you with killing your husband
I never did, nor never saw you before
   You sent for Goody Gale to cut your head off
   What do you say to that?
I never sent for her upon that account.
What do you say about killing your husb^d.
Susan: Sheldon ~~came~~ also charged her ~~that~~ that she came in with two cats, & brought me the
book, {& fell into a fit} & told me your name was ~~a~~ Goody Bukly.
No, I never did, I never saw them before.
What black cats were those you had?
   I had none.

May 2, 1692

Mary Walcot, Susan: Sheldon, & Abigail Williams said they saw a black man whispering in her ears.

Oh! you are liars, & God will stop the mouth of liars

You are not to speak after this manner in the Court.

I will speak the Truth as long as I live.

Mary Walcot & susan: Sheldon & Eliz: Hubbard said again there was a man whispering in her ear, & said she should never confess.

Goody Bibber free from fits hitherto said there was a black man with her & fell into a fit.

What do you say to those cats that suckt your breast, what are they?

I had no cats.

You do not call them cats, what are they that suck you?

I never suckt none, but my child.

Why do you say, you never saw Goody Bukly?

I never knew her.

Goodm: Bukly testifyed that she had been at the house often.

I know you but not the woman.

You said you did not know the Name.

Many by-standers testifyed she disowned that she knew the name

I did not know the name so as to goe to the woman

Susan: Sheldon & Abig: Williams cryed there was a blew bird gone into her back.

The Marshall struck, & several of the by-standers testifyed that they saw a fly like a Millar.

What did you see Goody Bibber. who was looking up.

Goody Bibber was taken ~~up~~ dumb.

What can you have no heart to confess

I have nothing to do with Witchcraft

They say the Devil is whispering in your ear.

I cannot help it if they do se it.

Cannot you confess what you think of these things?

Why should I confess that I do not know.

Susan: Sheldon cryed O Goody Hoar do not kill me, & fell into a fit, & when she came to her self she said, she saw a black man whispering in her ear, & she brought me the book.

I have no book, but the Lords book.

What Lords book.

The Lords book.

Oh said some of the afflicted there is one whispering in her ears.

There is some body will rub your ears shortly, said the Examinant

Immediately they were afflicted, & among others Mercy Lewes.

Why do you threaten they should be Rubb'd?

I did not speak a word of Rubbing.

Many testifyed she did.

My meaning was God would bring things to light.

Your meaning for God to bring the thing to light would be to deliver these poor afflicted ones, that would not Rubb them. This

[Reverse] This is unusual impudence to threaten before Authority. Who hurts them now.

I know not.

They were rubbed after you had threatened them.

May 2, 1692

Mary Walcot, Abigail Williams, & Eliz: Hubbard were carried towards her, but they could not come near her

What is the reason these cannot come near you

I can not help it, I do them no wrong, they may come if they will

Why you see, they cannot come near you.

     I do them no wrong

Note. The afflicted were much distressed during her examination.

This is a true account of the Examination of Dorcas Hoar without wrong to any party according to my original from Characters at the moments thereof

Witness my hand

Sam: Parris.

    Dorcas Hoars Examination

Notes: The claim by Abigail Williams that Dorcas Hoar was the first to afflict her is no more reliable than any of her testimony. The reference to "a fly like a Millar" may have been an embellishment of Parris's, drawing from Joseph Glanvil's *Sadducismus Triumphatus*, II, 1681, a work very well known to those with any interest in witchcraft. Glanvil writes that "a fly like a great Millar flew out from the place", the fly being a witch's "familiar" (p. 144). Goody Gale may be Sarah Gale of Beverly, although no further mention of her in the documents occurs. Later in the month, Wilmot Redd was arrested, and one of the people who testified against her was Ambrose Gale of Marblehead, married to Deborah Gale. "Bukly" is apparently Sarah Buckley, arrested on May 14. ◊ "rub your ears": "rub": 'to affect painfully or disagreeably; to annoy, irritate. Chiefly in various phrases' (*OED* s.v. *rub* 3.a). ◊ Hand 1 = Samuel Parris

Essex County Court Archives, vol. 1, no. 206, Massachusetts Supreme Judicial Court, Judicial Archives, on deposit James Duncan Phillips Library, Peabody Essex Museum, Salem, MA.

103. Deposition of Thomas Putnam & Edward Putnam v. Dorcas Hoar‡

See also: Sept. 6, 1692.

[Hand 1] The Deposistion of Thos putnam aged 40 years and Edward putnam aged 36 years who testifie and saith. that we haueing been conversant with Diuers of the afflected parsons as mary walcott Eliza Hubbrd Ann putnam and others: and we haue seen them most greviously tortored by ~~plaine~~ biting and pinching and their bones. almost put out of joynt greviously complaineing of one gooddy Hore of Beuerly for hurting them but on the :2: day of may 1692 being the day of the Examination of Darcass ^{Hoar} of Beuerly the aboue said afflected parsons ware most grevi⟨of⟩ously tormented dureing the time of hir Examination for upon the glance of hir Eies they ware strucken down or allmost choakd: also seuerall times sence we ~~seen~~ haue seen the aboue named parsons most greviously tormented and the marks of plaine bits on there flesh and complaining of gooddy Hoar for hurting them: and we beleue that Darcas Hoare the prisoner att the barr has often hurt the affore named parsons by acts of wicthcraft

[Hand 2] Jurat in <u>Curia</u>.

[Reverse] Tho: Putman & Edward Putman

Notes: The manuscript is on the lower part of a sheet cut from the top where some illegible parts of words appear. Whether there is a connection to the deposition from the other portion is unknown. ◊ Used at trial. ◊ Hand 1 = Thomas Putnam

May 2, 1692   *Essex County Court Archives, vol. 1, no. 218, Massachusetts Supreme Judicial Court, Judicial Archives, on deposit James Duncan Phillips Library, Peabody Essex Museum, Salem, MA.*

104. Examination of Susannah Martin

[Hand 1] The Examination of Susan: Martin. 2. May <u>1692</u>

As soon as she came in many had fits.

Do you know this Woman

Abig: ^{Williams} saith it is Goody Martin she hath hurt me often.

Others by fits were hindered from speaking.

Eliz: Hubbard said she hath not been hurt by her.

John Indian said he hath not seen her

Mercy Lewes pointed to her & fell into a little fit.

Ann Putman threw her Glove in a fit at her

The examinant laught.

What do you laugh at it?

Well I may at such folly.

Is this folly? The hurt of these persons?

I never hurt man woman or child.

Mercy Lewes cryed out she ha⟨th⟩ hurt me a great many times, & pulls me down

Then Martin laught againe

Mary Walcot saith this woman hath hurt me a great many times.

Sus: Sheldon also accused her of afflicting her.

What do you say to this?

I have no hand in Witchcraft.

What did you do? Did not you give your consent?

No, never in my life.

What ails this people?

I do not know.

But w^t do you think?

I do not desier to spend my judgm^t upon it.

Do not you think they are Bewitcht?

No, I do not think they are?

Tell me your thoughts about them.

Why my thoughts are my own, when they are in, but when they are out they are anothers.

You said their Master – Who do you think is their Master?

If they be dealing in the black art, you may know as well as I.

Well what have you done towards this?

Nothing.

Why it is you, or your appearance.

I cannot help it.

That may be your Master

I desire to lead my self according to the ~~will of God.~~ word of God.

Is this according to Gods word?

If I were such a person I would tell you the truth.

How comes your appearance just now to hurt these.

How do I know?

Are not you willing to tell the Truth?

⟨I⟩ cannot tell: He that appeared in same ⟨s⟩hape a⟨s⟩ glorifyed saint can appear in any ⟨o⟩ne⟨s⟩ sh⟨a⟩pe.

Do you beleive these do no⟨t⟩ say true?

      They may lye for ought I know

May not you lye?

I dare not tell a lye if it would save my life.

Then you will speak the Truth.

⟨I⟩ have spoke nothing else, I would do them any good.

I do not think you have such affections for them, whom just now you insinuated ha⟨d⟩ the Devil for their Master.

Eliz: Hubbard was afflicted & then the Marshal w° [= who] was by her said she pincht her hand.

Severall of the afflicted cryed out they [Lost] [= saw] her upon the beam.

Pray God discover you, if you be guilty.

Amen. Amen. A false tongue w⟨ill⟩ never make a guilty person.

You have been a long time coming to the Court to day, you can come fast enough in the night. Said Mercy Lewes

No, sweet heart, said the Examinant

And then Mercy Lewes, & all, or many of the rest, were afflicted

John Indian fell into a violent fit, & said it was that woman, she bites, she bites, ⟨&⟩ then sh⟨e⟩ was biting her lips

Have you not compassion for these afflicted

No, I have none

Some cryed out there was the black man with her, & Goody Bibber who had not accused her before confirmed it.

Abig: William upon trial could not come near her: Nor Goody Bibber: Nor Mary Walcot.

John Indian cryed he would kill her if he came near her, but he ⟨was⟩ flung down in his approach to her

What is the reason these cannot come near y⟨ou⟩

I cannot tell. It may be the Devil bea⟨rs⟩ me more malice than an other.

D⟨o⟩ no⟨t⟩ y⟨ou⟩ s⟨ee⟩ h⟨ow⟩ God ⟨evi⟩dently [Lost] you?

No, not a bit for that.

All the congregation think so.

Let them think w^t they will.

What is the reason these cannot come near you

I do not know but they can if they will ⟨or⟩ else if you please, I will come to them

What is the black man whispering to you?

There was none whispered to me.

[Reverse] [2 words illegible] of Susa⟨na⟩ Martin

Notes: This is a Parris draft copy of the examination. The reference by Susannah Martin to "glorifyed saint" is to the Bible, 1 Samuel 28. The witch of Endor raises to Saul what appears as the spirit of Samuel. Martin's point, one that was crucial to claims of innocence, is that the Devil can appear in someone else's shape. This argument represented the strongest one against the use of spectral evidence. ◊ Hand 1 = Samuel Parris

Essex County Court Archives, vol. 1, no. 174, Massachusetts Supreme Judicial Court, Judicial Archives, on deposit James Duncan Phillips Library, Peabody Essex Museum, Salem, MA.

105. Examination of Susannah Martin, Second Version

[Hand 1]The Examination of Susannah Martin. 2. May: <u>1692</u>
As soon as she came into the meeting-house many fell into fits
Hath this Woman hurt you?
Abig: Williams said it is Goody Martin, she hath hurt me often.
Others by fits were hindered from speaking.
Eliz: Hubbard said she had not hurt her.
John Indian said he never saw her.
Mercy Lewes pointed to her & fell into a fit.
Ann Putman threw her Glove in a fit at her
What do you laught at it?
Well I may at such folly.
Is this folly, to see these so hurt?
I never hurt man, woman, or child
Mercy Lewes cryed out, she hath hurt me a great many times & plucks me down.
Then Martin laught againe
Mary Walcot said this woman hath hurt her a great many times
Susannah Sheldon also accused her of hurting her
What do you say to this?
I have no hand in Witchcraft⟨s⟩.
What did you do? Did you consent these should be hurt?
No never in my life.
What ails these people?
I do not know.
But what do you think ails them
I do not desire to spend my judgment upon it.
Do you think they are Bewitcht?
No I do not think they are.
Well tell us your thoughts about them?
My thoughts are mine own when they are in, but when they are out they are an others.
You said their Master
Who do you think is their Master?
If they be dealing in the black art, you may know as well as I.
What have you done towards the hurt of these.
I have done nothing.
Why it is you, or your appearance.
I cannot help it.
That may be your Master that hurt them
I desire to lead my life according to the word of God.
Is this according to the word of God?
If I were such a person I would tell you the Truth.
How comes your appearance just now to hurt these?
How do I know?
Are you not willing to tell the Truth?
I cannot tell: He that appeared in sam⟨e⟩ shape can appear in any ones shape.
Do you beleive these afflicted persons do not say true?

May 2, 1692

The⟨y⟩ ⟨may⟩ lye for ought I know.

May not you lye?

I dare not tell a lye ~~to~~ ^{if it would} save my life.

Then you will not speak the truth will you?

I have spoken nothing else. I would do them any good.

I do not think that you have such affections for these whom just now you insinuated had the Devil for their Master.

The Marshall said she pincht her hands, & Eliz: Hubbard was immediately afflicted.

Severall of the afflicted cryed out they saw her upon the Beam.

Pray God discover you, if you be g⟨u⟩ilty?

Amen, Amen. A false tongue will never make a guilty person.

You have been a long time coming to day said Mercy Lewes, you can come fast enough in the night.

No Sweet heart

And then said Mercy, & all the afflicted beside almost were afflicted

John Indian fell into a fit, & cryed it was that woman, she bites, she bites.

And then said Martin was biting her lips

Have not you compassion on these afflicted

No I have none.

They cryed out there was the black man along with her, & Goody Bibber confirmed it

Abig: Williams went towards her, but could not come near her: nor Goody Bibber thô she had not accused her before: also Mary Walcot could not come near her.

John Indian said he would kill her, if he came near her, but he fell down before he could touch her

What is the reason these cannot come near you?

I cannot tell it may be the Devil bears me more malice than an other.

Do you not see God evidently discovering you?

No, not a bit for that.

All the congregation besides think so.

Let them think what they will.

What is the reason these cannot come to you?

I do not know but they can if they will or else if you please I will come to them.

What was that the black man whispered to you?

There was none whispered to me.

[Reverse] The Examinãon of Susannah Martin:

Notes: This is Parris's completed version of the examination. ◊ Hand 1 = Samuel Parris

Essex County Court Archives, vol. 1, no. 175, Massachusetts Supreme Judicial Court, Judicial Archives, on deposit James Duncan Phillips Library, Peabody Essex Museum, Salem, MA.

106. Deposition of Sarah Bibber v. Susannah Martin†

See also: June 29, 1692.

[Hand 1] The Deposistion of Sarah viber agged about 36 years: who testifieth and s[Lost] [= says] that on the 2: may 1692: the Apperishtion of Susannah martin of Amsbery di⟨d⟩

May 2, 1692   most greviously torment me dureing the time of hir examination for if she did but look
personally upon me she would strik me down or allmost cho⟨a⟩[Lost] [= choke] me: and also
the same day I saw the Apperishtion of Susannah ^{martin} most g[Lost]ously [=
grievously] afflect the bodyes of mary walcott: mercy lewes and Ann putn[Lost] [= Putnam]
by pinching and almost choaking them: and seuerall times sence the App[Lost]tion [=
apparition] of Susannah martin has most greviously Afflected me by beating and pinching
me and almost choaking me to death:
[Hand 2] & yᵗ She beleiues She Sd Martin is a witch & yᵗ she is bewiched by her

                     Jurat in Curia

[Reverse] [Hand 1] Sarah viber against Susan: martin

Notes: Although there is no ink change in this and the following document, both carry what may be a later addition of
"and seuerall times sence." ◊ Used at trial. ◊ Hand 1 = Thomas Putnam; Hand 2 = Stephen Sewall

*Essex County Court Archives, vol. 1, no. 197, Massachusetts Supreme Judicial Court, Judicial Archives, on deposit James Duncan
Phillips Library, Peabody Essex Museum, Salem, MA.*

107. Deposition of Elizabeth Hubbard v. Susannah Martin†

[Hand 1] The Deposistion of Elizabeth Hubburd agged about :17: years: who testifieth and
saith that I haue often seen the Apperishtion of Susannah Martin amongst the wicthes but
shee did not hurt me tell the :2 day of may being the day of hir examination: but then she did
afflect me most greviously dureing the time of hir Examination for if she did but look
parsonally upon me she would strike me down or allmost choak me: and seuerall times sence
the Apperishtion of Susannah martin has most greviously afflected me also on the day of hir
Examination I saw the Apperishtion of Susannah martin goe and afflect and allmost choak
Mary walcott Miry Lewes Abigaill williams and Ann putnam junr

                   mark
                Eliz:  Hubburds

[Reverse] Eliz: Hubburd againt Susannah Martin

Notes: Although similar to the previous record, No. 106, this one was not used at the trial. ◊ Hand 1 = Thomas Putnam

*Essex County Court Archives, vol. 1, no. 196, Massachusetts Supreme Judicial Court, Judicial Archives, on deposit James Duncan
Phillips Library, Peabody Essex Museum, Salem, MA.*

108. Deposition of Mercy Lewis v. Susannah Martin†

[Hand 1] The Deposistion of Mircy lewes aged about 19 years who testifieth and sath that
in the latteer end of April 1692 there appered to me the Apperishtion of a short old woman
which tould me hir name was gooddy mat⟨i⟩[Lost] [= Martin] and that she came from
Ambery who did most greviously torment me by by biting and pinching me urging me
vehemetly to writ in hir book but on the 2 may 1692 being ["ing" written over "the"] the day

May 2, 1692

of hir examination Susannah Martin did torment and afflect me most greviously in the time of hir Examin⟨a⟩tion for wⁿ she looked upon me parsonally she would strike me down or almost choake ^{me} and seuerall times senc the Apperishtion of Susannah martin has most greviously affleted me by pinching and almost choaking me to death urging me to writ in hir book: and also on the day of hir Examination I saw the Apperishtion of Susannah Martin goe and hurt the bodyes of Mary walcott Elizabeth Hubburd Abigail williams and Ann putnam junr.

mercy lewes

[Reverse] mircy lewes againt Susannah martin

Notes: The manuscript shows an ink change beginning with "and also on the day . . ." that strongly suggests Putnam adding information at a later time. It is not possible to tell whether the signature of Mercy Lewis is authentic or not. ◊ Hand 1 = Thomas Putnam

Essex County Court Archives, vol. 1, no. 195, Massachusetts Supreme Judicial Court, Judicial Archives, on deposit James Duncan Phillips Library, Peabody Essex Museum, Salem, MA.

109. Deposition of Samuel Parris, Nathaniel Ingersoll, & Thomas Putnam v. Susannah Martin‡

See also: June 29, 1692.

[Hand 1] The Deposition of Sam: Parris aged about 39. years, & Nathanael Ingersoll aged about fifty & eight yeares & also Tho: Putman aged about fourty yeares all of Salem testifyeth & saith that Abigail Williams, Mercy Lews, Mary Walcot, Susannah Sheding & John Indian were much afflicted at the Examination of Susannah Martin of Almsbury Widdow – before the honoured Magistrates the .2. May. 1692 & that Goody Bibber (who before had not accused her) & some other of the afflicted then & there testifyed that there was a black man whispering in her ear, & also that the said Bibber Abigail Williams, & Mary Walcot & John Indian could not come near ^{said Martin} when upon triall they were ordered by the Magistrates to attempt it, & their agonies & tortures they charged said Martin as the cause of, & also we farther saw that when she ^{said Martin} bit her lips they were bitten, & when the afflicted were ordered to go towards her they were knockt down

[Hand 2] Jurat in Curia

[Reverse] [Hand 1] The Depoͭion of Sam: Parris &c agsᵗ Susan: Martin

Notes: Used at trial. ◊ Hand 1 = Samuel Parris

Essex County Court Archives, vol. 1, no. 194, Massachusetts Supreme Judicial Court, Judicial Archives, on deposit James Duncan Phillips Library, Peabody Essex Museum, Salem, MA.

110. Deposition of Ann Putnam Jr. v. Susannah Martin†

[Hand 1] The Deposistion of Ann putnam ^{junr} who testifieth and saith sume time in April 1692 ther⟨e⟩ appered to me the Apperishtion of an old short woman that toald me hir

May 2, 1692

name was martin and that she came from Amsbery who did Immediatly afflect me urging me to writ in hir book but on the 2: may 1692 being the day of hir examination Susannah martin did most greviously afflect me dureing the time of hir examination for when she did but look parsonaly upon she would strike me down or almost choak and seuerall times senc the Apperishtion of Susannah martin has most greviouly affleted me by pinching me & allmost choaking me urging me vehemently to writ in hir book: also on the the day of hir Examination I saw the Apperishtion of Susannah martin goe and Afflect the bodys of mary wallcott Mircy Lewes Elizabeth Hubburd and Abigail williams

[Reverse] Ann putnam Junr aganst Susannah Martin

Notes: Hand 1 = Thomas Putnam

Essex County Court Archives, vol. 1, no. 198, Massachusetts Supreme Judicial Court, Judicial Archives, on deposit James Duncan Phillips Library, Peabody Essex Museum, Salem, MA.

111. Deposition of Thomas Putnam v. Susannah Martin and Testimony of Nathaniel Ingersoll v. Susannah Martin‡

See also: June 29, 1692.

[Hand 1] The deposistion of Tho. putnam agged 40 years & ~~Ed. putnam~~ agged 38 yers ~~we whose names are under writ~~⟨e⟩n who testifie and say that we haue ben conversant with the afflected parsons or the most of them as namly mary walcott mercy lewes Eliz: Hubburd Abigail williams and ^{Saraı vibber} Ann putnam {Jn⟨r⟩} {and} haue often heard the afforementioned parsons complain of Susannah martin of Amsbery tortoring ["i" written over "e"] them and we haue seen the marks of seuerall bittes and pinches which they said Susannah martin did hirt them ^{with} and also on the 2 day of may 1692 being the day of the Examination of Susannah martin the afformed ["n" written over "e"] parsons ware most greviously tortored dureing the time of hir Examination for upon the glance of hir eies they ware strucken down or allmost choak and upon the motion of hir finger we took notis they ware afflected ~~ad~~ and if she did but clench ⟨?⟩ hir hands or hold hir head asid⟨e⟩ the afflected parsons affor mentioned ware most greviouly tortored in like maner and seuerall times sence we haue seen them tortored complaing [= complaining] of Susannah martin for hirting them

Thomas putnam
~~Edward Putnam~~

[Hand 2] Nathaniel Ing^ɛsoll Testifieth to all y^e aboue & both of them do Say On Oath that they beleiue it is done by Witchcraft

Jurat in Curia

[Reverse] Nathan^ll Ing^ɛsoll & Tho: Putman
[Hand 3] Susannah Martin

Notes: Nathaniel Ingersoll's confirming testimony was probably added to the original document at the time of the trial where, perhaps, Edward Putnam did not appear as planned. ◊ Used at trial. ◊ Hand 1 = Thomas Putnam; Hand 2 = Stephen Sewall

Essex County Court Archives, vol. 1, no. 193, Massachusetts Supreme Judicial Court, Judicial Archives, on deposit James Duncan Phillips Library, Peabody Essex Museum, Salem, MA.   May 2, 1692

112. Deposition of Mary Walcott v. Susannah Martin†

See also: June 29, 1692.

[Hand 1] The Deposistion of Mary walcott agged about 17 years who testifieth and saith that in the latter end of April 1692 there Appered to me the apperishtion of a short old woman which tould me hir name was gooddy martin and that she came from Amsbery who did most greviously torment and affflect me by pinching and allmost choaking me to death urging me to writ in hir booke or elce threating to kill me: but on the 2ᵈ may being the day of hir examination she did most greviously torment and afflect me dureing the time of hir examination for when she did ∧{but} look parsonally upon me she would strik me down or allmost choak me to death: and seuerall times sence the Apperishtion of Susannah Martin has most greviously afflected me by biting pinching and allmost choaking me to de{a}th threating to kill me if I would not writ in hir book: also on the :2 day of may 1692 being the day of hir Examination I saw the Apperishtion of Susannah martin goe {⟨?⟩} and afflect and hutt [= hurt] the bodyes of Mircy Lewes Elizabeth Hubburd Abigaile williams and Ann putnam Junr.

hir marke

mary 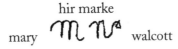 walcott

[Reverse] mary walcott against Susannah martin
[Hand 2] Court Oyʳ & Ter by Adjournmᵗ June. 29. 92
[Hand 3] Martin
[Hand 1] Susannah martin

Notes: Thomas Putnam in another ink adds the part beginning with "also on the" at a later time. This trial document does not carry Stephen Sewall's usual "Jurat in Curia," but the reference to it as used at the Court of Oyer and Terminer, in Sewall's hand, makes clear that it was used at the trial. ◊ Used at trial. ◊ Hand 1 = Thomas Putnam; Hand 2 = Stephen Sewall

MS Am 45, Rare Books & Manuscripts, Boston Public Library. Boston, MA.

113. Testimony of Abigail Williams v. Susannah Martin†

[Hand 1] The Testimony of Abigail Williams witnesseth & saith that she hath severa⟨l⟩ times seen, & been afflicted by the apparition of Susannah Martin of Almsbury widow at & before the .2. May. 1692

Notes: Hand 1 = Samuel Parris

Essex County Court Archives, vol. 1, no. 178, Massachusetts Supreme Judicial Court, Judicial Archives, on deposit James Duncan Phillips Library, Peabody Essex Museum, Salem, MA.

May 2, 1692

114. Mittimus for Susannah Martin, Lydia Dustin, Dorcas Hoar & Sarah Morey

[Hand 1] To the Keeper of theire Majes^ts Goale in Boston

You are in theire Majes^ts names hereby required to take into, your care and safe Custody the Bodys of Susanah Martin of Amesbury Widdow, Lydia Dastin of Reding Wi[Lost] [= widow], Dorcas Hoar of Beverly widdow and Sarah Murrill also of Beverly who all stand Charged with high Suspition of Sundry acts of Witchcraft donne or Committed by them vpon the Bodys of Mary Walcot Marcy Lewis Abigail Williams Ann Putnam Elizabeth Hubbert and Susannah Sheld[Lost] [= Sheldon] and Goody Viber of Salem Village or ffarmes whereby great hurt and dammage hath benne donne to y^e bodys ⟨of⟩ said persons according to Complaint of Capt Jonathan Walcot and Serj^ε Thomas Putnam of Salem Village Yeoman Exhibited Salem Aprill the 30th 1692: whome you are to secure in order to theire further Examination or Tryall and hereof you are not to faile. Dated Salem Village May 2^d 1692

John Hathorne ⎫
                           ⎬ Assis^ts
Jonathan. Corwin ⎭

Notes: Hand 1 = John Hathorne

Essex County Court Archives, vol. 1, no. 177, Massachusetts Supreme Judicial Court, Judicial Archives, on deposit James Duncan Phillips Library, Peabody Essex Museum, Salem, MA.

115. Letter of Elisha Hutchinson to John Hathorne & Jonathan Corwin Regarding Apprehension of George Burroughs

[Hand 1] Portsmouth. May .2. 1692

Gentlemen

I Rec^d an order from ye Gov^ε & Council to aprehend m̄^r George Buroughs at present preacher at Wells, to be Sent to Salem their to be Examened, being Susspected to have Confedracy with the devil in opressing Sundry persons about yo^ε Towne of Salem, accordingly I have Sent him by John Partredg Marshal of this provence, Except he meet with any other Authority that will com̄it him to Some other officer to be Convayed as above, he pleading it will be to his dam̄age to go So far, I am

yo^ε humble Servant
Elisha Hutchinson

[Reverse] To Jn° Hauthorn ⎫
            or Jon^a Curwin ⎬   Esq^εs
      In Salem ⎭

[Hand 2] Maj^oε Hutchesons Letter Concern^ε Burrough

Notes: Hutchinson had signed the warrant for the arrest of Burroughs. ◊ Hand 1 = Elisha Hutchinson; Hand 2 = John Hathorne

Witchcraft Papers, no. 2, Massachusetts Historical Society. Boston, MA.

Tuesday, May 3, 1692   May 3, 1692

116. Examination of Deliverance Hobbs in Prison

[Hand 1] Deliverance. Hobbs. Exam$^\varepsilon$ May. 3. 1692. Salem ⟨pri⟩son
Q. W^t have you done Since whereby y^r is further Trouble in your appearance? An. Nothing
att all. Q. but have you nott Since bin Tempted? An. yes S$^\varepsilon$, but I have nott done itt, nor will
nott doe itt. Q. here is a great Change Since We last Spake to you, for now you Afflict &
Torment againe; now Tell us y^e Truth Whoe Tempted you to Sighne againe? An. itt was
Goody Olliver; she would have me⟨e⟩ to Sett my hand to y^e book, butt I would nott neither
have ⟨I⟩ neither did consent to hurt y^m againe. Q. was y^t True y^t Goody W⟨ilds⟩ appeared to
you & Tempted you? An. yes, that was True. Q. have y⟨ou⟩ bin Tempted Since? ~~ye~~ An. yes,
about fryday or Saturday nig⟨ht⟩ [Lost] [*Woodward* = last] Q. did y^a [= they] bid you y^t you
should nott Tell? An. yes, thay Tould me ⟨soe.⟩ Q. but how farr did thay draw you or Tempt
you, & how f[Lost] [*Woodward* = farr did] you yeild to y^e Temptation? but doe nott you
acknowledge y^t [Lost] [*Woodward* = that] was True y^t you Tould us formerly? An. yes. Q.
and you did sig⟨h⟩[Lost] [= sign] then att y^e ffirst, did you Nott? An. yes, I did itt is True.
Q. did you [Lost]miss [= promise] y^n to deny att last what you Said before? An. yes, I did
[Lost] [*Woodward* = and itt] was Goody Oliver [Hand 2] ^{Alias Bishop} [Hand 1] y^t
Tempted me to deny all y^t I had Confessed before. Q. doe you nott know y^e man wth y^e
Wenne? ⟨A⟩n. noe I doe nott know whoe itt is; all y^t I Confessed before is True. Q. Whoe
Were y^a you Named formerly? An. Osburne, Good, Burrough⟨s,⟩ Olliver, Wiles, Cory & his
Wife, Nurse, Procter & his Wife. Q. ⟨who⟩ Were wth you in ye Chamber? (itt being informed
y^t Some were Talking wth hir there). An. Wilds and Bushop or Olliver, Good & Osburne, &
y^a had a ffeast Both of Roast & Boyled meat & did eat & drink & would have had me to have
eat & drank wth y^m, but I wou⟨ld⟩ nott; & y^a would have had me Sighned, but I would nott
y^n Nor whe[Lost] [= when] Goody. Olliver came to me. Q. Nor did nott you Con[Lost]
[*Woodward* = consent to hurt these] children in your likeness? An. I doe nott know ⟨y^t⟩ I
did. Q. W[Lost] [= what] is y^t you have to Tell, wch you cañott Tell ye⟨t⟩ you Say?

[Reverse] Mary. Warrens Examination. May. [Lost]
Q. Whether you did nott Sett your hand
[Hand 2] Warren ve. Procter
[Hand 3] Deliu$^\varepsilon$ Hobs her Examination & Testimony ag^t procter & wife & others

Notes: The reverse begins with an examination of Mary Warren, almost certainly in prison, by Jonathan Corwin, probably
on May 12. For whatever reasons, Corwin seems to have begun again on a separate document. Also, although the testimony
of Hobbs is most directly aimed at Bridget Bishop and Sarah Wilds, the notation on the reverse identifies only John
Procter and Elizabeth, his wife, this probably related to the Warren portion. Deliverance Hobbs confirmed previous
accusations against others. The further examination of confessors in prison had become a pattern by May 3. ◊ "Wenne":
'protuberance' (*OED* s.v. *wen* 1a). ◊ Hand 1 = Jonathan Corwin; Hand 2 = Stephen Sewall; Hand 3 = John Hathorne

*Essex County Court Archives, vol. 1, no. 140, Massachusetts Supreme Judicial Court, Judicial Archives, on deposit James Duncan
Phillips Library, Peabody Essex Museum, Salem, MA.*

Wednesday, May 4, 1692

Officer's Return: Warrant for the Apprehension of George Burroughs
2nd of 2 dates. See No. 97 on April 30, 1692.

Friday, May 6, 1692

117. Warrant No. 2 for the Apprehension of Philip English, and Officer's Return

See also: May 30, 1692.

[Hand 1] To the Marshall Generall or his Lawfull Deputie

Whereas Complaint hath bin made by Capt Jonathan Walcott and Thomas Putnam of Salem Village vpon the 30th of Aprill Last past ^{in behalfe of theire Majesties} against Phillip English of Salem Merchant for high Suspition of Diuers acts of Witchcraft donne or Committed by him vpon the Bodys of Ann Putnam Marcy Lewis Susannah Sheldon &c ^{of Salem village or farmes} and whereas Warrant hath benne for Some tyme Since granted out for the apprehending of the Said Phillip English to bring him vpon Examinati[Lost] [= examination] and he not appeareing or found ^{since} in y^e County of Essex You ["You" written over "These"] are therefore in their Majes^{ts} names hereby required to apprehend the S^d Phillip English of Salem Mer^{ct} and him Convey vnto Salem in y^e County of Essex and deliuer him into the Custody of the Marshall of S^d County of Essex or some Lawfull Authority there, that he may be Examined Relateing to y^e aboues^d premises Either by such as shall be appointed therevnto or to the Majestrates in S^d place and hereof you are not to faile Dated Boston May 6^t 1692

$ℙ$ vs   John: Hathorne   } Assis^{ts}
          Jonathan. Corwin

[Reverse] [Hand 2] In obedience to the within written warr^t the within menc̅oned [= mentioned] Phillip English was arrested & comitted by the Marshall Generall to the Marshall of Essex w̶e̶h̶ ⟨?⟩ on the 30th of May instant and in pursuance of the s^d warrant the s^d Phillipp English was brought before the within menc̅oned John Hathorne & Jonathan Corwin Esq^{Es} the 31st May 1692 to answer the within accusation by m⟨e⟩
$ℙ$ me⟨e⟩ Jacob Manning
marsell depay [= marshall deputy]

[Hand 3] Warrant P English

Notes: Although arrested, Philip English escaped with his wife, Mary, fled the colony, and returned when it was safe to do so. ◊ Hand 1 = John Hathorne; Hand 2 = Thomas Newton.

Essex County Court Archives, vol. 1, no. 170, Massachusetts Supreme Judicial Court, Judicial Archives, on deposit James Duncan Phillips Library, Peabody Essex Museum, Salem, MA.

Sunday, May 8, 1692

118. Warrant for the Apprehension of Sarah Dustin, and Officer's Return

See also: May 9, 1692.

[Hand 1] Whereas Complaint hath bin Exhibited before us ⟨by⟩ ⟨m^ε⟩ Thomas Putnam & ⟨m^ε⟩ Jno Putnam Jun^ε of Salem Village ⟨In⟩. y^e behalfe of theyr Majestys against Sarah Da⟨st⟩in of Redding Single Woeman for high su⟨s⟩pition o⟨f⟩ severall Acts of Witch=craft done or comitted ⟨b⟩y hir upon y^e Bodyes of Mercy Lewis, Mary Walcott, Anna Putnam & Abigall. Williams all of Salem Village & Craved Justice.

Therefore you are in theyre Majestyes Names Required forthwith to Apprehend the afores^d Sarah Da⟨s⟩tin of Redding Single woeman ⟨&⟩ hir Safely [Lost] [SWP = convey] unto y^e house of Le⟨u⟩^t Nathaniell Inger⟨solls⟩ o[Lost] [= of] Salem Village u⟨p⟩on y^e Ninth day of this In⟨st⟩ant May by Twelve of the Clock in y^e forenoone in o⟨r⟩der to hir examination ⟨&⟩hereof ff⟨a⟩ile n. upon y^e premises & hereof ffai⟨l⟩e nott att yo^ε perrill Salem. Dated. May 8th 1692.

To y^e Constable of Redding

> John: Hathorne
> ꝑ vs   } Assis^ts
> Jonathan. Corwin

[Reverse] [Hand 2] In obediance to this warant I haue brought the body of Sarah Dastin of Redding singal woman to y^e house of Leu^t Nathanall Ingerson of Salem. Villeg the nint of this Instant maye: 1692

John Parker Constable ꝑof Redding

Notes: Hand 1 = Jonathan Corwin

Essex County Court Archives, vol. 2, no. 99, Massachusetts Supreme Judicial Court, Judicial Archives, on deposit James Duncan Phillips Library, Peabody Essex Museum, Salem, MA.

119. Warrant for the Apprehension of Ann Sears, Bethiah Carter Sr., & Bethiah Carter Jr., and Officer's Return

See also: May 9, 1692.

[Hand 1] Whereas Complaint hath benne this day Exhibited (before vs) by Thomas Putnam and John Putnam {Jun^ε} both of Salem Village Yeoman ^{on behalfe of theire Majesties} Against [Hand 2] Ann[Lost] [= Annah?] [Hand 1] Seeres [Hand 2] the wife of John Seeres [Hand 1] of Woburne and [Hand 2] Bethia [Hand 1] Carter of s^d Towne of Woburne Widdow and [Hand 2] Bethya [Hand 1] Carter y^e daufter of s^d Carter Widdow. for high Suspition of Sundry acts of Witchcraft donne by them vpon the Bodys of Ann Putnam Marcy Lewis Mary Walcot &c of Salem Village wh[Lost] [= whereby?] much hurt & wrong is donne vnto them ^{there⟨f⟩[Lost] [= therefore?]} Crave⟨d⟩ [Lost] [SWP = Justice].

May 9, 1692

These are therefore in theire Majes^ts names to require you, to apprehend and forthwith bring the persons of the abouenamed before vs at Sal⟨em⟩ Village at y^e house of Lt Nathaniell Ingersalls in order to theire Examination Relateing to y^e abouesaid premises and hereof you are not to faile Dated Salem May 8th 1692

[Hand 3] To y^e Constable of Woburne.

$$\text{⅌ vs} \quad \left.\begin{array}{l} \text{John: Hathorne} \\ \text{Jonathan. Corwin} \end{array}\right\} \text{Assis}^{ts}$$

[Reverse] [Hand 4] I Ephraim bouck counstabel of Woburn haue sarued this warant acording to Law hau apurhanded [= apprehended] the parson of anah Sauris and of the wado cartter and hauf broit tham to Lautanant ingursons hois as warant due exprest

[Hand 5] In pursuance to the within specifyed warrant I haue apprehended the bodies of the within mentioned Anna Seers & Bethia Carter sen^ε & brought them to the place within ordered this 9 May 1692

Ephraim Bock Constable of woburn

[Hand 1] Whereas Complaint hath benne this day Exhibited (before vs) Against

Notes: Thomas Putnam filled in specific identities. Note that Samuel Parris wrote the return of the constable. ◊ Hand 1 = John Hathorne; Hand 2 = Thomas Putnam; Hand 3 = Jonathan Corwin; Hand 5 = Samuel Parris

Essex County Court Archives, vol. 2, no. 100, Massachusetts Supreme Judicial Court, Judicial Archives, on deposit James Duncan Phillips Library, Peabody Essex Museum, Salem, MA.

Monday, May 9, 1692

Officer's Return: Warrant for the Apprehension of Sarah Dustin
2nd of 2 dates. See No. 118 on May 8, 1692

Officer's Return: Warrant for the Apprehension of Ann Sears, Bethiah Carter Sr. & Bethiah Carter Jr.
2nd of 2 dates. See No. 119 on May 8, 1692

120. Examination of George Burroughs and Statement of Abigail Hobbs v. George Burroughs

See also: May 11, 1692.

[Hand 1] The Examination of Geo: Burrough. 9. May. 1692

$$\text{By } \cancel{\text{Before}} \text{ the Honoured} \quad \left\{\begin{array}{l} \text{W}^m \text{ Stoughton} \\ \text{John Hathorn} \\ \text{Sam: Sewall} \\ \text{Jonath: Corwin} \end{array}\right\} \quad \text{Esq}^{εs}$$

May 9, 1692

Being askt wⁿ he partook of the Lords Supper, he being (as he said) in full comunion at Roxbury.

He answered it was so long since he could not tell: yet he owned he was at meeting one Sab: at Boston part of the day, & the other at Charlstown part of a Sab: when that Sacrament happened to be at both, yet did not partake of either.

He denied that his house at Casko was haunted. Yet he owned there were Toads.

He denied that he made his ~~swear~~ wife Swear, that she should not write to her Father Ruck without his approbation of her letter to her Father.

He owned that none of his children, but the Eldest was Baptized.

The abovesd was in private none of the Bewitched being present.

At his entry into the Room, many (if not all of the Bewitched) were greivously tortured.

{1.} Sus: Sheldon testifyed that Burroughs two wives appeared in their winding sheets, & said that man killed them.

He was bid to look upon Sus: Sheldon.

He looked back & knockt down all (or most) of the afflicted, w^o stood behind him.

[Lost] [*Woodward* = Sus: Sheldon. .(one line gone)] the souldiers.

{2.} Mercy Lewes deposition going to be read & he lookt upon her & she fell into a dreadful & tedious fit.

{3.} Mary Walcot	
{4.} Eliz: Hubbard	Testimony going to be read & they all fell into fits.
Susan: Sheldon	

Susan: Sheldon	affirmed each of them that
{5.} Ann Putman jun^ε	he brought the Book & ⟨?⟩d [= would] have them write.

Bein⟨g⟩ askt w^t [Lost] [= he] thought of these things.

He answered it [Lost] [= was] an amazing & humbling Providence, but he understood nothing of ^{it}, ⟨&⟩ he said (some of you may observe, that) when they begin [Lost] name my name, they cannot name it

[Lost] [*SWP* = Ann Putnam Jun'r]	Testifyeth that his 2. Wi⟨ves⟩ & .2.
Susan: Sheldon	chil⟨dr⟩en ⟨did⟩ accus⟨e⟩ him.

The Bewitched were so tortured that Authority ordered them to be taken away Some of them.

{6.} Sarah Bibber testifyed that he had hurt her, thô she had not seen him personally before as she knew

Abig: Hobbs	
Deliverance Hobbs	Testimony read
Eliezar Keiser	

Capt Willard	
Jno Brown	Testimony about his great Strength & the Gun.
Jno Wheldon	

Capt. Putman testifyed about the Gun.

Capt. Wormwood testifyed about the Gun & the Mallassoes

He denied that about the Malassoes

About the Gun he said he took it before the lock & rested it upon his breast

JohnBrown~~test~~ testifyed about a b̄l̄l̄ [= barrel] Cyder.

May 9, 1692   He denyed that his family was affrighted by a white calf in his house.
Capt Putman testifyed that he made his wife enter into a Covenant

11. May .1692

Abig: Hobbs in prison affirmed that Geo: Burrou⟨ghs⟩ in his Shape appeared to her, &
urged her to set her hand to the Book, which she did; & afterwards in his own person he
acknowledged to her, that he had made her set her hand to the Book.

[Reverse] The [Lost] of Geo: Burrough

Notes: Burroughs's arrest having been ordered by the Governor and Council, his examination was conducted with William
Stoughton joining Hathorne and Corwin. All would serve as judges on the Court of Oyer and Terminer that condemned
him. The reverse of the manuscript printed here has some notations by Parris unrelated to the Salem witch trials that appear
to be citations from the Geneva Bible and are in a shorthand form. These are not printed in the edition. Confessors were
being used to support witchcraft claims against others, and Abigail Hobbs complied. Parris added her May 11 comments
to the document. The questions about the Lord's Supper and baptism raised the issue of whether Burroughs was a
dissident minister. A nineteenth-century copy of this examination, in the Essex County Court Archives, used by *SWP*,
has not been included in this edition. It appears in *SWP*, I,153–154. The copy carries in a later hand the following: "The
original minutes (of which the above is a true copy) is in the possession of I. F. Andrews Esq. & was found among Judge
Hathornes papers. – Aug. 8. 1843. *I B Curwen." *SWP* does not carry the original document. ◊ Hand 1 = Samuel Parris

UNCAT MS, *Miscellaneous Manuscripts (1692)*, Massachusetts Historical Society. Boston, MA.

121. Deposition of Sarah Bibber v. George Burroughs†
See also: Aug. 3, 1692 & Aug. 5, 1692.

[Hand 1] The deposistion of Sarah viber who testifieth and saith that on the 9th day of may
1692 as I was agoeing to Salem village I saw the apperishtio⟨n⟩ of a little man like a minister
with a black coat on ~~on~~ and he pinched me by the arme and bid me goe along with him but I
tould him I would not but when I came to the village I saw theire ⟨?⟩ Mr. Gorge Burroughs
which I neuer saw before and then I knew that it was his apperishtion which I had seen in
the morning and he tortured me seuerall times while he was in examination: also dureing the
time of his Examination I saw Mr. George Burroughs or his Apparance most greviously
torment and afflect mary walcott mercy [Hand 2] ^{Luis} [Hand 1] Elizabeth Hubburt Ann
putnam and abigaill williams by pinching ~~tiwi~~ twisting and al⟨m⟩[Lost] [= almost] choaking
them to death also seuerall times sence Mr George Burroughs or his Apperance has most
greviously tormented {me} with variety of tortors and I beleue in my heart that mr George
Burroughs is a dreadfull wizzard and that he has most greviously tormen⟨t⟩ed me and the
aboue mentioned parson by his acts of wicthcraft.

[Hand 3] Sarah Viber declared: to y^e Jury of inquest: that the: above written evidence is: the
truth: Aug^st :3: 1692 [Hand 2] the which she ownid one har oath

[Hand 4] Jurat in Curia

[Reverse] [Hand 5] Sarah Viber ag^t Burrough

Notes: Used at trial. ◊ Hand 1 = Thomas Putnam; Hand 2 = Simon Willard; Hand 4 = Stephen Sewall

Essex County Court Archives, vol. 2, no. 27, Massachusetts Supreme Judicial Court, Judicial Archives, on deposit James Duncan Phillips Library, Peabody Essex Museum, Salem, MA.

May 9, 1692

122. Statement of Elizabeth Hubbard v. George Burroughs
See also: Aug. 3, 1692 & Aug. 5, 1692.

[Hand 1] May yᵉ .9. 1692.

Elisabeth hubord aged about .17. yers saith that yᵉ last second day at night: There apeared a little blackheard [= black-haired] man to me in blackish aparill I asked him his name. & he told me his name was borrous, Then he tooke a booke out of his pocket: & opened it. & bid me set my hand to it I tould him I would not: yᵉ lines in this book was read as blod: then he pinched me twise & went away: The next morning. he apeared to me againe. and tould me he was aboue a wizard: for he was a conjurar {&} so went away but sins that he hath apeared to me euery day & night uery often: ~~and~~ and urged me uery much to set my hand to his book: and to run away telling me if I would do so I should be well & that I should need feare no body; & withall tormented me seuerall ways euery time he Came exept that time he told me he was a conjuror: This night he asked me very much to set my hand to his book or else he sayed he would kill me; withall tortoring me uery much by biting and pinching squesing my body & runing pins into me [Hand 2] also on the: 9ᵗʰ may 1692 being the time of his Examination Mr. George Burroughs or his Apperance did most greviously afflect and torment the bodyes of mary walcott. mercy lewes Ann putnam and Abigail williams for if he did but look upon them he would strick them down or almost choak them to death also seuerall times sence he has most dreadfully afflected and tormented me with variety of torments and I beleue in my heart yᵗ mr George Burroughs is a dreadfull wizzard and that he has very often tormented me and also the aboue named parsons by his acts of wicthcraft

[Hand 3] Jurat in Curia

[Hand 4] Eliz Hubbard: declared: yᵉ above written evedence: to be yᵉ truth: upon her oath: that she had: taken: this she owned: before yᵉ Jury of inquest: Augˢᵗ 3 1692

[Reverse] [Hand 5] Eliz: Hubbert agt Burroughs

Notes: Thomas Putnam's addition probably came later than May 9, presumably to strengthen the grand jury and/or trial case. ◊ Used at trial. ◊ Hand 2 = Thomas Putnam; Hand 3 = Stephen Sewall; Hand 4 = Simon Willard ◊ Facsimile Plate 3.

Essex County Court Archives, vol. 2, no. 30, Massachusetts Supreme Judicial Court, Judicial Archives, on deposit James Duncan Phillips Library, Peabody Essex Museum, Salem, MA.

123. Statement of Elizer Keyser v. George Burroughs†
See also: Aug. 3, 1692 & Aug. 5, 1692.

[Hand 1] Elizar Keysar aged aboute fourty fiue yeares sayth that on Thur⟨s⟩day last past being the fift day of this Instant moneth of May I was at yᵉ house of Thomas [1 word overstruck] in ⟨Sa⟩lem and Capᵗ Daniell King being there also at the same tyme, and in the Same Roome. Sᵈ Capᵗ Daniell King Asked mee whether I would not goe vp, and see mʳ Burrows and discourse with him: he being then in one of the Chambers in sᵈ House. I told

May 9, 1692

him itt did not belong to mee, and I was not willing to medle or make with itt, then s^d King sayd are you not a Christian if you are a Christian goe ⟨?⟩ see him and discourse with him, but I told him I did beleiue it did not belong to such as I was to discourse him he being a Learned man. then s^d King sayd I beleiue he is a Child of god, a Choice Child of god, and that God would Clear vp his Inocency; soe I told him my opinion or feare was, that he was, the Cheife of all the persons accused for witchcraft or the Ring Leader of them all, and told him also y^t [Lost] [= I] beleiued if he was such an one his Master ^{meaning ⟨y^e⟩ diuell} had told him before now, what I said of him; And s^d King seemeing to mee to be in a passion. I did afterward forbeare. ~~The same Euening after those words being alone in~~ ^{one Roome of} ~~my house and noe candle or light being in y^es^d Roome~~ the Same after noone I hauein⟨g⟩ occation to be at the s^d Beadles house ~~againe I was~~ {and being} in the Chamber where m^r George Burroughs Keept ~~and~~ I observed y^t s^d Burroughs did {stedfastly} [1 word overstruck] fix h⟨is⟩ Eyes vpon mee, the same Eueneing being in my own house, in a Roome [1 word overstruck] without any Light I did see very strange things appeare in y^e Chimney. I suppose a dozen of them. wch seemed to mee to b⟨e⟩ som⟨e⟩thing like Jelly y^t vsed to be in y^e water, and quic[Lost] [= quickly] with a strange Motion, and then quickly disappeared so⟨o⟩ne after which I did see a light vp in y^e chimney aboute y^e bigness of my hand something aboue the bar wch quivered & shaked. and seemed to {haue} a Motion vpward vpon which I called the Mayd, and she looking vp into the Chimney saw the same, and my wife l⟨o⟩[Lost] [= looking] vp could not see any thing, soe I did and doe [1 word overstruck] Consid[Lost] [= consider] it was some diabolicall apperition

[Hand 2] Jurat in Curia by Mr Keysor Sworne also by Eliz: Woodwell as to y^e Last night
[Hand 3] Mr Elizer Keyzer: declared: to y^e Jury of Inquest that y^e evidence: in this paper is y^e truth upon oath: Augst 3⟨?⟩ 1692
Mercy Lewis. also: s^d that M^{r⟨s⟩} Borroughs: told her: that: he made lights: in Mr Keyzers: Chimney

Notes: Used at trial. ◊ Hand 1 = John Hathorne; Hand 2 = Stephen Sewall; Hand 3 = Simon Willard

Salem Selections, Massachusetts Box, Essex Co., Manuscripts & Archives, New York Public Library. New York, NY.

124. Deposition of Mercy Lewis v. George Burroughs, and Statement of Thomas Putnam & Edward Putnam v. George Burroughs†

See also: Aug. 3, 1692 & Aug. 5, 1692.

[Hand 1] the deposistion of Mircy Lewes who testifieth and saith that one the 7th of may 1692 att evening I saw the apperishtion of Mr George Burroughs ^{whom I very well knew} which did greviously tortor me and urged me to writ in his Book and then he brought to me a new fashon book ~~to me~~ which he did not vse to bring and tould me I might writ in that book: for that was a book that was in his studdy when I liued with him ["him" written over "them"]: but I tould him I did not beleue him for I had been often in his studdy but I neur saw that book their: but he tould me that he had seuerall books in his studdy which I neuer saw ~~for he said he had counjuring books~~ in his studdy and he could raise the diuell: ~~and that he had bewicthed his Two first wiues to death:~~ and now had bewicthed Mr Sheppards daughter and I asked him how he could goe to bewicth hir now he was keept at Salem: and he tould mee that the divell was his sarvant and he sent him in his shap to doe it then he againe tortored me most dreadfully and threatened to kill me for he said I should not witnes against him also he tould me that he had made: Abigaill Hoobs: a wicth and severall more then againe he did most dreadfully ⟨?⟩ tortor me as if he would haue racked me all to peaces and urged me to writ in his book or elce he would kill me but I tould him I hoped my life was not in the power of his hands and that I would not writ tho he did kill me: the next nigh⟨t⟩ he tould me I should not see his Two wifes if he could help ^{it} because I should not witnes agast [= against] him: this 9th may mr Burroughs caried me up to an exceeding high mountain and shewed me all the kingdoms of the earth and tould me that he would giue them all to me if I would writ in his book. and if I would not he would thro me down and brake my neck: but I tould him they ware non of his to giue and I would not writ if he throde {me} down on 100 pichforks: allso on the 9th may being the time of his Examination mr. George Burroughs ⟨?⟩ did most dreadfully torment me: and also seuerall times sence

[Hand 2] marcy: luis uppon har oath did owne this har testimony to be the truth before the Juriars for Inquest: agust: 3. 92.

[Hand 1] we whose names are under writen being present hard mircy lewes declare what is aboue writen what she said she saw and hard from the Apperishtion of Mr George Burroughs: and also beheld hir tortors which we cannot exppress for sume times we ware redy to fear that euery joynt of hir body was redy to be displaced: allso we perceiued hir hellish temtations by hir loud outcries Mr. Burroughs I will not writ in your book tho you doe kil me

Thomas putnam

[Hand 3] Jurat in Curia

Ewward Putnam

[Reverse] [Hand 4] Mercy Lewis agst Burroughs

Notes: On the manuscript, a portion of a signature that has been cropped appears under the name of Edward Putnam and is not printed here. The name, represented as a signature, is probably Peter Prescott, written by Thomas Putnam. There is an ink change beginning with "allso on the 9th." Then, beginning with "we whose names" there is another ink change. ◊ Used at trial. ◊ "fashon": (in the phrase "a new fashon book") 'kind, sort' (*OED* s.v. *fashion* 4). Alternatively, "new-fashioned" 'of a new style or type' may be intended (*OED* s.v. *new-fashioned*); the 'ed' would have been dropped because of influence from pronunciation. ◊ Hand 1 = Thomas Putnam; Hand 3 = Stephen Sewall

Essex County Court Archives, vol. 2, no. 25, Massachusetts Supreme Judicial Court, Judicial Archives, on deposit James Duncan Phillips Library, Peabody Essex Museum, Salem, MA.

125. Deposition of Ann Putnam Jr. v. George Burroughs, and Statement of Edward Putnam & Thomas Putnam v. George Burroughs†

See also: Aug. 3, 1692 & Aug. 5, 1692.

[Hand 1] The deposition of Ann putnam who testifieth and saith that on the 8th of may {1692} at euening I saw the apperishtion of Mr George Burroughs who greviously tortored me and urged me to writ in his book which I refused then he tould me that his Two first wiues would appeare to me presently and tell me a grat many lyes but I should not beleue them: then Immediatly appeared to me the forme of Two women in winding sheats and napkins about their heads: att which I was gratly affrighted: and they turned their faces towards Mr Burroughs and looked very red and ang⟨u⟩ry and tould him that he had been a cruell man to them. and that their blood did crie for vengance against him: and also tould

May 9, 1692

him that they should be cloathed with white Robes in heauen when he should be cast into hell: and Immediatly he vanished away: and as soon as he was gon the Two women turned their faces towards me and looked as pail as as a white wall: and tould me that they ware mr. Burroughs Two first wiues and that he had murthered them: and one tould me that she was his first wife and he stabed hir under the left Arme and put a peace of sealing wax on the wound and she pulled aside the winding sheat and shewed me the place⟨?⟩ and also told me that she was in the house where Mr. parish now liued w^n it was don and the other tould me that Mr Burroughs and that wife which he hath now kiled hir ^{in the vessell as she was coming to se hir friends} because they would haue one another. and they both charged me that I should tell these things to the Majestraits before Mr Burroughs ^{face} and if he did not own them they did not know but that they should appere there ["re" written over "ir"]: thes moring [= morning] also Mis Lawson and hir daughter Ann appeared to me whom I knew: and tould me that Mr Burroughs murthered them: this morning also appered to me another woman in a winding sheat and tould me that she was goodman ffullers first wife and Mr. Burroughs kiled hir. because there was sum differance between hir husband and him: also on the 9th may dureing the time of his Examination he did most greviously torment and afflect mary walcott Mercy lewes Eliz Hubburd and Abigail williams by pinching prick^g and choaking them

[Hand 2] Jurat in Curia

[Hand 1] {we} ~~wee~~ whose names are under writen being present with ann putnam⟨?⟩ at the times aboue mentioned: saw hir tortured and hard hir refuse to writ in the book also hard hir declare what is aboue writen: what she said she saw and hard from the Apperishtion of Mr George ^{Burroghs} and from thos which ac⟨cu⟩[Lost] [= accused] ⟨h⟩[Lost] [= him?] for murthering of them

[Hand 3] ann putnam. ownid this har testimony to be the truth uppon har oath. before the Jariars of Inquest this: 3. dy. of agust 92

Edward putnam

~~Roburt Morrell.~~

Thomas putnam

[Reverse] [Hand 4] Ann putnam Con^t Geo: Burroughs Death of his wife & Lawsons Child

Notes: Putnam spells "deposition" differently from his usual "deposistion," but he is definitely the recorder. Robert Morrell had probably signed the document earlier, but Thomas Putnam substituted his own signature as the case advanced toward the grand jury. The part beginning with "also on the 9th" appears to have been added later. ◊ Used at trial. ◊ Hand 1 = Thomas Putnam; Hand 2 = Stephen Sewall.

Essex County Court Archives, vol. 2, no. 26, Massachusetts Supreme Judicial Court, Judicial Archives, on deposit James Duncan Phillips Library, Peabody Essex Museum, Salem, MA.

126. Deposition of John Putnam Sr. & Rebecca Putnam v. George Burroughs†

See also: Aug. 5, 1692.

[Hand 1] the Deposition of John putnam & Rebecah his wife testifieth and saith that in the yeare :80: m^ε Burros liued in our house nine month, there being a great differanc betwixt s:d Barros & his wife, the diffaranc was so great that they did ~~agree~~ Desier vs the deponants to com into their room to hear their differance, the contriuercy that was betwixt them was that

the afor s.d Burros did rquier his wife to giue him a writton couenant vnder ^{her} hand and   May 9, 1692
seall that shee would neuer reueall his secrits, our anser was that they had once made a
couenant before god and men which couenant we did conseiue did bind each other to keep
their lawfull secrits, and further saith that all the time that s.d Burros did liue att our house
he was a uery harch sharp man to his wife, not withstanding to our obseruation shee was a
uery good and dutifull wife to him,

[Hand 2] Jurat in Curia

[Reverse] Jn° Putm & Reb. his wife.

Notes: Used at trial.

Essex Institute Collection, no. 25, James Duncan Phillips Library, Peabody Essex Museum, Salem, MA.

127. Deposition of Thomas Putnam & Edward Putnam v. George Burroughs†

See also: Aug. 5, 1692.

[Hand 1] The deposistion of Tho: putnam aged 40: years and Edward putnam agged 38
years who testifieth and saith. that we haueing ben conversan⟨t⟩ with seuerall of the afflected
parsons ~~we~~ as mary walcott mercy lewes Eliz: Hubburt and we haue se⟨e⟩n them most
dreadfully tomented and we haue seen dreadfull marks in their fleesh which they said mr.
Burrough⟨s⟩ did make by hurting them: but on 9th may 1692: the day of the Examin[Lost]
[= examination] of mr. George Burroughs the afforesaid parsons ware most dreadfully
tormented ~~and~~ dureing the time of his ["s" written over "r"] Examination as if they would
haue been torne al to peaces ~~and~~ ^{or} all their bones putt out of joyn⟨t⟩ and with such
tortors as no tounge can express also seuerall times senc⟨e⟩ ~~seen~~ we haue seen the afforesaid
afflected parsons most dreadfully tormented and grevi⟨o⟩usly complainig of mr. Burroughs
for hurting th⟨em⟩ and we beleue that mr. George Burroughs the prizsoner att the ba⟨r⟩ has
severall times afflected and tormented the afforesaid persons by acts of wicthcraft

Thomas putnam.
[Hand 2] Jurat in Curia

[Reverse] Tho. Putman Ed. Putman

Notes: Used at trial. ◊ Hand 1 = Thomas Putnam; Hand 2 = Stephen Sewall

Witchcraft Papers, no. 11a, Massachusetts Historical Society. Boston, MA.

128. Statement of Susannah Shelden v. George Burroughs†

[Hand 1] The Complaint of Susannah Shelden against mᵉ burroos which brought a book to
mee and told mee if i would not set my hand too it hee would tear mee to peesses i told him i
would not then hee told mee hee would starue me to death then the next morning he told
mee hee could not starue mee to death but hee would choake mee that my uittals shou{l⟨d⟩}
doe me but litl good then he told mee his name was borros which had preached at the uilag
[= village] the last night hee came to mee and asked mee whether i would goe to the uillage

May 9, 1692

to morrow to witnes against him i asked him if hee was exsamened then hee told hee was then i told him i would goe then hee told mee hee would kil mee beefoar morning then hee apeared to mee at the hous of nathanniel ingolson and told mee hee had been the death of three children at the eastward and had kiled two of his wifes the first hee [1 word overstruck] [Hand 2] Smouthred [Hand 1] and the second hee choaked and killed two of his owne children

[Hand 3] Susannah Shelden against G. Burroughs

Notes: The word "complaint" in the document is misleading. This was not a formal complaint precipitating judicial action. The document represents something written by a sponsor of Shelden in the claim against Burroughs to present to the appropriate legal authority. On the probable dates of May 17, May 18, and May 22, the word "complaint" is used in connection with Shelden, as it is not with the other female accusers in the Salem cases. It is tempting to think that she wrote the documents herself, but the hands vary. Females could complain, as in the case of Mary Brown against Sarah Cole of Lynn, although she asked a male to present her complaint. See No. 681. The formal complaint against Burroughs was made on April 30. See No. 96. ◊ Hand 2 = Jonathan Corwin

Essex County Court Archives, vol. 2, no. 34, Massachusetts Supreme Judicial Court, Judicial Archives, on deposit James Duncan Phillips Library, Peabody Essex Museum, Salem, MA.

129. Deposition of Mary Walcott v. George Burroughs†
See also: Aug. 3, 1692 & Aug. 5, 1692.

[Hand 1] The Deposistion of mary walcott agged about 17 years who testifieth and saith that on the later end of April 1692: mr George Burroughs or his Apperance came to me whom I formerly well knew: and he did Immediatly most greviously torment me by biting pinching and almost choaking me urging me to writ in his book: which I Refusing he did againe most greviously torment me and tould me if I would but touch his book I sh⟨o⟩uld be well. but I tould him I would not for all the world and then he threated to kil me and sai⟨d⟩ I should neuer witnes againt him: but he continewed tortoring and tempting me tell the 8 may: and then he tould me he would haue kiled his first wife and child: when his wife was in travill but he had not power. but he keept hir in the ~~seller~~ [Hand 2] {kichin} [Hand 1] tell he gaue hir. hir deaths wound. but he charged me in the name of his God~~s~~ I should not tell of it: but Immediatly there appeared to me mr. Burroughs two first wiues ~~w⟨?⟩~~ in their winding sheets who⟨m⟩ I formerly well knew and tould me that mr. Burroughs had murthr⟨d⟩ them and that their blood did crie for vengance againt him: also on the 9th may being the day of his Examination he did most greviously torment me dureing the time of his Examination for if he did but look on me he would strick me down or allmost choake me: also dureing his Examination I saw mr. George Burroughs or his Apperanc most greviously torment mercy lewes Eliz Hubbrt ["t" written over "d"] Abigail william and Ann putnam and I beleue in my heart that mr. George Burroughs is a dreadfull wizza⟨r⟩d and that he has often afflated and tormented me and the affore mentioned parsons by his acts of wicthcraf[Lost] [= witchcraft]

[Hand 3] Mary Walcot: declared the writing to be a true evidence: to yᵉ Jury of inquest Augˢᵗ 3: 1692 upon yᵉ oath she has taken   [Hand 4] Jurat in Curia

Notes: Used at trial. ◊ Hand 1 = Thomas Putnam; Hand 3 = Simon Willard; Hand 4 = Stephen Sewall

Witchcraft Papers, no. 7a, Massachusetts Historical Society. Boston, MA.

130. Depositions of Simon Willard v. George Burroughs, and Testimony of William Wormall v. George Burroughs†

May 9, 1692

See also: Aug. 3, 1692 & Aug. 5, 1692.

[Hand 1] The: Deposition of Simon Willard aged: about fortytwo years sayth: I being att ye house of Mr Robt Lawrance: at ffalmoth in Casco Bay: in Septemb^{E} 1689 s^d Mr Lawrance was commending Mr George ~~Borroghs~~ Borroughs his strength: saying. that we none of us could do what he could doe: for s^d he Mr Borroughs can hold out this gun with one hand: Mr Borroughs being there: sayd I held my hand here behind ye lock: and took it up: and held it out. I s^d deponant saw Mr Borroughs: put his hand on ye gun: to show us: how he held it and where he held his hand: and saying there he held his hand when he held s^d gun out: but: I saw him not hold it out then:

S^d gun was about {or near} seven foot barrill: and very hevie: I then: tryed to hold out s^d gun with both hands: but could not do it long enough to take sight

                              Simon Willard   [Hand 2] Jurat in Curia

[Hand 1] Simon Willard owned: to y^e Jury of inquest: that y^e above {written} evidence: is y^e truth: Augst 3: 1692

[Hand 2] Capt Wm Wormall Sworne to y^e aboue & y^t he Saw him Raise it from y^e ground. himselfe

                                          Jurat in Curia

[Hand 1] The Deposition of Sim[Lost] [= Simon] W⟨i⟩ll[Lost] [= Willard] ⟨42⟩ years: saith I being at Sale. [= Salem?] in y^e year: [Lost]9 [= 1689?] some: in Capt Ed Sarjants garison was speaking of m^r George Borroughs his great strength: saying he could take: a barrill of mallasses out of a cannoo or boat alone: and that he could. take it in his hands or arms out of y^e cannoo or boat and carry it and set it on y^e shore: and Mr Borroughs being: there sayd that: he had carryed one barrill of mallasses. or sider: out {o}f a cannoo that had like to have done him a displeasure: s^d Mr Borroughs intimated: as if he did not want strength to do it but ye disadvantage of ye shore was such: that his foot slipping in the sand: he had like to have strained his legg

Simon Willard ownd: to y^e Jury of inquest: that y^e above written evidence: is y^e truth

                                    Simon Willard
                           [Hand 2] Jurat in Curia

[Reverse] [Hand 3] Simon Willard agst Burroughs

Notes: ◊ Used at trial. ◊ Hand 1 = Simon Willard; Hand 2 = Stephen Sewall.

Essex County Court Archives, vol. 2, no. 28, Massachusetts Supreme Judicial Court, Judicial Archives, on deposit James Duncan Phillips Library, Peabody Essex Museum, Salem, MA.

Tuesday, May 10, 1692

Death of Sarah Osburn in Prison

131. Warrant for the Apprehension of George Jacobs Sr. & Margaret Jacobs, and Officer's Return

[Hand 1] To: The Constables in Salem

You are in theire Majes^{ts} names hereby required to apprehend and forthwith bring before vs George Jacobs Sen^ε of Salem, And Margaret Jacobs the daufter of George Jacobs Jun^ε of Salem Single woman Who stands, accused, of high Suspition of Sundry acts of witchcraft by them both Committed on Sundry persons in Salem to theire great wrong and Injury and hereof faile not Dated Salem May 10th 1692

℈ vs   John: Hathorne   } Assis^{ts}

Jonathan. Corwin

To Constable Joseph <u>Neale</u>

[Hand 2] May ye 10th 1692
Then I Apprehended the Bodyes of George Jacobs Seni^ε and Margret Jacobs Daughter of George Jacobs Juni^ε Both of Salem, According to the Tenor of the Aboue warrants ℈ me
Joseph Neale Constable In Salem

[Reverse] [Hand 3] Warrant
George Jacobs.
Margaret Jacob⟨s⟩

Notes: Signature unreliability occurs often enough with Joseph Neal to suggest that he may not have been able to write his signature, thus perhaps having others writing returns for him as well as signing them. ◊ Hand 1 = John Hathorne

Essex County Court Archives, vol. 1, no. 220, Massachusetts Supreme Judicial Court, Judicial Archives, on deposit James Duncan Phillips Library, Peabody Essex Museum, Salem, MA.

132. Warrant No. 1 for the Apprehension of John Willard, and Officer's Return

See also: May 12, 1692.

[Hand 1] To ye Constable of Salem

You are in theyr Majestyes Names Required to Apprehend & Bring before ^{us} ye Body of John. Willard of Salem Village husbandman to morrow being the ~~Tenth~~ {Eleventh} day of this Instant May by one of ye Clock afternoone att ye house of Thomas. Beadle. in Salem, whoe Stand⟨s⟩ accused of high Suspition of Severall Acts of Witchcraft done or Committed

upon ye Bodyes of Sundry persons in Salem Village to theyr great hurt & Injury & hereof
You are nott to ffayle dated Salem May. 10th 1692

John Hathorne

Jonathan. Corwin

} Assis^ts

[Reverse] [Hand 2] ⟨2⟩ In prosecution of this warrant I went to the house of the vsuall abode of John Willards and made search for him, and in Seuerall other houses and places butt could not find him; and his relations and freinds then gaue mee accompt ["mp" written over "unt"] that to theire best knowledg he was ffleed Salem May 12th 1692

John Putnam Jun. Constable Salem

[Hand 3] John Willards Warr^t

Notes: Willard was brought in on May 18. ◊ Hand 1 = Jonathan Corwin; Hand 2 = John Hathorne; Hand 3 = Thomas Newton

Essex County Court Archives, vol. 1, no. 231, Massachusetts Supreme Judicial Court, Judicial Archives, on deposit James Duncan Phillips Library, Peabody Essex Museum, Salem, MA.

133. Examinations of George Jacobs Sr.

See also: May 11, 1692.

[Hand 1] The Examination of Geo: Jacobs. Senr 10 May. 1692

Here are them that accuse you of acts of witchcraft.
Well, let vs hear who are they, & what are they.
Abigail Williams
    Jacobs laught
Because I am falsly accused – Your worships all of you do you think this is true?
Nay: what do you think?
I never did it.
Who did it?
Don't ask me.
Why should we not ask you? Sarah Churchwell accuseth you, there she is.
I am as innocent as the child born to night, I have lived .33. yeares here in Salem.
What then?
If you can prove that I am guilty, I will lye under it.
Sarah Churchwell said last night I was afflicted at Deacon Ingersolls, & Mary Walcot said it was a man with .2. staves, it was my Master.
Pray do not accuse me, I am as clear as your Worships; You must do right judgment
What book did he bring you Sarah?
The same that the other woman brought.
The Devil can go in any shape.
Did he not he appear on the other side of the [Lost]er [= river] & hurt you, did not you see him.
[Lost]es [= Yes] he did.

May 10, 1692

[Lost]k [= Look] there, she accuseth you to your face, she [Lost]argeth [= chargeth] you that you hurt her twise.
[Lost]t [= It] is not true? What would you have me [Lost]y [= say]? I never wronged no man in word nor deed.
Here a [= are] 3. Evidences.
You tax me for a Wizard, you may as well tax me for a Buzard. I have done no harm.
Is it no harm to afflict these?
I never did it.
But how comes it to be in your appearance?
The Devil can take any likeness.
Not without their consent.
Please your worship it is untrue, I never showed the book, I am as silly about these things, as the child born last night.
That is your saying, you argue you have lived so long, but what then Cain might live long before he killed Abel, & you might live long before the Devil had so prevailed on you.
Christ hath suffered .3. times for me.
What three times
He suffered the Crosse & Gall

You had as good confesse (said Sarah Churchwell) if you are guilty.
Have you heard that I have any Witchcraft?
I know you lived a wicked life.
Let her make it out.
Doth he ever pray in his family?
Not unless by himself.
Why do you not pray in your family?
I cannot read.
Well but you may pray for all that. Can you say the Lords prayer? Let us hear you?
He mist in severall ~~peti~~ parts of it, & could not repeat it ~~rigtly~~ right after many trialls
Sarah Churchwell, when you wrote in the book you was showed your Masters name you said.
Yes Sr
If she say so, if you do not know it, what will you say?
But she saw you, or your likeness tempt her to write.
One in my likeness, the Devil may present my likeness.
Were you not frighted Sarah Churchwell, when ~~you~~ the Representation of your Master came to you?
Yes.
Well! burn me, or hang me, I will stand in the truth of Christ, I know nothing of it
Do you know nothing of getting your Son George & his daughter Margaret to signe?
No nothing at all.

The .2d Examination of said Geo: Jacobs.
11. May. 1692

The bewitched fell into most greivous fits & screkings when he came in.
Is this the man that hurts you?
Abig: Williams cryed out this is the man & fell into a violent fit.
Ann Putman said this is the man, & he hurts ^{her}, & brings the book to her, & would have her write in the book, & she should be as well as his Granddaughter.

May 10, 1692

Mercy Lewes is this the man?
This is the man (after much interruption by fits) he almost kills me.
Eliz: Hubbard said the man never hurt her till to day he came upon the Table.
Mary Walcot is this the man?
After much interruption by fits she said this is the man, he used to come with two staves & beat her with one of them.
What do you say, are you not a witch?
No, I know it not, if I were to dye presently
Mercy Lewes went to come near him but fell into great fits.
Mercy Lewes testimony read.
What do you say to this?
Why it is false, I know not of it, any more than the child that was born to night.
Ann Putman said yes, you told me so, that you had been so this .40. years.
Ann Putman & Abigail Williams had each of them a pin stuck in their hands, & they said it was this old Jacobs
Abig: Williams testimony read.
Are not you the man that made disturbance

[Reverse] at a Lecture in Salem?
No great disturbance. Do you think I use Witchcraft?
Yes indeed.
No I use none of them.

The Examīacon ⟨of⟩ Geo: Jacobs. Sen^ε

Notes: Sarah Churchill was the servant of the Jacobs family. ◊ "silly": 'ignorant' (*OED* s.v. *silly* 3.a.). ◊ Hand 1 = Samuel Parris

Essex County Court Archives, vol. 1, no. 224, Massachusetts Supreme Judicial Court, Judicial Archives, on deposit James Duncan Phillips Library, Peabody Essex Museum, Salem, MA.

134. Deposition of Mercy Lewis v. George Jacobs Sr.†

See also: May 11, 1692 & Aug. 4, 1692.

[Hand 1] The deposistion of mircy Lewes who testifieth and saith that on 20th: of April 1692: att or about midnight there appered to me the apperishtion of an old: very grayheaded man and tould me that his name was George Jacobs and that he had had Two ~~w⟨i⟩u⟨f⟩es w⟨hich⟩~~ ^{wiues and he} did tortor me and beate me with a stick which he had in his hand: and urged me to writ in his book which I refused to doe: and so he hath continewed euer sence by times coming sum times with Two sticks in his hands to afflect me still tempting me to writ in his book: but most dreadfull he fell upon ^{me} and did tortor me on the :9th of may at euenig after I came whom [= home] from the Examination of his maid: threating to kill me y^t night if I would not write in his Book: because I did witnes againt his maid and perswaded hir to confess:: but because I would not yeald to his hellish temtations he did tortor me most cruelly by beating me with the Two sticks which he had in his hands: and allmost Redy to pull all my bones out of joynt tell my strenth and har⟨t⟩ was Redy to faill but being upheld by an Allmighty hand and incouraged by them that stood by I indured his tortors that night: the 10th may he againe sett upon me and afflected me most greviouly a grat many times in the day: still urging me to writ in his book: but. att euening he againe tortored ^{me} most greviously by pinching me and beating me black and blue and threating to kill me if I would not writ in his Book but I tould him I would not writ in his book tho he he did kill me and tare me al to peaces: then he profered me to giue me gold and many figne things if I would writ in his book: but I tould him I would not writ in his book if he would giue me all the world. then againe he⟨d⟩ did tortor me most greviously but at last went away from me: also on the 11ᵗʰ may 1692 being the day of the Examination of George Jacobs then I saw that it was that very man that tould me his name ⟨was⟩ ⟨Ge⟩[Lost] [= George] Jacobs and then he did also most dreadfully torment me allmost Redy t⟨o⟩ kil me and I verily beleue in my heart that George Jacobs is a most dreadfull wizzard and that he hath very often afflected and tormented me ~~and mary walcott and Eliz: Hubbrd~~ by his acts of wicthcraft.

[Hand 2] Mercy Lewis declared to: yᵉ Jury. of Inquest that: yᵉ above written evidence [Lost] [= is the] truth::

[Reverse] [Hand 3] Marcy Lewis agᵗ Geo: Jacobs

Notes: The original deposition was probably written by Thomas Putnam on May 10, added to on May 11, and subsequently used at the grand jury, probably on August 4. Mary Walcott and Elizabeth Hubbard are subsequently crossed out, probably because, for whatever reason, they do not appear to have testified at this grand jury hearing. ◊ Hand 1 = Thomas Putnam; Hand 2 = Simon Willard

Essex County Court Archives, vol. 1, no. 229, Massachusetts Supreme Judicial Court, Judicial Archives, on deposit James Duncan Phillips Library, Peabody Essex Museum, Salem, MA.

135. Testimony of Abigail Williams v. George Jacobs Sr., Margaret Jacobs, George Jacobs Jr., Rebecca Jacobs, Sarah Churchill, Philip English, & Mary English

[Hand 1] Abigail Williams testifyeth & saith that an old man that goes with two sticks hath appeared to & hurt her many times by pinching & bringing the book for her to set her hands unto, & the man told her ["her" written over "me"] his name was Jacobs the Father of Geo: Jacobs & the Grandfather of Margaret Jacobs & he had made said Margaret set her hand to the book & Sarah Churchwell & his son Geo: Jacobs & his wife & another woman & her husband viz: Mʳ English & his wife: also that the said Margaret had hurt her pretty much to day & at other times & brought her the book several times to night but not before.

We whose names are underwritten testifye that we heard the abovesᵈ Abigail relate the charge aforesᵈ this .10. ~~Apr~~ May. 1692

Nathannel Ingersoll
Jonathan Walcott
John Lou⟨d⟩[Lost] [SWP = Louder]

[Reverse] [Hand 2] Abigail Williams agᵗ Geo. Jacobs

Notes: Hand 1 = Samuel Parris; Hand 2 = John Hathorne

Witchcraft Papers, no. 23b, Massachusetts Historical Society. Boston, MA.

Wednesday, May 11, 1692

Statement Added: Examination of George Burroughs and Statement of Abigail Hobbs v. George Burroughs
2nd of 2 dates. See No. 120 on May 9, 1692

Continued from May 10, 1692: Examinations of George Jacobs Sr.
2nd of 2 dates. See No. 133 on May 10, 1692

Continued from May 10, 1692: Deposition of Mercy Lewis v. George Jacobs Sr.†
2nd of 3 dates. See No. 134 on May 10, 1692

136. Deposition of Ann Putnam Jr. v. George Jacobs Sr.†

See also: Aug. 4, 1692.

[Hand 1] The Deposistion of Ann putnam who testifieth and saith that I haue ben most greviously afflected by George Jacobs sen but most dreadfully tomented by him on: 11th ~~may~~ of may 1692 dureing the time of his Examination also on the day of his Examination I saw George Jacobs or his Apperance most greviously torment mary walcott ~~mercy lewes~~ Eliz: Hubb⟨ru⟩d and I beleue in my hart that George Jacobs is a dreadfull wizzard and that he hath very often afflectd me and the affore mentioned pasons by his acts of wicthcraft

[Hand 2] ann putnam ownid this har testimony before the Juriars of Inquest: one har oath this .4. dy of agust: 1692

[Hand 3] Jurat in Curia

[Reverse] ~~David ff⟨urne⟩ss~~ Ann Putman

Notes: The crossed out name is probably David Ferneaux, age 23, who was an accuser in another case, that of Sarah Procter. See No. 210. ◊ Used at trial. ◊ Hand 1 = Thomas Putnam; Hand 3 = Stephen Sewall

Witchcraft Papers, no. 26b, Massachusetts Historical Society. Boston, MA.

137. Deposition of Thomas Putnam & John Putnam Jr. v. George Jacobs Sr.†

See also: Aug. 4, 1692.

[Hand 1] The Deposistion of Thomas putnam agged 40 years and Jno putnam aged 36 years who testifie and saith that we haueing been conuer⟨s⟩ant with diuers of the afflected parsons as mary walcott mercy lewes Eliz: Hubburd Abigail williams and Ann putnam and we haue seen them most dreadfully tormented and complaining of old Jacobe for hurting them but on: 11th may 1692 being the day of the Examination of George Jacobs sen^r the afforesaid parsons ~~most~~ ware most dreadfully tormented dureing the time of his Examination as if indeed their bones would haue ben disjoynted: ["te" written over "et"] being in such misery ["i" written

May 11, 1692

over "e"] as we could hardly hold them and wee beleue that George Jacobs the prizsoner att the barr as very often⟨?⟩ afflected and tormented the afforesaid persons by acts of wicthcraft

Thomas putnam

John putnam

[Hand 2] Jurat in Curia

[Reverse] Jnᵒ Putman Tho: Putman

Notes: Thomas Putnam signed John Putnam's name as well as his own. ◊ Used at trial. ◊ Hand 1 = Thomas Putnam; Hand 2 = Stephen Sewall

Witchcraft Papers, no. 26a, Massachusetts Historical Society. Boston, MA.

138. Testimony of Abigail Williams v. George Jacobs Sr.†

[Hand 1] The Testimony of Abigail Williams witnesseth & saith that she hath severall times seen, & been very much afflicted by the Apparition of Geo: Jacobs Senᵉ of Salem at & before the .11. May. 1692

[Reverse] Abig: ⟨Wil⟩liams agsᵗ Geo: Jacobs Senᵉ

Notes: By the time Jacobs's case went to the grand jury on August 4, Abigail Williams, one of the earliest accusers, had dropped out of the judicial proceedings. What became of her is unknown. For her grand jury appearance on June 30, her last testimony in the proceedings, see No. 245. ◊ Hand 1 = Samuel Parris

Essex County Court Archives, vol. 1, no. 223, Massachusetts Supreme Judicial Court, Judicial Archives, on deposit James Duncan Phillips Library, Peabody Essex Museum, Salem, MA.

139. Deposition of Bernard Peach v. Susannah Martin

[Hand 1] The deposion of Barnerd peache aged :43: or therabouts who testifying sayth That about six or seven year sinc this deponent Living at the house of Jacob morell in salsbury being in bed on a lords day night he heard a scrabling at the window he this deponent saw susana martin wif of Georg martin of Amsbury com in at the window & Jumpt downe vpon the flower shee was in her whud [= hood] & scarf and the same dress that shee was in before at meetting the same day
being com in shee was coming vp toward this deponents face but turned bak to {his} feet and took hold of them & drew vp his body into a heape & Lay vpon him about an hour & half or 2: hours in all wᶜʰ time this deponent cooled not stir nor speake but feelling him self begining to be Loosned or Lightned: he beginig to strive he put out his hand among the clothes and took hold of her hand and brought it vp to his mouth and bitt three of the fingers (as he Judg) to the breaking of the bones which don the sd martin. went out of the chamber downe the stayrs and out at the dore
And as soon as shee went away this deponent caled to the peop{l} of the house and told them wᵗ was don and that shee sd martin was now gon out of the dore this deponent did also follow her but the peopl did not see her (as thay sayd) but with{out} the dor{e} ther was a buket ~~of watter~~ on the Left hand ~~and:~~ and ther was a drop of blod in the buket ["buket"

May 11, 1692

written over "water"] {&} too more vpon the snow: for ther was a litle flight of snow: and ther wear the print of her :2: feett about a foot without the threshall but no more footting did appear

{2} he farther deposeth that somtime after this as he suposeth about 3 weeks after the sd martin desired this deponent to com and husk corne at her house the next Lords day night s<u>ay</u> that if I did not com it wear better that I did

but this deponent did not go: being then Living with w^m osgood of the sd salsbury: and that night Lodged in the barne vpon the hay: and about an hour or :2: in the night ye sd susana martin and another came out of the shop into the barne and on of them sd hear he is and then came tow⟨o⟩rds this deponent he hauing a quarter staf made a blow at them but the ruff of the barne prevented it: and thay went away but this deponent followed them and as thay wear going toward the window made another blow at y^m and struk them both down but away thay went out at the shop window & this deponent saw no more of them

and the Rumer went that the sd <u>martin</u> had a brokn head at y^t time but the deponent cannot speake to that vpon his owne kno<u>w</u>lig

sworne may the eleventh :1692:

before me Robt Pike Asis^t

[Reverse] [Hand 2] Barnard Peach⟨e⟩ ~~John All⟨en⟩~~

Notes: On May 11, Robert Pike took several sworn accusations against Susannah Martin, who had been examined on May 2. ◇ Hand 1 = Robert Pike; Hand 2 = Stephen Sewall

Essex County Court Archives, vol. 1, no. 184, Massachusetts Supreme Judicial Court, Judicial Archives, on deposit James Duncan Phillips Library, Peabody Essex Museum, Salem, MA.

140. Deposition of William Brown v. Susannah Martin

See also: May 16, 1692.

[Hand 1] The deposion of william Browne of salsbury aged :70: year{s} or ther about who testifying sayth That about on or to and thirty years ago Elizabeth his wif being a very rasional woman & sober & on that feard god as was well knowe to all that knew her & as prudently carefull in her family which woman going vpon a time from her owne house towords the mille in salsbury did ther meett{ing} with susana martin the then wif of Georg martin of Amsbury Just as thay came togather the sd susana martin vanisht away aut of her sight wch put the sd Elizabeth into a great fright

After which time the sd martin did many tims afterward appear to her {at her} house and did much troubl her in any of her accasions and this continued till about feb: ffollowing: and then when shee did com it was as birds peking her Legs or priking her with the mosion of thayr wings and then it woold rise vp into her stumak with priking payn as nayles & pines of wch shee did bitterly complain and cry out Lik a woman in trauil and after that it woold rise vp to her throt in a bunch Lik a pullets egg: and then shee woold turn back her head & say: wich ye shant chok me

In the time of this extremity the church appointed a day of humlaso [= humiliation] to seek god on her behalf & thervpon her trouble seas⟨e⟩d and shee saw goodwif martin no more: for a consideribl time for wch the church {in}steed of the day of humiliasion gaue thanks

for her deliveranc & shee came to meetting & went about her busnes as before this
continued till Aprill following: at wch time somonses wear sent to the sd Elizabeth brown &
goodwif Osgood by the court to give thayr evidences concernig the sd martin and thay did
befor the Grān Jury gaue a full ac̄compt [= account]

After wch time the sd Elizabeth told this deponent that as shee was milking of her cow the sd
susana martin came behind her and told her that shee woold make ^{her} the miserablest
creatur for defāmg [= defaming] her name at the court: & wep greevously as shee told it to
this deponent

About {2} month after this deponent came hom from hampton & his sd wif woold not
owne him but sd thay wear devorst and Asked him whether he did not mett with on m^ε
Bent of A{l}bery in England by whom he was divorst

And from that time to this very day haue ben vnder a straing kind of distemper & frensy
vncapibl of any rasional action though strong & helthy of body

he farther testifyeth that when {shee} came into that condition this deponent ꝑcur⟨e⟩d
docter fuller & Crosby to com to her for her relees but thay did both say that her distemper
was supernatural & no siknes of body: but that som evil ^{ꝑson} had bewiched her

sworne the eleventh day of may Anno Dom :1692:
before me Robt Pike Ass^t

[Hand 2] w^m Browne made Oath that ye aboue is a true relac̄on according to his wifes
Complaint in ye day of it

[Hand 1] concernig the truth of w^t is sworne by william Browne concerning his wif with
respect to her being a Rasional woman before shee was so handled and of her now present
condision & her so long continuanc all that then knew her and now know her can testefy to
the truth of it for shee yet remaines {a} miseribl cr⟨ea⟩t{r} of wch my self is on as wittnes my
hand :16: 3: 1692

Robt Pike

[Hand 2] Wm Browne

Notes: No reference to William Brown appears at the examination of Susannah Martin on May 2. It seems probable that
after she had been examined Brown decided to add his voice against her and, being from Salisbury, made a deposition
before the appropriate magistrate, Robert Pike. ◊ Hand 1 = Robert Pike; Hand 2 = Stephen Sewall

*Essex County Court Archives, vol. 1, nos. 179 & 180, Massachusetts Supreme Judicial Court, Judicial Archives, on deposit James
Duncan Phillips Library, Peabody Essex Museum, Salem, MA.*

141. Testimony and Deposition of John Pressy v. Susannah Martin

See also: June 29, 1692.

[Hand 1] The Testamony of J⟨o⟩hn Pressy of ~~sa~~ Amsbury age⟨d⟩ 53 years or ther abouts takn
before me at my house at salsbury the eleventh day of may Ano: Dom .1692. is as ffolloweth
That about twenty fower year ago: he this deponent was at Amsb⟨e⟩[Lost] [= Amesbury]
ferry vpon a Saterday in the evnig near about the shutting in of the day Light (wch was about
three mile ffrom his house) and as he was going home a litle beyond the field of Georg
martin at a hill caled goodals hill this deponent was bewildered and Lost his way & hauing

wandered a while he came bake againe to the sam place which he knew by stooping trees in that plac

wch ꝓceiving he set out againe & steerd by the moone wch shone brite and was againe Lost and came bake againe to the same place {And} then sett out the 3^d time in Lik manner and was bewildered and came bak but not so far as before: but knew whear he was and so sett himself in his way as before: and in Less then half a mile going he saw a Light stand on his Left hand about too rod out of the way: it seemd to be about the bignes of a half bushell but this deponent kept on his way & Left it: and in a matter of seven or eight rod going it appeared againe at the Lik distanc from him as before: & so it ^{did} againe the 3^d time: but the deponet past on his way: and in Less then twenty rod going the same or such another Light Lay in his way: and he hauing a stik in his hand did with the end of {it} indevered to stir it out of the plac and to give it som smale ["m" written over "h"] blows with it: and the Light seemd ^{to} brusl vp & waue from side to side as a turky cock when he spreds his tayle but went not out of the plac which ꝓceiving this deponent Layd it on with his stik with all his might he thinks he gaue her at Lest forty blows: and so was going away and Leave it: but as he was going his heals wear struk vp & he Layd on his bak on the ground & was sliding into a deep plac (as {to} him seemd) but taking hold of som brush or bushes & so recoverd himself: & hauig Lost his coat which he had vpon his Arme went bak to the Light saw his coate & took it vp & went home without any more disturbanc ther: he farther say that he do not know any such pitt to be in the plac that he ^{was} sliding into he also sayth that when he did strik at the Light he did certainly feel a substanc wth his stik he farther sayth that after his striking it & his recovering himself and going on his way as aforsd when he had gon about :5: or :6 rod he saw susana martine then wif of Georg martin of Amsbury standing on his Left hand as the Lights had don ther shee stood & Lookt vpon him & turned her face after him as he went along but sayd nothing nor did nothing to this deponent but that he went home as aforsd

only he againe ouerwent his owne house but knowing the ground he was vpon returned and found his owne house: but being then seazed with {fear} coold not speake till his wif spake to him at the dore & was in such condision that his family was afrayd of him

which story being caryd to the Towne the next day: it was vpon enquiry vnderstood (that the sd goodwif martin was in such a miseribl case and in such payn that thay swabbe her body (as was reported)

[Reverse] This deponent farther sayth that these things being noysed abroad maj^ɛ Pike sent for this deponent and had an acco⟨m⟩pt of the case: but seemd to be troubled that this deponent had not told him of it in season that shee might haue ben vewed to haue seen w^t her ayle was

John pressy aforsayd made oathe to the truth of what is writtn in these too sides of the paper the eleventh day of may Anno: Dom: 1692. before me

Robt Pike Asis^t

[Hand 2] Jurat in Curia

Notes: The testimony was sworn to by Pressy at an inferior court prior to the creation of the Court of Oyer and Terminer. ◊ Used at trial. ◊ "brusl vp": 'to rise like bristles, to become stiff and bristly' (OED s.v. *brustle* v^2 and *bristle* v^1). ◊ Hand 1 = Robert Pike; Hand 2 = Stephen Sewall.

May 12, 1692

142. Deposition of John Pressy & Mary Pressy v. Susannah Martin

See also: June 29, 1692.

[Hand 1] The deposion of John p̄resy aged 53 and marah his wif aged :46: or ther abouts testifying sayth

That som years after that the sd John pressy had givn his evidenc against the sd susana martin shee the sd mart⟨a⟩n came and took these deponents to do about it and revile⟨d⟩ them with many foule words saying wee had took a fals oathe and ^{sayd} that we shoold never prosper and that we shoold never prosper for our so doing: p̄ticulerly that we shoold never haue but too cows: & that if we wear never so likly to haue more yet {we} ~~thay~~ shoold never obtaine it we do farther testify that from that time to this day we haue never exeeded that nomber but somthing or other hau̅ prevented it tho never so likly (to obtaine it) tho thay had vsed all ordinary means for obtainig it by hiring cows of others that wea{r} not thayr owne
[Hand 2] this for Twenty yeares space

[Hand 1] John pressy made oathe to the truth⟨e⟩ of all that is aboue writtn at my house in salsbury the eleventh day of may Ano: Domin 1692 before me Robt Pike Asis^t
[Hand 2] Mary Pressy testifieth to all y^e aboue Except y̶^e Susanna her threatning of y^e not raising aboue Two Cowes.

Jurat in Curia by both

[Reverse] Jn⁰ Pressy of Salsbury Con. Martin

Notes: Used at trial. ◊ Hand 1 = Robert Pike; Hand 2 = Stephen Sewall

Essex County Court Archives, vol. 1, no. 183, Massachusetts Supreme Judicial Court, Judicial Archives, on deposit James Duncan Phillips Library, Peabody Essex Museum, Salem, MA.

Thursday, May 12, 1692

Officer's Return: Warrant No. 1 for the Apprehension of John Willard
2nd of 2 dates. See No. 132 on May 10, 1692

143. Warrant for the Apprehension of Alice Parker & Ann Pudeator, and Officer's Return

[Hand 1] To the Marshall of Essex or Constable in Salem

You are in theire Majes^ts names hereby required forthwith to apprehend and bring before vs [Hand 2?] Allce. [Hand 1] Parker the wife of John Parker of Salem and [Hand 2?] Ann [Hand 1] Pudeater of Salem Widdow who stand Charged with Sundry acts of Witchcraft by them Committed this day Contrary to ye Laws of our. Sou^ε Lord & Lady ffaile not Dated Salem May the .12th 1692

John: Hathorne
p̄ vs   } Assis^ts
Jonathan. Corwin

[Hand 2] May 12th 1692 I haue apprehended the aboue named persons and Brought them
att y^e place apointed by yo{u}r honers
P^ε mee George Herrick Marshall of Essex

[Reverse] [Hand 3] copied
[Hand 4] Warrant

Notes: It appears as if the first names of Alice Parker and Ann Pudeator may have been added by George Herrick, but the handwriting is inconclusive. ◊ Hand 1 = John Hathorne; Hand 2 = George Herrick

Essex County Court Archives, vol. 1, no. 261, Massachusetts Supreme Judicial Court, Judicial Archives, on deposit James Duncan Phillips Library, Peabody Essex Museum, Salem, MA.

Continued from April 20, 1692: Examinations of Abigail Hobbs in Prison

2nd of 2 dates. See No. 77 on April 20, 1692

144. Examination of Alice Parker

[Hand 1] The Examination of Alice Parker 12 May. 1692.

Q. Mary Warren Charges you with several acts off witchcraft, what say you to it Guilty or not Guilty: A. I am not Guilty. You told her this day you cast away Thomas Westgate – A. I know nothing of it – You told her John Laptho⟨rn⟩ was lost i⟨n⟩ [Lost] A I never spake a word to her in my Life. You told her also you bewitched her sister, because her father would not mo⟨?⟩w your grass. I nev^ε saw her – Warren desiring to go to strike her, was permitted, but Could not Come near so much as to touch her, but fel backward immediately into a dreadful fitt. Margaret Jacobs Charged her also to her face with seeing her in the North feild on fryday night last about ⟨nine a Clock⟩ an hour within Night in apparition – Marshal Herrick also affirmed to his face that she told him this day, after he had apprehended her and was bringing her to Examination, that there were threescore Witches of the Company, which he denyed not, But said she did not Remember, how many she said there was. But John Loader being by attested the same the Marshal had before. Mary Warren was grieviously afflicted dureing the whole time of her Examination. But being asked who told her there were threescore Witches, she answered she Could not tell. Mary Warren affirmd that Her Father having promised to mow the grass for her if he had time, which he not doeing she came to the house, and told him, he had better he had done it, presently after that Her sister fell ill and shortly after Her Mother was taken ill, and dyed. Mary Warren affirms that when Alice Parker brought the Poppet to her, she said if she would not Run the needle in, she would Run itt, into her heart. Mary Warren affirmd it to her face, but upon ye Glance of Parkers Ey she immediately struck her down into a fitt. being Examined upon these things, she wi⟨sh⟩ed God would open the Earth and swallow her up presently, if one word of this was true and make her an Example to Others – Thō att ye same times she practised her Witchcrafts before us on ye Body of Mary Warren, dreadfully tormenting her. Moreover Warren affirmed that she told her this day that she was att the Bloody sacrament in m^ε Parris's Pasture, and that they were about thirty of them. Mary Warren also affirms that she told her this day also, that she Ran after John Loader in the Common. Mary Warren affirms that the spectrum came direct from her Body and afflicted her dureing the whole time off her Examination. M^ε Noise in Time of Examination affirmed to her face, that he being with

May 12, 1692 her in a Time of sicknes, discoursing with about her witchcrafts whether she were not Guilty, she answered If she was as free from Other sins as from Witchcrafts she would not ask the Lord mercy. Mary. Warren being taken with a dreadful fit at the same time, w^{r}by her tongue hang out of h⟨e⟩r mouth until it was ⟨a⟩ black, Parker being present said warrens tongue would be blacker before she dyed. Parker being asked why she did thus afflict and torm^t her, answered If I do, the Lord forgive mee.

[Reverse] [Hand 2] Allice parkers Examin⟨a⟩[Lost] [= examination]
[Hand 3] Parker. & Wildes.

Notes: Although Margaret Jacobs later confirmed counterfeiting in the cases of George Burroughs and George Jacobs Sr., no confirmation of an admission of her counterfeiting against Alice Parker survives. ◊ Hand 2 = John Hathorne; Hand 3 = Stephen Sewall

Witchcraft Papers, no. 31, Massachusetts Historical Society. Boston, MA.

145. Examination of Mary Warren

[Hand 1] Mary Warrens Examination: May. 12th 1692
Q. Whether you did nott know, y^t itt was y^e Devill's book when you Sighned?
A. I did nott know itt y^n butt I know itt now, to be Sure itt was ye Devills book. in ye ffirst place to be Sure I did Sett my hand to ye Devills book; I have considered of itt, Since you were here last, & itt was ye Devills book, y^t my Master Procter brought to me, & he Tould me if I would Sett my hand to y^t book I should be well; & I did Sett my hand to itt, butt y^t wch I did itt was done wth my finger, he brought y^e Book & he Tould me if I would Take y^e book & Touch itt that I should be well & I thought then y^t itt was y^e Devill's Book.
Q. Was there nott your consent to hurt y^e Children, when y^a [= they] were hurt?
A. Noe S^e, but when I was Afflicted, my master Procter was in y^e Roome & said if y^a are Afflicted, I wish y^a were more Afflicted & you and all: I said ma⟨st⟩er, w^t make you Say soe? he Answered because y^a goe to bring out Innocent persones. I Tould him y^t that could nott bee & Whether ye Devill Took advantage att y^t I know nott to Afflict y^m and one Night Talking about y^m I said I did nott care though y^a were Tormented if y^a charged mee.
Q. Did you ever See any poppetts? An. yes once I saw one made of cloth in mistris Procters hand. Q. whoe was itt like or wch of ye Children was itt for? An. I cañott Tell, whether for Ann. Putnam or Abigall Williams, for one of y^m itt was I am Sure, itt was in my mistris's hand. Q. what did you stick into y^t poppitt? An. I did stick in a pin about ye Neck of itt as itt was in Procters hand. Q. how many more did you See afterwa⟨r⟩ds? An. I doe no⟨tt⟩ remember y^t ever I saw any more. yes I remember one and y^t Goody Parker brought a pop⟨p⟩itt unto me of Mercy. Lewiss & she gave me a need⟨l⟩e & I stook itt some where about y^e wasts & she appeared once more to me in y^e prison, & She Said to ⟨me⟩ what are you gott here? & she To⟨u⟩ld me y^t she was Comeing here hirsel⟨fe⟩. I had another person y^t a⟨pp⟩eared to mee, itt was Goody. Pudeator & Said she was Sorry to Se me [Lost]ere [= there], itt was in apparition & she brought me a poppitt, itt was like to Mary. Walcott & itt was a peice of Stick y^t she brought me to Stick into i⟨tt⟩ & Somewhere about hir armes I [Lost]took [= stuck] itt in. Q. where did she bring itt to you? An. up att Procters. G⟨oo⟩dy. ⟨Pa⟩rker Toul⟨d⟩ me she had bin a Witch the⟨se⟩.12. years & more; & Pudeator told me y^t

May 12, 1692

she had done damage, & Tould me y^t she had hurt Jame⟨s⟩ [Lost]⟨y⟩es [*Woodward* = Coyes] Child Takeing itt out of y^e mothers hand. Q. Whoe br⟨o⟩ught y^e last To [Lost]u [= you]? An. ⟨m⟩y mistris & when she brought itt, she ⟨b⟩rought itt in hir owne person & hir husband wth his owne hands brought me y^e book to Sighne, & he brought mee an Image wch looked yellow & I beleive itt was for Abigall Williames being like hir & I put a thing like a thorne into itt, this was done by his bodily person after I had Sighned ye night after I had Sighned ye book: While she was thus Confessing Parker appeared & bitt hir Extreamly on hir armes as she affirmed unto ⟨us⟩. Q. Whoe have you Sene more? An. Nurss & Cloys and Good's Child after I had Sighned. Q. What Sayd y^a to you? An. Thay Sayd y^t I should never Tell of y^m Nor anything about y^m & I have Seen Goody Good hirself. Q. was y^t True of Giles Cory y^t you Saw him & y^t he Afflicted yo⟨u⟩ ye other day? An. yes I have Sene him often & he hurts me very much & Goody ⟨Oll⟩iver hath appeared to me & Afflicted me & brought the Book to Tempt mee, & I have Seen Goody. Cory. the first night I was Taken, I saw as I thought ye Apparition of Goody Cory & Catched att itt as I thought & Caught my mas⟨t⟩er in my lap 'tho̅ I did nott See my master in y^t place att y^t Time, upon W^{ch} my master Said itt is noe body but I itt is my shaddow y^t you ⟨s⟩ee, butt my master was nott befor mee as I Could des⟨c⟩erne, but Catc⟨h⟩ing att ye Apparition y^t Looked li⟨ke⟩ Goody Cory I Caught hold of my master & pulled him downe into m⟨y⟩ Lap; upon W^{ch} he Said I see there is noe heed to any of you⟨r⟩ Talkings, for you are all possest With ye Devill for it is nothing butt m⟨y⟩ shape. I have Sene Goody Cory att my masters house in person, an⟨d⟩ she Tould mee y^t I should be Condemned for a Witch as well as sh⟨e⟩ hirself, itt was att my masters house, & she Said y^t ye Children Would cry out & bring out all. Q. was this before you had Sighned? An. yes, before I had any ffitts. Q. Now tell ye Truth about ye Mout⟨e⟩bank what Writeing was y^t? An. I don't know I asked hir what itt was about

[Reverse] but she would nott Tell mee Saying She had promised nott to Lett any body See itt. Q. well, but Whoe did you See more? An. I don't Know any more. Q. how long hath your Mast^ε & Mistris bin Witches? An. I don't know, they never Tould me. Q. ⟨w⟩hat likeness or appearance have you had to bewth [= bewitch] you? An. they never gave me any thing. While I was reading this over upon y^e Comeing in of m^ε Higginson & m^ε Hale as Soon as I read y^e Name Parker, She Im̅ediately ffell into dreadfull ffitts as she affirmed after hir ffitt was over by y^e appearance of Goody Parker: & m^ε Hathorne presently but nameing Goody Pudeator she alsoe appeared & Tormented hir very much. and Goody Parker in ye Time of hir Examination in one of Warrens ffitts Tould this Examinant y^t she had bewitched ye Examinants Sister & was ye Cause of hir dumbness as alsoe y^t she had lately killed a man aboard a vessell & Tould me ⟨y^t⟩ his name was Michaell Chapleman aboard ye vessell in the harbour after y^a Ware Come to Anchor & y^t he dyed with a paine in his Side & y^t she had done itt by strikeing Something into his Side & y^t she had strook this Examinan⟨t⟩s Sister dumb y^t she should never speak more. and Goody. Pudea⟨to⟩r att ye same Tyme appeared & Tould this Examinant y^t She had thr⟨o⟩wne Jno Turner off of a chery Tree & almost Killed ⟨h⟩im & Goody Parker s^d y^t s⟨h⟩e had Cast away Capt Prices Ketch, Thom⟨as⟩ Wes⟨t⟩gate m⟨a⟩ster & Venus Colefox in ⟨i⟩tt & presently Tould hir y^t Jno Lapthorne was lost in i⟨tt and⟩ that they W⟨e⟩re ffoundred in ye Sea. and she Saith ⟨y^t⟩ Goody Pudeator To⟨u⟩l⟨d⟩ hir y^t she went up to m^ε Corwins house to ⟨b⟩ewitch his mare y^t he should nott goe up to ye ffarmes to Exam̅ine y^e Witc⟨h⟩es, also⟨e⟩ m^ε Burroughs appearing ⟨att⟩ y^e Same Tim⟨e &⟩ A⟨ffl⟩ic⟨tin⟩g h⟨i⟩r ⟨T⟩ould hir y^t ⟨h⟩e Went to Tye m^ε H⟨a⟩thornes horses leggs when he went last to Boston & y^t he Tryed ⟨to⟩ bewi⟨t⟩ch him tho̅ he Could nott his horse: Goody ⟨P⟩udeat⟨or⟩

May 12, 1692

[Lost]⟨u⟩ld [= told] hir yᵗ sh⟨e⟩ Killed hir husband by g⟨iv⟩eing ⟨h⟩im Something whereby he ffell Sic⟨k⟩ and dyed, itt was she Tould hir about .7. or .8. years Since. and Goody Parker. Tould hir yᵗ she was Instrumentall to drowne Orns's Son in yᵉ harbour. alsoe she sᵈ she did bewitch Jnᵒ Searle's boy to death as his master was Carrying him out to ⟨S⟩ea soe yᵗ he was f⟨o⟩rced to bring him back againe: alsoe Burroughs Tould hir yᵗ he Killed his Wife off of Cape=Ann. ⟨P⟩arker tould hir al⟨ls⟩oe that Margarett Jacobs was a wittness again⟨st⟩ hir and did charge hir yesterday upon hir (that is Ja⟨co⟩bs's) examinatiō

Notes: By this time Mary Warren had crossed over and had become an accuser. The charge by Margaret Jacobs, appearing at the end of the document, refers to the examination of Margaret Jacobs on May 11, the record of which is not extant. ◊ Hand 1 = Jonathan Corwin

Essex County Court Archives, vol. 1, no. 116, Massachusetts Supreme Judicial Court, Judicial Archives, on deposit James Duncan Phillips Library, Peabody Essex Museum, Salem, MA.

146. Mittimus for George Jacobs Sr., William Hobbs, Edward Bishop Jr., Bridget Bishop, Sarah Bishop, Sarah Wilds, Mary Black, Mary English, Alice Parker, & Ann Pudeator

[Hand 1] To the Keeper of theire ⟨M⟩[Lost] [= Majesties]

You are in theire Majesᵗˢ names her[Lost] to take into your care and safe Custody [Lost] of George Jacobs senᵉ of Salem husbandman ⟨G⟩[Lost] of Salem ffarmes husbandman. William Hobs of [Lost] husbandman, Edward Bushop of Salem Village husband[Lost] [= husbandman] And Sarah Bushop the wife of sᵈ Edward Bushop, Bridg[Lost] [= Bridget] Bushop ^{Alias Olliuer} the wife of Edward Bushop of Salem Sawyer Sarah Wilde the wife of John Wilde of Topsfeild, Mary a Negro Woman of Lᵗ Nathaniell Putnam of Salem Village Mary English the wife of Phillip English of Salem Merchant; Allice Parker the wiffe of John Parker of Salem Seaman, And Ann Pudeatter ["Pudeatter" written over "Putnam"] of Salem Widdow, who all and Euery one of them; Stand Charged in behalfe of theire Majesᵗ With Sundry acts of Witchcraft Lately donne or Committed by them on the Bodys of Mary Walcot Abigail Williams Marcy Lewis Ann Putnam Eliz Hubbert S̶h̶usannah Shelden and Others of Sale⟨m⟩ Village and ffarmes, whereby great hurt hath bene donne them, Whome You are well to secure in sayd Goale vntill thay shall be thence deliuerd by due order of Law, and hereof you are not to faile Dated Salem May the 12th 1692

ꝑ vs

John: Hathorne }
                } Assisᵗˢ
Jonathan. Corwin }

Notes: The upper right corner of the manuscript is lost. However, the second person listed in this lost portion is identified as a husbandman from Salem Farms, probably Giles Cory. Edward Bishop is the husband of Sarah Bishop, not to be confused with the husband of Bridget Bishop, also named Edward but not accused. Mary Esty may have been in this group, her name in the lost portion. ◊ Hand 1 = John Hathorne

Witchcraft Papers, no. 25, Massachusetts Historical Society. Boston, MA.

147. Warrant for the Apprehension of Abigail Soames, and Officer's Return

[Hand 1] To Constable Peter Osgood.

You are in theire Majes^ts names hereby required to apprehend and forthwith bring before vs Abigaile Soames Single Woman, now Liueing at ye house of Saml Gaskill in Salem; who stand accused of Sundry acts of ~~Sundry~~ Witchcraft, (or high Suspition there of) donne or Committed by her Lately. on the Body of Mary Warren &c faile not Dated Salem May the. 13th 1692

John: Hathorne ⎫
ꝑ vs   ⎬ Assis^ts
Jonathan. Corwin ⎭

[Reverse] [Hand 2] I heaue Aprehended ye person of Abigall Soams Acordinge to warrante exprestt on ye other side and heaue broghte hir to ye howse of m^r Thomas Beadles

p^r me Peter Osgood constable in Sealem

May y^e 13 1692:

Cop

[Hand 3] Abigaile Soames

Notes: Why Mary Warren chose to accuse Abigail Soames is unclear. Perhaps Warren simply knew her by reputation. Soames, 37, had been in trouble for not attending church and was from a persecuted Quaker family. ◊ Hand 1 = John Hathorne

Essex County Court Archives, vol. 2, no. 103, Massachusetts Supreme Judicial Court, Judicial Archives, on deposit James Duncan Phillips Library, Peabody Essex Museum, Salem, MA.

148. Deposition of Jarvis Ring v. Susannah Martin, and Deposition of Joseph Ring v. Susannah Martin & Thomas Hardy

See also: June 29, 1692.

[Hand 1] Jarvis Ring of salsbury maketh oath as followeth

That about seven or eight years ago he had ben several times aflicted in the night time by sombody or som thing coming vp vpon him when he was in bed and did sorely aflict him by Lying vpon him and he coold neither moue nor speake while it was vpon him but somtimes made a kind of noyse that folks did hear him & com vp to him and as s⟨oo⟩n as any ⟨b⟩ody came it w⟨ool⟩d be gon this it did for a long time bother [= before] and sinc: but he did neu[Lost] [= never] see any body clearly but on time

but on time in the night it came vpon me as at other times and I did then see the ꝑson [Lost]na [*Woodward* = of Susana] martin of Amsbery I this deponent did ꝑsently see her [Lost] [*Woodward* = and shee] came to this deponent and took him by the hand and bitt him [Lost]inger [*Woodward* = by the finger] by fors and then came and Lay vpon him a while as [Lost] [*Woodward* = formerly] and after a while went away the print of the bite is

May 13, 1692

[Lost] [*Woodward* = yet to] be see{n} on the litle finger of his right hand for it was [Lost]le
[*Woodward* = hard to heale] (he farther sayth) That several times he was asleep [Lost]me:
[*Woodward* = when it came] But at that time when bitt his finger he was as [Lost]ked
[*Woodward* = fayerly awake] as ever he was: and plainly saw her shape and felt [Lost]
[*Woodward* = her teeth] ⟨a⟩s aforsayd

[Lost]e [= sworn] by Jarvis Ring abouesayd may the 13ᵗʰ 1692
[Lost]e [= before] me Robt Pike Assᵗ att salsbury

[Hand 2] Jurat in Curia

[Hand 1] The deposion of Joseph Ring of salsbury aged :27: years ⟨b⟩eing sworne sayth
⟨T⟩hat about the Latter end of september Last being in the wood wit⟨h⟩ his brother Jarvis
Ring hewing of timber his brother went home with his teame and Left this deponent alone
to finsh the hewing of the peec for him ∧{yᵗ is his brother} to cary wⁿ he came againe: but as
soon as his brother was gon ther came to this deponent the appearanc of Thomas Hardy of
the great Iland at puscataway and by som Impuls he was forsed to follow him to the house of
benouy tuker wᶜʰ was deserted and was about half a mile from the plac he w⟨a⟩s at work in
and in that house did appear susana martin of Amsbery and the aforsayd Hardy and another
female ꝑson wᶜʰ the dep⟨o⟩nent did not know: ther thay had a good fire & drink it seemd to
be sidᵉ [= cider] ther continud most part of the night ∧{sᵈ martan} being then in her natural
shape and talking as shee vse to do: but toward the mornig the sd martine went from the fire:
made a noyse and turned into the shape of a blak hoge & went away and: so did the other: to
{ꝑsons} go away and this deponent was strangly caryed away also: and the first plac he knew
was by sam⟨u⟩ll weeds h⟨o⟩us in Amsbery

[Hand 2] Jurat in Curia.

[Hand 1] sworne by Joseph Ring may yᵉ 13ᵗʰ :1692: before me Robt Pike Assᵗ

[Reverse] [Hand 2] Jaruis Ring & Joseph Ring

Notes: Robert Pike resumed hearing charges against Susannah Martin that he had begun on May 11. ◇ Used at trial. ◇
"peec": 'a measure of land' (*OED* s.v. *peck* n¹, 3). ◇ Hand 1 = Robert Pike; Hand 2 = Stephen Sewall

Essex County Court Archives, vol. 1, no. 181.1, Massachusetts Supreme Judicial Court, Judicial Archives, on deposit James Duncan
Phillips Library, Peabody Essex Museum, Salem, MA.

149. Deposition of Joseph Ring v. Susannah Martin & Thomas Hardy
See also: June 29, 1692.

[Hand 1] Joseph Ring of salsbury aged 27 years hauig ben str[Lost] [= strangely] ⟨h⟩andled
for the space of almost to year maketh this Relaṡon vpon oath as followeth viz
That in the month of Jun next after Casco bay fort was takn this deponent comig between
Sandy beach & hampton towne mett with Tho: Hardy of great Iland & a company of several
other cret.[Lost] [= creatures] with him wᶜʰ sd Hardy demanded of this deponent to
shillings: and with the dreadfull noyse & hidious shapes of these creaturs and firebale this
deponent was almost frited out of his witts: and in about som half an hour (or indeed he
coold not judg of the time) thay Left him & he came to hampton

About ten days after as yᵉ deponent came from boston between Rowly & new⟨b⟩[Lost] [=   May 13, 1692
Newbury] this deponent was overtakn with a compay of people on horsbak who pas⟨t⟩ by
him: and after thay wear past by him The aforsd Tho: Hardy tur⟨n⟩d about his horse alit &
came bak to this deponent with his hors in hand & desired this deponant to go to mᵉˢ whits
& drink with him: wᶜʰ being refused he turnd away to the company: & thay all came vp
togather such a breth that it seemd Imposibl to scape being trod down by them but th⟨a⟩y
went all past and then appeared no more

A⟨b⟩out oct: following comig from hampton in Salsbury pin plaine a company of horses with
men & wumen vpon them overtook this deponent & the aforsd Hardy being on of {them}
came to this deponent & before & demanded his :2s: of him an thretnd to tear him in peeces
to whom this depont made no answer & so he & the rest went away & Left this deponet.
After this this deponent had divers strang appearances wᶜʰ did fors him away with them into
vnknown places wʳ he saw meettings and festings and dancing and many strang sights: and
from Agust Last he was dom [= dumb] and coold not speake till this Last Aprill

he also relates th⟨at⟩ ther did vse to com to him a man that did present him a book to which
he woold haue him sett his hand with ℘mise of any thing that he woold haue & ther wear
presented all delectabl things ℘sons and places Imaginabl but he refusing it woold vsualy end
with most dreadfull shapes noyses ye⟨?⟩ing & sceeching [= screeching] that almost scared
him out of his witts & this was the vs⟨u⟩all manner of ℘seeding wᵗʰ him: & on time the book
w⟨a⟩s brought and a pen offerd him & to his aprehension ther was blod in the Ink horn but
he never toucht the pen

he farther say that thay never told him wᵗ he shoold writt nor he coold not speak to Ask
them wᵗ he shoold writ

he farther say in severall thair mery meetting he haue seen susanas marti⟨ns⟩ appearanc
among them

And that day that his speech came to him againe wᶜʰ was about [Lost] [Woodward = the end
of] Aprill La⟨s⟩t as he was in bed shee did stand by his beds sid [Lost] [Woodward = and
pincht him]

Joseph Ring abouesayd made oathe of ^{the} trut[Lost] [= truth] of all that is aboue
writtn this 13ᵗʰ day of may 1692 before me Robt Pike Assᵗ

[Hand 2] Jurat in Curia yᵉ Substance of it
viua voce

[Hand 1] [Lost] [Woodward = It is to] be vnderstood that the matter about the to shillings
demanded of sd [Lost] [Woodward = Ring] was this viz That when Casko was asalted before
it was takn [Lost] [Woodward = Capt] Cedrack walt was going from great Iland in
puscataway with [Lost]rty [Woodward = a party] for thayr releef of wᶜʰ party sd Ring was on
& sd [Lost]ng [Woodward = Hardy coming] vp into the Room wʳ sd Ring bilived before
thay sayled [Lost]ayd [Woodward = and playd] at shuffl bord or som such lik game & vrged
sd Ring play [Lost] [Woodward = sd] Ring told him he had no mony & sd hardy Lent him
2s and then [Lost] [Woodward = sd] Ring playd with him sd hardy who won his mony away
from [Lost] [Woodward = him] agane and so he coold not then pay him
this accopt was by sd Ring given to me Robt Pike Assᵗ

May 13, 1692

Notes: Used at trial. ◊ "bilived": 'lived, remained' (*OED* s.v. *beleave* or *belive*). ◊ Hand 1 = Robert Pike; Hand 2 = Stephen Sewall.

Essex County Court Archives, vol. 1, nos. 181.2 & 185, Massachusetts Supreme Judicial Court, Judicial Archives, on deposit James Duncan Phillips Library, Peabody Essex Museum, Salem, MA.

150. Examination of Abigail Soames

[Hand 1] Abigail Soams's Examination 13 May. 1692 att Salem
Upon the glance of her Eye she struck Mary Warren into a dreadful fit att her first appearance, and s^d Warren continually Crying out that it was this very Woman thō she knew her not before, only affirmed that she herself in apparition had told her that her name was Soams, and also did affirm that this was the very woman that had afflicted her all this day, and that. she met her as she was comeing in att the gate, and bit her Exceedingly. att her first Examining there was found in her Apron, a great Botching Needle, about the middle of it near her Belly, which was plucked out by one of the standers by, by ord^ε of the Magistrates, which the s^d Soams affirmed she knew not how it came there. Mary Warren affirmed that she never saw the s^d woman before only in apparition, and then she told her that her Name was Abigail Soams, and that she was sister to John Soams of Preston Cooper, and that she Lived att Gaskins, and that she had ^{lain} Bedrid a year. Being asked whether she was sister to John Soams she answered peremptorily she would not tell, for all was false that Warren said. furthermore Warren affirmed that she told her, that she viz the s^d Soams was the Instrumental Means of the death of Southwick, Upon which s^d Soams casting her Eye on Warren struck her into a dreadful fitt, and bitt her so dreadfully, that the Like was never seen on any of the afflicted, which the s^d Warren Charged the s^d Soams with doeing off, saying that the s^d Soams told her this day she would be the death of her. ffurther Warren Affirms that she the s^d Soams ran two pinns into her side this day, which being plucked out the blood ran out after them. Goody Gaskin being present att this Examination affirmed she had kept her Bed for most parts these thirteen months – Warren further affirms she told her that when she did goe abroad att any time it was in the Night which Goody Gaskin being present Confirmed the same, that that was the Usual time off her goeing abroad – furthermore Warren affirmed that this Abigail Soams would have had her to have made a bargain with her, telling her if she woud not tel of her being a sickly woman, she would not afflict her any more, and that then she should goe along with her, for the s^d Soams told her, she was her God, Upon wch Warren answered she would not keep the Devils Councel. Soams told her she was not a Devil but she was her God. after this appearing three times more to her, she s^d att one of those times she was as good as a God. Q. Mary Warren is this true? A. It is nothing but the truth. Soams being asked who hurt Warren in the time off her fits? she Answered it was the Enemy hurt her. I have been said I myself distracted many a time, and my senses have gone from mee, and I thought I have seen many a Body hurt mee, and might have accused many as wel as she doth. I Really thought I had seen many persons att my Mothers house at Glo⟨ce⟩ster, and they greatly afflicted mee as I thought: Soams being Commanded while Warren was in a dreadful ffit, to take Warren by the hand, the said Warren immediately recovered; this Experiment was tryed three times over and the Issue the same. Warren after a Recovery being commanded to touch the s^d Soams, althō she assayed

May 13, 1692

several times to do it with great Earnesteness she was not able, But fell down into a dreadful ffit, Upon which the s^d Soams being Commanded to take Warren by the hand, she immediately recovered her again, Warren affirming she felt some thing soft in her hand, (her Eyes then being fast shut) which revived her very heart. Warren being asked what the Reason was she could not Come to touch Soams affirmed she saw the apparition off Soams come from her Body, and would meet her, and thrust her with Violence back again, not suffring her to Come near her – sometimes Soams would say it was distraction in talking she would often Laugh, upon which Laughing the afflicted person would presently fal into a ffit. Soams being asked whether she thought this was witchcraft, or whether there were any Witches in the world, answered she did not know any thing but said itt was the Enemy, or some Other wicked person or the Enemy himself that forces persons to afflict her att this time, presently this Warren fell into a trance, comeing out of which she affirmed, that, Soams told her in the time of her trance, that she would thrust an Awl into her very heart and would kil her this night. Soams could never cast her Eye upon Warren, but immediately she struck her down, and one time she affirmed s^d Soams struck her such a Blow as almost killed, which made the s^d Warren break out into abundance of tears. Soams being Charged with it, instead of bewailing itt, Broke forth into Laughter. Warren being also afflicted by the wringing of her mouth after a strange, and prodigious manner, Soams being Command^d to look upon her in that fitt, peremptorily answered she would not, same being by being ordered to turn her face about to look on the afflicted, which being accordingly done, she shut her Eyes Close, and would not look on her being then ordered to touch her she did, and immediately Warren Recovered, which no sooner done but Soams opened her Eyes and looked on the afflicted, and struck her into another most dreadful and terrible fit, and in this manner she practised her Witchcrafts severall times before the Court. Mary Warren Looking on her affirmed this to be the very woman that had so often afflicted her dureing the Examination and Charged her with it to her face. sometimes dureing the Examination Soams would p⟨ut⟩ her own foot behind her Other leg, and immediately Warrens Legs would be twisted that

[Reverse] that it was impossible ffor the strongest man there to Untwist them, without Breaking her Leggs, as was seen by many present – After this Examination Warren saw the apparitions off Proctor Nurse and Burroughs that appeared before her, and Burroughs bitt her which bite was seen by many. Also Burroughs att the same time appeared to Margaret Jacobs who was then present, and told her as Jacobs affirmed, that her Grandfather would be hanged Upon which the s^d Jacobs wept. it was also Observed by the Revd Mr Noyse, that after the needle was taken away from Soams, that Warren was neither bit, nor pinched by the s^d Soams, but struck so dreadfully on her breast, that she cryed out she was almost killed.

[Hand 2] Abigail Soames Examination

Notes: Mary Warren's performance in her new role as an accuser revealed the extremes of affliction she could counterfeit, including the drawing of her own blood. She was probably the most self-harming of all the accusers. ◊ "Botching Needle": 'a mending needle' (see *OED* s.v. *botch* v^1, 1 'to patch, mend'). ◊ Hand 2 = John Higginson Jr.

Suffolk Court Files, vol. 32, docket 2703, p. 26, Massachusetts Supreme Judicial Court, Judicial Archives, Massachusetts State Archives. Boston, MA.

Saturday, May 14, 1692

151. Complaint of Nathaniel Ingersoll & Thomas Putnam v. Daniel Andrew, George Jacobs Jr., Rebecca Jacobs, Sarah Buckley, Mary Whittredge, Elizabeth Hart, Thomas Farrar Sr., Elizabeth Colson, & Bethiah Carter Jr.

[Hand 1] Salem. May the 14ᵗʰ 1692

Lᵗ Nathaniell Ingersall and Serjᵉ Thomas Putnam yeomen both of Salem Village personally appeared before [Lost] [= us] and made Complaint in behalfe of theire Majesᵗˢ, against Daniell Andrew of Salem Village Bricklayer. George Jacobs junᵉ of Salem Village husbandman, And [   ] Jacobs the wife of said George Jacobs, [   ] Buckley the wife of Wᵐ Buckley of Salem Village Cordwayner. and Mary Withridge of Salem Village daufter of Said Buckley [   ] Hart the wife of Isaac Hart of Lyn ^{husbandman} Thomas ffarrer senᵉ of Lyn. hubandman. Elizabeth Colson of Reding single Woman, And Bethya Carter of Ouburne daufter of Widdow Carter of sᵈ Towne. for high Suspition of Sundry acts of Witchcraft by them Committed or donne ^{Lately} on the body of Ann Puttnam Marcy ["M" written over "p"] Lewis Mary Walcot And Abigail Williams & others of Salem Village, whereby much hurt is donne to theire bodys, therefore Craues Justice.

Nathanail Ingersoll
Thomas putnam.

[Reverse] [Hand 2] Warrant agᵗ G. [1 word illegible]

Notes: Note the blanks where first names should appear. The omissions of first names in such cases give valuable insights into how well the accused were known by their accusers. ◊ Hand 1 = John Hathorne

Essex County Court Archives, vol. 1, no. 221, Massachusetts Supreme Judicial Court, Judicial Archives, on deposit James Duncan Phillips Library, Peabody Essex Museum, Salem, MA.

152. Warrant for the Apprehension of Daniel Andrew, George Jacobs Jr., Rebecca Jacobs, Sarah Buckley, & Mary Whittredge, and Officer's Return

[Hand 1] To the Constables in Salem

You are in theire Majesᵗˢ names hereby required to apprehend and bring before vs on Tusday next being the seauenteenth day of this Instant moneth of may aboute ten of yᵉ Clock in the forenoon at yᵉ house of Lᵗ Nathañll Ingersons ["Nathañll Ingersons" written over "Daniell Andrew"] of Salem Village, Daniell Andrew of Salem Village Bricklayer. George Jacobs Junᵉ of Salem Village husbandman And [Hand 2] Rebecka [Hand 1] Jacobs the wife of said George Jacobs [Hand 3]: and Sarah [Hand 1] Buckley the wife of Wᵐ Buckley of Salem Village Cordwayner, And ⟨M⟩ary Withridge the daufter of sayd Buckley. who all ⟨s⟩tand Charged ^{in behalfe of theire Majesties} with high Suspition of Sundry acts of witchcrafts by them donne or Committed on yᵉ Bodys of Ann Putnam Marcy Lewis Mary Walcot and

Abigail Williams and Others of Salem Village (Lately,) whereby great hurt hath benn donn   May 14, 1692
them. And hereof you are not to faile Dated Salem May the 14th 1692

John. Hathorne }
₱ vs   Assists
Jonathan. Corwin }

[Reverse] [Hand 3] In prosecution of this warant
I haue apprehended and brought the bodyes of Sarah Buckley and Marye Withredg and
Rebekah Jacobs all of Salem Velage according to the tener of the within written warrant: and
haue Likewise made delegant sarch at the house of Daniell Andrew and at the house of
Georg Jacobs for them Likewise but Cannot find them
⟨₱ me Jonathan Putnam Constable⟩
⟨in Salem⟩

Notes: If a date was written on the return, it is no longer legible on the manuscript. The most likely date would be the
same date as the warrant, but the search for Daniel Andrew and George Jacobs Jr. probably delayed the return. Andrew
and Jacobs escaped. ◊ Hand 1 = John Hathorne

*Essex County Court Archives, vol. 1, no. 270, Massachusetts Supreme Judicial Court, Judicial Archives, on deposit James Duncan
Phillips Library, Peabody Essex Museum, Salem, MA.*

153. Warrant No. 1 for the Apprehension of Elizabeth Colson, and Officer's Return

See also: May 16, 1692.

[Hand 1] To ye Constable of Redding
You are in theyr Majestyes Names ^{hereby} Required to Apprehend & bring before us
(upon Tuesday next being the Seavententh day of this Instant May by Tenne of ye Clock
aforenoone att ye house of Left Nathaniell Ingersolls in Salem Village) the body of Elizabeth
Colson of Redding Single woeman, whoe standeth charged ^{in behalfe of theyr Majestys}
wth high Suspition of Sundry Acts of Witchc[Lost] [= witchcraft] done or Comitted upon
ye Bodyes of Mary. Walcott, Mercy Lewis & others in Salem Village, whereby great hurt
hath bin done them: And hereof you are nott to faile
Salem datd May. 14th 1692.

John. Hathorne }
₱ vs   Assists
Jonathan. Corwin }

[Hand 2] May 16th 1692
I haue made Diligent Search for ye aboue named Elizabeth Collson and find shee is fled and
by the best Information shee is att Boston in order to bee shipt ofe; and by way of Escaped to
bee transported to some other Countery whereof I make my Returne
[Hand 3?] ₱ me John Parker Constable for Redding

Notes: Elizabeth Colson was complained against on May 14. Although eventually captured on September 14 and
imprisoned, she managed to stay in hiding long enough to avoid facing the Court of Oyer and Terminer. She was
in prison until her release on March 2, 1693. She was the granddaughter of Sarah Dustin, also arrested and imprisoned.
◊ Hand 1 = Jonathan Corwin; Hand 2 = George Herrick

May 14, 1692   *Essex County Court Archives, vol. 2, no. 104, Massachusetts Supreme Judicial Court, Judicial Archives, on deposit James Duncan Phillips Library, Peabody Essex Museum, Salem, MA.*

154. Warrant for the Apprehension of Elizabeth Hart & Thomas Farrar Sr., and Officer's Return

See also: May 15, 1692.

[Hand 1] To yᵉ Marshall of yᵉ County Essex or his deputy
You are in theyr Majestys Names hereby required ⟨to⟩ Apprehend & bring before us upon Tuesday next, bein[Lost] [= being] being yᵉ Seavententh day of this Instant May by [Lost] of yᵉ Clock in yᵉ forenoone att yᵉ house of Levᵗ Nath[Lost] [= Nathaniel] Ingersoll in Salem Village, the bodys of Thomas ff[Lost]rer [= Farrar] Senᵉ of Lin Husbandman and [Hand 2] Elizebeth [Hand 1] Hart yᵉ w[Lost] [= wife] of Isaac Hart of Lin Husbandman, whoe Stand C[Lost]ged [= charged] in behalf of theyr Majestys, with high Suspit[Lost] [= suspicion] of Sundry Acts of Witchcraft done or Comitted upo⟨n⟩ [Lost] Bodys of Ann. Putnam, Mercy Lewis & others in Sal[Lost] [= Salem] Village, whereby great hurt hath bin done them, And hereof you are nott to ffaile, Salem. datᵈ May. 14ᵗʰ 1692.

John. Hathorne ⎫
ꝑ vs   ⎬ Assisᵗˢ
Jonathan. Corwin ⎭

[Hand 2] May 1⟨5⟩ᵗʰ 1692 I haue apprehended yᵉ aboue named persons and brought them att att yᵉ time and place aboue written to answer as aboue

ꝑ George Herrick Marshall of Essex

Notes: Hand 1 = John Hathorne; Hand 2 = George Herrick

Essex County Court Archives, vol. 1, no. 201, Massachusetts Supreme Judicial Court, Judicial Archives, on deposit James Duncan Phillips Library, Peabody Essex Museum, Salem, MA.

155. Deposition of Rachel Tuck & Hannah Cox v. Dorcas Hoar

See also: Sept. 6, 1692.

[Hand 1] 14: 3ᵐᵒ 1692
The deposition of Rachell Tuck aged about 45. years and Hannah cox: aged about 30 years these deponants testifis and saith about three years before: the date aboue: named: that Darkis Hoar the wife of william Hoar seⁿ now deceaced/ being very sick in hir bed and seuerall being at that time to watch with hir: namly Christopher Read: hir son in law and his wife: and hir daughter Jone Hoard with seuerall others: these seuerall persons being there with said darkes Hoar to look after hir: and after some time went to the bede side to look after theyr mother and they found hir gon out of the: bead they knew not how and being affrighted they run out of dor and the last person that went out goodde Hoar seat vpon the stayrs or lader and held hir fast and the person that was held fast cried out
ffarther Hannah cox: one of the deponants before mentioned saith that the persons: that rune out of the hows in a fright weare affr⟨a⟩id ffor some time to goe into the hows: but after a while did go in and made a̶ ̶l̶i̶g̶h̶t̶ lite to se who it was that held the {person} that said shee

was held fast. and they found it to be goodde Hoar sitting upon the stayers or lader. dresed with hir clothes and hat & cloke on

{no⟨te⟩}: this aboue written was decleard to the two aboue said deponants at the hows of Thomas Cox by Jone Hoar doughter to dorkes: and farther saith not

May 15, 1692

[Hand 2] Jurat in Curia.

[Reverse] Rachell Tuck and Hannah Cox Contra G. Hoare

Notes: The initial "G" on the Reverse is either a clerical error or an abbreviation for "goodwife" or "Goody." The trial of Dorcas Hoar was on September 6, and Calef writes that she was condemned on September 9. Calef's two dates for the September condemnations, September 9 and 17, make sense in the cases he lists if one assumes a separate sentencing date from the conviction date. After condemnation she confessed and was not executed. ◊ Used at trial.

Essex County Court Archives, vol. 1, no. 207, Massachusetts Supreme Judicial Court, Judicial Archives, on deposit James Duncan Phillips Library, Peabody Essex Museum, Salem, MA.

Sunday, May 15, 1692

Officer's Return: Warrant for the Apprehension of Elizabeth Hart & Thomas Farrar Sr.
2nd of 2 dates. See No. 154 on May 14, 1692

156. Warrant No. 2 for the Apprehension of John Willard, and Officer's Return

See also: May 18, 1692.

[Hand 1] To The Marshall of the County of Essex or to the Constables in Salem or any other Marshal or Marshalls Constable or Constables within this theire Majes^{ts} Colony or Terretory of the Massachusetts in New England

You are in theire Majes^{ts} names hereby required to Apprehend John Willard of Salem Village husbandman, if he may be found in your precints who stands charged with sundry acts of Witchcraft by him donne or Committed on the Bodys of Bray Wilkins. and Daniell Wilkins the son͞ of Henery Wilkins both of Salem Village {and Others} – according to Complaint made before vs by Thomas ffuller Jun^ε and Benj^ε Wilkins sen^ε, both of s^d Salem Village afores^d Yeomen; who being found You are to Convey from Town to Towne from Constable to Constable vntill he be Brought before vs, or such as may be in Authority ~~There,~~ {in Salem} and hereof You are not to faile Dated Salem May the 15th 1692

John Hathorne
𝓅 vs   } Assis^{ts}
Jonathan. Corwin

To be prosecuted according
to the direction of Constable   }
John Putnam of Salem Village
who goes with the Same

May 16, 1692

[Reverse] [Hand 2] I haue apprehended John Wilard of Salam Veleg acorden to the tener of this Warrant and brought him before your Worsheps Date 18 may 1692

by me John Putnam Constoble of Salam

[Hand 3] Goody wheat
m$^{r\langle s\rangle}$ Hall of Gr$\langle$o$\rangle$tt$\langle$en$\rangle$

Notes: Goody Wheat and Mrs. Hall were witnesses, probably in support of wife-beating accusations against Willard. No other reference to Goody Wheat appears. In 1711 a Mary Hall received ten pounds compensation, and she is identified as formerly married to Burroughs. The Mrs. Hall in this document is not the same person. ◊ Hand 1 = John Hathorne

Essex County Court Archives, vol. 1, no. 238, Massachusetts Supreme Judicial Court, Judicial Archives, on deposit James Duncan Phillips Library, Peabody Essex Museum, Salem, MA.

Monday, May 16, 1692

Officer's Return: Warrant No. 1 for the Apprehension of Elizabeth Colson
2nd of 2 dates. See No. 153 on May 14, 1692

157. Deposition of Ann Putnam Jr., Thomas Putnam, & Robert Morey v. Thomas Farrar Sr.†

[Hand 1] the deposistion of Ann putnam who testifieth and saith that on the: 8th of may 1692: there appeard to me the Apperishtion of an old grayhead man with a great nose which tortored me and almost choaked me and urged me to writ in his book: and I asked him what was his name and from whence he came for I would complaine of him: and he tould ^{me} he came from linne and people used to call him old father pharo$\langle$ah$\rangle$ and he said he was my grandfather: for my father used to call him father: but I tould I would not call him grandfather: for he was a wizzard and I would complaine of him: and euer since he hath afflected me by times beating me and pinching me and allmost choaking me and urging me continewally to writ in his book

we whose names are underwriten haueing been conversant with Ann putnam haue hard hir declare what is aboue writen what she said she saw & heard from the apperishtion of old pharoah and also haue seen hir tortors: ^{and} perceiued hir hellish temtations by hir loud outcries I will not writ old pharoah I will not writ in your book

Thomas putnam
Roburt Morrell

[Reverse] [Hand 2] Ann. putnam ag$^{\langle st\rangle}$ Tho. ffarrer

Notes: Thomas Farrar and Elizabeth Hart were probably examined on May 16, since the day they were arrested, May 15, was a Sunday. Thomas Putnam signed the name of Robert Morrell (Morey). ◊ Hand 1 = Thomas Putnam; Hand 2 = Jonathan Corwin

Essex County Court Archives, vol. 2, no. 114, Massachusetts Supreme Judicial Court, Judicial Archives, on deposit James Duncan Phillips Library, Peabody Essex Museum, Salem, MA.

158. Deposition of Ann Putnam Jr. v. Elizabeth Hart†

May 16, 1692

[Hand 1] The Deposistion of Ann putnam who testifieth and saith that I haue often seen the apperishtion of gooddy heart among the wicthes but I did not know who she was: nor she did me no hurt tell the 13th of may 1692: that she came to my ffather house parsonally and tould me who she was and asked me if she had euer hurt me: but euer sence that day she has hurt me most greviously seuerall times and urgeth me greviously to writ in hir book

[Reverse] [Hand 2] Ann putnam agt G. Hart

Notes: As with Thomas Farrar, Elizabeth Hart was arrested May 15, a Sunday. ◊ Hand 1 = Thomas Putnam

Essex County Court Archives, vol. 1, no. 203, Massachusetts Supreme Judicial Court, Judicial Archives, on deposit James Duncan Phillips Library, Peabody Essex Museum, Salem, MA.

Witnessed: Deposition of William Brown v. Susannah Martin

2nd of 2 dates. See No. 140 on May 11, 1692

159. Deposition of John Kimball v. Susannah Martin

See also: June 29, 1692.

[Hand 1] The deposion of John kembal of Amsbury aged 45 or vpwards testifying sayth That about 23 years ago this deponent being about to remoue from newbery to Amsbery hauing bought a peec of Land of Georg martin of ⟨?⟩ Amsbery for which he was to pay him in catl or goods vpon a certaine day in the march next following & when the day of payment was come martin & his wif came for the pay and the sd kembal offered them the choyc of three cows and other catl but did res⟨er⟩[Lost] [= reserve] two cows wch thay wear not free to part with thay being the first that ever thay had but ["but" written over "And"] Martin {him}self was satisfyed with other pay {but} Susana his wif vnderstanding from this deponant and his wif that thay woold not part with on of these 2 cows the {sd} Susana martin {sayd} (you had ben as good you had) for s⟨h⟩ee will never do you any more good (and so it came to pass). for the next Aprill following that very cow Lay in the fayr dry yard with her head to her side (but starc dead) and when shee was fleaced no Impedement did appear in her for shee was a stout Lusty cow
and in a litle while {After} another cow dyed & then an ox and then other catle to the value of 30£ that sping [= spring]

sworne by John kembal may the 16 1692 before
                    Robt Pike Asist

                                                        [Hand 2] Jurat in Curia

[Reverse] John Kimball of Amesbury

Notes: Used at trial. ◊ Hand 1 = Robert Pike; Hand 2 = Stephen Sewall

Essex County Court Archives, vol. 1, no. 187, Massachusetts Supreme Judicial Court, Judicial Archives, on deposit James Duncan Phillips Library, Peabody Essex Museum, Salem, MA.

160. Deposition of John Kimball v. Susannah Martin
See also: June 29, 1692.

[Hand 1] John kembale of Amsbury afor mensiond farther deposeth That same year after he
was com to Live at Amsbery and was dwelling the house of E⟨a⟩dmund Elliat {he} was
mided [= minded?] to get a dog & hearing that the wif {of} sd Georg martin had a bich yᵗ
had whelps & this deponent went to her to get on of her but shee not Letting him haue his
choyc: he did not absolutly agree for any but sd he heard on blezdal had a bich by wᶜʰ he may
suply ⟨hmsef⟩ [= himself?] ^{but if not} ther nor nowhear els he woold haue hers {at her}
priz
but being vpon that accopt [= account] at sd blezdels v̶p̶o̶n̶ ̶t̶h̶a̶t̶ and marked the whelp that I
agreed ^{for} Georg martin coming by Askt me whether h̶e̶ I woold not haue {haue} on of
his wifes pupys to wᶜʰ this deponent made Answer on the negative
The same day Edmond Eliat sayd that he was at the house of the sd martins & heard the sd
martin Asked his wif whe [= why] this depent wear not to haue on of her pupys and {shee}
sd he was then sayd he he haue gott on at goodman blezdells & he saw him choose it and
mark it (to wᶜʰ his sd wif sayd) If I Live Ile give him pupys enough
within a few days after this I this deponent comig from his Intended hous in the woods to
Edmond Eliats house whear I dwelt ab⟨u⟩t the the sun sett or presently after {&} ther did
arise a litle blak cloud in the: n: w and a few drops of Raine and the wind blew prity hard in
going between the house of John wee & the meetting house the sd deponent came by seueral
stumps of trees by the way side he by Impuls he can give no reson {of} that made him tambl
[= tumble] ouer the stumps on after another though tho he had his ax vpon his shoulder wᶜʰ
put him in dang [= danger] & made him resolved to avoyd the next but coold not
And when he came a litl below the meetting house ther did appear a litl thing lik a pupy of a
darkish coler it shott betweene my Legs forward & bakward as on that wear dancin⟨g⟩ the
hay and this deponent being free from all fear vsed all posibl indevers to cut it with his ax but
coold not hurt it and as he was this Labering with his ax the pupy gaue a Litl Jump from
^{him} & seemed to go into the ground
in a litl farther going ther did appear a blak pupy som wᵗ bi⟨gger⟩ then the first but as blak
^{as a} cole to his apprehension which came agaist him wᵗ such violenc as its quik mosions
did exeed his mosions of his ax do wᵗ he coold. & it flew at his belly & away & then at his
throt & over his shoulder on way & go off & vp att it agane another way and with such
quiknes speed & violenc did it asalt him as if it {woold} tear out his throt or his ^{belly} a
good while he was without fear but at Last I felt my hart to fayle & sink vnder it that I
thought my Lif was going out & I recovered my self & gaue a start vp & ran to the fenc &
caling vpon god & naming the name Jesus christ & then it invisibly away my meaning is it
ceased at onc but this depont mad it not known to any body for frittng [= frightening] his wif

[Reverse] The next morning Edmond Eliat (as he told abrod and in his owne house) sayd
that he going toward the hous of sd martin to Look his oxn went in to Light his pipe & the
sd martins wif Asked ^{him} whear kembal was (sd Eliat sd abed with with his wif for ought
he knew then (sayd shee)
thay say he was frited Last night) with wᵗ sayd Eliat shee sayd with pupys Eliat replyd that
he heard nothing of it and Asked whear shee he⟨a⟩rd it and shee sayd about the Towne wᶜʰ
story sd Eliat hauing {told} it was all the Towne {ouer} when this deponent came hom at
night for he had ben all the day alone in the woods at work at his f⟨ar⟩mes

John kembale made oath to the truth of all that is writtn on both sides of this paper   May 17, 1692
may the 16th 1692 before me
    Robt Pike Asist

          [Hand 2] Jurat in Curia

Notes: Robert Pike continued taking depositions against Susannah Martin as he had on May 11 and May 13. Blezdell has not been identified. ◊ Used at trial. ◊ "the hay": 'a country dance' (*OED* s.v. *hay, hey* n[4]). ◊ Hand 1 = Robert Pike; Hand 2 = Stephen Sewall

Essex County Court Archives, vol. 1, no. 186, Massachusetts Supreme Judicial Court, Judicial Archives, on deposit James Duncan Phillips Library, Peabody Essex Museum, Salem, MA.

Tuesday, May 17, 1692

161. Warrant No. 2 for the Apprehension of Daniel Andrew, George Jacobs Jr., & Elizabeth Colson, and Warrant No. 3 for the Apprehension of Elizabeth Colson in Suffolk County, and Officer's Return

See also: Sept. 10, 1692.

[Hand 1] To the Marshall Generall or Lawfull Dep^t or Constables in Boston or elce where. You are in theire Majes^{ts} names hereby required to apprehend forthwith; or as soon as may be, Daniell Andrew And George Jacobs both of Salem Village, who Stand charged with high Suspition of Sundry acts of Witchcraft by them donne or Committed on the bodys of Mary Walot Abigail Williams Mary Lewis and Others of Salem Village Lately; whereby great hurt & dammage hath benne donne them, Contrary to ye Laws of theire Majes^{ts} who being found you are to convey vnto Salem & deliuer them vnto Authority in order to theire Examination Relating to ye premises and hereof you are not to faile Dated Salem. May. 17th 1692
        John Hathorne }
        Jonathan. Corwin } }
    By order of the Gouernour and Councill

You are likewise required to apprehend [   ] Coleson of Reding single woman who we are Informed is gone from Reding to Boston or Charlstowne, And who Also stands Charged wth sundry acts of witchcraft by her Committed on ye Bodys of Susannah Sheldon and Others of Salem Village. and send her also to Salem in order to her Examination there Relateing to ye premises afores^d
~~B~~ Salem. 17th 3mo 1692
        John Hathorne }
        Jonathan. Corwin }
         ℗ order of ye Gouern^o & Councill

[Hand 2] Complaint beinge made to me vnderwritten by william Arnold of Readinge that the {aboue} intended and mentioned Elizabeth Coleston is fled from the hands of Justice for which the warr^t aboue is directed to aprehhend her, and that ^{she} is now concealed in Bostone, These are in their Majesties name to require you to aprehend the said Elizabeth

May 17, 1692   Colstone & carry Before Lawfull Authority to be secured till she can be carried to Salem in order to her tryall there dated in Bostone the 10th of sept 1692

To the sherif of the Countie of Suffolke or his deputie

John Joyliffe Assis^t

Notes: Elizabeth Colson escaped, as did Andrew and Jacobs. Having been ordered arrested on May 14, May 17, and September 10, Colson was not captured until September 14. She remained in prison until March 2, 1693. Neither Andrew nor Jacobs were caught. ◊ Hand 1 = John Hathorne

MS Ch A, vol. 2, p. 67, Rare Books & Manuscripts, Boston Public Library. Boston, MA.

162. Return of the Coroner's Jury on the Inquest into the Death of Daniel Wilkins

See also: May 18, 1692.

[Hand 1] We whose names are underwriten being warned by Constable John putnam of Salem thes: 17 of may 1692 to veiw the body of daniell willknes of Salem village ^{late} deceased and we find seuerall bruised places upon the back of the said corps and the skin broken and many places of the gratest part of his back seemed to be ~~pri⟨ck⟩~~ prickt with an instriment about the bigness of a small awll and own side of his neck and ear seemed to be much bruised to his throat and turning the corps the blood Run out of his nose ⟨or⟩ mouth or both and his body nott sweld neither did he purge elce whare: and to the best of our judgments we cannot but ~~thinke~~ [Hand 2] ^{Apprhend} [Hand 1] but that he dyed an unnaturall death by sume cruell hands of wicthcraft or diabolicall art as is evident to us both by what we haue seen and hard consarning his death

Salem village this 17th of may 1692

Nathanell Patnam
Thomas ffuller sen
Jonathan Walcott Sen
Nathanail Ingersoll
Thomas Flint
William way
Thomas ffuller j
Joseph harrick
Thomas Haynes
Edward Putnam
Daniell Rea
John Putnam Jun

[Hand 2] all the abouenamed twelfe men the Jury of Inquest made Oath to y^e truth of theire aboues^d Returne Salem
May the 18th 1692

Before vs
John Hathorne
Jonathan Corwin
[Hand 3] ꝑ ord^ε of y^e Govern^ε & Councill

[Reverse] [Hand 4] Coron$^{\varepsilon s}$ Enquest ag^t [Hand 2?] Willard.   May 17, 1692

Notes: The circumstances of the death of Wilkins were prominent in the case of John Willard. ◊ Hand 1 = Thomas Putnam; Hand 2 = John Hathorne; Hand 3 = Jonathan Corwin; Hand 4 = Thomas Newton ◊ 1 wax seal.

MS Am 50, Rare Books & Manuscripts, Boston Public Library. Boston, MA.

163. Testimony of Susannah Shelden v. Elizabeth Colson, Mrs. White, John Willard, Philip English, Mary English, George Jacobs Jr., Rebecca Jacobs, Elizabeth Procter, Sarah Buckley, Mary Whittredge, & Elizabeth Hart

[Hand 1] may 17th ~~of~~ In the yeare 92
the Complainte of Sewzanah Shellten saith that Elizabeth Colson Remaynes in Afflicting of the {said} Shellten night & day. And Allso m$^{\varepsilon s}$ white also John willard Remaines in Afflic^{ng} of hur both day and night also m$^{\varepsilon}$ Inglish and. his wife Remaines afflicting of hure both night and day ~~J~~Googe Jacobs and his wife afflicting of hur the last lords day and tempting the said Shellten to sete hur ~~to sete~~ hand to the booke thay both appearing yesterday againe And would. haue hur sete hur hand to the booke the said Shelten said she would not then she she said she would stabb hur then sudenly she Res⟨ea⟩ued A sore wound one hur lifte side then: Ellizebeth Colson stabbing of hur one the back Right against the other woundes {soe that she spente blood} then goody prockter Appearing to hur and Afflicting of hur and tempting hur to sete hur hand to the bo{o}ke And last night goody prockter Appearing againe and would ha{u}e hu{r}e sete hur hand to the booke and towld hur that she hade sete hur ⟨ha⟩nd to the booke a grete while agooe

[Hand 2] moreou$^{\varepsilon}$ one the 1⟨7⟩th day aboue written 92 S⟨u⟩zana shelten saith that wife buckle did Aflicke me & her dat⟨e⟩r [= daughter] Mary & Misteres hart

[Reverse] [Hand 3] also s^d Shelden has se⟨ve⟩rall times seen Jno Procter {and his} afflic[Lost] [= afflict] Mary Warin since thay. s^d procter: & his wife were in prison

[Hand 4] Susannah Shelden ag^t Jno Willard Eliz Coleson Geo. Jacob & wife and Eliz. procter

S Shelden ag^t G Buckly & daufter &. G Hart

Notes: Mrs. White cannot be confidently identified. The use of the word "Complainte" in this document does not identify it as initiating a felony charge, the sense in which the word was formally used in legal matters. For the complaint against Elizabeth Colson, see No. 151. ◊ Hand 2 = Simon Willard; Hand 4 = Stephen Sewall

Essex County Court Archives, vol. 1, nos. 202 & 241, Massachusetts Supreme Judicial Court, Judicial Archives, on deposit James Duncan Phillips Library, Peabody Essex Museum, Salem, MA.

164. Statement of Susannah Shelden v. Philip English, Sarah Buckley, Mary Whittredge, Bridget Bishop, Giles Cory, Mary English, & Martha Cory‡

[Hand 1] The complaint of ssusanna Shelden against phillip english ~~for~~ the {sd} Susanah Shelden being ["i" written over "e"] at meeting on the sabboth day being the 24 of april shee

May 17, 1692

beeing aflicted in a uery sad manner she saw phillip english step ouer his pew and pinshed
her and a womand which Came from boston wich saith her name is good w^y when shee were
coming home again^t william shaws house their met her phillip english and a black man with
a hy crouned hatt on his head and a book in hish hand houlding the book to her and phillip
english told her that black man were her god and if shee would ~~thouch~~ touch that boock hee
would not pinsh her no more nor no bodie els should on the next day phillip english came
again and pinshed her and told her that if shee would not toutch the book hee would kill her
on the second day at night apered to her two women and a man and brought their books and
bid her touct [= touch] them she told them shee would not she did not know wher they
liued on of them told her they liued at the villadge and held the book to her again and bid
her touch it shee told her shee did not know their nams on of them told her shee was old
good man bucklyes wife and the other woman was her daughter mary and bid her touch the
book she told no shee had not told her hou long shee had beene a witch then shee told her
shee had been a witch ten years and then shee opened her brest and the black man gau her
two litl things lik{e} yong cats and she pit them to her brest and suckled them they had no
hair on ~~t~~ them and had ears like a man then they ofered her their books and shee refused
then then they pinsh her and the man struck her on the head and went away
on the third day their apeared a woman without the dore sat lafeing at her and came into the
house and hop⟨?⟩ed upandoun and profered her the book and told her if shee would touch it
shee would not pinsh her shee told her s [= she] wud. not she did not kno her [= where] s
liueed s told her she lie⟨u⟩ed at boston shee held her book to ⟨he⟩ her again shee told her shee
did not know her name shee told her her name was good wife whits
the same day came goody buckl⟨y⟩ and her daughter and brought books iwith [= in with]
them and told her if shee would touch their books they would not pinsh her but shee
refused then they pinshed her and went away
then i was siting on the inside of the dore sill and goody buckly came and stopeed my mouth
and Caried mee awai i know not how an near a mile and told mee that now shee had mee at
her Command if i would not set my hand to her booke shee would kil mee then
~~she did bit mee~~ william shaw beeing plowing in his fathers feild heard a fearfull Cry in a
thicket of yong wod went to it and found her in a terribl maner screaming and breacking of
sticks and fighting in a uiolent manner

[Hand 2] Susanah Shelden goody bucklie and her daughter
[Hand 3] Phillip English

[Hand 1] on the foarth~~aa~~ day at night Came goody olliuer and m^{ε}r english and good man
Cor[Lost] [= Corey] and a blak man with a hicrouned hatt with books in their hands goody
olliuer bad mee touch her booke i would not i did not know her name shee told me her name
was goody olliuer and bid me touch her booke now i bid her tel mee how long shee had been
a witch shee told mee shee told mee s [= she] had been a witch aboue twenti years then their
Came a streked snake creeping ouer her shoulder and crep into her bosom mrs english had a
yelo bird in her bosom and good man Core had two tircels hang to his Coat and hee opened
his bosom and put his turcls to his bres{t} and gaue them suck then good man core and
goody olliuer kneeled doune beefoar the blak man and went to prayer and then the blak man
told mee goody olliuer had been a witch twenti years and a ⟨?⟩ half then they all set to biteing
mee and so went away the next day Came good man Core mrs english in the morning and
told mee i should not eat no uittals i took a spoon and put on spoonful in my mouth and
good man Core gaue mee a blow on the ear and allmoast choaked mee then he laughed at

mee and told mee i would eat when he told mee i should not then he Clenched my hands that they Could not bee opened for more then a quarter of an our then Came phillip english and and told mee if i would touch his book hee would not bit mee but i refusid ["i" written over "e"] then hee did bite mee and went away

the sixth day at night Came goody olliuer and mrs english good man Core and his wife goodwy Core s profered mee a book i refused it and asked her whear she liued she told mee shee liued in boston prisson then shee puled out her brest and the blak man gaue her a thing like a blake pig it had no haire on it and she put it to her breast and gaue it suck and when it had sucked on brest shee put it the other and gaue it suck their then shee gaue it to the blak man then they went to praier to the blak man then goody olliuer told me that shee had kiled foar women two of them wear the fosters wifes and iohn trasks wife and did not name the other then they did all bitt mee and went away

then the next day Cam goody Core Choaked mee and told mee i would not eat when my dame bid mee but now i should eat none

[Hand 4] Susanna Sheldon
[Hand 3] ag^t oliver Englis {&} his wife Core & his wife good bucklie & her daughter & boston woman

Notes: Mary Whittredge is the daughter of Sarah Buckley, and "goody olliuer" is Bridget Bishop. This manuscript consists of three pieces of paper, archived separately in the Phillips Library. The document is reunited here. The use of "complaint" by Susannah Shelden, as elsewhere with her, is not in the sense of legal action initiating a felony charge. The document is speculatively placed on May 17 where there is a dated document connected to her. In this second of the two Shelden documents assigned to May 17, she describes events beginning on April 24 and concluding around the end of the month. For the complaint against Philip English, see No. 96, April 30, 1692. ◊ "tircels", "turcls": 'turtledoves' (*OED* s.v. *turtle* n^1). ◊ Hand 2 = Bartholomew Gedney

Essex County Court Archives, vol. 1, nos. 153, 154 & 168, Massachusetts Supreme Judicial Court, Judicial Archives, on deposit James Duncan Phillips Library, Peabody Essex Museum, Salem, MA.

165. Statement of George Herrick & Benjamin Wilkins v. John Willard & Sarah Buckley

[Hand 1] To: the Honble John Hathorne and Jonathan Corwin Esq^{rs} att Boston Humbly Thees Dated Salem village May 17th = 1692

This day Goeing to Salem village by yo^ε order I found all y^e fiue persons brought their which wee was in persute of wee had no sooner secured them in the wa{t}chhouse but Counstable John Puttnam came in with John willard haueing seized him att Nashaway hee beeing att worke wth a howe^ hee No sooner arriued, but ye afflicted persons made such an out Crye y^t I was forced to pinion him I haue an accompt from thees whoos names are under written that on the 14th day of Instant may Daniell Willkins aboute tenn {years:} of the clock in the morning was taken speechless and neuer spoak untell the 16th day^ in the interuale of time wee often Endeauoured to make {him} take something in A spoone but what hee tooke in which was but little hee spitt it out in our faces wth y^t wee sent to the french Doctor but hee sent word againe y^t it was not A naturall Cause but absolutly wichcraft to his Judgment that same day two of the afflicted persons Came up to vissett to Daniell Willkins ye last night beeing the 16th day Marcy Lewis and Mary Wallkott beeing their both did see y^e s^d John

May 18, 1692

Willard and Goodwife Buckley vpon y^e s^d Daniell willkins and said y^t thay would Kill him and in three hours after y^e s^d Daniell Departed this life in A most dolefull and solomne Condition Therefore wee humbley begg of yo$^\epsilon$ Honnors to Dispach A Returne for an Examination to preuent any farther murther in the afflicted Creatours who Continue in a lemetable Condition and so wee Remaine yo$^\epsilon$ Hon^{rs} most humble seruants

G Herrick

This breeiffe accomp^t was taken from Benj willkins by the Consent of wee whoes name are under written and sent by m$^\epsilon$ Ezekiell Cheeuers

    attest

        Geo: Herrick Marshall   Nathenell Putnam
        Joseph Neale Cos^{ll} John putnam sen
        John Putnam Cos^{ll} Jonathan Walcott
        Jonathan putnam Constable   Thomas fflint
                                   Eward Putnam
                                   John Buxton
                                   Thomas Putnam

                                  [Hand 2] mr ppariss is gon to Salem

[Reverse] [Hand 3] Nath^{ll} putnam {&^{c}} attesta$\overline{con}$ ag^t John Willard.

Notes: The signatures appear to be authentic except for Buxton's, which appears to have been written by Thomas Putnam. ◊ Hand 1 = George Herrick; Hand 2 = Thomas Putnam; Hand 3 = Thomas Newton

MS Am 51, Rare Books & Manuscripts, Boston Public Library. Boston, MA.

Wednesday, May 18, 1692

Officer's Return: Warrant No. 2 for the Apprehension of John Willard
2nd of 2 dates. See No. 156 on May 15, 1692

166. Warrant for the Apprehension of Roger Toothaker, and Officer's Return

[Hand 1] To: The Marshall of Essex or his dep^t or Constables in Salem.

You are in theire Majes^{ts} names hereby required to apprehend forthwith and bring before vs (Roger Toothaker of Bilrica who stands Charged with Sundry acts of Witchcraft by him Committed or donne on ye bodys of Eliz Hubert Ann Putnam Mary Walcot &c of Salem Village in order to his Examination Relateing to y^e premises faile not Dated Salem May 18th 1692

                            John Hathorne   }
                                        ~~Assis^{ts}~~
                            Jonathan. Corwin }

                              order of the Gouer$^{(nr)}$ and Councill.

[Hand 2] The parson spesefied in this warrante ^{was} Apprehended this day and broghte
befoore the corte Acrdinge to y^e tennor of this warrante by mee

Joseph Neall

constable in Salem i: May 18th :1692:

[Reverse] [Hand 3] Ag^st Toothaker

Notes: The authenticty of what appears as a signature by Joseph Neal has not been established. ◊ Hand 1 = John Hathorne

Essex County Court Archives, vol. 1, no. 273, Massachusetts Supreme Judicial Court, Judicial Archives, on deposit James Duncan Phillips Library, Peabody Essex Museum, Salem, MA.

167. Deposition of Elizabeth Booth v. Daniel Andrew & Mary Warren

[Hand 1] {Salem} May the 18th 1692
Elizabeth Booth Aged 18 Years or thereabouts Testifieth and saith that the three first fitts she had, she saw nothing: but afterwards in her fitts this Deponent saw Daniell Andross who told her though Mary Warren could not hurt her the night before now he would: and withall Broght: a Book and bid this deponent sett her hand to it: but the night before as she Lay in her Bed Mary warring went to her bed side and brought a little Baby to this Deponent and told her that she might sett her hand to the Book. and not know of it: but this Deponent told ye said Andross she would not: then he told the said Deponent that he would Afflicted Still since this Deponent hath been afflicted severall times by the said Andross: & others that she knows not.

[Reverse] [Hand 2?] Eliz Booth against Daniell Androw

Notes: A warrant for Daniel Andrew was issued May 14, but he escaped.

Essex County Court Archives, vol. 1, no. 118, Massachusetts Supreme Judicial Court, Judicial Archives, on deposit James Duncan Phillips Library, Peabody Essex Museum, Salem, MA.

168. Examination of Sarah Buckley

See also: Sept. 15, 1692.

[Hand 1] The Examination of Sarah Buckley .18. May. 1692

Abig: Williams said this is the Woman that hath bit me with her scragged teeth a great many times.
Mary Walcot, Ann Putman, & Susan: Sheldon unable to speak
Mercy Lewis said she see her upon her feet last night. Mary Walcots testimony read
Eliz: Hubbard said I see her last sab: day hurt Mary Walcot in the meeting house but I do not know that she hurt me.
Ann. Putmans testimony read
Mary Warren said that she saw this Woman & a great company & that this Woman would have her the said Warren go to their Sacrament up to Mr Parris

May 18, 1692

~~Eliz: Hubbard~~ Susan: Sheldon said this Woman hath tore her to peices & tempted her with
the book

Ann Putman carried to this Examinant in a fit was made well upon the Examinants grasping
her Arm

Susan: Sheldon the like.

Mary Warren the like.

When the Examinant was pressed to confess she said she did not hurt them: she was
Innocent

Susan: Sheldon said there is the Black man whispering in her ear.

This is a true Copy of the ~~Original~~ of the substance of the Original Examination of the
abovesᵈ

Sarah Buckley. Witness my hand upon my Oath taken this day in Court. 15. Septʳ 1692

Sam: Parris

[Reverse] [Hand 2] Sarah Buckley
Examināċon

⟨T⟩he Exa. of Sarah B

Notes: The copy sworn to on September 15 was used certainly at a grand jury, although Sarah Buckley was not tried
until January 4, 1693. ◊ "scragged": 'rough and irregular in outline' (*OED* s.v. *scragged* a. 1). ◊ Hand 1 = Samuel Parris;
Hand 2 = Anthony Checkley

Massachusetts Archives Collection, vol. 135, no. 22. Massachusetts State Archives. Boston, MA.

169. Deposition of Elizabeth Hubbard v. Sarah Buckley†

See also: Sept. 14, 1692 & Jan. 4, 1693.

[Hand 1] The Deposistion of Eliz. Hubbrud who testifieth and saith that I canot say that
eur goody Buckly hurt me but on the 18ᵗʰ may 1692 being the day of the Examin[Lost] [=
examination] of Sarah Buckly the wife of william Buckly I saw hir or Apperance torment and
afflete mary walcott and Ann putnam ^{&} ~~also seuerall times sence~~: [Hand 2] & I do
beleev: she sᵈ Buckly is a witch: & afflicted yᵉ ["y" written over "m"] above named persons ⟨ᵻ⟩
by witchcraft:

Eliz Hubbert: ownd to yᵉ grand Inquest that: yᵉ above written evidence ["i" written over "e"]
is yᵉ truth: Septᵋ 14 1692

[Hand 3] Elizᵃ Hubbard Jur in Cur

[Reverse] [Hand 4] Eliz Hobert agst Sarah Buckley

Notes: The grand jury heard evidence against Sarah Buckley on both September 14 and 15. ◊ Used at trial. ◊ Hand
1 = Thomas Putnam; Hand 2 = Simon Willard; Hand 3 = Jonathan Elatson; Hand 4 = Anthony Checkley

Massachusetts Archives Collection, vol. 135, no. 45. Massachusetts State Archives. Boston, MA.

170. Deposition of Ann Putnam Jr. v. Sarah Buckley†

See also: Sept. 15, 1692 & Jan. 4, 1693.

[Hand 1] The deposistion of Ann putnam who testifieth and that I haue a long time seen gooddy Buckly amongsts the wicthes but she did not doe me much hurt tell the 23th of April 1692 and then she fell upon me most greviously ~~to writ in hir bo⟨o⟩k~~ almost redy to kill me urging me vehemently to writ in hir book: also on the 18th may 1692 Sarah Buckly or hir Apperance did most greviously toment me dureing the time of hir Examinati [= examination] for if she did but look upon she would strick me down or allmost choak me: also on the day of hir Examination I saw Sarah Buckly or hir Apperanc most greviously afflect and torment mary walcott mercy lewes Abigail williams and Mary warren: and I beleue in my heart that Sarah Buckly is a wicth and that she has often afflected me and the afforesaid parsons by acts of wicthcraft.
[Hand 2] The aboue sd Deponant Ann Putnam acknowledged before y^e Grand inquest y^e truth of y^e aboue Euedence vpon her Oath this 15 of septem̄. 1692
[Hand 3] Ann putnam [Hand 4] Jur in Cur

[Reverse] [Hand 1] Ann Putnam against Sarah Buckly
[Hand 3] Ann Putn⟨am⟩
[Hand 5] [Lost]ry King & Quen

Notes: Used at trial. ◊ Hand 1 = Thomas Putnam; Hand 2 = Andrew Elliot; Hand 4 = Jonathan Elatson

Massachusetts Archives Collection, vol. 135, no. 44. Massachusetts State Archives. Boston, MA.

171. Testimony of Mary Walcott v. Sarah Buckley†

See also: Sept. 14, 1692 & Jan. 4, 1693.

[Hand 1] Mary Walcott Ageed sixteen yeares Testifieth and saith that on the 12th of may 1692 in the Euening I saw the Apparition of gooddy Buckly come to me and hurt me And tortor⟨e⟩d me most dreadfully by pinching and choaking of me and twesting of my nick seueral times and she brought me a book and would have ⟨me to⟩ write my name in it or elce giue my consent that she might d⟨o⟩ write it for me I told h⟨u⟩r that I would not touch her book nor write in it nor giue consent to her tho she killd me then she choaked me and many times she said ["said" written over "told"] that she would kill me that night if she had power for to do it I tould her that I did not fear hur I told her {y^t} god is aboue the deuil: and I hope that he would deliuer me out of her hands and the deuils to: {and} seueral times she has bet me and seueral others times sence she has tormented me [Hand 2] allso I being caried up to wills hill on the 16th of may to see the affletd persons there: I saw there the apperishtion of gooddy Buckly afflecting daniell willknes: also on the day of the Examination of of Sarah Buckly being the 18th may 1692 Sarah Buckly or hir Apperanc did most greviously torment me dureing the time of hir Exami[Lost] [= examination] ffor if she did but look upon me she would strick me down or allmost choak me also on the day of hir Examination I saw Sarah Buckly or hir Apperanc most greviously torment the bodyes of Abigail williams ⟨&⟩ ~~mercy lewes~~ and Ann putnam and I veryly beleue in my heart that Sarah Buckly is a wicth and that she has often affleted me and the afforesaid parsons by acts of wicthcraft.
[Hand 3] Mary Walcot ownd ye truth of ye above written evidence: to: ye grand ⟨?⟩ Inquest Septr 14: 1692 upon oath

[Reverse] [Hand 4] Mary Walcot ag^t G. Buckley
[Hand 5] Jur in Cur̄.

Notes: Thomas Putnam's addition beginning with "allso I being caried . . . ." may not be his only one in the document. After "Daniel Willknes" there appears to be an ink change by Putnam suggesting another addition by him at another time. A strong probability is that Putnam made one or both of these additions after May 18 in preparation for presentation at the grand jury on September 14 or 15. ◊ Used at trial. ◊ Hand 2 = Thomas Putnam; Hand 3 = Simon Willard; Hand 5 = Jonathan Elatson

Massachusetts Archives Collection, vol. 135, no. 43. Massachusetts State Archives. Boston, MA.

172. Deposition of Elizabeth Hubbard v. Rebecca Jacobs†

See also: Sept. 10, 1692.

[Hand 1] The deposistion of Eliz Hubbred who tetifieth and saith thaet one the beginig of may 1692 I was afflected by Rebecah Jacobs the wife of George Jacobs but on the 18th ~~Apr(i)l~~ {may} 1692: being the day of hir Examination I saw Rebekah Jacobs or hir Apperanc most greviously afflet mary wallcott Abigail williams and Ann putnam: tho when she began to confes she left ofe hurting of us but seuerall times sence that she has most greviously affleted me and I beleue in my heart that Rebecka Jacobs is a wicth and that she has often affleted me and the afforesaid parsons by acts of wicthcraf.
[Hand 2] Eliz Hubbard ownd: y^e truth of y^e above written evidence: before y^e Jury of Inques: Sept^{ε} 10: 1692

[Reverse] [Hand 3] eliz. hubard vs
[Hand 4] Reb⟨ec⟩ca Ja⟨co⟩bs.

Notes: Hand 1 = Thomas Putnam; Hand 2 = Simon Willard

Essex County Court Archives, vol. 1, no. 272, Massachusetts Supreme Judicial Court, Judicial Archives, on deposit James Duncan Phillips Library, Peabody Essex Museum, Salem, MA.

173. Examination of John Willard

[Hand 1] The Examina⟨tion⟩ of John Willard .18. ⟨M⟩ay. 1692
All the afflicted in most miserable fits when he came in, except John Indian.
When the warrant was read, he lookt upon severall & they fell into fits.
Here is a returne of the warrant that you were fled from Authority that is an acknowledgement of guilt, but yet notwithstanding this we require you to confesse the truth in this matter.
I shall, as I hope, I shall be assisted by the Lord of Heaven, & for my ~~flying away I~~ going away I was affrighted & I thought by my withdrawing it might be better, I fear not but the Lord in his due time will make me as white as snow.
What do you say? Why do you hurt them, it is you or your appearance?
I know nothing of appearance.
Was this the man?
Severall said yes.
They charge you, it is you or your appearance.

May 18, 1692

I know nothing of appearance, & the God of Heaven will clear me

Well they charge you not only with this but with dreadfull murthers, & I doubt not if you be guilty, God will not suffer evidences to be wanting.

Eliz: Hubbard testifyed against him & he lookt upon her, & she fell into a fit.

Mercy Lewes testimony read.

If you desire mercy from God, then confesse & give glory to God.

S^r as for sins I am guilty of if the Minister askt me I am ready to confess.

If you have ^{thus} revolted from God you are a dreadfull sinner

Mary Warren cryed out, oh! he bites me

Ann Putman cryed out much of him

Open your mouth, don't bite your lips

I will stand with my mouth open, or I will keep it shut, I will stand any how, if you will tell me how

An: Putmans testimony read.

Do you hear this evidence read?

Yes I do hear it

Sus: Sheldons testimony read.

What do you say to this murdering and bewitching your relations?

One would think (said he) that no creature except they belong to [Lost] [*SWP* = hell from] ⟨their⟩ Cradle would be guilty of such things.

You say you would bewitch your Grand-father because you, or your appearance saith he prays that the Kingdom of Satan may be thrown down.

He offered large talk

We do not send for you to preach

Benj^a Wilkins gave in evidence of his unnaturall usage to his wife.

You had much need to boast of your affections

There are a great many lyes told, I would desire my wife might be called

Peter Prescot testifyed that he with his own mouth told him of his beating of his wife

He urged Aaron Wey to speak

Aaron wey thereupon said if I must speak, I will, I can say you have been very cruell to poor creatures.

Let some person go to him

Ann Putman said she would go.

He said let not that person but another come

John Indian said cryed out he cuts me

Susan: Sheldon said there is the black man whispering in her ear, & he should not confesse

What do you say to this?

S^r I heard nothing nor see any thing.

Susan: Sheldon tryed to come to him, but fell down immediately.

What is the reason she cannot come near you?

They cannot come near any that are accused.

Why do you say so, they could come near Nehemiah Abbot, the children could talk with him

Mary Warren in a great fit carryed to him, & he clasping his hand upon her arm, she was well presently.

They all or most of the afflicted testifyed that the dead those that he had murdered were now about him.

Do you think these are bewitcht.

May 18, 1692

Yes, I really beleive it.

Well others they have accused it is found true that they are the guilty persons, why should it be false in you?

Susan: Sheldon & Mary Warren testifyed that now his appearance comes from his body & afflicts them.

How do you think of this, how comes it to pass?

It is not from me, I know nothing of it.

If you can find in your heart to confess it is possi[Lost] [= possible you] may [Lost] [*SWP* = obtain mercy] & therefore bethink your [Lost] [*SWP* = self]

S⟨r⟩ I cannot confesse that w[Lost] [*SWP* = which] I do not know

Well but if these things are true Heaven and Earth will rise up against you.

I am as innocent as the child that is now to be borne.

     Can you pray the Lords prayer?

Yes

     Let us hear you.

He stumbled at the threshhold & said Maker of Heaven & earth

     He began again & mist

It is a strange thing, I can say it at another time. I think I am bewitcht as well as they, & laught

     ~~Agg~~ Again he mist

     Again he mist, & cryed well this is a strange thing I cannot say it

     Again he tryed & mist

Well it is these wicked ones that do so overcome me.

Joshua Rea gave in testimony that last night [Lost] [*SWP* = he said] ⟨h⟩e hoped he should co⟨n⟩fesse, he had a hard heart, but he hoped he should confesse.

Well say what you will confesse

I am as innocent as the child unborne.

Do not you see God will not suffer you to pray to him? Are not you sensible of it?

Why it is a strange thing?

No it is no strange thing that God will not suffer a Wizard to pray to him. There is also the jury of Inquest that will bear hard against you – therefore confesse. Have you never wisht harm to your neighbours?

No never ~~in my life~~ since I had a being.

Well confesse & give glory to God, take counsell whilst it is offered

I desire to take good counsell, but if it was the last time I was to speak, I am innocent

[Hand 2] John Willards Examinācon
[Hand 3] ⟨E⟩xam[Lost]m [= Examination] agᵗ Willard

Notes: This is one of two versions of Willard's examination in Parris's hand. Since prosecutor Thomas Newton's hand is added later, it is presumably the one he chose in building his case. ◇ Hand 1 = Samuel Parris; Hand 2 = Thomas Newton

MS Am 46.2, Rare Books & Manuscripts, Boston Public Library. Boston, MA.

174. Examination of John Willard, Second Version

[Hand 1] The Examination of John Willard .18. May 1692

The afflicted in most miserable fits upon his this Examinants drawing near

After several of them were recovered, he lookt upon them, & they again fell into fits, whilst the warrant & returne was reading.

Here is a returne of the Warrant that you were fled from Authority that is an acknowledgment of guilt, but yet notwithstanding we require you to confess the truth in this matter.

I shall, as I hope, I shall be assisted by the Lord of Heaven, & for my going away I was affrighted, & I thought by my withdrawing it might be better, I fear not but the Lord in his due time will make me as white as snow.

What do you say? Why do you hurt these? It is you, or your appearance.

I know nothing of appearance.

Is this the man?

Several of the afflicted said yes.

They charge you, it is you or your appearance.

I know nothing of appearance, & the God of Heaven will clear me.

They charge you, not only with this, but with dreadfull murders, & I doubt not if you be guilty, God will not want evidence.

Eliz: Hubbard testifyed that he afflicted her, & then he lookt upon her & she fell into a fit.

Mercy Lewes testimony read.

If you desire mercy from God, then you must confesse & give Glory to God.

S^r as to sins I am guilty of, if the Minister asks me I am ready to confesse

If you have revolted from God you are a dreadful sinner.

Mary Warren cryed out, oh he bites me

Ann Putman cryed out much of him

Open your mouth, don't bite your lips.

I will stand with my mouth open, or I will keep it shut: I will stand any how, if you will tell me how.

Ann Putmans evidence read

Do you hear this evidence read?

Yes, I do hear it.

Susan: Sheldons testimony read

What do you say to this murdering & Bewitching your relations?

One would think (said he) that no creature except they belong to hell from their Cradle would be guilty of such things.

You say, you will bewitch your Grandfather because he prays that the Kingdom of Sathan may be thrown down

The Examinant began a large oration

We do not send for you to Preach.

Ben: Wilkins testifyed for all his natural affections he abused his wife much & broke sticks about her in beating of her

You had need to boast of your good affections

There are a great many lyes told, I could desire my wife might be called

Peter Prescot testifyed that he with his own mouth told him of his beating of his wife.

It seems very much one of your confidence & ability to speak, should be no more ~~in~~ couragious than to run away: by your running away you tell all that ~~world~~ you are afraid

May 18, 1692

The examinant called upon Aaron Wey & urged him ~~before~~ to speak if he knew any thing against him

Aaron Wey if I must speak I will, I can say you have been very cruel to poor creatures.

Let some persons goe to him

Ann Putman said she would go.

He said let not that person but another come.

John Indian cryed out Oh! he cuts me.

Susan: Sheldon said there is the black man whispering in his ear, & he should not confess What do you say to this?

S^r I heard nothing, nor see nothing.

Susan: Sheldon tryed to come near him but fell down immediately, & he took hold of her hand with a great deal of do, but she continued in her fit crying out, O John Willard, John Willard &

~~The ex~~ What was the reason you could not come near him?

The black man stood between us. They cannot come near any that are accused.

Why do you say they could not come near any that were accused: You know Nehemiah Abbet they could talk with him.

Mary Warren in a great fit carried to him & he clasping his hand upon her arm was well presently.

Why said he was it not before so with Susannah Sheldon?

Because said the standers by you did not Clasp your hand before.

The like said the Constable & others. They all or most testifyed that the dead those that he had murdered were now about him.

Do you think these are Bewitcht?

Yes, I verily beleive it.

Well others they have accused it is found true on & why should it be false in you?

Sus: Sheldon & Mary Warren testify that now h⟨i⟩[Lost] [= his] appearance comes from his body & afflicts them.

What do you think of this? How comes this to pass?

It is not from me, I know nothing of it

You have taxt your self wonderfully, it may be you do not think of it.

How so?

You cryed up your tender affections and here round about they testify your cruelty to man & beast, & by your flight you have given great advantage to the Law, things will bear hard upon you, if you can therefore find in your heart to repent it is possible you may obtain mercy & therefore bethink your self

S^r I cannot confess that I do not know

Well but if these things are true Heaven & Earth will rise up against you.

I am as innocent as the child that is now to be born.

Can you pray the Lords prayer?

Yes.

Well let us hear you.

{1.} He stumbled at the Threshold (that is the ~~beging~~ beginning) & said Maker of Heaven & Earth.

{2.} He began ~~against~~ again, & mist

It is a strange thing, I can say it at another time. I think I am bewitcht as well as they & laught

{3.} Again he began & said trespass against & mist us.

{4.} He begun again, & cryed being puzled

May 18, 1692

Well this is a strange thing I cannot say it.

He begun again & could not say it

Well it is these wicked ones that do so overcome me

Josh: Rea Senr gave in testimony that last night he said he hoped he should confess thô he had a hard heart, but he hoped he should confess.

Well say w^t you will confess.

I am as innocent as the child unborn.

Do not you see God will not suffer you to pray to him, are not you sensible of it?

Why it is a strange thing.

No it is no strange thing that God will not suffer a wizard to pray to him. There is also the jury of inquest for murder that will bear hard against you. Therefore confess. Have you never wisht harm to your Neighbours?

Never since I had a being.

Well confess & give glory to God. Take counsell.

I desire to hearken to all good counsell. If it was the last time I was to speak I am innocent.

This is a true account of the Examination ~~abovesai~~ of John Willard without wrong to any party according to my original from Characters at the moments thereof

Witness my hand Sam: Parris

John Willards Examination.

Notes: The possible offer of mercy to Willard if he confessed appears to present at an early stage a "plea bargain," an offer that became implicit in cases that would follow. Parris notes that he copied this record from "characters" he had written at the examination, so it seems likely that the actual record of the May 18 examination was written later, and this may be the case with other Parris recordings of examinations. ◊ Hand 1 = Samuel Parris

MS Am 46.1, Rare Books & Manuscripts, Boston Public Library. Boston, MA.

175. Deposition of Elizabeth Hubbard v. John Willard†

See also: June 3, 1692.

[Hand 1] The deposistion of Elizabeth Hubburd agged about 17 years w[Lost] [= who] testifieth and saith that on the 11 may 1692 I saw the Apperishtion of John willard of Salem villege who did Immediatly torment me and urged me to writ in his book: but on the 18th of may being the day of his Examination John willard did most greviously tortor me dureing the time of his Examination for if he did but look upon me he would Immediatly strick me down or allmost choak me: and also dureing the time of his Examination I saw the Apperishtion of John willard goe from him and afflect the bodys of mary walcott mircy lewes Abigaill williams and Ann putnam Junr

[Hand 2] elizabeth hubburt: did one this testimony aftar the Reding of it before us the Jurris for Inquest this .3. dy of June: 92

[Reverse] [Hand 3] Elizabeth Hubbard agt John Willard.

Notes: Hand 1 = Thomas Putnam; Hand 3 = Thomas Newton

Essex County Court Archives, vol. 1, no. 246, Massachusetts Supreme Judicial Court, Judicial Archives, on deposit James Duncan Phillips Library, Peabody Essex Museum, Salem, MA.

May 18, 1692

176. Deposition of Samuel Parris, Nathaniel Ingersoll, & Thomas Putnam v. John Willard†

See also: June 3, 1692 & Aug. 4, 1692.

[Hand 1] The Deposition of Samuel Parris aged about .39. years, & Nathanell Ingersoll aged about fifty & eight yeares & also Thomas Putman aged about fourty yeares all of Salem testifyeth & saith that Eliz: Hubbard, Mary Warren & Ann Putman & John Indian were exceedingly tortured at the Examination of John Willard of Salem Husbandman, before the honoured Magistrates the .18. May .1692. & also that upon his looking upon Eliz: Hubbard She was knockt down, & also that some of the afflicted & particularly Susannah Sheldon then & there testifyed that they saw a black man whispering him in the ear, & that said Sheldon could not come near to said Willard but was knockt down, & also that Mary Warren [Hand 2] ^{in a fit} [Hand 1] being carried to him the said Willard she said Warren was presently well upon his grasping her arm, & farther that severall of the afflicted also then testifyed, that divers of those he had murthered then rose up against ^{him}, & farther that he could by no means rightly repeat the Lords Prayer thô he made manifold assayes.

[Hand 3] mᵣ samuel parris and Nathaniel Ingerson and: thomas putnam did uppon the oath which they had taken did before us the Juris of inquest owne this their testimony: this .3. dy of June: 92.

[Hand 4] Sworn in Court by mᵣ Parris & Tho: Putnam

[Reverse] [Hand 1] The Depoͭion of Sam: Parris &c. agsᵗ John Willard

Notes: The "Court" where this was sworn was probably the trial court although "Jurat in Curia" would be a more likely signifier of that. The insertion of "in a fit" was probably added at a later date. Putnam's name, in a different ink, is also probably a later addition. ◊ Likely used at trial. ◊ Hand 1 = Samuel Parris; Hand 4 = Stephen Sewall

Essex County Court Archives, vol. 1, no. 242, Massachusetts Supreme Judicial Court, Judicial Archives, on deposit James Duncan Phillips Library, Peabody Essex Museum, Salem, MA.

177. Deposition of Thomas Putnam & Edward Putnam v. John Willard†

See also: Aug. 4, 1692.

[Hand 1] The deposistion of Thomas putnam agged 40. years and Edward putnam agged 38 years who testifie and say that we haueing ^{been} couersants with seuerall of the afflected parsons as namly mary walcott mercy lewes Elizabeth Hubbrut Abigail williams and ann putnam junr: and we haue seen them most greviously tormented by pinching and pricking and being allmost choaked to death most greviously complainig of John willard for hurting them: but on the 18th day of may 1692: being b̶e̶ the day of his Examination the afforesaid afflected parsons ware most greviously tormented dureing the time of his examinati⟨on⟩ for if he did but cast his eies upon them they ware strocken down or allmost choak: also seuer⟨a⟩ll times sence we haue seen the afforesaid afflected parsons most greviously tormented as if their bones would haue been disjoyned greviously complaining of John willard for hurting them: and ^{we} veryly beleue that John willard the prizsoner at the barr. has seuerall times tormented ⟨?⟩ and afflected the afforesaid parsons with acts of wicthcraft

Thomas putnam
Edward putnam

[Hand 2] Jurat in Curia   May 18, 1692

[Reverse] Thomas & Edward Putm^n y^r Euidence

Notes: Edward Putnam's signature was written by Thomas Putnam. ◊ Used at trial. ◊ Hand 1 = Thomas Putnam; Hand 2 = Stephen Sewall

Essex County Court Archives, vol. 1, no. 253, Massachusetts Supreme Judicial Court, Judicial Archives, on deposit James Duncan Phillips Library, Peabody Essex Museum, Salem, MA.

178. Testimony of Susannah Shelden v. John Willard†

[Hand 1] this this Is the first to bee Read

the 9th of may 1692

the testimony of susanah shelton Aged 18ten yers or there About testifieth And saith ye day of the date hereof I sawe At natt Ingersons house the Apparitions of thes 4 persons ⟨w⟩illiam shaws firs⟨t⟩ wife the ⟨w⟩iddow Cooke gooman Jons And his Child And Among these Came the Apparition of John Willard to whome these 4 said you haue murdere{d} vs thes 4 haueing said thus to willard thay turned As Red As blood And turning About to look on mee th⟨a⟩y turned As pale As deth these 4 desiered mee to tell M^ε hathorn J willard hering them pulled {out} A knif saying If I did hee would Cu⟨t⟩t my throote

Notes: This document, probably used on May 18, references either a previous use or previous claim for May 9 and probably used at the same time as No. 179.

Essex County Court Archives, vol. 1, no. 243, Massachusetts Supreme Judicial Court, Judicial Archives, on deposit James Duncan Phillips Library, Peabody Essex Museum, Salem, MA.

179. Statement of Susannah Shelden v. Elizabeth Colson & John Willard†

[Hand 1] the second to be Read

The sam day ther Apeared to mee ~~eleasad~~ eleasabath Coolson and shee took a book and would haue mee to set my hand to it and I would not and then shee Profered mee A blak Peas of monny and seaid I might touch that and I shall be well − − − may the 10 on tusday ther apeared to mee the sam apearatio{n} and another with them In the likns of a man and they seaid I should Gooe and tell mr hather{e⟨n⟩} of it then the seaid willard ⟨t⟩seaid he would break my head and stop my leegs that I shou{ld} not Gooe [Hand 2] there ~~And~~ did Appeared to Mee A shineing Man whoe tolde I should goe And tell w^t I had heard And seen to M^ε hathorn this willard being there present tould Mee If I did hee would Cutt my throote At this same time And place this shining man tolde Mee that If I did goe to tell this to M^ε hhathorn y^t I shoul{d} bee well goeing And Coming but I should bee Afflicted there then said I to the shining man hunt willard Away And I would Beleue w^t hee said y^t hee might not chock mee with that ye shining man held vp his hand And willard vanished Away [Hand 1] about two hours after the sam apeared to mee againe and the seaid willard with them and I asked the{m} wher ther wonds were and they seaid ther wou{ld} Com a angell from heauen and would show them and forth with the angell come I asked what the mans

May 18, 1692

name was that Apeared to mee last and yᵉ angell tould his name was southerek and the angell lifte⟨d⟩ up his winding sheet and out of his left sid hee Poolled out a Pichfork tiang and Pot it in ageain and lik wise he apened all ther win{d}ing sheets and shawed all ther wound and the whit man tould mee to tell Mʳ hatheren of It and I toulld him to hunt willard away and I would and he held up his hond and he uanished away

the second to be Read
[Hand 2] the Euening of the same day Came to mee the Apparitoⁿ of these three John Willard Elizabeth Colson And one old {man} which I knew not whom tempted her with their Boocks And money And Afflicted her sorely All the fore parte of the night I saw this willard suckle the Apparition of two black piggs on his breasts And this Colson suckled As It Appeared A yellow bird this old man Which I knew not suckled A black snake then willard tempted mee Again with his Boocke I said to willard how long haue you binn A wizard hee told mee twenty years [Hand 1] and forth with they kneelled to Prayer to the Black man with a loung Crouned hat which then was with them and then they uanished away
may the 11 being on wensday 1692
as I was coming to the tound [= town] by the brige I sawe the seaid willard and the olld man coming auere the water they landed by Gorge hakers In A dish and at the Preasan{t} writige thes three apeared with A booke tempting mee after the sam maner
[Hand 3] susanah shelton. did this 3. dy of June oned this har testimoy before us the Jurrers of Inquest: to be the truth

[Reverse] [Hand 4] Susanna Shelden agᵗ Jn⟨ᵒ⟩ Will⟨ar⟩d

Notes: Susannah Shelden here twice evokes the narrative of the Swedish trials, once with her reference to the shining angel who protected the children there, and the other to the Devil's "Crouned hat." Joseph Glanvil, *Saducismus triumphatus*, 1681, II. p. 316, 324. This document appears to have been used with No. 178. ◊ "tiang": 'tine, prong' (*OED* s.v. *tang* n¹). "hunt....Away": 'chase away' (*OED* s.v. *hunt* 4a). ◊ Hand 4 = Thomas Newton

Essex County Court Archives, vol. 1, no. 244, Massachusetts Supreme Judicial Court, Judicial Archives, on deposit James Duncan Phillips Library, Peabody Essex Museum, Salem, MA.

180. Deposition of Mary Walcott v. John Willard†
See also: June 3, 1692 & Aug. 4, 1692.

[Hand 1] The Deposistion of mary walcott ^{agged about 17 years} who testifieth and saith that ^{on} the 11ᵗʰ of may 1692 I saw the apperishtion of John willard who did Immediatly afflect me most greviously and urged me greviously to write in his book and so he hath continewed euer since greviously tortoring me by times and threating to kill me if I would not write in his book and he also tould me that he had bewiched his grandfather wilknes: and I being caried up to wills hill on the: 16ᵗʰ of may a litle before night I saw their the Apperishtion of John ~~willknes~~ willard a choaking Daniell willknes also on the 18ᵗʰ may being the day of his Examination I was most greviouly tortored by him dureing the time of his Examination for if he did but look parsonally upon me he would Immediatly strick me down or allmost choak me to death: also seuerall times dureing the time of his Examination I saw the Apperishtion of John ~~willi~~ willard goe from him and afflect the bodyes of mircy lewes Abigail williams Elizabeth Hubburd. and ann putnam junr

[Hand 2] Marry Wallcut: upone the Reading of this har testimony to har. did one the oath   May 18, 1692
she hath taken: owne it to be the truth before us the: Juriars for Inquest: this .3. dy of June. <u>92</u>
                                                                    [Hand 3] Jurat in Curia

[Reverse] [Hand 4] Mary Walcott ag^t John Willard

Notes: Beginning with "also on the 18th may…" an ink change shows that Thomas Putnam added to the document.
◊ Used at trial. ◊ Hand 1 = Thomas Putnam; Hand 3 = Stephen Sewall; Hand 4 = Thomas Newton

MS Am 49, Rare Books & Manuscripts, Boston Public Library. Boston, MA.

181. Testimony of Benjamin Wilkins & Thomas Flint v. John Willard & Sarah Buckley‡

See also: Aug. 4, 1692.

[Hand 1] The Testimony of benjamin wilkins ~~& Thom~~[Lost] {aged about .3[Lost]}
and Thomas fflint aged about :46: years Testifieth [Lost]
one y^e .16. day of may last :1692: we being at The hou[Lost] [= house]
henry wilkins where we saw his son danell wilkins [Lost]
we judged at y^e point of death & marcy luis & mary w[Lost]
being with us. Tould us That john willord & goody bucly [Lost]
upon his Throat & upone his brest and presed him & [Lost]
him) & to aur bes judgment he was presed and choked [Lost]
time we saw him almost to death
& the said benjamin wilkins continued with him till ⟨h⟩[Lost] [= he]
was about .3 howrs aftor & he altered not in the mannor [Lost]
Condisthtion only grew wors & wors till he died
                                          [Hand 2] Jurat in Curia
                                   by B⟨e⟩n: Wilk[Lost] [= Wilkins]

[Reverse] Ben. Wilkins Tho. fflintt.

Notes: In the manuscript there is a "mary w" followed by lost material. The reference here is most likely to Mary Walcott, who is referenced elsewhere as having come with Mercy Lewis to visit Daniel Wilkins. ◊ Used at trial. ◊ Hand 2 = Stephen Sewall

Essex County Court Archives, vol. 1, no. 255, Massachusetts Supreme Judicial Court, Judicial Archives, on deposit James Duncan Phillips Library, Peabody Essex Museum, Salem, MA.

182. Testimony of Benjamin Wilkins & John Putnam Jr. v. John Willard & Sarah Buckley‡

[Hand 1] The Testimony of benjamin wilkns aged about .36: years saith That about y^e .12:
of may last marcy lues being at my fathers hous tould us that she saw john wilard and goody
bucly upon my fathers wilkins presing his belly and my father complained of extreme paine
in his bely at ye same time: then John putnam struck at ye aperistions then marcy luis fel
down & my father had ease emediatly: John putnam testifieth to ye same aboue writen

[Reverse] [Hand 2] Benj Wilkins Contra Willard

May 18, 1692   *Essex County Court Archives, vol. 1, no. 257, Massachusetts Supreme Judicial Court, Judicial Archives, on deposit James Duncan Phillips Library, Peabody Essex Museum, Salem, MA.*

183. Testimony of Abigail Williams v. John Willard†

See also: June 3, 1692.

[Hand 1] The Testimony of Abigail Williams Witnesseth & saith that sundry times she hath seen & been almost killed by the Apparition of John Willard of Salem Village Husbandman at & before the .18. May. 1692
[Hand 2] abegall williams did deliuer this testimony to us the Jurriars for Inquest this 3. dy of June: 1692. and did afarme to the truth of it

[Reverse] [Hand 1] Abig: Williams ags^t John Willard

Notes: Hand 1 = Samuel Parris

MS Am 1147.3, Rare Books & Manuscripts, Boston Public Library. Boston, MA.

184. Deposition of Mercy Lewis v. John Willard†

[Hand 1] The Deposistion ⟨o⟩f Mircy Lewes who testifieth and saith that I haue often seen the Apperishtion of John willard amongst the wicthes with in this three weeks: but he did not doc mc much hurt tell the 11th of may 1692 and then he fell upon me most dreadfully and did most greviously afflect me allmost redy to kill me vrgeing me most vehemently to writ in his book: and so he hath continewed euer sence att times tortoring me most dreadfully beating and pinching me and allmost Ready to choak me threating to kill if I would not writ in his book: also I ^{being} caried to wi[Lost] [= Wills] hill on the 14th of may att euening to see the afflected parsons there I saw there the Apperishtion of John willard greviously afflecting his grandffather wilknes: and I also saw the apperishtion of John willard there greviously afflecting the body of Daniell willknes who laid speachles and in a sad condition and John willard tould me he would kill Daniell wilknes with in Two days if he could: also I was at Henry wilknes the 16 may a little before night and their I saw the apperish [= apparition] of John willard a choaking Daniell wilknes also on the 18th may beinging the day of his examination I was most greviously tortored by him dureing the time of his Examination for if he did but look upon me he struck me down or almost choaked me to death and seuerall times sence the Apperishtion of John willard has most greviously afflected me by beating pinching and allmost choaking me to death: also dureing the time of his Examination I saw the Apperishtion of John willard goe from him and afflect the bodyes of mary walcott Abigal ^{williams} Elizabeth Hubburd and Ann putnam Junr

[Reverse] [Hand 2] Mercy Lewis ag^t John Willard

Notes: On May 17 a Jury of Inquest reported on its examination of the body of Daniel Wilkins, suspecting witchcraft as the cause of his death. See No. 162. Beginning with "also on the 18th may" the ink changes as Thomas Putnam adds to the document. ◊ Hand 1 = Thomas Putnam; Hand 2 = Thomas Newton

Essex County Court Archives, vol. 1, no. 259, Massachusetts Supreme Judicial Court, Judicial Archives, on deposit James Duncan   May 18, 1692
Phillips Library, Peabody Essex Museum, Salem, MA.

185. Deposition of Ann Putnam Jr. v. John Willard†

See also: June 3, 1692 & Aug. 4, 1692.

[Hand 1] The Deposistion of Ann putnam who testifieth and saith that on the 23 of April
1692 att euening I saw the Aperishtion of John williard and I was very sory to se him so: that
one that had helpt to tend me was com to afflect me: and I bid him lett me alone and I
would not complaine of him: but on the 24 of Appril being Saboth day he did soe greviously
afflect me that he forced me to crie out against him before all them that ware with me: and
he being tould of it as he tould me one the 25th of may he came parsonally to my father
house to talk with me and I tould him to his face it was so that ⟨he⟩ ⟨did⟩ hurt ⟨?⟩ mee: ⟨?⟩
Butt he denyed it most dreadfully: but I also tould him that if he would leaue ofe and hurt
me no more that I would not complain of him: and for 3: or 4 days he did hurt me but very
little but then againe he did sett upon me most dreadfully and beat me and pinched and
almost choaked me to death: threatening to kill me if I would not writ in his book: for he
tould me he had whiped my little sister Sarah to death: and he would whip me to death if I
would not writ in his book. but I tould him I would not writ in his book tho he did kill me:
affter this I saw the apperishtion of my little sister Sarah who died when she was about ^{six}
weeks old crieing out for vengance against John willard. I also saw the Apperishtion of a
woman in in a winding sheat which tould me she was John willknes first wife and that John
willard had a hand in hir death: also I being caried to wills hill on the: 15th of may att
euening: to see the afflected parsons ~~ther~~⟨e⟩⟨I⟩ there I saw there the Apperishtion of John
willard afflecting of his grandfather willknes and Daniell willknes: and Rebecka willknes: &
he also tould me that he would kill daniell willknes if he could but he had not power enufe
yet to kill him: but he would goe to Mr Burroughs and gitt power to kill daniell willknes: and
also on the 18th may being the day of his Examination I was most greviously Afflected by
him dureing the time of his Examination for if he did but look upon me he would
Immediatly strick me down or almost choak me to Death and also att the time of his
examination I saw the Apperishtion of John willard goe from him and afflect the bodyes of
mary walcott Mircy lewes Abigaill williams and Elizabeth Hubburd
[Hand 2] ann putnam Jun: one har oath which she had taken did aftar the Reding of this to
har did owne it to be the truth: before us the Jurris for Inquest: this .3. dy of June: 1692. ["2"
written over "1"]

[Hand 3] Jurat in Curia.

[Reverse] [Hand 4] Ann puttnam ag^t Jo: Willard.

Notes: This deposition used at the grand jury was probably started on May 18. An ink change shows that Thomas Putnam
added to it, starting with "and also on the 18th may." ◊ Used at trial. ◊ Hand 1 = Thomas Putnam; Hand 3 = Stephen
Sewall; Hand 4 = Thomas Newton

MS Am 47, Rare Books & Manuscripts, Boston Public Library. Boston, MA.

May 20, 1692

186. Mittimus for Roger Toothaker, John Willard, Thomas Farrar Sr., & Elizabeth Hart

[Hand 1] To the Keeper of Theire Majes^ts Goale in Boston
You are in theire Majes^ts names hereby required to take into your care and safe Custody the Bodys of Roger Toothaker of Bilrica. John Willard of Salem Village, husbandman Thomas ffarrer ["e" written over "a"] of Lyn husbandman, and Elizabet Hart the wife of Isaac Hart of Lyn husbandman, who all stand charged with Sundry acts of Witchcraft, by them and Euery one of them Committed, on the Bodys of Mary Walcot Abigail Williams Mary Lewis Ann Putnam and others of Salem Village or farmes, whome you are well to secure in order to theire tryall for the same. and vntill thay shall be deliuered by due order of Law and hereof you are not to faile Dated Salem May 18th 1692

John Hathorne   } by order of y^e
Jonathan Corwin } Gouern̄ & couc̄ll [= council]

[Reverse] [Hand 2] Tookacher.
[Hand 3] Hart

Notes: The word "tryall" prior to the establishment of the Court of Oyer and Terminer and in the absence of grand jury proceedings, may suggest that at this point the examination in court was sufficient to lead directly to a trial. Other possibilities should be considered, but the significance of the word "tryall" under these authoritative circumstances should not be underestimated. ◊ Hand 1 = John Hathorne

Essex County Court Archives, vol. 1, no. 274, Massachusetts Supreme Judicial Court, Judicial Archives, on deposit James Duncan Phillips Library, Peabody Essex Museum, Salem, MA.

Sworn Before the Grand Jury: Return of the Coroner's Jury on the Inquest into the Death of Daniel Wilkins
2nd of 2 dates. See No. 162 on May 17, 1692

Friday, May 20, 1692

187. Complaint of John Putnam Jr. & Benjamin Hutchinson v. Mary Esty, with Warrant for the Apprehension of Mary Esty, and Officer's Return

[Hand 1] Salem May the 20th 1692

There being Complaint this day made before mee by John Putnam Jun^ɛ and Benjamin Hutcheson both of Salem Village, for themselfes and also for theire Neighbours, in behalfe of theire Majesties against Marah ["M" written over "S"] Easty the wife of Isaac Easty of Topsfeild for Sundry acts of Witchcraft by her Committed yesterday and this present day of the date hereof vpon the Bodys of Ann Putnam Marcy Lewis Mary Walcot and Abigail Williams of Salem village to ye wrong and Injury of theire bodys therefore Craued Justice

John Putnam Jun
Beniamin Huchinson

To the Marshall of the County of Essex or dep^t {or Constables of Salem}
You are in theire Majes^ts names hereby required to apprehend and forthwith bring before
mee at ye house of m^r Thomas Beadles in Salem the Body of Mary Easty the wife of Isaac
Easty of Topsfeild to [1 word overstruck] Be Examined Relateing to Sundry acts of
witchcraft by her Committed Yesterday and this present day according to Complaint
aboues^d and hereof you are not to faile Dated Salem May 20th 1692

John: Hathorne. Assis^t
ꝑ order of y^e Councill

[Hand 2] May 20th 1692
I haue taken the body of the aboue named Mary Estice and brought her att y^e time and place
aboue named

p^ε me Geo: Herrick
Marshall of Essex

Notes: Mary Esty's sisters, Sarah Cloyce and Rebecca Nurse, had already been arrested. ◊ Hand 1 = John Hathorne;
Hand 2 = George Herrick ◊ Facsimile Plate 1.

*Essex County Court Archives, vol. 1, no. 276, Massachusetts Supreme Judicial Court, Judicial Archives, on deposit James Duncan
Phillips Library, Peabody Essex Museum, Salem, MA.*

188. Deposition of Elizabeth Balch & Abigail Waldon v. Sarah Bishop‡

[Hand 1] The Depotion of Elizabeth Balch of Beuerly Aged aboute eight & thirty years &
wife vnto Beniamin Balch ju^ε
This Deponant Testifieth hereby & saith that she being at salem on ye very Day that Capt
Georg Curwin was buried & in ye euening of sd Day Cominge from sd Salem vnto sd
Beuerly on horse bac⟨k⟩ ~~with~~ with her sister then known by ye name of Abigaile Woodburie
[1–2 words illegible] now Abigaile Walden ~~now~~ Liuing in Wenham wife vnto Nathaniell
Walden Rideing behinde her & as they were Rideing [1 word illegible] before & were Come
soe far as Crane Riuer Common soe Called Edward Bishop & his wife ouertooke vs (on
horse back) who are both now in prison vnder suspition of witchcraft & had some wor⟨ds⟩ of
Difference it seemed vnto vs sd Bishop rideing into ye brook pretty hastily she finding fault
with his soe Doinge & said that he would throw her into ye water or words to that purpose
sd Bishop Answered her that it was noe matter if he Did or words to that effect: & soe wee
Rode along all togethe⟨r⟩ toward Beuerly & she blamed her husband for Rideing soe fast &
that he would Doe her a mischeife or words to that purpos⟨e⟩ & he Answered her that it was
noe matter what was Done vnto her or words to that purpose: And then sd Bishop Directed
hi[Lost] [= his] speech vnto vs as we Rode along & sd that she had ben a bad wife vnto him
euer since they were marryed & reckoned vp many of her miscarriages towards him but now
of Late [Lost]he [= she] was worse then euer she had ben vnto him before (and that the
Deuill Did Come bodyly vnto her & that she wa⟨s⟩ familiar with the ["the" written over
"him"] Diuill & that she sat⟨e⟩ vp all y^e night Long with y^e Deuill) or words to that purpose
& with such kinde of Discours he filld vp y^e time vntill we Came to sd Bishops Dwelling
house & this Deponant Did reprooue sd Bishop for speaking in such a manner vnto his wife

May 20, 1692

sd Bishop Answered it was nothing but what was truth & sd bishops wife made very Little
reply to all her husbands Discourse Dureing all ye time we were with them & farther saith not

[Hand 2] the mark of **E** elezebeth Balc⟨h⟩

the mark: **A** of: Abig⟨e⟩ll walden

[Hand 3] [Lost?] her Answer
if it be soe, you had neede pray. for <u>mee</u>

Notes: Sarah Bishop and her husband, Edward, both escaped from prison after having been "long Imprisoned." ◊ Hand
1 = Andrew Elliot; Hand 3 = John Hathorne

*Essex County Court Archives, vol. 1, no. 151, Massachusetts Supreme Judicial Court, Judicial Archives, on deposit James Duncan
Phillips Library, Peabody Essex Museum, Salem, MA.*

189. Deposition of John Hale v. Sarah Bishop

[Hand 1] John Hale of Beverly aged about 56 yeares tes[Lost] [= testifies] & saith that
about 5 or 6 yeares agoe Christian y^e wife of John Trask (living in Salem bounds bordering
on y^e abovesaid Bev⟨er⟩ly) beeing in full com̄union in o^ε Church came to me to desier y^t
Goodwife Bishop her neighb^ε wife of Edw: Bishop Ju^ε might not bee permitted to receive y^e
Lords supper in our chur⟨ch⟩ till she had given her y^e s^d Trask satisfaction for some offences
y^t were against her. viz because y^e said Bishop did en⟨t⟩[Lost]taine [= entertain] people in
her house at unseasonable houres in y^e nig[Lost] [= night] to keep drinking & playing at
shovell=board whereby dis⟨c⟩[Lost] [SWP = discord] did arise in other families & young
people were in dang[Lost] [= danger] to bee corrupted & y^t the s^d Trask knew these
th⟨i⟩ng⟨s⟩ & {ha⟨d⟩} once gon into y^e house & fynding some at shovel=board had taken y^e
peices they played w^th & thrown them into [Lost] [SWP = the] fyre & had reprooved y^e said
Bishop; for promoting such dis[Lost]ders [= disorders], But received no satisfaction from
her about it.
I gave s^d Christian Trask direction how to proceed farther in this matter if it were clearly
prooved. And indeed by y^e information I have had otherwise I doe fear y^t if a stop had not
been putt to those disorders s^d Edw. Bishops house would h⟨ave⟩ been a house of great
prophainness & iniquity. But as to C[Lost] [= Christian] Trask y^e next news I heard of her
was y^t she was dis[Lost]ted [= distracted] & asking her husband Trask when she was so
taken [Lost] [SWP = he told] me shee was taken distracted y^t night after shee came [Lost]
[SWP = from] my house when shee complained against Goody Bishop She continuing some
time distracted wee sought y^e Lord b⟨y⟩ fasting & prayer & y^e Lord was pleased to restore y^e
s^d [Lost] to y^e use of her reason agen. I was wth her often in [Lost] distraction (& took it
then to bee only distraction, yet fear[Lost] [= fearing] sometimes somw^t worse) but since I
have seen y^e fit[Lost] [= fits] of those bewitched at Salem village I call to mind some of hers
to be much like some of theirs.
  The s^d Trask when recovered (as I understood it did manif[Lost] [= manifest] strong
suspicion y^t shee had been bewitched by y^e s^d Bishops wife & shewed so much auerseness
from having any com̄erse [Lost] her that I was then trouble⟨d⟩ ⟨at⟩ ⟨it⟩ [Lost]⟨p⟩ing

May 20, 1692

[= hoping] better of s^d ⟨G⟩[Lost] [= Goody] Bishop, at that time ∧{for wee haue since p[Lost]}. At length s^d Christian Trask [Lost] [SWP = was] agen in a distracted fit on a sabboth day in y^e forenoon at ⟨y⟩[Lost] [= the] publck meeting to o^ε publick disturbance & so continued sometimes better sometimes worse unto her death, manifesting y^t she was under temptation to kill her selfe or somebod[Lost] [SWP = somebody else]. I enquired of Marget King who kept at or nigh y^e house w[Lost] [= what] shee had observed of s^d Trask before this last distraction shee told [Lost] Goody Trask was much given to reading & serch y^e prophecys {of scri[Lost]} [= scripture]. The day before shee made y^t disturbance in y^e meeting h[Lost] [= house] ⟨sh⟩[Lost] [= she] came home & said shee had been wth Goody Bishop & y^t they two were now freinds or to y^t effect.

[Lost] [SWP = I] was oft praying w^th & councelling of Goody Trask before her death [Lost] [SWP = and] not many days before her end beeing there shee seemed more [Lost]tionall [= rational] & earnestly desiered Edw: Bishop might be sent for y^t shee might make freinds with him, I asked her if shee had wronged Edw: Bishop she said not y^t she knew of unless it were in taking his shovel=board peices when people were at play wth them & throwing them into the fyre & if she did evill in it shee was very sorry for it & desiered he would be freinds with her or forgive her. this was y^e very day before she dyed, or a few days before. Her distraction (or bewitching) continued about a month [Lost] [SWP = and] in those intervalls wherein shee was better shee earnestly desired prayers & y^e sabboth before she dyed I received a note for prayers [Lost] [SWP = on] her behalf wch her husband said was written by her selfe & I judge was her owne hand writing beeing well acquainted wth her hand. As to y^e wounds she dyed of I observed 3 deadly ones; a peice of her wind pipe cutt out. & anoth^ε wound above y^t throw y^e windpipe, & Gullet & y^e veine they call jugular. So y^t I then iu⟨d⟩ged & still doe apprehend it impossible for her wth so short a pair of ⟨c⟩issars to mangle her selfe so without some extraordinary work of the devill or witchcraft signed. 20. may 1692 by John Hale.

[Hand 2] M^ε Jn° Hale ag^st Sarah Bushop

[Hand 1] To severall parts of this testemony can wittness Maj^ε Gidney. Mr Paris, Joseph Hirrek Ju^ε & his wife Thomas Raiment & his wife John Tras⟨k⟩ Marget King. Hanah wife of Cornell Baker, [   ] Miles & others As allso about y^e s^d Goody Bishop Capt Wm Raiment, his son Wm Raiment about creatures strangely dying. James Kettle, & y^e abovs^d Jos: Hirreck & Tho: Raiment about sundry actions y^t [Lost] y^e apearance of witchcraft.

[Hand 3] Deposition John Hale

Notes: The "drinking" and "shovel=board" activity has traditionally been confused by subsequent commentators who incorrectly attributed this to Bridget Bishop, confusing her with Sarah Bishop. ◊ Hand 1 = John Hale; Hand 2 = Jonathan Corwin; Hand 3 = Stephen Sewall

Essex County Court Archives, vol. 1, no. 142, Massachusetts Supreme Judicial Court, Judicial Archives, on deposit James Duncan Phillips Library, Peabody Essex Museum, Salem, MA.

190. Deposition of James Kettle v. Sarah Bishop†

[Hand 1] The deposition of James Kettle aged twenty seven: years or there about testyfieth & saith that I was att Docter Grigs his hous on the tenth of this instant may & there saw

May 20, 1692
Elizebeth Hubbard in severall Fitts: and after her ffits ware over she told me that she saw my too Childdren Laying before her & that thay cryd for vengance & that Sarah Bishop bid her Look on them & said that she kiled them & they were by her description much ⟨a⟩s they were ~~th~~ when they ware put in to there Coffins [Lost] [= to?] be buried & she told me that sarah bishop told her [Lost]⟨h⟩at [= that] I was going to burn a kiln of potts & that she would ⟨b⟩reak them if she Could: & i took notice that while she was in her Fits that she Cried & held her apron before her face saying that she would not se them Docter Grigs & his wife & John hues ware there present

[Reverse] [Hand 2] [Lost]ah. [= Sarah] Bishop

Notes: Hand 2 = Jonathan Corwin

Essex County Court Archives, vol. 2, no. 116, Massachusetts Supreme Judicial Court, Judicial Archives, on deposit James Duncan Phillips Library, Peabody Essex Museum, Salem, MA.

191. Deposition of Jonathan Putnam, James Darling, Benjamin Hutchinson, & Samuel Braybrook v. Mary Esty†

[Hand 1] The deposition of Jonathan Putman, James Darling, Benjᵃ Hutchinson & Sam: Braybrook wᵒ testify & say that we together with divers others the .20. May. 1692 between eight & eleven aclock at night being with Mercy Lewes whom we found in a case as if death would have quickly followed, & to whom Eliz: Hubbard was brought (said Mercy being unable to speak most of the day) to discover what she could see did afflict said Mercy, heard & observed that these two fell into fits by turns, the one being well whilst the other was ill, & that each of them complained much of Mary Eastie, who brought the book to said Mercy severall times as we heard her say in her trances, & vexed & tortured them both by choking & seemingly breathless fits & other fits, threatning said Mercy with a Winding Sheet & afterwards with a Coffin if said Mercy would not signe to her book, ~~m~~ with abundance more of vexations they both received from her.

[Reverse] [Hand 2] Jonath. Putman James Darlin &c [Hand 3] agaist Mary Esty

Notes: This and the following deposition, No. 192, highlight the role of Mercy Lewis in persisting, for whatever reason, in pursuing claims against Mary Esty, even when the others seemed ready to drop the accusations against her. ◊ Hand 1 = Samuel Parris

Essex County Court Archives, vol. 1, no. 279, Massachusetts Supreme Judicial Court, Judicial Archives, on deposit James Duncan Phillips Library, Peabody Essex Museum, Salem, MA.

192. Testimony of George Herrick & John Putnam, Jr. v. Mary Esty
See also: Sept. 9, 1692.

[Hand 1] May 20ᵗʰ 1692
The testimone of Geo: Herrick aged thirty four or thereaboutes and John Puttnam Junᵉ of Salem Village aged thity fiue yeares or there aboutes testifieth and saith yᵗ beeing att the house of yᵉ aboue sd John Puttnams both saw Mercy Lewis in A very Dreadfull and solemn

Condition: so y^t to our apprehention shee could not continue long in this world without A
mittigation of thoes Torments wee saw her ~~in~~ which Caused us to Expediate A hasty
dispacth to apprehend Mary Esstick in hopes if possable it might saue her Life and
Returneing ye same night to sd John Puttnam^s house aboute middnight wee found ye sd
Mercy Lewis in A Dreadffull fitt but her Reason was then Returned Againe shee said what
haue you brought me ye winding sheet Goodwife Essti⟨c⟩e, well I had rather Goe into y^e
winding sheet then sett my hand to ye Book but affter that her fitts was weaker and weaker
but still Complaining y^t shee was very sick of her stomake, aboute break of Day she fell a
sleep but still Continues Extream sick and was taken wth A Dread fitt Just as wee left her so
y^t wee perceaued life in her and that was all ~~Benj Huchison testefieth the same~~

[Hand 2] Jurat in Curia
Sepr 9th 92:
[Hand 1] as Atest Geo: Herrick
John. Putnam. Jun.

[Reverse] [Hand 2] George Herrick [Hand 3] agnist mary Estick

Notes: Used at trial. ◊ Hand 1 = George Herrick; Hand 2 = Stephen Sewall; Hand 3 = Thomas Putnam

Essex County Court Archives, vol. 1, no. 280, Massachusetts Supreme Judicial Court, Judicial Archives, on deposit James Duncan Phillips Library, Peabody Essex Museum, Salem, MA.

193. Deposition of Bernard Peach v. Susannah Martin

[Hand 1] The deposion of Barnard peache aged 42 or ther abouts testifyeth That about te⟨n⟩
year ago this deponant Living with w^m Osgood of Salsbury he sd Osgood had a⟨n⟩ ox hurt &
he kild him & Geor⟨g⟩ mart⟨a⟩n of Amsbery desired to haue som of the beef but was denyed
and went away discontent
And the next day on of the gentlest cows my sd master osgood had was in such a mad fright
that too men had much ado to gett her into ye hous w^r shee had vsually {ben} tide vp: shee
did run and fly about
The next day shee being Let out & went away wth the other catle (well & Lusty as far as we
coold desern) but came home at evening very Ill hauing Atter vnder her eyes as bigg as
wallnutts & dyed the same night

sworne at Salsbury the 20th day of may Ano 1692
before me Robt Pike Asst

[Reverse] [Hand 2] Barnard Peach

Notes: George Martin was the deceased husband of Susannah Martin, having died in 1686. ◊ "Atter": 'corrupt matter, pus' (*OED* s.v. *atter*). ◊ Hand 1 = Robert Pike; Hand 2 = Stephen Sewall

Essex County Court Archives, vol. 1, no. 189, Massachusetts Supreme Judicial Court, Judicial Archives, on deposit James Duncan Phillips Library, Peabody Essex Museum, Salem, MA.

May 21, 1692

194. Deposition of Elizabeth Booth v. Sarah Procter, John Procter, & Elizabeth Procter

[Hand 1] May 20th 1692

Elizabeth: Booth aged 18 years or thereabouts
Testifieth & saith
That: Sarah Procter apeared vnto her and brought her a Book and bid her sett her hand to it, this Deponent told her that she would not, ever sens⟨e⟩ this Deponent hath been greeviously afflicted by her ye said Procter: and John Procter and his wif⟨e⟩ hath Pinch't & Pricked this Deponent Likewise: severall times: / and still continues to Do so: Day[Lost]

[Reverse] [Hand 2] Eliz Booth against Sarah Procter

Notes: This deposition preceded the complaint against Sarah Procter, which came the next day. See No. 195.

Essex County Court Archives, vol. 1, no. 301, Massachusetts Supreme Judicial Court, Judicial Archives, on deposit James Duncan Phillips Library, Peabody Essex Museum, Salem, MA.

Saturday, May 21, 1692

195. Complaint of Thomas Putnam & John Putnam Jr. v. Sarah Procter, Sarah Bassett, & Susannah Roots

[Hand 1] Salem May the 21th 1691
Thomas Putnam and John Putnam, of Salem Village Yeomen made Complaint (before vs) on behalfe of theire Majests against [ ] Basset ye wife of Basset of Lyn husbandman and [ ] Roote of Beverly widow, and Sarah Procter of Salem ffarmes daufter of John procter of sayd place. for Sundry acts of Witchcraft by them donne and Committed on the Bodys of Mary Walcot Abigail Williams Marcy Lewis ann Putnam & others Lately whereby great hurt & Injury hath benne donne them therefore Craues Justice.

Thomas putnam
John. Putnam. Jun.

This Complt was Exhibited Salem 21th May 1692
          before vs

John Hathorne
Jonathan. Corwin
[Hand 2] ꝑ ordᵉ of ye Governᵉ & Councill

[Hand 3] Rebecka Walthom wife of Jnº Waltham
Bethya Lovett ye wife of Jnº Lovett Senᵉ

[Reverse] [Hand 4] Complt vs. S. Proctor

Notes: No record of indictments against Sarah Procter or Susannah Roots survives. Sarah Bassett, an aunt of Elizabeth Procter, in 1693 had an indictment returned with an "ignoramus." Bethia Lovett was the daughter of Susannah Roots, but why her name, or the names of the Walthams, appears here is not clear. Sarah Procter was the fifteen-year-old daughter of John and Elizabeth Procter. The "1691" date is simply a recording error. ◊ Hand 1 = John Hathorne; Hand 2 = Jonathan Corwin

Essex County Court Archives, vol. 1, no. 300, Massachusetts Supreme Judicial Court, Judicial Archives, on deposit James Duncan Phillips Library, Peabody Essex Museum, Salem, MA.

196. Warrant for the Apprehension of Susannah Roots, and Officer's Return

See also: May 23, 1692.

[Hand 1] Salem May 21=1692 To y^e Constabes of Beuerly.

Whereas Complaint hath been this day made before us, by Sergent Thomas Puttnam and John Puttnam: both of Salem village yeomen against Susannah Roots of Beuer[Lost] [= Beverly] widdow for Sundry acts of witchcrafft by her Commited on the bodys of Mary Wallcot Abigal William⟨s⟩ Marcy Lewis Ann Puttnam and others.

You are therfore in their Majesties names hereby Required to apprehend and forthwith bring before us Susannah Roots of Beuerly widdow, who stands charged with Committing Sundry acts of witchcrafft as aboue s^d to the wrong and Injury of the bodys of the abouenamed persons, in order to her Examination Relateing to ye aboue s^d premises faile not Dated Salem May the 21st 1692

To the Marshall of Essex   John Hathorne
or his Deputy   Jonathan Corwin
                                                                  p^ε order of y^e Gouerner & Councell

                                vera Copia attes^t Geo: Herrick Marshall of Essex

May 21=1692
I doe apoint m^ε Jonathan Biles to bee my Lawffull Depu⟨t⟩y to ser⟨v⟩e this warrant
                                                         Geo: Herrick Marshall of Essex

[Reverse] [Hand 2?] I [Hand 3] I haue prosecutted the within written warant and haue aprehended the person of the within mentioned Suzanah Roots and Brought her before awthority 23: may 1692

                                                              By mee Jonathan Biles
                                                              Cunstible of Beuerly

[Hand 4] Su⟨s?⟩ Roots

Notes: This is a contemporary copy of the original, and the "signatures" are by George Herrick. ◊ Hand 1 = George Herrick

Essex County Court Archives, vol. 1, no. 305, Massachusetts Supreme Judicial Court, Judicial Archives, on deposit James Duncan Phillips Library, Peabody Essex Museum, Salem, MA.

May 21, 1692

197. Deposition of Elizabeth Hubbard v. Mary Esty, John Willard, & Mary Whittredge

See also: May 23, 1692, Aug. 4, 1692 & Sept. 9, 1692.

[Hand 1] The Deposistion of Elizabeth Hubburt: who testifieth and saith I being caryed up to Constable Jn° putnams house on the 20th of may 1692: to se Mircy lewes who laid speachless and in a sad condition: I saw there the apperishtions of gooddy estick the very same woman that was sent whom the other day: and Jn° willard and mary witherridge Afflecting and tortoring of Mircy lewes in a most dreadfull maner. which did affright me most greviously: and Immediatly gooddy Estick did sett upon me most dreadfully and tortored me almost Ready to choak me to death and urged me vehemently to writ in hir book

[Hand 2] Sworne Salem Village May the 23d 1692

John Hathorne
Before vs   } Assis^ts
Jonathan. Corwin

[Hand 1] we whose names are under ^{writen} heauing: been along with Elizabeth. Huburd this time aboue mentioned hard hir declare what is aboue writen and we read it to hir when we came away and she said it was all true
this 21 may 1692

Thomas putnam
John. putnam Jun.
[Hand 3] Jurat in Curia Sepr 9th
1692

[Hand 1] Eliz Hubburd further testifieth that on the 23 may 1692 being the last day of the Examination of mary Estick she did most greviously afflect and torment me dureing the time of hir Examination allso dureing the time of hir examination I saw mary Estick most greviously aflet and torment mary walcott mercy lewes Abigail williams and ann putnam by twisting and allmost choaking them to death and I verily beleue in my heart that ma{r}y estick is a most dreadfull wicth and that she hath very often afflected and tormented me and parsons aboue named by hir acts of wicthcraft

[Hand 4] Eliz: Hubbard: declared: ye two above written evidences: in this paper before: ye Jury of Inquest: to be ye truth: upon oath: August 4: 1692

[Reverse] [Hand 3] El. Hubbard Contr. Easty

Notes: It appears as if Thomas Putnam wrote this document for Mary Esty's examination on May 21 and that the examination court, after adjourning for a Sunday recess, continued on May 23. Although others are mentioned, this testimony is primarily directed at Mary Esty. ◊ Used at trial. ◊ Hand 1 = Thomas Putnam; Hand 2 = John Hathorne; Hand 3 = Stephen Sewall; Hand 4 = Simon Willard.

Essex County Court Archives, vol. 1, no. 285, Massachusetts Supreme Judicial Court, Judicial Archives, on deposit James Duncan Phillips Library, Peabody Essex Museum, Salem, MA.

Monday, May 23, 1692

Officer's Return: Warrant for the Apprehension of Susannah Roots
2nd of 2 dates. See No. 196 on May 21, 1692

198. Complaint of Nathaniel Ingersoll & Thomas Rayment v. Benjamin Procter, Mary DeRich, & Sarah Pease

[Hand 1] Lt Nathaniell Ingersall and Thomas Rayment both of Salem village Yeoman Complained on behalfe of theire Majes^{ts} against Benjamin Procter the son of John Procter of Salem ffarmes, and Mary Derich y^e wife of Michall Derich and daufter of ~~John Procter of~~ ⟨?⟩ {William Basset of Lyn} and [   ] Pease the wife of Robert Pease of Salem {Weauer} for Sundry acts of Witchcraft by them Committed on y^e bodys of Mary Warren Abigaile Williames and Eliz Hub[Lost] [= Hubbard] &c of Salem Village, whereby great hurt is donne them therefore Craues Justice. Salem May 23^d 1692

          ꝉ Nathannil Ingersoll

          the mark   ⟋   of

          Thomas Rayment

[Reverse] [Hand 2] Benj. Proctor.

Notes: All three were imprisoned, but no record survives that any of them were brought to trial. ◊ Hand 1 = John Hathorne

Essex County Court Archives, vol. 1, no. 307, Massachusetts Supreme Judicial Court, Judicial Archives, on deposit James Duncan Phillips Library, Peabody Essex Museum, Salem, MA.

199. Warrant for the Apprehension of Mary DeRich, and Officer's Return

[Hand 1] To y^e Marshall of y^e County of Essex or his Lawfull Deputy or Constable in Salem

You are in theyr Majestys ⌃{Names} hereby req⟨ui⟩r⟨e⟩d to apprehend and forthwith bring before us, Mary de Rich y^e Wife of Michaell de Rich of Salem ffarmes Husbandman, whoe s⟨t⟩ands Charged wth Sundry Acts of Witch=craft by hir Comitted lately on the Bodys of Abigall Williames & Elizabeth Hubbard of Salem Village ⟨&⟩c. whereby greate hu⟨r⟩t & Injury hath bin done y^m in order to hir Examination relateing to y^e Same & hereof you are nott to fayle. Salem. Dat. May. 23. 1692.

          John Hathorne

          Jonathan. Corwin

       ꝑ ord^ε of y^e Govern^ε & Councill

[Hand 2] I haue apprehended y^e aboue named person and brought her as aboue

          ꝑ Josp Neal Counstable

Notes: The signature of Neal is probably not written by him. ◊ Hand 1 = Jonathan Corwin

May 23, 1692   *Essex County Court Archives, vol. 2, no. 105, Massachusetts Supreme Judicial Court, Judicial Archives, on deposit James Duncan Phillips Library, Peabody Essex Museum, Salem, MA.*

200. Warrant for the Apprehension of Sarah Pease, and Officer's Return

[Hand 1] To The Marshall of Essex or his dep^t or Constables of Salem
You are in theire Majes^ts names hereby required to apprehend and forthwith bring before vs (Sarah Pease ye wife of Robert Pease of Salem Weauer who stands charged with Sundry acts of Witchcraft by her Committed Lately on ye Body of Mary Warren of Salem Village [1 word overstruck] whereby great Injury was don̄ her. &c) in order to her Examination Relateing to ye same faile not Dated Salem May 23^d 1692

John Hathorne
Jonathan. Corwin
[Hand 2] ꝑ ord^ε of y^e Govern^ε & Councill

[Hand 3] I heaue Aprehended y^e parson mentioned within this warrant and heaue broghte hir

p^r me. Peter Osgood

Constable in Salem
May. y^e 23: 1692:

[Reverse] [Hand 4] S. Pease

Notes: Hand 1 = John Hathorne; Hand 2 = Jonathan Corwin

Essex County Court Archives, vol. 2, no. 106, Massachusetts Supreme Judicial Court, Judicial Archives, on deposit James Duncan Phillips Library, Peabody Essex Museum, Salem, MA.

201. Warrant for the Apprehension of Benjamin Procter, Mary DeRich, & Sarah Pease, and Officer's Return

[Hand 1] To: The Mar⟨s⟩hall of Essex or dep^t
or Const⟨a⟩bles in Salem
You are in theire Majes^ts names hereby required to apprehend and forthwith bring before vs Benja⟨m⟩ Procter the son̄ of John Procter of Salem ffarmes and Mary Derich the wife of Mic^l Derich of Salem ffarmes husbandman, and Sarah Pease the wife of Robert Pease of Salem Weauer who all stand charg[Lost] [= charged] of haueing Committed Sundry acts of Witchcraft on the Bodys of Mary Warren Abigail Williams and Eliz Hubbert of Salem Village whereby great hurt is donne them In order to theire Examination Relateing the abouesa⟨id⟩ premisses and hereof you are not to faile Dated Salem May the. 23^d 1692

John Hathorne
Jonathan. Corwin
ꝑ order of ye Gou^ε & Councill
[Hand 2] I doe apoint m^ε John Puttnam to bee my lawffull Deputy to serue this warrant p^ε
Geo: Herrick Marshall of Essex

[Reverse] [Hand 3] I haue sesed the body of Beniemin Prokter and haue brought him ⟨to⟩ ⟨t⟩h⟨e⟩ place wᵗ in expresed. by me John Putnam mashell Debety.

May 23, 1692

Notes: Hand 1 = John Hathorne; Hand 2 = George Herrick

Essex County Court Archives, vol. 1, no. 308, Massachusetts Supreme Judicial Court, Judicial Archives, on deposit James Duncan Phillips Library, Peabody Essex Museum, Salem, MA.

202. Statement of Susannah Shelden v. Daniel Andrew, Sarah Procter, George Jacobs Jr., & Philip English†

[Hand 1] the compaint of suanah shelden of m[Hand 2]ʳ [Hand 1] andras and sarah procter 20 of this may thay both aflicted me the next day sarah procter brought the book to me and sarah procter and andres and iorg gacobe thay mad me def and dum and blind al nigh and the next day tel 10 of clock then cam inges and brougt his book and drod [= drew] his knife and said if I would not touch it he would cut my throt. then thar Aperd to me A ded man ho told me his nam was Joseph rabson then he looked upon ingles and told him that he murderd him and drounded him in the se thar wos another man in the boot Along with me and the boot tosed up and doun and turend ouer and my handes ware clunched that I could not lay hold the other man layd hald and wos saued then he told me that I must tell mustr hatheren and told me that I should not [Lost]est [= rest] tel I had told it then inglish [Lost]ld [= told] me that if I did he would cut my ⟨l⟩eges of then ther apered to me a shiny ⟨m⟩an and told me I should tel of it to ⟨m⟩orah [= morrow] then inglesh told me that he wou⟨ld⟩ ⟨g⟩o kill the goue⟨r⟩nner {if he could} he would go try he wos the gretes ininemy he had the{r} he sayd that he would kil 10 folck in boston before next six day if he wos {not} tacken up ⟨t⟩he greter wiemen aflikt me stil

Notes: The word "complaint," as elsewhere with Susannah Shelden, is not used in the legal sense of a formal charge of felony. All the people named here had been previously complained against formally.

Essex County Court Archives, vol. 1, no. 304, Massachusetts Supreme Judicial Court, Judicial Archives, on deposit James Duncan Phillips Library, Peabody Essex Museum, Salem, MA.

203. Examination of Elizabeth Cary, as Published by Robert Calef‡

I having heard some days, that my Wife was accused of Witchcraft, being much disturbed at it, by advice, we went to Salem-Village, to see if the afflicted did know her; we arrived there, 24. May, it happened to be a day appointed for Examination; accordingly soon after our arrival, Mr. Hathorn and Mr. Curwin, &c. went to the Meeting-house, which was the place appointed for that Work, the Mininister began with Prayer, and having taken care to get a convenient place, I observed, that the afflicted were two Girls of about Ten Years old, and about two or three other, of about eighteen, one of the Girls talked most, and could discern more than the rest. The Prisoners were called in one by one, and as they came in were cried out of, &c. The Prisoner was placed about 7 or 8 foot from the Justices, and the Accusers between the Justices and them; the Prisoner was ordered to stand right before the Justices, with an Officer appointed to hold each hand, least they should therewith afflict them, and the Prisoners Eyes must be constantly on the Justices; for if they look'd on the afflicted, they

May 23, 1692

would either fall into their Fits, or cry out of being hurt by them; after Examination of the Prisoners, who it was afflicted these Girls, &c. they were put upon saying the Lords Prayer, as a trial of their guilt; after the afflicted seem'd to be out of their Fits, they would look steadfastly on some one person, and frequently not speak; and then the Justices said they were struck dumb, and after a little time would speak again; then the Justices said to the Accusers, which of you will go and touch the Prisoner at the Bar? Then the most courageous would adventure, but before they had made three steps would ordinarily fall down as in a Fit; the Justices ordered that they should be taken up and carried to the Prisoner, that she might touch them; and as soon as they were touched by the accused, the Justices would say, they are well, before I could discern any alteration; by which I observed that the Justices understood the manner of it. Thus far I was only as a Spectator, my Wife also was there part of the time, but no notice taken of her by the afflicted, except once or twice they came to her and asked her name.

But I having an opportunity to Discourse Mr. Hale (with whom I had formerly acquaintance) I took his advice, what I had best to do, and desired of him that I might have an opportunity to speak with her that accused my Wife; which he promised should be, I acquainting him that I reposed my trust in him.

Accordingly he came to me after the Examination was over, and told me I had now an opportunity to speak with the said Accuser, viz. Abigail Williams, *a Girl of* 11, *or* 12 *Years old; but that we could not be in private at Mr.* Parris's *House, as he had promised me; we went therefore into the Alehouse where an* Indian Man *attended us, who it seems was one of the afflicted: to him we gave some Cyder, he shewed several Scars, that seemed as if they had been long there, and shewed them as done by Witchcraft, and acquainted us that his Wife, who also was a Slave, was imprison'd for Witchcraft. And now instead of one Accuser, they all came in, who began to tumble down like Swine, and then three Women were called in to attend them. We in the Room were all at a stand, to see who they would cry out of; but in a short time they cried out,* Cary; *and immediately after a Warrant was sent from the Justices to bring my Wife before them, who were sitting in a Chamber near by, waiting for this.*

Being brought before the Justices, her chief accusers were two Girls; my Wife declared to the Justices, that she never had an knowledge of them before that day; she was forced to stand with her Arms stretched out. I did request that I might hold one of her hands, but it was denied me; then she desired me to wipe the Tears from her Eyes, and the Sweat from her Face, which I did; then she desired she might lean her self on me, saying, she should faint.

Justice Hathorn *replied, she had strength enough to torment those persons, and she should have strength enough to stand. I speaking something against their cruel proceedings, they commanded me to be silent, or else I should be turned out of the Room. The* Indian *before mentioned, was also brought in, to be one of her Accusers: being come in, he now (when before the Justices) fell down and tumbled about like a Hog, but said nothing. The Justices asked the Girls, who afflicted the* Indian? *They answered she (meaning my Wife) and now lay upon him; the Justices ordered her to touch him, in order to his cure, but her head must be turned another way, least instead of curing, she should make him worse, by her looking on him, her hand being guided to take hold of his; but the* Indian *took hold on her hand, and pulled her down on the Floor, in a barbarous manner; then his hand was taken off, and her hand put on his, and the cure was quickly wrought. I being extreamly troubled as their Inhumane dealings, uttered a hasty Speech* [That God would take vengeance on them, and desired that God would deliver us out of the hands of unmerciful men.] *Then her Mittimus was writ. I did with difficulty and charge obtain the liberty of a Room, but no Beds in it; if there had, could have taken but little rest that Night, she was committed to* Boston *Prison; but I obtained a* Habeas Corpus *to remove her to* Cambridge *Prison, which is in our County of* Midldesex.

May 23, 1692

Having been there one Night, next Morning the Jaylor put Irons on her legs (having received such a command) the weight of them was about eight pounds; these Irons and her other Afflictions, soon brought her into Convulsion Fits, so that I thought she would have died that Night, I sent to intreat that the Irons might be taken off, but all intreaties were in vain, if it would have saved her Life, so that in this condition she must continue. The Tryals at Salem *coming on, I went thither, to see how things were there managed; and finding that the Spectre-Evidence was there received, together with Idle, if not malicious Stories, against Peoples Lives, I did easily perceive which way the rest would go; for the same Evidence that served for one, would serve for all the rest, I acquainted her with her danger; and that if she were carried to* Salem *to be tried, I feared she would never return. I did my utmost that she might have her Tryal in our own County, I with several others Petitioning the Judge for it, and were put in hopes of it; but I soon saw so much, that I understood thereby it was not intended, which put me upon consulting the means of her escape; which thro the goodness of God was effected, and she got to* Road-Island, *but soon found her self not safe when there, by reason of the pursuit after her; from thence she went to* New-York, *along with some others that had escaped their cruel hands; where we found his Excellency* Benjamin Fletcher *Esq; Governour, who was very courteous to us. After this some of my Goods were seized in a Friends hands, with whom I had left them, and my self imprisoned by the Sheriff, and kept in Custody half a day, and then dismist; but to speak of their usage of the Prisoners, and their Inhumanity shewn to them, at the time of their Execution, no sober Christian could bear; they had also tryals of cruel mockings; which is the more, considering what a People for Religion, I mean the profession of it, we have been; those that suffered being many of them Church-Members, and most of them unspotted in their Conversation, till their Adversary the Devil took up this Method for accusing them.*

Per Jonathan Cary.

Notes: In the original publication in 1700 of *More Wonders of the Invisible World*, the narrative is indicated as "per Jonathan Cary" and is accordingly carried that way in this edition. Subsequent printings of *More Wonders* revised this line to read "per Nathaniel Cary," based on an errata sheet, a handwritten copy of which is contained in a copy of the 1700 edition in the collection of the Massachusetts Historical Society. The volume may have been owned by Cotton Mather, whose signature appears in it. Since the narrative is clearly from the point of view of Nathaniel Cary, attributing authorship to him seems logical and seems to support the change. However, there is no way to determine whether "per Jonathan Cary" was actually a printer's error or whether Jonathan Cary wrote or delivered the account from the point of view of his brother, Nathaniel. In this account, May 24 is the date given for her examination, the day that Mr. and Mrs. Cary arrived. However, according to No. 216, a census of prisoners, she was sent to prison in Boston on May 23 with the others examined that day, and prior to the formal complaint that came on May 28, No. 224. The assignment of May 23 as the date for this is based on what is known about her imprisonment. The most likely explanation of the May 24 inconsistency is that the date was recalled incorrectly. According to the diary of Samuel Sewall, she escaped on July 30. ◊ "at a stand": 'at a standstill' (*OED* s.v. *stand* 5a).

Robert Calef. More Wonders of the Invisible World, Display'd in Five Parts. (London: Nath. Hillard, 1700), pp. 95–98.

204. Deposition of Samuel Abbey and Testimony of Sarah Trask v. Mary Esty, John Willard, & Mary Whittredge†

See also: Sept. 9, 1692.

[Hand 1] The Deposistion of Samuell Abby aged about 45 years who testifieth [1st "i" written over "e"] and saith that on the 20th of may 1692 I went to the house of constable Jno putnam: about 9 a clock in the moring and when I came there: Mircy lewes lay on the bed in a sad condition and continewing speachless for about an hour: the man not being at whom:

May 23, 1692

the woman desired me to goe to Tho: putnams to bring Ann. putnam to se if she could ^{se} who it was that hurt Mircy lewes: accordingly I went: and found Abigail williams along with ann putnam: and brought them both to se mircy lewes: and as they ware a goeing along the way both of them said that they saw the Apperishtion of Gooddy Estick and said it was the same woman that was sent whom the other day: and said also that they saw the Apperishtion of the other woman that appered with gooddy estick the othr day. and both of them allso said that the Apperishtion of gooddy ^{Estick} tould them that now she was afflecting of mircy lewes: and when they came to Mircy lewes both of them said that they saw the Apperishtion of gooddy Estick and Jn° willard and mary witheridge afflecting the body of mircy lewes: and I continewing along with mircy who continewed in a sad condition the gratest part of the day being in such tortors as no toungue can Express: but not able to spake: but at last said Deare lord Receiue my soule and againe said lord let them not kill me quitt. but att last she came to hir self for a little whille and was uery sensable and then she said that Gooddy estick said she would kill hir before midnight because she did not cleare hir so as the Rest did. then againe pe{r}sently she fell very bad and cried out pray for the salvation of my soule for they will kil me

[Hand 2] Jurat in Curia Sep^t 9th 92

[Hand 1] Sarah Trask ageed about 19 years testifieth that she went along with Abigaill williams and ~~Mircy lewes~~ Ann putnam and also hard them say what is aboue writen. they said: and also hard mircy lewes declare what is aboue writen she said

[Reverse] [Hand 2] Sam. Abbey

Notes: Thomas Putnam added the comment on Sarah Trask's testimony, although when he did so is uncertain. "Jurat in Curia" can be found elsewhere to have been inserted in the middle of a document, or elsewhere in it, rather than at the end. ◊ Used at trial. ◊ Hand 1 = Thomas Putnam; Hand 2 = Stephen Sewall.

Essex County Court Archives, vol. 1, no. 290, Massachusetts Supreme Judicial Court, Judicial Archives, on deposit James Duncan Phillips Library, Peabody Essex Museum, Salem, MA.

Sworn Before a Justice of the Peace: Deposition of Elizabeth Hubbard v. Mary Esty, John Willard, and Mary Whittredge

2nd of 4 dates. See No. 197 on May 21, 1692

205. Deposition of Mary Walcott v. Mary Esty

See also: Aug. 4, 1692.

[Hand 1] The Depoestion of Mary Walcott: Who Testifieth and saith on the 20th of may 1692: about twelue of the clock: I saw the Apparition of gooddy: Eastieck come and pinch .&. choake me: and terrified me much and she told me that she had blinded al ["al" written over "my"] {.our.} eyes that ware afflicted olnly merey Lueies for she said. that {she} had not power anought to doe itt on that day she was clearid: on this.. {.20th} In⟨e⟩stante of may: 92 ⟨?⟩ about an hour by sun I went to m^r John Putnams to see mersey Lueis: and their I saw the apparition of the aboue said gooddy: Easteck: a choaking of mersey Lueis and pressing upon hur breast with her: hands and I saw hur put a chane aboute her nick and choaked her:

and all the while I was their I saw her hurting of her griueiously: and she told me that she would kill her this night if she could

May 23, 1692

[Hand 2] Sworne Salem Village May 23ᵈ 1692
      Before vs   John Hathorne
                          } Assisᵗˢ
             Jonathan. Corwin

[Reverse] [Hand 3] mary walcott ffurther testifieth yᵗ on 23 may 1692 mary Estick did most greviously torment me during the time of hir Examination also yᵉ day I saw hir or hir Apperanc most greviously toment mercy lewes Eliz Hubbrt and ann putnam and I veryly beleue in my hart that mary Estick is a most dreadfull wicth and that she hath very often most dreadfully tormented me and parsons aboue named by hir acts of wicthcraft.

[Hand 4] Mary: {walcot} declared: before yᵉ Jury of Inquest: yᵗ yᵉ above written evidence and that on yᵉ other side of this paper: is yᵉ truth: upon oath: Augˢᵗ 4: 1692

[Hand 5] Mary Wolcot ver. Easty

Notes: Hand 2 = John Hathorne; Hand 3 = Thomas Putnam; Hand 4 = Simon Willard; Hand 5 = Stephen Sewall

Essex County Court Archives, vol. 1, no. 284, Massachusetts Supreme Judicial Court, Judicial Archives, on deposit James Duncan Phillips Library, Peabody Essex Museum, Salem, MA.

206. Deposition of Abigail Williams & Ann Putnam Jr. v. Mary Esty, John Willard, & Mary Whittredge and Testimony of Ann Putnam Jr. v. Mary Esty

See also: Aug. 4, 1692.

[Hand 1] The Deposistion of Abigaill williams and Ann putnam who testifieth and saith that we both goeing along with goodman Abby and Sarah Trask the 20ᵗʰ of may 1692 to the house of Constable Jnᵒ putnam ^{to se mircy lewes.} as we ware in the way we ~~saw~~ both saw the Apperishtion of Gooddy Estick the very same woman that was sent whom the other day: and also the apperishtion of that woman that was with hir the other day: and the Apperishtion of Gooddy Estick tould us both that now she was afflecting of Mircy lewes because she would not clear hir as others did and wⁿ came to Mircy lewes who layd speachless and in a sad condition we saw there the Apperishtions of gooddy Estick and Jnᵒ willard and mary witheridge afflecting and choaking Mircy lewes in a most dreadfull maner. which did most greviouly affright us: and Immediatly gooddy Estick did fall upon us and tortor us allso Redy to choake us to death

[Hand 2] Abigail Williams and An putnam
Testified to yᵉ truth of the abouesᵈ Euedence
Salem {Village} May the 23ᵈ 1692
      Before vs   John Hathorne
                          } Assisᵗˢ
             Jonathan. Corwin

May 23, 1692

[Hand 1] Ann putnam further testifieth y^t on 23 may 1692 being the last day of the Examination of mary Estick ["i" written over "y"] she did most greviously torment me dureing the time of hir Examination also on the same day I saw mary Estick or hir Apperanc most greviously torment and afflect mary walcott mercy lewes Eliz Hubburd and abigail william and I veryly beleue in my hart that mary Estick is a most dreadfull wicth and that she hath very often afflected me and the parsons affore named by hir acts of wicthcra⟨ft⟩

[Hand 3] Ann putnam: declared: to ye Jury of Inquest: y^t y^e: her above written evidence: is ye truth upon her oath: Aug^st :4: 1692

[Reverse] [Hand 4] Anne Putman &c^a ver. Eastick

Notes: Abigail Williams, who had made her claims on May 23, did not appear at the grand jury hearing on August 4, she having disappeared from the proceedings by then. For her grand jury appearance on June 30, her last testimony in the proceedings, see No. 245. ◊ Hand 1 = Thomas Putnam; Hand 2 = John Hathorne; Hand 3 = Simon Willard; Hand 4 = Stephen Sewall.

Essex County Court Archives, vol. 1, no. 286, Massachusetts Supreme Judicial Court, Judicial Archives, on deposit James Duncan Phillips Library, Peabody Essex Museum, Salem, MA.

Sworn Deposition: Deposition of Samuel Parris, Thomas Putnam, & Ezekiel Cheever v. Sarah Good, Sarah Osburn, & Tituba

2nd of 3 dates. See No. 8 on March 1, 1692

207. Testimony of Abigail Williams v. Sarah Good, Sarah Osburn, & Tituba

[Hand 1] The testimony of ~~Eliz Parris jun^ε~~ & Abigail Williams testifyth ["th" written over "y"] & sayth ["th" written over "y"] that severall times last Febuary ^{she} ~~they~~ hath ["th" written over "ve"] been much afflicted with pains in ~~their~~ head & other parts & often pinched by the apparition of Sarah Good, Sarah Osburne & Tituba Indian all of Salem Village & also excessively afflicted by the said ^{apparition of said} Good, Osburne, & Tituba at their examination before authority the. 1st March last past 1691/2
Farther the said Abigail Williams testifyeth that
she saw the apparition of said Sarah Good at her
examination pinch Eliz: Hubbard & set her into
fits & also Eliz: Parris, & Ann Putman
　　　　The mark of

Abigail　𝒜·𝒲·　Williams.

[Hand 2] Testified before vs by Abigail^ε. Williams
Salem May: the. 23^d 1692
John Hathorne
Jonathan. Corwin
[Hand 3] ᵱ ord^ε of ye Govern^ε & Councill

Notes: Additions to the document were probably made on a different date from the original composition. It appears that when Samuel Parris wrote the deposition he planned on having his daughter testify. At what point Parris changed this document cannot be certain, but it seems likely that the original draft was written before March 25, at which time it is generally believed that she was residing at the home of Stephen Sewall. For more on Betty Parris, see the General Introduction. ◊ Hand 1 = Samuel Parris; Hand 2 = John Hathorne; Hand 3 = Jonathan Corwin

Essex County Court Archives, vol. 1, no. 31, Massachusetts Supreme Judicial Court, Judicial Archives, on deposit James Duncan Phillips Library, Peabody Essex Museum, Salem, MA.

208. Deposition of John Richards & Joseph Morgan v. Dorcas Hoar

See also: Sept. 6, 1692.

[Hand 1] The deposition of John Richards aged about 46 yeares saith that some time this last winter past I beeing Required by the constabell of Beuerly as one of the Jurores to vnderstand the Reason of the vntimely death of william Hoar beeing at the house of william hoar the Rest of the Jury beeing their I the said Richards said to the Rest of the Jury that it was nesesary that the naked body of the deceaced shoold bee veiued and darcus hoar the wife of the decaced brake out in a very greate pashtion wringing of her hands and stamping on the floore with her feete and said. you wiked wretch or wiked wretches what doe you think I haue murdered my husband: and the Rest of the Jury blaming her for beeing in such a pashon ^{and then} shee was some thing pasified

{[Hand 2] Joseph Morgan
Sworne to y^e same.
Jurat in Curia}

[Hand 3] Sworne Salem Village May 23^d 1692

Before vs.
John Hathorne
Jonathan. Corwin
} Assis^ts

[Reverse] [Hand 2] Jn° Richards Con. Hoar & Jos. Morgan

Notes: The role of Joseph Morgan, from Beverly, in this case has not been established. ◊ Used at trial. ◊ Hand 2 = Stephen Sewall; Hand 3 = John Hathorne

Essex County Court Archives, vol. 1, no. 208, Massachusetts Supreme Judicial Court, Judicial Archives, on deposit James Duncan Phillips Library, Peabody Essex Museum, Salem, MA.

209. Deposition of Elizabeth Booth v. Sarah Procter, Mary DeRich, John Procter, & Elizabeth Procter

[Hand 1] May ye 23 <u>1692</u>

Elizabeth Booth aged 18 yeares or thereabouts deposeth & saith

That Sarah Procter and Mary Derish the wife of Michell Derish apeared to this Deponent in the Night and Called her Jade, Mary Derish asked her what made ["e" written over "d"] her say any thing about ~~Ma Sarah Procter:~~ Sarah Procter ~~Replyed,~~ ^{said} it was well she did not come to the Villa⟨ge⟩ that Day:: and with all Afflicted, & Pinched, her, this Deponent most

May 23, 1692

greiveiously and so Continues to Afflict her this Deponet still and John Procter and his wife Likewise/ whos name is Elizabeth: Procter:

[Reverse] [Hand 2] Eliz. Booth ag^t Sarah procte⟨r &⟩ Mary Derich

Essex County Court Archives, vol. 1, no. 302, Massachusetts Supreme Judicial Court, Judicial Archives, on deposit James Duncan Phillips Library, Peabody Essex Museum, Salem, MA.

210. Deposition of David Ferneaux & Jonathan Walcott Jr. v. Sarah Procter†

[Hand 1] The Deposetion of Dauid Furneax Aged 23 or their abouts and Jonathan Walcott Junior aged 21: who testifieth and saith y^t on the 20th of may 1692 about 12 of the clock we hearde mary Walcott in one of her fitts say that she saw the apparition of Sarah Procttor come and hurte her by choak{ing} and pinching of her we both also heard her say that she brought the book to her and urged her to write in her book we ware then both presante and heard her say I would not write in your book though you kill me

dauid furneax
Jonathan Walcott Junior

[Reverse] [Hand 2] Dauid ffurnex

Essex County Court Archives, vol. 1, no. 299, Massachusetts Supreme Judicial Court, Judicial Archives, on deposit James Duncan Phillips Library, Peabody Essex Museum, Salem, MA.

211. Testimony of John Putnam Jr. v. Sarah Procter†

[Hand 1] John putnam Juner testifieth that very latly ~~she~~ he hath hard Elizabeth Hurburd complaine of Sarah proctor that she hath tortored hir very much and urgeth hir vehemently to writ in hir book

Notes: Hand 1 = Thomas Putnam

Essex County Court Archives, vol. 1, no. 298, Massachusetts Supreme Judicial Court, Judicial Archives, on deposit James Duncan Phillips Library, Peabody Essex Museum, Salem, MA.

212. Deposition of Thomas Putnam v. Sarah Procter†

[Hand 1] the Deposistion of Thomas putnam who testifieth and saith that with in these few days I haue hard Elizabeth Hubb⟨u⟩rd and Ann putnam Two of the afflected parsons greviously complaine of Sarah procter that she did tortor them very much ⟨a⟩nd urged them uehemently to writ in hir book⟨e⟩

Notes: Hand 1 = Thomas Putnam

Essex County Court Archives, vol. 1, no. 297, Massachusetts Supreme Judicial Court, Judicial Archives, on deposit James Duncan May 23, 1692
Phillips Library, Peabody Essex Museum, Salem, MA.

213. Deposition of Mary Walcott v. Sarah Procter

[Hand 1] The Depoestion of mary Walcott Who thestifieth and saith on the 20ᵗʰ omay [= of May] 1692 saw the apparition of Sarah Procter: come and choake me and pincht me and terrified me much and urged me greuiously to write in her book: but I told her I would not touch itt and then she tormented me dreadfully
[Hand 2] Sworne Salem Village May 23ᵈ 1692

Before vs. John Hathorne } Assisᵗˢ
Jonathan. Corwin }

[Reverse] [Hand 3] ~~Mary Waren agᵗ Procter~~

[Hand 4] Mary Walcutt
[Hand 5] against sara procktar

Notes: Hand 2 = John Hathorne; Hand 3 = Stephen Sewall

Essex County Court Archives, vol. 1, no. 303, Massachusetts Supreme Judicial Court, Judicial Archives, on deposit James Duncan
Phillips Library, Peabody Essex Museum, Salem, MA.

214. Statement of Andrew Elliott v. Susannah Roots†

[Hand 1] An information if it might ^{be} any help in the Examination of yᵉ person before ^{you} goode Roots I being in yᵉ house of mᵉ Laurence Dennis some time since she was suspected for what shee is now before you & there was Likewise Leonard Austen of ouᵉ Town of Beuerly sd Austen then sd that he thought she was a bad woman, his reason was that he Liuing in yᵉ house with sd Roots not Long since and when he went to prayer at any time with his wife & thought sd Roots would acompany them in sd Duty but Did not ^{at} any time but would withdraw & absent her selfe: & farther when my self & wife were gone to bed & she vnto her bed. she would rise in yᵉ night & we Could ^{here} her talk in yᵉ roome below I lying in yᵉ Chamber ouer sd roome a [= as] if there there were :5: or six persons with her more sd Austen might speak if Cal(l)ed therevnto as far as know more Concering Roots
Andrew Eliott

[Reverse] [Hand 2] Andrew Elliot agᵗ G: Rootes

Notes: Hand 1 = Andrew Elliot; Hand 2 = John Hathorne

May 23, 1692   *Essex County Court Archives, vol. 1, no. 306, Massachusetts Supreme Judicial Court, Judicial Archives, on deposit James Duncan Phillips Library, Peabody Essex Museum, Salem, MA.*

215. Deposition of Thomas Gage and Testimony of Elias Pickworth v. Roger Toothaker†

[Hand 1] The Deposition of Thomas Gage Aged aboute ~~six &~~ thirty six years ~~of Age~~ This Deponant saith & doth testifie that sometime this Last spring of ye year, that Docter Toothaker was in his house in Beuerly (vpon some occasion) & we Descoursed aboute John Mastons Childe of salem that was then sick & haueing vnwonted fitts: & Likewise another Childe of Phillip Whites of Beuerly who was then strangly sick I perswaded sd Toothaker to goe & see sd Children and sd toothaker answered he had seen them both allready, and that his opinion was they were vnder an Euill hand And farther sd Toothaker sd that his Daughter had kild a witch & I asked him how she Did it, & sd Toothaker answered readily, that his Daughter had Learned something from him I asked by what means she Did it, & he sd that there was a a Certaine person bewitched & sd person Complained of beeing afflicted by another person that was suspected by y^e afflicted person: & farther sd Toothaker sd that his sd Daughter gott some of y^e afflicted persons vrine & put it into an Earthen [Lost]ott [= pot] & stopt sd pott very Close & putt sd pott ~~vp Cl⟨ose⟩~~ [Lost]⟨to⟩ [= into] a hott ouen & stopt vp sd ouen & y^e next morning sd [Lost]⟨t⟩ch [= witch] was Dead other things I haue forgotten & farther saith not [Lost]ias Pickworth Aged aboute thirty foure years testifieth to all that is aboue written

[Reverse] [Hand 2]

                                      Sworne by Thomas Gage Salem Village May 2⟨3⟩^d [Lost]

                          John Hathorne ⎫
             before vs.   ⎬ Assis^ts
                          Jonathan. Corwin ⎭

[Hand 3] G⟨ou⟩ge Cont[Lost] [= contra] Toothaker

Notes: The digit after "2" following May is mostly lost in the manuscript, although "3" appears as the most likely number. No examination of Roger Toothaker is extant, so it is possible that this deposition came at an examination on May 23, although normally one would have expected an examination closer to the arrest date, May 18. Toothaker died in Boston prison June 16, 1692. ◊ Hand 1 = Andrew Elliot; Hand 2 = John Hathorne

Essex County Court Archives, vol. 1, no. 275, Massachusetts Supreme Judicial Court, Judicial Archives, on deposit James Duncan Phillips Library, Peabody Essex Museum, Salem, MA.

216. Census of Prisoners and Dates of Prison Transfers†

May 23, 1692

[Hand 1] Seuerall sent to Boston Goale on acc⁰ of witchcraft
Salem March 1ᵈ first Exaᵐ
sent boston

- Sarah Osburne
- Sarah Good
- Titiba Indian

———

- • Martha Cory
- • Rebecka Nurce
- • Dorothy Good   ⎫
- • Sarah Cloyce   ⎬   Aprill 12ᵗʰ sent to Boston
- • Eliz. Procter   ⎭
- • John. Procter

Salem May 12ᵗʰ ⅌ mittimas   •
wᶜʰ went May 13ᵗʰ, to Boston   •
1 George Jacobs senᵉ   •
2 Giles Cory   •
3 Wᵐ Hobs   •
4 Edwᵈ Bushop   ⎫   •
5 Sarah Bushop his wife ⎭   •
6 Bridget Bushop Alias Oliuer   •
7 Sarah Wild   •
8 Mary Lᵗ Nath putn⟨a⟩ms negro   •
9 Mary English   •
10 Allice. Parker   •
11 Ann. Pudeater   •

May 2ᵈ
- Lydea Dasting. Widᵒ of Redᵉ
- Susannah Martin of Amesᵇʳ
- Dorcas Hoar of Beverly Widᵒ
- Sarah Murrell of Bevᵉ

May 8th
- Bethya Carter ⎫ of Woburn ⎫
- Ann Seires   ⎭   ⎬ all sent to Boston
- Sarah Dasting   ⎪
- George Burrows   ⎭

In Salem prison

Delᵉ Abigail
- Easty.
- Hobs
- Hobs
- Mary. Waren

Churchwell   •
Jacobs Margret   •
Abigail Soames   •
Rebeca Jacobs   •
Sarah Buckley   •
Mary Witheridge   •
Sarah Procter   –X

Sent to Boston Wedensday the 18ᵗʰ May. 1692
- Thomas ffarror ⎫
- ⎧ Eliz Hart   ⎬ of lyn
- ⎨ John Willard of Salem Village
- ⎩ Roger Toothaker of bilrica

Sent to Salem Goale
yᵉ 23ᵈ May 1692
Sarah Pease
Sarah Procter

Sent to Boston Munday the 23ᵈ 1692
Mary Easty
Abigaile Soames
Susannah Rootes
Sarah Bassett

Mary Derich   ⎫
Benjamin Procter ⎬
Eliz: Cary   ⎭

May 25, 1692   [Reverse] [Hand 2] Salem Village the 23ᵈ May. 1692
Rootis
Bassett

Notes: Note "Dorothy Good" is used, and not the incorrect "Dorcas Good." ◊ Hand 1 = John Hathorne

Essex County Court Archives, vol. 2, no. 134, Massachusetts Supreme Judicial Court, Judicial Archives, on deposit James Duncan Phillips Library, Peabody Essex Museum, Salem, MA.

Wednesday, May 25, 1692

217. Mittimus for Martha Cory, Rebecca Nurse, Dorothy Good, Sarah Cloyce, John Procter, & Elizabeth Procter

[Hand 1] To the keeper of theire Majesᵗˢ Goale in Boston
You are in theire Majesᵗˢ names hereby required to take into your care and safe Custody the Bodys of Martha Cory the wife of Giles Cory of Salem ffarmes husbandman Rebecka Nurse the wife of ffranᶜˢ Nurce of Salem Village husbandman. Dorothy ["othy" written over "cas"] Good the daufter of Wᵐ Good aforesᵈ husbandman. Sarah Cloyce the wife of Peter Cloyce of Salem Village husbandman. John Procter of Salem ffarmes husbandman and Elizabeth the wife of sᵈ John Procter of Salem ffarmes Husbandman who all and every one of them, stand Chargcd on ["o" written over "i"] behalfe of theire Majesᵗˢ for feloniously Committeing sundry acts of witchcraft Lately, at Salem Village, on the Bodys of Ann Putnam the daufter of Thomas Putnam Abigail Williams Eliz. Hubbert & others of Salem Village aforesᵈ whereby great hurt hath benne donne to theire bodys Contrary to yᵉ peace of our Souᵋ Lᵈ & Lady Wᵐ & Mary of England &c King & Queen, whome you are all Well to secure. vntill thay shall be deliuered by due order of Law And hereof you are not to faile Dated Boston May 25ᵗ 1692.

$$
\left.\begin{array}{c}
\text{John Hathorne} \\
\text{℘ vs} \\
\text{Jonathan. Corwin}
\end{array}\right\} \text{Assis}^{\text{ts}}
$$

[Reverse] [Hand 2]
Sarah Good
Rebecca Nurs
Jnᵒ Willard
John Proctor
Eliza Proctor
Susanah Martin
Bridget Bishop all [= alias] Oliuer
Alice Parker
Tittuba Indian

Notes: The 'othy' written over 'cas' corrects the name from "Dorcas" to "Dorothy." Both the original error and the correction were made by Hathorne. Although the name "Dorcas" has been used universally by subsequent historians, nothing in the manuscripts or elsewhere indicates that anyone named Dorcas Good resided in the Salem area at the time. Sarah Good's daughter was named Dorothy Good. Dorcas is not a diminutive or variation of Dorothy. The error reminds us that people caught up in the various cases were often unknown to those who accused them and to those who recorded their experience. The movement of prisoners to Boston was probably based on local space limitations. ◊ Hand 1 = John Hathorne ◊ Facsimile Plate 7.

Essex County Court Archives, vol. 1, no. 36, Massachusetts Supreme Judicial Court, Judicial Archives, on deposit James Duncan Phillips Library, Peabody Essex Museum, Salem, MA.

218. Mittimus for Sarah Good & Tituba

[Hand 1] To the keeper of theire Majes^ts Goale in Boston

You are in theire Majes^ts names hereby required, to take into your care and safe Custody the Bodys of Sarah Good the wife of Wm Good of Salem ffarmes husbandman and Titiba an Indian Woman, belonging vnto m^r Samuell Parris of Salem Village Minester, who stand Charged on behalfe of theire Majes^ts for theire feloniou⟨s⟩ly Committeing Sundry acts of Witchcraft ^{at Salem Village} on ye Bodys of Elizabeth Parris Eliz Hubbert Abigail Williams And Ann Putnam of Salem Village. whereby great hurt hath benne donne to theire Body contrary to y^e peace of our Sou^ε L^d and Lady W^m & Mary of England &c King & Queen Whome you are well to secure vntill thay shall thence be deliuered by due order of Law and hereof you are not to faile Dated Boston May the 25^t 1692

$$\text{ꝑ vs}\qquad \left.\begin{array}{l}\text{John Hathorne}\\[1em]\text{Jonathan. Corwin}\end{array}\right\}\text{Assis}^{ts}$$

[Reverse] [Hand 2] Mittimus

Notes: Hand 1 = John Hathorne

Essex County Court Archives, vol. 1, no. 8, Massachusetts Supreme Judicial Court, Judicial Archives, on deposit James Duncan Phillips Library, Peabody Essex Museum, Salem, MA.

Thursday, May 26, 1692

219. Statement of George Herrick v. Mary Bradbury, Sarah Rice, Wilmot Redd, & Elizabeth Fosdick

[Hand 1] May 26th 1692
Beeing at Salem village wth Constable {Josp⟨h⟩} Neale the persons vnder written was afflicted much and Complained against viz Mary Walcott Ann Puttnam vpon Capt Bradberys wife of Salsbury & Mary Walcott Ann Puttnam: m^εs Marshall vpon Goodwife Rice of Reding & Mary Walcott ann Puttnam Marcy Lewis vpon Goodwife Read of

May 27, 1692

Marblehead & Mary Walcott Marcy Lewis Ann Puttnam vpon Goody Fosdick yᵉ same woemen tells them yᵗ shee afflicts mᵉ Tufts Negro

attest Geo: Herrick Marshall

[Reverse] [Hand 2] Goody B⟨rad⟩bery

Notes: Why the accusers chose these names from such distant locations, and what knowledge they had of those whom they accused, remains a subject for further investigation. ◊ Hand 1 = George Herrick

Essex County Court Archives, vol. 2, no. 71, Massachusetts Supreme Judicial Court, Judicial Archives, on deposit James Duncan Phillips Library, Peabody Essex Museum, Salem, MA.

Friday, May 27, 1692

220. Order for the Establishment of a Special Commission of Oyer and Terminer for Suffolk, Essex, and Middlesex Counties

[Hand 1] Upon consideration that there are many Criminal Offenders now in Custody, some whereof have lyen long & many inconveniences attending the thronging of the Goals at this hot season of the year; there being no Judicatories or Courts of Justice yet Established.

Ordered: That a Special Commission of Oyer and Terminer be made out unto William Stoughton, John Richards, Nathaniel ["i" written over "a"] Saltonstal, Wait Winthrop, Bartholomew Gedney, Samuel Sewall, John Hathorne, Jonathan Corwin, & Peter Sergeant Esqʳˢ. Assigning them the said William Stoughton, John Richards, Nathanael Saltonstal, Wait Winthrop, Barthᵒ Gedney, Samuel Sewall, John Hathorne, Jonathan Corwin and Peter Sergeant Esqʳˢ to be Justices, or any five of them (whereof the said William Stoughton, John Richards, or Bartholomew

Bartholomew Gedney Esqʳˢ to be one), to enquire of, hear and determine for this time according to the Law, & Custom of England, and of this their Majᵗⁱᵉˢ Province, all and all manner of Crimes and Offences had made, done or perpetrated within the Countys of Suffolke, Essex, Middlesex and of either of them.

William Phips.

Captain Stephen Sewall of Salem is nominated & appointed to Officiate as Clerke of the special Court of Oyer and Terminer.

William Phips.

Mr Thomas Newton is appointed to Officiate as Attourny for and on behalfe of their Majᵗⁱᵉˢ at the special Court of Oyer and Terminer.

William Phips.

Notes: The establishment of the Court of Oyer and Terminer makes no mention of witchcraft, and although the witchcraft issue dominated the Court's activity, it was not limited to it. This text is an excerpt from a copy of the Council Record for May 27, the entire entry of which begins on page 174.

221. Complaint of Joseph Holton & John Walcott v. Martha Carrier, Elizabeth Fosdick, et al.

323

Governor's Council Executive Records (1692), vol. 2, pp. 176–77. Massachusetts State Archives. Boston, MA. Certified copy from the original records at Her Majesty's State Paper Office, September 16, 1846. London, UK.

May 28, 1692

Saturday, May 28, 1692

221. Complaint of Joseph Holton & John Walcott v. Martha Carrier, Elizabeth Fosdick, Wilmot Redd, Sarah Rice, Elizabeth How, John Alden, William Procter, John Flood, Mary Toothaker, Margaret Toothaker, & Arthur Abbott

[Hand 1] Salem May the 28th 1692

Joseph Houlton and John Walcot both of Salem Village Yeomen made Complaint in behalfe of theire Majes^{ts} against [   ] Carrier of Andouer the wife of Thomas Carrier of s^d Towne husbandman [   ] ffosdick of Maulden or charlstown [   ] Re⟨e⟩d of Marblehead the wife of Samull Reed of s^d place [   ] Rice of Reding the wife of Nicholas Rice of s^d Towne [   ] How the wife of James How of Topsfeild Capt John Alden of Boston Mariner. William Procter of Salem ffarmes, Capt John fflood of ⟨Ramney⟩ {ma⟨rsh⟩ ⟨i⟩n boston} Mary Toothaker the wife of Roger toothaker of Bilrica, and [   ] Toothaker the daufter of s^d Roger Toothaker [   ] Abott y^t liues between Ip^s Topsfeild & wenham ffor Sundry acts of Witchcraft by them and Euery one of them Committed on the Bodys of Mary Walcot, Abigail Williams Marcy Lewis Ann Putnam and Others belonging to Salem Village or farmes Lately, to the hurt and Injury of theire bodys therefore Craues Justice

Joseph houlton
John Walcutt

Carrier of Andouer – Marshall Essex
Reed of Marblehead – Cons^t
Rice of Reding – Cons^t
How of Topsfeild – Con^s
Wm Procter – Cons^t

[Reverse] [Hand 2] Warant Carrer

[Hand 3?] Warrant

Notes: Mary Toothaker was the wife of Roger Toothaker, who had already been accused and imprisoned, dying there on June 16. Their daughter, Margaret, was nine years old. William Procter was the seventeen-year-old son of John and Elizabeth Procter. The others had no close relations in prison at the time, and the selection of this group was based on other factors. Who provided the list can only be a matter of speculation pending new discoveries, but the absence of first names strongly suggests that the people were not known personally by the accusers nor by those from whom they learned the names. It seems likely that the establishment of the Court of Oyer and Terminer the previous day influenced the timing of this set of accusations. The connection, if it exists, between the Arthur Abbott named here, and an Arthur Abbott who testified against Elizabeth Procter at her trial requires further investigation. ◊ Hand 1 = John Hathorne

Essex County Court Archives, vol. 1, no. 309, Massachusetts Supreme Judicial Court, Judicial Archives, on deposit James Duncan Phillips Library, Peabody Essex Museum, Salem, MA.

May 28, 1692

222. List of Accused and Accusers

[Hand 1] Complaint ["t" written over "d"] of [Hand 2] Seuerall May. 28th 1692

[Hand 1] gooddy Carier of Andevor }   [Hand 1] mary walcott
[Hand 2] Tho: Carriers wife   Abigail william

[Hand 1] gooddy fozdick of maldin   mary walcott
[Hand 2] Goody pain: mary Waren   Mircy lewes
                                  Abigall william
                                  Ann putnam

––––––––

[Hand 1] goody Read of marblehead   mary walcott
[Hand 2] vpon yᵉ hill by yᵉ meetᵉ house   Mircy lewes
                                  Abigall william
                                  Ann putnam

––––––––

[Hand 1] gooddy Rice of Reding   ––––––––
                                  Ed. marshals wife
–––––––   mary walcott
                                  Abigall william

gooddy How of Topsfeild or Ipswich bounds   Ma{r}y walcott
Capt Hows brother wife   }   Abigaill williams
[Hand 2] vis Ja. Hows wife   Two women there abouts much
                                  affleted and suspect hir but canot
                                  sartainly say

––––––––

[Hand 1] Capt Alldin complaind   Mary walcott
of a long time by   Mircy lewes
                                  Abigaill williams
                                  Ann putnam
                                  [Hand 2] Susana Sheldon

––––––––

[Hand 2] Wm procter: Mary. Walcot
                                  Susana. Shelden

Toothakers wife   }   Mary Walcot
& daufter   Abig. Williams

Capt fflood   Mary Walcot
                                  Abigail Williams
                                  & yᵉ rest

[Reverse] Arthur Abot liues in a by place something neere Majᵒ Appletons ffarme and liues between Ipᵉ Topsfeild & Wenham
Abott yt liues. between Ipswitch Topsfeild and Wenham

Complained of by Many

Notes: The changes of scribal hand have been marked separately in the two columns. In the first column, Hand 1 and Hand 2 frequently alternate while most of column two is written in Hand 1; Hand 2 only adds some names at the end. This list repeats the names of those accused in the previous document, although a new name appears, "Goody pain." This is Elizabeth Paine, but she was not complained against until May 30. Thus, the additions by Hand 2 were made on or after May 30. Of the accusers identified, only Mary Walcott appears in every instance. ◊ Hand 1 = Thomas Putnam; Hand 2 = John Hathorne

MS Am 44, Rare Books and Manuscripts, Boston Public Library. Boston, MA.

223. Warrant for the Apprehension of Martha Carrier, and Officer's Return

See also: May 31, 1692.

[Hand 1] To The Marshall of Essex or his dep^t or to the
Constables in Andouer

You are in theire Majes^{ts} names hereby required t[Lost] [= to] apprehend and forthwith secure, and bring befor⟨e⟩ [Lost] [*Woodward* = us] [Hand 2] martha [Hand 1] Carrier the wife of Thomas Currier of And[Lost] [= Andover] on Tuesday next being the 31^t day of this Instant m[Lost] [= month] of May aboute ten of the Clock in the forenoon ^{or as soon as may be afterwards} at [Lost] [*Woodward* = the] house of Lt Nathaniell Ingersalls in Salem Villag⟨e⟩ who stands Charged with haueing Committed Sundry [Lost] [*Woodward* = acts] of Witchcraft on the Bodys of Mary Walcot & abi[Lost] [= Abigail] Williams of Salem Village to theire great hurt & [Lost] [*Woodward* = injury] in order to her Examination Relateing to y^e prem[Lost] [= premises] aboue said: faile not Dated Salem May 28th 169⟨2⟩

⅌ vs
John Hathorne   ⎫
             ⎬ Assis^{ts}
Jonathan. Corwin ⎭

[Reverse] [Hand 2] I haue apperehend the w^t in named parson and brought her to the place appinted

by me John Ballard const andouer

[Hand 3] Martha Carrier

Notes: Arrest warrants were issued in connection with the May 28 accusations. Since warrants for all are not extant, the probability is that missing ones are simply lost rather than not issued. The arrest of Martha Carrier begins the Andover phase of events that would in July and August proliferate after John Ballard sought help from Salem Village accusers to identify who was bewitching his wife. ◊ Hand 1 = John Hathorne

Essex County Court Archives, vol. 1, no. 310, Massachusetts Supreme Judicial Court, Judicial Archives, on deposit James Duncan Phillips Library, Peabody Essex Museum, Salem, MA.

224. Complaint of Thomas Putnam & Benjamin Hutchinson v. Elizabeth Cary

[Hand 1] Salem. May. 28th 1692.

M^ε Thomas. Puttnam & Benjamin Hutchinson both of Salem Village Yeomen Complaine of Elizabeth Ca⟨r⟩y y^e wife of Capt Nathaniell Cary of Charls=Towne Ma⟨ri⟩ner, on behalfe

May 28, 1692

of theyr Majestyes, for Sundry Acts of Witch=craft by hir Comitted upon y^e Bodys of M[Lost] [= Mary] Walcott, Abigall. Willyams & Mercy Lewis all of Sa[Lost] [= Salem] Village, whereby great hurt & damage is done y^m, an⟨d⟩ therefore Crave Justice

Thomas putnam

Beniamin Huchinson

[Reverse] [Hand 2] Eliz Cary

Notes: This complaint is puzzling, since Elizabeth Cary was on the prisoners list on May 23. It may be that the formal complaint had been neglected and is here remedied. ◊ Hand 1 = Jonathan Corwin

Essex County Court Archives, vol. 2, no. 109, Massachusetts Supreme Judicial Court, Judicial Archives, on deposit James Duncan Phillips Library, Peabody Essex Museum, Salem, MA.

225. Warrant for the Apprehension of Elizabeth How, and Officer's Return

See also: May 31, 1692.

[Hand 1] To ye Constable of Topsfeild

You are in theyr Majestyes Names hereby Required to Apprehend & bring before us [Hand 2] Elizabeth [Hand 1] How y^e wife of James. How of Topsfeild Husbandman on Tuesday next being y^e thirty ffirst day of may about Ten of y^e Clock in y^e forenoone att y^e house of Lev^t Nathaniell Ingersolls of Salem Village, Whoe stands Charged wth Sundry Acts of Witch=craft done or Comitted on y^e Bodyes of Mary Walcott, Abigall. Williams & others of Salem Village, to theyr great hurt, in order to hir Examination, Relateing to y^e aboves^d premises. & hereof you are nott to fayle. Dat^d Salem. May. 28th 1692

℘ vs   John Hathorne   }
       Jonathan. Corwin } Assis^{ts}

[Reverse] [Hand 3] In obedence to this warant I haue ⟨?⟩d apprendeed [Hand 2?] {Elizabeth} [Hand 3] How the wife of Jems how ~~and brout~~ on the 29th of may 1692 and haue brought har unto the house of leftenant nathaniell englosons acording to⟨oe⟩ to warant as atested by me Ephraim Willdes constabell for the town of topsfelld dated may 31th 1692

[Hand 4] Eliz: Howe.

Notes: Hand 1 = Jonathan Corwin

Essex County Court Archives, vol. 1, no. 321, Massachusetts Supreme Judicial Court, Judicial Archives, on deposit James Duncan Phillips Library, Peabody Essex Museum, Salem, MA.

226. Warrant for the Apprehension of William Procter, and Officer's Return

May 28, 1692

See also: May 31, 1692.

[Hand 1] To yᵉ Constable of Salem

You are hereby Required in theyr Majestyes Names to Apprehend & bring before us William Procter of Salem ffarmes Son of John Procter of Sᵈ ffarmes Husbandman, upon Tuesday Next being yᵉ Thirty ffirst day of May about Tenne of the Clock in yᵉ morneing att yᵉ house of Levᵗ Nathˡˡ Ingersolls in Sᵈ Village, Whoe Stands Charged wᵗʰ Sundry Acts of Witch=craft done or Comitted upon the Bodys of Mary Walcott & Susañah Shelden & others of Salem Village to theyr great hurt, in order to his Examination, Relateing to yᴱ above Sᵈ premises. & hereof You are nott to fayle. dated. Salem. May. 28ᵗʰ 1692.

ẜ vs

John Hathorne
Jonathan. Corwin } Assisᵗˢ

[Hand 2] I haue apprehended the parson aboue named and brought him to the place apinted by me John Putnam Cunst of Salam

Notes: Hand 1 = Jonathan Corwin

Essex County Court Archives, vol. 2, no. 2, Massachusetts Supreme Judicial Court, Judicial Archives, on deposit James Duncan Phillips Library, Peabody Essex Museum, Salem, MA.

227. Warrant for the Apprehension of Wilmot Redd, and Officer's Return

See also: May 31, 1692.

[Hand 1] To The Constables of Marblehead

You are in theire Majesᵗˢ names hereby required to apprehend and bring before Vs willmut Reed the wife of Samuell Reed of Marblehead, on Tuesday next being the 31 day of this Instant moneth of May aboute ten of the Clock in the forenoon at yᵉ house of Lᵗ Nathanˡ Ingersalls in Salem Village; who Stands Charged wit⟨h⟩ haueing Committed Sundry acts of Witchcraft on yᵉ bodys of Mary Walcot and Marcy Lewis and Othe⟨r⟩[Lost] [= Others?] of Salem Village to theire great hurt &c, in order t⟨o⟩ her Examination Relateing to yᵉ abouesᵈ premises and hereof you are not to faile Dated Salem May 28ᵗʰ 1692

ẜ vs

John Hathorne
Jonathan. Corwin } Assisᵗˢ

May 28, 1692

[Reverse] [Hand 2] In answer to y⁰ withinmentioned warrant I haue apprehended Willmut Reed Wife to Sam^ll Reed of Marblehead & brought her to y⁰ house of Lt Ingersals May y⁰ <u>31th, 92</u>

James Smith Con^st
for Marblehead

Notes: Late in the publication stage a previously published transcription was located in Peleg Whitman Chandler's *American Criminal Trials* (1841), Vol. 1. p. 430. It reads as follows: "The deposition of Mercy Lewis, aged about eighteen years or thereabouts, testifieth and saith, that on the twenty-sixth day of this instant, May, that Goody Reed, of Marblehead, did pinch her, and she hath seen her severall times since, but she could not say she hurt her: and further saith nott." Whether anything else appeared on the manuscript to indicate its use cannot be determined. If it had been located in time, it would have been titled "Mercy Lewis v. Wilmot Redd" and would have carried a May 28, 1692 date. Unlike the depositions against Wilmot Redd at her examination on May 31, this one seems to have been prepared prior to it. ◊ Hand 1 = John Hathorne

Essex County Court Archives, vol. 2, no. 6, Massachusetts Supreme Judicial Court, Judicial Archives, on deposit James Duncan Phillips Library, Peabody Essex Museum, Salem, MA.

228. Warrant for the Apprehension of Sarah Rice, and Officer's Return

See also: May 31, 1692.

[Hand 1] To The Constables in Reding
You are in theire Majesties names hereby required to apprehend and bring before vs [Hand 2] Sarah [Hand 1] Rice the wife of Nicholas Rice of Reding on Tuesday next being the 31^t day of this Instant moneth. at the house of Lt Nathan^ε Ingersalls at Salem Village aboutc ten of the Clock in the forenoon. who stand charged with haueing Committed sundry acts of Witchcraft on y⁰ Bodys of Mary Walcot and Abigail Williams & others. to theire great hurt: &c in order to her Examination Relateing to y⁰ premis[Lost] [= premises] aboues^d faile not Dated Salem May <u>28th 1692</u>

John Hathorne
℘ vs   } Assis^ts
Jonathan. Corwin

[Reverse] [Hand 3] In obedence to this warant I haue brought the Body of Sarah Rice the wife of Nicolas Rice of Redding to the howse of Leu^t nath⟨a⟩nal Ingersons in Salem Viledg the :31: of this Instant May: 1692

Atest John Parker Constable for Redding

Notes: Hand 1 = John Hathorne

Essex County Court Archives, vol. 2, no. 108, Massachusetts Supreme Judicial Court, Judicial Archives, on deposit James Duncan Phillips Library, Peabody Essex Museum, Salem, MA.

Monday, May 30, 1692

Officer's Return: Warrant No. 2 for the Apprehension of Philip English
2nd of 2 dates. See No. 117 on May 6, 1692

229. Complaint of Nathaniel Putnam, Joseph Whipple, & Peter Tufts v. Elizabeth Fosdick & Elizabeth Paine

See also: June 2, 1692.

[Hand 1] Salem May the. 30th 1692
Lt Nathaniell Putnam and Joseph Whipple both of Salem Village made Complaint in behalfe of their Majes^{ts} against Elizabeth ffosdick of ~~Charlstown~~ Maulden the wife of John ffosdick. afores^d Carpenter And Elizabeth Paine of ~~Maulden~~ {Charlstown} the wife of ^{Stephen} Paine of S^d place husbandman for Sundry acts of witchcraft by them Committ{ed} Lately on the bbodys of Marcy Lewis and Mary Warren of Salem Village or farmes to theire great hurt therefore Craues Justice.

Nathanell Putnam
Joseph Whipple

The abouesayd Complaint was Exhibited before vs Salem May the. 30th 1692

John Hathorne }
                      } Assis^{ts}
Jonathan. Corwin }

Peter Tufts of Charlstowne also appeared before vs Salem June 2^d 1692. and also ~~made a~~ Comp⟨l⟩ained against both ye aboues^d for acts of Witchcraft by them Committed on his negro Woman

The Mark of

Peter Tuffts

[Reverse] [Hand 2] Elizabeth ffosdick

Notes: Elizabeth Fosdick had already been complained against on May 28. See No. 221. On May 26, George Herrick had attested that "Tufts Negro" was one of the afflicted. See No. 219. Here, the "Negro" is identified as female. She may have been "Nannee," mentioned in the probate of Tufts when he died a few years later. In the same document Herrick had included Elizabeth Fosdick as an afflicter. That another complaint in this record was added on June 2 may suggest that Fosdick and Paine had protectors. Although they were finally arrested, no record of further action against them survives. Whether Nathaniel Putnam is the same person who supported Rebecca Nurse (see No. 373) or his son has not been definitively established. ◊ Hand 1 = John Hathorne

Essex County Court Archives, vol. 2, no. 17, Massachusetts Supreme Judicial Court, Judicial Archives, on deposit James Duncan Phillips Library, Peabody Essex Museum, Salem, MA.

May 30, 1692   **230. Testimony of Samuel Gray v. Bridget Bishop**

[Hand 1] Samuell Gray of Salem Aged aboute 42 yeares Testifieth and sayth that aboute
~~twelfe~~ {fourteen} yeare agoe, he goeing to bed well one Lords Day at night, and after he had
ben⟨ne⟩ asleep some time, he awakened & looking vp, saw the house light as if a candle or
candles ware lighted in it and the dor locked & that little fire there, was Raked v⟨p⟩ he ["he"
written over "I"] did then see a woman standing between the Cradle i[Lost] [= in the?]
Roome. and the Bed side and seemed to look vpon ⟨him⟩ soe he ["he" written over "I"] did
Rise vp in his ["his" written over "my"] bed and it vanished or disapeared then he ["he"
written over "I"] went to yᵉ dor and found it locked. & vnlocking and Opening yᵉ dore he
["he" written over "I"] went to yᵉ Entry dore and looked out, and then againe did see the
same Woman he ["he" written over "I"] had a ["a" written over "just"] little before seene in yᵉ
Rome, and in the same garbe she was in before, then he ["he" written over "I"] said to her in
the name of God what doe you Come for. then she vanished away soe he ["he" written over
"I"] Locked yᵉ dore againe & went to bed and between sleepeing & wakeing he ["he" written
over "I"] felt some thing Come to his ["his" written over "my"] mouth or lipes cold, & there
vpon started & looked vp againe did see the same woman with some thing betweene both
her hands holding before his ["his" written over "my"] mouth vpon which she moued. and
the Child in the Cradle gaue a great screech out as if it was greatly hurt and she disappeared,
and takeing yᵉ child vp could not quiett it in some howres from which tyme, the child yᵗ
before was a very Likely thriueing Child ~~before~~ did pine away and was never well, althow it
Liued some moneths after, yet in a sad Condition and soe dyed; some tyme after within a
weeke ^{or less} he did see yᵉ same Woman in the same Garb and Cloaths, that appeared to
him as aforesaid, and althow he k⟨new⟩ not her, nor her name before, Yett ["Yett" written
over "her"] both by her Countenance & garb doth Testifie yᵗ it was the same Woman yᵗ thay
now Call Bridget Bishop Alias Oliuer. of Salem

                                                                    Samell Gray

                    Sworne Salem May 30ᵗʰ 1692
                    Before mee John Hathorne Assisᵗ

          [Reverse] Samˡˡ Grays Evede⟨nce⟩
          [Hand 2] Bridgett Bishopp

Notes: According to Robert Calef, Gray made a deathbed confession that his testimony against Bridget Bishop was
groundless. For whatever reason, his sworn testimony appears not to have been used at her trial. ◊ Hand 1 = John
Hathorne; Hand 2 = Thomas Newton

*Essex County Court Archives, vol. 1, no. 141, Massachusetts Supreme Judicial Court, Judicial Archives, on deposit James Duncan
Phillips Library, Peabody Essex Museum, Salem, MA.*

231. Deposition of William Stacy v. Bridget Bishop
See also: June 2, 1692.

[Hand 1] Bridgett [Hand 2] Bishop of the Towne of Salem aged [   ] Years or thereabouts
dep.

William Stacey Of the Towne of Salem Aged: Thirty Six Years or thereaboutes Deposeth   May 30, 1692
and Saith:/.

That about fo⟨u⟩rteene ^{years} agone this Deponant was Visited with the Small Pox, then
[Hand 1] Bridget [Hand 2] Bishop did give him a Visitt, and withall Proffessed a great Love
for this Deponant in his Affliction. more then ordinary, at which this Deponant admired,
some time after this Deponent was well, the said Bishop got him to do some work for her.
for which she gave hi⟨m⟩ three pence, which seemed to this Dep^t as if it had been good
Money,: but he had not gone not above 3 or 4 Rods before he Looked ~~on y^e~~ ~~Said mone~~
~~againe~~ in his Pockett where he put it. for it; but could not find any some time after this
deponent met the said [   ] Bishop: in ye Street agoeing to Mill; she askeing this Deponent
whether his ["his" written over "her"] father would grind her grist: he put it to ye said Bishop
why she Asked: she answered because folkes counted her a witch this Dep^t made answear:
he did not Question but that his fathe would grind it: but being gone about 6 Rod from her
ye said Bishop; with a small Load in his Cart: Suddenly ye Off wheele Slumped or Sunk
downe into a hole upon Plain grownd, that this Depon^t was forced to gett one to help him
gett ye wheele out afterwards this Depon^t went Back to look for said hole where his wheele
sunk in but could not find any hole Some time after in the winter about midnight ~~being~~
⟨awake⟩ this Deponent felt something betweene his lips Pressing hard ag^t his teeth: and
withall was very Cold: insomuch that it did awake him so y^t he gott up and sat upon his
beed: he at the same time seeing the said [Hand 1] Bridgett [Hand 2] Bishop sitting at the
foot of his bed: being to his seeming, it was then as light as if it had been day: or one in the
said Bishop⟨s⟩ shape: she haveing then a black cap, & a black hat, and a Red Coat with two
Eakes of two Coulers. then she the said Bishop or her shape clapt her coate close to her
Leggs. & hopt upon the bed and about the Roome and then went out: and then it was Dark:
againe some time after the s̄^{d} Bishop went to this Depon^t and asked him whither that
~~above written:~~ [Hand 3] {which he had reported} [Hand 2] was true, that he had told to
severall: he answered y^t was true & y^t it was she, and bid her denigh it if she dare, the said
Bishop ~~could~~ [Hand 3] {did} [Hand 2] not denigh it. and went away very Angry and said y^t
this Dep^t did her more Mi⟨s⟩chief: then any other body he asked Why: she answered because
folks would beleive him before anybody Elce: some time after the said Bishop thretned this
Deponent and told him he was the occasion of bringing her out about the brass she stole:
some time after this Dep^t in a dark night: was goeing to y^e Barn who was suddenly taken or
hoisted from y^e Ground & threw ag^t a stone wall after that taken up againe a throwed Down
a Bank at the End of his howse: some time after this Deponent mett the said Bishop by
Issaac Sternes Brick Kill [= kiln]: after he had Passed buy her: this Deponents Horse stood
still with a small load goeing ~~along~~ up the Hill so y^t the Horse striveing to draw All his Gears
& tacke^{ing} flew in Peices. and the Cart fell down⟨e⟩ afterward this Deponent went to lift
a Bagg of Corne of about 2 bushells but could not budge it with all his might: This
Deponent hath mett with severall other of her Pranks. at severall times: which would take up
a great time to tell of: This Deponet doth veryly beleive that the said [Hand 1] Bridget
[Hand 2] Bishop was Instumentall to his Daughter Prisillas Death: [Hand 1] aboute two
years agoe; the Child was a likely Thriueing Child. And sudenly Screaked out and soe
continued in an vnvsuall Manner for aboute. a fortnight & soe dyed in y^t lamentable
manner
          Sworne Salem May the 30th 1692

May 30, 1692

before vs
$$\left.\begin{array}{l} \text{John Hathorne} \\[1em] \text{Jonathan. Corwin} \end{array}\right\} \text{Assis}^{\text{ts}}$$

[Hand 4] Jurat in Curia June. 2^{d} 1692/
[Hand 5] William stacy

[Reverse] William Stacy
[Hand 6] May 30/92

Notes: This deposition of William Stacy, along with the preceding document, No. 230, the testimony of Samuel Gray, represents all that is extant of judicial activity on May 30 to hear evidence in connection with Bridget Bishop. She had been examined on April 19, and as the trials developed, this intervening step of what may have been a court hearing in addition to the examination court would disappear. The grand jury would respond to the indictment, and if a true bill resulted, as at least one always did against the accused tried in 1692, the trial would proceed. With this first of the trials, the judicial authorities were working out the procedures that they would follow. ◇ Used at trial. ◇ "Eakes": 'additions, pieces added on' (*OED* s.v. *eke* n^1). ◇ Hand 1 = John Hathorne; Hand 3 = Simon Willard; Hand 4 = Stephen Sewall; Hand 5 = Thomas Newton.

Essex County Court Archives, vol. 1, nos. 138 & 139, Massachusetts Supreme Judicial Court, Judicial Archives, on deposit James Duncan Phillips Library, Peabody Essex Museum, Salem, MA.

232. Warrant for Jurors for the Court of Oyer and Terminer

[Hand 1] To George Corwin Gent^{n} Sherriff of the
County of Essex –. Greeting.
You are Required in their Maties Names to publish and give notice within yo$^{\varepsilon}$ Bailiwick ~~of~~ in the best manner you can of the Sitting of their Maties Justices upon a Commissioner of Oyer and Terminer At the ["th" written over "Sa"] Town of Salem upon Thursday next the Second of June next at Eight in the morning, for the tryal of all Crimes and Offences done and perpetrated within the s^{d} County, Requiring all persons concerned as prosecutors or Evidences to give their attendance; And to Return Eighteen honest and lawfull men of yo$^{\varepsilon}$ Bailywick to Serve upon the Grand Enquest, and fforty Eight ["Ei" written over "Eg"] alike honest and lawfull men to Serve upon the Jury of Tryals at the said Court; hereof faile not. Dated in Boston. May. 30th 1692. In the ffourth year of their Maties Reign./.

William Stoughto⟨n⟩
Sam Sewall

[Reverse] [Hand 2] Precept to ye sheriff. & Return of ye Jury.

Notes: Samuel Sewall's signature is in a different ink. This warrant for jurors represents the first known document generated by the Court of Oyer and Terminer. Although transcribed here from the manuscript, a transcription appeared in print in 1841 in *American Criminal Trials*. See Note 143 in the General Introduction.

UNCAT MS, Karpeles Manuscript Archive. Santa Barbara, CA.

Tuesday, May 31, 1692

Officer's Return: Warrant for the Apprehension of Martha Carrier

2nd of 2 dates. See No. 223 on May 28, 1692

Officer's Return: Warrant for the Apprehension of Elizabeth How

2nd of 2 dates. See No. 225 on May 28, 1692

Officer's Return: Warrant for the Apprehension of William Procter

2nd of 2 dates. See No. 226 on May 28, 1692

Officer's Return: Warrant for the Apprehension of Wilmot Redd

2nd of 2 dates. See No. 227 on May 28, 1692

Officer's Return: Warrant for the Apprehension of Sarah Rice

2nd of 2 dates. See No. 228 on May 28, 1692

233. Warrant for the Apprehension of John Alden, and Officer's Return

[Hand 1] To the Constable of Salem

{Essex Ss} Whereas Complaint hath been made vnto us John Hathorne & Jonathan Corwin Esq^εs by severall persons of Salem Village that Capt John Alden of Boston Marrin^ε ~~that he~~ is guilty of witchcraft in cruelly tortureing & afflicting severall of their Children ^{& others} these are therefore in their Maj^ties King William & Queen Maryes name to Authorize & Comand you forthwith to Apprehend the body of the said John Alden and Imediately bring him before vs to Answer what shall be objected ag^t him in that behalfe and this shall be yo^ε sufficient warrant Given vnder our hands the 31st day of May 1692 And in the ffourth year of the Reigne of our Sovereigne Lord and Lady William & Mary now King & Queen over England &c

𝔭 vs   John Hathorne } Assis^ts

Jonathan. Corwin }

persons Complaining vizt
Mary Walcott
Mercy Lewis
Abigail Williams
Elizabeth Booth
Elizabeth Hubbard
Ann Putnam
Mary Warren

[Reverse] [Hand 2] In obediance to the within written warant I haue Apprehended the Body of Capt John Alden accordeing to the tener of this warant

May 31, 1692   [Hand 2?] John Alden

Notes: Newton lists those claiming affliction as "Complaining." It seems more likely that the formal complaint came from one or more adult males. Hand 1 = Thomas Newton

Essex County Court Archives, vol. 2, no. 107, Massachusetts Supreme Judicial Court, Judicial Archives, on deposit James Duncan Phillips Library, Peabody Essex Museum, Salem, MA.

234. Examination of John Alden, as Published by Robert Calef

John Aldin Senior, of Boston, *in the County of* Suffolk, *Marriner; on the 28th. Day of* May 1692, *was sent for by the Magistrates of* Salem, *in the County of* Essex, *upon the Accusation of a company of poor distracted or possessed Creatures or Witches; and being sent by Mr. Stoughton, arrived there the 31st of* May, *and appeared at* Salem-Village, *before Mr.* Gidney *Mr.* Hathorn, *and Mr.* Curwin.

Those Wenches being present, who plaid their juggling tricks, falling down, crying out, and staring in Peoples Faces; the Magistrates demanded of them several times, who it was of all the People in the Room that hurt them? one of these Accusers pointed several times at one Captain Hill, *there present, but spake nothing; the same Accuser, had a Man standing at her back to hold her up; he stroped down to her Ear, then she cried out,* Aldin, Aldin *afflicted her; one of the Magistrates asked her if she had ever seen* Aldin, *she answered no, he asked how she knew it was* Aldin? *She said, the Man told her so.*

Then all were ordered to go down into the street, where a Ring was made; and the same Accuser cried out there stands Aldin, *a bold fellow with his Hat on before the Judges, he sells Powder and Shot to the* Indians *and* French, *and lies with the* Indian *Squaes, and has* Indian *Papooses. Then was* Aldin *committed to the Marshal's Custody, and his Sword taken from him; for they said he afflicted them with his Sword. After some hours* Aldin *was sent for to the Meeting-house in the Village before the Magistrates; who required* Aldin *to stand upon a Chair, to the open view of all the People.*

The Accusers cried out that Aldin *did pinch them, then, when he stood upon the Chair, in the sight of all the People, a good way distant from them, one of the Magistrates bid the Marshal to hold open* Aldin's *hands, that he might not pinch those Creatures.* Aldin *asked them why they should think that he should come to that Village to afflict those persons that he never knew or saw before? Mr.* Gidney *bid* Aldin *confess, and give glory to God;* Aldin *said he hoped he should give glory to God, and hoped he should never gratifie the Devil; but appealed to all that ever knew him, if they ever suspected him to be such a person, and challenged any one, that could bring in any thing upon their own knowledge, that might give suspicion of his being such an one. Mr.* Gidney *said he had known* Aldin *many Years, and had been at Sea with him, and always look'd upon him to be an honest Man, but now he did see cause to alter his judgment;* Aldin *answered, he was sorry for that, but he hoped God would clear up his Innocency, that he would recall that judgment again, and added that he hoped that he should with* Job *maintain his Integrity till he died. They bid* Aldin *look upon the Accusers, which he did, and then they fell down.* Aldin *asked Mr.* Gidney, *what Reason there could be given, why* Aldin's *looking upon him did not strike him down as well; but no reason was given that I heard. But the Accusers were brought to* Aldin *to touch them, and this touch they said made them well.* Aldin *began to speak of the Providence of God, in suffering these Creatures to accuse Innocent persons, Mr.* Noyes *asked* Aldin *why he would offer to speak of the Providence of God, God by his Providence (said Mr.* Noyes*) governs the World, and keeps it in peace; and so went on with Discourse, and stopt* Aldin's *mouth, as to that.* Aldin *told Mr.* Gidney *that he could assure him that there was a lying Spirit in them, for I can assure you that there is not a* *word of truth in all these say of me. But* Aldin *was again committed to the Marshal, and his Mittimus written, which was as follows.*

To Boston Aldin *was carried by a Constable, no Bail would be taken for him; but was delivered to the Prison-keeper, where he remained Fifteen Weeks; and then observing the manner of Tryals, and Evidence then taken, was at length prevailed with to make his Escape, and being returned, was bound over to Answer at the Superiour Court at* Boston, *the last* Tuesday *in* April, Anno, 1693. *And was there cleared by Proclamation, none appearing against him.*

Per. John Aldin.

Notes: Calef introduces this as "Mr. Aldin himself has given account of his Examination, in these Words." The ending of "Per. John Aldin," further supports the probability that although this narrative appears in the third person, Alden himself either narrated it or wrote it. He was examined on May 31, and although this account was obviously written much later, it is placed here to coincide with his examination date. He was cleared on April 25, 1693. See No. 837. A mittimus copied and used by Calef in the narrative has been extracted and shown separately. See No. 252.

Robert Calef. More Wonders of the Invisible World, Display'd in Five Parts. *(London: Nath. Hillard, 1700), pp. 98–100.*

235. Examination of Martha Carrier

[Hand 1] The Examination of Martha Carrier. 31. May. <u>1692</u>

Abigail Williams, w° hurts you?
Goody Carrier of Andover.
Eliz: Hubbard who hurts you?
Goody Carrier
Susan: Sheldon, who hurts you?
Goody Carrier, she bites me, pinches me, & tells me she would cut my throat, if I did not signe her book.
Mary Walcot said she afflicted her & brought the book to her.
What do you ^{say} to this you are charged with?
I have not done it:
Sus: Sheldon cried she looks upon the black man.
Ann Putman complained of a pin stuck in her.
What black man is that?
I know none
Ann Putman testifyed there was.
Mary Warren cryed out she was prickt.
What black man did you see?
I saw no black man but your own presence.
Can you look upon these & not knock them down?
They will di⟨ssem⟩ble if I look upon them
You see you look upon them & they fall down.
It is false the Devil is a liar.
I lookt upon none since I came into the room but you.
Susan: Sheldon cryed out in a Trance I wonder what could you murder .13. persons?
Mary Walcot testifyed the same that there lay .13. Ghosts
All the afflicted fell into most intollerable out-cries & agonies.

May 31, 1692   Eliz: Hubbard & Ann Putman testifyed the same that she had killed 13. at Andover.

It is a shamefull thing that you should mind these folks that are out of their wits.

Do not you see them?

If I do speak you will not beleive me?

You do see them, said the accusers.

You lye, I am wronged.

There is the black man whispering in her ear said many of the afflicted.

Mercy Lewes in a violent fit, was well upon the exam⟨i⟩nants grasping her arm.

The Tortures of the afflicted was so great that there was no enduring of it, so that she was ordered away & to be bound hand & foot with all expedition the afflicted in the mean while almost killed to the great trouble of all spectators Magistrates & others.

Note. As soon as she was well bound they all had strange & sodain ease.

Mary Walcot told the Magistrates that this woman told her she had been a Witch this .40. yeares.

[Reverse] [Hand 2] Martha Carrie^{εs} Examina͞con
[Hand 3] Carrier

Notes: Martha Carrier was 38 years old, her age inconsistent with Mary Walcott's invention. ◊ Hand 1 = Samuel Parris

Essex County Court Archives, vol. 1, no. 311, Massachusetts Supreme Judicial Court, Judicial Archives, on deposit James Duncan Phillips Library, Peabody Essex Museum, Salem, MA.

236. Deposition of Elizabeth Hubbard v. Martha Carrier‡

See also: July 1, 1692 & Aug. 3, 1692.

[Hand 1] The deposistion of Eliz: Hubburd agged about 17 years who testifieth and saith that I haue been a long time afflected by a woman that tould me hir name was Carrier and that she came from Andevovr but on the 31: may 1692 martha Carrier did most greviously tortor me dureing the time of hir Examination for if she did but look upon me she would strick me down or almost choak me and also I saw martha Carrier most greviously torment mary walcott mercy lewes Abigail williams and ann putnam junr with such dreadfull tortor as no tongue can express: that had not the Honr^d Majestrats commanded hir to be fast bound I beleue she would haue quickly kiled sume of us: and I verily beleue in my hart that martha Carrier is a most dreadfull wicth for seuerall times sence martha caririe [2nd "r" written over "e"] {or hir Apparenc} has been in prison she hath ^{or hir Apperance} com to me and most greviously tortored me by pinching pricking and and almost choaking me to death: which I beleue she could not doe if she ware not a wicth
[Hand 2] Elizabeth Hubburd: owned: ye above written evidence: to be ye truth: to ye Jury of inquest: upon: ye oath: she hath taken: July:1: 1692

[Hand 3] Jurat in Curia

[Reverse] [Hand 4] elizabeth hubard

Notes: The assignment of May 31 as the first use of this document is speculative. Arguing against such an assignment is the comment by Elizabeth Hubbard that Martha Carrier afflicted her while in prison. For an assignment of May 31 as the date of first use, the part before Carrier's imprisonment would have to have been written after May 31, the date of her examination. Since the document conforms so much to similar examination documents, the speculation is that it was first written immediately after the examination when Carrier was indeed in prison. Its use on July 1 is certain. ◊ Used at trial. ◊ Hand 1 = Thomas Putnam; Hand 2 = Simon Willard; Hand 3 = Stephen Sewall

Witchcraft Papers, no. 17a, Massachusetts Historical Society. Boston, MA.

237. Deposition of Mary Walcott v. Martha Carrier‡

See also: July 1, 1692 & Aug. 3, 1692.

[Hand 1] The deposistion of mary walcott agged about 18 years who testifieth and {saith} that I haue ben a long time afflected by a woman which tould me hir name was carrier and that she came from Andevor but on the 31ᵗʰ may 1692: martha Carrier of Andeuer did most greviously torment me dureing the time of hir Examination by biting pricking pinching and allmost choakin⟨g⟩ me to death for if she did but look upon me she would strik me down or allmost choak me to death also on the day of hir Examination I saw martha Carrier most greviously torment and afflect mercy lewes Elizabeth Hubburd abigail williams and ann putnam jur by most dreadfully pricking and claping hir hand on their throats and allmost choaking them to death and with such cruell tortors as no toung can Express: that had not The Honᵉ majestrats command hir to be bound fast {heart} I beleue ʌ{I belieue} she would haue quickly kild sum of us: and I beleue in my ha{e}rt that martha ʌ{carrier} is a most dreadfull wicth and that she hath tormented me and the parsons affore named by hir acts of wicthcraf

[Hand 2] Mary Walcot owned: to: yᵉ Jury of inquest that yᵉ above written evidence: is yᵉ truth: upon yᵉ oath she hath taken: July 1: 1692

[Hand 3] Jurat in Curia

[Reverse] [Hand 4] Depostion of Mary Walcott
[Hand 5] Mary Walcot

Notes: The confidence level of the May 31 dating is reduced because of the uncertainty regarding the deposition of Elizabeth Hubbard, probably first used at the same time as this one. See No. 236. ◊ Used at trial. ◊ Hand 1 = Thomas Putnam; Hand 2 = Simon Willard; Hand 3 = Stephen Sewall

Witchcraft Papers, no. 17b, Massachusetts Historical Society. Boston, MA.

238. Statement of Susannah Shelden v. Giles Cory, Elizabeth Procter, Sarah Buckley, & John Willard [?]

[Hand 1] Susanna. Shelden saith yᵗ yᵉ spectre of [1 word overstruck] Giles Corey Murdered his first wife & would haue murdered this to only she if she had not been a Witch yᵗ his first wife ⟨g⟩aue him nothing but skim Milke. {& yʳfor s⟨o⟩e} he did it & yᵗ Goody Procters spectre told her she Murdered her owne child & yᵗ it was sick & she did it because she would not be troubled wᵗʰ it & yᵗ she allsoies ["so" written over "waies"] saies yᵗ Goody Buckley & Jnu Willard appᵈ wᵗʰ Hen. Wilkins appᵉ

[Reverse] [Hand 2] [Lost] Shelden

May 31, 1692   Notes: The date assignment is speculative. John Willard was the latest of the group to be arrested, this on May 18. See No. 156. Because of the number of claims made on May 31, including testimony against Elizabeth Procter, this document is assigned here. ◊ Hand 1 = Stephen Sewall

Essex County Court Archives, vol. 2, no. 90, Massachusetts Supreme Judicial Court, Judicial Archives, on deposit James Duncan Phillips Library, Peabody Essex Museum, Salem, MA.

239. Deposition of Mercy Lewis v. Martha Cory‡

[Hand 1] The Deposistion of Mircy lewes ^{agged about 19 years} who ^[caret overstruck] testifieth and saith that I veryly beleue I was bewiched by gooddy Cory on the: 14ᵗʰ of March 1691/92 for she then came to the house of Thomas putnam to se ann putnam whom I was atending and I was Immediatly taken whill gooddy ^{Cory} was their: and Ann putnam said she {se} gooddy Cory bewich me: but I could not se parfitly who they ware that hurt me tell the 26ᵗʰ of march and sence that I haue often seen the Apperish⟨t⟩tion of gooddy Cory com and afflect me by biting pinching and almost choaking me urging me vehemently to writ in hir book allso ["ll" written over "s"] I was most dreadfully tortored whill martha Cory was in Examination being the 21 march and Mary walcott and Elizabeth Hubburd said th{a}y ^{saw} the Apperishtion of martha Cory tortor me: and I beleue in my heart that martha Cory is a most dreadfull wicth and yᵗ she hath very often affletid me a seuerall othrs by hir acts of wicthcraft

[Reverse] [Hand 2] Mercy. Lewis against Martha Cory

Notes: The ink changes with ": and I beleue in my heart....", indicating Thomas Putnam's later entry. ◊ Hand 1 = Thomas Putnam; Hand 2 = Jonathan Corwin

Witchcraft Papers, no. 22a, Massachusetts Historical Society. Boston, MA.

240. Testimony of Abigail Williams v. Martha Cory

[Hand 1] The testimony of Abigail Williams Witnesseth & saith that divers times in the months of March last past particularly .14. 20. 21. & 23. dayes of that month, & also in the month of April Last past at several times, particularly on the .12. 13. & .14. dayes of that month she the said Abigail was much disquieted by the apparition of Martha Kory, by which apparition she was somtimes haled to & fro, & somtimes pinched, & somtimes tempted to put her hand to the Devils book, & that she hath several times seen her at the Devils Sacrament.
[Hand 2] May 31ˢᵗ 1692, attested before

[Reverse] [Hand 1] Abig: Williams agsᵗ Martha Kory

Notes: Stephen Sewall's involvement, noting the date the testimony was attested to, suggests a connection of this record with the Court of Oyer and Terminer, but no further steps appear to have been taken against Martha Cory at this time. ◊ Hand 1 = Samuel Parris; Hand 2 = Stephen Sewall

Witchcraft Papers, no. 16b, Massachusetts Historical Society. Boston, MA.

241. Examination of Elizabeth How

[Hand 1] The Examination of Eliz: How .31. May. <u>1692</u>

Mercy Lewes & Mary Walcot fell in a fit quickly after the Examinant came in
Mary Walcot said that this woman the examinant had pincht her & choakt thi[Lost] [= this] month. Ann Putman said she had hurt her three times.
What say you to this charge? Here are them that charge you ~~of~~ ^{with} Witchcraft
~~If(?)~~ If it was the last moment I was to live, God knows I am innocent of any thing in this nature
Did not you take notice that now when you lookt upon Mercy Lewes she was struck du[Lost] [= dumb]
I cannot help it.
You are chargid here, what doe you say?
I am innocent of any thing of this natur⟨e⟩.
Is this the first time that ever you were accused?
Yes Sʳ
Do not you know that one at Ipswitch hath accused you?
This is the first time that ever I heard of it
You say that you never heard of these folks before.

Mercy Lewes at length spake, & charged this woman with hurting & pinching her: And then Abigail Williams cryed she hath hurt me a great many times, a great while & she hath brought ~~the~~ me the book.
Ann Putman had a pin stuck in her hand
What do you say to this?
I cannot help it.
What consent have you given?
Mary Warren cryed out she was prickt
Abig. Williams cryed out that she was pincht, & great prints were seen in her arm
Have not you seen some apparition?
No, never in all my life
Those that have confessed, they tell us they used images & pins, now tell ⟨us⟩ what you have used.
You would not have me confess that which I know not
She lookt upon Mary Warren, & said Warren violently fell downe.
Look upon this maid viz: Mary Walcot, her back being towards the Examinant
Mary Warren & Ann Putman said they saw this woman upon her.
Susan: Sheldon saith this was the woman that carryed her yesterday to the Pond
Sus: Sheldon carried to the Examinant in a fit & was well upon grasping her arm.
You said you never heard before of these people
Not before the warrant was served upon me last sabbath day
John Indian cryed out Oh she bites, & fell into a grievous fit, & so carried to her in his fit & was well upon her grasping him.
What do you say to these things, they cannot come to you?
Sʳ I am not able to give ac⟨c⟩ount of it

May 31, 1692

Cannot you tell what keeps them off from your body?

I cannot tell, I know not what it is?

That is strange that you should do these things & not be able to tell how.

This a true account of the examination of Eliz: How taken from my characters ^{written} at the time thereof Witness my hand Sam: Parris

[Reverse] [Hand 2] Eliza. How Exam̄

Adjour^t
June .30 92.

[Hand 3] How

Notes: "June .30." was the day of How's trial. ◊ Hand 1 = Samuel Parris ◊ Facsimile Plate 2.

Essex County Court Archives, vol. 1, no. 322, Massachusetts Supreme Judicial Court, Judicial Archives, on deposit James Duncan Phillips Library, Peabody Essex Museum, Salem, MA.

242. Deposition of Sarah Bibber v. Elizabeth How†
See also: June 30, 1692.

[Hand 1] the depozition of sarah beber aged 36 year testifieths and saith. the day that elizabeth how. was examnd I saw her hurt elizabeth hubbort and ann putna{m} and abegel williams. and emediately. she fell apon me and Choked {me} and thru me down and hurt one of my leags. uery. much. [Hand 2] and elizabeth how did aflicte mary walcot seuarall tims. and one the day of har examination
[Hand 3] Sarah. Vibber: owned to yᵉ Jury of inquest: yᵉ above written to be a true evidence of hers:: upon oath: June: 30ᵗʰ 1692

[Hand 4] Jurat in Curia

[Reverse] Sarah Vibbe

Notes: Used at trial. ◊ Hand 1 = Edward Putnam; Hand 3 = Simon Willard; Hand 4 = Stephen Sewall

Witchcraft Papers, no. 22b, Massachusetts Historical Society. Boston, MA.

243. Deposition of Joseph Safford v. Elizabeth How & Bridget Bishop‡
See also: June 30, 1692.

[Hand 1] ⟨T⟩he deposishtion of Joseph safford aeged ab⟨o⟩ut 60 he testefyeth and saith ⟨t⟩[Lost]⟨t⟩ [= that] my wife wa⟨s⟩ much afr[Lost]⟨d⟩ [= afraid] of Elisabeth how {the wife of Jams [Lost]w [= How]} upon the Reports that were of her about Samuell Perlleys Child but apon a tim after th⟨e⟩s Reportes Jams how and his wife Coming to my hous⟨e⟩ J̶a̶m̶ neither myselfe nor my wife were at home and goodwife how asked my Chi⟨ldr⟩en wher ther

May 31, 1692

mother w⟨a⟩[Lost] [= was] and thay said at the next [Lost]gbouers [= neighbour's] hous she disired them Coll ther mother which thay did: when my wife ca⟨m⟩ whom my wife told me that she was much startled to s⟨e⟩ goode how but she took her by the hand and said go⟨o⟩[Lost] [= goody] Safford I beliue that you are not ignorant [Lost] [*SWP* = of the] g⟨r⟩ete scandall: that I Ly under upon the evill Report that is Raised upon me about Samuell Perlleys ch⟨i⟩ld and other things Joseph Safford saith that affter this his wife wa⟨s⟩ ⟨t⟩e⟨k⟩en beyond Rason and all parswasion to tek the part of this woman after this the wife of this Jams how propounded ⟨h⟩erselfe to com into the chu⟨rc⟩h of ⟨Ips⟩wich wher upon sum objection arose by sum unsa⟨ti⟩sfied ⟨bre⟩tharen wher upon ⟨t⟩her was a meeting apinted b⟨y⟩ our elders of the church to Considar ⟨i⟩f ⟨things⟩ brought in again[Lost] [= against] her my wife was more then orde⟨n⟩ery ernist to goe to L[Lost]r [= lecture] th⟨e⟩ church mee⟨ti⟩ng being on that day notwithstanding the meny arguments I used to perswed her; to the contrery: yet I obtained a promis of her that shee would not goe to the ch⟨urc⟩h meeting but meeting with som of the naybourhood thay persweded her to go with them to the church meeting at eldar pains and ~~t⟨h⟩~~ told her that shee need say nothing ther: but goodwife how then being Rether Rendred guilty then cleered my wife took here by the hand after meeting and told her though shee wer condemned before men shee was Justefyed befor god: the next Saboth after this ["i" written over "e"] my son that caried my wife to Lectur was teken aftar a strang manar: the Satarday. aftar that my wife was teken aftar a Reuing franzy manar expresing in a Reging manar that goode how must Com into the church and that shee was a precious saint and though shee wer Condemned befor men shee was Justefyed befor god and Continued in this frem for the spece of thre or four hours aftar that my wife fell into a kind of a tranc for {the} spec of two or thre mi⟨n⟩[Lost]ts [= minutes]

[Reverse] shee then Coming to herselfe opened har ays and said t[Lost] [= that] ⟨I⟩ w⟨as⟩ ⟨m⟩[Lost]eken [= mistaken]: no answ⟨a⟩[Lost] [= answer] ⟨w⟩as med by the standars by: and ⟨a⟩gai⟨n⟩ shee ~~she~~ said ha I w⟨a⟩s misteken: majar appletons w⟨i⟩fe standing by said: wherin art misteken: I was misteken said she for I thought goode h⟨o⟩w had bene a precious saint of god but now I see shee is a witch for she hath bewitched mee and my Child and we s[Lost]ll [= shall] neuer be well till theer ⟨i⟩s te⟨st⟩emoney for her that she ⟨m⟩[Lost]⟨y⟩ [= may] be teken into the church⟨:⟩ [Lost]⟨f⟩ter [= after] this ther was a meeting of t⟨h⟩e eldars at my hous and thay [Lost]sird [= desired] that g⟨o⟩ode how might be at the meeting. insign wallis ⟨w⟩ent⟨e⟩ with myselfe to inuit goode how to this meeting. she c[Lost] [*SWP* = coming] in discours at that tim shee said two or thre tims shee w⟨a⟩s ⟨s⟩ory to se my wife at the church meeting at eldar pa⟨i⟩ns af⟨te⟩r ⟨t⟩hi⟨s⟩ she said she⟨e⟩ was aflicted by: the aparishtion of goode ho⟨w⟩ [Lost] a few days after shee was teken shee said the cous of h⟨e⟩r Changing her apinion co⟨n⟩sar⟨nin⟩g goode how was becaus she⟨e⟩ ape⟨a⟩rd to her throug a creuic ⟨o⟩f ⟨t⟩he clambouerds which she knew no good person cowld do and at thre seuerall tims after was aflicted by the aperishtion ⟨of⟩ ⟨g⟩oode how and goode olleuer
and furder this deponit s[Lost] [= says] ⟨t⟩hat R[Lost]⟨sin⟩g [= rising] erlly in the moring and kindl⟨i⟩{ng} ⟨a⟩ fir in the other Room ⟨mi⟩ wife shricked out I presently Ran into the Rom wher my wife was and a⟨s⟩ ⟨s⟩on as euer I opened the dore m⟨y⟩ [Lost] said ther b⟨e⟩ ⟨th⟩e euill ons teke [Lost]m [= them] whervpon I Replyed whe[Lost] [= where] are thay I will teke them if I can shee said you w⟨i⟩ll not ⟨tek⟩ the[Lost] [= them] and then sprang out of the bed herselfe and went to the wi[Lost]ow [= window] and said ther thay went out th⟨a⟩y wer both biger then she and thay went out ther but shee c⟨o⟩uld not: then I Replyed

who be thay she said goode how and go⟨od⟩e olleuer. goode olleuer said I you nauer saw the womon in you⟨r⟩ Life no said she I neuer saw her in my Life but so she is Represented to me goode olleuer of Sallam that hurt william stace of Sallam the mill⟨ar⟩

[Hand 2] Joseph Safford declared to yᵉ Jury of inquest: that: yᵉ evidence above written: & on yᵉ other side ⟨o⟩f this paper is yᵉ truth upon oath June: 30ᵗʰ 1692
[Hand 3] Jurat in Curia
Joseph Safford

Notes: Elizabeth How was examined on May 31 (see No. 241), and the reference in this document to Bridget Bishop ("goode olleuer"), who had been executed by the time of Elizabeth How's grand jury date, suggests that this document was first used at the examination of How on May 31, prior to the trial of Bridget Bishop. Other June 30 documents against Elizabeth How, preceding this one, may also have been used on May 31. It remains possible though less likely, however, that the document was created only for June 30 with the Bridget Bishop reference made after her execution. ◊ Used at trial. ◊ "ha": This may be an expression of laughter or it may be a variant spelling of *how*. "clambouerds": 'clapboards'(?) (*OED* s.v. *clapboard*). Henry Alexander, "The Language of the Salem Witchcraft Trials," *American Speech* 3 (1928): 398 suggests that the 'm' is due to influence from *clamp*. ◊ Hand 2 = Simon Willard.

Essex County Court Archives, vol. 1, no. 337, Massachusetts Supreme Judicial Court, Judicial Archives, on deposit James Duncan Phillips Library, Peabody Essex Museum, Salem, MA.

Sworn Before a Justice of the Peace: Deposition of Ann Putnam Sr. v. Martha Cory & Rebecca Nurse, and Testimony of Ann Putnam Jr. v. Rebecca Nurse, Martha Cory & Sarah Cloyce
2ⁿᵈ of 3 dates. See No. 30 on March 24, 1692

244. Testimony of Abigail Williams v. Rebecca Nurse & Sarah Cloyce
See also: June 3, 1692.

[Hand 1] The testimony of Abigail Williams witnesseth & saith that divers times in [Lost] [*Woodward* = the month] of March last past, particularly on the .15 .16 .19 .20 .21 .23 .31. dayes of that m[Lost] [= month and] in the month of April following at severall times, particularly on the 13. & 1[Lost] [*Woodward* = 1⟨?⟩ of] that month, & also in this present month of May, the .4ᵗʰ .& .29. dayes, sh[Lost] [*Woodward* = she the said] Abigail has been exceedingly perplexed with the apparition of Rebek[Lost] [*Woodward* = Rebecka Nurse of] Salem Village, by which apparition she hath been pulled violently [Lost] [*Woodward* = and] often pinched & almost choaked, & tempted somtimes to leap into the [Lost] [*Woodward* = fire and] somtimes to subscribe a book the said apparition brought, & als[Lost] [*Woodward* = also she saith] that she hath seen this apparition at a sacrament sitting next to [Lost] [*Woodward* = the man?] with an high crowned hat, at the upper end of the Table, & fa[Lost] [*Woodward* = farther saith that] said apparition hath somtimes confessed to her the said Abigail its g[Lost] [*Woodward* = guilt in] committing severall murders together with her sister Cloyse as upon old Goodm: Harwood, Benjᵃ Porter, & Rebek Shepard & said Shepards [Lost] [= child?]
[Hand 2] May 31ˢᵗ 1692 attested before
[Hand 3] abegall williams did one this har testimony [Lost] [*Woodward* = on the] oath which she had taken: to be truth: before u[Lost] [*Woodward* = us the] Juriors of Inqueste this 3. dy of June: 92

[Reverse] [Hand 4] [Lost]gail [= Abigail] Williams
[Hand 5] 4

Notes: *SWP*'s conjectural readings appear to be based on Woodward. The "high crowned hat" is probably from the Swedish trials. The grand jury heard the case of Rebecca Nurse on June 3. The naming of Sarah Cloyce appears incidental to that. ◊ Hand 1 = Samuel Parris; Hand 2 = John Hathorne; Hand 4 = Thomas Newton

Essex County Court Archives, vol. 1, no. 73, Massachusetts Supreme Judicial Court, Judicial Archives, on deposit James Duncan Phillips Library, Peabody Essex Museum, Salem, MA.

245. Testimony of Abigail Williams v. Elizabeth Procter
See also: June 30, 1692.

[Hand 1] The Testimony of Abigail Williams witnesseth & saith that divers times in the month of March last past, particularly on the .14. 21. & .29. dayes of the same month, & also divers times in the month of April last past, particularly, on the 2. & .13. dayes, she the said Abigail hath been greivously vexed with the apparition of Eliz: Proctor the wife of John Proctor of Salem, by which apparition she has been greivously pinched, had also her bowels almost pulled out, by this together with the apparition of Rebekah Nurse, & by the aforesd apparition of Elizabeth Proctor has been tempted by the offer of fine things to subscribe to a book the said apparition tendered her the said Abigail Williams.

The Mark of

A W

Abigail.   Williams.

[Hand 2] May 31: 1692 attested before
[Hand 3] Abigeil Williams owned to ye Jury of inquest: that ye above writen evidence is ye truth:
June 30: 92

[Reverse] [Hand 1] Abig: Williams ag^st Eliz: Procter.
A. W.

Notes: It may be that the May 31 court sessions were in preparation for trials in early June, which were delayed while the implications of Bridget Bishop's conviction and execution were assessed. After June 30 Abigail Williams disappears from the judicial record. ◊ Hand 1 = Samuel Parris; Hand 3 = Simon Willard

Essex County Court Archives, vol. 1, no. 94, Massachusetts Supreme Judicial Court, Judicial Archives, on deposit James Duncan Phillips Library, Peabody Essex Museum, Salem, MA.

246. Testimony of Abigail Williams v. John Procter

[Hand 1] The Testimony of Abigail Williams witnesseth & saith that divers times in the month of April last past & particularly on the .4. 6. ^{eleven} & .13. dayes of the same month, she the said Abigail hath been much vexed with the apparition of John Proctor Senior of Salem Husbandman, by which apparition she the said Abigail hath been often pinch't & otherwise tortured.

May 31, 1692   [Hand 2] May 31. 1692 attested before

[Reverse] [Hand 1] Abig: William⟨s⟩ ags^t John Proctor Senr

Notes: This may have been prepared in anticipation of a trial of John Procter in early June. Why this was not sworn before the grand jury on June 30 is puzzling, since Williams did so against his wife Elizabeth that day. See No. 245. ◊ Hand 1 = Samuel Parris; Hand 2 = John Hathorne

Essex County Court Archives, vol. 1, no. 54, Massachusetts Supreme Judicial Court, Judicial Archives, on deposit James Duncan Phillips Library, Peabody Essex Museum, Salem, MA.

247. Examination of Wilmot Redd

[Hand 1] The examination of Wilmot Redd. [Hand 2] {Wife of Sam͞l Red of marblehed ffisherman.} [Hand 1] 31. May. 1692

When this Examinant was brought in Mercy Lewes Mary Walcot & Abigail Williams fell into fits
Mercy Lewes said this Woman hath Pincht me a great many times.
Mary Walcot sais this Woman brought the Book to her.
Ann Putman jun^E saith she never hurt her, but ~~she hath seen~~ ^{she hath seen} her once upon Mercy Lewes & once upon Mary Walcot the last fast day. Eliz: Hubbard said this Examinant had brought the book to her, & told her she would knock her in the head, if she would not write.
Ann Putman said she brought the Book to her just now
Eliz: Booth fell into a fit, & Mary Walcot & Ann Putman said it was this Woman afflicted her.
Susan: Sheldon was ordered to goe to the Examinant but was knock down before she came to her, & being so carryed to said Redd in a fit, was made well after said Redd had graspt her arm.
Eliz: Hubbard dealt with after the same manner
This Examinant was bid by the Magistrates to Look upon Eliz: Hubbard, & upon the examinants casting her eye upon said Hubbard, she the said Hubbard was knockt down.
Abig: Williams & John Indian being carried to the Examinant in a grevious fit were made Well by her grasping their arms.
This examinant being often urged what she thought these Persons ailed; would reply, I cannot tell.
Then being askt if she did not think they were Bewitcht: she answered I cannot tell And being urged for her opinion in the case
All she would say was: my opinion is they are in a sad condition.

[Reverse] [Hand 2] Willmott Redd Examination
[Hand 1] The Examination of Wilmot Redd

Notes: Hand 1 = Samuel Parris; Hand 2 = Anthony Checkley

Essex County Court Archives, vol. 2, no. 8, Massachusetts Supreme Judicial Court, Judicial Archives, on deposit James Duncan Phillips Library, Peabody Essex Museum, Salem, MA.

May 31, 1692

248. Deposition of Elizabeth Hubbard v. Wilmot Redd†

See also: Sept. 14, 1692.

[Hand 1] The deposistion of Eliz: Hubburd who testifieth and saith that I was a a considerable time afflected by a woman wch tould me hir name was Redd: and that she came from marblehead: but on the 31 may 1692 being the day of the Examination of willmott Redd then I saw that she was ye very same woman that tould me hir name was Redd: and she did most greviously afflect and torment me dureing the time of hir Examination for if she did but look upon me she would strick me down or almost choake me: also on the day of hir Examination I saw willmott Redd or hir Apperance most dreadfully afflect and torment mary walcott Abigaill williams Eliz: Booth and Ann putnam and I beleue that willmott Redd is wicth and that she hath often affleted me and the affore said parsons by acts of wichcraft

[Hand 2] Eliz Hubbert: upon her oath: to ye grand Inquest: to ye truth of ye above written: evidence:; Sept^ε :14: 1692

[Hand 3] Jurat in Curia

[Reverse] [Hand 4] Eliz^a Hobert depo. agst: Willmott Redd

Notes: That Wilmot Redd's case was not heard by a grand jury until the middle of September exemplifies further the continuing puzzle as to what criteria were used for the selection of people to be tried and the timing of those trials. ◊ Used at trial. ◊ Hand 1 = Thomas Putnam; Hand 2 = Simon Willard; Hand 3 = Stephen Sewall; Hand 4 = Anthony Checkley

Essex County Court Archives, vol. 2, no. 12, Massachusetts Supreme Judicial Court, Judicial Archives, on deposit James Duncan Phillips Library, Peabody Essex Museum, Salem, MA.

249. Deposition of Ann Putnam Jr. v. Wilmot Redd†

See also: Sept. 14, 1692.

[Hand 1] The deposistion of Ann putnam who testifieth and saith that I was for a considerable time afflectid by a woman that tould me hir name was Redd and that she came from marblehead but on the 31 May 1692 being the day of the Examination of wilmott Redd then I saw that she was the very same woman that tould me hir name was Redd and she did most greviously torment me dureing the time of hir Examination for if she did but look on me she would strick me down or almost choak me: also on the day of hir Examination I saw willmott Redd or hir Apperan⟨c⟩e most greviously afflet and torment mary walcott Eliz: Hubburd: Eliz: Booth and Abigail williams: and I very beleue that ⟨?⟩ willmott Redd is a wicth and that she has often affletid me and the afforesaid parsons by acts of wicthcraft

[Hand 2] An Putnam ownd y^e truth of y^e above written evidence: to y^e grand Inquest: Sept^ε :14: 1692: upon oath

[Hand 3] Jurat in Curia

May 31, 1692   [Reverse] [Hand 4] An Puttnam Evidence Against Willmott <u>Redd</u>

Notes: Used at trial. ◊ Hand 1 = Thomas Putnam; Hand 2 = Simon Willard; Hand 3 = Stephen Sewall; Hand 4 = Anthony Checkley.

Essex County Court Archives, vol. 2, no. 13, Massachusetts Supreme Judicial Court, Judicial Archives, on deposit James Duncan Phillips Library, Peabody Essex Museum, Salem, MA.

250. Deposition of Mary Walcott v. Wilmot Redd†

See also: Sept. 14, 1692.

[Hand 1] The deposistion of mary walcott who testifieth and saith that I was for a considerable time afflectid by a woman which tould me hir name was Redd: and that she came from marblehead but on the 31: may 1692 being the day of the Examination of willmott Redd then I saw that she was the very same woman that tould me hir name was Redd: and she did most dreadfully afflect and torme⟨t⟩ me dureing the time of hir Examination. for if she did but look upon me she would strick me down or almost choak me: also on the day of hir Examination I saw willmott Redd: or hir Apperance most greviously afflet and torment marcy lewes Eliz: Hubburd ~~Eliz: Booth~~ and Ann putnam and I beleue in my heart that willmott Redd is a wicth and that she has often afflet⟨e⟩d and tormented me & the afforesad parsons by acts of wicthcraft.

                                                            [Hand 2] Jurat in Curia

[Hand 3] Mary: Walcot: upon her oath: Affirmd to y^e grand Inquest y^t y^e above written evidence is y^e truth: Sept^ε 14: 1692

[Reverse] [Hand 4] Mary Walcott Euidence against Willmott <u>Redd</u>

Notes: Used at trial. ◊ Hand 1 = Thomas Putnam; Hand 2 = Stephen Sewall; Hand 3 = Simon Willard; Hand 4 = Anthony Checkley

Essex County Court Archives, vol. 2, no. 11, Massachusetts Supreme Judicial Court, Judicial Archives, on deposit James Duncan Phillips Library, Peabody Essex Museum, Salem, MA.

251. Deposition of Mary Warren v. Wilmot Redd†

See also: Sept. 14, 1692.

[Hand 1] The deposistion of mary warren who testifieth and saith that I canott say that ~~e⟨ur⟩I canot say that~~ willmott Redd eur hurt me but I saw willmott Redd on the 31 may 1692 most: greviously afflect and torment mary walcott Abigaill williams and Eliz: Booth [Hand 2] ^{& Elizabeth Hubbard} [Hand 1] and Ann putnam and I verily beleue in my heart that wilmott Redd is [Hand 2] ^{a} [Hand 1] wicth ^{&} that she has often hurt the aboue said parsons by accts of wicthcraft

[Hand 3] Mary: Warin upon oath: affirmd to y^e grand Inquest: to y^e truth of y^e above written evidence: Sept^ε 14th 1692

[Hand 2] & this day, she hath aflicted this deponant most Greuiously [Hand 4] Jurat in Curia

[Reverse] [Hand 4?] Mary Warren dep° agst Willmot Redd

Notes: Used at trial. ◊ Hand 1 = Thomas Putnam; Hand 2 = John Hathorne; Hand 3 = Simon Willard; Hand 4 = Stephen Sewall.

Essex County Court Archives, vol. 2, no. 10, Massachusetts Supreme Judicial Court, Judicial Archives, on deposit James Duncan Phillips Library, Peabody Essex Museum, Salem, MA.

252. Mittimus for John Alden & Sarah Rice

To Mr. *John Arnold,* Keeper of the Prison in *Boston,* in the County of *Suffolk,*

Whereas Captain John Aldin *of* Boston, *Marriner, and* Sarah Rice, *Wife of* Nicholas Rice of Reding, *Husbandman, have been this day brought before us,* John Hathorn, *and* Jonathan Curwin, *Esquires; being accused and suspected of perpetrating divers acts of Witchcraft, contrary to the form of the Statute, in that Case made and provided; These are therefore in Their Majesties, King* William *and Queen* Marys *Names, to Will and require you, to take into your Custody, the bodies of the said* John Aldin, *and* Sarah Rice, *and them safely keep, until they shall thence be delivered by due course of Law; as you will answer the contrary at your peril; and this shall be your sufficient Warrant. Given under our hands at* Salem *Village, the 31st. of* May, *in the Fourth Year of the Reign of our Sovereign Lord and Lady,* William *and* Mary, *now King and Queen over* England, *&c. Anno. Dom. 1692.*

John Hathorn,   }
                }   Assistants.
Jonathan Curwin }

Notes: The section on this mittimus is part of Calef's entry in Alden's narrative. However, since this portion is copied from a court document it is treated as a separate record here. The manuscript from which Calef copied this is not extant.

Robert Calef. More Wonders of the Invisible World, Display'd in Five Parts. (London: Nath. Hillard, 1700), pp. 98–100.

253. Letter of Thomas Newton to Isaac Addington, with Mittimus v. Sarah Good, Rebecca Nurse, John Willard, John Procter, Elizabeth Procter, Susannah Martin, Bridget Bishop, Alice Parker, & Tituba

See also: May 31, 1692.

[Hand 1] Salem 31: May 1692

Worthy Sᵉ

I have herewith sent you the names of the persons that are desired to be transmitted hither by habeas Corpus & have pᵉsumed to send you a Coppy thereof being more as I pᵉsume ~~were~~ accustomed to that practise then yoᵉselfe and beg pardon if I have infringed vpon you therein, I fear we shall not this weeke try all that we have sent for, by reason the tryalls will be tedious, & the afflicted persons cannot readily give their testimonyes, being

May 31, 1692   struck dumb & senceless for a season at the name of the accused, I have been all this day at the village with the Gent⟨ᵐ⟩ of the Council at the Exaicon of 7: persons where I have beheld most strange things scarce credible but to the spectatoᵉˢ ⟨and⟩ too tedious here to relate, and amongst the rest Capᵗ Alden & Mᵉ English have their Mittimus & I must say according to the pᵉsent appearance of things, they are as deeply concerned as the rest, for the afflicted spare no person of what quality soever neither conceale their Crimes tho: never soe hainous, we pray that Tittuba the Indian & M̄ᵉˢ Thatchers maid may be transferred as Evidences but desire they may not come amongst the prison̄ᵉˢ but r⟨a⟩ther by themselves with the records in the Court of Assig̅ˢᵗˢ 1679. agᵗ Bridgett Olliver & the records relating to the first persons com̄itted left in Mᵉ Webbs hands by the order of the Council I pray pardon that I cannot now further enlarge & with my Cordiall service only add that I am

                                          Sᵉ

                                    Yoᵉ most humble servᵗ
                                    Tho: Newton

William & Mary by the Grace of God of England Scottland ffrānce & Ireland King & Queen defend̄ᵉˢ of the faith &c To our sherriffe of our County of Suffolke Greeting We Comānd you that the bodyes of Sarah Good the wife of William Good of Salem farmes husb: ~~Rebec⟨?⟩~~ Rebeckah Nurse the wife of ffrāncis Nurse of Salem Village husb̄. John Willard of the same place husb̄ John Procter of Salem farmes husb̄. Elizabeth his wife Susanna ^{Martin of} Almesbury widdow Bridgett Bishop āls Olliver the wife of Edwᵈ Bishop of Salem sawyer Alice Parker the wife of John Parker of Salem seaman & Tittuba Indian in our prison vndᵉ yoᵉ Custody as it is said detained together with the day & Cause of the taking & detaining of the s̄ᵈ Sarah &c you have before our Justices of our Court of Oyer & Terminer to be held at Salem on thursday the second day of June next for the County of Essex to do & receive what the same our Justices then & there shall thereof consider in that bhaffe [= behalf] & have with you then & there this writt wittness Wᵐ Stought⟨on⟩ Esqᵉ the 31ˢᵗ day of May in the ffourth year of our Reigne

                                    Addington

[Reverse] These To Isaac Addington Esqᵉ at Boston
post hast   pᵉsent

[Hand 2] Mʳ Tho: Newton.
May: 3̄1° 1692.

Notes: Of the seven examinations mentioned for May 31, records for four of them survive: John Alden (in Calef), Martha Carrier, Elizabeth How, and Wilmot Redd. The evidence from the returns strongly suggests that the other three were Philip English, William Procter, and Sarah Rice. Thomas Newton was Attorney General, Isaac Addington was Secretary of the Province. Christopher Webb was an attorney and clerk. Why Newton wanted Tituba and Mrs. Thatcher's maid sent separately is not clear, but certainly warrants further research, as does the interest in the 1679 documents. Others against whom testimony was heard on May 31 include Sarah Cloyce, Rebecca Nurse, and Elizabeth and John Procter. These people, however, were in jail in Boston. The document strongly supports the idea that at some point various trials were planned for early June. Of the nineteen people hanged in the Salem witch trials seven are named in this document. An eighth, Elizabeth Procter, was condemned but survived because of her pregnancy. ◊ "post hast": 'with all possible haste or expedition' (OED s.v. post-haste adv). ◊ Hand 1 = Thomas Newton ◊ 1 wax seal.

Massachusetts Archives Collection, vol. 135, no. 25. Massachusetts State Archives. Boston, MA.

Unknown Date in May 1692

254. Petition of Israel Porter et al. for Rebecca Nurse [?]

[Hand 1] We whos nams Are heareunto subscribed being desiered by goodman nurse to declare what we knowe concerning his wiues conuersation for time past: we cane testyfie to all whom it may co{n}cerne that we haue knowne her for: many years and Acording to our obseruation her Life and conuersation was Acording to hur ["ur" written over "er"] profession and we neuer had Any: cause or grounds to suspect her of Any such thing as she is nowe Acused of

Israel Porter	Samuell Sibly
Elizibeth porter	heph⟨z⟩ibah Rea
Edward beshep {sen}	Daniell Andrew
hana beshep	sara andrew
Jo⟨s⟩hua Rea	Jonathan Putnam
Sarah Rea	lydia putnam
Sarah leach	Walter Phillipps senior
John putnam sen	Nathaniel ffellton Sen:
Rebeckh putnam	margaret Philips
Joseph hucheson sen	T⟨a⟩itha phillipps
leada hucheson	Joseph houlton Junior
Joseph holten sen	Sam^ll Endecott
sarah holten	Elzibeth buxtston ["s" written over "o"]
beniaman putnam	samuel aborn senr
sarah putnam	Isaack Cooke
Job Swinerton	Elisabeth Cooke
Esther Swinerton	William Osborne
Joseph herrick sen	hanah osborne
Daniell Rea	Joseph Putman ⟨?⟩
Sar{a}h putnam	

Notes: The document was written and first signed no later than May 14, when Daniel Andrew, a signatory, fled. The ink changes suggest that the document was signed by others over a period of time. It was probably not used at the trial of Rebecca Nurse, since a petition with the name of Daniel Andrew on it would work against her. She was arrested on March 23, and no good evidence can place the dating for this anywhere except between March 23 and May 14. The document is placed in May simply because it is the latest plausible month when it could have been written unless it was used at the trial of Rebecca Nurse in spite of carrying the name of Daniel Andrew.

Witchcraft Papers, no. 30, Massachusetts Historical Society. Boston, MA.

June 1692

Wednesday, June 1, 1692

255. Deposition of Abigail Hobbs, Deliverance Hobbs, & Mary Warren v. George Burroughs, Sarah Good, Sarah Osburn, Bridget Bishop, Giles Cory, Rebecca Nurse, Elizabeth Procter, Alice Parker, Ann Pudeator, Abigail Soames, John Procter, & Lydia Dustin

[Hand 1] 1st June 1692

Abigaile Hobbs then confessed before John Hathorn Jonathan Corwin Esq$^{\varepsilon}$ There at the generall meeting of the Witches in the feild near Mr Parrisses' house she saw M$^{\varepsilon}$ George Burroughs, Sarah Good, Sarah Osborne Bridgett Bishop a$\overline{ls}$ Olliver & Giles Cory, two or three nights agone. Mr Burroughs came & sat at the window & told her he would terribly afflict her, for saying so much ag^t him & then pinched her, Deliverance Hobbs then saw s^d Burroughs & he would have tempted her to sett her hand to the book & almost shooke her to pieces because she would not doe it,

Mary Warren Testifyeth that when she was in prison in Salem about a fortnight agone Mr George Burroughs, Goody Nurse Goody Procter, Goody Parker, Goody Pudeator, Abigail Soames, Goodman Procter ^{Goody Dasting & others vnknowne} came to this depon^t &. M$^{\varepsilon}$ Burroughs had a trumpett & sounded it, & they would have had this depon^t to have gone vp with them to a feast at M$^{\varepsilon}$ Parrisses & Goody Nurse & Goody Procter told her this depon^t they were Deac$\overline{ons}$ & would have had her eat some of their sweet bread & wine. & asking them what wine that was one of them said it was blood & better then our wine but this depon^t refused to eat or drink with them & they then dreadfully afflicted her at that time. Sworne the first of June 1692

Before vs

John Hathorne

Jonathan. Corwin
} Assis^{ts}

[Hand 1] M^d [= memorandum] that at the time of her taking of this deposicon Goody Nurse appeared in the roome & afflicted the Depon^t Mary & Deliverance Hobbs as they attested & alsoe almost Choaked Abigaile Hobbs as alsoe testified, & Mr English then run a pin into Maryes hand as she attested

[Reverse] [Hand 2] Abigail Hobs and Mary Warren and Geo. Burroughs

Notes: Hand 1 = Thomas Newton; Hand 2 = John Hathorne

Witchcraft Papers, no. 6a, Massachusetts Historical Society. Boston, MA.

256. Deposition of Samuel Perley & Ruth Perley v. Elizabeth How, and List of Witnesses v. Elizabeth How

See also: June 30, 1692.

June 1, 1692

[Hand 1] the first of iune 1692

the deposition of Samuel perley and his wife
aged about 52 an his wife about 46 years of age
we hauing a dafter about ten years of age being in a sorowful condition this ~~faling ought~~
{being} sone after a faling ou⟨t⟩ ["t" written over "g"] that had bene betwen ieams how and
his wife and and miself our daughter tould us that it was ieams hous wife that afflicted her
both night and day som times complainig of being pricked with pins and somtimes faling
doun into dredful fits and often sai i could neuer aflict a dog as goode how aflicts me mi wife
and i did often chide her for naming goode how being loth her name shold be defamed but
our daughter would tel us ~~the⟨w⟩e would tel us~~ that though we would not beleue ~~us~~ {her}
now yet yow wil know it one day ~~me~~ we went to seueral docters and thai tould us that she
was under an euil hand: our ~~daf~~ daughter tould us that when s{h}e came nere the fire or
water this witch puls me in and was often soreli burnt and she would tel us what cloaths she
wore and ~~s⟨a⟩~~ would sai there she goes and there she goes and now she is gone in to the ouen
and after these sights faling doun into dredful fits and thus our daughter continuing {about}
two or three years constantli afirming to the ⟨?⟩ last that this goode how that is now seised
was the cause ~~of~~ of her sorows and so pined awai to scin and bone and ended her sorowful
life, and this we ["we" written over "i"] can atest upon oath

ruth perleys mark   ⟨mark⟩
[Hand 2] Sam^ll Pe⟨a⟩rly ⟨&⟩ his wife decla⟨r⟩es ye above written. to b⟨e⟩ ye truth. upon oath
[Hand 1] after this the aboue said goode how had a mind to ioyn to ipswich Church thai
being unsatisfied sent to us to bring in what we had against her and when we had decleared
to them what we knew thai se cause to put a stop to her coming into the Church
~~withk~~ within a few dais after I had a cow wel in the morning as far as we knew this cow was
taken strangli runing about like a mad thing a litle while and then run in to a great pon [=
pond] ad [= and] drouned her self and ~~when she~~ {as sone as she} was dead mi sons and mi
self towed her to the shore and she stunk so that we had much a doe to flea [= flay] her
[Hand 2] Sam^ll Pearly: ~~and his w~~ declared to: y^e Jury of inquest: that all y^e above written: is
y^e truth: upon oath: June: 30th 92

[Hand 1] as for the time of our daughters being taken ill it was in the yere of our lord 1682

[Hand 3]
other Euidences.
ag^t Goody How

Deacon Cummins wife of Topsfield.
Tho: Heasins wife Box^d
Jos: Andrews & wife Box^d
Jno Sherrin. Ispwich
Jos. Safford of Ispw^ch
Abr. How's wife Tops^d

June 1, 1692

Ab. ffosters wife Ispwich
Francis. Leaue

memorandum
Widow Dutch
& Sam. ⟨S⟩ibley & wife
Against Goody Parker
Euidences. ag^t How

Notes: "Goody Parker" is Alice Parker. The named people presumably presented evidence to the grand jury. No evidence indicates that this document was used at the trial of Elizabeth How, although one can reasonably speculate that the people named here also gave evidence against Elizabeth How when she was tried June 30. ◊ Hand 2 = Simon Willard; Hand 3 = Stephen Sewall

Essex County Court Archives, vol. 1, no. 325, Massachusetts Supreme Judicial Court, Judicial Archives, on deposit James Duncan Phillips Library, Peabody Essex Museum, Salem, MA.

257. Deposition of Timothy Perley & Deborah Perley v. Elizabeth How
See also: June 30, 1692.

[Hand 1] the first of iune 1692.

the deposition of timothi perley and deborah perley his wife timothi perley aged about 39 and his wife about 33
there be{ing} som diferance betwene goode how that is now seised [Hand 2] {namely Elizebeth: How: wife to James How: Jun^ε} [Hand 1] and timothi perli aboue said about some bords the night folowing three of our cous lay out and finding of them the next morning we went to milk them and one of them did not giue but two or thre spoone fuls of milk and one of the other cous did not giue aboue half a pinte and the other gaue about a quart and these cous used to giue three or four quarts at a meale two of thes cous continued to giue litle or nothing four or fiue meals and yet thai went in a good inglesh pasture and within four dais the cous gaue ther ful proportion of milk that thai used to ~~doe~~ giue

furder deborah perley testifieth
a{n}d {and} as conserning hanah perley Samuel perleys daughter that was so sorli aflicted her mother and she coming to our house hanah perley being sudainli scared ~~leaped ouer a chest~~ and said the{r}s that woman she goes into the ouen and out again and then fel in to a dredful fit and when I haue asked her when she said that woman what woman she ment she tould me ieams hows wife sometime hanah perley went along with me to ieams hows an sone fell in to a fit goode how was ueri louing to her and when the garl and I came away i asked her whi she talked so of goode how being she was so louing to her she tould me that ~~if she afflicte~~ if i were aflicted as she was that i would talk as bad ⟨on⟩ of her as she did at another time i saw goode how and hanah perley together and thai were ueri louing together and after goode how was gone i asked her whi she was so louing to good⟨e⟩ how when thai were together she tould me that she was afraid to doe other wise for then goode how would kil her

deborah Perley

[Hand 2] ⟨Th⟩ Timothy Pearly: And ["A" written over "D"] Deborah his wife declared to yᵉ   June 1, 1692
Jury of inquest to all of yᵉ above written Evidence: on this side of this paper: that: it is yᵉ
truth upon oath: June 30ᵗʰ

[Reverse] [Hand 3] De

Notes: "meale," "meals": 'time, occasion' (*OED* s.v. *meal* n², 2). ◊ Hand 2 = Simon Willard

Essex County Court Archives, vol. 1, no. 323, Massachusetts Supreme Judicial Court, Judicial Archives, on deposit James Duncan Phillips Library, Peabody Essex Museum, Salem, MA.

258. Testimony of Sarah Churchill v. Ann Pudeator and Testimony of Mary Warren v. Bridget Bishop, Elizabeth Cary, George Jacobs Sr., & Ann Pudeator.

See also: Sept. 10, 1692.

[Hand 1] Sarah Churchwell confesseth that Goody Pudeater brought the book to this Examinᵗ and she signed it, but did not know her at that tyme but when she saw her she knew her to be the same and that Goody ^{Bishop a̅l̅s} Olliver appeared to this Examinᵗ & told her she had killed John Trasks Child, (whose Child dyed about that tyme) & said Bishop a̅l̅s Olliver afflicted her as alsoe did old George Jacobs, and before that time this Examinᵗ being afflicted could not doe her service as formerly and her sd Master Jacobs called her bitch witch & ill names & then afflicted her as ~~before~~ {above} and that Pudeater brought 3: Images like Mercy Lewis, Ann Putnam, Elizᵃ Hubbard & they brought her th⟨o⟩rnes & she stuck them in the Images & told her the persons whose likeness they were, would be afflicted, & the other day saw Goody Olliver ~~sitt~~ sate vpon her knee,
this Confession was taken before John Hathorne
and Jonathan Corwin Esqᴱˢ 1° Junij 1692, as attests
                    Tho: Newton
                              [Hand 2] Jurat in Curia
                                    by Sarah Churchill

[Reverse] [Hand 1] Mary Warren aged 20: yeares or thereabouts testifyeth & saith That severall times after the Nyneteenth day of April last when Bridgett Bishop a̅l̅s Olliver ⟨who⟩ w⟨a⟩s in the Gaol at Salem she did appear to this deponᵗ tempting her to signe the book & oft times during her being there as aforesᵈ the sᵈ Bridgett did torture & afflic⟨t⟩ this deponᵗ & being in Chaines said tho: she could not do it, she would bring ^{one that} ^{mᴱ} C̶⟨ar⟩y̶ ⟨t⟩⟨o⟩ ^{should} doe ⟨it⟩ {which now {she} knowes ⟨to⟩ be mᴱ Cary that then came & afflicted her,} Sworne before vs the 1. day of June 1692

            John Hathorne ⎫
                           ⎬ Assisᵗˢ
        Jonathan. Corwin   ⎭

[Hand 3?] Sarah Churchw[Lost] [= Churchwell] agᵗ pudeater

June 1, 1692

Notes: Although others are named in the document, this trial document is identified here as directed at Ann Pudeator, since the only notation on it indicates that it belongs to her case. ◊ Used at trial. ◊ Hand 1 = Thomas Newton; Hand 2 = Stephen Sewall

Essex County Court Archives, vol. 1, no. 262, Massachusetts Supreme Judicial Court, Judicial Archives, on deposit James Duncan Phillips Library, Peabody Essex Museum, Salem, MA.

259. Summons for Witnesses v. Rebecca Nurse, and Officer's Return†

[Hand 1] William & Mary by yᵉ Grace of God of England &cᵃ

To Abigall Williams Ann Putnam Mercy Lewis Elizabeth Hubbard Mary Walcott Ann Putnam Senᵉ Susanna Shelden ^{wee Comand} that they & Euery of Them all Excuses Set aside appear ~~at~~ befor thier Majᵗⁱᵉˢ Justices of Court of Oyer & Terminer Holden this present Thursday being {2. June} at Eight of yᵉ Clock in yᵉ Morning to Testifie yᵉ Truth of what they know vpon certain Endictments Exhibited at Our sᵈ Court on behalfe of Our Soueragne agᵗˢ Rebecka Nurse hereof fail not

at your perill   ⎫   Stephen Sewall Cleⁱ
& make return   ⎭
To yᵉ Constable of <u>Salem</u>

[Reverse] [Hand 2] I have summuned the with in written persons
by me John Putnam of Salem constable
[Hand 1] Subpana for Euidences Agᵗ Reb. Nurse

Notes: Hand 1 = Stephen Sewall

Essex County Court Archives, vol. 1, no. 65, Massachusetts Supreme Judicial Court, Judicial Archives, on deposit James Duncan Phillips Library, Peabody Essex Museum, Salem, MA.

260. Summons for Witnesses v. John Willard, and Officer's Return

[Hand 1] William & Mary by yᵉ Grace of God of England [Lost] &a. King &cᵃ.
To Abigall Williams ["iams" written over "ard"] Mary Walcott Susanna Shelden Nathaniil Putnam Ann Putnam Mercy Lewis Greeting: Wee comand you all Excuses laid aside to be & personaly appear ⟨?⟩ befor Our Justices of Court of Oyer & Terminer Held at Salem for yᵉ County of Essex on Thursday yᵉ second of this Instant June at Nine of yᵉ Clock in yᵉ Morning there to Testifie yᵉ Truth of your knowledge vpon certai⟨n⟩ Endictments to be Exhibited at Our said Court ⟨?⟩ agᵗ John Willard of Salem Villiage hereof you are not to fail. 1ˢᵗ June 1692. & in yᵉ fourth year of Our Reigne: Stephen Sewall Cleᵉ
& Benj: Wilkins.
To yᵉ Constable of Salem

[Reverse] Subpena agᵗ Willard

[Hand 2] I haue warned the parsons within Named
℟ me Jonathan putnam Constable in Salem

[Hand 1] <u>Wittnesses</u> agᵗ Jnᵒ Willar⟨d⟩

Notes: It seems likely that the trial of Willard, though eventually delayed, was originally expected in early June. ◊ Hand
1 = Stephen Sewall

June 1, 1692

*Essex County Court Archives, vol. 1, no. 237, Massachusetts Supreme Judicial Court, Judicial Archives, on deposit James Duncan
Phillips Library, Peabody Essex Museum, Salem, MA.*

261. Statement of Sarah Ingersoll & Ann Andrews Regarding Sarah Churchill [?]

[Hand 1] The diposition of Sarah Ingelson Aged about 30 yers: saith that seing Sarah
Church after hur exsamination she Came to me Crieng and wringing hur hands seming to
be mutch trobeled in sparet [= spirit] I asked hur what she ailed she answered she had
undon hur salf I asked hur in what she saied in belieng hur salfe and others in saieng she had
seat hur hand to the diuells Book whair as she saied she nauer did I told hur I beleued she
had saet hur hand to the Book she answered Crieng and saied no no no: I nauer I nauer did I
asked then what had maed hur say she did she answered because thay thratoned hur: and told
hur thay would put hur in to the dongin and put hur along with m^r Borows: and thus sauerall
times she folowed me up and downe tealing me that she had undon hur salfe in belieng hur
salf and others I asked hur why she did ~~not~~ [1–2 words illegible] writ it she tould me because
she had stood out so long in it that now she darst not she saied allso y^t If she told m^r Noys
but ons she had sat hur hand to ye Book he would beleue hur but If she told the truth and
saied she had not seat hur hand to ye Book a hundred times he would not beleue hur:

Sarah Ingrsol
AnnA. AndRusse

Notes: This narrative offers a telling insight into the pressures used to elicit accusations. As Mary Warren struggled not
to accuse the Procters in whose home she was a servant, so Sarah Churchill, servant to George Jacobs Sr., tried not to
implicate him. Both capitulated to the pressures and joined the counterfeiting, pretending to be attacked by spectres,
although Churchill much less so than Warren. Ann Andrews was the daughter of George Jacobs Sr. Pinning down the
date of this document has not succeeded, and it is here placed at its earliest possible time, June 1, when Sarah Churchill
was examined.

*Essex County Court Archives, vol. 2, no. 113, Massachusetts Supreme Judicial Court, Judicial Archives, on deposit James Duncan
Phillips Library, Peabody Essex Museum, Salem, MA.*

262. Testimony of Edward Bishop Jr., Sarah Bishop, & Mary Esty Regarding Mary Warren†

[Hand 1] Edward Bisshop Aiged Aboute 44: Yeares Sarah Bisshop Aiged Aboute 41: yeares
And Mary Eastey Aiged Aboute 56: Yeares all Testifie and say that Aboute three weekes
Agoe to say when wee ~~In~~ was In Salem Goale then and There wee Heard Mary warrin
seuerall Times say that the Majestrates Might as well Examine Keysars Daughter that had
Bin Distracted Many Yeares And take Noatice of what shee said: as well as any of the
Afflicted p^e sons for said/ Ma^e y warrin when I was Aflicted I thought I saw the Apparission
of A hundred persons: for shee said hir Head was Distempered that shee Could Not tell
what shee said, And the said Mary Tould vs that when shee was well Againe shee Could Not
say that shee saw any of the Apparissions at the Time Aforesaid

June 2, 1692

[Reverse] [Hand 2] Edward Bishop Sarah Bishop Mary Eastey dep° as ⟨?⟩ Mary Warrin
[Hand 3] Coppie

Notes: The dating here is based on a claim by Mary English on June 1 indicating that this episode had occurred about a month earlier. See No. 263. Also, the date comes close to three weeks after May 12, the date when the Bishops and others were transferred from Salem jail (see No. 146), and likely on the same day when Mary English testified against Mary Warren. ◊ "to say": 'that is to say' (*OED* s.v. *say* v[1], 4c).

Essex County Court Archives, vol. 1, no. 120, Massachusetts Supreme Judicial Court, Judicial Archives, on deposit James Duncan Phillips Library, Peabody Essex Museum, Salem, MA.

263. Testimony of Mary English Regarding Mary Warren

[Hand 1] 1 June 1692

Mary English Aged about 39 ["9" written over "5"] years Testifyeth that about a Month agoe at Sallem That I heard the Said Mary Warrine to Spake the Same words (as is Testifyed too by Edward Bishop Sarah Bishop And Mary Easty) that She Said that the Majestrats might as well Examen Keysers Daughter that had bene Distracted many years And take Notice of what She Said as well as any of the Eflicted persons &c
as witnes my hand Mary English

[Reverse] [Hand 2] Mary English
[Hand 3] Mary Waren

Notes: The circumstances of this record are puzzling. The Court of Oyer and Terminer was about to begin, and why a person arrested as an accused witch would be giving testimony that appears to be sworn remains unresolved.

Essex County Court Archives, vol. 1, no. 119, Massachusetts Supreme Judicial Court, Judicial Archives, on deposit James Duncan Phillips Library, Peabody Essex Museum, Salem, MA.

Thursday, June 2, 1692

Grand Jury of Bridget Bishop
Trial of Bridget Bishop

264. Oaths of Thomas Newton as Attorney General & Stephen Sewall as Clerk of the Court of Oyer and Terminer

[Hand 1] You Thomas Newton Gen[t] being apointed to perform the Office of their Maj[s] Attorny-Gen[l] in the prosecution of the several persons to be indicted and Tryed before their Maj[s] Justices of Oyer and Terminer now sitting, and from time to time to Sit, by vertue of the Comission now published, and in all other matters that may be requisite in the Execution of the same [   ] Do Swear, that according to your best skill, you will act truly and faithfully on their Majesties behalf, as to Law and Justice doth appertain, without any favour or Affection.
So help you God

[Hand 2] Salem. June 2ᵈ ^{1692} Thomas Newton
tooke the oath abouesayd in open
Court before me
                    Wᵐ: Stoughton.

[Hand 1] You being Appointed to officiat as Clerk of this Court, [   ] Do Swear ~~by the~~ that
you will carefully, uprightly & truly execute and perform whatsoever unto your Duty in that
Place of a Clerk doth appertain
                                        So help you God.

[Hand 2] Salem. June 2ᵈ. 1692
Stephen Sewall in open Court made
oath as aboue to doe the duty of his
place as clerke. coram me
                    Wᵐ Stoughton.

[Reverse] [Hand 3] The Oathes Giuen to Mʳ Tho: Newton & Step. Sewall
[Hand 4] Ju⟨n⟩ 2 1692

Notes: The oaths of Thomas Newton and Stephen Sewall begin the formal phase of the prosecutions that would come
to be known as the Salem Witch Trials. Although other signatures by William Stoughton appear in the records, this is
the only record in this edition that contains a segment of text in Stoughton's handwriting. ◊ Hand 1 = Samuel Sewall;
Hand 2 = William Stoughton; Hand 3 = Stephen Sewall

*Essex County Court Archives, vol. 1, no. 2, Massachusetts Supreme Judicial Court, Judicial Archives, on deposit James Duncan
Phillips Library, Peabody Essex Museum, Salem, MA.*

Complaint of Nathaniel Putnam, Joseph Whipple & Peter Tufts v. Elizabeth Fosdick & Elizabeth Paine

2ⁿᵈ of 2 dates. See No. 229 on May 30, 1692.

265. Warrant for the Apprehension of Elizabeth Fosdick & Elizabeth Paine, and Officers' Returns

See also: June 3, 1692.

[Hand 1] To The Marshall or sheriff of The County of Middlesex or depᵗ:

You are in theire Majesᵗˢ names hereby required to apprehend and bring before vs at Salem.
forthwit⟨h⟩ or as soon as may be: Elizabeth ffosdick the wife of John ffosdick of ~~Charlstown~~
{Maulden} Carpenter. and Elizabeth Paine the wife of ~~William~~ ^{Stephen} Paine of
Charlstownē husbandman, for Sundry acts of Witchcraft by them Committed Lately on yᵉ
Bodys of Marcy Lewis Mary Warren &c of Salem Village or ffarmes. to theire great hurt and
Injury accordᵉ to Complaint Exhibited before vs. appeares. faile not Dated Salem June the
2ᵈ 1692

                              John Hathorne   ⎫
              ℘ vs   ⎬ Assisᵗˢ
                              Jonathan Corwin   ⎭

June 2, 1692

[Hand 2] I doe Appoint Sam^ll Gibson of Cambridge To Serue this warrent To Effect
Sam^ll Gookin Marsh^ll for Mddx

June 2^d 1692
[Hand 3] June 2^d {1692} I haue apprehended the aboue named Elizebeth Paine and
Deliuered her unto the sheriff of the County of Essex att Salem in ye County afores^d in order
to her Examination and waite in Expectation of the aboue s^d Elizabeth Fiosdick by mee
[Hand 4] June 3 92
I haue allso apprehended the body of Elizbeth ffosdick of mauldin & deliu{⟨e⟩}red har to the
aboue said sheriff of Essex.

Sam^ll Gibson y^e mar{sh}
dep⟨t⟩

[Reverse] [Hand 5]
E. J. osdick 29
E Paine. 30

Notes: Hand 1 = John Hathorne; Hand 3 = George Herrick

Essex County Court Archives, vol. 2, no. 16, Massachusetts Supreme Judicial Court, Judicial Archives, on deposit James Duncan Phillips Library, Peabody Essex Museum, Salem, MA.

266. Deposition of Sarah Andrews v. Elizabeth How

[Hand 1] The deposicon of Sarah Andrew of Boxford aged 27. years about Seuen yeares.
Since going to see my Sister Hanah Pearly of Ipswich ffarmes. who was in a Strange
Condicon Sick of fitts & ye Like She told me when she⟨?⟩ came Out of her fitts that it was
Eliz. How [Hand 2] {wife to James How Junr} [Hand 1] of Ipswich ffarmes that Hurtt her
& that she would feign throw her into ye fire & into ye water. & y^t though her father had
Corrected her for charging So pious a woman yet she was sure twas ~~Se~~ true & should stand
to it to her death

Sworn in Court
June. 2^d 1692
attest St: Sewall Cler

Jno Cookes Euidence

[Reverse] Sarah Andrews   Hanah And.
Euidence agt   Contr^a El. How
How

Notes: The deposition makes clear that at the beginning of the Court of Oyer and Terminer sworn testimony was being taken against people who would not be tried till later. It appears that the Court was uncertain at this stage as to whose case would be addressed by a grand jury and when. It is not clear whether this deposition was subsequently used at the trial of Elizabeth How. The taking of such sworn testimony began at the end of May prior to the establishment of the Court of Oyer and Terminer. The name of "John Cook" appears upside down on the manuscript and has no known connection

to the deposition. Cook, 18 years old, testified against Bridget Bishop at her trial. See No. 277. ◊ Possibly used at trial. June 2, 1692
◊ "feign": 'gladly' (*OED* s.v. *fain* a. and adv). ◊ Hand 1 = Stephen Sewall; Hand 2 = Simon Willard

Witchcraft Papers, no. 23a, Massachusetts Historical Society. Boston, MA.

267. Deposition of Ann Putnam Sr. v. Rebecca Nurse, Sarah Cloyce, Sarah Bishop, & Elizabeth Cary‡

[Hand 1] The Deposistion of Ann putnam the wife of Thomas putnam who testifieth and saith that on the first day of June 1692 the Apperishtion of Rebekah ^{nurs} did again fall upon me and almost choak me and she tould me that now she was come out of prison she had power to afflet me and that now she would afflect me all this day long and would kil me if she could for she tould me she had kiled benjamine Holton and John ffuller and ~~re~~ Rebekah shepard: and she also tould me that she and hir sister Cloyes and Ed: Bishops wife of Salem village had kiled young Jn° putnams child because yong Jn° putnam had said y^t it was no wonder they ware wicthes for their mother was so before them and because they could not aveng themselues on him they ~~would~~ {did} kill his child: and Immediatly their did appere to me: six childeren in win⟨d⟩ing sheets which caled me aunt: which did most greviously affright me: and they tould me that they ware my sisters Bakers children of Boston and that gooddy nurs and Mistris Cary of Chalstown and an old deaf woman att Boston had murthered them: and charged me to goe and tell thes things to the majestrats ["a" written over "i"] or elce they would tare me to peaces for their blood did crie for vengance also their Appeared to me my own sister Bayley and three of hir children in winding sheets and tould me that gooddy nurs had murthered them

[Reverse] Ann putnam sen^r against Rebekah n⟨irs⟩

Notes: The reference to Rebecca Nurse being "out of prison" does not mean that she was free. It probably refers to her transfer from Boston jail to Salem in closer proximity to Ann Putnam Sr. At the end of the month, after her trial Rebecca Nurse reportedly did have a brief reprieve from Governor Phips, but it was quickly withdrawn. ◊ Hand 1 = Thomas Putnam

Essex County Court Archives, vol. 1, no. 83, Massachusetts Supreme Judicial Court, Judicial Archives, on deposit James Duncan Phillips Library, Peabody Essex Museum, Salem, MA.

268. Deposition of John Westgate v. Alice Parker

See also: Sept. 7, 1692.

[Hand 1] Jn° Wesgate aged about forty years This deponent Testifieth thatt about Eight years since he being att the house of m^ɛ Sam^ll Beadle In the company of Jn° Parker and severall others, the wife of said Jn° Parker came into the company and scolded att and called her husband all to nought whereupon I the said deponent tooke her husbands part telling of her itt was ~~and~~ vnbeseeming thing for her to come after him ["him" written over "me"] to the taverne and raile after thatt rate wth thatt she came up to me and call'd me rogue and bid me mind my owne busines and told me I had better have said nothing sometimes afterwards I ye s^d deponent going ffrom the house of m^ɛ ~~Th°Beadle~~ {Dan^ll King}, w⟨n⟩ I came over against Jn° Robinsons house I heard a great noyce coming ffrom towards m^r Babage his house then there apeared a black hogg running towards me wth open mouth as though he would have devoured me att thatt {Instant} time I the said deponent ffell downe vpon my hipp and my knife runn into my hipp up to the haft w^n I came home my knife was in my s^{h}eath w^n I drew itt out of the sheath ~~and~~ then imediatly the sheath fell all to peaces, ~~of⟨f⟩~~ and further this deponant Testifieth thatt after he gott up from his fall his stockin and shew was full of blood and thatt he was forc't to craule along by the fence all the way home and the hogg follow'd him ~~all the way home~~ and never left him tell he came home, [Hand 2] and haueing a stout dog then with him ["him" written over "mee"], the dog run then away from him ["him" written over "mee"] Leapeing ouer ye fence and Cryeing much, which at other times vsed to Wory any hog well or sufficiently

[Reverse] which hog I then apprehended, was Either ye Diue⟨l⟩l or some Euell thing not a Reall hog, and did then Really Judge or determine in my mind that it was Either Goody parker or by her meenes {& procureing}, feareing y^t she is a Witch,

Sworne Salem June 2^d 1692
Before John Hathorne Assis^t

[Hand 3] Jno Wastgate declared ye above written & what is written on the other side of this paper to be a true evidence before ye Jury of Inquest upon: ye oath he hath taken: Septem^ε 7: 1692

[Hand 4] Jurat in Curia

[Hand 5] John Westgate ag^t parker
[Hand 6] ~~Mary~~ Parker Alice
[Hand 7?] [2–3 words illegible]

Notes: This record was incorrectly carried in *SWP* in the case of Mary Parker. The crossout of "Mary" suggests confusion between Alice and Mary Parker even in 1692. ◊ Used at trial. ◊ Hand 2 = John Hathorne; Hand 3 = Simon Willard; Hand 4 = Stephen Sewall.

Essex County Court Archives, vol. 2, no. 66, Massachusetts Supreme Judicial Court, Judicial Archives, on deposit James Duncan Phillips Library, Peabody Essex Museum, Salem, MA.

269. Testimony of Ann Putnam Sr. v. John Willard, William Hobbs, & Martha Cory

[Hand 1] Hanah Putnam aged 30 years
{Saith y^t} ye Shape of Sam^ll Fuller & Lidia Wilki⟨n⟩s this day told me at my Owne house by y^e ⟨f?⟩ bed side. ~~y^t~~ who appeared in winding sheets y^t if I did not Goe & tell m^r Hathorne y^t John Willard had Murdered them. they would tare Me ["Me" written over "her"] to peices. I knew y^m when they were liuing & it was Exactly thier resemblance & Shape
& at ye Same Time ye apparic͞on of John Willard told me y^t he had killd Sam^ll Fuller Lidia Wilkins Goody S⟨ha⟩w & Fullers Second wife & Aron Ways Child & Ben: ffullers Child & this deponents Child. Sarah 6 weeks old & Phillips Knights Child wth ye help of Wm Hobbs. & Jonathan Knights ["Knig" written over "Hobbs"] Child & 2 of Ezek: Cheeuers Children with ye help of Wm Hobbs. Anna Elliott & Isack Nicholls wth help of Wm Hobbs:

& y^t if mr Hathorne would not beleiue y^m (ie) Sam. Fuller & Lida Wilkins shaps they would appear to ye Majistrartes

June 2, 1692

ye Same day

Joseph Fullers apparicon also came to me & told me y^t Goody Corey. had Killd him ⟨?⟩ ye Spect⟨o⟩r ^{afors^d} told me y^t vengeance vengeanc was Cried by s^d ffuller

Sworne in Court June 2^d 1692

This Relacon is <u>true</u>

Marke

Ann *aac* Putnam

[Reverse] Ann Putnams Relacon Sworne

Notes: This appears to be sworn testimony in preparation for presentation to grand juries. Willard's case was heard by a grand jury the next day. Martha Cory's case was heard on August 4. William Hobbs was in prison till December 14, when he was freed on recognizance. He was cleared by proclamation on May 11, 1693. See No. 720. ◊ Hand 1 = Stephen Sewall

Essex County Court Archives, vol. 1, no. 240, Massachusetts Supreme Judicial Court, Judicial Archives, on deposit James Duncan Phillips Library, Peabody Essex Museum, Salem, MA.

270. Deposition of Henry Wilkins Sr. v. John Willard‡

[Hand 1] The Deposition of Henery Wilkins Se⟨n⟩

aged 41 yeares

Who testefieth and sayth. that vpon the third of may last John Willard came to my house: and very earnestly entr⟨e⟩ated me to go with him to Boston wch I at lenght consented to go with him, my son Daniel comeinge and vnderstanding I was go⟨i⟩nge with him to Boston. and. seemed to be much troubled that I would go with the sayd Willard: and. he sayd he thought it were wel If the sayd Willard were hanged: wch made me admire for I neuer heard. such. an expressaen {come} from him. to any. one Liuinge. since he came to yeares of discreti⟨o⟩n but. after. I was gone. in a few dayes. he was taken. sicke: and. grew euery day worse & worse where vpon we made aplication to a phisition who. affirmed. his sicknes. was by some preternatural cause. & would make no aplication of any phisicke. sometymes after this. our neighbours comeinge to visit my son. mercy Lewis came wth the⟨m⟩ and affirmed that she saw the apperition of John Willard aflicting him. quickly after came An Putnam. and she saw the same apperition and then my eldest daughter was taken in a sad manner. & the sayd An: saw the sayd Willard aflicting her. at Another tyme mercy lewes. and mary Walcut came to visit him. and they. saw. the same apparition of Willard aflicting him. and this was but a litle tyme before his death.

[Hand 2] Sworne in Court

[Reverse] Henry Wilkins ag^t Willard.

Notes: This is dated here to June 2, when sworn testimony was being taken as the Court of Oyer and Terminer was beginning. It is possible that this is a trial document for August 5, although the "Sworn in Court" as opposed to the usual trial "Jurat in Curia" by Sewall argues for the earlier date. Also, there is no indictment against Willard for afflicting Daniel Wilkins, thus arguing against the idea that Willard was ever tried for his death. For other uses of "Sworn in Court" on June 2 by Sewall, see No. 266 and No. 269. ◊ "admire": 'wonder' (*OED* s.v. *admire*). ◊ Hand 2 = Stephen Sewall

Essex County Court Archives, vol. 1, no. 254, Massachusetts Supreme Judicial Court, Judicial Archives, on deposit James Duncan Phillips Library, Peabody Essex Museum, Salem, MA.

June 2, 1692

271. Physical Examinations No. 1 & No. 2 of Bridget Bishop, Rebecca Nurse, Elizabeth Procter, Alice Parker, Susannah Martin, & Sarah Good

[Hand 1] 1692 Salem June 2^d aboute 10 in Morning

Wee whose names are vnder written being Comanded by Capt George Corwine Esqr Sherriffe of ye County ~~of~~ of Essex this 2^d day of June 1692 for to vew ye bodyes of Brigett Bishop alias Oliver

> Rebecah Nurse
> Elizabeth Procter
> Alice Parker
> Susanna Martine
> Sarah Good

The first three Namely; Bishop: Nurse: Procter, by diligent search haue discouered a preternaturall Excresence of flesh between y^e pudendum and Anus much like to tetts & not vsuall in women, & much vnlike to y^e other three that hath been searched by vs [Hand 2] & y^t they were in all y^e three women neer y^e same place

J Barton Chyrurg$^\varepsilon$

[Hand 1] Salem aboute 4 afternoon June 2⟨^{d} 1692⟩
We whose names are Subscribed to y^e wthin mentioned, vpon a second search aboute 3 or 4 houres distance, did find y^e said Brigett Bishop alias Oliver, in a clear & free state from any p$^\varepsilon$ternaturall Excresence, as formerly seen by vs as alsoe Rebecah Nurse instead of that Excresence wthin Mentioned it appears only as a dry skin wthout sence, & as for Elizabeth Procter which Excresence like a tett red & fresh, not any thing appears, but only a proper procedentia Ani, & as for Susanna Martine whose breast in y^e Morning search appeared to vs very full; y^e Nibbs fresh & starting, now at this searching all lancke & pendant which is all at p$^\varepsilon$sent from y^e wthin Mentioned Subscribers, (that that piece of flesh of Goodwife Nursis formerly seen is gone & only a dry skin nearer to y^e anus
[Hand 2]   in another place
[Hand 1]

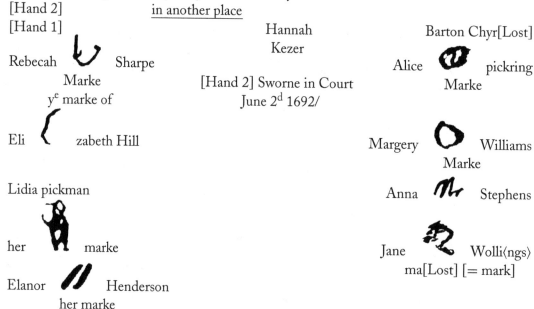

Rebecah   Sharpe   Hannah   Barton Chyr[Lost]
         Marke   Kezer
       y^e marke of   Alice   pickring
                                        [Hand 2] Sworne in Court   Marke
Eli   zabeth Hill   June 2^d 1692/

                                                          Margery   Williams
Lidia pickman   Marke

                                                           Anna   Stephens

her   marke   Jane   Wolli⟨ngs⟩
                                                          ma[Lost] [= mark]
Elanor   Henderson
       her marke

[Reverse]

Alice Pickering
    her Marke

Jane   Woolings
    her marke

Marjery   Williams
    her marke

Anna   Stephens
    her marke

Elizabeth   Hill
    her marke

Elanor   Henderson
    her marke

Rebecah   Sharpe
    her marke

Lydia   pickman
    Hannah Kezer

[Hand 2] Sworne in Court June 2^d 1692.
Att Step. Sewall Cle

[Hand 2] Jury of Womens Return
[Hand 3] B. Bishop

Notes: The search was for evidence of "Familiars" of the Devil sucking from witches. All of these women were eventually condemned, regardless of the outcome of the searches. The report on this and other body searches probably went to grand juries when such searches implicated a person. ◊ "procedentia Ani": *Latin* 'prolapsus or slipping down of the rectum' (*OED* s.v. *prolapsus* and s.v. *procidence*). ◊ Hand 2 = Stephen Sewall

Essex County Court Archives, vol. 1, no. 136, Massachusetts Supreme Judicial Court, Judicial Archives, on deposit James Duncan Phillips Library, Peabody Essex Museum, Salem, MA.

272. Physical Examinations of John Procter & John Willard

[Hand 1] We whose names vnder written haueing searched y^e bodyes of John Procter sen^r & John Williard now in y^e Goale & doe not find any thing to farther suspect them

    Dated June 2 1692
    Rondel ap^{re} testis   J. Barton Chyr$^{\varepsilon}$g
    John Rogers   Jno Gyles
    Joshua Rea Jun$^{\varepsilon}$ William Hine
    John C[Lost] Cooke   Ezekiel Cheever

June 2, 1692   [Hand 2] [Reverse] Return of Doctor Barton & other men y^t Search^t Willard & Procter.

Notes: The results, favorable to the accused, did not alter Procter and Willard's eventual condemnation. Whether these results delayed it or not can only be a matter of speculation. ◊ Hand 2 = Stephen Sewall

Essex County Court Archives, vol. 1, no. 50, Massachusetts Supreme Judicial Court, Judicial Archives, on deposit James Duncan Phillips Library, Peabody Essex Museum, Salem, MA.

273. Indictment No. 1 of Bridget Bishop, for Afflicting Mercy Lewis†

[Hand 1] Anno Regni Regis et Reginæ ⟨W⟩[Lost][= William]
Mariæ nunc Angliæ &^{c} Quarto:
Essex ss
The J̄ūrō$^\varepsilon$ for our Sovereigne Lord & lady the King & Queen p$^\varepsilon$sents that [Hand 2] **Bridgett Bishop aⁱs Olliver the wife of Edward Bishop of Salem in the County of Essex Sawyer** [Hand 1] the [Hand 2] **Nyneteenth** [Hand 1] Day of [Hand 2] **April** [Hand 1] in the [Hand 2] **ffourth** [Hand 1] Year of the Reigne of our Sovereigne Lord and Lady William and Mary by the Grace of God of England Scottland ffrance & Ireland King & Queen Deffenders of the faith &^{c} and Divers other Dayes & times a [= as] well before as after. certaine Detestable Arts ~~of~~ {called} Witchcrafts & Sorceries. wickedly, and felloniously ~~ag^t~~. hath vsed Practised & Exercised, at and within the Towneship of Salem ~~ab~~ in the County of Essex afore$\overline{\text{es}}$^{d} in ~~and~~ vpon, and ag^t one, [Hand 2] **Mercy Lewis of Salem Village in the County afores^d singlewoman** [Hand 1] by which said wicked Arts the said [Hand 2] **Mercy Lewis** [Hand 1] the [Hand 2] **s^d Nyneteenth** [Hand 1] Day of [Hand 2] **April** [Hand 1] in the [Hand 2] **ffourth Y⟨ear⟩** [Hand 1] above$\overline{\text{es}}$^{d} and divers other Dayes and times as well before as after, was & is hurt Tortured Afflicted. ~~tormented~~ Pined, Consumed, wasted: & tormented, ag^t the Peace of our ^{said} Sovereigne Lord And Lady the King & Queen and ag^t the forme of the Statute in that Case made & provided/
[Hand 2] wittnesses
Mercy. Lewis
Nathan^{ll} Ingersoll
Mr Sam^{ll} paris
Thomas puttnam J⟨u⟩n$^\varepsilon$
Mary Walcott.
Ann puttnam Jun$^\varepsilon$
Elizabeth Hubbard
Abigail Williams.

[Reverse] [Hand 3] N^o (1) Bills ag^t Bishop
Olliuer
[Hand 2] Billa vera
[Hand 4] John Rucke fforeman in the name of the Rest of ^{the} Grand Jurie

Notes: As was generally the case with the indictments, the document was prepared in advance with spaces left to be filled in as appropriate. Because two adult witnesses to witchcraft were required for conviction, in the absence of a confession, the indictments centered heavily on the day of the examination rather than on the original complaint. At the examinations, people could see accusers claiming affliction by the spectres of those being accused. Indictment No. 3, probably for afflicting Mary Walcott, is missing. The order of these indictments in the edition is not alphabetical, and the name of

Mercy Lewis on the first indictment perhaps reflects her significant influence on the core accusers. ◊ Hand 2 = Thomas   June 2, 1692
Newton; Hand 3 = Stephen Sewall

*Essex County Court Archives, vol. 1, no. 121, Massachusetts Supreme Judicial Court, Judicial Archives, on deposit James Duncan
Phillips Library, Peabody Essex Museum, Salem, MA.*

274. Indictment No. 2 of Bridget Bishop, for Afflicting Abigail Williams†

[Hand 1] Anno Regni Regis et Reginæ Willim et
Mariæ nunc Angliæ &ᶜ Quarto./

Essex ss

The Juroᴱ for our Sovereigne Lord & Lady the King & Queen pᴱsents that [Hand 2]
**Bridgett Bishop āls Olliver the wife of Edward Bishop of Salem in the County of Essex
Sawyer** [Hand 1] the ~~Day~~ [Hand 2] **Nyneteenth** [Hand 1] Day of [Hand 2] **Aprill** [Hand 1]
in the [Hand 2] **ffourth** [Hand 1] Year of the Reigne of our Sovereigne Lord & Lady
William & Mary by the Grace of God of England Scottland ffrance & Ireland King &
Queen Defendᴱ of the faith &ᶜ and Divers other dayes & times as well before as after.
certaine Detestable Arts ~~of~~ ^{called} Witchcrafts & Sorceries. wickedly and felloniously hath
vsed Practised & Exercised. at and within the Towneship of Salem in the County of Essex
aforesᵈ in vpon and agᵗ one [Hand 2] **Abigail Williams of Salem Village in the County of
Essex aforesᵈ singlewoman** [Hand 1] by which said wicked Arts yᵉ said [Hand 2] **Abigail
Williams** [Hand 1] the [Hand 2] **Nyneteenth** [Hand 1] Day of [Hand 2] **April aforesᵈ**
[Hand 1] in the [Hand 2] **ffourth Year** [Hand 1] abovesᵈ and divers other Dayes and times
as well before as after, was, and is Tortured Afflicted. Pined Consumed wasted & tormented
agᵗ the Peace of our said Sovereigne Lord & Lady the King & Queen and agᵗ the forme of
the Statute in that Case made and Provided

[Hand 2] Wittnesses

Abigail Williams

Mᴱ Samˡˡ paris [Hand 3] Sworne

[Hand 2] Nathanˡˡ Ingersoll [Hand 3] Sworne

[Hand 2] Thomas puttnam [Hand 3] Sworne

[Hand 2] Mercy Lewis

Ann puttnam Junᴱ [Hand 3] Sworne.

[Hand 2] Mary ~~Warren~~ Walcott [Hand 3] Sworne

[Hand 2] Elizabeth Hubbard [Hand 3] Sworne.

Jnᵒ Bligh & Rebeka ["Rebeka" written over "Sworne"] his wife Sworn

Samuel Shattock & Sarah his wife Sworn

William Bligh Sworne

William Stacey Sworne

John Loader Sworne.

[Reverse] [Hand 2] Billa vera

[Hand 4] John Ruck fforeman in the name of the Rest

[Hand 3] (2)

Notes: Hand 2 = Thomas Newton; Hand 3 = Stephen Sewall

*Essex County Court Archives, vol. 1, no. 122, Massachusetts Supreme Judicial Court, Judicial Archives, on deposit James Duncan
Phillips Library, Peabody Essex Museum, Salem, MA.*

June 2, 1692

275. Indictment No. 4 of Bridget Bishop, for Afflicting Elizabeth Hubbard†

[Hand 1] Anno Regni Regis et Reginæ Willim et
Mariæ nunc Angliæ &c Quarto./.

Essex ss

The Juroᵉ for our Sovereigne Lord & Lady the King & Queen pᵉsents that [Hand 2] **Bridgett Bishop a̅l̅s Olliver the wife of Edward Bishop of Salem in the County of Essex Sawyer** [Hand 1] the [Hand 2] **Nyneteenth** [Hand 1] Day of [Hand 2] **April** [Hand 1] in the [Hand 2] **ffourth** [Hand 1] year of the Reigne of our Sovereigne Lord & Lady William & Mary by the grace of God of England. Scottland ffrance. & Ireland King and Queen Defendᵉ of the ffaith &c and Divers other Dayes & times as well before, as after certaine Detestable Arts, called Witchcraft⟨s⟩ & Sorceries, Wickedly and ffelloniously hath vsed Practised, & Exercised, at and within the Towneship of Salem in the County of Essex afore̅s̅d in and upon and agᵗ one [Hand 2] **Elizabeth Hubbard of Salem Village in the County afores^d singlewoman** [Hand 1] by which said wicked arts the said [Hand 2] **Elizabeth Hubbard** [Hand 1] the [Hand 2] {sᵈ} **Nyneteenth** [Hand 1] Day of [Hand 2] **April** [Hand 1] in the [Hand 2] ffourth year [Hand 1] above̅s̅d and divers other dayes, and times as well before as after was & is hurt tortured Afflicted Pined Consumed, wasted, and tormented agᵗ the Peace of our sᵈ Sovereigne Lord & Lady the King and Queen, and agᵗ the forme of the Statute in that Case. made and Provided./.

[Hand 2] Wittnesses
Elizabeth Hubbard
Mercy Lewis
Mᵉ Samˡˡ paris
Nathanˡˡ Ingersoll
Thomas puttnam
Ann puttnam Junᵉ
Mary Walcott
abigail Williams,

[Reverse] [Hand 3] (4)
[Hand 2] Billa vera:
[Hand 4] John Rucke ^{formane} in the name of the Rest

Notes: Indictment No. 3 has not been located. Presumably it was for afflicting Mary Walcott. ◊ Hand 2 = Thomas Newton; Hand 3 = Stephen Sewall

Essex County Court Archives, vol. 1, no. 123, Massachusetts Supreme Judicial Court, Judicial Archives, on deposit James Duncan Phillips Library, Peabody Essex Museum, Salem, MA.

276. Indictment No. 5 of Bridget Bishop, for Afflicting Ann Putnam Jr.†

[Hand 1] Anno Regni Regis et Reginæ Willim et
Mariæ nunc Angliæ &c Quarto:

Essex ss

The Juroᵉ for our Sovereigne Lord & Lady the King & Queen pᵉsents that [Hand 2] **Bridgett Bishop a̅l̅s Olliver the wife of Edward Bishop of Salem in the County of Essex**

Sawyer [Hand 1] the [Hand 2] **Nyneteenth** [Hand 1] Day of [Hand 2] **April** [Hand 1] in   June 2, 1692
the [Hand 2] **ffourth** [Hand 1] Year of the Reigne of our Sovereigne Lord & Lady William
and Mary By the Grace of God of England Scottland ffrance & Ireland King & Queen
Defend$^\varepsilon$ of the ffaith &^{c} and divers other Dayes & times as well before as after. certaine
Detestable Artes called Witchcraft⟨s⟩ & Sorceries, Wickedly and felloniously hath vsed
Practised & Exercised at and within the Towneship of Salem, afores^d in vpon and ag^t one.
[Hand 2] **Ann puttnam of Salem Village in the County** afores^d **singlewoman** [Hand 1] by
which said wicked Arts the said [Hand 2] **Ann puttnam** [Hand 1] the [Hand 2] s^d
Nyneteenth [Hand 1] Day of [Hand 2] **April** [Hand 1] in the [Hand 2] **ffourth Year** [Hand
1] aboves^d and divers other Dayes & times as well before as after was & is hurt, tortured,
Afflicted Pined Consumed wasted & Tormented ag^t the Peace of our said Sovereigne Lord
& Lady the King and Queen and against the forme of the Statute in that Case made &
Provided./.
[Hand 2] Wittnesses
Ann puttnam Jun$^\varepsilon$
M$^\varepsilon$ Sam^{ll} paris
Nathan^{ll} Ingersoll
Thomas puttnam
Mercy Lewis
Mary Walcott
Abigail Williams
Elizabeth Hubbard

[Reverse] [Hand 3] (5) 5. Bills ag^t Brid^t Bishop alias Olliuer found by y^e Grand Inquest
[Hand 3?] ~~9~~⟨2⟩ ["2" written over "9"]
folio 966
[Hand 2] Billa vera
[Hand 4] John Rucke fforeman in the name of the Rest

Notes: Hand 2 = Thomas Newton; Hand 3 = Stephen Sewall

*Essex County Court Archives, vol. 1, no. 124, Massachusetts Supreme Judicial Court, Judicial Archives, on deposit James Duncan
Phillips Library, Peabody Essex Museum, Salem, MA.*

277. Testimony of John Cook v. Bridget Bishop

[Hand 1] John Cooke aged about 18 yeares Testifieth
that about fiue or Six yeares agoe One Morning about Sun rising as I was in bed before I rose
I Saw goodwife Bishop alias Olliuer Stand in ye Chamber by ye window and she looked On
me & Grinn'd On me & presently Struck me on ye Side of ye head wch did very much hurt
me & Then I Saw her goe Out under ye End ⟨of⟩ window at a little Creuiss about So bigg as
I Could thrust my hand into [   ] I Saw her again ye Same day wch was ye Sabath day about
noon walke across ye room & hauing at y^t time an apple in my hand it flew Out of my hand
into my mothers lapp who Sate Six or Eight foot distance from me & then She disapeard &
though my mother & Seuerall others were in ye Same room yet they afirmed they Saw her not
[Hand 2] John Cooke apearid before us the Jarris of inquest and did owne this to be his
testimony [1 word overstruck] one the oath that he hath taken: this 2: dy of June 92.
                                        [Hand 1] Jurat in Curia

June 2, 1692

[Reverse] John Cookes Witnis
[Hand 3] 2ⁿᵈ June 92

Notes: Used at trial. ◊ Hand 1 = Stephen Sewall

Essex County Court Archives, vol. 1, no. 148, Massachusetts Supreme Judicial Court, Judicial Archives, on deposit James Duncan Phillips Library, Peabody Essex Museum, Salem, MA.

278. Testimony of John Louder v. Bridget Bishop

[Hand 1] John Louder of Salem Aged aboute thurtey two Yeares, Testifieth and sayth yᵗ aboute seauen or Eight yeares since I then Liueing wᵗʰ Mʳ John Gedney in Salem and haueing had some Controversy with Bridgett Bushop yᵉ wife of Edwᵈ Bushop of Salem ∧{Sawyer} aboate her fowles yᵗ vsed to Come into our orchard or garden. Some little tyme after which, I goeing well to bed; aboute yᵉ dead of yᵉ night felt a great weight vpon my Breast and awakening looked and it being bright moon: light did clearely see sᵈ Bridget Bushop – or her likeness sitting vpon my stomake and puting my Armes of of yᵉ bed to free myselfe from yᵗ great oppression she presently layd hold of my throat and almost Choa[Lost] [= choked] mee and I had noe strenth or power in my hands to resist or help my selfe, and in this Condittion she held mee to almost day, some tyme after this, my Mistress Susannah Gedney was in our orchard and I was then with her. and sᵈ sᵈ Bridget Bushop being then in her Orchard wᶜʰ was next adjoyneing to ours my Mistress told sᵈ Bridget. yᵗ I said or afirmed yᵗ she cume one night & satt vpon my brest as aforesᵈ which she denyed and I Afirmed to her face to be tru and yᵗ I did plainely see her. vpon wᶜʰ discourse with her she Threatened mee. And some tyme after that I being not very well stayed at ~whome on a Lords day and on yᵉ after noon of sᵈ day the dores being shutt I did see a black pig in the Roome Comeing towards mee soe I went towards itt to kick it and it vanished away Immediatly after I satt down in a Narrow Bar and did see a black thing Jump into yᵉ window and came & stood Just before my face, vpon yᵉ bar yᵉ body of itt looked like a Munky only yᵉ feete ware ∧{like} a Cocks feete wᵗʰ Claws and yᵉ face somewhat more like a mans yⁿ a Munkies. and I being greatly affrighted not being able to speake or help my selfe by Reason of feare I suppose, soe the thing spake to mee and said I am a Messenger sent to yᵘ for I vnderstand you are trobled in mind, and if you will be Ruled by mee you shall want for Nothing in this world vpon which I Endeauered to clap my hands vpon itt, and sayd You devill I will Kill you. but could feale noe substan⟨ce⟩ and itt Jumped out of yᵉ window againe. and Imediatly Came in by yᵉ porch althow yᵉ dores ware shutt. and sayd you had Better take my Councill, where vpon I strook at it with a stick butt strook yᵉ Groundsill and broak yᵉ stick,

[Reverse] but felt noe Substance, and yᵗ arme with which I strook was presently disenabled, then it vanished away and I opened yᵉ back dore and Went out and goeing towards yᵉ house End I Espied sᵈ Bridget Bushop in her orchard goeing towards her house, and seing her had not power to set one foote forward but returned in againe and goeing to shutt yᵉ dore. I Againe did see yᵗ or yᵉ like creture yᵗ I before did see within dores, in such a posture as it seemed to be agoeing to fly at mee, vpon which I cryed. out; yᵉ whole armo⟨r⟩ of god be between mee and You. soe itt sprang back and flew ouer yᵉ apple tree flinging yᵉ dust wᵗʰ its feet against my stomake, vpon which I was struck dum⟨b⟩ and soe Continued for aboute three days tyme and also shook many of yᵉ apples of, from the tree wᶜʰ it flu ouer:

[Hand 2] John louder apearid before us this 2. dy of June 1692 and one the oath that he had taken did owne this testimony to be the truth before us the Jarris of Inquest
[Hand 3] Jurat in Curia

Euidences ag^t Br. Bishop.
Jno Loader

+ On her Tryall Bridget Bishop alias Olliue⟨r⟩ denied y^t she knew this deponent though ~~their~~ y^e orchard of this depon^t & y^e orchard of s^d Bishop Joined & they often had difference for Some yeares together

[Hand 4] John Loader

Notes: Used at trial. ◊ Hand 1 = John Hathorne; Hand 3 = Stephen Sewall

Essex County Court Archives, vol. 1, no. 145, Massachusetts Supreme Judicial Court, Judicial Archives, on deposit James Duncan Phillips Library, Peabody Essex Museum, Salem, MA.

279. Deposition of Samuel Shattuck & Sarah Shattuck v. Bridget Bishop

[Hand 1] Sam^{ll} Shattock aged 41 years testifieth y^t in y^e year 1680 Bridged Oliuer formerly wife to old Goodman Oliuer: now wife to Edward Bishop did Com⟨e⟩ to my hous pretending to buy an old hh^d [= hogshead] wch tho I asked verry little for: & for all her pretended want She went away wthout it: & Sundry other tymes she came in a Smooth flattering maner in very Slighty Errants; wee have thought Since on purpos to work mischeif: at or very near this tyme ~~aft~~ o^r Eldest Child who promised as much health & vnderstand{ing} both by Countenance and actions as any other Children of his years: was taken in a very drooping Condition and as She Came oftener to the hous he grew wors & wors: as he would be standing at ye door would fall ~~and~~ out & b⟨?⟩{r}uis his face vpon a great ^{Step} Stone. ⟨?⟩ as if he had bin thrust out bye an invissible hand: often tymes falling & hitting his face agst ye Sides of ye h⟨?⟩ hous: bruising his face in a very misserable maner: after this ye abouesaid Oliuer brought me a pair of Sleeues to dye & after y^t Sundry peeces of lace Som of wch were Soe Short y^t i could not judge y^m fit for any uce: She p^d me 2^d for dying y^m wch 2^d I ⟨a⟩ gaue to Henery Will^{ms} wch liued wth me he told me he put it in a purs among Som other mony wch he locked vp in a box & y^t ye purs & mony was gon out of ye Box he Could not tell how; & neuer found it after just after ye dying of these ~~things~~ things this child was taken in a terrible fit; his mouth & Eyes drawne aside and gasped in Such a maner as if he was vpon ye point of death; after this he gre⟨w⟩ wors in his fits: and out of y^m would be allmost allways crying y^t for many months he would be crying till natures strenght was Spent & then would fall asleep and {y^n} awake & fall to crying & moaning; y^t his very Countenance did bespeak Compassion; and at lenght wee p^{r}ceiued his vnderstanding decayed Soe y^t wee feared (as it has Since proued) y^t he would be quite bereaft of his witts; for Euer Since he has bin Stupified and voide of reason his fitts Still following of him; after he had bin in this ["i" written over "e"] kind of Sicknes Som tyme he has gon into the garden & has got vpon a board of an inch thick wch lay flat vpon ye ground & wee haue Called him; he would Com to the Edge of ye board & hold out his hand & make as if {he} would Com but Could not till he was helped of y^e board; other tymes when he has got vpon a board as

June 2, 1692

aforesaide my wife has Said She has ofered him a Cake & mony to Com to her and he has held out his ~~reach~~ hand & reach^t after it but Could not Com till he has bin help^t of y^e board; by wch i Judge Som inchantm [= enchantment] kep^t him on

about 17 or 18 months after, y^e first of this Ilnes there Came a Stranger ~~Came~~ to my hous & pittyed this Child and Said among other word^s wee are all borne Som to one thing & Som to another; I asked him & w^t doe you Say this Child is borne too he replyed he is born to be bewitched and is bewitched I told him he did ^{not} know; he said, he did know & Said to me you haue a neighbo^r y^t liues not far of y^t is a witch: I told him wee had noe neighb^r but w^t was honest folke; he replyed you haue a neighb^r y^t is a witch & She has had a falling out wth yor wife. & Said in her hart y^r wife is a proud ~~proud~~ woman & ~~Sheld~~ would bring downe her pride in this Childe: I paused in my Selfe & did rememb^r y^t my wi⟨f⟩

[Reverse] mye wife had told me y^t goodwife Oliuer had bin at ye hous & spoke to ^{her ⟨to⟩} beat He⟨nry⟩ Will^{ms} y^t liued wth vs & y^t She went away muttering & She thought threatning; but little before o^r child was taken ill; I told ye aforesaid Stranger y^t there was Such a woman as he Spoke of; he asked where She liued for he would goe & See her if he knew how: I gaue him m⟨o⟩ny & bid him ask her for a pot of Syd^r; away he went & i Sent my boy wth him who afte^r a short tyme: both returned; ye boys face bleeding & i asked w^t wa⟨s⟩ ye matter they told me ye man ~~kn~~ knock^t at ye door & goody oliuer Came to ye door & asked ye Stranger w^t he would haue he told her a pot of Syd^r She Saide he Shewld haue none & bid him get out & took vp a Spade & made him goe out She followed him & when She came wthout ye poarch She Saw mye boy & run to him & Scratched his face & made it bleed; Saying to him thou roague w^t dost thou bring this fellow here to plague me; now this man did Say before he went; y^t he would fetch blood of her

And Euer Since this Child hath bin followed wth greuious fitts as if he would neuer rcouer moor: his hed & Eyes drawne aside Soe as if they would neuer Come to rights moor lying as if ^{he} were in a maner dead falling any where Either into fier or water if he be not Constantly looked too, and generally in Such an vneasie and restles frame allmost allways runing too & fro acting Soe Strange y^t I cannot judge otherwise but y^t he is bewitched and {by} these circumstances doe beleiue y^t ye aforesaide Bridged Oliuer now Called Bishop is ye Caus of it and it has bin ye Judgem^t of Docters Such as liued here & forreigners: y^t he is vnder an Euill hand of witchcraft

[Hand 2] Eued. Against Bridget Bishop. 9   [Hand 1] Sam^{ll} Shattock & Sarah Shattock
℈ Saml Shadock & wife   affirmeth vpon ye oath they haue taken to the
                                           truth of w^t is aboue written

                                           [Hand 3] Jurat in Curia June 2^d 92
                                                  attest Steph: Sewall Cler

Notes: Used at trial. ◊ hh^d: 'a hogshead', 'a large cask for liquids' (*OED* s.v. *hogshead*). ◊ Hand 2 = John Hathorne; Hand 3 = Stephen Sewall

Essex County Court Archives, vol. 1, no. 144, Massachusetts Supreme Judicial Court, Judicial Archives, on deposit James Duncan Phillips Library, Peabody Essex Museum, Salem, MA.

280. Testimony of John Bly Sr. & William Bly v. Bridget Bishop

[Hand 1] June 2th 1692
Jno Blye Senio^r aged about 57 yeers & William Blye aged about 15 years both of Salem
Testifieth and saith y^t being Imployed by Bridgitt Bushup Alies Oliuer of Salem To help
take downe y^e Celler wall of The owld house she formerly Liued in wee y^e s^d Deponants in
holes of y^e s^d owld wall Belong{ing} To y^e s^d sellar found seuerall popitts made vp of Raggs
And ["And" written over "wth"] hoggs Brusells [= bristles] wth headles pins in Them wth y^e
points outward & This was about seauen years Last past

[Hand 2] Jurat Curia

[Reverse] [Hand 3] [Lost]pers [= papers] ag^t B: B: n° 16: 10
[Hand 4] John Bly and Wm Bly
[Hand 2] Court Oy^r & Term^r held at Salem 2^d June. 92
[Hand 3?] poppets.
[Hand 5] Olliuer

Notes: Used at trial. ◊ Hand 2 = Stephen Sewall; Hand 3 = Thomas Newton

*Essex County Court Archives, vol. 1, no. 147, Massachusetts Supreme Judicial Court, Judicial Archives, on deposit James Duncan
Phillips Library, Peabody Essex Museum, Salem, MA.*

281. Deposition of John Bly Sr., & Rebecca Bly v. Bridget Bishop†

[Hand 1] John Bly sen^r and Rebecka Bly his wife of Salem, both⟨e⟩ Testifie and say y^t s^d Jno
Bly Bought a Sow of Edwd Bushop of Salem ~~Labourer~~ ^{Sawyer} and by agreement with s^d
Bushop was to pay y^e price agreed vpon, vnto Lt Jeremiah Neale of Salem, and Bridgett y^e
wife of said Edward Bushop because she could n⟨ot⟩ haue the mony or vallue agreed for,
payd vnto her, she [Lost] to the house of the deponents in Salem and Quarrelled wth
⟨t?⟩[Lost] [= them] aboute it. ~~and also then Threatened them sayeing~~
    soon after which the Sow haueing piged she was taken with Strainge fitts Jumping vp.
and knocking hir head against the fence and seemed blind and deafe and would not Eat
neither Lett her pigs suck but foamed at the mouth, which goody hinderson heareing of sayd
she beleiued she was ouer-looked, and y^t thay had theire cattle ill in such a manner at y^e
Eastward when she liued there, and vsed to cure them by giueing of them Red Okar & Milk.
which wee also gaue the Sow. Quickly after eating of which she grew Better. and then for the
Space of Neere Two howre[Lost] [= hours] togather she g⟨e⟩tting into y^e street did sett of
Jumping & runing betweene y^e house of s^d deponents and s^d Bushops as if she ware stark
mad; and after that was well againe and wee did then Apprehend. or Judge & doe still y^t s^d
Bishop had bewitched s^d Sow

[Hand 2] Jurat in Curia

[Reverse] [Hand 1] John Bly and wife

[Hand 2]
Jno Bligh
Wm Bligh
Rob. Bligh

June 2, 1692   Notes: Used at trial. ◊ Hand 1 = John Hathorne; Hand 2 = Stephen Sewall

Essex County Court Archives, vol. 1, no. 150, Massachusetts Supreme Judicial Court, Judicial Archives, on deposit James Duncan Phillips Library, Peabody Essex Museum, Salem, MA.

282. Testimony of Richard Coman v. Bridget Bishop

[Hand 1] Richard Coman aged aboute 32 years Testifieth that sometime aboute Eight yeares Since: I then being in bed with my wife at Salem. one fift day of the Weeke at night Either. in ye Latter end of May or ye Begining of June. and a light burneing in our Roome I being awake, did then see Bridget Bishop of Salem Alias Olliuer come into ye Roome wee Lay in and two Women more with her. wch Two Women ware strangers to mee I knew them not. but s^d Bishop came in her Red paragon Bodys and the rest of her cloathing y^t she then vsually did ware, and I knowing of her well also ye garb she did vse to goe in. did clearely & plainely know her, and Testifieth that as he locked the dore of the house when he went to bed soe he found it after wards w^n he did Rise, and quickly after thay appeared the light was out, and the Curtaines at ye foote of ye bed opened where I did see her and presently came ~~and as I~~ And lay vpon my Brest or body and soe oppressed him y^t he could not speake nor stur noe not soe much as to awake his wife althow he Endeauered much soe to doe itt; y^e next night thay all appeared againe in like manner an⟨d⟩ she s^d Bishop Alias Oliu⟨er⟩ tooke hold of him by [Lost] [*Woodward* = the] throate and almost haled him out of the bed the Satterday night followeing; I haueing benne y^t day telling of what I had seene and how I suffered the two nights before, my Kinsman Wm Coman told mee he would stay with mee & Lodg with mee and see if thay would come againe and aduised mee to lay my Sword on thurt [= athwart] my body. quickly after Wee Went to bed y^t s^d night and both well awake and discourseing togather in came all the three women againe and s^d Bishop was the first as she had benne the Other two nights, soe I told him; W^m heere thay be all Come againe & he ~~he~~ was Immediatly strook speechless & could not moue hand or foote and Immediatly thay gott hold of my sword & striued to take it from mee but I held soe fast as thay did not gett it away; and I had then Liberty of sp[Lost]ch [= speech] and called W^m. also my wife & Sarah phillips y[Lost] [*Woodward* = y^t lay] [Lost]ith [= with] my wife. who all told mee ⟨af⟩[Lost] [*Woodward* = afterwards thay heard] mee, but had not power to Spe⟨a⟩[Lost] [*Woodward* = speak or stur]

[Reverse] {afterwards} And the first y^t spake was Sarah phillips. and said in y^e name of god Goodm̄ Coman w^t is y^e Matter with you, soe thay all vanished away

> Sworne Salem June 2^d 1[Lost] [= 1692]
> Before mee John Hathorn[Lost] [= Hathorne]
>
> [Hand 2] Jurat in Curia

[Hand 3] Richar⟨d⟩ ⟨C⟩[Lost] [= Coman]
als Olliver.

Notes: Richard McNally, Professor of Psychology at Harvard University and author of many papers on sleep paralysis, in correspondence has described Richard Coman's account as consistent with the syndrome of sleep paralysis, which could support the idea that Coman "experienced" this visit by Bridget Bishop. See the General Introduction on this issue. ◊ Used at trial. ◊ Hand 1 = John Hathorne; Hand 3 = Thomas Newton

Essex County Court Archives, vol. 1, no. 146, Massachusetts Supreme Judicial Court, Judicial Archives, on deposit James Duncan Phillips Library, Peabody Essex Museum, Salem, MA.   June 3, 1692

283. Deposition of Susannah Shelden v. Bridget Bishop

[Hand 1] The Deposistion of Susannah Shelldin aged about 18 years who testife and saith that on this 2 June 1692 I saw the Apperishtion {of} Bridgit Bishop. and Immediatly [2nd "m" written over "e"] appered to little children and said that they ware Thomas Greens two tiwins and tould Bridget Bishop to hir face that she had murthered them in seting them into fits wherof they dyed

[Reverse] [Hand 2] Susanna Sheldon Evid^s ag^t Bridgett Bishop

Notes: Susannah Shelden generally lacked credibility, and this deposition offered on the day of Bridget Bishop's grand jury and trial was used at neither procedure. The Court's response to Susannah Shelden supports the view that to a limited extent that the issue of counterfeiting was addressed. ◊ Hand 1 = Thomas Putnam; Hand 2 = Thomas Newton

Essex County Court Archives, vol. 1, no. 149, Massachusetts Supreme Judicial Court, Judicial Archives, on deposit James Duncan Phillips Library, Peabody Essex Museum, Salem, MA.

Sworn at Trial: Deposition of William Stacy v. Bridget Bishop
2nd of 2 dates. See No. 231 on May 30, 1692

Friday, June 3, 1692

Grand Juries of Rebecca Nurse & John Willard

Officers' Returns: Warrant for the Apprehension of Elizabeth Fosdick & Elizabeth Paine
2nd of 2 dates. See No. 265 on June 2, 1692

284. Testimony of Samuel Phillips & Edward Payson for Elizabeth How

[Hand 1] The testimony of Samuel Phillips aged about 67, minister of the word of God in Rowly, who sayth, that mr payson (minister of gods word alsoe in Rowly) and my self. went, being desired, to Samuel pearly of ipswich to se their young daughter who was viseted with strang fitts & in her fitts (as her father & mother affirmed) did mention goodwife How the wife of James How Junior of Ipswich, as if she was in the house & did affl⟨ic⟩te her; when we were in the house the child had one of her fitts but made noe mention of goodwife how; & when the fitt was over & she come to her self, goodwife ^{How} Went to the child and ⟨?⟩ took her by the hand & askt her whither she had ever done her any hurt And she answered noe never, and if I did complain of you in my fitts I know not that I did soe; I further can affirm vpon oath that young Sam⟨uel⟩ P⟨earl⟩y Brother to the afflicted Girle looking out of a chamber window (I and the afflicted child being without dores together) and sayd to his sister say goodwif⟨e⟩ ⟨How is⟩ a witch, say she is a witch. & the child spake not a word that way, but I lookt vp to the window wher the youth stood & rebuked him for his boldness to

June 3, 1692   stirr vp his sister to accuse the sayd goodw: How whereas she had cleared her from doing any hurt to his sister in both our hearing. & I added noe wonder that the child in her fitts did mention Goodwife How, when her nearest relations were soe frequent in expres⟨si⟩ng their suspitions [1 word overstruck], in the childs hearing when she was out of her fitts, that the sayd Goodwife How, was an Instrument of mischeif {to} the child:

Rowley 3 June 1692.

Samuel phillips

[Hand 2] I Edward Paison of ye Town aboves^d thô present at ye place & time afores^d, yet cannot evidenc in all the particulars mentioned: Thus much is yet in my remembranc {viz^t} being in ye aboves^d Pearley's house some considerable time before ye s^d Goodw. How came in; their afflicted Daughter, upon something that her Mother spake to her with tartnes⟨s⟩, she presently fell into one of her usu⟨a⟩ll strange fitts, during which, she made no mention (as I observed) of ye above s^d How her name, or any thing relating to her. some time after, the s^d How came in, when s^d Girl had recovered her capacity, her fitt being over, s^d How took s^d Girl by y^e hand, asked her whether she had ever done her any hurt,? y^e child answ^{ε}d no never; with several expressions to y^t purpose which I am not able particularly to recount &c.

Rowley J$\overline{\text{un}}$ -3- 1692.

Edward Paison

[Reverse] [Hand 3] m^r Philips & m^r Paison in behalfe of Eliz: How

Notes: Phillips and Payson were ministers from Rowley. Their testimony may have delayed the grand jury hearing the case of Elizabeth How, which eventually came on June 30.

Essex County Court Archives, vol. 1, no. 326, Massachusetts Supreme Judicial Court, Judicial Archives, on deposit James Duncan Phillips Library, Peabody Essex Museum, Salem, MA.

285. Indictment No. 1 of Rebecca Nurse, for Afflicting Ann Putnam Jr., with Memorandum by Stephen Sewall Concerning Nurse Trial Papers†

See also: June 29, 1692 & July 4, 1692.

[Hand 1] Anno Regni Regis et Reginæ et
Mariæ Nunc: Angliæ &^{c} Quarto:

Essex ss

The J$\overline{\text{uro}}$^{ε} for our Sovereigne Lord & Lady the King and Queen. p^{ε}sents that [Hand 2] **Rebecca Nurse of the wife** [Hand 3] ⌃{**ffrancis Nurse S**⟨e⟩[Lost] [= senior]} [Hand 2] **of Salem Villag**[Lost] [= village] **in the County of Essex husb** [Hand 1] the [Hand 2] **four & twentieth** [Hand 1] Day of [Hand 2] **March** [Hand 1] in the [Hand 2] **ffourth** [Hand 1] Year of the Reigne of our Sovereigne Lord & Lady William & Mary by the Grace of God of Englan⟨d⟩ Scotland ffrance & Ireland King & Queen Def⟨e⟩[Lost] [= defenders] of the ffaith &^{c} and divers other dayes & times as w[Lost] [= well] before as after certaine detestable Arts of Called Witchcraft & Sorceries: wickedly & ffelloniously hath vsed Practised ["s" written over "c"] & Exercised. at & within the Towneship of Salem in the County of Essex afore$\overline{\text{es}}$^{d} in upon & ag^t one: [Hand 2] **Ann puttnam Jun**^{ε} **of Salem Village afores**^{d} **in the County afores**^{d} **singlewoman** [Hand 1] by wch said wicked Arts the said [Hand 2] **Ann puttnam J$\overline{\text{un}}$**^{ε} [Hand 1] the [Hand 2] **s**^{d} **four & twentieth** [Hand 1] Day of [Hand 2] **March** [Hand 1] in the [Hand 2] **ffourth** [Hand 1] year above$\overline{\text{es}}$^{d}: and Divers other dayes & times as well before as after. was and is hurt. tortured Afflicted consumed Pined

wasted & tormented ag^t the Peace of our said Sovereigne Lord &: Lady the King & Queen, June 3, 1692
and ag^t the fforme of the Statute in that case made and Provided./
[Hand 2] Wittnesses
Ann Puttnam Jū$n^ε$
Abigail Williams
Mary Walcott
Elizabeth Hubbard

[Reverse] [Hand 4] N° 1 [Hand 3] Reb. Nurse
[Hand 4] Bill Avara
John Ruck fforeman in the name of the Rest
[Hand 3] Memorand^m
In this Tryall are Twenty papers besides this Judgment & these were in this Tryall as well as
other Tryalls of y^e Same Nature Seuerall Euidences viva voce which were not written & so I
can giue no Copies of them Some ffor & Some against y^e parties Some of y^e Confessors did
alsoe Mention this & other persons in their Seuerall declara$\overline{con}$s which being promised. &
Considered y^e sd 20 papers herewith fild is y^e whole Tryall attest Steph Sewall Cl⟨r⟩
    Copy of y^t aboue wrote on y^e Judgm^t wch I Gaue out to y^e Nurses

Notes: No record survives of any other family requesting or receiving trial documents. The memorandum is dated in the
edition on July 4, the day that the jury foreman, Thomas Fisk, explained the reason for the jury's decision to find Rebecca
Nurse guilty. See No. 416. ◊ Hand 2 = Thomas Newton; Hand 3 = Stephen Sewall

*Essex County Court Archives, vol. 1, no. 69, Massachusetts Supreme Judicial Court, Judicial Archives, on deposit James Duncan
Phillips Library, Peabody Essex Museum, Salem, MA.*

286. Indictment No. 2 of Rebecca Nurse, for Afflicting Mary Walcott†

    See also: June 29, 1692.

       [Hand 1] Anno Regni Regis et Reginæ et.
       Mariæ nunc: Angliæ &^{c} Quarto:
Essex ss
The Juro^ε for our Sovereigne Lord & Lady. the King & Queen p^{ε}sent̶s̶ that, [Hand 2]
Rebecca Nurse the wife of ffr̄ancis Nurse ^{Sē$n^ε$} **of Salem Village in the County of Essex**
husb [Hand 1] the [Hand 2] **four & twentyeth** [Hand 1] Day of [Hand 2] **March** [Hand 1]
in the [Hand 2] **ffourth** [Hand 1] Year of the Reigne of our Sovereigne Lord & Lady
William & Mary by the Grace of God of England Scottland ffrance & Ireland: King &
Queen Defend^ε of the ffaith &^{c} and Divers other Dayes & times as well before, as after,
certaine detestable Arts Called Witchcrafts & Sorceries: wickedly & ffelloniously vsed
Practised & Exercised at & within the towneship of Salem in the County of Essex afor$\overline{es}^d$ in
and upon and ag^t one [Hand 2] **Mary Walcott of Salem Village** afores^d **in the County**
afores^d **hus̄b** [Hand 1] by wch said wicked Arts y^e said [Hand 2] **Mary Walcott** [Hand 1] the
[Hand 2] **s^d four & twentieth** [Hand 1] Day of [Hand 2] **March** [Hand 1] in the [Hand 2]
ffourth [Hand 1] Year abov$\overline{es}^d$ and Divers other Dayes & times: as well before as after. was
& is hurt tortured Afflicted. consumed Pined wasted & tormented ag^t the Peace of our
[Hand 2] {s^d} [Hand 1] Sovereigne Lord & Lady. the King & Queen and. ag^t the forme of
the Statute in that Case made and Provided.

June 3, 1692

[Hand 2] Wittnesses
Mary Walcott
Abigaile Williams
Ann puttnam J̄un̄ᵋ
Elizabeth Hubbard

[Reverse] [Hand 3] Nº 2
Bill Avara
John Rucke fforman in in the nam of the Rest

Notes: Hand 2 = Thomas Newton

Essex County Court Archives, vol. 1, no. 68, Massachusetts Supreme Judicial Court, Judicial Archives, on deposit James Duncan Phillips Library, Peabody Essex Museum, Salem, MA.

287. Indictment No. 3 of Rebecca Nurse, for Afflicting Elizabeth Hubbard†
See also: June 29, 1692.

[Hand 1] Anno Regni Regis et Reginæ et
Mariæ nunc: Angliæ &ᶜ Quarto/
Essex ss
The Jur̄oᵋ for our Sovereigne Lord & Lady the King & Queen pᵋsent̶s̶. that [Hand 2] **Rebecca Nurse the wife of ffrāncis Nurse** [Hand 3] {Senᵋ} [Hand 2] **of Salem Village in the County of Essex hus̄b** [Hand 1] the [Hand 2] **four & twentyeth** [Hand 1] Day of [Hand 2] **March** [Hand 1] in the [Hand 2] **ffourth** [Hand 1] year of the Reigne of our Sovereigne Lord & Lady William & Mary ⟨ꝯ⟩ by the Grace of God of England Scottland france & Ireland King & Queen Defenders of the ffaith &ᶜ and Divers Day⟨e⟩s & times as well before as after. certaine Detestable Arts of witchcraft & Sorceries. wickedly & ffelloniously hath vsed Practised & Exercised at & within the towneship of Salem in the County of Essex afor̄esᵈ in upon & agᵗ one [Hand 2] **Elizabeth Hubbard of Salem Village afor̄esᵈ in the County afor̄esᵈ singlewoman** [Hand 1] the [Hand 2] **sᵈ four & twentieth** [Hand 1] Day of [Hand 2] **March** [Hand 1] in the [Hand 2] **ffourth** [Hand 1] year abor̄esᵈ and divers other Dayes & times as well before as after. was and is hurt tortured Afflicted Pined wasted consumed. & tormented agᵗ the Peace of our said Sovereigne Lord. and Lady yᵉ King & Queen and agᵗ the forme of the Statute in that case made & Provided/
[Hand 2] Wittnesses
Elizabeth Hubbard
Mary Walcott
Abigail Williams
Ann puttnam J̄un̄ᵋ

[Reverse] [Hand 4] Nº 3.
Bill Avara
John Rucke fforman in the name of the Rest

Notes: Hand 2 = Thomas Newton; Hand 3 = Stephen Sewall

Essex County Court Archives, vol. 1, no. 66, Massachusetts Supreme Judicial Court, Judicial Archives, on deposit James Duncan Phillips Library, Peabody Essex Museum, Salem, MA.

288. Indictment No. 4 of Rebecca Nurse, for Afflicting Abigail Williams†

June 3, 1692

See also: June 29, 1692.

[Hand 1] Anno Regni Regis et Reginæ et
Mariæ nunc Angliæ &ᶜ Quarto./

Essex ss

The Juroᵉ for our Sovereigne Lord & Lady the King & Queen pᵉsents That [Hand 2] **Rebeckah Nurse the wife of ffrancis Nurse** ^{Senᵉ} **of Salem Village in the County of Essex** husb [Hand 1] the [Hand 2] **ffour & twentyeth** [Hand 1] Day of [Hand 2] **March** [Hand 1] in the [Hand 2] **ffourth** [Hand 1] Year of the Reigne of our Sovereigne Lord & Lady William & Mary by the Grace of God of England Scottland ffrance & Ireland. King & Queen Defendᵉ of the ffaith &ᶜ and Divers other Dayes & times as well before as after. certaine detestable Arts called Witchcrafts & Sorceries wickedly and ffelloniously hath vsed Practised & Exercised at and within the Towneship of Salem in the County of Essex aforesᵈ in upon and agᵗ one [Hand 2] **Abigail Williams of Salem Village aforesᵈ in the County aforesᵈ singlewoman** [Hand 1] by which said wicked Arts. the said [Hand 2] **Abigail Williams** [Hand 1] the [Hand 2] sᵈ **four & twentieth** [Hand 1] Day of [Hand 2] **March** [Hand 1] in the [Hand 2] **ffourth** [Hand 1] Year abovesᵈ and divers other dayes & times as well before as after was & is hurt tortured. Afflicted consumed Pined wasted: & tormented agᵗ the Peace of our Sovereigne Lord & Lady the King & Queen and agᵗ the forme of the Statute in that Case made & Provided

[Hand 2] Wittnesses
Abigail Williams
Mary Walcott
Elizabeth Hubbard
Ann puttnam Junᵉ

[Reverse] [Hand 3] Nº 4
Bill Avara
John Ruck fforeman in the nam of the Rest

Notes: Hand 2 = Thomas Newton ◊ Facsimile Plate 5.

Essex County Court Archives, vol. 1, no. 67, Massachusetts Supreme Judicial Court, Judicial Archives, on deposit James Duncan Phillips Library, Peabody Essex Museum, Salem, MA.

289. Deposition of Johanna Childen v. Rebecca Nurse‡

[Hand 1] The deposision of Johannah Childin testieth and saieth that upon the: 2ᵈ of June: 1692 that the aparition of goody nuss and goodman Harrwood did apeare to her and the said Harrwood did look goody nuss in the face {and} said to her: that she did murder him by pushing him off the Cart and strock the breath out of his body

Notes: This may have been prepared for a grand jury, but it was not used.

Essex County Court Archives, vol. 1, no. 76, Massachusetts Supreme Judicial Court, Judicial Archives, on deposit James Duncan Phillips Library, Peabody Essex Museum, Salem, MA.

June 3, 1692

290. Deposition of Elizabeth Hubbard v. Rebecca Nurse

[Hand 1] The Deposistion of Elizabeth Hubburd: agged about 17 years who testifieth and saith that about the 20th march 1692 I saw the Apperishtion of Rebekah nurs the wife of frances nurs sen^r senr. tho she did not hurt me tell the 24th march being the day of hir examination and then she did hurt me most greviously duering the time of hir examination for if she did but look upon me she would strick me down or allmost choak me and also severall times sence the Apperishtion of Rebekah nurs has most greviously afflected me by pinching pricking and almost choaking me urging me to writ in hir book and also on the day of hir examination I saw the Apperishtion of Rebeckah nurs goe and hurt the bodys of Ann putnam sen^r and mary walcott and Abigaill williams and Ann putnam Junr
[Hand 2] elizabeth hubard upon har oath she had taken did owne this testimony before us the Juriars of Inquest: this 3 dy of June: 1692

[Reverse] [Hand 3] 3
[Hand 1] Eliz: Hubburd againt Rebekah nurs

Notes: No evidence survives that this was used at the trial, although one would have expected it to be. This was probably first prepared on or near March 24. ◊ Hand 1 = Thomas Putnam

Essex County Court Archives, vol. 1, no. 78, Massachusetts Supreme Judicial Court, Judicial Archives, on deposit James Duncan Phillips Library, Peabody Essex Museum, Salem, MA.

291. Deposition of Ann Putnam Jr. v. Rebecca Nurse

See also: June 29, 1692.

[Hand 1] The Deposistion of Ann putnam ^{junr} who testifieth and saith that on the 13th march {1691/92} I saw the Apperishtion of gooddy nurs: and she did Immediatly afflect me but I did not know what hir name was then: tho I knew whare she used to sitt in our Meetinghouse: but sence that she hath greviously afflected me by biting pinching and pricking me: urging me to writ in hir book and allso on the 24th of march being the day. of hir Examination I was greviously tortored by hir dureing ["ur" written over "ru"] the time of hir Examinatio⟨n⟩ and also seuerall times sence and also dureing the time of hir Examination I saw the Apperishtion of Rebekah nurs goe and hurt the bodys of mircy lews mary walcott Elizabeth Hubbrd and Abigaill ["A" written over "a"] williams.
[Hand 2] ann putnam Jurn: did one the oath which she hath taken. this har euidens to be the truth. before us the: Juriers for Inquest this 3. dy of June: 1692

[Hand 3] Jurat in Curia

[Reverse] [Hand 4] Ann puttnam

Notes: This was probably first prepared on or near March 24. Used at trial. ◊ Hand 1 = Thomas Putnam; Hand 3 = Stephen Sewall

Essex County Court Archives, vol. 1, no. 81, Massachusetts Supreme Judicial Court, Judicial Archives, on deposit James Duncan Phillips Library, Peabody Essex Museum, Salem, MA.

293. Deposition of Clement Coldum Regarding Elizabeth Hubbard, in Support of Rebecca Nurse [?]

379

June 3, 1692

Sworn Before the Grand Jury in the case of Rebecca Nurse: Deposition of Ann Putnam Sr. v. Martha Cory & Rebecca Nurse, and Testimony of Ann Putnam Jr. v. Rebecca Nurse, Martha Cory & Sarah Cloyce
3rd of 3 dates. See No. 30 on March 24, 1692

292. Deposition of Mary Walcott v. Rebecca Nurse

[Hand 1] The Deposistion of Mary walcott aged about 17 years who testifieth and saith that on the 20th march 1691/92 I saw the Apperishtion of Rebekah nurs the wife of frances nurs senr: but she did not hurt me tell the 24 march being the day of hir Examination but then the Apperishtion of Rebekah nurs did most greviously torment me dureing the time of hir Examination: and also seuerall times since she hath most greviously afflected me by biting pinching and almost choaking me urging me vehemently to writ in hir book or elce she would kill me: and on the 3d of may in the euening the Apperishtion of Rebekah nurs tould me she had a hand in the deaths of Benjamin Holton John Harrod Rebekah Sheppard. and seuerall others and allso att the time of hir examination I saw the Apperishtion of Rebekah nurs goe and hurt the bodys of Ann putnam mircy lewes Elizabeth Hubburd and Abigaill williams [Hand 2] marcy woulcok on the oath which she hath taken did owne this har testimony to be truth before us the Juriars of Inquest: this 3 dy of June 1692

[Reverse] [Hand 3] 2 [Hand 4] Mary Walcott

Notes: The reference to May 3 probably comes from Rebecca Nurse, among others, having been named that day at the examination of Deliverance Hobbs. See No. 116. Sarah Bibber in another deposition, No. 357, made an accusation against Nurse for afflicting her on May 2. Beginning with "and also at the time . . ." there is an ink change by Thomas Putnam, suggesting that the deposition was prepared prior to June 3 before being expanded by Putnam. ◊ Hand 1 = Thomas Putnam; Hand 4 = Thomas Newton

Essex County Court Archives, vol. 1, no. 80, Massachusetts Supreme Judicial Court, Judicial Archives, on deposit James Duncan Phillips Library, Peabody Essex Museum, Salem, MA.

Sworn Before the Grand Jury: Testimony of Abigail Williams v. Rebecca Nurse & Sarah Cloyce
2nd of 2 dates. See No. 244 on May 31, 1692

293. Deposition of Clement Coldum Regarding Elizabeth Hubbard, in Support of Rebecca Nurse [?]

[Hand 1] The deposition of Clement Coldum aged 60 years or yr about; saith; yt on ye 29th of May; 1692; being at Salem Village carrying home Elizabeth Hubbard from ye Meeting behind me; she desired me to ride faster, I asked her why; she said ye woods were full of Deuils, & said yr & there they be, but I could se none; then I put on my horse, & after I had rid a while, she told me I might ride softer, for we had outrid them. I asked her if she was not afraid of ye Deuil, she answered me no, she could discourse with ye Deuil as well as with me, & further saith not; this I am ready to testifie on Oath if called thereto, as witness my hand;

~~Clement Coldum~~
Clement Colddom

[Hand 2?] Against Eliz: Hubbard

June 3, 1692   Notes: The evidence for dating this is not adequate. However, the deposition may be part of the Nurse case for the grand jury that met on June 3.

Essex County Court Archives, vol. 2, no. 122, Massachusetts Supreme Judicial Court, Judicial Archives, on deposit James Duncan Phillips Library, Peabody Essex Museum, Salem, MA.

294. Statement of Rebecca Preston & Mary Tarbell for Rebecca Nurse‡

[Hand 1] we whos nams are under written: can⟨e⟩ testiefie if cald to it that goodde nurs haue bene trobled with an Infirmity of body for many years which the Juree of wemen seme to be Afraid it should be some{thing} Elce

Rebcah preson.
Mary Tarbel

Notes: This appears to be a response to the physical examination of Rebecca Nurse the previous day. See No. 271. Rebecca Preston and Mary Tarbell were daughters of Rebecca Nurse. The possibility that this document was used for Rebecca Nurse's trial on June 29 rather than, or in addition to, its apparent use on June 3 remains. The names of Rebecca Preston and Mary Tarbell are written by the recorder of the document. ◊ Possibly used at trial.

Essex County Court Archives, vol. 1, no. 85, Massachusetts Supreme Judicial Court, Judicial Archives, on deposit James Duncan Phillips Library, Peabody Essex Museum, Salem, MA.

295. List of Witnesses v. John Willard‡

[Hand 1] Evidences ag^t John Willard.

Exaicon vide.

abigail Williams. ["iams" written over "ard"]
Mary Walcott
Susanna Shelden
Nath^{ll} Putnam &c vpon murder
Ann Puttnam

Coron^{es} Enquest

Mercy Lewis
Ann puttnam sen^r
[Hand 2]
Sarah Churchill   }
                            } y^t Willard diswaded from confession
Margaret Jacobs   }

[Reverse] [Hand 1] Evidences ag^t John Willard

Notes: This appears to be Thomas Newton's list of evidence to be presented against Willard at the grand jury and is here dated to that hearing. ◊ Hand 1 = Thomas Newton; Hand 2 = Stephen Sewall

Essex County Court Archives, vol. 1, no. 239, Massachusetts Supreme Judicial Court, Judicial Archives, on deposit James Duncan Phillips Library, Peabody Essex Museum, Salem, MA.

296. Indictment No. 1 of John Willard, for Afflicting Mercy Lewis†

See also: Aug. 4, 1692.

June 3, 1692

[Hand 1] Anno Regni Regis et Reginæ et Mariæ
nunc Angliæ &ᶜ Quarto:

Essex ss

The Juroᵉ for our Sovereigne Lord and Lady the King & Queen pᵉsents That. [Hand 2] **John Willard of Salem Village in the County** ~~aforesᵈ~~ **of Essex husb:** [Hand 1] the [Hand 2] **Eighteenth** [Hand 1] Day of [Hand 2] **May** [Hand 1] in the [Hand 2] **ffourth** [Hand 1] Year of the Reigne of our Sovereigne Lord and Lady William & Mary by the Grace of God of England Scottland ffrance & Ireland King & Queen Defenders of the ffaith &ᶜ and Diuers other Dayes & times as well before as after, certaine detestable arts called Witchcrafts & Sorceries wickedly & feloniously {hath} vsed, Practised & Exercised at & within the Towne of Salem in the County of Essex aforesᵈ in. upon. and agᵗ one [Hand 2] **Mercy Lewis of Salem Village aforesᵈ in the County aforesᵈ singlewoman** [Hand 1] by which said wicked arts the sᵈ [Hand 2] **Mercy Lewis** [Hand 1] the [Hand 2] sᵈ **Eighteenth** [Hand 1] Day of [Hand 2] **May** [Hand 1] in the [Hand 2] **ffourth** [Hand 1] Year abovesᵈ and divers other Dayes & times as well before as after was & is hurt. tortured Afflicted consumed Pined wasted & tormented. agᵗ the Peace of our Sovereigne Lord & Lady the King & Queen. and agᵗ the forme of the Statute in that case made ~~for~~ & Provided

[Hand 2] Wittnesses
Mercy Lewis
Abigail Williams
Mary Walcott
Susanna Sheldon
Ann puttnam senᵉ
Ann puttnam Junᵉ
Elizabeth Hubbard

[Reverse] Nº 1.
[Hand 3] bill Avaro
John Rucke fforeman in the name of the Rest
[Hand 4] Jnº Willard

Notes: Hand 2 = Thomas Newton

Essex County Court Archives, vol. 1, no. 234, Massachusetts Supreme Judicial Court, Judicial Archives, on deposit James Duncan Phillips Library, Peabody Essex Museum, Salem, MA.

297. Indictment No. 2 of John Willard, for Afflicting Ann Putnam Jr.†

See also: Aug. 4, 1692.

[Hand 1] Anno Regni Regis et Regine Willim et
nunc Angliæ &ᶜ Quarto.

Essex ss

The Juroᵉ for our Sovereigne Lord & Lady the King pᵉsent That: [Hand 2] **John Willage [= Willard] of Salem Village in the County of Essex husb:** [Hand 1] the [Hand 2] **Eighteenth** [Hand 1] day of [Hand 2] **May** [Hand 1] in the [Hand 2] **ffourth** [Hand 1] year

June 3, 1692

of the Reigne of our Sovereigne Lord, & Lady, William and Mary by the Grace of God of England, Scottland ffrance and Ireland King & Queen Defender of the faith &ᶜ and Divers other Dayes & times as well before as after. certaine detestable Arts called Witchcrafts & Sorceries. Wickedly and felloniously hath Vsed and Exercised at and within the Towne of Salem in the County of Essex afores̄ᵈ in ~~and~~ upon and against one [Hand 2] **Ann puttnam Junᵋ of Salem Village aforesᵈ in the County aforesᵈ Singlewoman** [Hand 1] by which said Wicked arts the said [Hand 2] **Ann puttnam Jūnᵋ** [Hand 1] the [Hand 2] sᵈ **Eighteenth** [Hand 1] Day of [Hand 2] **May** [Hand 1] in the [Hand 2] **ffourth** [Hand 1] year abou̅es̄ᵈ and Divers other dayes & times as well before as after was and is hurt tortured, afflicted, pined Consumed Wasted & Tormented against yᵉ Peace of our said Sovereigne Lord [Hand 2] ˄{and Lady} [Hand 1] the King and Lady the King & Queen, and agᵗ the forme of the Statute in that Case made and Provided.
[Hand 2] Wittnesses
Ann puttnam Jūnᵋ
Abigaile Williams
Mary Walcott
Susanna sheldon
Mercy Lewis
Ann puttnam s̄enᵋ
Elizabeth Hubbard

[Reverse] Nᵒ 2.
[Hand 3] billa vera
[Hand 4] John Rucke foreman in the name of the Rest
[Hand 5] Jnᵒ Willard

Notes: Hand 2 = Thomas Newton

Essex County Court Archives, vol. 1, no. 233, Massachusetts Supreme Judicial Court, Judicial Archives, on deposit James Duncan Phillips Library, Peabody Essex Museum, Salem, MA.

298. Indictment No. 3 of John Willard, for Afflicting Susannah Shelden (Returned Ignoramus)†

See also: Aug. 4, 1692.

[Hand 1] Anno Regni Regis et Regine Willim et
Mariæ nunc Angliæ &ᶜ Quarto:
Essex ss
The Jūroᵋ for our Sovereigne Lord & Lady the King & Queen pᵋsentᵋThat [Hand 2] **John Willard of Salem Village in the County of Essex husb:** [Hand 1] the [Hand 2] **Eighteenth** [Hand 1] Day of [Hand 2] **May** [Hand 1] in the [Hand 2] **ffourth** [Hand 1] year of the Reigne of our Sovereigne Lord & Lady William & Mary by the Grace of God of England Scottland ffrance and Ireland King & Queen Defenders of the ffaith &ᶜ and Divers other Dayes & times as well before as after. certaine detestable arts called Witchcrafts, & Sorceries, wickedly and felloniously, hath used practised & Exercised at & within the Towne ~~of~~ Ship of Salem in the County of Essex afores̄ᵈ in & upon and against one [Hand 2] **Susanna Sheldon of Salem Village aforesᵈ in the County aforesᵈ singlewoman** [Hand 1] by which said wicked

June 3, 1692

arts the said [Hand 2] **Susanna sheldon** [Hand 1] the [Hand 2] s^d **Eighteenth** [Hand 1]
Day of [Hand 2] **May** [Hand 1] in the [Hand 2] **ffourth** [Hand 1] year aboues̄^d and Divers
other Dayes & times as well before as after, was and is hurt. tortured afflicted pined
consumed Wasted & tormented ag^t the Peace of our Souereigne Lord and Lady King &
Queen. and ag^t the forme of the Statute in that case made and Provided
[Hand 2] Wittnesses
Susanna sheldon
Abigail Williams
Mary Walcott
Ann puttnam sen^ε
Ann puttnam Jun^ε
Mercy Lewis
Elizabeth Hubbard

[Reverse] N° 3.
[Hand 3] :Ignoram⟨o⟩s
[Hand 4] Jn° Willard.

Notes: The notations of "ignoramus" that appear from time to time on indictments reflect the willingness of grand jurors to evaluate cases and not simply to assume guilt. Although in all the grand jury witchcraft cases at least one true bill was returned, the ignoramuses remain as evidence of serious deliberation. Susannah Shelden in general seems to have lacked credibility with her contemporaries, and this suggests that grand juries may have been alert to counterfeiting. ◊ Hand 2 = Thomas Newton

Essex County Court Archives, vol. 1, no. 232, Massachusetts Supreme Judicial Court, Judicial Archives, on deposit James Duncan Phillips Library, Peabody Essex Museum, Salem, MA.

299. Indictment No. 4 of John Willard, for Afflicting Abigail Williams†

See also: Aug. 4, 1692.

[Hand 1] Anno Regni Regis et Reginæ Willim
et Mariæ nunc Angliæ et Quarto,
Essex ss
The Jūro^ε for our Sovereigne Lord & Lady the King & Queen p^εsent^s that [Hand 2] **John Willard of Salem Village in the County of Essex husb:** [Hand 1] the [Hand 2] **Eighteenth** [Hand 1] Day of [Hand 2] A̶p̶r̶ **May** [Hand 1] in the y̶ [Hand 2] **ffourth** [Hand 1] year of the Reigne of our Sovereigne Lord & Lady William & Mary by the Grace of God of England Scottland ffrance and Ireland King & Queen Defender of the ffaith &^c and divers other Days & times. as well before as after certaine detestable arts called Witchcrafts & Sorceries Wickedly and felloniously hath Vsed practised & Exercised at and within the Towneship of Salem, in the County of Essex afores̄^d in upon and ag^t one [Hand 2] **Abigail Williams of Salem Village in the County** ^{**afores^d singlewoman**} [Hand 1] by which said wicked arts. the said [Hand 2] **Abigail Williams** [Hand 1] the. [Hand 2] s^d **Eighteenth** [Hand 1] Day of [Hand 2] **May** [Hand 1] in the [Hand 2] **ffourth** [Hand 1] Year aboues̄^d and Divers other Dayes, & times. as well before as after, was and is hurt tortured. Afflicted Pined Consumed, wasted and Tormented ag^t the Peace of our said Sovereigne Lord & Lady the King & Queen and ag^t the forme of the Statute in that Case made and Provided
[Hand 2] Wittnesses

June 3, 1692

Abigail Williams
Mary Walcott
Susanna Sheldon
~~Nathani:ll puttnam~~
Ann puttnam Jun^ε
Mercy Lewis
Ann puttnam s̄ēn^ε
Elizabeth Hubbard

[Reverse] N° 4 [Hand 3] bill Avarr⟨o⟩
John Rucke fforeman in the name of the Rest
[Hand 4] Jn° Willard

Notes: Hand 2 = Thomas Newton

Essex County Court Archives, vol. 1, no. 236, Massachusetts Supreme Judicial Court, Judicial Archives, on deposit James Duncan Phillips Library, Peabody Essex Museum, Salem, MA.

300. Indictment No. 7 of John Willard, for Afflicting Elizabeth Hubbard†

See also: Aug. 4, 1692.

[Hand 1] Anno Regni Regis et Reginæ et
Mariæ nunc Angliæ &^c Quarto:

Essex ss

The Jūrō^ε for our Sovereigne Lord & Lady the King & Queen p^εsents That [Hand 2] **John Willard of Salem Village in the County of Essex husb** [Hand 1] the [Hand 2] **Eighteenth** [Hand 1] Day of [Hand 2] **May** [Hand 1] in the [Hand 2] **ffourth** [Hand 1] Year of the Reigne of our Sovereigne Lord & Lady William & Mary by the Grace of God of England. Scottland ffrance & Ireland King & Queen Defend^ε of the ffaith &^c and Divers other Dayes & times as well before as after certaine Detestable Arts called Witchcraft & Sorceries wickedly & ffelloniously hath vsed Practised & Exercised at & within the Towneship of Salem in the County of Essex afores^d in upon, and ag^t one [Hand 2] **Elizabeth Hubbard of Salem Village afores^d in the County afores^d singlewoman** [Hand 1] by which said wicked arts the said [Hand 2] **Elizabeth Hubbard** [Hand 1] the [Hand 2] s^d **Eighteenth** [Hand 1] Day of [Hand 2] **May** [Hand 1] in the [Hand 2] **ffourth** [Hand 1] year abovēs^d and divers other Dayes & times as well before as after. was & is hurt: tortured: Afflicted consumed Pined. wasted & tormented ag^t the Peace of our [Hand 2] ^{said} [Hand 1] Sovereigne Lord & Lady the King & Queen and ag^t the fforme of the Statute in that Case made & Provided [Hand 2] Wittnesses
Elizabeth Hubbard
Mary Walcott
Abigail Williams
Susanna sheldon
Ann puttnam sen^ε
Ann puttnam Jun^ε
Mercy Lewis.

[Reverse] N° 7. ["7" written over "5"?]
[Hand 3] bill Avaro
John Rucke fforeman in the name of the Rest
[Hand 4] Jn° Willard

Notes: Indictments 5 and 6 are missing. They were probably for afflicting Ann Putnam Sr. and Mary Walcott. No evidence survives as to whether true bills on them were returned or not, although it seems likely that they were. ◊ Hand 2 = Thomas Newton

Essex County Court Archives, vol. 1, no. 235, Massachusetts Supreme Judicial Court, Judicial Archives, on deposit James Duncan Phillips Library, Peabody Essex Museum, Salem, MA.

301. Testimony of Sarah Bibber v. John Willard

See also: Aug. 4, 1692.

[Hand 1] june the .3. 1692:

[Hand 2] Sarah vibber aged 36 years or thear abouts testefie and saith the day befor Jn° Welard was exammend at the ui(?) uilleg [Hand 1] I being in left Engorsols Chambor I saw yᵉ aporishtion of john willard com to mary walcot & marcy luis & hurt them griuosly & almost choked Them Then I tould of it & emediatly yᵉ sayd wiliord fel upon me & tormented me greuesly & pinched me & threw me down
[Hand 3] sarah uibber: ownid this har testimony before us the Jurriars for Inquest: this .3. of June: 1692

[Hand 4] Jurat in Curia

[Reverse] Sarah Vibber

Notes: Used at trial.

Essex County Court Archives, vol. 1, no. 245, Massachusetts Supreme Judicial Court, Judicial Archives, on deposit James Duncan Phillips Library, Peabody Essex Museum, Salem, MA.

Sworn Before the Grand Jury: Deposition of Elizabeth Hubbard v. John Willard

2nd of 2 dates. See No. 175 on May 18, 1692

Sworn Before the Grand Jury: Deposition of Samuel Parris, Nathaniel Ingersoll & Thomas Putnam v. John Willard

2nd of 3 dates. See No. 176 on May 18, 1692

Sworn Before the Grand Jury: Deposition of Ann Putnam Jr. v. John Willard

2nd of 3 dates. See No. 185 on May 18, 1692

Sworn Before the Grand Jury: Deposition of Mary Walcott v. John Willard

2nd of 3 dates. See No. 180 on May 18, 1692

June 4, 1692

302. Deposition of Benjamin Wilkins, John Wilkins, & Nathaniel Richardson v. John Willard‡

[Hand 1] The deposition of benjamin Wilkins aged 36 years and John Wilkins aged 26 years these deponents testifieth and say that Lidia Wilkins wiffe of John: Wilkins was well delivered ^{with child.} and was well the next day after but the 2 day after shee was deleivered shee was taken with a violent feaver and flux as we supposed and in a litle time the flux abated but the feaver continued till shee died which was about four dayes

[Reverse] [Hand 2] Nath: Richison tells of a Nashway man y^t speak⟨s⟩ of a profound sleep. y^t that Willard w⟨a⟩s in

Notes: As with No. 270, the possibility remains that it is an unused document prepared for the trial rather than for the grand jury on June 3. The Wilkins family played a significant role in charging Willard. The Richardson connection has not been established. ◊ Hand 1 = Ezekiel Cheever; Hand 2 = Jonathan Corwin

Essex County Court Archives, vol. 2, no. 127, Massachusetts Supreme Judicial Court, Judicial Archives, on deposit James Duncan Phillips Library, Peabody Essex Museum, Salem, MA.

Sworn Before the Grand Jury: Testimony of Abigail Williams v. John Willard
2nd of 2 dates. See No. 183 on May 18, 1692.

Saturday, June 4, 1692

303. Complaint of Edward Putnam, Thomas Rayment, Elizabeth Booth, Abigail Williams, & Ann Putnam Jr. v. Mary Ireson

[Hand 1] Deacon Edward Putnam and Thomas Rayment both of Salem Village Complained ^{on behalfe of theire Majesties} against Mary Ireson the wife of Benjamen Ireson of Lyn husbandman for Sundry acts of Witchcraft by her Committed Lately on y^e bodys of Mary Waren Susana Shelden & Mary Walcot & others {also Eliz both [= Booth] Abi Williams Ann Putnam also} of Salem Village whereby great hurt hath beane donne to theire bodys. therefore Craued Justice Salem June 4^t 1692

Edward Putnam

The Mark **L** of
Thomas Rayment

[Reverse] [Hand 2] Ireson.

Notes: Hand 1 = John Hathorne

Essex County Court Archives, vol. 2, no. 19, Massachusetts Supreme Judicial Court, Judicial Archives, on deposit James Duncan Phillips Library, Peabody Essex Museum, Salem, MA.

304. Warrant for the Apprehension of Mary Ireson, and Officer's Return

June 4, 1692

See also: June 6, 1692.

[Hand 1] To The Sherriffe of The County of Essex or his deputie or Constable in Lyn You are in theire Majes^ts names hereby required to apprehend and bring before vs Mary. Ierson ye wife of Benjamin Ireson of Lyn husbandman on Munday next aboute ten of ye Clock in the forenoon at ye house of Thomas Beadles in Salem who stands Charged ∧{on behalfe of theire Majes^ts} with haueing Committed Sundry acts of Witchcraft on y^e Bodys of Mary Waren Susannah Shelden Mary Walcot and Others whereby great hurt is donne to their bodys.) in order to her Examination Relateing to the abouesayd premises faile not Dated Salem June 4^t 1692

℘ vs $\left\{ \begin{array}{l} \text{John Hathorne} \\ \text{Barth}^o \text{ Gedney} \\ \text{Jonathan. Corwin} \end{array} \right\}$ J: pea⟨ce⟩

[Reverse] [Hand 2] According to this warrant I haue Aprehended the person of mary Ierson and wife of B⟨e⟩njemen Ierson of Lyn and brought her to the plase apoynted in order to for her exemination as atest my hand Henery Collings Constabll for y^e town of Lyn

Notes: Hand 1 = John Hathorne

Essex County Court Archives, vol. 2, no. 18, Massachusetts Supreme Judicial Court, Judicial Archives, on deposit James Duncan Phillips Library, Peabody Essex Museum, Salem, MA.

305. Statement of Mary Warren v. Mary Ireson & Mary Toothaker‡

[Hand 1] one may the 24 m⟨ary⟩ waren being in a feet and greuosly aflecte{d} then was in a tranc for sum tim we har{d} her say who ar ye wha{⟨t⟩} is your name and again. she said what totheker Doktr toothekers wiffe wee often her{d} her say I wont i wonte i will not touch y^r book an⟨d⟩ then the fet was ouer then she told us that Dockter toothekers wiff brought the boo{k} to her and a kofen ["n" written over "r"?] and a winding shet and grau cloths and said that she must set her hand to the book or elce she would kil her and stil she urged to touch the bo{o}k o{r} elc be wrapt in that sheet this haue ben Done this Day by toothekers wiff mary iyerson, wiff to bengemin iyerson at lin ha [= have?] in the sam maner hau tormented almost to Deth and brought the book to he{r}

[Reverse] [Hand 2] Mary Warren ag^t Ierson Toothaker &c

Notes: *SWP* misreads this document as "Mary Warren and Mary Ireson v. Jerson Toothaker" (III, 765). No such person as "Jerson Toothaker" appears in the records. Woodward (II, 202) introduced the erroneous reading of "Jerson Toothaker." ◊ Hand 2 = Jonathan Corwin

Essex County Court Archives, vol. 2, no. 117, Massachusetts Supreme Judicial Court, Judicial Archives, on deposit James Duncan Phillips Library, Peabody Essex Museum, Salem, MA.

June 4, 1692

306. Statements of Mary Warren, Susannah Shelden, Ann Putnam Jr., Sarah Bibber, Mary Walcott, Elizabeth Hubbard, Elizabeth Booth, James Darling, & John Louder v. Job Tookey, with Examination of Job Tookey

See also: Jan. 5, 1693.

[Hand 1] June the 4. 1692

Mary Waren. Susanah Shelden Ann Putnam: Sarah Viber Mary Walcot, Eliz Hubert. and Eliz booth

    all accused Job Tuckey y^t he came in person; also in his shape to them and this day afflicted them; and also in our presence greatly afflicted them. as they all declared # and told Mary Warren and Ann Putnam ^{and Susanah shelden} y^t he had Learneing and coald Raise the Diuell W^n he pleased

Susanah Shelden sayth y^t he told her he was not onely a Wizard but a Murtherer to

                     [Hand 2] Mary walcot ann Putnam Ju̅r̅ in Cur

                     [Hand 1] Job Tuckey sayth its not he but ye diuell in his shape y^t hurts ye people

present
Maj^ε Bar^t Gedney
Jona^t Corwin
Jno Hathorne   }

Mary Warren and Ann Putnam and Susannah Shelden all Made Oath before Vs that Job Tukey did this day tell them y̶^t in his owne person that he had Learneing and could Raise the diuele when he pleased

Sworne ⅌ all three aboues^d Salem June the 4th 1692

[Hand 2] Mary Walcot   [Hand 1] Before Vs

[Hand 2] & Ann Putnam

Jur in Cur.

[Hand 1] Susannah Shelden Mary Warren and Ann Putnam all Testified y^t this 4th of June when Job Tuckey was Examined before y^e Majestrats wee did all see fiue people y^t [Lost]ose [= arose] from y^e dead two of them men two Women & one Child. wch all Cryed Vengance vengance

Job Tuckey being asked before Vs w^t child y^t was y^t arose and Cryed Vengance he Answerd, it was Jno Trasks child.

And Ann Putnam. told her y^t it was John Trasks child

       [Hand 1?] Before

                            John Hathorne Jus^t peace

[Reverse] [Hand 3] James Darling Sworne Saith That Job Tookey Said he was not the Deuills Seruant but the Deuill was his

Jno Loader Sworn Saith

[Hand 4] Euidences ver. Tookie

Notes: Used at trial. ◊ Hand 1 = John Hathorne; Hand 2 = Jonathan Elatson; Hand 3 = Anthony Checkley; Hand 4 = Stephen Sewall

Massachusetts Archives Collection, vol. 135, no. 26. Massachusetts State Archives. Boston, MA.   June 6, 1692

307. Testimony of John Louder, Samuel King, Daniel Bacon, John Stacy, & John Putney Jr. v. Job Tookey

See also: Jan. 5, 1693.

[Hand 1] John Lauder aged aboute 32 yeares testifieth that Job Tuckey ^{of Beverly Labourer} did this day say; that he can ~~could~~ as freely discourse the Diuell as well as he speaking to him s^d Lauder, ~~Capt Jona~~ {Samuell} ~~Walcot~~ ^{King} & Daniell Bacon ^{sen^ε} also Testifieth y^t thay heard him say soe to John Lauder as aboues^d

Sworne by all the three aboue named
Salem J[Lost] [= June] the 4 1692

[Hand 2] Jur̄ in Cur
Jon^a Elatson Cler

[Hand 1] John Stacy aged aboute 30 Testifieth and sayth that this day wee heard Job Tuckey of Beverly Labourer say y^t he would take m^r Burrows his part. and then the afflicted persons (vis) Mary Warren Mary Walcot & others ware greately afflicted and did then Complaine of him – for afflicting them John Pudney Jun^ε aged aboute 28 yeares testifieth to all y^e aboues^d

Sworne ℘ both y^e aboue named
Salem June 4th 1692

[Hand 2] Jur in Cur

[Reverse] [Hand 3] Jno Laud^ε &c^a
Euidence ve. Job Tookie

Notes: Used at trial. ◊ Hand 1 = John Hathorne; Hand 2 = Jonathan Elatson

Massachusetts Archives Collection, vol. 135, no. 27. Massachusetts State Archives. Boston, MA.

Monday, June 6, 1692

Officer's Return: Warrant for the Apprehension of Mary Ireson†
2nd of 2 dates. See No. 304 on June 4, 1692

308. Warrant for the Apprehension of Ann Dolliver, and Officer's Return

[Hand 1] Essex ss.
> To. The Sheriffe of the County of Essex or his deputie or Constable in Salem or Beuerley –

June 6, 1692

You are in theire Majes^ts names, hereby required to apprehend and forthwith bring before vs Ann Dalibar the wife of Wm Dalibar of Glocester who stands Charged this day with haueing Committed sundry acts of Witchcraft on the Bodys of Mary Warren & Susannah Shelden to the hurt of theire Bodys ⟨?⟩ in order to her Examination Relateing to the premises faile not Dated Salem June the 6^t 1692

Barth° Gedney

ʒp vs   John. Hathorne

Jonathan. Corwin

[Hand 2] Just^Es of ye peace.

[Reverse] [Hand 3] In obediance to this warant I haue aprehended ye person with in Named and brought her to the plase apoynted in order to her examinaton as atest

my hand   Peter Asgood

Constabell for the town of <u>Salem</u>

[Hand 3?] Ann [Hand 4] Dalibar

Notes: Having been deserted by her husband, Ann Dolliver was probably living in Salem at the home of her father, Reverend John Higginson. Her brother was Justice of the Peace John Higginson Jr., and these strong connections appear to have protected her in spite of the arrest. ◊ Hand 1 = John Hathorne; Hand 2 = Jonathan Corwin

Essex County Court Archives, vol. 2, no. 110, Massachusetts Supreme Judicial Court, Judicial Archives, on deposit James Duncan Phillips Library, Peabody Essex Museum, Salem, MA.

309. Examination of Ann Dolliver

[Hand 1] M^rs An Dolliver was examined before Maj^r Gedney: Mr Hawthorn & Mr Corwin June 6: 1692

Mrs Dolliver: Did you never act witch craft: answerd: Not ^{with intent} to hart any body with it but you implicitly confess will: you goe on to confess: but she asked where be my accusers I am not willing to accuse my selfe. She ownd she had often been out in ye woods all night: once she was in a fainting fitt: & could not get ~~hom~~ home other times she would rather ly in ye woods & goe round them come over with ye ugly fellow that kept ye fferry ~~man:~~ her: mother also was not pleased with her & she went from home on y^t acco^t some {times}. but she had not seen any thing that affrighted her: nor spirits as she knew once a negro affrighted her & she knew not a spirit from a man in ye night for she had heard y^t ye devill sometime was in ye shape of a man: & some times she went alone to pray: but Susanna Sheldon Mary Walcot Mary Warin came. being cald & {they} fell down: they all afirmd that this was the person y^t afflicted them this day: she had other cloaths but it was ye same face: some of them s^d: there was a little child: y^t was Just now dead: y^t cryed for vengeance: for she had pressed ye breath out of its body: Some of them s^d she had tryed seven or eight houses: her spectre s^d: to afflict but could do it no where else: her spectre: they s^d: told them she would have kild her father if she could: for: she had more spite at him y^n she had: at ye childe: also her spectre s^d: y^t she knew: where: to finde ye devil at any time: if she did goe but to such a ditch: ~~they~~ afflicted s^d also: y^t she had poppits in a secret place that she afflicted with: Mrs Dolliver was asked whether she had not made poppits of waxe: she s^d yes ~~she s^d~~ one: afterward she ownd two popits & it was becau⟨s⟩ she thought she was bewitched & she

had read in a book: that told her: that that: was ye way to afflict: them y^t had afflicted her: June 6, 1692
she s^d she was not very well upon it but her mother: and her brother Jno were ill ~~were ill~~ upon
it when she was afflicted as she thought she s^d she was much pinched
the afflicted persons: then charged her with afflicting them: & they: every one s^d they saw
her afflict: ye others: s^d Dolliver was asked: what she had bin doing: this day y^t these persons
were afflicted: she s^d nothing but spinning: she had stuck pins in nothing but her cloaths to
dress her & she had stuck a pin to fasten her distafe ye afflacted: told her she had bin some
times in Tho Putnams window at ye Village but she owned it not: also that she had bin at
goodwife Nurses: but she s^d it was but once when she mist her way going round becaus she
would not goe over with ye ferry man:
but being bid to shake hands with ye afflicted: she did it & they were not hurt
The waxe poppits: were made about fourteen year agoe:
The standers by: took notice that once s^d Dollivers eyes: were fixed: ye afflicted s^d ye black
man was: before her: in ye time of her examination this was

I und^ε written: being appointed by Authority to take: ye Above written examination doe
testify: ~~y^t this~~ upon oath taken in Court: y^t this is a true coppy of y^e ~~subst⟨ane⟩~~ substance of it
to y^e best of my knowledge
Simon Willard

[Reverse] [Hand 2] Ann Dolliuer's Examinacon

Notes: Nothing survives regarding what followed from this examination. ◊ Hand 1 = Simon Willard

MS Ch K 1.40, vol. 2, p. 194, Rare Books & Manuscripts, Boston Public Library. Boston, MA.

310. Examination of Mary Ireson

[Hand 1] Mary Ireson was examined: before Maj^r Gedney: & other their Majest^ε Justices
June: 6th 1692
before s^d Ireson was brought: into y^e roome: ~~y~~ in prayer time ye afflicted fell into a fitt &
complayned of Mary Ireson
when s^d Ireson came in her sister came with her: & ye Justices: cald to ye afflicted: to come &
look on her sister: & see if that was she y^t afflicted them but they s^d that was not she. that hurt
them: it was she w^t a whood on s^d Ireson had a ~~whoo~~ riding whood on: it was asked s^d Ireson
doe you not see how you are discovered: she s^d she: might be left: to this afflictions for her
other sins for she had: bin of a bad temper: ~~for~~ but for witch craft she had not y^t sin to answer
for: Eliz Boothe Susana Sheldon Mary Warin & Mary Warin fell down when she looke on
them: & were well again when she touched them with her hand seval [= several] times it was
so: they charged her with afflicting them: when some of them were well they charged her
with hurting y^e others y^t were afflicted: they three of them: all but Mary Walcot s^d they never
had seen her in person: before: but they knew y^t this was y^e woman y^t had afflicted them:
Mary Warin s^d she had brought the book: her to sign: a monthe before: Susana Sheldon s^d
she brought ye book at that pressent time of her examination: & s^d if she would not sign it
she would tear her throat out: s^d Iresons: eyes being fixed: it was asked her: what she fixed
her eyes upon: ye afflicted s^d ye black man was before her & bid her not confess both: y^e
Justices: & s^d Iresons unkle: ffuller: that was there urged her to confess & breake ye snare of

ye devill: but she s^d she knew not y^t she was in it: she asked wheither she might be a witch & not know it: but was answerd no: She s^d then she could not confess till she had more light

I und^r written being appointed by Authority to: take: y^e above examination doe testify upon oath taken in Court: that this is a true coppy of y^e substance of it to y^e best of my knowledge:

Simon Willard

[Reverse] [Hand 2] Mary Ireson's
~~Confession~~ Examination

Notes: No record of whether Ireson was indicted or tried survives. ◊ Hand 1 = Simon Willard

MS Ch K 1.40, vol. 2, p. 210, Rare Books & Manuscripts, Boston Public Library. Boston, MA.

Tuesday, June 7, 1692

311. Deposition of John Allen v. Susannah Martin

See also: June 29, 1692.

[Hand 1] The deposion of {Left} John Allen of salsbury aged 4⟨5⟩ years testifying sayth That in or about the year [   ] this deponent was haling timber for m^ε Georg Car for building a vesell at Amsbery at m^ε goodins building plac & haueing don & about to go home susana martin then wif of Georg martin desired this deponent to cart staves for them which this deponent refused to do because of his oxn which wear weake & needed now to gett flesh, but shee seemed to be discontent (and as Jams freez and others then present told this Deponent) (that shee sayd) I had had ben as good I had (for my oxn shoold never do me much more servis) vpon wch this deponent sayd d⟨o⟩st thretn me thou old wich or words to that efect resoluing to throw her into a brook that was fast by: which to avoyd shee flew ouer ye bridg & so esc⟨a⟩ped: but as he was going home on of his oxn tired that he was forst to vnyok him to get him home And after thay wear com home: put the sd oxn to salsbury beach whear several other oxn whear catl vsualy ar⟨e⟩ putt whear thay had Lang rang of medows to feed on & whear catle did vse to get flesh: but in a few days al the oxn vpon the beach we found by thayr tra{c}ks wear gon to the mouth of the River merimak but not returned from whenc we thought thay wear run into the sd river: but the next day sending to pl⟨a⟩m Iland found thayr ⟨t⟩racks ther to be com ashore wch traks thay followed to the other end of the sd Iland & a consideribl way bak againe & the⟨n⟩ sate down wch being espyed by those that sought {⟨y^m⟩} thay did vse all Immaginable gentlnes to them to som aqaintanc wch som of them seemed to attend but all on a sudaine away thay all run with such violenc as if thay their mosion had ben dyabolical: till thay came neer the mouth of merimak river and then: turned to the right hand & run right in to the sea all but to old oxn (wch had befor Left thayr company) and all the rest went to sea a far as thay coold see them: & then {on} of them came bak again with such swiftnes as was amazing to the beholders who stood redy to Imbrac him & help his tyerd carcase vp: but Letting him Loose away he runs vp into the Iland & from there through the marshes vp in to newbery towne & so vp into their woods and ther was after a while faund about hartechok river over against Amsbery so that of :14: good oxn only that was saued the

rest were all cast vp som at cap an som in on plac and som in ather of thay [= them] thay
only had the hids: he farther sayth that the abouesd James freez did often moue the ꝓsecuting
of the sd Susana martin in the case being vndoutedly confident that shee was a wich

    Left John Allin made oathe to the truth of all that is above writtn Jun y^e 7th 1692
before me   Robt Pike As⟨s⟩^t

               [Hand 2] Jurat in Curia

[Reverse] Jn° Allen

Notes: Used at trial. ◊ "gett flesh," "get flesh": approx. 'get in good condition' (*OED* s.v. *flesh*). ◊ Hand 1 = Robert Pike;
Hand 2 = Stephen Sewall

*Essex County Court Archives, vol. 1, no. 188, Massachusetts Supreme Judicial Court, Judicial Archives, on deposit James Duncan
Phillips Library, Peabody Essex Museum, Salem, MA.*

312. Examination of Job Tookey

[Hand 1] 7 June 1692
Before Major Gidney Mr Hauthorn & m^r Corwin
The examination of Job Stuky

After propounding Severall questions and negative answers returned q. Did you not say the
other day that yow saw the Devil. Answer I knew not then what I said. – The said Stuky
lookeing upon the afflicted persones struck them down with his eyes & recovered them by
takeing of th[Lost] [= them] Severally by the hand or wrist
Mary warrin in a trance said that Gamaliel Hawkins was dead in Barbados and Job Stuky
~~had~~ did stick a great pin into him
Being out of her trance she affirmed as before and added one Andrew woodberry more. And
that Stuky had bewitched Betty Hews
Susanna Shelden said that Stuky had killed one Androw woodberry And one Gamaliel (but
was just then choakt) A litle efter she proceeded & said that Tuky had murdered Trasks
child And that he run a great pin into a poppets heart which killed the said Hawkins.
Warrin said she saw a yo⟨u⟩ng child under the table cryeing out for vengean⟨?⟩e upon Stuky
[Hand 2] {Elizabeth} jnr ["jnr" written over Hand 1 "Mary"] [Hand 1] booth pointed to the
same place but could not speake Shelden said that Stukyes apparition told her. he ["h"
written over "s"] would never reveale again what he had said before.
Mary warrin then saw a man rise up also before Stuky
Mary walcot saw 3 men 3 women and two childrens Apparitions who all cryed for
vengeance. against Stucky (and then her mouth was stopt) within a litle while she said she
knew not the persones, but they appeared in their winding sheets and looked pale upon her
but Red upon Stuky
[Hand 2] {Elizabeth} [Hand 1] ~~Mary~~ ⟨walcot⟩{Booth} & Sus: Shelden saw the same 8
persones cryeing out for vengeance upon Stuky and looked as red as blood
Shelden said that John Trasks child was one, As also Gamaliel Hawkins and Andrew
woodberry
Shelden said that Stuky had pinched & choaked her this day

June 8, 1692

Mary warrin saw the apparitions of Hawkins and severall more but knew them not, She saw also the apparitions of seargin & her child; had [Lost]n a fitt & cryed out upon one Burse.
I under subscrybing being appointed by the justices of the Peace in Salem to take down in writing the Examination of Job Tooky Doe testify the above written to be a true coppy of the originall as to the substance of it

Wm Murray

[Reverse] [Hand 3] Examinat⟨o⟩n of Job ⟨ꝛ⟩Tookie
7: June 1692

Notes: Mary Warren's charge against "Burse," Reverend John Busse, represents the first recorded charge against him. Claims against him continue through the summer, although no record of his having been arrested exists. He had been a preacher in Wells, Maine, and was the son-in-law of Mary Bradbury, who was first accused of witchcraft on May 26 (see No. 219). In some of the subsequent narratives he is associated with George Burroughs in leading the meetings of witches. See No. 428 & No. 525. ◊ Hand 1 = William Murray; Hand 2 = Andrew Elliot

Massachusetts Archives Collection, vol. 135, no. 28. Massachusetts State Archives. Boston, MA.

Wednesday, June 8, 1692

313. Warrant for the Execution of Bridget Bishop, and Officer's Return
See also: June 10, 1692.

[Hand 1] To George Corwin Gent^m high Sherriffe of the County of Essex Greeting Whereas Bridgett Bishop a̅l̅s̅ Olliver the wife of Edward Bishop of S[Lost] [= Salem] in the County of Essex Sawyer at a speciall Court of Oyer and Terminer [Lost] [*SWP* = held at] Salem the second Day of this instant month of June for the Countyes of Essex Middlesex and Suffolk before William Stoughton Esq^ε and his Associates Ju[Lost] [*SWP* = Justices] of the said Court was Indicted and arraigned vpon five severall Ind[Lost] [= indictments] for vseing practis⟨s⟩ing and exerciseing [Lost] [*SWP* = on] the Nynete[Lost] [*SWP* = Nyneteenth day of April] last past and divers other dayes and times before and after [Lost] [*SWP* = certain acts of] Witchcraft in and vpon the bodyes of Abigail Williams, Ann puttnam Jun Mercy Lewis, Mary Walcott and Elizabeth Hubbard of Salem village singlewomen, whereby their bodyes were hurt, afflicted pined, cons[Lost] [= consumed] Wasted and tormented contrary to the forme of the Statute in that Case [Lost] [= made and] provided To which Indictm^ts the said Bridgett Bishop pleaded not [Lost] [*SWP* = guilty] and for Tryall thereof put her selfe vpon God and her Country, where she was found guilty of the ffelonyes and Witchcrafts whereof she stood Indicted and sentence of Death accordingly passed ag^t her as the Law directs, Execution whereof yet remaines to be done These are theref[Lost] [= therefore] in the Name of their Maj^ties William and Mary now King & Queen ove⟨r⟩ England &c to will and Comand you That vpon fryday next being t[Lost] [= the] Tenth Day of this instant month of June between the houres of Eight and twelve in the aforenoon of the same day You safely conduct the s^d Bridge⟨t⟩ Bishop a̅l̅s̅ Olliver from their Maj^ties Gaol in Salem afores^d to the place [Lost] [*SWP* = of] Execution and there cause her to be hanged by the neck vntill she be d[Lost] [= dead] and of your doings herein make returne to the Clerk of the s^d Court and p^εcept And hereof you are not to faile at your peril

And this shall be [Lost] [= your] sufficient Warrant Given vnder my hand & seal at Boston   June 16, 1692
the Eig[Lost] [= eighth] of June in the ffourth Year of the Reigne of our Sovereigne Lord &
[Lost] [= lady] William & Mary now King & Queen over England &c Annoꝗ Dn̄i 1692
Wm Stoughton

[Hand 2] June 10th = 1692
Ac{c}ording to the Within Written precept I haue taken the body of the within named
Brigett Bishop out of their Majest[Lost] [= majesties'] Goale in Salem and Safely conueighd
her to the place prouid[Lost] [= provided] for her Execution and Caused y^e sd Brigett to be
hange[Lost] [= hanged] by the neck untill Shee was dead ~~and buried in the pla⟨ce⟩~~ all which
was according to the time Within Required and So I make Returne by me
George Corwin Sheriff

[Reverse] [Hand 3] Bridget Bishop
Death Warrant

Notes: Hand 1 = Thomas Newton; Hand 2 = George Herrick ◊ 1 wax seal. ◊ Facsimile Plate 9.

Essex County Court Archives, vol. 1, no. 71, Massachusetts Supreme Judicial Court, Judicial Archives, on deposit James Duncan Phillips Library, Peabody Essex Museum, Salem, MA.

Friday, June 10, 1692

Execution of Bridget Bishop

Officer's Return: Warrant for the Execution of Bridget Bishop
2nd of 2 dates. See No. 313 on June 8, 1692

Thursday, June 16, 1692

Death of Roger Toothaker in Prison

314. Warrant of Coroner of Suffolk County for an Inquest into the Death of Roger Toothaker, and Return of the Coroner's Jury
See also: Nov. 29, 1692.

[Hand 1] {Suffolke}
To ye Constables of Boston, or either of them
By Vertue of mine office, These are in ye names of our soueraigne Lord and Lady, King
William & Qvenne Mary of England etc^t to will and Require you Immediatly, vpon y^e
Recept and sight hereof to summons, & warne, twenty fouer able and suffitient men to be
and apear before me at ye prison forthwith, then and there, to doe and execute such things,
As on there Majes^{ts} {behalfe} shall be giuen them in charge, whereof faile ye not, as you and

June 20, 1692

euery of you, will answer ye contrary at your perills, Dated Vnd^ɛ my hand, & seal, the 16th day of June, in ye year of our Lord: <u>1692</u>

By me Edw Wyllys: one of
the Corroners of ye County
of <u>Suffolke</u>

[Reverse] [Hand 2] Wee whose names are underwritten being sommoned by vertue of a Warrant from M^ɛ Edward Williss one of their Maj^{sts} Coroners of ye County of Suffolk to veiw the Body of Roger Toothacker who dyed in ye Goal of Boston, in obedyence to which we haue veiwed ye same & obtaind ye best Information we can from ye persons near & present at his death & doe finde he came to his end by a naturall death as witness our hands this 16 of June 1692

The s^d Toothacker was an Inhabitant of ye Town of Bellricky in the County of Essex

Benj^a Walker fore man
Enoch Greenleafe
Thomas Barnard
Dan^{ll} Powning
Robert Gubberidg
James Thornberei
William Paine
Andrew Cūningham
William Man
John Kilby
John Roulston
Abraham Blith
John Higgs
Sam^{ll} Wentworth
ffrancis Thresher

[Hand 3] The Coroners Return of untimely deaths Nou^ɛ 29: 1692.

Notes: It is probable that Toothaker died the same day as the Coroner's warrant indicates. As noted on the document, the Coroner's Return did not come until November 29. ◊ 1 wax seal.

Suffolk Court Files, vol. 32, docket 2690, p. 18, Massachusetts Supreme Judicial Court, Judicial Archives, Massachusetts State Archives. Boston, MA.

Monday, June 20, 1692

315. Testimony of William Hubbard for Sarah Buckley

[Hand 1] These may certifye whom it may

These are to certyfye whom it may or shall concerne that I haue known Sarah ye wife of William Buckly of Salem Uillage more or lesse eu⟨e⟩r since she was b̶⟨o̶r̶n̶e̶⟩ brought out of ⟨?⟩ England wch is aboue fifty yeares agoe and during all ye time I neuer knew nor heard of any euill in her carriage or conuersation unbicomming a christian: likewise she was bred up by christian parents all yᵉ time she liued here att Ipswich ^{I} further ⟨S⟩atisfye yᵗ yᵉ said Sarah was admitted as a member into yᵉ church of Ipswich abo⟨u⟩e f⟨or⟩ty yeares since: and that I neuer heard from others or obserued by my ~~my~~ selfe any thing of her that was inconsist⟨e⟩nt with her profession or unsuitable to christianity either in word deed or conuersation and am straingly surprized that any person should speake or thinke of her as one worthy to be Susspected of any such crime that she is now charged with in testimony hereof I haue here sett my hand this 20ᵗʰ of June 1692

William: Hubbard

[Reverse] [Hand 2?] mʳ Hubbards Certifficate

Notes: Sarah Buckley was examined May 18 (No. 168), but a grand jury did not hear her case until September 15, when a true bill was returned on an indictment for afflicting Ann Putnam Jr. (No. 618). However, she was not brought to trial until the following January, probably January 4, when she was found not guilty. See No. 755.

Massachusetts Archives Collection, vol. 135, no. 29. Massachusetts State Archives. Boston, MA.

Friday, June 24, 1692

316. Deposition of Deborah Hadley for Elizabeth How

[Hand 1] The Deposision of Debory Hadley aged about 70 yeares: this Deponant testifieth & sʰ that I haue liued near to Elizabeth How (yᵉ wife of James How Junior of Ipswich) {24 ⟨y⟩ear} & haue found her a Neighbourly woman Consciencious in her dealing faithfull to her pmises [= promises] & Christian=like in her Conuersation so far as I haue obs⟨er⟩ued & further saith nᵗ June 24 .1692.

Deborah Hadley

Notes: The deposition appears to have been prepared for How's grand jury, June 30. Her trial and conviction came that same day, and the document was probably used then. Documents similarly supporting her followed on June 25. ◊ Likely used at trial.

Essex County Court Archives, vol. 1, no. 327, Massachusetts Supreme Judicial Court, Judicial Archives, on deposit James Duncan Phillips Library, Peabody Essex Museum, Salem, MA.

Saturday, June 25, 1692

317. Testimony of Simon Chapman & Mary Chapman for Elizabeth How

[Hand 1] Ipswich June: th: 25th: 1692

The testimony of Simon Chapman agid. About 48 yers testifieth and sayth that ~~heth~~ heth bin Aquayntid with the wiuef of James houe ^{iunr} as a naybar for this 9 or 10 yers and he

June 25, 1692

neuar Sau eny harm by hur but that That hath bin good for I found hur Joust In hur delling faythfooll too hur prommisis [2nd "m" written over "i"]

I haue had acation to be in the ⟨p⟩ compiny of goodwiuf houe by the fortnight to gathar at Thayar hous: and at othar Tims and I found at all Tims by hur discors shee was a woman of afliktion and ⟨a⟩morning for sin in hur seluef And othars And when shee met with eny Afliktion she semid to iostifi god and say that Itt was all bett{⟨er⟩} then she desarfid [= deserved] thof [= though] it war By falls aq{u}sations ~~men~~ from men: and she yust To bles god that she got good by afliktions for it med hur exsamin hur oun hart

I neuar herd hur refil [= revile] eny parson that heth akusid hur with wichcraft but pittied them and sayid i pray god forgiue them for thay harm them selues mor then me Thof i am a gret sinar yit i am cler of that sayid she. and such kind of afliktions doth but set me aexsamining my oun hart and I find god wondarfolly seportining [= supporting] me and Confarting me by his word and promisis She semid to be a woman throu in that gret work of conuiktion and conuartion which I pray god mak us all: ⅄

Simon Chapman

My wiuef Mary Chapman cane Testifi to the most of this abouritan as witnes my hand

Mary Chapman

Notes: Likely used at trial. ◊ "throu": 'thorough' (*OED* s.v. *through* a.). "iostifi": 'prove or find [God] to be righteous or just' (*MED* s.v. *justifien* 3; *OED* s.v. *justify* 3).

Essex County Court Archives, vol. 1, no. 328, Massachusetts Supreme Judicial Court, Judicial Archives, on deposit James Duncan Phillips Library, Peabody Essex Museum, Salem, MA.

318. Statement of Daniel Warner, John Warner, & Sarah Warner for Elizabeth How

See also: June 30, 1692.

[Hand 1] from Ipswich Jū yᵉ :25: 1692
this may sertify hom it may conserne ~~I~~ ^{we} being desierd to wright some thing in yᵉ behalfe of yᵉ wife of Jeams how Junior of Ipswich hoe is aprehended: upon susspitiō of being gilty of yᵉ sin of wichcraft & nou in Salam prissoon upon yᵉ same acount for ~~my~~ ^{ouer} oun partes. ~~I~~ ^{we} haue bin ~~a~~ well aquainted wᵗ hur for aboue twenty yeers ~~I~~ ^{we} neuer see but yᵗ she cared it uery wel & yᵗ both hur wordes & actions wer always such as well become a good cristian: ~~I~~ ^{we} oftē spake to hur of some things yᵗ wer reported of hur yᵗ gaue som susspition of yᵗ she is now charged wᵗ & she always profesing hur Iinosency yᵗ in offen desiring ~~my~~ ^{ouer} prayers to god for hur ~~in his fear & supporte hur under yᵗ burdin~~ yᵗ god would keep hur in his fe⟨ar⟩ & yᵗ god would support hur under hur burdin ~~I~~ ^{we} haue offen herd hur speeking of thos persons yᵗ raisd thos reportes of hur and ~~I~~ ^{we} neuer heerd hur ~~euelly~~ speake badly of ~~of~~ ȳ for yᵉ same: but ~~rather~~ in ~~my~~ ^{ouer} {hering} hath offen said yᵗ she desired god that he would santtify [1st "t" written over "k"] yᵗ afflicktion as wel as others for hur spirituel good:

⟨D⟩ Daniel Warner: senʳ

John Warner. senʳ

Sarah Warner

Notes: Elizabeth How's grand jury case and trial came on June 30, shortly after this statement. ◊ Likely used at trial. ◊ "cared it": 'behaved' (*OED* s.v. *carry* v. 22c.).

Essex County Court Archives, vol. 1, no. 329, Massachusetts Supreme Judicial Court, Judicial Archives, on deposit James Duncan   June 25, 1692
Phillips Library, Peabody Essex Museum, Salem, MA.

319. Petition of William Milborne

To the Grave and Juditious ye General Assembly of the Province of ye Massachusets Bay in New-England the humble petitions of several Inhabitants of the Province afore^{sd} may it please the honorable Assembly that whereas several persons of good fame and of unspotted reputation stand committed to several gaols in this Province upon suspistion of sundry acts of witchcraft only upon bare specter testimonies many whereof we cannot but in Charity Judge to be Innocent and are sensible of their great Affliction and if sd. specter testimonie pass for evidence have great grounds to fear that the Innocent will be condemned upon ———. A woeful chain of consequences will undoubtedly follow besides the uncertaintie of ye exemption of any person from ye like accusation in ye said Province—the serious consideration whereof WE HAVE HUMBLY TENDERED TO YOU IN OUR HUMBLE ADDRESS IN ANOTHER PAPER; such peculiar matter of fact therein asserted and we have suffcent testimonie ready to aver ye same: therefore request that ye validitie of specter Testimonie may be weighed in ye balance of your grace and solid Judgments it being the womb that hath brought forth inextricable damage and misirie to this Province and to order by your votes that no more credence be given thereto than the word of God alloweth by which means God will be glorified their Majesties honored and the Interest and welfare of the Inhabitants of ye Province promoted and your Petistioners in duty boune shall dayly pray.

Notes: Although written earlier in June, this record is dated to the day when Governor Phips had Milborne arrested. See No. 320. He was ordered to post bond as a guarantee for good behavior or to be jailed. He apparently posted the bond. Milborne was a Baptist minister in Boston.

New England Historical and Genealogical Register and Antiquarian Journal, vol. 27 (1873), p. 55.

320. Order for the Arrest of William Milborne

Saturday June 25th 1692./.

There being laid before his Excy. and Council, Two Papers directed unto the Assembly, One of them Subscribed by William Milborn of Boston and Several Others, conteining very high Reflections upon the Administrations of Publick Justice within this their Majesties Province; The said William Milborne was sent for, and upon Examination Owned that the said Papers were of his writing, and that he Subscribed his Name to One of them.

Ordered. That the said William Milborne be committed to Prison, Or give Bond of Two hundred pounds, with two Sureties for his personal appearance at the next Superiour Court, or Court of Goal delivery to be held at Boston, to Answer what shall be Objected against him. on their Maties behalfe for framing, contriving, writing and publishing the said Seditious and Scandalous Papers or writings, and in the meantime to be of good Behaviour:/.

William Phips./.

Colonial Office 5/785, pp. 336–37. National Archives, UK.

Monday, June 27, 1692

321. Deposition of Isaac Cummings Sr. v. Elizabeth How

See also: June 30, 1692.

[Hand 1] Jun 27. 1692

The disposition of Isaac commins Sy{e}n^r [= senior] aged about sixty yers or thare abouts ⟨h⟩ who testyfieth and saith that about aight yers agon James how iun^r of ipswech. came to my hous to borow a hors I not being at home my son isaac told him {⟨?⟩ my son told me wh⟨e⟩n i cam home} i hade no hors to ride on. but my son isaac did tell the said how that his father hade no hors to ride on but he hade a mare the which he thought his father would not be wiling to lend this being upon a thursday the next ~~fr~~ day being fryday I took the ma{e}re and my self and my wif did ride on this maer abute half a mile to an naighbours hous and home again and when we came home I turnd the maer out the maer being as well to my thinking as ever she was next morning it being saterday about sun rising this said maer stood neer my doore and the said maer as i did aperehand did ⟨?⟩ show as if she head bin much abused by riding and here flesh a⟨s⟩ I thoug much wasted and her mouth ~~much~~ [Hand 2] {read} [Hand 1] semenly to my aperehantion much abused and hurt with ye bride⟨l⟩ ⟨b⟩its I seing ye maer in such a sad condition I toke up the said maer and put her in to my barn and she wold eate no maner of thing as for provender or any thing w^c i gave her then i sent for my brother thomas andros which was living in boxford the said anderos came to my hous. I not being at home when I came home a litil afore night my brother anderos told me he head giving ⟨?⟩ the said mear somthing for the bots but as he could purseve it did do her no good but said he I can not tell but she may have ~~y~~ the baly ach and said he i wil try one thing more ⟨?⟩ my brother anderos said he wold take a pipe of tobaco and lite it and but [= butt] itt in to ~~y~~ the fu{n}dement of the ~~mar~~ maer I told him that I thought it was not lawfull he said it was lawfull for man or beast then I toke a clen pipe and filled it with tobaco and did lite it and went with the pipe lite to ~~y^e~~ the barn then the said and{e}ros used the pipe as he said before he wold and the pip of tobaco did blaze and burn blew then I said to my brother anderos you shall try no more it is not lawful he said I will try again once mor which he did and then thar arose a blaze from ~~y~~ the pipe of tobaco which seemed to me to cover the butocks of the said mear the blaz went up ward towards the roof of the barn and {in} the roof of the barn thar was a grate crackling as if the barn would have falen or bin bu{r}nt which semed so to us which ware with in and som that ware with out ~~the~~ and we hade no other fier in the barn but only a candil and a pipe of tobaco and then I said I thought my barn or my mear ~~be~~ must go the next day being Lords day I spoke to my brother anderos at noone to come to see the said mear and said anderos came and what h [= he] did I say not the same Lords day {at} night my naig{h}bour John hunkins came to my hous and he and I went in to my barn to see this mear said hunkins said and if I ware as you i wolud cute of a pece of this mear and burn it I said no not to day but if she lived til {tomorow} morning he might cut of a pece ["p" written over "b"] off of⟨e⟩ her and burn if he would presently as we hade spoken these words we stept out of the barn and emedeiotly this said mear fell downe dade and never stured as we [Lost]o{u}ld [= could] purseve after she fell down but lay ~~stone~~ dead

[Hand 3] Isa^c Commings Senr declared: to y^e Jury of inquest: that y^e above written evidence: June 27, 1692
is y^e truth: upon oath June: 30th 1692

[Reverse] [Hand 4] Isaach Cumins

Notes: Even for the Salem witch trials, this comes as an unusual piece of evidence. It was not used at the trial of Elizabeth
How. ◊ "the bots": 'disease in horses caused by parasitical worms in the stomach' (*OED* s.v. *bot*, *bott*). ◊ Hand 3 = Simon
Willard

*Essex County Court Archives, vol. 1, no. 330, Massachusetts Supreme Judicial Court, Judicial Archives, on deposit James Duncan
Phillips Library, Peabody Essex Museum, Salem, MA.*

322. Three Depositions of Mary Cummings v. Elizabeth How

See also: June 29, 1692 & June 30, 1692.

[Hand 1] Jun 27 1692

The disposition of mary commings {y^e wif of isac commins syn^r} aged about sixty yers or
thare abouts ~~ho~~ who teseifieth and saith my husband not being at home I was sent to by som
parsons of ipsweg sent to me for to have me to write what I cold {say} of James how iun^r his
wife [Hand 2] {elesbeth} [Hand 1] conscarning her life or conversation and that I would say
what I cold say for or against her when the said hows wife sought to aioyn with y the church
at ipsweg and I spoke to my son Isaac to write that we hade used no brimston nor oyl ^{nor
no combusteblss to} to give to our maer becaus thare was a report that ~~y~~ the said hows wife
hade said ~~y~~ thay we hade givin the mear ⟨?⟩ brimston and oyl and ~~y~~ the like and a short time
after I hade writen my testemony consarning this hows wife my son Isaac his maer was
mising that [2nd "t" written over "y"] he could not find her in to or thre days. and in a short
time after my son isaacs maer came in sight not fare from the hous and my son isaac praid
me to go out and look ~~of~~ on his maer when I came to her ~~I~~ he asked me what I thought on
her and I said if he wold have my thoughts i could not compair it to nothing elce but that she
was riden with a hot bridil ~~I said also to isaac that I hered that the said~~ for she hade divirses
bruses as if she had bin ru͞ning over rocks an much wronged and where the bridel went was as
if it hade bin burnt with a ~~reede~~ hot bridel then I bide isaac take ye mare and have her up
amongst ~~our~~ the naghbours that peopl might see her for I hered that James how iun^r or his
wife or both hade said that we kepe up our maer that popel might not see her and isaac did
show his mear to saveril and then ⟨&⟩ the sai{d} how as i hered did report that isac had riden
to Lin ["i" written over "e"] ~~and~~ spring and caryed his ga⟨u⟩rl ["u" written over "i"] ^{and so
surfited the maer} the which was not so
[Hand 3] Mary Comins owned this har testimony to be truth before the Juryers for Inques:
this .29. of June: 1692
                                                                                    [Hand 4] Jurat in Curia

[Hand 1] Jun 27 1692

I mary co͞mins ~~the~~ ageed about sixty yers or thar abouts the wife of isaac comins syne^r I being
at my naigbour samel parlys hous samuel parlys daugter hannah being in a straing condition
asked me if i did not see goodee how in the hous going round upon the wall as the gur⟨l⟩
dricted her finger along round in won place and another of the hous {~~and the g⟨u⟩rl~~

June 27, 1692

~~asked me if i did nott~~} I teled her no. I loked as dilegently as i cold and i could see nothing of her the gurls mother then did chek her and told her she was alwas full of such kind of notions and bid her hold her toung the{n} she told her mother she would belive it one day and somthing mor which shold have bin mantio{ned} as ⟨?⟩ the g{a}ur⟨l⟩ poynted to show me whare goode how was she ask⟨ed⟩ me if I did not se her go out at that crak which she poynted at

[Hand 3] Mary Comins owned this har testimony one har oath to be the truth before the Juriars of Inquest: this 29. of June :92

[Hand 4] Jurat in Curia

Mary Comming

[Hand 1] Jun 27 1692

The disposition of mary commins aged about sixty. yers. or there abouts ho testefieth and saieth that about too yeres agon I went to viset my naigbour sherins wife and she told me that James how iun[r] had bin thare to give her a viset and he did sharply talk to her asking her what hopes she hade of her salveation her answer was to him that she did bild her hopes upon that suer rock Jesus christ this ~~y[e]~~ the said serins wife did tell me and she told me also that she had never talked of ~~Ja~~ the said how or his wife but she was the wors for it after wards. and she said also when she lay sick of the same sikness whareof she ~~dy~~ dyed that ⟨?⟩ the said how would come som times in to the roome to see her but s{h}e could not tell how to bare to se him nor that he should be in the hous.

[Hand 3] Mary Comins: ownid. that this har testimony on har oath before the Juryars for Inques: this 29. of June 1692

[Hand 4] Jurat in Curia

[Reverse] [Hand 5] Mary Cum̄ins

Notes: All three documents were used at the grand jury hearing and trial of Elizabeth How. "sherins wife" is presumably the wife of John Sherrin who appears as a sworn witness on both indictments against her, No. 347 & No. 348. The depositions here are dated to a grand jury on June 29, while other grand jury documents in her case are June 30. Either the grand jury met on Elizabeth How's case two days in a row, or there was a dating error. ◊ Used at trial. ◊ "surfited": 'exhausted, overstrained' (cf. *OED* s.v. *surfeit*). ◊ Hand 4 = Stephen Sewall

Essex County Court Archives, vol. 1, no. 331, Massachusetts Supreme Judicial Court, Judicial Archives, on deposit James Duncan Phillips Library, Peabody Essex Museum, Salem, MA.

323. Summons for Witnesses v. Sarah Good, and Officer's Return

See also: June 28, 1692.

[Hand 1] W[m] & Mary By y[e] grace of God of England Scotland ffrance & Ireland King & Queen def[rs] of y[e] faith &c[a]

To Samuel Abbey & his Wife. Joseph Herrick & his Wife goodwife Bibber Abigall Williams Elizabeth Hubbard. Mary Wolcott Ann Putman Marcey. Lewis. – [Hand 2] Samuel Braybrook [Hand 3] ~~Thom gage Zachriah herek~~

[Hand 1] Wee comand:

You and Euery of you all Excuses set apart to appear at yᵉ special Court of Oyer & Terminer to be held at Salem for yᵉ County of Essex on yᵉ 28ᵗʰ of this Instant month at Nine of yᵉ Clock in yᵉ Morning there to testify yᵉ truth to yᵉ best of your knowledge on seuerall Indictments then & there to be Exhibited against Sarah Good for sundry acts of Witchcrafts by her Comitted & done. hereof make return fail not dated in Salem June .27. 1692

Step: Sewall Clerc

To yᵉ Constables of Salem or any of them Greeting
[Hand 3] Dat: 28 Jun 1692
I haue warned ^{the.} parsens. aboue named
accorden to tener of this summonce by
me. John putnam. Cunst of salam

[Reverse] [Hand 1] Subpena versus. Sa: Good.

Notes: In the manuscript, Mercy Lewis's name appears to be an insertion after the document had been completed. The same is true regarding Zachariah Herrick, Thomas Gage, and Samuel Braybrook, although "herek" and "Gage" are crossed out. Numerous instances of such adjustments appear among the documents. ◊ Hand 1 = Stephen Sewall; Hand 2 = Thomas Putnam ◊ 1 wax seal. ◊ Facsimile Plate 8.

Essex County Court Archives, vol. 1, no. 10, Massachusetts Supreme Judicial Court, Judicial Archives, on deposit James Duncan Phillips Library, Peabody Essex Museum, Salem, MA.

324. Summons for Witnesses v. Susannah Martin, and Officer's Return

See also: June 28, 1692 & June 29, 1692.

[Hand 1] William & Mary By yᵉ Grace of God of England Scotland ffrance & Ireland King King & Queen defendᴱˢ of yᵉ faith &cᵃ. To John Allen Barnard Peache Joseph Ringg William Browne Jaruis Ringg James {ffreeze} John Kimball John Pressy Ensigne Joseph Knight mʳ John Atkison & his wife & Son [Hand 2] & mary the wif of nathanell whitteer the wife John pressy & Joⁿ kembal

[Hand 1] Greeting

Wee Comand you and Euery of you all Excuses Set apart to be and appear at yᵉ Speciall Court of Oyer & Terminer holden at Salem yᵉ 28ᵗʰ of this Instant month then & There to testify yᵉ truth to yᵉ best of their knowledge On Seuerall Indictments to be Exhibited against Susanna Martin of Amesberry hereof make Return fail not dated in Salem June. 27ᵗʰ 1692 & in yᵉ fourth year of Our Reign.

Step: Sewall Cler

To yᵉ Sheriff of Essex or deputy or Constables of Newbury Salsbury & Amesbury Greeting also warn those persons that wᵗʰ James ffreeze or at any other time heard Susanna Martin Threaten relating to John Allens Oxen or any other thing whatso{e}uer & make return as aboue

Step: Sewall Cler

[Hand 3] 28. June ⟨?⟩ ^{92} by uertue of this supeny. then was. warned mʳ John. Atkinson. his wife. and his son. nathaniel to make theire. parsnall. apperance ~~at Salem~~ ⟨a⟩t yᵉ Court of

June 27, 1692

oyer & term⟨iner⟩ ~~to be~~ holden at Salem. 28:: of this instant. June: ensigne Joseph ~~dated 29 of~~ Knight. was warned before

> by me Samuel hills co[Lost][= constable]
> for newbury

[Reverse] [Hand 4] This or these supenys weare obserued & serued upon the seuerall persons therin mentioned according to yᵉ tenour there of namly upon Mʳ John Allin: & Barnard Peach & Joseph Ring & william Browne & Jaruiss Ring & Mary yᵉ wife of Nathaniell Whitcher: & yᵉ same read to them the twenty ninth of this Instant ~~may~~ {June} Anño: 1692

> ℈ me Joseph Eaton Constable
> ffor sallisbury

This supeny was serued according to yᵉ tenor theare of upon yᵉ persons thearin mentioned belonging to our towne Namly upon John Pressy & his wife & ⟨J⟩[Lost]⟨h⟩n [= John] Kimball & his wife & the same read to them yᵉ: 29ᵗ[Lost] [= 29th] ⟨of⟩ this Instant June Anño: 1692:

> ℈ me Joseph Lankister senʳ
> Constable ffor Amsbury

[Hand 1] Subpena Con Susan Martin

Notes: Hand 1 = Stephen Sewall; Hand 2 = Robert Pike ◊ 1 wax seal.

Essex County Court Archives, vol. 1, no. 176, Massachusetts Supreme Judicial Court, Judicial Archives, on deposit James Duncan Phillips Library, Peabody Essex Museum, Salem, MA.

325. Statement of Joseph Knowlton & Mary Knowlton for Elizabeth How
See also: June 30, 1692.

[Hand 1] from Ipswich June 27:. 1692 Joseph knoulton being aquainte with the wife of James How {Junʳ}. as a neighbour & somtims bording in the house: and at my first coming to liue in those parts which was about ten years ago, I hard ⟨Ꝫ⟩ a bad Report of her about Samuell perleys garle. which caused me to take speshall noates of her life & conuersation euer sence and I haue asked her if she could freely forgiue them that Raised such Reports of her she tould me yes with all her heart desiering that god would giue her a heart to be more humble vnder such a prouidences and further she sayd she was willing {to doe} any good she could to them as had don vnneighbourly by her also this I haue taken notes of that she would deny her self to doe a neighbour a good turn. and also I haue known her to be faithfull in her word and honest in her dealeings as fare as euer I saw

> [Hand 2?] Jos⟨u⟩ph knoulton eaged forty tu
> mary knowlten eaged thury tu

[Reverse] [Hand 3] in behalfe of Eli. How

Notes: Likely used at trial. ◊ Hand 3 = Stephen Sewall

Essex County Court Archives, vol. 1, no. 332, Massachusetts Supreme Judicial Court, Judicial Archives, on deposit James Duncan Phillips Library, Peabody Essex Museum, Salem, MA.

Tuesday, June 28, 1692

Grand Jury of Sarah Good

Trial of Sarah Good (Day 1)

Officer's Return: Summons for Witnesses v. Sarah Good
2nd of 2 dates. See No. 323 on June 27, 1692

Officer's Return: Summons for Witnesses v. Susannah Martin
2nd of 3 dates. See No. 324 on June 27, 1692

326. Deposition of Johanna Childen v. Sarah Good‡

[Hand 1] The deposition ["t" written over "s"] of Johanna Childin testifieth and saieth that upon 2^d of June: 1692: that the aparition of Sarah good and her least Child did apear to her: and the Child did tell its mother that she did murrder it: to which Sarah ~~replied~~ Good replyed that she did it becaus that she Could ^{not} atend it ~~and~~ and the Child tould its mother that she was A witch: and then Sarah good said she did giue it to the diuell

[Reverse] [Hand 2] Childrin

Notes: The assignment of a date here is speculative. The deposition is a June document and appears to have been in preparation for Sarah Good's grand jury case or for her trial. It was used at neither.

Essex County Court Archives, vol. 1, no. 22, Massachusetts Supreme Judicial Court, Judicial Archives, on deposit James Duncan Phillips Library, Peabody Essex Museum, Salem, MA.

327. Testimony of Isaac Cummings Jr. v. Elizabeth How

[Hand 1] June 28th 1692.
The testimony of Isack Comings ^{Juner} aged about 27. yeers Testifieth & saith y^t James Hough Juner came to my fathers house when he was not att home he asked me if my father had Euer a hors & I told him no he asked me if he had Euer a maer & I told him yesh he asked me if I Thought my father would Lend him his maer & I told him I Did not Think he would vpon wch wth in a short Tyme after my father & mother Ridd their maer to Their neighbours house ye same maer wch s^d hough would haue Borowed wch semingly was well when my fath^r & moth^r came home I seeing ye same s^d maer ye nex morning Could Judge noe other butt. y^t she had bin Rid ye other part of y^t night or oth^r wayes horibly abuzed vpon wch my fath^r seeing w^t a Condition his maer was in sent for his Broth^r Thomus Andros wch when he came he giu her seuerall Things wch he Thought to be good for her butt did her not any good vpon wch he s^d he would try one Thing moer wch was a pipe & some Tobacou wch he applid to her Thinking itt might doe her good against ye Belly ake Thinking y^t might be her diszease wch when they vzed ye pipe wth Tobacco in itt abought ye s^d maer ye pipe being Litt itt Blazed so much y^t itt was as much as Two persons Could putt itt ought wth both of Their hands vpon wch my father said wee will Trye no more brother my vncle s^d he would trye on⟨c⟩e more ye wch he did ye pipe being Litt ye fyer Blazed out of ye same s^d pipe more

June 28, 1692   vehemently the⟨n⟩ before vpon wch my father answerd he had Rather Looze his maer y^n his barn ye uery nex night folloing ye s^d maer folloing my father in his barn from one side to ye other side fell down imediatly Dead against ye sell of ye barn befor my fath^r had well Cleerd him selfe from her. furth^r saith not

[Reverse] [Hand 2] Isak Cumins

Notes: As with other Cummings family testimony against Elizabeth How, the story of the mare continues. See No. 321, No. 322 & No. 396. This document was not used at the grand jury or trial, and the "testimony" apparently was written in advance of those procedures.

Essex County Court Archives, vol. 1, no. 333, Massachusetts Supreme Judicial Court, Judicial Archives, on deposit James Duncan Phillips Library, Peabody Essex Museum, Salem, MA.

328. Summons for Witnesses v. John Willard & Martha Carrier, and Officer's Return, Copy

See also: June 29, 1692.

[Hand 1] William & Mary By ye Grace of god of England Scotland ffrance & Ireland King Defenders of ye faith &^{c}

~~Greeting~~

To John Rogers Allen Toothaker Ralph ffarnum ~~Senr~~ Jun^ε John ffarnum Son of Ralph Farnū Sen^ε Benjamin Abbott & His Wife Andrew ffoster Mark Graues & his wife and Daughte⟨r⟩ Sarah Whight Phebe Chandler daughter of Will Chandler

Greeting

Wee Comand you & Euery of you to appear at ye p^{ε}sent Court of Oyer & Terminer holden Att Salem wthout delay There to Testifie ye truth of ye Best of yo^ε Knowledge on Certain Indictments Then & There to Be ~~indicted~~ Exhibited Against John Willard & Martha Carrier Hereof Make return fail not
Dated in Salem June 28^t 1692 And in ye 4^t year of ~~ye reign~~ Our Reign

Stephen Sewall
Cleric

To ye Constables of Andov^ε & Bilrica

~~This is A Trew Coppey Compared~~
~~w^ε~~ vera Copia. Comperata &^{c}
This is A trew Coppey Compared with the
Origionall &^{c}
June 29th 1692

[Reverse] [Hand 2] In obedienc to this writ I haue sumanc those parsones [   ] hose names are hearein written/
This 29 day of iune: 1692
By mee John Ballard constable of andouer

[Hand 1] Subpena Carr^r & Willard

Notes: John Ballard was to become a crucial figure in helping to precipitate the Andover phase of the witchcraft episode.
◊ Hand 1 = Stephen Sewall

Witchcraft Papers, no. 16a, Massachusetts Historical Society. Boston, MA.

329. List of Witnesses v. Sarah Good‡

[Hand 1] ~~Aboue~~ witnesses against Sarah Good
William Allen
John Hughes
Samuell Brabrooke
Mary walkut
Mercy Lewis
Sarah Vibber
Abiga^ll Williams
Elizabeth Hubberd
Ann Putman
    Tittube indian
Richard Patch

[Reverse] [Hand 2] Sarah Good

Notes: *SWP* carries this document as part of a mittimus for Sarah Good, May 25, incorrectly dated in *SWP* as May 24. However, this manuscript is a separate document from the mittimus, No. 218, and is more likely to be a record of witnesses at her grand jury or trial on June 28 and 29.

Essex County Court Archives, vol. 1, no. 7, Massachusetts Supreme Judicial Court, Judicial Archives, on deposit James Duncan Phillips Library, Peabody Essex Museum, Salem, MA.

330. Indictment No. 1 of Sarah Good, for Afflicting Sarah Bibber†

[Hand 1] Anno: Regis et Reginæ Willm̄ et
Mariæ: nunc Angliæ &^c Quarto.

Essex ss:

The Juro̅ᵉ for our Sovereigne Lord and Lady the King and Queen: pᵉsents That Sarah Good wife of William Good of Salem [Hand 2] ^{Villiage} [Hand 1] in the County of Essex Husbandman the Second Day of May in the forth year of the Reigne of our Sovereigne Lord and Lady William and Mary by the Grace of God of England Scottland ffrance & Ireland King and Queen Defenders of the ffaith &^c and Divers other Dayes and times as well before as after, certaine Detestable Arts, called Witchcrafts, and Sorceries, Wickedly, & ffelloniously, hath vsed Practised, & Exersised, at and within the Township of Salem: in the County of Essex aforesaid in vpon and against one Sarah Vibber wife of John Vibber of Salem aforesaid Husbandman, by which said Wicked Arts: the she [= she the] said Sarah ["S" written over "M"] Vibber, the said Second Day of May in the fourth Year abovsaid and divers other Dayes and times as well before as after was and is Tortured Afflicted Pined Consumed wasted and Tormented,- and also for Sundrey other Acts of witchcraft by said Sarah Good ["G" written over "g"] committed and done before and Since that time ag^t the Peace of our Sovereigne Lord & Lady the King & Queen, their Crowne and Dignity and ag^t the forme of the Statute in that case made and Provided:/

[Hand 2] Witnesses.

June 28, 1692

Sarah Vibber Jurat
Abigall Williams Jurat
Elizabeth Hubbard.
Ann Putman Jurat
Jnº Vibber – Sworne

[Reverse] Nº 1. Ind^t of Sarah Good.
[Hand 3] billa uera

Notes: Hand 2 = Stephen Sewall

Essex County Court Archives, vol. 1, no. 3, Massachusetts Supreme Judicial Court, Judicial Archives, on deposit James Duncan Phillips Library, Peabody Essex Museum, Salem, MA.

331. Indictment No. 2 of Sarah Good, for Afflicting Elizabeth Hubbard†

[Hand 1] Anno Regis et ^{Reginæ} Willm̄ et
Mariæ. nunc: Angliæ &: Quarto

Essex ss

The Juro̅^{ɛ} for our. Sovereigne Lord and Lady the King and Queen: p^{ɛ}sents That Sarah Good wife of William Good: of Salem Villiage in the County of Essex husbandman the first Day of March in the forth year of the Reigne of our Sovereigne Lord. and Lady William & Mary by the Grace of God of England Scottland ffrance and Ireland Defenders of the faith &^{c} and divers other Dayes, and times, as well before as after certaine Detestable Artes called witchcrafts & Sorceries: wickedly and ffellioniously hath vsed Practised & Exercised: at and within the Towne ship of Salem in the County of Essex aforesaid. in upon and ag^t one Elizabeth Hubbard: of Salem aforesaid single woman: by wch said wicked Arts the said Elizabeth Hubbart, the said first Day of March in the fourth year aforesaid: and at Divers other Dayes and times as well before as affter, was and is Tort⟨v⟩red Afflicted: Pined. wasted and Tormented. as also for Sundery other Acts of Witchcraft by s^d Sarah Good Committed and done before and since that time ag^t the Peace of our Sovereigne Lord and Lady King & Queen of England, and ag^t the forme of the statute in that Case made & Provided.

Wittnesses

Elizabeth Hubbard

Anne Puttman [Hand 2] Jurat

[Hand 1] Mary Wallcott [Hand 2] Jurat in Curia June. 28th 1692.

[Hand 1] Abigaill Williams [Hand 2] Jurat

[Reverse] Nº 2: ag^t Sarah. Good
[Hand 3] bila uera
[Hand 2?] Sarah Good

Notes: The use of "Jurat in Curia" to confirm grand jury testimony is unusual, as is the dating of an indictment. It may suggest some use of this document at the trial beyond the presentation of it to the trial jury and even the possibility that Sarah Good's trial began on June 28. But if so, it remains unclear as to how this indictment might have been used differently at the trial. ◊ Possibly used at trial. ◊ Hand 2 = Stephen Sewall

Essex County Court Archives, vol. 1, no. 6, Massachusetts Supreme Judicial Court, Judicial Archives, on deposit James Duncan Phillips Library, Peabody Essex Museum, Salem, MA.

332. Indictment No. 3 of Sarah Good, for Afflicting Ann Putnam Jr.† June 28, 1692

[Hand 1] The Jurors for our Soveraigne Lord & Lady. King William & Queen Mary. Doe present; That Sarah Good yᵉ Wife. of william Good, of Salem. Villiage In yᵉ County of Essex husbandman, upon, yᵉ first day of March, In yᵉ fourth Year of yᵉ Reigne of our Soveraigne, Lord & Lady Wᵐ & Mary, by yᵉ Grace of god of England, Scotland ffrance & Ireland. King & Queen, defendᵉ of yᵉ faith &⟨c⟩ & Diuers other dayes, & Times. as well before as after, Certaine Detestable Arts, Caled Witchcrafts, & Sorceries, wickedly & ffeloniously, hath vsed; practiced & Exersised. at & within yᵉ Township of Salem aforesaid In, vpon & against An̄. Puttman, Singlewom⟨an⟩ of Salem Village, by which said Wicked arts, ~~of~~ {the} said, An̄ Puttman yᵉ said first day of March in yᵉ fourth, Year, abouesaid & diuers other dayes & times, as well before, as after, was & is hurt, Tortured afflicted, Pined, Consumed, wasted, & Tormented, & also for Sundry acts, of Witchcraft by said Good, Com̄itted & done before & since that time, against yᵉ peace of our Soveraigne Lord & Lady yᵉ King & Queen, Thair Crowne & dignity & against yᵉ forme of, yᵉ Statutes; ~~made~~ In that Case made & provided.
[Hand 2] Witnesses.
Ann Putman Jurat
Eliz: Hubbard
Abigall Williams: Jurat

[Reverse] [Hand 3] Nᵒ 3 [   ] bila uera
Sarah Goodˢ

Notes: Hand 2 = Stephen Sewall

Essex County Court Archives, vol. 1, no. 5, Massachusetts Supreme Judicial Court, Judicial Archives, on deposit James Duncan Phillips Library, Peabody Essex Museum, Salem, MA.

333. Testimony of William Batten, William Shaw, & Deborah Shaw v. Sarah Good
See also: June 29, 1692.

[Hand 1] The testiminy of William Batten aged ⟨65⟩ 76 years or there abouts and william Shaw aged about 50 years and Deborah his wife aged about 40 years these all testifie and say that this day was a weeke agoe. Susannah shelding being at the house of william shaw shee was tied her hands acrosse in such a manner that we were forced to cut the string before we could git her hands loosse and when shee was out of her fit shee told us it Goode dastin that did tye her hands after that manner and 4 times shee hath been tyed in this manner in toue weeks time the 2 first times shee sayth it was goode Dostin and the 2 Last times it was Sarah Goode that did ~~afflict~~ tye her we furder testifie that when ever shee doeth but touch this string shee is presently bit
we furder testifie that in this time there was a broome carried away out of the housse invisibble to us and put in a apple tree two times and a shirt once and a milke tube once was carried out of the house three poles from the house into the woods and shee ~~testifieth that~~ say{e}th tha⟨t⟩ it
[Hand 2] thes parsons aboue named upon their oath ownid this their testimony to be the trus before us the Juriars for Inquest this. 28. of Jun: 1692
[Hand 3] Jurat in Curia.

June 28, 1692   [Reverse] [Hand 2] Wm Batten
                        Con. Good

Notes: Used at trial. ◊ Hand 1 = Ezekiel Cheever; Hand 3 = Stephen Sewall

Essex County Court Archives, vol. 1, no. 17, Massachusetts Supreme Judicial Court, Judicial Archives, on deposit James Duncan Phillips Library, Peabody Essex Museum, Salem, MA.

334. Deposition of Sarah Bibber v. Sarah Good

[Hand 1] The deposition of Sarah Biber aged 36 years testifieth and sayeth that the
^{saterday} night before ~~Sarah~~ goode Dostin ^{of Reding} was examined I saw the
appariton of Sarah goode standing by my bedside, and shee ~~pll~~ pulled aside the curtain and
turned down the sheet and Looked upon my child about 4 years old and presently upon it
the child was stracke into a great fit that my housband and I could hardly hold it
[Hand 2] Sara biber one har oath did owne this har testimony before the Jurriars for Inquest:
this .28. of June: 1692
[Hand 3] Jurat Sarah Viber

[Hand 4] G. Vibber ags^t Goody. Good

Notes: Hand 1 = Ezekiel Cheever; Hand 3 = Stephen Sewall; Hand 4 = Jonathan Corwin

Essex County Court Archives, vol. 1, no. 25, Massachusetts Supreme Judicial Court, Judicial Archives, on deposit James Duncan Phillips Library, Peabody Essex Museum, Salem, MA.

335. Deposition of Sarah Bibber v. Sarah Good
See also: June 29, 1692.

[Hand 1] The Deposistion of Sarah viber aged about 36 years who testifieth and saith that
sence I haue ben afflected I haue often seen the Apperishtion of Sarah Good but she did not
hurt me tell the 2 day of may 1692 tho I saw hir Apperishtion most greviously tortor ^{mircy
lewes &} Jno. Indian att {Salem} on the 11th April 1692: but on the 2: may 1692 the
Apperishtion of Sarah good did most greviously torment me by presing my breath almost
out of my body and also she did Immediatly afflect my child by pinceig of it that I could
hardly hold it and my husband seing of it took hold of the Child but it cried out and twisted
so dreadfully by reson of the torture that the Apperishtion of Sarah Good did afflect it with
all that it gott out of its fathers Armes to: also seuerally times ^{sence} the Apperishtion of
Sarah Good has most greviously tormented me by beating and pinching me and almost
choaking me to death and pricking me with pinnes after a most dreadfull maner

[Hand 2] Sara uiber ownid this har testimony to be the truth one the oath she had taken:
before us the Juriars for Inquest: this: 28 dy of June: 1692

[Hand 3] Sworne. in Court June. 29th 1692.

[Hand 4] And further Add^s that shee very beleiues upon her Oath that Sarah Good had
bewitched her

[Reverse] [Hand 1] Sarah viber against Sarah good   June 28, 1692
[Hand 4?] ~~Sarah Goods Examination~~

Notes: The use of "Sworne in Court" by Sewall is unusual for a trial notation, but nevertheless seems to indicate that Sarah Bibber's testimony is a trial document. Likely used at trial. ◊ Hand 1 = Thomas Putnam; Hand 3 = Stephen Sewall

Essex County Court Archives, vol. 1, no. 26, Massachusetts Supreme Judicial Court, Judicial Archives, on deposit James Duncan Phillips Library, Peabody Essex Museum, Salem, MA.

336. Depositions of Sarah Gage & Thomas Gage v. Sarah Good

[Hand 1] The deposition of Sarah Gadge y^e wife of thomas Gadge aged about 40 years this deponent testifieth & saith that about two years & an halfe agone; Sarah Good Came to her house & would have come into ye house, but sd Sarah Gadge told her she should not come in for she was afraid she had been with them that had ye smallpox; & with that she fell to mutring & scolding extreamly & soe; told sd Gadge if she would not let her in ~~she~~ she should give her somthing; & she answered she would not have any thing to doe with her & the next morning after to sd Deponents best remembrance one ^{of} sd Gadges Cowes Died in A sudden, terible, & strange, unusuall maner soe y^t some of ye neighbors & said Deponent did think it to be done by witchcraft & farther saith not

And Thomas Gadge husband of sd Sarah: testifieth y^t he had a Cow soe Died about ye time abovmentioned & though he & some neighbors opened y^e Cow yet they Could find no naturall Cause of s̄d Cowes Death & farther saith not

[Hand 2] Thomas gadge and sara gadge owned this to be the truth one theire oath. before us: the Juriars for Inquest this 28. of June: 92

[Reverse] [Hand 3] Thomas Gauge & his wife ver. Good

Notes: Hand 3 = Stephen Sewall

Essex County Court Archives, vol. 1, no. 15, Massachusetts Supreme Judicial Court, Judicial Archives, on deposit James Duncan Phillips Library, Peabody Essex Museum, Salem, MA.

337. Deposition of Joseph Herrick Sr. & Mary Herrick v. Sarah Good
See also: June 29, 1692.

[Hand 1] The Deposistion of Joseph Herrick ^{senr} who testifieth and saith that: on the first day of march 1691/92: I being then Constable for Salem: there was deliuered to me by warrant ffrom the worshipfull Jno Hathorne and Jonathan Corwine Esqrs: Sarah good: for me to cary to Their majesties Gaol at Ipswich and that night I sett a gard to wacth hir at my own house ⟨Sa⟩ namely Samu^l Braybrook michaell dunell Jonathan Baker:: and the affore named parsons Informed me in the morning that: that night Sarah good was gon for sume time from them both bare foot and bare legde: and I was also informed that: that night Elizabeth Hubburd one of the Afflected parsons complaned that Sarah Good came and afflected hir:: being bare foot and barelegded and Samuell Sibley that was one that was

June 28, 1692

attending of Elizā Hubburd strock Sarah good on the Arme as Elizabeth Hubburd said and mary Herrick the wife of the abouesaid Joseph Herick testifeth that {on:} the 2ᵗʰ march 1691/92 in the morning I took notis of Sarah good in the morning and one of hir Armes was blooddy from ^{a little below} the Elbow to the wrist: and I also took notis of hir armes on the night before and then there was no signe of blood on them

[Hand 2] Joseph. herrik senr and mary harrik appearid before us the Jary for Inquest: and did on the oath which the [= they] had taken owne this their euidens to be the truth: this 28. of June 1692

[Hand 3] Sworne in Court

[Reverse] [Hand 1] Joseph Herrick and his wife against Sarah Good
[Hand 3] Memento.
Sam. Sibley to be Serued
Michˡˡ ⟨≱⟩ Dunwill
Jona. Bacar

ver. Sa. Good

Notes: As with Document 335, Sewall's notation is unusual for a trial document, which this appears to be. Likely used at trial. ◊ Hand 1 = Thomas Putnam; Hand 3 = Stephen Sewall

Essex County Court Archives, vol. 1, no. 16, Massachusetts Supreme Judicial Court, Judicial Archives, on deposit James Duncan Phillips Library, Peabody Essex Museum, Salem, MA.

Deposition of Samuel Parris, Thomas Putnam, & Ezekiel Cheever v. Sarah Good, Sarah Osburn, & Tituba

3ʳᵈ of 3 dates. See No. 8 on March 1, 1692

Sworn Before the Grand Jury: Deposition of Ann Putnam Jr. v. Sarah Good

2ⁿᵈ of 2 dates. See No. 9 on March 1, 1692

338. Deposition of Susannah Shelden v. Sarah Good

[Hand 1] The Deposistion of Susannah Shelden agged about 18 years who testifieth and saith that sence I haue ben afflected I haue uery often ben most greviously tortored by the Apperishtion of Sarah Good who has most dreadfully afflected me by bitting pricking and pinching me and almost choaking me to death but on the 26. June 1692 Sarah good most violently pulled down my head behind a cheast and tyed my hands together with a whele band & allmost choaked me to death. and also seuerall times sence the Apperishtiō of Sarah good has most greviously tortored me by biting pinching and almost choaking me to death: also william Battin and Thomas Buffington juner ware fforced to cutt the whele band from ofe my hands for they could not unty it

[Hand 2] And farther sᵈ Sheldon upon giving in this testimony to the grand jury was seized with sundry fits wᶜʰ when she came to her self she told the sᵈ jury being askt that it was sᵈ Good that afflicted her & a little after M̶e̶r̶c̶y̶ ̶L̶e̶w̶e̶s̶ ^{Mary Warren} falling into a fit sᵈ Sheldon affirmed to the Grand jury that she saw sᵈ Good upon her, & also a sauser being by

invisible hands taken of from ~~the~~ ^{a} Table ~~at which the jury sat~~ & carried out of doors s^d   June 28, 1692
Sheldon affirmed she saw said Sarah Good carry it away & put it where it was found abroad
[Hand 3] Susanah Shelden: oned this har testimony to be the truth before the Juriars of
Inquest on the oath which she had taken this .28. of June 1692.

[Reverse] [Hand 4] Susannah Shelden ag^t Sarah Good

Notes: It appears as if Parris made his addition after the grand jury testimony of Shelden, but the document was not used at the trial. ◊ Hand 1 = Thomas Putnam; Hand 2 = Samuel Parris; Hand 4 = Stephen Sewall

Essex County Court Archives, vol. 1, no. 23, Massachusetts Supreme Judicial Court, Judicial Archives, on deposit James Duncan Phillips Library, Peabody Essex Museum, Salem, MA.

339. Deposition of Mary Walcott v. Sarah Good

[Hand 1] The Deposistion of Mary walcott agged about 17 years who testifieth and saith
that sence I haue been afflected I haue often seen the Aperishtion of Sarah good amongst the
wicthes who has also afflected me and urged me to writ in hir book

[Hand 2] The mark of
Mary Walcot.

[Hand 3] mary welcott ownid this har testimony to be the truth one har oath. before the
Juriars for Inquest this 28. of June 1692
[Hand 1] also mary walcott testifieth that I haue seen Sarah good afflicting mercy lewes and
Elizabeth Hubberd and Abigail williams and I uerily beleue she bewicthed me

[Reverse] [Hand 4] Mary Walcott ag^t Sarah Good

Notes: Hand 1 = Thomas Putnam; Hand 2 = Samuel Parris; Hand 4 = Thomas Newton

Essex County Court Archives, vol. 1, no. 24, Massachusetts Supreme Judicial Court, Judicial Archives, on deposit James Duncan Phillips Library, Peabody Essex Museum, Salem, MA.

340. Petition of Rebecca Nurse

[Hand 1] To y^e Honou^ɛd Cou^ɛt of Oryn and Terminer now sitting In Salem
this 28 of June An° 1692
The humble petission of Rebecca Nurse of Salem Village//
Humbley Sheweth//
That whareas sum Women did sarch Yo^ɛ Petission^ɛ At Salem as I did then Conceiue for
sum supernaturall Marke, And then one of the s^d Women which is Known to be, the Moaste
Antient skillfull prudent person of them all as to Any such Concerne: did Express hir selfe to
be: of A contrary opinion from the Rest And did then Declare, that shee saw Nothing In or
Aboute yo^ɛ Hono^ɛs poare pettissione^ɛ But what might Arise from A naturall Cause: And I

then Rendered the said persons a sufficient Knowne Reason as to my selfe of the Moueing Cause Thereof: which was by Exceeding Weaknesses: decending partly from an ouerture of Nature And difficult Exigences that hath Befallen me In the Times of my Trauells: And therefore Yo^ε pettission^ε Humbley prayes/ That yo^ε Honou^{ε}s would be pleased to Admitt of sum other Women to Enquire Into this Great: Concerne, those that are Moast Graue wise and skillfull: Namely Ms: Higginson sen^ε Ms Buckstone Ms: Woodbery two of them Being Midwiues: Ms: Porter Together with such others, as may be Choasen on that Account: Before I am Brought to my triall: All which I hoape yo^ε Honou^{ε}s: will take Into yo^ε prudent Consideration And find it Requisite Soe to doe: for my Life Lyes Now In yo^ε Hands vnder God: And Being Conscious of My owne Innocency I Humbley Begg that I may haue Liberty to manifest it to the wourld partly by the Meanes Abouesaid

And Yo^ε Poare pettissio^ε shall Euermore
pray as In duty Bound &c//

Rebecca Nurse

hir Marke

[Reverse] [Hand 2] Rebecca Nurse Peticõn

Notes: According to Robert Calef, Rebecca Nurse received a reprieve from Governor Phips that was quickly withdrawn after objection to it, probably by one or more of the Court's judges. Calef gives no details as to when it was given or when it was withdrawn. *More Wonders*, p. 103. ◊ Hand 2 = Stephen Sewall

Essex County Court Archives, vol. 1, no. 88, Massachusetts Supreme Judicial Court, Judicial Archives, on deposit James Duncan Phillips Library, Peabody Essex Museum, Salem, MA.

341. Statement of James How Sr. for Elizabeth How

See also: June 30, 1692.

[Hand 1] information for elizebath How the wife of Jams How Junr
Jams How sen^r aged about 94 sayth that he liueing by her for about thirty years hath taken notes that she hath caried it well becoming her place as a daughter as a wife in all Relation seting aside humain infirmitys as becometh a Christion with Respact to my self as a father very dutyfully & a wifife to my son uery Carfull loueing obediant and kind Considering his want of eye sight tenderly leading him about by the hand {now} desiering god may guide your honours to se a differans between predigous [= prejudice] and Consentes [= conscience] I Rest yours to sarue

James How sen^r of Ipswich

dated this 28 day of June 1692

[Reverse] [Hand 2] S⟨?⟩no⟨?⟩[Lost]

Notes: Likely used at trial. ◊ "caried it": 'behaved' (*OED* s.v. *carry* v. 22c.).

Essex County Court Archives, vol. 1, no. 339, Massachusetts Supreme Judicial Court, Judicial Archives, on deposit James Duncan Phillips Library, Peabody Essex Museum, Salem, MA.

Wednesday, June 29, 1692

Grand Juries of Elizabeth How (Day 1) & Susannah Martin

Trials of Sarah Good (Day 2), Susannah Martin & Rebecca Nurse

Officer's Return: Summons for Witnesses v. Susannah Martin
3rd of 3 dates. See No. 324 on June 27, 1692

Officer's Return: Summons for Witnesses v. John Willard & Martha Carrier, Copy
2nd of 2 dates. See No. 328 on June 28, 1692

342. Fragment of the Examination of Deliverance Hobbs‡

[Hand 1] Deliverance Hobs Confession
That they were both at the generall meeting of the Witches in Mr Parisses fiel[Lost]
[= field] Mr Burroughs preached & administred to them

[Reverse] [Hand 2] [Lost]⟨s.⟩ Procter

Notes: The document is degraded but appears to match a summary of evidence against Sarah Good, and it is accordingly
dated June 29, the date assigned to that summary against Sarah Good. See No. 345. ◊ Hand 1 = Thomas Newton

*Essex County Court Archives, vol. 2, no. 31, Massachusetts Supreme Judicial Court, Judicial Archives, on deposit James Duncan
Phillips Library, Peabody Essex Museum, Salem, MA.*

343. Deposition of Sarah Stevens & Margery Pasque v. Rebecca Nurse, Sarah Cloyce, & Faith Black‡

[Hand 1] The Deposition of Sarah Stephens aged [   ] & about Margery Pasque aged [   ]
testify & say that the 21. June last past they being improved in the holding of Jemima Rea
sodainly seized with strange fits, they heard the said Jemima in her fits cry out much upon
Goody Nurse, Goody Cloyce & Goody Black, & said, what you cannot do it alone, & you
brought this woman to help you; why did you bring her? She was never complained of.
Goody Cloyce (as these Deponenents suppose) answered that the Devil would not suffer her
any longer to be a Witch, she must be brought out: And the said Jemima complained that
Goody Cloyce Prickt & Pincht her, & the said Jemima (as they understood by her discourse)
was told by the said Cloyce that one Lords day when she run out of the meeting-house from
the Sacrament in a great rage, had her Master met her at the garrison gate just before the
Fore-door of the meeting house, to which Master she made a Courtesy, & at that time set
her hand to his book, & when she took her leave of him she made another Courtesy And
farther these Deponents say that the said Jemima spake to this purpose in six or seven fits
one after another, & that the said Cloyce would have her the said Jemima do as she the said
Cloyce had done, & bid these two deponents hold her hands that she might not so do; &
also the said Jemima when recovered of her fits confirmed what she had spoken in her fits to
these Deponents & farther saith not.

June 29, 1692   [Reverse] [Hand 2] Sarah Stev[Lost] [= Stevens] Marjery Pa[Lost] [= Pasque] y^r
Euid[Lost] [= evidence] Ver: [Lost]

Notes: Jemima Rea was eleven years old. The reference to "Goody Black" is probably to Faith Black. The deposition was probably prepared for the trial of Rebecca Nurse but not used. It is here dated to the trial although it could have been prepared as early as June 22. ◊ Hand 1 = Samuel Parris

MS Ch K 1.40, vol. 2, p. 110, Rare Books & Manuscripts, Boston Public Library. Boston, MA.

344. Examination of Abigail Hobbs

[Hand 1] Examina$\overline{con}$ of Abigall Hobbs [Lost]
Maj^{ties} Justices June. 29. 1692.
Saith y^t On Friday last John Procter Sen[Lost] [= senior] being in a room wth her alone told her y^t she had better to aflict then be aflicted & y^t she should not be hanged ⟨&⟩ but Enjoyned her to aflict Ann Putman & perswaded her to set her hand to y^e Booke. & Guided her hand personaly to do it & after this his appearance brought me a poppe[Lost] [= puppet] & a Thorne wch I stuck into y^e poppet to aflict s^d Ann Putman a friday

[Reverse] ⟨martha⟩ ~~Carrier~~
George Jacobs
[Hand 2] Jno⟨?⟩

Notes: As previously, Abigail Hobbs is questioned in prison to support a charge, this time against Procter. What appears as the reverse of the document is apparently part of another document written on the other side of the paper, and now mostly lost. ◊ Hand 1 = Stephen Sewall

Essex County Court Archives, vol. 1, no. 156, Massachusetts Supreme Judicial Court, Judicial Archives, on deposit James Duncan Phillips Library, Peabody Essex Museum, Salem, MA.

345. Summary of Evidence v. Sarah Good‡

[Hand 1] Titabe's Confession & Examina$\overline{con}$ ag^t her selfe & Sara⟨h⟩ Good abstracted
Charges Sarah Good to hurt the Children & would have ~~her~~ had her done it
5. were with her last night & would have. had her hurt the Children wch she refuse[Lost] [= refused] & that Good was one of them
Good with others are very strong & pull her with them to M^r putnams & m⟨a⟩[Lost] [= make] her hurt the Child~~ren~~
Good &^{c} rode with her vpon A poole behind her, takeing hold of one another doth not know how they goe for she never sees trees nor path but are p^{ε}sently t[Lost] [= there]
Good &^{c} tell her she must kill some body with a knife & would have had her killed Tho: putnams Child last night the Child at the same time afirmed s⟨he⟩ would have had her cutt of her own head if not Titabe would doe it & compla[Lost] [= complained] of ~~kn~~ a knife cutting her
Good came to her last night when her M^r was at prayer & would not let her hear hath one yellow bird & stopped her Eares in prayer time, the yellow bird hath been seen by the

June 29, 1692

Children & Titabee saw it suck Good between the forefinger & l[Lost] [= long] finger vpon the right hand

Saw Good &ᶜ practise ~~wh~~ witchcraft.

Saw Good have a Catt besides the bird, & a thing all over hairy &ᶜ

Sarah Good appeared like a wolfe to Hubbard going to proctors & saw it sent ⟨b⟩[Lost] [= by] Good to Hubbard.

Good &ᶜ hurt the Children again & the Children affirme the same Hubbard knew ⟨t⟩[Lost] [= them?] not being blinded by them & was once or twice taken dumb her selfe/: & Titabe [Lost]

Good caused her to pinch the Children all in their own persons

Saw Goods name in the booke, & the. divell told her they made these marks & said to her she made ther makke [= mark] & {it} was the same day she went to prison

Good &ᶜ come to ride abroad with her. & the man shewed her Goods mark in the [Lost] [= book]

Good &ᶜ pinched her on the leggs & being searched found it soe. after confession

{Nota S: G: mumbled when she went away from Mʳ Parriss & the Children after hurt.}

     Dorothy Goods Charge agᵗ her mother Sarah Good

That she had three birds one black, one yellow & that these birds hurt the Children & afflicted persons

     her owne Confession

{Nota} None ~~here~~ sees the witches but the afflicted & themselves Charges Sarah Osburne with hurting the Children looking vpon them at the same {time} & not being afflicted must consequently be a Witch

     Deliverance Hobs Confession

being at a meeting of the witches in Mʳ parisses feild when Mʳ Burroughs preached. administred the sacramᵗ to them saw Good amongst the rest & {this} fully agrees wit⟨h⟩ what the afflicted persons relate. 22ᵗʰ Aprˡ (92)

     Abigaile Hobs confession

was in Company with Sarah Good & knowes her to be a witch, ~~the divell told her to~~ & afterwards was taken deafe & Mary walcott &ᶜ saw Good & Osburn run their fingers into this Exaīts ears & a little after she spoke & sᵈ Good told her she shᵈ not speake.

     Mary Warrens Confession

That Sarah Good is a Witch & brought her the booke to signe to ~~wᶜʰ she did~~

[Reverse] Elizabeth Hubbard

Mary Walcott

Ann puttnam

Mercy Lewis

Sarah Vibber

Abigail Williams aflicted by S. Good & saw her shape.

Richard. Patch

Wᵐ Allen yᵗ she appᵉd to him when abed.

Wᵐ Good. yᵗ she hath a strange Tett or wort vnder her sholder

John Hughes yᵗ he saw strange sights.

Sam: Braybrooke. yᵗ she said she would not confess unless prooued agᵗ her & yᵗ yʳ was but One Euidence & yᵗ an Indian & yʳfor did not fear

June 29, 1692

Evidences ag^t Sarah Good | V. Sarah. Good
Extract of y^m | Witnesses to ye Indictm^{ts}
[Hand 2] no 1. Ind^t | N° 1
Sarah Vibber | Sarah Vibber
Abigall Williams | Abigall Williams
Eliz. Hubbard | Elizabeth Hubbard
Ann Putman | Ann Putman
No. 2 | N° 2. versas Good
Eliz: Hubbard | Marcy Lewis.
Ann Putman | ⟨?⟩ ~~Parris~~
Mary Wolcott | Ann Putman
Abigall Williams. | Sarah Bibber
3 | ~~Eliz. Hubbard~~
Ann Putman | Mary Wolcott
El. Hubbard | abigall Williams
Abigall Williams. | N° 3
Sarah Davis of wenham | ———
widow of Jno Davis

Notes: This summary of evidence appears to be a record of Sarah Good's case compiled after her trial on June 29, and is placed here on that date. However, for its possible earlier use, see "Legal Procedures," p. 52. ◊ Likely used at trial. ◊ Hand 1 = Thomas Newton; Hand 2 = Stephen Sewall

Essex County Court Archives, vol. 1, no. 13, Massachusetts Supreme Judicial Court, Judicial Archives, on deposit James Duncan Phillips Library, Peabody Essex Museum, Salem, MA.

346. List of Witnesses v. Elizabeth How‡

[Hand 1] Witnesses against ^g⟨o⟩ody How

Samuell Pearly & his wife
Timothy Pearly
deborah Pearly
Sarah Andrews
deacon Cummins his wife
Thomas Hea⟨s⟩ons wife of boxford
Joseph Andrews & his wife Boxford
John sherring of Ipswich
Joseph Safford Ipswich
Abram Howe⟨s⟩ wife
~~John Andrews~~   ~~Boxford~~

[Reverse] [Hand 2]
Warrants & Euidences ag^t seu^{ell}

[Hand 3] How.

Notes: Whether this is a list of witness for the grand jury case of Elizabeth How, or for the trial, or both, is not clear, but   June 29, 1692
both seems the most probable, and the document is dated here to June 30, the date of both her grand jury and trial. ◊
Hand 2 = Stephen Sewall

*Essex County Court Archives, vol. 1, no. 320, Massachusetts Supreme Judicial Court, Judicial Archives, on deposit James Duncan
Phillips Library, Peabody Essex Museum, Salem, MA.*

347. Indictment No. 1 of Elizabeth How, for Afflicting Mary Walcott†

See also: June 30, 1692.

[Hand 1] Anno Regis et Reginæ Willm̄ et
Mariæ nunc Angliæ &ᶜ Quarto:

Essex ss

The Juroᵉ for our Sovereigne Lord and Lady the King and Queen pᵉsents That: [Hand 2]
Elizabeth How wife. of James How. of Ipswich [Hand 1] the [Hand 2] **thirty first** [Hand 1]
Day of [Hand 2] **May** [Hand 1] in the forth Year of the Reigne of our Sovereigne Lord and
Lady William and Mary by the Grace of God of England Scottland. ffrance, and Ireland
King and Queen Defenders of the ffaith &ᶜ and Divers other Dayes and times. as well before
as after Certaine Detestable Arts called Witchcraft⟨s⟩ and Sorceries wickedly and
ffelloniously. hath vsed Practiced and Exercised at and within the Towneship of [Hand 2]
Salem [Hand 1] in the County of Essex aforēsᵈ in upon and against one [Hand 2] **Mary
Wolcott of Salem Villiage Singlewoman** [Hand 1] by which said wicked Arts the said
[Hand 2] **Mary Wolcott** [Hand 1] the [Hand 2] **31ˢᵗ** [Hand 1] Day of [Hand 2] **May**
[Hand 1] in the forth Year as abovesaid and Divers other Dayes and times as well before as
after was and is Tortured Afflicted Pined Consumed wasted & Tormented and also for
Sundrey other Acts of witchcraft by said [Hand 2] **Elizabeth How** [Hand 1] Committed
and Done. before and Since that time, agᵗ the Peace of our Sovereigne Lord & Lady the
King and Queen, and against the forme of the Statute in that Case made & Provided/.
[Hand 2] Mary Wolcott Jurat
Ann Putman Jurat
Abigall Williams.
Samˡˡ Pearly & wife. Ruth. Jurat
Joseph Andrews & wife. [Hand 3] Sarah [Hand 2] Jurat
Jnᵒ Sherrin Jurat
Jos: Safford. Jurat
ffrancis L⟨e⟩ane. Jurat
Abraham ffosters wife Lydia Jurat
Isack Cumins Junᵉ Jurat

[Reverse] nᵒ 1. Ind. El. How
[Hand 4] billa [Lost]a [= vera]

Notes: Hand 2 = Stephen Sewall

*Essex County Court Archives, vol. 1, no. 324, Massachusetts Supreme Judicial Court, Judicial Archives, on deposit James Duncan
Phillips Library, Peabody Essex Museum, Salem, MA.*

June 29, 1692

348. Indictment No. 2 of Elizabeth How, for Afflicting Mercy Lewis†
See also: June 30, 1692.

[Hand 1] Anno Regis et Reginæ Willm̄ et
Mariæ nunc Angliæ: &ᶜ Quarto

Essex ss

The Jūroᵉ for our Sovereigne Lord and Lady the King & Queen pᵉsents That [Hand 2] **Elizabeth How Wife of James How of Ipswich** [Hand 1] the [Hand 2] **29ᵗʰ** [Hand 1] Day of [Hand 2] **May** [Hand 1] in the forth Year of the Reigne of our Sovereigne Lord and Lady ᵞᵉ William and Mary by the Grace of God of God of England Scottland ffrance and Ireland King and Queen Defendᵉ of the ffaith &ᶜ and diverss other Dayes and times as well before as after certaine Detestable Arts called witchcraft & Sorceries wickedly & ffelloniously hath vsed Practised and Exercised at and within the Towne ship of [Hand 2] **Salem** [Hand 1] in the County of Essex aforesaid in upon and against one: [Hand 2] **Marcy Lewis of Salem Villiage Single woman** [Hand 1] by which said wicked Arts ["r" written over "c"] the said [Hand 2] **Marcy Lewis** [Hand 1] the [Hand 2] **29ᵗʰ** [Hand 1] Day of [Hand 2] **May** [Hand 1] in the forth Year abouēˢᵈ and Divers other Dayes & times as well before as after was and is Tortured. Afflicted: Pined Consumed wasted & Tormented and also for sundrey other Acts of witchcraft by the said [Hand 2] **Elizabeth How** [Hand 1] Committed & done before and since that Time. agᵗ the Peace of our Sovereigne Lord and Lady the King & Queen, and agᵗ the forme of the Statute in that case made and Provided

[Hand 2] Witnesses.

Mercy Lewis. Jurat

Mary Wolcott Jurat

Abigall Williams.

Ann Putman Jurat

Samˡˡ Pearly & wife Jurat

Isack Cumins Junᵉ

Samˡˡ Pearly & wife Ruth. Jurat

Joseph Andrews & wife Sarah Jurat

Jnᵒ Sherrin Jurat

Jos. Safford Jurat

ffrancis Leane Jurat

Abraham ffosters wife Lydia J[Lost] [= jurat]

[Reverse] Nᵒ ⟨2⟩ (2) Eli H⟨o⟩[Lost] [= How]
[Hand 3] billa uera

Notes: Hand 2 = Stephen Sewall

Essex Institute Collection, no. 28, James Duncan Phillips Library, Peabody Essex Museum, Salem, MA.

Sworn Before the Grand Jury: Three Depositions of Mary Cummings v. Elizabeth How
2ⁿᵈ of 3 dates. See No. 322 on June 27, 1692

349. Indictment No. 1 of Susannah Martin, for Afflicting Mary Walcott†

June 29, 1692

[Hand 1] Anno Regis et Reginæ Willm̄ et
Mariæ. nunc Angliæ: &c Quarto

Essex ss

The Juroᵉ for our Sovereigne Lord & Lady the King and Queen pᵉsents That Susanah
Martin of Amsbury in the County of Essex widdow the Second Day of may in the forth year
of the Reigne of our Sovereign⟨e⟩ Lord and Lady William and Mary by the Grace of God of
England Scottland: ffrance and Ireland King. and Queen: Defenders of the faith &c and
divers other Dayes and Times as well before as after certaine Detestable Arts called
witchcrafts & Sorceries wickedly and ffelloniously hath vsed Practised & Excercised at and
within the Towneship of Salem in the County of Essex aforesaid. in vpon and agᵗ one Mary
Wallcott of Salem Village Single Woman, by which said wicked arts the s̄d Mary Wallcott
the second day of May: in the forth year aforesᵈ and at Divers other Dayes & times as well
before as after was, and is Tort⟨u⟩red ["u" written over "o"] Afflicted Pined wasted and
Tormented: as also for s⟨u⟩ndery other acts of witchcraft by Said Susanah Martin committed
and Done before and since that time agᵗ yᵉ Peace of our Sovereigne Lord & Lady william
and Mary King and Queen of England theire Crowne and Dignity and agᵗ the fforme of the
statute in that case made & Provided/

Wittnesses

[Hand 2] Sarah Vibber Sworn

Mary Wolcutt Sworn

[Lost]ᵉ [= Mr] Samˡˡ Parris. Sworn

Elizabeth Hubbard.

Marcy Lewis

[Reverse] Nᵒ ⟨1⟩ ⟨I⟩nd[Lost]⟨s⟩ [= indictments] ver. Martin.

[Hand 3] ⟨b⟩ila uera

Notes: Hand 2 = Stephen Sewall

Essex County Court Archives, vol. 1, no. 173, Massachusetts Supreme Judicial Court, Judicial Archives, on deposit James Duncan Phillips Library, Peabody Essex Museum, Salem, MA.

350. Indictment No. 2 of Susannah Martin, for Afflicting Mercy Lewis†

[Hand 1] Anno Regis et Regina Willm̄ et
Marie: nunc Angliæ &c Quarto

Essex ss

The Juroᵉ for our Sovereigne Lord & Lady the K[Lost] [= king] and Queen: pᵉsents That
Susanah Martin of Amsbury in the County of Essex widdow the D̶ Second day of may in the
forth Year of the Reigne of our Sovereigne Lord & Lady William and Mary by the Grace of
God of England Scottland ffrance & Ireland King and Q[Lost] [= queen] Defenders of the
faith &c and divers other Dayes & times as well before as after. certaine Detestable Arts
called witchcrafts and Sorceries Wickedly: and ffelloniously hath vsed Practised & Exercised
at and within the Township of Salem in the County of Essex afores̄d in and vpon and agᵗ one
Marcy Lewis: of Salem Villiage single woman by which said wicked Arts yᵉ said Marcy

June 29, 1692

Lewis, the said second day of may in the forth year aforesaid and at Divers othe⟨r⟩ dayes and times as well before as after was and is Tortured: Afflicted Pined wasted and Tormented as also for sundrey other Acts of Witchcraft by said Susanah Martin Committed and done before and since that time ag^t the Peace of our Sovereigne Lord. and Lady. William & Mary King & Queen of England there Crowne and Dignity. and ag^t the fforme of the Statute in that case made and Provided./
Wittnesses
Marcy Lewis
Mr Sam^ll Parris [Hand 2] Sworn
[Hand 1] Anne Puttman [Hand 2] Sworn
[Hand 1] Sarah Bibber [Hand 2] Sworne
[Hand 1] Elizabeth: Hubbard
Mary wallcott [Hand 2] Sworne in Court June. 2⟨9⟩. 92.

[Reverse] [Hand 2?] N° 2. I[Lost] [= indictment] ⟨ag⟩[Lost] [= against] [Lost]⟨rtin⟩ [= Martin]
[Hand 3] ⟨bi⟩[Lost] [= billa vera]
[Hand 4] S. Martin.

Notes: This is a dated document, but the date can be interpreted as either June "28" or "29." The 29 seems more likely, and it is dated here accordingly.

Essex County Court Archives, vol. 1, no. 172, Massachusetts Supreme Judicial Court, Judicial Archives, on deposit James Duncan Phillips Library, Peabody Essex Museum, Salem, MA.

351. Deposition of Joseph Knight & Elizabeth Clark v. Susannah Martin

[Hand 1] The Depossittion of Joseph knight aged about 40 yers

This Deponant doe testifie & saye that on the 20th Daye of october or thereabouts in the yere of o^r Lord 1686 Nathanill Clarke Junj^r of ~~Ipswich~~ Newbery together with this Deponant goeing out into. the woods together to fetch vp horses there met with Susana Martaine of Amsbury with a litle Dog Runing by hir syde & in my sight ^{she} tooke vp s^d Dog vnder hir arme but Comeing vp nere to hir she had a Kegg or a halfe feirkin vnder the same arme; this Deponant then lookt hir in the face & told hir that that Kegg was a litle Dogg but nowe Nath^ll Clarke said soe it was: & then passing from hir we found our horses & brought them to a small Causwaye but Could not git them ouer but there being a small knowle of land nere; our horses ran round about it the greatist parte of that daye we oftn bringing them vp to the Causwaye but then they turnd to that knowle & Ran about it the same waye but at length there Came a young man with a yoak of oxen to go⟨e⟩ ouer the Causwaye who with some dificaultie got them ouer ~~& then we dr⟨a⟩ue our horses after them~~ for altho the Causwaye was very good yet one of ~~the⟨m⟩~~ the oxen hung back as though he were frighted but at length were forct ouer & then we gat ouer our horses [Hand 2]) Joseph knight ownid this his testimony to be the truth: on his oath. before the Juryers of Inquest this 29. of June: 1692 [Hand 1] Elizabeth Clark: who then was the wife of the abous^d Nathaniell Clarke doe testifie that when my s^d husband Nath^ll Clarke Came home he told me this Deponant the matter mentiond ⟨?⟩ in Joseph knights testimony & he related to me the wholl of the matter

& all the sircumstances related in s^d testimony; excepting that my husband told Joseph   June 29, 1692
knigh⟨t⟩ that the Kegg vnder goodwif martains arme wa[Lost] [= was] or had bi⟨n⟩ a d⟨o⟩gg
This Deponant doe further testifie that goodwife martain abous^d Came to our house the
same daye ~~abo~~ mentiond in Joseph knights testimony before my husband Came home &
Comeing into the house our dog bit hir by the leg as she said wherevpon she being angry
said: that he was a Chuer^ll~~lish C⟨arle⟩~~ lik his master
[Hand 2] Elizabeth ~~m~~ Clark ownid this har testimo to be the truth: on the oath which she
had taken before: the Jary for Inquest: this 29. of June 1692

[Reverse] Joseph knight elizabeth clark

[Hand 3] El. Clarke

Notes: This manuscript had been cut in half and catalogued separately by an archivist. It is here restored.

Essex County Court Archives, vol. 1, nos. 190 & 192, Massachusetts Supreme Judicial Court, Judicial Archives, on deposit James Duncan Phillips Library, Peabody Essex Museum, Salem, MA.

352. Deposition of Samuel Abbey & Mary Abbey v. Sarah Good†

[Hand 1] Samuel Abbey of Salem Villiage Aged 45. Years or thereabouts and
Mary Abbey his wife aged 38 years or thereabout: Deposeth and saith:

That about this Time Three Years past Wm Good and his wife Sarah Good being Destitute
of an howse to dwell in these Deponents out of Charity, they being Poor. lett them live in
theirs some time, vntill that the said Sarah Good was ~~of~~ so Turbulant a Spirritt, Spitefull,
and so Mallitiously bent, that these Deponent⟨s⟩ could not Suffer ^{her} to Live in their
howse any Longer; and was forced for Quiettness sake to turne she ye said Sarah, with her
husband, out of theire howse, ever since, which is about two Years 1/2 agone; the said Sarah
Good, ~~hath~~ {not} [1–2 words overstruck] ~~to the s^d deponents hat⟨?⟩~~ hath carried it very
Spitefully & Mallitiously, toward them, the winter following after the said Sarah was gone
from our howse, we began to Loose Cattle, and Lost severell after an vnusall Manner: in a
drupeing Condition and yett they would Eate: and your Deponents have Lost after that
manner 17 head of Cattle within this two years, besides Sheep, and Hoggs: and both doe
beleive they Dyed by witchcraft, the said William Good ["William Good" written over
"Samuel Abbey"] on ["on" written over "in"] the last ^{of} may, was twelve months, went
home to his wife the s^d Sarah Good, and told her, what a sad Accident had fallen out, she
asked what:, he answered that his neighbour Abbey had lost two Cowes, both dyeing within
halfe an hower of one another, the s^d Sarah good said she did not care if he the said Abbey
had Lost all the Cattle he had, {as ye said Jno Good told vs} Just that very Day, that the said
Sarah good was taken up, we yo^ε Deponents had a Cow that could not rise alone, but since
presently after she was taken up, the said Cow was well and could rise so well, as if she had
ailed nothing: she the said Sarah good: ever since these Dponants turned ^{her} out of their
howse she hath ~~carried~~ behaveed her selfe very crossely & Mallitiously, to them & their
Children calling their Chillren Vile Names and hath threetened them often./.
                                                                    [Hand 2] Jurat in Curia.

June 29, 1692

[Reverse] Sam. Abbey & wife.
Sworne.
[Hand 1] Sarah Good.

Notes: "Jn° Good" is a recording error for William Good. Used at trial. ◊ Hand 2 = Stephen Sewall

Essex County Court Archives, vol. 1, no. 18, Massachusetts Supreme Judicial Court, Judicial Archives, on deposit James Duncan Phillips Library, Peabody Essex Museum, Salem, MA.

Sworn at Trial: Testimony of William Batten, William Shaw & Deborah Shaw v. Sarah Good†

2nd of 2 dates. See No. 333 on June 28, 1692

Sworn at Trial: Deposition of Sarah Bibber v. Sarah Good

2nd of 2 dates. See No. 335 on June 28, 1692

353. Deposition of Henry Herrick & Jonathan Batchelor v. Sarah Good†

[Hand 1] The deposition of Henery Herrick Aged about 21 one years, this deponent testifieth & saith that in Last march was two yeare; Sarah Good came to his fathers house & desired to Lodge there; & his father forbid it; & she went away Grumbling & my father bid us follow her & see y^t she went away clear lest she should lie in ye barn; & by smoking of her pipe should fire ye barn; & sd deponent wth Jonathan Batchelor seing her make ^{a stop} near ye barne bid her be gone; or he would set her fa⟨r⟩ther [1st "r" written over "t"] of; to which she replied that then it should Cost his father Zachariah Herick one; or two of ye best Cowes which he had;
And Jonathan Batchelor aged 14 year testifieth ye same abovewriten; & doth farther testifie that about a weeke after two of his grandfathers: Master Catle were removed from their places: & other younger Catle put in their rooms & since that severall of their Catle have bene let Loose in a strange maner

[Hand 2] Jurat in Curia

[Reverse] [Hand 3] H. Herrick
[Hand 4] Sarah Good

Notes: Used at trial. ◊ Hand 2 = Stephen Sewall

Essex County Court Archives, vol. 1, no. 21, Massachusetts Supreme Judicial Court, Judicial Archives, on deposit James Duncan Phillips Library, Peabody Essex Museum, Salem, MA.

Sworn at Trial: Deposition of Joseph Herrick Sr. & Mary Herrick v. Sarah Good†
2nd of 2 dates. See No. 337 on June 28, 1692

354. Testimony of Samuel Sibley v. Sarah Good†

[Hand 1] Samuell Sibly aged about :34: years Testefieth and saith that .I. being at the house of doctter grides that night after that Sary good was examened and Elizebeth Hubbard said that ther sands [= stands] Sary good stands apon the tabel by you with all hear naked brast and bar footed bar lagded and said .o. nast slout [= nasty slut?] if .I. had sum thingg .I. wood kill hear then .I. struck with my staf wher she said Sary good stud and Elizabath hubbard cried out you haue heet har right acors the back you haue amost killd hear if any body was there they may see it

[Hand 2] Jurat in Curia

[Reverse] [Hand 3] Sibley dep^t

Notes: Used at trial. ◊ Hand 2 = Stephen Sewall

Essex Institute Collection, no. 30, James Duncan Phillips Library, Peabody Essex Museum, Salem, MA.

Sworn at Trial: Deposition of John Allen v. Susannah Martin†
2nd of 2 dates. See No. 311 on June 7, 1692

355. Testimony of John Atkinson v. Susannah Martin†

[Hand 1] John Attkinson aged fifty six years or thereabout; Testifieth thatt some time about five years since; One ["O" written over "o"] of the sons of Susanna Martin sen^ε of Amsbury, Exchanged a cow of his wth me ffor a cow wch I bought of m^ε Wells the minister; wch cow he tooke ffrom m^ε Wells his house; About ["A" written over "a"] a weeke after I went to the house of Susanna martin to receive the cow of the young man her son; W^n I came to bring the cow home nottw^thstand hamstringi⟨ng⟩ of her an [= and] haltring her, she was so madd thatt we could scarce gett her along, butt she broke all the ropes ffastened to her, we putt the halter two or three times round a tree wch she broke and ran away, and w^n we came downe to the fferry, we were forct to run up to our ~~armpitt~~ [Hand 2] {wastes} [Hand 1] in water, she was so firce, butt after wth much adoe we gott her into the boat, she was as tame as any creature w^tsoever.
[Hand 2] & further this deponent Saith y^t Susanna Martin Muttered & was Unwilling this depon⟨e⟩nt should haue y^e Cow

Jurat in ℭ⟨?⟩ Curia

[Reverse] John Atkinson

Notes: Used at trial. ◊ Hand 2 = Stephen Sewall

Essex County Court Archives, vol. 1, no. 199, Massachusetts Supreme Judicial Court, Judicial Archives, on deposit James Duncan Phillips Library, Peabody Essex Museum, Salem, MA.

June 29, 1692

356. Testimony of Sarah Atkinson v. Susannah Martin†

[Hand 1] Sarah Attkinson aged forty Eight years or thereabouts testifieth thatt some time in the spring of the year⟨s⟩ about Eighteen years since {Su}sanna Martin came vnto our house att Newbury from Amsbury in an Extraordinary dirty season wⁿ itt was nott ffitt ffor any ꝑson to travell she then came on foot, wⁿ shee came into our ["our" written over "my s"] house I asked her whether she came ffrom Amsbury ["A" written over "a"] affoot she say'd she did I asked how she could come in this time affoott and bid my children make way ffor her to come to the fire to dry her selfe she replyed she was as dry as I was and turn'd her Coats on side, and I could nott ꝑceive thatt the soule of her shews were wett I was startled att itt. yᵗ she should come soe dry and told her thatt I should have been weett up to my knees If I should have come so ffarr on ffoott. shee replyd thatt she scorn'd to have a drabled tayle ["t" written over "d"]

[Hand 2] Jurat in Curia

[Reverse] Sarah Atkinson

Notes: Used at trial. ◊ Hand 2 = Stephen Sewall

Essex County Court Archives, vol. 1, no. 200, Massachusetts Supreme Judicial Court, Judicial Archives, on deposit James Duncan Phillips Library, Peabody Essex Museum, Salem, MA.

Sworn at Trial: Deposition of Sarah Bibber v. Susannah Martin†
2ⁿᵈ of 2 dates. See No. 106 on May 2, 1692

Sworn at Trial: Deposition of John Kimball v. Susannah Martin†
2ⁿᵈ of 2 dates. See No. 159 on May 16, 1692

Sworn at Trial: Deposition of John Kimball v. Susannah Martin†
2ⁿᵈ of 2 dates. See No. 160 on May 16, 1692

Sworn at Trial: Deposition of Samuel Parris, Nathaniel Ingersoll, & Thomas Putnam v. Susannah Martin [?]
2ⁿᵈ of 2 dates. See No. 109 on May 2, 1692

Sworn at Trial: Testimony and Deposition of John Pressy v. Susannah Martin†
2ⁿᵈ of 2 dates. See No. 141 on May 11, 1692

Sworn at Trial: Deposition of John Pressy & Mary Pressy v. Susannah Martin†
2ⁿᵈ of 2 dates. See No. 142 on May 11, 1692

Sworn at Trial: Deposition of Thomas Putnam v. Susannah Martin and Testimony of Nathaniel Ingersoll v. Susannah Martin†
2ⁿᵈ of 2 dates. See No. 111 on May 2, 1692

Sworn at Trial: Deposition of Jarvis Ring v. Susannah Martin†
2ⁿᵈ of 2 dates. See No. 148 on May 13, 1692

Sworn at Trial: Deposition of Jarvis Ring v. Susannah Martin and Deposition of Joseph Ring
v. Susannah Martin & Thomas Hardy†

2nd of 2 dates. See No. 149 on May 13, 1692

Sworn at Trial: Deposition of Mary Walcott v. Susannah Martin

2nd of 2 dates. See No. 112 on May 2, 1692

Billa Vera: Indictment No. 1 of Rebecca Nurse, for Afflicting Ann Putnam Jr.†

2nd of 3 dates. See No. 285 on June 3, 1692

Billa Vera: Indictment No. 2 of Rebecca Nurse, for Afflicting Mary Walcott†

2nd of 2 dates. See No. 286 on June 3, 1692

Billa Vera: Indictment No. 3 of Rebecca Nurse, for Afflicting Elizabeth Hubbard†

2nd of 2 dates. See No. 287 on June 3, 1692

Billa Vera: Indictment No. 4 of Rebecca Nurse, for Afflicting Abigail Williams†

2nd of 2 dates. See No. 288 on June 3, 1692

357. Deposition of Sarah Bibber v. Rebecca Nurse†

[Hand 1] The Deposistion of Sarah viber agged about :36: years who testifieth and saith: that on the 2 day of may 1692: I saw the Apperishtion of Rebekah nurs the wife of ffrances nurs sen^r most greviously tortor and afflect the bodyes of mary walcott mercy lewes and ~~Eliz:~~ Abigaill williams by pinching them and almost choaking them to death: but I doe not know that she hurt me tell the 27th June 1692: and then the: Apperishtion of Rebekah nurs did most greviously torment me by pinching me and almost choaking me seuerall times.

[Hand 2] Jurat in Curia.

[Reverse] [Hand 1] Sarah viber against Rebekah nurs

Notes: Used at trial. ◊ Hand 1 = Thomas Putnam; Hand 2 = Stephen Sewall

Essex County Court Archives, vol. 1, no. 74, Massachusetts Supreme Judicial Court, Judicial Archives, on deposit James Duncan Phillips Library, Peabody Essex Museum, Salem, MA.

358. Deposition of Sarah Holton v. Rebecca Nurse†

[Hand 1] The Deposis[Lost] [= deposition] [Lost] [= of Sarah Holton] Relique of benjamine Holton Deceased who testifieth and saith that about this time three years my deare and loueing Husband Benjamine Holton Deceased: was as well as euer I knew him in my life: tell one Saterday morning that Rebekah nurs who now stands charged for wicthcraft: came to our house and fell arailing at him because our piggs ["p" written over "b"] gott into hir feild: tho our piggs ware suffisiently yoaked and their fence was down in seuerall places: yett all we could say to hir could no ways passifie hir: but she continew{ed} Railing and scolding a grat while together calling to hir son Benj̄. nurs to goe and git a gun and kill our

June 29, 1692

piggs ["p" written over "b"] and lett non of them goe out of the feild: tho my poor Husband gaue hir neuer a missbeholding word: and within a short time affter this my poor Husband goeing out uery early in the morning: as he was acoming in againe he was taken with a strainge ffitt in the entery be^{ing} struck blind and strucken down. Two or three times. so that when he came to himself he tould me he thought he should never haue com into the house any more: and all summer affter he continewed in a languishing condition being much pained at his stomack and often struck blind: but about a fortnight before he dyed he was taken with strange and violent ffitts acting much like to our poor bewicthed parsons when we thought they would haue dyed and the Doctor. that was with him could not find what his distember was: and the day before he dyed he was very chearly but about midnight he was againe most violently sezed upon with violent ffitts tell the next night about midnight he departed this life by a ~~eu~~ cruel~~l~~ death

[Hand 2] ~~Jurat in Curia~~
Jurat in Curia

[Reverse] Sarah Holton

Notes: The issue about the pigs may have been related to swine laws that set rules for such matters. Why the original "Jurat in Curia" was crossed out and replaced with the same words can only be speculative. ◊ Used at trial. ◊ "Relique": 'widow' (cf. *OED* s.v. *relic*). "missbeholding": 'disrespectful, impolite' (*OED* s.v. *misbeholden*). ◊ Hand 1 = Thomas Putnam; Hand 2 = Stephen Sewall

Essex County Court Archives, vol. 1, no. 84, Massachusetts Supreme Judicial Court, Judicial Archives, on deposit James Duncan Phillips Library, Peabody Essex Museum, Salem, MA.

359. Deposition of Nathaniel Ingersoll & Hannah Ingersoll v. Rebecca Nurse†

[Hand 1] The Deposistion of Nathaniell Ingersoll and Hannah his wife who: testife and say that we ware conversant with Benjamin Holton for aboue a week before he died and he was acted in a very strange maner with most violent fittes acting much like to our poor: bewicthed parsons w^n we thought they would haue died tho: then we hade no suspition of wicthcraft. amongst us and he died a most violent death with dreadfull fitts and the Docktor that was with him said he could not tell what his disteber [= distemper] was and he died about Two days before Rebekah Sheepard:

[Hand 2] Jurat in Curia
attest Steph Sewall Cle.

[Reverse] [Hand 2?] Nath. & Hanah Ing^εsll

Notes: That the deposition was attested to by Stephen Sewall may mean that the Ingersolls were not present at the trial but had submitted their deposition. ◊ Used at trial. ◊ Hand 1 = Thomas Putnam; Hand 2 = Stephen Sewall

Essex County Court Archives, vol. 2, no. 124, Massachusetts Supreme Judicial Court, Judicial Archives, on deposit James Duncan Phillips Library, Peabody Essex Museum, Salem, MA.

360. Deposition of Samuel Parris & John Putnam Sr. v. Rebecca Nurse & Martha Carrier†

[Hand 1] The Deposition of Sam: Parris aged about .39. years & John Putman Sen$^{\varepsilon}$ aged about 63. years both of Salem Village testifyeth & saith that this 18. instant June being at the house of Jonathan Putman whom we found very ill, after a little while Mercy Lewes sent for on purpose came into said Jonathan Putmans ^{house}, & was presently struck dumb, but being bid to hold up her hand if she saw any of the Witches afflict said Jonathan, whereupon she presently lift up her hand, & after fell into a Trance, & when said Mercy came to her self, she said she saw Goody Nurse & Goody Car⟨r⟩ier holding said Jonathans head, & farther saith not

[Hand 2] Jurat in Curia

[Reverse] [Hand 1] Sam: Parris & Capt Putman Contra Reb: Nurse
[Hand 2] Mr Parris
Capt Putman

Notes: The manuscript reveals that Parris likely prepared the body of the document in advance. Subsequently he completed it, filling in his and Putnam's names and ages. This document was probably used only at Rebecca Nurse's trial. ◊ Used at trial. ◊ Hand 1 = Samuel Parris; Hand 2 = Stephen Sewall

Essex County Court Archives, vol. 1, no. 77, Massachusetts Supreme Judicial Court, Judicial Archives, on deposit James Duncan Phillips Library, Peabody Essex Museum, Salem, MA.

361. Deposition of Samuel Parris, Nathaniel Ingersoll, & Thomas Putnam v. Rebecca Nurse†

[Hand 1] The Deposition of Sam: Parris aged about .39. years & Nathanael Ingersoll aged about fifty & eight yeares & Thomas Putman aged about fourty yeares all of Salem testifyeth & saith that Ann Putman Sen$^{\varepsilon}$, & her daughter Ann, & Mary Walcot & Abigail Williams were severall times & greivously tortured at the Examination of Rebekah Nurse wife to Francis Nurse of Salem before the Honoured Magistrates the .24. March. 1691/2 & particularly that when her hands were at liberty some of the afflicted were pinched, & upon the motion of ^{her} head & fingers some of them were tortured; & farther that some of the afflicted then & there affirmed that they saw a black man whispering in her ear, & that they saw birds fluttering about her, ~~& particularly Mary Walcot~~

[Hand 2] Jurat in Curia

[Reverse] 6 [Hand 1] The Depotion of Sam: Parris &c. ags^t Rebek: Nurse

Notes: Used at trial. ◊ Hand 1 = Samuel Parris; Hand 2 = Stephen Sewall

Essex County Court Archives, vol. 1, no. 79, Massachusetts Supreme Judicial Court, Judicial Archives, on deposit James Duncan Phillips Library, Peabody Essex Museum, Salem, MA.

Sworn at Trial: Deposition of Ann Putnam Jr. v. Rebecca Nurse†
2nd of 2 dates. See No. 291 on June 3, 1692

June 29, 1692   *Sworn at Trial: Deposition of Edward Putnam v. Rebecca Nurse†*
2nd of 2 dates. See No. 32 on March 25, 1692

362. Deposition of John Putnam Jr. & Hannah Putnam v. Rebecca Nurse, Mary Esty, & Sarah Cloyce†

[Hand 1] The Deposistion of John putnam weavere: and Hannah his wife who testifieth and saith that our child which dyed about the middle of April 1692: was as well ~~as~~ and as thriueing a child as most was: tell it was about eight weeks old: but a while affter ^{that} I the said Jno: putnam had Reported sum thing which I had hard consarning the mother of Rebekah nurs: Mary Estick and Sarah Cloyes I myself was taken with strange kind of fitts: but it pleased Allmighty God to Deliuer me from them: but quickly affter this our poor yong child was taken about midnight with strange and violent fitts: which did most greviously affright us acting much like to the poor bewicthed parsons when we thought they would Indeed haue died: where upon we sent for our Mother putnam in the night Immediatly: and as soon as she came and se our child she tould us that she feared there was an euell hand upon it: and also as fast as posiblely could be we gott a Docktor to it: but all he did giue it could doe it no good: but ^{it} continewed in ^{a} strange and violent fitts for about Two days and Two nights and then Departed this life by a cruell and violent death being enuf to pears ["a" written over "i"] a stonny hart. for to the best of ^{our} understanding ^{it was} near fiue hours a dying

[Hand 2] Jurat in Curia

[Reverse] John Putman Hannah Putman
[Hand 1] John Putnam weauer and his wife.

Notes: This deposition against the three Towne sisters is a trial document most likely used at the trial of Rebecca Nurse. However, it may also have been used at the trial of Mary Esty on September 9. ◊ Used at trial. ◊ Hand 1 = Thomas Putnam; Hand 2 = Stephen Sewall

Essex County Court Archives, vol. 1, no. 82, Massachusetts Supreme Judicial Court, Judicial Archives, on deposit James Duncan Phillips Library, Peabody Essex Museum, Salem, MA.

363. Deposition of Thomas Putnam & Edward Putnam v. Rebecca Nurse†

[Hand 1] The Deposition of Tho: Putman aged about 40. years & Edward Putman aged about .38. years

witnesseth & saith that having been several times present with Ann Putman jun^ε in & after her fits & saw her much afflicted, being bitten, pinched, her limbs distorted, & pins thrust into her flesh, which she charged on Rebekah Nurse that she was the Acter thereof & that she saw her do it

The deponents farther testify that on the ~~day of~~ 24. March [   ] last past at the publick examination of said Nurse We saw the said Ann Putman ^{Abigail Williams & Eliz: Hubbard} often struck down upon the glance of the said Nurse eye [   ] upon said William⟨s⟩ Putman & Hubbard several times & the said Putman Williams & Hubbard was

then afflicted according to the various motions of said Nurse her body in time of examination
as when said Nurse did clinch her hands, bite her lip, or hold her head aside the said Putman
Hubbard & Williams was set in the same posture to her great torture & affliction.

June 29, 1692

Thomas putnam

Edward Pututnam

[Hand 2] Jurat in Curia

[Reverse] [Hand 3] Thomas Putman
Edward Putman

Notes: The words preceding "witnesseth" although in Parris's hand appear to have been written at a separate time. Parris
frequently recorded the names of people to be deposed prior to writing what they said. The document may have been
first created just after the examination of Rebecca Nurse. ◊ Used at trial. ◊ Hand 1 = Samuel Parris; Hand 2 = Stephen
Sewall

*Essex County Court Archives, vol. 1, no. 86, Massachusetts Supreme Judicial Court, Judicial Archives, on deposit James Duncan
Phillips Library, Peabody Essex Museum, Salem, MA.*

364. Testimony of Joseph Fowler Regarding Sarah Bibber, in Support of Rebecca Nurse‡

[Hand 1] The Testimony of Joseph fowler, who Testifieth that Goodman Bibber & his wife,
Liued at my howse, And I did obserue and take notice, that Goodwife Bibber was a woman,
who was uery idle in her calling And uery much giuen to tatling & tale Bareing makeing
mischeif amongst her neigbo‍ᵉˢ, & uery much giuen to speak bad words and would call her
husband bad names, & was a woman of a uery turbulent unruly spirit

[Reverse] [Hand 2] Against Bibber & Wife
Joseph fowler

Notes: This appears to have been used on Rebecca Nurse's behalf. ◊ Likely used at trial.

*Essex County Court Archives, vol. 2, no. 120, Massachusetts Supreme Judicial Court, Judicial Archives, on deposit James Duncan
Phillips Library, Peabody Essex Museum, Salem, MA.*

365. Testimony of Thomas Jacobs & Mary Jacobs Regarding Sarah Bibber, in Support of Rebecca Nurse, and Testimony of Richard Walker Regarding Sarah Bibber, in Support of Rebecca Nurse‡

[Hand 1] The testymony of Thomas Jacob and mery his wife doth testyfy and say that good
bibbor ~~and~~ now that is now counted aflicke{t⟨e⟩d} parson she did for a time surgin [=
sojourn] in our hou⟨s⟩ and good bibber wood be uery often spekeking against won and
nother uery obsanely [= obscenely] and thos things that were uery falls. and wichshing uery
bad wichchis and uery often and she wichs that wen hor chill fell into the reuer that she had
neuer pull ~~out~~ hor chilld out and good bibbor yous to wich ill wichches to horselfe and hor
chilldren and allso to others: the nayborhud were she liueued [2nd "u" written over "d"]

June 29, 1692 amonkes aftor she bered: hor fust ho{u}sbon hes tolld us that this John bibbor wife coud fall into {ffitts} as often as she plesed ["d" written over "s"]

[Hand 2] The Testimony of Richard Walker; who Testifieth; that Goodwife Bibber Somtimes, Liuing neare to me, I did obserue her to be a woman of an unruly turbulent spirit, And would often fall into strange fitts: when any thing crost her humor

[Reverse] [Hand 3] Tho. Jacobs
[Hand 4] goody fiber

Notes: This appears to have been used on Rebecca Nurse's behalf. ◊ Likely used at trial. ◊ Hand 3 = Jonathan Corwin

Essex County Court Archives, vol. 2, no. 121, Massachusetts Supreme Judicial Court, Judicial Archives, on deposit James Duncan Phillips Library, Peabody Essex Museum, Salem, MA.

366. Testimony of Sarah Nurse Regarding Sarah Bibber, in Support of Rebecca Nurse

[Hand 1] the testimony of Sarah Nurs aged 28 years or th[Lost] [= there]
abouts who testifieth and saith that being in the Cour[Lost] [= court] this 29 of June 1692 I
sawe goodwife bibber pull o[Lost] [= out?]
pins out of her Close and held them betwene h[Lost] [= her]
fingers and Claspt her hands round her knese and
then she Cryed out and said goody Nurs prict
her this I can testifie if Calld as witnes my mark

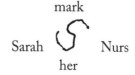

Sarah   Nurs
mark
her

[Reverse] [Hand 2] Euidences in behalfe of yᵉ prisonᵉˢ

Notes: Many documents note the claims of the accusers that spectres were attacking them with pins, but Sarah Nurse's testimony offers the only extant observation of an accuser at a judicial proceeding having brought the pins to it. Whether she succeeded in giving this as trial testimony remains speculative. Her statement strongly suggests that Sarah Bibber was performing at the trial as well as previously. The plural reference to prisoners may mean that such documents were collected together and noted. ◊ Likely used at trial. ◊ Hand 2 = Stephen Sewall

Witchcraft Papers, no. 37b, Massachusetts Historical Society. Boston, MA.

367. Testimony of John Porter & Lydia Porter Regarding Sarah Bibber, in Support of Rebecca Nurse‡

[Hand 1] T⟨he⟩ Testimony of John Porter: And Lidia Porter These

The Testimony of John Porter, who Testifieth & Sayth that Goodwife Biber Somtime
liuing amongst us I did obserue her to be a woman of An unruly turbulent Spirit; And shee
would often fall into strange fitts; when shee was crost of her humor: Likewise Lidia Porter
Testifieth, that Goodwife Bibber And her Husband would often quarrel & in their quarrels
shee would call him, uery bad names, And would haue strange fitts when shee was crost,
And a woman of an unruly turbulent spirit, And double tongued

June 29, 1692

[Reverse] [Hand 2] Jn⁰ Porters Euidence in behalfe of yᵉ pʳsonᴱˢ in Inualidating Sarah vibber
[Hand 3] copy
copied

Notes: This appears to be part of the defense of Rebecca Nurse. Since this is a copy, it was almost certainly made after
June 29, and the original may have been made well before that date. The Nurse supporters had early on worked at a
defense for her, but specifically dating most such Nurse documents is unreliable. Thus, the June 29 date, since it seems
likely that such evidence would have been presented on her behalf at the trial. ◊ Likely used at trial.

*Essex County Court Archives, vol. 2, no. 119, Massachusetts Supreme Judicial Court, Judicial Archives, on deposit James Duncan
Phillips Library, Peabody Essex Museum, Salem, MA.*

368. Testimony of James Kettle Regarding Elizabeth Hubbard, in Support of Rebecca Nurse [?]

[Hand 1] the testimony of James Cetel being of age who testi{fie}[Lost] [= testifieth] and
saith i being at docter grigses one a saba{th} day about the last of may in 1692 hauing some
discource with elizabeth hubberd and I found her to speack seuerall untruthes in denying the
sabath day and saying she had nat ben to meting that day but had onely bea⟨?⟩{n} up to
James houlltons this I can testifie to if called: as witnes my han{d}

James Ketle

[Reverse] [Hand 2] James Ceetel

Notes: Good evidence for dating this has not been established. It is possible that in joining Clement Coldum (see No.
293) in speaking against Elizabeth Hubbard he was seeking to discredit her in the same way that Nurse supporters sought
to discredit Sarah Bibber. This is placed in June as possibly connected to that. Ironically, in a deposition against Sarah
Bishop on May 20 (No. 190), Kettle had recalled the suffering of Elizabeth Hubbard on May 10 at the house of Dr.
Griggs, where she was a servant. The connection of this document to the Nurse case remains speculative.

*Essex County Court Archives, vol. 2, no. 123, Massachusetts Supreme Judicial Court, Judicial Archives, on deposit James Duncan
Phillips Library, Peabody Essex Museum, Salem, MA.*

369. Statement of William Bradford, Rachel Bradford & William Rayment Jr. Regarding Mercy Lewis, in Support of Rebecca Nurse [?]

[Hand 1]
[Lost]⟨l⟩ william Bradford & Rachell his wife
[Lost] ⟨t⟩hat about two years and half since Marcy

June 29, 1692

[Lost]licted persons did Live with us about
[Lost] quarter of a year: & we {did} then Judg that
[Lost] ⟨m⟩atter of consienc of speaking yᵉ truth
[Lost] and untruth she would stand stifly to
[Lost] William Rayment Junior testifieth
[Lost] the aboue sd Marcy Luis I Knew her when
[Lost] of my ~~of~~ neibours and I all wayes took her to
[Lost]⟨n⟩ as the aboue ^{writen} evidences hath dscribed

Notes: This badly torn document, with much text missing, nevertheless shows an attack on the credibility of Mercy Lewis. This may be part of the Nurse defense, but in part because of the condition of the manuscript the evidence is insufficient for anything other than speculative dating. The connection to the Nurse case is similarly speculative.

Witchcraft Papers, no. 29a, Massachusetts Historical Society. Boston, MA.

370. Testimony of Robert Moulton Sr. Regarding Susannah Shelden, in Support of Rebecca Nurse‡

[Hand 1] the testimony of Robart Moulton sener who testifit{h} and saith that I waching with Susannah Sheldon sence she was afflicted I heard her say that the witches halled her vpone her bely through the yeard like a snacke and halled her ouer the stone walle & presently I heard her Controdict her former: discource and said that she Came ouer the stone wall her selfe and I heard her say that she Rid vpone a poole to boston and she said the diuel Caryed the poole

Robart Mouelton

Samuel Nurs and Joseph Trumball saw Robart moulton sine this wrighting

Notes: Likely used at trial.

Essex County Court Archives, vol. 2, no. 128, Massachusetts Supreme Judicial Court, Judicial Archives, on deposit James Duncan Phillips Library, Peabody Essex Museum, Salem, MA.

371. Deposition of Joseph Hutchinson Regarding Abigail Williams, in Support of Rebecca Nurse [?]

[Hand 1] The deposition of Joseph Huchinson aged 59: year doe testifie as foueth Abigaill Williams I ha⟨w⟩e heard yow spake often of a booke that haue bin offred to yow. she said that thare wos two Books one wos a short thike booke & the other wos a Long booke: I asked her wᵗ Coler the booke war of: she said the bookes ware as Rede as blode I asked her if she had sene the booke opned: shee said that shee had sen it opned many times: I asked her if shee did see any Ritinge in the in the booke: shee said thar wos many lins Riten & at the End of Euary line thar wos a seall: I asked her whoe brought the booke to her: shee towld me that it wos the blacke man
I asked her whoe the blacke man wos: shee towld mee it wos the deuell: I asked her if shee wos not afraid to see the deuell

shee said at the first shee wos and did goe from him but now shee wos not afraid but Could   June 29, 1692
talke with him as well as shee Could with ~~him~~ mee

Notes: Evidence for dating is not sufficient. This could be part of the Nurse defense, but that is speculative.

Witchcraft Papers, no. 37a, Massachusetts Historical Society. Boston, MA.

Statement of Samuel Nurse & John Tarbell for Rebecca Nurse‡
2nd of 2 dates. See No. 35 on March 29, 1692

372. Testimony of John Putnam Sr. & Rebecca Putnam for Rebecca Nurse‡

[Hand 1] the testemoney of John putnam: sen and rebecke his wife saith that our son in law John fuller: and our dafter rebecke Shep{a}rd did both of them dy ~~a most~~ a most uiolent death and did acting uerey strangly at the time of ther death.) farder saith that wee did Judg then that thay both diead of a malignant feuer and had no suspicion of wichcraft of aney nether Can wee acues the prisner at the bar of aney such thing

Notes: Possibly used at trial.

Essex County Court Archives, vol. 2, no. 125, Massachusetts Supreme Judicial Court, Judicial Archives, on deposit James Duncan Phillips Library, Peabody Essex Museum, Salem, MA.

373. Statement of Nathaniel Putnam Sr. for Rebecca Nurse‡

[Hand 1] Nathaniell putnam {sen^{or}} being desire⟨d⟩
by francis nurse sen^{or} to giue informa[Lost] [= information]
of what i could say concerning his wifes [Lost]
and conuersation: I the abouesayd ha[Lost] [= have]
known this sayd aboue sayd woman fou[Lost]
years & what i haue obserued of her human
frailtys excepted; her life & conuersation hath
been according to her proffession: & she hath
brought up a great family of children & educated [Lost] [= them?]
well soe that there is in some of them apparent s[Lost] [= signs?]
of godliness: i haue known her differ with her neig[Lost] [= neighbors]
but i neuer knew nor heard of any that did accus[Lost] [= accuse]
of what she is now charged with

Notes: Possibly used at trial.

Witchcraft Papers, no. 29b, Massachusetts Historical Society. Boston, MA.

Thursday, June 30, 1692

Grand Juries of Elizabeth How (Day 2), Elizabeth Procter, John Procter & Sarah Wilds

Trial of Elizabeth How

374. Depositions of Robert Downer, Mary Andrews, & Moses Pike v. Susannah Martin

[Hand 1] The deposion of Robert ~~Pike~~ downer of salsber⟨y⟩ aged 52 years who testif~~ying~~ and say

That several years ago susana martin the the⟨n⟩ wif of Georg martin being brought to court for a wich the sd downer hauig [= having] som words with her (sh⟨e⟩ at that time attending mrs Light at salsbury) This [Lost]ponent [= deponent] among other things told her he beleeved that shee was a wich by w^t was sd or wittnesd agans⟨t⟩ {her} at wch shee seeming not well afected sd that a {or som} shee divel woold fech him away ~~in a short time~~ shortly at wch this deponent was not much moved: but at ~~nig⟨?⟩~~ night as he Lay in his bed in his owne house alone ther came in at his window the Liknes ⟨?⟩ of a catt and by an by com vp to his bed took fast hold of his throt and Lay hard vpon him a consideribl while and was lik to throtl him at Length he minded w^t susana martin thretned him with the day before he strove w^t he coold and sayd avoyd thou shee divell in the name of the father & the son & the ho⟨l⟩y Ghost & then it Lett him go & slumpt down vpon the flower and went out at window againe he farther sayth that the next morning befor ever he he had sayd any thing of it som of that family asked him about it (as from her owne)

mrs mary Andras aged :40: year testify that shee did heer the sd susana martin threatn or tell the sd Robt downer that a shee divell woold fech him away shortly: shee furth⟨er⟩ sayth that from som of her fathers family shee did hear that that the sd su martin told them how sd downer was served y^e night that he was aflicted as abovsd

moses pike aged :26: years or more testify that he did he[Lost] [= hear] susana martin tell how R̄ō downer was handled and as he [Lost]members [= remembers] it ⟨w⟩as ["w" written over "t"] the next day after it was don at nigh⟨t⟩

sworne by Robt downer mr^s mary ~~Andr~~ Allin & moses p[Lost] [= Pike]

Jun 30 1692 before me Robt Pike Ass^t

[Reverse] [Hand 2] Robt Downer &c^a ver. Martin

Notes: This deposition was sworn after the trial of Susannah Martin, presumably because Robert Pike at an inferior court was not yet aware that Susannah Martin had been convicted the previous day. ◊ "avoyd": 'go away, depart' (*OED* s.v. *avoid* 6). ◊ Hand 1 = Robert Pike

Essex County Court Archives, vol. 1, no. 191, Massachusetts Supreme Judicial Court, Judicial Archives, on deposit James Duncan Phillips Library, Peabody Essex Museum, Salem, MA.

375. Deposition of Mary Warren v. Elizabeth Procter

See also: Aug. 5, 1692.

[Hand 1] The deposistion of mary warrin aged about 20 years ho testifieth and saith I haue often seen the apparition of Elizabth procter ["p" written over "El"] the wife of John procter

among the witches and she hath often tortored me most greuiously. by biting me and
Choakeing me and pinching me and presing my stomack tell the blood Came out of my
mouth. and allso apon the day. of her examingnation I saw her tortor mary walcoot marcy
lues. ann putnam. Elizabeth hubbort abigell. williams.
and she hath euer sence at times tortored me mest greuiously
[Hand 2] Mary warewin ownid this har testimony to be the truth before the Juriars of
Inquest this 30 of June 1692

[Hand 3] Jurat in Curia

[Reverse] Mary Warren Con El. Pro

Notes: Used at trial. ◊ Hand 1 = Edward Putnam; Hand 3 = Stephen Sewall

Essex County Court Archives, vol. 1, no. 102, Massachusetts Supreme Judicial Court, Judicial Archives, on deposit James Duncan Phillips Library, Peabody Essex Museum, Salem, MA.

376. Testimony of Nehemiah Abbott Sr. v. Elizabeth How

[Hand 1] The testimony of Nahamiah Abot Aged about 60 yers: saith that after any
difrencis with James Hows wif [Hand 2] ^{elizabeth how} [Hand 1] ofen ⟨?⟩ Euill acurents
[= occurrences] did falow som straing l⟨a⟩sis I met withall amongst our Catill: I had one ox
gat into thair fild and James Hows wife was uary aingry and wished he was Choked and
some short time after his falow [= fellow?] was choked with a turnop: and goodwif
how[Hand 2]s [Hand 1] s⟨a⟩nt her dafter [Hand 2] ^{came} [Hand 1] to borow my hors but
I could not spare him: and the night {day} after my hors was Cast in the barne with his head
under him as my saruants tould me and I want and saw the plac whair he lay and I had a kow
was so wake and lame y^t she could not go without the halp of thre or fouer men to hold hur
up and I put hur in my barne and put up the Raills to kep hur from other Catill and about
one ouer after the kow was gone the Raills being up and was in the mier about forty Rods of
and I was f⟨a⟩rst to gat the same halpe to get hur thathe⟨r⟩ againe
[Hand 3] Nehamiah Abbot: declared: to: y^e Jury of inquest: y^e above written to: be y^e truth:
upon oath: June: 30: 1692

[Hand 4] Jurat in Curia

[Reverse] Nathan^ε Abot

Notes: Used at trial. ◊ Hand 3 = Simon Willard; Hand 4 = Stephen Sewall

Essex Institute Collection, no. 5, James Duncan Phillips Library, Peabody Essex Museum, Salem, MA.

Sworn Before the Grand Jury and at Trial: Deposition of Sarah Bibber v. Elizabeth How
2nd of 2 dates. See No. 242 on May 31, 1692

Sworn Before the Grand Jury: Deposition of Isaac Cummings Sr. v. Elizabeth How
2nd of 2 dates. See No. 321 on June 27, 1692

June 30, 1692

377. Deposition of Jacob Foster v. Elizabeth How

[Hand 1] The deposion of Jacob foster aged about 29 years this doponant saith that some years agoe good wife How ^{the wife of Jeames how} was about to Joyne with the church of Ipswich My father was an instrumentall means of her being deny{ed}ing admision quickly after my mare was turned out to grass on the tusday: and on thursday I went to seek my mare to go {to} lecture I sought my mare and could not find her I sought all friday and found her not on Saturday I sought till noon & I found my mare standing leaning with her butocks against a tree I hit ["i" written over "e"] her with a small whip she gaue a heaue from a tree and fell back to the tree: again then I took of her fetters and strouk her again she did the same againe ["e" written over "d"] then I set my shoulder to her side and thrust her af from the tree ⟨?⟩ and moued her feet then she went home and leapt into the pausture and my mare lookt as if she had been miserably beaten and abused
[Hand 2] Jacob ffoster: declared: y^e evidence: to be y^e truth before y^e Jury of inqust: on oat⟨h⟩ June 30: 92.

[Reverse] [Hand 3] Jacob ffostar

Notes: Hand 2 = Simon Willard

Essex County Court Archives, vol. 1, no. 336, Massachusetts Supreme Judicial Court, Judicial Archives, on deposit James Duncan Phillips Library, Peabody Essex Museum, Salem, MA.

378. Testimony of John How v. Elizabeth How

[Hand 1] The Testimony of John How aged about 50 yers.
saieth that one that day that my brother James his Wif [Lost] [*Woodward =* was] Caried to Salem farmes upon exsamination she was at my [Lost] [*Woodward =* house] and would a haue had me to go with hur to Salem farmes I tould hur: that If she had ben sant for upon allmost any acount but witch Craft I would a haue gone with hur but one that acount I would not for ten pounds:: but said I If yow are a witch tell me how long yow have ben a witch and what mischeue yow haue done and then I will go with yow for said I to hur yow haue bin acusied by Samuell Pearlys Child and saspacted by Daken Cumins for witch craft: she semed to be aingry with me: stell she asked me to Come one the morow I told hur I did not know but I might Com to morow but my ocashons Caled me to go to Ipswich one the morow and Came Whome about sunsaet: and standing Nere my dore talking with one of my Naibours: I had a sow with six. small Pigs in the yard the sow was as wall so fare as I know as Euer: one a suding she leaped up about thre or fouer foot hie and turned about and gaue one squeake and fell downe daed. I told my naibour: that was with me I thought my sow was bewitched: for saied I I think she is daed he lafed at me but It proued true for she fell downe daed: he bed me Cut of hur Eare the which I did and my hand I had my knif in was so nume and full of paine that night and sauerall days after that I Could not doe any work and is not wholy wall now [Hand 2?] and I sospacted no other parson but my s^d sister ~~How~~ [Hand 3] elizabeth How

Capt Jno How: declared: y^e abovewritten: evidence: to be y^e truth: before: y^e Jury of inquest: June: 30th 1692 upon his oath: in Court

[Reverse] [Hand 4] Jo^n How

Notes: Hand 3 = Simon Willard

Essex County Court Archives, vol. 1, no. 335, Massachusetts Supreme Judicial Court, Judicial Archives, on deposit James Duncan Phillips Library, Peabody Essex Museum, Salem, MA.

379. Testimony of Francis Lane v. Elizabeth How

[Hand 1] Francis Laue aged 27 yeares testifyeth & saith that about seauen yeares agoe James How the Husband of Elizabeth How of Ipswich farmes hired s^d Laue to get him a parcell of posts & railes & s^d Laue hired John Pearly the son of Samuell Pearly of Ipswich to help him in getting of them And after they had got said Posts & railes. the said Laue went to the said James How that he might goe with him & take deliuery of said Posts & railes. & Elizabeth How the wife of s^d James how told said Laue that she did not beleiue that s^d Posts & railes would doe because that s^d John Pearly helped him & she t⟨ou⟩ld said that if he had got them alone & had not got s^d ["s^d" written over "John"] John Pearly to help him she beleiued beleiued ["be" written over "sh"] that they would haue done but seing that said Pearly had helped about them she beleiued that they woul⟨d⟩ not doe. so s^d James How went with said Laue for to take deliuery of s^d Posts & railes & the s^d James How toke seuerall of the said railes as they lay in heaps up by the end & they broke of. so many of them broke that said Laue was ["Laue was" written over "was forced"] forced to get thirty or forty more & when said How came home he told his wife thereof & she said to him that she had told him before that they would not doe because said Pearly helped about them which railes said Laue testifyeth that in his Aprehention were ["w" written over "th"] good sound railes
[Hand 2] ffrancis Laue: declared: to y^e Jury of inques: to: y^e truthe of y^e abovewritten: evidence: upon oath: June: 30th 1692

[Hand 3] Jurat in Curia.

[Reverse] ffrances Lane

Notes: Used at trial. ◊ Hand 2 = Simon Willard; Hand 3 = Stephen Sewall

Essex County Court Archives, vol. 1, no. 334, Massachusetts Supreme Judicial Court, Judicial Archives, on deposit James Duncan Phillips Library, Peabody Essex Museum, Salem, MA.

Sworn Before the Grand Jury: Deposition of Samuel Perley & Ruth Perley v. Elizabeth How and List of Witnesses v. Elizabeth How

2nd of 2 dates. See No. 256 on June 1, 1692

Sworn Before the Grand Jury: Deposition of Timothy Perley & Deborah Perley v. Elizabeth How

2nd of 2 dates. See No. 257 on June 1, 1692

Sworn Before the Grand Jury and at Trial: Deposition of Joseph Safford v. Elizabeth How & Bridget Bishop

2nd of 2 dates. See No. 243 on May 31, 1692

June 30, 1692

380. Indictment No. 1 of Elizabeth Procter, for Afflicting Mary Walcott†
See also: Aug. 5, 1692.

[Hand 1] Anno Regis et Reginæ Willm̄ et
Mariæ nunc Angliæ &ᶜ Quarto

Essex ss

The Juroᵉ for our Sovereigne Lord and Lady the King and Queen pᵉsents That: [Hand 2] **Elizabeth Procter Wife of John Procter of Salem** [Hand 1] the [Hand 2] **11**ᵗʰ [Hand 1] Day of [Hand 2] **Aprill** [Hand 1] in the fourth Year of the Reigne of our Sovereigne Lord and Lady William and Mary: by the Grace of God of England Scottland ffrance and Ireland King and Queen Defenders of the faith &ᶜ and Divers other Dayes and times. as well before, as after, certaine Detestable Arts called witchcraft & sorceries wickedly and ffelloniously hath vsed Practised and Exercised, at and within the Towneship of [Hand 2] **Salem** [Hand 1] in the County of Essex aforesaid in upon and agᵗ one [Hand 2] **Mary Walcott of Salem Villiage Singlewoman** [Hand 1] by which said wicked arts the said [Hand 2] **Mary Wolcott** [Hand 1] the [Hand 2] **11**ᵗʰ [Hand 1] Day of [Hand 2] **Aprill** [Hand 1] in the forth Year as abovesᵈ and Divers other Days and times. as well before; as after was and is Tortur⟨d⟩ed afflicted Pined Consumed wasted & Tormented: and also for sundry other Acts of witchcraft. by said [Hand 2] **Elizabeth Procter.** [Hand 1] Committed and done before and since that time agᵗ the Peace of our Sovereigne Lord & Lady, the King and Queen and agᵗ the fforme of the Statute in that case made and Provided

[Hand 2] Wittnesses.

Mary Wolcutt   ⎫
Ann Putman   ⎬   Sworn
Mercy Lewis.   ⎭

[Reverse] [Hand 2?] No. (1) El. Procter bila uera Procter & wife

Notes: Although this indictment is only against Elizabeth Procter, the notation mentioning her husband, John Procter, may suggest the possibility that the two cases were heard together. ◊ Hand 2 = Stephen Sewall

Essex County Court Archives, vol. 1, no. 90, Massachusetts Supreme Judicial Court, Judicial Archives, on deposit James Duncan Phillips Library, Peabody Essex Museum, Salem, MA.

381. Indictment No. 2 of Elizabeth Procter, for Afflicting Mercy Lewis†
See also: Aug. 5, 1692.

[Hand 1] Anno Regis et Reginae Willm̄ et
Mariæ nunc Angliæ &ᶜ Quarto:

Essex ss

The Juroᵉ for our Sovereigne Lord and Lady the King and Queen⟨e⟩ pᵉsents That [Hand 2] **Elizabeth Procter. Wife of John Procter of Salem husbandman** [Hand 1] the ~~Day of~~ [Hand 2] **11**ᵗʰ [Hand 1] Day of [Hand 2] **Aprill** [Hand 1] in the forth Year of the Reigne of our Sovereigne Lord and Lady William and Mary by the Grace of God of England Scottland ffrance and Ireland King and Queen Defenders of the ffaith &ᶜ and Divers other Dayes and times as well before as after, certaine Detestable Arts called Witchcrafts and Sorceries Wickedly and ffelloniously hath vsed Practised and Exercised at and within the Towneship of [Hand 2] **Salem** [Hand 1] in the County of Essex aforesᵈ in vpon and agᵗ one [Hand 2]

Marcy Lewis of Salem villiage in ye County afores^d Singlewoman [Hand 1] by which said Wicked Arts, the said [Hand 2] **Marcy Lewis** [Hand 1] the ~~Day~~ [Hand 2] **11th** [Hand 1] Day of [Hand 2] **Aprill** [Hand 1] in the forth Year abouesaid and Divers other Dayes and times as well before as after was and is Tortured Afflicted Pined Consumed wasted & Tormented, And also for Sundrey other Acts of Witchcraft by the said [Hand 2] **Elizabeth. Procter** [Hand 1] Committed and Done before and sience that time. ag^t the peace of our Sovereigne Lord and Lady the King and Queen and ag^t the fforme of the Statute, in that case made, and Provided.

June 30, 1692

[Hand 2] Witnesses.

Mercy Lewis.
Ann Putman } Sworn
Eliz. Hubbard }

[Reverse] N^o (2) Eli. Procter
[Hand 3] billa uera

Notes: Hand 2 = Stephen Sewall

Essex County Court Archives, vol. 1, no. 89, Massachusetts Supreme Judicial Court, Judicial Archives, on deposit James Duncan Phillips Library, Peabody Essex Museum, Salem, MA.

382. Deposition of Stephen Bittford v. Rebecca Nurse & Elizabeth Procter

See also: Aug. 5, 1692.

[Hand 1] The Deposistion of Steephen Bittford agged about 23 years who testifieth and saith that about the begining of April 1692 about midnight as I was abed att the house of James Darling of Salem I being parfittly awake I saw standing in the chamber Rebekah ["kah" written over "ce"] nurs and Elizabeth proctor [Hand 2] ^{the wife of John prockter} [Hand 1] whom I uery well knew and I was in uery grate paine in my neck and could not stir my head nor spake a word but I cannot say that it was they that hurt me and for .2. or 3 dayes after I could not stir my neck but as I moued my whol body

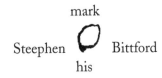

mark
Steephen ◯ Bittford
his

[Hand 2] Stephen bittford owned this his testimony to be
the truth on his oath before the Juriars of Inquest this .30. of June: 1692

[Hand 3] Jurat in Curia

[Reverse] [Hand 2] Stephen bittford testimony

Notes: Rebecca Nurse had been tried the previous day, and although her name appears on the document, the date of the grand jury places it in the case against Elizabeth Procter. ◊ Used at trial. ◊ Hand 1 = Thomas Putnam; Hand 3 = Stephen Sewall

Essex County Court Archives, vol. 1, no. 100, Massachusetts Supreme Judicial Court, Judicial Archives, on deposit James Duncan Phillips Library, Peabody Essex Museum, Salem, MA.

June 30, 1692

383. Deposition of Elizabeth Booth v. Elizabeth Procter

[Hand 1] The Deposistion of Eliz: Booth agged about 18: years who testifieth and saith that on the 27 June Elizabeth proctor came to me and did most greviously tortor me by biting pinching and pricking me and allmost choak{ing me:} and tould me that my mother nor I would not beleue that she w⟨a⟩s a wicth but she said she would make me know she was a wicth before she had don with me.

Eliz: Booth

[Hand 2] elizabeth booth owinid this har testimony to be the truth one har oath before the Juriars of Inquest this 30. dy of June 1692

[Hand 3] Jurat in Curia

[Reverse] El. Booth

Notes: Elizabeth Booth's name was signed by Thomas Putnam. ◊ Used at trial. ◊ Hand 1 = Thomas Putnam; Hand 3 = Stephen Sewall

Essex County Court Archives, vol. 1, no. 103, Massachusetts Supreme Judicial Court, Judicial Archives, on deposit James Duncan Phillips Library, Peabody Essex Museum, Salem, MA.

384. Testimony of Elizabeth Booth v. Elizabeth Procter, John Procter, & Martha Cory

[Hand 1] The testimony of Elesebeth Booth Aged 18 years or their about testifie{th} & saith y^t one y^e 8 day of June fath{er} Law. Shafling. Apered vnto me & sai⟨d⟩ y^t Elesebeth prockter Kiled him Because my mother woold not seand for doctor grigs to giue him feseke [= physic] & also Because she was not sent for when he was. first taken sicke

Elesebeth Booth

The testimony of Elesebeth Booth. Aged 18 ye{a}rs or their about testifieth y^t one y^e 8 day of June Robert Stone. Sinyer Apered vnto me. & told me y^t John proctor Sinyer & Elesebeth his wife Kiled him Because they. had som diferance in a rekninge & also. at ye same time Robert Stone Juner Apered vnto me & told me that John prockter & Elesebeth. his wife Kiled him because he tooke his fatheirs part.

Elesebeth Booth.

The testimony of Elesebeth. Booth Aged 18 yers or their about testifieth y^t one y^e 8 of June Geiorg nedom Apeired vnto me & saide y^t mattha Goerie kiled him Because he wold not mend her Lening [= linen] wheal

Elesebeth Booth.

The testimony of Elesebeth Booth Aged 18 yers or their about testifieth y^t on y^e 8 day of June Thomas Goold Senyer Apered vnto. me & told me y^t ~~she~~ {mattha Corie} kiled him because he told her she did not doe weel by Goodman parkers Childringe

Elesebeth Booth

[Hand 2] Elizabeth Booth owned {vpon Oath} all that is aboue written before & vnto ye June 30, 1692
Grand inquest on ye 30th Day of June 1692

[Reverse] [Hand 3] Booth. gs^t procters.
[Hand 4] M Corie

Notes: Booth's "signature" is by Hand 1. June 30 is known as the date when a grand jury heard the cases against John and Elizabeth Procter. Although Elizabeth Booth accuses three people in this document it was likely only used against the Procters. For the reference to Martha Cory see p. 98 of Chronological Arrangement. ◊ Hand 2 = Andrew Elliot

Essex County Court Archives, vol. 1, no. 104 & vol. 2 no. 112, Massachusetts Supreme Judicial Court, Judicial Archives, on deposit James Duncan Phillips Library, Peabody Essex Museum, Salem, MA.

385. Testimony of Elizabeth Booth v. Elizabeth Procter & John Willard

[Hand 1] The testimony of Elesebeth. Booth Aged 18 yers. or ther about testifieth. y^t one ye 8 of June. hugh. Joanes Apered vnto me & told me that Elesebeth. prockter Kiled him because he had a poght of sider of her which he had not paid her for.

Elesebeth Booth.

The testimony of Elesebeth. Booth. Aged 18 yer{s} or their about testifieth y^t one ye 8 of June Elesebeth Shaw apered vnto me & told me y^t Elesebeth proctor & John wilard Kiled Her Because she did not vse those doctors. she Advised her too.

Elesebeth. Booth

The testimony of Elesebeth Booth Aged 18. yers. or their about testifieth y^t one ye 8. of June ye wife of John felton Apered vnto me & told me that Elesebeth proctor Kiled her Because she wold not giue her Aples. when she sent for sum

Elesebeth Booth

The testimony of Elesebeth Booth Aged 18. yers or. their about testifieth y^t one y^e 8 of Jun⟨e⟩ Doc^r Serubabel Endecot Apered vnto me & told me Elesebeth. proctor Kiled him because thay difered in their Judgments. about thomas veries wife & lickwis y^e saide Eleseb⟨e⟩[Lost]{h} [= Elizabeth] proctor woold haue kiled doc^t Endecots. wife But Cold not But lamed her a Good while

Elesebeth Booth

[Hand 2] ⟨⩴⟩ All the Depotitions of Elizabeth Booth written in this side of paper were acknowledge by said Booth before & vnto the Grand inquest on the: 30th Day of June 1692 vpon Oath

[Reverse] [Hand 3] Procter

Notes: Although Willard is accused, this document was probably used only at the grand jury hearing the case of Elizabeth Procter. Elizabeth Booth's "signature" is Hand 1. ◊ Hand 2 = Andrew Elliot; Hand 3 = Stephen Sewall

June 30, 1692   *Essex County Court Archives, vol. 1, no. 105, Massachusetts Supreme Judicial Court, Judicial Archives, on deposit James Duncan Phillips Library, Peabody Essex Museum, Salem, MA.*

Sworn Before the Grand Jury: Deposition of Mercy Lewis v. Elizabeth Procter
2nd of 2 dates. See No. 51 on April 11, 1692

Sworn Before the Grand Jury: Deposition of Samuel Parris, Nathaniel Ingersoll, & Thomas Putnam v. Elizabeth Procter
2nd of 2 dates. See No. 52 on April 11, 1692

Sworn Before the Grand Jury: Deposition of Ann Putnam Jr. v. Elizabeth Procter
2nd of 3 dates. See No. 53 on April 11, 1692

386. Deposition of Mary Walcott v. Elizabeth Procter
See also: Aug. 5, 1692.

[Hand 1] The Deposistion of mary walcott agged about 17 years who testifeth and saith that I neuer saw the Apperishtion of Elizabeth proctor: the wife of Jno: proctor before the day of hir Examination being the 11th April 1692: but senc that time the Apperishtion of Elizabeth proctor has most greviously afflect⟨ed⟩ me by biting pinching and almost choaking me urging me to writ in hir book

mark

mary 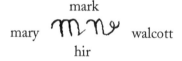 walcott

hir

[Hand 2] Mary Walcutt owned her Deposition aboue written vpon her Oath before & vnto yᵉ Grand inquest on yᵉ 30th Day of June 1692

[Hand 3] Jurat in Curia

[Reverse] [Hand 1] Mary walcott againt Eliz: proctor

Notes: Used at trial. ◊ Hand 1 = Thomas Putnam; Hand 2 = Andrew Elliot; Hand 3 = Stephen Sewall

Essex County Court Archives, vol. 1, no. 95, Massachusetts Supreme Judicial Court, Judicial Archives, on deposit James Duncan Phillips Library, Peabody Essex Museum, Salem, MA.

Sworn Before the Grand Jury: Testimony of Abigail Williams v. Elizabeth Procter
2nd of 2 dates. See No. 245 on May 31, 1692

387. Indictment No. 1 of John Procter, for Afflicting Mary Walcott (Returned Ignoramus)†

[Hand 1] Anno Regis et Reginæ Willm̄. et
Mariæ nunc Angliæ &ᶜ Quarto:
Essex ss

June 30, 1692

The Juro͞ᵉ for our Sovereigne Lord and Lady the King. and Queen pᵉsents That: [Hand 2] **John Procter of Salem Husbandman in yᵉ County of Essex** [Hand 1] the [Hand 2] **Eleuenth** [Hand 1] Day of [Hand 2] **Aprill** [Hand 1] in the [Hand 2] **fourth** [Hand 1] Year of the Reigne of our Sovereigne Lord & Lady Willia⟨m⟩ and Mary by the Grace of Godd of England Scottland ffrance and Ireland King and Queen Defenders of t[Lost] [= the] ffaith &ᶜ and divers other Dayes and times as well befor⟨e⟩ as After Certaine Detestable Acts, called Witchcraft and Sorceries Wickedly. and ffelloniously hath. used. Practised and Excercised at and within the Towneship of [Hand 2] **Salem** [Hand 1] in the County of Essex afore͞sd. in upon, and agᵗ one [Hand 2] **Mary Wolcott of Salem Villiage in yᵉ County of Essex Single Woman** [Hand 1] by which said wicked Arts the said: [Hand 2] **Mary Wolcott** [Hand 1] the [Hand 2] **11ᵗʰ** [Hand 1] Day of [Hand 2] **April** [Hand 1] in the Year abovesaid and Divers other Dayes and times as well before. as after was and is Tortured, Afflicted, Pined, Consumed wasted, and Tormented, agᵗ the Peace of our Sovereign[Lost] [= sovereign] Lord & Lady the King and Queen, and agᵗ the form of the Statute in that case made and Provided/.
[Hand 2] Witnesses.
Mary Wolcot Jurat
Mercy Lewis Jurat.
Ann Putman Jurat.

[Reverse] Nᵒ 1. Jnᵒ Procter
[Hand 3] Ignoramos
[Hand 2] Procter & wife

Notes: As elsewhere, grand juries were willing, although infrequently, to reject charges from the core accusers whose claims they normally accepted. ◊ Hand 2 = Stephen Sewall

Essex County Court Archives, vol. 1, no. 46, Massachusetts Supreme Judicial Court, Judicial Archives, on deposit James Duncan Phillips Library, Peabody Essex Museum, Salem, MA.

388. Indictment No. 2 of John Procter, for Afflicting Mercy Lewis†
See also: Aug. 5, 1692.

[Hand 1] Anno Regis et Reginae Will͞m et
Mariæ nunc Angliæ &ᶜ Quarto
Essex. ss.
The Juroᵉ for our Sovereigne Lord and Lady the King and Queen pᵉsents That [Hand 2] **John Procter of Salem in yᵉ County of Essex in New England {husbandman}** [Hand 1] the [Hand 2] **11ᵗʰ** [Hand 1] Day of [Hand 2] **April** [Hand 1] in the forth Year of the Reigne of our Sovereigne Lord and Lady William & Mary by the Grace of God of England Scottland ffrance & Ireland King and Queen Defenders of the ffaith &ᶜ and Divers other Dayes and times as well before as after. certaine Detestable Arts called witchcrafts and Sorceries wickedly and ffelloniously hath vsed Practised and Exercised at and with in the Towneship of [Hand 2] **Salem** [Hand 1] in the County of Essex afore͞sᵈ in upon and agᵗ one [Hand 2] **Mercey Lewis of Salem Villiage in yᵉ County of Essex afore͞sᵈ Singlewoman** [Hand 1] by which said wicked Arts the said [Hand 2] **Mercey Lewis** [Hand 1] the D̶a̶ [Hand 2] **11ᵗʰ** [Hand 1] Day of [Hand 2] **April** [Hand 1] in the forth Year above͞sᵈ, and divers other

June 30, 1692

Dayes and times. as well before as after was and is Tortured afflicted Pined: Consumed wasted and. Tormented, and also for sundrey other acts of witchcraft by said [Hand 2] **John Procter** [Hand 1] Committed and done before and since that time. ag^t the Peace of our Sovereigne Lord & Lady the King and Queen, and ag^t the fform of the Statute in that case made and Provided:/

[Hand 2] Witnesses.

Mercy Lewis
Ann Putman   } Sworne.

[Reverse] Jn° Procter N° 2. On M: Lewis
[Hand 3] bila uera

Notes: Hand 2 = Stephen Sewall

Essex County Court Archives, vol. 1, no. 45, Massachusetts Supreme Judicial Court, Judicial Archives, on deposit James Duncan Phillips Library, Peabody Essex Museum, Salem, MA.

389. Indictment No. 3 of John Procter, for Afflicting Mary Warren†

See also: Aug. 5, 1692.

[Hand 1] Anno Regis et Reginæ Willm et
Mariæ nunc Angliæ &^c Quarto

Essex. ss:

The Juro^e for our Sovereigne Lord and Lady the King and Queen p^esents That [Hand 2] **John Procter of Salem in ye County of Essex husbandman** [Hand 1] the D [Hand 2] **26**^th [Hand 1] Day of [Hand 2] **March** [Hand 1] in the [Hand 2] **fourth** [Hand 1] Year of the Reigne of our Sovereigne Lord and Lady William and Mary by the Grace of God of England Scottland ffrance and Ireland King and Queen Defenders of the ffaith &^c and Divers other Dayes and times as well before as after certaine Detestable Arts called witchcrafts and Sorceries wickedly and ffelloniously. hath Vsed, Practised and Excercised at, and within the Township of [Hand 2] **Salem** [Hand 1] in the County of Essex afores^d in, Vpon and ag^t one [Hand 2] **Mary Warren of Salem in ye County of Essex Singlewoman** [Hand 1] by which said wicked arts the said [Hand 2] **Mary Warren** [Hand 1] the [Hand 2] **Twenty Sixth** [Hand 1] Day of [Hand 2] **March** [Hand 1] in the [Hand 2] **fourth** [Hand 1] Year abovesaid and Divers other Dayes & times as well before, as after, was and is Tortured, Afflicted, Pined: Consumed wasted and Tormented, ag^t the Peace of our Sovereigne Lord & Lady the King and Queen and agt. the fform of the Statute in that case made and Provided /.

[Hand 2] Witnesses.

Mary Warren {Jurat.} Jur
Mary Wolcott. Jurat

[Reverse] N° 3. Jn° Procter Ind^t vp^n M: Wa:
[Hand 3] bila uera

Notes: Hand 2 = Stephen Sewall

Essex County Court Archives, vol. 1, no. 44, Massachusetts Supreme Judicial Court, Judicial Archives, on deposit James Duncan Phillips Library, Peabody Essex Museum, Salem, MA.

390. Deposition of Sarah Bibber v. John Procter

See also: Aug. 5, 1692.

[Hand 1] The Deposistion of Sarah vibber agged about 36 years who testifieth and saith that on the 3 June 1692 Jno: proctor. sen^r came to me and did most greviously torment me by pinching pricking and almost presing me to death urging me to drink: drink as Red as blood which [1st "h" written over "ic"] I refusing ⟨s⟩he did tortor me with variety of tortors and Immediatly he vanished away also on the same day I saw Jno: proctor most greviously tortor Susannah Shelden by claping his hands on hir throat and almost choaking hir. also seuerall times sence Jno: proctor sen^r has most greviously tortored me a grat many times with variety of tortors.

[Hand 2] Sara uibber. ownid this har testimony to be the truth on har oath before the Juriars of Inquest this: 30. of June 1692

[Hand 3] Jurat in Curia

[Reverse] Sarah Vibber

Notes: Used at trial. ◊ Hand 1 = Thomas Putnam; Hand 3 = Stephen Sewall

Essex County Court Archives, vol. 1, no. 56, Massachusetts Supreme Judicial Court, Judicial Archives, on deposit James Duncan Phillips Library, Peabody Essex Museum, Salem, MA.

Sworn Before the Grand Jury: Testimony of Joseph Pope v. John Procter‡
2nd of 2 dates. See No. 58 on April 11, 1692

Sworn Before the Grand Jury: Deposition of Ann Putnam Jr. v. John Procter
2nd of 2 dates. See No. 59 on April 11, 1692

391. Deposition of Mary Warren v. John Procter

[Hand 1] the deposistion of mary warrin [Hand 2] {agegd 20 ys} [Hand 1] ho testifieth I haue seen the apparition of John proctor [Hand 2] {senr} [Hand 1] among {siner} the wiches. and he hath often tortrdtoread: me by penching. me. and biting me and Choakeing me and presing. me one my. stomack. tell the blood [1st "o" written over "u"] Came out of my mouth and allso I saw him tortor mes poop and marcy. lues. and John Indian: apon the day of his examinnation and he hath allso temted me to right in his book. [Hand 2] and to eat bread which he brought to me which I Refuseing to doe: Jno procter ["t" written over "k"] did most greviously tortor me with variety of torturs allmost Redy to kill me

[Hand 3] Mary Warren owned the aboue written vpon her Oath before ⟨a⟩ & vnto y^e Grand inquest on the 30th Day of June 1692

Notes: The document was probably written before June 30. Thomas Putnam made his addition probably to strengthen it for the grand jury. "mes poop" is Mrs. Bathshua Pope. ◊ Hand 1 = Edward Putnam; Hand 2 = Thomas Putnam; Hand 3 = Andrew Elliot

Essex County Court Archives, vol. 1, no. 59, Massachusetts Supreme Judicial Court, Judicial Archives, on deposit James Duncan Phillips Library, Peabody Essex Museum, Salem, MA.

June 30, 1692

392. Indictment No. 1 of Sarah Wilds, for Afflicting Mercy Lewis†

See also: July 2, 1692.

[Hand 1] Anno Regis et Reginæ Willm̄ et
Mariæ nunc Angliæ &ᶜ Quarto

Essex ss

The Juroᴱ for our Sovereigne Lord and Lady the King and Queen pᴱsents That [Hand 2] **Sarah Willes wife of John Willes of Topsfield Husbandman** [Hand 1] the [Hand 2] **Twenty Second** [Hand 1] Day of [Hand 2] **Aprill** [Hand 1] in the forth Year of the Reigne of our Sovereigne Lord and Lady William and Mary by the Grace of God of England Scottland ffrance and Ireland King and Queen Defenders of the ffaith &ᶜ and divers other Dayes and times as well before as after, certaine Detestable Arts called Witchcrafts and Sorceries wickedly and ffelloniously hath vsed Practised and Excercised at and within the Towneship of [Hand 2] **Salem** [Hand 1] in the County of Essex aforesaid in upon and against one [Hand 2] **Marcy Lewis of Salem Villiage Singlewoman** [Hand 1] by which said wicked Acts the said [Hand 2] **Mercey Lewis** [Hand 1] the [Hand 2] **Twenty Second** [Hand 1] Day of [Hand 2] **Aprill** [Hand 1] aforesaid in the forth Year abovēsᵈ and Divers other Dayes and times as well before and after, was and is Tortured Afflicted Pined Consumed wasted & Tormented and also for Sundery orther Acts of Witchcraft by said [Hand 2] **Sarah Willes.** [Hand 1] Committed and Done before and since that time agᵗ the Peace of our Sovereigne Lord & Lady the King and Queen, and agᵗ the form of the Statute in that Case made and Provided.

[Hand 2] Witnesses.

Marcy Lewis

Ann Putman

Mary Wolcott

[Reverse] Sar⟨ah⟩ Wills

Indᵗ Contr. Willes Nᵒ (1)

[Hand 3] bila uera

Notes: Hand 2 = Stephen Sewall

Essex Institute Collection, no. 14, James Duncan Phillips Library, Peabody Essex Museum, Salem, MA.

393. Deposition of John Andrews & Joseph Andrews v. Sarah Wilds

See also: July 2, 1692.

[Hand 1] The deposistion of John Andrew aged about. 37 years and Joseph Andrew agged about 33 years: ^{both of Boxford} who testifieth and saith that in the year 1674: we ware amowing together and one of us broak our sith [= scythe] and not haueing oppertunity jest then to mend that nor by another wee went to the house of John willes senʳ of Topsfeild to borow a sith: but when we came there there was no man att whom: but the said willes wife who is now charged with {acts} ^{of} wicthcraf: was with in: and we asked hir to lend us a sith but she said they had noe siths to lend: but one of hir neighbors being also there said to us there is John willes junʳˢ sith hanging in that tree which stood by the house you may take that and spake ["a" written over "e"] with him as you goe to your work for he is at worke

neare the way as you goe along: and accordingly we took down the sith out of the tree and
tould the old woman that we would ask leaue of John willes jun^r for his sith before we used
{it}: but she was very angery and said it was a braue world that euery one did what they
would. however we went away with the sith: but we had not been gon very fare from the
house but a litle lad came affter. us whose name was Efraime willes: and tould us that his
mother said we had best bring the sith back againe: or Elce it should be a dear sith to us:
however. we went on our way with the sith and asked the Right. owner of it leaue for it
before we used it and went to our work and cutt down as much gras⟨s⟩ that day as made about
three load of hay: and Returned the sith to the owner: and afterwards made up our hay: and
afterwards went to carting of our hay and went into the meadow and loaded up one load very
well and caried it whom: and went againe into the meadow and loaded a second load and
bou⟨nd⟩ it and went to Driue it whom: but when we came to drive our oxen wee could not
make them stire the load tho we had six good oxen and the Two foremost oxen ware on the
upland and the meadow very firme where we carted constantly: but we striued a while to
make our oxen goe but could not git them along: att last one of our wheales fell in up to the
stock altho the meadow was feirme: then we threw allmost all the hay from ofe our cart and
thought to trie to git out the cart with sum hay upon it but we could not. then we said one to
another. it was in vain to ⟨s⟩riue [= strive] for we thought gooddy willes was in the cart. and
then we threw of all the hay and then we tried to make our oxen draw out the emty cart
which at first they could not doe: but att last the whele jumpt up at once w⟨e⟩ know not how
almost redy to thro down our oxen on their ~~heads~~. {knees} then againe we loaded up our
load of hay very well and bound it: and away wee went with it very well tell we came near to a
very dangerous hill to goe dow[Lost] [= down] with a load of hay: and ^{then I} the said
Joseph Andrew was by the foremost oxen an[Lost] [= and] saw sumthing about as bigge as a
dogge glance from a stump or root of a tree along by me and the oxen and the oxen began to
jump: but I coul⟨d⟩ not stire ["i" written over "u"] fom [= from] the place for I know not how
long: and I the said John Andrew being by the hindmost oxen saw nothing but the oxen
begining to jump I caft [= caught] hold of one of the oxen bowes as was caried down
viollently that dangerouse hill I know not how: where was a brooke at the bottom of it with a
bridge and a fford: and the oxen ran into the for⟨d⟩ and ouer thrue the load of hay their: and
when I came to [Reverse] To understand where I was and saw the oxen ware all well I
bega[Lost] [= began] to bethinke my self of my Brother Joseph: and Immediatly called him
but he gaue me no answer. and I began to be trobled for him and went backward towards the
place where the oxen were affrighted and I called seuerall times but he gaue me no answer att
last I calle[Lost] [= called] and said the load is ouerthron then immediatly he answered me
and came unto me: but how the load should keep upon the wheles runing so violently down
that dangerous hill: ⟨?⟩ ^{&} being ouer throne whare it was we can giue no account unles it
was don by summ diabolicall art: then againe we gott up our cart and loaded up our hay very
firme in resouling to gitt hom our load if we could tho it was night: and wh[Lost] [= when]
we had loaded we went to bind our load: but ^{by} all the skill an⟨d⟩ strenth we had we could
now wayes bind our load with our cart rope but it would hang lose on our load: howeuer we
went awa⟨y⟩ whom with our load and it laid very well for all it was night and o[Lost] [= our]
load unbound: also before we got whom many of our friends and neighbors meet us being
consarned for us because we ware so latte & they also saw our cart Rope hang lose and tould
us of it. and wee tould them what mishap we had that day: and they also tried to fasten the
Rope but could not: {all} which made us then to think and euer sence haue thought: and still
doe thinke that Gooddy willes who ~~had~~ now stand⟨s⟩ charged w⟨ith⟩ ^{High} suspition of
seuerall acts of wicthcraft had a hand in our Mishap at that time⟨?⟩

June 30, 1692

[Hand 2] Jn° Andrew: and Joseph Andrew. declared: yᵉ evidence: written: on these two sides to: be yᵉ truth on: their oathes: declared: before yᵉ Jury of inquest: Juni 30. {92}

[Hand 3] Jurat in Curia by both ꝑsons

[Hand 4] Jn° & Joseph. Andre⟨w⟩ agˢᵗ Wilds

Notes: Used at trial. ◊ Hand 1 = Thomas Putnam; Hand 2 = Simon Willard; Hand 3 = Stephen Sewall; Hand 4 = Jonathan Corwin

Essex Institute Collection, no. 6, James Duncan Phillips Library, Peabody Essex Museum, Salem, MA.

Sworn Before the Grand Jury: Deposition of Ann Putnam Jr., v. Sarah Wilds
2ⁿᵈ of 2 dates. See No. 92 on April 22, 1692

Sworn Before the Grand Jury: Deposition of Mary Walcott v. Sarah Wilds
2ⁿᵈ of 3 dates. See No. 93 on April 22, 1692

Billa Vera: Indictment No. 1 of Elizabeth How, for Afflicting Mary Walcott†
2ⁿᵈ of 2 dates. See No. 347 on June 29, 1692

Billa Vera: Indictment No. 2 of Elizabeth How, for Afflicting Mercy Lewis†
2ⁿᵈ of 2 dates. See No. 348 on June 29, 1692

Sworn at Trial: Three Depositions of Mary Cummings v. Elizabeth How†
3ʳᵈ of 3 dates. See No. 322 on June 27, 1692

394. Testimony of Martha Wood v. Elizabeth How†

Among others, *Martha Wood*, gave her Testimony, That a little after her Father had been employed in gathering an account of *How's* Conversation, they once and again lost great Quantities of Drink out of their Vessels, in such a manner, as they could ascribe to nothing but Witchcraft. As also, That *How* giving her some Apples, when she had eaten of them, she was taken with a very strange kind of Amaze, insomuch that she knew not what the said or did.

Notes: A manuscript of Martha Wood's testimony is not extant, and Cotton Mather's account is used here for that reason. ◊ Used at trial.

Cotton Mather. Wonders of the Invisible World: Being an Account of the Tryals of Several Witches, Lately Executed in New-England: And of several remarkable Curiosities therein Occuring. . . . (London: John Dunton, 1693), p. 78.

Presented at Trial: Statement of Daniel Warner, John Warner & Sarah Warner for Elizabeth How‡
2ⁿᵈ of 2 dates. See No. 318 on June 25, 1692

Presented at Trial: Statement of Joseph Knowlton & Mary Knowlton for Elizabeth How‡
2ⁿᵈ of 2 dates. See No. 325 on June 27, 1692

Presented at Trial: Statement of James How Sr., for Elizabeth How‡
2ⁿᵈ of 2 dates. See No. 341 on June 28, 1692

July 1692

Friday, July 1, 1692

Grand Jury of Martha Carrier†

395. Complaint of John Putnam Jr. & Thomas Putnam v. Margaret Hawkes & Candy

[Hand 1] Essex John Putnam {Ju:} & Thomas Putnam of Salem Complaines o[Lost]
[= of?] Margret Hawkes Late of Barbados now of Salem [1 word overstruck] and her Negro
Woman ⟨for⟩ ^{upon suspption} that they doe Afflict & Torment by Witchcraft the bodeys
of Mary Walcott & Mary Warren, Ann Putnam, All of Salem Spinstᵉs And Pray that the
said Margret Hawkes & her Negro Woman may be apprehended & Comitted according to
Law – to Answer the Complaint of the aboue said Putnems
Salem: 1̄: July 1692

Thomas putnam
John putnam Jun

Notes: Hand 1 = Stephen Sewall

MS Ch K 1.40, vol. 1, p. 154, Rare Books and Manuscripts, Boston Public Library. Boston, MA.

396. Deposition of Thomas Andrews v. Elizabeth How

[Hand 1] July 1ᵗʰ 1692.

The Testimony of Thomas Andrews of Boxford aged about 50. yeers This Deponant
Testifieth & saith yᵗ Isack Comings Senioᵋ of Topsfield sent for me To healp a mare yᵗ was
not well & when I came There yᵉ mare was in such a Condition yᵗ I Could not tell wᵗ she
ailed for I neuer sawe yᵉ Like her Lips ware Excedingly swelled yᵗ yᵉ Incides of Them
Turned outward & Looked Black & blew & gelled her Tung was in yᵉ same Condition I
told yᵉ sᵈ Comings I Could not tell wᵗ to doe for her I perceiued she had not yᵉ Botts wᶜʰ I
Did att first think she had butt I sᵈ she might haue some great heat in her Body & I would
applie a pipe of Tobacco to her & yᵗ was Concented to & I Litt a pipe of Tobacco & putt itt
vnto her fundiment & there Came a Blew flame out of yᵉ Bowle & Run along yᵉ stem of sᵈ
pipe & took hold of yᵉ haer of sᵈ maer & Burnt itt & we tryed itt 2 or 3 times together & itt
did yᵉ same itt semed to Burn Blew butt Run Like fyer yᵗ is sett on yᵉ gras to Burn itt in yᵉ
spring Tyme & we struck itt out wᵗʰ ouᵋ hands & yᵉ sᵈ Comings sᵈ yᵗ he would trye no more
for sᵈ he I had Rather Loose my mare yⁿ my barn & I this Deponant doe testife yᵗ to yᵉ Best
of my vnderstanding was yᵉ same mare yᵗ James Hough Junio⟨r⟩ Belonging to Ipswich farmes
husband To Elizabeth Hough. would haue haue Borowed of yᵉ sᵈ Comings

Tho Andrews

[Reverse] [Hand 2] Thomas Andrew Deposition

July 1, 1692

Notes: For whatever reason, Andrews gave a deposition the day after the trial of Elizabeth How was concluded. This is not the only instance of evidence presented after a trial's conclusion. For example, on September 15, Thomas Greenslit gave testimony against George Burroughs after Burroughs had already been executed. See No. 634 & No. 635. Greenslit, however, did so under oath. Andrews did not. ◊ "gelled": 'cold as ice' (*OED* s.v. *gelid*), or 'stiffened as of cold, congealed' (*OED* s.v. *geal* and *gell*). "yᵉ Botts": 'disease in horses caused by parasitical worms in the stomach' (*OED* s.v. *bot*, *bott*).

Essex County Court Archives, vol. 1, no. 338, Massachusetts Supreme Judicial Court, Judicial Archives, on deposit James Duncan Phillips Library, Peabody Essex Museum, Salem, MA.

397. Indictment No. 1 of Martha Carrier, for Afflicting Mary Walcott†

See also: Aug. 3, 1692.

[Hand 1] Anno Regis et Reginæ Willm̄ et
Mariæ nunc Anglia &ᶜ Quarto./.

Essex ss

The Juro̅ᵋ for our Sovereigne Lord & Lady the King and Queen pᵋsents That ~~Bridgett~~ [Hand 2] **Martha Carrier wife. of ~~Richard~~ ^{Thomas} Carrier of Andouer ^{in yᵉ County of Essex.} husbandman** [Hand 1] the [Hand 2] **thirty first** [Hand 1] Day of [Hand 2] **May** [Hand 1] in the [Hand 2] **fourth** [Hand 1] Year of the Reigne of our Sovereigne Lord and Lady William and Mary by the Grace of God of England Scottland ffrance and Ireland King, and Queen Defenders of the faith &ᶜ and divers other Dayes and times. as well before, as after, certaine Detestable Arts called Witchcrafts and Sorceries, Wickedly and ffelloniously hath Vsed, Practised, and Exercised, at and within the Towneship of [Hand 2] **Salem** [Hand 1] in the County of Essex afore̅e̅sᵈ in, Vpon, and against, one [Hand 2] **Mary Walcott of Salem Villiage Singlewoman in yᵉ County of Essex aforesᵈ** [Hand 1] by which said wicked Arts the said. [Hand 2] **Mary Walcott** [Hand 1] the [Hand 2] **thirty first** [Hand 1] Day of [Hand 2] **May** [Hand 1] in the [Hand 2] **fourth** [Hand 1] Year abovesaid and divers other Dayes and times as well before, as after, was and is Tortured Afflicted, Pined, Consumed wasted & Tormented agᵗ the Peace of our Sovereigne Lord and Lady the King and Queen and against the forme of the Statute in that case made and Provided./.

[Hand 2] Witnesses.

{Juᵗ} Mary Walcott
{Ju⟨r⟩ᵗ} Elizabeth Hubbard
Ann. Putman

[Reverse] Martha Carrier (Nᵒ 1)
[Hand 3] bila uera
[Hand 2] Nᵒ 1. Martha. Carier

Notes: Ann Putnam Jr.'s name appears on this and on the second indictment of Martha Carrier, but not as sworn. It may be that she was expected but not present when the grand jury met to hear the case of Martha Carrier. It remains puzzling as to why Martha Carrier was not tried until the beginning of August. ◊ Hand 2 = Stephen Sewall

Witchcraft Papers, no. 15, Massachusetts Historical Society. Boston, MA.

398. Indictment No. 2 of Martha Carrier, for Afflicting Elizabeth Hubbard†

July 1, 1692

See also: Aug. 3, 1692.

[Hand 1]Anno Regis et Reginæ Willm et
Mariæ nunc Angliæ &c Quarto:

Essex ss.

The Juroᵉ of our Sovereigne Lord and Lady the King and Queen: pᵉsents That [Hand 2] **Martha Carrier wife of** ~~Richard~~ ^{**Thomas**} **Carier of Andouer** ^{**in yᵉ county of Essex**} **husbandman** [Hand 1] the [Hand 2] **31** [Hand 1] Day of [Hand 2] **May** [Hand 1] in the forth Year of the Reigne of our Sovereigne Lord and Lady William and Mary by the Grace of God of England Scottland ffrance and Ireland King and Queen Defenders of the ffaith: &c And Divers other Dayes and Times as well before as after, certaine Detestable Arts called Witchcrafts: and Sorceries, Wickedly and ffelloniously hath vsed Practised and Excercised at and within the Towneship of Salem in the Couny of Essex aforesᵈ in and vpon and agᵗ one [Hand 2] **Elizabeth Hubbard of Salem in yᵉ County of Essex aforesᵈ** [Hand 1] by which said Wicked Arts. the said [Hand 2] **Elizabeth Hubbard** [Hand 1] the [Hand 2] **thirty first** [Hand 1] Day of [Hand 2] **May** [Hand 1] in the fforth Year abouesᵈ and Divers other Dayes, and times, as well before as after was and is Tortured Afflicted Pined Consumed Wasted and Tormented agᵗ the Peace of our Sovereigne Lord and Lady the King and Queen: and agᵗ the fforme of the Statute in that case made and Provided

[Hand 2] Witnesses

Elizabeth Hubbard Jurat

Mary Walcutt Jurat

Ann Putman

Mary Warren Jurat

[Reverse] Nᵒ 2 Martha Carier

Nᵒ (2)

[Hand 3] bila uera.

Notes: Hand 2 = Stephen Sewall

Essex County Court Archives, vol. 1, no. 312, Massachusetts Supreme Judicial Court, Judicial Archives, on deposit James Duncan Phillips Library, Peabody Essex Museum, Salem, MA.

Sworn Before the Grand Jury: Deposition of Elizabeth Hubbard v. Martha Carrier

2nd of 3 dates. See No. 236 on May 31, 1692

Sworn Before the Grand Jury: Deposition of Mary Walcott v. Martha Carrier

2nd of 3 dates. See No. 237 on May 31, 1692

Saturday, July 2, 1692

Grand Jury of Dorcas Hoar

Trial of Sarah Wilds

399. Examination of Ann Pudeator

[Hand 1] An Puddeater: examined before ye Majestrates of Salem July 2: 92 Sarah: Churchwell: was bid to: say what she: had to say of her: you have charged her with bringing: ye book to you: A: Yes. s^d Churchwell have you seen her since. A no: goodwife Puddeater: you have: formerly: bin complaynd of: we now further enquire: here is one person: saith you brought her: ye book which is Sarah Churchell: look on ye person: ses Churchell: you did bring me ye book: I was at goodman Jacobses Puddeater s^d I never saw ye woman before now:: it was told Puddeater this mayd charged you with: bringing her: ye book: at ye last examinati^n Puddeater s^d I never saw: ye devils book nor knew: that he had one

Lt Jer: Neal: was asked what he could say of this woman

Neal s^d she had bin an ill carriaged woman: & since my wife has bin sick of ye small pox: this woman has come to my hous pretending kindnes: and I was glad to see it: she: asked: whether she might use our morter: which was used: for my wife: and I consented to it: but I afterward repented of it: for ye nurs told. me: my wife was ye wors: for since she was very ill of a flux: which She had not before

When the officer came: for: Puddeater: ye nurs s^d you are come to late for. my wife grew wors. till she dyed: s^d Pudeater had often thretned my wife:

Eliz Hubard: s^d she: had seen s^d Pudeater: ~~but she~~ s^d Mary Walcut: but she had not hurt her she had seen her with goodwife Nurs

goody Puddeater what did you doe with ye ointments that you had in yor hous so many of them:: she s^d I never had ointment nor oyl {⟨b⟩ut neats ⟨foo⟩t ⟨oyl⟩} in my hous since my husband dyed: but the Constable Joseph Neal affirmd she had: she had near 20 that had oynment or greas: in them: a little in a thing: she s^d she never had any oyntment but neats foot oyl: in ye hous

but what was in these things ye Constabl. speakes. of.

A: it was greas: to make sope of:: but: why: did you put them in so many things when one would have held all: but answerd not to ye porpose: but the constabl. s^d o. oyntments were of several sorts

Sarah Vibber did you ever se this woman: before now answerd no An Putnum s^d she had never seen: her but since she come: to Salem Town last: s^d Putman fell into a fitt: & s^d Puddeater: was commanded to take her by ye wrist: & did & s^d Putnum was w⟨e⟩ll presently: Mary Warin: fell into: two fitts quickly after. one another: & both times was helped: by: s^d Puddeaters: taking her by ye wrist

Notes: That Ann Pudeator was not examined earlier is unusual, unless there was an examination with no confirming document extant. She was arrested on May 12. See No. 143. In court on June 1 Sarah Churchill in her confession gave sworn testimony against Ann Pudeator with Thomas Newton attesting so. See No. 258. Since her arrest was done on the verge of the Court of Oyer and Terminer beginning, and since Attorney General Newton was involved in gathering testimony against her, the possibility seems real that her case was considered for trial then. However, the inaction against

her simply continued until the July 2 examination, and subsequently at her trial in September. Her son, Thomas Greenslit, July 2, 1692
perhaps in a vain attempt to save his mother's life, testified against George Burroughs after Burroughs had been executed.
See No. 634 and No. 635. ◊ Hand 1 = Simon Willard

Essex County Court Archives, vol. 1, no. 264, Massachusetts Supreme Judicial Court, Judicial Archives, on deposit James Duncan Phillips Library, Peabody Essex Museum, Salem, MA.

400. Indictment No. 1 of Dorcas Hoar, for Afflicting Elizabeth Hubbard†

See also: Sept. 6, 1692.

[Hand 1]   [Hand 2]
Prouince of yᵉ Mattathuset⟨s⟩   Anno ^{Regni} Regis et Reginæ:Willm̄ et Mariæ nunc
Bay in New England   Angliæ &ᶜ Quarto
Essex ss
The Juroᵉ for our Sovereigne Lord and Lady the King and Queen pᵉsents That [Hand 1]
Dorcas Hoar of Beuerly in yᵉ County of Essex Widow [Hand 2] the [Hand 1] **Second**
[Hand 2] Day of [Hand 1] **May** [Hand 2] in the forth Year of the Reigne of our Sovereigne
Lord and Lady William and Mary by the Grace of God of England Scotland ffrance &
Ireland King and Queen Defenders of the ffaith &ᶜ and Divers other Dayes and times as
well before as after. certaine Detestable ~~called~~ Arts called Witchcrafts and Sorceries
Wickedly and felloniously hath vsed Practised: and Exercised, at and within the Towneship
of [Hand 1] **Salem** [Hand 2] in the County of Essex aforesaid, in and upon, and agᵗ one
[Hand 1] **Elizabeth Hubbard of Salem Singlewoman** [Hand 2] by which said Wicked Arts
the said [Hand 1] ⟨ȝ⟩ **Elizabeth Hubbard** [Hand 2] the [Hand 1] **Second** [Hand 2] Day of
[Hand 1] **May** [Hand 2] in the forth Year abouesd: and Divers other Days and times as well
before as after, was and is Tortured ⟨ȝ⟩ Afflicted Pined Consumed wasted & Tormented agᵗ
the Peace of our Sovereigne Lord and Lady the King and Queen, and agᵗ the fforme of the
Statute; in that case made and Provided
[Hand 1] Witnesses
Elizabeth Hubbard
Mary Wolcott
Ann Putman

[Reverse] nᵒ(1) Dorcas Hoar
[Hand 3] billa uera

Notes: Hand 1 = Stephen Sewall

Essex County Court Archives, vol. 1, no. 205, Massachusetts Supreme Judicial Court, Judicial Archives, on deposit James Duncan Phillips Library, Peabody Essex Museum, Salem, MA.

401. Indictment No. 2 of Dorcas Hoar, for Afflicting Mary Walcott†

See also: Sept. 6, 1692.

[Hand 1]   [Hand 2]
Prouince of yᵉ Mattath⟨s⟩   Anno ^{Regni} Regis et Reginæ:Willm̄ et Mariæ nunc
Bay in New England   Angliæ &ᶜ Quarto

July 2, 1692

Essex ss

The Juro⁶ for our Sovereigne Lord & Lady the King and Queen: p⁶sents That [Hand 1] **Dorcas. Hoar of Beuerly in yᵉ County of Essex Widow** [Hand 2] the [Hand 1] **Second** [Hand 2] Day of [Hand 1] **May** [Hand 2] in the forth year of the Reigne of our Sovereigne Lord and Lady William and Mary by the Grace of God of England Scottland ffrance and Ireland King and Queen Defenders of the ffaith &ᶜ And Divers other Dayes and times as well before as affter, certaine Detestable Arts called witchcraft and Sorceries: wickedly and ffelloniously hath vsed Practised, and Exercised, at and within the Towneship of [Hand 1] **Salem** [Hand 2] in the County of Essex aforesaid in and upon and agᵗ one [Hand 1] **Mary Wolcott of Salem Villiage Single woman** [Hand 2] by which said wicked arts the said [Hand 1] **Mary Wolcott.** [Hand 2] the [Hand 1] **Second** [Hand 2] Day of [Hand 1] **May** [Hand 2] in the fourth year as aboues⁴ and Divers other Dayes and times, as well before as after was and is Tortured Afflicted Pined Consumed wasted and Tormented. agᵗ the Peace of our Sovereigne Lord and Lady the King and Queen: and agᵗ the forme of the statute in that case made and Provided:/

[Hand 1] Witnesses.
Mary Wolcott
Elizabeth Hubbard
Ann Putman

[Reverse] nº(2) Dorcas Hoar
[Hand 3] billa uera
[Hand 1?] Hoar
Hoar

Notes: Hand 1 = Stephen Sewall

Essex County Court Archives, vol. 1, no. 204, Massachusetts Supreme Judicial Court, Judicial Archives, on deposit James Duncan Phillips Library, Peabody Essex Museum, Salem, MA.

402. Deposition of Sarah Bibber v. Dorcas Hoar

See also: Sept. 6, 1692.

[Hand 1] The Deposistion of Sarah viber agged about 36 years who testef⟨th⟩ and saith that darcas Hoar of Beurly has most greviouly tomentd [= tormented] me a grat many times with variety of tortors: allso on the 2 may 1692 being the day of hir Examination I saw Darcas Hoar or hir Appearanc most greviouly torment mary walcot Elizabeth Hubbrd Abigaill williams ann putnam jnr and Susannah Shellden by biting pinching and almost choaking them: and I verily beleue in my heart that Darcas Hoar is wicth for sence she went to prison she has most dreadfully torto⟨r⟩d me with variety of tortors: which I beleue if she ware a wicth she could not doe

[Hand 2] Jurat in Curia

[Hand 3] Sarah Vibber: owned to yᵉ Jury of inquest that yᵉ abowe written evidence: is truth: upon yᵉ oath she hath taken: ~~Jly.~~ July 2: 92

Mary Warin: testifieth ["th" written over "d"] before yᵉ Jury of inquest: that: she saw. Dorcas Hoare: of Beaverly: hurt and afflict: Susanah: Sheldon: then in yᵉ presence of yᵉ sᵈ Jury July: 2: 1692

[Reverse] [Hand 4] Sara. viber ag: hoar
[Hand 2] Sarah Vibber

Notes: Although the grand jury returned true bills on the indictments against Dorcas Hoar on July 2 (No. 400 & No. 401), she was not tried until September 6. ◊ Used at trial. ◊ Hand 1 = Thomas Putnam; Hand 3 = Simon Willard

Essex County Court Archives, vol. 1, no. 209, Massachusetts Supreme Judicial Court, Judicial Archives, on deposit James Duncan Phillips Library, Peabody Essex Museum, Salem, MA.

403. Deposition of Elizabeth Hubbard v. Dorcas Hoar

See also: Sept. 6, 1692.

[Hand 1] The deposistion of Eliz: Hubburd agged about 17 years who testifieth and saith I haue been a long time afflected by a woman that tould me hir name was Hoar but one ^{the} :2: may 1692 Darcas Hoar of Beuerly did most greviously torment me dureing the time of hir Examination and then I saw that it was the very same woman that tould me hir name was Hoar and if she did but look upon me she would strick me down or allmost choak me allso on the day of hir Examination I saw Darcas Hoar or hir Appearance most greviously torment and Afflect the bodys of mary walcott Abigaill williams Ann putnam ~~and Susannah Shelden~~ by biting pinching and almost choaking them to death. also seuerall time senc Darcas Hoar or hir Apperance has most greviously tormented me with variety of tortors and I verily beleue that Darcas hoar the prisoner att the barr is a wicth for sence she has been in prison she or hir Appearance has com to me and most dreadfully tormented with veriety of tortors: which I beleue she could not doe without she ware a wicth

[Hand 2] Eliz: Hubburd: owned to y^e Jury of inquest: that y^e above written evidence: is y^e truth July: 2: 1692

[Hand 3] Jurat in Curia

[Reverse] [Hand 4] elizabeth hubart ag: hoar

Notes: Used at trial. ◊ Hand 1 = Thomas Putnam; Hand 2 = Simon Willard

Essex County Court Archives, vol. 1, no. 210, Massachusetts Supreme Judicial Court, Judicial Archives, on deposit James Duncan Phillips Library, Peabody Essex Museum, Salem, MA.

404. Deposition of Ann Putnam Jr. v. Dorcas Hoar

See also: Sept. 6, 1692.

[Hand 1] The deposistion of Ann putnam Junr who testifieth and saith that on the latter end of April 1692 ther came an old woman and did most greviosly torment me and tould me hir name was Hoar: but on the 2 may 1692 Darcas Hoar did most dreadfully torment me during the time of hir Examination and then I saw that it was the very same woman that tould me hir name was Hoar: alls{o} on the day of hir Examination I saw Darcas Hoar or hir Apperanse most greviously torment and afflect mary wallcott Eliz: Hubbred Sarah vibber Abigail williams ~~and Susannah Shelden~~ and I verily beleue in my heart that Darcas Hoar is a wicth for sence she went to prisson she or hir Apperanc⟨e⟩ has com to me and most greviously tormented me by biting pinching and almost choaking me to death

July 2, 1692

[Hand 2] ann putman ownid this har testimony to be the truth one har oath before the Juriers of Inques: this 2. dy of July: 1692.

[Hand 3] Jurat in Curia

[Reverse] [Hand 2] ann putman ag hoar.
[Hand 3] Ann. Putman

Notes: Used at trial. ◊ Hand 1 = Thomas Putnam

Essex County Court Archives, vol. 1, no. 213, Massachusetts Supreme Judicial Court, Judicial Archives, on deposit James Duncan Phillips Library, Peabody Essex Museum, Salem, MA.

405. Deposition of Mary Walcott v. Dorcas Hoar

See also: Sept. 6, 1692.

[Hand 1] The deposistion of mary walcott agged about 17 years who testifieth and saith I haue been a long time afflected by a woman that tould me hir name was Hoar: but on the :2 may 1692. Darcas Hoar of Be⟨u⟩verly did most greviousl torment me dureing the time of hir Examination for if she did but look parsonally upon me she would strick me down or allmost choak me to death: allso on the day of the Examination of darcas Hoar I saw hir: or hir Apperanc most greviously torment and afflect the bodyes of Eliz: Hubburd Abigaill williams Ann putnam and Susannah Shelding also seuerall times senc the afforesaid darcas hoar or hir Apperance has most greviously tormented me by biting pineching and allmost choaking me to death and I verily beleue in my heart that Darcas Hoar is a most dreadfull wicth for she or hir Apperance has come and most dreadfully tormented me sence she was put in prison which I beleue she could not doe if she ware not a wicth.

[Hand 2] Mary Walcot: owned: to y^e Jury of inquest: y^e above written evidence: to be y^e truth: upon: oath: July 2: 92

[Hand 3] Jurat in Curia

[Reverse] [Hand 4] mary walcot ag: hoar

Notes: Used at trial. ◊ Hand 1 = Thomas Putnam; Hand 2 = Simon Willard

Essex County Court Archives, vol. 1, no. 212, Massachusetts Supreme Judicial Court, Judicial Archives, on deposit James Duncan Phillips Library, Peabody Essex Museum, Salem, MA.

406. List of Witnesses v. Sarah Wilds, and Notation Concerning Sarah Good‡

[Hand 1] ⟨?⟩ Sarah Wilds

John Andrews
William Perkins
Joseph Andrews

[Hand 2] & also for Sundry other Acts of Witchcraft by S^d Good Comitted & done before & Since y^t tim⟨e⟩

[Reverse] Complaints Warrants &⟨c⟩
[Hand 3] Sarah Wilds.

Notes: This seems not to be a document used in the legal proceedings, but simply notations, perhaps used as a wrapper for other documents. Placing it on July 2 is speculative, and it is put there because of its proximity to the trial of Wilds along with the fact that the names on the document other than Good are names associated with the Wilds case. The name "Sarah Wilds" on the verso may be a more modern notation. ◊ Hand 2 = Stephen Sewall

Essex County Court Archives, vol. 1, no. 167, Massachusetts Supreme Judicial Court, Judicial Archives, on deposit James Duncan Phillips Library, Peabody Essex Museum, Salem, MA.

Billa Vera: Indictment No. 1 of Sarah Wilds, for Afflicting Mercy Lewis†
2nd of 2 dates. See No. 392 on June 30, 1692

Sworn at Trial: Deposition of John Andrews & Joseph Andrews v. Sarah Wilds†
2nd of 2 dates. See No. 393 on June 30, 1692

407. Deposition of Humphrey Clark v. Sarah Wilds†

[Hand 1] ye deposition of humpry Clark aged about 21 yere saith y^t about a yere agoo I was asleep and about midnight y^e bed shook & I awaked and saw a woman stand by y^e bed side which when I well Looked semed to me to be goodwif wills which jumpid to y^e tother corner of y^e house & then I saw hir no more

[Hand 2] Jurat in Curia

[Reverse] Humphey Clerk

Notes: Used at trial. ◊ Hand 2 = Stephen Sewall

Essex Institute Collection, no. 8, James Duncan Phillips Library, Peabody Essex Museum, Salem, MA.

408. Deposition of Thomas Dorman v. Sarah Wilds†

[Hand 1] the deposition of Thomas Dorman aged 53 yers saith ~~than~~ goody wils was arnest with me to by one hiue of beese ~~of⟨m⟩e and I~~ and sins goodwife wils had thes beese I lost many Creturs and she Came to my hous one day and said she how doth your ~~doe~~ {geese thriue} and she went to the pen whare thay were fatting, and thay were uery fat and we Cept ~~the~~ them a grat while longer feding them with {Corne} and thay pind away so as thay were good for litle and I lost six braue Cattle six yere agoe which was frozen to death in the midell of jenewary now sum time this summer my wif went to salem uili{d}g and my wife tould me that an putman the aflicted parsun tould hur that ~~goodf⟨?⟩~~ goodwif wils had whoried away my Cattell and I wondred an putman should know I lost my Cattle so long agoe

[Hand 2] Jurat in Curia

[Reverse] [Hand 3] Thomas Dorman.

July 2, 1692   Notes: Used at trial. ◊ Hand 2 = Stephen Sewall

Essex Institute Collection, no. 7, James Duncan Phillips Library, Peabody Essex Museum, Salem, MA.

409. Deposition of John Gould & Zacheus Perkins v. Sarah Wilds†

[Hand 1] The Depotion of John Gould aged about 56 yeares or theire about
Testifeth and saith that some time sence whether it be fiufteen or sixteene yeares agoe I am
not sarting but it [= I] toke it to be theire abouts sister Mary Redington tould mee as she
was Coming from Salam with her Brother Redington that Goodwife Wilds did striue two or
three times to pul her doune of her horse one time she did striue to pul her doune in a brooke
but she did set her selfe with all her strenke ^{to set her selfe} she Could and did git out of y^e
brook and ~~as~~ soone after she was got out of y^e brooke she said that Goodwife Wilds did pul
her doune bakwords of her horse and held her doune so as she Could not helpe her selfe tell
her Brother Redington and sarg^t Edmon Towns did Come and helper [= help her] / and my
sister did desier mee to Come and wright what she Could say how Goodwife wilds did
aflicte her for she would Leafe it in wrighting so as it might be seene when she was dead and
I did goe doune to wright it once or twise but when I was redy to wright it sister was taken so
as she Could not declare any thing/ also sister Mary tould mee that when Johanthan Wilds
was ele at her house in a straing maner so as he Could goe out at y^e Chimey tops ~~in~~ into y^e
barne hed git her henes and put them in to his briche[Lost] [= breeches] and kiled them/
sister Mary did aske Goodwife Wilds to take som of y^e dead henes and Let her haue som
Liueing henes and she did but sister said thay went moping about tell thay died and so shall I
said sister Redington and y^e Last words I hard sister Redington say was that it was Goodwife
Wilds that brought her into y^t Condition she did stand to it tell her death
ffarder I doe testifi~~eth~~ that as I was afeching two or thr⟨ee⟩ Load of hay for Zacheus perkins/
ye sd perkins tould mee ⟨t⟩hat I must Lay ye hay fast or eles his ant Wilds would not Let mee
Cary it for she was angrey with him and as I went with one Load it did slipe doune in plaine
way and I Lay it up againe and ⟨w⟩hen I Came almost at home with it it fell doune againe
and I went and feched him another Load and when I Came wheare ye first Load sliped y^e
seckond did slipe doune then I got some of our frinds to helpe me vp with it and wee bound
it with two Cart ropes but i⟨t⟩ did slipe vp and doune so as I did neuer see hay doe soe in my
Life and when I came wheare I Left ye first Load ye hay went all of ye Cart apon ye ground
and did bring ye Cart ouer and it was rising ground I ~~Could~~ ^{did} thinke that it was don by
wichcraft.

              [Hand 2] Jurat in Curia
Zacheus Perkins made Oath to the latter part of this Euidence relating to the Hay
Jurat in Curia

[Reverse] Jno Jno. Gould ⟨?⟩ Zacheus Perkins

Notes: Used at trial. ◊ Hand 2 = Stephen Sewall

Essex Institute Collection, no. 12, James Duncan Phillips Library, Peabody Essex Museum, Salem, MA.

410. Testimony of John Hale v. Sarah Wilds

July 2, 1692

[Hand 1] I John Hale of Beverly aged 56 years beeing sumõned to appeare & giue evidence against Sarah Wiles of Topsfeild July .2. 1692;

Testify y^t about 15 or 16 yeares agoe came to my house y^e wife of John Hirrek of Beverly wth an aged woeman she said was her mother Goody Reddington of Topsfeild come to me for counsel beeing in trouble of spirit. when y^e said Reddington opned her greifs to me this was one that she was assaulted by witchcraft y^t Goody wiles her neighb$^\varepsilon$ bewitched her & afflicted her many times greiviously, telling me many particular storys how & when she troubled her, wch I have forgotten. She said allso y^t a son in law of said Wiles, did come & visit her (shee called him an honest young man named John as I take it) & did pitty her y^e said Reddington, signifying to her that he beleived his mother wiles was a witch & told her storys of his mother. I allso understood by them, that this Goody Wiles was mother in law to a youth named as I take it Jonathan Wiles who about twenty yeares agoe or more did act or was acted very strangly Insomuch y^t I was invited to joyn with Mr Cobbet & others at Ipswich to advize & pray for ye said Youth; whome some thought to counterfeit, others to be possessed by y^e devill. But I remember Mr Cobbet thought he was under Obsession of y^e devil. Goody Reddingtons discourse hath caused me to have farther ~~thoug~~ thoughts of y^e said Youths case whether he were not bewitched.

[Hand 2] Jurat in Curia

Notes: Used at trial. ◊ Hand 1 = John Hale; Hand 2 = John Hathorne

Essex Institute Collection, no. 21, James Duncan Phillips Library, Peabody Essex Museum, Salem, MA.

Sworn at Trial: Deposition of Nathaniel Ingersoll & Thomas Putnam v. Sarah Wilds†
2nd of 2 dates. See No. 91 on April 22, 1692

411. Deposition of Elizabeth Symonds v. Sarah Wilds†

[Hand 1] The Depotion of Elizabath Symons aged about 50 yeares

Whoe testifieth and saith that about ~~tweuelue~~ twelue ^{or thurtieene} yeares sence ^{theire abouts} being in Company with my Mother Androus/ after a Lecter~~day~~ in Topsfeild my mother and I ware agoeing to giue Goodwife Redington a visiat and as wee went wee ouertooke Goodwife Wilds and my mother fell into discourse about a syee [= scythe] that my Brother John and Joseph Androus had borede of Goodman Wilds for one day: and my mother tould Goodwife Wilds how John and Joseph Androus ware trobled about gitting home a Load of hay/ then goodwife Wilds replied and said all that might bee and I know ⟨?⟩ nothing of it/ then my mother replied and said to her whie did y^u threaten them and tould them thay had better alet [= have let] it alone

then she did threaten my mother and tould her that she wou[Lost] [= would] make her proue it and then my mother caaled to mee and bid mee bare witnes Elizabath what she saith/ and then she di⟨d⟩ Looke bake apon mee and Emedatly I did fale into such a trembling Condition that I was as if all my joynts did knoke togather so tha⟨t⟩ I Could hardly goe along/ and the night faling ~~as~~ ^{after} I was ~~agoeing to~~ bed I did see somthing stand betwe⟨e⟩ne ye wale and I/ I did see somthing stand theire and I did Looke apon it a

July 2, 1692

Considradabell time so Long that I was afraid to Ly one that sid of y^e bed and asked my husban to Let mee Ly one y^e other sid of y^e bed and he did/ and then I did feele it Come apon my feete as if it had bin a Cat and crope vp t⟨o⟩ my breast and Lay apon mee and then I Could not moue nether h[Lost] [= hand] nor ffoot nether Could I speeake a word I did striue to caled to m[Lost] [= my] husban but I Could not speake and so I Lay all night/ and in y^e moring I Could speeake and then I tould ~~him~~ ^{my husban} thay talke of y^e old w[Lost] [= witch] but I thinke she has ride mee all this night and then I tould [Lost]ban [= my husband] h⟨o⟩w it had bin with mee all y^e night/ we had a Lec⟨t⟩[Lost] [= lecture] once a ~~fortnight~~ {month} in Topsfeild and y^e next Lectter day after y^e first ab[Lost] [= above] named/ as I was sitting in my seate ~~God~~ Goodwife Wilds Coming by y^e End of y^e seeat I sat in I was Emedatly taken with such a pay [= pain] in my bake that I was not abell to bare it and fell doune in y^e see[Lost] [= seat] and did not know wheaire I was and some pepall tooke me vp an[Lost] [= and] Caried mee out of y^e meeting house but I did not know nothing of i[Lost] [= it] tell afterwards when I Came to my selfe I did wonder how I Come theire vp to m^r Hubbard house and when I did Come to my selfe a[Lost] [= and] a great many pepall Come about mee to aske mee what was y^e matter with mee Goodwife Wilds Come and stood at y^e End of y^e tabell and I Replied and said theire she is and my mother bid mee goe and ser[Lost] [= serve] her but I Could not sture/[= stir] and so I haue contined at times Euer senc som times with paynes in one plase and som times in another plas soe ^{as} I have not bin abell to doe any thing in my fameliey at seueri[Lost] [= several] times I haue bin at y^e Docters but thay Cannot giue mee any thin⟨g⟩ that ~~doe~~ dos mee any good this is in short of what I Can say b[Lost] [SWP = being] ~~some of y^e~~ heire in y^e heart of what I Can speeake too. I am verey willing to Come and ateste to all aboue wrighteen and if y^e Lord giu[Lost] [= give] mee streanke but at present I am not abell to Come

[Hand 2] Jurat in Curia

[Reverse] [Hand 3] Elisabeth Symons agt Sarah Wiles
to be Sumoned
Abraham Reddington Sen
Joseph Bixbey Jun^ε

Notes: Used at trial. ◊ Hand 2 = Stephen Sewall

Essex Institute Collection, no. 13, James Duncan Phillips Library, Peabody Essex Museum, Salem, MA.

Sworn at Trial: Deposition of Mary Walcott v. Sarah Wilds†

3rd of 3 dates. See No. 93 on April 22, 1692

412. Ephraim Wilds for Sarah Wilds†

[Hand 1] This may inform this Honred cort that I: Ephraim willdes being constabell for topsfelld this yere and the marshall of sallem coming to fetch away my mother he then shued me a warant from athority derected to the constabll of topsfelld wherin was william hobs and deliueranc his wife with maniey others and the marshall did then require me forthwith to gow and aprehend the bodies of william hobes and his wife which acordingly I ded: and I haue had serous thoughts maniey tims sence whether my sesing of them might not be some case of hare thus acusing my mothe thereby in some mesuer to be reuenged of me the woman ded show a ueriey bad sperit when I sesed: on [= one] might allmost se reuenge in har face she looked so molishesly on me: as for my mother I neuer saw aniey harm by har upon aniey sutch acout naither in word nor action as she is now acused for she hath awlwais instructed me well in the cristion religon and the wais of god euer sence I was abell to take instructions: and so I leue it all to this honred cort to consider of it = Ephraim willdes

July 4, 1692

Notes: The warrant mentioned for the apprehension of William and Deliverance Hobbs and others in Topsfield, No. 79, does not bear a return by any of the officers who apprehended the people named in it. ◊ Likely used at trial.

Essex County Court Archives, vol. 1, no. 165, Massachusetts Supreme Judicial Court, Judicial Archives, on deposit James Duncan Phillips Library, Peabody Essex Museum, Salem, MA.

413. Testimony of John Wilds & Ephraim Wilds for Sarah Wilds†

[Hand 1] John Wiells testifieth y^t he did hear y^t Mary the wife of Jno Reddinton did [1 word overstruck] raise a report y^t my wife had Bewitched her and i went to y^e Saide Jno Reddinton & told him I would arest him for his wife^s defaming of my wife but y^e Said Reddinton desiered me not to doe it for it would but waste his Estate & y^t his ^{wife} would a [= have] done wth it in tyme: and y^t he knew nothing She had agst mye wife = after this I got my Bro: Auerell to goe to y^e Said Sarah Reddinton & my said Bro^r told me y^t ^{he} told y^e Said Sar: Reddinton y^t if She had any thing agst my wife y^t he would be a means & would help her to bring my wife out; and y^t y^e Said Sarah Reddinton replyed y^t She knew no harm mye wife had don her: y^t

[Hand 2] The testimonny of Ephraim Willdes eged about 27 or the'abouts testifieth and saith that about ~~fow~~ fouer yers agow there was som liklyhode of my haueng one of goodiey Simonds dafter and as the maid towld me har mother and father were ueriey willing I shoulld haue hare: but after some time I had a hint that goodiey Simonds had formerlly said she beleued my mother ~~h(?)d har~~ had done har wrong and I went to hare and tock marke how that is now deed who dyed at the estward. along with me and before both of us {shee} denied that euer she had eniey grounds to think eniey harme of my mother only from what goodiey redington had saide and afterwards I left the hous and went no mor and euer sence she bene ueriey angriey with me and now she will reward mee   Ephraim willdes

[Reverse] [Hand 3] Behalfe Sarah Wills

Notes: Likely used at trial.

Essex County Court Archives, vol. 1, no. 166, Massachusetts Supreme Judicial Court, Judicial Archives, on deposit James Duncan Phillips Library, Peabody Essex Museum, Salem, MA.

Monday, July 4, 1692

414. Examination of Candy

SALEM, Monday, July 4, 1692. The examination of Candy, a negro woman, before Bartholomew Gedney and John Hawthorne Esqrs. Mr. Nicholas Noyes also present.

July 4, 1692   Q. Candy! are you a witch? A. Candy no witch in her country. Candy's mother no witch. Candy no witch, Barbados. This country, mistress give Candy witch. Q. Did your mistress make you a witch in this country? A. Yes, in this country mistress give Candy witch. Q. What did your mistress do to make you a witch? A. Mistress bring book and pen and ink, make Candy write in it. Q. What did you write in it? — She took a pen and ink and upon a book or paper made a mark. Q. How did you afflict or hurt these folks, where are the puppets you did it with? — She asked to go out of the room and she would shew or tell; upon which she had liberty, one going with her, and she presently brought in two clouts, one with two knots tied in it, the other one; which being seen by Mary Warren, Deliverance Hobbs and Abigail Hobbs, they were greatly affrighted and fell into violent fits, and all of them said that the black man and Mrs. Hawkes and the negro stood by the puppets or rags and pinched them, and then they were afflicted, and when the knots were untied yet they continued as aforesaid. A bit of one of the rags being set on fire, the afflicted all said they were burned, and cried out dreadfully. The rags being put into water, two of the of forenamed persons were in dreadful fits almost choaked, and the other was violently running down to the river, but was stopped.

Attest.   John Hawthorne, Just. Peace.

Notes: Slaves, both "Negro" and "Indian," were part of the Puritan community, although slavery as an institution had much more support among merchants than among clergy. That Candy identifies herself as from Barbados may be useful in considering the origin of Tituba, an "Indian" slave but not a "Negro." Although Tituba is widely believed to be from Barbados, no firm evidence, as in the case of Candy, supports that belief even though circumstantial evidence offers reasonable arguments for that origin.

Thomas Hutchinson, The History of the Province of Massachusetts-Bay, from the Charter of King William and Queen Mary, in 1691, Until the Year 1750, vol. 2, ed. Lawrence Shaw Mayo. (Cambridge, MA: Harvard University Press, 1936), p. 26.

415. Examination of Candy, as Told by John Hale†

Among the Confessors, *Anno* 1692. was a Negro Woman, who charged two women to make her a Witch, describing how she see her mark in the Devils Book. And said, if she might be permitted, she would fetch the things whereby she tormented the afflicted complainers. And accordingly brought an Handkerchief, wherein several knots were tyed, raggs of Cloth, a piece of Cheese and a piece of grass And as I was credibly informed, some compelled her to swallow the grass, & that night was burned in her flesh; and one took a piece of her ragg and burnt it in the fire, and one of the Afflicted that had complained of her, was presently burned on the hand. Another piece of her rags was put under water, and then others complaintants were choaked, and strived for breath as if under water; And another ran to the River as if she would drown her self.

Notes: Although Hale does not name her, he is describing the examination of Candy. No original manuscript of her examination is extant, but this account contains a few details not included in the version that appeared in transcription in Hutchinson's *History*. See No. 414. Whether these differences were based solely on stories heard by Hale in the years following the trials as he wrote his book or if they were details taken directly from a manuscript available to him at the time that has not survived is impossible to tell.

John Hale. A Modest Enquiry into the Nature of Witchcraft (Boston: Green & Allen, 1702), pp. 80–81.

Memorandum by Stephen Sewall: Indictment No. 1 of Rebecca Nurse, for Afflicting Ann
Putnam Jr.‡
3rd of 3 dates. See No. 285 on June 3, 1692

416. Declaration of Thomas Fisk, Juryman†

I Thomas Fisk, *the Subscriber hereof, being one of them that were of the Jury the last week at* Salem-*Court, upon the Tryal of* Rebecka Nurse, &c. *being desired by some of the Relations to give a Reason why the Jury brought her in Guilty, after her Verdict not Guilty; I do hereby give my Reasons to be as follows,viz.*

When the Verdict not Guilty was, the honoured Court was pleased to object against it, saying to them, that they think they let slip the words, which the Prisoner at the Bar spake against her self, which were spoken in reply to Goodwife Hobbs *and her Daughter, who had been faulty in setting their hands to the Devils Book, as they have confessed formerly; the words were* [What do these persons give in Evidence against me now, they used to come among us.] *After the honoured Court had manifested their dissatisfaction of the Verdict, several of the Jury declared themselves desirous to go out again, and thereupon the honoured Court gave leave; but when we came to consider of the Case, I could not tell how to take her words, as an Evidence against her, till she had a further opportunity to put her Sense upon them, if she would take it; and then going into Court, I mentioned the words aforesaid, which by one of the Court were affirmed to have been spoken by her, she being then at the Bar, but made no reply, nor interpretation of them; whereupon these words were to me a principal Evidence against her.*

Thomas Fisk.

Notes: This is probably one of the documents that Stephen Sewall gave to the Nurse family after her conviction. See No. 285. Precisely when this happened has not been established. Calef dates this July 4.

Robert Calef. More Wonders of The Invisible World, Display'd in Five Parts. (London: Nath. Hillard, 1700), pp. 102–3.

417. Appeal of Rebecca Nurse‡

These presents do humbly shew, to the honoured Court and Jury, that I being informed, that the Jury brought me in Guilty, upon my saying that Goodwife Hobbs *and her Daughter were of our Company; but I intended no otherways, then as they were Prisoners with us, and therefore did then, and yet do judge them not legal Evidence against their fellow Prisoners. And I being something hard of hearing, and full of grief, none informing me how the Court took up my words, and therefore had not opportunity to declare what I intended, when I said they were of our Company.*   Rebecka Nurse.

Notes: Rebecca Nurse responded to the statement of Thomas Fisk as to why the jury had found her guilty. See No. 416. Presumably this was done quickly, and the assigned date here represents a speculation that it happened the same day.

Robert Calef. More Wonders of The Invisible World, Display'd in Five Parts. (London: Nath. Hillard, 1700), p. 103.

Tuesday, July 12, 1692

418. Warrant for the Execution of Sarah Good, Rebecca Nurse, Susannah Martin, Elizabeth How & Sarah Wilds, and Officer's Return
See also: July 19, 1692.

[Hand 1] To George Corwine Gent^n High Sheriff of y^e County of Essex Greeting

Whereas Sarah Good Wife of William Good of Salem Villiage Rebecka Nurse wife of Francis Nurse of Salem Villiage Susanna Martin of Amesbury Widow Elizabeth How wife of James How of Ipswich Sarah Wild Wife of John Wild of Topsfield all of y^e County of Essex in thier Maj$^{ti⟨e⟩}$[Lost] [= majesties'] Prouince of y^e Massachusets Bay in New England Att A Court of Oyer & Terminer held by Adjournment for Our Soueraign Lord & Lady King William & Queen Mary for y^e said County of Essex at Salem in y^e s^d County On y^e 29th day of June ⟨last⟩ ⟨paste⟩ were Seuealy Arrai⟨g⟩ned On Seuerall Indictments for ye horrible Crime of Witchcraft by them practised & Comitted On Seuerall persons and pleading not guilty did for thier Tryall put themselu⟨es⟩ On God & Thier Countrey whereupon they were Each of them found & brought in Guilty by y^e Jury that passed On them according to thier respectiue Indictm[Lost] [= indictments] and Sentence of death did then pass vpon them as the Law directs Execution whereof yet remains to be done: These are Therefore in thier Maj^{ties} Names William & Mary now King & Queen Over England &c^a to will & Coma[Lost]⟨d⟩ [= command] you that vpon Tuesday Next being y^e 19th day of [Lost] [= this?] Instant July between y^e houres of Eight & ⟨twelue⟩ in [Lost] [= the] forenoon y^e Same day you Safely conduct y^e s^d Sarah [Lost] [= Good] Rebecka Nurse Susanna Martin Elizabeth How & Sara⟨h⟩ Wild from thier Maj^{ties} Goal in Salem afores^d to y^e place of Execuc̄on & There Cause them & Euery of them to be hanged by y^e Necks vntill they be dead and of yo^ε doings herein make return to y^e Clerke of y^e said Court & this p^{ε}cept and hereof you are not to fail at your perill and this Shall be your Sufficient Warrant Giuen under my hand & Seale at Boston the 12th day of July in ye fourth yeare of ye Reign of Our Soueraign Lord & Lady W^m & Mary King & Queen &c^a
Anno q̄ Dom. 1692   Wm Stoughton.

[Reverse] Salem July. 19th <u>1692</u>
I Caused y^e within mentioned persons to be Executed according to y^e Tenour of y^e with⟨in⟩ warrant

                                                            George Corwin Sherif⟨f⟩

Notes: Hand 1 = Stephen Sewall ◊ 1 wax seal.

MS Am 48, Rare Books & Manuscripts, Boston Public Library. Boston, MA.

Friday, July 15, 1692

419. Examination of Ann Foster

See also: July 16, 1692, July 18, 1692, July 21, 1692 & Sept. 10, 1692.

[Hand 1] The Examination & Conffesion of Ann ffoster at Salem Vilage 15 July 1692 after a while Ann ffoster conffesed that the diuill apered to her in the shape of a bird at seurall Times, such a bird as she neuer Saw the like before, & that she had had this gift (viz of striking ye aflicted downe wth her eye euer) since, & being ask^t why she thought y^t bird was the diuill she answred because he came white & vanished away black, & y^t the diuill told her {y^t} she should haue this gift & y^t she must beleiue hi⟨m⟩ & told her she should haue prosperity. & ~~that~~ She Said y^t he had apeared to her three times & was alwayes as a bird & the last time was as about halfe a yeare since, & sat upon a table had two legs & great eyes & y^t it was the Second time of his apearance that he promised her prosperity & y^t it was Cariers wife about three weeks agoe y^t came & perswaded her to hurt these people
16: July. 1692 Ann Foster Examined conffesed y^t it was Goody Carier y^t made her a witch y^t she came to her in person about six yeares agoe & told her if she would not be a witch ye diuill should tare her in peices & Cary her away at wch time she promised to serue the diuill, y^t she had bewitched a hog of John Loujoyes to Death & that she had hurt Some persons in Salem Vilage, y^t goody Carier came to her & would haue her bewitch two children of Andrew Allins & that she had then two popets made & Stuck pins in them to bewitch ye said Children by which one of them dyed ye other very sick, that she wa⟨s⟩ at the meeting of the witches at Salem Villige, y^t Goody Carier came & told her of the m⟨e⟩eting & would haue her goe so they gat upon Sticks & went Said Jorny & being ther⟨e⟩ did see m^r Buroughs ye minister who Spake to them all, & this was about two months agoe that ther was then twenty fiue persons meet together, that she tyed a knot in a Rage & threw it into the fire to hurt ~~a weoman~~ {Tim^o Swan} ~~at Salem Village & that she was hurt by her & y^{t}her name is Goody Vibber~~ & that she did hurt the rest y^t complayned of her by Squesing popets like them & so almost choaked them 1692 18 July Ann ffoster Examined confesed y^t ye diuill in shape of a ~~black~~ man apeared to her wth Goody carier about six yeare since when they made her a witch & that she promised to Serue the diuill two yeares upon wch the Diuill promised her prosperity & many things but neuer performed it, that she & Martha Carier did both ride on a stick or pole when they went to the witch meeting at Salem Village & that the Stick broak: as they ware caried in the aire aboue the tops of the trees. & they fell but she did hang fast about the neck of Goody Carier & ware presently at the Vilage, that she was then much hurt of her Leg, she further Saith that she hard Some of the witches say that their was three hundred & fiue in the whole Country. & that they would ruin that place ye Vilige, also Saith ther was present at that metting two men besides m^r Buroughs ye minister & one of them had gray haire, she saith y^t she formerly frequented the publique metting to worship god. but the diuill had Such power ouer her y^t she could not profit there & y^t was her undoeing: she saith y^t about three or foure yeares agoe Martha Carier told her she would bewitch James Hobbs child to death & the child dyed in twenty four howers
21. July: 92 Ann. ffoster Examined Owned her former conffesion being Read to her and further conffesed that the discourse amongst y^e witches at y^e meeting at Salem Village was

that they would afflict there to set up the Diuills Kingdome This conffesion is true as wittnese my hand:

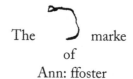

The ⟩ marke
of
Ann: ffoster

Ann ffoster: Signed & Owned the aboue Examination & Conffesion before me
Salem: 10th Septem^ɛ 1692

John Higginson
Just^ɛ peace

[Reverse] [Hand 2] Ann ffosters Examinaion And Conffession

Notes: The examination of Ann Foster picks up the Andover phase begun earlier with the issuing of a warrant for the arrest of Martha Carrier on May 28. See No. 223. Who first complained against Ann Foster is not clear, but the accusation may have grown from the summoning of two accusers from Salem Village to help discover witches connected with the suffering of Elizabeth Ballard, the wife of Andover's constable, John Ballard. The grand jury did not consider Ann Foster's case until September 13. Unlike the Salem Village and Salem phase, the Andover phase produced many confessions. There has been much speculation as to who the accusers from Salem Village were. The only two who claim to have been afflicted by Ann Foster on July 15 are Elizabeth Hubbard and Mary Walcott. See No. 615 & No. 616. Although not conclusive, this makes them leading candidates. Mary Warren claimed affliction by her, but at the grand jury hearing in September. See No. 617. ◊ Hand 1 = John Higginson Jr.; Hand 2 = Anthony Checkley

Essex County Court Archives, vol. 2, no. 48, Massachusetts Supreme Judicial Court, Judicial Archives, on deposit James Duncan Phillips Library, Peabody Essex Museum, Salem, MA.

Saturday, July 16, 1692

Continued from July 15, 1692: Examination of Ann Foster
2nd of 5 dates. See No. 419 on July 15, 1692

Monday, July 18, 1692

Continued from July 16, 1692: Examination of Ann Foster
3rd of 5 dates. See No. 419 on July 15, 1692

Tuesday, July 19, 1692

Executions of Sarah Good, Elizabeth How, Susannah Martin, Rebecca Nurse, & Sarah Wilds

Officer's Return: Warrant for the Execution of Sarah Good, Rebecca Nurse, Susannah Martin, Elizabeth How & Sarah Wilds   July 19, 1692

2nd of 2 dates. See No. 418 on July 12, 1692

420. Docketed Cover Paper Used to Contain the Warrant for the Execution of Sarah Good, Elizabeth How, Susannah Martin, Rebecca Nurse, & Sarah Wilds [?]

[Hand 1] Warrant ⟨for⟩ Execuc̄on of Sarah Good Rebecka Nurse Eliz. How Susanna Martin & Sarah Wildes
On Tuesday 19th July 1692

Notes: Hand 1 = Stephen Sewall

Essex County Court Archives, vol. 2, no. 135, Massachusetts Supreme Judicial Court, Judicial Archives, on deposit James Duncan Phillips Library, Peabody Essex Museum, Salem, MA.

421. Complaint of Joseph Ballard v. Mary Lacey Sr. & Mary Lacey Jr.

[Hand 1] Joseph Ballard of Andouer husbandman Complaineth of Mary. Lacy wife of Lawrence Lacy of Andouer husbandm and of Mary Lacy, daughter of sd Lawrence Lacy of Andouer aforesd Singlwoman: as followeth that whereas in ⟨ye⟩ this Complainers Wife Elizabeth Ballard hath been this Seuerall monthes Sorely aflicted & visited wth Strange pains and pressures & remains So to this day which I verily beleiue is Occasioned by Witchcraft and haue cause to Suspect ye aboue Mencioned Mary Lacy & her daughter Mary to be ye Actors of it & accordingly Enter this my Complaint against them. & acknowledge my Selfe Indebted to Our Soueraign & Lord & Lady ye King & Queen One hundred poundes Currant money of New England On Condic̄on to prosecute this my Complaint to Effect as ye law directs. in witness whereof I haue hereunto Set my hand this 19th day July: 1692.

                                                                 Joseph Ballard

[Hand 2] This Complt was Exhibited Salem July the 19th 1692 ᵱ Josᵉ Ballard abouesayd before

| Barth Gedney. | Jno Hathorne | ⎫ |
| Jonah Corwin | Jno Higginson | ⎬ Jus peace |

Notes: Joseph Ballard posted bond for his complaint, consistent with the law that was regularly violated in all earlier cases, with one exception, and regularly followed in all subsequent cases. John Higginson Jr.'s presence, for the first time in hearing a formal complaint in the witchcraft episode, perhaps accounts for Corwin, Gedney, and Hathorne subsequently following appropriate procedure. The other case where bond was posted occurred in March 29. It was an Ipswich case, involving Rachel Clinton, with none of the three above magistrates involved. See No. 34. In No. 421 Hathorne signed the names of all the magistrates. ◊ Hand 1 = Stephen Sewall; Hand 2 = John Hathorne

MS Ch K 1.40, vol. 2, p. 400, Rare Books and Manuscripts, Boston Public Library. Boston, MA.

Wednesday, July 20, 1692

422. Warrant for the Apprehension of Mary Lacey Jr., and Officer's Return

See also: July 21, 1692.

[Hand 1] To: The Sherriffe of the Coanty of Essex or dep^t or Constable in Andouer

You are in theire Majes^{ts} names hereby required to apprehend and forthwith bring before vs, Mary Lacy. daufter of Lawrance Lacy of Andouer single womun. who Stands Charged ⌃{on behalfe of theire Maj^{es}} with haueing Committed Sundry acts of Witchcraft on. Eliz ballerd the wife of Jos Ballerd of Andouer. to her great hurt and that in order to her Examination Relateing to ye abouesayd premises faile not
Dated Salem July 20th 1692

You are likewise required to Search   Barth^o Gedney
diligently in ye house & aboute it for popetts   John Hathorn
&c   Jonathan. Corwin
                                                          John Higginson
                                                               Jus^{ts} peace

[Hand 2] In obediance unto this warant I haue Seased the body of the aboue Riten person: & and brought hur to the place apoynted: & deliuered hur: and allso made Serch for popetts or the like: ~~w(?)~~ with Two Men and Two wimin: and ffound a persol of Rags yearn tape and a parsell of quils tied up that none of the famely knew what it {was} done ffor and brought them to yur honers:: this 21: of July 1692

℘ ⟨?⟩ Ephraim ffoster Constable of Andouer

[Reverse] Mary Lacy Jun^e

21:5:92

Notes: Mary Lacey Jr. was the granddaughter of Ann Foster. ◊ Hand 1 = John Hathorne

MS Ch K 1.40, vol. 2, p. 400, Rare Books & Manuscripts, Boston Public Library. Boston, MA.

Thursday, July 21, 1692

Officer's Return: Warrant for the Apprehension of Mary Lacey Jr.
2nd of 2 dates. See No. 422 on July 20, 1692

423. Warrant for the Apprehension of Richard Carrier & Andrew Carrier, and Officer's Return

See also: July 22, 1692.

[Hand 1] To the Sherriffe of the County of Essex or Deputy or Constable of Andouer

You are in their Majesties names herby required to Apprehend and forthwith bring before us Richard Carier ^{and Andrew Carrier} Sons of Thomas Carier of Andiuor Husbandman who Stands charged on behalfe of their Majesties with haueing Cometted Sundry acts of wichcraft ^{on the body of Mary Warren of Salem &c} & that in order to his Examination relating to the abouesaid premisses and herof faile not & you are likewise to inquire after & make Serch for any paper or popetts. y^t may relate to witchcraft dated in Salem 21: July 1692:

July 21, 1692

Barth^ll Gedney
John Hathorne
Jonathan. Corwin
John Higginson
Jus^ts Peace

[Hand 2] in obedience to This warant I haue sesed the body. of richard carier and andrew carier and haue ~~broth~~ brought them to the house of Mr Thomas bedell: 22 iuly 1692

By me John Bullard Constable
[Hand 1] in Andouer

[Reverse] [Hand 1] Rich^d & Andrew Carier

Notes: Hand 1 = John Higginson Jr.

MS Ch K 1.40, vol. 2, p. 208, Rare Books & Manuscripts, Boston Public Library. Boston, MA.

424. Examinations of Ann Foster, Mary Lacey Sr., & Mary Lacey Jr.

21st July, '92. Before Major Gedney, Mr. Hathorne, Mr. Corwin and Capt. Higginson.

Goody Foster, you remember we have three times spoken with you, and do you now remember what you then confessed to us? Her former confession was read, which she owned to be all true.

You have been engaged in very great wickedness, and some have been left to hardness of heart to deny; but it seems that God will give you more favor than others, inasmuch as you relent. But your daughter here hath confessed some things that you did not tell us of. Your daughter was with you and Goody Carrier, when you did ride upon the stick. A. I did not know it. Q. How long have you known your daughter to be engaged? A. I cannot tell, nor have I any knowledge of it at all. Q. Did you see your daughter at the meeting? A. No. Q. Did not you know your daughter to be a witch? A. No. Q. Your daughter said she was at the witches meeting, and that you yourself stood at a distance off and did not partake at that meeting; and you yourself said so also; give us a relation from the beginning until now. A. I know none of their names that were there, but only Goody Carrier. Q. Would you know their faces if you saw them? A. I cannot tell. Q. Were there not two companies in the field at the same time? A. I remember no more.

Mary Warren, one of the afflicted, said that Goody Carrier's shape told her, that this Goody Foster had made her daughter a witch. Q. Do not you acknowledge that you did so about thirteen years ago? A. No, and I know no more of my daughter's being a witch than what day I shall die upon. Q. Are you willing your daughter should make a full and free confession? A. Yes. Q. Are you willing to do so too? A. Yes. Q. You cannot expect peace of conscience without a free confession. A. If I knew any thing more, I would speak it to the utmost. Goody Lacey, the daughter, called in, began thus; Oh, mother! how do you do? We have left Christ, and the Devil hath gat hold of us. How shall I get rid of this evil one? I desire God to break my rocky heart that I may get the victory this time. Q. Goody Foster, you cannot get rid of this snare, your heart and mouth is not open. A. I did not see the Devil, I was praying to the Lord. Q. What Lord? A. To God. Q. What God do witches pray to? A. I cannot tell, the Lord help me. Q. Goody Lacey, had you no discourse with your mother in your riding? A. No, I think I had not a word. Q. Who rid foremost on that stick to the village? A. I suppose my mother. Goody Foster said that Goody Carrier was foremost. Q. Goody Lacey, how many years ago since they were baptized? A. Three or four years ago, I suppose. Q. Who baptized them? A. The old serpent. Q. How did he do it? A. He dipped their heads in the water, saying they were his, and that he had power over them. Q. Where was this? A. At Fall's river. Q. How many were baptized that day? A. Some of the chief; I think there were six baptized. Q. Name them. A. I think they were of the higher powers. These were then removed.

Mary Lacey, the grand-daughter, was brought in, and Mary Warren in a violent fit. Q. How dare you come in here, and bring the Devil with you, to afflict these poor creatures? A. I know nothing of it. Lacey laying her hand on Warren's arm; she recovered from her fit. Q. You are here accused for practising witchcraft upon Goody Ballard; which way do you do it? A. I cannot tell. Where is my mother that made me a witch, and I knew it not? Q. Can you look upon that maid, Mary Warren, and not hurt her? Look upon her in a friendly way. She trying so to do, struck her down with her eyes. Q. Do you acknowledge now you are a witch? A. Yes. Q. How long have you been a witch? A. Not above a week. Q. Did the Devil appear to you? A. Yes. Q. In what shape? A. In the shape of a horse. Q. What did he say to you? A. He bid me not to be afraid of any thing, and he would not bring me out; but he has proved a liar from the beginning. Q. When was this? A. I know not; above a week. Q. Did you set your hand to the book? A. No. Q. Did he bid you worship him? A. Yes; he bid me also afflict persons. You are now in the way to obtain mercy if you will confess and repent. She said, The Lord help me. Q. Do not you desire to be saved by Christ? A. Yes. Then you must confess freely what you know in this matter. She then proceeded. I was in bed, and the Devil came to me, and bid me obey him and I should want for nothing, and he would not bring me out. Q. But how long ago? A. A little more than a year. Q. Was that the first time? A. Yes. Q. How long was you gone from your father, when you run away? A. Two days. Q. Where had you your food? A. At John Stone's. Q. Did the Devil appear to you then, when you was abroad? A. No, but he put such thoughts in my mind as not to obey my parents. Q. Who did the Devil bid you afflict? A. Timothy Swan. Richard Carrier comes often a-nights and has me to afflict persons. Q. Where do ye go? A. To Goody Ballard's sometimes. Q. How many of you were there at a time? A. Richard Carrier and his mother, and my mother and grandmother. Upon reading over the confession so far, Goody Lacey, the mother, owned this last particular. Q. How many more witches are there in Andover? A. I know no more, but Richard Carrier.

Tell all the truth. A. I cannot yet. Q. Did you use at any time to ride upon a stick or pole? A. Yes. Q. How high? A. Sometimes above the trees. Q. Your mother struck down these afflicted persons, and she confessed so far, till at last she could shake hands with them freely and do them no hurt. Be you also free and tell the truth. What sort of worship did you do the Devil? A. He bid me pray to him and serve him and said he was a god and lord to me.

Q. What meetings have you been at, at the village? A. I was once there and Richard Carrier rode with me on a pole, and the Devil carried us. Q. Did not some speak to you to afflict the people there? A. Yes, the Devil. Q. Was there not a man also among you there? A. None but the Devil. Q. What shape was the Devil in then? A. He was a black man, and had a high crowned hat. Q. Your mother and your grandmother say there was a minister there. How many men did you see there? A. I saw none but Richard Carrier. Q. Did you see none else? A. There was a minister there, and I think he is now in prison. Q. Were there not two ministers there? A. Cannot tell. Q. Was there not one Mr. Burroughs there? A. Yes.

Notes: W. F. Poole had access to draft material not published by Hutchinson. For clarification, see Richard Trask's essay in this edition. The entry into the Massachusetts witchcraft narrative of 1692, among the extant documents, of the Devil baptizing children begins here. It was a feature of the Swedish witch trials.

William Frederick Poole. The Witchcraft Delusion of 1692. By Gov. Thomas Hutchinson, From an Unpublished Manuscript (An Early Draft of His History of Massachusetts) in the Massachusetts Archives. New England Historical and Genealogical Register, vol. 24: no. 4 (October 1870), pp. 399–401.

Continued from July 18, 1692: Examination of Ann Foster

4th of 5 dates. See No. 419 on July 15, 1692

425. Examinations of Mary Lacey Jr., Mary Lacey Sr., & Ann Foster, Andover Examinations Copy

[Hand 1] Seuerall Examinations Before Barth° Gidny John Hathorne

Jonat Corwin & John Higginson Esqᵉ

21: July 1692:

Mary Lacy Junʳ Exaᵉ She was brought in & mary warren in a violen⟨t⟩ fit: Q. how dare you come in here & bring the diuill wᵗʰ you to aflict these pore creatures. A. I know nothing of it, but upon lacys layi⟨n⟩g her hand on warrins arme she was then recouered from her fit. q you are here accused for practising witchcraft upon goody Ballard wᶜʰ way doe you doe it. A. I canot tell, where is my mother yᵗ made me a witch and I knew it not. Q. can you look on Mary Warrᵉ & not hurt her look upon her now in a freindly way, she tryed so to doe struck her downe q. doe you acckn⁽ˡ⁾ now you are a witch A. yes. q. how long haue you ben a wictc[Lost] [= witch] A not aboue a week. Q. did the diuill apeare to you. A: yes: Q. In what shape. A in the shape of a horse Q. where. A in the House. Q. what did he say to you. A he bid me to be afraid of nothing. & he would not bring me out. but he has proued a lyer from the begining Q. what did he order you to doe. A. he set me to kill a tinker in the Towne and I would not. yⁿ he said he would kill me if I did not. I said I hoped god would he⟨lp⟩ me. Q. what other shap: did he apeare in A. in the shape of a round Gray thing & bid me set my hand to his book & I would not, − Q did he bid you worship him A ye⟨s⟩ and bid me also afflict persons. − Q. how many times did the diuill apeare to you A. twice & both times in the night I was in my bead & he awaked me by making a strange noyse Q what did he say to you A he bid me obey him & he would neuer bring me out q. did you not worship him A. yes I doe not question it sometimes Q. you may yet be deliue⟨rd⟩ if god giue you

repentance A. I hope he will Q. haue you neuer ben molested. till abou⟨t⟩ a week agoe A no.
but my mother has wished Seuerall times yᵉ diuill woul⟨d⟩ [Lost]
all away. Q. but how did you aflict the persons. A. I squesed m[Lost]
Q. was it Somthing in the liknese of them yᵗ you squesed A yes [Lost]
thing yᵗ came to hand. Mary lacy being desired Now [Lost]
she Struck her downe wᵗʰ her looks. Q. mary war[Lost]
but pointed at Mary lacy Q. Mary lac[Lost]
A a yeare & I haue ben a disobed[Lost]
good, the diuill apeared to m[Lost]
& mother & neuer doe as the [Lost]
{every night} She then as⟨ke⟩d dot⟨h⟩[Lost]

and Richᵈ Carier did one time draw cider ther, Q. how many of you ware there a[Lost][= at]
a time A. Richᵈ Carier & his mothʳ & my grandmother & monther [= mother], NOATE.
upon reading ouer the confesion so farr goody lacy yᵉ mother owned yᵉ last perticuler Q how
many more witches are in Andiuer A I know no more but Richᵈ Carier Q wᵗ time was it you
drunk yᵉ cider A. Sometime this Spring Q had you any feasting there A we eate nothing but
drunk. Q. tell all yᵉ truth A. I canot yet Q had you no victualls A. no. Q wᵗ other persons
haue you hurt A. none else Q. did not you hurt yᵗ maid their Mary warren wᶜʰ way did you
doe it was it her liknes A the diuill doth it & I know ^{it} not Q did not you Squese
Somthing to hurt her A I lay on a forme yesterday & Squesed yᵗ [Hand 2] Q. how Maney
year is it since You had familliarty wᵗʰ yᵉ diuel A a year and quarter agoe Q Were You neuer
at Salem Village. A⟨?⟩ No Q how many haue You afflicted A. Non but Tim͠ᵒ Swan ~~and this~~
Ballard & Mary Warren Q did You nott afflict Jeames ffrys Child A yes and Rᵈ Carrier Was
wᵗʰ me and told me yᵗ Jeames ffry, had beat his brother & he would fitt him for it & soe he
afflicted sᵈ fryˢ Child & gott me to assist him Q did You vse at any Time {to ride} vpon a
Stik or poll A Yes Q how high A Somtimes aboue yᵉ trees Q doe not ye Anoynt yᵋ Selues
before ye fflye A no but yᵉ diuell Carried vs upon hand poles Q Yᵋ Mothᵋ Stuck dwon these
afflicted pᵋsons sorely and she Confesed Soe far till at last she could shake hands wᵗʰ yᵐ frely
& doe yᵐ noe harm Now therfore be You ^{also} free and tell us all yᵉ truth what kind of
Worship did You doe yᵉ Diuell A he bid me pray to him & serue him & said he was a god &
lord to me qᵋ what did he promise to giue you A he said I should want nothing in this world
& yᵗ I should obtain glory wᵗʰ him Q Why wou^{ld} they hurt the Village people A yᵉ Diuell
~~told me he~~ would sett vp his Kingdome their & we sho^{u}ld haue happy days & it wo^{u}ld
then be bettᵋ times for me if I would obay him Q wᵗ Mettings haue You bin at, at yᵉ Village
[Lost] was once there, and ther was Rᵈ Carrier who rod wᵗʰ me upon a poll
[Lost] Carried us and ther was also my Granmothᵋ my mothᵋ & good{e}
[Lost] two poles or one A two Q how many were ther at yᵗ
[Lost] A I beleue there was a hundred & they were in
[Lost] Q were you not in two Companys A we
[Lost] Came ffirst but we were in two
[Lost] ⟨d⟩iuell there A I know nott yᵗ I did
[Lost] bout afflicting pᵋsons Q wᵗ tim[Lost]

Noate yᵗ mary Warren then Saw on the table a Young man & was Just then herself afflicted
And this Mary Lacy said she saw Young Carrier Sitt vpon Warrens Stomack yᵉ Sᵈ Lacy Said
ffurther there is a little Boy at Deacon ffrys yᵗ is an vnhappy Boy & I think he Joynes in this

Witchcraft his Name Is Andrew Carrier & he hurts frys Child because fry beat him Q Doth yᵉ Diuell require any thing of You besides hurting pᵉsons A Yes to Serue him & make more witches if we can & says if we will not make other pᵉsons Sett there hand to yᵉ Book he will tear us in peaces qᵉ haue you this Book A no yᵉ Diuel Keeps it, & he goes along with us, & we pᵉswade pᵉsons, & then he Setts Dwone ther Names in Blood, qᵉ wᵗ doe you write wᵗʰ all A wᵗʰ penns & Granmothᵉ & all of us Sett our Hands to yᵉ Book qᵉ did you See this Andrew Carrier afflictt ffreyˢ Child A he went wᵗʰ us when Rᵈ and I went She Sᵈ further yᵗ Rᵈ Carrier had a thing of his Mothᵉs wᵗʰ She Charged him Neuer to ⟨?⟩ Show to any pᵉson qᵉ wᵗ thing is it A a writting Q what writting is this A it is a w̶r̶⟨?⟩ writting yᵗ yᵉ Diuel gaue to goodᵉ Carrier and She has bin a witch Euer Since She Liued at Bilrica. Q wᵗ Murthers has She done A two Brothᵉ of her own and a Brothᵉ In Law Andrew Allin Jnᵒ Allin & Jeames Holt – here this Mary Lacey Spake at Larg of a difference betwen Goodᵉ Carrier & Jeams Holt @ [= about] a days work & yᵗ goodᵉ Carriᵉ Said She would ffitt him for itt Q wᵗ Children has She Killed A Goodᵉ ffryˢ Child & Christophᵉ osgoodˢ Wife & yᵗ this osgood & Carrier had a falling out before, She also killed Jeames Holts Child & a Child of andᵉ Allins Q wᶜʰ way did She kill them A She Stabbed yᵐ to yᵉ hart wᵗʰ pinns Needles & knitting Needles Q was this in ther bodyes or Somthing in there liknes A it was on there bodye A̶ And othᵉ things also Q did they vse to doe itt By Poppetts A Yes Q did you Euer hear what was in that ["th" written over "yᵗ"] paper yᵗ Goodᵉ Carrier Gaue to Richᵈ A no but Goodᵉ Carrier g̶a̶u̶ told her yᵗ She had giuen him a paper yᵗ would make him as good as her Self Q did You Euer ask him where he putt this paper A No but I k̶w̶o̶u̶ know he Is a wicked wretch {Q –} was You not at mʳ Ballards house on thanskgiu⟨i⟩g day at night A this Goodᵉ Carrier Came to us in her Spirit & to Granmothᵉ and would not lett her alone till She went wᵗʰ her and afflict pᵉsons Q how Doth She Come when She Comes In her Spiritt A Somtimes in yᵉ Likness of a Catt Somtimes In yᵉ Likness of a bird & tells us it is She Q w⟨ᵗ⟩ Coulor are these Catts A Blak Q where or in wᵗ pᵗ doe these Catts or Shapes Suck A I Cannott tell but beleue they Doe Suck her body Q did you hear the 77 witches Names Called ouer A Yes the Diuel Called yᵐ to him Q wᵗ Speech did he use to them A he bid them obey him and doe his Commands & it would be Bettᵉ for them & they Should obtain Crownes In hell, & Goodᵉ Carrier told me the Diuell Said to her She Should be a Queen In hell, Q how [= who] was to ^{be} King? {A} yᵉ Ministᵉ Q wᵗ kind of Man Is Mʳ Burroughs A a prettᵉ little Man and he has Come to Vs Somtimes In his Spiritt in yᵉ Shape of a Catt & I think Somtimes In his propᵉ Shape Q doe You hear the Diuel hurts in yᵉ Shap of any pᵉson without there Consents A no Q did yᵉ Diuel then bid yᵐ hurt yᵉ people at yᵉ Village A yes Q were ye Euer baptized A Yes Q did not yᵉ Diuel desire You to Renounce yᵉ Baptiz⟨?⟩ᵉ & to Renounce God A he bid me Neuer to keep Gods word but to Ser[Lost] [= serve] him & Said that he was god & also made me deny my baptizᵉ Q wᵗ words did he Say A he would haue me baptized again & I would not Q did you Neuer See him baptize Any A No Q did You Neuer Se yᵗ Sacrement at yᵉ Village; tell us truly A Yes Q wᵗ Coulor was yᵉ Bread A yᵉ bread was brownish & ⟨yᵉ⟩ wine Red they had also a table and Erthen Cups & there was So many that there was no⟨t⟩ bread Enough for yᵐ all Some of them Stole bread and Some brought bread wᵗʰ them and Some of yᵉ bred lookᵗ of a Reddish Couler Q how Drew yᵉ Sidᵉ when You were at Josᵉ Ballards A Goodᵉ Carriers Spiritt Q did you drink of yᵗ Sidᵉ bodyly A Yes Q in what posture was her body in when her Spirit was gone A it was dead Q are they Sensible when they goe for yᵉ Sidᵉ A Yes Q. did You goe bodely to yᵉ Vil[Lost] [= village] A Yes Q were you ⟨e⟩uer out in Yᵉ Spirit [Lost] Yᵉ [Lost] ⟨An⟩d [Lost]

{A} Yes and Good^ε Carrier fetches me away wth her Imps Q doe You then vnd^{ε}stand w^t you doe in y^e Spirit A Yes and can tell in moring when I come home what I haue don and Can tell y^e p^{ε}sons I haue Conuersed wth Q what time of ye day was y^t metting at ye Village A about twelue a Clock in the ~~morning~~ day Q if You ware there ⟨In⟩ Y^e p^{ε}sons how came it to pase y^t oth^ε p^{ε}sons did not See You A Somtimes we leaue our bodyes at home but at other times we goe in our bodyes & ye Diuel puts a Mist before there Eyes & will not lett them See us Q when any p^{ε}son Striks wth a Sword or Staf at a Spirit Or ["Or" written over "for"] Specter will y^t hurt ye body A Yes Q did any Euer any Strik at You A no Q did You Euer here of any that were thus hurt A Yes My Granmoth^ε was hurt in here arme Q how long agoe A arely this Spring {Q} where was she then A at ye Village Q did you here of any other A Yes my own Mother was hurt in ye hip by a blow Q and where was She Struck A at y^e Village Q you Say y^ε Moth^ε was hurt this Spring at y^e Village A Yes {Q} how Came You to know y^ε Moth^ε was hurt A She told me Soe that She was hurt Q and why will they Venture again after they are hurt {A} the Diuell Makes Y^m ["Y^m" written over "goe"] goe again and tells y$^{⟨m⟩}$ y^m that if they will not he will afflict y^m worse After this Confession Mary Warrin Came and took her by y^e hand & was No way hurt & She Viz Mary Lacy did Ernestly ask Mary Warren fforgiuenese for afflicting of her and both fell a weeping Together etc {Good^ε} Lacey y^e Moth^ε brought into y^e Chamber, To whome ye court S^d thus, Here is a Poor Miserable Child a Wretched Moth^ε & Granmother; Vpon Which Mary Lacey ye Daughter Brook forth into these Expressions, o Moth^ε Why did You giue Me to ye Diuell twice or thrice ever The Mother S^d She was Sorry at ye hart for it, it was through that wicked one, The Daughter Ernestly bid her repent and Cal Vpon God, O Mother Your wishes are Now Come to pase for Haue often wished y^t ye Diuel Would ffetch Me away aliue O My hart will break within me O y^t Moth^ε Should haue Euer giuen me to ye Diuel thus She weept Bitterly Crying out bitterly o lord Comfort Me and bring out all y^t are witches Then was Good^ε ffostter ye Granmoth^ε Brought in To whom ye Grandaughter S^d thus, O Granmother why did you Giue Me to ye Diuel why did You p^{ε}swade me and o Granmoth^ε doe ^{not} You deny it you haue bin a verry bad Woeman in Your time I must Needs Say Court here Is an Argument of hope for this poor creature y^t she Will be Snatched out of y^e Snare of y^e Diuel because there Semes to be somthing of repentance, But as for You Old Woeman though You haue Shown Somthing of Relenting Yet you r⟨t⟩ain a lye in Y^ε Mouth We desire You therefore to be free in y^e prence [= presence] of ⟨go⟩ god and tell us ye truth in this Matter Will You play wth Deuow^{ring} [= devouring] Fire & wil not you Shun Euerlasting fflames & y^e Society of this Deuowring Lyon y^t has Soe Ensnared Y^ε, y^e Grandaughter prayed her to tell all The old Woeman then S^d y^t Jeames ffryes Child was Killed by Good^ε Carrier but She her Self had no hand In it & Ch$^{⟨r⟩}$ Osgoods Child was Killed by S^d Carrier & Jeames holts Child also, & heard y^t Toothakers wife Came hither but doe Not Remember She did any Mishchif, and S^d further y^t toothak^{ε}s wife & Daughter was at y^e Village Me^{e}tting of Witches Q did not know Richd Carrier A he is Naught I Doubt Q did he goe to ye Village Metting at y^t time A I doe not Remember but Mary Lacey affermed he did & Ernestly Desired he might be taken hold of Goody Lacey did you know Richd Carrier to be a witch A Yes he Came to Stephen Osgoods ⟨ffild⟩ ffeild ^{one time} where was a teem of Oxen and S^d if he pleased he Could mak⟨e⟩ all these cattle Drop Dwon Dead p⟨resa⟩ntly [Lost]

Marey Lacey what tricks doe You know hee has Done A he has done worser then any for he and ^{his} Mother was a Means of killing Christoph^ε Osgoods Child wife Old woeman

what time was it y^t you Entred upon this work A⟨?⟩ not @ [= about] Six Years agoe Q why
did not you tell y^e truth at y^e first A the Diuel would not lett me Noate y^t Vpon y^e Reading
ouer Mary Laceys Confession the Mother & Granmoth^ε owned their Signing y^e Diuels book
at y^e Village Metting which Mary Lacey Spake of Q was it Red you wrote withal A Yes like
blood & Mary Lacy S^d they Vsed a penn Mary Warren then had a fitt and Cried out Vpon
Richd Carrier & Mary Lacey prayed ~~they~~ ^{he} Might be Sent for & goody Lacey owned y^t
Carrier told her also y^t She Shold be Queen of hel The old woeman owned & Conffesed y^t
She was hurt at ye Village Metting and Goody Lacey also Conffesed y^t She was Struck there
at y^t time & She Conffesed further y^t ye Diuel forced y^m to goe again & afflict though they
Haue been hurt before, & ye old woeman S^d ye Same Mary Lacey S^d her Granmother had
been a witch these Seauen Years And ye old woman s^d She did not ^{know} but it might be
Soe Good^ε Lacey wch way did you goe to ye fals Riuer to ye baptizing of Bradbery A ye Diuel
Carried me in his armes She also S^d y^t Andrew Carrier was a Witch Q w^t did you wth those
Images or likneses A ye Diuel fetched them all away She S^d further y^t when She rolled a
Rage or any Such thing & so Imagine it to Represent Such & Such p^εsons & what Euer She
did ~~thing~~ to y^t thing In ye Same Manner ye p^εson Represented by ye Likness Is
afflicted

Notes: Sometime after September 17, the date is unknown, a copy of several Andover related examinations was made. Although the practice for *Records of the Salem Witch-Hunt* has been not to split manuscripts, but to show them in their entirety for each record, this document created insurmountable difficulties for presenting it intact and at the same time giving the reader a continuing chronology. Accordingly, the manuscript, consisting of ten sheets with writing on both sides, has been split into chronological segments. The titles used in the edition for each of these records reflects the main person being examined. However, interspersed within these segments are questions directed to or volunteered by others. Subsequent records from this manuscript will refer the reader back to this note for the *Andover Examinations Copy*. The first sheet of the manuscript, containing the examination recorded here, has been torn and a significant portion of the content lost. ◊ "fitt," "ffitt": 'to visit (a person) with a fit penalty, to punish' (*OED* s.v. *fit* v[1], 12). ◊ Hand 1 = John Higginson Jr.

Essex Institute Collection, No. 24, 1r–3r,, James Duncan Phillips Library, Peabody Essex Museum, Salem, MA.

426. Examination of Mary Lacey Sr.

[Hand 1] 21 July 1692.
A part of Goody Laceyes {2^d} Examination and confession to be added to {the first.}
Before mag^ε [= major] Gidney Mr Hauthorn & m^r Corwin

When Goody foster was upon examination the second tyme, Goody Lacey was brought in also, who said to her mother foster, we have forsaken Jesus christ And the devil hath got hold of us. how shall we get cleare of this evil one:
She confesses that her mother foster, Goody Carryer & herself rid upon a pole to Salem Village meeting, and that the pole broke a litle way off from the village: She sayth further that about 3 or 4 yea^εs agoe she saw mistriss Bradburry Goody How and Goody Nurse baptised by the old serpent at newburry falls And that he dipped theire heads in the water and then said Thay wer his and he had power over them, she sayes ther wer six baptised at that tyme who were some of the chieff or heigher powe^εs, and that the⟨i⟩r might be neare

about a hundred in company at that tyme. It being asked her, after what maner she went to Newberry falls answered the devil carryed her in his armes, And sayth further that if she doe take a ragg, clout or any such thing and Roll it up together And Imagine it to represent such & such a persone, Then whatsoever she doth to that Ragg or clout so rouled up, The persone represented thereby will be in lyke manner afflicted.

It being again asked her if what she had said was all true, she answered affirmatively, confessing also that Andrew Carryer was a witch

She confesses. that she afflicted Timothy Swan in Comp^a [=company] with mistriss Bradbury Goody Carryer Richard Carryer and her own daughter mary lacey, They afflicted him with an Iron spindle and she thinks they did once with a tobacko pipe she said she was in Swans chamber and it being askd which way she got in answered the devil helpt her in at the window, she also remembe^ᵉs the afflicting of Ballards wife, and y^t Richd Carryer was yr [= there] also

She said further the devil takes away her memory and will not let her remember

[Reverse] [Hand 2] Mary Lacey's further confession
[Hand 3] part of y^e Examin͞acon of Mary Lacey

Notes: Mary Lacey Sr. was examined on July 21 with her daughter, Mary Lacey Jr., and her widowed mother, Ann Foster (age 72), who had been examined first on July 15 and had confessed, accusing Martha Carrier. Ann Foster was also examined on July 16 and 18 and swore to her testimony on September 10. See No. 419. Richard and Andrew Carrier, ages 18 and 16 respectively, were examined on July 22, denying witchcraft. They were removed from the room and upon returning confessed. See No. 428, No. 429, & No. 430. According to John Procter, writing from jail in Salem on July 23, they were tied "Neck and Heels till the Blood was ready to come out of their noses. . . ." See No. 433. Mary Lacey Jr. is listed in *Andover Vital Records* as age 18 years, and in a recognizance on October 6, 1692 as 15 years old. See No. 690. ◊ Hand 1 = William Murray; Hand 2 = Stephen Sewall; Hand 3 = Anthony Checkley

Essex County Court Archives, vol. 2, no. 51, Massachusetts Supreme Judicial Court, Judicial Archives, on deposit James Duncan Phillips Library, Peabody Essex Museum, Salem, MA.

Friday, July 22, 1692

Officer's Return: Warrant for the Apprehension of Richard Carrier & Andrew Carrier
2nd of 2 dates. See No. 423 on July 21, 1692

427. Warrant for the Apprehension of Martha Emerson, and Officer's Return

[Hand 1] To the Sheriff of the County of Essex or his dept or Constable of Hauerhill

You are in theire Majes^{ts} names hereby required forthwith or as soon as may be to. Bring before vs Martha Emerson the wife of [Hand 2] Joseph [Hand 1] Emerson of Hauerhill ~~Husband~~, who was daufter of Roger toothaker of Belrica, Late Deceased; who stands accuused of haueing Committed Sundry acts of Witchcraft Lately on ye Bodys of Mary Warren Mary Lacy & others to theire great hurt And y^t in Order to her Examination

Relateing to the abouesaid premisses and hereof ffaile not Dated Salem July the 22 1692 You   July 22, 1692
are likewise required to make diligent search for any Images or popetts &c in s^d house or
aboute itt
Salem:

> Barth^o Gedney
> John Hathorne
> Jonathan. Corwin
> John: Higginson
> Justices peace

[Hand 3] by uertiue of the of thes warant I haue Seased ~~the~~ martha Emerson of hauerill and
haue brought her heare to Answer to what shall be Charged Against her
dat this 22 of July 1692

> ℞ me wiliam Starling
> Constable

[Reverse] [Hand 4] Martha Emerson 23. 5. 1692.

Notes: The date of July 23 on the reverse is tentative, since the document is covered with paper for preservation. ◊ Hand
1 = John Hathorne

MS Ch K 1.40, vol. 2, p. 28, Rare Books & Manuscripts, Boston Public Library. Boston, MA.

428. Examinations of Richard Carrier, Mary Lacey Jr., Mary Lacey Sr., & Andrew Carrier, Copy

[Hand 1] 22th July 1692 Richard Carrier Aged 18 Years & His Brother
Andrew @ 16 Years Richd Carrier & his brother brought into Court who vnto Many
Qestions propounded returned Negatiue Answers to all & y^e afflicted p^εsons S^d they Saw y^e
black Man & there Mother wth others Stand before y^m on y^e Table to Hinder there
Conffesion
{Q M.L. [= Mary Lacey]} did Not Richd Joyne⟨?⟩ wth You In Seuerall things A Yes & he
burned Tim^o Swan wth his Tobacc^o pipe Q Where was Rich^d when he did it A In Swans
Chamber In Spirit Q who Else Joyned In it A Good^ε Carrier My Granmother & Mother &
Rich^d Q Was Rich^d there bodyly A his body Came to ye house & his Spirit went In & did it
Q were ye all bodyly in ye Chamber A Somtimes we ware in Shapes & Somtimes in body but
they did not See vs She S^d further y^t they rod upon hand poles & ye Diuel also was there in
ye Shape of a black Man & high Crowned hatt & bid us Kill Swan by Stabing him to Death
& we also Stick pinns Into his Liknes Q and what Else had You any hott Irons or knitting
knedles A Yes we had an Iron Spindle & Richd Carrier run it through or Into Swans knee Q.
wher had you y^t Spindle A ye Diuel Brought it to us Q had you any Quarrell wth him A we all
Came in Vpon Mrs Bradberys acc^o or Quarrel She had wth him Q Good^ε Lacey did not you
hurt Swan A No The Daughter S^d Yes Mother doe not deny it Q Goody Lacy who was in y^t
Company A Goody Carrier & her Son Mrs Bradbery & we⟨e⟩ Q were not Y^e Mother there
Viz ffoster A I know not but She Might be there Q did You hurt ᷃{him} A ye Diuel Made

July 22, 1692

his Imps doe it Q wch way did you hurt him A there was hott Irons & ye Diuel ^{held} y^m Q
Y^e Daughter S^d it was an Iron Spindle A Yes Yes it was a Spindle Q did you practise wth a
Tobac^o pipe A I think once Q who was it y^t you hurt A Tim^o Swan Q who held ye pipe A y^e
Diuel & his Imps Q had You any thing for his licknes A ther was a thing before us as it were
Good^ε Lacey were You in ye Chamb^r wth him A Yes Q wch way did you gett in A y^e Diuel
helped us in at y^e window And Mary Lacey S^d She went in at y^e ~~win~~ door Mary Lacey how
Maney was there A granmoth^ε Good^ε Carrier Richd Carrier Mother & G & Mrs Bradbery
& we went upon y^e Diuel & Mrs Bradb^ε acc^ε who Came to ⟨u⟩[Lost] [= us] & brought us
ffrom our own homes. And we Consented to Kill him if we were not brought out before, &
here [Lost] Marey Lacey Related Somthing of y^e Qarrell betwext Bradb^ε & Swan @
Thatching of a house – Now Richd Carrier w^t Say you to these two Euidences y^t saw You
wth Tim^o Swan, but Still he Denyed al Q^{u}estions – Mary Lacey when you went to afflict
Ballard was not this man wth You Viz Richd Carrier A Yes & it was @ a fortnight Since we
went Vpon poles in ye Night we got into ye house & this Rich^d afflicted Ballard by pinching
~~him~~ & Choaking her & I was ther also when ye Sider was Drawn Good^ε Lacey doe You
Remember any thing of afflicting this Ballard A Yes. and this Rich^d was there and afflicted
by pinching choaking & Laying his hand on her Stomak Mary Lacey Vrged Richd Very
Much to Confes & S^d further y^t he bid her help to kill Swan & y^t they Vsed to discourse
togeth^ε on ["on" written over "of"] ther Jorneys & Vsed to tell her ^{he} would goe and
afflict p^εsons, telling him he had a hart as hard as a Rock to Deny it. She S^d further y^t this
Rich^d told her he would Kill Goody ballard also Mary was it Richard ["Richard" written over
"Ballard"] pipe y^t burnt Swan {A} Yes and it he did him Self & Run ye Spindle into Swans
knee he told me also y^t he would make his Broth^ε one & afflict p^εsons Mary Warrin in a bad
ffitt & blood Runing out of her Mouth. Mary Lacy S^d that this Andrew did it The afflicted
p^εsons were Greuously tormented y^t Rich^d and Andrew were Carried out to another
Chambber – And there feet & hands bound a Little while after Rich^d was brought In again
Q Rich^d though you haue been Verry Obstinate Yett tel us how Long agoe it is Since You
ware taken in this Snare A a year Last May and Noe More Vnto Many Qestions Propounded
he Answered Affermatiuly As ["As" written over "Viz"] ffolloweth Viz he Saw ye Shape of a
man In ye Night, he had been in twone & was Goeing home ye man was ⟨bl⟩ Black & had a
high Crowned hat he told me I was afrayd to goe home & asked me what I Should be afraid
of & proffered to goe a little way wth me, he bid me Serue him & he would Gett Me New
Cloaths & giue Me a horse, he told me also y^t he was Christ, & I must beleue him, & I think
I did Soe. I Sett My hand to his book it was a little Red book ^{I wrought w^t a Stick & mad
a red Colour w^t it} & I promised to Serue him & at parting hee bid bid Me Goodnight – the
2nd time he Apeared to me was in ye Shape of a Yellow Bird And told me he had not
p^εformed his promise but wo^{u}ld & y^t Shortly – I was to doe Seruice @ ye Children &
afflicted p^εsons he told Me also of Tim^o Swan & y^t I must Giue him leaue to afflict him he
asked my Consent also to afflict Ballards Wife – I also hurt y^e Images of p^εsons or y^e liknes
of y^m by Squezing any thing I had a mind to, betwene My hands – The 2nd Aperance was
last January, It is not aboue a moth [= month] Since y^t I began to afflict Swan, I can not tell
how long it is Since y^t I rod to Salem Village, I was ther twice & Rod wth Mary Lacey y^e
Diuel Carried us Somtimes in y^e Shape of a horse Somtimes In y^e Shape of a Man the 1^rst
time he was a horse the 2nd time a Man, when he was a horse our pol lay across ye horse,
when he was a man our pol was on his Sholder – when We ["We" written over "he"] went to
ballard he was a Man. we ware at ballards house and went in Somtimes at ye Window &

Somtimes at yᵉ Door, I goot yᵉ Sider out of yᵉ Sellᵋ & Drew it in a pot belonging to yᵉ house & Drank it in yᵉ Orchard I fetcht yᵉ Sider my Self & went in my Spirit for it here Mary Lacey Sᵈ he went in his Spirit & his body lay dead yᵉ while & ^{out of doors} he Sᵈ it was true

I hurt Swan in my Spirit & Struck him in yᵉ knee wᵗʰ a Spindle yᵉ Diuel brought it & was then in the Shape of A black Man & high Crowned hatt I afflicted frys Child by Squezing of it & I did it upon any thing I had a mind Should represent yᵉ Child, my m⟨oth⟩ Mothᵋ was wᵗʰ me Somtimes but not often, – Mother was bodyly wᵗʰ me – I haue {Seen} her once in her Spirit Since her Imprissenment & in yᵉ Shape of a Catt I was pᵋsent when brother Signed yᵉ book & I think Mothᵋ was there also & yᵉ Diuel. – I rod yᵉ 1ʳˢᵗ time on a horse & yᵉ 2ⁿᵈ time on a man to Salem Village & I think there might be @ Seuenty there at Each Mettings, we mett in a Green wᶜʰ was yᵉ Ministers paster And we were in two Companys at yᵉ Least ["L" written over "l"], I think there was a few Men wᵗʰ yᵐ I heard Sarah Good talk of a Minister or two – one of yᵐ was he yᵗ had ben at yᵉ Estward & preached once at yᵉ Village, his Name Is Burroughs and he Is a little Man – I Remember not yᵉ other Ministers Name I Saw yᵉ {Diuel} Open a Grate Booke & We all Sett or hands & Seales ["S" written over "it"] to it, yᵉ Ingagement was to afflict pᵋsons & to ouer Come yᵉ Kingdome of Christ, & Set Vp the Diuels Kingdome & we ware to haue happy Days – Marey Lacey Sᵈ She heard yᵐ talk of throwing Dwone yᵉ Kingdome of Christ & Setting up yᵉ Diuel on his throwne – they ware to Doe Soe throughout all yᵉ Whole Country – & were Enjoyned by yᵉ Diuel to Make as Many witches as we Could – I know Marthra Toothaker & her Mother to be witches & they ware in Company both times ~~In Goeing~~ In Goeing to yᵉ Village Metting – Goodᵋ Lacey Sᵈ all this was true – Richᵈ Sᵈ that Toothakᵋ yᵗ Dyed in prison was one too, Mary Lacey then in a bad fitt afflictted, this Richᵈ Could ["Could" written over "Sᵈ"] Then See Toothakᵋ Vpon her – Q Richᵈ Can You Name any yᵗ ware at the Mettings A Jnᵒ Willard Jnᵒ Procter & his Wifeˡ Goodᵋ Nurse Goodm̄ Cory & his Wife Goodᵋ how Mʳˢ Bradbery & Goodᵋ Oliuer &c – Jnᵒ Willard Is a black ^{hared} Man of a Midle Statture & he told me his Name – we heard a drum & Mary Lacey heard yᵉ Same Mary Lacey In a bad fitt Richᵈ Saw on Burse upon her & Sᵈ further yᵗ yᵗ man was at Salem Village Metting – I was wᵗʰ ballards wife I Think on Moonday or Tuesday I Think I haue afflicted 3 at yᵉ Village – 2 in yᵉ Ministers house one of yᵐ a grown pᵋson yᵉ other a Child yᵉ growne pᵋson was yᵉ Mʳˢ of yᵉ house, yᵉ Younger pᵋson was one abigall Williams also Mary Walkutt on Wednesday last, I doe it by Roling Vp a handcherchif & Soe Imagining to be a representation of a pᵋson – the Diuel Doth it Sometimes yᵉ Diuell Sturred Me Vp to hurt yᵉ Ministers Wife – I Was Baptized at yᵉ falls at Nᵋberry in yᵉ Riuer he dipt my head into yᵉ Wattᵋ but doe not Remembʳ wᵗ he Sᵈ ther were not aboue 6 Baptizᵋ Viz Mʳˢ Bradbᵋ Goodᵋ Nurse Goody How When they Signed the book the Diuel told yᵐ they Should ouer Come & Preuail the witches are all afaird they Shall al Come out & yᵉ Diuel threatens if I come not Unto this Quarrell he will tear me in peaces – After this Richᵈ would take yᵉ afflicted pᵋsons by yᵉ hand wᵗʰout hurting of yᵐ & asked fforgiueness

Andrew Carrier brought In & his brother told him yᵗ he had acknowledged all: Court – tell us plainly &c – Vnto Many Questions asked he Returned these ffollowing Answers it Is aboue ~~aboue~~ a month agoe Since he Signed yᵉ Diuelˢ

July 22, 1692

Booke – the Diuel is a black Man – his Mother & brother Came wth the d⟨?⟩ Diuel when he Signed – he was to Serue ye Diuel fiue Years and ye Diuel was to giue him house and land in Andeauor the Diuel did not tell him Who ["Who" written over "he"] he was, but he Set his hand to his book {w^th ⟨a⟩ pen ye ink was Red But cannot tell ye Coll^ɛ} – he Saw a pretty many Names in it – he put to a Seal & ye Stamp was a little thing he knows not what – it was in ye Night Time & up at Deacon ffrys in ye Oarchard which Richard Owned The Diuel told him he Must Serue him, keep his Councel & afflict p^ɛsons Som times – Memorandum this Andrew in his ffirst Examination Stammered & Stuttered Excedinly in Speaking which Some of his Neighbours p^ɛsent S^d he was not want to doe but now In his Confession h⟨e⟩ [Lost]

He further Sayes y^t ye Diuel p^ɛswaded him to hurt frys Child a little The way Thus, the man Came & asked me what he Should doe for me And I S^d he Should afflict y^t Child, & Richd S^d Andrew had assisted a little in afflictting Swan Andrew S^d he had not afflicted any Since ye Child but Mary Warrin he Says ye Diuel baptized him w^thin this Month at Shawshin Riuer, ye Diuel put his head into ye Watt^ɛ Richd Saw baptized & ye Diu^l ⟨?⟩ S^d that Andrew was his & he had Command Ouer him wch Andrew Owned ther were two at y^t Metting besides his brother baptized but he has forgat there Names – Rich^d was at ye Sacrement at ye Village, did Drink of ye wine but not Eate of ye Bread he Remembers not ye words Vsed at ye administration but goody Nurse handed ye bread about. ye wine & bread were both Red – Noate y^t Richd Conffesses nothing of ye paper or writting wch ye Diuel gaue his Mother & as Mary Lacey S^d his Mother gaue to him

Notes: From *Andover Examinations Copy*. See No. 425. Richard Carrier was 18. Andrew was 16. Accusations were circulating around Reverend John Busse and Reverend Francis Dane, perhaps the ministers he could not name, although he soon came up with "Burse," John Busse. Richard's comment about the "high Crowned hatt" evokes the "high-crown'd hat" the Devil wore in the account of the Swedish outbreak (Joseph Glanvil, *Sadducismus triumphatus*, ll, p. 316). His comment on hurting the "Ministers Wife" appears to reference Elizabeth Parris Sr., Samuel Parris's wife. Timothy Swan's name had first been introduced on July 15 at the examination of Ann Foster (No. 419), and he is often referenced in the Andover cases. Richard Carrier's conversion to becoming a confessor is unusual in that it was clearly related to his being tortured.

Essex Institute Collection, no. 24, 3r–4v, James Duncan Phillips Library, Peabody Essex Museum, Salem, MA.

429. Examination of Richard Carrier

[Hand 1] Richard: Carriers: Confession July 22: 1692
{Q} have you bin in ye devils s⟨n⟩are A: yes.
{Q} is yor bro: Andrew: ensnared by ye devils snare: A: Yes how long: has yor brother bin a wich: A: Near a monthe how long: have you bin a witch: A: not long: Q have you Joined in aflicting: ye aflicted persons: A: Yes: Q you help⟨t⟩ to hurt: Timo Swan: did you A: yes: Q how long: have yo^u bin a wich: A abo^t five weeks: who was in company when you Covnanted with ye devill: A Mrs Bradbery did she help {yo^u aflict yes:} what was ye ocasion: Mrs Bradbery: would have to aflict Timo Swan: A becaus: her husband & Timo Swan fell out about a scyth: I think: Q did they not fall out abo^t thaching of a barn: to A no not as I know of {Q} who was att the villadge meeting when you was there A. goodwife How: goodwife Nurs

g. Wildes Procter: & his wife Mrs Bradbery: & Gory.s wife: Q was any of Boston there A no: Q how many was there in all: A: a duzzen I think: was Jn° Willard there A I think he was: {Q} what kind of man is Jn° willard: a yong man or an old man A he is not an old man: he had black hair

{Q} what meeting was this meeting: was this: that: that was near: Ingersals: A yes I think Q what did they do there

{A} the: eat: & they drank wine: was there. a minister. there

{A} no: not as I know of: whence had you your wine: A from Salem I think. was {from} Q: goodwife Olliver there: yes I knew her

Notes: Hand 1 = Simon Willard

Essex County Court Archives, vol. 2, no. 111, Massachusetts Supreme Judicial Court, Judicial Archives, on deposit James Duncan Phillips Library, Peabody Essex Museum, Salem, MA.

430. Fragment of the Examination of Richard Carrier‡

We met in a green, which was the minister's pasture – we were in two companies at last. I think there was a few men with them. – I heard Sarah Good talk of a minister or two. – One of them was she that had been at the eastward; his name is Burroughs, and is a little man. – I remember not the other's name.

Notes: This fragment, appearing in Poole's article, offers no clear basis for dating. Carrier was examined on July 22, and the fragment is dated here accordingly, but it may be from an examination on a later date.

William Frederick Poole. The Witchcraft Delusion of 1692. By Gov. Thomas Hutchinson, From an Unpublished Manuscript (An Early Draft of His History of Massachusetts) in the Massachusetts Archives. New England Historical and Genealogical Register, vol. 24: no. 4 (October 1870), p. 401.

431. Petition in Support of Mary Bradbury

[Hand 1] July 22^d 1692

Concerning m^s Bradburies life & conversation

Wee the Subscribers doe testifie: that it was such as became ye gosp⟨el⟩ shee was a louer of ye ministrie [Hand 2] ^{in all appearanc} [Hand 1] & a dilligent attender vpon gods holy ordinances, being of a curteous, & peaceable disposition & cariag: neither did any of vs (some of whom haue lived in ye town {w^th her} aboue fifty yeare) ever heare or know that shee ever had any difference or falling oute wth any of her neighbo^εs man woman or childe but was allwayes readie & willing to doe for them w^t laye in her power night & day, though wth hazard of her health: or other danger: more might be spoken in her comendačon but this for the p^εsent

July 22, 1692

Mar⟨t⟩ha Pike
Willam Buswell
Sarah Buswell
Samuell ffelloes senᵉ
Rodger Easman
Sarah Easman
Joseph ffletcher & his wyfe
Joseph ffrench
John. ffrench senᵉ
Mary ffrench his wyfe
Abigayl ffrench
John Allin
Mary Allin
William Carr
Elizabeth Carr
Samˡˡ Colby
Samuel ffrench & his wyfe
Henry Ambros & his wyfe
Nathanel Stevens & his wyfe
Ephraim Severans
Lidia Severans
Joanna Stevens
Sarah Hacket
Marthe Carter
Elizabetch Gettchell
Benj: Eastman
Ann Easman
Benony Tucker
Ebenezer Tucker
Nathanel Brown
Hannah Brown
Tho: Evens
Hannah Evens

Samˡˡ ffelloes junᵉ
⟨A⟩bigail ffelloes
Samˡ Easman
Elizabeth Easman
Joseph Eaton
Mary Eaton his wyfe
Robert Downer
Sarah Downer
Richard Long & his wyfe
Richard Smith & his wyfe
Joseph True, & his wyfe
Andrew Greley ⟨&⟩ his
    wyfe
William Hooke
Elizabeth Hooke
Benjamin Allin & Rachel his
    wyfe
Benj: Allin, & Rachill his
    wyfe
Isaac Buswell, & his wyfe
William Allin
Nathanel Eastman
Elizabeth Easman
John Eastman: & Mary
    Eastman his wife
Sarah Shepherd
Willi: Osgood
Abigayl osgood
Susanah Severance
Onesiphris Page & his wyfe
Samˡˡ Gill & his wyfe
John Clough & his wyfe
Abraham Brown & his wyfe

Ephraim Eaton
Ephraim Winsley
Mary Winsley his wyfe
Philip Grele and his wyfe
Richard Hubbard
Matthew Hubbard his wyfe
Daniell Moody
Elizabeth Moody
Isaac Morrill
Phœbœ Morrill
John Maxfeild
Jarves Ring
Hannah Ring
Nathanel Whitter
Mary Whitther
Jacob Morrill
Susannah Morrill
Elizabeth Maxfeild
Hanah Stevens widdow
John Stevens
Dorethie Stevens
Tho: Clough & his wyfe
Sarah Connor widow
John Tomson
John Watson & his wyfe
Steven Tongue & his wyfe
John Connor & his wyfe
Joseph Page
Meres Tucker & his wyfe
Henry Brown Senᵉ & his
    wyfe

Notes: The strong network of support for Mary Bradbury did not save her from condemnation in September. However, she escaped. The details of that escape are unknown except that she had powerful support. The dated document comes well before her indictment and trial in September. She was examined on July 2, according to the depositions against her, probably arrested that day or the day before, although neither a warrant for her arrest nor an examination are extant. Given that the petition came in July, it is possible that a grand jury hearing was anticipated earlier than September. All of the "signatures" were written by Thomas Bradbury, but there is no reason to doubt that he recorded them with the knowledge of the people named. The repetition of Benjamin Allin and his wife, Rachel, may be a recording error. No record of two Benjamin Allins, each married to Rachel, has been located. ◊ Hand 1 = Thomas Bradbury; Hand 2 = Robert Pike

Essex County Court Archives, vol. 2, no. 83, Massachusetts Supreme Judicial Court, Judicial Archives, on deposit James Duncan Phillips Library, Peabody Essex Museum, Salem, MA.

Saturday, July 23, 1692

432. Examination of Martha Emerson

See also: Jan. 10, 1693.

[Hand 1] Martha Emorson {was} examined before Maj$^\varepsilon$ Gedney & other their Majest$^\varepsilon$ Justices in Salem July 23: 1692

Martha Emorson: you are here accused for afflicting: of Mary Warin & Mary Lascy: by witchcraft: what say you: Answer: I never saw them

Richard Carrier: s^d he see her hurt them both yesterday: but he had never seen her at y^e witch meeting: but Mary Lascy sen$^\varepsilon$ s^d y^t she had seen both Martha Emorson & her ~~moth~~mother at y^e witch meeting: Mary Warin & mary Lacy ~~were~~ fell down when s^d martha Emorson looked on them: & Mary Lasy was presantly well when s^d Emorson took her by y^e wrist: two more also fell down with her looking on them: but: she denyed that she knew any thing of witchcraft

Mary Warin s^d y^t s^d Emorsons spectre told her: that: she had rid a man with an inchanted bridle: & Matthew Herriman: was called: to say: whether he had bin ridden: so or no: who answerd. that last monday night: he was in a strange condision: and heard it rain & blow: as I thought: but in y^e morning there had bin no rain: but in y^e morning my tongue was sore & I could not speak till son [= sun] two hours high: & Martha Emorson came to our hous: that morning: as soon as it was light for fire: Mary: Warin being in a long dumb fitt: signified by holding up her hand that this Harriman was y^e man that she s^d Emerson s^d she had ridden: but Emerson s^d she knew nothing of it

Emorson was told: that her father: had s^d he had taught his daughter Martha so that she had killed a witch: and: that was to take ye afflicted persons water & put it in a glass or bottle: & sett it into an oven: emorson ownd she had stopt a womans urin: in a glass: Emorson was asked: who hindred her from confessing she answered that her Aunt Carrier: & good wife Green of Haverill: were before her: goodwife Green: was angry with her: becaus she: would not be like her selfe for Green had Inticed her a fortnight: to afflict & she would not: she s^d Greens wife would have her be of: that number: she was asked what Number: she s^d ye number of devils: She complaynd: that: greens wife & her Aunt Carrier: took her by ye throat: & y^t they would not lett her confess. She s^d Greens wife had a pigg y^t use to follo her: but after ward she denyed all. & s^d what she had s^d was in hopes to have favour: & now she could not deny god: that had keept her from that sin: & after s^d though he slay me I will trust in him

[Reverse] [Hand 2] Mar. ⟨E⟩merson Exam^{ns}
[Hand 3] Mary Warren Owned before the Grand iury Jan$^\varepsilon$ 10th 1692 that Martha Emerson had aflicted her severall times before & at this time when she was p$^\varepsilon$sent with vs
Attests
[Hand 4] Robert. Payne foreman.

Notes: The January 10 date appears on the manuscript as 1692 rather than 1693, reflecting the old calendar usage. ◊ Hand 1 = Simon Willard; Hand 2 = Stephen Sewall

July 23, 1692   *Suffolk Court Files, vol. 32, docket 2708, p. 32, Massachusetts Supreme Judicial Court, Judicial Archives, Massachusetts State Archives. Boston, MA.*

433. Petition of John Procter from Prison

Mr. *Mather*, Mr. *Allen*,
Mr. *Moody*, Mr. *Willard*, and   } Salem-*Prison*, July, 23. 1692.
Mr. *Bailey*

Reverend Gentlemen.

The Innocency of our Case with the Enmity of our Accusers and our Judges, and Jury, whom nothing but our Innocent Blood will serve their turn, having Condemned us already before our Tryals, being so much incensed and engaged against us by the Devil, makes us bold to Beg and Implore your Favourable Assistance of this our Humble Petition to his Excellency, That if it be possible our Innocent Blood may be spared, which undoubtedly otherwise will be shed, if the Lord doth not mercifully step in. The Magistrates, Ministers, Jewries, and all the People in general, being so much inraged and incensed against us by the Delusion of the Devil, which we can term no other, by reason we know in our own Consciences, we are all Innocent Persons. Here are five Persons who have lately confessed themselves to be Witches, and do accuse some of us, of being along with them at a Sacrament, since we were committed into close Prison, which we know to be Lies. Two of the 5 are (Carriers Sons) Young-men, who would not confess any thing till they tyed them Neck and Heels till the Blood was ready to come out of their Noses, and 'tis credibly believed and reported this was the occasion of making them confess that they never did, by reason they said one had been a Witch a Month, and another five Weeks, and that their Mother had made them so, who has been confined here this nine Weeks. My Son William Procter, *when he was examin'd, because he would not confess that he was Guilty, when he was Innocent, they tyed him Neck and Heels till the Blood gushed out at his Nose, and would have kept him so 24 Hours, if one more Merciful then the rest, had not taken pity on him, and caused him to be unbound. These Actions are very like the* Popish *Cruelties. They have already undone us in our Estates, and that will not serve their turns, without our Innocent Bloods. If it cannot be granted that we can have our Trials at* Boston, *we humbly beg that you would endeavour to have these Magistrates, changed, and others in their rooms, begging also and beseeching you would be pleased to be here, if not all, some of you at our Trials, hoping thereby you may be the means of saving the shedding our Innocent Bloods, desiring your Prayers to the Lord in our behalf, we rest your Poor Afflicted Servants,*   John Procter, &c.

Notes: John Procter's petition follows a day after the torture of Andrew and Richard Carrier. His reference to the torture at the examination of his son, William, is intriguing in that the only extant record of a formal examination of William is on September 17. See No. 663. Either the record of an earlier examination is missing, which is probable, or Procter is referencing torture not specifically tied to a Court examination. William Procter had been in jail since May 31. See No. 226. Whether "Mather" is Cotton or Increase cannot be established conclusively, although Increase seems more likely. The other ministers are James Allen, John Bailey, Joshua Moody, and Samuel Willard.

Robert Calef. More Wonders of The Invisible World, Display'd in Five Parts. (London: Nath. Hillard, 1700), pp. 104–5.

Tuesday, July 26, 1692

434. Summons for Witness v. George Burroughs, and Officer's Return

[Hand 1] W^m & Mary by ye Grace of God of England Scotland ffrance & Ireland King defend^r of ye faith &c^a

To James Greenslit Greeting.

Wee comand you all Excuses set apart to be & personaly app^e at ye Next Court of Oyer & Terminer. held at Salem on ye first Tuesday in August Next There to Testify ye Truth on certain Indictments to be Exhibited against George Burroughs & not depart ye Court without lycense or leaue of s^d Court hereof fail not On penalty of One hundred pounds money to be leuied on your Goods Chattels &c^a Dated in Salem July 26th 1692. Step: Sewall Cler

To y^e Sheriffe of Essex.

[Reverse] [Hand 2] July 26th 1692 I haue Sumoned the within named James Greinslett according to this within Subpena to Giue in his Euidence att the time and place ⟨?⟩ith⟨?⟩ [= within] mentioned by mee Geo: Herrick Dep^t Sheriff

[Hand 1] James Greens^t Subpena

Notes: Hand 1 = Stephen Sewall; Hand 2 = George Herrick ◊ 1 wax seal.

Essex County Court Archives, vol. 2, no. 21, Massachusetts Supreme Judicial Court, Judicial Archives, on deposit James Duncan Phillips Library, Peabody Essex Museum, Salem, MA.

435. Appointment of Anthony Checkley and Payment to Stephen Sewall

[Hand 1] At a Council held at his Ex^cy's house in Boston, upon Tuesday July 26. 1692.

Present.

His Excellency Sr William Phips Kn^t &c^a
William Stoughton Esqr Lt Govr

Wait Winthrop	John Foster	John Joyliffe
Samuel Sewall Esq^rs	John Walley	Adam Winthrop Esqr
Richd Middlecott	John Richards {Esq^rs}	Joseph Lynde.
	James Russell	

Ordered: That Mr Anthony Checkley be & is hereby Appointed and Impowred to Officiate as Attourney for and on behalfe of their Maj^ties at the special Court of Oyer and Terminer.

William Phips.

Ordered: That Mr Treasurer do deliver unto Capt^in Stephen Sewall Clerke of the Special Court of Oyer and Terminer or his order, the sum of Forty pounds for the present answering of the necessary charges of the said Court.

William Phips.

July 27, 1692   *Governor's Council Executive Records (1692), vol. 2, p. 191. Massachusetts State Archives. Boston, MA. Certified copy from the original records at Her Majesty's State Paper Office, September 16, 1846, London, UK.*

Wednesday, July 27, 1692

436. Commission from William Phips to Anthony Checkley as Attorney General

[Hand 1] Sr William Phips K^{nt} Captaine Generall and Governour in Chief in and over their Maj^{ties} Province of the Massachusetts Bay in New England. To Anthony Checkley Gent. Greeting, Whereas by their Maj^{ties} Speciall Commission of Oyer and Terminer there are certain Justices Assigned to Enquire of hear & Determi⟨ne⟩ for this time, all and all manner of Felonies, Witchcrafts, Crimes and Offences how or by whomsoever done, comitted or perpetrated within the Severall Countys of Suffolke Essex or Middlesex, or Either of them Wherefore reposing speciall Trust and Confidence in your Loyalty, ffaitfulness, Learning, and Ability. These are in their Maj^{ties} Names (with the Advice and Consent of the Councill) to Authorize and Impower you the said Anthony Checkley to Appear before the said Justices, at such times and places as they shall appoint, And for and on behalfe of their s^d Maj^{ties} to implead and prosecute all Offenders Capitall or Criminall then and there to be brought upon their Tryall. And therein to do Execute and perform all and whatsoever to the Office of the Kings Attourney Generall in any wise belongeth; Taking accustomed ffees. For which doing this shall be your warrant. Given under my hand and Seal at Boston thc Twenty Seaventh day of July 1692 In the ffourth yeare of their Maj^{ties} Reigne.

William Phips

By Order of his Excellency
the Governo$^\varepsilon$ and Councill

Notes: Anthony Checkley takes over from Thomas Newton as Attorney General. The "seal" referenced in the document does not appear on this manuscript.

Judicial Volume 40 (1683–1724), p. 264. Massachusetts State Archives. Boston, MA.

Thursday, July 28, 1692

437. Warrant for the Apprehension of Mary Bridges Sr., and Officer's Return

[Hand 1] To The Sherriff of ye County of Essex or dep^t or Constable in Andouer
You are in theire Majes^{ts} names hereby required to apprehend & forthwith, or as soone as May be, bring before vs, Mary Bridges the wife of John Bridges of Andouer who stands Charged ^{in behalfe of theire Majes^{ts}} wth haueing Committed Sundry acts of Witchcraft Lately on the Body of Tymothy Swan of Andouer and Others to theire great hurt, And y^t in order to her Examination Relateing to the abouesaid premises and hereof You are not to faile Dated Salem July the 28th 1692

Barth° Gedney
John: Hathorne
Jonathan. Corwin
John Higginson
Just$^{\varepsilon s}$ peace.

[Hand 2] in obedience to this writ I haue Se{a}sed the Body of Marie Bridges wife of John Bridges and haue brought her to ~~the worshifull~~ answer ~~John hathron esq~~ at Sailom what shall be {aledged} ^{against her} this 28 of iuly 1692

By mee John Ballard constable of andouer

Notes: Hand 1 = John Hathorne

MS Ch K 1.40, vol. 2, p. 349, Rare Books & Manuscripts, Boston Public Library. Boston, MA.

438. Warrant for the Apprehension of Mary Green & Hannah Bromage, and Officer's Return

[Hand 1] [Lost]⟨e⟩r⟨iff⟩[Lost] [= sheriff] of Essex or his dep^t or [Lost]⟨s⟩tables [= constables] in Haverhill
⟨Y⟩ou are in theire Majes^{ts} names hereby Required to apprehend and forthwith or a⟨s⟩ soon as may be bring before vs. mary. Green y^e wife of Peter Green of Ha⟨ve⟩rhill Weau⟨e⟩r and [Hand 2?] Hanah [Hand 1] Bromage the wife of Edward Bromage of haverhi⟨l⟩[Lost] [= Haverhill] husbandman who both stand Charged on behalfe of theire Majes^{ts} with haueing Committed Sundry acts of Witchcraft on the Bodys [Hand 2?] ^{Timothy Swan} [Hand 1] of Mary Walcot Ann Putnam &c whereby great hurt hath benne donne them, In order to theire⟨?⟩ Examination Relateing to the aboues^d premises faile not Dated Salem July the 28th 1692

Barth° Gedney
John Hathorne
Jonathan. Corwin
John: Higginson

[Hand 3] by vertue of this ⟨w⟩arant I have Se⟨a⟩sed Hanah Br⟨u⟩mig⟨e⟩ ⟨a⟩nd mary gree⟨n⟩ [1 word illegible] pe⟨r⟩son⟨s⟩ mentione⟨d⟩ ⟨ꝑ⟩ me wi⟨l⟩li[Lost] [= William] [Lost] Cons⟨t⟩[Lost] [= Constable]

Notes: Hand 1 = John Hathorne

William L. Clements Library, University of Michigan, Ann Arbor, MI.

439. Testimony of Thomas Bradbury for Mary Bradbury

[Hand 1] July y^e 28: <u>1692</u>
Concerning my beloued wife Mary Bradbury this is that I haue to say: wee haue been maried fifty fiue yeare: and shee hath bin a loueing & faithfull wife to mee, vnto this day shee hath been wonderfull: laborious dilligent & industryous in her place & imployment, about the bringing vp o$^\varepsilon$ family (wch haue bin eleven childeren of o$^\varepsilon$ owne & fower grand=children:

shee was both prudent, & provident: of a cheerfull Spiritt liberall & charitable: Shee being now very aged & weake, & greiued vnder her affliction may not bee able to s^{p}eake much for her selfe, not being so free of Speach as some others may bee: I hope her life and conversation hath been such amongst her neighbours, as giues a better & mo^{re} reall Testimoney of her, then can bee exprest by words

own'd by mee Tho: Bradbury

[Reverse] [Hand 2] Capt Bradberys testamony of his wif

Notes: It is not clear under what circumstances Bradbury gave his testimony other than its proximity to Mary Bradbury's examination on July 26. ◊ Hand 1 = Thomas Bradbury; Hand 2 = Robert Pike

Essex County Court Archives, vol. 2, no. 73, Massachusetts Supreme Judicial Court, Judicial Archives, on deposit James Duncan Phillips Library, Peabody Essex Museum, Salem, MA.

Saturday, July 30, 1692

440. Examination of Hannah Bromage

[Hand 1] 30 July 92.
The Examination of Hannah Broomage taken before Major Gidney Esq$^{\varepsilon}$ & other their majesties justices.

Severall persones present who had not accused her being privatly desyred to look on her & take her by the hand, They did the same without receiveing any harme. But mary walcot & ann Putnam who had accused her being called, and s^{d} Broomage being requyred to look on y^{m}, She Essayeing so to doe they wer struck into fitts. & she recovered them again by her touch.
S^{d} Mary walcot & ann Putnams testimonyes wer read. Ann putnam being ~~affected~~, in a fitt. the rest of the afflicted s^{d} they saw Broomage upon her
Goody Bridges said that ^{Broomage} was in her society at Ballards, {house} telling her to her face she was there in her spirit & urged her to confess, that being the way to eternal life.
S^{d} Bridges said further that broomage hurt ballards wife by sitting on her breast. And Ann putnam being in a violent fitt, said Bridges & Lacey s^{d} they saw Broomage upon her and walcot s^{d} she saw broomage stabb Putnam wth a Spear
Said Bridges told Broomage that the devil would not Leave her untill she did confess, and therefore urged her so to doe /.
S^{d} Broomage said she had been under some deadnes wth respect to the ordinances for the matter of 6 weeks, And a Sudden suggestion came in to her heart sayeing I ~~sh(a)~~ Can help thee with strenth., To which she answered avoid Satan.
She being asked what shap the devil appeared to her, answered she beleeved the devil was in her heart And being asked severall other questiones, She returned negative answe$^{\varepsilon}$s /.

[Reverse] [Hand 2] Hannah Bromage Examination

Notes: "avoid Satan": 'go away, Satan!' (*OED* s.v. *avoid* 6). ◊ Hand 1 = William Murray; Hand 2 = Anthony Checkley

Suffolk Court Files, vol. 32, docket 2670, p. 3, Massachusetts Supreme Judicial Court, Judicial Archives, Massachusetts State Archives. Boston, MA.

441. Examination of Mary Toothaker

July 30, 1692

See also: Jan. 6, 1693.

[Hand 1] 30 July 92

The Examination and confession of widow Toothaker Taken before Majo᷎ Gidney m͏ʳ Hauthorn m͏ʳ Corwin & Cap͏ⁿ Higginson.

After many questiones propounded and negative answe᷎s return⟨e⟩d and her stricking down of severall of the afflicted persones with her looks, she was desyred to tell the truth in this matter She then said that this may last she was under great discontentednes & troubled w͏ᵗ feare about the Indians, & used often to dream of fighteing with them. Being asked what was the devils temptation under her discontentm͞t She said she would confess ⟨if⟩ she could But that there was something at her breast that hindered her. she said she had often prayed but thought she was the worse for prayeing and knows not but that the devil hes tempted her not to pray, for ~~my~~ {her} breath has been often stopt as it was ⟨?⟩ just now; Being asked ⟨i⟩f the devil did not Desier her to renounce her baptisme, she answered that she had thought, she was rather the worse for her baptisme and has wished she had not been baptised because she had not improved it as she ought to have done She saith she used to get into a corner alone and desyred to pray but her mouth would be stopt but sometymes she had been helped to say Lord be mercifull to me a sinner. Being again asked how far she had yeilded to Satan she said the devil promised her she should not be discovered and if {she} wer discovered & brought down yet she should goe home Innocent & cleare but now finds he hes deluded her Being again asked how long it is since Satan first wrought with her in this manner she said she could not well tell how long but thinks it is not two year⟨s⟩

And confesses that she went in her spirit to Timothy Swans, and did often think of him & her hands would be clinched together, And that she would grip the dishclout or any ~~thg⟨e⟩lse~~ thing else. and so think of the persone; And by this & afflicting of othe᷎s since she came down she is convinced she is a witch – she saith now, the devil appeared to her in the shape of a Tawny man and promeised to keep her from the Indians & she should have happy dayes with her sone – she was asked if she did not signe the devills book; answered he brought something which she took to be a peece of burch bark, and she made a mark with her finger by rubbing off the whit Scurff. And he promised if she would serve him she should be safe from the Indians (she was then a litle stopt again & beleeved it was the devil that did it) Being asked if the devil did not say she was to serve him Answered yes, and signed the mark upon that condition & was to praise him w͏ᵗʰ her whole heart, And it was to that appearance she prayed at all tymes for he said he was able to delyver her from the Indians And it was the feare of the Indians y͏ᵗ put her upon it

She confesses she hurt Timothy Swan and thinks she was twice at salem Village witch meeting and that goody bridges was one of her company – she said as she came along in order to examin͞an she promised herself twenty tymes by the way (but fea᷎s it was to the devil) That if she should dye upon the Gallowse yet she would not say any thing but that she was Innocent And rejoiced In the thought of it that she should goe home Innocent, – she saith that Goody Green and Goody Broomage were also her companions and that Broomage afflicted Swan by squeezeing his armes, And is afrayd that she the s͏ᵈ toothaker squeezed his throat – she said further that when Goody Bridges (who had confessed before) urged her also to confess she had then no remembrance of this but with the justices discourse & the help of god it came into her mynd

July 30, 1692

She saith she thought that that appearance was God her creator & being asked if she did not know otherwise answered The devil is so subtil that when she would confess he stops her and deluds also by scripture and being asked what scripture he made use of to her she mentioned that in the psalmes where it is said Let my enemies be confounded, And so she⟨e⟩ hes wished them all destroyed that raised such reports of her – She confesses y^t her sister was with her at all the meetings & particularly at Salem Village & there went with her Goody Bridges Goody foster Goody Green & goody Broomage – Severall afflicted persones said they saw the black man before her in the tyme of her examination And she now herself confesses she saw him upon the table before her She sayes further there was a minister a litle man whose name is Burroughs that preache⟨d⟩ at the village meeting of witches, and she heard that they used bread & wyne at those meetings And that they did talk of 305 witches in the countrey. she sayth their discourse was about the pulling down the Kingdome of christ and setting up the Kingdome of Satan, And also Knew Goody How among the rest Being asked if their was not a woman that stirred them up to afflict swan Answered yes there was a pretty elderly woman that was most busie about him and encouraged the rest to afflict him.

She thinks she set hir hand to that book at Salem Village meeting And thinks the end of all their setting their hands to that book was to come in, and afflict & set up the Devils Kingdome She being asked if her husband did not speak to his daughter to Kill one Bulton a reputed witch, Answered yes, and that they used to read many historyes, especially one book that treated of the 12 signes, from which book they could tell a great deale. – she saith she never knew her daughter to be in this condition before this summer, But that she was at Sallem village meeting once with her, she cannot tell that her daughter did then signe the book but a great many did. Being asked how many were of her Society she said Goody Broomage, foster, green, the two mary Laceyes older & younger, Richard Carryer, her sister Carryer and another aged woman.

She sayth she heard the Beating of a drum at the village meeting And think⟨s⟩ also she heard the sound of a trumpet

⟨2⟩ I underwritten being appointed by authority to take the above & within examinat⟨?⟩ in wryting Doe testify upon oath taken in court That this is a true coppy of the substance of it, to the best of my knowledge; 6^t Jan^ε in 1692/3

Wm Murray

[Hand 2] The within named Mary Toothaker was examined
by their Majesties Justices of the peace in Salem

Mary Toothaker:Examined 30 July 1692:	atest Jno Higginson Just^ε peace. owned before the Grand Jurey: 6 January 1692 atest.

Robert Payne
foreman.

acused	Goody Bridges	2 lacys
	Goody Gren	R^d Carier
	Goody Brumage	
	Goody Carier	
	Goody ffoster	
	Mr Burroughs.	
	Goody How.	
	Math. Emerson	
fflicted Tim^o Swan		

Notes: The sister referred to is Martha Carrier, the daughter, Martha Emerson. The list of names at the end recapitulates   July 30, 1692
those accused by Mary Toothaker. "Bulton" is probably "Button" as she is called in the *Andover Examinations Copy*. See
No. 425. ◊ Hand 1 = William Murray; Hand 2 = John Higginson Jr.

*Suffolk Court Files, vol. 32, docket 2713, p. 50, Massachusetts Supreme Judicial Court, Judicial Archives, Massachusetts State
Archives. Boston, MA.*

442. Examination of Mary Toothaker, Copy

[Hand 1] 30th July <u>1692</u> The Examination & Confession of Widow Toothaker Taken
Before Maj^E Gidney M^E Hathorn M^E Corwin Jno Higginson
After Many Questions propounded & Negative Answers ~~propo⟨un⟩ded~~ Return^d & her
Stricking Dwone of Seueral of ye afflicted p^{E}sons wth Her looks, She was Desired to tell the
truth in this Matter, She then S^d y^t this May last She was vnder great Discontentednes &
troubled wth fear @ y^e ~~Deuil(l)~~ Ind^s & vsed often to Dream of fighting wth y^m being asked
what was ye Diuels Temptation vnder her Discontentment She Said She would confes if She
Could But y^t their was Somthing at her breast y^t hindred her, She S^d She had often prayed
but thought She was ye worse for praying & knows not but that ye Diuel has tempted her
Not to pray for her breath was almost Stopt as it was Just Now, Being asked if ye Diuel did
not tempt her to renounce her baptizm She answered y^t She had ~~that~~ thought She was
reather ye worse for her baptizin & has wished She had not ben bapt^{E}ed because She had not
Improued it as She ought to haue done She Saith ["th" written over "d"] She used to gett
into a Corner alone & Desired to pray but her mouth was Stopt but Somtimes She has ben
helped to Say Lord be Mercyfull to me a Siner being asked again how far She had yelded to
Sattan, She S^d the Diuell Promised her She Should not be Discouered, And if She were
Discouered & brought Dwone yett She Should goe home Innocent & Clear but now finds
he has Deluded her, Bing again asked how long it is Since Satan first wrought wth her in this
Manner She S^d She could not tell how long but thinks it is not two Years & Conffessed y^t
She went In her Spirit to Tim^o Swans & did often think of him & her hands Would be
Clinched together and y^t She would grip the Dishclout or any thing Else & Soe think of
p^{E}sons And by this & afflicting of others Since She Came Dwone She is Conuinced She is a
witch – She Saith now the Diuel apeared to her in ye Shap of a Tawny Man & promised to
Keep her from ye Indians & Should haue happy Dayes wth her Son – She was asked if She
did not Signe ye Diuels booke Answ^E he brought me Something ~~like~~ ^{which She to Be a
peice} of burch bark & She made a mark wth her finger by Rubing of ye white Scruf & he
promised if She would Serue him She Should be Safe from ye Ind^E (She was then a litle
Stopt again & beleued it was ye Diuel y^t did it) being asked if ye Diuel did not Say She was to
Serue him A Yes and Signed ye Mark vpon that Condition & was to praise him wth her
whole hart & it was to y^t aperance She prayed at all tymes for he Said he was able to Deliuer
her from ye Indians. & it was y^e ^{fear of y^e} Ind^E y^t put her upon it She Conffesses She hurt
Tim^o Swan & & thinks She was ^{twice} at Salem Village Witch Metting & that Good^E
Bridges was one of her Company She S^d as She Came along in order to her Examination She
promised her Self twenty times By ye way (but feales it was to ye Diuel) that if She Should
Dye upon ye Gallows. Yett She would not Say any thing but y^t She was Innocent & rejoyced
In ^{y^e thoughts of} it that She ["She" written over "they"] Should goe home Inocent – She
Saith y^t Good^E Green & Good^E Broomage were also her Companyons & y^t broomage
afflicted Swan by Squesing his armes And is afraid that She the S^d Toothaker Squeezed his

July 30, 1692

Throate – She S^d further y^t when Good$^\varepsilon$ bridges (who Had Conffesed befor) Vrged her also to Confes She had no Remembrance of this but wth y^e Justices Discourse & y^e help of god it Came into her mind She Saith She thought y^t that apperance was god her Creator & being asked if She did not now otherwise A y^e Diuel is Soe Subtil y^t when She wo^{u}ld Confes he Stops her & Deluds also by Scripture & being asked w^t Scipture he made Vse of to her She mentioned y^t In the ~~Samle~~ Psalmes where it is Said Lett My Enimies be Confounded And So She has wished y^m all desto^{r}yed y^t raised such reports of her She Conffesses y^t her Sister was wth her at ^{all} y^e Mett$^\varepsilon$s & p$^\varepsilon$ticularly at Salem Village & their went wth her Good$^\varepsilon$ Bridges ffoster Green & Good^e Broomage – Seuerall of y^e afflicted p$^\varepsilon$sons Said thay Saw y^e black man before her In y^e time of her Examination & She Now her Self Conffeses She Saw him Vpon y^e table befor her She Says further ther was a Minister a little man Whose Name Is Burroughs y^t preached at y^e Village Metting of witches, & She He^{a}rd y^t they Vsed bread & wine at thes Metting & y^t they did talk of 305 Witches in ye Country She Saith their Discourse was about pulling Dwone ye Kingdome of Christ. & Setting Vp the Kingdome of Satan And also knew Goody How among the Rest Being asked if their was not a woeman that Stared y^m Vp to afflict Swan – A Yes their was a pretty Elderly woeman y^t was most busie about him & Encouraged ye rest to afflict him She thinks ~~She ⟨?⟩ing~~. She Sett her hand to that book at Salem Village Metting & thinks ye End of all ther Setting their hands to y^t Book was to Come In & afflict & Sett Vp ye Diuel Kingdome She being asked if her husband did not Speak to his Daughter to Kill on Button a reputted witch A Yes & y^t thay Vsed to read many ~~Histo~~ Histories Especially one book y^t treated of ye 12 Signes from wch book they could ~~Could~~ tell. a greate Deal, She Saith She Neuer New her Daughter to be in y^t Condision before this Sumer Butt y^t She was at Salem Village Metting once wth her She can not tell y^t her Daughter then Did Signe y^e book but a great many ^{did} being asked how many ware of her Society She S^d Good$^\varepsilon$ Broomage ffostter & Green the two Mary Laceys Richd Carrier her Siste Carr$^\varepsilon$ & another aged Woeman She Saith She heard y^e bettinge of a Drum at y^e Village Metting & Thinks also She heard y^e Sound of a Trumpet

Notes: From *Andover Examinations Copy*. See No. 425.

Essex Institute Collection, no. 24, 4v–5r, James Duncan Phillips Library, Peabody Essex Museum, Salem

443. Summons for Witnesses v. Martha Carrier, and Officer's Return

See also: Aug. 1, 1692.

[Hand 1] W^m & Mary by y^e Grace of God of England Scotland ffrance & Ire⟨lan⟩d King & Queen defend$^{\varepsilon s}$ of y^e faith &c^a

To y^e Constable or Constables of Andover Greeting.
Wee Comand you to Warn & giue Notice vnto. Allen Toothaker Ralph ffarnum Jun$^\varepsilon$ John ffarnum Son of Ralph ffarnum sen$^\varepsilon$ Benjamin Abbot & his wife Andrew ffoster ~~Sarah⟨?⟩~~ Phebe Chandler daughter of Wm Chandler: [Hand 2] Saml Holt sen$^\varepsilon$ Samuel Preston Jun$^\varepsilon$

[Hand 1] ~~Greeting~~ that they & Euery of them be and personaly appear at y^e Court of Oyer & Terminer to be held by adjournment on Tuesday Next at Ten of y^e Clock in y^e Morning there to testifie ^{y^e truth} to y^e best of thier knowledge on certain Indictments to be

Exhibited against Martha Carrier of Andover hereof fail not at your vtmost perill & make
return of your doings herein

Stephen Sewall Clar

Dated in Salem July 30th <u>1692</u>

[Reverse] [Hand 3] In obedenc to this writ I have timely warned the persons hose names are
herein writ⟨en⟩ and euery one of them/ this 1 day ~~of ag august 169~~ of august 1692

By mee John Ballard
constable of andouer

Notes: Hand 1 = Stephen Sewall ◊ 1 wax seal.

*Essex County Court Archives, vol. 1, no. 313, Massachusetts Supreme Judicial Court, Judicial Archives, on deposit James Duncan
Phillips Library, Peabody Essex Museum, Salem, MA.*

444. Summons for Witnesses v. Martha Carrier, and Officer's Return

See also: Aug. 1, 1692.

[Hand 1] William & Mary by ye Grace of God of England Scotland France & Ireland King
& Queen defend^ε of ye faith &^c

To ye Constable of Billrica Greeting
Wee Comand you to Warn & giue Notice vnto Capt [   ] Danforth John Rogers &

that they & Every of them be and personaly appear at ye Court of Oyer & Terminer to be
held by Adjurnment Att Salem on Tuesday Next at Ten of ye Clock in ye Morning there to
testify ye truth to ye best of thier knowledge on Certaine Indictments to be Exhibited against
Martha Carrier of Andover and hereof They nor you are to fail at your vtmost perill making
return hereof vnder your hand.
Dated in Salem July 30th 1692 & in ye fourth yeare of Our Reign

Stephen Sewall Cler

[Reverse] [Hand 2] According to this warrant I haue shew{d} ^{it} to Capt Danforth, & his
Answ^ε is, that hee can say nothing in ^{y^e} case that is worth mentioning, I haue warned
John Rogers, & he saith he will attend if his garison may guarded in his absence.
Billerica ~~A⟨?⟩gu~~ August. 1st 92.

James paterson, Const:

Notes: The first name of Captain Danforth was Jonathan, and he was the brother of Thomas Danforth, who as Deputy
Governor had presided over the examinations of April 11. That Stephen Sewall did not know the first name of Danforth's
brother perhaps gives some perspective as to how tightly knit, or not, the leaders of the colony were. ◊ Hand 1 = Stephen
Sewall ◊ 1 wax seal.

Witchcraft Papers, no. 18, Massachusetts Historical Society. Boston, MA.

August 1692

Monday, August 1, 1692

Officer's Return: Summons for Witnesses v. Martha Carrier
2nd of 2 dates. See No. 443 on July 30, 1692

Officer's Return: Summons for Witnesses v. Martha Carrier
2nd of 2 dates. See No. 444 on July 30, 1692

Tuesday, August 2, 1692

445. Warrant for the Apprehension of Mary Post, and Officer's Return
See also: Aug. 3, 1692.

[Hand 1] To the Constable of Rowley

Essex Whereas Timothy Swan of Andover, & Mary Walcutt, & Ann Puttman of Salem Village have this day appeared before me Dudley Bradstreet of Andover one of their Majestyes Justices of yᵉ Peace, for yᵉ County of Essex; and made complaint in writeing: That Mary Post of Rowley hath sorely Afflicted them the sᵈ Swan, Walcut, & Putman by witchcraft &c contrary to the peace of our Sovereigne Lord & Lady King William & Queen Mary of England: and to the statutes in that case provided: And also Sᵈ Swan haveing given bond, according to Law, of twenty pounds ~~of~~ in currant mony of New England for prosecu⟨?⟩tion of sᵈ complaint to Effect. before the Worshipˡ Bartholome[Lost] [= Bartholomew] Gedney, John Hathorn, J[Lost]th[Lost]n [= Jonathan] Corwin, & John Higginson Esqᵉs, their Majesty[Lost] [= Majesties'] Justices of yᵉ Peace at S[Lost]m [= Salem] in the County of Essex.

These therefore require you in their Majestyes names to Apprehend and Seise the body of Mary Post aforesᵈ fort{h}with, and her Safely convey to Salem, before the Sᵈ worshipfˡˡ Barthol. Gedney, John Hathorn &c Esqᵉ, there to be Examined, and proceeded with accord to Law: for which this shall be your Justification. Given under my hand and seal this 2ᵈ day of August 1692 & in the fourth year of yᵉ Reighn of our Sovereign Lord. &. Lady William and Mary King & Queen of England. Scotland &c.

Dudley Bradstreet justice of yᵉ peace

[Hand 2] [2 words overstruck] by vertue of the abouesaid warrant I haue Seized the Body of Mary Post of Rowley & brought her to Salem beffore the abouesaid Barthᵒ Gidny John Hathorne Jonᵃ Corwin &c Esqᵉs
Salem. 3: August 1692   Joseph jewett Constable of [Lost]owley. [= Rowley]

[Reverse] [Hand 3?] Mary post

2:6:92

Notes: Justice of the Peace Dudley Bradstreet handled numerous warrants in the Andover cases and followed the law in requiring the posting of bond by those making formal complaints. ◊ Hand 1 = Dudley Bradstreet ◊ 1 wax seal.

August 2, 1692

MS Ch K 1.40, vol. 2, p. 204, Rare Books & Manuscripts, Boston Public Library. Boston, MA.

446. Testimony of Mary Webber v. George Burroughs

[Hand 1] Mary Webber ^{wid} aged aboute 53 years
Testifieth and sayth y^t she liueing at Casco Bay aboute six or seauen years agoe, when George Burroughs was Minester at s^d place, and liueing a neere Neighbour to s^d Burroughs, was well aquainted with his wife wch was daufter to m^r John Ruck of Salem she hath heard her tell much of her husbands vnkindness to her and y^t she dare not wright to her father to aquaint her how it was with her, and soe desired mee to wright to her father y^t he would be pleased to send for her and told mee she had benne much affrighted, and y^t something in ye night made a noise in ye chamber where she lay as if one Went aboute ye Chamber, and she calling Vp the negro. to come to her; ye negro not Comeing sayd y^t she could not Come some thing stopt her, then her husband being called he came vp. something Jumped down from betweene ye Chimney & ye side of ye house and Run down ye staires and s^d Burroughs followed it down, and ye negro then s^d it was something like a white calfe: another tyme lyeing with her husband some thing came into ye house and stood by her bed side and breathed on her, and she being much affrighted at it, would haue awakened her husband but could not for a considerable tyme, but as soone as he did awake it went away., but this I heard her say. and know nothing of it myselfe otherwise Except by common report of others also concerning such things. Salem August. 2th 1692

mary webber

[Reverse] [Hand 2] Mary Webber ve. Burro^ε

Notes: Mary Webber's testimony was not used at the trial of Burroughs although her son's was. Her signature seems to be in the same hand as his. The court had direct testimony from Samuel Webber to use. See No. 447. ◊ Hand 1 = John Hathorne; Hand 2 = Stephen Sewall

Witchcraft Papers, no. 9, Massachusetts Historical Society. Boston, MA.

447. Testimony of Samuel Webber v. George Burroughs

See also: Aug. 5, 1692.

[Hand 1] Samuell Webber aged aboute 36 yeares Testifieth and sayth y^t aboute Seauen or Eight Yeares agoe I Liued at Casco Bay and George Burroughs was then Minester there, and haueing heard much of the great Strenth of him s^d Burroughs; he Comeing to our house wee ware in discourse aboute the Same and he then told mee y^t he had put his fingers into the Bung of a Barrell of Malasses and lifted it vp, and carryed it Round him and sett it downe againe. Salem August 2^d 1692.

Samuell Webber
Jurat in Curia

[Reverse] [Hand 2] Sam. Webber Cont: Burroughs

August 2, 1692

Notes: Although used at the trial of Burroughs, this testimony was not sworn to the grand jury, which certainly met on August 3, but may also have also met on August 2. ◊ Used at trial. ◊ Hand 1 = John Hathorne; Hand 2 = Stephen Sewall

Essex County Court Archives, vol. 2, no. 22, Massachusetts Supreme Judicial Court, Judicial Archives, on deposit James Duncan Phillips Library, Peabody Essex Museum, Salem, MA.

448. Deposition of John Rogers v. Martha Carrier

[Hand 1] The deposition of John Rogger of Billreca aged fifty yeares or Thereabouts saith

That about seuen yeares since Martha Carrier being a Nigh Neigbour vnto this depon^t and there hapening some difference betwixt vs she gaue forth seuerall threatninge words as she often vsed to doe and in a short time after this deponent had two large lusty sowes wch frequented home daily that were lost & this deponent found one of them dead Nigh ye s^d Carriers house wth both Eares cut of & ye other ^{sow} I Neuer heard of to this day: & ye same summer to ye best of my rembrance I had a Cow wch vsed to giue a good Mess of ^{milke} twice a day & of a sudden she would giue little or None Euery Morning though a Nights she gaue as formerly and this Continued about ye space of a month in wch time I had three Meals milke ⟨not⟩ on three seuerall Mornings not successiuely: and no more though One Night three of vs Watched ye Cow all night ~~one night~~ – yet I could haue no milke in ye morning of her & about ye monthes End she gaue milke as formerly she vsed, by all wch I did in my Conscience beleiue then in ye day of it & haue so done Euer since & doe yet beleiue that Martha Carrier was ye occasion of those Ill accidents. by Meanes of Witchcraft {she} being a very Malicious Woman & further saith Not

marke of

John ʃ Rogger

Inq^E Sam Holt ^{Andouer} about M.C.
Capt Danforth Billreca

[Reverse] Court O. & Ter by Adjt
Augt 2. 92

Jno Rogger of Billrica ver: Marth: Carrier

[Hand 2] Carrier

Notes: The deposition was prepared for the Court, but it is not clear as to whether it was sworn to at the trial. ◊ Possibly used at trial. ◊ Hand 1 = Stephen Sewall

Essex County Court Archives, vol. 1, no. 315, Massachusetts Supreme Judicial Court, Judicial Archives, on deposit James Duncan Phillips Library, Peabody Essex Museum, Salem, MA.

449. Testimony of William Beale v. Philip English

See also: Jan. 12, 1693.

[Hand 1] William Beale of Marbllee Head aged upward of sixty yeares testifieth & sayeth that last March past was twelue moe⟨n⟩th towards the latter end of the moenth then my self beeinge in the house of George Bonfeilds of Marbllee Head whither I repaired that I mighte haue helpe to nurse or looke after mee because of A very greate & wracking paine had seized uppon my body & ye distemper of the small pox then beeing in my house & my son James at the same time then in my house lying sick then towards the latter end of that moenth Aforesayed in that house as as I lay in my bed in y^e morneinge presently after it was faiere lighte abroade in the roome where I lay in my bed which was layed low & neire unto the fire towards the Norward parte of the roome; I beeing broade Awake I then saw up on the the south iaume [= jamb] of that chimny A darke shade wch couered the iaume of that chimney aforesayed from y^e under floore to y^e upper fIloore & alsoe A darness more then it was beefore in y^e southerne part of the house & also⟨e⟩ in the middllee of the darknes in the shade upon the iaume of the chimny aforesayed I beeheld somthinge of the forme or shape of A man I tooke most notice of his legs because they weere of A very greate statute [= stature] or bigness I wondred at the sighte & therefore I turned my head as I lay in my bed & cast my eyes towards the south side of the house to see if the sun weere risen or whethe⟨r⟩ there weere any person or anythinge in the house wch by y^e r̶e̶⟨?⟩ help of y^e sun mi⟨g⟩[Lost] [= might] cause such ["u" written over "h"] A shade or shape but I saw non nor any lighte of y^e sun in that room then; & then turned my head upon the pillow where it was before I saw in y^e darkness aforesayed the plaine shape or els the person of phillip English of Salem the wch reports say married with william hollingworths daughter of Salem ackcordinge to my best iudgment knoledg & understandeinge of him as I had formerly knoledg & ackquaintance with him; my coniecktures of him & these passages aforesayed were as followeth what is this mans buisness heere now I remember not that euer I bought or sould with him either more or less or wch way came hee hither so soone this morneinge by land or by water or hath hee been at marbllee Head all nighte; & then laboreing to correckt my [Lost] not to thinke that hee was A wich; & flyinge to Our ["O" written over "to"] omnipotent Jehouah for his blessing & protecktion by secret eiaculations; instantly the roome aforesayed became cleare & ye shape shade or person vanished, & this was abou⟨t⟩ the time that newes was brought to mee in ye morneinge that my son James was very like to recouer of the small pox wch I left at home Sick; & ye same day in ye aftornoone came news that hee was suddenly strooke with A paine on his side & did not expeckt to liue three houres & ackcording to my iudgment before three houres weere ended newes came that hee was departed this life at wch docktor Jackson wch was his docktor & william dagget wch was his nurse both of marblle he[Lost] [= Head] told mee y^t they admired & wondred, & it was not many moenths before that my son George Beale departed this life in y^e same house & complained of A stoping in his throate after he was Recouered of the small pox hee
^{deceased} ianuary y^e 23 before my [Lost] [*SWP* = son] James Beale aforesayede
Marbllee head Agust y^e 2Cond [= second]

16:92

Attested to this truth by mee William Beale

far this deponent testifieth that in y^e springe of y^e yeare before th[Lost] [= the] new england for⟨e⟩ces went for cannady; phillip english aforesayed came i⟨nt⟩o A neighbors house where this deponent then was present & then in A fauneing ⟨&⟩ flattering manner sayed to mee; you are him wch can giue mee A good euidenc⟨e⟩ in shewing mee the bounds of my lande; this deponent replyed, & sayed I know not of any you haue; phillip english replyed yes you doe & if you will Ile pa[Lost] [= pay] you well I haue a peice of eighte in my pocket for you & named A peice of land by A certaine distance from my house wch I think m^ε Richard Reede of marblle was then & is now in possession of it; this deponent replyed, doe not tell mee of your peice of eight for if I bee called I must giue euidence again⟨s⟩[Lost] [= against] you & told him what I must ^{say} at wch hee seemed to bee moued & told mee y^t I lyed. with more discourse aboute & ["&" written over "I"] so then wee departed; thene the next fa[Lost] [= fall?] ensuing wch was about y^e time that the forces began to com from Cannady I then haueinge heard that phillip english aforesayed had arrested m^ε Reade aforesayed aboute the land aforesayed I then as I thought it my duty in concience ackquainted m^ε Reeds son wit[Lost] [= with] what I could say concerninge the titllee of y^e lande aforesayed & withall told him of another witness as namely Thomas ffarrar {sen'^ε} of Linn; then afterward uppon ~~re~~ their request I rode to Lin & at Lin Mill there I found Thomas ffarar Aforesayed & as wee rode alonge Lin Commons; then beetwixt the reuerende m^ε Sheapards house & m^ε Leytons ^{then beeinge in discours aboute the titllee of y^e lande aforesayed} my nose gushed out bleedeinge in A most extraordinary manner so y^t I bllodyed A hankershiff of an considerablle biggnes & allsoe ran downe uppon my cloaths & uppon my horse mane; I ~~lighed~~ lighted of my ^{hors} thinking the iodginge [= jogging?] of my horse mighte cause it but it kept on Allthough not alltoger [= altogether] so bad till I came to m^ε Reades at marbllee head & ~~so~~ it hath ^{blead} not ~~bled~~ as I can Remember neuer since I was a boy; exept about that time nor since that time exept by ackcident that it was hurt thiese things that are set downe ^{last} were before the former euidence;

William Beale

[Hand 2] owned the Abov written before the Grand iury
vpon the Oath ^{hee} had taken in Court Jēn^ε [= January] 12th 1692
Robert: Payne fforeman
[Hand 3] Beale ag^t Phillip English

Notes: The context of this unsworn testimony on August 2, 1692 is unknown. Philip English had already fled, and no grand jury met on his case until 1693. See No. 790 & No. 791. ◊ "peice of eighte": 'spanish dollar or piastre' (*OED* s.v. *eight*). "eiaculations": 'prayers' (*OED* s.v. *ejaculation* 4b).

Thomas Madigan Collection, Manuscript & Archives, New York Public Library. New York, NY.

Wednesday, August 3, 1692

Grand Juries of George Burroughs & Mary Esty

Trial of Martha Carrier

Officer's Return: Warrant for the Apprehension of Mary Post
2nd of 2 dates. See No. 445 on Aug. 2, 1692

450. Complaint of Robert Swan & John Swan v. Mary Clark

August 3, 1692

[Hand 1] The Complaint of Roburt Swane and John Swane of Andevor against mary Clarke ~~of Haverill~~ the wife of Edward Clarke of Haverill: In behalf of Their Majesties: for themselves and severall of their neighbors: for High suspition of sundry acts of wicthcraft by hir ^{latly} commited on the bodys of Timothy Swwane of Andevor and mary walcott and Ann putnam of Salem village wherby much hurt hath ben don the affore said affleted parsons and theirfore they Carue [= crave] justis

Robert Swan

[Hand 2] This Complaint was brought to me (by Robert Swan of Andou$^\epsilon$) the 3^d day of August Anno Domini 1692. & bond giuen for y^e prosecution thereof before, y^e Worship^l justices of peace att Salem: upon which I gaue, a writt of Apprehension:

Dudley Bradstreet jus^{ts} peace

Notes: Hand 1 = Thomas Putnam; Hand 2 = Dudley Bradstreet

MS Ch K 1.40, vol. 2, p. 156, Rare Books & Manuscripts, Boston Public Library. Boston, MA.

451. Warrant for the Apprehension of Mary Clark, and Officer's Return

[Hand 1] Essex   To y^e Constable of Hauerhill:
This day Complaint being made to me y^e subscriber, by Robert Swan of Andou$^\epsilon$ in y^e County of Essex, Against Mary Clark of Hauerhill in y^e County afores^d, (~~that~~ the wife of Edward Clerk,) that she is Highly suspected to be guilty of seuerall acts of witchcraft & more lately some comitted on y^e bodys of Timothy Swan of Andou$^\epsilon$ & Mary Wallcutt & Anne Putman of Salem Village in y^e County afores^d Contrary to y^e peace of o$^\epsilon$ Souereigne Lord & Lady William & Mary King & Queen of England Scotland &c: & to y^e statutes in that Case prouided, & s^d Robert Swan hauing giuen bond according to Law, to prosecute s^d Complaint (as he desires) before y^e Worship^{ll} Bartholmew Gedney John Hathorne: Johnathan Corwin & John Higginson Esqs: their Majests: Justices of ye peace in Salem ⟨?⟩&c

These therefore require you, upon sight hereof, to apprehend & seise y^e body of s^d Mary Clerk, & ~~here~~ her forthwith safely Conuey to Salem, before y^e abouesd Justices of y^e peace there/: there to be examined, & proceeded with according to Law, for which this shall be yo$^\epsilon$ warrant

Giuen und$^\epsilon$ my hand & seal this 3^d day of August Anno Domini 1692: & in y^e 4th year of their Majes^{ts} reigne &c:

Dudley Bradstreet justice of Peace

[Hand 2] By Vertue of this Warrant I have Seised the Body of Mary Clark and Brought her down   ℈ mee Wm Sterling Constable of haveril

[Reverse] [Hand 3] Mary Clarke of Hauerhill
4:6.-92

Notes: Hand 1 = Dudley Bradstreet ◊ 1 wax seal.

MS Ch K 1.40, vol. 2, p. 244, Rare Books & Manuscripts, Boston Public Library. Boston, MA.

August 3, 1692

452. Indictment No. 1 of George Burroughs, for Afflicting Mary Walcott†
See also: Aug. 5, 1692.

[Hand 1] Anno Regis et Reginæ Willm et
Mariæ nunc Angliæ &c Quarto
Essex ss The Juroε for our Sovereigne Lord and Lady the King and Queen pεsents That
[Hand 2] **George Burroughs** ~~of late of ffalmouth in yᵉ province of yᵉ Massachᵗˢ Bay in New
England. Clark** [Hand 1] the [Hand 2] **Ninth** [Hand 1] Day of [Hand 2] **May.** [Hand 1] in
the fourth Year of the Reigne of Our Sovereigne Lord and Lady William and Mary by the
Grace of God of England Scottland france and Ireland King and Queen Defenders of the
faith &c and Divers other Dayes and times, as well before, as after, Certaine Detestable Arts
called Witchcrafts, and Sorceries, Wickedly, and ffelloniously, hath used Practised. &.
Exercised at and within. the Towneship of [Hand 2] **Salem** [Hand 1] in the County of Essex
aforesaid in vpon and agᵗ one [Hand 2] **Mary Walcott of Salem Villiage in yᵉ County of
Essex Singlewoman** [Hand 1] by which said wicked Arts the said [Hand 2] **Mary Walcott**
[Hand 1] the [Hand 2] **Ninth** [Hand 1] Day of [Hand 2] **May** [Hand 1] in the forth Year
abovesᵈ and Divers other Dayes and times. as well before as after was and is Tortured
afflicted Pined Consumed wasted and Tormented. agᵗ the Peace of our Sovereigne Lord and
Lady the King and Queen and agᵗ the fforme of the Statute in that case made and Provided:
[Hand 2] Wittnesses
Mary Walcott
Sarah Vibber Jurat
Mercy Lewis
Ann Putman
Eliz. Hubbard

[Reverse] Geor. Burroughs ~~Case~~ Nᵒ (1)
[Hand 3] billa uera

Notes: Hand 2 = Stephen Sewall

Witchcraft Papers, no. 4, Massachusetts Historical Society. Boston, MA.

453. Indictment No. 2 of George Burroughs, for Afflicting Mercy Lewis†
See also: Aug. 5, 1692.

[Hand 1] Anno Regis et Reginæ Willm et
Mariæ nunc: Angliæ &c Quarto
Essex ss The Juroε for our Sovereigne Lord and Lady the King and Queen pεsents That
[Hand 2] **George Burroughs late of falmouth in yᵉ province of yᵉ Massachusets Bay in New
England{Clarke}** [Hand 1] the [Hand 2] ~~Second~~ ^{ninth} [Hand 1] Day of [Hand 2] **May**
[Hand 1] in the forth Year of the Reigne of our Sovereigne Lord and Lady William and
Mary by the Grace of God of England Scottland ffrance and Ireland King and Queen
Defenders of the ffaith &c and Divers other Dayes and times, as well before as after certaine
Detestable Arts called Witchcrafts and Sorceries. Wickedly and ffelloniously, hath vsed
Practised and Excercised at and within the Towneship of [Hand 2] **Salem** [Hand 1] in the

County of Essex afores̄ᵈ in. vpon. and agᵗ one [Hand 2] **Marcy Lewis. of Salem Villiage in yᵉ County of Essex in New England** [Hand 1] by which wicked Arts the said [Hand 2] **Marcy Lewis** [Hand 1] the [Hand 2] **Ninth** [Hand 1] Day of [Hand 2] **May** [Hand 1] in the fourth Year afores̄ᵈ and Divers other Dayes and times as well before as after was and is Tortured Afflicted Pined Consumed Wasted and Tormented: agᵗ the Peace of our Souereigne Lord and Lady the King. and Queen, and agᵗ the forme of the Statute in that case made and Prouided./.
[Hand 2] Witnesses.
Marcy Lewis
Mary Walcott.
El. Hubbard
Ann Putman

[Reverse] George Burroughs Nᵒ (2)
George Burroughs
[Hand 3] billa uera

Notes: Hand 2 = Stephen Sewall

Witchcraft Papers, no. 5, Massachusetts Historical Society. Boston, MA.

454. Indictment No. 3 of George Burroughs, for Afflicting Elizabeth Hubbard†

See also: Aug. 5, 1692.

[Hand 1] Anno Regis et Reginæ Willm̄ et
Mariæ nunc Angliæ &ᶜ Quarto
Essex ss The Juroᵋ for our Sovereigne Lord and Lady the King and Queen pᵋsents That [Hand 2] **George Burroughs. Late of Falmouth** wᵗʰⁱⁿ yᵉ **province of yᵉ Mattathusets Bay in New England Clerke** [Hand 1] the ~~Day~~ [Hand 2] **Ninth** [Hand 1] Day of [Hand 2] **May** [Hand 1] in the [Hand 2] **fourth** [Hand 1] Year of the Reigne of our Sovereigne Lord and Lady William and Mary by the Grace of God of England Scottland ffrance and Ireland King and Queen Defenders of the ffaith &ᶜ and Diver [= diverse] other Dayes and times as Well before as after, certaine Detestable Arts called Wicthcraft & Sorceries Wickedly and ffelloniously hath vsed Practiced & Exercised at and within the Township of [Hand 2] **Salem** [Hand 1] in the County of Essex aforesaid, in vpon & agᵗ one [Hand 2] **Elizabeth Hubbard of Salem in yᵉ County of Essex Singlewoman** [Hand 1] by which said Wicked Arts the said [Hand 2] **Elizabeth Hubbard** [Hand 1] the [Hand 2] **Ninth** [Hand 1] Day of [Hand 2] **May** [Hand 1] in the [Hand 2] **fourth** [Hand 1] Year abovēs̄ᵈ and Divers other Dayes and Times. as well before as after. was. and is Tortured afflicted Pined Consumed wasted and Tormented. also for Sundrey other Acts of Witchcrafts by said [Hand 2] **George Burroughs.** [Hand 1] Committed and done agᵗ the Peace of our Sovereigne Lord & Lady the King & Queen their Crowne and Dignity and agᵗ the fforme of the Statute in that case made & Provided:
[Hand 2] Witnesses.
Elizabeth Hubbard

August 3, 1692

Mary Wolcott
Ann Putman

[Reverse] Nº 3) ve. Gea. Burroughs
[Hand 3] billa uera

Notes: Hand 2 = Stephen Sewall

Witchcraft Papers, no. 3, Massachusetts Historical Society. Boston, MA.

455. Indictment No. 4 of George Burroughs, for Afflicting Ann Putnam Jr.†
See also: Aug. 5, 1692.

[Hand 1] Anno Regis et Reginæ Willm̄ et
Mariæ nunc: Angliæ &c Quarto
Essex. ss: The Jūroᵉ for our Sovereigne Lord and Lady the King & Queen pᵉsents That
[Hand 2] **George Burroughs Late of ffalmouth within yᵉ Province of yᵉ Mattathusets Bay in New England Clarke** [Hand 1] the [Hand 2] **Ninth** [Hand 1] Day of [Hand 2] **May** [Hand 1] in the [Hand 2] **fourth** [Hand 1] Year of the Reigne of our Sovereigne Lord & Lady William and Mary by the Grace of God of England Scottland ffrance and Ireland King and Queen Defendᵉ of the ffaith &ᶜ and Diver [= diverse] other Dayes and times as well before as After certaine Detestable Artes called Witchcrafts & Sorceries: Wickedly and ffelloniously hath vsed Practised & Exercised at and within the Towne of [Hand 2] **Salem** [Hand 1] in the County afor̄esᵈ in upon and agᵗ one: [Hand 2] **Ann Putman of Salem Villiage Singlewoman** [Hand 1] by which said wicked arts the said [Hand 2] **Ann Putman** [Hand 1] the ~~Da~~ [Hand 2] **Ninth** [Hand 1] Day of [Hand 2] **May** [Hand 1] in the [Hand 2] **fourth** [Hand 1] Year abovesaid and Divers other Dayes and times as well before as after. was and is Tortured Afflicted Pined Consumed Wasted and Tormented also for Sundery other Acts of Witchcrafts by said [Hand 2] **George Burroughs.** [Hand 1] Committed and Done agᵗ the Peace of our Sovereigne Lord and Lady the King and Queen their Crowne & Dignity and agᵗ the fform of the Statute in tha⟨t⟩ case made and Provided:
[Hand 2] Witnesses.
Ann Putman
Mary Wolcott
Elizabeth Hubbard
Mary Warren

[Reverse] Geo. Burroughs
[Hand 3] billa [Lost] [= vera]

Notes: Hand 2 = Stephen Sewall

Essex Institute Collection, no. 3, James Duncan Phillips Library, Peabody Essex Museum, Salem, MA.

Sworn Before the Grand Jury: Deposition of Sarah Bibber v. George Burroughs
2ⁿᵈ of 3 dates. See No. 121 on May 9, 1692

456. Fragment of a Statement of Richard Carrier, Mary Lacey Sr., & Mary Lacey Jr. v. George Burroughs

Richard Carrier affirmed to the jury that he saw Mr. George Burroughs at the witch meeting at the village and saw him administer the sacrament. Mary Lacey, Senr. and her daughter Mary affirmed the Mr. George Burroughs was at the witch meetings and witch sacraments, and that she knows Mr. Burroughs to be of the company of witches. Aug. 3, 1692.

Notes: Since this is taken from a printed extract it is not possible to determine whether this was subsequently used at the trial of Burroughs. It possibly was, but no clear evidence supports this.

Thomas Hutchinson, The History of the Province of Massachusetts-Bay, from the Charter of King William and Queen Mary, in 1691, Until the Year 1750, vol. 2, ed. Lawrence Shaw Mayo. (Cambridge, MA: Harvard University Press, 1936). p. 29 & p. 42n.

Sworn Before the Grand Jury: Statement of Elizabeth Hubbard v. George Burroughs
2nd of 3 dates. See No. 122 on May 9, 1692

Sworn Before the Grand Jury: Statement of Elizer Keyser v. George Burroughs
2nd of 3 dates. See No. 123 on May 9, 1692

Sworn Before the Grand Jury: Deposition of Mercy Lewis v. George Burroughs, and Statement of Thomas Putnam & Edward Putnam v. George Burroughs
2nd of 3 dates. See No. 124 on May 9, 1692

457. Deposition of Ann Putnam Jr. v. George Burroughs, and Statement of Thomas Putnam, Peter Prescott, Robert Morey, & Ezekiel Cheever v. George Burroughs
See also: Aug. 5, 1692.

[Hand 1] The Deposition of Ann putnam: who testifieth and saith that on 20th of April 1692: at euening she saw the Apperishtion of a Minister at which she was greviouly affritted ["it" written over "gh"] and cried out oh dreadfull: dreadfull here is a minister com: what are Ministers wicthes to: whence com you and what is your name for I will complaine of: you tho you be ~~a mi~~ A minister: if you be a wizzard: and Immediatly I was tortored by him being Racked and allmost choaked by him: and he tempted ^{me} to write in his book which I Refused with loud outcries and said I would not writ in his book tho he tore me al to peaces but tould him that it was a dreadfull thing: that he which was a Minister that should teach children to feare God should com to perswad poor creatures to giue their souls to the⟨ɟ⟩ diuill: oh dreadfull dreadffull tell me your name yᵗ I may know who you are: then againe he tortored me & urged me to writ in his book: which I Refused: and then presently he tould me that his name was George Burroughs and that he had had three wives: and that he had bewicthed the Two first of them to death: and that he kiled Mⁱˢᵗ Lawson because she was so unwilling to goe from the village and also killed Mr Lawsons child because he went to the eastward with Sir Edmon and preached soe: to the souldiers and that he had bewicthed a grate many souldiers to death at the eastward when Sir Edmon was their. and that he had {made} ^{Abigail Hobbs a wicth and:} seuerall wicthes ^{more:} and he has continewed euer sence: by times tempting me to write in his book and greviouly tortoring me by beating pinching and almost choaking me seuerall times a day and he also tould me that he was aboue a wicth for he was a cunjurer

[Hand 2] Jurat in Curia

[Hand 1] wee whose names are under writen being present with Ann putnam att the time aboue mentioned hard hir declare what is aboue writen what she said she saw and hard from the Apperishtion of Mr. George Burroughs: and allso beheld hir tortors: and pereeiceiued hir hellish temtations by hir loud outcries I will not I will not writ tho you torment me al days of my life: and being conversant with hir euer sence haue ~~every day~~ seen hir tortored and complaining that Mr. Burroughs hirt hir. and tempts hir to writ in his Book

Thomas putnam
peter prescott
Roburt Morrell

[Hand 3] Ann Puttnam declared: her above written evidence: to be ye truth: before ye Jury of inquest: Aug^st :3: 92: upon her oath

[Hand 2] Ezekiel Cheuer made Oath to y^e latter part of this paper

Jurat in Curia

[Reverse] [Hand 4] Ann putnam ag^st Burroughs

Notes: The "Sir Edmon" is Sir Edmund Andros. The "signatures" of Prescott and Morrell are written by Thomas Putnam, whose own signature is authentic. ◊ Used at trial. ◊ Hand 1 = Thomas Putnam; Hand 2 = Stephen Sewall; Hand 3 = Simon Willard

Essex County Court Archives, vol. 2, no. 24, Massachusetts Supreme Judicial Court, Judicial Archives, on deposit James Duncan Phillips Library, Peabody Essex Museum, Salem, MA.

Sworn Before the Grand Jury: Deposition of Ann Putnam Jr. v. George Burroughs, and Statement of Edward Putnam & Thomas Putnam v. George Burroughs

2nd of 3 dates. See No. 125 on May 9, 1692

Sworn Before the Grand Jury: Deposition of Mary Walcott v. George Burroughs

2nd of 3 dates. See No. 129 on May 9, 1692

458. Testimony of Mary Warren v. George Burroughs, John Alden, Elizabeth Cary, & Ann Pudeator

[Hand 1] againe
The Testimone of Mary Warren aged twenty yeares or thereaboutes Testefeyeth and Saith that Sometime in July Last m^e Burrougs pinched mee uery much and choaked [Hand 2] me almost to death: and I saw and hard him sound a Trumpitt and Immediatly I saw seuerall com to him as namely capt Allding Mis Cary ⟨A⟩nd gooddy pudeater and seuerall othrs and they urged me to goe along with them to their sacrementall meeting. and mr Burroughs brought to: me bread to eat and wine to drink which I Refuseing he did most greviously torment me urging me vehemently to writ in his book: also I haue seen mr George Burroughs

or his Apperance most greviously tormenting mary walcott and Ann putnam and I verily beleue in my heart that Mr. Geooge Burroughs is a dreadfull wizzard and that he has seuerall times tormented me and the affore said parsons by his acts of wicthcr⟨a⟩[Lost] [= witchcraft] August 3, 1692

[Hand 3] Mary Warrin declared: upon: her oath; to y^{e} Jury of inquest that y^{e} above written evidence: is y^{e} truth. Augst 3: 1692

[Reverse] [Hand 4] Mary Warren
[Hand 5] Deposition

Notes: This testimony was not used at the trial of Burroughs, perhaps because of the naming of three other people. The circumstances under which Thomas Putnam continued recording his document after the brief beginning by George Herrick remain undetermined. However, the document helps highlight Putnam's continuing activity and influence. ◊ Hand 1 = George Herrick; Hand 2 = Thomas Putnam; Hand 3 = Simon Willard; Hand 4 = Stephen Sewall

Witchcraft Papers, no. 8, Massachusetts Historical Society. Boston, MA.

Sworn Before the Grand Jury: Depositions of Simon Willard v. George Burroughs; Testimony of William Wormall v. George Burroughs
2nd of 3 dates. See No. 130 on May 9, 1692

459. Indictment No. 1 of Mary Esty, for Afflicting Mercy Lewis†

See also: Sept. 9, 1692.

[Hand 1]	Anno [Hand 1] ^{Regni} [Hand 2] Regis et Reginæ
Prouince of ye Massachusetts	[Hand 1] Gullielmi ["Gullielmi" written over "Willim"]
Bay in New England [Hand 2]	[Hand 2] et Mariæ nunc Angliæ &^{c} Quarto: [Hand 1]
Essex ss	Anoqȝ Dom 1692

[Hand 2] The Jūro^{ε} for our Sovereigne Lord & L⟨a⟩dy the King and Queen p^{ε}sents That [Hand 3] **Mary Easty wife of Isaack Easty of Topsfield husbandman⟨~~in~~⟩ on the twenty{third}** ⟨~~?~~⟩ [Hand 2] Day of [Hand 3] **May** [Hand 2] in the [Hand 3] **fourth** [Hand 2] year of the Reigne of our Sovereigne Lord and Lady William and Mary by the Grace of God of England Scottland ffr⟨a⟩nce and Ireland King and Queen Defenders of the ffaith &^{c} and Divers other Dayes and times as well before as After certaine Detestable arts called Witchcrafts and Sorceries Wickedly and ffelloniously hath vsed Practised and Exercised at and within the Towneship of [Hand 3] **Salem** [Hand 2] in the County of Essex aforesaid in vpon and against one [Hand 3] **Marcy Lewis of Salem Villiage Singlewoman** [Hand 2] by which said wicked Arts the said [Hand 3] **Marcy Lewis** [Hand 2] the ~~Day~~ [Hand 3] **Twenty third** [Hand 2] Day of [Hand 3] **May** [Hand 2] in the Year abovesaid and Divers other Dayes and times as well before as after, was and is Tortured Afflicted Pined Consumed wasted & Tormented. ag^{t} the Peace of our Sovereigne Lord & Lady the King and Queen and ag^{t} the form of the statute in that case made and Provided
[Hand 3] Witnesses.
Marcy Lewis Jurat
Ann Putman Jurat
Eliz. Hubbard Jurat
Mary Wolcott Jurat

August 3, 1692

[Reverse] [Hand 1] Indictm[t] [Hand 3] Mary Easty [Hand 1] for bewitching Mary Lewiss
[Hand 3] N° (1)
[Hand 4] Billa Vera
[Hand 3] N° 1
[Hand 5?] Ponet Se

Notes: Hand 1 = Anthony Checkley; Hand 3 = Stephen Sewall

Essex County Court Archives, vol. 1, no. 278, Massachusetts Supreme Judicial Court, Judicial Archives, on deposit James Duncan Phillips Library, Peabody Essex Museum, Salem, MA.

460. Indictment No. 2 of Mary Esty, for Afflicting Elizabeth Hubbard†

See also: Sept. 9, 1692.

[Hand 1]   Anno [Hand 1] ^{Regni} [Hand 2] Regis et Reginæ
Province of the Massathusetts   [Hand 1] Gullielmi ["Gullielmi" written over "Willim"]
Bay in New England [Hand 2]   [Hand 2] et Mariæ nunc Angliæ &[c] Quarto: [Hand 1]
Essex ss   Anoq[z] Dom 1692

The Jūro[ε] for our Sovereigne Lord and Lady the King and Queen p[ε]sents That: [Hand 3]
Mary Easty wife of Isaack Easty of Topsfeild husbandman [Hand 2] the [Hand 3] **twenty third** [Hand 2] Day of [Hand 3] **May** [Hand 2] in the [Hand 3] **fourth** [Hand 2] Year of the Reigne of our Sovereigne Lord and Lady William & Mary by the Grace of God of England Scottland ffrance & Ireland King and Queen Defenders of the ffaith &[c] and Divers other Dayes and times as well before as after certaine Detestable Arts called Witchcrafts & Sorceries Wickedly and ffelloniously hath vsed Practised and Exercised at and within the Towneship of [Hand 3] **Salem** [Hand 2] in the County of Essex afore̅s[d] in upon and ag[t] one [Hand 3] **Elizabeth Hubbard of Salem Singlewomen** [Hand 2] by which said Wicked Arts the said [Hand 3] **Elizabeth Hubbard** [Hand 2] the [Hand 3] **twenty third** [Hand 2] Day of [Hand 3] **May** [Hand 2] in the [Hand 3] **fourth** [Hand 2] Year abou̅es[d] and Divers other Dayes and times as well before. as after was, and is, Tortured Afflicted Pined Consumed wasted and Tormented ag[t] the Peace of our Sovereigne Lord and Lady the King and Queen and ag[t] the fform of the Statute in that case made and Provided./.
[Hand 3] Witnesses
Eliz: Hubbard Jurat
Marcy Lewis Jurat
Ann Putman Jurat

[Reverse] Mary Easty [Hand 1] Indictm[t] for bewitching Eliz Hobard
[Hand 3] N° (2)
[Hand 4] Billa: Vera
[Hand 5?] Ponet Se

Notes: Hand 1 = Anthony Checkley; Hand 3 = Stephen Sewall

Essex County Court Archives, vol. 1, no. 277, Massachusetts Supreme Judicial Court, Judicial Archives, on deposit James Duncan Phillips Library, Peabody Essex Museum, Salem, MA.

461. Statement of Sarah Bibber v. Mary Esty

August 3, 1692

[Hand 1] Sarah: Viber: afirmed upon her oath: that she saw: Mary: ye wife of Isaac Esty: ~~hurt~~ {upon}: Jno Nortons: ~~by~~ bed: when s^d Norton: was: ill: and s^d goody Esty: flew out upon her: & afflicted her: s^d Vibber; and s^d Vibber affirmed: that since ye time of the⟨?⟩ last: examination of s^d Esty: s^d Esty: has hurt & afflicted Mercy Lewis: and Mary Walcot & Ann: Putman: she or her ~~apperation~~ Apperition: & she s^d Esty has some times: hurt & afflicted her: s^d Vibber also: since s^d Esty. her last examination: also: s^d Vibber: ~~has~~ s^d that: s^d Esty or her apperition has Afflicted: Eliz: Hubbard: this s^d Vibber owned: to be: y^e truth: before y^e Jury of inquest: Aug^st: 3: 1692

[Reverse] [Hand 2] Sara Wiber
[Hand 3] Mary Eastey

Notes: Hand 1 = Simon Willard

Essex County Court Archives, vol. 1, no. 282, Massachusetts Supreme Judicial Court, Judicial Archives, on deposit James Duncan Phillips Library, Peabody Essex Museum, Salem, MA.

462. Statement of Mary Warren v. Mary Esty

[Hand 1] Mary: Warin: affirmd: before: the ~~grand~~ Jury: of Inquest: that: Goodwife Esty of Topsfeild: has: afflicted her: she or: her Apperition: And that s^d Esty: hath afflicted Marcy Lewis: Elizabeth: Hubbard: & Mary Walcot and Ann Putnam: upon: y^e oath: y^t she has: taken:

Aug^st :3: 1692

Notes: Hand 1 = Simon Willard

Essex County Court Archives, vol. 1, no. 283, Massachusetts Supreme Judicial Court, Judicial Archives, on deposit James Duncan Phillips Library, Peabody Essex Museum, Salem, MA.

Billa Vera: Indictment No. 1 of Martha Carrier, for Afflicting Mary Walcott†
2nd of 2 dates. See No. 397 on July 1, 1692

Billa Vera: Indictment No. 2 of Martha Carrier, for Afflicting Elizabeth Hubbard†
2nd of 2 dates. See No. 398 on July 1, 1692

463. Testimony of Benjamin Abbott and Deposition of Sarah Abbott v. Martha Carrier

[Hand 1] The teastymony of Beniamin Abbutt aged about 31 years Saith: last march was twelfe months: then haueing Some land granted to mee by the Touwne of Andouer. Near to goodman Carriers his land, & when this land Came to be laied out goodwiffe Carrier was very Angery, & said that she would stick as Closs to Beniamin Abbut as the bark stooke to the Tree. & that I ["I" written over "he"] should Repent of it afore seauen years Came to an

August 3, 1692

E{a}nd & that doctor prescott Could Neuer Cure ~~hime~~: These words were heard by Allin Toothaker She also Said to Ralph farnam Jun^ε that she would hold my noss so Closs to the grindstone ⟨a⟩s Euer it was held since my Name was Beniamin Abbut: presently after I was taken with a swelling in my ffoott & then was taken with a payne in my side Ecksidiengly Tormented, wich bred to a sore: which was lancit by doctor prescott & seuerall gallons of Corruption did Run out ^{as was Judged} & so Continued about six weeks Very bad, & then one other sore did breed in my grine wich was lancit by doct. prescott also: & Continued very bad a while & then on other sore breed in my grine which was also Cutt: & putt me to very great missery, So that it brough me almost to Deaths doore, & Continued, untill goodwiffe Carrier was Taken & Carried awaye by the Constable, & that very day I begun to grow better, my soers grew well & I grew better Euery day: & so heue been well Euer since: [Hand 2] & haue great Cause to think that the s^d Carrier had a great hand in my sickness & misery.

beniamen Abbut

[Hand 3] Jurat in Curia Augt 3^d 1692. attes^t Step. Sewall Cle⟨r⟩

[Hand 2] The deposition of Sarah Abbott aged about 32 years Testifieth that since my husband had a parcell of land graunted by ye Towne, lying near ye land of Thomas Carrier, (which as I haue heard) his wife Martha Carrier was greatly troubled att & gaue out threatining words) that my husband Benjamin Abbott has not been only afflicted in his body, as he testifies, but alsoe that strange & unusuall ~~char~~ things has happened to his Cattle, for some haue died suddenly & strangely, which we Could not tell any naturall reason for, & one Cowe Cleaued a fourthnight before she Calued, but ye Cowe died afterwards strangely though she Calued well soe far as we Could p̴ceiue, & some of ye Cattle would Come out of ye woods wth their tounges hanging out of their mouths in a strange & affrighting manner, & many such things, which we Can give noe ~~ace~~ account of y^e reason of, unless it should be y^e effects, of Martha Carriers threatnings

her mark.
Sarah  Abbott

[Hand 3] Jur⟨?⟩at: in Curia.
Augt 3^d 1692. attes^t Steph: Sewall Cler.

[Reverse] Ben Abbo⟨t⟩ & wife

Notes: Used at trial. ◊ Hand 3 = Stephen Sewall

Essex County Court Archives, vol. 1, no. 314, Massachusetts Supreme Judicial Court, Judicial Archives, on deposit James Duncan Phillips Library, Peabody Essex Museum, Salem, MA.

464. Deposition of Phoebe Chandler and Testimony of Bridget Chandler v. Martha Carrier†

[Hand 1] The deposition of Phœbe Chandl^ε aged about 12 years:

{Testifieth} That about a fourthnight before Martha Carrier, was sent for to Salem to be examined, upon ye Sabbath day when y^e ~~psl~~ psalm was singing, s^d Martha Carrier took me s^d

August 3, 1692

deponent by ye shoulder & shaked me, in ye meeting house & asked me where I liued: but I made her noe answere, (not doubting but that she knew me, hauing liued some time the next door to my fathers house, on one side of ye way) & that day that s^d Martha Carrier was Ceased, my mother sent me to Carry some bear to ye folks y^t were att work in ye lott, & when I came within ye fence, there was a uoice in ye bushes (which I thought was Martha Carriers uoice, which I knowe well) but saw noe body, & ye uoice asked me, what ~~she~~ I did there & whether I was going: which greatly frighted me, soe that I run as fast as I could to those att work, & told them what I had heard, about an hour & half, or two hours after, my mother sent me again upon ye same occasion, to ye workmen aboues^d and Comming home, near ye place aboues^d where I heard that uoice before, I heard ye same uoice, as I iudged, ouer my head, saying I should be poysoned within two or three days, ~~which~~ {which} accordingly happened, as I Conceiue, for I went to my sister Allens farm ye same day, and on friday following, about one half of my right hand was greatly swolen & exceeding painfull, & allsoe part of my face, which I Can giue noe account how it Came, & Continued ~~b~~ uery bad some days, & seuerall ~~d~~ times since I haue been troubled with a great weight upon my breast, & upon ~~a~~ my leggs, when I haue been going about, soe that I Could hardly, goe, which I haue told my mother of: And ye last Sabbath day was seauen night, I went to meeting uery well in ye morning, & went to my place where I used to sitt (ye ministers not being Come) & Richard Carrier son of aboues^d Martha looked uery earnestly upon me, & imediately my hand which had formerly been poysoned as aboues^d began to pain me greatly, & I had a strange burning att my stomake, & then was struck deaf that I Could not hear any of ye prayer, nor singing, tell ye two or three last words of ye singing:

her mark

Phœbe   VM   Chandler

[Hand 2] Jurat in Curia

Bridget Chandler aged 40 years Mother to y^e s^d Phœbe Testifieth y^t in y^e day of it her daughter Complained as aboue is Expressed.

Jurat in Curia

[Reverse] Phebe Chandler

Notes: Sister Allen is Elizabeth Allen, Phoebe Chandler's older half-sister. Used at trial. ◊ Hand 2 = Stephen Sewall

Essex County Court Archives, vol. 1, no. 316, Massachusetts Supreme Judicial Court, Judicial Archives, on deposit James Duncan Phillips Library, Peabody Essex Museum, Salem, MA.

465. Testimony of Andrew Foster v. Martha Carrier†

[Hand 1] The tistimony of Andrew ffoster aged about 55 who saith that some time Last may I being at the hous of Thomas Carrier I was saieing that I hard that when Timothy Osgood and his Brother Samuell want to Salam the other day thay goeing to Let Engersons one of the aflicted maides lucked [= looked] out and asked what thay brought them three woman behind them fore thay asked what woman the maid sayd Goodwife carrier goodwife Touthacor and hir dughter and thay goeing into Engerson hous thay askeed the maide where goodwife carrier was shee Answered ther shee sits by you vpon the table vpon which the

August 3, 1692

maide had a fit: which ~~almost~~ twisted hir nick almost ^{round} of. then Goodwife carrier
Answered me it is no matter if hir nicke had ben quite of if shee sayd I was thiere ["ere"
written over "re"]

[Hand 2] Jurat in Curia

Notes: Although Martha Carrier's sister, Mary Toothaker, and her nine-year-old niece, Margaret Toothaker, are also
mentioned by Foster, there is no indication that this document was used against anybody other than Martha Carrier. Mary
Toothaker was arrested, probably on May 28 (see No. 221), but not tried until January, 1693. See No. 830. Margaret was
arrested at the same time as her mother, Mary Toothaker, and was probably imprisoned but not tried. ◊ Used at trial. ◊
Hand 2 = Stephen Sewall

Witchcraft Papers, no. 21b, Massachusetts Historical Society. Boston, MA.

Sworn at Trial: Deposition of Elizabeth Hubbard v. Martha Carrier†
3rd of 3 dates. See No. 236 on May 31, 1692

466. Statement of Samuel Preston v. Martha Carrier†

[Hand 1] Samuel Preston aged about 41: years saith y^t about 2 yeares since I had some
difference wth Martha Carrier wch also had hapened seuer^ll Times before and soon after I lost
a Cow in a strange manner being Cast vpon her back wth her heels vp in firm ground when
she was very Lusty it being in June {& about} ⟨?⟩ ~~after this~~ & within abo^t month after this y^e
s^d Martha & I had some difference again at which Time she told me I had ⟨a⟩ lost a Cow
lately & it Would not or should not be long before I should loose Another wch accordingly
came to pass. for I had a Cow y^t was well kept wth English Hay & I could not p⟨er⟩ceiue y^t she
aild any thing & yet she pined & quickley lay downe as if she was asleep & dyed

Jurat in Curia.

[Reverse] [Hand 2] Ag^t Martha Carrier
[Hand 1] Sam. Preston

Notes: Used at trial. ◊ Hand 1 = Stephen Sewall

*Essex County Court Archives, vol. 1, no. 318, Massachusetts Supreme Judicial Court, Judicial Archives, on deposit James Duncan
Phillips Library, Peabody Essex Museum, Salem, MA.*

467. Deposition of Thomas Putnam & John Putnam Jr. v. Martha Carrier†

[Hand 1] The Deposistion of Thomas putnam agged 40 and Jno putnam aged 36 years who
testifie and saith that we haueing ben conuersant with divers of the afflected parsons as
namely mary walcott mercy lewes Abigail williams Eliz. Hubburt and Ann putnam and we
haue seen them often most greviously tormented by biting pinching and being almost choak
to death often complaining of one gooddy carrier for hirting them: but on the 31: may 1692
being the day of the Examination of martha carrier the afforementioned parsons ware most
dreadfully tormented dureing the time of hir examination that had not the Hon^d majestrats
commanded hir to be bound we ware redy to think she would quickly haue kiled sum of

August 3, 1692

them: also seuerall times sence we haue seen the affore mentioned most dreadfully affleted and tormented as if all their bones would haue been disjoyned or bodyes twisted all to pe⟨ice⟩s complaining most dreadfully of martha Carier for hurting them and we beleue in our hearts ["a" written over "r"] that martha Carrier the prizsoner att [1st "t" written over "s"] the barr has most dreadfully tormented and most greviously afflected the affore mentioned parsons by acts of wicthcraft

Thomas putnam

Jno putnam

[Hand 2] Jurat in Curia

[Reverse] Tho. Putman Jnº Putman

Notes: The deposition did not originally carry the name of John Putnam, nor his age. Both later additions appear in a different ink. John's "signature" was written by Thomas Putnam. The deposition originally had a blank space where the name and age of John were subsequently filled in by Thomas. It appears that when creating the deposition Thomas Putnam was uncertain as to who would be his other witness, so he temporarily left it blank. ◊ Used at trial. ◊ Hand 1 = Thomas Putnam; Hand 2 = Stephen Sewall

Witchcraft Papers, no. 21a, Massachusetts Historical Society. Boston, MA.

468. Deposition of Allen Toothaker v. Martha Carrier†

[Hand 1] The deposition of Allin Toothaker aged about 22 years saith, I heard martha Carrier say that Beniamin Abbutt would wish he had not medled with that land so Near our houwse for she would stick as Cols [= close] to him as the barck to the tree, afore seauen years Com abaut, & that doctor prescott should Neuer Cure him, & about last march Richard Carrier & my selfe had som difference, & said Richard pulled me downe by the haer of my head to the ground for to beat me: I desired him to lett me Risse, when I was up, I went to strick at him, but I fell downe flate upon my back ^{to the ground} & had not power to ster hand Nor foote, then I toold sayd Richard I would yeald to him & owne him the best man, & then I saw Martha Carrier goe of from my brest, butt when I was Rissen up I saw non of her, I was wounded in the warre, Martha Carrier toold me I Would ["W" written over "sh"] Neuer be Cured, afore she was Aprehended I Could thrust in my wound a knitting nedle four Inches ^{deep} but, ⟨?⟩ since she haue been Taken I am thorowly healed: and haue had more Ease then I haue had in halfe a year before somtimes when Martha Carrier & I had some difference she would Clap her hand at me & say I should gett. Nothing by it: & ~~still~~ with in a day or two: I lost a thre year old heffer: Next a yealin: & then a Couw; & then had som litle difference againe, & lost a yearlin, [Hand 2], ⟨?⟩ ~~wh⟨?⟩~~ ~~these aboues^d Creatures which died, I could g⟨?⟩ e not knowe of any reason for their ⟨?⟩ld~~ And I knowe not of any naturall Causes of yᵉ death of the aboues^d Creatures, but haue always feared it hath been yᵉ effect of my Aunt Martha Carrier her malice: /

his mark.

Allen  Toothaker

[Hand 3] Jurat in Curia

[Reverse] Allen Toothaker

August 4, 1692   Notes: Allen Toothaker was the nephew of Martha Carrier. ◊ Used at trial. ◊ Hand 3 = Stephen Sewall

Essex County Court Archives, vol. 1, no. 317, Massachusetts Supreme Judicial Court, Judicial Archives, on deposit James Duncan Phillips Library, Peabody Essex Museum, Salem, MA.

Sworn at Trial: Deposition of Mary Walcott v. Martha Carrier†
3rd of 3 dates. See No. 237 on May 31, 1692

Thursday, August 4, 1692

Grand Juries of Martha Cory, Mary Esty & George Jacobs Sr.

Trials of George Jacobs Sr. and John Willard

469. Examination of Mary Clark

[Hand 1] 1692. 4. Aug.
[Hand 2] 4⟨?⟩ Agust 1692
The Examination of Mary Clark. of. Haverhill Taken before. Jnᵒ Hauthorn Esqᵉ and other their majesties justices of the peace.
The accused mary Clark being called, it was enquyred of Mary walcot if ever Clark had afflicted her, she answered yes, that is the very woman, And upon mary Clarks ~~aflicting of~~ Lookeing upon walcott and otheᵉs of the afflicted they wer struck into fitts.
The Justices haveing used severall arguments. (for the good of her soul) to confess if she knew her self guilty. she absolutely denyed
And then the constable of ~~Andover~~ {Haverhill} was called, and being asked of what fame & reputation mary Clark was off; He answered they had ~~had~~ ^{he⟨ar⟩d} ~~guilty~~ she was or had been guilty of such things, but as to any thing in particular he could not say.
The justices. asked mary walcot if she wer not mistaken in this woman /. walcot answered this is the very woman I saw afflict Timothy swan, and she has aflicted me severall tymes and after a fitt she was then Imediatly in, she said, she saw the above mary Clark afflict Betty hubbard & Ann putnam
The said mary Clark Lookeing upon Walcott, hubbard Putnam, warrin, they wer in fitts.
Mary walcott haveing a pinn run into her arme suddenly; said that mary Clark did it,
At the same tyme mary warrin, had a pinn run into her throat under her chin which Mʳ Noice took out,
Susanna shelden upon sᵈ examination had 4 pinns taken out, of her hand sayeing that, sᵈ Clark put in two of them & mr usher the other two.
Mary Post said she saw the sᵈ Clark afflict Timothy swan Richard Carryer a former confessor said he beleeved he saw the sᵈ mary Clark with some otheᵉs & and himself baptised at Newburry falls.
Betty hubbard was struck down by {her} lookeing upon her
It was asked if she could say the lords prayer perfectly she erred much.

Ann putnam said that s^d Clark had aflicted her by pincheing choakeing & stricking her in the face, & told her, that her name was Mistriss Mary Clark. but that people used to call her goody Clark.

Ann putnam said further that She saw the s^d Clark stabb Timothy Swan with a square ragged Speare as long as her hand

August 4, 1692

[Reverse] and being asked why she called it a Ragged speare, she said ~~it~~ because it was ragged Like a file.

Mary post said she saw this mary Clarks spirit at the village witch meeting & y^t she did eat & drink there as the rest did And further she has seen the s^d Mary Clark afflict Timothy swan /

I underwritten being appoynted by authority to take the within examination in wryting Doe testify upon oath taken in court, that this is a true coppy of the substance of it, to the best of my knowledge. ____

[Hand 1] Mary Clarks Examinaci

Notes: A record of the final disposition of this case is not extant. ◊ Hand 1 = William Murray

Salem Selections, Massachusetts Box, Essex Co., Manuscripts & Archives, New York Public Library. New York, NY.

470. Testimony of George Herrick & William Dounton v. George Jacobs Sr.

[Hand 1] The testimone of George Herrick aged thirty fouer yeares or theireabouts Testyfeyeth and Saith that Sometime in May Last by order of their Majesties Justies I Went to the prisson in Salem to Search George Jacob Sen^ɛ and likewise William Dounton the Goale keeper and Joseph Neale Constable Was in presence and Concerned with mee in the Search where under ye s^d Jacobs his Right Sholder wee found A tett aboute A quarter of an Inch longue or better with A Sharpe point Drupeing downewards so that I tooke A pinn from s^d Dounton and Run: it through the s^d tett but their {was} n{e}ither watter blood nor Curruption nor any other matter and so wee made Returne: William Dounton tesstifeyeth the aboue written

and wee farther Testefy and Say that ye s^d Jacobs was not in the least Senceable in wha⟨t⟩ wee had done for affter I had made Returne to the majestrates and Returned I tould ye s^d Jacob And hee knew nothing before

[Hand 2] Sworne in Court Aug^t .4. 92.

[Reverse] [Hand 3] Harik downton Nele.

[Hand 4] ⟨Ha⟩r⟨e⟩k

Notes: "Sworne in Court" is unusual for a trial document, as is the dating of sworn trial testimony. This nevertheless appears as if it may be a trial document. Somewhat less likely is that it was a grand jury document not used at the trial. ◊ Possibly used at trial. ◊ Hand 1 = George Herrick; Hand 2 = Stephen Sewall

Essex County Court Archives, vol. 1, no. 228, Massachusetts Supreme Judicial Court, Judicial Archives, on deposit James Duncan Phillips Library, Peabody Essex Museum, Salem, MA.

471. Deposition of Mary Daniel v. Margaret Scott & Goodwife Jackson

See also: Sept. 15, 1692 & Sept. 16, 1692.

[Hand 1] The Deposition of Mary Daniel aged nineteen yeers or there ab^{ts} s^d Deponent testifyeth y^t upon ye 2^d day of the ~~last~~ week last past, towards night, I was suddenly taken very ill and went to lye down on a bed, soon after which, there appeared to me the shape of some woman, who seemed to look and speak most feircly ["e" written over "i"] & angrily, and beat; pinch'd & afflicted me very sorely telling me I should not have said ["a" written over "d"] so, or told such things & to y^t purpose; I cannot positively say whose shape it was y^t I saw ye first fitt. ye next night after, I was taken very ill again all over & felt a great pricking in ye soles of my feet, and after a while I saw apparently the shape of ~~widow~~ [Hand 2] {margret} [Hand 1] Scott, who, as I was sitting in a chair by ye fire pulled me with ye chair, down backward to ye ground, and tormented and pinch'd me very much, and I saw her go away at ye door, in which fit I was dumb and so continued 'till ye next morning, finding a great load and heaviness upon my tongue. In some of ye fitts y^t I had afterwards, I was sensless and knew not y^t I saw who it was y^t afflicted me. In one fitt (upon ye beginning of it) I thought I saw goodw Jackson and widow Scott come walking into the chamber with y^r staves, one of y^m came and sat upon me so y^t I could not stirr; Goodw Jackson I saw no more, nor know I y^t she did me any harm. In another fitt I saw [Hand 2] ^{y^e appearanc of} [Hand 1] s^d Scott in ye room who afflicted me, and being speechless, I continued so, untill I went to ye s^d Scott, who taking me by ye hand, I had ye liberty of speech again as formerly. The last fitt I had was upon the last Sabb^th day, in which I saw ye shapes of four women or five, of whom widow Scott was one, ye rest I knew not, nor knew y^t any did hurt me, unless s^d widow Scott.

Rowley August 4 .1692

[Hand 2] Mary Daniell owned: ye truth of ye above written evidence ~~upon a:~~ to ye Jury of Inquest Sept^ε 15: 1692
[Hand 3] Mr Edward Paison Made Oath that Mary Daniil did declare as aboue is written. attes^t St: Sewall Cler in Court at Salem Sepr 16. 92

[Reverse] [Hand 4] Mary Daniell dep^o Agst Mary Scott

Notes: Goodwife Jackson's relationship to John Jackson Sr., if any, is uncertain, as is her identity. Jackson's wife had died in 1671. He and John Jackson Jr. were both indicted and cleared in the January session. See No. 771 & No. 772. Both from Rowley, they were in jail from August 27, 1692 to January 12, 1693. See No. 859. No evidence survives to indicate that Elizabeth Jackson was also arrested, although the possibility remains. ◊ Likely used at trial. ◊ "apparently": 'clearly, plainly' (OED s.v. apparently). ◊ Hand 2 = Simon Willard; Hand 3 = Stephen Sewall; Hand 4 = Anthony Checkley

Private Collection. Access provided by William Reese Company. New Haven, CT.

472. Deposition of Elizabeth Booth & Testimony of Susannah Shelden v. John Willard [?]

[Hand 1] The Deposistion of Eliz: Booth agged about. 18 years who testifieth and saith that severall times sence the later(?) end of June 1692. I haue ben most greviously afflicted and

tormented by John willard or his Apperanc by pinch⟨in⟩g pricking and almost choaking me
to death: also I haue often seen John willard or his apperanc most greviously tormenting and
afflecting my Brother Gorge Booth almost Redy to kill him: Susannah Shelden also
Testifieth that within this fortnight she hath seen John willard or his Appera⟨nce⟩ most
greviously torment and afflect George Booth allmost Redy to prese him to death.

Notes: There is no good evidence for dating this document other than "the later⟨?⟩ end of June 1692" reference that
precludes an earlier date. It may have been prepared for the trial of Willard, on or around August 4. It is assigned to
August 4 on the speculation that it was planned for Willard's trial, although not used. Neither Booth nor Susannah
Shelden had much credibility. ◊ Hand 1 = Thomas Putnam

*Essex County Court Archives, vol. 1, no. 247, Massachusetts Supreme Judicial Court, Judicial Archives, on deposit James Duncan
Phillips Library, Peabody Essex Museum, Salem, MA.*

473. Summons for Witnesses John Pierce & John Lane v. George Burroughs, and Officer's Return

[Hand 1] W^m & Mary by y^e Grace of God of England Scotland ffrance & Ireland King &
Queen defend$^\varepsilon$ of y^e faith &c^a
Wee Comand you to Warn & giue Notice vnto John Peirce [Hand 2] and John lane

[Hand 1] that they & Euery of them be & personaly app$^\varepsilon$ forthwith at y^e p$^\varepsilon$sent Court of
Oyer & Termin$^\varepsilon$ holden at Salem to Testify y^e truth to y^e best of thier knowledge on certain
Indictm^{ts} Exhibited against m^r George Burrough hereof Make return fail Not dated in
Salem Augt 4th 1692 in y^e fourth yeare of Our Reign
                                                                    Stephen Sewall Cler

To y^e Constable of Manchester
[Hand 3] August 4th I haue sumoned the aboue named that thay and Each of them att time
and place aboue written by me
                                                                    John Ley

[Reverse] [Hand 1] A Sumons for John Pearce John Lane and and Sumoned Contra m$^\varepsilon$
Geo Burroughs

Notes: Hand 1 = Stephen Sewall; Hand 3 = George Herrick ◊ 1 wax seal.

Witchcraft Papers, no. 7b, Massachusetts Historical Society. Boston, MA.

474. Physical Examination of George Burroughs & George Jacobs Sr.‡

[Hand 1] wee whoes names are under written haueing reciued an order from y^e sreife for to
search y^e bodyes of George Burroughs and George Jacobs. wee find nothing upon y^e body of
y^e aboue sayd burroughs but w^t is naturall: but upon y^e body of George Jacobs wee find 3
tetts. wch according to y^e best of our Judgements wee think is not naturall for wee run a pinn
through 2 of y^m and he was not sinceible of it: one o[Lost] [= of] them being within ~~the~~ his

mouth upon y^e Inside of his right Cheake and 2^d upon his right shoulder blade and a 3rd upon his right hipp

Ed: Weld	sworne
Tom Flint	[Hand 2] Jurat
[Hand 1] Will Gill	sworne
Tom West	sworne
Zeb Hill	[Hand 2] Jurat
[Hand 1] Sam Morgan	sworne
John Bare	[Hand 2] Jurat

[Reverse] Jury men Return about Ja⟨co⟩bs & Burroughs.

Notes: The "signatures" are in the same hand. The original date of the document is uncertain, but it was probably presented to the grand jury on August 4. ◊ Hand 2 = Stephen Sewall

Essex County Court Archives, vol. 2, no. 23, Massachusetts Supreme Judicial Court, Judicial Archives, on deposit James Duncan Phillips Library, Peabody Essex Museum, Salem, MA.

475. Summons for Witnesses v. George Jacobs Sr.

[Hand 1] W^m & Mary by y^e Grace of God of England &c^a King and Queen &c^a
To ye Sheriff of Essex or deputy Greeting or Constables of Salem.
Wee Comand you to Warn & giue Notice vnto Joseph fflintt John Waters Sen^ε John Deritch Corpo^ll John ffoster [Hand 2] Capt putnam & {his Rebeca his wife} [Hand 1] that they & Euery of them be & appear forthwith Att ye Court of Oyer & Terminer holden at Salem there to Testifie y^e truth to y^e best of your knowledge on certain Indictments Exhibited against George Jacobs Sen^ε hereof Make Return fail not dated in Salem Augt 4th 1692. & in y^e fourth yeare of Our Reign

Stephen Sewall Cle⟨r⟩

[Reverse] [Hand 3] G. Jacob⟨s⟩

Notes: Hand 1 = Stephen Sewall; Hand 2 = Thomas Putnam ◊ 1 wax seal.

Essex County Court Archives, vol. 1, no. 225, Massachusetts Supreme Judicial Court, Judicial Archives, on deposit James Duncan Phillips Library, Peabody Essex Museum, Salem, MA.

476. Indictment No. 1 of Martha Cory, for Afflicting Elizabeth Hubbard†

See also: Sept. 8, 1692.

[Hand 1]	[Hand 2]
Province of ye Mattathusets Bay in New England.	Anno Regis et Reginæ Will͞m et Mariæ nunc: Angliae &^c Quarto

Essex ss The Juro^ε for our Sovereigne Lord and Lady the King and Queen p^εsents That [Hand 1] **Martha Corey Wife of Gyles Corey of Salem husbandman**[Hand 2] the [Hand 1] **21.** [Hand 2] Day of [Hand 1] **March** [Hand 2] in the [Hand 1] **fourth** [Hand 2] Year of the Reigne of our Sovereigne Lord and Lady William and Mary by the Grace of God of England Scottland ffrance and Ireland King and Queen Defend^ɛ of the faith &^{c} and Divers other Dayes and times as well before as After Certaine Detestable Arts called witchcrafts & Sorceries wickedly and ffelloniously hath vsed, Practised & Exercised. at and within the Towneship of [Hand 1] **Salem** [Hand 2] in the County of Essex afores^d in vpon and ag^t one [Hand 1] **Elizabeth Hubbard of Salem Singlewoman** [Hand 2] by which said wicked Arts the said [Hand 1] **Elizabeth Hubbard** [Hand 2] the [Hand 1] **21.** [Hand 2] Day of [Hand 1] **March** [Hand 2] in the Year aboves^d and Divers other Dayes & times as well before as after was and is Tortured afflicted Pined Consumed and Tormented and also for sundery other Acts of witchcrafts by said [Hand 1] **Martha Corey** [Hand 2] Committed and Done before and since that time ag^t the Peace of our Sovereigne Lord & Lady the King and Queen their Crowne and Dignity and ag^t the fform of the statute in that case made and Provided/

[Hand 1] Witnesses
El: Hubbard & Jury of womens return
Marcy Lewis
Ann putman
Edward Putman
Ezek. Cheever

[Reverse] N° 1) Martha. Corey
[Hand 3] Billa Vera
[Hand 1?] Martha Corey
[Hand 4] [2 words illegible]

Notes: ◊ Hand 1 = Stephen Sewall

Essex County Court Archives, vol. 1, no. 37, Massachusetts Supreme Judicial Court, Judicial Archives, on deposit James Duncan Phillips Library, Peabody Essex Museum, Salem, MA.

477. Indictment No. 2 of Martha Cory, for Afflicting Mercy Lewis†

See also: Sept. 8, 1692.

[Hand 1]
Province of the Massacus(s)tts Bay
in New England.

[Hand 2]
Anno Regis et Reginæ Willm̄ et Mariæ nunc:
Angliæ &^{c} Quarto

Essex ss The Juro͞^{ɛ} of our Sovereigne Lord and Lady the King & Queen p^{ɛ}sents That [Hand 3] **Martha Corey wife of Giles Corey of Salem husbandman** [Hand 2] the [Hand 3] **21** [Hand 2] day of [Hand 3] **March** [Hand 2] in the [Hand 3] **fourth** [Hand 2] Year of the Reigne of our Sovereigne Lord and Lady William & Mary by the Grace of God of England Scottland ffrance and Ireland King & Queen Defend^ɛ of the faith &^{c} and Divers other Dayes & times, as. well before as after. certaine Detestable Arts called Witchcrafts & Sorceries. Wickedly and ffelloniously hath vsed Practised & Exercised at and within the Towneship of [Hand 3] **Salem**[Hand 2] in the County of Essex aforesaid in upon & ag^t one. [Hand 3] **Marcey Lewis of** ∧{**Salem Village**} **Singlewoman** [Hand 2] by which said Wicked Arts the said [Hand 3] **Marcy Lewis.**[Hand 2] the [Hand 3] **21** [Hand 2] Day of [Hand 3] **March** [Hand 2] in the [Hand 3] **fourth** [Hand 2] Year abovesaid. & Divers other Dayes &

August 4, 1692

times as well before as after, was and is Tortured afflicted Pined Consumed wasted &
Tormented and also for Sundrey other Acts of Witchcrafts by said [Hand 3] **Martha Corey**
[Hand 2] Committed & Done before & Since that time ag^t the Peace of our Sovereigne
Lord and Lady the King and Queen their Crowne and Dignity. and ag^t the fform of the
Statute in that case made and Provided
[Hand 3] Marcy Lewis
Eliz. Hubbard
Ann Putman
Edward Putman
Ezek. Cheeuer

[Reverse] N. (2) Martha Corey
[Hand 4] Billa: Vera
[Hand 3] Martha Corey

Notes: Hand 1 = Anthony Checkley; Hand 3 = Stephen Sewall; Hand 4 = Simon Willard

Witchcraft Papers, no. 14, Massachusetts Historical Society. Boston, MA.

Sworn Before the Grand Jury: Deposition of Ezekiel Cheever & Edward Putnam v. Martha Cory†

2nd of 3 dates. See No. 18 on March 21, 1692

Sworn Before the Grand Jury: Deposition of Elizabeth Hubbard v. Martha Cory

2nd of 3 dates. See No. 19 on March 21, 1692

Sworn Before the Grand Jury: Deposition of Elizabeth Hubbard v. Mary Esty, John Willard, & Mary Whittredge

3rd of 4 dates. See No. 197 on May 21, 1692

Sworn Before the Grand Jury: Deposition of Mary Walcott v. Mary Esty

2nd of 2 dates. See No. 205 on May 23, 1692

Sworn Before the Grand Jury: Deposition of Abigail Williams & Ann Putnam Jr. v. Mary Esty, John Willard, & Mary Whittredge and Testimony of Ann Putnam Jr. v. Mary Esty

2nd of 2 dates. See No. 206 on May 23, 1692

478. Indictment No. 1 of George Jacobs Sr., for Afflicting Mary Walcott†

[Hand 1] Anno Regis et Reginæ Will$\overline{m}$ et
Mariæ nunc Angliæ &^{c} Quarto
Essex ss The Juro$^\varepsilon$ for our Sovereigne Lord and Lady the King and Queen p$^\varepsilon$sents That
[Hand 2] **George Jacobs Sen$^\varepsilon$ of Salem husbandman**[Hand 1] the [Hand 2] **11**th [Hand 1]
Day of [Hand 2] **May** [Hand 1] in the [Hand 2] **fourth** [Hand 1] Year of the Reigne of our
Sovereigne Lord and Lady William and Mary by the Grace of God of England Scottland
ffrance and Ireland King and Queen Defend$^\varepsilon$ of the faith &^{c} and Divers other Dayes and

Times as well before as after Certaine Detestable Arts called Witchcrafts and Sorceries   August 4, 1692
Wickedly and ffelloniously hath vsed. Practised and Exercised at and within the Towneship
of [Hand 2] **Salem**[Hand 1] in the County of Essex aforesd. in upon. and ag^t one [Hand 2]
Mary Walcott of Salem Villiage Singlewom [Hand 1] by which said Wicked Arts the said
[Hand 2] **Mary Walcot** [Hand 1] the [Hand 2] **11**^th [Hand 1] Day of [Hand 2] **May** [Hand
1] in the [Hand 2] **fourth** [Hand 1] Year abovesaid and Divers other Dayes and times as well
before as after was and is Tortured Afflicted. Pined Consumed wasted & Tormented: and
also for sundrey other Acts of witchcraft⟨s⟩ by said [Hand 2] **George Jacobs.** [Hand 1]
Committed and Done before and Since that time ag^t the Peace of our Sovereigne Lord and
Lady the King and Queen their Crowne and Dignity and ag^t the forme of the Statute in that
Case made and Provided./.
[Hand 2] Witnesses.
Marcy Lewis.
Mary Walcott
Eliz. Hubbard
Ann Putman
Sarah Churchill

[Reverse] George Jacobs N^o (1)
[Hand 3] billa uera

Notes: Hand 2 = Stephen Sewall

Witchcraft Papers, no. 24, Massachusetts Historical Society. Boston, MA.

479. Indictment No. 2 of George Jacobs Sr., for Afflicting Mercy Lewis (Returned Ignoramus)†

[Hand 1] Anno Regis et Reginæ Willm̄ et
Mariæ nunc Angliæ &^c Quarto:
Essex ss The Juro͞ᵋ for our Sovereigne Lord and Lady the King and Queen p^ᵋsents That
[Hand 2] **George Jacobs. Sen**^ᵋ **of Salem** in ye County of Essex [Hand 1] the [Hand 2]
11th [Hand 1] Day of [Hand 2] **May** [Hand 1] in the [Hand 2] **fourth** [Hand 1] Year of the
Reigne of our Sovereigne Lord and Lady William and Mary by the Grace of God of
England Scottland ffrance and Ireland King and Queen Defend^ᵋs of the ffaith &^c and:
Divers other Dayes & times as well before as after certaine Detestable Arts called witchcrafts
and sorceries Wickedly and ffelloniously hath vsed Practised and Exercised at and withwin
[= within] the Towneship of [Hand 2] **Salem** [Hand 1] in the County of Essex aforesaid in,
~~and~~ upon, and ag^t one [Hand 2] **Marcy Lewis. of Salem Villiage Singlewoman** [Hand 1] by
which said Wicked Arts the said [Hand 2] **Marcy Lewiss.** [Hand 1] the [Hand 2] **11**^th
[Hand 1] Day of [Hand 2] **May** [Hand 1] in the [Hand 2] **fourth** [Hand 1] Year abovesaid
and, Divers other Dayes and times as well before as after was and is Tortured Afflicted Pined
Consumed wasted and Tormented and also for sundery other Acts of witchcraft by said
[Hand 2] **George Jacobs.** [Hand 1] Committed and Done before and since that time ag^t the
Peace of our Sovereigne Lord and Lady the King and Queen their Crowne and Dignity and
ag^t the form of the statute in that Case made and Provided:/.

August 4, 1692

[Hand 2] Witnesses
Marcy Lewis
Mary Walcott
Eliz. Hubbard
Sarah Churchill

[Reverse] George Jacobs nᵒ(2)
[Hand 3] Indictment
[Hand 4] Ignoramus

Notes: The grand jury rejected the claims of one of the core accusers. ◊ Hand 2 = Stephen Sewall

Essex County Court Archives, vol. 1, no. 222, Massachusetts Supreme Judicial Court, Judicial Archives, on deposit James Duncan Phillips Library, Peabody Essex Museum, Salem, MA.

480. Statements of Sarah Bibber, Sarah Churchill, Elizabeth Hubbard, Mary Walcott, & Mary Warren v. George Jacobs Sr.

[Hand 1] Mary: Warin. afirmd: before yᵉ Jury of Inquest: that George Jacobs Senᵉ has: afflicted her: sᵈ Warin: & beat: her with his staffe he or his Apperition: sᵈ Warin ses she has seen sᵈ Jacobs or Appearition afflict: Mary Walcot: & beat her with his staffe: she sayd also: that sᵈ Jacobs has: afflicte Ann Putman sᵈ Warin verily: thinks: sᵈ George Jacobs is a wizard ["wizard" written over "witch"] Augˢᵗ: 4: 1692 upon her oath

[Hand 2] Jurat in Curia

[Hand 1] Elizabeth Hubbard Affirmd to yᵉ ~~grand~~ Jury of Inquest: that she hath seen: George Jacob Senᵉ afflict: Mary Walcot Ann Putnam & Abigail Williams: and sᵈ Jacobs: or his Appearition has sorely afflicted her sᵈ Eliz Hubbard: August: 4: 1692 upon her oath

[Hand 2] Jurat in Curia

[Hand 1] Mary Walcot Affirmd before: yᵉ Jury of Inquest that she hath seen George: Jacobs Senᵉ afflict Mary Warin & Ann Putnam and Elizabeth Hubbard: and sᵈ Jacobs or his Apperition: hath hurt her sᵈ Mary Walcot and beat her with his staffe: Augˢᵗ 4: 92 upon her oath sᵈ Walcot sᵈ she verily beleevs: sᵈ Jacobs is a wizerd: and: that on yᵉ day & time of sᵈ Jacobs his examination: he afflicted: her & Ann Putman & Elizabeth Hubard

[Hand 2] Jurat in Curia

[Hand 1] Sarah Churchwell: Affirmd. to yᵉ Jury of Inquest: that George Jacobs Senᵉ or his Apperition: has afflicted: her sᵈ Churchell: by choaking of her. and she ["she" written over "I"] veryly thinks: that sᵈ Jacobs: did it by witch craft

[Hand 2] Jurat in Curia

Sarah Vibber ^{made Oath} yᵗ she saw him ^{yᵗ George Jacobs} at yᵉ Gallows when Goody Olliuer was Executed & yᵉ black man help him ["im" written over "er"] vp. & yᵗ she saw him aflict Mary Walcot & beat hir with his Staff

Jurat in Curia

[Hand 1] Mercy Lewis

Mary Walcot
Eliz Hubbard
Ann: Putnam

[Reverse] Seuerall Evidences Contra. Georg: Jacobs.

Notes: While the grand jury certainly heard the case of George Jacobs Sr. on August 4, the trial date is less certain. It was probably concluded on August 4, but may have extended to August 5. ◊ Used at trial. ◊ Hand 1 = Simon Willard; Hand 2 = Stephen Sewall

Essex County Court Archives, vol. 1, no. 226, Massachusetts Supreme Judicial Court, Judicial Archives, on deposit James Duncan Phillips Library, Peabody Essex Museum, Salem, MA.

Sworn Before the Grand Jury: Deposition of Mercy Lewis v. George Jacobs Sr.†

3ʳᵈ of 3 dates. See No. 134 on May 10, 1692

Sworn Before the Grand Jury and at Trial: Deposition of Ann Putnam Jr. v. George Jacobs Sr.

2ⁿᵈ of 2 dates. See No. 136 on May 11, 1692

481. Testimony of John DeRich v. George Jacobs Sr. et al.†

[Hand 1] John Deritch aged 16 years or thereabouts
    Testifieth and saith:
That John Small and his Wife Anne both Deceased and formerly of the Towne of Salem doth both appear to this Deponent and told him that they would tare him to peices if he did not goe and Declare to Mᵉ Harthorne that George Jacobs senier: Did Kill them: and Likewise that Mary Warrens Mother Did appeare to this Deponent this Day with a white Man and told him that woodwife [= goodwife] Parker & Oliver did Kill her: and Likwise Core Procter & his Wife: Sarah Procter Joseph Procter & John Procter did all afflict this Deponent and do continually every day sense he hath began to be afflicted: and would have him this Deponent to sett his hand to a Booke but this Depon^t told them he would not: Likewise Phillip English & his Wife Mary Doth appeare to this Deponent & afflict him and all the aboves^d Persons Thretten to tare this Deponent in peices: if he doth not Signe to a Booke: Likewise goodwife Pease & Hobs ["b" written over "p"] and her Daughter Abigail. doth afflict him: and thretten the same: and Likewise a woman appeares to this Deponent who Lives at Boston at yᵉ Vper End of the Towne whose name is Mary: she goes in black Clothes hath: but one Eye: with a Crooked Neck and she saith there is none in boston like her. she did ["did" written over "doth"] afflictt this Deponent but saith she will not any more: nor tell him her Name/

                                                     [Hand 2] Jurat all relating to yᵉ
                                                       prisoner at yᵉ barr

[Reverse] [Hand 3] John Dericth ag⟨n⟩ist Georg Jacobs

Notes: Likely used at trial. ◊ Hand 2 = Stephen Sewall

August 4, 1692   *Essex County Court Archives, vol. 1, no. 227, Massachusetts Supreme Judicial Court, Judicial Archives, on deposit James Duncan Phillips Library, Peabody Essex Museum, Salem, MA.*

482. Testimony of John DeRich v. George Jacobs Sr.†

[Hand 1] The testimoney of John derich {Agged bout 16 yeares} testifieth and saith that somtim in may last paste: Gorge ~~ga~~ Jacobs sin^r Cam to me and bid me goe to my wife and tell her that she muste send me some money: and he bid me that I should not Eate aney of his Cheires: and diuers times sence he hath bin⟨e⟩ in prissone hee hath afflictted me sereual. ways by pinching and by sraching and bitting and told me that if ~~he~~ I would not sett mi hand to his boocke he would destroye me and lead me in to the water and would haue drownded me and natheinnil watter⟨e⟩ tooke me out of the water. and ~~the~~ [Hand 2] ^{y^e prisoner} [Hand 1] knockt me downe with his stafe: the 3 day of this instant Augst: and while I wase ~~I~~ writting mi testimoney he told me that he did not Care for that writting and told me that ~~th~~ He had bin⟨n⟩ a wizard this fortie yeares

                                                                    [Hand 2] Jurat in Curia

[Reverse] [Hand 3] Jno Derich ags^t Jacobs.

Notes: Used at trial. ◊ Hand 2 = Stephen Sewall

Witchcraft Papers, no. 27, Massachusetts Historical Society. Boston, MA.

483. Deposition of Joseph Flint v. George Jacobs Sr.†

[Hand 1] The deposicon of Joseph Flintt aged 30 yeares
Saith y^t being at y^e house of m^r Thomas Beadles on y^e 11th of May 1692. when y^e Majestrates. were Examining George Jacobs his Grandaughter and understanding that She had Confessed ~~that she had Confessed.~~ I this deponent went into ye other room where George Jacobs was & Told him y^t his Grandaughter had Confessed ~~wh⟨o⟩~~ he asked me what She had Confessed I told him y^t She Confesst She was a Witch or that She had Set her hand to ye Deuils Booke whereupon s^d Jacobs Said that She was Charged not to Confess & then I asked him ~~what She was~~ {who} Charged ^{her} not to Confess. he then ~~make~~ made a Stop & at last Said y^t if She were Innocent & yet Confest She would be accessary to her owne death.

                                                                    marke
                              Jurat in Curia   Joseph ✑ fflintt

[Reverse] [Hand 2]
[Lost]se⟨p⟩[Lost] [= Joseph] ⟨ff⟩lint agst
Geo. J⟨a⟩cobs Sen^ε

Notes: Used at trial. ◊ Hand 1 = Stephen Sewall; Hand 2 = Jonathan Corwin

Essex County Court Archives, vol. 1, no. 230, Massachusetts Supreme Judicial Court, Judicial Archives, on deposit James Duncan Phillips Library, Peabody Essex Museum, Salem, MA.

August 4, 1692

Sworn at Trial: Deposition of Thomas Putnam & John Putnam v. George Jacobs Sr.†
2nd of 2 dates. See No. 137 on May 11, 1692

Billa Vera: Indictment No. 1 of John Willard, for Afflicting Mercy Lewis†
2nd of 2 dates. See No. 296 on June 3, 1692

Billa Vera: Indictment No. 2 of John Willard, for Afflicting Ann Putnam Jr.†
2nd of 2 dates. See No. 297 on June 3, 1692

Billa Vera: Indictment No. 3 of John Willard, for Afflicting Susannah Shelden (Returned Ignoramus)†
2nd of 2 dates. See No. 298 on June 3, 1692

Billa Vera: Indictment No. 4 of John Willard, for Afflicting Abigail Williams†
2nd of 2 dates. See No. 299 on June 3, 1692

Billa Vera: Indictment No. 7 of John Willard, for Afflicting Elizabeth Hubbard†
2nd of 2 dates. See No. 300 on June 3, 1692

484. Deposition of Elizabeth Bailey v. John Willard†

[Hand 1] The Testimonie of Elizabth Bayly aged twenty seauen years or there aboutes testifeyeth and saith that John Willard lookeing his oxen mett wth this deponant and to{u}ld her that all the way from Francis Eliotts hous to his owne home hee ~~uer~~ veryly thought that the Diuell ["i" written over "e"] Came before him or behind him all the way Which dreadffully frigted him the s^{d} Deponant asked him why he thought so he answered hee could not tell and Emediately fell a singing

The marke of + Elizabeth Bayly
[Hand 2] Jurat in Curia

[Reverse] El. Bayley
[Hand 3?] ~~Againest Elliet⟨h⟩~~

Notes: No hard evidence confirms the date of Willard's trial, but it was no earlier than August 4. Robert Calef is slightly off in writing that the Court of Oyer and Terminer resumed on August 5 (*More Wonders*, p. 103), since there is firm evidence of activity on August 4. Willard's trial date cannot be certain and is dated in this edition to the initial court activity in August. ◊ Used at trial. ◊ Hand 1 = George Herrick

Essex County Court Archives, vol. 1, no. 251, Massachusetts Supreme Judicial Court, Judicial Archives, on deposit James Duncan Phillips Library, Peabody Essex Museum, Salem, MA.

485. Deposition of Thomas Bailey v. John Willard†

[Hand 1] The deposition of Thomas Baly aged 36 yeares who testefieth and sayth.
That I being at Groaton. some short tyme after John Willard. as the report went had beaten
his wife I went to cal him home. and comeinge home with him in the night I heard such a
hideaus noyse of strang creatures I was much affrighted for I neuer had heard the like noyse I
fearinge they might be some euil spirits I enquired of the sayd Willard what might it be that
made such a hideous noys⟨e⟩ the sayd Willard sayd they were Locust: the next day as I
suppose the sayd Willards ~~bringing his wife~~ {wife} with a younge child and her mather
being vpon my mare. ridinge. betweene Groaton Mil and Chensford. they. being willing to
g⟨o⟩e on foote a litle desired me to ride: then I taking my mare being willing to let her feed a
litle: there as I remember I may aprehend I heard the same noyse agayne where at my mare.
started: and got from me.

[Hand 2] Jurat in Curia

[Reverse] Tho. Bayley ag^t Willard

Notes: Used at trial.

*Essex County Court Archives, vol. 1, no. 250, Massachusetts Supreme Judicial Court, Judicial Archives, on deposit James Duncan
Phillips Library, Peabody Essex Museum, Salem, MA.*

Sworn at Trial: Testimony of Sarah Bibber v. John Willard†
2nd of 2 dates. See No. 301 on June 3, 1692

486. Deposition of Philip Knight & Thomas Nichols v. John Willard [?]

[Hand 1] The deposition of Philip knight aged 46 yeares and of Thomas Nicols 22 yeares
who do testefy and say

That sometymes in April last there was discourse at the house of the sayd Philip Knight.
about seuerall of the village that were taken vp vpon suspition of witch craft. John ~~Willard~~
willard being present then replyed: hang them. they ar all witches

[Reverse] [Hand 2] Phillip Knight

Notes: This is speculatively dated to the trial of Willard as a deposition prepared for the trial but not used.

*Essex County Court Archives, vol. 1, no. 256, Massachusetts Supreme Judicial Court, Judicial Archives, on deposit James Duncan
Phillips Library, Peabody Essex Museum, Salem, MA.*

487. Deposition of Lydia Nichols & Margaret Knight v. John Willard [?]

[Hand 1] The deposition of Lydia Nicols aged. 46 yeares and of Margaret knight. aged .20.
yeares ~~and of Margaret~~ who testefy and say.

That the wife of John Willard being at her fathers house. when the sayd Willard liued at Gr⟨o⟩aton. she made. a lamentable complaynt. how cruelly her husband had beaten her: she thought her selfe that she should neuer recouer of the blows he had giuen her: the next morninge he was got into a litle hole vnder the stayers. and then she thought some thinge extraordinary had befallne him. then: he ran out at the doore: and ran vp. a steep hill. almost impossible. for any man to run vp: as she sayd: then she tooke her mare and rid away. fearing some euil had ben intended agaynst her. and when she came to the house of Henery ^{or Beniamin} Willard. she told how it was with her and the sayd Henery Willard. ^{or both} went to looke after him and met him com⟨e⟩inge in a strange destracted frame

August 4, 1692

[Reverse] [Hand 2] Lidia Nicols

Notes: This appears to be a deposition prepared for the grand jury on June 3 but not used. In the absence of clear evidence it is speculatively dated to Willard's trial date, for which it may have been prepared but not used.

Essex County Court Archives, vol. 1, no. 248, Massachusetts Supreme Judicial Court, Judicial Archives, on deposit James Duncan Phillips Library, Peabody Essex Museum, Salem, MA.

Sworn at Trial: Deposition of Samuel Parris, Nathaniel Ingersoll & Thomas Putnam v. John Willard†

3rd of 3 dates. See No. 176 on May 18, 1692

Sworn at Trial: Deposition of Ann Putnam Jr. v. John Willard†

3rd of 3 dates. See No. 185 on May 18, 1692

Sworn at Trial: Deposition of Thomas Putnam & Edward Putnam v. John Willard†

2nd of 2 dates. See No. 177 on May 18, 1692

Sworn at Trial: Deposition of Mary Walcott v. John Willard†

3rd of 3 dates. See No. 180 on May 18, 1692

Sworn at Trial: Testimony of Benjamin Wilkins & Thomas Flint v. John Willard & Sarah Buckley†

2nd of 2 dates. See No. 181 on May 18, 1692

488. Deposition of Bray Wilkins v. John Willard‡

[Hand 1] The Deposition of Bray Wilkins of Salem Village aged about eighty & one years with reference to John Willard of s^d Salem, lately charged with Witchcraft, when he was at first complained of by the afflicted persons for afflicting of them he came to my house greatly troubled, desiring me with some other Neighbours to pray for him: I told him I was then going from home, & could not stay, but if I could come home before night I should not be unwilling, but it was near night before I came home, & so I did not answere his desire, but I heard no more of him upon that account. Whither my not answering his desire did not offend him, I cannot tell, but I was jealous afterwards that it did. A little after my wife & I went to Boston at the last Election, when I was as well in health as in many yeares before, & the Election day coming to my brother Lf^t Richard Way's house, at noon there were many

August 4, 1692

freinds to dine there, they were sat down at the Table, Mr Lawson & his wife & severall more, John Willard came into the house with my Son Henry Wilkins before I sat down, & s^d Willard to my apprehension lookt after such a sort upon me as I never before discerned in any, I did but step into the next room, & I was presently taken in a strange condition, so that I could not dine, nor eat any thing, I cannot express the misery I was in for my water was sodainly stopt, & I had no benefit of nature, but was like a man on a ~~wrack~~ Rack, & I told my wife immediately that I was afraid that Willard had done me wrong, my pain continuing & finding no releif my jealousie continued: Mr Lawson, & others there, were all amazed, & knew not what to do for me: There was a Woman accounted skilfull came hoping to help me, & after she had used means, she askt me whither none of those evil persons had done me damage. I said, I could not say they ^{had}, but I was sore afraid they had, she answered she did fear so too, as near as I remember. I lay in this case. 3. or. 4. dayes at Boston, & afterwards with the jeopardy of my life (as I thought) I came home, & then some of my freinds coming to ~~se⟨?⟩~~ see me, (& at this time John Willard was run away) One of the afflicted persons Mercy Lewes came in with them, & they askt whither she saw any thing: She said yes, they are looking for John Willard but there he is upon his Grandfathers Belly (& at that time I was in greivous ~~parts~~ pain in the small of my Belly) ~~I sent my~~ I continued so in greivous pain & my water much stopt till s^d Willard was in chains, & then as near as I can guess I had considerable ease, but on the other hand in the room of a stoppage, I was vexed with a flowing of water, so that it was hard to keep my self dry. On the . 5. July last talking with some freinds about John ^{Willard}, some pleading his innocency & my self & some others arguing the contrary, within about 1/4 of an hour after~~w~~ that I had said it was not I, nor my son Benj^a Wilkins, but the testimony of the afflicted persons, & the jury concerning the Murder of my Grandson Dan: Wilkins that would take away his life if any thing did, & within about 1/4 hour after this I was taken in the sorest distress & misery my water being turned into real blood, or of a bloody colour & the old pain returned excessively as before which continued for about 24. houres together

[Reverse] Bray Wilkins Testim⟨?⟩ ags^t John Willard

Notes: The document is docketed as testimony, but that may be a recording error. It was apparently prepared as a deposition for the trial but not used. Another possibility is that the recorder simply made no distinction between a deposition and testimony. ◊ "jealous" and "jealousie": 'suspicious, fearful' and 'suspicion' (*OED* s.v. *jealous* and *jealousy* 5). ◊ Hand 1 = Samuel Parris

Essex County Court Archives, vol. 1, no. 258, Massachusetts Supreme Judicial Court, Judicial Archives, on deposit James Duncan Phillips Library, Peabody Essex Museum, Salem, MA.

489. Testimony of Rebecca Wilkins v. John Willard†

[Hand 1] The testomony of Rebeckah wilkins aged ninteen years Doe testifie that 29th July at night shee se John wilard seting in the Corner and hee said that hee wold afflick me that night and forthwith hee ded afflick me: and the nax day I ded se him afflick me soer by Choaking & Polling me ear into Peases the nex day being the Lords day I being Going to meting I se John wilard and hee afflickted me uery soer

[Hand 2] Jurat in Curia

[Reverse] Rebeckah Wilkins

[Hand 3?] Rebecka Wilkins vs. Willard   August 5, 1692

Re

Notes: Used at trial. ◊ Hand 2 = Stephen Sewall

Essex County Court Archives, vol. 1, no. 252, Massachusetts Supreme Judicial Court, Judicial Archives, on deposit James Duncan Phillips Library, Peabody Essex Museum, Salem, MA.

490. Deposition of Samuel Wilkins v. John Willard†

[Hand 1] The Deposistion of Samuell wilknes agged about 19 years who testifieth and saith that sence Jno: willard has ben in prizson I haue been afflected in a strange kind of maner for about the later end of June or begining of July as I was a weaveing the yarn broak exceeding fast: and as I was a tying a thread I had a stroak on my hand like a knife the blood being almost Redy to com out and I was also pinched seueral times by an unseen hand: also Riding to marblehead Just as I came to forrist Riuer Bridge I was Immediatly seazed with a violent wait [= weight] on my back and I saw a black hate [= hat]: and was Immediatly pulled ofe my horse or mare and almost pulled into the Riuere: but: holding fast at last I gott up againe: a while affter as I was once in the woods and a goeing hom ∧{&} a little boy with me: I thought I must run: and I said: to the boy let us Run: and as soon as I Ran there was a black hate Run along by me: a while affter one mornig about an hour by sun I was afflected and I saw John willard or his Apperance with a darke collored coot: and a black hate very like that hate which I formmorly saw: a llitle while affter this one night as soon as I was abed John willard whom I very well knew or his Appearanc came in to the Room where I was abed: and another man and woman along with him which I did not know and they tould me they woold cary me away before morning.

[Hand 2] Jurat in Curia

[Reverse] Sam Wilkins

Notes: Used at trial. ◊ Hand 1 = Thomas Putnam

Essex County Court Archives, vol. 1, no. 249, Massachusetts Supreme Judicial Court, Judicial Archives, on deposit James Duncan Phillips Library, Peabody Essex Museum, Salem, MA.

Friday, August 5, 1692

Trials of George Burroughs, Elizabeth Procter, & John Procter

491. Summons for Witnesses v. George Burroughs, and Officer's Return

[Hand 1] William & Mary by yᵉ Grace of God of England Scotland ffrance & Ireland King & Queen defend\^{Es} of yᵉ faith &cᵃ
        mʳ Jnᵒ Ruck mˢ Eliz: Ruck mʳ Thomas Ruck & Samuel Ruck

August 5, 1692

To Capt William Worwood Greeting.

Wee Comand you all Excuses set apart to be and personaly appear at y^e present Court of Oyer & Terminer held at Salem there to Testify y^e Truth to y^e best of your knowledge On certain Indictm^{ts} Exhibited against m^r George Burrough: hereof fail not dated in Salem. Augt 5th 1692. & in ye fourth yeare of Our Reign

Stephen Sewall Cler

[Hand 2] August 5th The persons aboue Named where all Euery of them sumoned ~~by~~ to appeare as aboue by me

[Hand 3] by me Joseph Neale
Cons^{ll} in in Sale⟨m⟩

[Reverse] [Hand 4] G. Burroughs Sumons Ruck ⟨&⟩[Lost]

Notes: A summons for witnesses on the day of the trial could possibly indicate that the Burroughs case was not concluded on August 5. However, it is not unreasonable to expect that it could all have been handled on the same day. ◊ Hand 1 = Stephen Sewall; Hand 2 = George Herrick

Essex County Court Archives, vol. 2, no. 29, Massachusetts Supreme Judicial Court, Judicial Archives, on deposit James Duncan Phillips Library, Peabody Essex Museum, Salem, MA.

Billa Vera: Indictment No. 1 of George Burroughs, for Afflicting Mary Walcott†
2nd of 2 dates. See No. 452 on Aug. 3, 1692

Billa Vera: Indictment No. 2 of George Burroughs, for Afflicting Mercy Lewis†
2nd of 2 dates. See No. 453 on Aug. 3, 1692

Billa Vera: Indictment No. 3 of George Burroughs, for Afflicting Elizabeth Hubbard†
2nd of 2 dates. See No. 454 on Aug. 3, 1692

Billa Vera: Indictment No. 4 of George Burroughs, for Afflicting Ann Putnam Jr.†
2nd of 2 dates. See No. 455 on Aug. 3, 1692

Sworn at Trial: Deposition of Sarah Bibber v. George Burroughs†
3rd of 3 dates. See No. 121 on May 9, 1692

492. Deposition of Hannah Harris v. George Burroughs†

[Hand 1] The depotion of Hannah Harres Aiged twenty seuen ⟨?⟩ yeares or thareabout⟨s⟩ Testifieth and saith that she Liued at ye houc of Georg Burros [Hand 2]{a⟨t⟩ falmouth} [Hand 1] ~~ad~~ & the aboue said hannah harres many times hath taken notis that when she hath had anny Discorce with the aboue said burross wife when the aboue said burros was from hom that apone his Returne he hath often scolded wife and told her that⟨t⟩ he knew what thay said when he was abroad and further saith that apone a time when his wife had Laine In Not aboue one weake that he fell out with his wife and kept her by Discorce at the Dore till she fell sike In ye place and grew wors at ~~knight~~ so that ye aboue said hannah⟨?⟩ harres was afraid she would Dye and thay Called In thare Naibo{u}rs and the aboue said burroses

August 5, 1692

Daughter told One of yᵉ women that was thare yᵉ Cause of her mothers Ellnes and yᵉ aboue said burros Chid his Daughter for telling. and yᵉ aboue said burros Came to the aboue said hannah harres and told her If that his wife Did otherwise then well she should not tell of It & the abousaid hannah harres Told him that she would not be confined to anny such thing
[Hand 2] Jurat in Curia

[Reverse] Hannah Harris agt Burroughs

Notes: Used at trial. ◊ Hand 2 = Stephen Sewall

Essex County Court Archives, vol. 2, no. 32, Massachusetts Supreme Judicial Court, Judicial Archives, on deposit James Duncan Phillips Library, Peabody Essex Museum, Salem, MA.

Sworn at Trial: Statement of Elizabeth Hubbard v. George Burroughs†

3ʳᵈ of 3 dates. See No. 122 on May 9, 1692

Sworn at Trial: Statement of Elizer Keyser v. George Burroughs†

3ʳᵈ of 3 dates. See No. 123 on May 9, 1692

Sworn at Trial: Deposition of Mercy Lewis v. George Burroughs, and Statement of Thomas Putnam & Edward Putnam v. George Burroughs†

3ʳᵈ of 3 dates. See No. 124 on May 9, 1692

Sworn at Trial: Deposition of Ann Putnam Jr. v. George Burroughs, and Statement of Thomas Putnam, Peter Prescott, Robert Morey & Ezekiel Cheever v. George Burroughs†

2ⁿᵈ of 2 dates. See No. 457 on Aug. 3, 1692

Sworn at Trial: Deposition of Ann Putnam Jr. v. George Burroughs, and Statement of Edward Putnam & Thomas Putnam v. George Burroughs†

3ʳᵈ of 3 dates. See No. 125 on May 9, 1692

Sworn at Trial: Deposition of John Putnam Sr. & Rebecca Putnam v. George Burroughs†

2ⁿᵈ of 2 dates. See No. 126 on May 9, 1692

Sworn at Trial: Deposition of Thomas Putnam & Edward Putnam v. George Burroughs†

2ⁿᵈ of 2 dates. See No. 127 on May 9, 1692

493. Testimony of Thomas Ruck v. George Burroughs†

7. One Mr. *Ruck*, Brother-in-law to this *G.B.* testified, that *G.B.* and himself, and his Sister, who was *G.B.*'s Wife, going out for two or three Miles to gather Straw-berries, *Ruck* with his Sister, the Wife of *G.B.* Rode home very Softly, with *G.B.* on Foot in their Company, *G.B.* stept aside a little into the Bushes; whereupon they halted and Haloo'd for him. He not answering, they went away homewards, with a quickened pace, without expectation of seeing him in a considerable while; and yet when they were got near home, to their Astonishment, they found him on foot with them, having a Basket of Straw-berries. *G.B.* immediately then

fell to Chiding his Wife, on the account of what she had been speaking to her Brother, of him, on the Road: which when they wondred at, he said, *He knew their thoughts.* Ruck being startled at that, made some Reply, intimating, that the Devil himself did not know so far; but *G.B.* answered, *My God makes known your Thoughts unto me.* The Prisoner now at the Bar had nothing to answer, unto what was thus witnessed against him, that was worth considering. Only he said, *Ruck, and his Wife left a Man with him, when they left him.* Which *Ruck* now affirm'd to be false; and when the court asked *G.B. What the Man's Name was?* his Countenance was much altered; nor could he say, who 'twas.

Notes: This document does not appear elsewhere, and although Mather is using this material to justify the trials, there is no reason to doubt the basic validity of this as a report of a court record. ◊ Used at trial.

Cotton Mather. Wonders of the Invisible World: Being an Account of the Tryals of Several Witches, Lately Executed in New-England: And of several remarkable Curiosities therein Occuring. . . . (London: John Dunton, 1693), pp. 64–65.

Sworn at Trial: Deposition of Mary Walcott v. George Burroughs†

3rd of 3 dates. See No. 129 on May 9, 1692

Sworn at Trial: Testimony of Samuel Webber v. George Burroughs†

2nd of 2 dates. See No. 447 on Aug. 2, 1692

Sworn at Trial: Depositions of Simon Willard v. George Burroughs; Testimony of William Wormall v. George Burroughs†

3rd of 3 dates. See No. 130 on May 9, 1692

Billa Vera: Indictment No. 1 of Elizabeth Procter, for Afflicting Mary Walcott†

2nd of 2 dates. See No. 380 on June 30, 1692

Billa Vera: Indictment No. 2 of Elizabeth Procter, for Afflicting Mercy Lewis†

2nd of 2 dates. See No. 381 on June 30, 1692

494. Deposition of Joseph Bailey & Priscilla Bailey v. Elizabeth Procter & John Procter†

[Hand 1] the deposition of Joseph Bayley aged forty four years testifyeth and saith, that I on the: 25th day of may last my self & my wife being bound to Boston, on the road when I came in sight of the house where John procter did liue, there was a uery hard blow strook on my brest which caused great pain in my stumoc & amasement in my head but did see no person near me only my wife behind me on the same hors, and when I came agains sd procters house according to my understanding I did se John procter & his wife att sd house procter himself loocked out of the windo & his wife did stand Just without the dore, I tould my wife of it, {&} shee did loock that way & could see nothing but a littell maid att the dore. I saw no maide there but procters wife according to my understanding did stand att the dore, afterwards about half a mile from the afore sd house I was taken spechles for sum short time. my wife did ask me seuarall questions and desiered me that if I could not speak I should

hould up my hand which I did. and immediatly I could speak as well as euer, and when we   August 5, 1692
came to the way where Salem Road cometh into Ipswich road there I receiued another blow
on my brest which caused much pain that I could not sitt on my hors and when I did alite off
my hors, to my understanding I saw a woman coming towards us about sixteen or twenty
pole from us but did not know who it was, my wife could not see her when I did get up on
my hors againe to my understanding there stood a cow where I saw the woman, after that we
went to Boston without any farther molestation but after I came home againe to newbury I
was pinched and nipt by sumthing inuisible for sum=time but now through gods goodnes to
me I am well again

                             [Hand 2] Jurat in Curia by both p{er}sons.

[Reverse] Joseph Bayley & wife

Notes: The docket does not indicate whether this is John or Elizabeth Procter, but the context suggests Elizabeth even
though the possibility that it is John cannot be ruled out. ◊ Used at trial. ◊ Hand 2 = Stephen Sewall

*Essex County Court Archives, vol. 1, no. 106, Massachusetts Supreme Judicial Court, Judicial Archives, on deposit James Duncan
Phillips Library, Peabody Essex Museum, Salem, MA.*

Sworn at Trial: Deposition of Stephen Bittford v. Rebecca Nurse & Elizabeth Procter†
2nd of 2 dates. See No. 382 on June 30, 1692

Sworn at Trial: Deposition of Elizabeth Hubbard v. Elizabeth Procter†
2nd of 2 dates. See No. 50 on April 11, 1692

Sworn at Trial: Deposition of Ann Putnam Jr. v. Elizabeth Procter†
3rd of 3 dates. See No. 53 on April 11, 1692

Sworn at Trial: Deposition of Thomas Putnam & Edward Putnam v. Elizabeth Procter†
2nd of 2 dates. See No. 54 on April 11, 1692

Sworn at Trial: Deposition of Mary Walcott v. Elizabeth Procter†
2nd of 2 dates. See No. 386 on June 30, 1692

Sworn at Trial: Deposition of Mary Warren v. Elizabeth Procter†
2nd of 2 dates. See No. 375 on June 30, 1692

495. Petition in Support of John Procter & Elizabeth Procter‡

[Hand 1] We whose names ar vnder written hauinge seueral yeares knowne John Procter and
his wife do testefy. that we neuer heard or vnderstood that ^{they} were euer suspected to be
guilty of the crime now charged vpon ^{them} and seueral of v⟨s⟩ being their neare
neighbours do testefy that to our aprehension they liued christian life in their famely and
were euer ready to helpe such. as stood in need of their helpe/
Nathaniel ffelton sen: ⟨?⟩[Lost]
and mary his wife

August 5, 1692

Samuel Marsh
and Priscilla his wife
James Houlton and
Ruth his wife
John ffelton
Nathaniel ffelton iun
ssamuell ffrayll
and an his wife
Zachriah marsh
and mary his wfe
ssamuel Endecott
and hanah his wife
Samuell Stone
George Locker
Samuell Gaskil
& provided his wife
George Smith
Ed Edward: Gaskile

Notes: This show of support for the Procters seems most likely to be a supporting document for them at their trial on August 5. The possibility that it was prepared for the grand jury, June 30, however, cannot be ruled out. None of the people signing the petition were subsequently accused of witchcraft. Some of the signatures are signed by spouses, some by people in the group other than the "signatories." George Locker had been the constable ordered on February 29 to arrest Sarah Good, which he did on March 1. See No. 1. ◊ Likely used at trial. ◊ Facsimile Plate 6.

Essex County Court Archives, vol. 1, no. 110, Massachusetts Supreme Judicial Court, Judicial Archives, on deposit James Duncan Phillips Library, Peabody Essex Museum, Salem, MA.

496. Petition in Support of John Procter & Elizabeth Procter‡

[Hand 1] The Humble, & Sincere Declaration of us, Subscribers, Inhabitants, in Ipswich, on yᵉ Behalf of oᵉ Neighbᵉs Jnᵒ Procter & his wife now in Trouble & undᵉ Suspition of Witchcraft.
To the Honᵉable Court of Assistants now Sitting In Boston.
⟨?⟩ Honᵉed, & Right Worshipfull⟨?⟩!
The foresd John Procter: may have Great Reason ⟨?⟩ to Justifie the Divine Sovereigntie of God undᵉ thes S⟨e⟩vere Remarqᵉˢ of Providenc upon his Peac & Honᵉ; undᵉ A due Reflection upon his Life Past; And so the Best of us have Reason to Adoar the Great Pittie & Indulgenc of Gods Providenc, that we are not a⟨s⟩ Exposed to the utmost Shame, yᵗ the Divell Can Invent undᵉ the pᵉmissions of Sovereigntie, tho not for yᵗ Sin fore Named; yet for oᵉ many Transgretions; for we Do at present Suppose that it may be A Method wᵗʰin the Seveerer, But Just Transactions of the Infinite Majestie of God; yᵗ he Some times may pᵉmitte Sathan to pᵉsonate, Dissemble, & therby abuse In̄ocents, & Such as Do in the fear of God Defie the Devill & all his works. The Great Rage he is pᵉmitted to attempt holy Job wᵗʰ The Abuse he Does the famous Samuell, In Disquieting his Silent Dust, by Shaddowing his venerable Pᵉson in Answer to the Charmes of witch Craft, & other Instances from Good

hands; may be Arg^{t⟨s⟩} Besides the unsearcheable footstepps of Gods Judgments y^t are
brought to Light Every Morning y^t Astonish o^ε weaker Reasons, To teach us Adoration,
Trembling, & Dependanc, &c^a But

    We must not Trouble y^ε Hon^ε s by being Tedious, Therfore we being Smitten with the
Notice of what hath happened, we Reccon it w^{th}in the Duties of o^ε Charitie, that Teacheth
us to do, as we would be done by; to offer thus much for the Clearing of o^ε Neighbo^ε s
Inocencie; viz That we never had the Least Knowledge of Such a Nefandous wickedness In
o^ε Said Neighbours, Sinc they have been w^{th}in our acquaintanc; Neither do we remember
any Such Thoughts in us Concerning them; or Any Action by them or either of them
Directly tending that way; no more then might be in the ⟨li⟩ves of any other p^ε sons of the
Clearest Reputation as to Any Such Evill⟨s⟩
What God may have Left them to, we Cannot Go into Gods pavilions Cloathed w^{th}
Cloudes of Darknesse Round About. But as to what we have Ever ~~heard~~ seen, or heard of
them [] upon o^ε Consciences we Judge them Innocent of ye Crime objected.
His Breading hath been Amongst us; and was of Religious Parents in o^ε place; & by Reason
of Relations, & Prop^ε ties w^{th}in o^ε Towne hath had Constant Intercourse wth us.
We speak upon o^ε p^ε sonall acquaintanc, & observation: & So Leave our Neighbours, & this
our Testimonie on their Behalfe to the wise Thoughts of y^ε Honours & Subscribe &c^a

> Jno Wise
> William Story Senr
> Reienallde ffoster:
> Thos: Chote
> John Burnum S^r
> william: Thomsonn.
> Tho. Low. sanor
> Isaac ffoster
> John Burnum jun^ε
> William Goodhew
> Isaac perkins
> Nathanill Perkins
> Thomas Lovkine.
> William Cogswell
> Thomas Warny
> John ffellows
> william Cogswell Sen
> Jonathan cogswell
> John Cogswell J̄^u
> John Cogswell
> Thomas Andrews
> Joseph Andrews
> Benjamin marshall
> John Andrews Ju^r
> william Butler
> William Andrews
> John ~~Andr~~ Andrews
> John Chote Se^r
> Joseph prockter

August 5, 1692

Samuell Gidding
Jseph Euleth
Jems: White.

Notes: The argument in the petition emphasizes an issue at the heart of the witchcraft debate, whether the devil could impersonate an innocent person. As with the previous petition, No. 495, this was probably used at the trial. The two separate petitions show a remarkable range of support for the Procters, with no retaliation against those who signed. But the support proved futile in regard to the verdicts. The signatures generally reflect different hands, although Thomas and Joseph Andrews were signed by the same hand. Both of them had been witnesses against Elizabeth How. See No. 346 & No. 396. ◊ Likely used at trial. ◊ "Nefandous": 'unmentionable, abominable' (*OED* s.v. *nefandous*).

Essex County Court Archives, vol. 1, no. 60, Massachusetts Supreme Judicial Court, Judicial Archives, on deposit James Duncan Phillips Library, Peabody Essex Museum, Salem, MA.

497. Testimony of William Rayment Jr. for Elizabeth Procter†

[Hand 1] ⟨t⟩he testimony of william Rayment aged 26 years or there abouts testifieth & saith that I being at the house of leftint Ingesone: some time in the later end of marth: there discoursing conserning. the examying of sererall person suspected for wiches: I was saying that I hard that goody procter was to be examyned to morrow to which goody ingesone replyed she did not beleue it for she heard nothing of it: some of ⟨t⟩he afflict{ed} persons being present one of them or more cryed out there is goody procter there is goody procter and old wich Ile haue har hang goody ingerson sharply reprou{ed} them: then they sem⟨e⟩d to make. a Jest of it

[Reverse] [Hand 2] Wm Rayment

Notes: This appears to have been used in defense of Elizabeth Procter at her trial. The document following this one, No. 498, appears to be a copy, but some ambiguity exists as to which is the original and which is the copy. ◊ Likely used at trial.

Essex Institute Collection, no. 26, James Duncan Phillips Library, Peabody Essex Museum, Salem, MA.

498. Testimony of William Rayment Jr. for Elizabeth Procter, Copy‡

[Hand 1] The testimony of William Rayment aged 26 years or there about testifieth and saith that I being at the hous of Left^nt Ingarsels some time in the Later end of march; there discoursing conserning the examyning of severall person⟨s⟩ suspected for wiches: I was saying that I hard that goody procter ~~t~~was to be examyned to morrow to which goody Ingarsell replyed she did not beleve it for she heard nothing of it: som of the afflicted persons being present one of them or more cryd out there goody procter there goody procter and old ~~which~~ wich Ile have her hang goody Ingersell sharply reproved them then they semed to make a Jest of it

[Reverse] [Hand 2] william rayment

Notes: Likely used at trial.

August 5, 1692

Essex County Court Archives, vol. 1, no. 98, Massachusetts Supreme Judicial Court, Judicial Archives, on deposit James Duncan Phillips Library, Peabody Essex Museum, Salem, MA.

499. Testimony of Samuel Barton for Elizabeth Procter, and Testimony of John Houghton for Elizabeth Procter†

[Hand 1] the testimony of Samuel Barton aged 28 years or thearabouts who testifieth and saith that I being at Thomas Putnams ahelping to tend the aflickted follks i heard them talking who the ~~Child~~ Children Complained of and I heard them teel mercy lewes that she Cryed out of goody Procter and mercy lewes said that she did not Cry out of goody procter nor nobody she said she did say thear she is but did nat teel them who and Thomas Putnam & his wife & others told her that she Cryed out of goody pro{c}ter and mercy lewes said if she did it was when she was out in her head for she said she saw nobody this being the 29 of march in the year. 1691/2

[Hand 2] John Hou⟨lt⟩on aged 23 testefieth and saith I this Deponent. was present at the same tyme. {aboue written} and I heard Thomas Putnam, and his wife sayd that mercy. Lewis saw. or named the wife of John Procter. in her fits. and we heard the sayd mercy Lewis affirme that she neuer sayd that euer she saw her

[Reverse] ⟨In⟩ behalfe Procter

Notes: Likely used at trial.

Essex County Court Archives, vol. 1, no. 107, Massachusetts Supreme Judicial Court, Judicial Archives, on deposit James Duncan Phillips Library, Peabody Essex Museum, Salem, MA.

500. Testimony of Daniel Elliott for Elizabeth Procter†

[Hand 1] the testimony of daniel elet aged 27 years or thear abouts who testifieth & saith that I being at the hous of leutennant ingasons one the 28 of march in the year: 1692 thear being preasent one of the aflicted persons which cryed out and said thears goody procter william raiment iuner being theare present told the garle he beleued she lyed for he saw nothing then goody ingerson told the garl she told a ly for thear was nothing: then the⟨?⟩ garl said that she did it {for} sport they must haue some sport

Notes: Likely used at trial.

Essex County Court Archives, vol. 1, no. 109, Massachusetts Supreme Judicial Court, Judicial Archives, on deposit James Duncan Phillips Library, Peabody Essex Museum, Salem, MA.

August 5, 1692

Billa Vera: Indictment No. 2 of John Procter, for Afflicting Mercy Lewis†
2nd of 2 dates. See No. 388 on June 30, 1692

Billa Vera: Indictment No. 3 of John Procter, for Afflicting Mary Warren†
2nd of 2 dates. See No. 389 on June 30, 1692

Sworn at Trial: Deposition of Sarah Bibber v. John Procter†
2nd of 2 dates. See No. 390 on June 30, 1692

Sworn at Trial: Deposition of Elizabeth Booth v. John Procter†
2nd of 2 dates. See No. 55 on April 11, 1692

Deposition of Elizabeth Hubbard v. John Procter†
2nd of 2 dates. See No. 56 on April 11, 1692

Sworn at Trial: Deposition of Thomas Putnam & John Putnam Jr. v. John Procter†
2nd of 2 dates. See No. 60 on April 11, 1692

501. Statement of Samuel Sibley v. John Procter, as Recorded by Samuel Parris†

[Hand 1] The morning after ye examination of Goody Nurse Sam: Sibly met John Proctor about Mr Phillips wo called to said Sibly as he was going to s^d Phillips & askt how ye folks did at the village, He answered he heard they were very bad last night but he had heard nothing this morning Proctor replyed he was going to fetch ^{home} ⟨ₐ⟩ his jade he left her there last night & had rather given 40^s than ^{let} ~~left~~ her ~~here~~ ^{come up} S^d Sibly askt why he talkt so Proctor replyed if they were let alone so we should all be Devils & Witches quickly they should rather be had to the Whipping post but he would fetch his jade home & thresh the Devil out of her & more to the like purpose crying hang them, hang them. And also added that when she was first taken with fits he kept her close to the Wheel & threatened to thresh her, & then she had no more fits till the next day he was gone forth, & then she must have her fits again firsooth &c.

[Hand 2] Jurat in Curia
Procter Ownes he meant Mary Warren
attest St. Sewall Cle

[Reverse] Sam Sibleys Euidence

Notes: This document is a record by Samuel Parris of what he had heard from Samuel Sibley about John Procter's threat against his servant, Mary Warren. It could have been written as early as March 25, the day after the examination of Rebecca Nurse. Subsequently, Procter himself confirmed that he had meant Mary Warren. ◊ Used at trial. ◊ "jade": 'a term of reprobation applied to a woman' (*OED* s.v. *jade* n^1, 2). ◊ Hand 1 = Samuel Parris; Hand 2 = Stephen Sewall

Essex County Court Archives, vol. 1, no. 52, Massachusetts Supreme Judicial Court, Judicial Archives, on deposit James Duncan Phillips Library, Peabody Essex Museum, Salem, MA.

502. Deposition of Mary Walcott & Elizabeth Hubbard v. John Procter, Elizabeth Procter, Benjamin Procter, & Sarah Procter and Testimony of James Holton v. John Procter & Elizabeth Procter†

[Hand 1] The Deposion of mary Walcutt and elizabeth Hubbord sd that one the 29 of may 1692 we came to see James holten how [= who] lay greuesely tormented and we then saw John Prockter and his Wife his son beni procter sarah procter and ~~Wiluam procter~~ all of them a presing of ~~them~~ him ~~w^t~~ him {w^t} there hands one his stomack and tormenting of him most greuesoly and then quckly after they fell vpon vs and afflecked vs most Dredfuly for a Considerable time

[Hand 2] Jurat in Curia by
both

[Hand 1] James holten testifieth ["f" written over "e"] and sd that as soon as mary ["y" written over "gr"] Walcutt and elizebeth hubard was afflicked that at that same time I had ease of my pains.

[Hand 2] Jurat in Curia

[Reverse] [Hand 3] Mary. Walcott & Elizabeth ag^st Jno procter & Wife &c.
[Hand 4] & James Holton

Notes: The deposition was apparently used as trial testimony against both John and Elizabeth Procter in spite of the additional people named, perhaps because they were the Procter children or because no immediate trial action was planned against them. Indeed, although Benjamin and Sarah Procter were both imprisoned, no record of them being tried, even in 1693, survives. ◊ Used at trial. ◊ Hand 2 = Stephen Sewall; Hand 3 = Jonathan Corwin

Essex County Court Archives, vol. 1, no. 58, Massachusetts Supreme Judicial Court, Judicial Archives, on deposit James Duncan Phillips Library, Peabody Essex Museum, Salem, MA.

Wednesday, August 10, 1692

503. Examination of Sarah Carrier, Copy†

[Hand 1] {Sarah Carrier /}
The Examination of Sarah Carrier Taken before Dudly Broadsteat
Sarah Carrier ^{being accused of witchcraft} Confeseth as ffolloweth y^t She hath been a witch Euer Since She was Six Years Old y^t her moth^ε brought a ^{red} book to her and She touched it y^t her Moth^ε Baptizd her in Andrew ffostters pauster [= pasture] y^e day before She went to prison. & y^t her Moth^ε promised her She Should not be hanged y^t her Mother taught her how to afflicte p^εsons by pinching y^m or Setting on y^m y^t She began to afflict Sarah Phelps last Satterday & y^t Betty Johnson was wth her y^t her Moth^ε gaue her a Spear Last Night & y^t She precked Sarah Phelps & Ann Puttnam wth it

Notes: From *Andover Examinations Copy.* See No. 425. Sarah Carrier was eight years old. Dudley Bradstreet examined her on the same day as Thomas Carrier Jr. and Elizabeth Johnson Jr.. The Collections of the Massachusetts Historical Society, Third Series, vol. 1 (1825), pp. 124–126, includes transcriptions of these three examinations that were likely

August 10, 1692

made from the same originals as these copies in the *Andover Examinations Copy*. The differences between these and the 1825 transcriptions are minor, except for the inclusion of the following text after the examinations in the 1825 publication:

> Gentlemen,
>
> I Thought it meet to give you this broken account, hoping it may be of some service. I am wholly unacquainted with affairs of this nature neither have the benefit of books for forms &c. but being unadvisedly entered upon service I am wholly unfit for, beg that my ignorance and failings may be as much covered as conveniently may be; which will ever be acknowledged by
>
> Your poor and unworthy servant,
> DUDLEY BRADSTREET.
>
> I know not whether to make any returns. Bonds I have taken. The custos rotulorum I know not, &c.
>
> *To the Honoured* Bartholomew Gedney, John Hathorne, Esq., *or any of their Majesties' Justices of the Peace in Salem these humbly present.*

Notes: "custos rotulorum": *Latin* 'Keeper of the Rolls,' 'the principal justice of the peace in a county, who has the custody of the rolls and records of the sessions of the peace' (*OED* s.v. *custos*)

Essex Institute Collection, no. 24, 5v, James Duncan Phillips Library, Peabody Essex Museum, Salem, MA.

504. Examination of Thomas Carrier Jr., Copy†

[Hand 1] {Tho$^\varepsilon$ Carrier – /}
The Examination of Tho$^\varepsilon$ Carrier Taken before Dudly Broadstret Esq$^\varepsilon$ on of their.
Majesties Justices of y^e Peace
Tho̅ Carr$^\varepsilon$ ^{being acused of witchcraft} Conffeseth that he was Giulty of witchcraft & y^t he had been a witch a weak & y^t his Mother taught him witchcraft That a Yellow bird apeared to him & Spoke to him at wch She being affrighted his Mother apeared to him & brought him a book & bid him ~~a book~~ Sett his hand to it telling him it would doe him good if he did Soe & y^t She would tear him in peices if he would not That his Mother baptized him in Shaw Shin Riuer pulled of his Cloths & putt him into y^e Riuer & y^t his Mother then told him he was hers for Euer That his Moth$^\varepsilon$ bid him afflict Mary walkutt Ann puttman & Sarah Phelps And y^t he went y^e 9th Instant at Night to Jno Chandlers, y^t their were 10 in Company wth him Who rid upon 2 Poles y^t there were 3 Men in y^e Company & 2 of y^e woemen belomged to Ipswich whose names ware Mary & Sarah & y^t he Saw Betty Johnson in ye Company & Conffesed y^t he ~~a~~ Did ye 9th Instant at night afflict Sarah Phelps & Ann puttnam by pinching y^m

Notes: From *Andover Examinations Copy*. See No. 425. Thomas Carrier was ten years old.

Essex Institute Collection, no. 24, 5v, James Duncan Phillips Library, Peabody Essex Museum, Salem, MA.

505. Examination of Elizabeth Johnson Jr., Copy

[Hand 1] The Examination of Elizabeth Jonson ^{Jun^r} Taken Before Dudley Broadstre[Lost] [= Bradstreet]
the 10 August 1692 // She Confeseth as ffolloweth That Good^ε Carrier brought a book to her & She Set her hand to it That Good^ε Carrier baptized her when She Baptized her Daughter Sarah & y^t Good^ε Carr^ε told her She Should be Saued if She would be a witch That She had bin at Salem Village wth C⟨?⟩ Good^ε Carr^ε & y^t She had been at ye Mock Sacrement theire & Saw Mr Burroughs their She Conffesed She had afflicted Seuerall p^εsons y^t ye first She afflicted was Lawrence Lacey & y^t She & Tho Carrier aflected Sarah phelps & Mary Walcutt & Ann Puttman, ye 9th Instant & y^t She afflicted y^m this day as She Came to Twone And y^t afflicted. and y^t She hath afflicted ^{a Child of} Ephrahim Dauis ye 9 Instant & this day by pinching him it and y^t she afflicted Ann puttnam wth a Spear That She and Good^ε Carrier afflicted Benj^a Abbott – That Good^ε Toothaker & 2 of her Children ware wth her ye last Night when She afflicted ye Children – She also Conffesed y^t one Dan^ll Ems of Boxford was wth her one ye 8th & 9th Instant at Night & he afflicted Sarah Phelps, & told her he had been a witch Euer Since he ran away And y^t She had a hand in afflicting Tim^o Swan

Notes: From *Andover Examinations Copy*. See No. 425. Elizabeth Johnson Jr. was twenty-two years old.

Essex Institute Collection, no. 24, 5v, James Duncan Phillips Library, Peabody Essex Museum, Salem, MA.

Thursday, August 11, 1692

506. Examination of Sarah Carrier

Sarah Carrier's confession Aug. the 11th, 1696.
It was asked Sarah Carrier by the Magistrates or Justices John Hawthorne Esq; and others: How long hast thou been a witch? A. Ever since I was six years old. Q. How old are you now? A. Near eight years old, brother Richard says, I shall be eight years old in November next. Q. Who made you a witch? A. My mother, she made me set my hand to a book. Q. How did you set your hand to it? A. I touched it with my fingers and the book was red, the paper of it was white. She said she never had seen the black man; the place where she did it was in Andrew Foster's pasture and Elizabeth Johnson junr. was there. Being asked who was there beside, she answered her Aunt Toothaker and her cousin. Being asked when it was, she said, when she was baptized. Q. What did they promise to give you? A. A black dog. Q. Did the dog ever come to you? A. No. Q. But you said you saw a cat once. What did that say to you? A. It said it would tear me in pieces if I would not set my hand to the book. She said her mother baptized her, and the devil, or black man was not there, as she saw, and her mother said when she baptized her, thou are mine for ever and ever and amen. Q. How did you afflict folks? A. I pinched them, and she said she had no puppets, but she went to them that she afflicted. Being asked whether she went in her body or her spirit, she said in her spirit. She said her mother carried her thither to afflict. Q. How did your mother carry you

when she was in prison? A. She came like a black cat. Q. How did you know that it was your mother? A. The cat told me so that she was my mother. She said she afflicted Phelp's child last saturday, and Elizabeth Johnson joined with her to do it. She had a wooden spear, about as long as her finger, of Elizabeth Johnson, and she had it of the devil. She would not own that she had ever been at the witch meeting at the village. This is the substance.

Attest.

Simon Willard.

Notes: The incorrect date of 1696 appears in Hutchinson's publication. The *Andover Examinations Copy* (See No. 425) includes the text of an examination of Sarah Carrier on August 10 by Dudley Bradstreet (see No. 503), but this indicates that she was examined again the following day by John Hathorne.

Thomas Hutchinson, The History of the Province of Massachusetts-Bay, from the Charter of King William and Queen Mary, in 1691, Until the Year 1750, vol. 2, ed. Lawrence Shaw Mayo. (Cambridge, MA: Harvard University Press, 1936). p. 34.

507. Examinations of Abigail Faulkner Sr.

See also: Aug. 30, 1692.

[Hand 1] Abig^l: ffolkner examined: Augst 11: 1692
Mr Hauthorn.: Mr Corwin: & Cap: Higginson pressent

When she was brought into ye room: ye afflicted persons fell down {m^r Ha:} you are: heare: aprehended: for: witchcraft: but Answ^d: I know nothing of it with: ye cast of her eye: Mary: Walcot: & ye rest of ye afflicted: Mary Waren & others fell do⟨w⟩n: it was s^d to her do you not see:
she s^d yes but it is ye devill dos it in my shape: Mary Walcot s^d she had {2 monthes} seen her: a good wh⟨i⟩l⟨e⟩ agoe but was not hurt by her till last night: An Putnam sayd she had seen {s^d} ff⟨olk⟩n^ε ~~2 monthes~~: but was not hurt by her till last night & then she pulld me off my hors: Mary Warin s^d she had seen: her in company with other witches: but was not hurt by her till lately {~~night~~}
Mary Warin & others of ye afflicted: were struck down into: fitts & helped up out of their fitts by a touch of Abig^{il} ffolkn^{εs} hand: she was urged to confes ye truth: for ye creddit of her Town: her Couz̄ Eliz Jonson urged her: with that: but: she refused to do it saying god would not: require her to confess that: y^t she was not gilty of: ~~ff⟨e⟩l~~ Phelpses daughter complayned her afflicting her: but: she: denyed: that she had any thing to doe vith witchcraft she s^d ffolkn^ε had a cloth in her hand: that when she squeezed in her hand ye afflicted: fell into greevous fits: as was observed: ye afflicted sayd Dan^{ll} Eames & Capt ffloyd was upon that cloth when it was upon ye table
she s^d she was sorry: they were afflicted: but: she was told & it was observd she did not shed a tear: Mary Waren was pulld und^ε ye table & was helpd out of her fitt by a touch of s^d ffolkn^ε: she s^d she had looked on some of these afflicted: when they came to Andov^ε & hurt them not: but she was told it was before she began to afflict them: she was told that it was reported she used to conjure with a seiv: but she s^d it was not so that story: was cleard up: &

August 30: 92: Abig^l ffol⟨ro⟩er: before: their Majest^{ts} Justices at first deny⟨e⟩d witchcraft as she had done before: but afterward: she ~~ownd~~ owned: that: she was Angry at what folk s^d:

when her Couz̄ Eliz Jonson was teken up: & folk laught & s^d her sister Jonson would come
out next: & she did look with an evil eye on ye afflicted persons: & did consent that they
should be afflicted: becaus they were ye caus of bringing her kindre{d} out: and she did wish
them ill. & her spirit being raised she did: pinch her hands together: & she knew not but
that ye devil might take that advantage but it was ye devil not she that afflicted: them: this
she s^d she did at Capt Chandlers garison: ye Night after: Eliz Jonson had bin examined
before Capt Bradstreet in ye day

      this is ye substance of what s^d Abig^l ffolkners: examina{tion} ^{was;} taken out of
      my charactors: Attest

                                           Simon Willard

          [Hand 2] The aboues^d Examination was before John Hathorne Jus^t peace

[Reverse] [Hand 3] Abigaiel ffalkners Examination

Notes: Hand 1 = Simon Willard; Hand 2 = John Hathorne; Hand 3 = Anthony Checkley

Essex County Court Archives, vol. 2, no. 40, Massachusetts Supreme Judicial Court, Judicial Archives, on deposit James Duncan
Phillips Library, Peabody Essex Museum, Salem, MA.

508.   Examination of Elizabeth Johnson Jr.

See also: Jan. 5, 1693.

      [Hand 1] Eliz Jonsons: {Jun^ε} Confession: August: ye 11th 1692
before: Jno Hawthorn Esq^ε & others: their majes^ts Justices
:ye Majestrates: s^d to her: you have alredy confessed: you are a witch: how long have you bin
soe. A: four year: she s^d ye devill like {a black man} & goodwife Carrier perswaded: her to be
a witch: & that she was att goodwife Carriers hous when: thay perswaded her: and they
promised her she should be safe: and should not be found: out: they also promised her: a
shilling in money: but she s^d she never had it she s^d she did not presently afflict persons: ~~but~~
not till she had bin babtized: by ye devill: which was about 3 years agoe: in goodwife Carriers
well: she s^d she scratcht ye devills book with her finger when she signed to it so she signed it
she s^d ye devill never apeared to her from ye time she signed: till she was babtized: after she
was babtized he appeared like two black Catts: she forgott: what ye devill s^d to her when she
was babtized by him: but he dipt her head over in water: she owned she had bin at y^e
witcheses meeting: & that she saw Capt ffloyd there: and she saw goodwife Carrier: &
goodwife toothaker & two of Toothakers children: one of them was Martha Emorson she s^d
she saw Capt ffloyd in ye room: when she was examined & that goodwif Toothaker: &
daghter: & goodwife Carrier: were there & intended kill her: for they threatned to tere her to
peices: being asked how old she was: she s^d 22 years: she s^d there were: about six score att y^e
witch meeting att ye Villadge that she saw: she s^d ye ocasion of her first signing ye devils book
was: the devill & goodwife Carrier threatned to tere in peices if she did not doe it: she s^d she
wrought then att s^d Carriers hous: she s^d they had bread & wine att ye witch sacrement att y^e
Villadge & they filled ye wine out into cups to drink she s^d there was a minister att that
meeting & he was a short man & she thought his name was Borroughs: She s^d they agreed
that time to afflict folk: & to pull downe ye kingdom of Christ & to sett up ye devils
kingdom: & y^t ye first she afflicted was Benj^a Abbit or Lawrance Lascy: she s^d she had also

August 11, 1692

afflicted Phelpses daughter: she s^d she knew also: that Richd Carrier: & mary Lascy: had afflicted by witchcraft: but she knew it not till a little before they were taken up: she s^d she had aflicted Law^r Lascy: by setting on his stumack: & that goodwife Carier & goodwife Lascy Joined w^t her in afflicting Law^r Lascy: & that Dan^{ll} Eames: & Sarah Carrier Joynd w^t her to afflict Sarah Phelps also toothakers wife Joynd with: her: to afflict s^d Phelps: she s^d she afflicted s^d Phelps by poppets she brought out 3 poppits: made of: rags or stripes of clothe: two of them: the other was made of a birch Rhine [= rind]: one poppet: had: four peices or stripes of cloth: rapt one upon another: which she s^d was to afflict four persons with thare was thread in y^e middle und^r y^e rags Lawr Lascy & ephraim Davises child were two that: she afflicted by pinching that popet: a second popet had two such peices of rags rolld up together: & 3 pins stuck into it: & she afflicted be Abitt & James ffryes two children: & Abra: ffosters childred: with that poppet & other. she afflicted: An Putnam with a spear: & was asked whether ye spear was Iron or wood: she s^d either of them would doe: she was asked: where her ffamillier suckt: her: she showd one of her knuckles of her finger & s^d there was one place: & it looked: red: she s^d she had two places more whe⟨re⟩ they suckt her: &: women were ordered to search: them out: & they found two little red specks y^t s^d Jonson s^d were all that: there was to be seen: they were playn to be seen when they were: newly sucked: one of s^d places was behin⟨d⟩ her arm: R^d Carrier & Mary lascy Jn^r s^d thay saw goody Carier: lascy: & toothaker an ye poppits

This is ye substance of what I took in Characters from her mouth

Attest: Simon Willard

She owned: that she did renounce: god & Christ: & her former babtisme: when: y^e devill babtized her

she s^d that Martha toothaker goodwife Carrier goodwife Lascy: Capt ffloyd & she had Joiynd: together: to hurt &⟨?⟩ Jos Ballards wif

[Reverse] [Hand 2] I underwrytten being appointed by au$\overline{to}^ε$ to tak in wryteing the within examina^{ε}n Doe testify upon oath taken in court that this is a true coppy of the substance of itt to the best of my knowledge. 5 Jan^{ε}y 1692/3

Simon Willard

owned bef⟨or⟩e the Grand Jury
5 January 1692/3

[Hand 3] Robert. Payne foreman:

[Hand 4] Eliz Johnson was Examined before theire Maj^{εs} Justices att Salem

attests John Hathorne Jus^t P^ε

[Hand 5] Eliz Johnson Junr

Notes: This subsequent examination by Hathorne is much more extensive than the one by Dudley Bradstreet included in the *Andover Examinations Copy* (See No. 425), dated August 10. See No. 505. ◊ Hand 1 = Simon Willard; Hand 2 = John Higginson Jr.; Hand 4 = John Hathorne

Massachusetts Archives Collection, vol. 135, nos. 33 & 34. Massachusetts State Archives. Boston, MA.

Saturday, August 13, 1692

509. Examination of Daniel Eames

[Hand 1] 13: 6: 1692
the Exā of Dan^ll Emes:
Eliz: Johnson owned her confesion against Dan^ll Emes & y^t he was wth her 3 nights before she owned it. & aflicted phelps Child wth popets. puting pins in it & she se him Yesterday in the prison.
he fell upon. mary lacy & Ell: Johnson & Richd Carier said he saw him aflict y^m
mary walcot afirmed Emes aflicted her last night at aslots house at andiuor & she se him aflict ~~dan^ll Emes~~ Tim^o Swan. & Inga⟨ll⟩s {child.}
An. puttman & mary warren afirme y^t Dan^ll Emes aflicted them seuerall times
ye aflicted all fell downe w^n he came in
Q Dan^ll Emes. what doe you act your witch craft before us.
tell us how long is it sence you first began. y^e Euiden⟨c⟩es say you haue be a wi⟨tch⟩ euer sence you ran away.
A I neuer went away but w^n I went to the Southward & stayd a yere & 3 or 4 months. it was in June. about.
I am 28 yeres old:
I haue be maried 8. or. 9 yeres.
I first & formost am aran⟨?⟩d [= arraigned] afore y^ε hon^r I am her before you. I desire in y^e presents of Jx [= Jesus Christ] y^t you w⟨o⟩uld pray for me y^t I may spek y^e truth. he y^t is y^e Grat Judge knows y^t I neuer did couen^t wth y^e diull:. & doe not know any thing of it
I neuer signed to no book nor neuer se satan or any of his Instrum^ts y^t I know of
Q. her is mary warren. y^t neuer saw you personaly y^t afirmes you haue aflicted her aboue a month. se if you can look upon her; he turnd about & 5 fell downe & wth his touch he raised y^m
A I did ^{drem.} I se Goody Tooaker & some others who did tempt me: to signe to Sattan but I resisted Q are you certain you ware asleep; A. I was asleep. to be sure
Sam^ll Varnum. afirmes ~~y^tDan^ll Emes. told me that he~~
y^t Eph. Steuens. told me y^t Dan^ll Emes. said y^t he followed ye Diuell in the shap of a horse ouer 5 mile pond. & Bridges.
Richd Carier afirmed y^t Dan^ll Emes shap knock⟨t⟩ him downe:
A. as I was once on a progrese Jno wilson Jno lull. was goeing to Salsbory & I went wth y^m & came againe together:
Jno Lull. came up along wth me till we came against @ 5 mil⟨e⟩ pond. I had ben long from home: & was not willing y^e man should goe wth me: home:
Bridges: sai⟨d⟩: y^e report y^t he inuited this man & Cheated him, told y^e man that ther was y^e diuel in y^e 5 mill pond: & said he would goe to him, but he rid away. home & shut y^e doe [= door]:
y^e brook by Sam^ll bratlebooks. house. when I was a litle boy: my fath^r left me at home & I got a botle of rom & Drank more y^n might doe me good.
mary waren afirmed that this dan^ll Emes. aflicted. me w^n falkner was Exā & ther was a young man. apered & y^e bl [= black] man. stood upon his shoulder:

mary post doe you know DE: yes I know him his is my neighbr did you euer know him to aflict: no. did you know him to be a witch. no.

Goody bridges doe you know him yes doe you know him to be a witch no:

An: putman said he was made a witch at a broo⟨k⟩:

at yᵗ time at yᵉ Brook: wᵗ ingagmᵗ [= engagement] did you make to yᵉ diuill::

Bridges: I beleue ther is euidence Enough. yᵗ he said the diull caried him & his pack to yᵉ brook. at yᵉ Sabath day:

I doe not know but I might say so, but I bely my selfe

Eliz Johnson afirmes yᵗ the young man yᵗ stood before Emes wᵗ yᵉ bl man is Deane Robinson. & mary lacy said yᵗ young man. hurt mary warren::;.

I se him personaly. at ffr [= Francis] Deanes lane & he told me he was a wizard & a⟨t⟩ [ ] ga⟨t⟩e in his shap & a bl cat wᵗʰ him. yᵗ told me yᵗ {he} was Danˡˡ Emes: & said he would goe along wᵗʰ me to aflict folkes

[Reverse] EJ: the 3 time was yᵉ nite afore I owned ~~he said~~ he appeared. in his shap & I went with him to aflict [ ] child & aflictᵈ wᵗʰ pinching & prickᵋ wᵗʰ a speare Emes pricked wᵗʰ a pin, it is all. true:

post. said her compᵃ was. Sc⟨o⟩t. Chandler. tootaker. Carier. ffoster: ~~R⟨?⟩sse~~. Nurse:.

mary lacy said she saw the aperition of Danˡˡ Emes. yᵉ day before. her father came to done & told her father she doubted he would be sent for in away:

This Examination was taken the 13ᵗʰ August 1692 before ther majesties of yᵉ peace in Salem

atest John Higginson Justᵋ peace

Notes: "progrese": 'the action of stepping or marching forward or onward' (*OED* s.v. *progress* 1a). ◊ Hand 1 = John Higginson Jr.

UNCAT MS, Miscellaneous Manuscripts (1692), Massachusetts Historical Society. Boston, MA.

Thursday, August 18, 1692

510. Warrant for the Apprehension of Frances Hutchins & Ruth Wilford, and Officer's Return

See also: Aug. 19, 1692 & Aug. 20, 1692.

[Hand 1] Essex/ To the Constable of Hauerhill

Complaint being made to me this day, by Timothy Swan of Andouer: & Mary Wallcott, & Anne Putman of Salem Village, Against Mʳˢ ffrances Hutchins & Ruth Willford, of Hauerhill, & that yᵉ sᵈ Mʳˢ ffrances Hutchins ^{&} Ruth Willford, hath sorely afflicted them, yᵉ sᵈ Timothy Swan mary Wallcott & Anne Putman in their bodies, by witchcraft ^{Seuerall times} Contrary to yᵉ Peace of oᵋ Souereigne Lord & Lady King William & Queen Mary, of England &c: & to their Majesᵗˢ Laws in that Case prouided: & sᵈ Timothy Swan hauing, according to Law, giuen suffitient bond, to Prosecute sᵈ Complaint, before their Majesᵗˢ: justices of Peace att Salem yᵉ 19ᵗʰ or 20ᵗʰ Instant:

These therefore require you in their Majes^ts names to Apprehend & Seise ye bodies of ye afores^d ffrances Hutchins & Ruth Willford, upon sight hereof, & them safely Conuey to to Salem afores^d, to their Majes^ts justices of y^e peace there, to be examined, & proceeded with according to law: for which this shall be yo^ε warrant: Giuen und^ε my hand & seal this eighteenth day of August Anno Domini 1692: In y^e 4th year of their Majes^ts Reigne. &c:

                    Dudley Bradstreet Justice of Peac[Lost] [=peace]

[Reverse] [Hand 2] according to this warrant I haue seased and brought don M^r frances huchins: but sought with dilligenc for Ruth Wilford and she canot be found datt August 19: 1692

                    by me Wilam Starlin Constble for hauerhill

hauerhill ⌃{August} ~~the~~ the 20 1692
I seased the ~~the~~ body of Ruth wilfor[Lost] [= Wilford] of hauerhill to answer the Complant within menshoned

                    ꝑ me William: Strlin of hauerhill Constable

[Hand 3] Ruth Wilford Exa^ε. 22: 6: 92

Notes: The referenced examination of August 22 is not extant. ◊ Hand 1 = Dudley Bradstreet ◊ 1 wax seal.

MS Ch K 1.40, vol. 2, p. 92, Rare Books & Manuscripts, Boston Public Library. Boston, MA.

Friday, August 19, 1692

Executions of George Burroughs, Martha Carrier, George Jacobs Sr., John Procter, & John Willard

Officer's Return: Warrant for the Apprehension of Frances Hutchins & Ruth Wilford
2nd of 3 dates. See No. 510 on Aug. 18, 1692

511. Examination of Rebecca Eames

[Hand 1] Rebecca: Eames: examined: before Salem Majestrates: Aug^st 19: 1692

She ownd she had bin in ye snare a monthe: {or 2:} & had bin perswaded ⟨?⟩ to it: 3 monthes: & that ye devil: apeared to her like a colt. very ugly: ye first: time: but she would not ⟨?⟩own: y^t she had bin babtized by him. she did not know but y^t ye devil did perswade her: to renounce god & christ & ffolow his wicked wayes & that she did take his counsell: and that she did afflict Timo: Swan: she did not know but that ye devil might ask: her body & soul: & she knows not but y^t she did. give him soul & body: afterward she s^d she did do it & that she would forsake god & his works: & ye devil promised her: to give her powr: to avenge her selfe on them that offended her afterward she s^d ye devil apeared to her 7 year agoe: & that he had tempted her to: ly: and had made her to afflict persons. but she could not tell th⟨e⟩ir names that she first afflicted: Q who came w^t ye devil when he made you a witch A: a ragged girl: they came togethe^r and they perswaded me to afflict: & I afflicte Mary Warin & an

August 19, 1692

other fayr face: it is abo^t a quarter of a year agoe: I did it by sticking of pins. but did you afflict Swan: yes but: I am sorry for it: Q where had you your spear A I had nothing but an all [= awl] but was it with yor body or spirit you came to hurt these mayds: {A} with my spirit: Q but can you ask them forgivnes: A: I wil fall down on my knees: to ask it: of them: She would not own: that she signd y^e devils book when he askd her body & soul: but he would have had her done it nor. to a burch Rign [= birch rind]: nor nothing: she s^d y^e devil was in y^e shape of a hors when: he caried her to afflict. but would not own any body went with her to afflict: but y^e afflicted s^d her son Dan^{ll} went with her: to afflict: Q did you not say: y^e devil babtized yor son daniell. A he told me so: but: did you not touch the book nor lay yor hand on book nor paper: A I layd my hand on nothing without it was a peice of board: and did you lay yor hand on ye board when he bid you. A yes: Mary Lascy: s^d she had given her son Dan^{ll} to ye devil: at 2 years old: & y^t her aperition told her so: but: she could not remember it: she was bid to take Warin & lascy by ye hand & beg forgivnes & did so. & they forgave her. she s^d if she had given her son Dan^{ll} to ye devil it was in an Angry fitt she did not know but she might do it nor I do not know he is a wich but I am afrayd he is: Mary lascy saw her son Dan^{ll} stand before her & s^d Dan^{ll} bid his mother not confess he was a Wich: his mother: did not know she s^d but: she might se him for she saw a burlling: thing: before her: Mary Lascy s^d she had babtized her: son Dan^{ll} & y^t she had bin babtized in five mile Pond: she s^d ye reason she feard Dan^{ll} was a witch: was becaus he used dredfull bad words when he was Angry: and bad wishes

being asked: the ["t" written over "s"] s^d her age of Dan^{ll}: s^d he was 28 years old: she was told she had bin long a witch: then. if she gave her son to ye devil at 2 years old. she owned she had bin discontented since she had bin in league: with ye devil: she knew not but ye devil might come once a day: lik a mous: or ratt: she s^d she knew Sarah Parker but did not know: her to be a wich: but she heard she had bin crosd in love & ye devil had come to her & kisd her who was with you when you afflicted Swan: A. no body but my son Dan^{ll} he was there when I came: theether: she would have Dan^{ll} perswaded to confes: but was told she: were: best. to perswa⟨d⟩ him becaus she knew him to be a wich: she was askt if she was at ye execution: she s^d she was at ye hous below: ye hill: she saw a few folk: the woman of ye hous had a pin stuck into her foot: but: she s^d she did not doe it:. but how do you afflict:

{A} I Consent to it: but have you bin a wich 26 years: A no I can remember but 7: years & have afflicted: about a quarter of a year: but: if you have bin a wich so long: why did you not afflict before seing you promisd to serv ye devil A:. others: did not Afflict before: and the devil: did not require it:

but: doth not ye devil threaten: ~~to t~~⟨ere⟩ you ~~in peices~~: if you not do what he ses: A yes he thretens to tere me in peices but did you use: to goe to meeting on Sabath dayes:

yes: but not so often as I should have done; what shape did the devil com in when you layd yor hand on ye board:

A: I cannot tell exept it was a mous ~~or ratt~~

[Reverse] [Hand 2] R Eames [Hand 3] Examination

Notes: "Mary Lacey" is probably Mary Lacey Jr. A main Andover accuser, she was apparently being asked at the examination of Rebecca Eames to accuse Sarah Parker, daughter of Mary Parker who was examined and executed in September. See No. 540. Mary Lacey Jr. seemed reluctant to do so. Sarah Parker was imprisoned but survived. See No. 949. Rebecca Eames was convicted but survived. See No. 712 & No. 888. ◊ "burlling": 'whirling, rotating' (*OED* s.v. *burling* vbl. n.^{3}). ◊ Hand 1 = Simon Willard

Essex County Court Archives, vol. 2, no. 52, Massachusetts Supreme Judicial Court, Judicial Archives, on deposit James Duncan   August 20, 1692
Phillips Library, Peabody Essex Museum, Salem, MA.

Saturday, August 20, 1692

Officer's Return: Warrant for the Apprehension of Frances Hutchins & Ruth Wilford
3rd of 3 dates. See No. 510 on Aug. 18, 1692

512. Letter of Margaret Jacobs to George Jacobs Jr., from Prison

From the Dungeon in *Salem*-Prison, *August* 20. 92.

Honoured Father,
After my Humble Duty Remembred to you, hoping in the Lord of your good Health, as Blessed be God I enjoy, tho in abundance of Affliction, being close confined here in a loathsome Dungeon, the Lord look down in mercy upon me, not knowing how soon I shall be put to Death, by means of the Afflicted Persons; my Grand-Father having suffered already, and all his Estate Seized for the King. The reason of my Confinement is this, I having, through the Magistrates Threatnings, and my own Vile and Wretched Heart, confessed several things contrary to my Conscience and Knowledg, tho to the Wounding of my own Soul, the Lord pardon me for it; but Oh! the terrors of a wounded Conscience who can bear. But blessed be the Lord, he would not let me go on in my Sins, but in mercy I hope so my Soul would not suffer me to keep it in any longer, but I was forced to confess the truth of all before the Magistrates, who would not believe me, but tis their pleasure to put me in here, and God knows how soon I shall be put to Death. Dear Father, let me beg your Prayers to the Lord on my behalf, and send us a Joyful and Happy meeting in Heaven. My Mother poor Woman is very Crazey, and remembers her kind Love to you, and to Uncle, viz. D.A. So leaving you to the protection of the Lord, I rest your Dutiful Daughter,

Margaret Jacobs.

Notes: Margaret Jacobs had been accused on May 10 and examined May 11. See No. 131. On May 12, she joined the others in pretending to be afflicted by Alice Parker (see No. 144) and participated in the accusations against George Burroughs at the examination of Abigail Soames on May 13 (see No. 150). Unwilling to sustain the fraud, she wrote her retraction. Her father had fled, so it is unclear as to when and if this letter reached him. "D.A." refers to her uncle, Daniel Andrew, who had fled with her father. Her mother, Rebecca Jacobs, was also accused and tried. See No. 152 & No. 752. Two petitions by Margaret's grandmother, Rebecca Fox, appealed to Chief Magistrate William Stoughton in September and Governor William Phips in December for leniency, refering to Rebecca's longstanding mental difficulties. See No. 611 & No. 715.

Robert Calef. More Wonders Of The Invisible World, Display'd In Five Parts. (London: Nath. Hillard, 1700), pp. 105–106.

Thursday, August 25, 1692

513. Warrant for the Apprehension of William Barker Sr., Mary Marston, & Mary Barker, and Officer's Return

See also: Aug. 29, 1692.

[Hand 1] Essex To ye Constables of Andou^ε

Complaint being made to me this day, by Saml Martin of Andouer & Moses Tyler sen^ε of Boxford, against Williã Barker sen^ε Mary Marstone ye wife of John Marstone jun^ε & Mary Barker ye daughter of Lef^t John Barker, all of Andou^ε in y^t ye aboues^d William Barker Mary Marstone & Mary Barker, haue woefully afflicted & abused, Abigail Martin & Rose ffoster of Andou^ε & Martha Sprague of Boxford by witchraft, Contrary to ye peace of o^ε souereigne Lord & Lady ~~King~~ William & Mary King & Queen of England &c: & to their Majes^ts Laws in y^t Case prouided:

These therefore require you in their Majes^ts names upon sight hereof, to apprehend & seise ye bodies of William Barker sen^r Mary Marstone ye wife of John Marstone jun^ε & Mary Barker ye daughter of Lef^t John Barker all of Andou^ε & them safely Conuey to Salem, before their Majes^ts justices of ye peace there, to be examined & proceeded with according to law, for which this shall be yo^ε warrant: giuen und^ε my hand & seal this ~~eighteenth~~ {25^th 25} day of August Anno Domini 1692: in ye fourth year of their Majes^ts Reigne:/

Dudley Bradstreet justice of Peace

The s^d Martin & Tyler haue giuen suffitient bond to prosecute s^d persons to effect, which bond remains with me:

[Reverse] [Hand 2] In Obediance Two this warant I haue aprehended the within Riten persons and haue brought them to Salom the 29th of August 1692 Before ~~y~~ their honours mentined in the Rit:

℘ me Ephraim ffoster
Constable of Andouer

[Hand 3] Wm Barker
Mary Marston
Mary Barker
Exa^ε 29: 6. 92

Notes: Hand 1 = Dudley Bradstreet ◊ 1 wax seal.

MS Ch K 1.40, vol. 2, p. 108, Rare Books & Manuscripts, Boston Public Library. Boston, MA.

514. Complaint of Ephraim Foster & Joseph Tyler v. John Jackson Jr., John Jackson Sr., & John Howard

[Hand 1] Ephriam ffoster. of Andiuor. & Joseph Tyler of Boxford Complaine to their majesties Justices of the peace in Salem against John Jackson Senr & his Son John Jackson Junr & John Howard. all of the Towne of Rowley. Labourers ffor that they & Euery of them haue Comited Seuerall acts of witchcraft upon the bodys martha Sprage of Boxford & Rose ffoster of Andiuor Singleweomen to their Great hurt, & the Said Eph^r ffoster & Joseph Tyler doe by these presents oblige themselues Joyntly & Seuerally to our Souer^{e}s Lord & Lady King William & Quen mary in the full & whole Sume of one hundred pounds Bond Currant mony of New England The Condition is that they will prosecut the abouesaid Complaint to Effect as the law directs – 25 Augs^t 1692

Ephraim ffost⟨e⟩r

Joseph Tiler

this Recognizance taken before me
John Higginson Just^e peace

Notes: Hand 1 = John Higginson Jr.

MS Ch K 1.40, vol. 2, p. 196, Rare Books & Manuscripts, Boston Public Library. Boston, MA.

515. Warrant for the Apprehension of John Jackson Sr., John Jackson Jr., & John Howard, and Officer's Return

See also: Aug. 26, 1692.

[Hand 1] Essex/ To the Sheriff of the County of Essex or his deputy
Complaint being made this day to us by Ephriam ffoster of Andiuor & Joseph Tyler of Boxford against John Jackson Senr & his son John Jackson Junr & John Howard all of Rowley Labourers that they the said John Jackson Senr John Jackson Junr & John Howard haue sorely afflicted Martha ["M" written over "th"?] Sprage of Boxford & Rose ffoster of Andiuor Singleweomen by witchcraft contrary to the peace of our Souerain Lord & Lady william & Mary King & Quen of England &c & to their Majesties Laws in that case prouided, & said Ephriam ffoster & Joseph Tyler haueing giuen Sufficient bond to procecut their Complaint to Effect
These are therfore to require you in their Majesties names forthwith to aprehend & seize the Bodys of the said John Jackson Senr John Jackson Junr & John Howard of Rowley & them safely conuey to Salem before vs their Majesties Justices of the peace to be examined & proceded wth according to Law. for wch this shall be ye warrant dated In Salem: 25th August 1692:

Barth^o Gedney ⎫
John Hathorne ⎪
Jonathan: Corwin ⎬
John Higginson ⎪
Just^e peace ⎭

[Reverse] [Hand 2] August 26 1692 I haue apprehended the three within nam⟨ed⟩ John Jackson Sen^e John Jackson Jun^e and John Howard: and haue brought them before yo^e honnors to Answer as wthi[Lost] [= within]
by me Geo Herrick Dep^t Sheriff

[Hand 3] Jno Jackson Senr
Jno Jackson Junr

August 25, 1692   John Howard
                     26. 6 1692
                     Exa$^\varepsilon$

Notes: A portion of text at the beginning of this manuscript is lost. ◊ Hand 1 = John Higginson Jr.; Hand 2 = George Herrick ◊ 1 wax seal.

MS Ch K 1.40, vol. 2, p. 222, Rare Books & Manuscripts, Boston Public Library. Boston, MA.

516. Examination of Mary Bridges Jr.
See also: Jan. 10, 1693.

[Hand 1] Mary Bridges: an Andover Maid was examined before: Jno Hawthorn Esqr & other of [Lost] Majest^s in Salem: August 25 1692

Mary Bridges you are acused here for acting witchcraft upon Martha Spre⟨ag⟩ & Rose ffoster how long have you bin in this snare: she Answered about a month but afterward s^d ever since ye spring: she s^d a yellow bird apeared to her: out of dores: & bid her serve him: he promised me mony s^d she and fine cloathes & I promised to serv him: & I was to afflect: Martha Spreag & but: he gave me neither mony nor fine cloathes: she s^d she thought when he appeared: it was ye devil & she was to serve him two years: & then was to be his body & soul she owned she had bin babtized by him {the⟨?⟩} Then she was bid to goe take ye two afflicted persons by ye hand & she did & they were not hurt
She s^d ye next time she saw any such shape: it was a black bird & he would have her serve him & would have her to touch a paper: which she did with her finger & it made a red mark: she s^d she did not dip her finger in any thing when she made ye Mark {then she saw next a blak man} she: ownd she was at ye witch meeting at Chandlers at Andover ~~near a fortnigh agoe~~ last week & she thought there were near a hundred at it she s^d her shape was there: she s^d she knew not that her mother was a witch but she kne⟨w⟩ her sisters Susanna Post & Sarah Bridges were so: y^e way of her afflicting was by sticking pinse into things any cloathes & think of hurting them: & she s^d y^e devi⟨l⟩ tought her this way of afflicting or y^e blak man; she s^d she had afflicted only these 2: that complayned: only she afflected one y^e other night she knew not but y$^{⟨t⟩}$ it might be Mary Warin: she thouht it might be she: y^e devil told her she should never be brought out: she s^d they drank sack at y^e witch meeting at Andover: it stood y^r in pots & they drawed it out of a barrill. she knew but few there but s^d goodwife ffoster & Carrier was there: she also s^d she rid to Salem Village meeting upon a pole & the black man carried y^e pole over y^e tops of y^e trees & there they promised one another to afflict persons

I und$^\varepsilon$ written being appointed by Authority to take y^e above examination doe testify upon oath taken in Court: that this is a true coppy of the substance of it to y^e best of my knowledge Jan$^\varepsilon$ 10th 1692

                                       Simon Willard

[Hand 2] Mary Bridges was Examind before their Majesties Justices of the peace in Salem atest

                                   John Higginson Just$^\varepsilon$ peace

[Hand 1] Simon Willard owned: y^e above: written: to be y^e truth: to y^e best of his knowledge   August 25, 1692
before: y^e grand Inquest Jan^ε 10th 1692

Robert Payne
foreman.

[Reverse] [Hand 2] Mary Brid[Lost][= Bridges]
Junio^ε

Notes: Mary Bridges Jr. was twelve years old. ◊ "sack": 'a general name for a class of wine formerly imported from Spain and the Canaries' (*OED* s.v. *sack* n^3). ◊ Hand 1 = Simon Willard; Hand 2 = John Higginson Jr.

Suffolk Court Files, vol. 32, docket 2729, p. 73, Massachusetts Supreme Judicial Court, Judicial Archives, Massachusetts State Archives. Boston, MA.

517. Examination of Sarah Bridges, Copy

[Hand 1] August 25th 1692
{+} Sarah Bridges of Andiuor Examined before y^e Justices of Salem
She was told She was Charged for Hurting martha Sprage by witchcraft but denied it & hoped God would Clear her Inocencey ye afflicted p^{ε}sons were Struck Dwone into a fitt & helped up by ye touch of her hand Richd Carrier S^d it was She that was Vpon ye afflicted in there fitt She disowned witchcraft Saying She had Neuer Sett her hand to ye Diuels book nor been baptized by him though She ^{was} told y^t her Sister Hannah Post had Confesed that She was one of ye Company y^t had been baptized wth her at 5 Mile pond yett denyed y^t She had any thing to doe wth ye Diuel or y^t She had Seen or heard any thing {y^t way} tending She was throwne of her horse. once Indeed Coming from Ipswich & frighted by it but She thought it was by her aunt How, know knothing of Witchcraft She was Sencible ye afflicted were Strangly Struck Dwone but She knew not ye Mening of it – Yett after ~~She owned~~ She owned She had been in ye Diuels Snare Euer Since ye last ~~year~~ winter & y^t ye Diuel Came to her lik⟨e⟩ a man would haue her Signe to his book & told His name was Jesus & y^t She must Serue & worship him She did Sign ye book & ye Mark was Red he told me I must goe and afflict Some body & ye Diuel prickt her finger & She made a Red mark in ye book ye Diuel told her She ["She" written over "her"] Must Renounce god & Christ & promis to Serue him & I did S^d She, & She S^d ye Diuel Came Somtimes like a bird Somtimes like a bare Som times like a man but most frequently like a man. he told me Since I Came here he would kill me if I Conffesed She S^d her Comp^a was Mary Post her Sister hanah & Mary Bridges y^t She used to afflict p^{ε}sons by Squezing her hands & Sticking pins in her Cloths She owned She had been baptized by ye Diuel wth her Sister Susana post⟨e⟩ Mary Bridges & y^t She was to Serue ye Diuel 4 Years
Brought from ouer leafe
& he was to haue body & Soul She owned She had been & ye witch Metting at Chandlers Garrison at Andiuor & y^t She thought there ware @ 200 witches their & y^t they Eat bred & Drank wine & y^t Some of ye prisoners were there She S^d She had heard of but one Inocent man Imprisoned Yet for witchcraft & y^t was abbott of Ipswich being asked w^t She thought of ye afflicted whether they Ware witches She S^d no they were Honest p^{ε}sons y^t helpd to bring out y^e witches She owned She had Some times Rid upon a pole & bing bid to goe and

August 25, 1692

ask foregiuenes of y^e afflicted She did & owned She had afflicted y^m but would Doe it No
More but would Renounce y^e Diuel & his Works & y^e afflicted p$^\varepsilon$sons forgaue her & She
~~cold~~ could talk wth them & not hurt them

These two p$^\varepsilon$sons Hanah Post & Sarah Bridges haue Conffesed y^e Carcumstances of what y^e
afflicted S^d of y^m & not laying falswhood to y^m ⟨?⟩ any one of their Charging of y^m as that
they haue afflicted the time when y^e Way how they afflicted y^m y^e place where ^{all}
agreeing wth what y^e afflicted haue Charged y^m as thus ye afflicted would Say did not you
afflict me Such a time in Such a place in Such a maner they did answer Yes I did I am Sorry
for it pray forgiue me & forgiuenes they asked wth plenty of tears whereas they Could not
Shed on tear before as was well obserued Hannah Post owned her being Struck at her unkle
Tilers by y^e Constab$^\varepsilon$ as y^e afflictd had Said and as to {y^e} Number of witches y^e afflicted S^d
their Saw ["Saw" written over "was"] @ 200 at Chandlers Metting Soe S^d these two they
thought their was @ 200, Soe also Susana Post in her Confession Sayth She Saw @ 200, at a
witch Metting at y^e Village. Mary Bridges Said in her Conffession Sayd She Saw @ 100 at a
^{witch} Metting y^t She was at

Notes: From *Andover Examinations Copy*. See No. 425.

Essex Institute Collection, no. 24, 6r–v, James Duncan Phillips Library, Peabody Essex Museum, Salem, MA.

518. Examination of Hannah Post, Copy

[Hand 1] August y^e 25th 1692

Hannah Post of Boxford Examined before y^e Justices of Salem when She was a Coming into
y^e Roome y^e afflicted p$^\varepsilon$sons Some of y^m ware afflicted & S^d She was Coming y^e Maj$^\varepsilon$strets
told her She was acused for hurting of two p$^\varepsilon$sons, but She Denyed y^t She had any thing to
doe wth y^e Diuel, the Constable told her of Somthing She had owned tending y^t way y^e
afflicted p$^\varepsilon$sons were afflicted by her looking on y^m

And were well again by her taking y^m by y^e hand yet She denyed y^t She was a Witch & S^d
She Neuer Signed y^e Diuels book nor neuer was baptized by him She S^d She disowned y^t
Euer She had ben at any of their Mettings, She disowned y^t She had been Struck at Namely
her aperition: & y^t She had been almost Cripled by her aperition. being Struck wch She
afterwards ~~Struck~~ Owned also She afterwards Confesed y^t ye Diuel had apeared to her
Seueral times ye first time in ye Shape of a pige but She S^d did not Speak to her but She was
much hurried in her mind with it & next he apeared like a Catt afterward like a bird flying at
ye window of her Master Chamber wher She was at work & ye bird Spoke to her promised
her new Cloths if She would Serue & worship him & She did bargain to ~~worship~~ Serue him
Soe Long as She liued She s^d ye Diuel ^{has} Come to her Som times like a black Man & y^t
She was baptiz⟨e⟩d by ye Diuel at five Mile pond & y^t her Sister Susanna Post & Sarah &
Mary bridges were baptized there when She was, & She owned that She made a Marke wth
her finger in ye Diuels book & y^t ye marke was Red She also Showed her finger top where it
had been Cut & S^d She made ye Red mark in ye Diuels book wth ye blood of y^t She owned
She had been at Some of ye witch Mettings & y^t She thought their Meight be about 200 at
ye witch metting at Chandlers Garison at Andiuor She also told of ye 2 Jaxons & Jno
Howard of Rowly ["R" written over "r"] y^t they ware witches & 13 of Ipswich as She heard

August 25, 1692

y^m Say & of abigal ffalkner of Andiuor now in prison & y^t Martha Emerson afflicted her there in y^e ~~Ro⟨m⟩e~~ Room, & then She could goe Shake hands & beg pardon of ye afflicted p^{ε}sons & not afflict y^m – Mary Post ~~a freind of hers~~ at ye Same time aff-^{i}rmd y^t She had Seen Church Clark Good^ε Green Good^ε Hutchins of Hauerill & abigall fforkner of andiuor & wifford & Good^ε Eames & her Son Dan^{ll} at a witch Metting at andiuor & y^t She knew them to be witches

Notes: From *Andover Examinations Copy*. See No. 425. "Church" is Sarah Churchill.

Essex Institute Collection, no. 24, 6r, James Duncan Phillips Library, Peabody Essex Museum, Salem

519. Examination of Susannah Post

See also: Jan. 7, 1693.

[Hand 1] Susanah Post was examined: before Maj^r Gedney: & other y^r Majest^s Justices..
August 25. 1692
The Justices told her she was acused for afflicting: Martha Spreag & Rose ffoster by witchcraft
when Susanah was Brought in before: them: ye afflicted: was greatly afflicted: Mary Warin & was recovered by her touching with: her hand: her sister Hannah Post s^d she was babtized: with her at five mile pond
the afflicted persons. then charged her with afflicting: them: & that they saw her afflict & but she denyed it & s^d she knew not of it: nor that she had made a covnant with ye devill but afterward: she confessed she had bin in ye devils snare three years: ye first time she saw him he was like a {gray} catt: he told her he was a prince: & I was to serve him I promised him to doe it ye next shape was a yellow bird it s^d I must serv him: & he s^d I should live well: ye next time he appeared like a black man y^t time he brought a book: & she s^d she touched it with a stick y^t was dipt in an Inkhorn & it made a red mark: & Jno Jaxon sen^r was there when she signed: he y^t was y^e great Eater: she would own but three times: y^t she had seen y^e devil: but it was told her it could not but be more in 3 years time: she was unwilling to own y^t she had afflicted: Martha Spreag & Rose ffoster: but Mary Bridges s^d she use to afflict y$^{⟨m⟩}$ by sticking pins into cloaths: which she then owned: she s^d she s^d she was now willing to renownce y^e devil & all his works: & she went: when bid & begged forgivnes of y^e of y^e afflicted & could come to y^m & not hurt them she ownd she had been babtized at 5 mile pond about halfe a year agoe & ye devil dipt her head in ye water & s^d she must serv him she s^d there were a great many at ye witchmeeting at Andover: but knew not exactly how many there ["re" written over "ir"] might be 200: ~~& they eat white bread & drank wine that was red:~~ & there ["re" written over "ir"] was a minister: there that sayd he ⟨w⟩as to be excicuted: but he was ~~Jolly~~ Joyfull enough: he bid them doe as he did not confess & they should be happy: she ownd y^t once she had bin at ye Villadge meeting of witches & they ⟨had⟩ a sacrement: & there was 200 there & they eat bread y^t was white & drank wine that was red: she s^d she heard there were 500 witches in ye country she s^d she & two of her sisters went to ye Villadge meeting & rod upon a stik: ye devil carried it & she rode before she s^d y^t ffolkner Wilford of Haverell Sarah Parker was at ye witch meeting & that she knew ye two Jaxons goodwife ⟨S⟩cott & Jno Howard of Rowly to be witches:

I und^r written being appinted to: take ye Abave examination: Doe testifie upon oath taken in Court that is a true coppy of y^e of Substance of it: to ye best of my knowledge.
Janu^ε 7th 1692

Simon Willard

[Reverse] [Hand 2] the within Hanah post was Examined befor their Majesties ^{Justies} of peace in Salem

atest John Higginson. J: peace

owned before ye Grand Jury
January 1692

[Hand 3] Robert Payne foreman:

[Hand 4] Examinacon of Susanah Post -

Notes: Ruth Wilford had been arrested August 20. See No. 510. A warrant was issued for John Jackson Jr., John Jackson Sr., and John Howard the same day of Post's examination, and they were arrested August 26. See No. 515. ◊ Hand 1 = Simon Willard; Hand 2 = John Higginson Jr.; Hand 4 = Anthony Checkley

Suffolk Court Files, vol. 32, docket 2705, p. 28, Massachusetts Supreme Judicial Court, Judicial Archives, Massachusetts State Archives. Boston, MA.

Friday, August 26, 1692

Officer's Return: Warrant for the Apprehension of John Jackson Sr., John Jackson Jr. & John Howard
2nd of 2 dates. See No. 515 on Aug. 25, 1692

Saturday, August 27, 1692

520. Examination of John Jackson Jr.
See also: Jan. 7, 1693.

[Hand 1] Jno Jaxon Jun^ε was examined before Jno Hawthorn Esqr & other their Majest^s Justices August 27th 1692

When s^d Jaxon was brought into ye room ye Afflicted persons fell down: & he was asked: can you tell why: these fall down: he s^d Jaxon s^d he was bewitched by his Ant How: about four year agoe: Q: & did ye devill appear to yo^u then he Answered yes: in ye shape of a black man & would disturb him & not lett him sleep a nights: but he would not own: that ever he brought him a book he could say nothing about a book: being asked: when he was babtized: Answerd in Mr Phillips his meeting hous: but would not own y^t ever: ye devill babtized him nor: that ever: he had signed: to ye devils book: he s^d when asked y^t ye devil next appeared to him in ye shape of a woman: he was asked what woman: he s^d his Aunt How: he s^d she asked: whether he would not set his hand to ye devils book but he sayd he did not see ye devils book: Ques: what other shapes did ye devil appear to you in: Answered: in ye shape of catts: he owned y^t ye black man had bid him serve hi⟨m⟩ ye afflicted: s^d his father stood by him & bid him not confess: which he owned & cryed Quest: was yor Aunt How a witch: A: yes she Afflicted me: when I was at work in ye faild she come & looked on me & tore down ye fence & my head fell of aking when: she looked on me there was a black spott on my hatt as if it was burnt but you say yor Aunt How & yor father bewitched you; when did yor father bewitch you: but answerd not: it was s^d to him if you will not confess: witnes should be called i⟨n⟩ Mary Warin: was asked if this was one of them: men she saw: ye other night: & s^d ye⟨s⟩ but was struck down into a fit: & s^d Jaxon ~~was~~ towched her & she was well: she s^d s^d Jaxon afflicted her: then: & she had seen him afflict others: Mary Lascy s^d she knew: s^d Jaxon: at Tilers: & she had seen him afflict others of ye afflicted

Mary Warin: Mary Lascy Martha Spreag: & Rose ffoster fell into a fitt: & Jaxo⟨n⟩ cryed out: much like a fooll when: he was mad to touch ye afflicted: but: they were all well: when he touched them: hannah Post sayd s^d Jaxon was at ye witch meeting att Andover she saw him there: Sarah Bridges: & Susana Post s^d Jaxon d⟨oth⟩ at this present hurt them

[Hand 2] I underwrytten being appointed by authority to take in wryting the above examina^εn Doe testify upon oath taken in court That this is a true coppy of the substance of it to the best of my knowledge.
[Hand 1] Janu^ε 7th 1692   Simon Willard

[Hand 3] owned before the Grand Jury 7 Jan^ε 1692
Robert Payne Foreman.

[Reverse] [Hand 4] Griggs pet^n
[Hand 5] Jno Jaxon
Jun^ε Ex__ama__

Notes: "Mr Phillips" is Reverend Samuel Phillips, minister at Rowley. Jackson's "Aunt How" is Elizabeth How, executed on July 19. ◊ Hand 1 = Simon Willard; Hand 2 = William Murray; Hand 3 = John Higginson Jr.

MS Ch K 1.40, vol. 2, p. 448, Rare Books & Manuscripts, Boston Public Library. Boston, MA.

521. Examination of John Jackson Sr.

See also: Jan. 7, 1693.

[Hand 1] Jno Jaxon Sen^ε examined before their Majest^s Justices In Salem August 27th 1692 Jno Hawthorn Esqr & others
The afflicted persons fell into a bad fitt: before s^d Jaxon came into the room & s^d he is coming
Ques. Jno Jaxon why. do you afflict these person A I desire to cry to god to keep both me & mine from this sin: I never: did it since the day I was born
Jno Jaxon you are here acused for hurting Martha Spreag & Rose ffoster: by witchcraft: A I am inocent
Mary Warin was asked if ever s^d Jaxon had afflicted: her: she s^d yes.

August 29, 1692

Martha Spreag: is this: yᵉ man: that afflicted you: A. Yes he hurt my throat last night he hath afflicted me: ever since I came downe with: yᵉ three: that confessed one night it was sᵈ to sᵈ Jaxon if you be Inocent: you can look upon them yᵗ are afflicted but: Martha Spreag was struck down: when he looked: & was recovered out of her fitt ~~when~~ with sᵈ Jaxons touch of his hand: the like was done by Mary Warin.

it was sayd to him: look how you afflict them: but he sᵈ no indeed I never did it but: here is witnes against you: & Hannah Post was called: but sᵈ Jaxon sᵈ he never: knew, nothing of it: but Hannah Post: sayd she had seen him at yᵉ witch meeting at Andoverr & that he drank there: she ~~said~~ sayd: that he & his son was in hast to be gone: and away: they went: sᵈ Post was a little afflicted when sᵈ Jaxon looked on her: for he was to look right on her: when he was bid: but looked downward Mary Walcot: sayd. she saw sᵈ Jaxon at: the witch meeting at Chandlers of Andover: but he never had hurt her: but ~~hee~~ was at yᵗ meeting wher: Mʳ Borroughs: had exorted them: & puld off his hatt & took his leave of them & sᵈ Jaxon took his leav of Mʳ Borroughs: Ann Putman: sᵈ & hoped he shoul⟨d⟩ see him. again: but Mʳ Borroughs thout not: but Mary Walcot & Ann Putnum both fell into a fitt: Sarah Bridges was brought in: & fell into a fitt and sᵈ Jaxon took her by: yᵉ hand & she was well pressently: but sᵈ she kne⟨w⟩ not yᵉ man: Mary Lascy wˢ asked:: doe you know this man: sᵈ yes I saw him last night: & fell into a fitt: Richard Carrier sᵈ he saw sᵈ Jaxon last night: but Jaxon sᵈ he was at work at Capᵗ Wicoms of Rowly last night he sᵈ these persons was not in their Right mind: Mary Warin was struck down & sᵈ she was struck on yᵉ head: a bloud was seen to come. through her head cloathes Jaxon was charged with acting wich craft before them but he sᵈ he did it not nor would not own: yᵗ ever yᵉ devill had babtized him but when sᵈ Jaxon was carried out yᵉ afflicted was much hurt: & Richᵈ Carrier: was halled almost undᵋ yᵉ bed

[Hand 2] I underwritten being appoynted by authority: to testi⟨fy⟩ in wryting the above examination Doe testify upon oath taken in court that this is a true coppy of the substance of it to the best of my Knowledge. 7ᵗ Jaᵋy 1692/3

Simon Willard

[Hand 3] owned before yᵉ Grand Jury
7. Janʳ 1692 Robert Payne foreman:

Notes: Hand 1 = Simon Willard; Hand 2 = William Murray; Hand 3 = John Higginson Jr.

Suffolk Court Files, vol. 32, docket 2704, p. 27, Massachusetts Supreme Judicial Court, Judicial Archives, Massachusetts State Archives. Boston, MA.

Monday, August 29, 1692

Officer's Return: Warrant for the Apprehension of William Barker Sr., Mary Marston, & Mary Barker

2ⁿᵈ of 2 dates. See No. 513 on Aug. 25, 1692

522. Warrant for the Apprehension of Elizabeth Johnson Sr. & Abigail Johnson, and Officer's Return

See also: Aug. 30, 1692.

August 29, 1692

[Hand 1] Essex:/ To the Constable of Andiuor
Complaint being made this day to us by Sam^ll Martin of Andiuor & Moses Tyler of Boxford. against Elizabeth Johnson widow and Abigall Johnson Singleweoman of Andiuor that they the Said Elizabeth Johnson & Abigall Johnson hath greuiously afflicted & abused Martha. Sprage of boxford & Abigall Martin of Andiuor Singleweomen by witchcraft contrary to the peace of our Souer^ε Lord & Lady william & Mary King & Quen of England &c & to their Majesties Lawes in that case prouided, and Said Sam^ll Martin & Moses Tyler haueing giuen Sufficient bond to prosecut their Said Complaint to Effect/ These are therfore to require you in their Majesties name fforthwith to aprehend & Seize the Bodys of the Said Elizabeth Johnson widow & Abigall Johnson her dafter Singleweoman of Andiuor & them Safely conuey to Salem before us their Majesties Justices of the peace to be examinied & proceded with according to law, for wch this shall be your warrant.
dated in Salem 29: August 1692.

Barth° Gedney
John Hathorne
John Higginson
Just^ε peace

[Reverse] [Hand 2] in obedenc to this writ i haue seased the Bodies of Elizabeth jonson widow and abegell ionson hur dafter Both of andouer this 30 day of agust 1692
By me John Ballard constable of andouer

Notes: Gedney and Hathorne broke from their original handling of the bond issue. They now follow the law and require bond. The new variable is the presence of John Higginson Jr. It seems reasonable to speculate that the presence of Higginson brought about the change. ◊ Hand 1 = John Higginson Jr. ◊ 1 wax seal.

MS Ch K 1.40, vol. 2, p. 350, Rare Books & Manuscripts, Boston Public Library. Boston, MA.

523. Examination of Mary Barker

See also: Sept. 17, 1692.

[Hand 1] 29 Agust 1692.
Before Maj^ε Gidney Mr Hauthorn and m^r Corwin
The Examination and confession of Mary Barker of Andover
After severall questiones propounded and negative answe^εs Returned she at last acknowledged that Goody Johnson made her a witch, And that ~~this~~ ^{sometine} last ~~spring~~ ^{sumer} she made a red mark in the devils book with the forefinger of her Left hand, And the Devil would have her hurt martha Sprague Rose foster and Abigail martin which she did upon Saturnday and Sabath day last, she said she was not above a quarter of an hour in comeing down from Andover to Salem to afflict, she sayes she afflicted the above three persones by⟨e⟩ squeezeing her hands.

August 29, 1692

she confesses she was at the witch meeting at Salem Village with her unkle, there was a great many theire, and of her company their was only her uncle, Wm Barker, and mary marston Martha Sprague said that Mary Barkers apparition told that she was baptised at five myle pond.

said mary Barker said there was such a load & weight at her stomack that hindered her from speakeing And is afrayd she hes given up her self soul & body to the devil

she sayes she promised to serve worship and beleeve in him And he promessed to pardone her sins, but finds he hes deserved her, and that she was Lost of god and all good people, That Goody Jonson and Goody falkner appeared at the same tyme and threatned to teare her in peeces if she did not doo what she then did. she further sayth that she hes seen no appearance since but a ffly which did speake to her, and bid her afflict these poor creatu^εs. which she did by pincheing with, and Clincheing of her hands for which she is sorry, And further the devil told her it would be very brave and cliver for her to come down here to Salem among these accused persones. And that she should never be brought out.

She promises to confess what more she shall hereafter remembe⟨r⟩

[Hand 2] Mary Barker Signed & owned the abouesaid
Examination & Confesion
17 Sept 1692 before me John Higginson Jus^ε peace

The marke

✗

of

Mary. Barker:

[Reverse] [Hand 1] Confession of Mary Barker
[Hand 2] acused.   w^m Barker Senr
                           Goody Johnson
                           Goody ffalkner
                           Goody Marston

aflicted   Martha Sprage
                Rose ffoster
                Abigall Martin

Notes: Mary Barker was thirteen years old. On January 13 she was released on bond (see No. 818), and was subsequently tried and found not guilty, probably on May 10 (see No. 850). Her indictments were probably presented that day, but the possibility that they had been drawn as early as September 1692 cannot be ruled out. See No. 801 & No. 802. ◊ Hand 1 = William Murray; Hand 2 = John Higginson Jr.

Suffolk Court Files, vol. 32, docket 2678, p. 10, Massachusetts Supreme Judicial Court, Judicial Archives, Massachusetts State Archives. Boston, MA.

524. Examination of Mary Barker, Copy

See also: Sept. 17, 1692.

[Hand 1] 29th August 1692 Before Maj^ε Gidney M^ε Hathorne M^ε Corwin
The Examination And Confession of Mary Barker of Andiuor afte Seueral Questions Propounded & Neagatiue ans^ε Returned She at last acknowledged y^t Good^ε Johnson Made her a witch & y^t Some time last Sumer She made a Red Mark in y^e Diuels book wth y^e

forefinger of her left hand & y^e Diuel would haue her hurt Martha Sprage Rose ffoster & Abigall Martin wch She did on Satterday & Sabbath day last. She Said She was not aboue a Quart$^\varepsilon$ of an hour a Coming Dwone from Andiuor to Salem to afflict She S^d She afflicted y^e aboue S^d 3 p$^\varepsilon$sons by Squezing her hands She Conffesses She was at y^e witch Metting at Salem Village wth her Vnckle, there was a grate many there & of her Company was only her Vnkle W$\overline{m}$ Barker &. Mary Marston Martha Sprage S^d y^t Mary Barkers apperition told y^t She was baptized at 5 Mile pond – S^d Mary Barker S^d ther was Such a load & weight at her Stomack y^t Hindred her from Speaking & is afrayd She has Giuen up herself Soul & body to Y^e Diuel She Says She promised to Serue worship & beleiue in him & he promised to pardon her ⟨?⟩ Sins but finds he has deceiued her & y^t She was left of god & all good people & y^t Good$^\varepsilon$ Johnson & Good$^\varepsilon$ falkner apeared at y^e Same time & threatned to tear her in peices if She did not doe what She then did She further Said y^t She had Seen no aperance Since but a fly ~~y^t had~~ {w^{ch} did} Speak to her & bid her afflict these poor Creaturs wch She did by pinching With Clin{c}hing of her hands for wch She is Sorry & furthe y^e Diuel told her it would be Very braue & Cliuer for her to Come Dwone to Salem among these acused p$^\varepsilon$sons & y^t She Should Neuer be brought out She promised to Confese w^t more She Shall hearafter Rememb^r

Mary Barker Signed & owned the abouesaid Examination & Conffession before me Jno Higginson Justice of Peace 17th Sep^t 1692 /

The X Marke
of
Mary Barker

Notes: From *Andover Examinations Copy*. See No. 425.

Essex Institute Collection, no. 24, 6v-7r, James Duncan Phillips Library, Peabody Essex Museum, Salem, MA.

525. Examination of William Barker Sr.

See also: Sept. 5, 1692 & Sept. 16, 1692.

[Hand 1] 29. agust. 92.
Coram [= before] Mag$^\varepsilon$ [= major] Gidn⟨e⟩y m^r hathorn m^r Corwin Capt higginson
William Barker of Andove$^\varepsilon$s examination & confession

He confesses he hes been in the snare of the devil three yeares, that the devil first appeared to him lyke a black man and perceived he had a cloven foot, That the devil demanded of him to give up himself soul & Body unto him, which he promesed to doe, He said he had a great family, the world went hard with him and was willing to pay every man his own, And the devil told him he would pay all his debts and he should live comfortably. – He confesses he hes {afflicted} ⟨?⟩sed Sprague foster and martin, his three accusers. That he did syne [= sign] the devils book with blood brought to him in a thing lyke an Inkhorn that he dipt his finger y^{r}in and made a blott in the book which was a confirmation of the Covenant with the devil. He confesses he was at a meeting of witches at Salem Village where he judges there was about a hundred of y^m, that the meeting was upon a green peece of ground neare the ministe$^\varepsilon$s house, He said they mett there to destroy that place by reason of the peoples being divided & theire differing with y^r ministe$^\varepsilon$s

August 29, 1692

Satans design was to set up his own worship, abolish all the churches in the land, to fall next upon Salem and soe goe through the countrey, He sayth the devil promeised y^t all his people should live bravely that all persones should be equall; that their should be no day of resurection or of judgement, and neither punishment nor shame for sin. – He sayth there was a sacrament at y^t meeting, theire was also bread & wyne m^r Burse was a ringleader in that meeting and named several persones that were there at the meeting, It was proposed at the meeting to make as many witches as they could, And they were all by m^r Burse and the black man exhorted to pull down the Kingdome of christ and set up the Kingdome of the devil, He said he knew mr Burroughs and Goody How to be such persones, And that he heard a trumpet sounded at the meeting and thinks it was Burse that did it, The sound is heard many myles off, And then they all come one efter another – In the spring of the yeare the witches came from Connecticut to afflict at Salem Village but now they have left it off And that he hes been informed by some of the grandees y^t y^r is about 307 {witches} in the country, – He sayth the witches are much disturbed with the afflicted persones because they are discovered by y^m, They curse the judges because their Society is brought under, They wold have the afflicted persones counted as witches But he thinks the afflicted persones are Innocent & y^t ⟨t⟩h⟨e⟩y doe god good service And that he hes not known or heard of one Innocent persone taken up & put in prisone – He saith he is heartily sorry for what he has done and for hurting the afflicted persones his accuse^εs, prayes their forgiveness, desyres praye^εs for himself⟨f⟩, promises to renounce the devil and all his works, And y^n he could take them all by the hand without any harme by his eye or any otherwise

[Hand 2] 5.7:92 the aboue Said is the Truth as wittnese my hand: William Barker

he owned this is [= in] y^e Court of Oyre & Terminer as on y^e back Side

[Reverse] Wm Barkers Exā.
acused.
      m^r Buse
      m^r Buro⟨u⟩ghs
      Goody How
      Coneticot witches
      & Seuerall others

aflicted
      martha Sprage
      Rose foster
      Abigall martin

[Hand 3] ⟨at⟩ A Court of Oyer & Termine^ε held at Salem
Sepr 16 92.
owned in Court at Salem Sepr. 16. 1692
attest St: Sewall

Notes: William Barker Sr. fled before he could be brought to trial. As a confessed witch he could not swear in court, and thus "he owned" his account. Note the reference to the Connecticut "witches." The Connecticut cases, involving Elizabeth Clawson and Mercy Disborough and others named by the accuser, Katherine Branch, were handled in the traditional New England way by the authorities proceeding cautiously and not choosing to expand cases as in the Salem episode. As in Massachusetts Bay, a Special Court of Oyer and Terminer dealt with the matter. Both Clawson and Disborough were tried on September 14, 1692, with other cases being dismissed, but the jury could not reach agreement on the indictments. The court met again on October 28, when Clawson was found not guilty. Disborough was found guilty, but the judges asked the jury to reconsider. The jury, however, stood by its verdict. Still, Disborough was not executed, and she was released from prison in 1693 in part because the authorities in Connecticut saw the Salem trials as an example of how not to handle witchcraft cases. No executions occurred in Connecticut during this "witchcraft" phase. ◊ Hand 1 = William Murray; Hand 2 = John Higginson Jr.; Hand 3 = Stephen Sewall

Massachusetts Archives Collection, vol. 135, no. 39. Massachusetts State Archives. Boston, MA.

526. Examination of William Barker Sr., Copy

See also: Sept. 5, 1692.

[Hand 1] 29 August 1692 Wᵐ Barker {Senʳ} of Andiuers Examination & Conffession Before Majᵉ Gidney Mᵉ Hathorne Mᵉ Corwine Jnᵒ Higginson Esqᵉˢ
He Conffesses he has been in yᵉ Snare of yᵉ Diuel @ Three Years yᵗ yᵉ Diuel first apeared to Him ["im" written over "er"] in yᵉ Shape of a black man & perceiued he had a Clouen ["n" written over "d"] foott yᵗ yᵉ Diuel demand of him to giue up himself Soul & body to him wᶜʰ he promised to doe he Said he had a greate family yᵉ world went hard wᵗʰ him & was willing to pay Euery Man his owne & yᵉ Diuel told him he would pay all his Debts & he Should liue Comfortably He Conffesses he has afflicted Sprauge ffostter & Martin his three akusers yᵗ he did Sign yᵉ Diuel book wᵗʰ blood brought to him In a thing like an Inkhorn yᵗ he dipt his finger therin and made a bloot ~~therein~~ in yᵉ book wᶜʰ was a Confermation ^{of yᵉ Couenant} Made wᵗʰ yᵉ Diuel – He Conffesses he was at a metting of yᵉ witches at Salem Village where he Judges there was about a hundred of yᵐ yᵗ yᵉ Metting was Vpon a green peice of ground Near yᵉ Ministers house he Says they Meet ⟨?⟩ their to destroy yᵗ place by reason of yᵉ peoples being deuided & yʳ differing wᵗʰ there Ministers – Satans desire was to Sett ^{up} his one [= own] worship, abolish all yᵉ Churches in yᵉ Land to fall next Vpon Salem & Soe goe through yᵉ Country he Saith yᵉ Diuel promised al his people Should liue Brauely yᵗ al pᵉsons Should be Equal yᵗ their Should be no day of resurection or Judgment And Nither Punishment nor Shame for Sin – he Saith their was a Sacrement at yᵉ Metting there was also bread & wine Mʳ Burse~~ughs~~ was a Ring Leader in yᵗ Metting & Named Seueral pᵉsons yᵗ ware there at yᵉ Metting It was proposed at yᵉ Metting to Make as Many witches as they Could & they ⟨?⟩ were al by Mʳ Burse~~ughs~~ & yᵉ black Man Exhorted to pull dwone yᵉ Kingdome of of Christ & Sett Vp yᵉ Kingdome of yᵉ Diuel, He Sᵈ he knew Mʳ Buroughs & Goode How to be Such pᵉsons & yᵗ he heard a trumpet Sounded at yᵉ Metting & thinks it Was Burse yᵗ did it yᵉ Sound is heard Many miles of and then they all Come one after another – In yᵉ Spring of yᵉ Year yᵉ witches Came from Connecticut to afflict at Salem Village butt now they haue left it of, & yᵗ he has been Informed by Some of yᵉ Grandees yᵗ there is @ 307 witches in yᵉ Country
He Saith yᵉ wi^{c}t^{c}hes are much disturbed wᵗʰ yᵉ afflicted pᵉsons because they are Discouered by yᵐ, they Curse yᵉ Judges because their Society is brought under they would have yᵉ afflicted pᵉsons Counted as witches but hee thinks ~~they~~ ^{yᵉ afflicted pᵉsons} are Inocent & yᵗ they doe god good Seruice & yᵗ he has not knowne or heard of one Inocent pᵉson taken up And ["And" written over "Yett"] putt In prison – he Saith he is hartly Sorry for wᵗ he has done & for hurting yᵉ afflicted pᵉsons his accusers, prays there forgiuenes: desire prayers for him Self promises to Renounce yᵉ Diuel & al his works & yⁿ he could take

August 29, 1692 y^m all by y^e hand w^{th}out any harme by his Eye or otherwise y^e aboue S^d is y^e truth as wittnesse my hand – William Barker
5^d $7^{m\langle o\rangle}$ <u>92</u>

Notes: From *Andover Examinations Copy.* See No. 425. The copyist flounders between Burse, who is John Busse, and Burroughs, before correcting to 'Burse.' Subsequently, he correctly references Burroughs. Why John Busse was not arrested remains an untold story.

Essex Institute Collection, no. 24, 7r, James Duncan Phillips Library, Peabody Essex Museum, Salem, MA

527. Examination of William Barker Sr. in Prison [?]

Nextly, I will insert the Confession of a man about Forty years of Age, *W. B.*, which he wrote himself in Prison, and sent to the Magistrates, to confirm his former Confession to them, *viz. God having called me to Confess my sin and Apostasy in that fall in giving the Devil advantage over me appearing to me like a Black, in the evening to set my hand to his Book, as I have owned to my shame. He told me that I should not want so doing. At* Salem Village, *there being a little off the Meeting-House, about an hundred five Blades, some with Rapiers by their side, which was called and might be more for ought I know by* B *and* Bu. *and the Trumpet sounded, and Bread and Wine which they called the Sacrament, but I had none; being carried over all on a Stick, never being at any other Meeting. I being at Cart a* Saturday *last, all the day, of Hay and English Corn, the Devil brought my Shape to* Salem, *and did afflict* M. S. *and* R. F. *by clitching my hand; and a Sabbath day my Shape afflicted* A. M. *and at night afflicted* M. S. *and* A. M. E. I. *and* A. F. *have been my Enticers to this great abomination, as one have owned and charged her to her Sister with the same. And the design was to Destroy* Salem *Village, and to begin at the Ministers House, and to destroy the Church of God, and to set up Satans Kingdom, and then all will be well. And now I hope God in some measure has made me something sensible of my sin and apostasy, begging pardon of God, and of the Honourable Magistrates and all Gods people, hoping and promising by the help of God, to set to my heart and hand to do what in me lyeth to destroy such wicked worship, humbly begging the prayers of all Gods People for me, I may walk humbly under this great affliction and that I may procure to my self, the sure mercies of* David, *and the blessing of* Abraham.

Notes: The date of this prison confession is uncertain and is placed here with Barker's other confessions in the absence of a verifiable date. Two indictments against him survive, one for covenanting with the Devil and the other for afflicting Abigail Martin. See No. 805 & No. 806. The indictments against him came in January although he had fled by then. The references to "B" and "Bu" are to George Burroughs and John Busse, although in what order is impossible to determine. Other initials include MS = Martha Sprague, RF = Rose Foster, AM = Abigail Martin, EI = Elizabeth Johnson Sr., and AF = Abigail Faulkner Sr.

John Hale. A Modest Enquiry into the Nature of Witchcraft (Boston: Green & Allen, 1702), pp. 33–34.

528. Examination of Mary Marston
See also: Sept. 15, 1692 & Jan. 6, 1693.

[Hand 1] ⟨2⟩9 Agust ⟨1692⟩
Before Maj$^\varepsilon$ Gidney Mr Hauthorn & Cap^n Higginson

The Examination & confession of mary marston wife of Jn° marston Jun° of Andover: August 29, 1692

Being asked how long she had practised witchcraft, Answered a week agoe since she gave
consent or Leave to afflict, she said she heard a voice in the night tyme which desyred leave
of her to afflict & she answered yes. and being asked if she had not afflicted Abigail martin
she said the devil did it for her

Said Abigail martin being in a choakeing fitt, mary Lacey saw William Barker and this mary
marston afflicting of her. sd lacey saw them also afflict martha Sprague – The said mary
marston being again asked how long it is since she was first seduced, she said sometyme in
the last winter, And that being at home in her own house, & her husband absent, she saw
the appearance of a black man in the evening a litle after it was dark. The said black man bid
her serve him and beleeve in him, He also offered a paper book without covers to signe,
which she did with a pen dipt in Ink and therewith made a stroake, He told her ["her"
written over "she"] sh⟨e⟩ should not be discovered, he also told her he was the devil and that
she should li⟨v⟩e happil[Lost] [= happily]

She again said it is not above a week agoe since the devil asked her consent to afflict and that
yesterday being sabath day and the 28th of the month she afflicted Abigail martin, And
martha Sprague on the Saturnday before, she again said that on the munday before that she
only heard a voice and that if it was any body it was the devil that taught her this witchcraft.
Being asked what she was to doe when the persones should be afflicted Answered to pinch
and squeeze her hands together and so to think upon the persones to be afflicted

She saith that Wm Barker & she afflicted in company together the last saturnday And it was
by their spirits they conversed and aggreed so to doe, And they mett at mr Tylers house for
that end, And further they began their affliction first upon martha Sprague; next upon Rose
foster and then upon Abigail martin

Martha Sprague said that she was afflicted upon Saturday at Salem by sd mary marston &
othe°s, The said marston being asked how long she was comeing from Andover to Salem
upon saturnday in her Spirit, Ansred not long.

Q: how [= who] brought yow. A. the black man. and said als⟨o⟩ yr came along with her
William Barker & mary Barker And that she ["she" written over "said"] viz marston for her
part Squeezed Spragues neck

Being asked what moved her to afflict any persone she said the devil made her doe it, And
when she refused he looked angry, and threatned her very much

{Noate,} That hitherto she still struck down the afflicted persones wt her eyes and recovered
them again by Layeing her hand upon their wrist or arme

Being again asked how long since the devil seduced her answered about thre[Lost] [= three]
yea°s agoe (noate, Lacey & Sprague saw the apparitions of the black man and Wm Barker
standing before said mary marston)

~~She now saith that about the tyme when her mother dyed and she was over come with
melancholly~~ [Hand 2] ^{about three yere since} [Hand 1] the black man appeared to her in
the great Roome and told her she must serve and worship him And so she did And that was
the first tyme she signed the devils book, she saith Wm & mary Barkers were her
companiones, she acknowledges the hurting of the aflicted persones, & was sorry for it But
yet could not Look upon them without Strykeing of them down.

A litle efter she ₉fessed [= confessed] she was at the witchmeetng at Salem Village and yt she
did ryde upon a pole and the meeting was upon a green

August 29, 1692   Martha Sprague said the apparitions told marston. she ~~should not~~ had confessed too much already and therefore would not Let her speak any more.

[Hand 2] Mary Marston Signed & owned the abouesaid   The mark
Examination & Conffession 15 Sept 1692:
before me: John Higginson Just^ε peace   of ✍
                                                                        Mary Marsto⟨n⟩

[Reverse] [Hand 3] Confession of Mary marston wife of John marston Jun^ε of Andover.
[Hand 2] accused: Wm Barker
                           Mary Barker

           afflicted   Martha Sprage
                           Rose foster
                           Abigall Martin
[Hand 4] Billa uera
Robert: Payne
foreman:

Notes: No original indictment of Mary Marston survives, although copies of two indictments appear in the record of her trial on January 6, 1693. See No. 768. A notation of a true bill, probably written on January 6, 1693, appears on the back of this examination and confession document, unusual, but not the only instance. Mary Marston was tried and found not guilty on January 6, 1693. Others who confessed were similarly found not guilty even though, as with Mary Marston, there is every reason to believe that the confessions were presented to the jurors as evidence. ◊ Hand 1 = William Murray; Hand 2 = John Higginson Jr.

Massachusetts Archives Collection, vol. 135, no. 47. Massachusetts State Archives. Boston, MA.

529. Examination of Mary Marston, Copy

See also: Sept. 15, 1692.

[Hand 1] August 29th 1692 Before Maj^a Gidney Mr Hathorne Mr Corwin & John Higginson Esq^{ε}s
The Examination & Conffession of Mary Marston wife of Jno Marston Junr of Andiuor
Being asked how long She had practised witchcraft A a week agoe Since She gaue ^{consent or} leaue to afflict She S^d heard a uoyce in y^e night time which desired leaue ^{of her} to afflict & She answerd Yes & bing asked if She had not afflicted abigall Martin She S^d y^e Diuel did it for her, S^d Abigall Marttin being in Choaking fitt Mary lacy Saw W$\overline{m}$ Barker Brought from Ouer leafe
{1692} & this Mary Marston afflicting of Her S^d lacey Saw y^m also afflict Martha Sprauge –
The S^d Mary Marston being agin asked how long it was Since She was first Seduced She S^d Somtime in y^e last Winter, & y^t being at home in her owne house & her husband absent She Saw ye apearance of a black Man In ye Eueni^{n}g a litle after it was dark She Said ye black man bid her Serue him & beleeue ^{in} him, he also offered a paper book wthout Couers to Signe wch She did wth a pen dipt in Ink & therwith made a Stroake He told her She Should not be discouerd & he also told her he was ye Diuel & y^t She Should liue happily, She again

S^d it was not above a week agoe Since ye Diuel asked her Consent to afflict & y^t Yersterday   August 30, 1692
being Sabbath day & ye 28th of ye M^o She afflicted abigal Martin, & Martha Sprauge y^e
Satterday before, She again S^d y^t on ye Mooday before y^t She only heard a Voice & y^t if it
was any body it was ye Diuel y^t tavght her this witchcraft Being asked what She was to doe
when ye p^esons Should be afflicted Answered to pinch & Squeez her hands tog⟨e⟩~~ther~~ gether
& Soe think vpon ye p^esons to be afflicted She Saith y^t Wm Barker & She afflicted in Comp^a
Togeth^e ye Last Satterday & it was by their Spirits they Conuersed & agreed So to doe &
they mett at Mr Tylers House for y^t End, & fu^{r}ther they began their affliction Vpon
Martha Sprauge Next Vpon Rosse foster & yⁿ Vpon Abigal Martin
Martha Sprauge S^d y^t She was afflicted last Satterday at Salem By S^d Marston & others y^e S^d
Marston being asked how long She was Coming from Andiuor to Salem upon Satterday in
her Spirit A Not long. Q how brought you A y^e black man and S^d also y^r Came along wth
her W͞m & Mary Barker^s & y^t She Viz Marston for He [= her] part Squeezed Sprauges
Neck being asked w^t Moved her to afflict ^{any} p^eson She S^d y^e Diuel Made her do it &
when She Reffused he looked angry & Threatned her Much. {Noate}, y^t Hitherto She Still
Struck Downe y^e afflicted p^esons wth her Eyes & recouered them again by laying Her Hand
upon there Riste [= wrist] or armes – Being asked how long it was Since y^e Diuel Seduced
Her A @ 3 Years agoe (Noate Lacey & Sprauge Saw y^e apparittions of y^e black Man & Will^e
Barker Standing before S^d Mary Marston) the black man appeared to her in y^e Greate
roo⟨m⟩ @ 3 Years Since & told her She must Serue & Woship him & So She did & y^t was y^e
first time She Signed y^e Diuels book, She Saith y^t W͞m & Mary Barkers were her
Companians She acknowledges y^e Hurting of y^e afflicted p^esons & was Sorry for it butt Yett
Could not look on y^m without Stricking y^m downe – a little after She Conffesed She wa [=
was] at y^e witch meeting at Salem Village & y^t She did Rid Vpon a pole & y^e Metting was
Vpon a Green Martha Spauge Said y^e aperitons told Marston She had Conffesed to Much
already & Therfore would not Lett her Speak any More

Mary Marston Signed & owned the aboue S^d Examination &   The X Mark
Conffession before me John Higginson Just^e pease   of
15 Sep^t 1692   Mary Marston

Notes: From *Andover Examinations Copy.* See No. 425.

Essex Institute Collection, no. 24, 7r–v, James Duncan Phillips Library, Peabody Essex Museum, Salem, MA.

Tuesday, August 30, 1692

Officer's Return: Warrant for the Apprehension of Elizabeth Johnson Sr. & Abigail Johnson
2nd of 2 dates. See No. 522 on Aug. 29, 1692

Continued from Aug. 11, 1692: Examinations of Abigail Faulkner Sr.
2nd of 2 dates. See No. 507 on Aug. 11, 1692

August 30, 1692   **530. Examination of Elizabeth Johnson Sr., Copy**

[Hand 1] Eliz^ε Johnson Examined Before The Justices of Salem
August 30th 1692
{1692} Eliz^ε Johnson You are here Charged for acting Witchcraft Come tell how long You
haue ben a witch A I cannot tell butt Since y^e~Diuel {my Daught^ε} Came heither & Stopt Q
w^t ye Diuel Come to You did he not A Yes Q was it in ye Day A no in ye Night when I was
aslep & awaked me & S^d he would goe & afflict in my Shape but I Neuer Sett my hand to
his book – Come be thorow in all licklyhood you haue been long in this Snare ye Sundry
Years She S^d o pray for me for it is true I haue bin Long in this Snare but Yett would owne
but 3 Year or not aboue 4 w^t Shape did ye Diuel ^{appear} to You at first A a white bird wel
what would he haue You to doe A Serue & worship him well y^t time Then ^{you} Signed to
his book how did You doe it A wth my finger Q w^t Spott did itt Make A black q what bignes
was ye book A pretty big Q did you Promise ["Promise" written over "Serue"] to Serue &
worship him A Yes Q When & where did y^e {bird} Diuel apear to You A In ye day time in
my owne house Q. has he not apeared to You Like a black man A Yes he mostly apears to me
Like a black man Was you alone when he appeare^d to You A Yes I haue been to Much alone
how Long has Y^e Child y^t Is here been a witch A 5 Yeares I Suppose for liued at Good^ε
Carriers @ y^t time who Came w^t ye Diuel when he Came to You first did W͞m Bark^ε No he
has not been on Soe long it was my Sister abigall ffalkner – who stands before you now is it
not Y^e Sister falkner A Yes She Threattens to Tear me in peices if I Conffes Q how long
hath She ben one A No longer then I where did ye Diuel baptize you A at 5 Mile pond who
ware baptized when You was A My Sister falkner & a great Many More Jeames How was
one how many times haue you been at y^e witch metting at y^e Village A butt once V^{n}lese I
was Their in my Spirit Q how did you goe thither one Horse back as far as I know but
afterwards S^d She was Carried thither upon a pole & y^t her Sister falkner ^{was there} &
William Barker others She new [= knew] not for She did not know folk Q but did You giue
Y^e Children to y^e Diuel A No I do not know y^t this Girle is a witch w^t number of witches be
there in all A a 100 it may be I doe not know w^t did they agre to doe at y^e Metting at y^e
Village A to afflict people & make as many witches as they Could as they Could how many
haue you made witches A none Q was they to Sett up ye diuels Kingdome A Yes but why
doe ^{they} afflict now they Soe they are daly brought out A y^e Diuel makes y^m doe it Q
how Many ~~Might~~ ^{was} their ~~be~~ at that Metting at Chandlers A @ 20 or 30 I dont know
how Many whatt did you doe their A drink wine, where did you gett Your wine A from
Boston I think butt I doe not know how [= who] brought it M^r busse was Their did You
drink A Yes how did it tast A it has been bitt^ε to me I am Sure butt Who were y^e Company
A I do not ~~kn⟨o⟩w~~ know any but y^m that are brought out Q was Martha Emerson there A I
know not Was Dan^ll Eames ~~th⟨e⟩re~~ ^{of Y^ε Comp^a} A yes he was She S^d also Hannah Mary
& Susana Posts were baptized when She was & y^t ye Diuel dipt there heads in ye watt^ε & S^d
thou art mine Soul & body Come You y^t haue been a witch Soe long you doe not Thouroly
Conffes~~d~~ you {know} who you haue Afflicted She owned She had afflicted Sarah Phelps &
3 of Martins Children & y^t her Sister & Sarah parker Joyned wth her in afflicting them Q
then doe you know Sarah parker to be a witch A I know She afflicted these [1 word
overstruck] {or} Else I afflicted none She owned Sh⟨e⟩ ⟨h⟩ad afflicted Rose ffostter but I
know not y^t I haue afflicted Martha Sprauge I know not what ~~th⟨e⟩y~~ my Spirit did Q how are
you when Your Spirit is Gone out of You A In a Cold Dumpish Mallancolly Condition She

would not own y^t She had afflicted Swan She was askt how She knew She Should be Sent   August 31, 1692
for A My Son Told me I Should be Sent for Yesterday She owned he had afflicted Martin &
Martha Sprauge Yesterd^ɛ & y^t ye actions of body y^t She Vsed to afflicte by was ye pinching
her hand. & y^t ye Diuel had Made her promis to renounce god & ~~crist~~ Christ & She did Soe
being ask how long she had a ^{ben} witch she Said She knew nott, butt She was 30 Years
old when She was Married & now She was 51 & when She had had 3. Childr⟨e⟩n ye Diuel
Came to her & it might be @ 26 Years & y^t ye Diuel Appeared to her like a bird a black bird
& then She did not Signe ~~then~~ butt @ a year after She Signed & y^t ye Diuel came alone
when She Signed She S^d her Sister Abigl had been a witch as long as She, She would not
own y^t She was baptized before ye time fornamed nor y^t She had been baptized by him aboue
once nor that She had Set her Seal to ye book but She had Sett her hand to ye book at Salem
Village when ye Combination was She owned She had Eat & drink & ye Mett^ɛ at Chand^ɛ
butt no where Else She S^d Burroughs & Buss ware at the Village Metting & Buss was at y^e
Mett^ɛ at Chand^ɛ & bid y^m Stand to y^e ^{faith &} truth She S^d ye Diuel propound^ɛed 30
Years to her to Serue him & he had promised her al glory & happines & Joy But as yett
performed Nothing She S^d her familliar was like a Browne puppee & y^t he also Sucks her
breast She also Conffes^ɛ She was afrayd her Son Stephen was a witch butt She did not
Ceartainly know it but Conffes^ɛ his apperance was then before her & y^t was ye young man y^e
afflicted Saw before Her & before She had Conffesed of her Son She could not Shake hands
wth afflicted but affterward^s She could
  This is ye Substance of Eliz^ɛ Johnson Sen^rs
Conffession & Examination out of my Carrect^ɛ
  Attest Simond Willard

Notes: From *Andover Examinations Copy*. See No. 425. ◊ "Dumpish": 'sad, dejected' (*OED* s.v. *dumpish*).

Essex Institute Collection, no. 24, 8r-v, James Duncan Phillips Library, Peabody Essex Museum, Salem, MA.

Wednesday, August 31, 1692

531. Second Examination of Rebecca Eames

See also: Sept. 15, 1692.

[Hand 1] August 31^t 1692 Present Jno Hathorne Jona^t Corwin E⟨sq⟩^⟨?⟩
Rebeca Eames further acknowledgeth & declareth that she was baptized aboute thr⟨e⟩e years
agoe in five Mile pond and that her son D⟨a⟩niell was also then baptized by the Diuell, and y^t
her son Daniell hath be⟨n⟩ne a ⟨W⟩izard aboute thurteene Yeares and y^t [] Toothaker
Widow. and Abig⟨a⟩il faulkner are both Witches and y^t her son an⟨d⟩ ⟨bo⟩th them haue
benne in Company with her in Andouer afflicteing of Timothy Swan and further Confirmes
What she formerly acknowl⟨edg⟩ed (viz) that she hath benne a with [= witch] this 26 yeares
and y^t the Diuell then appeared to her in y^e likeness of a black man and she then gaue
h⟨er⟩selfe she sayth soule and body to y^e Diuell and promised to searve & obey him and
Keepe his ways. and further declares y^t she did then at that tyme signe to a paper the Diuell

August 31, 1692	then had y^t she would soe doe and sayth she made a Mark vpon said paper with her finger, and the spott or Mark she made was black. and that she was then in such horror of Conscienc y^t she tooke a Rope to hang her selfe and a Razer to cutt her throate, by Reason of her great sin in Committeing adultery & by that the Diuell Gained her he promiseing she should not be brought out or eve[Lost] [= ever] discouered.

the abouesaid Conffesion is the truth as wittnese my hand

T⟨he⟩ m[Lost] [= mark of]

𝐟

Rebecka [Lost]es [= Eames]

[Hand 2] Rebecka. Emes. signed & owned the abouesaid Conffesion to be the trut⟨h⟩ before me John Higginson Justice of peace.
15 Sep^t 1692
[Reverse] [Hand 3] Wm Rayment

Notes: Rebecca Eames was condemned in September but not executed. See No. 712. She was released from prison, probably in February 1693, after having been there seven months. See. No. 888. The relation of William Rayment to Document 531 is not clear. ◊ Hand 1 = John Hathorne; Hand 2 = John Higginson Jr.

Essex Institute Collection, no. 29, James Duncan Phillips Library, Peabody Essex Museum, Salem, MA.

532. Warrant for Jurors for the Court of Oyer and Terminer

[Hand 1] To the Sherriffe of the County of Essex./

You are Required in their Maties Name to Impannel and return Forty good and lawful men of the ffreeholders and other Freemen of yo^ε Bailiwick duely qualified, to Serve on the Jury of Tryals of life and death at the next Session of their Maties Special Court of Oyer and Terminer, in Salem upon ~~the~~ Tuesday the Sixth day of Septemb^ε next at nine in the morning; whome you are by your Selfe, Undersherriffe, or Deputy, to Summon to attend the said Court, at the time abovespecified;
You are alike Required in their Maties Name to give Notice and Summon the Grandjuro^εs that were Impanneled and Sworn at the last Session of said Court, to attend again upon Tuesday the said Sixth of September next by the time abovementioned; Hereof you may not faile; Given under my Hand and Seal, At Boston the 31th day of August. 1692. In the ffourth year of their Maties Reign
Wm Stoughton

[Reverse] [Hand 2] Precepts to y^e Sheriffe for Impa^ε a Jury
Adj^t Deputy

Notes: Hand 2 = Stephen Sewall ◊ 1 wax seal.

Essex County Court Archives, vol. 1, no. 1, Massachusetts Supreme Judicial Court, Judicial Archives, on deposit James Duncan Phillips Library, Peabody Essex Museum, Salem, MA.

September 1692

Thursday, September 1, 1692

533. Examination of William Barker Jr.†

[Hand 1] ⟨?⟩ Sep^t 92
Before Maj^r Gidney m^r Hawthorn m^r Corwin & Capt Higginsone.

The Examination and confession of Wm Barker aged 14 yeares or ~~there~~about

He is accused for exerciseing acts of witchcraft upon the bodyes of Martha Sprague Rose foster and Abigail Martin, which he did not deny but could not remember it.
He confesses now that he hath not been in the snare of the devil aboue six dayes, That as he was goeing in the woods one evening to look efter cowes he saw the shape of a black dog which looked very fiercely upon him And he was much disturbed in his mynd about it and could not sleep well that night
And betymes next morneing he mett with a black man (he calls him a black man because he had black cloaths and thinks he had a black skin) who bid him set his hand to a book and serve him as long as he the said Barker Lived, which he promeised
And thereupon set his hand to the book by putting his finger thereon, He saith the black man brought red stuff along with him in an Inkhorn
And he the said Barker dipt his finger into it and therewith made a red mark on the paper
He Confesses he was to doe any service the black man appoynted him and was to have a sute of cloaths for it. he said further the black man would have him baptised but he never was.
He saith further that Goody Parker went with him last night to afflict martha Sprague, And that he afflicts by clincheing his hands together. He now Saith he is sorry & hates the devill but yet struck down the afflicted with his eyes,
And martha Sprague being recovered out of a fitt said that Barkers apparition and Goody Parker [1 word overstruck] rid upon a pole. and was baptised at five myle pond, – He now sayes there was such a load upon his Stomack that he could not speak,
A litle after he owned he was baptised by the black man at five myle pond and did also renounce his former baptisme, he knowes Goody Parker to be a witch
And sayes the devil dipt his head into the water & spoke these words that he the said Barker was his for ever and ever.
He said he could not think of his baptisme before,
And that the load that was upon his stomak is not so heavy as it was but just before
He ~~said~~ still afflicted martha Sprague & shut her mouth but by layeing his hand thereon opened it again. – and afterwards confessed that there were of his Company Goody Parker Goody Johnson Samuel Wardwell & his wife and two daughte^rs.
And then could take the afflicted persones by the hand without doeing ym any harme.

September 1, 1692   [Hand 2] Wm Barker Junr Signed & owned the abouesaid   The marke
                     Examination & Confession.
                     before me John Higginson Just^ε peace: ✗ of
                                                                                   William Barker Junr

                     [Reverse] [Hand 3?] Confession of William Barker Jun^ε
                     [Hand 2] acused.   Goody parker.
                                           Goody Johnson
                                           Sam^{ll} wardell.
                                           his wife
                                           & 2 daughters
                              aflicted
                                           martha. Sprage

Notes: The dating on this document simply indicates "Sep^t 92," but the copy of it in the *Andover Examinations Copy*
(see No. 425) has a September 1 date that is probably accurate for this one. See No. 534. ◊ Hand 1 = William Murray;
Hand 2 = John Higginson Jr.

*Suffolk Court Files, vol. 32, docket 2761, p. 103, Massachusetts Supreme Judicial Court, Judicial Archives, Massachusetts State
Archives, Boston, MA.*

534. Examination of William Barker Jr., Copy

See also: Sept. 15, 1692.

[Hand 1] 1 Sep^ε ["S" written over "s"] 92 Before Maj^ε Gidney Mr Hathorne Mr Carwin Jno
Higginson Esq^ε
The Exam̄ & Conff^εon of Wm̄ Barker Jun^ε aged 14 Yeares or their about He is accused for
Exercising acts of Witchcraft Vpon ye bodyes of Martha Sprauge Rosse ffostter & abigall
Martin wch he did not deny but Could Not Rememb^ε it –
He Conffesses now y^t he hath not been in ye Snare of ye Diuel aboue Six ~~Years~~ days, y^t as he
was Goeing into the Woods one Euening to loeck after Cows he Saw ye Shape of a black dog
wch looked Verry fercly Vpon Him & he was Much disturbed in his Mind about it & Could
not Sleep well y^t Night & betimes Next Morning he Mett wth a black Man (he Calls him a
black man because he had black Cloaths & thinks he had a black Skin) Who bid him Sett his
hand to his book & Serue him as long as he ye s^d Barker liued wch he promised And ~~Soe~~
^{theirupon} Sett Hi⟨s⟩ hand to thi⟨s⟩ book by putting his fing^ε Theron he Saith ye black
man brought Red Stuf along wth him in an Inkhorn & he ye S^d Barker dipt his finger into it
and ther wth Made a Red Mark on ye paper He Conffesses he was to doe any Seruis ye black
man appointed him ~~to doe~~ & was to haue Suite of [1 word overstruck] Cloaths for it he S^d
further ye black man would haue him baptized but he Neur was – he Saith further y^t good^ε
Parker went wth him last Night to afflictt Martha Sprauge & y^t he afflicts by Clinching
["Clinching" written over "pinching"] his hands Together he Saith he Now is Sorry & hates
ye Diuel but Yett Struck dwone ye afflicted wth his Eyes – and Marth^ε Sprauge being

Recouered out of a fitt S^d y^t barkers apperition & Good^ε Parker rod Vpon a pole & was
baptized at 5 Mile pond – He Now Says there was Such a load Vpon his Stomach y^t he
Could Not Speak a little affter he owned he was baptized by y^e black man at 5 Mile
pond & Renounced his former baptizime he Knows Good^ε parker to be a witch & Says y^e
Diuel dipt his head into y^e Watter & Spook these words y^t he y^e S^d Barker was his for Euer
& Euer He S^d he Could not think of his baptizime before & y^t y^e Load y^t was Vp[Lost] [=
upon] his Stomach Is not Soe heauy as it was Just now He Stil afflicted Martha Sprauge &
Shut her Mouth but by ^{laying} his hand Theron open⟨e⟩d i⟨t⟩ again – and afterwards
Confessed y^t ther ware of his Comp^a Good^ε parker Good^ε Johnson Sam^{ll} Wardwel his wife
& two Daughters & y^n Could take y^e afflicted p^{ε}sons by y^e Hand wthout doeing y^m any
harm

W$\overline{m}$ Barker Jun^ε Signed & owned y^e aboue S^d Exam^ε &
Conffession
before Me John Higginson Just^ε peace

The Marke
X of
W$\overline{m}$ Barker Jun^ε

Notes: From *Andover Examinations Copy*. See No. 425.

Essex Institute Collection, no. 24, 10r–v, James Duncan Phillips Library, Peabody Essex Museum, Salem, MA.

535. Examination of Sarah Hawkes, Copy

See also: Sept. 17, 1692.

[Hand 1] 1 Sep^ε 1692 Before Maj^ε Gidney Mr Hathorne Mr Corwin Jno Higginson Esq^{ε}s
The Examination & Confession of Sarah Hawks Daughter in law to Sam^{ll} Wardwell of
Andiuor After ye afflicted p^{ε}sons had accused her & ye Rest of Her Comp^a wth aflicting of
y^m and p^{ε}ticularly Making y^m da^{u}nce & Sing Seuerall houres at Mr Tylers House And
after her Stricking y^m dwone wth ye Glance of her Eyes in ye Court & Recouering y^m again
She Confesses as ffollowes Viz That this last Spring after She had turned ye Siue & s⟨e⟩issers
Sissers ye Diuel Came to her and gott a promise of her but She Neuer had any thing of him
She Saith She went to Salem Village Metting of Witches wth Good^ε Carryer She promised
to Serue ye Diuel 3 or 4 Years & to giue him her Soul & body & y^t She Signed a paper He
offered to her by Making a black Sc^{r}aule or Mark wth a Stick as a Confermation of y^e
Couenant & he promised She Should have w^t She Wanted but neuer had any thing of him
She Saith She Neuer afflicted till last night, when She afflicted Martha Sprauge & Rose
ffostter – She Saith She knoweth y^t When She pulled of her Gloue In Court She afflicted
y^m – Noate y^t Sarah Hawks in Recou^ε Sprauge out of her fitt gript her wrist Soe hard y^t
p^{ε}esently it Swelled & Sprauge Could not Stir it but upon Hawks laying her hand Gently
Vpon it it was p^{ε}sently wel again – She Saith ye paper She Signed Seemed to her to hang
Vpon Nothing at y^e 1^{rst} & 2nd aperance of y^e Diuel he was like a man but y^e 3rd aperance was
like a Shadow She Saith y^e Diuel doth Carry Things out of her mind Strangly for when She
Came Vp Stairs She had a mind to Confese but Now Cannot – She Saith further y^t W$\overline{m}$
Barker was one of her Company when they Daunced at Mr Tylers house & y^t they Caused

September 1, 1692

Ephraim ffostter Wife to Daunce at home & Martha Sprauge Sung at Mr Tylers almost all day till She was almost killed She Conffesses y^t Stephen Johnson Her ffathar & Mother & her Sister Mercy ware of her Company She was baptized a little aboue a month agoe in fiue Mile pond & Renounced her former baptizime y^e Diuel dipt her face in y^e Watt$^\varepsilon$ & he was then in y^e Shape of a black Man & has Seen him Seueral times Since – as to y^e Witch Metting at y^e Village She Saw there a doz^n of Strangers riding upon poles but knew y^m not, ther was a man or 2 y^e Rest ware Woemen one of y^e Men ware tall⟨e⟩ y^e other Short & fatt Noate here y^t when She had Conffessed all as aboue, Except y^e Renounceing of her former baptizme She Could not Come Near any of y^e afflicted p$^\varepsilon$sons without Tormenting y^m wth her Eyes but when She did Remember & Conffesed that She had Renounced her former baptiz$^\varepsilon$ then they ware are Reconciled & Could all take one another by y^e hand frely

Sarah Hawks Signed & owned the aboue S^d Examination &   The Mark
Conffession before Me John Higginson   X of
17 Sept$^\varepsilon$ 1692   Sarah Hawks

Notes: From *Andover Examinations Copy*. See No. 425. In the Swedish witch trials, one feature was that people danced after a meal with the Devil. ◊ "She had turned y^e Siue & . . . Sissers": Probably the same idiom as "sieve and shears," 'used for purposes of divination' (*OED* s.v. *sieve* sb. 2b).

Essex Institute Collection, no. 24, 9v, James Duncan Phillips Library, Peabody Essex Museum, Salem, MA.

536. Examination of Stephen Johnson, Copy

See also: Sept. 15, 1692.

[Hand 1] 1th Sep$^\varepsilon$ 92 Before Maj$^\varepsilon$ Gidney M$^\varepsilon$ Hathorne Mr Corwin & Jno Higginson Esq$^\varepsilon$
The Examination & Confession of Steph$^\varepsilon$ Johnson aged 14 Yeares
In y^e time of his Examinat$^\varepsilon$ he afflicted Marth$^\varepsilon$ Sprauge Mary Lacy & Rose ffostt$^\varepsilon$ by looking on y^m & Recouered y^m again by laying his hand Vpon There Rist or arme & at last Conffesed thus – y^t @ hilling time this Sum̄er being allone he Saw a Speckled bird not Soe big as a pigeon which Spake to him & y^e Next day he Saw a black Catt & after y^t Came a black man who told him he must Se⟨?⟩t his hand to a book & Soe p$^\varepsilon$sented him a Single paper to which he Sett his hand being asked after w^t maner he did it he Said he prickt his fing$^\varepsilon$ & blood Came out & he Stampt his fing$^\varepsilon$ Vpon y^e paper & Made a re⟨d⟩ Mark He S^d ~~S~~ y^t he was also to Serue y^e black man one Year & his Seruis was to afflict p$^\varepsilon$sons & further y^t y^e Diuel asked hin [= him] to giue up him Self Soul & body to him & Soe he did & thinks also y^t y^e Diuel was to H[Lost]⟨u⟩e [= have] him at y^e Years End being asked w^t he was to haue of y^e Diuel for his Seruice A a pair of french fall Shouses wch he Neuer yett had He Saith also y^t he was baptized at Shaw Shim Riuer a little after he Saw y^e Diuel y^e first time The Man̄er was thus hauing ben at work at Benj^a abbotts he went alone in the Euening to Swim In y^e Watt$^\varepsilon$ & there mett wth y^e black Man who told him he must be his Seruant &

Must be ^{also} baptized & Soe y^e black man took him Vp & flung in his Whole body ouer   September 1, 1692
y^e bank into y^e Watt^ε, being Ready Stript before to goe in him Self, & y^n then this black
man told him he must be his & must Renounce his first baptizime & Soe he did he Saith
their was also a couple of Mades [= maids] & 2 Men he Conffes^ε y^t Yersterday he afflicted
Martha Sprauge & y^t he did it by Squeezing his hands together he Conffesses also y^t he and
y^e Rest of his Comp^a did Daunce at Moses Tylers house & Made Martha Sprauge Sing he
Says he is Sorry for w^t he has done Renounces y^e Diuel & all his Works & y^n Could Take y^e
afflicted by ye Hand w^thout hurting of y^m

Stephen Johnson Signed & owned ye aboue S^d   The Marke
Examination & Conffesion Before Me Jno Higginson Just^ε peace   X of
15 Sep^t 92   Stephen Johnson

Notes: From *Andover Examinations Copy*. See No. 425.

Essex Institute Collection, no. 24, 10r, James Duncan Phillips Library, Peabody Essex Museum, Salem, MA.

537. Examination of Mercy Wardwell, Copy

See also: Sept. 15, 1692.

[Hand 1] 1th Sep^t 1692. Before Maj^ε Gidney Mr Hathorne ^{M^r Corwin} & Jno Higginson
Esq^ε The Examination & Conffession of Mercy Wardwel Daughter of Sam^ll Wardwell of
Andiuor She Conffesses She hath be⟨e⟩n in ye Snare of ye Diuel @ a quartter of a Year y^e
Cause of her being Inticed was her discontent & ye occation of her discontent was because y^t
people told her y^t She Should Neuer haue Such a Young Man who Loued her & he finding
no Enco^{u}ragment threatned to drowne himself at wch She was much troubled Somtime
after to her Apprehenction he y^t mad loue to her Came & Intreated her to be his & She did
not then Consent & Soe dismist him wth y^t Awnswer y^e Next time he appeared in y^e Shame
[= shape] of a dogg & told her She Must be his for he was god & Christ & She Should want
for no thing if She would Serue him ^{and She did y^n beleue him. & promised to Serue him}
He told her She must always wish y^e Diuel had this or that & y^t She must Curse & lye She
Conffeses She Cueuanted to Serue ye Diuel twenty Years & he promised y^t She Should be
happy & She Made a red Mark Vpon a peece of Paper wher She Saw no other Names And
thinks he keeps thee paper because He ~~paper~~ {Carried it away} wth him, She owned She
Afflicted Martha Spraug & Rose ffostter butt Neuer any before – Here Companians ware
her ffather Mother Sister Sarah hawks & W^m̄ Barker She S^d furth^ε (wch is Remarkable) y^t
when She lookt dwone Vpon ye Table She Could Conffese Nothing – She Conffesses She
was Baptized at home in a pale of Watt^ε in Which He dipt her face telling her She must
Serue him & y^t it is about a Quarter of a Year agoe Since She was Baptized She Say⟨s⟩ also y^t
She afflicted Tim^o Swan by Squeezing her hands & Thinking Vpon him & ye Diuel made
~~him~~ her doe it whome She hath not seen @ 4 Times – Noate Here a thing Remarkable y^t
notwithstanding all this Conffession yett ye afflicted p^εsons Could Nott Come Near her But
upon ye Maj^ε asking of her if ye Diuel had not made her Renounce her former baptizime
And She Answering Yes then they Could all take one another by ye Hand without
any hurt

September 1, 1692

Mercy Wardwell Signed & owned the
aboue S^d Examination & Conffession
before Me Jn° Higginson Just^ε peace
15 Septemb^r 1692

Marcy Wardwell owned all y^e
aboue S^d Examination &
Conffession (only S^d She did not
know her ffarther & Mother
ware witches as witness her hand
The Mark
X of
Ma^{r}cy Wardw⟨e⟩l

Notes: From *Andover Examinations Copy*. See No. 425.

Essex Institute Collection, no. 24, 9r, James Duncan Phillips Library, Peabody Essex Museum, Salem, MA.

538. Examination of Samuel Wardwell

See also: Sept. 13, 1692.

[Hand 1] The Examination and Confession of Sam^ll wardwell. [Hand 2] taken Sept 1st 92.
before John Higginson Esq one of their maj^ties, Justices of peace for the County of Esse⟨x⟩
[Hand 1] After the returneing of negative answe^εs to severall questions He said he was
sensible he was in the snare of the devil, He used to be much discontented that he could get
no more work done, and that he had been foolishly Led along with telling of fortunes, which
sometymes came to pass, He used also when any creature came into his field to bid the devil
take it, And it may be the devil took advantage of him by that,
Constable foster of Andover said that this wardwell told him once in the woods that when
he was a young man he could make all his cattell come round about him when he pleased.
The said wardwell being urged to tell o truth he proceided thus, That being once in a
discontented frame he saw some catts together with the appearance of a man who called
himself a prince of the aire and promised him he should live comfortably and be a captain
and requyred said wardwell to honor him which he promised to doe, and it was about twenty
yeares agoe. He said the reason of his discontent then was be⟨c⟩ause he was in love with a
maid named Barker who slighted his love, And the first appearance of the catt then was
behind Capt bradstreets house, about a week after that A black man appeared in the day
tyme at the same place and called himself prince and lord and told him the said wardwell he
must worship and beleeve him, and promeised as above, with this addition that he should
never want for any thing but that the black man had never performed any thing, And further
that when he would goe to prayer in his family the devil wold begin to be angry He saith also
that at that tyme when the devil appeared & told him he was prince of the aire that then he
syned his book by makeing a mark like a square with a black pen and that the devil brought
him the pen & Ink He saith furth⟨er⟩ he Covenanted with the devil untill he should arryve to
the age of sixty yea^εs And that he is now about the age of 46 yea^εs. And at that tyme the
devil promeised on his part as is above exprest,
he said it was about a 4^tnight agoe since he began to afflict, And confesses that mary Lilly
and Hannah Tayler of Ridding were of his company Furth⟨e⟩r he saith that martha
Sprague was the first he afflicted, that the devil put him upon it and threatned him

September 1, 1692

yrunto [= thereunto] And that he did it by pincheing his coat & buttons when he was discontented, and gave the devil a com̄ission so to doe, He sayes he was baptised by the black man at Shaw shin river alone and was dipt all over. And beleeves he renounced his former baptisme.

~~⟨noate⟩, that he still afflected notwithstanding the former confession~~
att^st John Higginson ~~Just~~ ⁿ̃peace

[Hand 3] Sam^ll Wardwell. owned: to: ye grand Inquest: that: ye above written: conffession: was: taken: from: his mouth. & that he had s^d it: but: he s^d he belyed: himselfe:: he also s^d it was alone one: he: knew he should dye for it: wheither: he ownd it or no
Sept^ε 13th: 1692

[Reverse] [Hand 4] Samuel Wardell his Examination & Confesion

Notes: When Wardwell originally confessed, confessors were not being tried. Wardwell abandoned his false confession after the court began grand jury hearings in response to confession. He was executed on September 22. ◊ Hand 1 = William Murray; Hand 3 = Simon Willard

Essex County Court Archives, vol. 2, no. 59, Massachusetts Supreme Judicial Court, Judicial Archives, on deposit James Duncan Phillips Library, Peabody Essex Museum, Salem, MA.

539. Examination of Sarah Wardwell, Copy

See also: Sept. 15, 1692.

[Hand 1] The 1^rst Septemb^r 1692.
Before Maj^ε Gidney Mr Hathorne Mr Corwin Jno Higginson Esq^εs The Confession of Sarah Wardwel wife of Sam^ll Wardwel of Andiuor after many Denials of w^t She was accused for & p^εticularly of tormenting ye afflicted p^εsons by loocking on y^m wth her Eyes before ye Justices wch notwithstanding was Euident to ye behold^εs She was required to declare ye truth in ye fear of god, & then She Conffeses & followeth y^t She thinks She has been in ye Snare of ye Diuel 6 Years at wch time ~~y^eDiuel~~ ^{a man} appeared to her & required her to Worship him & doe him Seruice he Said he was god & Should be worshiped & promised Me Such thing as I wanted as Cloathing & ye like She Saith She Signed a peice of paper by putting her fing^ε to it which (as She thinks) made a black mark being asked why She did not weep & lament for it She answered She could not Weep She S^d She was baptized in Shawshin Riuer & he dipt her face in ye Watt^ε & at her baptizme She gaue her Self Soul & body to him & he told her She was his Seruant She Says She both went & Retturned on foot & was alone She was also once at Salem Village Witch metting where their ware many people & y^t She ^{was} Carried upon a pole in Comp{a}ny wth 3 more Viz Good^ε ffostter Good^ε Carrier & Good^ε Lawrence their was also a minister there & Some Men wth pretty handsome apparell & y^t She Saw a w⟨e⟩aman Cary wine @ amongts y^m She S^d She knew Good^ε Carrier to be a witch She S^d She afflicted none butt Martha Sprauge last night being asked how She did it Said y^t Marth^ε Spraue was a means of taking up her husband & because he was gone from home & She much Vext at it & therupon Suddenly Catcht up her Child in her armes & wished Sprauge Might be afflicted & little after S^d She Squezed her Child wth an Intention y^t y^e p^εsons Should be afflicted She S^d She Neuer New [= knew] her husband to be a witch

till She was Such an one her Self & thinks her daughters haue been so butt a little while not aboue a month She ownes She is Sorry for w^t She has done & promises to renounce y^e Diuel all his works & Serue y^e true Liueing god – Noate She is accused for afflicting Sprauge Marttin & Rosse ffostt^E & In ye time of her Examination Struck y^m dwone w^th ^{her} Eyes & Recouered y^m by her touching of their armes as also Struck dwone Sarah Bridges & Hanah Post & Mary Warren Mary Lacy Junr & Martha Sprauge Testified they Saw her afflict Abigal Martin in ye Court & Hannah post S^d She Saw her afflict Sarah Bridges

Sarah Wardwell Signed & owned the aboue S^d   The X Mark
Examination & Conffession   of
Before Me John Higginson Justice peace   Sarah Wardwel

Notes: From *Andover Examinations Copy*. See No. 425.

Essex Institute Collection, no. 24, 8v–9r, James Duncan Phillips Library, Peabody Essex Museum, Salem, MA.

Friday, September 2, 1692

540. Examination of Mary Parker

[Hand 1] 2 Sep^E 1692.
The Examination of mary Parker of Andover widow [Hand 2] taken before Barth° Gidny John Hathorne Jona^t Corwin & John Higginson Esq^E ther majesties Justices of the peace for the County of Essex in the forth yeare of their majestes Reigne
[Hand 1] upon mentioneing of her name, severall afflicted persones wer struck down as Mary warrin Sarah churchhill. hannah post. Sarah Bridges Mercy wardwell, And ^{when} she came before the Justices, she recovered all the afflicted out of their fitts by the touch of their hand
She is accused for ~~bewitching~~ acting of witchcraft upon martha Sprague And Sarah Philps.
Q. how long have ye been in the snare of the devil. Ansr. I know nothing of it
There is another woman of the same name in Andover But martha Sprague affirmed that that this is the very woma⟨n⟩ that afflicted her
The said mary Parker Lookeing upon Sprague struck her down, and recovered her again out of her fi⟨t⟩t,
Mary Lacey being in a fitt, cryed out. upon mary Parker, & s^d Parker recovered her out of her fitt
Mercy wardwell was twice afflicted by Parker & recovered again by her
William Barker ~~Jun~~^E lookeing upon mary Parker said to her face That she was one of his company And that the last night she afflicted martha Sprague in company with him
Mercy wardwell said that this mary Parker was also one of her company. And that the said parker afflicted Timothy Swan in her company
Mary Warrin in a violent fitt was brought neare haveing a pin run through her hand. and blood runeing out of her mouth she was recovered from her fitt by s^d mary Parker,

The said mary warrin said that this mary Parker afflicted & t⟨o⟩rmented her, And further   September 3, 1692
that she saw the said Parker at ane examination up at Salem village sitting, upon one of the
Beams. of the house./

> I underwritten being appointed by the Justices of the peace in Salem to wryt down
> the Examination of Mary Parker abovementioned. Doe testify this to be a true
> coppy of the originall examination As to the substance of it
>
> Wm Murray

[Reverse] [Hand 3?] Exam^n of Mary Parker

Notes: Little survives on the case of Mary Parker, with neither a complaint nor an arrest warrant extant. Her case came before the grand jury on September 16, and she was probably tried that day. She was executed on September 22. In a letter dated the day of Mary Parker's examination, but apparently not related to it, Cotton Mather wrote William Stoughton for an account of the trials, sending along part of *Wonders of the Invisible World* and indicating his plans to include in that book an account of the Swedish trials, particularly those parts that he saw as in accordance with the Salem trial cases. ◊ Hand 1 = William Murray

Essex County Court Archives, vol. 2, no. 63, Massachusetts Supreme Judicial Court, Judicial Archives, on deposit James Duncan Phillips Library, Peabody Essex Museum, Salem, MA.

Saturday, September 3, 1692

541. Warrant for the Apprehension of Elizabeth Dicer & Margaret Prince, and Officer's Return

See also: Sept. 5, 1692.

[Hand 1] To the Constable of Gloster.
complaint haueing ben made to us their Majesties Justices of the peace in Salem by Ebenezer Babson of Gloster against Elizabeth Dicer wife of Wm Dicer and Margret Prince widow of Gloster for that they haue griueously hurt & Tortured. Elonor Babson widow & Mary Sarjent wife of Wm Sarjant Just^e of Gloster by witchcraft & has giuen Bond to their Majesties to procecut Said Complaint to Effect These are therfore in their Majestes name to require you to Aprehend & Seize the Bodys of Elizab: Dicer wife of william Dicer of Boston Seaman & Margret Prince widow of Gloster & them bring before their Majesties Justices of the peace in Salem their to be Examined about the premises ffor wch this shall be your warrant Salem 3: September 1692.

Barth^o Gedney
John. Hathorne
Jonathan. Corwin
John Higginson
Just^e peace

September 5, 1692

[Reverse] in obedience to this within warrant I haue Seized the bodys of Elizabeth Dicer &
Margret Prince widow & brought them to Salem before their Majestes Justies of the peace
5 Sep^ᵉ 1692   Thom griggs Jun^or
                                                                                    Cnstta of glostr

Eliz: dicer
Margret Prince

Notes: Hand 1 = John Higginson Jr.

MS Ch K 1.40, vol. 2, p. 50, Rare Books & Manuscripts, Boston Public Library, Boston, MA.

Monday, September 5, 1692

Officer's Return: Warrant for the Apprehension of Elizabeth Dicer & Margaret Prince
2nd of 2 dates. See No. 541 on Sept. 3, 1692

542. Complaint of Thomas Dodd v. Nicholas Frost, and Complaint of Simon Willard & Elizer Keyser v. Joseph Emons

[Hand 1] Thomas Dod of Marblehead complaineth to their Majesties Justices of the peace
in Salem against Nicholas ffrost of pascataque for that the Said Nicholas ffrost hath Sorely
afflicted Johana Dod daughter of the Said Thomas Dod by witchcraft. to her great hurt: &
prays that a writ of Aprehention may be Granted against him & the Said Thomas Dod doth
herby oblige himselfe to our Souer^ᵉˢ William & Mary King & Queen of England &c in the
ffull &. whole Sume of one hundred pound Curant mony of New Engld the Condition is
that the Said Dod shall procecut the abouesaid complaint against Nich^o ffrost to Effect
dated. 5th Sep^t 1692:

The  marke
of
Thomas. Dod.

This Recognizance taken before me
5 Sep^t 1692   John Higginson Just^ᵉ peace

Sim^o: Wiliard & Eliz: Kesor Complaineth to their Majesties Justices of the. peace in Salem
against Joseph Emens of Manchester. for that the Said Emins hath Sorely afflicted Mary
warren by witchcraft to her great hurt & prays that a writ of Aprehention may be giuen out
against him/. & the. Said Simon wiliard & Eliz^r Kesor doe by these presents oblige
themselues to our Soueraines William & Mary King & Quene of England &c in the ffull
Sume of one hundred pounds Currant mony of New England / The Condition i⟨s⟩ ["is"
written over "of"] that the Said willard & Kesor shall procecut the Said Complaint to Effect
5 Sept 1692

                                                                                    Simon Willard
                                                                                    Elizur Keysar

This Recognizance taken before me John Higginson Just$^\varepsilon$ peace
5 Sep^t 1692

September 5, 1692

[Reverse] Nich° ffrost
Joseph Emins
5-7-92

Notes: Whatever the reason for these complaints nothing further is extant in connection with them. ◊ Hand 1 = John Higginson Jr.

MS Ch K 1.40, vol. 2, p. 44, Rare Books & Manuscripts, Boston Public Library, Boston, MA.

Sworn Before a Justice of the Peace: Examination of William Barker Sr.

2nd of 3 dates. See No. 525 on Aug. 29, 1692

Sworn Before a Justice of the Peace: Examination of William Barker Sr., Copy

2nd of 2 dates. See No. 526 on Aug. 29, 1692

543. Testimony of John DeRich v. Margaret Jacobs‡

[Hand 1] The testemeny af John derech Eaged about sixten years testefieth and sayeth that marget Jacobs Came and aflicted me this 5 af September as she heth many ~~a~~ tims {before} she also teleth me that she will kill me if ~~she~~ I woul not yeld to hur she also bringeth the book to me tempen me to set my hand to it ^{she} teleth me that i shal be wel if i will set my hand to the boob [= book] she teleth me that she will run a scuer [= skewer] thoraw me and ~~thre~~ threteneth me to Cut me with a knife beger then an ordnery knife {is} as ~~he~~ she heth don wonse before

[Reverse] [Hand 2] Margaret Jacobs.

Notes: The circumstances of this testimony are not clear. It was not used by the grand jury hearing Margaret Jacobs's case on September 14.

Essex County Court Archives, vol. 2, no. 118, Massachusetts Supreme Judicial Court, Judicial Archives, on deposit James Duncan Phillips Library, Peabody Essex Museum, Salem, MA.

544. Examination of Jane Lilly & Mary Colson

See also: Jan. 5, 1693.

[Hand 1] Jane Lilly examined: before: their Majest^s Justices: att Salem Sept$^\varepsilon$ 5th 1692
Jn° Hawthorn Esqr: & others
When: s^d Lilly was brought into: y^e Court of Justices: Mary Warin. Eliz Boothe and others of y^e afflicted were struck down into a dredfull fitt: & recovered again by a touch of s^d Lillyes hand: Mary Warin Allice Booth. & Susanna Post & Mrs Mary Marshall was asked who struck them down: they answered y^t it was s^d Lilly

September 5, 1692

It: was s^d to her: Jane Lilly you are acused for afflicting Mrs Mary Marshall by witchcraft: & now you have hurt many others: now you hav⟨e⟩ oppertunity to: tell ye truth: in this matter: but she answered: the truth was she knew nothing of it nor was she sencible y^t she was in ye devills snare Mary Warin s^d she had sometimes ~~used~~: come to Procters hous but: she denyed that ever she had: had: any conferrance with Procter or his wife: she wou⟨d⟩ not own: that she had any hand in killing of Wm Hooper: or in firing the hous: while he lay dead in it: or y^t she knew of his being killed with a spear she: was bid to speak ye truth: & she s^d she would for god was a god of truth: & she pressently spoke very hoars: Mary Warin coming out of a fitt & other of ye afflicted sayd that ye black man choaked her: when she say god was a god of truth: Sam^ll Wardwell: also s^d there was sever^l Gallans of wine that was prepared for Wm Hoopers buriall: that was drunk up: and there was five shouts made in triumph at what they had done: Jno Brown sen^ᵉ s^d he heard a shouting about y^t time: that Hoopers hous was fired: ye hous was on fire in the roofe first: both Maj^r Swayn & Jno Brown Sen^ᵉ declared: it was told {Tayler &} s^d Lilly that she {& Tayler} s^d when: goodwife Rice was taken up now we shall be deprived of drinking of sider: Sarah Churchell s^d she had seen s^d Lilly att prison w^t Procters wife but she denyed it: s^d Lilly looked on ye afflicted persons again & severall of them fell down: being struck down with her look & by a touch of her hand were helped up again & was well: Wardwell also s^d that s^d Lilly: did triumph: when she went away from ye firing of Hoopers hous but she s^d she was in her own hous all that time & that she never went: in body nor spirit nor ~~ever~~ ever had any inclynation to witchcraft: Maj^r Sway told her she had bin a frequenter of Dostins hous: but she s^d if she confessed any thing of this she shou{d} deny y^e truth & wrong her own soul.
this is y^e substance of ~~what~~ Jane Lillyes: examination: Attest Simon Willard

Mary Coultson examined before Sall̄ [= Salem] Justices {for y^r Maj^st} Sept^ᵉ 5^ᵉ 1692 Jno Hathorn Esqr
Mary Coultson. you are here acused for afflicting Mrs Mary Marshall by witchcraft Mrs Marshal with others fell down at her coming into y^e Court s^d Coultson helped M^rs marshall up by a touch of her hand: but s^d Coultson s^d she never hurt s^d marshall in her life: M^rs marshal was asked how long Coul⟨t⟩son had afflicted her: she s^d at times: she had afflicted her ever since her Mother Dostin had bin in prison & that she did it in vindication of her mothe⟨r⟩ These 3: Tayler: Lilly & Coultson came to me & s^d though Mr Pearpoint sang that ~~psl~~ Psalm: god will be a husband to ye widdow: but ^{he} would be none to me they sayd: they told me also: if I had served their god my husband had bin alive yett: but s^d Coultson was bid to look on ye afflicted persons: ~~and~~ and: some of the afflicted was bid to look on her: and Eliz Booth: & George Boothes wife & Allice Booth: with others: was struck down with her look & afflicted: & helped up: & was well by a touch of Coultsons hand: the were asked when they were well agayn who hurt: them & s^d it was s^d Coultson it was told Coultson it was evident that she acted witchcraft now before them: & it was like to apear that she had a hand in Wm Hoopers Death & in Ed Marshals death: but she s^d if she should confes she should be by her selfe: examined before Jno. Hawthorn Esqre others their Majest^s Justice
this is y^e substance of what Mary Coultson s^d at her examination:

Attest Simon Willard

[Reverse] I und$^\varepsilon$ written: being appinted by Authority: to take y^e within examination: doe   September 5, 1692
testifie upon oath taken in Court that this is a true Coppy of y^e substance of it to: y^e best of
my knowledge
Janu$^\varepsilon$ 5: 1692/3:

                                                                                        Simon Willard

            [Hand 2] the within Jane Lilie was Examined before their Majestes Justices of the
            peace in Salem

                                                        atest John Higginson Just$^\varepsilon$ peace
                        Owned before the Grand Jury
                        5 January 1692/3 Robert: Payne foreman:

[Hand 1] I und$^\varepsilon$ written: being appinted by Authority: take y^e within examination: doe
testifie upon oath taken in Court: that this is a true Coppy of y^e Substance of it: to y^e best of
my knowledge
Jan$^\varepsilon$ 5 1692/3:   Simon Willard

[Hand 2] the within Mary Colson was Examined before their Majesties Justies of the peace
in Salem

                                                        atest John Higginson Just$^\varepsilon$ peace

owned before the Grand Jury
5: January 1692/3   Robert Payne foreman

[Hand 3] Lillie & Colson
Middlisex

Notes: No complaint or arrest warrant for either is extant. Mary Colson was the mother of Elizabeth Colson, who had
been so difficult to catch after having been accused. See No. 153 & No. 161. ◊ Hand 1 = Simon Willard; Hand 2 =
John Higginson Jr.

*Suffolk Court Files, vol. 32, docket 2714, p. 52, Massachusetts Supreme Judicial Court, Judicial Archives, Massachusetts State
Archives, Boston, MA.*

545. Examination of Margaret Prince

See also: Jan. 5, 1693.

[Hand 1] Margret Prince of Capan [= Cape Ann] examined Sept$^\varepsilon$ 5: 1692 before. Jno
Hawthorn Esq$^\varepsilon$ & other y^e majest^s Justices
Margret Prince you are Complayned of for afflicting of the Widdow Babson: & Wm Serjants
wife of Capan. what say you.
She answered I am: inocent
Mr Serjant of Capan was asked: what: he could say. of this woman: he s^d his sister. was
greivously afflicted: & y^e Afflicted persons s^d that this woman hurt her: but he: knew
nothing but that Her conversation was: well: & good:
Eliz Hubert & mary warin were struck down into a fitt and helped up: & was well by a touch
of s^d Princes hand mary warin was helped another time so: Eliz Boothe & George Boothes

September 5, 1692

wife: were asked if ever ^{they had} seen this woman: they s^d no not before but both they: & two more were struck down into a fit & recovere⟨d⟩ by a touch of s^d Princes hand: & they s^d ye woman at ye bar hurt them. Some of ye afflicted s^d they saw ye black man on: ye table:: divers of them: having their eyes fixed was asked what they saw. & when: they could speake: s^d they saw a coffin: Elizabeth Hubberd s^d that Margret Princes spectre. had told her that she killd Mrs Duncun of Capan but s^d Prince s^d she had never hurt s^d Duncun nor Babson nor would not hurt anybody for a thousand worlds

Eliz Hubbert: was dumb: for a while. & yong Babson s^d Eliz Hubbert told him as they came from Capan. that goodwife prince: told her she should not speak anything against her. when she came to Salem

this is the substance: of what was sayd: to. & by Margret Prince: att: her exam⟨i⟩nation

Attest Simon Willard

I und^εwritten bei⟨n⟩g. appinted: by Athority to take ye above: examination doe testifie upon oath taken in Court: that this: is a tru Coppy: of y^e substance of it: to y^e best of my knowledge

Janu^ε 5: 1692/3   Simon Willard

[Hand 2] owned before the Grand Jury

5 January 1692/3   Robert: Payne

foreman:

the aboue Margret prince was Examined befor their majesties. of peace in Salem

atest Jno Higginson Just^ε peace

Notes: Hand 1 = Simon Willard; Hand 2 = John Higginson Jr.

Goodspeed Bookshop Catalogue no. 271, Boston, Nov. 1936.

546. Examination of Mary Taylor

See also: Jan. 5, 1693.

[Hand 1] Mary Tayler examined before their Majest^s Justices: at Salem Septr 5th 1692 Jno Hawthorn Esqr & others

It was sayd to her: you are here acused for afflicting Mrs Mary Marshall by witchcraft: but she s^d she knew nothing of it

Mrs Marshall did you acuse this woman or do you acuse her for hurting you by by witchcraft: A. Yes. she has beat me & came to perswade me to worship her god: & told me my god could not save me & she has brought images to me

S^d Tayler was bid to look on Mrs Mary Marshall: & did & s^d Marshall was struck down by it & s^d when she could speak it was s^d Tayler y^t struck her down: Mary lascy s^d also y^t s^d Tayler was upon s^d Marshall Tayler was told she had a dangerous eye: that struck folk down: which gives ground to think she was a witch: but she s^d she was not sencible she was one

S^d Tayler: look^t on Hannah Post: & Mary Lascy: & they fell down & Susa^n Post s^d Tayler was upon them: Mary Warin fell down also when she was b⟨id⟩ to look on: s^d whether Tayler

September 5, 1692

hurt: Post & Lascy: s^d Tayler was asked how she kild w^m Hooper: but she disownd any
knowledge of it: but Sam^ll Wardwel asked her: if she never had fallen out with: his bro
Hooper: Maj^r Swayn s^d her falling out with Hooper would easyly be proved: Wardwel s^d
their falling out was becaus s^d Hooper took his child from s^d Tayler: that she had to suckle:
Mary Waren fell into a fitt: & was helped up again: by a touch of Taylers hand: she was
asked if she had bin babtized: she s^d ye at Charlstown: when she was a ch⟨ild⟩ but ownd
nothing of witchcraft exept: she had in a passion wished bad wishes becavs Mrs Marshall had
complaynd: of her

Maj^r Swayn told her she had used thretning words both to his sister & others. s^d Tayler was
asked about burning Hoopers hous: where ye fire began first: but s^d she knew nothing of it
she was att home in her ~~bed~~ hous: but Sam^ll Wardwell told s^d Tayler: they had a meeting: in
Tryumph after: ye hous of Hoopers was burnt & drank ye wine that was provided for Hoopers
funerall: & that s^d Tayler & Jane Lilly was there: at ye drinking of it & one from Billerica:
Maj^r Swayn s^d ye wine for ye buriall of Hooper was drunk: Sam^ll Wardwell told Tayler: she
might remember ye stroke & ye stroke and ye double stroke: ye stroke was ye killing: ye man
ye other stroke was: ye firing ye hous: being asked what ye duble stroke was s^d Wardwell knew
not but y^t it might be ye destroying ye rest of Hoopers familly: the Reddin Constable s^d that:
s^d Tayler yesterday s^d who ever lived to se it would finde Mrs Marshals cace like Mary Warins
& that there was a hott pott now: & a hott^r pott preparing for her here after & being asked
what she men⟨t⟩ by ye hotter pott s^d that if Mrs Marshall wronged her hell would be prepared
for her: but after ward she s^d she would tell: & desired prayers that she might tell y^e truth:
but was much hindred: but was asked if y^e last Sabath was seven night. was not y^e first time
of her hurting Mary Marshall: which at last she in a manner owned: & she s^d to Mr Nois &
Mr Keyzer. {:} the Devill ∧{& goodi Dustin} brought her a birch Rhine [= rind; "R" written
over "b"] which she signed to: she owned she had promised y^e devill to serv him ~~worship~~ him
& trust in him: & to give up soul & body to him but: y^e first of her being a witch was her
frequenting: goodwife Dastins hous & goodwife Dastin had bin twice at her hous in y^e night
to her: but she would not own that ye devill had babtized her: nor that she Joyned in killing
Hooper: nor burning his hous ye time of her frequenting Dastins hous was ye last winter she
owned she had bent her fist & wished ill to Mrs Marshall: & that goodwife Dastin & her
Daughter was with her: & it was at Jane Lillyes hous so she begd forgivn^s of ye afores^d
this is ye substance of what: Mary Tayler: s^d at her examination: & of what was s^d there.
taken out of my characters: Simon Willard
I und^ε writen: being appinted by Authority: to take. y^e [Hand 2] {aboue} [Hand 1] ~~within~~
examinatio⟨n⟩ doe testifie upon oath taken in Court that this is a tru Coppy of the substance
of it to ye best of my knowledge: 5 Janu^ε 1692/3

                                                                                    Simon Willard

[Reverse] [Hand 2] The within Mary Tayler was Examined before their Majestes Justice of
the peace in Salem

                                                                    atest John Higginson Just^ε peace

Owned before the Grand Jury
5 January 1692/3

                                                                                    Robert Payne foreman:

September 5, 1692   [Hand 3] ~~This is Eved~~

Maj^ε Jeramiah Swaine ^{~~in Court~~} and M^ε William Arnold Swoarn ^{in Court} to the
truth of the within Confession being present at her Examination.

Test

Jon^a Elatson Cler

[Hand 2] Mary Tayler of Reding in midlesex

Notes: Mary Taylor's case came before a grand jury on January 5, 1693, but then went before another grand jury on January 31, 1693, the day of her trial. She was found not guilty. See No. 831. ◊ Hand 1 = Simon Willard; Hand 2 = John Higginson Jr.; Hand 3 = Jonathan Elatson

Suffolk Court Files, vol. 32, docket 2710, p. 43, Massachusetts Supreme Judicial Court, Judicial Archives, Massachusetts State Archives, Boston, MA.

547. Statement of John Parker & Joshua Eaton v. Mary Taylor†

[Hand 1] {Sworne in Court}

{ Jno Parker
{ Josuah Eaton } say that Mary Taylor thretened. them saying they were high but they
should haue a downefall and vsed other thretening words and allso thretened Goodwif
Marshall saying shee was the Cause of her displeasure aginst them and they should see what
would becom of her for her ~~And parting~~ god would deceiue her the said Parker said her god
what do you mean by her god I doubt you haue been somewhere to often / but afterward
goeing home ~~his sone~~ ward one came runing and sed his son was redy to dy and he was prest
allmost Choked and his wife s^d that if he the s^d Parker did not goe to Mary ~~tootheaker~~
Taylor ⟨?⟩ her husband would die and ~~he Imediately went and~~ ^{and so soone as shee had
named⟨ed⟩ her s^d Parkers name} his son became well Imediately and sundry times his son
was ~~sundry~~ strangly handled and was som times blind on one Ey and som times ⟨?⟩ on the
other Ey // And ye s^d Eaton swears to all but what relates to s^d Parkers ~~son~~ son

Suffolk Court Files, vol. 32, docket 2710, p. 43, Massachusetts Supreme Judicial Court, Judicial Archives, Massachusetts State Archives, Boston, MA.

548. Summons for Witnesses v. Mary Bradbury

[Hand 1] W^m & Mary by ye Grace of God of Eng⟨l⟩and Scotland ffrance & Ireland King &
Queen defend^{εs} of ye faith &c^a

To Thomas Ring of Amesbury or Salsbury Timothy Swann of Andover Richard Carr &
James Carr of Salsbury.

Greeting Wee Com̄and you all Excuses Set apart to be and personaly appear at ye Next.
Court of Oyer & Terminer holden at Salem On Tuesday Next at Twelue of ye Clock or as
Soon after as possible There to Testify ye Truth On Seuerall Indictments to be Exhibited
against m^{εs} Mary Bradbury & other prisoners to be Tried for ye horrible Crime of
Witchcraft, hereof Make return fail not dated in Salem Sepr 5th 1692 & in y^e fourth year of

Our Reign {To yᵉ Sheriff of Essex: or} Constables of Andouer Hauerill {Salsbury}   September 5, 1692
Amesbery. Bradford or Newbury.

Stephen Sewall Cler

[Reverse] Zerub. Endecot
Sam. Endecot
James Carr
Richᵈ Carr
Timᵒ: Swan
Jos: Ringg

Notes: Hand 1 = Stephen Sewall ◊ 1 wax seal.

Essex County Court Archives, vol. 2, no. 74, Massachusetts Supreme Judicial Court, Judicial Archives, on deposit James Duncan Phillips Library, Peabody Essex Museum, Salem, MA.

549. Summons for Witnesses v. Mary Esty, Sarah Cloyce, Giles Cory, & Martha Cory, and Officer's Return

[Hand 1] Wᵐ & Mary by yᵉ Grace of God of England Scotland ffrance & Ireland King & Queen defenders of yᵉ faith &cᵃ

To yᵉ Sheriffe of Essex or deputy or Constable or Constables of Salem Topsfield & Boxford Greeting
Wee Comand you & Either of you to warn and giue Notice vnto Jonathan Putman James Darlin Samuel Abbey of Salem Daniel Clarke of Topsfield & Samuel Smith of Boxford Edward Putman Ez: Cheeu⟨er⟩ Jnᵒ Parker Senʳ Samˡˡ Braybrooke Mary Wolcot Ann Putman Sarah Vibber Marcy lewis Eli: Hubbard that they & Euery of them be at yᵉ Next Court of Oyer & Terminer holden at Salem on Tuesday Next at Twelue of yᵉ Clock or as soon after as may be there to Testify yᵉ truth to yᵉ best of thier knowledge on Seuerall Indictments Exhibited against Mary Easty & Sarah Cloyce Giles Corey & Martha Corey his wife hereof Make Return fail not dated in Salem: Sepʳ 5ᵗʰ 1692. & in yᵉ fourth year of Our Reign
Stephin Sewall Cler⟨?⟩

[Reverse] [Hand 2] To the clark of Salem I haue acordenely To warent Som{m}and
[= summoned] danile clake of topsfeld And Samuel Smith of Boxfrd.
Joseph. Andrews Constebele
of Boxferd

Notes: Sewall uncharacteristically spells an "i" in "Stephin" but the hand is definitely his. ◊ Hand 1 = Stephen Sewall ◊ 1 wax seal.

Essex County Court Archives, vol. 1, no. 40, Massachusetts Supreme Judicial Court, Judicial Archives, on deposit James Duncan Phillips Library, Peabody Essex Museum, Salem, MA.

September 5, 1692

550. Summons for Witnesses v. Alice Parker & Ann Pudeator, and Officer's Return

[Hand 1] W^m & Mary by ye Grace of God of England Scotland ffrance & Ireland King & Queen defend^s &c

To ye Sheriff of Essex or deputy Greeting
Wee Comand you to Warn John Wesgate John Bullock Martha Dutch Susanna Dutch Lt Jeremiah Neale John Beckett John Best Jun^ε [Hand 2] Jno Loader Sarah parott [Hand 1] That they & Euery of them appear at ye Next Court of Oyer & Terminer holden at Salem on ye Next Tuesday at Twelue of ye Clock There to Testify ye Truth to ye best of thier knowledge On certain Indictments to be Exhibited against Alce Parker & Ann Pudeater hereof make return fail not dated in Salem Sepr 5th 1692. in ye fourth yeare of Our Reign Stephen Sewall Cl⟨r⟩

[Reverse] [Hand 3]
Sep^⟨t⟩ 5th 1692
I haue Sumoned ⟨a⟩nd haue Warned all the within named persons John Best Jun^ε Exep^t sd Best beeing Remoued to Ipswich that thay and Euery of them appeare to Giue in their Euid: &c: att time and place within written

ꝑ me Geo. Herrick
Dep^t sheriff

Notes: Hand 1 = Stephen Sewall; Hand 3 = George Herrick ◊ 1 wax seal.

Essex County Court Archives, vol. 1, no. 263, Massachusetts Supreme Judicial Court, Judicial Archives, on deposit James Duncan Phillips Library, Peabody Essex Museum, Salem, MA.

551. Testimony of John DeRich v. Giles Cory, and Statement of Hannah Small & Martha Adams v. Giles Cory‡

[Hand 1] the testomeny af John derech Eaged about sixten years testefieth ~~that that~~ and sayeth that gils Cory also Came to me and aflicted me this 5 af ~~dese~~ September as wel before as after he also threteneth me to kill me if I will not yeld to him he also ["l" written over "s"] ~~told~~ Came about the 20 of oges [= August] and told me that he wanted som platers for he was gowen to a feast he told me that he had a good mind to ask my dame but he ~~th~~ sayd that she wouled not let him haue them so he took the platers and Cared them ~~a~~ away being gown about half a ~~nowr~~ oure {with} them then he brot them againe gowen away and sayd no thing also Sary pese afliceth me at seuerel times she Came to me af the fast day Last at Salam she pinched me then and i haue not sene hur sencs

~~the⟨p⟩~~	these howes nams are under reten were there and saw the
~~the⟨p⟩~~	platers were gown as John derich sayed
	hanah Smal
	Martha Adams

[Reverse] [Hand 2] Jno Derich ag^t Giles Cory

Notes: The grand jury met on Giles Cory September 9, and perhaps this document was intended for use then, but was   Sept. 6, 1692
not. The two "signatures" of Small and Adams appear to be in the same hand as the recorder of the document.

Essex County Court Archives, vol. 2, no. 92, Massachusetts Supreme Judicial Court, Judicial Archives, on deposit James Duncan
Phillips Library, Peabody Essex Museum, Salem, MA.

552. Statement of Thomas Fosse & Elizabeth Fosse for Mary Esty

See also: Sept. 9, 1692.

[Hand 1] thes may sartifie home it may c[Lost] [= concern]
that wee hows names are vndorrit[Lost] [= underwritten]
Being dasired by sume of the Realeations o⟨f⟩
marey estweke to giue our obsarvation how
she behaued hur salf while she Reamai⟨ned⟩
in Ipswech prison we dow afarme th[Lost] [= that]
wee sowe noe ell carreg or behau[Lost] [= behavior] [Lost?]
th⟨a⟩m {hure} but thare {that hure} daportment wos⟨e⟩
sobor and ciuell as wittnes our ha[Lost] [= hands]

thomos Ŧ [Lost]
his mar[Lost] [= mark]

5. Saptem 92

elesebeth ꓕ [Lost]
hur m[Lost] [= mark]

[Reverse] thomos ffosse tastimoney about marey. Ast⟨e⟩y

Notes: This appears to have been prepared for Esty's trial on September 9. Thomas Fosse was the prison keeper in Ipswich,
and Elizabeth was his wife. ◊ Likely used at trial.

Essex County Court Archives, vol. 1, no. 289, Massachusetts Supreme Judicial Court, Judicial Archives, on deposit James Duncan
Phillips Library, Peabody Essex Museum, Salem, MA.

Tuesday, September 6, 1692

Grand Jury of Ann Pudeator (Day 1)

Trial of Dorcas Hoar

553. Deposition of Thomas Putnam & William Murray v. Alice Parker†

See also: Sept. 7, 1692.

[Hand 1] the deposistion of Tho: putnam aged 40: years and william murry aged 36: year.
who: testifieth and saith: that seuerall of the afflected: parzons ware as mary walcott and

September 6, 1692   mary warren and seuerall other ~~and~~ were much afflected on the: 6ᵗʰ Septr. 1692 dureing the time of the Examination of Elce parker: and we obsarved that upon the glan⟨c⟩e of hir Eies they ware strucken down: and upon hir laying hir hand on them they ware Recouered and we beleue ⟨?⟩ that Elce parker the prisoner att the barr has often hurt the ⟨ab⟩[Lost] [= above] said parsons by acts of wicthcraf

                                                                                                Thomas putnam
         [Hand 2] Jurat in Curia   Wᵐ Murray

         [Reverse] [Hand 3] Tho: Putnam & Wᵐ Murray
         [Hand 4] Elec Parker

Notes: Alice Parker was first examined on May 12. See No. 144. An account of another examination on September 6 is not extant, but this deposition and the indictments against her all indicate that she was examined again on this date. ◊ Used at trial. ◊ Hand 1 = Thomas Putnam; Hand 2 = Stephen Sewall

Essex County Court Archives, vol. 2, no. 97, Massachusetts Supreme Judicial Court, Judicial Archives, on deposit James Duncan Phillips Library, Peabody Essex Museum, Salem, MA.

554. Summons for Witnesses v. Mary Esty, and Officer's Return

[Hand 1] Wᵐ & Mary by yᵉ Grace of God of England Scotland ffrance & Ireland King & Queen defendᴱ of yᵉ faith &cᵃ

To yᵉ Constable of Topsfield Greeting Wee Comand you to Warn & Giue Notice vnto yᵉ Wife of Abraham Reddington Mary Towne Widow William Towne & Samuel Towne ~~her~~ Sons of sᵈ Mary Towne Rebecka & Elizabeth Towne ~~also~~ of sᵈ Widow Towne that they & Euery of them all Excuses Set apart be and personaly appear at yᵉ Court of Oyer & Terminer {holden at Salem} to Morrow by Twelue of yᵉ Clock hereof Make return fail not dated in Salem Sepʳ 6ᵗʰ 1692 & in yᵉ fourth yeare of Our Reign

                                                                           Stephen Sewall Cle⟨r⟩

[Reverse] [Hand 2] I haue somensed and warned al the parsons with in nemed as ~~as~~ atested by me
Ephraim Willdes constabell o topsfelld

Notes: Even though Mary Esty is not named, the dating is consistent with the grand jury consideration of her case, and a deposition by Margaret Reddington, No. 87, helps clarify that this summons was for the Mary Esty case. ◊ Hand 1 = Stephen Sewall ◊ 1 wax seal.

Witchcraft Papers, no. 36, Massachusetts Historical Society, Boston, MA.

555. Testimony of Sarah Churchill, Mary Warren, Elizabeth Hubbard, Ann Putnam Jr., Sarah Bibber, & Mary Walcott v. Ann Pudeator

September 6, 1692

See also: Sept. 7, 1692 & Sept. 10, 1692.

[Hand 1] Sarrah Churchel: affirmd: to: ye Jury of inquest: that Ann Puddeate: her has: greatly afflicted her s^d Churchel by: choaking her pinching her & sticking pinse into her: & by pressing of her: &: making her sett her hand to: ye book upon: ye oath she hath: taken: Sept: 6: 1692

[Hand 2] & brought poppets to her to   } Sworne in Court.
Stick pins to wch she did   }   & y^e ꝑsons aflicted by it

[Hand 1] Mary {Warin} upon her oath: y^t she ⟨ɔ⟩ hath taken affirms: to ye Jury of inquest: that Ann Puddeater:: hath often: afflicted me: by biting me pinching me sticking pins in me: & choaking me: and perticulerly on ye 2: day of. July: att her. examination: s^d Puddeater did: afflict⟨e⟩ me greatly: also she or her Apperition: did offer: me the book to sign to: she told: me also y^t she was ye caus of Jno Turners ffalling off: ye cherry tree: to his great: hurt: & which: amazed him in his head & allmost kild him: she told me also: she was the caus of: Jerimiah Neals. wifes death: & I saw her hurt: Eliz Hubbard: Mary Walcot: & An Putnam: ye last night she: afflicted: me also: last night: by her wichcrafts & I doe veryly: beleev: s^d Ann Puddeater is a: wich: she affirms Puddeater: told her: she kild her husband Puddeater: & his first wife and that she was an instrument of Jno Bests: wifes death: Sept^ɛ 7: 1692

[Hand 2] Sworne in Court

[Hand 1] Eliz Hubberd affirmd: upon: ye oath she hath taken: thatt: she hath seen: Ann: Pudeater: Afflicted Mary: Warin: & that she her or her Apperition: did hurt me and Mary Warin ye last night before. ye Jury of inquest. Sept^ɛ: 7: 1692

[Hand 2] & that she hath aflicted her since she came into Court
Jurat in Curia.

[Hand 1] An Putnam affirmed: upon: her oath: to: ye Jury of inquest: that: she: hath seen Ann Puddeater: afflict: Mary Warin: Mary Walcot: & Eliz Hubbard: often: and perticulerly: atte att ye time: of her: last examination: before ye Majestrates: at Mr Tho. Beadles: she also: hath afflicted me: both then: and at other times: Sept^ɛ 7: 1692

[Hand 2] Owned her Euidence in Court

[Hand 1] Sarah Vibber: upon: her: oath: affirmed to ye Jury of inquest: that: shee: hath seen: An Puddeater afflict: Mary Warin: Mary Walcot & An Putnam: both at ye time of her examination. at Mr Tho Beadles; and ye last night she: together with goodwife Parker. did afflict: ye forenamed: Warin Walcot & Putnum: s^d Puddeater: hath afflicted: me: to: and i do beleev she is a wich. Sept^ɛ: 7: 1692

Mary Walcot: upon oath: affirmd to ye Jury of inquest: that: she hath seen An Puddeater: afflict Mary: Warin: An Putnam: & Eliz Hubbard: at ye time of her examination: at Mr Tho Beadles: and also ye last night: I saw: her: afflict Mary Warin Mercy Lewis: An Putman & Eliz Hubbard: by wichcraft: & I verily beleev: s^d Pudeater: is a witch [Hand 3] September: 7: 92. [Hand 2] & that this day she hath aflicted this deponent.

Jurat in Curia Sepr 10. 92. attest SSewall

September 6, 1692

[Hand 1] I find: by: my Charracters: which I: took: ~~from:~~ at yᵉ examination {of} An Puddeat⟨er⟩ that it: was on yᵉ 2 day of July: that she was examined: {at mʳ Tho ⟨?⟩ Beadles} thay bearing: date so: Septᴱ 7: 1692   Simon Willard:

[Reverse] [Hand 3] Several Wittnesses Against An Pudeator

Notes: Sewall's "Jurat in Curia" on September 10 is puzzling in that an earlier "Jurat in Curia" by him indicated September 7 as the trial date. It may be that the trial did not conclude until September 10, or there may be some other explanation for this anomaly. ◊ Used at trial. ◊ "amazed": 'put out of one's wits; stunned or stupefied' (*OED* s.v. *amaze* v, 1). ◊ Hand 1 = Simon Willard; Hand 2 = Stephen Sewall; Hand 3 = Anthony Checkley

Essex County Court Archives, vol. 1, no. 265, Massachusetts Supreme Judicial Court, Judicial Archives, on deposit James Duncan Phillips Library, Peabody Essex Museum, Salem, MA.

Billa Vera: Indictment No. 1 of Dorcas Hoar, for Afflicting Elizabeth Hubbard†

2ⁿᵈ of 2 dates. See No. 400 on July 2, 1692

Billa Vera: Indictment No. 2 of Dorcas Hoar, for Afflicting Mary Walcott†

2ⁿᵈ of 2 dates. See No. 401 on July 2, 1692

Sworn at Trial: Deposition of Sarah Bibber v. Dorcas Hoar†

2ⁿᵈ of 2 dates. See No. 402 on July 2, 1692

Sworn at Trial: Deposition of Rachel Tuck & Hannah Cox v. Dorcas Hoar†

2ⁿᵈ of 2 dates. See No. 155 on May 14, 1692

556. Deposition of Mary Gage v. Dorcas Hoar, Sarah Wilds, & Sarah Bishop †

[Hand 1] The deposition of Marie Gadge aged about 48 years this deponent testifieth & saith that about mine [= nine] years agon sd Deponent & her son Josiah Wood being at yᵉ house of John Giles in Beverly & Dorcas hoare being there alsoe; the sd Hoare told her that her Child was not Long lived & sd Deponent asked her how she knew; the Child being well then: sd Hoare replied it would not live Long & bade her: marke the end of it; & about a month after that time her sd Child was taken sick & died sudenly and about halfe a year after sd Deponent asked sd Hoare how she could fortell yᵉ death of yᵉ Child her answer was she had acquaintaince wᵗʰ a doctor that taught her to know & had a doctors booke by her And sd Deponent saith farther yᵗ about 2 year agon sd Deponent being often Concerned at yᵉ house of Benjamin Balch Sⁿʳ (wᵗʰ his son David being then sick; she heard sd David Balch often Complaine yᵗ he was tormented by witches: sd Deponent asked him whether he knew who they were & sd David balch onswered it was Goody wiles & her Daughter & Goody Hoare. & one of marblehead he knew not by name: saying alsoe there was a Confederacy of them & they were then whispring together at his beds feet, and desired Gabriell Hood to strike them: & when he did strike at yᵉ place where sd Balch sd they sate, sd Balch said that he had struck Goody wiles & she was Gone presently: and at Severall other times sd Balch Cried out of Goody Hoares tormenting him & prayed earnestly to yᵉ Lord to bring them out & discover them & farther saith not

[Hand 2] Jurat in Curia.

[Reverse] Mary Gage   September 6, 1692
[Hand 3] m$^{\varepsilon}$ Gild

Notes: "Gild", at the end of the document appears very faintly on the manuscript. Who that is has not been identified.
The "Daughter" of Sarah Wilds is her step-daughter, Sarah Wilds Bishop. ◊ Used at trial.

Essex County Court Archives, vol. 1, no. 217, Massachusetts Supreme Judicial Court, Judicial Archives, on deposit James Duncan
Phillips Library, Peabody Essex Museum, Salem, MA.

557. Testimony of John Hale v. Dorcas Hoar

[Hand 1] John Hale aged 56 yeares Testifieth 6. 7. 1692

That for severall yeares ^{agoe} formerly were storys told concerning Dorcas Hoar her
beeing a fortune teller. And y^t shee had told her owne fortune. viz y^t shee should live poorely
so long as her husband will͞m Hoar did live, but ye said will should dye before her, & after y^t
shee should live better. Allso ye fortune of Ens: Corning & his wife who should dye first. &
y^t she had a book of fortune telling. About twenty two y̶a̶ yeares agoe ye s^d Dorcas minifested
to me great repentance for ye sins of her former life & y^t she had borrowed a book of
Palmstry, & there were rules to know what should come to pass. But I telling her y^t it was an
evill book & evill art shee seemed to me to renounce, or reject all such practices; whereupon I
had great charity for her severall yeares. But 14 yeares agoe last spring I discovered an evill
practice had been between a servant of mine & some of s^d Hoars chilldren in conveying
goods out of my house to ye s^d Hoars. & I had a daughter Rebecca then between 11 & 12
yeares old, whome I asked if she knew of ye Hoars stealing; she told me yea. But durst not
reveale it to me, & one reason was, She was threatened y^t Goody Hoar was a witch & had a
book by wch shee could tell what s^d Rebecca did tell me in my house & if ye s^d Rebecca told
me of ye stealing, ye said Hoar would raise ye devill to kill her, or bewitch her, or words to y^t
effect. (but whether she said y^t Dorcas her selfe or her chilldren told Rebecca those words I
remember not). I asked Rebecca if she saw ye book she said yea, she was shewed ye book &
their were many strea⟨ks⟩ & pictures in it by w^{ch} (as she was told) ye said Hoar could reveale
secrets & work witchcrafts. I Asked her how big ye book was, she said it was like a gram͞er, y^t
lay on ⟨y⟩^{e} table. And said shee now I have told you of the stealing Goody Hoar will bewitch
me. I perswaded my daughter not to think so hardly of Goody Hoar: But shee replyed I
know Goody Hoar is a witch (or to y^t effect) & then told storys of strange things y^t had been
acted in or about my house, when I & my wife were abroad, to fright s^d Rebecca into silence
about the theft, wch s^d Rebecca judged to be acts of s^d Hoars witchcraft: the particulars I
have now forgotten. I called to minde y^t ye s^d Hoar had told me of a book of Palmstry she
had, but not ye bigness of it; therefore y^t I might be better satisfyed I asked Thomas Tuck if
he knew Goody Hoar to have a book of fortune telling & he said yea shee had, such a kind of
book wch he had seen wth streaks & pictures in it & y^t it was about y^e bigness of such a book
poynting to a gram͞er, or book of like magnitude. this confirmed me in y^e opinion y^t my
daughter had seen such a book. And after my daughters death a freind told me y^t my
daughter said to her she went in fear of her life by y^e Hoars till quieted by y^t script$^{\varepsilon}$ [=
scripture]. Feare not them wch can kill y^e boady &c.

September 6, 1692

[Reverse] About those times other things were spoken of yᵉ sᵈ Hoares suspicians of her witchcraft whereupon a frend of mine did as I was informed ac⟨q⟩uaint Majᴱ Denison wᵗʰ them, for his consideration & as I was informed Majᴱ Denison took an opportunity to examine sᵈ Wᵐ Hoare about a fortune book his wife had & Wᵐ Hoar answered yᵉ book was John Samsons & his wife had returned yᵉ book long agoe & so yᵉ matter was left for yᵗ time. When discourses arose about witchcrafts at yᵉ Village then I heard discourses revived of Goody Hoars fortune telling of later times, & she beeing comīted to Boston I did last may speak wᵗʰ her of many things that I had known & heard of her. Shee told me yᵗ her owne fortune yᵗ she spake of, She was told by a shipmaster when she was first marryed. & Ens: Cornings fortune. viz yᵗ his first wife should dye before him (wᶜʰ is since come to pass) she spake it from observing a certain streak under yᵉ eye of sᵈ Corning or his wife: But as I take it it was his wife had yᵉ streak. And for seeing yᵉ devill (wᶜʰ was one thing I spake to her of) She said she never saw yᵉ devill, ~~but~~ or any spirit but ones, & yᵗ was soon after old Thomas Tuck dyed (wᶜʰ I take to be about ten yeares since) & yᵗ shee took it to be yᵉ Ghost of Thom: Tuck coming to speak wᵗʰ her about some land sᵈ Tuck had told her of before his death. But yᵗ shee fled from yᵉ Ghost & got away.

The fortune book she sai⟨d⟩ was about yᵉ bigness of a chids [= child's] Psalter (wᶜʰ agrees wᵗʰ yᵗ of a gramēr). But owned no other but yᵗ of John Samsons wᶜʰ he had from her as she said above 20 years agoe & yᵗ shee had not told fortunes since yᵉ time I had layd before her yᵉ evill of it. wᶜʰ is about 20 or 22 years since.

I lately spake wᵗʰ John Samson & he told me yᵗ he had a book of Palmstry when he lived at Goody Hoars wᶜʰ shee had seen; But yᵗ it was a book in quarto. & he sold it at Casco=Bay about 30 yeares since & had not seen it since.

[Hand 2] Jurat in Curia

[Hand 3] mʳ Jnᵒ Haile

Notes: Although found guilty at her trial, Dorcas Hoar escaped the gallows through confessing and thereby precipitating a successful petition, September 21, for a one month or longer stay of execution. John Hale was the first signatory on this petition, also signed by Nicholas Noyes, Daniel Epes Jr., and John Emerson Jr. All the petitioners were ministers. ◊ Used at trial. ◊ Hand 1 = John Hale; Hand 2 = Stephen Sewall

Essex County Court Archives, vol. 1, no. 211, Massachusetts Supreme Judicial Court, Judicial Archives, on deposit James Duncan Phillips Library, Peabody Essex Museum, Salem, MA.

558. Deposition of Edward Hooper v. Dorcas Hoar†

[Hand 1] The depersision of Edward hooper aged about .15. years being with John neal at Dorkus ~~whore~~'s house when the .sd. neal brought a hin [= hen]: ~~of a~~ of the .sd. whors which he had kiled doing damage in his master whitredgs Corn the .sd. ~~whore~~ did say then to the .sd. John: neall: ~~I the sd deponant did then hear.~~ that he should be neuer the beter for it before the weak was out

[Hand 2] Jurat in Curia

[Reverse] Edward Hooper

Notes: Used at trial. ◊ Hand 2 = Stephen Sewall

Essex County Court Archives, vol. 1, no. 215, Massachusetts Supreme Judicial Court, Judicial Archives, on deposit James Duncan
Phillips Library, Peabody Essex Museum, Salem, MA.

Sept. 6, 1692

Sworn at Trial: Deposition of Elizabeth Hubbard v. Dorcas Hoar†

2nd of 2 dates. See No. 403 on July 2, 1692

559. Deposition of John Lovett v. Dorcas Hoar†

[Hand 1] The depersision of John Louet aged about .25. years this deponant destifi[Lost] [= testifies] & say that he the .sd. deponant being at bostan. sume time in June last past wen[Lost] [= went] into the prisan to see my granmother then goodee ~~w~~hore asked me the .sd. depna[Lost] [= deponent] whether .I. knew of any ~~of~~ witnesses that would Come in ~~against~~ or be brought in against hear .&. I the said deponant told her I did not know of any and then the .sd. ~~w~~hore asked me whether goodma{n} witredg would not ["t" written over "d"] Come in against her about his Cow .I. the .sd. debonant tould the sd whore I did belieue he Would ["W" written over "he"] the sd ~~w~~hore rplyed. she did not know that he had ar a Cow furder saith not

[Hand 2] Jurat in Curia

[Reverse] Jnº Louett

Notes: Lovett's grandmother was Susannah Roots, who had been arrested on May 23. See No. 196. ◊ Used at trial. ◊ "ar": "ar" is probably a reduced form of *ever* (*OED* s.v. *ever*) or it might possibly be a form of *ere* 'formerly' (*OED* s.v. *ere*). Henry Alexander, "The Language of the Salem Witchcraft Trials," *American Speech* 3 (1928): 398 interprets the form "ara" (taking "ar" with the indefinite article "a") as a form of *any*, but this interpretation seems improbable.

Essex County Court Archives, vol. 1, no. 219, Massachusetts Supreme Judicial Court, Judicial Archives, on deposit James Duncan
Phillips Library, Peabody Essex Museum, Salem, MA.

560. Depositions of Joseph Morgan & Deborah Morgan v. Dorcas Hoar†

[Hand 1] The depotion of ~~Thomas~~ {Joseph} morgin aged abought 46 yerrs or thair aboughts Testifyeth and saith that gooday hoer being at my hous did pretend sum thing of forting [= fortune] telling and thair said that I shuld dy before my wife and that my ⟨e⟩ldest dafter shuld not Liue to be a woman and f⟨e⟩rther saith that my self being caled to sit on the Juery to sarch the body of goodman hore he dyeng uery sudingly: that then on desiering to haue ~~the~~ his body stript shee: said goody hoer did fly out in a great pation and said what do you think that I haue kild my husband you retches you and

The depotion of Debrough morgin aged 43: years or thair aboughts testifyeth and saith that goody hoer being at ouer hous said that my eldst dafter shuld neur liue to be a woman: and I asking her how shee knew: shee told me that she obserued sum ueins abought her eys by which shee knew: and ferther saith not

[Hand 2] Jurat in Curia:

[Reverse] Joseph & Deborah Morgan

Sept. 6, 1692

Notes: Used at trial. ◊ Hand 2 = Stephen Sewall

Essex County Court Archives, vol. 1, no. 214, Massachusetts Supreme Judicial Court, Judicial Archives, on deposit James Duncan Phillips Library, Peabody Essex Museum, Salem, MA.

Sworn at Trial: Deposition of Ann Putnam Jr., v. Dorcas Hoar†

2nd of 2 dates. See No. 404 on July 2, 1692

Sworn at Trial: Deposition of Thomas Putnam & Edward Putnam v. Dorcas Hoar†

2nd of 2 dates. See No. 103 on May 2, 1692

Sworn at Trial: Deposition of John Richards & Joseph Morgan v. Dorcas Hoar†

2nd of 2 dates. See No. 208 on May 23, 1692

561. Deposition of John Tuck v. Dorcas Hoar, and Statement of Joseph Tuck v. Dorcas Hoar†

[Hand 1] The depersision of John tuck aged about 18 years this deponant doth testif and say that I the .sd. deponant being at the hous of Dorkas ~~whore~~ {about .3 year agone} with John neal which was then thomas whitredgs seruant then the .sd. neal brought a hin [= hen] of the said whors which he the .sd. neal had kiled doing damage in his .sd. masters Corn .&. I the sd deponant being thare when the .sd. neal presented the hen to hear: the .sd. ~~whore~~ did then breake out in grreat pashan and tould the .sd. John neal that it should be the worst weaks worke that Euer he did farder saith not

[Hand 2] Jurat in Curia

[Hand 1] Joseph tuck aged about .15. years doth say that he being with his brother John tuck doth say that he Can witnes to the uery same aboue writen

[Hand 2] Jurat in Curia

[Reverse] Jn° Tuck Joseph Tuck

Notes: Used at trial. ◊ Hand 2 = Stephen Sewall

Essex County Court Archives, vol. 1, no. 216, Massachusetts Supreme Judicial Court, Judicial Archives, on deposit James Duncan Phillips Library, Peabody Essex Museum, Salem, MA.

Sworn at Trial: Deposition of Mary Walcott v. Dorcas Hoar†

2nd of 2 dates. See No. 405 on July 2, 1692

Wednesday, September 7, 1692

Grand Juries of Alice Parker & Ann Pudeator (Day 2)

Trials of Alice Parker & Ann Pudeator

562. Examination of Rebecca Johnson Sr.‡
See also: Jan. 7, 1693.

[Hand 1] ⟨?⟩ Sept^ε
The Examination of Rebecka Johnson, widow. Taken 1692. before Jn° Hauthorn Esq^ε &
other their majesties Justices.

She denyed what she was accused of, But she acknowledged the turneing of the sieve, in her
house by her daughter, whom she desyred to try if her brother Moses Haggat was alive or
dead And that If the sieve turned he was dead, and so the sieve did turn, And my daughter
said that Mr Bernards maid told her the way The⟨r⟩ words used were, By Saint Peter & Saint
Paul, if Haggat be dead Let this sieve turn round; & so it did.
Elizabeth the wife of George Booth was struck down by the said widow Johnsons lookeing
upon her, and martha Sprague s^d she saw the s^d widow Johnson afflict her. and Rose foster
saw the same And further that said Johnsons apparition told them she Intended to spoyle
George boot⟨h⟩s wifes child
The s^d widow Johnson upon her examination as was Judged afflicted Sprague & foster into
fitts and by her touc⟨h⟩ recovered them againe.
Martha Sprague and Rose foster said thay saw the s^d Rebeck[Lost] [= Rebecca] Johnson
afflict Abigail Martin & Alice Booth
Alice Booth said she sawe s^d Johnson afflict her sister booth and that she saw her at our
house partake of the sacram^t.
Rose foster; Alice booth. & martha Sprague said They saw the devill. stand before her and
also before her daught⟨e⟩[Lost] [= daughter]

I underwritten being appoynted by authority to take the above examination in wryting Doe
testify upon oath taken in court That this is a true coppy of the substance of it to y^e best of
my knowledge 7^t Jan^εy 1692/3 Wm Murray

[Hand 2] The aboue Reb^ε Johnson was Examined before ⟨th⟩eir Majest^ε Justies of peace. in
Salem atest John Higginson Jus^⟨t⟩ Peace.
Owned before the Grand Jury
7 Jan^r 1692
Robert: Payne foreman

Notes: Although the smudged date on the manuscript may be a "7," it remains inconclusive. September 8 is another
possibility. ◊ Hand 1 = William Murray; Hand 2 = John Higginson Jr.

*Suffolk Court Files, vol. 32, docket 2707, p. 30, Massachusetts Supreme Judicial Court, Judicial Archives, Massachusetts State
Archives, Boston, MA.*

September 7, 1692

563. Examination of Henry Salter

See also: Jan. 5, 1693.

[Hand 1] 7. Sep^t 92

The Examination ~~and confession~~ of Henry Salter. Taken before Jn° Hauthorn Esqr & other their majesties Justices.

In the tyme of his Examination He struck down with his eye Mary warrin mary walcot Rose foster {&} mary Lacey And recovered them by touching of them with his hand

mary walcot said he hurt her the last thursday, & almost choaked her to death upon the last Sabath day she saw him afflict Timothy swan [   ] Barnam and Goody Bigsby

Mary warrin ^{and mary walcot} saw him afflict Martha Sprague and martha Sprague saw him afflict hannah post.

Mary warrin said he told her he used his witchcraft by the Key & bible & sometymes by the sieve & scisse^εs. – she also saw the black man 2 women one man and a company of Litle ones before him.

{q} when was it that the company of witches were at yo^ε house and the whyt{e} men drove them away A. I never knew of any such thing, but afterwards said he had told one Goody Lovejoy something but knew not what

He ownes he has told Lyes before now and been in drink also.

~~This is a true~~cop   ___

I underwritten being appointed by auhe to take in wryteing the above examination Doe testify upon oath taken in court that this is a true coppy of the substance of it, to the best of my knowledge

5 January 1692/3   Wm Murray

[Hand 2] the above Hen^r Salter was Examined before their majesties Justices of peace in Salem

atest John. Higginson Just^ε peace.

[Reverse] Hen^r Salter Exā 7. 7. 92

afflicted: Mary Walcot
                  Mary Warren
                  Rose ffoster
                  Mary lacy
                  Tim° Swan
                  Goody Bigsby
                  Martha Sprage

Owned before the Grand Jury 5: January 1692/3

atest: Robert: Payne
                  foreman:

Notes: Hand 1 = William Murray; Hand 2 = John Higginson Jr.

Suffolk Court Files, vol. 32, docket 2702, p. 24, Massachusetts Supreme Judicial Court, Judicial Archives, Massachusetts State Archives, Boston, MA.

564. Summons for Witnesses v. Giles Cory, and Officer's Return

September 7, 1692

[Hand 1] W^m & Mary by y^e Grace of God of England Scotland ffrance & Ireland King & Queen defend^{Es} of ye faith &c

To ye Constable of Salem Greeting.

Wee Comand you to Warn & giue Notice vnto Jno Derich ye wife of Stephen Small ye Widow Adams & Goody Golthite that they & Euery of them be and personaly Appear at ye p^Esent Court of Oyer & Terminer holden at Salem fforthwith there to Testify ye Truth to ye best of thier knowledge On Certain Indictments Exhibited against Giles Cory hereof make return fail not

Salem Sepr 7th 1692:   Stephen Sewall Cl

[Reverse] [Hand 2] Sep^t 7th 1692
I Depute m^{ll} John Tomkins to serve this within Sumons and Make Returne therof by me Peter osgood Constable in Salem

[Hand 3] I haue warned the w^{th}in persons to appeare att the time and place within written by Jno Tomkin
Deputed

Notes: Hand 1 = Stephen Sewall; Hand 3 = George Herrick ◊ 1 wax seal.

Essex County Court Archives, vol. 2, no. 84, Massachusetts Supreme Judicial Court, Judicial Archives, on deposit James Duncan Phillips Library, Peabody Essex Museum, Salem, MA.

565. Indictment of Alice Parker, for Afflicting Mary Walcott†

[Hand 1] Essex in y^e Prouince of the Massachusetts Bay in New England ss/

Anno $\overline{RR}$^s & Reginæ Gulielmi & Mariæ Angliæ &c Quarto Annoqʒ Domini 1692//

The Juriors for our Sou^E Lord and Lady the King and Queen doe present That Alice Parker wife of John Paker of Salem in y^e County Essex Fisherman ~~In the County of Essex~~ the Sixth day of Septemb^r ~~in the yeare afore^{sd}~~ In the yeare aforesaid and diuers other days and times as well before as after Certaine detestable Arts called Witchcraft and Sorceries Wickedly Mallitiously and felloniously hath used practised and Exercised At and [Hand 2] **in the Towne of Salem in the County of Essex** [Hand 1] Aforesaid in upon and against one [Hand 2] **Mary Walcott of Salem Village in the County** [Hand 1] Aforesaid [Hand 2] **Single Woman** [Hand 1] by which said Wicked Acts the said [Hand 2] **Mary Walcot the day & yeare** [Hand 1] Aforesaid and diuers other days & Times both before and after was and is Tortured Aflicted Consumed Pined Wasted & Tormented and also for sundry other Acts of Witchcraft by the said [Hand 2] **Allice Parker Comitted** [Hand 1] and done before and Since that time against the peace of our Sou^E Lord and Lady the King and Queen theire Crowne and Dignity and the form [Hand 2] **of** ["of" written over "in"] [Hand 1] the Stattute in that case made and Prouided

September 7, 1692   [Hand 2] Wittnesses
Ann Putman
Mary Warren
Eliz: Hobard

[Reverse] Allice Parker Mary Walcot
[Hand 3] billa uera

Notes: Alice Parker had been examined on May 12 (see No. 144). Normally, an indictment would have referenced this examination date, but presumably the events of September 6 were considered more useful for making a case against her. ◊ Hand 2 = Anthony Checkley

Witchcraft Papers, no. 33, Massachusetts Historical Society, Boston, MA.

566. Indictment of Alice Parker, for Afflicting Mary Warren†

[Hand 1] Essex in the Prouince   Anno⟨q⟩ $\overline{RR}^s$ and Reginæ Gulielmi & Mariæ Angliæ
of the Massachusetts Bay in New   &c Quarto Annoqʒ Domini 1692.
Engl^d ss

The Juriors for our Sou^ε Lord and Lady the King and Queen doe ꝑsent That [Hand 2] **Allice Parker Wife of John Parker of Salem** [Hand 1] In the County of Essex [Hand 2] **aforsaid ffisherman, the** ~~Twelfth~~ [Hand 3] {**sixt**} [Hand 2] **day of** ~~May~~ [Hand 3] **September** [Hand 1] ⟨In⟩ the yeare aforesaid and diuers other days and times as well before [Lost] [= as] ⟨a⟩fter Certaine detestable Arts called Witchcraft and Sorceries Wickedly Mallitiously & felloniously hath used practised & Exercised At and [Hand 2] **in the Towne of Salem** ~~aforesaid~~ [Hand 1] Aforesaid in upon & against one [Hand 2] **Mary Warren of Salem** [Hand 1] Aforesaid [Hand 2] **Single Woman** [Hand 1] by which said Wicked Acts the said [Hand 2] **Mary Warren ye Day & year** [Hand 1] Aforesaid and diuers other days & times both before and after was and is Tortured Aflicted Consumed Wasted Pined and Tormented, and also for Sundry Acts of Witchcraft by the said [Hand 2] **Allice Parker** [Hand 1] Comitted and done before and Since that time against the peace of Our Sou^ε Lord & Lady the King and Queen theire Crowne and dignity and the forme [Hand 2] **of** ["of" written over "in"?] [Hand 1] the Stattute ^{in that case} made and Prouided

[Hand 2] Wittness

[Reverse] Allice Parker: Mary Warre⟨n⟩
[Hand 3] bila uera

Notes: May 12, a date that one would expect in such an indictment, the day of Alice Parker's first examination (see No. 144), is crossed out, and September 6 is substituted as the day of the affliction. Since Mary Warren was a key accuser against Alice Parker on May 12, it makes sense that the indictment would have been originally prepared to reference that date. The deposition of Mary Walcott against Alice Parker is similarly corrected. ◊ Hand 2 = Anthony Checkley

Witchcraft Papers, no. 32, Massachusetts Historical Society, Boston, MA.

567. Depositions of Sarah Bibber, Mary Walcott, Elizabeth Hubbard, Ann Putnam Jr., & Mary Warren v. Alice Parker, and Statement of Abigail Hobbs v. Alice Parker

September 7, 1692

[Hand 1] Sarah Vibber upon oath affirmeth: to ye grand Jury of inquest: that she hath seen Alice Parker: afflict: Mary. ^{.Warin} Mary Walcot: & An Putnam: & that s^d Parker did: choke s^d Warin ye last night & griped her: abo^t ye waste. Septem^r 7: 1692
[Hand 2] & y^t she hath aflicted this deponent

Jurat in Curia

[Hand 1] Mary Walcot: upon oath: affirmeth: to ye Jury of inquest: that she hath: seen: Alice Parker: afflict: Mary Warin: Eliz Hubbard Mercy Lewis: An Putnum: perticulerly: ye last night: by choaking of them & squeezing of them Septem^ε 7: 1692
[Hand 2] & y^t she aflicted this deponent Jurat in Curia

[Hand 1] Eliz Hubard: on oath affirmed to ye Jury of inquest. that Alice Parker: hath once afflicted her: & that was last night: Sept^ε 7: 1692

An Putnum: upon oath: affirmed: to ye Jury of Inquest: that she hath seen: Alice Parker aflict: Mary: Warin: Mary Walcot: goodwife Vibber: & Sara Churchell by choking: of them & squeezing. Mary Warin: this they did ye last night in ye Court:
Septem^ε 7: 16:92

Mary: Warin: upon oath: tha {afirms} to ye Jury of Inquest: that: she hath seen Alice Parker afflict: Mary Walcot: Eliz Hubbard An Putnam: & goodwife Vibber: {y^e last night} by choking: them & squeezing them: s^d Parker: has afflicted me: has brought me ye book to sign to she brought: me a poppit: & a needle: & thretned: to stab: me if I would not stick ye needle into ye poppit: & she did run: ye needle a little way into me: s^d Parker s^d she was a caus: of ye death of Tho Wastgate: and crew: y^t was fowndred in ye sea: she was also a caus: of ye death of goodwife Ormes her son: y^t was drown^d be⟨fo⟩re there dore: and was a caus of ye death of Jno Serlse his barbadian boy: she was ye caus also of: Mich⟨a⟩el: Chapmans. {Death} in Boston harbour: she also told me she: bewiched my mother: & was a caus of her death: also that: she: bewiched my sister: Eliz: y^t is both deaf: & dumb [Hand 3] Septemb^r 7. 92
[Hand 2] Jurat in Curia

Abigail: Hobs: afirms: she has seen. Alice Parker: afflict: Mary: Warin: when: s^d Warin was at prison. also. I have seen her: afflict. An Putnam: by choking: of them:
Septem^ε 7: 1692: before y^e Jury of Inquest

[Reverse] [Hand 4] Seuerall Afflicted ꝑsons Euidences

Notes: The hand change of "Septem^r 7" reflects the later insertion of that date and seems to be the filling in of a date that had inadvertently been omitted. ◊ Used at trial. ◊ Hand 1 = Simon Willard; Hand 2 = Stephen Sewall; Hand 4 = Anthony Checkley

Witchcraft Papers, no. 34, Massachusetts Historical Society, Boston, MA.

Sworn Before the Grand Jury and at Trial: Deposition of John Westgate v. Alice Parker
2nd of 2 dates. See No. 268 on June 2, 1692

September 7, 1692

568. Indictment of Ann Pudeator, for Afflicting Mary Warren†

[Hand 1] Essex in the Prouince   }   Anno $\overline{RR}$s & Reginæ Gulielmi & Mariæ Angliæ &c
of the Massachussetts Bay In   }   Quarto Annoqȝ Domini 1692//
New England ss   }

The Juriors for our Sou$^{\varepsilon}$ lord and Lady the King & Queen ꝑsent That Ann Pudeator of
Salem in the County of Essex ~~Widow~~ aforesaid [Hand 2] ^{Widdow} [Hand 1] The second
day in July in the Yeare Afore Said and diuers others days and times as well before as after
Certaine detestable Arts called Witchcraft & Sorceries Wickedly Mallitiously and
felloniously hath used practised and Exercised At and within the Township of Salem
aforesaid {in & upon & against one Mary Warren of Salem aforesaid} Single Woeman, by
which said Wicked Acts the said Mary Warren the second day of July aforesaid and diuers
other days and times both before and after was and is Tortured Afflicted Pined Consumed
Wasted & Tormented, and also for Sundry other Acts of Witchcraft by the Said Ann
Pudeator Comitted and done before and Since that time Ags^t the peace of Our Sou$^{\varepsilon}$ lord &
Lady the King & Queen theire Crowne and Dignity and {ags^t} the forme of the Stattute in
y^t Case made and Prouided
[Hand 2] Witnesses
Mary Warren [Hand 3] Jurat
[Hand 2] Sarah Churchel [Hand 3] Jurat
[Hand 2] An Putman [Hand 3] Jurat

[Reverse] [Hand 2] Ann Pudeat⟨o⟩r on Mary Warren
[Hand 4] bila uera

Notes: Hand 2 = Anthony Checkley; Hand 3 = Stephen Sewall

Essex County Court Archives, vol. 1, no. 260, Massachusetts Supreme Judicial Court, Judicial Archives, on deposit James Duncan Phillips Library, Peabody Essex Museum, Salem, MA.

569. Testimony of John Best Sr. v. Ann Pudeator

[Hand 1] The Testimony of Jno Best. Senio$^{\varepsilon}$ aged about 48 yeers Testifieth & saith y^t some
yeers Last past y^t I this Deponat did often hear my wife saye y^t Ann pudeater would not Lett
her alone vntill she had killd her By her often pinching & Bruseing of her Till her Earms &
other parts of her Body Looked Black By Reson of her soer pinching of her in y^e Tyme of
her sickness & my wife did affarne [= affirm] y^t itt was an pudeater y^t did afflict her & stood
in y^e Belefe of itt as Long as she Liued
[Hand 2] Sepr 7th <u>92</u>   Jurat in Curia
S Sewall Cler

[Hand 3] Jno Best: afirmed: to y^e truth of y^e above written:
befor: y^e Jury of inquest Septr 7: 1692

[Reverse] [Hand 4] Jnᵒ Best Oath agsᵗ An: Pudeator   September 7, 1692

Notes: Sewall dated this trial document as September 7. In another trial document, No. 555, he gave a date of September
10. "Jurat in Curia" on September 10 seems puzzling in that this earlier "Jurat in Curia" by him indicated September 7 as
the trial date. However, the trial continued on September 10. Other trial documents in the case of Ann Pudeator, except
for the one dated September 10, are dated in the edition as September 7 with the understanding that a September 10
dating on these is plausible. In a later petition, No. 655, Ann Pudeator said that John Best Sr. was a known liar. ◊ Used
at trial. ◊ Hand 2 = Stephen Sewall; Hand 3 = Simon Willard; Hand 4 = Anthony Checkley

*Essex County Court Archives, vol. 1, no. 268, Massachusetts Supreme Judicial Court, Judicial Archives, on deposit James Duncan
Phillips Library, Peabody Essex Museum, Salem, MA.*

***Continued from Sept. 6, 1692: Testimony of Sarah Churchill, Mary Warren, Elizabeth
Hubbard, Ann Putnam Jr., Sarah Bibber, & Mary Walcott v. Ann Pudeator***

2ⁿᵈ of 3 dates. See No. 555 on Sept. 6, 1692

570. Testimony of Samuel Pickworth, and Statement of Ann Putnam Jr. v. Ann Pudeator

[Hand 1] The testimony of samuall pikworth: Whou testifieth that about six weckes agoo: I
this deponant was coming along salim strete: betwen ann pudeaters hous and Captin higison
hous. it being in the euening: and I this deponant saw a woman: neare Captin higisonn
Cornar. the which I sopposed to be ann pudeatar. and in a moment of time she pasid by me
as swifte as if a burd flwe by me and I saw said woman goo in to ann pudeateaters hous

[Hand 2] Jurat in Curia
SSewall Cl

[Hand 3] Samˡˡ Pickworth: affirmeth: yᵗ yᵉ above written evidence is yᵉ truth: upon oath: to:
yᵉ Jury. of Inquest: Septᴱ 7: 92

[Reverse] [Hand 1] september: the 7. 92
ann putnam afarmid to the grand Inquest that ann pudeatar: towld har that she flu by a man
in the neight in to a hous
[Hand 2?] Sam Pickwᵗʰ

Notes: In her petition, Pudeator accused Pickworth, along with the two John Bests, of lying. See No. 655. Ann Putnam
Jr.'s testimony before the grand jury was probably also used at the trial. ◊ Used at trial. ◊ Hand 2 = Stephen Sewall;
Hand 3 = Simon Willard

*Essex County Court Archives, vol. 1, no. 266, Massachusetts Supreme Judicial Court, Judicial Archives, on deposit James Duncan
Phillips Library, Peabody Essex Museum, Salem, MA.*

571. Testimony of James Allen, Robert Pike, & John Pike for Mary Bradbury

[Hand 1] Being desired to give my testimony concerning the life & conversation of mʳˢ
Bradbury of Salisbury amongst us. wᶜʰ is as followeth. viz.
{I} having lived nine years at Salisbury in the work of the ministry & now four years in the
office of a Pastour; to my best notice & observation of mʳˢ Bradbury she hath lived according

Sept. 7, 1692

to the rules of the gospell, ^{amongst us.} was a constant attender upon the ministry of ye word; & all the ordinances of the gospell; full of works of charity & mercy to the sick & poor neither have I seen or heard any thing of her unbecoming the proffession of the gospell:

James Allin

[Hand 2] m^ε James Allin made oathe to the truth of w^t is above writtn septem̅^ε ye 7th 1692: before me Robt Pike Ass^t

I do also aferm to the truth of ["of" written over "w^t"] w^t ^{is} aboue testifyed vpon vpward of fifty years experienc and shall so testify if opertunity do present wch I shall indever

Robt: Pike

[Hand 3] Having lived many years in Salisbury & been much Conversant there, according to my best notice & observation of mrs Bradbury must needs affirm to what is abovewritten, & add my oath to it if Called therto

John Pike

Notes: An oath is here given in support of an accused person by three people, one of whom is the person who administers the oaths. One can only guess that Robert Pike hoped he would have the opportunity to present these sworn statements at the trial of Mary Bradbury, which began the next day. However, there is no reason to believe that sworn testimony on her behalf would have been accepted at her trial, although one may speculate that he might have given unsworn testimony at the trial. ◊ Hand 2 = Robert Pike

Essex County Court Archives, vol. 2, no. 75, Massachusetts Supreme Judicial Court, Judicial Archives, on deposit James Duncan Phillips Library, Peabody Essex Museum, Salem, MA.

572. Deposition of William Carr for Mary Bradbury†

[Hand 1] The testamony of william Car⟨e⟩ aged: 41: or ther abouts is That my brother John Car when he was yong was a man of as goo⟨d⟩ capasity as most men of his age but faling in Love with Jan⟨e⟩ Tru (now wif of Capt John march) and my father being ꝑswaded by [Lost] [*SWP* = some] of the family (wch I shall not name) not to Let him mary so yong: my fa⟨th⟩[Lost] [= father] woold not give him a porsion w^r vpon the mach broke of wch my ⟨b⟩[Lost] [= brother?] Layd so much to hart that he grew melencoly & by degrees much craze⟨d⟩ not being the man that he was before to his dying day

I do farther testify that my s^d brother was sick about a fortnight ⟨or⟩ three weeks & then dyed & I was present with him w^n he dyed & I do aferm that he dyed peacibly and quietly never manifesting the Lest troubl in ⟨y^e⟩ world about any body nor did not say any thing of mr^s Bradbur⟨ly⟩ n⟨o⟩r nor any body else doing him hurt & yet I was with him till the brea⟨th⟩ & Lif was out of his body

[Hand 2] Jurat in Curia

[Reverse] [Hand 1] william Cars testamony

Notes: The "Jurat in Curia," a standard notation by Stephen Sewall for trial documents, is here not written by him. It was probably sworn at an inferior court held on September 7, independent of the trial. It is highly unlikely that this would have been used at Bradbury's trial. September 7 was the day James Allen, John Pike, and Robert Pike swore on her behalf. See No. 571. ◊ Hand 1 = Robert Pike

Essex County Court Archives, vol. 2, no. 82, Massachusetts Supreme Judicial Court, Judicial Archives, on deposit James Duncan   Sept. 7, 1692
Phillips Library, Peabody Essex Museum, Salem, MA.

573. Testimony of John Bullock & Martha Dutch v. Alice Parker

[Hand 1] Jn° Bullvck aged 36 years testifieth y^t aboute ye middle of January last past one of my neighbo^{rs} told me y^t m^{es} park^r did: lay vpon ye durt & Snow if I did not take Care of her y^t She would perish wherevpon I did desire Som men y^t were in mye hous to goe & help her: & when they Came to he⟨r⟩ y^t they would not meddle because they thought She was ded there being a neighbo^r {by} Said She Saw her before in Such kind of fits: then I p^{r}swaded one man bye; to take her vpon his Shoulders & Carrye her ho⟨m⟩e but ⟨in⟩ a l⟨it⟩tle [Lost] [B&N = way] going he let her fall vpon a place of Stones: wch did not awake her wch Caused me to thinke She was really dead after {y^t} wee Carryed her into her hous & Caused her Cloaths to be taken of & while wee [Hand 2] {were} [Hand 1] taking of her Cloaths to put her into bed She rises vp & laughs in o^r faces: [Hand 2] Martha Dutch aged abo^t 36 years: testifieth: to ye Above written [Hand 3] and farthar saith that I haue sene said parker in such a Condition seuerall othar tims

[Hand 4] Jurat in Curia. Sep^r .7. 92.
S Sewall Cle

[Reverse] [Hand 5] John Bullock dep°

Notes: This was incorrectly carried in *SWP* (II, p. 634) in the case of Mary Parker. ◊ Used at trial. ◊ Hand 2 = Simon Willard; Hand 4 = Stephen Sewall

Essex County Court Archives, vol. 2, no. 67, Massachusetts Supreme Judicial Court, Judicial Archives, on deposit James Duncan
Phillips Library, Peabody Essex Museum, Salem, MA.

574. Testimony of Martha Dutch v. Alice Parker

[Hand 1] The Testimony of Martha Dutch aged about 36 yeers This Deponant Testifieth and saith y^t about 2 yeers Last past Jn° Jarman of Salem Coming in from sea I This Deponant & Alice parker of Salem Both of us standing Together said vnto her w^t a great mercy itt was for to see Them Come home well and Through mercy I said my husband had gone & Came home well many Times & I This deponant did saye vnto ye s^d parker y^t I did hope he would Come whome This voyage well allso & ye s^d parker made answer vnto me & said no Neuer more in This world y^e wch Came to pass as she y^n told me for he died abroad as I sertinly heare

[Hand 2] Jurat in Curia Sepr 7. 92.
attest Step. Sewall Cle

[Reverse] [Hand 3] Martha Dutch dep° [Hand 4] against J⟨ohn⟩ Jarman

Notes: Used at trial. ◊ Hand 2 = Stephen Sewall; Hand 3 = Anthony Checkley

Sept. 7, 1692   *Essex County Court Archives, vol. 2, no. 93, Massachusetts Supreme Judicial Court, Judicial Archives, on deposit James Duncan Phillips Library, Peabody Essex Museum, Salem, MA.*

Sworn at Trial: Deposition of Thomas Putnam & William Murray v. Alice Parker†
2nd of 2 dates. See No. 553 on Sept. 6, 1692

575. Testimony of Samuel Shattuck v. Alice Parker†

[Hand 1] Sam^ll Shattock aged 41 years testifieth y^t in the year 1685: Goodwife ⟨?⟩ Parker wife to Jn° Parker Mariner Came to my hous: & went into the room where my wife & Children were & fauned vpon my wife wth very Smooth words in a Short tyme after that Child wch was Supposed to haue bin vnder an ill hand for Seuerall years before: was taken in a Strange & vnuceall maner as if his vitalls would haue broak out his breast boane drawn vp to gather to the vper part of his brest his neck & Eys drawne Soe much aside as if they would neuer Come to right againe he lay in So Strange a maner y^t the Docter & others did beleiue he was bewitched Soom days after Som of the vissiters Cut Som of his hair of to boyle wch they Saide altho they ^{did} wth great tendernes ye Child would Shreek out as if he had bin tormented: they put his hair in a Skillet ouer a fier: wch Stood plaine on the hearth and as Son as they were gon out of ye room it was throwne downe & i came immediatly into ye room & Could See no Creature in ye room they put it on againe & after it had boyled Som tyme the aboue Said Goodwife Parker Came in & asked if i would buye Soom Chic⟨k⟩eens I told her no: the women y^t were aboue in the Chamber Said to me it is pitty you did {not} ask to See her chickens for they did beleiue she had none to Sell: and aduised me ⟨to⟩ Send to her hous to buy Som wch i did & ye messenger brought me word y^t She told him She had none & y^t ye woman y^t liued in the Same hous told him y^t ye Said Parker had not had any in three weeks before: Soom days after She wth her husband & two men moor Came to mye hous & to answer their request i went to them: She asked me if i Saide She had bewitched mye Child I told her I did beliue She had: She Said to me {yow} are a wicked man: ye lord avenge me of you ye lord bring vengance vpon you for ʸ⟨ᵗ⟩ this wrong: one of ye men asked her w^t made you Com to this hous last Saturday She Saide to Sell Chicken: why did not yow let him haue y^m when he Sent for y^m Said he: She Said becaus She had Sold y^m he asked to whome She Saide to Such a one: wee Sent presently to y^e party: & the answer was brought vs y^t he neuer bought any of h⟨e⟩[Lost] [= her] well you {See} Saide they you haue told vs y^t wch is not true w^t did yow wth y^m She was at a Stand but at last Said her Son Carryed y^m to Sea wth him: her husband told her y^t was not true for her Son went to Sea last fryday: & if he̶d̶ had Carryed y^m to Sea She Could not brough y^m here ye Saturday following She could not giue {any} true account w^t She did w^t them: but went into ye room where ye Child ⟨was⟩ & told my wife y^t She was a wicked woman for Saying Soe of her: & to⟨ld⟩ my wife in these words I hope I Shall See the downfall of you {my wife told me} and Soe went away in a great anger: & this is all true & reall to ^{the} vttermost of my remembrance & after this threatning or Euill [1 word overstruck]

[Hand 2] Jurat in Curia

[Reverse] [Hand 1] Euill wishing the Child has Continued in a very Sad Condition fowllow[Lost] [= followed] wth very Solem fits wch hath taken away his vnderstanding

[Hand 2] Jurat in Curia

[Hand 3] Sam^ll Shattock ag^st parker.

Notes: This was incorrectly carried in *SWP* (II, pp. 635–36) in the case of Mary Parker. ◊ Used at trial. ◊ Hand 2 = Stephen Sewall

Sept. 8, 1692

Essex County Court Archives, vol. 2, no. 65, Massachusetts Supreme Judicial Court, Judicial Archives, on deposit James Duncan Phillips Library, Peabody Essex Museum, Salem, MA.

576. Excuse of Mary Towne

[Hand 1] To the Honered Court now seting in Salam
Right honered: the Constabll of Topsffild hath sarued a warent one me and too of my sons and too of my dafters: to Apere this day at Salem I humbly baig that your honers will not Impuet any thing concarning our not Coming as Contampt of athoryty for ware I my salf or any of my famely sant for in any Capasete of Coming we would Com but we are in a straing Condicion and most of us can scars git of of our beads we are so wake and not abell to Ried at all: as for my dafter Rebaka she hath straing ffits somtimes she is knoked downe of a sodin: ~~and that espachaly If hur ant Easty be but named~~:
Dat yᵉ 7ᵗʰ of Septembr 1692

Mary Towne

Notes: It is highly unlikely that Mary Towne wrote this herself, since the same hand appears in recording other documents in other cases. The reason for the crossout is not clear. Mary Towne was Mary (Browning) Towne, widow of Sarah Cloyce's and Mary Esty's late brother. Sarah Cloyce was accused of afflicting Rebecca Towne on September 9, but it is not clear whether the accusation was for afflicting her in court, or at home to prevent her from coming to court. See No. 809.

Essex County Court Archives, vol. 1, no. 287, Massachusetts Supreme Judicial Court, Judicial Archives, on deposit James Duncan Phillips Library, Peabody Essex Museum, Salem, MA.

Thursday, September 8, 1692

Grand Jury of William Procter

Trial of Martha Cory

577. Fragment of the Examination of Deliverance Dane‡

Deliverance Deane being asked why she and the rest brought in Mr. Deane as afflicting persons, she answered, it was Satan's subtility, for he told her he would put a sham upon all these things, and make people believe that he did afflict. She said Mrs. Osgood and she gave their consent the devil should bring Mr. Deane's shape to afflict. Being asked again if Mrs. Osgood and she acted this business, she said yes.

Notes: The arrest warrant for Deliverance Dane and the full record of her examination have not been found. Very little on her case is extant. ◊ "put a sham upon all these things": 'put a shadow of deceit over all these things,' 'use trickery' (cf. *OED* s.v. *sham* n. 1).

Sept. 8, 1692   *Thomas Hutchinson, The History of the Province of Massachusetts-Bay, from the Charter of King William and Queen Mary, in 1691, Until the Year 1750, vol. 2, ed. Lawrence Shaw Mayo (Cambridge, MA: Harvard University Press, 1936), p. 29.*

578. Examination of Mary Osgood

See also: Jan. 5, 1693.

The examination and confession (8. Sept. 92.) of Mary Osgood, wife of Captain Osgood of Andover, taken before John Hawthorne and other their Majesties justices.

She confesses, that about 11 years ago, when she was in a melancholy state and condition, she used to walk abroad in her orchard; and upon a certain time, she saw the appearance of a cat, at the end of the house, which yet she thought was a real cat. However, at that time, it diverted her from praying to God, and instead thereof she prayed to the devil; about which time she made a covenant with the devil, who, as a black man, came to her and presented her a book, upon which she laid her finger and that left a red spot: And that upon her signing, the devil told her he was her God, and that she should serve and worship him, and, she believes, she consented to it. She says further, that about two years agone, she was carried through the air, in company with deacon Frye's wife, Ebenezer Baker's wife, and Goody Tyler, to five mile pond, where she was baptized by the devil, who dipped her face in the water and made her renounce her former baptism, and told her she must be his, soul and body, forever, and that she must serve him, which she promised to do. She says, the renouncing her first baptism was after her dipping, and that she was transported back again through the air, in company with the forenamed persons, in the same manner as she went, and believes they were carried upon a pole. Q. How many persons were upon the pole? A. As I said before, viz. four persons and no more but whom she had named above. – She confesses she has afflicted three persons, John Sawdy, Martha Sprague and Rose Foster, and that she did it by pinching her bed clothes, and giving consent the devil should do it in her shape, and that the devil could not do it without her consent. – She confesses the afflicting persons in the court, by the glance of her eye. She says, as she was coming down to Salem to be examined, she and the rest of the company with her, stopped at Mr. Phillips's to refresh themselves, and the afflicted persons, being behind them upon the road, came up just as she was mounting again and were then afflicted, and cried out upon her, so that she was forced to stay until they were all past, and said she only looked that way towards them. Q. Do you know the devil can take the shape of an innocent person and afflict? A. I believe he cannot. Q. Who taught you this way of witchcraft? A. Satan, and that he promised her abundance of satisfaction and quietness in her future state, but never performed any thing; and that she has lived more miserably and more discontented since, than ever before. She confesses further, that she herself, in company with Goody Parker, Goody Tyler, and Goody Dean, had a meeting at Moses Tyler's house, last monday night, to afflict, and that she and Goody Dean carried the shape of Mr. Dean, the minister, between them, to make persons believe that Mr. Dean afflicted. Q. What hindered you from accomplishing what you intended? A. The Lord would not suffer it so to be, that the devil should afflict in an innocent person's shape. Q. Have you been at any other witch meetings? A. I know nothing thereof, as I shall answer in the presence of God and his people; but said, that the black man stood before her, and told her, that what she had confessed was a lie; notwithstanding, she said that what she had confessed was true, and thereto put her hand. Her husband being present was asked, if he judged his wife to be any way discomposed. He answered, that having lived with her so long, he doth not judge her to be any ways discomposed, but has cause to believe what she has said is true. When Mistress Osgood was first called, she afflicted Martha Sprague and Rose Foster, by the glance of her eyes, and recovered them out of their fits by the touch of her hand. Mary Lacey and Betty Johnson and Hannah Post saw Mistress Osgood afflicting Sprague and Foster. – The said Hannah Post and Mary Lacey and Betty Johnson, jun. and Rose Foster and Mary Richardson were afflicted by Mistress Osgood, in the time of their examination, and recovered by her touching of their hands.

Sept. 8, 1692

> I underwritten, being appointed by authority to take this examination, do testify upon oath, taken in court, that this is a true copy of the substance of it, to the best of my knowledge, 5th Jan. 1692–3. The within Mary Osgood was examined before their Majesties' justices of peace in Salem.
>
> Attest.   John Higginson, Just. Peace.

Owned before the Grand Jury 5 Jan. 1692–3. Robert Payne, Foreman.

Notes: The line at the end of the manuscript, "Owned before the Grand Jury 5 Jan. 1692–3. Robert Payne, Foreman." was found by William Frederick Poole in Hutchinson's draft, and did not appear in Hutchinson's book. For the connection of Poole to Hutchinson, see Trask's "Legal Procedures."

Thomas Hutchinson, The History of the Province of Massachusetts-Bay, from the Charter of King William and Queen Mary, in 1691, Until the Year 1750, vol. 2, ed. Lawrence Shaw Mayo (Cambridge, MA: Harvard University Press, 1936), pp. 24–25.

579. Summons of Mary Towne & Rebecca Towne, and Officer's Return

[Hand 1] W^m & Mary by ye Grace of God of England Scotland ffrance & Ireland King & Queen defend^{rs} of y^e ⟨?⟩ith faith

To Mary Towne Widow & Rebecka Towne her Daughter Greeting.
Wee Comand you all Excuses Set apart to be & appear at ye Court of Oyer & Terminer holden at Salem to morrow morning at Eight of ye Clock precisely There to Testify y^e {truth} to ye best of your knowledge on Seuer^{ll} Indictments Exhibited against Mary Easty hereof fail not at your vtmost perill Dated in Salem Sep^ε 8th 1692 & in ye fourth yeare of Our Reign

Stephen Sewall Cler

To ye Constable of Topsfield hereof Make return fail not.

[Reverse] [Hand 2] I haue Warned the Widow town and hare dafter to apere at. ⟨t⟩he corte. acording to time spoken of in the warant as atested by me Ephraim. Wildes {constabl} of topsfeld

Notes: No indictment survives to indicate that Rebecca Towne claimed affliction by her aunt, Mary Esty, although one does survive claiming affliction by Esty's sister, Sarah Cloyce. See No. 809. ◊ Hand 1 = Stephen Sewall ◊ 1 wax seal.

Essex County Court Archives, vol. 1, no. 288, Massachusetts Supreme Judicial Court, Judicial Archives, on deposit James Duncan Phillips Library, Peabody Essex Museum, Salem, MA.

September 8, 1692

580. Deposition of Ann Putnam Jr. v. Mary Bradbury

[Hand 1] [Lost] ⟨d⟩eposistion of Ann putnam who testifieth and saith that I being [Lost] [= at?] [Lost]vovr [= Andover] on the 26 day of July 1692 I saw there Mis mary [Lost]bery [= Bradbury] the wife of Capt Tho: Bradbery of Salisbury or hir [Lost]erance [= Appearance] most grevious afflecting and tormenting of Timothy Swan of Andevor allmost Redy to kill him also seurall times before and ⟨s⟩ence that time I haue seen mis^t Bradbery or hir Apperance ⟨mo⟩st greviously ~~aff~~ afflecting Timothy Swan and I beleue that Mis [Lost]radbery [= Bradbury] is a most dreadfull wicth for sence she has been in prison she or hir Apperance has com to me and most greviously affle⟨c⟩d me
[Hand 2] ann putnam ownid before the grand Inquest this har euidens to be the ⟨t⟩ruth one the oath that she hath taken: this: 8 dy of Siptember 1692

[Reverse] [Hand 3] Anna Putnam

Notes: Ann Putnam Jr. swore to this deposition on September 8 before the grand jury. She also swore against Mary Bradbury before the grand jury on September 9. See No. 588. No other record of grand jury activity against Mary Bradbury on September 8 is extant. ◊ Hand 1 = Thomas Putnam

Essex County Court Archives, vol. 2, no. 77, Massachusetts Supreme Judicial Court, Judicial Archives, on deposit James Duncan Phillips Library, Peabody Essex Museum, Salem, MA.

581. Indictment of William Procter, for Afflicting Elizabeth Hubbard (Returned Ignoramus)†

[Hand 1]
[Lost] [= Essex in] the Prouince   Anno $\overline{RR}$s & Reginæ Gulielmi & Mariæ Angliæ &c
[Lost] [= of the] Massachusetts   }   Quarto Annoq̄ Domini 1692
[Lost] [= Bay in] New England
Ss/
The Juriors for our Sou^ε Lord and Lady the King and Queen doe present That [Hand 2] **William Procter of Salem** [Hand 1] In the County of Essex [Hand 2] **Husbandman In & vpon the Thirty first day of May** [Hand 1] In the yeare aforesaid and diuers other days and times as well before as after Certaine detestable Arts called Witchcrafts [Hand 2] ∧{**&**} [Hand 1] Sorceries Wickedly Mallitiously & felloniously hath used practised and Exercised at and ~~& upon & Against~~ [Hand 2] **in the Towneship of Salem** [Hand 1] Aforesaid in upon and against one [Hand 2] **Elizabeth** ∧{**Hobert**} **of Salem aforesaid Single Woman** [Hand 1] ~~Aforesaid~~ by which said Wicked Acts the said [Hand 2] **Elizabeth Hobart, the day & yeare** [Hand 1] Aforesaid and diuers other days and times both before and after was and is Tortured Afflicted Consumed pined Wasted and Tormented, and also for sundry other Acts of Witchcraft by the said [Hand 2] ~~**Elizabeth Warren**~~ [Hand 3] {**William procter**} [Hand 1] Comitted and done before and since that time against Our Sou^ε Lord and Lady the King and Queen theire Crowne and Dignity And the forme in the Stattute in that Case made & Prouided.
[Hand 2] Wittness
Mary Warren

[Reverse] [Hand 3] Wm Pr⟨oc⟩[Lost] [= Procter]   September 8, 1692
[Hand 4] Igno Ram⟨a⟩ [= ignoramus]

Notes: The three indictments against William Procter were all returned ignoramus, but by two separate grand juries. The grand jury's return of "Igno Rama" on the two indictments for afflicting Elizabeth Hubbard and Mary Warren is in the same hand that recorded Elizabeth Hubbard's deposition against him dated September 8, No. 583, indicating that those two were decided in September. The third, No. 776, is signed by January grand jury foreman, Robert Payne, confirming that the third was decided four months later by a different grand jury, for allegedly afflicting Mary Walcott during William Procter's examination on September 17, No. 663. ◇ Hand 2 = Anthony Checkley

Essex County Court Archives, vol. 2, no. 1, Massachusetts Supreme Judicial Court, Judicial Archives, on deposit James Duncan Phillips Library, Peabody Essex Museum, Salem, MA.

582. Indictment of William Procter, for Afflicting Mary Warren (Returned Ignoramus)†

[Hand 1] Essex in the Prouince of the Massachusetts Bay in New England Ss/   } Anno $\overline{RR}^s$ Reginæ Gulielmi & Mariæ Angliæ &c Quarto Annoqȝ Domini 1692.

The Juriors for our Sou^ε Lord and Lady the King and Queen doe present that [Hand 2] **William Procter of Salem** [Hand 1] In the County of Essex [Hand 2] **Husbandman in & vpon the thirty first day of May** [Hand 1] In the yeare aforesaid and diuers other days & times as well before as after Certaine detestable Art called Witchcrafts and Sorceries Wickedly Mallitiously and felloniously hath used practised & Exercised At and [Hand 2] **in the Towneship of Salem** [Hand 1] Aforesaid in upon & against one [Hand 2] **Mary Warren of Salem** [Hand 1] Aforesaid [Hand 2] **Single Woman** [Hand 1] by which said Wicked Acts [Hand 2] **Mary Warren aforsaid the day & yea^ε** [Hand 1] the aforesaid and diuers other days and times both before & after was and is Tortured Aflicted Consumed Pined Wasted & Tormented & also for sundry other acts of Witchcraft by the said [Hand 2] **William Procter** [Hand 1] {Comitted} and done before & Since that time against Our Sou^ε Lord and Lady the King & Queen theire Crowne and Dignity and the forme in the Stattute in that Case made & Prouided.
[Hand 2] Wittness
Eliz Hobert

[Reverse] [Hand 3?] Wm Procter
[Hand 4] Igno Rama [= ignoramus]

Notes: Hand 2 = Anthony Checkley

Essex County Court Archives, vol. 2, no. 3, Massachusetts Supreme Judicial Court, Judicial Archives, on deposit James Duncan Phillips Library, Peabody Essex Museum, Salem, MA.

583. Deposition of Elizabeth Hubbard v. William Procter

[Hand 1] elizabeth hubart douth testify one: har oath before the grand Inquest that william procter did aflicte me this deponant the 31. day of may 92. at the time of his examination: and allso I did see said william procter aflicte mary warrin at the time of his examination: and said william procter hath affliktid me this deponant seuerall tims sins: septembr the .8. day 1692

[Reverse] [Hand 2] William Proctor

Essex County Court Archives, vol. 2, no. 4, Massachusetts Supreme Judicial Court, Judicial Archives, on deposit James Duncan Phillips Library, Peabody Essex Museum, Salem, MA.

Billa Vera: Indictment No. 1 of Martha Cory, for Afflicting Elizabeth Hubbard†
2nd of 2 dates. See No. 476 on Aug. 4, 1692

Billa Vera: Indictment No. 2 of Martha Cory, for Afflicting Mercy Lewis†
2nd of 2 dates. See No. 477 on Aug. 4, 1692

Sworn at Trial: Deposition of Ezekiel Cheever & Edward Putnam v. Martha Cory†
3rd of 3 dates. See No. 18 on March 21, 1692

Sworn at Trial: Deposition of Elizabeth Hubbard v. Martha Cory†
3rd of 3 dates. See No. 19 on March 21, 1692

Sworn at Trial: Deposition of Edward Putnam v. Martha Cory†
2nd of 2 dates. See No. 21 on March 21, 1692

Friday, September 9, 1692

Grand Juries of Mary Bradbury & Giles Cory

Trials of Mary Bradbury & Mary Esty

Sworn Before a Justice of the Peace: Examination of Abigail Hobbs
2nd of 2 dates. See No. 67 on April 19, 1692

584. Indictment of Mary Bradbury, for Afflicting Sarah Bibber†

[Hand 1] Essex in the Prouince of the Massachusetts Bay in New England Ss// } Anno $\overline{RR}$s & Reginæ Gulielmi & Mariæ Angliæ &c Quarto Annoqʒ Domini 1692.

The Juriors for our Soueᵉ Lord & Lady the King and Queen doe present That [Hand 2] **Mary Bradbury Wife of Capt Thomas Bradbury of Salisbury** [Hand 1] In the County of

Essex [Hand 2] **Gen^tm̄ vpon the Second day of July** [Hand 1] In the yeare aforesaid and   September 9, 1692
diuers other days and times as well before as after certaine detestable Arts called Witchcraft
and Sorceries. Wickedly Mallitiously and felloniously hath used practised and Exercised At
and [Hand 2] **in the Towne of Salem in the County of Essex** [Hand 1] Aforesaid in upon &
against one [Hand 2] **Sarah Vibber Wife of John Vibber of Salem** [Hand 1] Aforesaid
[Hand 2] **Husbandman** [Hand 1] by which said wicked acts the said [Hand 2] **Sarah Vibber
the** ^{**second**} **day of July** [Hand 1] aforesaid & diuers other days and times both before and
after was and is Tortured Afflicted Consumed Pined Wasted & Tormented & also for
sundry other Acts of Witchcraft by the said [Hand 2] **Mary Bradbury Comitted Acted**
[Hand 1] and done before and Since that time against [Hand 2] ^{**the peace of**} [Hand 1]
Our Sou^ε Lord & Lady the King and Queene theire Crowne and Dignity and the forme
[Hand 2] **Of** ["Of" written over "in"] [Hand 1] the Stattute In that case made and Prouided
[Hand 2] **Wittness**
Mary Walcott
Eliz Hobard
Eliz: Booth
Mercy lewis

[Reverse] Indictmt. Bradbury: = Vibber
[Hand 3] bila uera

Notes: This dating is probable but not certain in view of the fact that the grand jury heard an accusation from Ann Putnam
Jr. on September 8, so other indictments regarding Mary Bradbury may also have been presented that day. The issue is
further complicated by Ann's testimony on both September 8 and 9. See No. 580 & No. 588. ◊ Hand 2 = Anthony
Checkley

*Essex County Court Archives, vol. 2, no. 70, Massachusetts Supreme Judicial Court, Judicial Archives, on deposit James Duncan
Phillips Library, Peabody Essex Museum, Salem, MA.*

585. Indictment of Mary Bradbury, for Afflicting Timothy Swan†

[Hand 1] Essex in the Prouince   } Anno R̄R̄^s & Reginæ Gulielmi & Mariæ Angliæ &c
of the Massachusetts Bay in New   } Quarto Annoqȝ Domini 1692/
England
Ss/
The Juriors for our Sou^ε Lord and Lady the King and Queen doe present That [Hand 2]
Mary Bradbury Wife of⟨C⟩ap^t Thomas Bradbury of Salisbury [Hand 1] In the County of
Essex [Hand 2] **Gen^t vpon the Twenty Sixth day of July** [Hand 1] In the yeare aforesaid and
diuers other days and times as well before as after Certaine detestable Arts called Witchcraft
& Sorceries Wickedly Mallitiously and felloniously hath used practised and Exercised At
and [Hand 2] **in the Township of Andivor in the County of Essex** [Hand 1] Aforesaid in
upon & against one [Hand 2] **Timothy Swann of Andivo^r In** ["In" written over "af"] **the
County** ~~aforesaid~~ [Hand 1] Aforesaid [Hand 2] **Husbandman** [Hand 1] by which said
Wicked Acts the said [Hand 2] **Timothy Swann vpon the 26th day of July** [Hand 1]
Aforesaid and diuers other days & times both before and after was and is Tortured Afflicted
Consumed Pined Wasted and Tormented, and also for Sundry other Acts of Witchcraft by

the said [Hand 2] **Mary Bradbury** [Hand 1] Comitted and done before and Since that time against the peace of our Sou^E Lord & Lady the King and Queen theire Crowne and dignity And the forme [Hand 2] **Of** ["Of" written over "⟨in⟩"] [Hand 1] the Stattute In that case made and Prouided.
[Hand 2] Wittness
Mary Walcott
Ann: Puttnam

[Reverse] Indictm^t v^{E}s Bradbury for Bewitching Swan.
[Hand 3] bila uera

Notes: Hand 2 = Anthony Checkley

Essex County Court Archives, vol. 2, no. 69, Massachusetts Supreme Judicial Court, Judicial Archives, on deposit James Duncan Phillips Library, Peabody Essex Museum, Salem, MA.

586. Deposition of Sarah Bibber v. Mary Bradbury†

[Hand 1] [Lost] ⟨D⟩eposistion of Sarah vibber who testifieth and saith [Lost] haue a long time ben afflected by a woman which tould ⟨m⟩e hir name was Mis Bradbery and that she came from Salisbury but on th⟨e⟩ 2 day of July 1692 being the day of the Examin [Lost] [= examination] of m^{is} Bradbery I was most greviously tormented by hir dureing the time of hir Examination: tho for a good while she would not let me se hir parsonally but at last I saw hir and then I saw that it was the very same woman that tould me hir name was m^{is} Bradbery and she has most greviously affleted me senc that time allso I haue ₮ seen m^{is} Bradbury or Hir [Lost]⟨pp⟩erance [= appearance] seuerall times afflecting the bodyes of mary walcott and [Lost]tnam [= Putnam] and I beleue in my heart that m^{is} Bradbery is a [Lost]nd [= witch and?] that she has often afflected and tormented me and the [Lost]amed [= aforenamed?] parsons by hir acts of wicthcraft
[Hand 2] [Lost]bber [= Bibber] ownd: to: Jury of Inquest. y^t y^e above written evidence. is y^e truth upon her oath [Lost] 1692

[Reverse] [Hand 3] Sarry wibber
[Hand 4] Deposition
[Hand 5] Sarah [Lost]

Notes: Hand 1 = Thomas Putnam; Hand 2 = Simon Willard

Witchcraft Papers, no. 13, Massachusetts Historical Society, Boston, MA.

587. Deposition of Elizabeth Hubbard v. Mary Bradbury

[Hand 1] The [Lost]⟨t⟩ion [= deposition] of Eliz: Hubberd who testifieth and saith that I along [Lost]⟨b⟩en afflected by a woman which tould me hir name was Mis^t Bradbery of Salisbury ⟨₴⟩ but on the :2. day of July 1692 being the day of the Examination of mis^t mary

Bradbery I then saw that it was the very same woman that tould me hir name was miˢᵗ   September 9, 1692
⟨B⟩radbery: and she did most greviously torment me dureing the time of hir Examination for
if she did but look upon me she wou⟨ld⟩ s⟨tr⟩ick me down or allmost choake ^{me} also on
the day of hir Examinat[Lost] I saw miˢᵗ Bradbery or hir Apperance most greviously afflect
& torment mary walcott Sarah vibber and Ann putnanam and I beleue in my hart that misᵗ
Bradbery is a wicth and that she has very often afflected and tormented me and the
afformentiond parsons by hir acts of wicthcraf for sence she has ben in prison she or hir
Apperance has com to me and most grevio⟨u⟩sly tomented me which if she ware not a wicth
she cold not doe
[Hand 2] elizabeth huberd on hear ownid this har testimony to be the truth before the grand
Inquest this 9. dy of September 92

Notes: The manuscript has been silked onto another sheet for preservation, and the reverse, which has some writing on it, cannot be accessed. The bleedthrough shows the name of "Elizabeth" as well as a "b." Nothing else can be read. ◊ Hand 1 = Thomas Putnam

Witchcraft Papers, no. 11b, Massachusetts Historical Society, Boston, MA.

588. Deposition of Ann Putnam Jr. v. Mary Bradbury

[Hand 1] The deposistion of Ann putnam who testifieth and saith that euer sence the
begining of may 1692 I haue ben afflected by a woman which tould me hir name was Mⁱˢ
Bradbery and that she came from Salisbury but on the 2ᵗʰ day of July 1692 being the day of
the Examination of Mⁱˢ Mary Bradbery I then saw that ⟨ꝛ⟩ {she} was the very same woman
that tould me hir name was Mⁱˢ Bradbery and she did most greviously afflect and and
torment me dureing the time of hir Examination. for if she did but look upon me she would
strick me down or almost choak me also on the day of hir Examination I saw miˢ Bradbery
most greviously afflet and torment mary walcott Sarah vibber and Eliz: Hubburd and I
beleue in my hart that mⁱˢ Bradbery is a wicth & & that she has often affleted me and
seuerall othrs by hir acts of wicthcraft: also there Apper⟨e⟩d to me my uncle Jnᵒ Carr in a
winding sheet: whom I very well knew in his life time: and he tould me that mⁱˢ Bradbery
had murthered him and that his blood did crie for venjance againt hir.: also miˢ Bradbery or
hir Apperance tould me that it was she that made my ffathers sheep to run a[Lost]ll [= away
till?] they ware all lost and that she had kiled my ffathers ⟨cowe⟩ and also kiled that horse he
took such delight in
[Hand 2] An: Putnam: affirmd to yᵉ Jury of inquest: to yᵉ truth of yᵉ above written evidence:
on oath Septᴱ :9: 1692

[Reverse] [Hand 3] Ann Put⟨m⟩[Lost][= Putnam]
[Hand 4] ann putnam

Notes: Hand 1 = Thomas Putnam; Hand 2 = Simon Willard; Hand 3 = Stephen Sewall

Witchcraft Papers, no. 12a, Massachusetts Historical Society, Boston, MA.

589. Deposition of Mary Walcott v. Mary Bradbury

[Hand 1] [Lost]sistion [= The deposition] of mary walcott who testifieth and saith that I being at [Lost] [*Woodward* = Andeur] on the later end of July 1692: and on the 26 day of the sam⟨e⟩ [Lost]nth [= month] I saw there Mis mary Bradbery the wife of Capt Tho: Bradbery of Salisbury ["u" written over "e"] or hir Apperance most greviously affleting and tormenting of Timothy Swan of Andeuor⟨e⟩ allmost Redy to kill him: also before and sence that time I haue seen m^is Bradbery or hir Apperance most greviously afflecting and tormenting Timothy ⟨ə⟩ Swan and I doe beleue in my heart that M^ist Bradbery is a most dreadffull wicth for sence she has been in prison ["s" written over "z"] she or hir Apperance has come to me and most greviously tormented me

[Hand 2] mary Walcot: affirmd: y^e truth of y^e above written evidence before y^e Jury of Inquest: upon oath ~~Augus~~ Sept^ɛ 9: 1692

[Reverse] [Hand 1] Mar[Lost] [= Mary Walcot]

Notes: Hand 1 = Thomas Putnam; Hand 2 = Simon Willard

Essex County Court Archives, vol. 2, no. 81, Massachusetts Supreme Judicial Court, Judicial Archives, on deposit James Duncan Phillips Library, Peabody Essex Museum, Salem, MA.

590. Deposition of Mary Walcott v. Mary Bradbury†

[Hand 1] [Lost]posistion [= deposition] of mary walcott who testifieth and saith that I
[Lost]een [= been] a long time afflected with a woman which tould me hir
[Lost] ⟨w⟩as Mis: Bradbery: and that hir husband was capt of Salisbury
[Lost]⟨n⟩ [= on] the 2 day of July 1692: being the day of the Examination
[Lost]{ery} [= Mary] Bradbery of Salisbury I then saw that she was the very
[Lost] woman that tould me hir name was Mis^t Bradbery and then
[Lost]⟨d⟩ [= did] most greviously afflect and torm⟨en⟩t me dureing the time
[Lost] ⟨E⟩xamination for if she did but look upon me she would strick
[Lost]wn [= down] or allmost choak me: also on the day of hir Examination
[Lost]⟨w⟩ [= saw] mis^ti mary Bradbery or hir Apperance most griviously afflect
[Lost] torment ~~mercy lewes~~ Eliz: Hubbrd mary warren ~~Sarah vibber~~
[Lost]d [= and] Ann putnam: and I verily beleue that mistris mary Bradbery is a
[Lost] most dread wicth and that she hath very often affleictd me and the
[Lost]re [= afore] named parsons by acts of wicthcraf for sence she has been in
[Lost]⟨ss⟩on [= prison] she or hir apperanc has come to me and has most greviose
tor[Lost]ed [= tortured] me: also their appeared to me a yong man in a winding sheet
[Lost]⟨h⟩ [= which] tould me his name was Jno Carr and that mi^s Bradbery had murth
[Lost] [= murdered]
[Lost] that his blood did cry for venjance against hir
[Hand 2] [Lost] [= Mary] Walcot affirmd: to y^e truth of y^e aboue written evidence: before:
y^e Jury of Inquest: upon her oat[Lost] [= oath]
[Lost] 1692

Notes: It is not clear why Mary Walcott gave two depositions in this case to the grand jury. See No. 589. ◊ Hand 1 = Thomas Putnam; Hand 2 = Simon Willard

Sept. 9, 1692

Witchcraft Papers, no. 12b, Massachusetts Historical Society, Boston, MA.

591. Deposition of Mary Warren v. Mary Bradbury

[Hand 1] The Deposistion of mary warren who testifieth and saith ^{⟨?⟩} th⟨at⟩
I haue ben a long time afflected by a woman which tould me Hir
name was Mis Bradbery and that she came from Salisbury but on
the 2th day of July 1692: being the day of the Examinat[Lost] [*Woodward* = examination of]
m^is mary Bradbery I then saw that she was the very [Lost] [*Woodward* = same]
woman which tould me hir name was m^is Bradbery and [Lost] [*Woodward* = she did]
most ⟨gre⟩viously Afflect and torment me dureing ⟨t⟩[Lost] [*Woodward* = the time of hir]
Examination for if she did but ~~strick~~ look upon ⟨m⟩[Lost] [= me] [*Woodward* = she would]
strick me down or allmost choak me also on the da⟨y⟩ [Lost] [*Woodward* = of her]
[Lost]mination [= examination] I saw mi^s Bradbery or hir Apperance mo⟨s⟩[Lost]
[*Woodward* = most greviously]
afflect and torment mary walcott Sarah vibber E[Lost] [*Woodward* = Eliz Hubbard]
and Ann putnam and I beleue in my heart that m^i[Lost] [*Woodward* = mi^s Bradbery]
is ⟨a⟩ ⟨wicth⟩ and that she has very often affleted an[Lost] [*Woodward* = and tormented me]
and seural othrs by hir acts of wicthcraft
[Hand 2] mary warrin ownid this har testimony one the oath whic⟨h⟩ [Lost] [*Woodward* =
she hath]
taken before the grand Inquest this.9[Hand 3]th ["th" written over "dy"] [Hand 2] of
Septemb⟨e⟩r 92

[Reverse] [Hand 4] Mary Warren
[Hand 5] Depostion

Notes: *SWP*'s conjectural readings are consistent with Woodward's transcription. ◊ Hand 1 = Thomas Putnam

Essex County Court Archives, vol. 2, no. 78, Massachusetts Supreme Judicial Court, Judicial Archives, on deposit James Duncan Phillips Library, Peabody Essex Museum, Salem, MA.

592. Deposition of Sarah Bibber v. Giles Cory

[Hand 1] The deposistion of Sarah vibber who testifieth and saith that I haue ben most
greviously affleted by Giles Cory or his ["s" written over "r"] Apperance
~~also on the day of his Examination if he did but looke on me he would strick me down or~~
~~or allmost choake me~~ and allso I haue seen Giles Cory or his Apperance most greviously
affleting and tormenting the bodyes of mary walcott mercy lewes and ann putnam and I
beleue in my heart that Giles Cory is a wizzard and that he has very often afflected and
torme⟨nt⟩^d [Lost] [= me] and the parsons aboue mentioned by his actts of wicthcraft

September 9, 1692

[Hand 2] I testifie y^t on y^e fourteenth of August⟨e⟩ & ever since: at times s^d Cory [Lost] [= has] afflicted me by whipping me ⟨?⟩ & beating me: & urgeing me Vehemently: to read [Lost] [= and] write in his book: [Hand 3] and cote me with his knife

[Hand 2] Sarah Vibber: affirmd to y^e Jury of Inquest: y^t y^e above written evidence: is y^e truth upon oath: Sept^ε 9: 1692

[Reverse] [Hand 1] Sarah Vibber ag[Lost] [= against] Giles Cory:

Notes: Although dated to the grand jury, this document, as well as Documents 593 and 594, were almost certainly recorded earlier. Hand 1 = Thomas Putnam; Hand 2 = Simon Willard

Essex County Court Archives, vol. 2, no. 87, Massachusetts Supreme Judicial Court, Judicial Archives, on deposit James Duncan Phillips Library, Peabody Essex Museum, Salem, MA.

Sworn Before the Grand Jury: Deposition of Benjamin Gould v. Giles Cory, Martha Cory, & John Procter†

2nd of 2 dates. See No. 66 on April 19, 1692

593. Deposition of Mercy Lewis v. Giles Cory

[Hand 1] The Deposistion of Mircy Lewes ~~who~~ agged about 19 years who testifieth and saith that on the 14th April 1692 I saw the Apperishtion of Giles Cory com and afflect me urging me to writ in his book and so he continewed most dreafully to hurt me by times beating me & almost braking my back tell the day of his examination being the 19th April and then allso dureing the time of his examination he did afflect and tortor me most greviously: and also seuerall times sence urging me vehemently to writ in his book and I veryly beleue in my heart that Giles Cory is a dreadfull wizzard for sence ⟨h⟩e has been in prison ["s" written over "z"] he or his Appearanc has com and most greviously tormented me

[Hand 2] Mercy Lewis: ⟨?⟩ affirmd to. y^e Jury of Inquest: y^t y^e above written evidence: is the truth upon y^e oath: she has formerly taken: in y^e Court of oyer & terminer: Sept^ε 9: 1692

[Reverse] [Hand 3] Mercy Lewis [Hand 4] again[Lost] [= against] Geoyles Cory
[Hand 5] Giles Cory

Notes: Hand 1 = Thomas Putnam; Hand 2 = Simon Willard

Essex County Court Archives, vol. 2, no. 85, Massachusetts Supreme Judicial Court, Judicial Archives, on deposit James Duncan Phillips Library, Peabody Essex Museum, Salem, MA.

594. Deposition of Ann Putnam Jr. v. Giles Cory

[Hand 1] The Deposistion of Ann putnam who testifieth and saith that on 13th of April 1692 I saw the Apperishtion of Gilles Cory com and afflect me urging me to writ in his book: and so he continewed hurting me by times tell the 19th April being the day of his

Examination: and dureing the time of his Examination ~~the Apperishtion of~~ Giles Cory did   September 9, 1692
tortor me a grat many times and allso seuerall times sence ~~the Apperishtion of~~ Giles Cory
^{or his Apperance} has most greviously afflected me by beating pinching and allmost
choaking me to death urging me to writ in his book also on the day of his Examination I saw
Giles Cory or his Apperance most greviously afflect and torment mary walcott mercy lewes
and Sarah vibber and I veryly beleueue that Giles Cory is is a dreadfull wizzard for senc he
has ben in prizon he or his Apperanc⟨e⟩ has com to me a grat many times and afflected me
[Hand 2] An Putnam ownd upon her. oath that: yᵉ above written evidence. is yᵉ truth to yᵉ
Jury of inquest Septᴱ 9: 92

[Reverse] [Hand 3] Ann. puttnam ag⟨s⟩[Lost] [= against] Giles Cory

Notes: Hand 1 = Thomas Putnam; Hand 2 = Simon Willard; Hand 3 = Jonathan Corwin

Essex County Court Archives, vol. 2, no. 86, Massachusetts Supreme Judicial Court, Judicial Archives, on deposit James Duncan Phillips Library, Peabody Essex Museum, Salem, MA.

595. Statements of Mary Warren, Elizabeth Woodwell, Mary Walcott, & Elizabeth Hubbard v. Giles Cory

[Hand 1] Mary Warin, affirmd: to yᵉ Jury of Inquest: that: she hath been: ~~Giles~~ afflicted by
Giles Cory or his appearition and that by beating of me with his staffe: & by: biting me &
pinching & choaking me greatly torturing me ["me" written over "her"] & cutting me with a
knife. & perticulerly at yᵉ time of his examina{tion} he did greivously torment me: also: at
the time of his examination. I saw: sᵈ Cory or his appearition most: dredfully afflict: Mary
Walcot An Putnam: Mercy lewis & Sarah: Vibber Septᴱ 9: 1692

Eliz Woodwell upon yᵉ oath she formerly has taken in this Court: did affirm to yᵉ Jury of
Inquest: that: she saw Giles Cory at meeting at Salem on a lecture day. since he has bin at
prison he or his apearition: came in & sat, in yᵉ middlemost seat: of yᵉ mens seats: by yᵉ post
this was yᵉ lecture day before: Bridget Bishup was hanged and I saw him come out: with yᵉ
rest of yᵉ people: ~~at yᵗ time~~ Mary Walcot: affirmed: yᵗ {she} saw sᵈ Cory: as above. sit in yᵉ
same place at yᵉ same time he or his appearance & yᵗ she did se him goe out: with yᵉ rest of yᵉ
people: this she affirmd to yᵉ Jury of Inquest: Septᴱ 9: 1692

Eliz Hubbard: to yᵉ Jury of Inquest: that Giles Cory hath several times afflicted me ["me"
written over "her"] with several sorts of torments. I veryly think he is a wizard & afflicted me
by wichcraft Septᴱ 9 ["9" written over "8"]:: 1692

Notes: Hand 1 = Simon Willard

Essex County Court Archives, vol. 2, no. 89, Massachusetts Supreme Judicial Court, Judicial Archives, on deposit James Duncan Phillips Library, Peabody Essex Museum, Salem, MA.

596. Petition of Sarah Cloyce & Mary Esty‡

[Hand 1] The humble Request of Mary Esty and Sarah Cloys to the Honoured Court, Humbly sheweth, that whereas we two sisters Mary Esty & Sarah Cloys stand now before the Honoured court charged with the suspition of Witchcraft, our humble request is first that seing we are neither able to plead our owne cause, nor is councell alowed to those in our condicion, that you who are our Judges, would please to be of councell to us, to direct us wherein we may stand in neede. Secondly that wheras we are not conscious to our selves of any guilt in the least degree of that crime, wherof we are now accused (in the presence of yᵉ Living God we speake it, before whose awfull Tribunall we know we shall ere Long appeare) nor of any other scandalouse evill, or miscaryage inconsistant with Christianity, Those who haue had yᵉ Longest and best knowledge of vs, being persons of good report, may be suffered to Testifie upon oath what they know concerning each of vs, viz Mʳ Capen [Hand 2] ⌃{the ⟨P⟩astour and} [Hand 1] those of yᵉ Towne & Church of Topsfield, who are ready to say somthing which we ~~beg~~ [Hand 2] ⌃{hope} [Hand 1] may be looked upon, as very considerable in this matter; with the seven children of one of us, viz Mary Esty. and [Hand 2] ⟨wᵗ⟩ ["wᵗ" written over "it"] [Hand 1] may be produced of Like nature in reference to the wife of Peter Cloys, her sister. Thirdly that the Testimony of witches, or such as are afflicted, as is supposed, by witches may not be improved to condemn us, without other Legal evidence concurring. we hope the Honoured Court & Jury will be soe tender of the lives of such [Hand 2] ⌃{as we are} [Hand 1] who have for many yeares lived vnder the vnblemished reputation of Christianity [Hand 2], ⌃{as not to condemne them} [Hand 1] without a fayre and equall hearing of what may be sayd for us, as well as against us. And your poore supplyants shall be bound always to pray. &c

[Reverse] [Hand 3] Easty & Cloyce peticon̅
[Hand 4] the pertison

Notes: Mary Esty went to trial on September 9. This document appears not as a formal plea, but as a petition to allow sworn testimony on behalf of both. A grand jury was scheduled to hear the case of Sarah Cloyce on that same day. It appears as if this petition was for those two events on the same day, and is dated to September 9 accordingly. For Sarah Cloyce, see the General Introduction. ◊ Hand 3 = Stephen Sewall

Essex County Court Archives, vol. 1, no. 295, Massachusetts Supreme Judicial Court, Judicial Archives, on deposit James Duncan Phillips Library, Peabody Essex Museum, Salem, MA.

597. Plea of Mary Bradbury†

[Hand 1] The answer of Mary Bradbury in yᵉ charge of wichcraft or familliarity with
   yᵉ divell I doe plead not guilty:/
I am wholly inocent of any such wickedness through the goodness of god that haue kept mee hitherto) I am yᵉ servant of Jesus Christ & haue giuen my self vp to him as my only lord & saviour: and to the dilligent attendance vpon him in all his holy ordinances, in vtter contempt & defiance of the divell, and all his works as horid & detestible: and accordingly haue endevoᵋed to frame my life: & conversation according to yᵉ rules of his holy word, & in that faith & practice resolue by yᵉ help and assistance of god to contineu to my lifes end:

for ye truth of what I say as to matter of practiss I humbly refer my self my selfe; to my   September 9, 1692
brethren & neighbo^{εs} that know mee and vnto ye searcher of all hearts for the truth &
vprightness of my heart therin (human frailties, & vnavoydable infirmities excepted) of
which j bitterly complayne every day:/

                                                                        Mary Bradbury

Notes: This is probably Mary Bradbury's plea at her trial. The "signature" is by Thomas Bradbury. ◊ Hand 1 = Thomas
Bradbury

*Essex County Court Archives, vol. 2, no. 72, Massachusetts Supreme Judicial Court, Judicial Archives, on deposit James Duncan
Phillips Library, Peabody Essex Museum, Salem, MA.*

598. Deposition of James Carr v. Mary Bradbury

[Hand 1] The Deposistion of James carr. who testifieth and saith that about 20 years agoe
one day as I was accidently att the house of mr wheleright and his daughter the widdow
maverick then liued there: and she then did most curtuously invite me to com oftener to the
house and wondered I was grown such a strangr and with in a few days affter one euening I
went thether againe: and when I came thether againe: william Bradbery was y^r who was then
a suter to the said widdow but I did not know it tell affterwards ~~he~~ affter I came in the
widdow did so corsely treat the s^d william Bradbery that he went away semeing to be angury:
presently affter this I was takn affter a strange maner as if ~~euery~~ liueing creature did run
about euery part of my body redy to tare me to peaces and so I ~~hau~~ continewed for about 3
qurters of a year ^{by times &} I applyed my self to doctor {crosbe} who gaue me a grate
deal of visek [= physic] but could make non work tho he steept tobacko in bosit drink he
could make non to work where upon he tould me that he beleued I was behaged: and I tould
him I had thought so a good while: and {he} asked me by hom I tould him I did not care for
spaking for one was count⟨e⟩d an honest woman. but he uging [= urging] I tould him and he
said he did beleue that m^{is} Bradbery was a grat deall worss then goody mertin ["e" written
over "i"]: then presentely affter this one night I being abed & brod awake there came
sumthing to me ⟨~~lik~~⟩ which I thought was a catt and went to strick {it} ofe the bed and was
sezed fast that I could not stir hedd nor foot but by and by coming to my strenth I hard
sumting a coming to me againe and I prepared my self to strick it: and ^{it} coming upon
the bed I did strick at it and I beleue I hit it: and affter that visek would work on me and I
beleue in my hart that mis Bradbery the prisonr att the barr has often affle⟨ct⟩d me by acts of
wicthcraft [Hand 2] Jurat in Curia Sepr 9th 92

[Reverse] [Hand 3] James Carr Depo͞ition
[Hand 4] Bradbury

Notes: Used at trial. ◊ "behaged": 'bewitched' (not recorded in *OED*). "bosit": 'posset, a medicinal drink of hot milk mixed
with beer or wine, flavored with spices' (*OED* s.v. *posset*). ◊ Hand 1 = Thomas Putnam; Hand 2 = Stephen Sewall

*Essex County Court Archives, vol. 2, no. 79, Massachusetts Supreme Judicial Court, Judicial Archives, on deposit James Duncan
Phillips Library, Peabody Essex Museum, Salem, MA.*

September 9, 1692

599. Deposition of Richard Carr & Zerubable Endicott v. Mary Bradbury

[Hand 1] The deposistion of Richard: Carr who testifieth and saith: that about {13:} years ago presently affter sume Diferance that happened to be between my Hon^d ffather mr. George Carr: and m^{is} Bradbery the prisoner at the barr upon a Sabboth at noon as we ware riding hom by the house of Capt Tho: Bradbery I saw m^{is} Bradbery goe into hir ~~house~~ {gate} and {turne the corner of} Immediatly there derted out of hir gate a blue boar and darted at my ffathers horses ledgs which mad him stumble but I saw it no more and {my} ffather said boys what doe you se: we both answed a blue bore:

Zorobabell Endecott testifieth and saith that I liueed att mr George Carr: now deceased att the time aboue mentioned and was present with mr George Carr and mr Richard Carr and I also saw a blue bore dart out of mr Brdbery gate to mr Gorge Carrs horses ledges which mad him stumble affter a strange manr and I also saw the blue bore dart from mr carrs horses ledgs in att m^{is} Bradberys window: and mr carr Immediattly said boys what did you see and we both said a blue bore then said he from whence came it and we said out of mr Bradberys gate. then said he I am glad you see it as well as well as I

[Hand 2] Jurat in Curia Sep^r .9th 92

& They both further say on y^r Oathes that m^r Carr discoursed wth them as they went home about what had happened & ^{yy [= they] all} concluded that it was m^{εs} Bradbury that so app^εd as a blue boar.

[Reverse] [Hand 1] Richard Carr. Zorobable Endcot

Notes: Used at trial. ◊ Hand 1 = Thomas Putnam; Hand 2 = Stephen Sewall

Essex County Court Archives, vol. 2, no. 80, Massachusetts Supreme Judicial Court, Judicial Archives, on deposit James Duncan Phillips Library, Peabody Essex Museum, Salem, MA.

600. Deposition of Samuel Endicott v. Mary Bradbury

[Hand 1] Sam^{ll} Endecott aged thirty one years or thereabout Testifieth Thatt about eleven years since being bound upon a vioage to sea wth Capt ~~Th°~~ Sam^{ll} Smith Late of Boston Deceas'd, just before we sayl'd m^{εs} Bradbery of Salisbury the prisoner now att the barr came to Boston wth some firkins of butter of wch Capt Smith bought two, one of y^m proved halfe way butter and after we had been att sea three weekes our men were nott able to eat itt, itt stanck soe and runn wth magotts, wch made the men very much disturb'd about itt and would often say thatt they heard m^{εs} ["m" written over "G"] Bradbury was a witch and thatt they verily beleived she was soe or else she would ^{nott} have served the Capt soe as to sell him such butter. And further this deponent Testifieth y^t in four dayes after they sett sayle they mett wth such ⟨a⟩ violent storm y^t we Lost our main mast and riggin and Lost fifteen horses and thatt about a fortnight after we sett our jury mast and thatt very night there came up a shipp by our side and Carried ^{away} two of the mizon shrouds and one of the Leaches of the mainsaile, And this deponent further sayth thatt after they arived att Barbados and went ^{to} Saltitudos and had Laden their vessell the next morning she sprang a leake in the hold w^{ch} ~~dam⟨ne⟩f⟨ied⟩~~ wasted sev^εall tunns of salt in soe much thatt we were forct to unlade our vessell again wholy to stopp our leake there was then four foot [Hand 2] ^{of} [Hand 1]

water in the hold after we had taken in our lading again we had a good passage home butt   September 9, 1692
when we came near the Land the Capt sent this deponent forward to looke out for land in a
bright moone shining night and as he was

[Reverse] sitting upon the windless he heard a Rumbling noise under him w⟨t⟩ʰ thatt he the
sᵈ deponent Testifieth thatt he looked one the side of the windless and saw the leggs of some
ꝑson being no wayes frighted ^{&} thatt presently he was shook and looked over his
shoulder, and saw the appearan⟨c⟩{e} of a woman from her middle upwards, haveing a white
Capp and white neckloth on her, wᶜʰ then affrighted ⟨h⟩i⟨m⟩ very much, and as he was
turning of the windless he saw the aforsaid two leggs.
                                        [Hand 3] Jurat in Curia Sepʳ 9ᵗʰ 1692

[Hand 4] Sam. Endecott

Notes: Used at trial. ◊ Hand 3 = Stephen Sewall

Essex County Court Archives, vol. 2, no. 76, Massachusetts Supreme Judicial Court, Judicial Archives, on deposit James Duncan Phillips Library, Peabody Essex Museum, Salem, MA.

Billa Vera: Indictment No. 1 of Mary Esty, for Afflicting Mercy Lewis†
2ⁿᵈ of 2 dates. See No. 459 on Aug. 3, 1692

Billa Vera: Indictment No. 2 of Mary Esty, for Afflicting Elizabeth Hubbard†
2ⁿᵈ of 2 dates. See No. 460 on Aug. 3, 1692

Sworn at Trial: Deposition of Samuel Abby and Testimony of Sarah Trask v. Mary Esty, John Willard, & Mary Whittredge
2ⁿᵈ of 2 dates. See No. 204 on May 23, 1692

Sworn at Trial: Testimony of George Herrick & John Putnam Jr. v. Mary Esty†
2ⁿᵈ of 2 dates. See No. 192 on May 20, 1692

601. Deposition of Edward Putnam v. Mary Esty†

[Hand 1] the deposistion of Eward Putnam aged abought 38 year ho testifieth and saith
abbought 18 day of may 1692. mary easty the prisner now at the bar being then seat at libarty
but one the 20: and: 21: days of may. marcy lues. was so greuiously. aflicted and tortred. by
her (as she her self and mary walcott: ann putnam Elizabeth hubbart abigel williams) said) I
my self being ther present with seueral others with marcy lues locked for nothing. else. but
present death with marcy lues. for allmost the space of two days. and a night. she was Choked
allmost to death in so much we thought sumtimes she had ben dead her mouth and teath
shut and all this uery often. untell shuch time as we understood mary easty was laid in Irons
allso apon the second day of mary estys examminnation at the uilag. marcy lues mary walcott
elizabeth hubbart ann putnam mary warrin and abigell williams when mary e{a}sty Came to
the mar. [= bar?] was Choked in shuch a most greuious. maner that the honred magestrats
Cold not proseed to her examminnation untell they desired mee haile to go to prayer and in

September 9, 1692

prayr time and sumtime after it they ~~#~~ remaned in this sad Condition of being allmost Choked to death. and when they ware abul again to spaek they all with one Consent Charged her that she ded them that mis⟨c⟩hef⟨f⟩ I allso haue. hard sum of them Complain uery often of hur hurting them with the spindell of a wheel.

Edward Putnam.
[Hand 2] Jurat in Curia

[Reverse] Edwd Putm^n

Notes: On May 18 Mary Esty had briefly been released from prison, but the accusers, led by Mercy Lewis, complained enough to have her imprisoned again on May 20. See No. 187. ◊ Used at trial. ◊ "haile": 'call out (to attract attention)' (*OED* s.v. *hail* v^2 4). ◊ Hand 1 = Edward Putnam; Hand 2 = Stephen Sewall

Essex County Court Archives, vol. 1, no. 291, Massachusetts Supreme Judicial Court, Judicial Archives, on deposit James Duncan Phillips Library, Peabody Essex Museum, Salem, MA.

Used at Trial: Deposition of Elizabeth Hubbard v. Mary Esty, John Willard, & Mary Whittredge†

4th of 4 dates. See No. 197 on May 21, 1692

Presented at Trial: Statement of Thomas & Elizabeth Fosse for Mary Esty†

2nd of 2 dates. See No. 552 on Sept. 5, 1692

602. Statements of John Arnold & Mary Arnold for Mary Esty & Sarah Cloyce‡

[Hand 1] These May Cartify home it may. Consarne that wee hous names are vnderritten bein⟨g⟩ dasired by sum of the Realeations of {Mary} estwek and Sareh Cleise to giue ou[Lost] [= our] obsarvation how thay behaued t⟨h⟩am salus while thay ~~ware~~ {Ramained} in B[Lost]torn [= Boston] prison we dow affirme ⟨th⟩at wee [2 words illegible] sow noe ill carreg or Behauor in tham But that thare daportmont wose varey s⟨a⟩bere and ciuell as wittnes our hands

John Arnold
Marey
Arn⟨o⟩ld

this is truee cop⟨i⟩e

[Reverse] [Hand 2] Cloyse

Notes: Sarah Cloyce had been sent from Salem to prison in Boston on May 25. See No. 217. Her name appears on a witness list, September 5, of people to address indictments against her and others, so this document almost certainly comes after that date. See No. 549. Presumably it was prepared for the grand jury and trials of Esty and Cloyce in September, although no grand jury acted on an indictment against Cloyce until January 1693, and there is no indication that it was used against either. The copyist indicates that the document belongs to the Cloyce case. Also referenced on the witness list were Mary Esty, Giles Cory, and Martha Cory. ◊ Possibly used at trial.

Essex County Court Archives, vol. 1, no. 296, Massachusetts Supreme Judicial Court, Judicial Archives, on deposit James Duncan Phillips Library, Peabody Essex Museum, Salem, MA.

Saturday, September 10, 1692

Grand Juries of Abigail Hobbs & Rebecca Jacobs

Trial of Ann Pudeator (Day 2?)

Warrant for the Apprehension of: Warrant No. 2 for the Apprehension of Daniel Andrew, George Jacobs Jr., & Elizabeth Colson, and Warrant No. 3 for the Apprehension of Elizabeth Colson in Suffolk County
  2nd of 2 dates. See No. 161 on May 17, 1692.

603. Warrant for the Apprehension of Hannah Carroll & Sarah Cole (of Salem), and Officer's Return

See also: Sept. 15, 1692.

[Hand 1] To the Sheriffe of the County of Essex or ~~their~~ his deputy
Complaint haueing ben made to us their Majesties Justices of the peace in Salem by Henery Brage of Salem labourer. against Hanah. Carrell wife of Nathaniell Carell ^{of Salem wheleright}. & Sarah Coale. wife of Abraham Coale of Salem Taylor. for that the Said Hannah Carrell & Sarah Coale Did Sometimes one of them & Sometimes Both. together Seuerall Times ^{ffeloniously} afflict Torture & Torment william Brage Son of ^{s^d} Hen^ε Brage by that diabollicall art of witchcraft, & the Said Hen^ε Brage hath giuen in bond to procecut his said Complaint to Effect. These are therfore in their majesties names to. require you fforthwith to Aprehend & Seize the Bodyes of the Said Hanah Carrell & Sarah Coale & Bringe them before their Majesties ^{Justices} of the peace in Salem in order to their Examination for wch this shall be your Sufficient warrant
Dated in Salem: 10th Sep^t 1692.

Barth° Gedney
John Hathorne
Jonathan. Corwin
John Higginson

[Reverse] [Hand 2] Sep 15th 1692
By virtue hereof I haue apprehended the body of Sarah Cole within named and left her under Guard in the town of Salem in order to her Examination

by me Geo. Herrick Dep sheriff

Sara: Coale.
Exa: 16:7 92

Notes: No record of an officer's return for the arrest of Hannah Carroll exists. ◊ Hand 1 = John Higginson Jr.; Hand 2 = George Herrick

MS Ch K 1.40, vol. 2, p. 12, Rare Books & Manuscripts, Boston Public Library, Boston, MA.

604. Report of William Arnold, Regarding Elizabeth Colson

[Hand 1] William: Ar⟨no⟩[Lost] [= Arnold] ⌃{Redding} forty three years of age or thereabouts testefieth and Saith tha⟨t⟩ on yᵉ Sabbath day last being the 4ᵗʰ Instant 7ᵇʳ :92 early in yᵉ morning [Lost] being Com̄a⟨?⟩d [= commanded] by yᵉ Constable of said Redding. Jnᵒ Parker by [Lost] to assist hi⟨m⟩ in the Execution of his office ꝑsuant to a [Lost]nt [= warrant] from: ⟨ma⟩j⟨o⟩r Wᵐ Johnson [1 word illegible] to apprehend Elisabeth Colsen &c: under Suspicion of yᵉ Sin of Witchcraft Then they Coming to yᵉ house of Widow Dastin the Constable opening yᵉ out most dore, and finding yᵉ inner dore fast that he Could not gett in, calld me to him and Said he Could not gett in and as soon as ~~I Came~~ I Came to him, we heard yᵉ back dore open then I ran behind yᵉ house & ~~then~~ then I saw said Elisab: Colsen run from yᵉ back dore and gott over into John Dixes field. and I called to her being not far from her and asked why she ran away for I would Catch her. she said nothing, but run away and ~~at last~~ quickly fell down and got up againe and ran again shaking her hand behinde her as it were striking at me. and I ran and seeing I could not gaine ground of her. I sett. my dog. at her, and he ran round about her: but would not touch her. and runing litle further there was a Stone wall and on yᵉ other [1 word overstruck] side of it a few bushes yᵗ took my sight from her a litle, being but litle behinde her, and when I came up to said Bushes I lookt into them, and ~~Could~~ Could see nothing of her, and running on further there was great Cat Came running towards me, and Stared up in my face, being but a litle distance from me, near a fence. I Endeauoured to sett my dog ~~up~~ upon her, and yᵉ dog would not minde her but went yᵉ Contrary way, and yn [= then] I offering to Strike at her wᵗʰ my Stick she seemed to run under yᵉ fence and so disappeared. and I could get sight of maid nor cat neither any more. Spending Some litle time looking about for her & further Saith not 7ᵇʳ .10ᵗʰ :92

William Arnoll

[Reverse] [Hand 2?] Wᵐ Arnold⟨ˢ⟩ Euid⟨ᵉ⟩

Notes: A later jail bill indicates that Elizabeth Colson was imprisoned in Cambridge on September 14, and was released on March 2, 1693. See No. 856. She was sixteen years old at the time of her arrest.

Suffolk Court Files, vol. 1212, docket 162281, p. 82, Massachusetts Supreme Judicial Court, Judicial Archives, Massachusetts State Archives, Boston, MA.

605. Testimony of Mary Marshall v. Elizabeth Colson

[Hand 1] 10 Septʳ 1692

The Testemony of Mary Marshall of Moldin aged fortie six yeare or there abouts Testefieth and sayth that about the Eaighth day of Aprill Last past: Elizebeth ⟨?⟩ ⌃{Coleson of Reding was} knocking me downe strikeing of Me deafe and Dumm Tortering my body in most parts; Chokeing of me quite dead for some time Likewise beating of me apon my head and bruseing of itt much; & Ringing of my Neck aboutt that my Chinn was behinde my soulder and stabing of me in the shoulders sides and brests, Likewise that this Creture aboue sᵈ did

and hes put my soulder out of Joynt, and att Often times Comeing to my howse and abroad
and at the Meeting howse in time of publick worship frighted me and Knocked me down

Sept. 10, 1692

[Hand 2] These taken from ther own mouth of said Mary Marshell before four or fiue
wittness⟨e⟩s: by yᵉ sherriff of yᵉ County of Meddˣ 7ᵇʳ 10ᵗʰ["0" written over "9"] 92

MS Ch K 1.40, vol. 2, p. 186, Rare Books & Manuscripts, Boston Public Library. Boston, MA.

Sworn Before a Justice of the Peace: Examination of Ann Foster
5ᵗʰ of 5 dates. See No. 419 on July 15, 1692

606. Indictment of Abigail Hobbs, for Covenanting†

[Hand 1] Essex in the Prouince of the Massachusetts Bay in New England Ss// ⟩ Anno R̅R̅ˢ & Reginæ Gulielmi & Mariæ Angliæ &cᵃ Quarto Annoqꝫ Domini 1692//

The Juriors for our Souᵋ Lord and Lady the King and Queen doe present That Abagaile
Hobbs of Topsfeild in the County aforesaid Single Woeman In the yeare of our Lord 1688.
In Cascoe Bay In the Prouince of Mayne in New England, Wickedly and felloniously A
Couenant with the Euill Spirritt the Deuill did make, Contrary to the peace of our Souᵋ
Lord and Lady the King & Queen theire Crowne and Dignity, and the forme of the Stattute
In that case made and Prouided.

[Reverse] [Hand 2] Indictmᵗ agst Abigail Hobbs for Couenanting with yᵉ Devill
[Hand 3] bila uera
[Hand 2?] Cogn̅

Notes: In September 1692, the Court of Oyer and Terminer in a dramatic shift of policy began trying confessors. The
grand jury hearing of Abigail Hobbs's case on September 10 appears to have been the first step in this change. Only
one dated document survives (see No. 69) to indicate that the grand jury heard the indictment on September 10, so it is
possible that the jury also met on her the day before or the day after. ◊ Hand 2 = Anthony Checkley

Essex Institute Collection, no. 23, James Duncan Phillips Library, Peabody Essex Museum, Salem, MA.

607. Indictment of Abigail Hobbs, for Afflicting Mercy Lewis†

[Hand 1] Essex in the Prouince of the Massachusetts Bay in New England Ss// ⟩ Anno R̅R̅ˢ & Reginæ Gulielmi & Mariæ Angliæ &c Quarto Annoqꝫ Domini 1692//

The Juriors for our Souᵋ Lord and Lady the King and Queen doe ꝑsent That [Hand 2]
Abigaill Hobbs of Topsfeild [Hand 1] In the County of Essex [Hand 2] **Single Wom̄a At
Salem aforesaid in the County of Essex aforsaid the Ninteenth day of Aprill** [Hand 1] In the
Yeare aforesaid and diuers other days and times as well before as after Certaine detestable

September 10, 1692

Arts Called Witchcraft and Sorceries Wickedly Mallitiously and felloniously hath used practised and Exercised At and [Hand 2] **in the Towne of Salem** [Hand 1] Aforesaid in upon and against one [Hand 2] **Mercy lewiss of Salem in ye County of Essex** [Hand 1] Aforesaid [Hand 2] **Single Woman** [Hand 1] by which said Wicked Acts the said [Hand 2] **Mercy lewis the day & yeare**[Hand 1] Aforesaid & diuers other days and times both before and after was and is Tortured Afflicted Consumed Pined Wasted and Tormented, and also for Sundry other Acts of Witchcraft by the said [Hand 2] **Abigail Hobbs** [Hand 1] Comitted and done before and Since that time against our Sou^E Lord and Lady the King and Queen theire Crowne and dignity and the forme in the Stattute in that case made and Prouided. [Hand 3] witnes
mercy lewes
mary walcott
Eliz Hubbrd
Ann putnam

[Reverse] [Hand 2] Indictm^t Ags^t Abigail Hobbs for bewitching Mercy lewis
[Hand 4] bila uera
[Hand 2?] Coḡn

Notes: Hand 2 = Anthony Checkley; Hand 3 = Thomas Putnam

Essex Institute Collection, no. 2, James Duncan Phillips Library, Peabody Essex Museum, Salem, MA.

Sworn Before the Grand Jury: Deposition of Elizabeth Hubbard v. Abigail Hobbs
2nd of 2 dates. See No. 69 on April 19, 1692

608. Indictment of Rebecca Jacobs, for Covenanting (Returned Ignoramus)†

[Hand 1] Essex in the Prouince of the Massachusetts Bay in New England Ss/ } Anno, R̄R̄^{S} & Reginæ Gulielmi & Mariæ Angliæ &c^a Quarto Annoqȝ Domini 1692

The Juriors for our Sou^E Lord and Lady the King and Queen ~~theire~~ doe ꝑsent That Rebeccah Jacobs the Wife of George Jacobs of Salem Villadge in the County of Essex ^{afors^d} husbandman In the Yeare aforesaid In Salem Villadge in the County of Essex, ^{afors^d} Wickedly and felloniously A Couenant with the Euill Spiritt the Deuill did make Contrary to the Peace of our Sou^E Lord and Lady the King and Queen theire Crowne and Dignity, And the forme in the Stattute In that Case made and Prouided.

[Reverse] [Hand 2] Indictm^t Agst Rebeckah Jacobs. for Couenanting with the Devill
[Hand 3] Igno Rama [= ignoramus]

Notes: That the grand jury did not return a true bill for covenanting and did for afflicting Elizabeth Hubbard appears inconsistent. However, a plausible possibility is that the grand jury accepted the reasoning of Rebecca Jacobs's mother that her daughter was not of sound mind (see No. 611) and concluded that the confession of Rebecca Jacobs was insufficient.
◊ Hand 2 = Anthony Checkley

Essex County Court Archives, vol. 1, no. 271, Massachusetts Supreme Judicial Court, Judicial Archives, on deposit James Duncan Sept. 10, 1692
Phillips Library, Peabody Essex Museum, Salem, MA.

609. Indictment of Rebecca Jacobs, for Afflicting Elizabeth Hubbard‡

See also: Jan. 4, 1693.

[Hand 1] Essex in the Prouince of the Massachusett Bay in New England Ss//

Anno R̄R̄ˢ & Reginæ Gulielmi & ⟨M⟩[Lost]⟨æ⟩ [= Mariae] Angliæ &cᵃ Quarto Annoqȝ Domini 1692//

The Juriors for our Souᵉ Lord & Lady the King and Queen doe present That [Hand 2] **Rebechah Jacobs Wife of** ^{**Georg⟨e⟩**}J̶o̶h̶n̶ **Jacobs of Salem Village** [Hand 1] In the County of Essex [Hand 2] **aforsaid Husbandman vpon the Eighteenth day of May** [Hand 1] In the yeare afor⟨e⟩said and diuers other days and times as well before as after C[Lost]⟨t⟩aine [= certain] detestable Arts called Witchcraft and Sorceries ⟨W⟩[Lost]edly [= wickedly] Mallitiously and felloniously hath used practi⟨s⟩[Lost] [= practised] [Lost]nd [= and] Exercised At and [Hand 2] **in Salem Village** [Hand 1] Aforesaid in upon ⟨&⟩ aga⟨in⟩st one [Hand 2] **Elizabeth Hobert of Salem** [Hand 1] aforesaid [Hand 2] **Single Woman** [Hand 1] by which said Wicked Acts the said [Hand 2] **Eliz⟨ᵃ⟩ Hobart the day & yeare** [Hand 1] Aforesaid and diuers other days and times as well before and after was and is Tortured Aflicted Consumed Pined Wasted and Tormented, a̶n̶d̶ ̶a̶l̶s̶o̶ ̶f̶o̶r̶ ̶S̶u̶n̶d̶r̶y̶ ̶o̶t̶h̶e̶r̶ ̶A̶c̶t̶s̶ o̶f̶ ̶W̶i̶t̶c̶h̶c̶r̶a̶f̶⟨t̶⟩ ̶b̶y̶ [Lost]⟨e⟩ [= the] s̶a̶i̶d̶ [Hand 2] R̶e̶b̶e̶c̶k̶a̶h̶ ̶J̶a̶c̶o̶b̶s̶ [Hand 1] C̶o̶m̶i̶t̶t̶e̶d̶ ̶a̶n̶d̶ ̶d̶o̶n̶e̶ ̶b̶e̶f̶o̶r̶e̶⟨a̶n̶d̶⟩ ̶S̶i̶n̶c̶e̶ ̶t̶h̶a̶t̶ ̶t̶i̶m̶e̶, against ^{the peace of} our Souᵉ Lord & Lady ⟨th⟩[Lost]⟨e⟩ [= their] Crowne and Dignity and the forme in the [Lost] [= statute] In that case made and Prouided

[Hand 3] ⟨wi⟩tnes

Eliz: H[Lost] [= Hubbard] [Hand 4] Jur. in Cuia [= jurat in curia]

[Hand 3] Mary [Lost] [= Walcott]

Ann p[Lost] [= Putnam]

Notes: It appears that the September grand jury returned a true bill on Rebecca Jacobs, but the case did not come to trial until January when Rebecca Jacobs was tried for afflicting Elizabeth Hubbard, who had testified against her at the September grand jury. On January 4, 1693, Rebecca Jacobs was tried and found not guilty and ordered released upon paying her fees. See No. 752. However, if her husband, George Jacobs Jr., is to be believed (see No. 913), she spent eleven months in prison, meaning that she was not released until April 1693. The claim is plausible, since the Jacobs family may indeed have not had the money to pay her fees, having had possessions taken by Sheriff Corwin. ◊ Hand 2 = Anthony Checkley; Hand 3 = Thomas Putnam

Massachusetts Archives Collection, vol. 135, no. 98. Massachusetts State Archives, Boston, MA.

Sworn Before the Grand Jury: Deposition of Elizabeth Hubbard v. Rebecca Jacobs

2ⁿᵈ of 2 dates. See No. 172 on May 18, 1692

September 10, 1692

610. Testimony of John Best Jr. v. Ann Pudeator†

[Hand 1] The testimony of John best Junear hou testifieth uppon his oath before the grand Inquest that his mother did seuerall tims in har siknis complain of ann pudeatar of salim the wife of Jacob pudeatar hou she did captur had beewiched har and that she did beleue she would kill har before she had dun: and soo she said seuerall tims duering hear siknis: until har death: allso I this deponant: did seuerall tims goo in to the wouds to fech my fathars Cowes: and I did driue goode pudeatars Cow back from. our Cowes: and I being all alone: ann pudeatar: would Chide me when I Came houm: for turning the Cow bak: by Reson of which I this deponant did Conclude said pudeater was a wich

[Hand 2] Jurat in Curia

[Reverse] [Hand 1] John best: [Hand 3] ^{Junior} [Hand 1] against pudeatar

Notes: Used at trial. ◊ Hand 2 = Stephen Sewall

Essex County Court Archives, vol. 1, no. 269, Massachusetts Supreme Judicial Court, Judicial Archives, on deposit James Duncan Phillips Library, Peabody Essex Museum, Salem, MA.

Sworn at Trial: Testimony of Sarah Churchill, Mary Warren, Elizabeth Hubbard, Ann Putnam Jr., Sarah Bibber, & Mary Walcott v. Ann Pudeator

3rd of 3 dates. See No. 555 on Sept. 6, 1692

Sworn at Trial: Testimony of Sarah Churchill v. Ann Pudeator and Testimony of Mary Warren v. Bridget Bishop, Elizabeth Cary, George Jacobs Sr., & Ann Pudeator†

2nd of 2 dates. See No. 258 on June 1, 1692

611. Petition of Rebecca Fox for Rebecca Jacobs‡

[Hand 1] To the Honble William Stoughton Esqr Cheif Judge of Their Maj^ties
Special Court of Oyer & Terminer holden at Salem &c
The Humble Petition of Rebeccah Fox Sheweth

That Whereas Rebeccah Jacobs (daughter to y^ε ["y^ε" written over "the"] Humble Petitioner) has long lyen in Prison for Witchcraft, & she at some times has uttered hard words of her self as thō she had killed her Child, which words are much accounted of as is famed

These may acquaint Your Hon^r y^t the S^d Rebeccah Jacobs is a Woman broken & distracted in her mind, & that she has been so at times above these 12 Years, & this I am ready to take my oath to, & I can bring Several Others that will do the Same, & therefore

Your Humble Petitioner thought her self bound in Conscience for your Hon^r's Informatiō to declare the same to Your Hon^r & Prays that due regard may be had thereto, that ⟨?⟩so there may not be stresse laid on the Confession of a Distracted Woman to the Prejudice of her life; So not doubting of your Hon^r's Integrity in this Matter Your Petitioner

prays to God Almighty, y^t Wisedome may not be withholden from Yo⟨w⟩r Hon^r who is
Wise, & subscribes her Self
Honble S^r

September 12, 1692

Your Hon$^{r's}$
Dutiful Serv⎯at
and
Humb^l Petition^r
Rebecca Fox

[Reverse] [Hand 2] Rebecka Fox in behalf of Rebecka Jacobs her daughter.

Notes: Arrested on May 14 (see No. 152), Rebecca Jacobs had her case heard by the grand jury on September 10. The petition to Stoughton probably places this at the time of an anticipated trial in September. She was not tried, however, until January 4, 1693, when she was found not guilty. See No. 752. The date here of the petition is approximate.

Witchcraft Papers, no. 28, Massachusetts Historical Society, Boston, MA.

Monday, September 12, 1692

612. Account for Payment Submitted by John Arnold, Jailkeeper

[Hand 1]

Boston	The Countrey is	D^r [= debtor]
1691/2:		
March 9.	To Chaines for Sarah Good & Sarah Osbourn	£ —14 —
14.	To Keeping Lewis Hutchins 8 weeks 2^s 6^d	£ 1 ———
1692. Apr. 5.	To 2 blanketts for Sarah Goods Child ⍣ order	£ —10 —
29.	To 500 foot boards to mend the Goal & prison house	£ 1 10 —
	To 4 locks for the Goal	£ —8 —
	To 2^C [= 200] Nails	£ —3 —
	To repairing the prison house	£ 2 8 —
May 10th	To 3 large Locks for the Goal	£ —9 9
23.	To Shackles for 10 prisoners	£ 2 ———
29.	To 1 p$^\varepsilon$ [= pair] of Irons for Mary Cox	£ —7 —
	To Sarah Good of Salem villedge from the 7th of March to ditto 1st June 12 weeks at 2^s 6^d	£ 1 10 —
	To Rebecca Nurse of same place from the 12th April 7 Weeks and one day at 2^s 6^d	£ —17 10.
	To George Jacob 6 weeks & 4 dayes from y^e 12th May	£ —16 4.
	To John Procter & Elizabeth his Wife from the 12th April. to the 1st of June at 5^s	£ 1 15 —
	To Susanna Martin of Amsbury from ye 2^d May to the 1st of June 4 weeks & 2 days	£ —10 8.

September 13, 1692

To Bridget Bishop als Oliver of Salem from ye 12th of May 20 days at 2s 6d ℔ week	£ —7 —
To Alice Parker of Salem from ye 12th of May to the 1st of June 20 days at 2s 6d	£ —7 —
To George Burroughs 7 weeks from 9th of May	£ —17 6.
To Sam Passanauton an Indian 8 weeks & 4 days from the 28th of Aprill at 2s 6d ℔ week	£ ⟨1⟩ 1 5.
To Roger Toothaker of Salem villidge } 5 week & 5 days from 18th May at To John Willard of Salem villidge } 2s 6d ℔ week	£ 1 8 —
To the Keeping of Sarah Osbourn from the 7th of March to the 10th of May when she died being 9 weeks & 2 days	£ 1 3 —
To yearly Salery	£ 20 ———
To mending the Prison	£ —13 —

40   16   6

John: Arnald

[Hand 2] Jnᵒ Arnald Prison [Lost?]

[Reverse] [Hand 3] [Lost?] £40:16.6. allowd
1693

Notes: The date has been confirmed from the Governor's Council Executive Records. A certified copy, dated September 16, 1846, of the original records held at Her Majesty's State Paper Office, London, exists in the Massachusetts Archives Collections, Governor's Council Executive Records, Vol. 2, 1692, p. 149. ◊ "500 foot boards": 500 foot of boards, not *footboards*.

Massachusetts Archives Collection, vol. 135, no. 24. Massachusetts State Archives, Boston, MA.

Tuesday, September 13, 1692

Grand Jury of Ann Foster

613. Complaint of Zebulon Hill v. Joan Penny
See also: Sept. 20, 1692.

[Hand 1] Zebulon Hill Complaineth in the behalfe of Our Sovereigne Lord and Lady William and Mary King and Queen vnto this Honorable Court now Assembled and sitting in Salem this 13 Day of September 1692./
Against one Goodwife Piney wife of [ ] Piney of the Towne of Gloster vpon Cape an Anne in the County of Essex for that shee the said [ ] Piney Did on the Tenth and Eleventh Day of this Instant September Afflict, torture, and Torment, your Honours Complaints Daughter

Mary; by that Diabollical Art of Witchcraft. by which the said Mary is in great Paine, and   September 13, 1692
Torture, as will be made appear:/

Zebulon Hill

[Reverse] [Hand 2] Zebulon Hill Obliges himselfe to our Souerains W^m & Mary King &
Quen of England &c. in the full & whole Sume of one hundred pounds Currant mony of
New England The Condition is that the said Zeb^l Hill shall & will procecut the within
mentioned Complaint against [ ] peney of Gloster to Effect

before me John Higginson Just^s peace

20: Sep^t 1692:

Notes: Hand 2 = John Higginson Jr.

MS Ch K 1.40, vol. 2, p. 198, Rare Books & Manuscripts, Boston Public Library, Boston, MA.

614. Summons for Witnesses v. Wilmot Redd, and Officer's Return

See also: Sept. 14, 1692.

[Hand 1] {Essex ss.} W^m & Mary by y^e Grace of God. of England Scotland ffrance &
Ireland King & Queen defend^{εs} of ye faith &c^a

To ye Sheriff of Essex Or deputy or Constable of Marblhead Greeting
Wee Comand you to Warne & giue Notice vnto ye Wife & [Hand 2] daughter of Thomas
Dodd ye Wife & daughter of Thomas Ellis John Caley Dauid Shapley wife & daughter John
Chinn. Marthah Beale, Elias Henly jun̄^r & wiffe. Benjamin Gale, Joane Bubbee, Charitty
Pittman, [Hand 3] & Jacob Wormwood,
[Hand 1] That they & Euery of them be and personaly appear at ye Court of Oyer and
Terminer holden at Salem to morrow at Eight of ye Clock in ye Morning ~~to morrow~~ there to
Testify ye Truth to ye best of your knowledge on Seuerall Indictments Exhibited against
Wilmot Redd hereof Make return fail not dated in Salem Sepr 13th 1692. & in ye fourth
yeare of Our Reign:

Stephen Sewall Cle

[Reverse] [Hand 4] Wilmot Redd/

[Hand 3] I haue warn & sumonsed all y^e persons withinmentiond accordingly except John
Calley & Ellis henly who are at sea, & beni: gale not well

sep^tber y^e 14th	℘ mee James Smith
by 7 aclock in	Cons^t in Marblehead
y^e morning	

Notes: Hand 1 = Stephen Sewall ◊ 1 wax seal.

Sept. 13, 1692   *Essex County Court Archives, vol. 2, no. 7, Massachusetts Supreme Judicial Court, Judicial Archives, on deposit James Duncan Phillips Library, Peabody Essex Museum, Salem, MA.*

615. Indictment of Ann Foster, for Afflicting Elizabeth Hubbard†

[Hand 1] Essex in the Prouince of the Massachusetts Bay in New England ss./   } Anno $\overline{RR}^s$ & Reginæ Gulielmi & Mariæ Angliæ &c^a Quarto. Annoqȝ Domini 1692.

The Juriors for o$^\varepsilon$ Sou$^\varepsilon$ Lord and Lady the King and Queen doe present that. [Hand 2] **Ann ffoster of Andivor**[Hand 1] In the County of Essex [Hand 2] **Widdow In & vpon the fifteenth Day of July** [Hand 1] In the year Afores^d and diuers other days and times as well before as after Certaine Detestable arts called Witchcrafts and Sorceries wickedly and Mallitiously and felloniously hath vsed practised and Exercised at and [Hand 2] **in the Towne of Salem in the County of Essex** [Hand 1] aforesaid in vpon & against one [Hand 2] **Eliz^a Hobert of Salem in the County of Essex** [Hand 1] aforesaid [Hand 2] **Single Woman** [Hand 1] by which Said wicked arts the Said [Hand 2] **Elizabeth Hobert the day & yeare** [Hand 1] aforesaid and diuers other days and times both before and after Was and is Tortured aflicted Consvmed Pined wasted and Tormented and also for Svndry other acts of withcraft by the Said [Hand 2] **Ann ffoster** [Hand 1] Comitted and done before and Since that time against the peace of o$^\varepsilon$ Sou$^\varepsilon$ Lord and Lady the King and Queen theire Crowne and Dignity and the forme of the Stattute in that Case made and Prouided,

[Reverse] [Hand 2] Indictm^t Agst An ffoster for bewitching Eliz^a Hobert
[Hand 3] Billa vera

Notes: Ann Foster pled guilty at her arraignment on September 17 and was condemned, but she died in prison, probably in late December 1692 or early January 1693. No person holding to a confession was executed. ◊ Hand 2 = Anthony Checkley; Hand 3 = Andrew Elliot

Essex County Court Archives, vol. 2, no. 47, Massachusetts Supreme Judicial Court, Judicial Archives, on deposit James Duncan Phillips Library, Peabody Essex Museum, Salem, MA.

616. Indictment of Ann Foster, for Afflicting Mary Walcott†

[Hand 1] Essex in the Prouince of the Massachusetts Bay in New England ss/   } Anno $\overline{RR}^s$ & Reginæ Gulielmi & Mariæ Angliæ &c$^{(a)}$ Quarto. Annoqȝ Domini 1692

The Jvriors for our Soueraigne Lord and Lady the King and Queen doe present that [Hand 2] **Ann ffoster of Andivor** [Hand 1] In the County of Essex [Hand 2] **Widow, in & vpon the fiftenth day of July** [Hand 1] In the year aforesaid and diuers other days and times as well before as after Certaine Detestable Arts called Witchcraft and Sorceries Wickedly and. Mallic̄iously and felloniously hath Vsed practised and Exercised at and [Hand 2] **in The**

Towne of Salem in the County of Essex [Hand 1] aforsaid in vpon & against one [Hand 2]
Mary Walcott of Salem [Hand 1] aforesaid [Hand 2] **Single Woman** [Hand 1] by which
Said wicked Acts the Said [Hand 2] **Mary Walcott the day & yeare** [Hand 1] aforesaid. and
diuers other dayes and times both before and after Was and is Tortured aflicted Consumed
Pined Wasted and Tormented and also for Sundry other Acts of Witchcraft by the said
[Hand 2] **Ann ffoster** [Hand 1] Comitted and done before and Since that time against the
peace of our Soueraigne Lord and Lady the King and Queen ~~and~~ theire Crowne and Dignity.
and the forme Of ["Of" written over "in"] the Stattute in that Case made and Prouided

[Reverse] [Hand 2] Indictm^t agst Ann ffoster for bewitching Mary Walcott
[Hand 2?] Cogn̄:
[Hand 3] Billa vera

Notes: Hand 2 = Anthony Checkley; Hand 3 = Andrew Elliot

MS Am 52, Rare Books & Manuscripts, Boston Public Library, Boston, MA.

617. Statements of Mary Warren, Mary Walcott, & Elizabeth Hubbard v. Ann Foster

[Hand 1] ⟨~~Ma~~⟩~~ry~~ Mary Walcot: affirmed to y^e Jury of Inquest: that Ann ffoster: of Andouer:
has afflicted. her: both: before her examination: and at her examination & since: that time:
by biting pinching & choaking of her s^d Walcot also: sayth she has: seen her s^d ffoster:
afflict: Eliz Hubbert: ~~both:~~ at ye time of her examination: by choaking & pinching of her: &
~~that~~ I beleev: s^d ffoster: is a wicth: & that: she hath afflicted me & Eliz Hubbard by
witchcraft:: ~~Sept^ε 13: 16~~ upon: her oath: Sept^ε 13: 1692

Mary: Warin affirmd to ye Jury of Inquest: that she saw Ann ffoster or her Apperition:
afflict: Mary Walcot: & Eliz Hubbert: & she also: afflicted me s^d Warin: before ye Jury of
Inquest: & I veryly believ s^d ffoster: is a witch & y^t she Afflicted: me &: ye persons
mentioned: by Witchcraft upon her oat: Sept^ε

Eliz Hubburt. Affirmed to ye Jury of Inquest: y^t Ann ffoster: both: before: and at her
examination & after: hath afflicted her: she also affirmd: that she saw s^d Ann ffoster: or her
apperition afflict. Mary Walcot. & Ann Putnum: & she ses she verily beleeves: An ffoster is
a witch: & that: she s^d ffoster: did afflict hur & y^e ~~a~~ above named persons by witch craft upon
her oath: Sept^ε 13 1692

Notes: Hand 1 = Simon Willard

MS Am 1147.1, Rare Books & Manuscripts, Boston Public Library, Boston, MA.

Retracted Before Grand Jury: Examination of Samuel Wardwell
2nd of 2 dates. See No. 538 on Sept. 1, 1692

Wednesday, September 14, 1692

*Grand Juries of Sarah Buckley (Day 1), Margaret Jacobs, Mary Lacey Sr.,
Wilmot Redd & Samuel Wardwell*

Trials of Wilmot Redd & Samuel Wardwell

Officer's Return: Summons for Witnesses v. Wilmot Redd
2nd of 2 dates. See No. 614 on Sept. 13, 1692

618. Indictment of Sarah Buckley, for Afflicting Ann Putnam Jr.†
See also: Jan. 4, 1693.

[Hand 1] Essex in the Prouince of the Massachusetts Bay in New England Ss//	Anno $\overline{RR}^s$ & Reginæ Gulielmi & Mariæ Angliæ &c Quarto Annoqʒ Domini 1692.

The Juriors for our Sou^E Lord and Lady the King and Queen doe present That [Hand 2] **Sarah Buckley Wife of William Buckley of Salem** [Hand 1] In the County of Essex [Hand 2] **Shoomaker In & vpon the Eighteenth day of May** [Hand 1] In the yeare aforesaid and diuers other days and times as well before as after Certaine detestable Arts called Witchcraft or Sorceries Wickedly Mallitiously and felloniously hath used practised and Exercised At and [Hand 2] **in the Towne of Salem in the County of Essex** [Hand 1] Aforesaid in upon & against one [Hand 2] **Ann: Puttman of Salem** [Hand 1] aforesaid [Hand 2] **Single Woman** [Hand 1] by which said Wicked Acts yᵉ said [Hand 2] **An Puttnam yᵉ Day & yeare** [Hand 1] Aforesaid and diuers other days and times both before and after was and is Tortured Aflicted Consumed Pined Wasted & Tormented, and also for sundry other Acts of Witchcraft by the said [Hand 2] **Sarah Buckley Comitted** [Hand 1] and done before and Since that time against Our Sou^E Lord and Lady the King & Queen theire Crowne & Dignity and the forme in the Stattute In that case made and Prouided.

[Reverse] [Hand 2] Sarah Buckley An Putman
[Hand 3] Billa vera
[Hand 2] Pone Se
[Hand 4] the jury finds the person by this indittement not gilty
[Hand 5] non Cull [= not guilty]

Notes: Sarah Buckley's case was heard by the grand jury on September 14 and 15, but she was not tried until January 4, 1693, when she was found not guilty. See No. 755. The notation of a true bill was written in September 1692 in the same handwriting that recorded the true bills on the indictments of Ann Foster, Rebecca Eames, Samuel Wardwell, Margaret Scott, Wilmot Redd, Mary Whittredge, and Margaret Jacobs between September 13 and 15. There is no record of Eames's trial, but she affirms that she was tried and condemned but remained in prison (see No. 888). Wardwell, Scott, and Redd went to trial that September and were executed. Jacobs and Whittredge, like Buckley, were tried in January 1693 and found not guilty. See No. 754 & No. 756. For Foster see note to No. 615.◊ Hand 2 = Anthony Checkley; Hand 3 = Andrew Elliot

Massachusetts Archives Collection, vol. 135, no. 23. Massachusetts State Archives, Boston, MA.

Sworn Before the Grand Jury: Deposition of Elizabeth Hubbard v. Sarah Buckley September 14, 1692
2nd of 3 dates. See No. 169 on May 18, 1692

Sworn Before the Grand Jury: Testimony of Mary Walcott v. Sarah Buckley
2nd of 3 dates. See No. 171 on May 18, 1692

619. Indictment of Margaret Jacobs, for Afflicting Elizabeth Hubbard‡
See also: Jan. 4, 1693.

[Hand 1] Essex in the Prouince of the Massachusetts Bay in New England Ss// } Anno R̅R̅ˢ & Reginæ Gulielmi & Mariæ Angliæ &cᵃ Quarto Annoqȝ Domini 1692.

The Juriors for our Soueraigne lord & lady the King & Queen doe present That [Hand 2] **Margarett Jacobs of Salem Single Woman** [Hand 1] In the County of Essex [Hand 2] **aforesaid Att or vpon the Eleuenth day of May** [Hand 1] In the yeare aforesaid and diuers other days and times as well before as after Certaine detestable Arts called Witchcrafts & Sorceries Wickedly Mallitiously and felloniously hath used practised and Exercised At and [Hand 2] **in the Towne of Salem in the County of Essex** [Hand 1] Aforesaid in upon & against one [Hand 2] **Elizabeth Hobert of Salem** [Hand 1] Aforesaid [Hand 2] **Single Woman** [Hand 1] by which said Wicked Acts the sa⟨i⟩d [Hand 2] [1 word overstruck] **Elizabeth Hobert the day & yeare** [Hand 1] aforesaid & diuers othe[Lost] [= other] days and times both before and after was and is Tortured Aflicted Consumed Wasted Pined and Tormented, and also for sundry other Acts of Witchcraft by the said [Hand 2] **Margarett Jacobs Comitted** [Hand 1] and done before and since that time against our Souᵉ Lord and Lady the King & Queen their Crowne and Dignity and the forme in the Stattu{t}e in that Case made and Prouided.

[Reverse] [Hand 2] Indictmᵗ Margarett Jacobs, bewiching Elizabeth Hobert
[Hand 3] Billa vera
[Hand 4] Ponet Se.
[Hand 5] Not guilty
2
Salem Court 3ᵈ Januᵉ 1692/3
[Hand 6] Entered on record

Notes: Based on the handwriting of "Billa vera" on the indictment, this was presented in September 1692. As with other cases, the trial was not held till the following January. The indictment date is an approximation based on the probability that the grand jury met on Margaret Jacobs between September 13 and 15. She was tried on January 4, 1693, and found not guilty. See No. 754. The January 3 date on this document probably refers to when the indictment was noted for the trial the next day. ◊ Hand 2 = Anthony Checkley; Hand 3 = Andrew Elliot

Massachusetts Archives Collection, vol. 135, no. 100. Massachusetts State Archives, Boston, MA.

September 14, 1692

620. Indictment of Mary Lacey Sr., for Afflicting Elizabeth Hubbard†

[Hand 1] Essex in the Prouince 　　　Anno $\overline{RR}^s$ & Reginæ Gulielmi & Mariæ Angliæ &
of the Massachusetts Bay in New 　　Quarto. Annoqȝ Domini 1692
England

The Jvrors for o^ɛ Sou^ɛ Lord and Lady the King and Queen doe Present that [Hand 2] **Mary lacey Wife of lawrence lacey of Andivor** [Hand 1] in the County of Essex [Hand 2] **Husbandman vpon the Twentieth day of July** [Hand 1] In the year aforesaid and diuers other dayes and times as well before as after Certaine detestable Arts called Witchcraft and Sorceries wickedly Mallitiously and felloniously hath Vsed Practised and Exercised at and [Hand 2] **in the Towne of Salem in the County of Essex** [Hand 1] aforesaid in vpon and against one [Hand 2] **Elizabeth Hobert of Salem** [Hand 1] aforesaid [Hand 2] **Single Woman** [Hand 1] by which Said wicked Acts the said [Hand 2] **Eliz^a Hobert ye day & yea^ɛ** [Hand 1] aforesaid and diuers other dayes and Times Both Before and after was and is Tortured aflicted Consum^d Pined Wasted and Tormented and also for Sundry other Acts of witchcraft by the Said [Hand 2] **Mary lacey** [Hand 1] Comitted and done Before and Since that Time against the Peace of o^ɛ Sou^ɛ Lord and Lady the King and Queen theire Crowne and Dignity and the forme of Stattute in that Case made and Prouided.

[Reverse] [Hand 2] Indictm^t ags^t Mary lacey for bewitching Eliz^a Hobert
[Hand 3] Billa vera

Notes: Mary Lacey Sr. pled guilty at her arraignment and was condemned on September 17, but released in January or February, 1693 after having spent seven months in prison. See No. 918. ◊ Hand 2 = Anthony Checkley; Hand 3 = Andrew Elliot

Essex County Court Archives, vol. 2, no. 49, Massachusetts Supreme Judicial Court, Judicial Archives, on deposit James Duncan Phillips Library, Peabody Essex Museum, Salem, MA.

621. Indictment of Mary Lacey Sr., for Afflicting Mercy Lewis

[Hand 1] Essex in the Prouince 　　　Anno $\overline{RR}^s$ & Reginæ Gulielmi & Mariæ Angliæ &c^a
of the Massachusetts Bay in New 　　Quarto Annoqȝ Domini 1692//
England
ss//

The Jurors for our Sou^ɛ Lord and Lady the King and Queen doe ꝑsent That [Hand 2] **Mary Lacey Wife of Lawrence Lacey of Andivo^ɛ** [Hand 1] In the County of Essex [Hand 2] **Husbandman The Twentieth day of July** [Hand 1] In the Yeare aforesaid and diuers other days and times as well before as after Certaine detestable Arts Called Witchcraft & Sorceries Wickedly Mallitiously and felloniously hath used practised and Exercised At and [Hand 2] **in the Towne of Salem in the County of Essex** [Hand 1] Aforesaid in upon and against one [Hand 2] **Mercy Lewis of Salem** [Hand 1] Aforesaid [Hand 2] **Single Woman** [Hand 1] by which said Wicked Acts the said [Hand 2] **Mercy lewis the day & yea^ɛ** [Hand 1] Aforesaid and diuers other days and times both before and after was and is Tortured Aflicted Consumed Pined Wasted and Tormented, and also for Sundry other Acts of Witchcraft by

the said [Hand 2] **Mary lacey** [Hand 1] Comitted and done before and Since that time   September 14, 1692
against the Peace of Our Sou$^{\varepsilon}$ Lord & Lady the King and Queen theire Crowne and
Dignity and the forme of the Stattute In that case made and Prouided.
[Hand 2?] Cogn̄:

[Reverse] [Hand 2] Indictm^{t} ags^{t} Mary lacey for bewitching Mercy lewis
[Hand 3] Billa vera
[Hand 2?] Cogn̄.

Notes: Hand 2 = Anthony Checkley; Hand 3 = Andrew Elliot

Essex Institute Collection, no. 31, James Duncan Phillips Library, Peabody Essex Museum, Salem, MA.

622. Depositions of Elizabeth Hubbard, Mercy Lewis, & Mary Warren v. Mary Lacey Sr.

[Hand 1] Eliz: Hubert affirmd to y^{e} grand Inquest: that: she hath: seen Mary lascy sen^{r}
afflict: Joseph Ballards wife of Andover: she sayth also: that: s^{d} Mary Lascy did at y^{e} time of
her examination: afflict her s^{d} Eliz Hubbert: & Mercy Lewis: & she ["she" written over "I"]
dos beleev: s^{d} Mary lascy was a witch: & afflicted me & y^{e} above s^{d} persons: by witchcraft:
but: she never afflicted her: s^{d} Hubberd since: she Confessed::   upon oath: Sept$^{\varepsilon}$ 14: 1692

Mercy lewis: affirmd to y^{e} grand Inquest: that se [= she] saw: Mary Lascy sen^{r} afflict Joseph
Ballards: wife of Andover: she saith also: that Ma[Lost] [= Mary] Lascy: sen^{r} {afl⟨i⟩ct⟨e⟩d}
her s^{d} Lewis: & Eliz Hubbert: at y^{e} time of her examina[Lost] [= examination] but since she
has not hurt h⟨e⟩r she ["she" written over "I"] sayth: she beleeves s^{d} Lacy wa[Lost] [= was] a
witch: & afflicted: her: & y^{e} above named persons: by witchc⟨raft⟩
Sept$^{\varepsilon}$ y^{e} 14: 1692 upon oath

Mary Warin affirmd to y^{e} grand Inquest: that she saw Mary Lascy sen$^{\varepsilon}$ ⟨E⟩ Afflict: Eliz
Hubbert: & Mercy Lewis: at y^{e} time o⟨f⟩ her examination she ownd it:
upon her former oath Sept$^{\varepsilon}$ 14: 1692,

[Reverse] Wittneses [Hand 2] ag^{t} Mary Lacey.

Notes: Hand 1 = Simon Willard; Hand 2 = Stephen Sewall

*Essex County Court Archives, vol. 2, no. 50, Massachusetts Supreme Judicial Court, Judicial Archives, on deposit James Duncan
Phillips Library, Peabody Essex Museum, Salem, MA.*

623. Indictment of Wilmot Redd, for Afflicting Elizabeth Booth (Returned Ignoramus)†

| [Hand 1] Essex in the Prouince of the Massachusetts Bay in New England Ss// | Anno $\overline{RR}^s$ & Reginæ Gulielmi & Mariæ Angliæ &c^a Quarto Annoqʒ Domini 1692 |

The Juriors for our Sou^ε Lord and Lady the King & Queen doe present That [Hand 2] **Willmott Redd Wife of Samuel Redd of Marblehead** [Hand 1] In the County of Essex [Hand 2] **ffisherman vpon the Thirty first day of May** [Hand 1] In the Yeare afores^d and diuers other days and times as well before as after Certaine detestable Arts called Witchcraft and Sorceries Wickedly Mallitiously and felloniously hath used practised and exercised At and [Hand 2] **in the Towne of Salem in the County of Essex** [Hand 1] Aforesaid in upon and against one [Hand 2] **Eliz^a Booth of Salem** [Hand 1] Aforesaid [Hand 2] **Single Woman** [Hand 1] by which said Wicked Acts ye said [Hand 2] ~~Elizabeth Booth~~ ["Elizabeth Booth" written over "Willmott Redd"] ∧{**Eliz^a Booth**} **The day & yeare** [Hand 1] Aforesaid and diuers other days and times both before and after was and is Tortured Aflicted Consumed Pined Wasted and Tormented and also for Sundry other Acts of Witchcraft by the said [Hand 2] **Willmott Redd.** [Hand 1] Comitted and done before and Since that time against [Hand 2] ∧{**the peace of**} [Hand 1] our Sou^ε Lord & Lady the King & Queen theire Crowne and Dignity and the forme [Hand 2] **Of** ["Of" written over "in"] [Hand 1] the Stattute in that case made and Prouided.

[Reverse] [Hand 2] Indictm^t v^εs Willmott Redd for: bwitching Eliz^a Booth
[Hand 3] Ignoramus

Notes: Hand 2 = Anthony Checkley; Hand 3 = Andrew Elliot

Essex County Court Archives, vol. 2, no. 5, Massachusetts Supreme Judicial Court, Judicial Archives, on deposit James Duncan Phillips Library, Peabody Essex Museum, Salem, MA.

624. Indictment of Wilmot Redd, for Afflicting Elizabeth Hubbard†

| [Hand 1] Essex in the province of the Massachusetts Bay in New England ss | Anno $\overline{RR}^s$ & Reginæ Gulielmi & Mariæ Angliæ , &c^c Quarto Annoqʒ Domini 1692. |

The Jvriors for our Sou^ε Lord and Lady the King & Queen doe present that [Hand 2] **Willmott Redd wife of Samuel Redd of Marblehead** [Hand 1] In the County of Essex [Hand 2] **ffisherman vpon the Thirty first day of May** [Hand 1] In the year aforesaid and diuers other days and times as well before as after Certaine Detestable Arts. called Witchcraft and Sorceries Wickedly Mallitiously and felloniously hath vsed practised and Exercised at and [Hand 2] **in the Towne of Salem in the County of Essex** [Hand 1] aforesaid in Vpon and against one [Hand 2] **Eliz^a Hobert of Salem aforsaid in the County of Essex** [Hand 1] aforesaid [Hand 2] **Single Woman** [Hand 1] by which said wicked Acts the said [Hand 2] **Eliz^a Hobert the day & yeare** [Hand 1] aforesaid and Diuers other dayes and times

both before and after was and is Tortured aflicted Consumed Pined Wasted and Tormented   Sept. 14, 1692
and also for Svndry other Acts of Witchcraft by the said [Hand 2] **Willmott Redd** [Hand 1]
Comitted and done before and Since that time against the peace of oᵉ Soueraigne Lord and
Lady the King and Queen theire Crowne and Dignity And the forme [Hand 2?] **Of** ["Of"
written over "in"] [Hand 1] the Stattute in that Case made and Prouided.

[Reverse] [Hand 2] Indictmᵗ agst Willmott Redd for bewitching Elizᵃ Hobert
[Hand 3] Billa vera
[Hand 4] Ponet se

Notes: Hand 2 = Anthony Checkley; Hand 3 = Andrew Elliot

Essex County Court Archives, vol. 2, no. 9, Massachusetts Supreme Judicial Court, Judicial Archives, on deposit James Duncan Phillips Library, Peabody Essex Museum, Salem, MA.

Sworn Before the Grand Jury and at Trial: Deposition of Elizabeth Hubbard v. Wilmot Redd
2ⁿᵈ of 2 dates. See No. 248 on May 31, 1692

Sworn Before the Grand Jury and at Trial: Deposition of Ann Putnam Jr. v. Wilmot Redd
2ⁿᵈ of 2 dates. See No. 249 on May 31, 1692

Sworn Before the Grand Jury and at Trial: Deposition of Mary Walcott v. Wilmot Redd
2ⁿᵈ of 2 dates. See No. 250 on May 31, 1692

Sworn Before the Grand Jury and at Trial: Deposition of Mary Warren v. Wilmot Redd
2ⁿᵈ of 2 dates. See No. 251 on May 31, 1692

625. Statements of Sarah Dodd & Ambrose Gale v. Wilmot Redd

[Hand 1] Sarah Dod: Affirmd: upon her oath to yᵉ grand Inquest: that: she heard: Mʳˢ
Simse threatned to have Wilmot Redd: before a Majestrate. for some of sᵈ Redds
misdemeanures. sᵈ Redd. wisht sᵈ Simse might never any wayes ease nature before she did it:
& soon after; to this deponanᵗˢ knowledge it fell out with: Mʳˢ Simse: acording: sᵈ Redds
wish this she ownd before: sᵈ Jury of inquest: Septʳ 14: 1692

Mʳ Ambros Gale: Affirmd that: Mʳˢ Simse was: aboᵗ that time {or soon after}: so: afflicted:
as was then Reported & ~~upon that~~ [1–2 words overstruck]: Septemᵉ 14: 1692
[Hand 2] Juriat in Curia

[Reverse] [Hand 3] Sarah Dodd: euidence Agst: Willmott Redd

Notes: Used at trial. ◊ Hand 1 = Simon Willard; Hand 2 = Stephen Sewall; Hand 3 = Anthony Checkley

Essex County Court Archives, vol. 2, no. 15, Massachusetts Supreme Judicial Court, Judicial Archives, on deposit James Duncan Phillips Library, Peabody Essex Museum, Salem, MA.

626. Indictment of Samuel Wardwell, for Covenanting†

[Hand 1] Essex in the province of the Massachusetts bay in New England ss// } An° $\overline{RR}$s & Reginæ Gulielmi & Mariæ Angliæ &c Quarto, Anoq₃ $\overline{Dom}$ 1692

The Jurio^{E}s for o^r Sov^r lord & lady the King & Queen p^{E}sent Samuel Wardell of Andivor In the County of Essex Carpent^E About Twenty years agoe in the Towne of Andivor In the County of Essex aforesaid Wickedly & felloniously he the Said Samuel Wardell with the Evill Speritt the Devill ∧{A Couenant} did make Wherin he promised to honor Worship & beleiue the devill Contray to the Stattute of King James The first in that behalfe made & provided. And Against the peace of Soveraigne Lord & Lady the King & Queen their Crown & dignity

[Reverse] Indictm^t agst Saml Wardell for Couenanting wth y^e Devill 1692 [1 word overstruck]
[Hand 2] Billa vera
[Hand 3] Ponet se.

Notes: Hand 1 = Anthony Checkley; Hand 2 = Andrew Elliot

Essex County Court Archives, vol. 2, no. 55, Massachusetts Supreme Judicial Court, Judicial Archives, on deposit James Duncan Phillips Library, Peabody Essex Museum, Salem, MA.

627. Indictment of Samuel Wardwell, for Afflicting Martha Sprague

[Hand 1] Essex in the Prouince of the Massachusetts Bay in New England ss/ } Anno $\overline{RR}$^{s} & Reginæ Gulielmi & Mariæ Angliæ &c Quarto Annoq₃ Domini 1692.

The Juriors for our Sou^E Lord and Lady the King and Queen doe present That [Hand 2] **Samuel Wardell of Andivor** [Hand 1] In the County of Essex [Hand 2] **Carpenter on or about the fifteenth day of August** [Hand 1] In the yeare aforesaid and diuers other days and times as Well before as after Certaine detestable Arts called Witchcraft and Sorceries Wickedly Mallitiously and felloniously hath used practised & Exercised At and [Hand 2] **in the Towne of Boxford in the County of Essex** [Hand 1] Aforesaid in upon and against One [Hand 2] **Martha Sprague of Boxford in the County of Essex** [Hand 1] Aforesaid [Hand 2] **Single Woman** [Hand 1] by which said Wicked Acts the said [Hand 2] **Martha Sprague the day & yeare** [Hand 1] Aforesaid and diuers other days and times ~~both~~ both before and after was and is Tortured Aflicted Consumed Pined ~~an~~ Wasted and Tormented, and also for sundry ∧{other} Ac⟨ts⟩ of Witchcraft by the said [Hand 2] **Samuel Wardell** [Hand 1] Comitted and done before and Since that time against the peace of Our Soueraigne Lord and Lady the King and Queen theire Crowne and dignity And the ["the" written over "in"] forme in the Stattute ∧{in that case} made and Prouided.

[Reverse] [Hand 2] Indictm^t against Samuel Wardell for bewitching Martha Sprague
[Hand 3] Billa vera
[Hand 4] Ponet se

Notes: Hand 2 = Anthony Checkley; Hand 3 = Andrew Elliot   September 14, 1692

Essex County Court Archives, vol. 2, no. 56, Massachusetts Supreme Judicial Court, Judicial Archives, on deposit James Duncan Phillips Library, Peabody Essex Museum, Salem, MA.

628. Depositions of Martha Sprague, Mary Walcott, & Mary Warren v. Samuel Wardwell

[Hand 1] Martha Spreag: Aged 16: years Affirmd to ye grand Inquest: that Sam^{ll} Wardwell: has afflicted her: both before: his examination & at ye time of it: by ~~biti~~ pinching & sticking pinse into her & striking: her downe: & yesterday: when I had a warant to come to Court s^d Wardwell: did greivously afflict~~e~~ {me}: I also {have} seen s^d Wardwell afflict Rose ffoster & her mother: & I veryly beleev he is a wizzard & that he afficted me &: y^e above mentioned by acts of witchcraft⟨s⟩ Sept$^{\varepsilon}$ 14:, 1692

[Hand 2] Jurat

[Hand 1] Mary Warin: affirmd: to: Jury of Inquest that Sam^{ll} Wardwell: hath: often afflicted her & that: he now: {before} ~~with~~: y^e grand Inquest hath: afflicted her: also: she s^d that y^t on y^e day & at y^e time of s^d Wardwels examination ~~s^d war~~ {he} d⟨i⟩d afflict Martha Spreag: & she veryly beleevs: s^d Wardwell is a wizzard and y^t he afflicted her and martha Spreag: by witch craft. ~~sep~~

Sept$^{\varepsilon}$ 14: 1692. upon her oath

[Hand 2] Jurat.

[Hand 1] Mary Walcot: affirmd to y^e grand Inquest: that she saw Sam^{ll} Wardwell or his Apperition pull Martha Spreag off from her horse: as she was ~~going~~ riding out of Salem: & ~~verily~~ beleevs he did it by witchcraft: ⟨S⟩ Septr 14: 1692: upon oath   [Hand 2] Jurat

[Reverse] [Hand 3] Wittnesses ver Wardwell Martha Sprague Mary Warren Mary Wallcott

Notes: Possibly used at trial. ◊ Hand 1 = Simon Willard; Hand 2 = Stephen Sewall

Essex County Court Archives, vol. 2, no. 57, Massachusetts Supreme Judicial Court, Judicial Archives, on deposit James Duncan Phillips Library, Peabody Essex Museum, Salem, MA.

629. Testimony of Charity Pitman v. Wilmot Redd†

[Hand 1] The Testimony of Charity Pitman of Marblehead

This deponent aged twenty nine years affirms, that about five years agoe, Mrs Syms of ye Towne having lost some linnen which she suspected Martha Laurence the girle which then lived with Wilmott Redd had taken up, desired the deponent to goe with her to Wilmott Redds, and demanding the same, having many words about the same, Mrs Syms told her, that if she would not deliver them, she would go to Salem ∧{to mr Hathorne,} and gett a speciall warrant for her servant girle; upon which the s^d Redd told her in my hearing, that she wished that she might never mingere [= urinate], nor cacare [= defecate], if she did not goe, and some short time after the deponent observed that the s^d Mrs Syms was taken with the distemper of the dry Belly=ake, and so continued many monethes during her stay in the Towne, and was not cured whilst she tarryed in the Cowntrey,

September 14, 1692   [Hand 2] Jurat in Curia

[Reverse] [Hand 3] Charity Pittman agst Willmott Redd

Notes: Used at trial. ◊ Hand 2 = Stephen Sewall; Hand 3 = Anthony Checkley

Essex County Court Archives, vol. 2, no. 14, Massachusetts Supreme Judicial Court, Judicial Archives, on deposit James Duncan Phillips Library, Peabody Essex Museum, Salem, MA.

630. Deposition of Joseph Ballard v. Samuel Wardwell†

[Hand 1] The testimony of Joseph Ballard of andouer eaged about 41 yeares saith that my brother John ballard told me that Samuel Wardel told him that I had reported that he had bewich{ed} my wife these wordes weare spoken before I had ⟨f⟩ any knolidg of my wife being aflicted by wichcraft after I meting with said Samuel Wardel prisnor at the bar I told him that I douteed that he was gilty of hurting my wife for I had no sutch thoughts nor had spoken any sutch wordes of him or any other parson and thearefore I ~~was~~ doe not know but you are gilty
[Hand 2] & further yᵗ Samˡˡ Wardwell Owned to this deponent that he had Spoke it to my Brother.

Jurat in Curia.

[Reverse] [Hand 3] Joseph Ballard. depo agst Samˡ Wardwell

Notes: Used at trial. ◊ Hand 2 = Stephen Sewall; Hand 3 = Anthony Checkley

Essex County Court Archives, vol. 2, no. 61, Massachusetts Supreme Judicial Court, Judicial Archives, on deposit James Duncan Phillips Library, Peabody Essex Museum, Salem, MA.

631. Deposition of Thomas Chandler v. Samuel Wardwell†

[Hand 1] The tistimony of Thomas Chandler aged about 65 who saith that I haue often hard Samuell wardle of Andour till yung person thire fortine and he was much adicted to that and mayd sport of it and farther saith not

[Hand 2] Jurat in Curia.

[Reverse] [Hand 3] Thomas Chandler depo agst Samˡ Wardwell

Notes: Used at trial. ◊ Hand 2 = Stephen Sewall; Hand 3 = Anthony Checkley

Essex County Court Archives, vol. 2, no. 60, Massachusetts Supreme Judicial Court, Judicial Archives, on deposit James Duncan Phillips Library, Peabody Essex Museum, Salem, MA.

632. Deposition of Ephraim Foster v. Samuel Wardwell†

[Hand 1] The deposetion of Ephraim ffoster of Andovr: aged about thirty fiue ["fiue" written over "six"] years this deponant testifyeth and sayeth: that he heard: Samuell wardwall: the prisoner now at the bare ~~tell:~~ tell my wife: that she should haue fiue gurls: before: she should:

haue: a son: which thing is Come to pase: and I heard him tell dority Eames hur forten [= fortune]: ~~which he did~~: and I have heard: said dority: say after that she beliued wardwall was a: witch. or Els he Cold neuer tell what he did: and I tooke knotes: that: said wardwall: would look in their hand: and then would Cast his Eyes down: [Hand 2?] ^{vpon y^e ground} [Hand 1] allways before he told Eny thing this I haue both seen and heard seuerall times: and about seuerall persons [Hand 2] & y^t he Could make Cattle come to him when he pleased

Jurat in Curia

[Reverse] [Hand 3] ⟨f⟩foster & Martin Vs Wardw^ell

Notes: Used at trial. ◊ Hand 2 = Stephen Sewall

Essex County Court Archives, vol. 2, no. 58, Massachusetts Supreme Judicial Court, Judicial Archives, on deposit James Duncan Phillips Library, Peabody Essex Museum, Salem, MA.

633. Deposition of Abigail Martin & John Bridges v. Samuel Wardwell†

[Hand 1] the deposetion of Abigell Marten of Andaer Aged about sixteen years this deponan[Lost] [= deponent] Testifyeth and sayeth that some time last winter: Samuell wardwall being at my fat⟨he⟩r⟨s⟩ hows: with John ffarnom: I heard said John farnom ask: said wardwall his forteen [= fortune]: whi[Lost] [= which] he did: and told him that: {he} was in love with a gurll: but: should be crost: & should goe to the Sutherd: which said farnom oned to be his thought: said wardwall furthr: told he had like to be shot with a gon: & should haue a foall of from his hors or should haue: which: said farnom: after: oned that he told Right:

And further I heard him tell Jeams bridges his forten: that he loued a gurll at forteen years ould: which: said bridges: oned to be the truth: but Cold not imagin how said wardwall knew: for he never: spake of it: John bridges father of said ieams: bridges sayeth: he heard Jeam say I wonder how wardwall cold teell: so true

[Hand 2] Jurat in Curia, By both

[Reverse] [Hand 3] Abiga^l Martin & James Bridges dep^o v^e s Saml Wardwell
[Hand 4?] ⟨p?⟩

Notes: Used at trial. ◊ Hand 2 = Stephen Sewall; Hand 3 = Anthony Checkley

Essex County Court Archives, vol. 2, no. 62, Massachusetts Supreme Judicial Court, Judicial Archives, on deposit James Duncan Phillips Library, Peabody Essex Museum, Salem, MA.

Thursday, September 15, 1692

Grand Juries of Sarah Buckley (Day 2), Rebecca Eames, Margaret Scott, Job Tookey, & Mary Whittredge

Officer's Return: Warrant for the Apprehension of Hannah Carroll & Sarah Cole (of Salem)
2nd of 2 dates. See No. 603 on Sept. 10, 1692

634. Deposition of Thomas Greenslit v. George Burroughs

[Hand 1] Th° Greenslitt: aged about forty years [Hand 2] ^{being deposed} [Hand 1] Testifieth y^t about the first breaking out of th{e} ["the" written over "these"] last Indian warre ["e" written over "s"] {he} being att the house of Capt [Hand 2] {Joshua} [Hand 1] Scotto att Black point, ~~this deponent saith y^t~~ he saw m$^\varepsilon$ [Hand 3] ^{George} [Hand 1] Burrow's [Hand 2] ^{who was lately Executed at Salem} [Hand 1] lift a gunn of six ffoott Barrell [Hand 3] ^{or thereabouts} [Hand 1] putting the ["the" written over "his"] forefinger of his right hand into the muzell of s^d gunn and [Hand 2] ^{that he} [Hand 1] held ~~her~~ [Hand 2] ^{it} [Hand 1] out att arms end only wth ^{thatt} finger, and further this deponent testifieth that ~~about~~ [Hand 2] {at} [Hand 1] the same time he saw the s^d Burrows Take up a full barr^{ll} ofe molasses wth butt two of ~~his~~ fingers [Hand 2] ^{of one of his hands} [Hand 1] in the bung and carry itt from ye stage head to the door att the end of the stage wthout letting itt downe [Hand 3] & that Liu^t Richd Hunniwell & John Greinslett were then present & some others y^t are dead.

Sepr. 15. 92.   Thomas † Greinslit
                                        his Marke.
                                        Jurat.

Notes: The circumstances of this deposition remain unclear, but the document helps affirm the centrality of the Burroughs case to the proceedings as they developed. Burroughs had already been tried and executed when this deposition was sworn before the Court of Oyer and Terminer. Charles W. Upham maintained, without supplying evidence, that many depositions were taken after the trials and "surreptitiously" placed in the records (II, 797–798). Greenslit may have cooperated here with the court in a vain attempt to save the life of his mother, Ann Pudeator, who was executed

September 22. The document appears very much like a trial document, although it obviously is not. Of the extant comments regarding the feats of strength demonstrated by Burroughs, Greenslit's account is the only one not based on hearsay claims. Whether the account is credible or not is impossible to determine. See note for No. 635. ◊ Hand 3 = Stephen Sewall

Essex County Court Archives, vol. 2, no. 33, Massachusetts Supreme Judicial Court, Judicial Archives, on deposit James Duncan Phillips Library, Peabody Essex Museum, Salem, MA.

635. Deposition of Thomas Greenslit v. George Burroughs, Second Version

[Hand 1] Prouince of y^e Mattathusets Bay in New England Essex Sc.

The deposition of Thomas Greinslitt aged about forty yeares Testifieth

That about the breaking Out of this last Indian Warr being at ye house of Capt Scottow's at black point he Saw m^r George B⟨?⟩arroughs lift and hold Out a gunn of Six foot barrell or thereabouts putting ye forefinger of his right hand into ye Muzle of S^d gunn and So held it Out at Armes End Only with y^t finger and further this deponent Testifieth that at ye Same ^{time} he Saw the Said Burroughs take vp a full barrell of Malasses wth but two fingers of one of his hands in the bung & Carry it from ye Stage head to ye Door at ye End of the Stage without letting it downe & that Liu^t Richard Hunniwell & John Greinslitt & Some other persons that are ~~dead~~ Since dead Were then present.
Salem Sepr 15th 1692. Thomas Greinslitt appeared before Thier Maj^ties Justices of Oyer & Terminer in Open Court & Made Oath that ye aboue Mentioned perticulars & Euery part of them were True

attest Step. Sewall Clr

[Reverse] Thomas Grein Euidence ver. Burr

[Hand 2] Court O & T by As^t Aug^e 2. 92

Notes: This appears to be a cleaned-up version of the previous document. The August 2 date may suggest that Greenslit prepared the deposition for the trial of Burroughs in August but that for some reason it was not introduced. If this is the case, it may indicate that Greenslit's deposition was sworn in September after Burroughs had been executed so that the record would be clarified. This offers an alternative hypothesis to the idea that he gave the deposition in an attempt to save his mother, Ann Pudeator. See note for No. 634. ◊ Hand 1 = Stephen Sewall

Witchcraft Papers, no. 10, Massachusetts Historical Society. Boston, MA.

636. Memorandum: Major Brown, Thomas Evans, Thomas Ruck, Martha Tyler, & Sarah Wilson Jr. v. George Burroughs‡

[Hand 1] Memorand^m in m^r George Burroughs Tryall besides y^e written Euidences y^r was Sworne Seu^ll who gaue y^rs by word {of} mouth
Majo^e Browne holding Out a heauy Gun wth One hand
Thomas Ruck of his Sudden coming in after y^m & y^t he could Tell ~~y^e~~ his thoughts.
Thomas Euans. y^t he Carried Out Barr^lls Molossus & Meat &c out of a Canoo.
Whilst ~~y^e~~ ⟨?⟩⟨of⟩ his mate. went to y^e fort for hands to help Out wth y^m
{These Since y^e Execuīon of mr Burro:} Sarah Wilson Confesst y^t y^e night before mr Burroughs was Executed. y^t y^r was a great Meeting of y^e witches Nigh Sarj^t Chandlers y^t mr

September 15, 1692   Bur. was y^r & y^y had y^e Sac^t [= sacrament] & ~~at his going away he~~ after y^y had done he
tooke leaue & bid y^m Stand to y^r faith & not own any thing
Martha Tyler Saith y^e Same wth Sarah Wilson & Seuerall others

[Reverse] [Hand 2] Mr Burr$\bar{s}$

Notes: As with the previous documents, No. 634 & No. 635, this was used after the execution of Burroughs, probably on the same date. ◊ Hand 1 = Stephen Sewall

Essex County Court Archives, vol. 2, no. 36, Massachusetts Supreme Judicial Court, Judicial Archives, on deposit James Duncan Phillips Library, Peabody Essex Museum, Salem, MA.

Sworn Before the Grand Jury: Examination of Sarah Buckley

2nd of 2 dates. See No. 168 on May 18, 1692

637. Deposition of Benjamin Hutchinson v. Sarah Buckley & Mary Whittredge

[Hand 1] The deposistion of benjamine Hutchinson who testifieth and saith that my wife was much affleted presently affter the last Exeicution w^t violent paines in hir head and teeth and al parts of hir body but on Sabath day was ~~thre~~ fortnight in the morning she being in such Excesciue mesiry that ^{she} said she beleued that she had an euell hand upon hir whereupon I went: to mary walcott one of ovr next neighbors to com and look to se if she could se any body upon hir {and} as soon as she came into the house she said that our Two next neigh[Lost] [= neighbors] Sarah Buckly and mary witheridge ware upon my wife: and Immediatly my wife had Ease and mary walcott was torment⟨e⟩d: whereupon I ^{went} dow[Lost] [= down] to the shrieff and desired him to take sume course with thos women that they might not haue such power to torment: and presently he ordered them to be ffettered and eur senc that my wife has ben tolorable well and I beleue in my hart that Sarah Buckly and mary withridge has hurt my wife and seurall othrs by acts of wicthcraft [Hand 2] Beniamin Huchenson ["Hu" written over "ann"] owned y^e aboue written Euidence to be the truth vpon Oath before y^e grand Inquest 15–7 1692

[Reverse] [Hand 3] Ben: Hutchinson depo Agst Sarah Buckley & Mary Withridg

Notes: Hand 1 = Thomas Putnam; Hand 2 = Andrew Elliot; Hand 3 = Anthony Checkley

Massachusetts Archives Collection, vol. 135, no. 35. Massachusetts State Archives. Boston, MA.

Sworn Before the Grand Jury: Deposition of Ann Putnam Jr. v. Sarah Buckley

2nd of 3 dates. See No. 170 on May 18, 1692

638. Indictment of Rebecca Eames, for Covenanting†

[Hand 1] Essex in the province of the Massachusetts Bay in New England ss.	An^o $\overline{RR}$s & Reginæ Gulielmi & Mariæ Angliæ &c quarto Anoqʒ Do$\bar{m}$ 1692

The Jurio^εs for o^r Sov^ε lord & lady the King & Queen doe present That Rebeckah Eames
Wife of Robert Eames of Boxford in y^e County {afords^d} About Twenty Six years past in
the Towne of Boxford in the County aforesaid Wickedly & felloniously A Couenant with
The evill Speritt the Devill did make in & by which Wicked Couenant Shee the Said
Rebeckah Eames hir Soule & body to the Deuill did giue & promised to Serve & obey him
& Keep his Wayes, Contrary to the Stattute Of ["Of" written over "in"] the first yeare of y^e
Reigne of King James the first in that Case made & provided And C⟨?⟩ary Against the peace
of o^r Soveraigne lord & lady the King & Queen their Crowne & dignity

Sept. 15, 1692

[Hand 1?] Cogn̄

[Reverse] [Hand 1] Indictm^t ags^t Rebecka Eames for Couenanting with y^e Devill
[Hand 2] Billa vera
[Hand 1?] Cogn̄

Notes: The records of a trial for Rebecca Eames do not survive, but she affirms that she was tried and condemned seven
months after being imprisoned in August. According to her account, she was reprieved by Governor Phips. See No. 888.
◊ Hand 1 = Anthony Checkley; Hand 2 = Andrew Elliot

*Essex County Court Archives, vol. 2, no. 54, Massachusetts Supreme Judicial Court, Judicial Archives, on deposit James Duncan
Phillips Library, Peabody Essex Museum, Salem, MA.*

639. Indictment of Rebecca Eames, for Afflicting Timothy Swan†

[Hand 1] Essex in the Prouince
of the Massachusetts. Bay in   Anno R̄R̄^s & Reginæ Gulielmi & Mariæ Angliæ &c^t
New England.   Quarto Annoq̃ Domini. 1692.
ss/

The Juriors for our Sou^ε Lord and Lady the King and Queen doe. present. That. [Hand 2]
Rebeckah Eames Wife of Robert Eames of Boxford [Hand 1] in the County of Essex. [Hand
2] **aforesaid** [Hand 1] In the Yeare afores^d and diuers other dayes and times as well before as
After Certaine detestable Arts Called Witchcraft & Sorcereis Wickedly Mallitiously and
felloniously hath vsed practised and. Exercised at and. [Hand 2] **in the Towne of Andivor in
the County of Essex** [Hand 1] afores^d in vpon and against one. [Hand 2] **Timothy Swan**
[Hand 1] afores^d [   ] by which said wicked Acts the Said [Hand 2] **Timothy Swan the day
& yeare** [Hand 1] Afores^d and diuers other dayes and times both before and after was and Is
Tortured aflicted Consvmed. Wasted Pined and Tormented and also for Svndry other Acts
of Witchcraft by the Said [Hand 2] **Rebeckah Eames Comitted** [Hand 1] and done. before
and Since that time against the peace of our Sou^ε Lord and Lady the King and Queen theire
Crowne and dignity and the forme in the Stattute In that Case made and prouidd⟨e⟩d.

[Reverse] [Hand 2] Indictm^t agst Rebecka Eam⟨es⟩ for bewitching Tim° Swan
[Hand 3] Billa vera
[Hand 1?] She acknowledged y^t She aflicted Tim° Swann

Notes: Hand 2 = Anthony Checkley; Hand 3 = Andrew Elliot

Sept. 15, 1692   *Essex County Court Archives, vol. 2, no. 53, Massachusetts Supreme Judicial Court, Judicial Archives, on deposit James Duncan Phillips Library, Peabody Essex Museum, Salem, MA.*

640. Statements of Mary Walcott, Mary Warren, & Ann Putnam Jr. v. Rebecca Eames

[Hand 1] Mary Walcot. Affirmed to yᵉ grand Inquest: that Rebbecca Eames: hath afflicted her at yᵉ time of her examination this she ownd: Septᴱ 15: 1692

Mary Warin: & Ann Putnam: affirmed: that: Rebecca: Eames: did afflict Mary Walcot at yᵉ time of her examination: this they ownd Septᴱ 15: 1692

Notes: Hand 1 = Simon Willard

MS Am 1147.2, Rare Books & Manuscripts, Boston Public Library. Boston, MA.

641. Indictment of Margaret Scott, for Afflicting Mary Daniel†

See also: Sept. 16, 1692.

[Hand 1] Essex in the Prouince of the Massachusetts Bay in New England Ss// } Anno R̅R̅ˢ & Reginæ Gulielmi & Mariæ Angliæ &cᵃ Quarto Annoqȝ Domini 1692//

The Juriors for our Souᴱ Lord and Lady the King and Queen th⟨eire⟩ C⟨rowne⟩ doe present That [Hand 2] **Margarett Scott of Rowley** [Hand 1] In the County of Essex [Hand 2] ~~Single~~ **widdow** ["widdow" written over "woman"] **About the latter end of July or the beginning of August** [Hand 1] In the yeare aforesaid and diuers other days and times as well before as after Certaine detestable Arts called Witchcraft and Sorceries Wickedly Mallitiously and felloniously hath used practised and Exercised At and [Hand 2] **in the Towne of Rowley in the County of Essex** [Hand 1] Aforesaid in upon and against one [Hand 2] **Mary Daniell of Rowley** [Hand 1] Aforesaid [Hand 2] **single Woman** [Hand 1] by which said Wicked Acts the said [Hand 2] **Mary Daniell yᵉ day** ^{**& yeare**} [Hand 1] Aforesaid and diuers other days and times both before and after was and is Tortured Aflicted Consumed Pined Wasted and Tormented and also for Sundry ^{other} Acts of Witchcraft by the said [Hand 2] **Margrᵗ** ["g" written over "y"] ~~Daniel~~ **Scott** [Hand 1] Comitted and done before and Since that time against ^{the Peace of} our Souᴱ Lord & Lady the King and Queen theire Crowne and Dignity and the forme of the Stattute in that case made and Prouided.

[Reverse] [Hand 2] Indictmᵗ agst. Margarett Scott: for bewitching Mary Daniell
[Hand 3] Billa vera
[Hand 4] Ponet se

Notes: Hand 2 = Anthony Checkley; Hand 3 = Andrew Elliot

Private Collection. Access provided by William Reese Company. New Haven, CT.

642. Indictment of Margaret Scott, for Afflicting Frances Wycomb†

See also: Sept. 16, 1692.

Indictm^t. ag^st Margaret Scott, for bewitching Frances Wijcomb.

Essex in the Province	Anno RR^S & Reginae Gulielmi
of the Massachusetts	& Mariae &c^a Quarto Annoq;
Bay in New Engl^d	Domi 1692.
ss.	

The Jurors for our Sou^e Lord and Lady the King and Queen doe Present That Margarett Scott, of Rowley, In the County of Essex, Widdow: Upon the fifth day of August In the yeare aforesaid and divers other days and times as well before as after Certaine detestable Arts Called Witchcraft and Sorceries Wickedly Mallitiously and felloniously hath used practised and Exercised At and in the towne of Salem in the County aforesaid in upon and against one Frances Wijcomb, of Rowley, aforesaid Single Woman by which s^d Wicked Acts the said Frances Wijcomb, ye day and yea^e aforesaid and divers other days and times both before and after was and is Tortured Afflicted Consumed Pined Wasted and Tormented, and also for sundry other Acts of Witchcraft by the said Margaret Scott, Committed and done before and since that time against the Peace of our Sou^e Lord and Lady the King and Queen their Crowne and Dignity and the forme of the Stattute In that case made and Provided.
Billa Vera.
Ponet Se.

Thomas Gage. The History of Rowley, anciently including Bradford, Boxford and Georgetown, from 1639–1840. (Boston: Ferdinand Andrews, 1840), pp. 170–171.

Sworn Before the Grand Jury: Deposition of Mary Daniel v. Margaret Scott & Elizabeth Jackson

2nd of 3 dates. See No. 471 on Aug. 4, 1692

643. Deposition of Sarah Coleman v. Margaret Scott

The Deposition of Sarah Coalman, who saith, about the fiuetenth of August last past that she was tormented three or four times by Marget Scot, of Rowly, or her apearance, by pricking, pinching, and choaking of me, and I do uerily believe that she is a witch.
Sarah Coleman affirmed before ye Grand Inquest, that the above written Evidence is truth, vppon her oath 15th September, 1692.

Thomas Gage. The History of Rowley, anciently including Bradford, Boxford and Georgetown, from 1639–1840. (Boston: Ferdinand Andrews, 1840), pp. 174–75.

September 15, 1692

644. Testimony of Philip Nelson & Sarah Nelson v. Margaret Scott

See also: Sept. 16, 1692.

[Hand 1] ~~also~~ phillip nellson ^{and} Sarah his wife doe testifie and say that for Two or three years before ~~the said~~ Robert Shilleto dyed we haue often hard him complaining of margerit Scott for hurting of him and often said that she was a wicth and so he continewed complaing of magarit Scott saying he should neuer be well so long as margerit Scott liueed [Hand 2] & so he Complayned of Margret Scott: att times untill he dyed
Phillip Nelson: and Sarah his wife affirmed: upon their oath: to yᵉ grand Inquest that: yᵉ above written evidence: is yᵉ truth: Septᴱ 15: 1692

[Hand 3] Jurat in Curia

[Reverse] [Hand 4] Sarah Nelson depᵒ agst Mary Scott

Notes: Used at trial. ◊ Hand 1 = Thomas Putnam; Hand 2 = Simon Willard; Hand 3 = Stephen Sewall; Hand 4 = Anthony Checkley

Essex County Court Archives, vol. 2, no. 95, Massachusetts Supreme Judicial Court, Judicial Archives, on deposit James Duncan Phillips Library, Peabody Essex Museum, Salem, MA.

645. Deposition of Thomas Nelson v. Margaret Scott

See also: Sept. 16, 1692.

The Deposition of Thomas Nelson, who saith, that, about six yeares ago the last winter, Margaret Scot, of Rowley, widow, desired me to bring her some wood, and spake to me seuerall times for wood, and I told her, that I owed her ten shillings and I would bring her wood for it, and she was not willing to set of that. Earnest she was for me to bring her wood: denied her; soon after this one of my cattell was dead in the stantiall, and stood up on his hind feet, and kneeled on his knees [afore], and little after this another of my cattell was ded in the yard, his neck under a plank at the barn side as if he were chok'd; and after this, and ever since, had hard thoughts of this woman and my neighbours told me, something more then ordinery that my cattell died so. And I do uerily believe that she is a witch.
Tho: Nelson, one of yᵉ Grand Inquest gave in this evidence to yᵉ grand Inquest, September 15, 1692.

Jurat in Curia.

Notes: Thomas Nelson's comment offers a reminder that grand jurors could and sometimes did take an active role in addressing cases before them. ◊ Used at trial.

Thomas Gage. The History of Rowley, anciently including Bradford, Boxford and Georgetown, from 1639–1840. (Boston: Ferdinand Andrews, 1840), p. 174.

646. Statements of Mary Warren, Elizabeth Hubbard, & Ann Putnam Jr. v. Margaret Scott

See also: Sept. 16, 1692.

September 15, 1692

Mary Waren: and Eliz. Hubbert both: Affirmed upon their oathes: that: they saw: Margret Scott: afflict Mary Daniell: of Rowley: before ye grand Inquest this they owned to : ye grand Inquest Sept^r : 15 : 1692.

Mary Warin s^d : s^d Scott hurt: her s^d Warin also: before: ye grand Inquest.
15*

Eliz. Hubbert sayd that Margret Scott: afflicted her: before ye grand Inquest: Sept^r : y^e : 15 : 1692.

Jurat in Curia.

An: Putnam: and Mary Warin affirmed to ye grand Inquest: that: they saw Margret : Scott: afflict: Frances Wycom : in presence of ye grand Inquest: Sept^r : 15: 1692 upon their othes also y^t s^d Scott: afflicted: s^d Frances Wycom : before in Salem.

Jurat in Curia by Ma. Warrin.

Notes: Used at trial.

Thomas Gage. The History of Rowley, anciently including Bradford, Boxford and Georgetown, from 1639–1840. (Boston: Ferdinand Andrews, 1840), pp. 173–74.

647. Deposition of Daniel Wycomb & John Burbank v. Margaret Scott

See also: Sept. 16, 1692.

Jno Burbanke   Dep^o agst Margret Scott.
Daniel Wycomb

the testymony of Daniell Wicom ayged aboue fifty years Who sayth that abought fiue ore sixs years a go Margret Scot of Rowlah came to my hous and asked me if she might gleane corne in my felld i towld hir she might if she woulld stay whilst my corne was ought of the feeld s^d Scot s^d you will not get youer corne ought to night it may be i tould hir i would s^d Scot s^d may be not: at that, time my wife gaue s^d Scot sum corne and then Scot went a way and presently after s^d Scot was gon i went with my cart and oxsen into the feeld for corne and when i had lodid my cart i went to go home with my corne but the oxsen would not draw the cart any ways bout from home thof i wear not twenty Rod from my Door and i coulld not get any corne ought of my felld that day the next Day i touck the same oxsen and put them to the cart and the s^d cart and the same lode of corne they did draw a way with ease.

Jurat in Curia.

Capt. Dan^{ll} Wycom owned: ye above written evidence to : be ye truth before grand Inquest upon his oath Jno : Burbank and Frances Wycom, attested: to : substance of this above written: evidence:: as: that: s^d Scott s^d it may be you will not gett: yor corn in to night therefor let me glean to night: and that ye oxen would not goe forward: but backward with ye load of corn: nor: ye corn: could: none of it be gott in that night: before: s^d Inquest: Sept^r: 15: 1692.

Sworne in Court also by John Burbanke.

Sept. 15, 1692   Notes: Used at trial.

Thomas Gage. The History of Rowley, anciently including Bradford, Boxford and Georgetown, from 1639–1840. (Boston: Ferdinand Andrews, 1840), pp. 171–72.

648. Deposition of Frances Wycomb v. Margaret Scott

See also: Sept. 16, 1692.

[Hand 1] The deposistion of ffra{n}ces wycum who testifieth and saith that quickly affter the first court att Salme about wicthcraft margerit Scott whom I very well knew: or hir Apperance came to me and did most greviously torment ^{me} by choaking and almost presing me to death: and so she did continu affleting me by times tell the 5th August 1692 being the day of hir Examination allso during the time of hir Examination margerit Scott did most greviously affl⟨ec⟩t me: and also seurall times sence: and I beleue in my heart that margerit Scott is a wicth and that she has often affleted me by acts of wicthcraft

[Hand 2] ffrances Wycom ownd: to y^e grand Inquest. that y^e above written evidence: is y^e truth upon oath: Sept^ε 15. 1692
                [Hand 3] Jurat in Curia.

[Reverse] [Hand 4] ffrances Wycomb dep^o Agst ~~MM~~Margarett Scott

Notes: Used at trial. ◊ Hand 1 = Thomas Putnam; Hand 2 = Simon Willard; Hand 3 = Stephen Sewall; Hand 4 = Anthony Checkley

Essex County Court Archives, vol. 2, no. 94, Massachusetts Supreme Judicial Court, Judicial Archives, on deposit James Duncan Phillips Library, Peabody Essex Museum, Salem, MA.

649. Indictment of Job Tookey, for Afflicting Elizabeth Booth (Returned Ignoramus)‡

[Hand 1] Essex in the Prouince of the Massachusetts Bay in New England ss//   } Anno $\overline{RR}$^s & Reginæ Gulielmi & Mariæ Angliæ &c^a Quarto Annoq̄ʒ Do͞m: 1692//

The Jurors for our Sou^ε Lord & Lady the King & Queen ~~th~~ doe ꝑsent That [Hand 2] **Job Tukie of Beverly** [Hand 1] In the County of Essex [Hand 2] **Waterman vpon the fowerth day of June** [Hand 1] In the Yeare aforesaid and diuers other days and times as well before as after Certaine detestable Arts Called Witchcraft & Sorceries Wickedly Mallitiously & felloniously hath used practised and Exercised At and [Hand 2] **in the Towne of Salem in the County of Essex** [Hand 1] Aforesaid in upon and against one [Hand 2] **Eliz^a Booth of Salem** [Hand 1] Aforesaid [Hand 2] **Single Woman** [Hand 1] by which s^d Wicked Acts the said [Hand 2] **Elizabeth Booth the day & yeare** [Hand 1] Aforesaid and diuers other days and times both before & after was and is Tortured Aflicted Consumed Pined Wasted and Tormented, & also for sundry other Acts of Witchcraft by the said [Hand 2] **Job Tukey** [Hand 1] Comitted and done before and Since that time against the Peace of Our Sou^ε

Sept. 15, 1692

Lord & Lady the King & Queen theire Crowne & Dignity and the forme of the Stattute In that case made and Prouided.

[Reverse] [Hand 2] Indictm^t ags^t Job Tookey for Bewitching Eliza: Booth
[Hand 3] ⟨B⟩ Ignoramus

Notes: This references George Booth's sister and not his wife with the same name. Although the trial of Tookey took place on January 5, 1693, the indictment came to the grand jury between September 13 and 17, 1692. See No. 760. ◊ Hand 2 = Anthony Checkley; Hand 3 = Andrew Elliot

Suffolk Court Files, vol. 32, docket 2670, p. 2, Massachusetts Supreme Judicial Court, Judicial Archives, Massachusetts State Archives. Boston, MA.

650. Indictment of Job Tookey, for Afflicting Susannah Shelden (Returned Ignoramus)‡

[Hand 1] Essex in the Prouince of the Massachusetts Bay in New England Ss } Anno R̄R̄^s & Reginæ Gulielmi & Mariæ Angliæ &^c Quarto. Annoq̃ Domini 1692

The Jvrors for o^ε Sou^ε Lord and Lady the King & Queen doe Present That. [Hand 2] **Job Tookie** ["T" written over "St"] **of Beverly** [Hand 1] in The County of Essex [Hand 2] **Waterman vpon the Seauenth day of June** [Hand 1] In the year aforesaid and diuers other dayes and Times as wel before as after Certaine Detestable Arts Called Witchcraft and Sorceries Wickedly Mallistiously and felloniously hath vsed practised and Exercised at and [Hand 2] **in the Towne of Salem in the County of Essex** [Hand 1] aforesaid in vpon and against one [Hand 2] **Susana Shelden of Salem** [Hand 1] aforesaid [Hand 2] **Single Woman** [Hand 1] by which Said Wicked acts the Said [Hand 2] **Sarah Shelden the day** ^{& yeare} [Hand 1] aforesaid and diuers other dayes and Times both before and after was and is Tortured aflicted Consvmed Pined Wasted and Tormented ~~and also for Sundry other Acts of Witchcraft by the Said~~ [Hand 2] ^{**Job Stooky**} ~~**Robert**~~ ["Robert" written over "Susanah"] **S̶ ⟨?⟩ford** ["S⟨?⟩ford" written over "Shelden"] [Hand 1] ~~Comitted and done before and Since that time~~ against the peace of o^ε Sou^ε Lord and Lady the King and Queen Theire Crowne and Dignity and the ~~forme of~~ ["of" written over "in"] ~~the Stattute~~ [Hand 2] {**laws**} [Hand 1] in that Case made and Prouided,

[Reverse] [Hand 2] Indictm^t agst Job Stookey For bewitching S̄ūs̄. Shelden
[Hand 3] Ignoramus

Notes: Hand 2 = Anthony Checkley; Hand 3 = Andrew Elliot

Suffolk Court Files, vol. 32, docket 2670, p. 3, Massachusetts Supreme Judicial Court, Judicial Archives, Massachusetts State Archives. Boston, MA.

September 15, 1692

651. Indictment of Job Tookey, for Afflicting Mary Warren‡

See also: Jan. 5, 1693.

[Hand 1] Essex in the Prouince [Lost]f [= of] the Massachusett⟨s⟩ Bay in New England Ss/   Annoq R̄R̄ˢ & Reginæ Gulielmi & Mariæ Angliæ &c Quarto Annoqȝ Dom̄ 1692//

The Jurors for our Souᵉ Lord and Lady the King and Queen [Hand 2] **doe present That Job Tookey** ["T" written over "St"] **of Beverly** [Hand 1] In the County of Essex [Hand 2] **Waterman The Seaventh day of June** [Hand 1] In the Yeare aforesaid and diuer⟨s⟩ other days and times as well before as after Certaine detestable Arts Called Witchcraft and Sorceris Wickedly Mallitiously and felloniously hath used practised and Exercised At and [Hand 2] **in the Towne of Salem in the County of Essex** [Hand 1] Aforesaid in upon and against one [Hand 2] **Mary Warren of Salem** [Hand 1] Aforesaid [Hand 2] **Single Woman** [Hand 1] by which said Wicked Acts the said [Hand 2] **Mary Warren the day** ˄{**& yeare**} [Hand 1] aforesaid and diuers other days and times ~~as~~ both before and after was and is Tortured Aflicted Consumed Pined Wasted and Tormented, and also for Sundry other Acts of Witchcraft by the said [Hand 2] **Job Stuky** [Hand 1] Comitted and done before and Since that time against the Peace of our Souᵉ Lord and Lady the King and Queen theire Crowne and Dignity and the forme of the Stattute In that case made and Prouided

[Reverse] [Hand 2] Ponet Se
[Hand 3?] Non Cul̄: [= not guilty]
5

Notes: Part of this document is missing, so no true bill or ignoramus appears. Since a grand jury heard Tookey's case in September 1692 and no extant "true bill" was returned against him, it seems probable that in 1692 a true bill was returned in this case and originally appeared on the missing part of the document. He was tried and found not guilty on January 5, 1693. See No. 760. ◊ Hand 2 = Anthony Checkley

Massachusetts Archives Collection, vol. 135, no. 32. Massachusetts State Archives. Boston, MA.

652. Indictment of Mary Whittredge, for Afflicting Elizabeth Hubbard†

See also: Jan. 4, 1693.

[Hand 1] Essex in the Prouince of the Massachusetts Bay in New England: ss/   Anno R̄R̄ˢ & Reginæ Gulielmi & Mariæ Angliæ &c Quarto Annoqȝ Domini 1692

The Jurors for oᵉ Souᵉ Lord and Lady. the King and Queen doe present That [Hand 2] **That Mary Witheridg of Salem Village Alias Salem** [Hand 1] in the County of Essex [Hand 2] **The Eighteenth day of May** [Hand 1] in the Year aforesaid and diuers other dayes and times as well before as after Certaine Detestable Arts called witchcraft and Sorceries Wickedly Mallitiously and felloniously hath vsed practised and Exercised at and [Hand 2] **in the Towne of Salem in the County of Essex** [Hand 1] Aforesᵈ in vpon and against one

[Hand 2] **Elizabeth Hobert of Salem** [Hand 1] afores^d [Hand 2] **Single Woman** [Hand 1]   Sept. 15, 1692
by which said wicked Acts the said [Hand 2] **Elizabeth Hobert the day & yeare** [Hand 1]
aforesaid and diuers other dayes and times both before and after was and is Tortured aflicted
Consvmed Wasted Pined and Tormented and also for Svndry other Acts of Witchcraft by
the said. [Hand 2] **Mary Witheridg** ~~the day & yeare~~ **Comitted** [Hand 1] and done before
and Since that Time against the peace of o^ε Sou^ε Lord and Lady the King & Queen theire
Crowne & dignity and the forme in the ~~Stat~~ Stattute. In that Case made and prouided.

[Reverse] [Hand 2] Mary Witheridg: ~~Eliz Hobert~~
[Hand 3] Billa vera
[Hand 2] Pone Se
found not Guilty
[Hand 4?] <u>4</u>

Notes: Fortunately for Mary Whittredge, her trial was delayed till January 1693. See No. 756. ◊ Hand 2 = Anthony
Checkley; Hand 3 = Andrew Elliot

Massachusetts Archives Collection, vol. 135, no. 21. Massachusetts State Archives. Boston, MA.

653. Deposition of Elizabeth Hubbard v. Mary Whittredge

[Hand 1] The deposistion of Eliz: Hubburd who testifieth and saith that I haue a
considerable time ben affletid by Mary Witheridge: but on the 18th May {1692} being the
day of hir Examination mary witheridge did most greviously torment me dureing the time of
hir Examination for if she did but look upon me she would strick me down or almost choake
also on the day of hir Examination I saw mary witheridge or hir Apperance most greviously
afflet a⟨n⟩d torment mary walcott ~~Sarah vibber~~ and Ann putnam and I beleue in my heart
that mary witheridge is a wicth and that she has often affleted and tormented me and the
afforesaid parsons by acts of wicthcraft.
[Hand 2] Eliz Hubbert: ownd: y^e truth of y^e above written evidence to y^e grand Inquest
Sept^ε 15: 1692 upon oath
          [Hand 3] Eliz^a Hubbard ["d" written over "J"] Ju̅r. in Cur.

[Reverse] [Hand 4] Eliz^a Hobert dep° agst Mary Witheridg

Notes: Used at trial. ◊ Hand 1 = Thomas Putnam; Hand 2 = Simon Willard; Hand 3 = Jonathan Elatson; Hand 4 =
Anthony Checkley

Massachusetts Archives Collection, vol. 135, no. 46. Massachusetts State Archives. Boston, MA.

654. Petition of Mary Esty‡

[Hand 1] The humbl petition of mary Eastick unto [Hand 2] ˄{his Excellencyes S^r W^m
Phipps and to} [Hand 1] the honourd Judge and Bench now stting In Judi⟨?⟩cature in Salem
and the Reuerend ministers humbly sheweth

September 15, 1692

That wheras your poor and humble Petition being condemned to die Doe humbly begg of you to take it into your Judicious and pious considerations that your Poor and humble petitioner knowing my own Innocencye Blised be the lord for it and seeing plainly the wiles and subtility of ^{my} accusers by my selfe can not but Judg charitably of others that are going ye same way of my selfe if the Lord stepps not mightily in i was confined a ~~my selfe if the lord~~ whole month upon the same account that I am condemned now for and then cleared by the ~~same~~ afflichid persons as some of your honours know and in ["in" written over "then"] ~~el cleared of~~ two dayes time I was cryed out upon by them and haue been confined and now am condemned to die the lord aboue knows my Innocencye then and likewise does kow [= know] ~~that~~ {as} ~~t~~att the great day will be known to men and Angells I Petition to your honours not for my own life for I know I must die and my appointed time is sett but the ~~the~~ Lord he knowes it is that if it be possible no more Innocen⟨t⟩t blood may be shed which undoubtidly cannot be Auoydd In the way and course you goe in I Question not but your honours does to the uttmost of your Powers in the discouery and detecting of witchcraft and witches and would not be gulty of Innocent blood for the world but by my own Innocencye I know you are in the wrong way the Lord in his infinite mercye {~~no more~~} direct you in this great work if it be his blessed will that ^{no more} Innocent blood be ~~not~~ shed I would humbly begg of you that your honours would be plesed to examine theis Aflicted Persons strictly and keepe them apart some time and likewise to try some of these confesing wichis I being confident there is seuerall of them has belyed themselue[Lost] [= themselves] and others as will appeare if not in this word [= world] I am sure in the world to come whither I am now {a}going and I question not ^{but} youle see an alteration of thes things they say my selfe and others hauing made a League with the Diuel w⟨i⟩ll we cannot confesse I know and ~~and~~ the Lord knowes as will ~~th⟨?⟩re~~ thorlly appeare they belye me and so I Question. not but they doe others the Lord aboue who is the searcher of all hearti [= hearts] knowes that as I shall answer it att the [Reverse] Tribunall seat that I know not the least thinge of witch{c}raft therfore I cannot I dare~~n~~ not belye my own soule I beg your honers not to deny this my humble petition from a ⟨I⟩ poor dying Innocent person and I Question not but the Lord will giue a blesing to yor endeuers

[Hand 2] To his Excellencye Sr Wm Phipps: Gouern^ε and to the honoured Judge and Magistrates now Setting in Judicature in Salem

[Hand 3] Mary Easty peticō̄n

Notes: Mary Esty was tried on September 9, and her formal sentencing would probably have been around September 12, with her execution on September 22. So the range of probable dates seems clear, and the document is dated arbitrarily to a few days after her probable sentencing. ◊ Hand 3 = Stephen Sewall ◊ Facsimile Plates 10 & 11.

Essex County Court Archives, vol. 1, no. 294, Massachusetts Supreme Judicial Court, Judicial Archives, on deposit James Duncan Phillips Library, Peabody Essex Museum, Salem, MA.

655. Petition of Ann Pudeator‡

[Hand 1] The humble Petition of Ann Poodeater unto ye honoured Judge and Bench now Setting in Judicature in Salem humbly sheweth:

That Wheras your Poor and humble Petitioner being condemned to die and knowing in my
own conscience as I shall shortly answer it before ye great God of heauen who is the₊ searcher
& knower of {all} hearts: That the Euidence of Jn° Best Sen^Ɛ and Jn° Best Jun^Ɛ and Sam^ll
Pickworth wch was giuen in against me in Court were all of them altogether false &
^{untrue} and besides the abouesaid Jn° Best hath been formerly whipt and likewise ⟨ᵻ⟩ is
reorded [= recorded] for A Lyar I would humbly begg of yo^Ɛ honours to Take it into your
Judicious and Pious consideratiō That my life may not be taken away by such false Euidences
and wittnesses as these be likewise y^e Euidence giuen in against me by Sarah church and
Mary Warren I am altogether ignorant off and know nothing in ye least measure about it nor
nothing else concerni͞g ye crime of witchcraft for wch I am condemned to die as will be
known to men and angells att the great day of Judgment begging and imploring your prayers
att the throne of grace in my behalfe and your poor and humble petition^Ɛ shall for euer pray
as she is bound in duty for yo^Ɛ hon^Ɛs health and happiness in this life and eternall felicity in
ye world to come

Sept. 16, 1692

[Reverse] [Hand 2] Ann Pudeaters Peticōn
[Hand 3] An Pudeater⟨s⟩ [1 word illegible]

Notes: Around the time of Ann Pudeator's failed petition, Dorcas Hoar offered the confession that saved her from joining
Ann Pudeator on the gallows on September 22. See No. 676. The exact day of the petition cannot be ascertained, but it
was certainly between September 10, when her trial concluded, and September 22, the day she was executed. The "whipt"
John Best was John Best Sr. The date of September 15 is arbitrary, chosen because it falls between the two possible dates.

*Essex County Court Archives, vol. 1, no. 267, Massachusetts Supreme Judicial Court, Judicial Archives, on deposit James Duncan
Phillips Library, Peabody Essex Museum, Salem, MA.*

Friday, September 16, 1692

Grand Jury of Mary Parker

Trials of Mary Parker & Margaret Scott

Sworn: Examination of William Barker Sr.
3rd of 3 dates. See No. 525 on Aug. 29, 1692

656. Deposition of Elizabeth Booth & Alice Booth v. Giles Cory‡

[Hand 1] The deposistion of Eliz: booth the wife of George booth ^{&} Allies Booth who
testifie and say that on the 12th of this Istant [= instant] sept^r [Hand 2] ^{at y^e widow
Shaflin's house in Salem} [Hand 1] their appeared to {us} a grate number of wicthes as
neare as we could tell about fifty thirteen of which we knew: who did Receiued the sacriment
in our sight amongst whicth we saw Giles Cory who brought to us bread and wine urging us
to pertake thereof: but because we Refused he did most greviously afflect and torment us:

September 16, 1692

and we beleue in our hearts that Giles Cory is a wizzard and that he has often affleted us and seurall othrs by acts of wicthcraft

[Hand 2] Elisabeth ⟨mark⟩ Booth's mark
Alice ⟨mark⟩ Booth's mark

[Reverse] [Hand 3] Boothes.

Notes: The grand jury heard Cory's case on September 9. Although no indictment survives, his subsequent execution makes clear that at least one true bill was returned. According to Calef, Cory pled not guilty to his indictment but refused to agree to a trial. In his diary entry of September 19, the day Cory was pressed to death, Samuel Sewall noted that the punishment was for standing mute. This strongly suggests that the Court treated his refusal to stand trial in the same way as English law normally treated a person who did so. It was treated as a guilty plea in spite of his having pled not guilty to the true bill, and under English law such a "plea" usually led to the punishment Cory received, being pressed to death (*peine forte et dure*). However, a deposition as late as this one, after September 12, strongly suggests that the Court was yet holding out for the possibility that Cory would change his mind and stand trial. Samuel Sewall makes clear in his diary that attempts to persuade Cory to do so had been made and had failed. Calef cites September 16 as the day Cory was pressed to death, but he does so in the context of listing dates on which people were condemned, and one strong possibility is that on that day the Court gave up in its attempts to get Cory to stand trial, and formally sentenced him to the form of death that followed soon after on September 19. Certainty as to what happened procedurally, however, remains elusive. The document is speculatively dated to September 16, the day it might have been used had there been a trial. ◊ Hand 1 = Thomas Putnam

Essex County Court Archives, vol. 2, no. 91, Massachusetts Supreme Judicial Court, Judicial Archives, on deposit James Duncan Phillips Library, Peabody Essex Museum, Salem, MA.

657. Summary of the Examinations of Dorothy Faulkner, Abigail Faulkner Jr., Martha Tyler, Johannah Tyler, Sarah Wilson Jr., & Joseph Draper v. Abigail Faulkner Sr.

See also: Sept. 17, 1692.

[Hand 1] ~~dori~~
dorritye fforknor: and Abigale fforknor ~~Confis⟨t⟩ed~~ Childern: to Abigall fforknor of Andouer now in prison confarsed befor the honoured majastrats vpon thire exsaminations heare in Salam the 16 day of this Enstant subtember: 1692 that thire mother apared and mayd them witches and also Marth⟨y?⟩ Tyler Johanah Tyler: and Sarih willson and Joseph draper all acknowlidge{ed} that thay ware lead into that dradfull sin of witchcrift by hir meanse: the foresd Abigale forknor

[Hand 2] The aboue named persons Each & Euery one of them Did affirm before y^e Grand inquest that the aboue written Euedences ar ["ar" written over "is"] truth 17 sep^t 1692

[Reverse] Dorety ffalkner v⟨s⟩ Abigail ffalkner

Notes: Hand 2 = Andrew Elliot

Essex County Court Archives, vol. 2, no. 45, Massachusetts Supreme Judicial Court, Judicial Archives, on deposit James Duncan Phillips Library, Peabody Essex Museum, Salem, MA.

658. Examination of Joannah Tyler, Copy

September 16, 1692

[Hand 1] The Exãm of Joanna Tyler taken Before Jnᵒ Higginson & Capᵗ Wade their Majesties Justices of yᵉ peace for yᵉ County of Essex 16ᵗʰ Sepᵉ 1692 about 2 Months agoe (but was Stopt) he Saith Somthing Speak to her & Sᵈ yᵗ She Should not Confes She Sᵈ Goodᵉ falkner pᵉswaded her first & yᵉ black Man wᵗʰ her & he asked me if I would Sett my hand to his book he would lett me haue fine Cloaths & when he Baptized Me he Sᵈ I Should be his for Euer & Euer She Sᵈ She promised to Serue the Diuel & if I wished So & So wᵗʰ Respect to afflicting pᵉsons it Should be done She made a Red Mark & he brought yᵉ trad wᵗʰ & She afflicted Sarah Wilson & Sarah Phelps She Saith She knows yᵉ Diuel went in her Shape to Mʳ Bernards Where Sarah Wilson was Conffesing to hindᵉ her – & asked Me if I was Willing he Should goe in my Shape She Sᵈ Goodᵉ falkner was before her Now on yᵉ table to hindᵉ her She was at a witch metting at Chandlerˢ pasture

John Higginson
Thõ Wade

Notes: From *Andover Examinations Copy*. See No. 425. ◊ "trad" : possibly *trade* 'commodities or produce used in barter' (*a Dictionary of American English on Historical Principles* s.v. *trade* n, 1).

Essex Institute Collection, no. 24, 10v, James Duncan Phillips Library, Peabody Essex Museum, Salem, MA.

659. Indictment of Mary Parker, for Afflicting Hannah Bixby†

[Hand 1] Essex in The Province of the Massachusetts Bay in New England } Anno R̄Rˢ & Reginæ Gulielmi & Mariæ Angliæ & Quarto. Annoqʒ Domini 1692

The Jvrors for oᵉ Souᵉ Lord and Lady the King and Queen do present That. [Hand 2] **Mary Parker of Andivor** [Hand 1] in [Hand 2] **the County of Essex Widdow vpon or about the first day of September** [Hand 1] In the year aforesaid and diuers other dayes and Times as well before as after Certaine detestable Arts Called Witchcraft and Sorceries wickedly Mallistiously & felloniously hath vsed Practised and Exercised at and [Hand 2] **in the Towne of Andiuoᵉ in the County** [Hand 1] aforesaid in vpon and against one [Hand 2] **Hannah Bigsbee of Andivor in the County** [Hand 1] aforesaid [Hand 2] ⟨Carpenter⟩ **Wife of Daniell Bigsby of Andiuor** {aforsᵈ **Carpenter**} [Hand 1] by whitch Said wicked acts the Said [Hand 2] **Hannah Bigsby** ^{**the Day & yeare**} [Hand 1] aforesaid and diuers other dayes and Times both before and after was and is Tortured aflicted Consvmed Pined Wasted and Tormented and also for Sundry othe Acts of Witchcraft by the Said [Hand 2] **Mary Parker** [Hand 1] Comitted and done Before and Since That time against the peace of oᵉ Souᵉ Lord and Lady the King and Queen theire Crowne and Dignity and the forome of the Stattute in That Case made and Prouided.
[Hand 2] Inquire of Capt Chandler

[Reverse] Mary Parker: Indictmᵗ for bewitching Hanah Bigsby
[Hand 3] Billa vera
[Hand 4] Ponet Se

Notes: "Capt Chandler" was the father of Hannah Bixby. ◊ Hand 2 = Anthony Checkley; Hand 3 = Andrew Elliot

Essex Institute Collection, no. 4, James Duncan Phillips Library, Peabody Essex Museum, Salem, MA.

660. Indictment of Mary Parker, for Afflicting Sarah Phelps†

[Hand 1] Essex in the Prouince of the Massachusetts Bay in New England ss// } Anno $\overline{RR}^s$ & Reginæ Gulielmi & Mariæ Angliæ &c^a Quarto Annoqȝ Domini 1692

The Jurors for our Sou^ε Lord and Lady the King and Queen ꝑsent That [Hand 2] **Mary Parker of Andivor** [Hand 1] In the County of Essex [Hand 2] **Widdow In or about the last day of August** [Hand 1] In the Yeare aforesaid and diuers other days and times as well before as after Certaine detestable Arts Called Witchcraft and Sorceries Wickedly Mallitiously and felloniously hath used practised & Exercised At and [Hand 2] **in The Towne of Andivor in the County of Essex** [Hand 1] Aforesaid in upon and against one [Hand 2] **Sarah Phelps of Andiuor** [Hand 1] Aforesaid [Hand 2] **Single Woman** [Hand 1] by which said Wicked Acts the ~~afo(r)esaid~~ [Hand 2] **Sarah Phelps the day & yeare** [Hand 1] aforesaid and diuers other days and times both before and after was and is Tortured Aflicted Consumed Pined Wasted and Tormented, & also for sundry other Acts of Witchcraft by the said [Hand 2] **Mary Parker** [Hand 1] Comitted and done before and Since that time against the Peace of our Sou^ε Lord and Lady the King and Queen theire Crowne and Dignity and the forme Of ["Of" written over "in"] the Stattute ~~Of~~ ["Of" written over "in"] ^{in} that case made and Prouided.
[Hand 2] Inquire of Capt Chandler

[Reverse] Mary Parker for bewitching Sarah Phelps of Andiuo^ε
[Hand 3] Billa vera
[Hand 4] Ponet se.

Notes: Sarah Phelps was nine years old and the granddaughter of Thomas Chandler. ◊ Hand 2 = Anthony Checkley; Hand 3 = Andrew Elliot

Witchcraft Papers, no. 35, Massachusetts Historical Society. Boston, MA.

661. Indictment of Mary Parker, for Afflicting Martha Sprague (Returned Ignoramus)†

[Hand 1] Essex in the Prouince of the Massachusetts. Bay in New England. ss// } Anno $\overline{RR}^s$ & Reginæ Gulielmi & Mariæ Angliæ &^c Quarto. Annoqȝ Domini 1692

The Jurors for o^ε Sou^ε Lord and Lady the King and Queen doe present That [Hand 2] **Mary Parker of Andivor** [Hand 1] In the County of Essex [Hand 2] **Widdow y^e first day of Septemb^ε** [Hand 1] In the year aforesaid and diuers other dayes and Times as well before as after Certaine detestable Arts called Witchcraft and Sorceries Wickedly Mallistiously and felloniously hath vsed Practised and Exercised At and [Hand 2] **in the Towne of Salem in y^e**

County of Essex [Hand 1] aforesaid in vpon and against one [Hand 2] **Martha Sprague of**   Sept. 16, 1692
Boxford in [Hand 1] aforesaid ["aforesaid" written over "Ra⟨?⟩d⟨?⟩"] [Hand 2] **the County of**
Essex aforesaid Single Woman [Hand 1] By which said wicked Acts the Said [Hand 2]
Martha Sprague yᵉ day & yeaᵋ [Hand 1] afore⟨s⟩aid and diuers other dayes and times both
before and after was and is Tortured aflicted Consumed Pined wasted and Tormented and
also for Sundry other Acts of Witchcraft by the Said. [Hand 2] **Mary Parker** [Hand 1]
Comitted and done. before and Since that Time against the peace of oᵋ Souᵋ Lord and Lady
the King and Queen theire Crowne & dignity and the forme of the Stattute, in that Case
made and. Prouided.

[Reverse] [Hand 2] Indictmᵗ agst Mary Parker for bewitching Martha Sprague
[Hand 3] Ignoramus

Notes: Hand 2 = Anthony Checkley; Hand 3 = Andrew Elliot

Essex County Court Archives, vol. 2, no. 64, Massachusetts Supreme Judicial Court, Judicial Archives, on deposit James Duncan
Phillips Library, Peabody Essex Museum, Salem, MA.

662. Statements of William Barker Jr. & Mercy Wardwell v. Mary Parker

[Hand 1] Wᵐ Barker Junᵋ affirmd to yᵉ grand Inquest: that: Mary Parker: did in Company
with him sᵈ Barker: afflict. Martha Sprage by: witchcraft: yᵉ night before: sᵈ Barker
confessed: which was: yᵉ 1 of Septᵋ 1692: this he owned: to yᵉ grand Inquest: Septᵋ 16: 1692
                                                                      [Hand 2] Owned in Court

[Hand 1] Mercy. Wardwell: owned to yᵉ grand Inquest: that she had seen: yᵉ shape of. Mary
Parker: when she: sᵈ Wardwell: afflicted: Timo Swan: also: she: sᵈ she saw: sᵈ Parkers shape:
when she sᵈ Wardwell afflicted Martha Sprage: but I did not certainly know: that sᵈ Parker
was a witch: this she owned: ~~to yᵉ~~ to yᵉ grand Inquest: Septᵋ 16: 1692

[Reverse] [Hand 3] William Barker & Mercy Wardw[Lost] [= Wardwell] euidence agst
Mary Parker

Notes: This document was probably used in the trial of Mary Parker. Sewall wrote "Owned in Court" because those
making the statement were confessed witches and could not be sworn. No other trial document is extant in the case of
Mary Parker. Calef says she was condemned on September 17. She was probably tried on September 16, the day that
the grand jury met on her case. ◊ Likely used at trial ◊ Hand 1 = Simon Willard; Hand 2 = Stephen Sewall; Hand 3 =
Anthony Checkley

Essex County Court Archives, vol. 2, no. 68, Massachusetts Supreme Judicial Court, Judicial Archives, on deposit James Duncan
Phillips Library, Peabody Essex Museum, Salem, MA.

Billa Vera: Indictment of Margaret Scott, for Afflicting Mary Daniel†
2ⁿᵈ of 2 dates. See No. 641 on Sept. 15, 1692

Billa Vera: Indictment of Margaret Scott, for Afflicting Frances Wycomb†
2ⁿᵈ of 2 dates. See No. 642 on Sept. 15, 1692

Sept. 17, 1692   *Sworn at Trial: Deposition of Mary Daniel v. Margaret Scott & Goodwife Jackson*
3ʳᵈ of 3 dates. See No. 471 on Aug. 4, 1692

Sworn at Trial: Testimony of Philip & Sarah Nelson v. Margaret Scott†
2ⁿᵈ of 2 dates. See No. 644 on Sept. 15, 1692

Sworn at Trial: Deposition of Thomas Nelson v. Margaret Scott†
2ⁿᵈ of 2 dates. See No. 645 on Sept. 15, 1692

Sworn at Trial: Statements of Mary Warren, Elizabeth Hubbard, & Ann Putnam Jr. v. Margaret Scott†
2ⁿᵈ of 2 dates. See No. 646 on Sept. 15, 1692

Sworn at Trial: Deposition of Daniel Wycomb & John Burbank v. Margaret Scott†
2ⁿᵈ of 2 dates. See No. 647 on Sept. 15, 1692

Sworn at Trial: Deposition of Frances Wycomb v. Margaret Scott†
2ⁿᵈ of 2 dates. See No. 648 on Sept. 15, 1692

Saturday, September 17, 1692

Grand Jury of Abigail Faulkner Sr.

Trial of Abigail Faulkner Sr.

Sentenced to Death: Rebecca Eames, Abigail Faulkner Sr., Ann Foster, Abigail Hobbs, Mary Lacey Sr., Mary Parker, Wilmot Redd, Margaret Scott, & Samuel Wardwell

Sworn Before a Justice of the Peace: Examination of Mary Barker
2ⁿᵈ of 2 dates. See No. 523 on Aug. 29, 1692

Sworn Before a Justice of the Peace: Examination of Mary Barker, Copy
2ⁿᵈ of 2 dates. See No. 524 on Aug. 29, 1692

Sworn Before a Justice of the Peace: Examination of Sarah Hawkes, Copy
2ⁿᵈ of 2 dates. See No. 535 on Sept. 1, 1692

663. Examination of William Procter
See also: Jan. 7, 1693.

[Hand 1] 17 Sep: <u>92</u>
The Examination of William Procter taken before Jnᵒ hauthorn Esqᵋ and other their majesties Justices. 17 Septembᵋ 1692.

He denyed what he was accused of   September 17, 1692

He lookeing upon mary warrin struck her down and by toucheing of her Recovered her again

Mary warrin said that Wm Proctor had almost murdered her to death this day by pains in all her bones and Inwards also. And that she saw him afflict Mary walcot Eliz^a booth, Eliz^a hubbard and Ann Putnam

The said Mary walcott & Ann Putnam being in dreadfull fitts Wm Proctor recovered them again,

Alice booth & Sarah Churchill in their fitts complained of Proctor

And he by toucheing y^m recovered y^m again

Mary Pickworth was in a fitt & the above afflicted persones said they saw Proctor afflict her; and he by his touch recovered her

Elizabeth Booth said she saw him twist and pinch poppets this very day. she also was afflicted and he recovered her by his touch

Betty hubbard said that Proctor afflicted her greivously this daye and made her promeise not to tell of him

Mary walcot said the same.

[Hand 2] Eliz Hubbard owned before the Grand iury vpon the oath she had taken that s^d Willm Proctor had aflicted her both before her examination, at that time, & since many times, notwithstanding his promise to her

as ates⟨t⟩

Robert: Payne

foreman:

[Reverse] [Hand 1] I underwritten being appoynted by authority to take the within examination in w^εting [= writing] Doe testify upon oath taken in court That this is a true coppy of the Substance of it, to the best of my knowledge 7^t Jan^εy 1692/3.

Wm Murray

[Hand 3] the within W^m procture was examin⟨ed⟩ before their Majesties Justies of peace in Salem

owned before the Grand Jury 7: Jan^r 1692

atest. Jn° Higginson Just^ε peace

Robert: Payne foreman:

Notes: William Procter had been arrested and imprisoned on May 31 (see No. 226) and was likely examined then for the first time. No record of that examination is extant, but indictments typically specified that the felonious acts of witchcraft were committed on the day of the examination, because there would be a crowd of witnesses to the claims of those saying they were afflicted. The two indictments against Procter earlier in the month were for afflicting Elizabeth Hubbard and Mary Warren on May 31, both of which were returned ignoramus on September 8. See No. 581 & No. 582. Complaints against him continued to be made, since in January a different grand jury would also return an ignoramus on an additional indictment for allegedly afflicting Mary Walcott during this examination. See No. 776. ◊ Hand 1 = William Murray; Hand 3 = John Higginson Jr.

Suffolk Court Files, vol. 32, docket 2706, p. 29, Massachusetts Supreme Judicial Court, Judicial Archives, Massachusetts State Archives. Boston, MA.

664. Indictment of Abigail Faulkner Sr., for Afflicting Sarah Phelps

[Hand 1] Essex in the Prouince   Anno $\overline{RR}^s$ & Reginæ Gulielmi & Mariæ Angliæ &c^a
of the Massachusetts Bay in New }   Quarto Annoqʒ Domini 1692//
England
ss//

The Jurors for our Sou^ε Lord and Lady the King & Queen doe ꝓsent That [Hand 2]
Abigaill ffalkner wife of ffrances ffalkner of Andivo^ε [Hand 1] In the County of Essex
[Hand 2] **Husbandman in & About** ["About" written over "vpon"] **the begining of August**
[Hand 1] In the Yeare aforesaid and diuers other days and times as well before as after
Certaine detestabl⟨e⟩ Arts called Witchcraft and Sorceries Wickedly Mallitiously and
felloniously hath used practised and Exercised At and [Hand 2] **in the Towne of Andivor in
the County of Essex** [Hand 1] Aforesaid in upon and against one [Hand 2] **Sarah Phelps
daughter of Samuel Phellps of Andivo^ε** [Hand 1] Aforesaid [Hand 2] **Husbandman** [Hand
1] by which said Wicked Acts the s^d [Hand 2] **Sarah Phellps the day & yeare** [Hand 1]
Aforesaid & diuers other days and times both before and after was and is Tortured Aflicted
Consumed Pined Wasted and Tormented, and also for sundry other Acts of Witchcraft by
the said [Hand 2] **Abigaill ffalkner** [Hand 1] Comitted and done before and Since that time
against the Peace of our Sou^ε Lord and Lady the King and Queen theire Crowne & Dignity
& the forme of ye Stattute In y^t case made & Prouided

[Reverse] [Hand 2] Abigaiell ffalkner Indictm^t for bewitching Sarah Phelps
[Hand 3] Billa vera

Notes: Copies of this indictment and the following one (Document 665) are in the Massachusetts Archives v. 135,
nos. 104 and 120. For other related copies in the Massachusetts archives see v. 135, nos. 48, 49, 50, 115, and 119.
Hand 2 = Anthony Checkley; Hand 3 = Andrew Elliot

*Essex County Court Archives, vol. 2, no. 37, Massachusetts Supreme Judicial Court, Judicial Archives, on deposit James Duncan
Phillips Library, Peabody Essex Museum, Salem, MA.*

665. Indictment of Abigail Faulkner Sr., for Afflicting Martha Sprague†

[Hand 1] Essex in the Prouince   Anno $\overline{RR}^s$ & Reginæ Gulielmi & Mariæ Angliæ &c^c
of ["of" written over "in"] the   }   Quarto Annoqʒ Domini 1692
Massachusetts Bay in New
England.
ss//

The Jurors for o^ε Sou^ε Lord and Lady King & Queen do⟨e⟩ present that. [Hand 2] **Abigaill
ffalkner Wife of ffrancis ffalkner of Andivor** [Hand 1] In the County of Essex [Hand 2]
afor̅sd Husband^m On or about the begining of August [Hand 1] In the year aforesaid and
diuers other dayes and times as well before as after Certaine Detestable Arts Called
Witchcraft and Sorceries Wickedly Mallistiously and felloniously hath vsed practised and
Exercised at and [Hand 2] **in the Towne of Boxford in the County of Essex** [Hand 1]
aforesaid in vpon and against [Hand 2] **One Martha Sprague of Boxford** [Hand 1] aforesaid
[Hand 2] **Single Woman** [Hand 1] by which Said wicked Acts the said [Hand 2] **Martha**

Sept. 17, 1692

Sprague the day & yea$^\varepsilon$ [Hand 1] aforesaid and diuers other dayes and times both before and after was and is Tortur^d Aflicted Consumed Pined Wasted and Tormented and also for Sundry other Acts of Witchcraft by the Said [Hand 2] **Abigaill ffalkner** [Hand 1] Comitted and done. ~~against~~ Before ⌃{&} Since that time against the Peace of o$^\varepsilon$ Sou$^\varepsilon$ Lord and Lady the King and Queen theire Crowne and dignity and the forme of the Stattute in that Case made and Prouided,

[Reverse] [Hand 2] Indictm^t ags^t Abagaill ffalkner for bewitching Martha Sprague
[Hand 3] Billa vera÷

Notes: Hand 2 = Anthony Checkley; Hand 3 = Andrew Elliot

Essex County Court Archives, vol. 2, no. 38, Massachusetts Supreme Judicial Court, Judicial Archives, on deposit James Duncan Phillips Library, Peabody Essex Museum, Salem, MA.

666. Depositions of Rose Foster & Martha Sprague v. Abigail Faulkner Sr., Copy, and Verdict and Sentence of Abigail Faulkner Sr., Copy

See also: Sept. 17, 1692.

[Hand 1] The Deposition of Rose Foster
Who Testefieth and saith I have beene most Greviously Aflicted & tormented by Abigall Faulkner of Andover Allso I have seene Abigall Faulkner or her appearence most Afflict & Torment Martha Sprague Sarrah Phelps: and hannah Bixbe since ye begining Agust & verrily believe that Abigall Faulkner is a witch & that she has often aflicted me and ye afores^d person by acts of Witchcraft

The above Named Rose Foster afirmed before ye grand Inquest that the above writen Evidence is Truth upon her Oath;

Copia Vera

The Deposition of Marthah: Sprague
Who testefieth and saith that I have beene Most greviously aflicted and tormented by Abigall Faulkner or her appearence Most Greviously torment and aflict hannah Bixbe & Rose Foster and Sarrah Phelps and i verrily believe in my hart that abigall Faulkner is a witch and that she has often aflicted me and severall others by act of Witchcraft

The above Named Martha Sprague afirmed before the grand Inquest that y^e above writen Evidence is truth upon her Oath

Copia Vera Septembr: 17: 1692

Att a Court of Oyer and Terminer holden att ⟨S⟩Salem by adjourment Septemb$^\varepsilon$ 17: 1692
Abigall Faulkner of Andover Indcated and Arraigned for the Crime of fellony by Witchcraft Comited on y^e bodyes of Martha Sprague Evidences being Called and sworne in open Court Matter of fact Comitted to y^e Jury

The Jury find Abigall Faulkner wife of Francis Faulkner of Andover guilty of ye fellony by Witchcraft Comited on ye body of Marthah Sprague allsoe on ye body of Sarrah Phelps

September 17, 1692   Sentence of Death pased on Abigall Faulkner
                                                                                    Copia Vera

Notes: This is a copy of two extant depositions and a copy of the verdict and death sentence. The original of the latter
does not survive. The originals of these depositions (see No. 667 & No. 668) were used as trial evidence. In a petition
dated December 3, Abigail Faulkner says she would have been put to death had she not been pregnant, but this is unlikely,
since she was a confessor. Pregnant or not, confessors were not executed. She did receive a reprieve from Governor Phips.
See No. 875. This manuscript is one of several copies of trial evidence in Faulkner's case in the Massachusetts Archives
Collection, Vol. 135, likely prepared when she petitioned for a reversal of attainder in 1700. See No. 875. ◊ Used at trial.

Massachusetts Archives Collection, vol. 135, no. 49. Massachusetts State Archives. Boston, MA.

Sworn Before the Grand Jury: Summary of the Examinations of Dorothy Faulkner, Abigail Faulkner Jr., Martha Tyler, Johannah Tyler, Sarah Wilson Jr., & Joseph Draper v. Abigail Faulkner Sr.

2nd of 2 dates. See No. 657 on Sept. 16, 1692

667. Deposition of Rose Foster v. Abigail Faulkner Sr.

[Hand 1] The deposistion: of Rose ffoster: who testifieth and saith I haue ben most
greviously afflected and tormented by Abigail ffalkner of Andeueo⟨ur⟩ also I haue seen
Abigail ffalkner or hir Apperance most greviously afflect and torment martha sprague Sarah
phelps and Hannah Bigsbe ^{sence the beginig Augst} and I veryly beleue that Abigail ⟨?⟩ll
ffalkner is a wicth and that she has offten affleted me and the afforesaid parson by acts of
wicthcraft:
[Hand 2] The aboue named Rose ffoster affirmed beffore y^e Grand inquest that y^e aboue
written Euidence is truth vppon her Oath sep^t :17: 1691

[Reverse] [Hand 3] Rose ffoster dep° ⟨a⟩gst: Abigaill ffalkn⟨o⟩r
[Hand 4] Jurat: in Curia

Notes: The "1691" in the document is simply a scribal error. ◊ Used at trial. ◊ Hand 1 = Thomas Putnam; Hand 2 =
Andrew Elliot

*Essex County Court Archives, vol. 2, no. 39, Massachusetts Supreme Judicial Court, Judicial Archives, on deposit James Duncan
Phillips Library, Peabody Essex Museum, Salem, MA.*

668. Deposition of Sarah Phelps v. Abigail Faulkner Sr.

[Hand 1] The depossistion of Sarah phelps who testifieth and saith that about the begining
of August 1692 I was most greviously afflected and tormented by Abigaill ffalkner or hir
Apperanc: but most dreadfull she did torment on the 11 August being the day of hir
Examination for if she did but loock upon me she would strick me down or almost choake
me: also sence the begining of August I haue seen Abigaill ffalkner or hir apperance most
greviously afflet and torment mary walcott Ann putnam and martha Sprague and I veryly

beleue in my heart that Abigail ffalkner is a wicth and that she has very offten affleted me   September 17, 1692
and the afforesaid parsons by accts of wicthcraft

[Hand 2] The aboue named Sarah Phelps affirmed before ye Grand inquest that ye aboue
written Euidence is ["s" written over "t"] T̶h̶ truth vpon her Oath ye 17 sep^t 1692
[Hand 3] Jurat. i̶n̶ ̶C̶u̶r̶i̶a̶ ̶a̶t̶t̶e̶s̶t̶⟨?⟩ ̶S̶t̶e̶p̶:̶ ̶S̶⟨e̶w̶⟩a̶l̶l̶ ̶C̶l̶⟨?⟩

[Reverse] [Hand 4] Sarah Phelps: dep^o v^{εs} Abagail ffalkner
[Hand 5?] Jurat
[Hand 6] M̶a̶r̶y̶ ̶P̶a̶r̶k̶e̶r̶

Notes: It is not clear whether this was used at the trial or not. Some clerical confusion occurred, as reflected in the crossouts
of Mary Parker and after "Jurat." ◊ Possibly used at trial. ◊ Hand 1 = Thomas Putnam; Hand 2 = Andrew Elliot; Hand
3 = Stephen Sewall; Hand 4 = Anthony Checkley

*Essex County Court Archives, vol. 2, no. 44, Massachusetts Supreme Judicial Court, Judicial Archives, on deposit James Duncan
Phillips Library, Peabody Essex Museum, Salem, MA.*

669. Deposition of Ann Putnam Jr. v. Abigail Faulkner Sr.

[Hand 1] The deposistion of Ann putnam who testifieth and saith that about the 9th of
August 1692 I was affleted by a woman which tould me hir w̶a̶⟨?h̶⟩ name was ffalkner: but on
the 11th of August being the day of the Examination of Abigail ffalkner she did most
dreadfully torment me during the time of hir Examinatin also on the day of hir Examination
I saw Abigaill ffalkner or hir Apperance most greviously afflect and torment mary walcott
Sarah phelps and I beleue⟨n⟩ that Abigal ffalkner is a wicth and that she has often affleted
me and seurall othrs by acts of wicthcraft
[Hand 2] The aboue named Ann Putnam affirmed before y^e Grand inquest that y^e aboue
written Euidence is the truth vpon her Oath Sep^t 17. 1692
[Hand 3] Sworne before y^e grand Jury

[Reverse] [Hand 4?] An Puttnam dep^{oε} v^{εs} Abig^l ffalkner [Hand 3] Jurat Coram Grand Jury

Notes: Hand 1 = Thomas Putnam; Hand 2 = Andrew Elliot; Hand 3 = Anthony Checkley

*Essex County Court Archives, vol. 2, no. 46, Massachusetts Supreme Judicial Court, Judicial Archives, on deposit James Duncan
Phillips Library, Peabody Essex Museum, Salem, MA.*

670. Deposition of Martha Sprague v. Abigail Faulkner Sr.

[Hand 1] The deposistion of martha Spreague who testifieth and saith that I haue ben most
greviously affleted and tormented by Abigail ffalkner of Andevor sen⟨c⟩e the beginig of
August 1692: also I saw Abigail ffalkner or hir Apperan⟨ce⟩s most greviously torment and
afflet Hannah Bigsbe and Rose ffoster and Sarah phelps and I verily beleuen in my heart that
Abigail ffalkner is a wicth & that she has often affletd me and seuerall othrs by acts of
wicthcraft

September 17, 1692   [Hand 2] The aboue named Martha sprague affirmed before y^e Grand inquest that y^e aboue written Euidence is truth vpon her Oath 17: sp^t 1692

[Reverse] [Hand 3] Martha Sprague dep° Agst Abigaill ffalkner
[Hand 4] Jurat in Curia

Notes: Used at trial. ◊ Hand 1 = Thomas Putnam; Hand 2 = Andrew Elliot; Hand 3 = Anthony Checkley; Hand 4 = Stephen Sewall

Essex County Court Archives, vol. 2, no. 41, Massachusetts Supreme Judicial Court, Judicial Archives, on deposit James Duncan Phillips Library, Peabody Essex Museum, Salem, MA.

671. Deposition of Mary Walcott v. Abigail Faulkner Sr.

[Hand 1] The deposistion of mary walcott who testifieth and saith that about the 9th August 1692 I wa⟨s⟩ most dreadfully afflected by a woman that tould me hir [Hand 2] ^{name} [Hand 1] was [Hand 2] ^{Abigail} [Hand 1] ffalkner. but on the 11th of August being the day of the Examination of Abigail ffalkner she did most dreadfully affle⟨ct⟩ me dvring the time of hir Examination I saw Abigail ffalkner or hir Apperance most greviously afflet and toment Sarah phelps and Ann putnam: and se [Hand 2] I [Hand 1] veryly beleue⟨s⟩ in my heart that Abigail ffalkner is a wicth and that she has often afflected me and the afforesaid said parsons by acts of wicthcrafft

[Hand 2] The aboue named mary Walcutt affirmed before y^e Grand inquest that y^e aboue written Euidence is truth vpon her Oath 17: sept: 1692

[Reverse] [Hand 3] Mary Walcott dep° agst: Aba: ffalkner
[Hand 4] Jurat in Curia

Notes: Used at trial. ◊ Hand 1 = Thomas Putnam; Hand 2 = Andrew Elliot; Hand 3 = Anthony Checkley; Hand 4 = Stephen Sewall

Essex County Court Archives, vol. 2, no. 42, Massachusetts Supreme Judicial Court, Judicial Archives, on deposit James Duncan Phillips Library, Peabody Essex Museum, Salem, MA.

672. Deposition of Mary Warren v. Abigail Faulkner Sr.

[Hand 1] The deposistion of marry warren who testifieth and saith that Abigail ffalkner of Andevor did most greviously afflet and torment me on 11th August 1692 dureing the time of hir Examination for if she did but look upon me she woold strick me down or almost choak me also on the day of hir Examination I saw Abigail ffalknr or hir Apperan⟨c⟩ most grevioully afflect and torment mary walcott Ann putnā and Sarah phelps and I veryly beleue that Abigail ffalkner is a⟨?⟩ wicth and that she has often afflected me and seurall othr by acts of wicthcraft

[Hand 2] Mary Waren: ownd: upon her oath:: to y^e grand Inquest that y^e above written evidence is y^e truth: Sep^ε 17: 1692

[Reverse] [Hand 3] Mary Warren dep° agst Abig⟨a⟩il ffal⟨k⟩ner
[Hand 4] Jurat in Curia

Notes: Used at trial. ◊ Hand 1 = Thomas Putnam; Hand 2 = Simon Willard; Hand 3 = Anthony Checkley; Hand 4 = Stephen Sewall

Essex County Court Archives, vol. 2, no. 43, Massachusetts Supreme Judicial Court, Judicial Archives, on deposit James Duncan Phillips Library, Peabody Essex Museum, Salem, MA.

Monday, September 19, 1692

Giles Cory Pressed to Death

673. Letter of Thomas Putnam to Samuel Sewall

The Last Night my Daughter *Ann*, was grievously Tormented by Witches, Threatning that she should be *Pressed* to Death, before *Giles Cory*. But thro' the Goodness of a Gracious God, she had at last a little Respite. Whereupon there appeared unto her (she said) a man in a Winding Sheet; who told her that *Giles Cory* had Murdered him, by *Pressing* him to Death with his Feet; but that the Devil there appeared unto him, and Covenanted with him, and promised him, *He should not be Hanged.* The Apparition said, God Hardned his heart; that he should not hearken to the Advice of the Court, and so Dy an easy Death; because as it said, *It must be done to him as he has done to me.* The Apparition also said, That *Giles Cory*, was carry'd to the Court for this, and that the Jury had found the Murder, and that her Father knew the man and the thing was done before she was born. Now Sir, This is not a little strange to us; that no body should Remember these things, all the while that *Giles Cory* was in Prison, and so often before the Court. For all people now Remember very well, (and the Records of the Court also mention it,) That about Seventeen Years ago, *Giles Cory* kept a man in his House, that was almost a Natural Fool; which Man Dy'd suddenly. A Jury was impannel'd upon him, among whom was Dr. *Zorobbabel Endicot*; who found the man bruised to Death, and having clodders of Blood about his Heart. The Jury, whereof several are yet alive brought in the man Murdered; but as if some Enchantment had hindred the Prosecution of the Matter, the Court Proceeded not against Giles
Giles Cory, tho' it cost him a great deal of Mony to get off. Thus the Story.

Notes: The letter is found in Cotton Mather's *The Wonders of the Invisible World* and is described there as "an Extract" of a letter from Thomas Putnam to Judge Samuel Sewall. Giles Cory was indicted on September 9 and died on September 19. ◊ "clodders": 'clots' (*OED* s.v. *clodder*).

Cotton Mather. The Wonders of the Invisible World: Being an Account of the Tryals of Several Witches, Lately Excuted [sic] in New-England: And of several remarkable Curiosities therein Occuring. (London: John Dunton, 1693), p. 47.

Tuesday, September 20, 1692

674. Warrant for the Apprehension of Joan Penny, and Officer's Return
See also: Sept. 21, 1692.

[Hand 1] To the Sherife of the County of Essex or his deputy or the Constable of ~~Gloster~~.
[Hand 2] Chebacco
[Hand 1] Complaint haueing ben made to us whose names are underwritten Justices of the peace in the County of Essex by Zebulon Hill of Salem against [Hand 2] Joan [Hand 1] Pen⟨e⟩y. widow of Thomas peney Late of Gloster for that she the Said [Hand 2] Joan [Hand 1] peney hath feloniously comitted Seuerall acts of witchcraft. on the Body of Mary Hill of Salem Singleweoman. To ⟨h⟩er great hurt & Torment. the Said ^{Zeb} Hill haueing giuen Sufficient bond for the procecution of the Said Complaint to Effect.
These are therfore in their Majesties name to require you fforthwith to Aprehend & seize. the Body of [Hand 2] Joane [Hand 1] peney widow as abouesaid & bring her. before their Majesties Justices of the peace to be examined & proceded wth according to law for wch this shall be your sufficient warant dated in Salem this 20: September 1692:

> Barth° Gedney
> John Hathorne
> Jonathan. Corwin
> John Higginson

[Hand 3] The: 21: of September 1692: I haue seased the body of wedowe peni and haue broghght hur to Salem by me
John Chote Counstabell of Ipswich

Notes: Hand 1 = John Higginson Jr. ◊ 1 wax seal.

MS Ch K 1.40, vol. 2, p. 248, Rare Books & Manuscripts, Boston Public Library. Boston, MA.

Sworn: Complaint of Zebulon Hill v. Joan Penny
2nd of 2 dates. See No. 613 on Sept. 13, 1692

Wednesday, September 21, 1692

Officer's Return: Warrant for the Apprehension of Joan Penny
2nd of 2 dates. See No. 674 on Sept. 20, 1692

675. Fragment of the Examination of Joan Penny

She was bid to say the Lord's Prayer. When she came to forgive us our trespasses as we forgive them that trespass against us, she said, so do I. No other mistake, in saying the prayer, remarkable.

Sept. 21, 1692

Notes: This fragment is from a note in Hutchinson in connection with Burroughs reciting the Lord's Prayer at his execution. The fragment probably concerns Joan Penny, widow, of Gloucester who was arrested on September 21. See No. 674. Late in the winter of 1692, she and others still in jail pleaded for release with bail and a willingness to stand trial. It remains unclear as to when they were released and whether they all survived the harsh winter. See No. 702. The attribution of this as associated with Penny is based on no record of anybody else being examined that day and is speculative.

Thomas Hutchinson, The History of the Province of Massachusetts-Bay, from the Charter of King William and Queen Mary, in 1691, Until the Year 1750, vol. 2, ed. Lawrence Shaw Mayo (Cambridge, MA: Harvard University Press, 1936), 43n.

676. Petition of John Hale, Nicholas Noyes, Daniel Epps Jr., & John Emerson Jr. for Dorcas Hoar

[Hand 1] To his Excellency Sr William Phips Governour of y^e Province of y^e Massachussetts Colony in Newe England or in his absence to y^e Honourable William Stoughton Esq$^\varepsilon$ Leiftenant Govern$^\varepsilon$

The Petition of y^e subscribers humbly sheweth

That it hath pleased y^e Lord wee hope in mercy to the soule of Dorcas Hoar of Beverly to open her hea[Lost] [= heart] out of distress of conscience, as shee professeth, to confess her selfe guilty of the heynous crime of witchcraft for wch shee is condemned, & how & when shee was taken in the snare of y^e devill, & y^t she signed his book with y^e forefinger of her right hand &c.
Allso she gives account of some other persons y^t shee hath: known to be guilty of ye same crime.
And beeing in great distress of Conscience earnestly craves a little longer time of life to realize & perfect her repentance for ye salvation of her soule.
These are therefore humbly to petition in her behalfe y^t their may be granted her one months time, ^{or more} to prepare for death & eternity unless by her relapse, or afflicting others shee shall give grounds to hasten her execution: And this wee conceive if y^e Lord sanctify it may tend to save a soule, & to give opportunity for her making some discovery of these mysterys of iniquity, & be presidentiall to y^e encouraging others to confess & give glory to God.
& y$^\varepsilon$ petitioners shall pray &c.
y$^\varepsilon$ Humble servants   John Hale.
Salem. September. 21: 1692.   Nicholas Noyes.
                                                                                      Daniel Epes.
                                                                                      John Emerson jun$^\varepsilon$

[Hand 2] Haveing Heard & taken the Conffession of dorcas Hoar doe Consent ^{y^t} her Execution be Respited untill further ord$^\varepsilon$
21. 7th 92   Barth^o Gedney

[Reverse] [Hand 3] Petition of John Hale Nich^o Noyes &c. 1692
[Hand 1] These for His Excellency Sr Wm Phips Govern$^\varepsilon$ &c at Boston or to y^e Honourable Wm Stoughton Esq$^\varepsilon$ Leift Gov$^\varepsilon$ at Dorchest$^\varepsilon$

Sept. 22, 1692   Notes: The plea by these four ministers for a stay was granted, and Dorcas Hoar escaped execution. She was eventually released from prison, probably in February 1693. Dorcas Hoar's daughter Annis, along with her husband John King in September 1710, asked compensation for the cost of going to Boston "to procure a repreive." See No. 910. The connection of this journey to the petition of the ministers, Hale, Noyes, Epps, and Emerson seems likely. Her attainder, along with several others, was removed October 17, 1711. See No. 931. ◊ Hand 1 = John Hale; Hand 2 = Bartholomew Gedney

Salem Selections, Massachusetts Box, Essex Co., Manuscripts & Archives, New York Public Library. New York, NY.

Thursday, September 22, 1692

Executions of Martha Cory, Mary Esty, Alice Parker, Mary Parker, Ann Pudeator, Wilmot Redd, Margaret Scott, & Samuel Wardwell

Monday, September 26, 1692

677. Petition of the Selectmen of Andover, Regarding the Children of Samuel Wardwell

[Hand 1] To the Hono^{ε}ed Court now sitting at Ipswich
The Petition of the Select men of Andover sheweth;

That wheras Samuel Wardwell and his wife of Andover, were lately apprehended and committed to prison for witchcraft, and have left severall small children who are vncapable of provideing for themselves, and are now in a suffering condition: we haue thought it necessary and convenient that they should be disposed of in some familyes where there may be due care taken of them.
We therefore humbly pray yo^ε Hon^{ε}s to inform us what is our duty in this case, and to give ~~us~~ order so to dispose of them that their necessityes may be releived, and to grant liberty to improve so much of their fathers Estate as is necessary for their present supply. And yo^ε Petition^{εs} shall ever pray &c

                                                                    John Abbott.
Sep^t 26. 1692   [Hand 2] {and} john Aslabee
                                                            by order of ye salekt men

[Reverse] [Hand 3] S⟨e⟩lect Men of Andouer peticon̄

Essex County Court Archives, vol. 2, no. 96, Massachusetts Supreme Judicial Court, Judicial Archives, on deposit James Duncan Phillips Library, Peabody Essex Museum, Salem, MA.

Tuesday, September 27, 1692

678. Judgment v. John Shepherd for Assisting Mary Green to Escape

[Hand 1] John Shepard of Rowley bound over by Thomas Wade Esq$^\varepsilon$ for Assisting and helping to Convey Mary Green a Prisoner for the Crime of Witchcraft out of their Maj^{tes} Goal in Ipswitch: Confest the fact./

The Courts Judgem^t is That he pay a fine of 30^{li} money and Costs of Court./

Vpon his Confession and Petition the Court Respits 25^{li} Till further Orders, y^t he stand Committed till the five pounds and Costs be paid/

Notes: The date of this session of the Court is given on page 4 of the record book.

Records of the Salem and Ipswich Court of General Sessions of the Peace (1692–1693), p. 8. Massachusetts Supreme Judicial Court, Judicial Archives, on deposit James Duncan Phillips Library, Peabody Essex Museum, Salem, MA.

679. Provision for the Support of the Children of Samuel Wardwell

[Hand 1] Att a Generall Sessions of ye Pease Holden at Ipswitch September 27th 1692:

Information being given to this Court by a Pettition layd before us from the Select Men of Andover shewing that Samuel Wardwell lately Convicted ∧{& Eccecuted} for Witchcraft, hath left severall Small Children that are Vncapable of Providing for themselves./.

This Court doth Order and Appoint that the Select Men of Andover for the time being doe place out and if Occation so Require bind out so many or all of Said Children into good and honest ffamilyes as they in their Prudence shall think meete Pursuant to Law in that case made and Provided./

Records of the Salem and Ipswich Court of General Sessions of the Peace (1692–1693), p. 5. Massachusetts Supreme Judicial Court, Judicial Archives, on deposit James Duncan Phillips Library, Peabody Essex Museum, Salem, MA.

Wednesday, September 28, 1692

680. Placement of the Wardwell Children by the Selectmen of Andover [?]

Wee ye subscribers selectmen of Andover ye abovesd year having informed ye Quarter Sessions at Ipswich ye 27th of ye aboves^d September that there was severall children of Saml Wardwels y^t was in a suffering condition begging their advice direction & order therein which they were pleased to Consider of & order as followes y^t ye Selectmen for ye time being should place out, or if need require binde out s^d children in good & honest families, referring to a law in that case provided. Persuant to this order of ye Court wee have placed them as follows; viz Samuel Wardwell we placed with John Ballard his uncle for one year, William we placed with Corpl Saml ffrie till he come to be of ye age of one and twenty years; s^d ffrie to learne him ye trade of a weaver. Eliakim we placed to Daniel Poor till he was twenty-one years of age & Elizabeth we placed with John Stevens till eighteen years of age, all ye abovesd were to find them with suites of apparel att ye end of s^d term of tyme.

Saml Frie
John Aslebe   }   Selectmen
John Abbot

Notes: The dating of this document is unknown, but is placed here immediately following the court order to which it responds, No. 679. It seems likely that the response to the court order would have been expeditious.

Sarah Loring Bailey. Historical Sketches of Andover, Comprising the Present Towns of North Andover and Andover, Essex County, Massachusetts. (Boston: Houghton, Mifflin and Company, 1880), pp. 220–221.

October–December 1692

Saturday, October 1, 1692

681. Complaint of Mary Brown & Benjamin Larobe v. Sarah Cole (of Lynn)

See also: Oct. 3, 1692.

[Hand 1] The Complaint Mary Browne of Reding widow // ⟨In⟩ against Sarah Colle wife of John Colle of Lyn Cooper // Complaineth as folowth

That the aboues^d Sarah Colle heth bodyly Appeared to mee and that In her full shepp and parson: both night and day: and heth thertened me soerly whot shee would do to me: heth Come to my beed sid & feet much disturbing of {me &} puting ^{me} to grat paine both strang and vnwonted such paines as In all my Illness that I heve gon through In all my lifetime pas{t} heve not mett wth such paines: // and I most say I. do think the s^d Sarah Colle (Is by gods purmition) Is the Cauess of this my Illness and that by acts of ~~witch~~ wicthcraftes done {me} [1 word illegible] and acted one my body & mind:/ this heth been h⟨er⟩ maner and Custome for the most part of th⟨e⟩ later part of september past: but I got some frineds to goe to speek to hur about a week ~~sin~~ past: & sinces that time I heve not seen her but Remaine vnder the lik Illness as befor and beleiue y^t she Is acting her part to the ⟨y⟩e roun{in}g [= the ruining?] of my famiely: as ferr as god doth give Leue// ~~and~~ my self and childern heve offten heard lik the throuing of stons against the hous and creatuers crying like catts vpon y^e Roffe of y^e house but there Runing there wes like dogs or biger creaturs for y^e [= they] med y^e Roff Crake.

Reeding

The 1st of

october 1692   Mary Browne

These mey Certifey that I Mary Browne with In nemed heve desiered goodman Beniemien   October 1, 1692
Larrobe to Carey this my Compliant to Authoury // how will act according to thier wisdom
for my Relief:// my son being Ille At This time// and my selfe a poor and afflected
person &c

Reeding
the 1ˢᵗ of October
1692   Mary Browne

[Hand 2] Benjᵃ Larobe Enters the within Complaint wᵗʰ their majesties Justices of the peace
of Salem in behalfe of the said Mary Browne of Reding widow.
3: October 1692

The marke

$\wp$ of

Benjᵃ Larobe:

Benjᵃ Larobe. of Lin in the County of Essex obligeth himselfe to our soueraines Wᵐ &
Mary King & Quen of Englᵈ &c in the ffull & whole sume of one hundred pounds Currant
mony of New England The Condition is that wheras the said Larobe hath Entred a
Complaint wᵗʰ their Majᵋ Justies of the peace at Salem in Behalfe of Mary Browne of
Reding widow against Sarah Coale wife of John Coale of Lin for that she hath sorly hurt the
said Mary Browne by witchcraft, &c that he the said Larobe will & shall procecut the said
Complaint to Effect as yᵉ law directs
3. october: 1692

The Marke

$\wp$ of

Benjᵃ Larobe.

this Recognizance was taken before me

John Higginson Justᵋ p⟨eace⟩

[Hand 3] Complaint of Mary Browne of Reding Agst Sarah Cole of Lynn

Notes: The complaint of Mary Brown is the only extant formal, legal complaint by a woman during the Salem witch
trials. ◊ Hand 2 = John Higginson Jr.; Hand 3 = Anthony Checkley

*Suffolk Court Files, vol. 32, docket 2712, p. 49, Massachusetts Supreme Judicial Court, Judicial Archives, Massachusetts State
Archives. Boston, MA.*

Monday, October 3, 1692

Complaint of Mary Brown & Benjamin Larobe v. Sarah Cole (of Lynn)
2nd of 2 dates. See No. 681 on Oct. 1, 1692

682. Warrant for the Apprehension of Sarah Cole (of Lynn) with Summons for Witnesses, and Officer's Return

[Hand 1] Essex: To the Constable of Lin
Complaint haueing ben made to us Barth° Gidny and John Higginson Esq^rs. their majesties Justices of the peace in Salem, by Benj^a Larobe of Lin in behalfe of Mary Browne of Reding widow against Sarah Coale wife of John Coale of Lin Cooper for that the Said Sarah Coale hath Greatly & feloniously hurt the Said Mary Browne by witchcraft to her great paine & damage & the Said Larobe hath giuen in bond to procecut the Said Complaint to Effect. These are therfor in their Majesties name to require you forthwith to Aprehend & Seize the Body of Sarah Coale the wife of John Coale of Lin Cooper & bring her before thier Majesties Justices of the peace in Salem ther to be Examined & proced with according to Law dated in Salem: 3. october 1692

Barth° Gedney
John Higgi⟨ns⟩on

To the Constable of Lin
you are required in their Majesties name to Sumon Maj^r Swain Mary Browne John Browne Elizabeth welman John Coale Benj^a Larobe ~~that~~ & the wife of Dan^{ll} Eaton that they & Euery of them doe forthwith apeare before their Majesties Justices of the peace in Salem their to giue in their testimony of what they know against Sarah Coale wife of John Coale who is complained of for comitting Seuerall acts of witchcraft upon ye body of mary Browne of Reding widow &c: & herof make returne faile not
dated in Salem 3. oct^r 1692

Barth° Gedney ⎫
John Higginson ⎬
                Justices peace

[Reverse] [Hand 2] In obedience to this Warrant I haue Seized the person wth in mentioned and brought her before Their Majesties Justices of y^e peace here in Salem Octob^r 3: 1692
The Mark of X [1 word illegible] Constable

[Hand 3] Sarah Coale
wife of Jn° Coale

Notes: Gedney signs his own name after the warrant, but Higginson signs Gedney's name after the summons. ◊ Hand 1 = John Higginson Jr. ◊ 2 wax seals.

MS Ch K 1.40, vol. 1, p. 88, Rare Books & Manuscripts, Boston Public Library. Boston, MA.

683. Examination of Sarah Cole (of Lynn)

[Hand 1] The Examination of Sarah Cole of Lynne
Octob^ε – 3 – 1692
She saith y^t y^e same night Capt Osgoods wife was Examined – She saw Eliz: Colstson & Abrah. Coles wife come into her house personally to her app^{ε}hension and ∧{Jn^o} Wilkinsons wife of Malden & one of her sister & a little Girle she did not know; about 10 years old one of them had a piece of board wth nails in it thro the board at the End about a foot long as broad as her hand, That one of her children was sorely afflicted at y^t time, and s^d one of them did strike her on ye head {wth s^d board} – They seemed to turn side ways and so were gone, wch was about midnight – The child was afflicted till Abr. Coles wife was take up – The begining of ye affliction in our family was upon a fast day about a month ago Abrah Coles wife was at my house she Commended my children much for pretty children & they w^r both taken sick my boy & girle, ye Girle s^d she saw A. Coles wife afflict her seuerall times, had pins thrust into her was bit & scratched had a blow on her nose wch caused her nose to run down wth blood ye last fit my child had and Complained of her aunt Cole was when s^d A. Coles wife was brought to Salem One night being in bed I was sorely afflicted, & saw a ball of fire I arose to see w^t was the matter before I got a light it went away – the last thing I saw was a dog wch I went to strike wth a spade and was beat down my self this was about a week ago The dog went out at a crack: in ye side of the house

[Reverse] [Hand 2] mary warren being aflicted was brought to Goody Coale & wth her touch. was. recouered. & looked on her twice & struck her downe & recouerd her wth her hand mary warren said y^t she had sen this Coale many ti⟨m⟩es wth goody hart & another weo. & goody & y^t she had not aflicted her till this night; & said y^t a weoman y^t said her name was baites & a Child both. Stood up before her & Cr⟨y⟩ed for vengance, coale owned y^t she & some others toyed wth a venus glase & an Egg. what trade their sweetharts should be of 3 oct^ε 1692 before. John Higginson Just$^{⟨ε⟩}$ peace

Notes: Hand 2 = John Higginson Jr.

Suffolk Court Files, vol. 32, docket 2712, p. 49, Massachusetts Supreme Judicial Court, Judicial Archives, Massachusetts State Archives. Boston, MA.

684. Deposition of John Brown Jr. v. Sarah Cole (of Lynn)

[Hand 1] The Deposistion of John Browne Junr Aged about twentyfiue Years saith. that a Mongth agoe Last Thursday knight, I was taken wth a shiuering cold, & full of paine. and full of Notions that Good^w Cole Hurt me, and Extraordinaryly prest vpon my Bowells; and my Coller bone prest, as if it would be broak, and could turn no wayes for Ease, and soe continued for two or three dayes; while my mother Carried whome a Barrell that we had of Good^m Coles, and then Imediatly I mended, & neuer haue had such violent fitts after But I neuer saw Good^w Cole But haue great Cause to thinke that Good^w Cole hurts mee and that because my mother see Good^w Cole and has been sadly Terrified by her and saith that I heard the Blows that was strock on the house at the same time when my Mother did, and heard my mother Crying out Imediatly of Good^w Coles afflicting of her. and heard my mother Cry out

October 3, 1692

much of Good^W Cole, hurting of her but Neuer saw her my self But heard ~~Nioy~~ Noyeses as if Catts ware ^{~~upon~~ woulling and crying} ~~walking~~ upon the House. but theire Tredings ware Like Great Doggs or of Bigger Creaturs which made the Rouffe to Crack. and once as I Lay on my Bedd I heard something ffly by my Ear as if it ware ~~i~~ a Bird But saw Nothing But heard grate Noyeses about the House. at that time. and Crackings of the House. uerry Much.

[Hand 2] Sworne in Court atest Jn° Higginson Justice peace 3: october: 1692:

[Reverse] [Hand 3] Jn° Brone Juni^E dep°

Notes: Although in retrospect it is clear that the Court of Oyer and Terminer that prosecuted the witchcraft cases would not continue, at the time of Sarah Cole's examination (see No. 683) she would have had no reason not to have seen herself in danger of execution, especially so soon after the hangings on September 22. This deposition, along with the following ones against her, was not sworn at the Court of Oyer and Terminer. ◊ Hand 2 = John Higginson Jr.

MS Ch F, vol. 1, p. 7, Rare Books & Manuscripts, Boston Public Library. Boston, MA.

685. Deposition of John Cole v. Sarah Cole (of Lynn)

[Hand 1] Jn° Cole Saith that Coming home to his house on Saturday night after his wife had seen strange sights That from y^t time his house hath been troubled wth Cats & dogs wch he saw often running up & down & one night he thinks he saw a ball of fire, & last munday night being a week ago he saith as he was at prayer in his family I heard somthing like a great thing flung against the house & on a sudden it was at ~~me~~ {him} & struck him on ye head & on~~e~~ one of his sides, and almost beat the breath out of his body so y^t I was forced to break of prayer for about half a quarter of an hour w^n he ["he" written over "I"] revived again he ["he" written over "I"] proceeded in his prayer
his wife being asked affirms she knew nothing of his being hindred in his prayer
W^th in a week or 8 days {after} s^d Cole saw a great Cat of an unusuall bignes at my door, staring me in ye face I pursued it wch went into the stalks near ye house and tho it was very calm all the stalks did wave as if there had been a ~~hurricane a~~ a strong wind and he thinks since this some of his children haue been afflicted by witchcraft
and s^d Cole saith y^t for this 3 nights he had not lodged in his own house being so affrighted that he was afraid to stay or lodge in it being sorely molested always about y^e dead of y^e night & was sorely handled last Saturday in his head & belly as if a string had been twisted about his head
[Hand 2] 3. oct^E 1692 Sworne in Court atest.

John. Higginson
Justices peace

[Reverse] [Hand 3] ⟨?⟩ Hathorne John

Notes: Hand 2 = John Higginson Jr.

Suffolk Court Files, vol. 32, docket 2712, p. 49, Massachusetts Supreme Judicial Court, Judicial Archives, Massachusetts State Archives. Boston, MA.

686. Deposition of Mary Eaton v. Sarah Cole (of Lynn)

October 3, 1692

[Hand 1] The, Deposistion of Mary Eaten Senr of Lyn: saith that upon a Time Sarah Cole wife of Jn° Cole of Lyn, and my self had some difference and with in a uerry ∧{Litle time} I had a Cow taken in a strange maner and at that same time ye afores^d Good^w Cole came to my house and stood at my window and said that she saw something on the Cow. in ye Barn and desired that my daughter would goe wth her to the Barn & they boath went but when they came to the Barn they saw nothing on the Cow but they Boath heard a great Noyes on y^e scaffald in the Barn and Sarah Cole said that she Beleiued the Cow was bewitched.

[Hand 2] 3. oct^ε 1692 Sworne in court atest Jn° Higginson Just^ε peace

[Reverse] [Hand 3] Mary Eaten lynn

Notes: Hand 2 = John Higginson Jr.; Hand 3 = Anthony Checkley

Suffolk Court Files, vol. 32, docket 2712, p. 48, Massachusetts Supreme Judicial Court, Judicial Archives, Massachusetts State Archives. Boston, MA.

687. Deposition of Elizabeth Wellman v. Sarah Cole (of Lynn)†

[Hand 1] The deposision of Eelizzebeth wellman aged forty fiue ~~I~~ testifieth and saith that she saw Sarah Cole the wif of John Cole the Cooper liueing in the bowns [= bounds] of linn going one in a plaine wood ~~with a the scirt of~~ in agust last past and she had Cast the scirt of hir garment ouer hir ~~head~~ neck and she saw a black thing of a Considerabl bigness goe by hir sid and as soon as Sarah Cole Came against a tree that lay vpon the ground this blacke {thing} was gon and be sene no more and Sarah Cole going a litle further turnd hir face about to me she Claspt hir hands togather and swong them twice ouer hir head was gon and I Coold se hir no mor and when I Cam to the place whar she toock hir flite I lookt for hir but Coold {not ~~be~~} se hir further saith not 1692

Elizzebeth
Wellman

[Reverse] [Hand 2] Eliz^a Wellman

Notes: The deposition appears to have been prepared for the October 3 examination of Sarah Cole, No. 683, but not being sworn nor dated was probably simply not used. The "signature" of Elizabeth Wellman is in the hand of the recorder. ◊ Hand 2 = Anthony Checkley

Suffolk Court Files, vol. 32, docket 2712, p. 48, Massachusetts Supreme Judicial Court, Judicial Archives, Massachusetts State Archives. Boston, MA.

Thursday, October 6, 1692

688. Recognizance for Dorothy Faulkner & Abigail Faulkner Jr. by John Osgood Sr. & Nathaniel Dane

[Hand 1] Know all Men by these presents That I John Osgood Senr of Andover in ye Cownty of Essex in New England And Nathan^{ll} Dean Senr of the Same Town & Cownty afforesaid Husbandmen Are holden & firmely Bownd Joyntly & Sevirally to theire Majesties King William & Queen Mary of England & Scottland France & Ireland King & Queen Defenders of the faith in the full & Juste Sum of five hundrid pownds Sterling for the True & Just payment of which s^d Sum of five hundrid Pownds to theire Majesties King William & Queen Mary wee do bind Our Selves Our heires Executtors Adminstrators & Assignes firmely & By these presents Dated in Salem the Sixth day Of October in ye year of Ou⟨r⟩ Lord One thousand Six hundrid & Ninety & two And in ye fourth Year of ye Reign Of Our Majesties King William & Queen Mary King & Queen of England Scottland france & Ireland, Deffenders of ye faith

The Condition of this Obligation is Such that whereas the Abovenamed John Osgood Senr & Nathan^{ll} Dean Senr Husbandmen Both of The Towne of Andover in the Cownty of Essex in New England have Taken into Theire Care and Custody the Bodyes of Dorothy Faukner Aged about Ten Yeares And Abigail Faukner Aged about Eight yeares who was both Committed to Theire Maiesties Goale in Salem in the Cownty of Essex in New England for Having Vsed practised & Committed Divers Acts of witchcraft Vpon the Bodyes of Sundrye persons who themselves also have Confessed the Same If y^t ye Aforesaid John Osgood Senr & Nathan^{ll} Dean Senr Aforesaid Husbandmen shall well ⟨&⟩ Truely Keep y^e Aforesaid Dorothy Faukner & Abigail Faukner & Them Secure Vntill they shall Receive Order from George Corwin Sherriff of the Cownty Of Essex to deliver y^e Aforesaid Dorothy Faukner & Abigail Faukner Vnto William Downton Now Keeper of theire Majesties Goale in Salem Or to Any Othe[Lost] [= other] Whome y^e Afforesaid George Corwin shall Appoint; that then they shall forthwith delliver the Same Dorothy Faukner & Abigail Faukner According to his Order – And if y^e Above bownd do performe y^e Above Mentioned Articles & shall pay Vnto George Corwin the Sherrif Aforesaid y^e forfieture of S^d Bond for there Maj^{ε}s vse in Case of Defaulte then this Obligation shall be void & of None Efect Or Otherwise to stan⟨d⟩ in full force & virtue – In Wittness hereof we have sett to Our hands & Seals this Six[Lost] [= sixth] Day of October in y^e Year of Our Lord One thowsand Six hundrid Ninety & two and in y^e fourth Year of y^r Majes^{ε}s Reigne

[Hand 2] Witnis Joshua Conant   John osgood
~~Eli~~ Elizur Keysar   Nathaniel Dane
Joseph Phippen Juner

Notes: Neither of the children went to trial, and both were cleared by proclamation on May 10, 1693. In October several Andover children were freed by recognizance. See No. 819. Prior to October 6 nobody is known to have been freed on bail. ◊ 2 wax seals.

Massachusetts Archives Collection, vol. 135, no. 56. Massachusetts State Archives. Boston, MA.

689. Recognizance for Stephen Johnson, Abigail Johnson, & Sarah Carrier by Walter Wright, Francis Johnson, & Thomas Carrier Sr.

October 6, 1692

[Hand 1] Know all Men by these presents that Wee Walter Wright weaver francis ⟨&⟩ Johnson Husbandman & Thomas Carrier Senr Husbandman All of The Town of Andover in the Cownty of Essex in New England, Are holden & firmely Bownd Joyntly & Sevirally to theire Maiesties King William & Queen Mary of England and Scottland france & Ireland King & Queen Defenders of the faith in the full & Just Sum of five hundrid pownds Sterling for ye True And ["And" written over "p⟨a⟩y"?] Juste paymente of which Said Sum of five hundrid pownds to theire Majesties King William And Queen Mary, wee do bind Our Selves Our heires Executtors Adminstra^{e}s And Assignes firmely by these presents Dated in Salem the Sixth day of Octo^e In ye Year of Our Lord One thowsand Six hundrid Ninety & Two & in ye fourth Year of ye Reigne of Our Majesties King William & Queen Mary King & Queen of England Scottland france & Ireland Defenders of ye faith

The Condition of this Obligation is Such that whereas the Above named Walter Wright weaver & francis Johnson & Thomas Carrier Husbandmē All of ye Town of Andover in ye Cownty of Essex in New England, havinge taken Into there Care & Custody the Bodyes of Stephen Johnson Aged About thirteen Years & Abigail Johnson Aged about Eleven Yeares & Sarah Carrier aged About Eight Yeares who weare all Committed to there Majesties Goale in Salem in ye Cownty of Essex in New England for havinge Vsed practised and Committed Divers Acts of Witchcraft Vpon the Bodyes of Sundry persons who Also themselves have all of them Confessed ye Same, If y^t ye Aforesaid Walter Wright weaver & Francis Johnson & Thomas Carrier husbandmen Shall well & Truly keep ye Aforesaid Stephen Johnson & Abigail Johnson & Sarah Carrier And them Secure Vntill they shall ⟨be⟩ Receive Order from George Corwin Sherrif of ye Cownty of Essex to deliver ye Aforesaid Stephen Johnson Abigail Johnson & Sarah Carrier Vnto William Downton Now keeper of theire Majes^{e}s Goale in Salem Or to Any Other Whome ye Afforesaid George Corwin shall Appoint; that then they shall forthwith deliver the Same Stephen Johnson Abigail Johnson & Sarah Carrier according to his Order And if ye above bownd do performe ye above mentioned Articles & Shall pay vnto George Corwin the Sherrif aforesaid ye forfieture of S^d Bond for there Maj^{e}s vse in Case of Default y^n This Obligation shall be Void & of None Effect Or Otherwise to Stand in full force & Virtue In Wittness hereof we ye above bownd have set to Our hands & Seles this Sixth of October in the year of Our Lord One thowsand Six hundrid ninety two In ye fourth year of y^r Majesties Reigne

Walter Wright ✝ his mark

[Hand 2] Witness Joshua Conant

ffrancis Johnson

⟨Elur⟩ Elizur Keysar
Joseph Phippen Juner

Thomas Carrier 𝕋𝐂 his mark

Notes: True bills were returned on the indictments against Stephen Johnson, probably on January 3, 1693. See No. 815 & No. 816. No record as to whether he went on trial or when he was released survives. No further record on Abigail Johnson or Sarah Carrier survives. ◊ 3 wax seals.

October 6, 1692

690. Recognizance for Mary Lacey Jr. by Francis Faulkner & John Barker

[Hand 1] Know all men by these presents that I Francis Faulkoner of Andouer in the County of Essex in new england husbandman & I ~~Francis~~ John Barke⟨r⟩ of the same towne and County aforesd husbandman: are holden & firmely bound Jointly & seuerally to their Majesties King William & Queen Mary of England Scottland France & Ireland King & Queen defenders of the faith: in yᵉ full & Just sum of fiue hundred pounds Sterling for the true & Just payment of wᶜʰ s̄d sum of fiue hundred to their Majesties King William & Queen Mary wee doe bind our selues our heires Executores Administratores & Assignes firmely by thees presen[Lost] [= presents] Dated in Salem the sixth day of october in the yeare of our lord one thousand six hundred ninety & two & in the fourth year of yᵉ Reigne of their Majesties King William & Queen Mary of Engla[Lost]d [= England] Scottland France & Ireland Deffenders of the faith

The Condition of this obligation is such that wheras the aboue named Francis Faulkoner of Andouer in the County of Essex in new england husbandman and John Barker of the towne & County aforesd husbandman: haue taken into their Care & Custody the body of Mary Laycy Junᵉ aged about fiueteen yeares who was Committed to their Majesties Goale in Salem in the County of Essex in new england for haueing used Practised & Committed diuers acts of wicthcraft vpon the bodys of sundrys persons who hath Conffess[Lost] [= confessed] the same: if that the aforesd Francis Faulkoner & John Barker senᵒ of the towne & County aforesd shall well & truely Keep yᵉ aforesd Mary Lacy and her secure untill thay shall Receiue order from George Corwin Sheriff of the County of Essex then to deliuer the aforesd Mary Laycy unto William Dounton now Keeper of their Majesties Goale in Salem or to any other who⟨m⟩ the aforesd George Corwin shall apoint that then thay shall according to his order forthwith Deliuer yᵉ aforesd Mary Lacy and if the aboue bound doe performe the aboue mentioned articles & shall pay unto George Corwin Sheriff aforesd yᵉ forfittur[Lost] [= forfeiture] of s̄d Bond for their Majesties use in Case of default Then this obligation to be voide of non effect or otherwise to Remaine in full force and virtue In Wittness hereof wee the aboue boun⟨d⟩ haue sett our hands & seales the sixth day of october & in the year⟨e⟩ of our lord one thousand ninety & one & in the fourth year of their Majesties Reigne
Signed Sealed & Deliuered
In presence of us   francis faulkner
Witnises Joshua Conant
Elizur Keysar   John Barker sen
Joseph Phippen Juner

Notes: Sources are conflicted on the age of Mary Lacey Jr., who played such a large role in the Andover phase of the witch-hunt. This record describes her as fifteen years old. *The Andover Vital Records* published in 1912 indicates that she was 18 in the summer of 1692 when she played her active role. ◊ Hand 1 = George Herrick ◊ 2 wax seals.

Massachusetts Archives Collection, vol. 135, no. 57. Massachusetts State Archives. Boston, MA.

691. Recognizance for John Sawdy by Walter Wright & Francis Faulkner

October 6, 1692

[Hand 1] Know all Men By these presents that I Walter Wright weaver of Andover in the Cownty of Essex in New England and I Francis Faukner of yᵉ Same Town and Cownty Afforesaid Husbandma⟨n⟩ Are holden & firmeley Bownd Joyntly & Sevirally to theire Majesties King William & Queen Mary of England Scottland france & Irelan⟨d⟩ King & Queen Defenders of yᵉ faith in yᵉ full & Juste Sum of five Hundrid pownds Sterling for yᵉ True & Just paymente of wᶜʰ Said Sum of five hundrid pownds to theire Majesties King William & Quee[Lost] [= Queen Mary] ⟨w⟩ee do Bind Our Selves our Heires Executtors administrators [Lost]⟨d⟩ [= and] Assignes firmely by these presents Dated in Salem the Sixth day of October in yᵉ Year of Our Lord One thowsand Six hundrid Ninety & Two and in yᵉ fourth Year of yᵉ Reigne of theire Majesties King Willia[Lost] [= William] And Queen Mary, King & Queen of England Scottland france & Irelan⟨d⟩ Deffenders of the faith

The Condition of this Obligation is Such that whereas the abovenamed Walter Wright weaver & francis ffaukner Husbandman of Andover in the Cownty Of Essex In New England have Taken into theire Care & Custody the body of John Sawdy Aged about thirteen Years who was Comitted to yʳ Majesties Goale in Salem In the Cownty of Essex in New England for having Vsed practised & Committed Divers Acts of witchcraft Vpon the bodyes of Sundrye persons who him Self hath also Confessed yᵉ Same. if that the Aforesaid Walter Wright weaver & Francis faukner of yᵉ Town & Cownty Aforesaid Shall well & Truly keep yᵉ Aforesaid John Sawdy & him Secure Vntill they shall Receive Order from George Corwin Sherriff of yᵉ Cownty of Essex to deliver yᵉ Aforesaid John Sawdy Vnto William Downton Now keeper of theire Majesties Goale in Salem Or to any Other Whome yᵉ Aforesaid George Corwin shall Appoint, And then they shall according to his Order forthwith delliver the Afforesaid John Sawdy, And if yᵉ Above bownd do performe yᵉ Abovementioned Articles & shall {pay} Vnto George Corwin the Sherriff aforesaid the forfieture of Sᵈ Bond for there Majᵉˢ Vse in Case of Default then this Obligation to ⟨be⟩ of None Effect & Void Or Otherwise to Stand in full force & Virtue, In Wittness Hereof we yᵉ Aboue bownd have Sett to Our hands & Seales, this Sixth of Octobʳ in yᵉ yʳ of Our Lord One thousand Sixhundrid ninety two and in yᵉ fourth Year of yʳ Majesᵉˢ Reigne

Walter Wright ✝ his mark

[Hand 2] Wittness
Joshua Conant
Elizur Keysar   ⟨F⟩
Joseph Phippen Juner   Francis Faukʳ

[Reverse] [Hand 3] Jnᵒ & Joseph Parkerˢ Petᶜᵒⁿ 1692

Notes: John Sawdy was thirteen. Material in his case is sparse. Mary Osgood confessed that she had afflicted him (see No. 578), but no record other than this one reveals his role as a confessor. No trial record survives. ◊ 2 wax seals.

Massachusetts Archives Collection, vol. 135, no. 55. Massachusetts State Archives. Boston, MA.

Friday, October 7, 1692

692. Receipt of Sheriff George Corwin to Samuel Bishop for the Seized Estate of Edward Bishop Jr. & Sarah Bishop

Received this 7th. day of October, 1692. of Samuel Bishop, of the Town of Salem, of the County of Essex, in New-England, Cordwainer, in full satisfaction, a valuable summ of Money, for the Goods and Chattels of Edward Bishop, Senior, of the Town and County aforesaid, Husbandman; which Goods and Chattels being seized, for that the said Edward Bishop, and Sarah his Wife, having been committed for Witchcraft and Felony, have made their Escape; and their Goods and Chattles were forfeited unto their Majesties, and now being in Possession of the said Samuel Bishop; and in behalf of Their Majesties, I do hereby discharge the said Goods and Chattles, the day and year above written, as witness my hand, George Corwin, *Sherrif.*

Notes: The reference to "senior" may have been an error by Corwin, or an indication that Edward Bishop Jr., whose property was taken, had a son named Edward.

Robert Calef. More Wonders Of The Invisible World, Display'd In Five Parts. (London: Nath. Hillard, 1700), p. 108.

Wednesday, October 12, 1692

693. Letter of William Phips to the Privy Council

[Hand 1] S[r]
When I first arived I found this Province Miserably Harrassed with a most Horrible witchcraft or Possesion of Devills w[ch] had broke in upon severall townes some scores of poor people were taken with preternaturall Torments, some scalded with brimstone some had pins stuck in their flesh others hurried into the fire and water and some dragged out of their houses and carryed over the tops of trees and hills for many miles togather, it hath been represented to mee much like that of Sweden about thirty years agoe, and there were many comitted to prison upon suspicion of witchcraft before my arrivall, the loud cries and clamours of the friends of the afflicted people with the advice of the Deputy Governour and many others prevailed with mee to give a Comission of oyer and Terminer for discovering what witchcraft might bee at the bottome or wheather it were not a possession the cheife Judge in this Comission was the deputy Governour and the rest were persons of the best prudence & figure that could then be pitched upon, when the court came to sitt att Salem in the County of Essex they convicted more then twenty persons of being guilty of witchcrafte, some of the Convicted were such as confessed their guilt, the court as I understand ~~were~~ began their proceedings with the accusations of the afflicted persons and then went upon other humane evidences to strengthen that, I was almost the whole time of the proceeding abroad in the service of their Maj[ties] in the easterne part of the Countrey and depended upon the Judgem[t] of the Court as to a right method of proceeding in cases of witchcrafte, but when I came home I found many persons in a strange ferment of disatisfaction, w[ch] was increase[d]

by some hott spirritts that blew up the flame, but on enquiry into the matter I found that the
devill had tak⟨en⟩ upon him the name and shape of severall persons who were doubtlesse
inocent and ^{to} my certaine knowledge of good reputation, for wch cause I have now
forbiden the Comitting of any more that shall be accused w^th⟨out⟩ unavoydable necessity; and
those that have b⟨ee⟩n Comitted I would shelter from any proceedings against them wherein
there may be the least suspicion of any wrong to be done unto the inocent I would alsoe waite
for any particular directions or Comands if their Maj^ties please to give mee any for the fuller
ordering this perplexed affaire. I have alsoe put a stop to the Printi⟨ng⟩ of any discourses one
way or other that may increase the needlesse disputes of people upon this occasion because I
saw a likelyhood of Kindling an inextinguishable flame if I should admitt any publique and
open Contests and I have grieved to see that some who should have done their Maj^ties and
this Province better service have soe farr taken Councill of Passion as to desire the
precipitancy of these matters, these things have been improved by some to give mee many
interuptions in their Maj^ties service and in truth none of my vexations have been greater then
this that their Maj^ties service has been hereby unhappyly clogged, and the persons who have
made soe ill improvement [Lost]f [= of] these matters here are seekeing to turne it all upon
mee, but I hereby declare that assoon as I c[Lost]⟨e⟩ [= came] from fighting against their
Maj^ties enemyes and understood what danger some of their inno[Lost] [= innocent]
[Lost]bjects [= subjects] might bee exposed to, if the evidence of the afflicted persons onely
did prevaile e[Lost] [= either to] the Comitting or trying any of them, I did before any
applycation was made unto mee about it, put a stop to the proceedings of the Court and they
are now stopped till their Maj^ties pleasure be knowne S^r I beg pardon for giveing you all this
trouble, the reason is because I know my enemyes are seeking to turne it all upon mee and I
take this liberty because I depend upon your friendship, and desire you will please to give a
true understanding of the matter if any thing of this kind be urged or made use of against
mee. Because the Justnesse of my proceeding herein will bee a sufficient defence.
Dated at Boston the 12th of   S^r
october 1692.   I am with all imaginable respect
                                               Your most Humble servant
                                                    William Phips

Notes: This account by Phips indicating that he was away while the Court of Oyer and Terminer was hearing cases is
inconsistent with Council minutes clearly showing that he was present at the time. In light of this, one can only speculate
as to the accuracy of various observations in the letter. His reporting of people carried over treetops comes more from
Sweden than from Massachusetts. The original letter and the official copy, used to confirm the editorial annotations
where the text has been lost in the original, are both found in the British National Archives. ◊ "assoon": 'as soon.' From
the fifteenth to the eighteenth century, this adverbial phrase was often written as one word (see *OED*, s.v. *as soon, assoon*
advb. phr.).

Colonial Office 5/857, p. 88. National Archives, London, UK.

694. Petition of John Osgood Sr., John Frye, John Marston, et al. for Their Wives & Daughters

[Hand 1] To the Honored Generall Court Now sitting in Boston This 12 of october 1692
Right honored Gentlemen and fathers we your humble petitioners whose Names are under
written petition as followeth: viz:

October 12, 1692

We would Not Trouble Your honours wth a Tedious diversion: but brieffly spread open our distressed Condition and beg your honors favour and pitty. in affording what Relieff may be Thought Convenient as for The matter of our Trouble: it is The distressed Condition of our wives and Relations in prison at Salem who are a Company of poore distressed creatures as full of inward grieff and Trouble as thay are able to bear up in life withall: and besides That ye agrivation of outward Troubles and hardships thay undergo: wants of food Convenient: and the Coldness of the winter season y^t is coming may soon dispatch such out of the way That have Not been used to such hardships: and besides this ["this" written over "that"] The exceeding great Charges and expences y^t we are at vpon many accounts which will be two [= too] Tedious to give a pertickular acount of which will fall heavy vpon us especially in a time of so great charge and expen⟨ce⟩ vpon a generall accout in the Country which is expected of us t⟨o⟩ bear a part as well as others which if put all together oure familys and estates will be brog⟨h⟩t to Ruin: if it Cannot in time be prevented: having spread open our Condition: we humbly make our address. To your honoo⟨rs⟩ to Grant y^t our wives and Relations being of such That have been ap⟨pr⟩o⟨v⟩ed as penitent Confessors. might be Returned home to us vpon what bond your honors shall see good we do not petition to take them out of the hands of Justice but to Remain as prisoners under bond in their own familys where thay may be more Tenderly Cared for: and may be redy to apear to Answer farther when the honored Court shall Call for them: we humbly Crave your honors favour and pitty for us and ours herin. having lett doun our Troubled state before you. we he⟨a⟩rtyly pray for your honors Petitioners:

John Osgood in behalf of his wife.

John ffry. in behalf of his wife.

John Maston. in behalf of his wife: mary maston

Christopher osgood. in behalf of his daughter mary maston

Joseph Willson: in behalf of his wife & children

John Bridges: in behalf of his wife and children

hope Tiler: in behalf of his wife and daughte⟨r⟩

Ebenezer Barker: for his wife

Nathaniel Dane for his Wife

[Hand 2] 1692 John Osgood et al̄. Petition.

Notes: Mary Bridges Jr. was released on recognizance October 15, 1692 (see No. 695), tried and cleared on May 10, 1693 (see No. 849). Eunice Frye and Mary Osgood were freed on recognizance on December 20, 1692 (see No. 725 & No. 726). Mary Marston was tried and freed on January 6, 1693 (see No. 768). Mary Barker, Martha and Joannah Tyler, and Sarah Wilson Sr. were freed on recognizance on January 13 (see No. 818, No. 820, & No. 821). All four were cleared on May 10, 1693, but only Mary Barker was tried (see No. 850). Deliverance Dane, according to a later petition (see No. 900), spent thirteen weeks in prison, but the record of the disposition of her case is not extant.

Massachusetts Archives Collection, vol. 135, no. 59. Massachusetts State Archives. Boston, MA.

Saturday, October 15, 1692

695. Recognizance for Mary Bridges Jr. by John Bridges & John Osgood Sr.

[Hand 1] Know All Men By these presents That I John Bridges of Andover in the Cownty of Essex in New England Blacksmith And John Osgood Senr of the Same Town & Cownty afforesaid Husbandman, Are Holden And firmeley Bownd Joyntly & Sevirally to there Maj^Es, King William And Queen Mary of England Scottland France And Ireland King & Queen Defenders of the faith in the full & Juste Sum of five Hundrid Pownds Sterling, for the True & Juste paymente of wch Said sum of five hundrid pownds to there Maj^Es King William And Queen M⟨a⟩[Lost] [= Mary] Wee do Bind Our Selves Our heires Executtors Adminstrators & Assignes firmely by these presents, Dated in Salem the fifteenth day of October In the year of Our Lord One thowsand Six hundrid Ninety And Two And in the fourth year of theire Maj^Es Reigne of King William & Queen Mary King & Queen of England Scottland France & Ireland Deffenders of the faith

The Condition of this Obligation is Such that whereas the abovenam⟨d⟩ Jno Osgood Senr & John Bridges Both of the Towne of Andever in the Cownty of Essex in New England have Taken into theire Care & Custodye The Bodyes of Mary Bridges Aged about Twelve Yeares who was Committed to theire Maj^Es Goale in Salem in the Cownty of Essex in Ne⟨w⟩ England for havinge Vsed practised & Comitted Divers Acts of witchcrafts Vpon the Bodyes of Sundry persons who her Selfe hath also Conffessed the Same, if that the Abovesaid John Bridges Blacksmith & John Osgood Senr Aforesaid husbandman Shall Well & Truely keep the Aforesaid Mary Bridges & Them Secure vntill they Shall Receive Order from George Corwin Sherriff of the Cownty of Essex to delliver the Aforesaid Mary Bridges Vnto William Downton Now keeper of theire Maj^Es Goale in Salem Or to Any Other Whome the Aforesaid George Corwin Shall Appointe, that then they Shall forthwith deliver the Same Mary Bridges According to his Order – And if the Aboue Bownd do perform the Above mentioned Articles, And shall pay Vnto George Corwin the Sherriff Afforesaid, the forfieture of Said Bond for there Maj^Es Vse in Case off Default then this Obligation shall be void & of None Effect Or Otherwise To Stand in full force & Virtue, In Wittness hereof we have Sett to Our hands & Seals this fi⟨ueteenth⟩ day of October One thowsand Six hundrid Ninety & Two And in the fourth year of there Maj^Es Reigne

Wittness
Jno Turner   John Bridges
Thomas Gardner Junr   John Osgood

Notes: A grand jury heard Bridges's case on May 10, 1693, and did not return a true bill. The change of dating at the head of her indictments from "1692" to "1693" (see No. 845 & No. 846) may be a scribal correction, but more likely it indicates that her case had been planned for an earlier hearing before being changed. ◊ 2 wax seals.

Massachusetts Archives Collection, vol. 135, no. 60. Massachusetts State Archives. Boston, MA.

Tuesday, October 18, 1692

696. Petition of Twenty-six Andover Men Concerning Townspeople Accused of Witchcraft

[Hand 1] To his Excellency the Governour, and Council, & Representatives, now
    Assembled at Boston. The Humble Address of the ministers, and of some of the
    Inhabitants of Andover.

We being deeply sensible of the heavy judgment that the Righteous God hath brought upon
this place, thought it our duty (after our earnest prayers to the God of Heaven, to give us
help from our trouble) to lay before this Honourable Assembly, our present distr⟨e⟩ssed
estate, and to crave a redress of our greivances.
It is well known that many persons of this Town, have been accused of witchcraft, by some
distempered persons in th⟨ese⟩ parts, and vpon complaint made have been apprehended and
committed to prison. Now though we would not appear as Advocates for any who shall be
found gvilty of so horrid a crime, but we heartily desire that this place, and the whole land,
may be purged from that great wickedness: yet if any of our ~~fre⟨i⟩{n}ds~~ friends and
neighbours have been misrepresented, as tis possible some of them have been; wee would
crave leave (if it might be without offen⟨ce⟩) to speak something in their behalf, have^{ing}
no other designh therein, then that the truth may appear. We can truly give this Testimony
of the most of them belonging to this Town, that have been accused, that they never gave the
least occasion (as we hear of) to their neerest relations or most intimate acquaintance, to
suspect them of witchcraft. Severall of the women that are accu⟨s⟩ed were members of this
church in full Communion, and had obtained a good report, for their blameless conversation,
and their walking as becometh women professing godliness. But whereas it may be alledged,
that the most of our people that have been apprehended for witchcraft, have vpon
Examination confessed it. To which we Answer that we have nothing to plead for those that
freely and upon conviction own themselves gvilty: but we apprehend the case of some of
them to be otherwise. for from the information we have had and the discourse some of us
have had with the Prisoners, we have reason to think that the extream urgency that was used
with some of them by their friends and others who privately examined them, and the fear
they were then under, hath been an inducement to them to own such things, as we cannott
since find they are conscious of; and the truth of what we now declare, we judge will in time
more plainly appear. And some of them have exprest to their neighbou$^\varepsilon$s, that it hath been
their great trouble, that they have wronged themselves and the truth in their confessions. ⟨ꝝ⟩
We are also very sensible of the disstressed condition of severall poor familyes, on whom this
great trouble is fallen; some ~~men~~ of our neighbo$^\varepsilon$s are like to be impoverished & ruin'd by
the great charge they are at to maintain, such of ⟨t⟩heir familyes as are in Prison, and by the
fees that are demanded of them, whose case we pray may be considered.
Our troubles which hitherto have been great, we foresee are like to continue and increase, if
other methods be not taken then ⟨ꝝ⟩ as yet have been, for there are more of our neighb$^\varepsilon$s of
good reputation & approved integrity, who are still accused, and complaints have been made
against them, And we know not who can think himself safe, if the Accusations of children
and others {who are} under a Diabolicall influence shall be received against persons of good
fame.

We thought meet also to Signifye that not only persons of good creditt among our selves, but October 19, 1692 some Hono^{ε}able & worthy men of other places, do suffer in their names by the acusations of afflicted people in this Town

Thus haveing given ⟨2h⟩ you^ε Hono^{ε}s Some account of our present troubles, we crave pardon for our boldness in this Address, and humbly pray this Hono^{ε}ed Court⟨?⟩ to take into their serious consideration our ⟨?⟩ low and d⟨i⟩stressed estate: And that the only wise God may bless yo^ε counsels & endeavo^{ε}s for the welfare of his people, shall be the prayer of

You^ε Humble Petitioners

Dated at Andou^ε 18th Oct. 1692.

Timothy Osgood	Samuel Martins	Francis Dane sen^ε
samuel Osgoode	William Chandler	Thomas Barnard
	William abbutts	John Osgood
	Thomas Chandler	Thomas Johnson
	Christopher osgood	Nathaniel Dane
	Ebenezer Barker	Hopestil Tiler
	Stephen Barn⟨e⟩tt	Ephraim Steeue⟨n⟩s
	Joseph Marble	John Aslebee
	Ephraim Daviss.	James Frie
	Andrew Peeters	Joseph Willson
	Walter Rite	Joseph Steeuens
	hooker osgood	Thomas Chandler Jun^ε

[Reverse] [Hand 2] 1692 Andover Pet^{con}
[Hand 3] Capt. Breadstreet

Notes: The authenticity of the signatures is uncertain. They are primarily written in two different inks with some signed by the same hand.

Massachusetts Archives Collection, vol. 135, no. 61. Massachusetts State Archives. Boston, MA.

Wednesday, October 19, 1692

697. Petition of Thomas Hart for Elizabeth Hart

[Hand 1] To the honoured Generall Court Now Sitting in Boston

The humble Petition of Thomas Hart Inhabitant at Linn
Sheweth that whereas Elizabeth Hart Mother to the petition^r was taken into Custody in the Latter end of May Last, and ever Since comitted a prison^ε in Boston Goal for witchcraft, Tho in all wch time nothing has Appeared against her whereby to render her deserving of Imprisonm^t or death, the petition^ε being obliged by all Christian duty as becomes a child to parents, to make application for the Inlargment of his said mother, being ancient and not able to undergoe the hardship that is Inflicted from lying in Miserie, and death rather to be Chosen then a life in her Circumstances, the father of the petition^ε being ancient and

decriped [= decrepit] was wholly unable to att⟨e⟩nd in this matter ~~but~~ and the petition^ε having lived from his childhood under the Same roofe wth his Said mother he dare presume to affirme that he never saw nor knew any Evill ["E" written over "ei"] nor Sinfull practice wherein there was any Shew of Impiety Nor ["N" written over "or"] witchcraft by her, and were it otherwise he would not for the world and all the Enjoyments thereof Nurrish or support any creature y^t he knew ingaged in the Drugery of Satan it is well knoune to all the neighbourhood that the petition^{εs} mother has Lived a sober and Godly life alwise ready to discharge the part of A good Christian and never deserving of Afflictions from ye hands of men for any thing of this nature

> May it humbly therefore please yo^ε hon^{εs} to take this
> Matter into yo^ε Consideration in order to the Speedy
> Inlargment of this person So much abused and the
> petition^ε as in duty bound shall Ever pray

dated the 19th octob^ε 1692   Thomas Hart

[Reverse] The humble petition of Thomas Hart of Linn {1692}

Notes: Elizabeth Hart was released from prison in Boston on December 7, 1692. See No. 841. An indictment was presented against her in early January 1693, but the grand jury returned an ignoramus and she was not brought to trial. See No. 814.

Massachusetts Archives Collection, vol. 135, no. 62. Massachusetts State Archives. Boston, MA.

698. Petition of Nicholas Rice for Restitution for Sarah Rice

[Hand 1] To The honoured Generall Court now Sitting in Boston

The humble Petition of Nicholas Rist of Reading

Sheweth that whereas Sara Rist wife to the petition^ε was taken into Custody the first day of June last and ever Since laine in Boston Goal for witchcraft, tho in all this time nothing has been made Appear for wch shee deserv^d Imprisonment or death, the petition^ε has been a husband to the Said woman above Tweinty years, in all wch time he never had reason to accuse her for any Impietie or witchcraft, but the Contrary Shee lived wth him as a good faithfull dutifull wife and alwise had respect ~~to the respect~~ to the ordinances of God while her Strength Remain^d and the petition^ε on that Consideration is obliged in Conscience and Justice ~~oblige~~ to use all lawfull means for the Support and preservation of her life, and it is deplorable that in old Age the poor decriped [= decrepit] woman Should ly under Confinment so long in a Stinching Goal when her Circumstances rather requires a Nurse to Attend her

> May it therefore please ["p" written over "b"] yo^ε hon^{εs} to
> take this matter in to yo^ε prudent Considerations. and
> derect Some speedy Methods whereby this ancient decriped
> person may not for ever ly in such Miserie wherein her life
> is made more afflictive to her then death, and the petition^ε
> Shall as ["a" written over "i"] in dutie bound
> Ever pray

Dated ye 19th october <u>1692</u>   October 19, 1692

[Reverse] 1692 The humble petition of Nicholas Rist of ~~Linn~~ Reading

Notes: Sarah Rice of Reading was arrested May 31. See No. 228. Since she is referred to throughout the records of the proceedings as "Rice" and not "Rist," and is identified as the wife of Nicholas Rice, it seems as if this petition was written by someone other than the signatory and that the petitioner in this case, and perhaps in others, was unknown to the recorder. No record of further court action in connection with this case survives.

Massachusetts Archives Collection, vol. 135, no. 63. Massachusetts State Archives. Boston, MA.

699. Recantations of Mary Osgood, Eunice Frye, Deliverance Dane, Abigail Barker, Mary Tyler, Sarah Wilson Sr., Mary Bridges Sr., Mary Marston, Sarah Churchill, Hannah Post, & Mary Post, as Reported by Increase Mather†

Mrs. Osgood freely and relentingly said, that the confession which she made upon her examination for witchcraft, and afterwards acknowledged before the honourable judges, was wholly false, and that she was brought to the said confession by the violent urging and unreasonable pressings that were used toward her; she asserted that she never signed to the devill's book, was never baptised by the devill, never afflicted any of the accusers, or gave her consent for their being afflicted. Being asked, why she prefixed a time and spake of her being baptised, &c.: about *twelve years* since; she replyed, and said, that when she had owned the thing, they asked the time; to which she answered, that she knew not the time; but being told that she did know the time and must tell the time, and the like; she considered that about twelve years before (when she had her last child) she had a fitt of sicknesse, and was melancholy; and so thought that that time might be as proper a time to mention as any, and accordingly did prefix the said time.

Being asked about the cat, in the shape of which she had confessed the devill appeared to her, &c.; she replyed, that being told that the devill had appeared to her, and must needs appear to her, &c.; (she being a witch) she at length did own that the devill had appeared to her; and being press'd to say in what creature's shape he appeared in, she at length did say, that it was in the shape of a cat; remembering that some time before her being apprehended, as she went out at her door, she saw a cat, &c.: not as though she any whitt suspected the said cat to be the devill in the day of *** but because some creature she must mention, and this came thus into her mind at that time.

Deacon Fry's wife said, that the confession she made she was frighted into, and that it was all of it false.

Mrs. Dean and Goodwife Barker said freely, that they had wronged the truth in making their confession; that they in their lives time never covenanted with the devill, or had seen him; that they were press'd, and urg'd, and affrighted; that at last they did say even any thing that was desired of them; they said that they were sensible of their great evill in giving way at last to own what was false, and spake all with such weeping, relenting, and bleeding, as was enough to affect the hardest heart; particularly G. Barker bewail'd and lamented her accusing of others, whom she never knew any evill by in her life time; and said that she was told by her examiners that she *did* know of their being witches and *must* confesse it; that she did know of their being baptised, &c.: and must confesse it; by the renewed urgings and chargings of

October 19, 1692

whom at last she gave way, and owned such things as were utterly false, which now she was in great horrour and anguish of soul for her complying with.

Goodwife Tyler did say, that when she was first apprehended, she had no fears upon her, and did think that nothing could have made her confesse against herself; but since, she had found to her great grief, that she had wronged the truth, and falsely accused herself: she said, that when she was brought to Salem, her brother Bridges rode with her, and that all along the way from Andover to Salem, her brother kept telling her that she must needs be a witch, since the afflicted accused her, and at her touch were raised out of their fitts, and urging her to confess herself a witch; she as constantly told him, that she was no witch, that she knew nothing of witchcraft, and begg'd of him not to urge her to confesse; however when she came to Salem, she was carried to a room, where her brother on one side and Mr. John Emerson on the other side did tell her that she was certainly a witch, and that she saw the devill before her eyes at that time (and accordingly the said Emerson would attempt with his hand to beat him away from her eyes) and they so urged her to confesse, that she wished herself in any dungeon, rather than be so treated: Mr. Emerson told her once and again, Well! I see you will not confesse! Well! I will now leave you, and then you are undone, body and soul forever: Her brother urged her to confesse, and told her that in so doing she could not lye; to which she answered, Good brother, do not say so, for I shall lye if I confesse, and then who shall answer unto God for my lye? He still asserted it, and said that God would not suffer so many good men to be in such an errour about it, and that she would be hang'd, if she did not confesse, and continued so long and so violently to urge and presse her to confesse, that she thought verily her life would have gone from her, and became so terrifyed in her mind, that she own'd at length almost any thing that they propounded to her; but she had wronged her conscience in so doing, she was guilty of a great sin in belying of herself, and desired to mourn for it as long as she lived: This she said and a great deal more of the like nature, and all of it with such affection, sorrow, relenting, grief, and mourning, as that it exceeds any pen for to describe and express the same.

Goodwife Wilson said, that she was in the dark as to some things in her confession; yet she asserted that knowingly she never had familiarity with the devill; that knowingly she never consented to the afflicting of any person, &c. However she said that truly she was in the dark as to the matter of her being a witch; and being ask'd how she was in the dark, she replyed that the afflicted persons crying out of her as afflicting them made her fearfull of herself, and that was all that made her say that she was in the dark.

Goodwife Bridges said, that she had confessed against herself things which were all utterly false, and that she was brought to her confession by being told that she certainly was a witch, and so made to believe it, though she had no other grounds so to believe.

Goodwife Marston said, that she had a burthen upon her conscience, and that she had been burthened ever since she had made her confession, for she had wronged the truth and belyed herself; she never was guilty of witchcraft, or having to do with the devill (as she knew of) in her life time.

Sarah Churchill knew not whether it was in the day time or night time, that she stuck the thorns in the three poppets.

Hannah Post said, that Margaret Jacobs was choking of S. Ch. and that she appeared as little as a child of two years old.

Mary Post told the old story of her spirit's riding upon the rail; but ***********

Notes: This report has long been attributed to Increase Mather, probably accurately. Hard evidence for this, however, has been elusive. There is a good possibility that Thomas Brattle was also present when the interview occurred in prison.

The comments at the end about Sarah Churchill, Hannah Post, and Mary Post, seem unrelated to the recantantations, but are included here since they appear on the published document, put there for unknown reasons. Material after the asterisks was not transcribed because it was deemed illegible at the time the manuscript was published.

Collections of the Massachusetts Historical Society, Boston, MA., 2nd ser., vol. 3 (Boston: John Eliot, 1815), pp. 221–225.

Tuesday, October 25, 1692

700. An Act for the Prevention of Juggling, Spells, Charms, etc.

[Hand 1] An act for ye prevention of Judgling ["d" written over "g"], spells, Charms &c.

Whereas notw^thstanding the light of ye Gospell which God hath been graciously pleased to Cause to shine so clearly in this Age, some p^ɛsons haue presumed to be Fortunetellers, Judglers ["d" written over "g"], and by unlawfull means to Tell where stollen goods. or other Lost things. and to tell fortunes, and some p^ɛsons haue unlawfully gone to such p^ɛsons either to know theire Fortunes or to be resolued. of Questions in such unlawfull manner, and by useing ^{such} unlawfull Arts some haue been drawn to ye horrid sin of Witchcraft to ye high displeasure of Allmighty ["Allmighty" written over "God"] God and theire own destruction For preuention whereof for ye future. Be it Enacted by ye Gouerno^ɛ Councill and Representatiues. That what p^ɛson so euer after ye Dublication hereof, that shall presume either by word or writing, or any other means to shew or declare any p^ɛsons fortune, or unlawfully to Resolue any Question, or to use any such unlawfull art or science, or to haue or keep any Books of Conjuration, witchcraft Judgling or ye like and shall not forthwith bring them forth before some Justice of ye Peace, who shall then Cause them to be burnt in Publick view, Every such p^ɛson so offending for ye first offence shall be publickly & severely whipt or shall pay a fine not Exceeding 20^ld, and for ye second offence of ye like kinde, shall stand upon ye Gallows, wth a Paper on his or her breast signifying ye Crime, and be whipt as aforesaid, and Imprisoned during ye Pleasure of ye Court. And be it further Enacted That if any p^ɛson after ye Publication hereof, shall presume to Enquire of any such Fortune teller or Judgler, or p^ɛson suspected to use any such unlawfull art as aforesaid to know his or her fortune, and to be unlawfully resolued of any Question, or to see or hear any such unlawfull art Craft or science used or shall know of any such unlawfull practice and not discover the same to ye next Justice of Peace, or conceal any p^ɛson that shall haue any such ⟨u⟩nlawfull Books, for ye first offence shall pay a fine of fiue pounds or be publickly whipt and for ye second offence^⟨?⟩, shall haue double punishment

Octob^ɛ 25. 92: This Bill read a first second & third time in this house of Rep^ɛsentatiues & voted. passed in ye Affirmatiue, & sent to his Excellency ye Gouern^ɛ and Councill for Consent

William Bond Speaker

[Reverse] [Hand 2] An act to p^ɛuent Judgling &c/ 1692.

October 26, 1692   Notes: Acts passed at this time against witchcraft, as with other legislation, needed approval in England. For whatever reason, the witchcraft acts did not receive that approval.

Massachusetts Archives Collection, vol. 47, nos. 97–98. Massachusetts State Archives. Boston, MA.

Wednesday, October 26, 1692

701. General Court Bill Proposing a General Day of Prayer and Fasting and Calling a Convocation of the Elders to Determine a Course of Action Due to the Recent Witchcraft Outbreak

[Hand 1] Whereas it hath pleased the Most High out of his Soveraign and holy will, in this Day of Tryall and Adversity, to Excercise his People with sore trouble and Affliction in divers Respects: more Especially in permitting the Grand Enemy of Mankind to prevaile so far, with great Rage, and Serpentine Subtilty; whereby severall persons have been Seduced, and drawn away into that horrid and most Detestable sin of Witchcraft; to the great vexation, and Amazeing affliction of many persons wch is Notoriously known beyond Expression; And that for the Due deserved punishment of the Nocent, cleaning the Reputation, & persons of the Inocent, and by Divine Assistance, in the use of meanes, to prevent the farther progress and prevailence of those Satanicall Delutions; a Speciall Comission hath been granted to Certaine Gentlemen of the Council and thereby a Court Errected by those persons of known Integrity, faithfullness and (according to man) Sufficiency who have Strenuously Endeavoured to Discharge their Duty to the utmost of their Power, for the finding out & Exterpation of that Diabollicall Evill; so much prevaileing amongst us, But finding (Notwithstanding the Indefatigable Endeavours of those Worthy Gentlemen, with Others, to Suppress that Crying [1 word overstruck] Enormity) the most Astonishing Augmentation and Increase of the Number of Persons Accused, by those Afflicted: many of whom (according to the Judgment of Charity) being persons of good Conversation Godliness and homesty [= honesty]; And on the Other hand severall persons have Come and Accused themselves before Authority, and by many Circumstances, confessed themselves Guilty of that most abominable Wickedness; with divers Other Strang & unaccountable Occurrances of this Nature through the Rage and malice of Sathan, greatly threatning the utter Ruine, and Distruction of this poor Country; if the Lord in his Tender Mercy, doth not wonderfully Appear for ye Salvation of his People: by Expelling those Dismall Clouds of Darkness, and Discovering the wiles of the Devil, and that mistry of Iniquity that doth so much abound; And by his Gracious guidance, and Divine Assistance, Direct his people in the Right way, that those That are guilty may be found Out, and brought to Condigne punishment, the Inocent may be Cleared, and our feares and troubles Removed.
To wch End, it is humbly Proposed by the Representatives ~~of~~ now Assembled, That a Generall Day of Humilliation may be Appoynted, Sollemnly to seek the Lord and to Implore his Ayd That he would be graciously pleased to shew unto his people what

[Reverse] What they Ought to doe at such a time as this; And that ~~in Order thereto~~ A Convocation of the Elders may be Called who with the Honble Council and Other persons, (whom they in their wisdoms shall Deem meet) may Seriously Consider the Premisses; and make Inspection into these Intricaces humbly Enquireing that they may know the mind of God in this Difficult Case; That so if it be his Blessed Will; all Dissatisfaction may be Removed, peace, Love, and Unity may be increased, and Continued amongst us, and ^{that} ye Gracious Presence of Our Blessed God may Remaine with us.

October 26, 1692

[Hand 2] Octob^Ɛ 26: 92: This Bill read a first second & third time in ye house of Rep^Ɛsentatiues & voted passed in ye Affirmatiue & Sent to his Excellency the Gouerno^Ɛ & Councill, for Consent

William Bond Speaker

[Hand 3] once Read since <u>returned by</u> ye Committe
[Hand 4] Motion for a Convocation 1692.

Massachusetts Archives Collection, vol. 11, nos. 69–70. Massachusetts State Archives. Boston, MA.

702. Petition of Ten Persons of Ipswich [?]

[Hand 1] To the Honourable Governer and Councell
and Generall Assembly now sitting at Boston

The humble petition of vs whose names are subscribed herevnto now prisoners at Ipswich humbly sheweth, that some of vs have Lyen in the prison many monthes, and some of vs many weekes, who are charged with witchcraft, and not being consciouse to our selues of any guilt of that nature lying upon our consciences; our earnest request is that seing the winter is soe far come on that it can not be exspected that we should be tryed during this winter season, that we may be released out of prison for the present upon Bayle to answer what we are charged with in the Spring. For we are not in this vnwilling nor afrayd to abide the tryall before any Judicature apoynted in convenient season of any crime of that nature; we hope you will put on the bowells of compassion soe far as to concider of our suffering condicion in the present state we are in, being like to perish with cold in lying longer in prison in this cold season of the yeare, some of us being aged either about or nere fourscore some though younger yet being with Child, and one giving suck to a child not ten weekes ["week" written over "month"] old yet, and all of us weake and infirme at th⟨e⟩ best, and one fettered with irons this ["this" written over "an"?] halfe yeare and allmost distroyed with soe long an Imprisonment. Thus hoping you will grant us a releas at the present that we be not left to perish in this miserable condicion we shall alwayes pray &c.

Widow Penny. Widow Vincent. Widow Prin⟨ce⟩ Goodwife Greene of Havarell, the wife of Hugh Roe of Cape Anne, Mehitabel Downing. The wif⟨e⟩ of T⟨h⟩ima⟨th⟩y Day, Goodwife Dicer of Piscataqua Hanah Brumidge of Havarell Rachel Hafield besides thre or foure men

[Reverse] [Hand 2] Prisoners Pit^con [= petition] in Ipswich.

Notes: The dating here is speculative, but the petition seems likely to have come in October, since winter was coming on, and is suggested by the dates when the people in the petition were arrested and the amount of time they state that various

November 1, 1692 of them have been imprisoned. The petition could have come no later than December 16, 1692, when Mary Green was released on recognizance. See No. 723. In the absence of a clearer date, the record is placed here. ◊ "bowells": 'the interiors of the body as the seat of the tender and sympathetic emotions' (*OED* s.v. *bowel* n^1, 3). Cf. The Authorized Version Col. 3:12 "Put on therefore . . . bowels of mercies"; 1 Jn. 3:15 "shutteth up his bowels of compassion from him."

No. 1740, John Davis Batchelder Autograph Collection, Library of Congress, Washington, DC.

Tuesday, November 1, 1692

703. Petition of Thomas Barrett for Martha Sparks

[Hand 1] To his Exc^y Sr William Phips Kn^t Cap^n Gen^{ell} and Governo$^\varepsilon$ in Cheife of their Maj^{ties} Province of the Massachusetts Bay in New England and to the Hon$^{\varepsilon d}$ Council thereof

The Humble Petition of Thomas Barrett of Chelmsford in New England, in behalf of his Daughter Martha Sparkes wife of Henry Sparkes who is now a Souldier in their Maj^{ties} Service att the Easterne Parts, and soe hath beene for a Considerable Time
Humbly Sheweth
That yo$^\varepsilon$ Petition$^{\varepsilon s}$ Daughter hath Layne in Prison in Boston for the Space of Twelve months and Five dayes, being Comitted by Thomas Danforth Esq$^\varepsilon$ the Late Dep^{ty} Governo$^\varepsilon$ upon suspicion of Witchcraft, Since which noe Evidence hath appeared against her in any Such matter, neither hath any Given bond to prosecute her nor doth any one att this day accuse her of any such thing as yo$^\varepsilon$ Petitio$^\varepsilon$ knows of.
That Yo$^\varepsilon$ Petition$^\varepsilon$ hath ever since kept two of her children the one of 5 Yeares y^e other of 2 yeares old, wch hath beene a considerable Trouble and charge to him in his poore & meane Condition, besides yo$^\varepsilon$ Petition$^\varepsilon$ hath a Lame antient & Sick wife who for these 5 yeares & upwards past hath beene soe afflicted; as that shee is altogether rendred uncapable of affording herself any help, wch much augments his Trouble,

        Yo$^\varepsilon$ Poore Petition$^\varepsilon$ Earnestly and humbly Intreates Yo$^\varepsilon$ Ex^{cy} & hon$^{\varepsilon s}$ to take his distressed Condition into Yo$^\varepsilon$ consideraç$\overline{on}$ And that You will please to order y^e releasem^t of his Daught^r from her confinem^t whereby shee may returne home to her poore children to Looke after them, haveing nothing to pay the charge of her confinem^t

        And Yo$^\varepsilon$ Petition$^\varepsilon$ as in duty bound shall ever pray &^{c}
Novr 1. 1692.

Notes: For the possible significance of Martha Sparks and for related information, see the General Introduction.

Massachusetts Archives Collection, vol. 135, no. 64. Massachusetts State Archives. Boston, MA.

Saturday, November 5, 1692

704. Warrant for the Apprehension of Esther Elwell, Abigail Row, & Rebecca Dike, and Officer's Return

See also: Nov. 7, 1692.

[Hand 1] To yᵉ Sheriffe of Our County of Essex, his vnder Sheriffe or Deputy. or Constable of: Glocester, or Constable

Where as Complaint Is made by Leuiᵗ James Stevens {& William Stevens} & Nathaniel Coyt ~~both~~ {all} of Glocester, In yᵉ County of Essex In behalfe of thair Majesties, vnto thair Majesties Justices. of yᵉ peace. against Esther Ellwell yᵉ wife of Samuel Elwell, & Abigail Roe daughter of Hugh Roe: & ~~Rebek~~ Rebecka Dike yᵉ wife of Richard Dike. all of Gloster, afforesaid, for that thay haue Grovnded suspicion that yᵉ Said Elwell Dike & Roe haue wickedly & felloniously Comitted Sundry acts of witchcraft upon yᵉ body of Mʳˢ Mary ffitch yᵉ wife of Mʳ John ffitch of Glocester afforesaid, unto yᵉ wasteing pineing & Consumeing of her body Contrary. to yᵉ peace of our soveraigne Lord & Lady yᵉ King & Queen & Contrary to yᵉ forme of yᵉ statutes in that Case made & provided, & haue Craved Justice & haue Entered into Recognisance, to prosecute yᵉ Said Complaint to Effect. yᵉ which is here with me. and of thair Majesties Justices of yᵉ Peace
This is therefore In thair Majesties Names. William & Mary of England &c king & Queen ^{to} Require ^{you} by Vertue hereof forthwith or as Soon as may be. to Apprehend Seize & Secure yᵉ Said Esther Ellwell Rebecka Dike & Abigall Roe, & them haueing So Secured You are yᵉ first Convenient time to bring before thair Majesties Justices of yᵉ Peace for yᵉ County of Essex that thay may be Examined & proceeded with as yᵉ Law directs of which You are not to faile at Your Perrill & for so doeing this shall be Your sufficient warrant. & make a true Returne vnder Your hand according to Law.
Ipswich Novembᵉ yᵉ 5ᵗʰ 1692. Giuen vnder my hand. Thoˢ Wade. J: P.

[Reverse] [Hand 2] This 7ᵗʰ of novembᵉ 1692
By vertue of this within ~~Within~~ Written warrant I have ~~yᵉ~~ Apprehended & Seized yᵉ persons therein ordered to be Seized Viz [   ] Esther Ellwell, Rebecka Dike & abigall Roe all of Glocester & haue Conveyed them all to Ipswich, & haue ordered a Guard to secure them In order to thair Examination as Justice shall Require
attests. Peter: Coffin Constabel

Notes: This document offers a reminder that witchcraft accusations continued after the special Court of Oyer and Terminer was dissolved, in this case even using the language of the indictments – "wasteing pineing & Consumeing." ◊ 1 wax seal.

Suffolk Court Files, vol. 32, docket 2689a, p. 17, Massachusetts Supreme Judicial Court, Judicial Archives, Massachusetts State Archives. Boston, MA.

Monday, November 7, 1692

Officer's Return: Warrant for the Apprehension of Esther Elwell, Abigail Row, & Rebecca Dike

2nd of 2 dates. See No. 704 on Nov. 5, 1692

705. Petition of John Parker & Joseph Parker for Restitution for Mary Parker

[Hand 1] To his Excellency the Governo$^\varepsilon$, and Councill and Representatives; now sitting in Boston
the humble Petition of John Parker, & Joseph Parker {of Andover} Sheweth,

That whereas our mother mary Parker of Andover, was apprehended vpon Suspition of witchcraft, and being brought to a tryall at Salem Court, was condemned: Since her Death the Sherriff of Essex sent an officer to seise on her Estate. The said officer required us in their majestyes name to give him an Account of our mothers Estate, pretending it was forfeited to ye King; we told him that our mother left no Estate; (which we are able to make appear) notwithstanding which, he seised vpon our Cattell, Corn & hay, to a considerable value; and ordered us to go down to Salem and make an agreement with ye Sherrif, otherwise the Estate would be Expos'd to sale. We not knowing to what advantage the Law might give him against us, and fearing we should Sustain greater Dammage by ye loss of our Estate, went to the sherriff accordingly, who told us he might take away all that was seis'd, if he pleas'd, but was willing to do us a kindness by giveing us an oppertunity to redeem it. He at first demanded ten pounds of us, but at length was willing to take six pounds which he has oblig'd us by Bill to pay him within a moneth. Now if our mother had left any Estate, we know not of any Law in force in this Province, by which it should be forfeited upon her condemnation; much less can we vnderstand that there is any Justice or reason, for y^e Sherriff to seise vpon our Estate And thō it is true ou$^\varepsilon$ own act has obliged us to pay him a Summ of money, yet we declare that we were drawn to it, partly by the officers great pretences of Law for what he did, partly to prevent y^e loss of our Estate which we feard would be immediately sold.
Now we humbly pray this Hon$^\varepsilon$ed Court to consider our case, and if it be judged that so much money ought not to have been demanded of us, vpon the formentioned account: we pray that we may be discharge'd from that obligation, which the Sherriff, takeing advantage of our ignorance hath brought us vnder And yo$^\varepsilon$ Petition$^\varepsilon$s as in duty bound ["o" written over "a"] shall ever pray &c
Dated at Andov$^\varepsilon$ John Parker
7th Novemb. 1692.   Joseph Parker

[Reverse] [Hand 2] Jno & Joseph Parker^s Pet^{con} 1692./.

Notes: The petition offers one of various pieces of evidence supporting the view that Sheriff George Corwin was seen as using the trials to extort money for himself.

Massachusetts Archives Collection, vol. 135, no. 65. Massachusetts State Archives. Boston, MA.

Tuesday, November 8, 1692

706. Testimony of James Stevens, in Support of Mary Fitch v. Esther Elwell

[Hand 1] James Steuens testifieth and saith that Mary fitch did say that she felt A woman upon ye bed, and put forth hir hand, and felt ye hair of hir head and A peg in it, also testifieth, that she said she was squesed to pieces, wheras I sa⟨w⟩ ~~noby~~ no body hurt hur. [Hand 2] Ipswich Now^br ye 8th 1692: sworne before us,

Daniell Epps: J:P
Thos Wade. J:P

Suffolk Court Files, vol. 32, docket 2689, p. 17, Massachusetts Supreme Judicial Court, Judicial Archives, Massachusetts State Archives. Boston, MA.

707. Deposition of Elizabeth Hubbard v. Abigail Row, Esther Elwell, & Rebecca Dike

[Hand 1] The Deposition of Elizabeth Hubburd aged seventeen years saith: that she saw Abigall Row Ester Elwell & Rebecca Dike [Hand 2] ^{or three in ther likeness} [Hand 1] a pressing squezeing & choaking of Mary ffitch the wife of John ffitch: which was done on thirsday the third of november ^{1692} and at severall other times, [Hand 2] & y^e {last} Night that. night she said, ffitch died she saw one on one side & another on ye other side & one at her back.
Ipswich 9^bᵉ ye 8th 1692. affirmed before us

Daniell Epps, J: P
Thos Wade. J: P.

[Reverse] Elizabeth: Hubard being asked wheither she thought that ye persons within named was ye Cause of ye death of Mary fitch she said she could not tell what to think about it.

Notes: Although Hathorne, Corwin, and Gedney had stopped taking depositions for witchcraft cases of 1692, Elizabeth Hubbard remained indefatigable in her involvement. Here, in a different jurisdiction, she gives evidence in a case before Justices of the Peace Daniel Epps and Thomas Wade of Ipswich. Rebecca Dike was the sister-in-law of Ann Dolliver, who had been arrested in June, 1692. See No. 308.

UNCAT MS, Miscellaneous Manuscripts (1692), Massachusetts Historical Society. Boston, MA.

Wednesday, November 9, 1692

708. Declaration of Arthur Abbott Concerning Testimony about Elizabeth Procter

[Hand 1] This may Certifie all whome this writting shall come before, that on the 15th of October 1692, Arthur Abbut sent for me Daniell Epps and Capt Thomas wade Esqr both of Ipswich, ffinding himselfe very weake and Ill bye Reason of some sad distempers vpon him, in Order to the makeing his will. And Leaueing something that might be to the veiw of the world Reffering to the Euidence that he had giuen in to the Honored Court of Oyer and terminer held at Sallem a Little before, which was as ffolloweth, Viz^t

I Arthur Abbut haueing a great impulse vpon me to declare vnto y^e Honored Court (as abouesayd sitting in Salem) some things that I had formaly discoursed with Goodwife Procter of Salem about and seen in her House, being after⟨?⟩sent for And gaue Euidence thereof vnto y^e s^d Honored Court, being a short time after sent for by y^e worll [= worshipful] Samuel Appleton Esqr, And by him accused for takeing a false Oath therein, I doe humblie acknowledg my weakenes and reale sorrow for mentioning stateing the time, or any way insisting vpon that, But being Extreordinarily Charged with fallshood as to the things I had both seen and heard in her House, I did with more then ordinarie Exprestion ⟨?⟩st ^{at⟨est⟩} the truth thereof And doe as in the presence of God, before whose Tribunall, both the accuser and the accused must appeare, Certinly afirme vpon good Consideration and deep meditation, that to be true, which I had before declared to the Court, neither did I intend any of those great and solem exprestions at Majore Appletons, should any way be vnderstood as to the time, but the things themselues, and this I desired to leaue to the world, not knowing how it might please God to deale with me /

This was taken from Arthur Abbut at his Earnest request, at the time aboue mentioned by {vs} [1 word overstruck] Dan

Daniell Epps, J:P

Dated this 9th of Nouember 1692 /

[Hand 2] I also affirme y^t I did hear ye said Arther Abbutt ye day aboue mentioned (when Capt Epps was present) declare & affirme y^t what he had before said was y^e Truth according as is aboue Exspressed. it being read. to him or y^e Like words after it was taken downe from his Mouth. speach

Wittness Thos Wade: J. P.

[Reverse] [Hand 3] Arthur. Abbott his declaracon when sick before Justices

Notes: Hand 3 = Stephen Sewall

Essex County Court Archives, vol. 1, no. 108, Massachusetts Supreme Judicial Court, Judicial Archives, on deposit James Duncan Phillips Library, Peabody Essex Museum, Salem, MA.

Monday, November 14, 1692

November 29, 1692

709. Statement of John Hale & Joseph Gerrish v. Mary Herrick

An Account Received from the mouth of Mary Herrick aged about 17 yeares having been Afflicted the Devill or some of his instruments, about 2 month. She saith she had oft been Afflicted and that the shape of M[rs] Hayle had been represented to her, One amongst others, but she knew not what hand Afflicted her then, but on the 5th of the 9th She Appeared again with the Ghost of Gooddee Easty, & that then M[rs] Hayle did sorely Afflict her by pinching, pricking & Choaking her. On the 12th of the 9th she Came again & Gooddee Easty with her & then M[rs]. Hayle did Afflict her as formerly. S[d] Easty made as if she would speake but did not, but on the same night they Came again & M[rs] Hayle did sorely Afflict her, & asked her if she thought she was a Witch. The Girl answered no, You be the Devill. Then said Easty s[d] and speake, She Came to tell her She had been put to Death wrongfully and was Innocent of Witchcraft, & she Came to Vindicate her Cause & she Cryed Vengeance, Vengeance, & bid her reveal this to M[r] Hayle & Gerish, & then she would rise no more, nor should M[rs] Hayle Afflict her any more. Memorand: y[t] Just before s[d] Easty was Executed, She Appeared to s[d] Girl, & said I am going upon the Ladder to be hanged for a Witch, but I am innocent, & before a 12 Month be past you shall believe it. S[d] Girl s[d] she speake not of this before because she believed she was Guilty, Till M[rs] Hayle appeared to her and Afflicted her, but now she believeth it is all a Delusion of the Devil.

> This before M[r] Hayle &
> Gerish 14th of the 9th 1692.

Notes: Mary Herrick was the niece of Joseph and Mary Herrick, both of whom testified against Sarah Good at her trial. See No. 337. Herrick was the constable who arrested Sarah Osborne and Tituba on March 1, 1692. See No. 2. The charge by their niece against Reverend Hale's wife has in popular culture been seen as instrumental in ending the Salem witch trials, but was in fact irrelevant to the ending of the Court of Oyer and Terminer. By the time the charge came, the Court of Oyer and Terminer trying the 1692 witchcraft cases had been disbanded. What impact the charge against Mrs. Hale had on Hale's attitude toward the trials and his subsequent book questioning some of the handling of the witchcraft issue can only be speculative. Gerrish was a minister from Wenham.

New England Historical and Genealogical Register and Antiquarian Journal, vol. 27 (1873), p. 55.

Tuesday, November 29, 1692

Coroner's Report: Warrant of Coroner of Suffolk County for an Inquest into the Death of Roger Toothaker
2nd of 2 dates. See No. 314 on June 16, 1692

December 3, 1692 **Saturday, December 3, 1692**

710. Recognizance for Ann Sears by Jonathan Prescott & John Horton

[Hand 1] Memorand^m
That on the Third day of December 1692 @ in the ffowerth year of the Reign of our
Soueraign Lord & Lady William & Mary by the Grace of God of Engld &c. King & Queen
defenders of the ffaith Personally Appeared before vs James Russell & Sam^ll Heyman Esq^℈s
of their Maies^ts Councill & Prouince of the Massachusets Bay in New Engld & Justices of
Peac[Lost] [= peace] within the Same Jonathan Prescot of Concord and John Horton of
Lancaster in y^e County of Middlesex & Acknowledged them selues & Each of them to be
indebted vnto our Said Lord & Lady the King & Queen & the Suruiuor of them their
Heires & Successo^℈s in the Some of Two hundred pounds to be leauied on their or Either of
their goods or Chattels Lands or Tennements for the vse of our Said Lord & Lady the King
& Queen or Suruiuor of them if default be made in the performance of the condition vnder
written viz
The Condition of the Aboue Recognizance is Such y^t whereas Ann Seers ye Wife of John
Seers of Wooburn in ye County Abouesd was committed to Cambridge Goal on Suspition
of Witchcraft, If therefore the Said Ann Seers shall make her personall Appearance before
the Justices of our Said Lord & Lady the King & Queen at ye next Court of Assize Oyer &
Terminer & Gen^ll Goall deliuery to be holden for or within the County. of Middlesex
Aforesd to Answere what shall be obiected against her in their Maies^ts behalf refering to
Witchcraft, and to do & receiue y^tt wch by sd Court shall be then & there injoined her & not
depart w^thout licen⟨c⟩ then ye Aboue Recognizance to be void or Elce to remain & abide in
fful fforce & virtue
Capt & Recognit die ꝑdict Coram

ꝑ Ja: Russell
Samuell Hayman

[Reverse] Recogn ꝑ Ann Seers appearance at Next Court in Middlesex

Notes: No further records on Sears's case survive.

Suffolk Court Files, vol. 32, docket 2694, p. 20, Massachusetts Supreme Judicial Court, Judicial Archives, Massachusetts State Archives. Boston, MA.

711. Petition of Abigail Faulkner Sr. for a Pardon

[Hand 1] The humble Petition of Abigall: ffalkner unto his Excellencye Sr Wm Phipps
knight and Gouern^℈ of their Majestyes Dominions in America: humbly sheweth

That your poor and humble Petitioner hauing been this four monthes in Salem Prison and
condemned to die hauing had no other Euidences against me but ye Spectre Euidences and
ye Confessors wch Confessors haue lately since I was condemned owned to my selfe and
others and doe still own that they wronged me and what they had sai⟨i⟩d against me was
false: and that they would not that I should haue been put to death for a thousand worldes

December 5, 1692

for they neuer should haue enjoyed themselues againe in this world; wch undoubtedly I sh⟨u⟩llld haue been put to death had it not pleased ye Lord I had been with child.: Thankes be to ye Lord I know my selfe altogether Innocent & Ignorant of ye crime of withcraft wch is layd to my charge: as will appeare at ye great day of Judgment (May it please yo^ε Excellencye) my husband about fiue yeares agoe was taken wth fitts wch did uery much impaire his memory and undestanding but wth ye blessin⟨g⟩ of ye Lord upon my Endeauours did recouer of them againe but now through greife and Sorrow they are returned to him againe as bad as Euer they were: I hauing Six children an⟨d⟩ hauing little or nothing to Subsist on being in a manner without a head to doe any thinge for my Selfe or them and I being closely confined can see no other wayes but we shull all perish: Therfore may it please you^ε Excellencye your poor and humble petition^ε doe humbly begge and Implore of yo^ε Excellencye to take it into yo^ε pious and Judicious consideration that some speedy Course may be taken wth me for my releasement that I and my children perish not throug⟨h⟩ meanes of my close confinement here wch undoubtedly we shall if ye Lord does not mightily preuent and yo^ε poor petitioner shall for euer pray for your health and happinesse in this life and eternall felicity in the world to come so prayes

ffrom Salem Prison   Your poor afflic{t}ed humble {Petition^⟨ε⟩ &} seru⟨ant⟩
Decem̄ ye 3^d 1692   Abigall: ffalkner

[Reverse] These: To his Excellencye Sr Wm Phipps knight and Gouern^ε of their Majestyes Dominions in America ꝑsent//

Notes: Abigail Faulkner had been condemned on September 17, but as with other confessors she was not executed. She had pled pregnancy, but it seems highly unlikely that she would have been executed whether or not she made that plea. How long she remained in prison after this petition is not clear.

Salem Selections, Massachusetts Box, Essex Co., Manuscripts & Archives, New York Public Library. New York, NY.

Monday, December 5, 1692

712. Petition of Rebecca Eames for a Pardon

[Hand 1] The humble Petition of Rebecka Eames unto his Excellency⟨e⟩ Sr Wm Phipps knight & Gouern^ε of their Majestyes Dominions in America humbly sheweth:

That wheras you^ε Poor and humble petitioner hauing been here closely confined in Salem prison neare four monthes and likewise condemned to die for ye crime of witchcraft, wch ye Lord aboue he knowes I am altogether innocent and ignorant off as will appeare att ye great day of Judgment hauing had no Euidences against me but ye Spectre Euidences and my owne confession wch ye Lord aboue knowes was altogether false and untrue I being hurried out of my Senses by ye A⟨ff⟩licted persons Abigall Hobbs and Mary Lacye who both of them cryed out against me charging me with witchcraft ye space of four dayes mocking of me and spitting in my face saying they knew me to be an old witch and If I would not confesse it I should uery Spe⟨e⟩dily be hanged for there was some such as myselfe gone before and it would not be long before I should follow them wch did so amaze and affright me that I knew not what I said or did wch was ye Occasion with my owne wicked heart of my saying what I did say: and ye reason of my standing to my confession: att my tryall was: That I know not one word w^t I said when I was upon my Tryall att what ye honour^d Magist⟨ra⟩tes said to me but onely ye Name of Queen Mary: But may it please yo^ε Excellencye: when m^r Matther and m^r Brattle were here in Salem they disowned w^t they before had said against me and doe still owne and say w^t they had sayd against me was Nothing but ye Diuells delusions and they knew nothing in ye least measure of any witchcraft by me: your poor and humble petition^ε doe begg and Implore of yo^ε Excellencye to Take it into yo^ε Pious and Judicious consideration To Graunt me A Pardon of my life Not diseruing death by man for witchcraft or any other Sin That my Innocent blood may not be shed and your poor and humble petitioner shall for euer pray as she is bound in duty for yo^ε health & happinesse in this life and eternall felicity in ye world to come So prayes

ffrom Salem prison   Your poor and humble petition^ε
Decem̄ ye 5th 1692.   Rebecka: Eames

Notes: Rebecca Eames was first arrested around August 19, 1692, and was in prison for seven months according to a statement by her, No. 888, that suggests she would have been released in February 1693. She had pled guilty and had been condemned in September.

Salem Selections, Massachusetts Box, Essex Co., Manuscripts & Archives, New York Public Library. New York, NY.

Tuesday, December 6, 1692

713. Recognizance for Martha Sparks by Thomas Barrett

[Hand 1] Memorandū
That on the Sixth day of Decemb^ε 1692 in the ffowerth year of the Reign of our Soueraign Lord &. Lady William &. Mary by the grace of God of England &.c King &. Queen Defenders of ye ffaith: Personally Appeared before vs James Russell & Samuell Heyman Esq^εs of their Majes^ties Councill &. Province of the Massachusetts Bay in new England, & Justices of peace within ye Same; Thomas Barrat of Chelmsford in ye County of Middle{sex}, Mason &. Acknowledged himselfe to be indebted unto our S^d Lord &. Lady the King &. Queen and the Surviuo^ε of them their Heires & Successo^εs in the Some of Two hundred pounds to be leauied on his Goods or Chattells Lands or Tennements for ye use of our said{e} Lord & Lady ye King & Queen or Surui^{u}er of Them if default be made in the performance of the Condition underwritten, viz

The Condition of the Aboue Recogn^{i}zance is Such y^t wheare as Martha Sparks of Chelmsford in the County of Middlesex was Committed to Boston Goall being Accused &. suspected of perpetrating or Com̄itting diuers Acts of Wichcraft; If therefore ye Afores^d Martha Sparks Shall make her personall Appearance before the Justices of our s^d Lord &. Lady the King &. Queen; at the next ^{Court} of Assi{z}es Oyer &. Terminer &. Generall Goall deliuery to be holden for, or within ye County of Middlesex Aboues^d to Answer what shall be Obiected Against her in their Mai^ties behalfe refering to Witchraft and to do &.

Receiue y^t which by said Court shall be then and there Inioined H̶e̶r̶ ["Her" written over   December 6, 1692
"and"] her, and not depart without Licence then the Aboues^{d}aid Recognizance to be void or
Elce to Abide in ffull fforce &. virtue
Capt &. Recognit die ꝑdict Coram

ꝑ Ja: Russell
Samuell Hayman

[Reverse] Thomas Barrets Recogn̄ ꝑ Martha Sparks apearanc at Middlesex Court

Notes: For Martha Sparks see the General Introduction. No record survives of a grand jury hearing her case. Neither is
there evidence of a trial or of any depositions in connection with this case.

*Suffolk Court Files, vol. 32, docket 2696, p. 21, Massachusetts Supreme Judicial Court, Judicial Archives, Massachusetts State
Archives. Boston, MA.*

714. Petition of John Osgood Sr. & Seven Other Andover Residents for the Accused

[Hand 1] To his Excellency the Governour, and Council now sitting at Boston. The humble
Petition, of severall of the Inhabitants of Andover, sheweth

That whereas our Wives and severall of our neighbours, sometime since, were committed to
Salem Prison, (for what cause your Hono^{εs} have been informed) and during their
imprisonment have been Exposed to great sufferrings, which daily Encrease by reason of the
winter comeing on; we had hoped that before this day they would have had a Goal delivery,
but since that hath been so long deferred, and we are very sensible of the Extream danger the
Prisoners are in of perishing, if they are not speedily released: have made bold to make our
humble Petition to t̶h̶i̶s̶ ̶H̶o̶n̶o̶^{ε}e̶d̶ ̶C̶o̶ yo^ε Honor^{εs}, to consider the present distressed and
suffering condition of our friends in Prison and grant them liberty to come home, vpon such
terms as yo^ε Hono^{εs} shall Judge most meet.
If we might be allowed to plead their Innocency, we think we have sufficient grounds to
make such a plea for them, and hope their Innocency will in time appear to the satisfaction
of others, however they are at present vnder vncomfortable circumstances.
So craveing pardon for the trouble we have now given your Ho⟨?⟩no^{εs}, and humbly
requesting that something may be speedily done for the releif of our friends. And yo^ε
Petition^{εs}, as in duty bound shall ever pray &c
Andover 6th Decemb^ε 1692

John Osgood
Christopher osgood
John ffrie
Nathaniel Dane
Joseph Willson
Hopestil Tiler
John Bridges
Ebenezer Barker

[Reverse] [Hand 2] 1692 Andover Pet^{con}

December 6, 1692 Notes: The petition is for the Andover women who had recanted on October 19, 1692: Mary Osgood, Eunice Frye, Deliverance Dane, Abigail Barker, Mary Tyler, Sarah Wilson Sr., Mary Bridges Sr., and Mary Marston. See No. 699. All were either freed on recognizance or tried and found not guilty, or both.

Massachusetts Archives Collection, vol. 135, no. 66. Massachusetts State Archives. Boston, MA.

715. Petition of Rebecca Fox for Rebecca Jacobs [?]

[Hand 1] To his Excellency Sr William Phips Kn^t Govern^r & the Honourable Council now
           setting at Boston, the Humble Petition of Rebeccah Fox of Cambrige
    Sheweth
    That whereas Rebecah Jacobs (daughter of Your Humble Petitioner) has a long time, even many Months now lyen in Prison for Witchcraft, & is well known to be a Person Craz'd, Distracted & Broken in mind, Your Humble Petitioner does most humbly & earnestly seek unto Your Excellency & to Your Hon^{rs} for releif in this case:
    Your Petitioner who knows well the Condition of her poor Daughter, together with severall others of good repute and creditt are ready to offer their Oaths, that the s^d Jacobs is a Woman Craz'd, Distracted & Broken in her mind, & that She has been so these twelve Years & upwards;
    However for (I think) above this half Year, ⟨y⟩ the s^d Jacobs has lyen in Prisō & yet remaines there attended with many sore Difficulties:
    Christianity & Nature do each of them oblige Your Petitioner to be very Solicitous in this matter, and althō many weighty cases do exercise Your thoughts, Yet Your Petioner can have no rest in her mind, till such time as she has offer'd this her addresse on behalf of her daughter:
    Some have dyed already in Prison, and others have been dangerously sick, & how soon Others, & among them my Poor Child by the Difficulties of this Confinem^t may be sick & dye, G^d only knows:
    She is uncapable of making that shift for her self that others can do, & such are her circumstances on other accounts that Your Petitioner who is her tender Mother has many great Sorrows & almost overcomīng burthens on her mind upon her account, but in the midst of all her ᵱplexities and Troubles (next to supplicating to a Good & Mercifull God) Your Petitioner has no way for help but to make this her afflicted conditiō known unto You, So not doubting but Your Excellency & Your Honours will readily hear the cries & Groans of a Poor Distressed Woman and grant what help and enlargem^t You may Your Petitioner heartily beggs God's gracious presence with You and Subscribes her self in all humble manner
                                                            Your Sorrowfull and
                                                            Distressed Petitioner
                                                            Rebeccah Fox

[Reverse] [Hand 2?] Rebecca Fox her Pet^{con}/.

Notes: Rebecca Jacobs was imprisoned May 14 (see No. 152) and according to this petition at the time had been there for more than six months. This probably places the petition in late November or in December 1692. In December much activity for seeking the release of prisoners occurred, and another petition to the Governor and Council, No. 714, is dated December 6. This document is placed here as only a guess as to the approximate dating. In 1710 George Jacobs Jr., husband of Rebecca Jacobs, claimed she had been in prison eleven months. See No. 913. If true, this would mean that

after being found not guilty at her trial in January 1693, she remained in prison, presumably unable to pay jail fees. Their   Dec. 8, 1692
daughter Margaret, according to the same claim, was in jail for seven months, which suggests that unlike her mother she
was released in January 1693 after being found not guilty.

Massachusetts Archives Collection, vol. 135, no. 76. Massachusetts State Archives. Boston, MA.

Thursday, December 8, 1692

716. Recognizance for Bethia Carter Sr. by John Pierson & George Lilly

[Hand 1] Memorandum
That on the 8th day of Decemb$^\varepsilon$ <u>1692</u> in the ffowert⟨h⟩ Year of the Reign of our Soueraign
Lord & Lady Wil⟨l⟩[Lost] [= William] & Mary by the Grace of God of England &c King
⟨&⟩ Queen Defenders of y^e ffaith personally Appeared before vs James Russell & Sam^{ll}
Heman Esq^{es} of their Maies^{ts} Councill & Prouince of the Massachu⟨s⟩[Lost] [=
Massachusetts] Bay in New England & Justices of peace within y^e Same John Pierson &
Georg Lylly of Lin in y^e Coun⟨t⟩y of Essex husbandmen, And acknowledged themselus &
Each of them to be indebted vnto our Said Lord & Lady the king & Queen & y^e Suruiuor of
them their Heires & Successors in the Some of Two hundred pounds to be leauied on their
or Either of their goods or Chattels Lands or Tennements for y^e vse of our Said Lord &
Lady the king & Queen or Suruivor of them if default be made in the ᵽformancce of the
Condition vnder written [Lost]i⟨z⟩ [= viz.]
The Condition of the Aboue Recognizance is Such y^t wher as Bethya Carter of Wooburn
Widdow in y^e County of Middlesex Stands charged ^{with Suspition} of y^e horrible Sin of
witchcraft & was Committed to Goale for y^e Same; If therfore the Aforesaid Bethya Carter
who is Suspected as Abouesd, Shall make her personall Appearance before ye Justices of our
Said Lord & Lady the King & Queen at ye Next Court of Assize Oyer & Terminer &
Generall Goale deliuery to be holden for & within y^e County of Middlesex Afores^d to
Answere what Shall be obiected against her ["er" written over "im"] in their Maies^{ts} behalf
refering to Witchcraft & to do & receiue y^t wch by Said Court shall be then & there inioned
her & not depart without licence then y^e Aboue Recognizan[Lost] [= recognizance] to be
void or Elce to remain in full force & virtue
Capt & Recognit die predict Coꝝ.

Ja: Russell
Samuell Hayman

[Reverse] Bethya Carters Recognizan[Lost] [= recognizance] ᵽ appearance at Middlesex C^t

Notes: No further record of Carter's case survives.

*Suffolk Court Files, vol. 32, docket 2697, p. 22, Massachusetts Supreme Judicial Court, Judicial Archives, Massachusetts State
Archives. Boston, MA.*

December 8, 1692

717. Recognizance for Jane Lilly by John Pierson, George Lilly, & Reuben Lilly

[Hand 1] Memorandū:
That on y^{e} Eighth day of Decem$^{\varepsilon}$b 1692 in y^{e} ffowerth Year of y^{e} Reign of our Soueriegn Lord & Lady William & Mary by y^{e} Grace. of God of Engld: &c King & Queen Defenders of y^{e} ffaith. personally Appeared before us Jame[Lost] [= James] Russell & Samu^{ll} Heman Esq$^{\varepsilon}$s of their Maies^{ts} Councill; & Province of y^{e} Massachusets bay in New Engld & Justices of peace within y^{e} Same; John; Peirson: George Lilly & Ruben Lilly All of Linn̄: husbandmen in y^{e} County of Essex And Acknowledged them selves and Each of them to be Indebted vnto Our s^{d} Lord & Lady y^{e} King & Queen &. y^{e} Survivo$^{\varepsilon}$ of them theire heires &. Successo$^{\varepsilon s}$ in y^{e} some of Two hundreds Pounds to be Leavied on their or Either of there Goods or Chattells Lands or Teneme̅nts for y^{e} use of S^{d} Lord & Lady y^{e} King & Queen or Suruivo$^{\varepsilon}$ of them if. defaullt be made in performance of y^{e} Condition vnd$^{\varepsilon}$ written: Viz:

The Condition of y^{e} Above Recognizance is Such y^{t} whera⟨s⟩ Jane Lilly of Reading ~~was~~ in y^{e} County of Middlssex wass Commited to [ ] Goall on Suspition of Witchcraft; If therefore y^{e} Abou[Lost] [= above] S^{d} Jane Lilly Shall make her personall Appearance before y^{e} Justices of Our s^{d} Lord & Lady y^{e} King &. Queen at y^{e} Next Court of Assizes Oyer & Terminer And Generall Goall deliue[Lost]y [= delivery] to be holden for & within y^{e} County of Middls^{x} to Answer what Shall be Obiected Against her in their Maies^{ts} behalfe Refering to Witchcraft And to do & Receiue y^{t} wch by s^{d} Court Shall be then & there Inioined her & not depart with out Licence then y^{e} Aboue Recognizance to be void or Elce to Remain in ffull fforce And Virtue

ꝑ Ja: Russell
Samuell Hayman

[Reverse] [Hand 2] Recogniz̄. ꝑ Jane Lilly her apearance at next Court in Middlesex

Notes: Whether Lilly was freed then or not is not clear. Around the end of January 1693, an ignoramus appeared on an indictment against her, and she was cleared by proclamation on February 3, 1693. See No. 827.

Suffolk Court Files, vol. 32, docket 2714, p. 52, Massachusetts Supreme Judicial Court, Judicial Archives, Massachusetts State Archives. Boston, MA.

718. Petition of George Herrick

[Hand 1] To his Excelency S$^{\varepsilon}$ William Phipps Knight Capt Gen^{ll} & Gouernor of their Majesties Teritores & Dominion of y^{e} Masachusetts Bay In New england
And To: the Honble William Stoughton Esq$^{\varepsilon}$ Leu^{t} Gouer$^{n\varepsilon}$ of said Prouince And To: the Rest of the Honored Councell

The Petition of yo$^{\varepsilon}$ Por~~re~~ Ser^{ut} [= servant] George Herrick

Most Humbly Sheweth

That Whereas your Excellency & Hon$^{\varepsilon s}$ Porre Pettition⟨e⟩r haueing been imployed as Marshall & Dep^{t} Sher⟨i⟩ff for the County of Essex for the Terme of nine months & vpward^{s}, in Serueing of Warrants and Appr⟨eh⟩ending many prisoners attending Examinations & Courts of Oyer & Terminer, as likewise by mitim⟨us⟩ and W⟨ri⟩tts of habeas Corpus haue often Conueighed [= conveyed] Prison⟨e⟩rs vnto Prison & from Prisson to Prisson it ha⟨th⟩

taken up my Whole time and made me Incapeable to gett any thing for the maintainance of
m⟨y⟩ Porre famally; & by that means become so impouerisht that Nesessity hath forcd me to
lay down⟨e⟩ my Place and must Certainly come to Wante if not in some Measure suplyd
Therefore I hum⟨b⟩ly beseech your Hon^Es to take my Case & Condition so fare into
Consideration That I may ⟨ha⟩ue some supply this hard winter that I and my Porre children
may not be destitute of sus⟨t⟩enance & so ineuitabley Perish for I haue been bread A Gen^t &
not much used To Worke and am becom⟨e⟩ Despicable in thees hard times and that yo^E
Exce^ll & Hon^Es may not immagine y^t I am Weary of seruing my King & Country where [=
were] but my habitation Grac⟨e⟩d with plenty in y^e roome of P⟨en⟩nury; there shall be no
seruis too dangerous & difficulte but your Porre Petition⟨e⟩r Will Gladly Except & to the
best of my Power accomplish: I shall Wholely ⟨?⟩gh ^{Lay} my selfe at⟨t⟩ your Honble feet
for Releife & shall allwayes Pray for yo^E Exce^ll and Hon^Es health & hapyness and s⟨u⟩bscribe
my selfe hopeing for S⟨r⟩ Gouner⟨i⟩s Returne

Da⟨t⟩ed in Salem   Yo^E Porre & Humble Pettitioner
This Eigth day of Decem^br   George Herrick
in ⟨t⟩he year of our Lord 1692

[Reverse] [Hand 2] Geo: Herrick his Petition./. 1692

Notes: A year later, on December 12, 1693, Herrick was awarded twenty-five pounds, although he probably received
other sums also. See No. 866. ◊ "Despicable": 'miserable, wretched' (*OED* s.v. *despicable* 1b). "in ye roome of": 'instead
of' (*OED* s.v. *room* n^1, 13c). "Except": 'receive, accept', possibly a mistake for *accept* (*OED*, s.v. *except* n, 6). "Returne": 'a
response to a demand, a reply to a letter' (*OED* s.v. *return* n, 9b).

Massachusetts Archives Collection, vol. 135, no. 67. Massachusetts State Archives. Boston, MA.

Saturday, December 10, 1692

719. Recognizance for Dorothy Good by Samuel Ray

[Hand 1] Memorandum
That On ye Tenth day of December 1692 Samuel Ray of Salem appeared before me
Underwritten One of ye Councill for Thier Maj^tis Province of ye Massachusets Bay in New
England and Acknowledged himselfe Indebted vnto Our Soueraign Lord & Lady ye King &
Queen ye Sume of fifty pounds Currant Money of New: England on ye Condicon hereafter
Named
[Hand 2?] {Vid^t} [Hand 1] That [ ] Good Daughter of [ ] Good of Salem Labourer being
Imprisoned On Suspicon of her being Guilty of ye Crime of Witchcraft & being Now Let to
Bail. That if The Said [ ] Good Shall & do appear at ye Next assize & Gener^ll Goal Deliuery
to be holden at Salem {& abide y^e Courts Judgment} Then y^e aboue Recognisance to be
void Elce to remain in force & vertue

[Reverse] [Hand 3] reecog
[Hand 4] Recog^ce not copied

Dec. 14, 1692   Notes: Dorothy Good was freed and not subsequently tried. ◊ Hand 1 = Stephen Sewall

Essex County Court Archives, vol. 2, no. 185, Massachusetts Supreme Judicial Court, Judicial Archives, on deposit James Duncan Phillips Library, Peabody Essex Museum, Salem, MA.

Wednesday, December 14, 1692

720. Recognizance for William Hobbs by John Nichols & Joseph Towne
See also: May 11, 1693.

[Hand 1] Memorand^m
That on ye fourteenth day of Decemb^ε 1692 in ye ffowerth year of the reign of our Soueraign Lord & Lady William & Mary by the Grace of God of England &c. King & Queen defenders of the ffaith Personally Appeared before vs James Russells & Sam^ll Heyman Esq^ε of their Maies^ts Councill & Prouince of the Massachusets Bay in New Engld, & Justices of Peace within the Same John⟨?⟩ Niccolls & Josep^{h⟨s⟩} Town of Topsfield in ye County of Essex Husbandmen Acknowledged them Selues & Each of Them to be indebted vnto our Said Lord & Lady the King & Queen & the Suruiuor of Them their Heires & Successors in ye Some of Two hundred Pounds to be leauied on their or Either of their goods or Chattells Lands or Tennements for the vse of our Said Lord & Lady the King & Queen or Suruiuor of them if default be made in the Performance of ye Condition vnd^εwritten ^{vi⟨z⟩}
The Condition of the Aboue Recognizance is Such y^t whereas William Hobs of Topsfield in y^e County of Esex Afor⟨e⟩said was committed to Boston Goal on suspition of witchcraft, If therefore the Said William Hobbs shal make his personall Appearance ~~Appearance~~ before y^e Justices of our Said Lord & Lady the King & Queen at y^e next Court of Assize Oyer & ___ Terminer & Generall Goal deliuery to be holden for or within the County of Essex Aforesd To Answere what Shall be obiected against her in their Maies^ts behalf refering to Witchcraft, and to do & receiue y^t wch by said Court shall be then & there inioined her in their Maies^ts behalf refering to Witchcraft, And to do & receiue y^t which by Said Court shall be then & there inioined h⟨er⟩ & not depart without licence, then the Aboue Recognizance to be void or Elce to remain & abide in full fforce & virtue
Capt & Recognit die ꝓdict Coram

Ja: Russell
Samuell Hayman

[Reverse] John Niccolls & Jos. Towns Recognizance ꝑ Wm Hobs of Topsfield
[Hand 2] Called
fforfeit for non Appearance
Apeard y^e 11th day of May & y^e fine remitted
11th day Cleared by proclam^os//

Notes: Hand 2 = Jonathan Elatson

Massachusetts Archives Collection, vol. 135, no. 70. Massachusetts State Archives. Boston, MA.

721. An Act Against Conjuration, Witchcraft and Dealing with Evil and Wicked Spirits

December 14, 1692

[Hand 1] A Bill against Conjuration, Witchcraft and dealing with evil and wicked Spirits.

For more particular direction in the Execution of the Law against Witchcraft. For Explan(ation) of the Law against Witchcraft, and more particular direction therein the Execution thereof and for the better restraining the said Offences, and more Severe punishing the Same, {&cte.} Be it Enacted by the Govern^ℇ Council and Representatives in General Court Assembled and by the Authority of the Same. That if any person or persons after shall use, practice or Exercise any Invocation or Conjuration of any evil and wicked Spirit, Or shall consult, covenant with Entertain, Employ, ffeed or reward any evil and wicked Spirit to or for any intent or purpose; Or take up any dead man woman or Child, out of his, her, or their grave, or any other place where the dead body resteth, or the Skin, bone, or any other part of any dead person to be Employed or used in any manner of Witchcraft, Sorcery, Charm ot {or} Inchantment, Or shall use, practice or Exercise any Witchcraft, Inchantment charm or Sorcery, whereby any person shall be killed, destroyed, wasted, consumed, pined or lamed in his or her body, or any part thereof, That then every such Offender or Offenders, their Aiders, Abetters, and Counsellors being of any the said Offences duly and lawfully convicted and attainted, shall suffer pains of death as a Felon or Felons.

And further to the intent that all manner of practice, use or exercise of witchcraft, Inchantment, charm or Sorcery, should be henceforth utterly avoided, abolished and taken away, Be it Enacted by the Authority afores^d That if any person or persons shall take upon him or them by witchcraft, Inchantment Charm or Sorcery to tell or declare in what place any Treasure of Gold or Silver should or might be found or had in the Earth or other Secret places or where goods or things lost or stoln should be found or become; Or to the intent to provoke any person to unlawful love; Or whereby any Cattel or Goods of any person shall be destroyed, wasted or impaired; Or to hurt or destroy any person in his or her body, although the same be not Effected and done; That then all and every such such ꝑson and ꝑsons so offending, and being thereof lawfully convicted, shall for the said offence suffer Imprisonment by the Space of one whole year without bail or mainprise and once in every Quarter of the s^d year shall in some

Shire Town

stand openly upon the pillory by the space of Six houres, and there shall openly confess his or her Error and offence, [Hand 2] which Said offence Shall be written in Capitall Letters & placed upon ye breast of Said offender [Hand 1] And if any person or persons being once convicted of the Same offence, and Shall again commit the like offence and being of any of the said offences the second time lawfully & duely convicted and attainted as is aforesaid shall Suffer pains of death as a ffelon or ffelons.

[Hand 2] xbr [= December]. 14. 92: This Bill read orderly in this house of Rep^ℇsentatives and voted passed in y^e Affirmatiue & Sent to his Excellency the Gouern^ℇ & Councill for Consent

William Bond speaker

December 15, 1692   [Hand 1] Read several times in Council, Voted, Ordered to be Engrossed and pass into an
Act, die predict.

And is consented unto
℘ William Phips

[Hand 3?] Bill against Conjuration [Lost]craf⟨t⟩ [= and witchcraft] and dealing ⟨wi⟩th Evil
and Wicked Spirits
Past Decemb^ɛ 1692

Notes: After the Court of Oyer and Terminer ended, it no doubt seemed important to reaffirm nevertheless the reality
of witchcraft. The legislation was passed on December 14 by the Governor, Council and Legislature, but was disallowed
when reviewed in England.

Massachusetts Archives Collection, vol. 135, nos. 68 & 69. Massachusetts State Archives. Boston, MA.

Thursday, December 15, 1692

722. Recognizance for Margaret Prince by Thomas Prince & Richard Tarr

[Hand 1] Memorandum
That on this fifteenth Day of December anno D$\overline{m}$: one Thousand Six hundred Ninty and
two in y^e fourth year of the Reigne of our Sovereigne Lord & Lady William & Mary by the
Grace of God of England Scottland &^{c} King & Queen Defend^{ɛs} of y^e ffaith &^{c} Personally
Came and Appeared before me George Corwin High Sherriffe of the County of Essex of the
Province of the Massathutetts Bay in New England Thomas Prince of Gloster in ye County
of Essex in New England Husbandman Richard Tarr of said Towne and County
Husbandman and Acknowledged them selves indebted to our said Sovereigne Lord & Lady
ye King & Queen, and the Surviver of them their Heires and Successers in the summe of two
hundred pounds to be Leavied on their Goods & Chattles Lands & Tennements for the vse
of our said Sovereigne Lord & Lady: King & Queen & the Surviver of them if Default be
made⟨?⟩ in y^e Performance of y^e Condition vnder written./.
Videlisitt
The Condition of this Aboue Recognizance is Such that Whereas Margerett Prince
Widdow Of Gloster aboue$\overline{es}$^{d} is Suspected & Accused of Committing Acts of Witchcrafts if
therefore Margerett Prince Widdow afore$\overline{es}$^{d} shall & do make her Personall Appearance
before the Justices of our $\overline{s}$^{d} Sovereigne Lord & Lady the King and Queen at y^e Next Court
of Assize Oyer & Terminer next: Generall Geoall Delivery to be held for or within the
County of Essex afore$\overline{es}$^{d} to answer w^t shall be Objected ag^t her on their Maj^{tes} behalfe: &
Referring to y^e Witchcrafts. & to do & Receive y^t by wch said Court shall be then & there
Injoyned & not depart without Lycence Then y^e above Recognizance to be void or Else to
abide & Remaine in full force and virtue: In Wittness⟨ꝛ⟩ whereof the above Named Persons
have herevnto sett their hand & Seales this fifteenth Day of December in the year of our

Lord one thousand six hundred Ninty & two and in the fourth year of our Maj^ties   December 16, 1692
Reigne
Wittness:

Benj^a Gerrish   Thomas $\mathcal{T}$ Prince
Naithaniel Beadle Sr   his Marke
Jn° Gyles   Richard Tarr
1692:

Notes: Margaret Prince's case was heard by the grand jury, probably on January 5, 1693, when an ignoramus was returned on her indictment. See No. 757. No record of a trial or other indictments survives. ◊ 2 wax seals.

Massachusetts Archives Collection, vol. 135, no. 71. Massachusetts State Archives. Boston, MA.

Friday, December 16, 1692

723. Recognizance for Mary Green by Peter Green & James Sanders

[Hand 1] Memorandum
That on this ⟨?⟩Sixteenth Day of December Anno D̄m̄ one thousands Six hundred Ninety & two In the fourth Year of the Reigne of our Sovereigne Lord & Lady William & Mary by the Grace of God of England Scottland &^c King & Queen Defend^Es of the faith &^c Personally came and Appeared before me George Corwin High Shirriffe of the County of Essex of the Province of the Massetuthetts Bay in New England Peter Green of Haverell in ye County afores^d Weaver. and James Sanders of the said Towne Husbandman And Acknowledged themselves & Each of them to be indebted vnto our s̄^d Sovereigne Lord the King and Lady the Queen or the Surviver of them their Heirs and Successo^Es in the Summe of two hundred pounds to be Leaved on their goods and Chattles Lands & Tenements for the vse of our Sovereigne Lord and Lady the King & Queen or the Survivor of them if Default be made in ye Performance of the Condition vnderwritten Videllisett
The Condition of ye Above written Recognizance is Such That Whereas Mary Green Wife of the above bounden Peter Greene of Haverell is Suspected and accused of Committing acts of Witchcrafts If therefore the said Mary Green aforesaid shall & do make her Personall Appearance before the Justices of our said Sovereigne Lord & Lady the King and Queen at ye Next Court of Assize Oyer & Terminer Next Generall Goal Delivery to be held for or within ye County of Essex afores̄^d to answear w^t shall be objected ag^t her on their Maj^tes behalfe Refering to the Witchcrafts & to do and Receive That by which said Court shall be then & there Injoyned and not Depart without Licence then the above Recognizance to be void or Else to abide and Remane in full force and virtue In Wittness whereof the abovenamed Persons Peter Green & James Sanders have here vnto sett their hand & seale this Sixteenth Day of December in ye Year of our Lord one Thousand six hundred Ninty & two and in the fourth year of their Maj^tes Reigne:/.

December 16, 1692

Wittnesse
Thomas beadle

⟨D⟩aniel L⟨u⟩nt
Jnᵒ Gyles
1692

Peter green

James 𝑖 🝰 Sanders

his Marke

[Reverse] [Hand 2] Mary Green Peter Green James Sanders Sur{e}ties

Notes: No record of a trial survives, but on September 13, 1710, Mary Green's husband, Peter, asked for compensation for expenses relating to her trial. See No. 908. When that might have been is unknown. ◊ 2 wax seals.

Massachusetts Archives Collection, vol. 135, no. 72. Massachusetts State Archives. Boston, MA.

724. An Act for Enabling the Justices of the Superior Court to Hold a Court of Assize and General Goale Delivery

[Hand 1] An Act for Enabling the Justices of the Superiour Court to hold a Court of Assize and General Goale delivery within the County of Essex upon Tuesday the third of January next [Hand 2] Upon Consideration that many pᵉsons Charged as Capitall offenders ∧{are}, now in Custody within yᵉ County of Essex, and yᵉ time prefixed by yᵉ act of yᵉ Generall Assembly Entitled an act [Hand 3] for the Establishing of Judicatories and Courts of Justice within this Province.

[Hand 2] For yᵉ Sitting of yᵉ Superiour Court and Goal Delivery within that County being past

It is Enacted by yᵉ Governoᵉ Councill & Repᵉsentatiues Convened in Generall Court [Hand 3] ∧{And by the authority of the same} [Hand 2] that for yᵉ Speedy Delivery of yᵉ Goals, the Justices of yᵉ Superioᵉ Court pro hāc vice, do hold and keep a Court of Assize, and Generall Goal delivery within yᵉ Sᵈ County of Essex upon [Hand 3] Tuesday [Hand 2] the Third [Hand 3] day [Hand 2] of [Hand 3] January. [Hand 2] next. [Hand 3] any thing in the sᵈ Act to the contrary notwithstanding

[Hand 2] xbr [= December] .16. 92. This bill orderly read in this house of Repᵉsentatiues and voted passed in yᵉ Affirmatiue & sent to his Excellency yᵉ Gouernoᵉ & Councill for Consent

William Bond Speaker

[Hand 1] Read in Council. Voted and Ordered to be Enacted, die predict.
Isᵃ Addington S̄ecr̄y

And is consented unto

𝔭 William Phips

[Reverse] A Bill for Impowring the Justices of yᵉ Superioᵉ Court pro hâc vice to hold a Court of Assize within yᵉ County of Essex.
past. xᵇʳ 16ᵗʰ 1692.
[Hand 4] Feb 16

Notes: The reason for the date of "February 16" is not clear and may be an insertion by a modern hand.

Massachusetts Archives Collection, vol. 47, no. 134. Massachusetts State Archives. Boston, MA.

Tuesday, December 20, 1692

725. Recognizance for Eunice Frye by John Frye & John Osgood Sr.

[Hand 1] Memorandum

That on y^e Twentieth Day of December Annoq$_3$ D$\overline{m}$ one thousand six hundred Ninty & two in y^e fourth year of the Reigne of our Sovereigne Lord & Lady William & Mary by the Grace of God of England &^{c} King & Queen Defenders of y^e ffaith &^{c} Personally came & Appeared before me George Corwin High Sherriffe for y^e County of Essex of y^e Province of the Massathuttets Bay in New England Deacon John ffry and John Ossgood both of Andavor. Yeomen and Acknowledged themselves & Each of them Indebted vnto our Sovereigne Lord & Lady the King & Queen or the Survivors of them their Heires & Success^{es} in the summe of two hundred pounds to be leaved on their goods & Chattles, Lands & Tenements for the vse of our Sovereigne Lord & Lady y^e King & Queen or y^e Survivor of them If default be made in the Performance of the Condition vnderwritten./. Visdellisett

The Condition of the above written Recognizance is such That whereas Vnis [= Eunice] ffry Wife to y^e above$\overline{es}$^{d} Decon John ffry of Andavor afore$\overline{es}$^{d} is suspected & Accused of Committing Divers Acts of Witchcrafts if therefore y^e $\overline{s}$^{d} Vnis ffry afore$\overline{es}$^{d} shall & do make her Personall Appearance before y^e Justices of our Sovereigne Lord & Lady y^e King & Queen at y^e Next Court of Assize of Oyer & Terminer next Generall Goal Delivery to be held for or within the County of Essex afore$\overline{es}$^{d} to answer w^t shall be objected ag^t her on their Maj^{tes} behalfe Refering to y^e Witchcrafts and to do & Receive y^t by which said Court shall be then & there Injoyned & not to depart without Lycence Then y^e above Recognizane to be void or Else to abide & Remaine in full force & virtue In Wittness whereof the above Named Persons: John ffry & John Ossgood have herevnto sett their hand & seals this Twentieth Day of December in the Year of our Lord one Thousand Six hundred Ninty & two & in ye forth year of their Maj^{tes} Reigne./.

Wittnessed

Joshua Conant }
Robert Gray }
Jno Gyles }
⟨1692⟩

John frie
John Osgood

Notes: Eunice Frye returned to court on January 12, 1693, where she was again set free on recognizance. See No. 795. She was finally brought to trial on May 10, 1693 and found not guilty. See No. 848. ◊ 2 wax seals.

Massachusetts Archives Collection, vol. 135, no. 73. Massachusetts State Archives. Boston, MA.

726. Recognizance for Mary Osgood by John Osgood Sr. & John Frye

[Hand 1] Memorandum

That on the Twentieth Day of Decemb^e anno. D$\overline{m}$ one thousand Six hundred Ninty & two in y^e fourth year of the Reigne of our Sovereigne Lord & Lady. William and Mary by y^e Grace of God of England Scotland &^{c} King and Queen Defenders of the ffaith &^{c} Personally came and Appeared before me George Corwin high Sherriffe of the County of

December 20, 1692

Essex of ye Province of the Massathutetts Bay in New England: John Osgood Yeoman and Deacon John ffry both of Andevor and Acknowledged them selves & Each of them Indebted vnto our Sovereigne Lord & Lady ye King & Queen or the Survivor of them their Heires & Successo^ɛs in the Summe of two hundred po⟨?⟩unds to be leaved on their goods & Chattles Lands & Tenements for ye vse of our Sovereigne Lord & Lady ye King & Queen or the S⟨u⟩rvivor of them if Default be made in ye Performance of the Condition vnder written./. Videllisett

The Condition of ye aboue written Recognizance is such That Whereas Mary ["Mary" written over "Sarah"] Ossgood wife of the aboue͞s^d John Osgood of Andevor afore͞s^d is Suspected & Accused of ~~witchcrafts~~ Committing Divers Acts of Witchcrafts if therefore ye Said Mary ["Mary" written over "Sarah"] Ossgood afore͞s^d shall and do make here Personall Appearance before ye Justices of our Sovereigne Lord & Lady the King & Queen at ye Next Court of Assize of O⟨y⟩er & Terminer Next Generall Goal Delivery to be held for or within ye County of Essex afore͞s^d to answear what shall be objected ag^t her on their Maj^tes behalfe Refering to ye Witchcrafts, & to do & Receive y^t by wch said Court shall be then & there Injoyned & not to Depart w^thout Lycence Then ye above Recognizance to be void or else to abide & Remaine in full force & virtue In Wittness Whereof the aboue Named Persons John Ossgood & John ffry have herevnto sett their hands & seals this Twentieth Day of December in y^e year of our Lord one Thousand Six hundred Ninty & two & in the fourt Year of their Maj^tes Reigne/:

Wittnesse

Joshua Conant   John Osgood
Robert Gr⟨a⟩y   John frie
Jno Gyles
1692

[Reverse] [Hand 2] Mary Osgood
Prin^c⟨p⟩ Suertes [= principal sureties] Jno Osgood Jno Frye

Notes: Mary Osgood was tried January 12, 1693, and found not guilty. See No. 800. ◊ 2 wax seals.

Massachusetts Archives Collection, vol. 135, no. 74. Massachusetts State Archives. Boston, MA.

727. Call for a Day of Prayer and Fasting

Province of the Massachusetts Bay in New England

By His Excellency and Council.

The Various Awful Judgments of God continued upon the *English* Nation, and the Dispersions thereof in Their Majesties several Plantations, by War, Sickness, Earth-quakes, and other Desolating Calamities; more especially, by permiting Witchcrafts and Evil Angels to Rage amongst his People: All which Loudly Call to Deep Humiliation and Earnest Application to Heaven as the best Expedient for Deliverance.

Upon Consideration thereof, His Excellency and Council have thought fit, and do hereby Appoint *Thursday*, the Twenty Ninth of *December* currant, to be Kept as a Day of Solemn

Dec. 21, 1692

PRAYER with FASTING in the several Towns throughout this Province, where this Order shall come seasonably to give Notice thereof. And in such other Towns, which it shall not reach soon enough, upon the *Thursday* following; Exhorting both Ministers and People fervently to Implore Heavens Blessings upon Their Majesties, their Three Kingdoms and Plantations Abroad, and upon the whole Protestant Interest; That a Spirit of Reformation may be Powred down from on High, and Gods Anger Diverted, That Divine Conduct may be vouchsafed to all the *English* Governments, and Success attend their Affairs.

And all Servile Labour on said Day is hereby Forbiden.

Boston, December 20, 1692.

Isaac Addington, Secr.

Notes: Although a printed document, it appears in a manuscript collection at the National Archives in Britain.

Colonial Office 5/857, p. 97. National Archives, London, UK.

Wednesday, December 21, 1692

728. Recognizance for Frances Hutchins by Samuel Hutchins & Joseph Kingsbury

[Hand 1] Memorandum
That on the Twenty one Day of Decemb$^\varepsilon$ Annoq$^\varepsilon$ D$\overline{m}$: one Thousand six hundred Ninty & two in y^e fourth year of y^e Reigne of our Sovereigne Lord & Lady William & Mary by the Grace of God of England &^{c} King & Queen Defenders of the faith &^{c} Personally came and Appeared before me George Corwin High Sherriffe for y^e County of Essex of the Province of the Massathutets Bay in New England. Samuel Hutchens of Haverell and Joseph Kingsbury of Haverell afores^d Husbandmen and Acknowledged themselves Indebted vnto our Sovereigne Lord & Lady the King & Queen or y^e Survivors of them their Heires & Successo$^{\varepsilon s}$ in the Summe of two hundred pounds to be leaved one [= on] their Goods & Chattles Lands & Tenements for the vse of our Sovereigne Lord & Lady the King & Queen or y^e Successors of them if Default be made in y^e Performance of the Condition vnderwritten./.
Videllisitt
The Condition of y^e above written Recognizance is Such That Whereas ffrancess Hutchens Widdow of Haverell afo$\overline{res}$^{d} is Suspected ~~of~~ and Accused of Committing Divers Acts of Witchcrafts If therefore the Said ffrancess Hutchens afo$\overline{res}$^{d} Shall & do make her Personall Appear⟨a⟩nce before the Justices of our Sovereigne Lord & Lady y^e King & Queen, at y^e Next Court of Assize of Oyer & Terminer Next Generall Goal Deliverey to be held for or ["o" written over "&"] within y^e County of Essex afo$\overline{res}$^{d} to answear w^t shall be objected ag^t her on their Maj^{tes} behalfe Refering to y^e Witchcrafts & to do & Receive y^t by wch said Court shall be then and there Injoyned & not Darpart [= depart] without Licence. Then y^e said Recognizance to be void: or Else to abide in full force & vertue In Wittness whereof y^e above Named Persons ~~have~~ Sam^{ll} Hutchings & Joseph Kingsberrey have herevnto sett our hands & seales this Twenty first Day of December in the Year of our Lord one Thousand six

December 22, 1692   hundred Ninty & two and in the fourth year of their Maj[ties] Reigne/
                          Wittnessed:
                          Thomas Beadle   Samuel hucthins
                          Joshua Conant   Joseph kingsbe⟨r⟩y
                          Jn° Gyles
                          1692

Notes: Frances Hutchins was arrested August 19, 1692. See No. 510. She probably remained in prison until December 21, 1692. No record of further legal action survives. ◊ 2 wax seals.

Massachusetts Archives Collection, vol. 135, no. 75. Massachusetts State Archives. Boston, MA.

Thursday, December 22, 1692

729. Appointment of the Justices and Clerk of the Superior Court of Judicature and Court of Assize

[Hand 1] At a Council held at the Council Chamber in Boston upon Thursday Dec[r] 22. 1692.

Present

His Excellency S[r] William Phips Kn[t] &c[a]

William Stoughton Esq[r] L[t] Gov[r]

Wait Winthrop	John Phillips	Peter Sergeant
Elisha Hutchinson Esq[rs]	Esq[rs]	Saml Sewall Esq[rs]
John Richards.	John Joyliffe	John Foster.

His Excellency delivered a Commission unto William Stoughton Esq[re] for Chief Justice of the Superiour Court of Judicature and Court of Assize and an Oath was administred unto him for the due Execution thereof according to Law.

William Phips.

John Richards, Wait Winthrop and Samuel Sewall Esq[rs] also received their Commissions for Justices of the Superiour Court ^{of Judicature and Court} of Assize, and were severally sworn to the due execution thereof according to Law.

William Phips.

M[r] Jonathan Ellatson was sworn Clerk of the Superiour Court of Judicature and Assize.

William Phips.

Governor's Council Executive Records (1692), vol. 2, p. 212. Massachusetts Archives Collection. Massachusetts State Archives. Boston, MA. Certified copy from the original records at Her Majesty's State Paper Office, September 16, 1846. London, UK.

Friday, December 23, 1692

730. Warrant for Jurors from Andover for the Grand Jury and Jury of Trials at a Court of Assize, and Town's Return

See also: Dec. 30, 1692.

[Hand 1] These are in Their Maj^{ties} Names to Require you forthwith to Assemble the ffree holders and other the Inhabitants of your Towne who are hereby allso required to Choose foure good and Lawfull men of the same Towne Each whereof to haue a reall Estate of fourty shillings ꝑ Annum or a ꝑsonall Estate of ffifty pounds to serue as Jurors Two vpon the Grand Jury and two vpon the Jury of Tryalls at a Court of Assises and Generall Goal Delivery to be held at Salem for the County of Essex on Tusday the third day of January next Ensuing the day of the date hereof wch ꝑsons so Chosen you are to summons to Attend the said Court by nine of the Clock in the morning of ye said Day and make returne hereof wth the names of ye said ꝑsons the day before the said Court and hereof not to faile Dated in Boston The Twenty third Day of Decemb̄ 1692
To The Constable or Constables of Andover or Either of them   ꝑ Cur̄
Jon^a Elatson Cler̄

[Hand 2] Andouer: Desember 30th 1692: In Obediance unto this Aboue Riten worant: I Haue Asembled the ffree holders & other the Inhabitance of Our Town Togither & thay Haue: Chosen ~~Samuell~~ Joseph Marble: sener: & henery holt sener: ffor the grand jury: & Left Cristiphur Ossgood & Samuell ffry sene ffor the Jury of Tryals for the aboue mentined Cort: & haue somonsed Them to apere acording to warant
As atest Ephraim ffoster Constable of Andouer

[Reverse] [Hand 1] Andover

Notes: This and the following warrants for grand jurors and trial jurors, in alphabetical order by town, were prepared for the initial session in 1693 of the Superior Court of Judicature in Salem. Warrants for jurors at the three subsequent sessions of this court (not included in this edition) were issued later, also in Jonathan Elatson's hand, with various officials from those towns writing the Returns. They were issued as follows: January 19, to Cambridge, Charleston, Concord, Malden, Medford, Newton, Watertown, and Woburn for the Middlesex sitting of the Court in Charleston on January 31; April 17 to Braintree, Roxbury, Milton, Medfield, Dorchester, Boston, and Weymouth for the Suffolk sitting of the Court in Boston on April 25; April 28 to Marblehead, Newbury, and Rowley for the Essex sitting of the Court in Ipswich on May 9; May 3, to Beverley and on May 4 to Andover, Bradford, and Topsfield for the May 9 sitting of the Court in Ipswich. A return from Salem dated May 6 indicated that the town sent jurors to this session, but no warrant is extant. This group of warrants and returns can be found in the Suffolk Court Files, Volume 32, Massachusetts Supreme Judicial Court, Judicial Archives. Hand 1 = Jonathan Elatson.

Massachusetts Archives Collection, vol. 135, no. 92. Massachusetts State Archives. Boston, MA.

731. Warrant for Jurors from Beverly for the Grand Jury and Jury of Trials at a Court of Assize, and Town's Return

See also: Jan. 2, 1693.

[Hand 1] These are in their Maj^{ties} Names to require you forthwith to assemble the ffree Holders and other the Inhabitants of your Towne who are hereby allso required to Choose

December 23, 1692

foure Good and Lawfull men of the same Towne Each whereof to haue a reall Estate of
fourty shillings ꝑ Annum or a ꝑsonall Estate of ffifty pounds to serue as Jurors two vpon yᵉ
Grand Jury and Two vpon the Jury of Tryalls at a Court of Assises & Genˡˡ Goal Delivery to
be held at Salem for the County of Essex on Tusday the third day of Jaⁿᵘᵃ next Ensuing the
day of the date hereof wᶜʰ ꝑsons so Chosen you are to sūmons to attend the said Court by
nine of the Clock ~~of~~ ^{in} the morning of the said Day. and make returne hereof with the
names of the said ꝑsons the day before the said Court and hereof not to faile. Dated in
Boston the Twenty third day of Decemb̄ 1692
To The Constable or Constables of Beverley or either of them   ꝑ Cur̄
                                                                      Jonᵃ Elatson Cler̄

[Reverse] [Hand 2] Beverly January yᵉ 2ᵈ 1692
these ar to certifie such Honoᵋd gentel men as may bee Concerned yᵗ in yᵉ persuance of the
within written yᵉ Inhabytance of our Towne beeing Asempled togeather on yᵉ 2ⁿᵈ of this
instant haue made choice of John Louit seᵋ and Roberd Cue for yᵉ grand Jury and Samuel
Morgan and Edmong Gale for yᵉ Jury of Tryals to attend yᵉ service of the Court within
named
{The aboue sd persons} I haue allso ~~sm~~ summonsᵈ to ated [= attend] acording to yᵉ within
written

                                                                      ꝑ John Conant
                                                                Constable of Beverly

Notes: Hand 1 = Jonathan Elatson

Massachusetts Archives Collection, vol. 135, nos. 88 & 89. Massachusetts State Archives. Boston, MA.

732. Warrant for Jurors from Gloucester for the Grand Jury and Jury of Trials at a Court of Assize, and Town's Return

See also: Dec. 31, 1692.

[Hand 1] These are in theire Majᵗⁱᵉˢ Names to require you forthwit⟨h⟩ to Asemble the free
holders and other the Inhabitants of your towne who are hereby also required to Choose
three good & lawfull men of the Same towne each whereof to haue a reall Esstate of fourty
shillings ꝑ Annum or a personall Estate of fifty pounds to Serue as Jurors one upon the
Grand Jury & two upon the Jury of Tryal[Lost] [= trials] at a Court of Assises & Genˡˡ Goal
deliuery to be held at Salem for the County of Essex on Tusday the third day of January next
ensueing the date hereof which persons so Chosen you are to Summons to attend the said
Court by nine of the Clock in the morning of the said day and make returne hereof with the
names of the said persons the day before the said Court and hereof not to faile Dated in
Boston yᵉ twenty third day of December 1692
To The Constable or constables of Glocester or either of them.   ꝑ Cur̄
                                                                      Jonᵃ Elatson Clerᵋ

[Hand 2] According to this warrant the free holders and other the Inhabetants of glocester
Asembled togather and Chose James persons to serue vpon the grand Jury and William
Stevens and John Davis to serue vpon the Jury of Tryals Att a Court of Assises to be held at

Salem the third day of January next Ensuing and these persons that are Chossen I did December 23, 1692
Summons to Attend the Said Court dated in glocester december the 31ᵗʰ 1692

Thomas Riggs Constable

[Reverse] [Hand 3] Glossester

Massachusetts Archives Collection, vol. 135, no. 83. Massachusetts State Archives. Boston, MA.

733. Warrant for Jurors from Haverhill for the Grand Jury and Jury of Trials at a Court of Assize, and Town's Return

See also: Dec. 31, 1692.

[Hand 1] These are in their Maj^ties Names to Require you forthwith to Assemble the ffree. holders and other the Inhabitants of yoᵉ Towne, who are hereby allso required to Choose Three good and Lawefull men of the same Towne, Each whereof to haue a reall Estate of ffourty shillings ⅌ Annum, or a ⅌sonall Estate of ffifty pounds, to serue as Jurors one vpon the Grand Jury, and two vpon the Jury of Tryalls, at a Court of Assises and Generall Goal Delivery to be held at Salem for the County of Essex on Tusday the third day of Janū̄ᵃ next Ensuing the day of the date hereof, wᶜʰ ⅌sons so Chosen you are to summons to Attend the said Court by nine of yᵉ Clock in yᵉ morning of yᵉ said Day, and make – Returne hereof wᵗʰ the names of yᵉ ^{said} ⅌sons the day before the said Court and hereof not to faile Dated in Boston yᵉ Twenty third day of Decemb̄ 1692
To The Constable or Constables of Haverill or either of Them　　　　⅌ Cur̄

Jonᵃ Elatson Cler̄

[Reverse] [Hand 2] Haverhill, 31ˢᵗ Decʳ 1692: at a meeting of the ffree-holders and other the Inhabitants of this Town, they then Chose: (according to the Tenor of this warrant) three Jury men, viz Cornᵗ Peter Aires to Serue on the grand-jury: and Sergᵗ Josiah Gage & James Sanders to Serue upon the Jury of Tryalls, and also haue summonsed the sᵈ three persons to attend the Court of Assises & Generˡˡ Goal Delivery to be held at Salem, for the County of Essex on Tuesday the third of Januᵉ next ensuing as attest

william Starlin
Constable of Haverhill

[Hand 1] Haverill

Notes: Hand 1 = Jonathan Elatson

Massachusetts Archives Collection, vol. 135, nos. 90 & 91. Massachusetts State Archives. Boston, MA.

December 23, 1692

734. Warrant for Jurors from Ipswich for the Grand Jury and Jury of Trials at a Court of Assize, and Town's Return
See also: Dec. 31, 1692.

[Hand 1] These are in their Maj^ties Names to require you forthwith to Assemble the free holders and other the Inhabitants of your towne who are hereby also required to Choose f(?)e {eleven} good & lawfull men of the Same towne each wherof to haue a reall estate of fourty shillings ⍵ Annum or a personall Estate of fifty pounds to Serue as Jurors three upon the Grand Jury & eight upon the Jury of Tryalls at a court of Assi⟨s⟩es and Gen^ll Goal delivery to be held at Salem for the County of Esex on Tusday the Third day of January next Ensueing the date hereof which persons So chosen you are to Summons to attend the Said Court by nine of the Clock in the Morning of the said day and make returne hereof with the names, of the said persons ye day before the Said Court And hereof not to faile Dated in boston y^e twenty third day of December 1692

To The Constable or Constables of Ipswich or eitheir of them   ⍵ Cur̄
                                                                                        Jon^a Elatson Cler̄

[Reverse] [Hand 2] Rec^d this warrant of Marshall Harris this 31.10^ber [= December] 1692

By Vertue of this warrant y^e Inhabitants of Ipswich being Lawfully assembled: according to notice before giuen In order to y^e Chooseing Eleven Good & Lawfull men to Serue on y^e Jury to attend at y^e Court of assizes & Generall Goal Deliuery to be holde[Lost] [= holden] at Salem In y^e County of Essex on Tuseday y^e Third day of January Instant. & These persons here under written were Vnanimously Chosen & had notice. thereof most of them personally Warned & y^e rest y^t ware not personally warned. Sum̄onses was read at thair dwelling houses. to Require them to attend accordingly ye which thair Severall families had notice of: January. ye 2^d 1692:

The Grand Jury are as ffollowes.   The Jury for Tryalls are
M^ε Robert Paine   Ens. Thos Jacob.
M^ε Richard Smith   Sarg^t Nathaniel Emerson sen^ε
M^ε Thomas Boareman,   M^ε Jacob. Perkins ju^ε
                                                    M^ε Matchew. Whipple sen^ε
                                                    John Pengery
                                                    Seth: Story
                                                    Thos Edwards
                                                    John Lamson

In Testemony whereof we hereto Subscribe our names
Joseph ffuller
Mathew Perkins ⎫
William Baker ⎬ Constabls of Ipswich
John Chote   ⎭

Massachusetts Archives Collection, vol. 135, nos. 79 & 80. Massachusetts State Archives. Boston, MA.

735. Warrant for Jurors from Lynn for the Grand Jury and Jury of Trials at a Court of Assize, and Town's Return

December 23, 1692

See also: Dec. 29, 1692.

[Hand 1] These are in their Maj^ties Names to require you forthwith to Asemble the free holders and other the Inhabitants of your towne who are hereby also required to Choose Six good and lawfull men of the Same towne each whereof to haue a reall Estate of ffourty Shillings ᵽ Annum or a personall Estate of fifty pounds to Serue as Jurors two upon the Grand Jury and four upon the Jury of Tryalls at a Court of Assises and Gen^ll Goal Delivery to be held at Salem for the County of Essex on tusday the third day of January next Ensueing the date hereof which persons so Chosen you are to Summons to attend ye Said Court by nine of ye Clock in the Morning of the said day and make returne hereof with the names of the said persons ye day before ye Said Court and hereof not to faile Dated in boston ye twenty third day of Decemb̄:
To The Constable or Constables of Lyn or either of them   ᵽ Cur̄
                                                                    Jon^a Elatson Cler.

[Reverse] [Hand 2] Lyn ye 29th of Desem^ε 92
Accoring to this warrant the town hathe Chose for gran Juryo^ε s Robert pottor sen^ε Benjemen Rednap ffor y^e Jury of tryalls Cornet Johnson Leften^t person John Witt & Benjemen Collins & I haue Warned them to appear acording to this within Mencioned Warrant as atest
                                                    Samuel Ingals Constabl of Lyn

[Hand 3] Lynn

Notes: Hand 3 = Jonathan Elatson

Massachusetts Archives Collection, vol. 135, nos. 77 & 78. Massachusetts State Archives. Boston, MA.

736. Warrant for Jurors from Marblehead for the Grand Jury and Jury of Trials at a Court of Assize, and Town's Return

See also: Dec. 30, 1692.

[Hand 1] These are in their Maj^ties Names to require you forthwith to Assemble the free holders and other the Inhabitants of your town⟨e⟩ who are hereby also required to Choose foure good and lawfull men of ye Same towne each whereof to haue a reall Estate of fourty shillings ᵽ Annum or a personall Estate of fifty pounds to Serue as Jurors two upon the grand Jury & two upon the Jury of Tryalls at a Court of Assises and Gen^ll Goal deliuery to be held at Salem for the County of Essex on Tusday the third day of January next ensueing the date hereof which persons So Chosen you are to Sumons to attend the Said Court by nine of the Clock in the morning of the Said day and make return hereof with the names of the said persons the day before y^e Said Court and hereof not to faile Dated in Boston the twenty third day of December 1692

December 23, 1692

To the The Constable or Constables of Marblehed or either of them   ℞ Cur

Jon^a Elatson Cler.

[Reverse] [Hand 2] The inhabitants {of our town} being assembled made thair Joyc [= choice] as followeth

for grand Jurors	[2–3 words overstruck]
	Wm Woods
	Ric: Reed
for Jury of tryals	Wm Beale
	Ric: Groce

Des: y^e 30th, <u>92</u>

James Smith Const:
for Marblehead

The persons aboue men^{ti} ware sumonsed according to Law
℞ mee James Smith

Massachusetts Archives Collection, vol. 135, nos. 84 & 85. Massachusetts State Archives. Boston, MA.

737. Warrant for Jurors from Newbury for the Grand Jury and Jury of Trials at a Court of Assize, and Town's Return
See also: Dec. 31, 1692.

[Hand 1] These are in their Maj^{ties} Names to requ⟨i⟩re you forthwith to Assemble the ffree Holders and other the Inhabitants of your Towne who are hereby allso required to Choose Nine good and Lawefull men of the same Towne. Each whereof to haue a reall Estate of ffourty shillings ℞ Annum or a ℞sonall Estate of ffifty pounds to serve as Jurors. Three vpon the Grand Jury and six vpon the Jury of Tryalls at a Court of Assises and Generall Goal Delivery to be held at Salem for the County of Essex on Tusday the third day of Janu^a next Ensuing the day of the date hereof w^{ch} ℞sons so Chosen you are to summons to Attend the said Court by nine of the Clock in the morning of ye said Day and make returne hereof wth the names of the said ℞sons the day before the said Court and hereof faile not Dated in Boston the Twenty third day of Decemb: 1692

To The Constable̶s̶ or Constables of Newbury or either of Them   ℞ Cur̄.

Jon^a Elatson Cler̄.

[Reverse] [Hand 2] To the ∧{high} Sheriff of ye County of essex Esqu^ε
29 desember 1692 then I warned ye freeholders & other inhabi^{ts} of Newbury to assemble together to Choose nine Jurars a̶s̶ {men} and according to waring y^e s^d freehol & inhabitants mett together and Cose ∧{nine} Jurors ∧{men} to Serue according ⟨?⟩ to y^e teneur of this warant

ffor yᵉ Grand Jury	Jury of trialls	December 23, 1692
thomas Hale	Sariant John Hale	
Richard Browne	Sarᵗ John kent sener	
Richard Bartlet sener	Jarᵗ [= sergeant] Joseph Little	
	Benayah titcomb	
	John Emery Juner	
	John Ordway	

I alsoe Sumoned the Jurors aboue named to make their a personall apperance at Salem on tusday next the thurd of Janawary According to yᵉ teneur of yᵉ with⟨in⟩ warant dated 31 desember 1692 by me   Samuel Hills Constable
                                                                                                   for Newbury

Notes: Hand 1 = Jonathan Elatson

Massachusetts Archives Collection, vol. 135, nos. 93 & 94. Massachusetts State Archives. Boston, MA.

738. Warrant for Jurors from Salem for the Grand Jury and Jury of Trials at a Court of Assize, and Town's Return

See also: Dec. 30, 1692 & Dec. 31, 1692.

[Hand 1] These are in their Majᵗⁱᵉˢ Names to require you forthwith to Assemble the ffree holders and other the Inhabitants of your towne who are hereby also required to Choose nine good & Lawfull men of yᵉ Same towne each whereof to haue a reall Estate of fourty Shillings ℔ Annum or a personall Estate of fifty pounds to Serue as Jurors three upon the Grand Jury & Six upon the Jury of Tryalls at a Court of Assises & Genˡˡ Goal Delivery to be held at Salem for the County of Essex on Tusday the third day of January next ensueing the date hereof which persons So Chosen you are to summons to attend the Said Court by nine of the Clock in the Morning of the said day and make returne hereof with the names of the said persons the day before the said [Hand 2] ∧{Court} [Hand 1] And hereof not to faile Datted In Boston the twenty third day of December 1692
To the Constable or Constables of Salem or either of them   ℔ Cuꝛ.
                                                                                          Jonᵃ Elatson Cleꝛ.

[Hand 3] In obedience to this warrante I hea⟨v⟩e warned the Inhabitants of this towne to mett together the 30 of Desember: 1692: who Acordingliey mett & In orderley prosedinge chose mʳ Benjamin Browne to be mediator the parsan⟨s⟩ then choson ear [= are] as falloeth

	This Don by me Joseph Neall and non of yᵉ
Chosen for Gran Jurors	parsans so choson in my ward I have
Joshua Ray ⎱	referred It to yᵉ Nex Constable by me
Job. Swinnerton ⎬ 3	Joseph Neale Const
Gilbert Tapley ⎰	in Salem

December 23, 1692

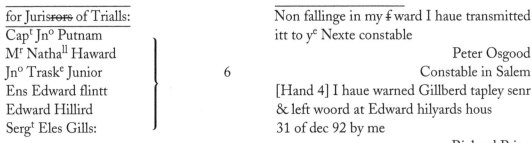

for Jurisrors of Trialls:
Capt Jno Putnam
Mr Natha^{ll} Haward
Jno Trask^e Junior   6
Ens Edward flintt
Edward Hillird
Serg^t Eles Gills:

Non fallinge in my f ward I haue transmitted
itt to y^e Nexte constable

                         Peter Osgood
                       Constable in Salem

[Hand 4] I haue warned Gillberd tapley senr
& left woord at Edward hilyards hous
31 of dec 92 by me

                         Richard Princ
                         constable

[Reverse] [Hand 5] This 31th of December 1692 Then warned m^r Edward fflint of Salem To Attend ye Court to be held att Salem on ye 3^d of January Incewing next vpon ye Jewry of Trials at nine of ye Clock   pr me Thomas Rucke Constable.
[Hand 6] ye 31 of december 1692 then I warned Eleaser Giles to se⟨?⟩rue {atend} on the Jury of tryales at y^e Cort to be heald at Salem on y^e 3 of January next insewing at nine of y^e Cloke by me

                         Samuel Stone Constobel
                         in Salem

[Hand 7] According to the tener of this warant I haue warned as Jueriours
Capt John Putnam   m$^\varepsilon$ Natheniell Howard
m$^\varepsilon$ Joshua Rea: John Trask Jun$^\varepsilon$
Capt putnam is Lame and he saith not able to   ꝑ me Jonathan Putnam
sarue   Constable in Salem
[Hand 8] Accorden to the tener of this warent I haue warned Job Sweneton to apere by nine a Clock in the morning on the 3 Day of Jenerey −1693−

                         by me. Jo^n Putnam Constable of Salam

[Hand 9] Returnes of the warr^{ts} for Choosing Jurymen

Notes: Hand 2 = Jonathan Elatson

Massachusetts Archives Collection, vol. 135, nos. 81 & 82. Massachusetts State Archives. Boston, MA.

739. Warrant for Jurors from Topsfield for the Grand Jury and Jury of Trials at a Court of Assize, and Town's Return

See also: Dec. 30, 1692.

[Hand 1] These are in their Maj^{ties} Names to require you forthwith to Assemble the free holders and other Inhabitants of your Towne who are hereby also required to Choose three good & lawfull men of the Same towne each whereof to haue a real Esstate of fourty Shillings ꝑ Annum or a personall Estat⟨e⟩ of fifty pounds to Serue as Jurors one upon the grand Jury & two upon the Jury of tryalls at a Court of Assises and Gen^{ll} Goal deliuery to be held at Salem for the County of Essex on Tusday ne The Third day of January next ensueing the date hereof which persons so Chosen you ar⟨e⟩ to summons to attend y^e Said Court by nine of the Clock in the morning of the Said day & make returne hereof with the names of the Said persons the day before the Said Court And hereof not to faile Dated in Boston the twenty third day of December 1692

To the Constable or Constable [= constables] of Topsfeild or either of them   ℗ Cur̄   Dec. 23, 1692
Jonᵃ Elatson Cler.

[Reverse] [Hand 2] At a lawfull Towne meeting by order of athoryty on yᵉ 30ᵗʰ of december. 1692: Enˢ Jacob Toune is Chosen to serue on the Grand Jury ^{at Salem} and John Prechet and Corpˡˡ John Curtio⟨u⟩[Lost?] [= Curtis?] are Chosen to serue on the Jury of Tryalls at yᵉ Court of assise[Lost?] [= assizes] to be houlden at Salem yᵉ 3ᵈ day of January 1692 or 93 This is a true Coppy taken out of yᵉ Towne book
℗ me Ephraim Dorman Recorder for Topsfield
[Hand 3] Thes men aboue m̶ menchened Ere chosen acording to the tener of this warant
as atested by me Ephraim Willdes
constabill of topsfelld

[Hand 4] Topsfield.

Notes: Hand 4 = Jonathan Elatson

Massachusetts Archives Collection, vol. 135, nos. 86 & 87. Massachusetts State Archives. Boston, MA.

740. Warrant for Jurors from Wenham for the Grand Jury and Jury of Trials at a Court of Assize, and Town's Return

See also: Dec. 30, 1692.

[Hand 1] These are in Theire Majᵗⁱᵉˢ names to require you forthwith to Asemble the ffree holders and other Inhabitants of your towne who are hereby also required to Choose foure good and lawfull men of y⟨ᵉ⟩ Same Towne each whereof to haue a reall Estate of ffourty Shilli[Lost] [= shillings] ℗ Annum or a personall Estate of fifty pounds to Serue as J[Lost] [= jurors] two upon the Grand Jury & two upon the Jury of Tryalls at a Court of assises and Generall Goal Delivery to be held at Salem for the County of Essex on Tusday the third day of January next Ens⟨u⟩eing the date heareof which persons So Chosen you are to Summons to attend the Said Court by nine of the Clock in the Morning of the [Lost]⟨d⟩ [= said] day and make returne hereof with the names of the Said pers⟨o⟩[Lost] [= persons] the day before the said Court And hereof not to faile Dated in Boston the Twenty Third day of December 1692 To the Constables or Constables of Wenham or either of them   ℗ Cur̄
Jonᵃ Elatson Cler.

[Hand 2] At a metting of the inhabitants of Wenham this: 30ᵗʰ of decembar: 1692: Richard hutten and Samuell Kimball ware chosen to sarve upon grand jurye and James freind and John abbye on the jurye of tryalls
as wittness my hand
William faierfeild
Constable of Wenham

[Reverse] [Hand 3] Wenham

Notes: Hand 3 = Jonathan Elatson

Massachusetts Archives Collection, vol. 135, no. 96. Massachusetts State Archives. Boston, MA.

Thursday, December 29, 1692

Town's Return: Warrant for Jurors from Lynn for the Grand Jury and Jury of Trials at a Court of Assize
2nd of 2 dates. See No. 735 on Dec. 23, 1692

Friday, December 30, 1692

Town's Return: Warrant for Jurors from Andover for the Grand Jury and Jury of Trials at a Court of Assize
2nd of 2 dates. See No. 730 on Dec. 23, 1692

Town's Return: Warrant for Jurors from Marblehead for the Grand Jury and Jury of Trials at a Court of Assize
2nd of 2 dates. See No. 736 on Dec. 23, 1692

Town's Return: Warrant for Jurors from Salem for the Grand Jury and Jury of Trials at a Court of Assize†
2nd of 3 dates. See No. 738 on Dec. 23, 1692

Town's Return: Warrant for Jurors from Topsfield for the Grand Jury and Jury of Trials at a Court of Assize
2nd of 2 dates. See No. 739 on Dec. 23, 1692

Town's Return: Warrant for Jurors from Wenham for the Grand Jury and Jury of Trials at a Court of Assize
2nd of 2 dates. See No. 740 on Dec. 23, 1692

741. Entry in Town Book of Newbury

[Hand 1] Newbury Decemb^ε 30: <u>1692</u>
At a Meeting of the ffreehold^εs & Inhabitan^{⟨t⟩s} of the Towne of Newbury, Convened by the Counstable, by vertue of a Warrant Dated Decemb^ε 23^d <u>1692</u>
    Then chosen to Serve as jurors at a Court of assises & Gen^ll Goale Delivery to be held at Salem for the County of Essex on the third of January next
    For the Grand Jury.
Thomas Hale Richard Bartlet sen^ε & Richard Browne
    For the Jury of Trialls
Serj^nt John Kent. Serj Joseph Little.
Serj. John Hale John Emery Ju^ε Benajah Titcomb & John Ordway
             Taken out of ye Towne Booke of Newbury ⅌ Henry Short cle^ε

Massachusetts Archives Collection, vol. 135, no. 97. Massachusetts State Archives. Boston, MA.

Saturday, December 31, 1692

Death of Ann Foster in Prison, between the End of December 1692 and Early January 1693

742. Town's Return for Jurors from Rowley for the Grand Jury and Jury of Trials at a Court of Assize

[Hand 1] sir In pursuance of a Warrant to mee derected from y^e [Lost]t [= court] Requireing mee to Call togather and Assemble the f⟨re⟩e h[Lost]⟨de⟩rs [= holders] of our town and other the inhabitants thereof to Choose Juriors to attend the Court of Assices and Gen^ll Goall deliuery to bee held att Salem the third day of January next Ensueing the date Hereof, and accordingly wee haue made Choyse of these men following viz̄:

Capt: Joseph Boynton
James Dickison   } for the Grand Jury

Jno pickard
Jno platts   } for the Jury of tryalls

Dated in Rowley ye 31th of decemb^ε 1692

℘ mee Robt Greenough Constable
for the Town of Rowley

[Reverse] To m^ε Jon^a Elatson Clark of the Court of Assices to bee held att Salem These With Care I pray

[Hand 2] Rowley
Summonses of Jury men to a Court at Salem the 3^d Janu^a 1692/3

Notes: The warrant has not been located. ◊ Hand 2 = Jonathan Elatson

Massachusetts Archives Collection, vol. 135, no. 95. Massachusetts State Archives. Boston, MA.

Town's Return: Warrant for Jurors from Gloucester for the Grand Jury and Jury of Trials at a Court of Assize
2nd of 2 dates. See No. 732 on Dec. 23, 1692

Town's Return: Warrant for Jurors from Haverhill for the Grand Jury and Jury of Trials at a Court of Assize
2nd of 2 dates. See No. 733 on Dec. 23, 1692

Town's Return: Warrant for Jurors from Ipswich for the Grand Jury and Jury of Trials at a Court of Assize
2nd of 2 dates. See No. 734 on Dec. 23, 1692

Dec. 31, 1692   *Town's Return: Warrant for Jurors from Newbury for the Grand Jury and Jury of Trials at a Court of Assize*
2nd of 2 dates. See No. 737 on Dec. 23, 1692

Notices of Warning: Warrant for Jurors from Salem for the Grand Jury and Jury of Trials at a Court of Assize
3rd of 3 dates. See No. 738 on Dec. 23, 1692

743. Mittimus for Lydia Dustin, Sarah Dustin, Mary Colson, Elizabeth Colson, & Sarah Cole (of Lynn), and Officer's Return

See also: Jan. 3, 1693.

[Hand 1] Province of the Massachusets Bay in New: England

Mid[x] ss[t] William and Mary by the Grace of God King and Queen of England Scottland ffrance and Ireland Defend[ᵉˢ] of y[e] ffaith &c to the Sheiriffe of the County of Midlesex Greeting Wee Command you that you haue the Body of Lidia Dastin of Reading widow Sarah Dastin single-woman Mary Coulson widow Elizabeth Colson single wo̅: All of Reading and Sarah Cole [ ] of Lyn in the prison of Cambridge vnder yo[ε] Custody as tis said Detained, and vnder safe and sure Conduct together wth the cause of their Caption vnder what name or names soever the said Lidia Dastin Sarah Dastin Mary Coulson Elizabeth Coulson and Sarah Cole be Censured in the same before o[ε] Justices of o[ε] Court of Assize and Goal Delivery at Salem in o[ε] County of Essex in o[ε] Province of the Massachusets Bay in New-England vpon Tusday the 3[d] Day of Jan⟨u⟩[a] next in y[e] fourth year of o[ε] Reigne To Do and receiue all and Every of those things w[ch] the Justices of o[ε] Court shall Consider of in that behalfe And then and there you haue this Writt Wittness W[m]illiam Stoughton Esq[ε] in Boston the 31st Decemb̅. In y[e] fourth year of o[ε] Reigne Annoqȝ Do̅m̅. 1692

Jon[a] Elatson Cle̅r:

[Reverse] [Hand 2] By Vertue of this Writt I haue hear Brought y[e] Bodyes of those persons within spesefyd and Deliuerd hear att Salem to the under Sheriffe

ꝓ me Tim[o] Phillips Sheriffe for Midd[x]

[Hand 1] The Returne of y[e] Habes Corpus From y[e] ~~Sher~~ Sheiriffe of Midlesex

Notes: Lydia Dustin was the mother of Sarah Dustin and Mary Colson, and Mary was the mother of Elizabeth Colson. Mary Colson's case came before the grand jury in Salem on January 5, 1693, but no record of a trial is extant. See No. 544. Sarah Cole (of Lynn), Lydia Dustin, and Sarah Dustin were tried February 1, 1693, in Charlestown, in Middlesex County, and found not guilty. See No. 832, No. 833, & No. 834. Lydia and Sarah Dustin, as well as Elizabeth Colson, were jailed again in Cambridge on February 11, 1693, but whether they had been briefly free or simply moved to another prison is unclear. Regardless, they remained in prison after February 11 for not paying jail fees. Elizabeth Colson was released on March 2, Lydia Dustin died in prison on March 10, and Sarah Dustin and Sarah Cole (of Lynn) were released on March 23. See No. 856. ◊ Hand 1 = Jonathan Elatson ◊ 1 wax seal.

Suffolk Court Files, vol. 32, docket 2700, p. 23, Massachusetts Supreme Judicial Court, Judicial Archives, Massachusetts State Archives. Boston, MA.

Dec. 31, 1692

744. Recognizance for John Alden by Nathaniel Williams & Samuel Checkley

See also: April 25, 1693.

[Hand 1] Suffolke sc./.

Memorandum, That on the Thirty ffirst day of Decemb$^{\varepsilon}$ 1692. In the Fourth year of the Reign of our Sovereign Lord & Lady William and Mary by the grace of God of England Scotland ffrance and Ireland King and Queen &⟨c⟩^{a} ꝑsonally came and appeared Before me John Richards Esq$^{\varepsilon}$ One of their Maties Justic⟨e⟩s of the Superiour Court of Judicature within the Province of the Massachusetts Bay in New=England, John Alden ~~of~~ Marrin$^{\varepsilon}$ Nathanael Williams & Samuel Chechley, Shopkeepers all of Boston within the said County of Suffolke.

and acknowledged themselves and each of them to be indebted unto our said Lord and Lady the King and Queen, and the Survivour of them, their heires and Successors in the Sum of Two hundred pounds To be levied on their or either of their Goods, Chattels, Lands or Tenements for the use of our said Lord & Lady the King and Queen or the Survivour of them, if default be made in the performance of the Condition underwritten.

The Condition of the above Recogniscance is such ["u" written over "i"] That whereas the abovebounden John Alden, being accused and Suspected of perpetrating divers Acts of Witchcrafts contrary to the forme of the Statute in that case made and provided, was taken up and committed for the same unto their Maties Goal in Boston, from whence he made his Escape If Therefore the said John Alden shall personally appear before their Maties Justices, at the next Superiour Court of Judicature And Court of Assize to be held at Boston within the said County of Suffolke, to answer what shall be objected against him on their Maj^{ties} behalfe referring unto the p$^{\varepsilon}$misses, And shall do and receive that which by the said Court shall then & there be Enjoyned him, Then this abovewritten Recogniscance to be void and of none Effect; Or else to abide and remain in full force and virtue./.

Recognit die predict.
Cor. me. John Richards;//

Notes: John Alden was cleared by proclamation April 25, 1693. See also No. 837. He had earlier escaped the colony.

MS Ch F, vol. 10, p. 47, Rare Books & Manuscripts, Boston Public Library. Boston, MA.

1693

Monday, January 2, 1693

Town's Return: Warrant for Jurors from Beverly for the Grand Jury and Jury of Trials at a Court of Assize
2nd of 2 dates. See No. 731 on Dec. 23, 1692

745. Statement of Francis Dane Sr., Regarding Some of the Andover Acccused

[Hand 1] Rnd S^r

Wheras there haue been divers reports raysed, how, and, by what hands I know not, of the Towne of Andover, and the Inhabitants, I thought it my bounden duty to giue an account to others, so farr as I {ha} had the vnderstanding of any thing amongst us. Therfore doe declare, that I beleeue the reports haue been Scandalous, and unjust, neither will bear. ye light, As for that, of the Siue, and Cisers I never heard of it, till this last Summer, and the Sabboth after I spake publiqly concerning ^{it} Since which I beleeue it hath not been tryed, As for such things of Charmes, and way's to find their cattle, I never heard, nor doe I know any Neighbour that ever did So, neither haue I any grounds to beleeue it. I haue lived aboue Fortie fower yeares in the Towne, and haue been frequent among ye Inhabitants, and in my healthfull yeares oft at their habitations, and Should certainely heard if so it had been. That there was a Suspicion(s) of Goodwife Carrier among Some of us before she was apprehended, I know. [3 words overstruck]. As for any other persons, I had no Suspicion of them, and had Charity been put on, the Divel would not haue had Such an advantage against us, and I beleeue many Innocent persons haue been accused, & Imprisoned, ye Conceit of Spectre Evidence as an infallible mark did too far prevaile with us Hence we So easily parted with our neighbours, of honest, & good report, & members in full Comunion, hence we So easily parted with our Children, when we knew nothing in their liues, nor {any of} our neighbours ^{to Suspect them} and thus things were hurried on; hence Such strange breaches in families, Severall that came before me, that Spake with much Sobrietie, professing their innocency, though through the Devils Subtilty they were too much urged to Confesse, and we thought we did doe well in so doeing, yet they stood their ground professing they knew nothing, never Saw ye deuil, never made a covenant with him, & ye like; & Some Children, that we haue cause to feare that dread has overcome them to accuse themselues in that they knew not. Stephen Johnson Mary Barker ye Daughter of Lieftenant Barker, and some others did(?) by what we had from them, with Suitable affections we haue cause to beleeue they were in the truth, and {So} held to it, if after many indeauours they had been dismissed not been overcome to Say w^t they never knew

[Reverse] This hath been a trouble to me, considering how oft it hath been Sayd, you are a witch, you are guilty, & who afflicts this maid or the like, & more then this hath been Sayd, charging persons with witchcraft, and what flatteries haue past from; & threats and telling

them they must goe to prison et. this I Say, I feare haue caused many to fall. our Sinne of   January 2, 1693
Ignorance wherin we thought we did well, will not excuse us when we know we did amisse
but what ever might be a Stambling block to others must be removed, else we shall procure
divine displeasure, & Euills will unavoidably breake in upon us.
Andover Jan 2.

      92   Yours S^r who am ^{though unworthie} a friend to them y^t are friends to Sion
              Francis Dane Se⟨n⟩[Lost] [= Senior]

Concerning my Daughter Elizabeth Johnson, I never had ground to Suspect her; neither
haue I heard any other to accuse her, till b[Lost] [= by] Spectre evidence she was brought
forth, but this I must Say, She was weake, and incapacious, fearfull, and in that respect I
feare she hath falsely accused her self ^{& others.} she Not log long before ^{that} she was
sent for ^{she} Spake as to her owne particular, that she was sure she was no witch, and for
her Daughter Elizabeth, she is but Simplish at ye best, and I feare the com̄on speech that was
frequently spread among us, of their liberty, if they would confesse, and the like expression,
used by some, haue brought many into a snare, the Lord direct & guide those that are in
place, and giue us all Submissiue wills, & let the Lord doe with me, & mine, what Seems
good in his owne eys.

[Hand 2] Memorial
Francis Dane

Notes: The exact circumstances of this statement have not been established, although it was clearly in anticipation of the
cases to be heard by the Superior Court of Judicature.

*Essex County Court Archives, vol. 1, no. 319, Massachusetts Supreme Judicial Court, Judicial Archives, on deposit James Duncan
Phillips Library, Peabody Essex Museum, Salem, MA.*

746. Testimony of John Higginson Sr. & Samuel Cheever for Sarah Buckley

[Hand 1] Being desired by goodman Buckly to give my test^{im}omy to his wiues
conversation before this great Calamity befell her, I cannot refuse to bear witnes to the truth,
viz that during ye time of her living in Salem for many years in Communion with this
Church having occasionally frequent converse & discourse with her, I haue neuer obs⟨e⟩ved
my selfe nor heard from any other any thing y^t was vnsuitable to a Conversation becoming
the Gospel; & ⟨h⟩aue allwayes looked vp⟨o⟩n her as a serious Godly woman.

                                    John Higginson.

[Hand 2] Marblerhead: Jan: 2: 1692/3:
Vpon the same request, having had the like opportunity by her residence many years att
Marble=head, I can do no less th⟨e⟩n give the alike testimony for her pious conversation;
during her abode in this place and com̄union w⟨i⟩th us

                                    Samuel Cheever

[Reverse] [Hand 3] Mr Higgison &^{⟨c⟩} their Certiffi[Lost]

January 3, 1693   Notes: This appears to have been written in preparation for the trial of Sarah Buckley, which took place on January 4. See No. 755. Both Higginson and Cheever were ministers. ◊ Possibly used at trial.

Massachusetts Archives Collection, vol. 135, no. 99. Massachusetts State Archives. Boston, MA.

Tuesday, January 3, 1693

747. Superior Court of Judicature Record Book: Court of Assize and General Jail Delivery Held at Salem, Essex County

[Hand 1] {Suffolk. ss.} Att Their Maj^ties Superiour Court of Judicature Court of Assizes & Generall Goal Delivery Holden at Sallem In The County of Essex in Their Maj^ties Province of the Massacsets Bay in New England in Amirica. Unde⟨r⟩ the Goverment of his Excellancy Sr William Phips Kn^t &c the 3^d January Anno RR^s et Reginæ Gulielmi et Mariæ nunc Angliæ &c Qu[Lost] [= Quarto] Annoqȝ Domini 1692

Grand Jury Sworn	Present
Robert Paine fforeman	The Honble Willam Stoughton Esq^ε Cheif Justice
Job Swinerton	Thomas Danforth Esq^ε ⎫ John Richards Esq^ε
Gilbert Tapley	Wait Winthrop Esq^ε ⎭ Samuel Sewell Esq^ε
William Wood	
Richard Read	The Court being opened the Grand Jury was sworn
Richard Hutton	
John Lovit Senr	Severall Bills of Indictment against divers persons ⟨for⟩
Robert Cue	ffelony by witchcraf were committed to the Grand Jury a⟨nd⟩
Joseph Marble Sen^ε	then the Court Adjourned to nine of the Clock next morn[Lost]
James Persons	[= morning]
Benja Rednap	
Robert Potter Sen^ε	
Richard Browne	
Thomas Borman	
Joseph Bointon	
James Dickeson	
Richard Smith.	

Notes: The cases in 1693 addressed by the Superior Court of Judicature are here transcribed from the original record book, which was discovered in a filing cabinet in the Suffolk County Court House in 1996. Previous transcriptions have used a nineteenth-century copy.

Records of the Superior Court of Judicature (1692/3), p. 1, Massachusetts Supreme Judicial Court, Judicial Archives, Massachusetts State Archives. Boston, MA.

Officer's Return: Mittimus for Lydia Dustin, Sarah Dustin, Mary Colson, Elizabeth Colson, January 3, 1693
& Sarah Cole (of Lynn)
2nd of 2 dates. See No. 743 on Dec. 31, 1692

748. Indictment of Sarah Bassett, for Afflicting Mary Walcott (Returned Ignoramus)

[Hand 1] Prouince of the Massachusetts Bay in New England Essex } Año R̄R̄s & Reginæ Gulielmi & Mariæ Angliæ &c Quarto Anoqʒ Dom̄ 1692

ss

The Juro$^\epsilon$s for o^r Sou$^\epsilon$ lord & lady the King & Queen p$^\epsilon$sent That Sarah Bassett wife of William Basett of lyn in the County of Essex aforesaid vpon or about the 23^d day of May last Anno: 1692 aforsaid And D⟨i⟩uers other days & Times as well before ~~and~~ as after Certaine detestab⟨le⟩ Arts Called Witchcraft & Sorceries wickedly mallitiously & ffelloniously hath vsed practised & Exercised at & in the Towne of Salem in the County of Essex aforesaid vpon & Against One Mary ["M" written over "⟨El⟩"] Walcott of Salem Single Woman By which Wicked Arts The Said Mary Walcott is Tortured aflicted Tormented Consumed wasted & pined the day & yeare aforesaid & diuers other days & times as well before as after Contrary to the peace of o$^\epsilon$ Sou$^\epsilon$ lord & lady the King & Queen their Crowne & dignity & the Laws in that Case made & prouided
Wittness
An Putnam
Marcy lewis

[Reverse] Sarah Bassett
[Hand 2] Ignoramus
Robert: Payne foreman
[Hand 3] Salem Court 3^d Janu^a 1692/3

Notes: Hand 1 = Anthony Checkley

Suffolk Court Files, vol. 32, docket 2701, p. 24, Massachusetts Supreme Judicial Court, Judicial Archives, Massachusetts State Archives. Boston, MA.

749. Declaration of Mary Osgood, Mary Tyler, Deliverance Dane, Abigail Barker, Sarah Wilson Sr., & Hannah Tyler‡

We whose names are under-written, inhabitants of Andover; whenas that horrible and tremendous judgment beginning at Salem village in the year 1692, by some called witchcraft, first breaking forth at Mr. Parris's house, several young persons, being seemingly afflicted, did accuse several persons for afflicting them, and many there believing it so to be, we being informed that, if a person was sick, the afflicted person could tell what or who was the cause of that sickness: Joseph Ballard, of Andover, his wife being sick at the same time, he, either

January 3, 1693

from himself or by the advice of others, fetched two of the persons, called the afflicted persons, from Salem village to Andover, which was the beginning of that dreadful calamity that befel us in Andover, believing the said accusations to be true, sent for the said persons to come together to the meeting house in Andover, the afflicted persons being there. After Mr. Barnard had been at prayer, we were blindfolded, and our hands were laid upon the afflicted persons, they being in their fits and falling into their fits at our coming into their presence, as they said; and some led us and laid our hands upon them, and then they said they were well, and that we were guilty of afflicting them: Whereupon, we were all seized, as prisoners, by a warrant from the Justice of the peace and forthwith carried to Salem. And, by reason of that sudden surprizal, we knowing ourselves altogether innocent of that crime, we were all exceedingly astonished and amazed, and consternated and affrighted even out of our reason; and our nearest and dearest relations, seeing us in that dreadful condition, and knowing our great danger, apprehended there was no other way to save our lives, as the case was then circumstanced, but by our confessing ourselves to be such and such persons as the afflicted represented us to be, they, out of tenderness and pity, persuaded us to confess what we did confess. And indeed that confession, that it is said we made, was no other than what was suggested to us by some gentlemen, they telling us that we were witches, and they knew it, and we knew it, which made us think that it was so; and our understandings, our reason, our faculties, almost gone, we were not capable of judging of our condition; as also the hard measures they used with us rendered us incapable of making our defence, but said any thing and every thing which they desired, and most of what we said, was but, in effect, a consenting to what they said. Some time after, when we were better composed, they telling us what we had confessed, we did profess that we were innocent and ignorant of such things; and we hearing that Samuel Wardwell had renounced his confession, and quickly after condemned and executed, some of us were told we were going after Wardwell.

| Mary Osgood, | Deliverance Dane, | Sarah Wilson, |
| Mary Tiler, | Abigail Barker, | Hannah Tiler. |

Notes: This seems likely to have been presented in early January 1693, when these women were facing trial. On the following document, No. 750, four of these six women are supported in a petition by a large group of people. It seems likely that the two documents are related in time as well as purpose. ◊ "surprizal": 'surprise' (*OED* s.v. *surprisal*).

Thomas Hutchinson, The History of the Province of Massachusetts-Bay, from the Charter of King William and Queen Mary, in 1691, Until the Year 1750, vol. 2, ed. Lawrence Shaw Mayo (Cambridge, MA: Harvard University Press, 1936), pp. 31–32.

750. Petition for Mary Osgood, Eunice Frye, Deliverance Dane, Sarah Wilson Sr., & Abigail Barker‡

To the honoured court of Assize held at Salem,
    The humble address of several of the inhabitants of Andover.

May it please this honoured court,

We being very sensible of the great sufferings our neighbours have been long under in prison, and charitably judging that many of them are clear of that great transgression which hath been laid to their charge, have thought it our duty to endeavour their vindication so far as our testimony for them will avail. The persons in whose behalf we are desired and concerned to speak something at present are Mrs. Mary Osgood, Eunice Frye, Deliverance Dane, Sarah Wilton and Abigail Barker, who are women of whom we can truly give this character and commendation, that they have not only lived among us so inoffensively as not to give the least occasion to any that know them to suspect them of witchcraft, but by their sober godly and exemplary conversation have obtained a good report in the place, where they have been well esteemed and approved in the church of which they are members.

We were surprized to hear that persons of known integrity and piety were accused of so horrid a crime, not considering, then, that the most innocent were liable to be so misrepresented and abused. When these women were accused by some afflicted persons of the neighbourhood, their relations and others, tho' they had so good grounds of charity that they should not have thought any evil of them, yet, through a misrepresentation of the truth of that evidence that was so much credited and improved against people, took great pains to persuade them to own what they were, by the afflicted, charged with, and, indeed, did unreasonably urge them to confess themselves guilty, as some of us who were then present can testify. But these good women did very much assert their innocency, yet some of them said they were not without fear least Satan had some way ensnared them, because there was that evidence against them which then was by many thought to be a certain indication and discovery of witchcraft, yet they seriously professed they knew nothing by themselves of that nature: Nevertheless, by the unwearied sollicitations of those that privately discoursed them both at home and at Salem, they were at length persuaded publickly to own what they were charged with, and so submit to that guilt which we still hope and believe they are clear of. And, it is probable, the fear of what the event might be, and the encouragement that it is said was suggested to them, that confessing was the only way to obtain favour, might be too powerful a temptation for timorous women to withstand, in the hurry and distraction that we have heard they were then in. Had what they said against themselves proceeded from conviction of the fact, we should have had nothing to have said for them, but we are induced to think that it did not, because they did soon privately retract what they had said, as we are informed, and, while they were in prison, they declared to such as they had confidence to speak freely and plainly to, that they were not guilty of what they had owned, and that what they had said against themselves was the greatest grief and burden they laboured under: Now, though we cannot but judge it a thing very sinful for innocent persons to own a crime they are not guilty of, yet, considering the well ordered conversation of those women while they lived among us, and what they now seriously and constantly affirm in a more composed frame, we cannot but in charity judge them innocent of the great transgression that hath been imputed to them. As for the rest of our neighbours, who are under the like circumstances with these that have been named, we can truly say of them that while they lived among us, we have had no cause to judge them such persons as, of late, they have been represented and reported to be, nor do we know that any of their neighbours had any just grounds to suspect them of that evil that they are now charged with.

January 3, 1693

Dudley Bradstreet
Francis Dane, sen.
Thomas Barnard
Tho. Chandler, sen.
John Barker
Henry Ingolls, sen.
Wm. Chandler, sen.
Samuel Martin
Stephen Parker
Samuel Ingolls
Ephraim Stevens
Daniel Poore
John Ingolls
Henry Ingolls, jun.
John Frie, sen.
James Frie
John Aslebee
Samuel Holt

John Abbot, sen.
Samuel Blanchard
Wm. Ballard
Thomas Hooper
John Hooper
Wm. Abbot
James Russell
Oliver Holt
John Presson
Francis Dane, jun.
George Abbot
Wm. Chandler, jun.
John Chandler
Joseph Robinson
Thomas Johnson
Tho. Johnson, jun.
Andrew Peters
Mary Peters,

Elizabeth Rite
Wm. Peters
Sam. Peters
Walter Wright
Hooker Osgood
Benj. Stevens
Ann Bradstreet
Joanna Dane
Eliza. Stevens
Eliza. Barnard
Phebe Robinson
Hannah Chandler
Hannah Dane
Bridget Chandler
Mary Johnson
Robert Russel
Mary Russel.

Notes: As the petition indicates, the women were free and preparing to face the Superior Court of Judicature. Recognizances for Eunice Frye and Mary Osgood are extant for December 20, 1692. See No. 725 & No. 726. From this record, it appears that all were similarly free, although the other recognizances are not extant. The earliest known trial date from this group is for Abigail Barker on January 6. See No. 770. Since the petition is to a sitting court, the document is dated to the first day of that court sitting in Salem, January 3, 1693, and could not be dated after January 6. Records on Deliverance Dane are sparse. She spent thirteen weeks in prison (see No. 900) and was probably released on a recognizance that is not extant. She apparently never went to trial.

Thomas Hutchinson, The History of the Province of Massachusetts-Bay, from the Charter of King William and Queen Mary, in 1691, Until the Year 1750, vol. 2, ed. Lawrence Shaw Mayo (Cambridge, MA: Harvard University Press, 1936), pp. 32–33.

751. Account for Payment Submitted by Timothy Phillips, Sheriff and Order for His Payment

See also: Dec. 18, 1697.

[Hand 1] Midd^x Ss 1692/3 Jan^e y^e 3^d
An Acount of Charges Expended upon Prizoners Accused for Witchcraft and tryed att Charlstowne

	l̄ s d
To Carying Elizebeth Coleson to Salem by warant from Charlstowne ^{& Expenses} & assistance:	01:11:00
To Remoueing 6 prizoners from Camebridge to Salem by habeasorpas [= habeas corpus] 5 Men & 5 horses Vitcwall [= victual] & drink upon y^e Road 22^s	09:08:00
To Expences for prizoners when Brought by habeascorpas from Salem to Charlstown for Tryall, for Vict⟨e⟩walls & Drink & a keeper for them at Charlstowne	2:04:00

To Mony for Wood when in Charlstowne Prizon	00:09:00	January 4, 1693
To 8 persons Tryals for my ffees as alowed att Salem 15ˢ pʳ peice	06:00:00	
To Transporteing of Them after Tryall to Camebridg with Cart		
& 4 men to guard	01:00:00	
To 7 dayes my self spent with a guard to seize and pursue with huencry		
[= hue and cry] after them:	4:00:00	
To the County Prizon keeper for Diott [= diet] as appears in peticulers	15:07:08	
To Mʳ Henery Summers Mony Due for yᵉ Prizoners	00:19:08	
To yᵉ keeper 6 Bushells of Corn att 2ˢ pʳ bushell	00:12:00	
To yᵉ Cryers fees 16ˢ 6ᵈ To yᵉ Cunstabels Ringing yᵉ bell 6ˢ	01:02:06	
	42:13:10	

℘ me Timᵒ Phillips sherriffe

[Hand 2] ~~March 22ᵈ 1696 Read~~
~~26ᵗʰ Read a Second time.~~
~~Decembʳ 17ᵗʰ 1697.~~
~~Voted; That the Consideration hereof be referred to the Court Quarter Sessions in the~~
~~County of Middlesex, That if any thing be their due, it be discharged as the Law provides~~
~~Sent up for Concurrance~~
                               Penn Townsend speaker.

[Reverse] Decembʳ 17ᵗʰ 1697. In the House of Representatives
Ordered, That in Answer to the within Petition and Account Ten pounds be allowed and
paid out of the Publick Treasury towards sᵈ Account; and ~~that~~ the Quarter Sessions of the
^{Peace in sᵈ} County of Middlesex ~~be~~ {are} Ordered and impowered to raise on sᵈ County
the Remainder of sᵈ Account, and pay the Ballance thereof upon the petitioner their adjustmᵗ
Sent up for Concurrance   Penn Townsend speakʳ
[Hand 3] Decʳ 18ᵗʰ 1697.
In Council. Read & votᵈ a Concurrance
Isᵃ Addington Secry./.

Notes: A copy of this document is in the Middlesex County Court Archives.

Massachusetts Archives Collection, vol. 135, nos. 111 & 112. Massachusetts State Archives. Boston, MA.

Wednesday, January 4, 1693

Trials of Sarah Buckley, Margaret Jacobs, Rebecca Jacobs, & Mary Whittredge

Grand Juries of Sarah Bassett & Sarah Bridges

Billa Vera: Indictment of Rebecca Jacobs, for Afflicting Elizabeth Hubbard†
2ⁿᵈ of 2 dates. See No. 609 on Sept. 10, 1692

752. Court Record of the Trial of Rebecca Jacobs†

[Hand 1] Rebekah Jacobs wife of George Jacobs of Salem Vill⟨age⟩ in the County of Essex husbandman was Arraigned being Indicted by the Jurors for our Soveraigne Lord & Lady the [Lost] [*SWP* = King] & Queen vpon their Oathes For that the said Rebekah Jacobs vpon the Eighteenth day of May 1692 and divers other da[Lost] [*SWP* = days] and times as well before as after Certain detestable arts cal[Lost] [*SWP* = called] Witchcraft and Sorceries Wickedly Mallitiously and ffelone[Lost] [*SWP* = ffeloneously] hath used practised and Exercised at and in Salem Village aforesaid in vpon and against one Elizabeth Hobert of [Lost] [*SWP* = Salem] Single woman, by which said wicked Acts the said Elizab[Lost] [*SWP* = Elizabeth] Hobard the day & year aforesaid & divers other dayes and ti[Lost] [*SWP* = times] as well before as after was and is Tortured Afflicted Consumed pined wasted & Tormented against the peace of our Sovera[Lost] [*SWP* = Soveraigne] Lord & Lady their Crowne & dignity & the forme in the stattute in that Case made & provided.

	Vpon which Indictment the said Rebekah Jacobs [Lost] [*SWP*
<u>Jury of Tryalls</u>	= was] arraigned and to the Indictment pleaded not Guilty and
Sworn	[Lost] [*SWP* = put] her selfe upon Tryall by God & the Country
⟨Edw⟩ard fflint fforem.	The ffirst Jury of Tryalls being Called where of mᵉ Edward fflint is
Nathaniel Howard	fforeman and the prisoner making no challenge against any of
⟨Elie⟩zer Giles	them they were Sworn for her Tryall and past vpon her The Jury
⟨Joh⟩n Hall	Bring in their Verdict, that is to [Lost] [*SWP* = say] That they do
⟨John⟩ Kent	not find Rebekah Jacobs Guilty [Lost] [*SWP* = of] the ffelony by
⟨Jose⟩ph Litle	Witchcraft she hath been Indic[Lost] [*SWP* = Indicted].
⟨Bena⟩yah Tidcomb	The Court Ordered that the said Rebek[Lost] [*SWP* =
⟨Sa⟩muel Morgan	Rebekah Jacobs] be discharged upon her paying ffees
⟨Ed⟩mund Gale	
⟨Willi⟩am Stephens	
⟨John⟩ Lamson	
⟨Seth⟩ Story	

Records of the Superior Court of Judicature (1692/3), p. 1, Massachusetts Supreme Judicial Court, Judicial Archives, Massachusetts State Archives. Boston, MA.

Billa Vera: Indictment of Margaret Jacobs, for Afflicting Elizabeth Hubbard†

2ⁿᵈ of 2 dates. See No. 619 on Sept. 14, 1692

753. Plea of Margaret Jacobs†

The humble declaration of Margaret Jacobs unto the honoured court now sitting at Salem, sheweth,

That whereas your poor and humble declarant being closely confined here in Salem goal for the crime of witchcraft, which crime thanks be to the Lord I am altogether ignorant of, as will appear at the great day of judgment: May it please the honoured court, I was cried out upon by some of the possessed persons, as afflicting them; whereupon I was brought to my examination, which persons at the sight of me fell down, which did very much startle and affright me. The Lord above knows I knew nothing, in the least measure, how or who afflicted them; they told me, without doubt I did, or else they would not fall down at me; they told me, if I would not confess, I should be put down into the dungeon and would be hanged, but if I would confess I should have my life; the which did so affright me, with my own vile wicked heart, to save my life; made me make the like confession I did, which confession, may it please the honoured court, is altogether false and untrue. The very first night after I had made confession, I was in such horror of conscience that I could not sleep for fear the devil should carry me away for telling such horrid lies. I was, may it please the honoured court, sworn to my confession, as I understand since, but then, at that time, was ignorant of it, not knowing what an oath did mean. The Lord, I hope, in whom I trust, out of the abundance of his mercy, will forgive me my false forswearing myself. What I said, was altogether false against my grandfather, and Mr. Burroughs, which I did to save my life and to have my liberty; but the Lord, charging it to my conscience, made me in so much horror, that I could not contain myself before I had denied my confession, which I did though I saw nothing but death before me, chusing rather death with a quiet conscience, than to live in such horror, which I could not suffer. Where, upon my denying my confession, I was committed to close prison, where I have enjoyed more felicity in spirit, a thousand times, than I did before in my enlargement.

And now, may it please your honours, your declarant, having, in part, given your honours a description of my condition, do leave it to your honours pious and judicious discretions, to take pity and compassion on my young and tender years, to act and do with me, as the Lord above and your honours shall see good, having no friend, but the Lord, to plead my cause for me; not being guilty in the least measure of the crime of witch-craft, nor any other sin that deserves death from man; and your poor and humble declarant shall for ever pray, as she is bound in duty, for your honours happiness in this life and eternal felicity in the world to come. So prays your honours declarant.

Margaret Jacobs.

Notes: This appears to be the plea of Margaret Jacobs at her trial. ◊ Likely used at trial.

Thomas Hutchinson, The History of the Province of Massachusetts-Bay, from the Charter of King William and Queen Mary, in 1691, Until the Year 1750, vol. 2, ed. Lawrence Shaw Mayo (Cambridge, MA: Harvard University Press, 1936), pp. 30–31.

754. Court Record of the Trial of Margaret Jacobs

[Hand 1] Margaret Jacobs of Salem in the County of Essex Single woman was Arraigned being Indicted by the Jurors for our Soveraigne Lord and Lady the King and Queen vpon their Oaths For that the said Margaret Jacobs upon the Eleventh day of May in the year of our Lord One thousand six hundred Ninety and two and divers other dayes and times as well before as after Certain detestable arts called Witchcrafts and sorceries Wickedly mallitiously and ffeloniously hath used practised and Excised [= exercised] at and in the Towne of Salem in the County of Essex afores^d in vpon and against one Mary Wallcott of Salem afores^d singlewoman by which said wicked Arts the said Mary Wallcott the day and year aforesaid and divers other dayes and times both before and after was and is Tortured afflicted Consumed Wasted Pined & Tormented and allso for sundry other Acts of witchcrft by the

January 4, 1693

said Margret Jacobs Comitted and don before and since that time against ye peace of our Soveraigne Lord and Lady the King and Queen their Crowne and dignity and the forme in the Stattute in that Case made and provided.

And vpon one other Indictment That the said Margaret Jacobs on the Eleventh day of May aforesaid in the year afores^d and divers other dayes and times as well before as after Certain detestable arts called Witchcraft and Sorcerys wicked mallitiousely hath used practised and Exercised at and in the Towne of Salem in the County of Essex Afores^d in vpon & against one Elizabeth Hobert of Salem Single woman, by wch said wicked Acts the said Elizabeth ~th~ Hobard the day and year aforesaid and divers other dayes and times both before & after was and is Tortured Afflicted Consumed Wasted Pined and Tormented and allso for sundry other Acts of witchcraft by the said Margaret Jacobs Comitted and don before and since that time against our Soveraigne Lord and Lady the King and Queen their Crowne and dignity and the forme in the Stattute in that Case mad and Provided.

⟨Jur⟩y Swoarn
⟨Ja⟩mes Freind foreman
⟨R⟩ichard Gross
⟨J⟩ohn Emery
⟨Jo⟩hn ⟨Or⟩dway
⟨Jo⟩hn Abby
⟨J⟩ohn Witt
⟨J⟩osiah Gage
⟨J⟩ames Sanders
⟨N⟩athan^ll Emerson Sen^ε
⟨Th⟩omas Edwards
⟨Jo⟩hn Pritchard
⟨Jo⟩hn Plats

Vpon wch Indictments shee was Arraigned and to both the said Indictments pleaded not Guilty and put her selfe vpon Tryall by God and the Country The first Jury was Called Edward fflint fforeman, and and noe objection being made were Sworn to pass vpon her Tryall And the Evidences in the Case were read and the Case was Committed to the Jury. The Jury Gaue in their verdict vizt They find that Margaret Jacobs the Prisoner at y^e Barr is not guilty of the ffelon⟨y⟩ by witchcraft whereof Shee hath been Indicted.

The Court Ordered that the said Margaret Ja[Lost] [= Jacobs] be discharged paying her ffees.

Records of the Superior Court of Judicature (1692/3), p. 2, Massachusetts Supreme Judicial Court, Judicial Archives, Massachusetts State Archives. Boston, MA.

Billa Vera: Indictment of Sarah Buckley, for Afflicting Ann Putnam Jr.†
2nd of 2 dates. See No. 618 on Sept. 14, 1692

Sworn at Trial: Deposition of Elizabeth Hubbard v. Sarah Buckley†
3rd of 3 dates. See No. 169 on May 18, 1692

Sworn at Trial: Deposition of Ann Putnam Jr. v. Sarah Buckley†
3rd of 3 dates. See No. 170 on May 18, 1692

Sworn at Trial: Testimony of Mary Walcott v. Sarah Buckley†
3rd of 3 dates. See No. 171 on May 18, 1692

755. Court Record of the Trial of Sarah Buckley

January 4, 1693

[Hand 1] Sarah Buckley the wife of William Buckley [Lost] [*SWP* = of] Salem in the County of Essex Shoomaker Was Indicte⟨d⟩ by the Jur⟨or⟩s for our Soveraigne Lord and Lady the King & Queen vpon their oaths That the said [Lost] [*SWP* = Sarah] Buckley upon the Eighteenth day of May in the [Lost] [*SWP* = year] of our Lord One thousand six hundred ninety and [Lost] [= two] and divers other dayes and times as well before as after Certain detestable arts Called Witchcraft and Sorceries wickedly mallitiously and ffeloneously hath used practised and Exercised At and in the Towne of Salem in the County of Essex afores^d in vpon an⟨d⟩ against one Mary Walcott of Salem in the County [Lost] [*SWP* = of] Essex ^{afores^d} Singlewoman By which said wicked Acts the said Mary Walcott the day and year aforesaid and diver⟨s⟩ other dayes and times both before and after was and is Tortured Afflicted Consumed Pined Wasted and Tormented And allso for sundry other acts of witchcraft by the said Sarah Buckley Committed and don before and since that time against our Soveraigne Lord & Lady the King and Queen their Crowne and Dignity And the forme in the Stattute in that Case made & provided.

And vpon on other Indictment ffor that the said Sarah Buckley the wife of William Buckley aforesaid of Salem in the County of Essex afores^d in and vpon the Eighteenth day of May in the year of our Lord One thousand six hundred Ninety & Two and divers other dayes other dayes and times as well before as after Certa⟨in⟩ detestable arts called Witchcraft or sorceries wickedly malitiously and feloneousely hath used practiced and Exersised at and in the Towne of Salem in the County of Essex Aforesaid in vpon and against one Ann Putman of Salem aforesaid Singlewoman, by wch said wicked Acts the said Ann Putnam the day and year afores^d and divers other dayes and times both before and after was and is Tortured Afflicted Consumed Pined Wasted and Tormented, And allso for Sundry other Acts of witchcraft by the said Sarah Buckley Committed and don both before and since tha⟨t⟩ time against our Soveraigne Lord and Lady the King and Queen their Crowne and Dignity and the forme in the Stattute In that Case ^{made &} provided.

Petty Jury
James ffreind fform^ε
Rickard Gross
John Emery
John Ordway
John Abby
John Witt
Josiah Gage
James Sanders
Nathan^l Emerson
Thomas Edwards
John Pritchard
John Plats

Vpon wch Indictments the said Sarah Bukley was araigned and to both of them pleaded not Guilty & put her selfe vpon Tryall by God and the Country. The second Jury was Called James ffreind fforeman and noe objection being made ⟨w⟩ere swo⟨rn⟩ to pass vpon her Tryall & the Eviden⟨ces⟩ [2 words illegible] Case were read and the Wittnesses appeared The Prison⟨er⟩ made her Defence. The Jury Returne their verdict

The Jury Say that the said Sarah Bukley is not Guilty of the ffelony by witchcraft of which stands Indicted in the two Recited Indictments.

The Court Ordered that the said Sarah Buckle⟨y⟩ be discharged paying her ffees.

Records of the Superior Court of Judicature (1692/3), pp. 2–3, Massachusetts Supreme Judicial Court, Judicial Archives, Massachusetts State Archives. Boston, MA.

Billa Vera: Indictment of Mary Whittredge, for Afflicting Elizabeth Hubbard†

2nd of 2 dates. See No. 652 on Sept. 15, 1692

January 4, 1693

756. Court Record of the Trial of Mary Whittredge

[Hand 1] Mary Witheridge was Sett to the Barr and was Indicted by the Jurors for our Soveraigne Lord & Lady for that the said Mary Witheridge of Salem Village alias Salem in the County of Essex the Eighteenth day of May in the year of our Lord One thousand six hundred Nin⟨e⟩ty two and divers other dayes and times as well as aft⟨er⟩ Certaine detestable arts Called Witchcraft and Sorcerie⟨s⟩ wickedly mallitiously and ffeloniously hath used practi⟨s⟩ed and Exercised at and in the towne of Salem in the County of Essex aforesaid in vpon and against on⟨e⟩ Elizabeth Hobart of Salem afores^d Singlewoma⟨n⟩ by wch said Wicked Acts the said Elizabeth Hobert th⟨e⟩ day and year aforesaid and divers other dayes and ti⟨mes⟩ both before and after was and is Tortured Afflicted Consumed Wasted Pined & Tormented and allso for sund⟨ry⟩ other Acts of Witchcraft by the said Mary Witheridge Committed and don before and since that time against ye peace of our Soveraigne Lord and Lady ⟨the⟩ King and Queen their Crowne and dignity and the f⟨orm⟩ {of y^e} Stattute in that Case made and provided.

And the Jurors for our Soveraigne Lord and Lady the King and Queen doe allso vpon their Oaths ind⟨i⟩cte the said Mary Witheridge In or vpon the Eightee⟨nth⟩ day of May in the year of our Lord One Thousan⟨d⟩ six hundred Ninety & two and divers other dayes and times as well before as after Certain detestable Arts Called Witchcraft and Sorceries Wickedly Mallitiousely and feloniously hath used practised and Exercised at and in the Towne of Salem in the County of Essex afores^d In vpon and against one Sarah Vibber wife of John Vibber of Salem aforesaid Husbandman by wch said wicked Acts the said Sarah Vibber the day and year aforesaid and divers other dayes and times both before and after was and is Tortured Afflicted Cosumed Pined Wasted and Tormented, And allso for Sundry other Acts of Witchcraft by the said Mary Witheridge Committed and don before and since that time against our Soveraigne Lord and Lady the King and Queen their Crowne and dignity And the forme in the Stattute in that Case made and provided.

Petty Jury
James ffreind ffo:
Richd Gross
⟨J⟩ohn Emery
John Ardway
John Abby
John Witt
⟨Jos⟩iah Gage
James Sanders
⟨N⟩athan^l Emerson
Thomas Edwards
John Prichard
John Plats

Vpon both wch Indictem⟨ents⟩ the sa[Lost]ary [= said Mary] Witheridge was Areigned, and to th⟨e⟩ said Indictments pleaded not Guilty and put herselfe vpon Tryall by God and the Country. The second Jury was Called James ffreind fforeman and no Exception being made were swoarn to pass vp[Lost] [= upon] her tryall. The Evidences in the Cace being read and Wittness appearing The Prisoner made her defence. The Jury Returne their verdict. The Jury Say That Mary Witheridge is not Guilty of the felony by Witchcraft of whitch She stands Indicted in the two recitted Indictments.

The Court Ordered the said Mary Witheridge be Discharged paying her ffees.

Records of the Superior Court of Judicature (1692/3), pp. 4–5, Massachusetts Supreme Judicial Court, Judicial Archives, Massachusetts State Archives. Boston, MA.

Thursday, January 5, 1693

Grand Juries of Mary Colson, Elizabeth Johnson Jr., Jane Lilly, Margaret Prince, Henry Salter, Hannah Tyler

Trials of Job Tookey, & Hannah Tyler

Attested: Examination of Mary Osgood
2nd of 2 dates. See No. 578 on Sept. 8, 1692

Sworn Before the Grand Jury: Examination of Elizabeth Johnson Jr.
2nd of 2 dates. See No. 508 on Aug. 11, 1692

Sworn Before the Grand Jury: Examination of Jane Lilly & Mary Colson
2nd of 2 dates. See No. 544 on Sept. 5, 1692

757. Indictment of Margaret Prince, for Afflicting Elizabeth Booth (Returned Ignoramus)†

[Hand 1] Prouince of the Masachusets Bay in New England. Essex sc.

Anno $\overline{RR}$^s & Reginæ Gulielmi & Mariæ Anglia &c Quarto Annoqʒ Domini 1692

The Juriors for our Soueraigne Lord & Lady the King & Queen doe present that Margreet prince of Gloster alis Cap Ann in the County of Essex widow upon the fift day of September 1692 and diuers other dayes & Times as well before as after Certaine Detestable Arts Caled witch Craft and Sorceries wickedly Mallitiously & feloniously hath vsed practiced and Exersised at & in the Towne of Salem in the County of Essex upon & against one Elizabeth Booth of Salem aforsaid Singleweoman By which Said wicked Acts the Said Elizabeth Booth the day & yeare aboue said and diuers other dayes & times both before & after was & is tortured aflicted Consumed Pined wasted & Tormented Against the peace of our Soueraigne Lord & Lady the King & Queen their Crowne & Dignity & the Laws in that case made & prouided
Witnesses Elizabeth Huberd
Mary warren
Ebenz^r Babson.
Eliz. Booth.

[Reverse] Margret Prince, Eliz Booth
[Hand 2] Ignoramus
Robert. Payne foreman:

Notes: ◊ Hand 1 = John Higginson Jr.

Suffolk Court Files, vol. 32, docket 2676, p. 7, Massachusetts Supreme Judicial Court, Judicial Archives, Massachusetts State Archives. Boston, MA.

Sworn Before the Grand Jury: Examination of Margaret Prince
2nd of 2 dates. See No. 545 on Sept. 5, 1692

January 5, 1693

758. Indictment of Henry Salter, for Afflicting Rose Foster (Returned Ignoramus)†

[Hand 1] Essex in the Prouince of the Massachusett Bay in New England ss. } Anno $\overline{RR}^s$ & Reginæ Gulielmi & Mariæ Angliæ &c Quarto Annoqʒ Domini 1692

The Juriors for our Soueraigne Lord & Lady the King and Quen doe present that [Hand 2] **Henry Salter of Andover** [Hand 1] in the County of Essex [Hand 2] **husbandman** [Hand 1] upon or about [Hand 2] **yᵉ Seuenth Day of September** [Hand 1] In the yeare aforsaid and diuers other dayes and times as well before as after Certaine detestable Arts called witchcraft and Sorceries wickedly malitiously and feloniously hath vsed practised and Excercised at and in the Towne of [Hand 2] **Salem** [Hand 1] in the County of Essex in and upon and against one [Hand 2] **Rose ffoster of Andover Singlewoman** [Hand 1] by which said wicked acts. the Said [Hand 2] **Rose Foster** [Hand 1] The day and yeare aforsaid and diuers other dayes and Times both before & after was and is tortured afflicted Consumed wasted Pined and Tormented against the peace of our Souraigne Lord & Lady the King and Queen their Crowne & Dignity and the Law in that case made & prouided

[Hand 2] Witnesses Rose ffoster
Mary Wolcott
Mary Warren
[Hand 1] Martha. Sprage alis. Tyler.

[Reverse] [Hand 2] Henry Salter Aflic$^\varepsilon$ Rose ffoster
[Hand 3] Ignoramus
Robert: Payne foreman:
[Hand 4] Henry Salter delivered paying ffees

Notes: Hand 1 = John Higginson Jr.; Hand 2 = Stephen Sewall

Suffolk Court Files, vol. 32, docket 2702, p. 24, Massachusetts Supreme Judicial Court, Judicial Archives, Massachusetts State Archives. Boston, MA.

Sworn Before the Grand Jury: Examination of Henry Salter
2ⁿᵈ of 2 dates. See No. 563 on Sept. 7, 1692

Sworn Before the Grand Jury: Examination of Mary Taylor
2ⁿᵈ of 2 dates. See No. 546 on Sept. 5, 1692

759. Indictment of Hannah Tyler, for Afflicting Rose Foster‡

[Hand 1] Prouince of the Massachusetts Bay in New England Essex ss. } Anno $\overline{RR}$s & Reginæ Gulielmi & Mariæ Angliæ &c Quarto Anoqʒ Do$\overline{m}$ 1692.

The Juro$^\varepsilon$s for o^r Sou$^\varepsilon$ Lord & Lady the King & Queen Present That Hannah Tyler of Andivo$^\varepsilon$ in the County of Essex aforesaid Single Woman On or about the Seauenth Day of September last in the yeare of our lord 1692 aforesaid, And diuers other days & Times as Well before as after Certaine detestable Arts Called Witchcrafts & Sorceries, Wickedly

mallitiously & ffelloniously hath vsed practised & Excersised at and In the Towne of   January 5, 1693
Andivo^ε aforesaid, vpon & Against One Rose ffoster of Andiuor aforesaid [ ] by which Said
Wicked Arts The Said Rose ffoster The day & yeare aforesaid & diuers other days & times
as Well before as after, was & is aflicted Tortured Consumed pined Wasted & Tormented
Against the peace of o^ε Sou^ε lord & Lady the King & Queen Their Crowne & dignity And
the laws in that Case made & Prouided.

[Reverse] Hannah Tyler for bewitching Rose ffoster
[Hand 2] Billa uera:
Robert: Payne foreman:
[Hand 3] Ponet se
Not guilty

Notes: A true bill was returned. Tyler was tried and found not guilty. See No. 761, ◊ Hand 1 = Anthony Checkley

Massachusetts Archives Collection, vol. 135, no. 53. Massachusetts State Archives. Boston, MA.

Billa Vera: Indictment of Job Tookey, for Afflicting Mary Warren†
2nd of 2 dates. See No. 651 on Sept. 15, 1692

Sworn at Trial: Statements of Mary Warren, Susannah Shelden, Ann Putnam Jr., Sarah Bibber, Mary Walcott, Elizabeth Hubbard, Elizabeth Booth, James Darling, & John Louder v. Job Tookey, with Examination of Job Tookey†
2nd of 2 dates. See No. 306 on June 4, 1692

Sworn at Trial: Testimony of John Lauder, Samuel King, Daniel Bacon, John Stacy & John Putney Jr. v. Job Tookey†
2nd of 2 dates. See No. 307 on June 4, 1692

760. Court Record of the Trial of Job Tookey

[Hand 1] Jan^εry 5th Job Tookey of Beverley in the County of Essex Waterman was Indicted
by the Jurors for our Soveraign⟨e⟩ Lord and Lady the King and Queen upon their Oaths For
⟨that⟩ the said Job Tookey The seventh day of June In the year of our Lord One thousand
Six hundred Ninety and two and divers other dayes and times as well before as after Certaine
detestable Arts Ca[Lost] [*SWP* = Called] [Lost]hcraft [*SWP* = witchcraft] and Sorceries
Wickedly mall[Lost] [*SWP* = mallitiously and] [Lost]ly [*SWP* = feloniously] hath used
practised and Exercised at [Lost] [*SWP* = and in the] [Lost]owne [*SWP* = Towne] of Salem
In the County of Essex aforesaid In upon and against one Mary Warren of Salem aforesaid
Single woman by wch said wicked Acts the said Mary Warren the day and year aforesaid and
divers other dayes and times both before and after was and is Tortured Afflicted Wasted
^{Cons⟨umed⟩} pined ⟨&⟩ Tormented And al⟨so⟩ for Sundry other Acts of Witchcr⟨afts⟩ by
the said Job Tookey Committed and don before ⟨and⟩ since that time against the peace of
our Soveraigne Lord & Lady the King & Queen their Crowne & ⟨Di⟩gnity and the ^{forme
of y^e} Statute in that Case made and provided.

January 5, 1693

Jury of Tryalls
⟨E⟩dward fflint fform⁶
⟨N⟩athanˡ Howard
⟨E⟩liazer Gyles
John Hale
John Kent
Joseph Litle
Benayah Tidcomb
⟨S⟩amuel Morgan
⟨Ed⟩mund Gale
⟨Wil⟩liam Stephens
⟨Jo⟩hn Lampson
⟨Set⟩h Storey

Vpon wᶜʰ Indictment the said Job Tookey w⟨as⟩ Arraigned and vp⟨on his⟩ Arraignement plead⟨ed⟩ not Guilty to the Indictment and put himselfe vpon Tryall by God and the Country.
A Jury was called being the firs Jury Edward fflint fforeman and were accordingly Swore to pass vpo⟨n⟩ him (the prisoner makeing no Challeng) The Ind⟨ict⟩ment being read as allso the Evidences and Exa⟨min⟩ation the prisoner made his Defence the Jury ⟨retu⟩rne their Verdict.
The Jury Say that Job To[Lost] [*SWP = Tookey*] is not Guilty of the ffelony by witchcraft of w⟨ch⟩ he stood Indicted. The Court Ordered Job Too[Lost] [*SWP = Tookey to*] be discharg⟨e⟩d paying his ffees.

Records of the Superior Court of Judicature (1692/3), p. 5, Massachusetts Supreme Judicial Court, Judicial Archives, Massachusetts State Archives. Boston, MA.

761. Court Record of the Trial of Hannah Tyler

[Hand 1] Hannah Tyler of Andover in the County of of Essex Singlewom being Indicted by the Jurors for our Soveraigne Lord and Lady the King and Qeen vpon their Oaths by Two Severall Indictments, That is to say 1ˢᵗ That Shee the said Hannah Tyler of Andover in the County of Essex Singlewoman some time in the moneth of Aprill last in the year of our Lord One Thousand Six hundred ninety two af⟨ore⟩ˢᵈ in the Towne of Andover aforesᵈ wickedly mallitiousely and ffeloneously A Covenant with the Devill did make whereby she Gaue both her soule and body to the Devil and Signed his booke and by him was Baptized and owned the Devill to be her God and promised to hon⁶ and serve him forever And unto the Devill did renoun⟨ce⟩ her Christian Baptisme, and God and Christ By which Diababollicall ˄{&} wicked Covenanting with the Devill a⟨s⟩ aforesaid the said Hannah Tyler is becom a detestable Witch, Contrary to the peace of our Soveraigne Lord and Lady the King and Queen their Crowne and Dignity and the Law in that Case made and provided.
2ˡʸ For that she (the said Hannah Tyler) on or about the seventh day of September last in the year of our Lord One thousand Six hundred ninety Two aforesaid and [Lost]ther [*SWP = divers other*] dayes and times as well before as [Lost] [*SWP = after certaine*] [Lost]testable [*SWP = detestable*] arts called Witchcraft and [Lost] [*SWP = Sorceries*] [Lost]ickedly [*SWP = wickedly*] mallitiousely and feloneously ha⟨th⟩ used practised & Exercised in the Towne of Andover aforesᵈ vpon and against one Rose ffoster of Andover aforesᵈ By which said wicked arts the said Rose ffoster the day and year aforesaid and divers other dayes and times as well before as after, was and is afflicted Tortur⟨e⟩d Consumed pined wasted and tormented against the peace of our Soveraigne Lord and Lady the King & Their Crowne and dignity and the Lawes in that cas⟨e⟩ made and Provided.

January 6, 1693

3$\underline{^{rd}}$ Jury of Tryalls
⟨Na⟩thiell Howa⟨r⟩d
 fforem⟨n⟩
⟨J⟩ohn Ha⟨le⟩
James ffreind
⟨S⟩amuell Morgan
⟨J⟩ames Sanders
⟨Ri⟩chard Gross
John Witt
⟨N⟩athan^l Emerson
⟨John⟩ Emery
⟨Be⟩naiah Tidcomb
⟨Jo⟩hn Platts
⟨Jo⟩hn Lamson

Upon the aboues^d Indictments and each of them the said Ha⟨nn⟩ah Tyler was then & there ~~Indicted~~ before our Justices of Lord and Lady the King & Queen afores^d Arraigned & upon her arraignem^t th[Lost] [*SWP* = the said] Hannah did then and there the said day & year afores^d plead to them & each of them not Guilty & put her selfe vpon Tryall by God & her Country.

A Jury being called Nathaniel Howard fforema⟨n⟩ & accordingly Sworne no Exception made by the prisoner the Indictments being read together with Evidence & Examination and the Prisoners defence being heard the Jury went out to agre⟨e⟩ on their verdict who Returning did then and there in o⟨pen⟩ Court deliver their Verdict That the said Hannah Ty⟨ler⟩ was not Guilty of the ffelony by Witchcraft for ["for" written over "by"] wch she stood In[Lost] [*SWP* = indicted] in & by the said Indictm^{ts} & each of them

The Court Ordered Hannah Tyler aforesaid [Lost] [*SWP* = to] be discharged Paying her ffees//

Records of the Superior Court of Judicature (1692/3), p. 6, Massachusetts Supreme Judicial Court, Judicial Archives, Massachusetts State Archives. Boston, MA.

Friday, January 6, 1693

Grand Juries of Abigail Barker, Candy, Mary Marston, Abigail Soames, & Mary Toothaker

Trials of Candy, Mary Marston, Elizabeth Johnson Sr., & Abigail Barker

762. Indictment of Abigail Barker, for Afflicting Rose Foster‡

[Hand 1] Essex in the Prouince of the Massachusetts bay In New England ss// } Anno $\overline{RR}$s & Reginæ Gulielmi & Mariæ Angliæ &c Quarto Anoq$_3$ Do$\overline{m}$: 1692

The Juro^{ε}s for o^r Sou^ε lord & Lady the King and Queen present That Abigaill Barker Wife of Ebenezer Barker of Andivor In & vpon the Eighth day of September last in the yeare aforesaid & diuers other days & Times as well before as after Certaine detestable arts Called Witchcrafts & Sorcerys wickedly mallitiously & ffelloniously hath vsed practised & Exersised at & in the Towne of Andivor aforesaid in the County of Essex aforesaid ~~in~~ vpon & Against One Rose ffoster of Andivor [ ] by which Said Wicked Arts the Said Rose ffoster the day & yeare afor$\overline{s}$d & diuers others days & times both before & after was & is Tortured Aflicted Consumed pined Wasted & Tormented Against the peace of o^r Sou^ε lord & lady the King & Queen their Crowne & dignity & the laws & Acts in that Case made & prouided

[Reverse] Abigaill Barker for bewitching Rose ffoster

January 6, 1693   Notes: A true bill was returned on January 6, and that day Abigail Barker was tried and found not guilty. See No. 770. ◊
Hand 1 = Anthony Checkley

Massachusetts Archives Collection, vol. 135, no. 54. Massachusetts State Archives. Boston, MA.

763. Indictment of Candy, for Afflicting Ann Putnam Jr.†

[Hand 1] Essex In the prouince   } Annᵒ R̄Rs & Reginæ Gulielmi & Mariæ Angliæ &c
of the Massachusetts Bay in New   } Quarto Anoqʒ Dom 1692
England Ss//

The Juᵋors for oᵋ Souᵋ lord & lady the King & Queen present That Candy A negro Woman
Seruant to Margarett Hawkes of Salem in the County of Essex aforsd, In & vpon the Second
day of July last in the yeare 1692 And diuers other days & times as well before as after
Certaine detestable Arts Called Witchcrafts & Sorceries, Wickedly mallitiously &
ffelloniously hath vsed practised & exersised in the Towne of Salem aforesaid vpon &
Against One An Putnam of Salem Single Woman By which wicked Arts The Said Ann
Putnam the day & yeare aforsd & diuers other days & times both before & after Was & is
Tortured Aflicted Consumed Wasted pined & Tormented Contrary to the peace of our
Souᵋ lord & Lady the King & Queen Their Crowne & dignity and The laws in that Case
made & prouided

[Reverse] Candy Negro for bewitching Ann Putnam
[Hand 2] Billa uera
Robert: Payne foreman:
[Hand 3] ponet se
[Hand 4] the jury finds the person here inditted not gilty of ["of" written over "by"] this
indittment
[Hand 3?] 7

Notes: None of the three accused slaves, Candy, Mary Black, and Tituba, had their cases addressed by a grand jury in
1692. Mary Black was cleared by proclamation on January 11, 1693 (see No. 84). Tituba received an ignoramus on an
indictment on May 9, 1693 (see No. 844), and was thus not brought to trial. Candy was tried January 6, 1693, and found
not guilty on the two true bills against her, No. 763 for afflicting Ann Putnam Jr. and No. 764 for afflicting Mary Walcott.
◊ Hand 1 = Anthony Checkley

Massachusetts Archives Collection, vol. 135, no. 31.2. Massachusetts State Archives. Boston, MA.

764. Indictment of Candy, for Afflicting Mary Walcott†

[Hand 1] Essex in the prouince   } Anno R̄Rs & Reginæ Gulielmi & Mariæ Angliæ &c
of the Massachusett Bay in New   } quaᵋto Anoqʒ Dom̄ 1692.
England Ss

The Juroᵋs for oʳ Souᵋ lord & lady the King & Queen doe present That Candy A Negro
Woman Seruant ~~Seruant~~ of Margarett Hawkes of Salem, in & vpon the Second day of July
last in the yeare 1692 and diuers other days & times as well before as after Certaine
detestable Arts Called Witchcrafts & Sorceries wickedly mallitiously & ffelloniously hath

vsed practised & Exersised in the Towne of Salem aforsd vpon & Against One Mary
Wallcot of Salem Single Woman by which Wicked Arts The Said Mary Wallcot the day &
yeare aforesaid & diuers other times as well before as after was & is Tortured Aflicted
Consumed Wasted pined & Tormented Contrary to the peace of ou$^\varepsilon$ Sou$^\varepsilon$ lord & lady the
King & Queen their Crowne & dignity & The laws in that Case made & prouided

[Reverse] Candy Negro: for bewitching Mary Wallcott
[Hand 2] Billa uera
Robert Payne foreman
[Hand 3] Ponet se
[Hand 4] the juery find the person here inditted not gilty of ["of" written over "by"] this
indittement

Notes: Hand 1 = Anthony Checkley

Massachusetts Archives Collection, vol. 135, no. 31.1. Massachusetts State Archives. Boston, MA.

Endorsed by Grand Jury Foreman: Examination of Mary Marston†
3rd of 3 dates. See No. 528 on Aug. 29, 1692

765. Indictment of Abigail Soames, for Afflicting Mary Warren (Returned Ignoramus)

[Hand 1] Essex in y^e Province of y^e Anno $\overline{RR}$s Reginæ Gulielmi & Mariæ
Mattathusets Bay in New Eng^d Angliæ &c Quarto Annoq3 Domi: 1692
The Jurors for Our Soueraign Lord & Lady the King & Queen doe present That Abigaill
Soames of ~~Beuerly~~ Salem Late of Glosster in y^e County of Essex Singlewoman vpon the
thirteenth day of May in y^e yeare afores^d & Diuers other dayes & times as well before as after
Certain detestable arts Called Witchcrafts & Sorceries Wickedly and felloniously hath vsed
practised and Excercised att & in ye Towne of Salem in ye County of Essex afores^d in upon &
against One Mary Warren of Salem Single woman by which Said Wicked arts the Said Mary
Warren ye day & yeare afores^d and diuers other dayes & Times both before & after was & is
Consumed Pined Wasted & Tormented Against y^e peace of Our Soueraign Lord & Lady y^e
King & Queen Thier Crowne & dignity & the Laws in that Case made and prouided.
Witnesses. Mary Warren
Mary Wolcott
Eli. Hubbard

[Reverse] Abigail ⟨Soa⟩mes Aflict$^\varepsilon$ Mary [Lost] [= Warren]
[Hand 2] Ignoramus
Robert. Payne foreman:

Notes: Hand 1 = Stephen Sewall

Suffolk Court Files, vol. 32, docket 2703, p. 25, Massachusetts Supreme Judicial Court, Judicial Archives, Massachusetts State Archives. Boston, MA.

January 6, 1693

766. Deposition of Mary Warren v. Abigail Soames

[Hand 1] The Deposition of mary Warren who Testifieth & Saith that Abigaill Somes of Gloster hath often times aflickted mee by bitting pricking & pinching of mee & halling {mee} about vnder the Table & s^d ^{Somes s^d} she had been ~~half~~ bed Riden a twelvmoneth or their about & that she had never been out in the day time in s^d time but had been very often abroad in the night & when she was sent for to the village, I see her Aflict Ann Putnam & mary walcot

owned before the Grand iury vpon the
oath she had taken Jen^ε 6th 1692
Attests. Robert: Payn
foreman:

Notes: Although the deposition refers to Abigail Soames as from Gloucester, she had moved from there and had been living in Salem when arrested on May 13, 1692. An ignoramus was returned on the indictment for afflicting Warren. See No. 765.

Suffolk Court Files, vol. 32, docket 2703, p. 25, Massachusetts Supreme Judicial Court, Judicial Archives, Massachusetts State Archives. Boston, MA.

Sworn Before the Grand Jury: Examination of Mary Toothaker
2nd of 2 dates. See No. 441 on July 30, 1692

767. Court Record of the Trial of Candy

[Hand 1] Jan^ε ry 6th Candy a Negroe Servant to M^s Mary Hawk⟨es⟩ of Salem, in the County of Essex, being Indicted b⟨y⟩ the Jurors for our Soveraign Lord and Lady the King and Queen upon Oaths, by Two Severall Indictements; That is to Say, 1st For that the Said Candy Negroe Woman Servant to Mrs Mary Hawkes aforesaid of Salem in the County of Esse⟨x⟩ aforesaid, did upon the Second Day of July last in the Year 1692 And diverse other times before and after, certaine detestable Arts called witchcrafts and Sorceries, Wickedly, Malitiously, and ffelloniously, hath vsed, practised, and Exercised, in the Town of Salem aforesaid, vpon and against One Ann Putnam of Salem Single Woman, by which wicked Arts, the Said Ann Putnam the day and Year aforesaid, and divers other dayes and times both before and after was and is tortured, afflicted, consumed, wasted, pined, and tormented, contrary to the Peace of our Sovereign Lord and Lady the King and Quee⟨n⟩ their Crowne and dignity, and the Lawes in that case made, and Provided.

2dly For that she (the Said Candy) in and upon the Second Day of July last in the Year 169⟨2⟩ And divers other dayes and times, as well before ⟨and⟩ after Certaine detestable Arts called Witchcrafts and Sorceries wickedly malitiously and felloniously hath used practised and exercised in the Towne of Salem aforesaid upon and Against One Mary Wallcot of Salem Single Woman by which wicked arts, the Said Mary Wallcot the day and Year aforesaid and divers other times as well before as after was and is tortured, afflicted, consumed wasted, pined, and tormented contrary to the Peace of our Sovereign Lord and Lady the King and Queen their Crown and Dignity, and the Lawe⟨s⟩ in that case made and provided.

Petty Jurors
Richd Gross fforem^ε
John Emery
John Ardway
⟨J⟩ames friend
John Abby
John Witt
Josiah Gay
James Sanders
Nathaniel Emerson
Thomas Edwards
John Prick [*SWP* = Prickard]
John Platts

Upon the abovesaid Indictements and each of them the Said Candy was then and ∧{y^{re}} [= there] before the Jus⟨ti⟩ces of our Lord and Lady the King and Queen afores^{⟨d⟩} Arraigned, and upon her Arraignment the Said Candy did then and there the Day and Year afores^{⟨d⟩} plead to them and each of them Not Guilty and put her self upon triall by God and hur Countre⟨y⟩

A Jury being called Richard Gross foreman and A͞cordingly Sworne, no Exception made by the Prison⟨er⟩ the said Indictments and Every of them being rea⟨d⟩ together with Evidences and Examinations ⟨and the⟩ prisoners defence being heard, The Jury went ⟨out⟩ to agree on their verdict, who Returning, did ⟨then⟩ and there in open Court deliver there verdict, ⟨That⟩ the said Candy was not Guilty of the fellony ⟨by⟩ witchcraft for which she stood Indicted In and by the said Indictments and each of them.

The Court Ordered Cand⟨y⟩ the Negroe Servant abovesaid to be discharged, Paying her fee

January 6, 1693

Records of the Superior Court of Judicature (1692/3), pp. 7–8, Massachusetts Supreme Judicial Court, Judicial Archives, Massachusetts State Archives. Boston, MA.

768. Court Record of the Trial of Mary Marston

[Hand 1] Mary Marston wife of John Marston wife of John Marston Jun^ε of Andover In the County of Essex husbandman being Indicted by the Jurors for our Soveraigne Lord and Lady the King and Queen vpon their Oathes by Two severall Indictments, That is to say. 1st For that she the said Mary Marston wif of John Marston of Andover. husbandman about Three years since in the Towne of Andov^ε in the County of Essex afores^d A wicked and diabollicall Covenant wickedly mallitiousely and ffeloneously with the Devill did make and Signe the Devills book, and promis to worship the Devill and serue him by which wicked Covenant with the Devill the said Mary Marston is becom a detestable Witch Contrary to the Peace of our Soveraigne Lord & Lady the King and Queen their Crowne & Dignity and the Lawes in that Case made and provided.
2dly For that she the said Mary Marston on or about the twenty Eight day of August last in the year of our Lord one thousand Six hundred ninety two and divers other dayes and times as well before as after Certain detestable Arts Called Witchcraft and Sorceries wickedly mallitiously and ffeloneously hath used practised and Exercised at and in the Towne of Andover aforesaid in vpon and against one Abigail Martin of Andover aforesaid by wch said wicked Acts the said Abigail Martin the day & year aforesaid aforesaid and divers other dayes & times both before and after was and is Tortured afflicted Consumed Pined wasted and Tormented against the peace of our Soveraigne Lord and Lady the King and Queen their Crowne and Dignity and the forme of the stattute in that Case made & Provided.

January 6, 1693

Nath^ll howard forem^e
John Hale
Sam^ll Morgan
James Sanders
Richd Gross
John Witt
Natha^ll Emerson
John Emery
Benajah Titcomb
John Platts
John Lamson.
James Friend.

Vpon the aforesaid Indictments and Each of the⟨m the⟩ said Mary Marston was then and there before the Jus⟨tices⟩ of our Lord and Lady the King and Queen aforesaid Arraigned and vpon her arraignement did then and there th⟨e⟩ day and year aforesaid plead to them and each of them Not Guilty and put herselfe vpon tryall by God & hir Country
A Jury being Called Nathaniel Howard fforeman and accordingly Sworne no Exception being made by the prisoner the said Indictments and every of them being Read together with Evidences and Examination⟨s⟩ and the prisoners defence being heard. the Jury went out to agree on their verdict, Who Returning did then and there in open Court deliver their Verdict, That the said Mary Marston was not Guilty of the felony by witchcraft for which she stood Indicte⟨d⟩ In and by the said Indictments and each of them
The Court Ordered Mary Marston aforesaid to be discharged Paying ffees.

Records of the Superior Court of Judicature (1692/3), p. 8, Massachusetts Supreme Judicial Court, Judicial Archives, Massachusetts State Archives. Boston, MA.

769. Court Record of the Trial of Elizabeth Johnson Sr.

[Hand 1] Elisabeth Johnson of Andivor in the County of Essex Widdow, being Indicted by the Jurors for our Soveraigne Lord and Lady the King and Queen upon their Oathes, by two Severall Indictements,: That is to say; 1st For that shee the Said Elisabeth Johnson of Andover in the County of Essex afores^d Widdow on or about [ ] and dive⟨rs⟩ other times as well before as after in the Township of Andover aforesaid wickedly, malitiously, and ffelloniously, A covenant with the Devill did make, by which diabolicall Covenant, Shee gave he⟨r⟩ Selfe both Soule, and body, to the Devill and Sign⟨ed⟩ the Devills booke, and by him was baptized and un⟨to⟩ him renounced her Christian baptism, and God and Christ, And owned the Devill to be her God, and promised to Serve, and obey him for ever; by which wicked Covenant shee the Said Elisabeth Johnson is become a detestable witch, contrary to the Peace of our Soveraigne Lord and Lady the King and Queen, their Crowne, and dignity, and the Lawes in that case made, and Provided.

2dly For that shee the Said Elisabeth Johnson, of Andivor, in the County of Essex, aforesaid, Widdow, On or about the 30th Day of August, in the Year 1692 aforesaid, and diverse other days, and times, as well before, as after, certaine detestable Arts, called Witchcrafts, and Sorceries wickedly, Malitiously and fellloniously hath used, practised, and exercised, at and in the Towne of Andover, in the County of Essex aforesaid, upon, and against, one Sarah Phelps of [ ] by which Said wicked arts the Said Sarah Phelps the day, and Yeare aforesaid, and divers other dayes and times, as well before, as after, was, and is, tortured, consumed, wasted, pined, afflicted, and tormented; contrary to the Peace of our Soveraigne Lord and Lady the King and Queen, their Crowne, and dignity, and the Lawes in that case made, and Provided.

January 6, 1693

John Blaney forem$^\varepsilon$
Edward fflint.
Eleazar Giles.
John Kent Sen$^\varepsilon$
Joseph Litle
John Abby.
Edmund Gale.
Josiah Gay.
Seth Story.
John Ordway.
Thomas Edwards.
John Prikard.

Upon the aforesaid Indictments, and each of them, the said Elisabeth Johnson, was then & there, before the Justices of our Lord and Lady the King and Queen aforesaid, arraigned, and upon her arraignment, did then, and there, the day, and Year aforesaid, plead to them, and each of them, Not Guilty and put her Self upon tryall, by God, & her Country. A Jury being called John Blaney fforeman a$^\varepsilon$cordingly sworne, no exception made by the Prisoner, the said Indictments, and Every of them being read, together with Evidences, and Examinations, and the Prisoners defence being heard; the Jury went out to agree on their verdict, who returning, did then, and there, in open Court, deliver their verdict; That the said Elisabeth Johnson was Not Guilty of the ffellony by witchcraft, for wch she stood Indicted, in, and, by, the said Indictments and each of them

The Court Ordered Elisabeth Johnson aforesaid to be discharged, Paying her fees.

Records of the Superior Court of Judicature (1692/3), pp. 9–10, Massachusetts Supreme Judicial Court, Judicial Archives, Massachusetts State Archives. Boston, MA.

770. Court Record of the Trial of Abigail Barker

[Hand 1] Abigaill Barker wife of Ebenezar Barker of Andover in the County of Essex, being indicted by the Jurors, for our Soveraigne Lord and Lady the King and Queen, upon their Oathes; by three Severall Indictments; That is to Say: 1st

For that shee the Said Abigaill Barker wife of Ebenezar Barker of Andover in the County of Essex, about Two Yeares Since, at, & in the Towne of Andover aforesaid, wickedly malitiously, and ffelloniously, a Covenant with the De[Lost] [*SWP* = Devill] did make, and Signe the Devills Booke, and by the ⟨Devill⟩ was baptized, and renounced her former christian baptisme, and gave her Selfe up to the Devill, to Se⟨rve⟩ him, and for the Devill, to be her Lord and Master by which diabolicall, and wicked covenant Shee ⟨the⟩ said Abigaill Barker, is become a detestable wit⟨ch⟩ Contrary to the Peace of our Soveraigne Lord and Lady the King and Queen their Crowne, and Dignity, and the Lawes; in that case made, and provided.
2dly For that shee the Said Abigaill Barker, wife of Ebenezar Barker of Andover, in the County of Essex aforesaid, in and upon the Eighth Day of Septemb$^\varepsilon$ last, in the year of our Lord 1692, and diverse othe⟨r⟩ day's, and times, as well before, as after; certaine de⟨te⟩stable Arts, called witchcrafts, and Sorceries, wicked⟨ly⟩ malitiously, and ffelloniously, hath used, practis⟨ed⟩ and exercised, at, and in the Towne of Andover afores⟨d⟩ in the County of Essex aforesaid, upon, and against One Ralph ffarnum Senior of Andover aforesaid by which said wicked arts aforesaid, the said Ralph ffarnum the day and Yeare aforesaid, and diverse other dayes, and times, both before, and after was, ⟨&⟩ is, tortured, aflicted, consumed, wasted, pined, and tormented, contrary to the peace of our Soveraign⟨e⟩ Lord, and Lady, the King and Queen, their Crowne and, Dignity, and the Lawes in that case made, and provided.

3dly For that shee the said Abigaill Barker, wife of Ebenezar Barker, of Andover, in, and upon the Eighth day of September last in the Year of our Lord 1692 and divers other dayes and times as well before as after certaine detestable Arts, called witchcrafts, and Sorceries, wickedly, mallitiously, and ffellonious⟨ly⟩ hath used, practised, and Exercised, at, and in the towne of Andover aforesaid, in the County of Essex aforesaid, upon, and against, one Rose ffoster, of Andover [ ] by which Said wicked Arts, the Said Rose ffoster, the day, and year aforesaid, and diverse others dayes, and time⟨s⟩ both before, and after, was, and is, tortured, afflicted consumed, pined, and wasted, and tormented, against the Peace of o^ε Soveraigne Lord and Lady the King, and Queen, their Crowne and dignity, and the Lawes, and Acts in that case made, and, Provided.

Jury of Tryall
⟨N⟩athan^l Howard fform^ε
John Hale
Samuel Morgan
James Sanders
Richard Gross
John Witt
Nathan^l Emerson
John Emery
Benayah Tidcomb
John Platts
John Lamson
James ffreind

Upon the aforesaid Indictments, and each of them, the Said Abigaill Barker was then, and there, before the Justices of our Lord and Lady the King and Queen aforesaid, arraigned, and ⟨upon⟩ her arraignment, did then, and there, the day, and Y⟨ear⟩ aforesaid, plead to them, and each of them Not Guilty, and put her Selfe, upon triall, by God, and her Countrey. A Jury being called [ ] fforeman and a^εcordingly Sworne, no exception made by the Prisoner the said Indictments, and each of them, being read, together with Eudences, and Examinations and the Prisoners defence being heard; the Jury went out to agree on their verdict, who returning, did then, and there, in open Court, deliver there verdict; That the Said Abigaill Barker, was Not Guilty, of the ffellony by witchcraft, for which she stood Indicted, in, and by, the said Indictements, and each of them

The Court Ordered, Abigaill Barker aforesaid, to be discharged, paying her ffees.

Records of the Superior Court of Judicature (1692/3), pp. 10–11, Massachusetts Supreme Judicial Court, Judicial Archives, Massachusetts State Archives. Boston, MA.

Saturday, January 7, 1693

Grand Juries of John Jackson Jr., John Jackson Sr., Rebecca Johnson, Susannah Post & William Procter

Trial of Mary Tyler

771. Indictment of John Jackson Jr., for Afflicting Mary Warren (Returned Ignoramus)

[Hand 1] Province of the Massatuthetts Bay in New England Essex } Anno RRs.&: Reginæ Gulielmi & Mariæ Angliæ &^c Quarto: Annoq̨ Dͦm: 1692

The Juro^ε for our Sovereigne Lord & Lady the King & Queen Present That [Hand 2] **John Jaxon Jun^ε of Rowley on ye 27th day of August 1692** [Hand 1] And divers other Dayes & times as well before as after Certaine detestable Arts called Witchcrafts and Sorceries

January 7, 1693

Wickedly Mallishiously and ffelloniously hath vsed Practised. & Exercised at and in the
Towne of [Hand 2] **Salem** [Hand 1] in the County of Essex Affore͞s^d vpon and against one
[Hand 2] **Mary Warren of Salem Singlewoman** [Hand 1] by which Wicked Arts the said
[Hand 2] **Mary Warren** [Hand 1] the Day and year afores^d and Divers other Dayes and
Times as well before as after was & is Tourtered Afflicted Tormented Consumed & wasted
against the Peace of our Sovereigne Lord & Lady the y^e King & Queen their Crowne and
Dignity and the Lawes in that case ~~Provid~~ made & Provided
[Hand 2] Witnesses Martha Sprague
Rose ffoster

[Reverse] Jno Jaxon Jun^ε Afli. Mary Warr⟨en⟩
[Hand 3] ~~Billa vera~~ Ignoramus
Robert: Payne foreman:

Notes: Hand 2 = Stephen Sewall

*Suffolk Court Files, vol. 32, docket 2704, p. 26, Massachusetts Supreme Judicial Court, Judicial Archives, Massachusetts State
Archives. Boston, MA.*

Sworn Before the Grand Jury: Examination of John Jackson Jr.
2nd of 2 dates. See No. 520 on Aug. 27, 1692

772. Indictment of John Jackson Sr. for Afflicting Mary Warren (Returned Ignoramus)

[Hand 1] Province of y^e }   Anno RRs & Reginæ Gulielmi& & Mariæ Angliæ &^{c}
Massathusetts Bay in New }   Quarto Annoq҉ D͞o͞m 1692
England Essex }
The Juro^ε for our Sovereigne Lord & Lady the King & Queen Presents That [Hand 2] **John
Jaxon Sen^ε of Rowley in ye County of Essex on ye Twenty Seuenth day of August 1692**
[Hand 1] And Divers other Dayes and Times as well before as after Certaine Detestable Arts
called Witchcrafts & Sorceries wickedly Mallishiously & ffelloniously hath vsed Practised &
Exercised at & in the Towne of [Hand 2] **Salem** [Hand 1] in the County of Essex afore͞s^d
vpon and against One [Hand 2] **Mary Warren of Salem Singlewoman** [Hand 1] By which
Wicked Arts the said [Hand 2] **Mary Warren** [Hand 1] the Day & year afore͞s^d and Divers
other Dayes and Times as well before as after was & is Tortured Afflicted Tormented
Consumed Pined & wasted against the Peace of our Sovereigne Lord & Lady the King and
Queen their Crowne and Dignity and the Lawes in that Case made and Provided.
[Hand 2] Witnesses Rose Foster
Martha Sprague.

[Reverse] John Jaxon Sen Afli^ε Mar. Warren
[Hand 3] Ignoramus
Robert: Payne foreman:

Notes: Hand 2 = Stephen Sewall

January 7, 1693   *Suffolk Court Files, vol. 32, docket 2704, p. 27, Massachusetts Supreme Judicial Court, Judicial Archives, Massachusetts State Archives. Boston, MA.*

Sworn Before the Grand Jury: Examination of John Jackson Sr.

2nd of 2 dates. See No. 521 on Aug. 27, 1692

773. Indictment of Rebecca Johnson Sr., for Afflicting Alice Booth (Returned Ignoramus)†

See also: Jan. 9, 1693.

[Hand 1] Essex in the prouince of the Massachusets Bay in New England } Anno $\overline{RR}^s$ Reginæ Gulielmi & Mariæ Angliæ &c Quarto Annoqȝ Domini 1692

The Juriors for our Soueraigne Lord & Lady the King & Queen doe present that Rebecka Johnson widow, of Andiuor In the County of Essex upon the Seauenth day of September In the yeare aforsaid and diuers other dayes and times as well before as after Certaine detestable arts Called witchcraft and Sorcieres wickedly Malisiously [1st "s" written over "h"] and ffeloniously hath vsed practised and Exersiced at and in the Towne of Salem in the County of Essex in upon and against one Alice Booth of Salem aforsaid Singleweoman by which Said wicked Acts the Said Alice Booth the day and yeare abouesaid and diuers other dayes & Times both before & after was & is tortured afflicted Consumed Pined wasted and Tormented Against the peace of our Soueraigne Lord & Lady the King & Quen their Crowne & Dignity and the Laws in that case made & prouided.
Wittnesses
Ma⟨r⟩tha Sprage alis Tyler
Rose ffoster.

[Reverse] [Hand 2] Indictm^t Against Rebeckah Johnson of Andiuo^ε Widow
[Hand 3] Ignoramus
Robert: Payne foreman
[Hand 2?] Clered by proclama$\overline{co}$ 9: 11mo 1692

Notes: The "11" in the dating refers to the eleventh month in the old calendar. ◊ Hand 1 = John Higginson Jr.; Hand 2 = Anthony Checkley

Suffolk Court Files, vol. 32, docket 2707, p. 30, Massachusetts Supreme Judicial Court, Judicial Archives, Massachusetts State Archives. Boston, MA.

Sworn Before the Grand Jury: Examination of Rebecca Johnson

2nd of 2 dates. See No. 562 on Sept. 7, 1692

774. Indictment of Susannah Post, for Covenanting

See also: May 10, 1693.

[Hand 1] Province of the Massachusetts Bay in New England Essex ss } Anno $\overline{RR}^s$ Reginæ Gulielmi & Mariæ Angliæ &c Quarto Anoq3 Do$\overline{m}$ 1692

The Juro$^\varepsilon$s for o$^\varepsilon$ Sou$^\varepsilon$ lord & lady the King & Queen p$^\varepsilon$sent That Susanah Post of Andiuo$^\varepsilon$ In the County of Essex Single Woman About Three years Since In the Towne of Andiuo$^\varepsilon$ in the County of Essex aforesaid Wickedly mallitiously & ffelloniously A Couenant with the Deuill did make & Signed the Deuills Booke & was Baptized by the Deuill & promised to Serue the Deuill By which Diabollicall Couenanting with the Deuill (in maner & forme aforesaid by the Said Susannah ["Sus" written over "H"] Post made) Shee the [= the said] Hannah Post is become A Detestable Witch Against the Peace ⌃{of our Sou$^\varepsilon$ lord & lady the King & Queen} their Crowne & Dignity, & the laws in that Case made & prouided Wittness hir owne Confesion

[Reverse] Susanah Post for Couenanting with the Devill

[Hand 2] Billa vera

Robert: Payne foreman:

[Hand 3] Not Guilty

Notes: Post was tried in May 1693 and found not guilty. See No. 847. ◊ Hand 1 = Anthony Checkley

Suffolk Court Files, vol. 32, docket 2705, p. 28, Massachusetts Supreme Judicial Court, Judicial Archives, Massachusetts State Archives. Boston, MA.

775. Indictment of Susannah Post, for Afflicting Rose Foster

See also: May 10, 1693.

[Hand 1] Province of y^e Massathutetts Bay in New England Essex } Anno RRs Reginæ Gulielmi & Mariæ Angliæ &^{c} Quarto Annoq3 Dom 1692

The Jurro$^\varepsilon$ for our Sovereigne Lord & Lady the King & Queen Presents That [Hand 2] ~~Hannah~~ {Susannah} Postt of Andouer in y^e County of Essex Singlewoman on y^e 25th day of August in y^e yeare afores^d [Hand 1] And divers other Dayes and times as well before as after Certaine Detestable Artes called witch Crafts & Sorceries Wickedly Mallishiously & ffelloniously hath vsed Practised & Excercised at & in the Towne of [Hand 2] Salem [Hand 1] in the County afore$\overline{s}$^{d} vpon ~~the~~ and against one [Hand 2] Rose ffoster of Andover Singlewoman [Hand 1] By which Wicked Arts the said [Hand 2] Rose Foster [Hand 1] the Day and year afore$\overline{s}$^{d} and Divers other Dayes and Times as well before as after was and is Tortured Afflicted Tormented Consumed Pined and wasted against the Peace of our Sov$^\varepsilon$ Lord and Lady the King and Queen their Crowne and Dignity and the Lawes in Case made and Provided:

[Hand 2] Witness Martha Sprague alias Tyler & her Owne Confession

January 7, 1693

[Reverse] [Hand 3] Susanah Post for aflictin Rose ffoster
[Hand 4] Billa vera
Robert Payne foreman
[Hand 5] not Guilty
[Hand 6] The Jury finds Susannah Post not gilty
[Hand 7] ⟨?⟩ed

Notes: Hand 2 = Stephen Sewall; Hand 3 = Anthony Checkley

Suffolk Court Files, vol. 32, docket 2705, p. 28, Massachusetts Supreme Judicial Court, Judicial Archives, Massachusetts State Archives. Boston, MA.

Sworn Before the Grand Jury: Examination of Susannah Post

2nd of 2 dates. See No. 519 on Aug. 25, 1692

776. Indictment of William Procter, for Afflicting Mary Walcott (Returned Ignoramus)†

[Hand 1] Province of the Massathusetts Bay in New England Essex } Anno RRs & Reginæ Gulielmi Mariæ Angliæ &c Quarto Annoqʒ Dom 1692

The Juroᵉ for our Sovereigne Lord & Lady the King and Queen pᵉsents That [Hand 2] **William Procter of Salem in the County of Essex aforesaid On the Seauenteenth Day of September 1692** [Hand 1] And Divers other Dayes and Times as well before as after Certaine Detestable Artes called Witchcrafts & Sorceries Wickedly Mallishiously and ffelloniously hath vsed Preactised & Exercised at and in the Towne of [Hand 2] **Salem** [Hand 1] in the County of Essex aforēsᵈ vpon and against one [Hand 2] **Mary Walcott** ["M" written over "El"] **of Salem aforsaid Single Woman** [Hand 1] By which Wicked Arts the said [Hand 2] **Mary Walcott** [Hand 1] The Day and year aforēsᵈ and Divers other Dayes & Times as well before as after was and is Tortured Afflicted Tormented Consumed Pined & wasted against the Peace of our Sovereigne Lord and Lady the King and Qeen their Crowne and Dignity and against the Lawes in that case made & Provided
[Hand 2] Wittnesses
Elizᵃ Hobert
Ann Puttnam
Allice Booth
Elizᵃ Booth

[Reverse] Wᵐ Procter for Afliting Mary Wallcott
[Hand 3] Ignoramus
Robert: Payne foreman.

Notes: The allegation against William Procter in this indictment is for afflicting Mary Warren during his second examination on September 17 (see No. 663), after the first two indictments against him had been returned ignoramus by the grand jury on September 8 (No. 581 & No. 582). This different grand jury returned the additional indictment ignoramus also. ◊ Hand 2 = Anthony Checkley

Suffolk Court Files, vol. 32, docket 2706, p. 29, Massachusetts Supreme Judicial Court, Judicial Archives, Massachusetts State Archives. Boston, MA. January 7, 1693

Sworn Before the Grand Jury: Examination of William Procter
2nd of 2 dates. See No. 663 on Sept. 17, 1692

777. Court Record of the Trial of Mary Tyler

[Hand 1] {Jan^{εy} 7th} Mary Tyler, wife of hopestill Tyler of Andover, Blacksmith, being Indicted by the Jurors for o^ε Soveraigne Lord and Lady the King and Queen, upon their Oathes, by three Severall Indictments; That is to Say 1st

For that shee the Said Mary Tyler, wife of hopestill Tyler, of Andover in the County of Essex Blaksmith, about Seaven Yeares Since in the towne of Andover aforesaid, wickedly, malitiously and ffelloniously, a Covenant with the Devill ~~with the~~ did make, and Signed the Devills Booke, and promised to Serve the Devill, as long as shee Lived, and by the Devill was baptized; and renounced her former Baptisme, by which Diabolicall, And wicked Covenant with the Devill, shee the Said Mary Tyler is become a detestable witch, contrary to the peace of our Soveraigne Lord and Lady the King and Queen, their Crowne and dignity, and the Lawes in that case made, and Provided.

2dly For that shee the Said Mary Tyler, wife of Hopestill Tyler of Andover in the County of Essex Blaksmith, on, or about the Seventh day of Septem^r last in the Year 1692, and Divers others dayes And times, as well before, as after, certaine detes⟨ta⟩ble Arts called witchcrafts, and Sorceries, wickedly malitiously, and ffelloniously hath used, practised and Exercised, in the Towne of Andover aforesaid, upon, and against, one Ralph ffarnam Senio^ε of Andover aforesaid, by which wicked Arts, the Said Ralph ffarnam Senio^ε, the day and Yeare, aforesaid, and divers other dayes, and times, as we⟨ll⟩ before as after, was, and is, tortured, afflicted, consum⟨ed,⟩ wasted, pined, and Tormented contrary to the Peace of our Soveraigne Lord and Lady the King and Queen their Crowne and dignity, and the Lawes in that case made and Provided.

3dly For that shee the Said Mary Tyler, wife of Hopestill Tyler, of Andover, in the County of Essex Blaksmith, on or about, the Seaventh Day of Septemb⟨er⟩ last, in the Year 1692, and divers other dayes, and times, as well before, as after, certaine detestable arts, called witchcrafts, and Sorceries, wickedly, mali⟨ti⟩ously, and ffelloniously, hath used, practized, and exercised, in the Towne of Andover aforesaid, upon, and against, One Hannah Foster, wife of Ephraim Foster, of Andover aforesaid, by which wicked arts, the Said Hannah Foster, the day, and year aforesaid and divers other dayes, and times, as well before, as after, was, and is, tortured, afflicted, pined, wasted, consumed, and tormented, contrary to the Peace of our Soveraign Lord and Lady the King and Queen, their Crown and Dignity, & the lawes in that case made and provided.

January 9, 1693

The Jury Sworn
Nath: Howard ffore^ε
John Hall
James ffreind
Samuell Morgan
James Horner
Richd Gross
John Witt
Nathan^l Emerson
John Emery
Benay Tidcomb
John Platts
John Lampson

Upon the aforesaid Indictments, and each of them, the Said Mary Tyler, was then, and there, before the Justices of our Lord and Lady, the King and Queen aforesaid, arraigned and upon her arraignment, did then, and there, the day, and Year aforesaid plead to them, and each of them, Not Guilty, and put her Selfe, upon triall, by God, and her Countrey.
A Jury being called Nathaniel Howard – fforeman and Aͨordingly Sworne, no Exception made by the Prisoner, the Said Indictments, and each of them, being read, together with Evidences, and Examination⟨s⟩ and the Prisoners defence being heard; the Jury went out to agree on their verdict, who returning, ⟨did⟩ then, and there, in open Court deliver their verdict, That the Said Mary Tyler, was Not Guilty, of the ffellony by witchcraft, for which shee stood Indicted, in [Lost] [= and] by, the Said Indictments, and each of them.
        The Court Ordered, Mary Tyler aforesaid, to be discharged, paying her ffees.

Records of the Superior Court of Judicature (1692/3), pp. 12–13, Massachusetts Supreme Judicial Court, Judicial Archives, Massachusetts State Archives. Boston, MA.

Monday, January 9, 1693

Rebecca Johnson Cleared by Proclamation

Cleared by Proclamation: Indictment of Rebecca Johnson, for Afflicting Alice Booth (Returned Ignoramus)
2nd of 2 dates. See No. 773 on Jan. 7, 1693

Tuesday, January 10, 1693

Grand Juries of Mary Bridges Jr., Martha Emerson & Mercy Wardwell

Trials of Sarah Wardwell, Sarah Hawkes & Mercy Wardwell

Sworn Before the Grand Jury: Examination of Mary Bridges Jr.
2nd of 2 dates. See No. 516 on Aug. 25, 1692

778. Indictment of Martha Emerson, for Afflicting Mary Warren (Returned Ignoramus)†

January 10, 1693

[Hand 1] Province of the Massathutetts Bay in New England Essex } Anno RRs: & Regina Gulielmi & Maria Anglia &c Quarto Annoqʒ Dom 1692

The Juroᵉ for our Sovereigne Lord & Lady yᵉ King & Queen Presents ~~That~~ [Hand 2] **that Martha Emerson of Hauerhill in yᵉ County of Essex Married woman on yᵉ 23ᵈ of July 1692** [Hand 1] And Divers other Dayes and Times as well before as after Certaine Detestable Arts called Witchcrafts & Sorceries Wicked Mallishiously & ffelloniously hath vsed Practised & Exer⟨c⟩ised at & in the Towne of [Hand 2] **Salem** [Hand 1] in the County aforeˉsᵈ upon and against one [Hand 2] **Mary Warren of Salem Singlewoman** [Hand 1] By which Wicked Arts the said [Hand 2] **Mary Warren** [Hand 1] the Day & Year aforeˉsᵈ and Divers other Dayes & times as well before as after, was & is Tortured Afflicted Tormented Pined & wasted against the Peace of our Sovereigne Lord & Lady the King & Queen their Crowne and Dignity and the Lawes in that case made & Provided
[Hand 2] Mary Warren
~~Mary~~

[Reverse] Martha Emerson Aflicᵉ Mary Emerson
[Hand 3] Ignoramus
Robert: Payne foreman:

Notes: Hand 2 = Stephen Sewall

Suffolk Court Files, vol. 32, docket 2708, p. 31, Massachusetts Supreme Judicial Court, Judicial Archives, Massachusetts State Archives. Boston, MA.

Sworn Before the Grand Jury: Examination of Martha Emerson
2ⁿᵈ of 2 dates. See No. 432 on July 23, 1692

779. Indictment of Mercy Wardwell, for Covenanting†

[Hand 1] Prouince of yᵉ Massachusetts Bay in New England Essex ss } Annᵒ RˉRˉˢ & Reginæ Gulielmi & Mariæ Angliæ &c Quarto Anoqʒ Dom 1692

The Juᵉors for oʳ Souᵉ lord & Lady the King & Queen present That Mercy Wardwell daughteᵉ of Samuel Wardwell late of Andiuor in yᵉ County of Esssex oforesaid ~~Th~~ Sometime in this presant yeare 1692, Wikedly mallitiously & ffelloniously A Couenant with the Diuel Did make And Signed A paꝑ to the Diuill with A Red marke & Beleiued the Deuill & promised to Serue him & was Baptized by the Deiuill & vnto him Renounced hir formᵉ Baptizme By which Diabollicall Couenant With the Deuill by the Said Mercy Wardwell in forme aforsaid made She is become A detestable Witch Contrary to the peace of oᵉ Souᵉ lord & Lady the King & Queen Their Crowne & dignity & the Laws in that Case made & prouided.

January 10, 1693

[Reverse] Mercy Wardell for Couenanting with y^e Deuill
[Hand 2] Salem January 1692
[Hand 3] Billa u⟨e⟩ra
Robert: Payne foreman
[Hand 4?] ponet Se
[Hand 4] not Guilty
<u>14</u>
Salem Court of Oyer & Terminer Janu^⟨a⟩ 1692/3
N° 1
[Hand 1?] [4–5 words overstruck]

Notes: Hand 1 = Anthony Checkley; Hand 4 = Jonathan Elatson

Massachusetts Archives Collection, vol. 135, no. 101. Massachusetts State Archives. Boston, MA.

780. Court Record of the Trial of Sarah Wardwell

[Hand 1] {Janu^ey 10th All the Judges present Except Wait Winthrop who was not at any of y^e following Tryalls}
Sarah Wardwell of Andover in the County of Essex, being Indicted by the Jurors for o^ε Soveraigne Lord and Lady, the King and Queen, upon their oathes by two Severall Indictments.
That is to say; 1st
For that shee the Said Sarah Wardwell widow, about Six Yeares past, wickedly, mallitiously, and ffelloniously, a Covenant with, and Signed, a peece of paper to the Devill, and was Baptized, by the Devill, and gave her Self, Soule, and body to him, promised to be his Servant, by which diabolicall and wicked Covenant with the Devill, by her the Said Sarah Wardwell made, shee the Said Sarah Wardwell, is become a detestable witch, against the Peace of our Soveraigne Lord and Lady, the King and Queen, their Crowne, and Dignity, and the Lawes in that case made, and Provided.
2dly For that shee the said Sarah Wardwell widow, on, or about the first Day of Septemb^ε last, in the year 1692, aforesaid, and divers other dayes, and times, as well before, as after, certain detestable arts, called witchcrafts, and Sorceries, wickedly, mallitiously, and ffelloniously, hath used, practised and Exercised, in, upon, and against Martha Sprague, at, and in the towne of Salem, in the County of Essex aforesaid, by which Said wicked Arts, the Said Martha Sprague, the Day, and Year aforesaid, and divers other dayes, and times, as well before, as after, was, and is tortured, afflicted, and tormented, consumed, pined, and wasted, contrary to the Peace of our Souveraigne Lord and Lady, The King and Queen, their Crowne, and Dignity, and the Lawes, ~~and~~ in that case made, and Provided.

January 10, 1693

Jury Sworn
Nathan[l] Howard
John Hale
James ffreind
Samuel Morgan
John Kent
Richard Gross
John Witt
Nathan[l] Emerson
John Emery
Benayah Tidcomb
John Platts
John Lamson

Upon the aforesaid Indictments, and each of them, the said Sarah Wardwell, was then, and there, before the Justices of our Lord and Lady, the King and Queen, aforesaid, arraigned, and upon her arraignment, did then, and there, the day and year aforesaid, plead to them, and each of them, Not Guilty, and put her Selfe upon Triall, by God, and her Countrey. A Jury being called Nathan[ll] Howard fforeman and acordingly Sworne, no Exception made by the Prisoner, the said Indictements, and each of them, being read, together with Evidences, and Examination⟨s⟩ and the Prisoners defence being heard; the Jury went out to agree on their verdict, who returning did then, and there in open Court, deliver their verdict, that the said Sarah Wardwell was Guilty of covenanting with the Devill, for which she stood Indicted, in the first Indictment⟨s⟩, as also Guilty of the ffellony by witchcraft, for which she stood Indicted, in the second Indictment.

The Court Ordered the Keeper of the Goale to take care of the Prisoner, Acording to Law.

Notes: Although found guilty, Sarah Wardwell received a reprieve from Governor Phips. See No. 836.

Records of the Superior Court of Judicature (1692/3), pp. 14–15, Massachusetts Supreme Judicial Court, Judicial Archives, Massachusetts State Archives. Boston, MA.

781. Court Record of the Trial of Sarah Hawkes

[Hand 1] Sarah Hawkes of Andover in the County of Essex being Indicted, by the Jurors, for our Sovereigne Lord and Lady, the King and Queen, upon their Oathes, by Two Severall Indictments.
That is to Say; 1st
For that shee the said Sarah Hawkes, of Andover Single woman, Some time in the beginning of this present Yeare 1692, at, and in the towne of Andover aforesaid, wickedly, malitiously, and ffelloniously, a Covenant with the Devill did make, and Signed a Paper which he offered to her, and Promised to Serve the Devill, and gave to him her Soule and body, and afterwards about the latter end of July or beginning of August last was baptised by the Devill, and renounced her former christian Baptisme, by which diabolicall covenanting with the Devill, shee the Said Sarah Hawkes, is become a wicked, and detestable witch, against the peace of our Soveraign Lord and Lady, the King and Queen their Crown, and dignity, and the Lawes in that case made and Provided.
2[dly] For that shee, the said Sarah Hawkes, of Andover Single woman, On or about the first day of September last, A° 1692 certaine detestabl⟨e⟩ ⟨arts⟩ called witchcrafts, and Sorceries, wickedly, malitiously, and ffelloniously, hath used practized, and Exercised, in the Towne of Salem, in the County of Essex aforesaid, upon, and against Martha Sprague, by which wicked Arts, the Said Martha Sprague, was, and is tortured, afflicted, and tormented,

January 10, 1693

consumed, pined, and wasted, against the Peace of Our Soveraigne Lord and Lady, the King and Queen, their Crowne, and Dignity, and the Lawes, in that case made, and Provided.

Upon the aforesaid Indictements, and each of them the Said Sarah Hawkes, was then, and there, before the Justices of our Lord and Lady, the King and Queen aforesaid, arraigned, and upon her arraignment, did then, and there, the day, and year abovesaid, plead to them, and each of them, Not Guilty, and putt her Selfe upon Triall by God, and her countery.
A Jury being called Joseph Pike – fforeman and accordingly Sworne, no Exception made by the Prisoner, the said Indictements, and each of them, being read, together with Evidences, and Examinations, and the Prisoners defence being heard; the Jury went out to agree on their verdict, who returning, did then, and there, in Open Court, deliver their verdict That the said Sarah Hawkes was Not Guilty of the ffellony by witchcraft, for which she stood Indicted, in and by the said Indictements and each of them.

The Court Ordered Mary Hawkes aforesaid to be discharged, paying her ffees

Jury Sworn
Joseph Pike
Edward fflint
Eliazar Gyles
Joseph Li⟨tt⟩le
John Abby
Edmund Gale
Josiah Gage
Seth Storey
John Ordway
John Pickard
Edward Norris
William Becket

Records of the Superior Court of Judicature (1692/3), pp. 15–16, Massachusetts Supreme Judicial Court, Judicial Archives, Massachusetts State Archives. Boston, MA.

782. Court Record of the Trial of Mercy Wardwell

[Hand 1] Marcy Wardwell, daughter of Samuell Wardwell, of Andover, in the County of Essex, being Indicted by the Jurors, for oᵉ Soveraigne Lord & Lady, the King and Queen, upon their Oathes, by two Severall Indictments; That is to say: 1ˢᵗ
For that the said Marcy Wardwell, Daughter of Samuell Wardwell, of Andover, in the County aforesaid, some time in this present yeare 1692, wic⟨ked⟩ly, mallitiously, and ffelloniously, A Covenant wit⟨h⟩ the Devill did make, and Signed a paper to the Devill with a Red marke, and believed the Devill, and promised to serve him, and was baptized by the Devill, and unto him renounced her former Baptism, by which Diabolicall Covenant, with the Devill, by the said Marcy Wardwell, in forme aforesaid made, she is become, a detestable witch contrary to the Peace of our Soveraigne Lord and Lady, the King and Queen, their Crowne and Dignity, and the Lawes in that case made and Provided.
2ᵈˡʸ For that the said Marcy Wardwell, Daughter of Samuell Wardwell, of Andover in the County of Essex aforesaid, On, or about the month of Augᵉᵗ last past, in the yeare aforesaid, and divers other dayes, and times, as well before, as after, certaine detestable Arts, called witchcrafts, and Sorceries, wickedly, mallitiously, and ffelloniously, hath used, practized, and Exercised, upon, and against Timothy Swan, of Andover aforesaid, by which said wicked Arts, the said Timothy Swan, in the moneth of August afor^{e}said, and divers other dayes, and times, as well before, as after, was, {&} is tormented, afflicted, and tortured, consumed, wasted, and pined, contrary to the peac⟨e⟩ of our Soveraigne Lord and Lady, the King and Queen, their Crowne, and Dignity, and the Lawes, in that case made, and Provided.

Jury Sworn
Edward fflint
Thomas fflint
John Williams
Eliazer Gyles
Joseph Litle
John Abby
Edmund Gale
Seth Storey
John Ordway
John Pickard
Edward Norris
William Becket

Upon the aforesaid Indictements, and each of them, the said Marcy Wardwell, was then, and there, before the Justices of our Lord and the Lady, the King and Queen aforesaid, arraigned, and upon her arraignmen⟨t⟩ did then, and there, the day, and Yeare abovesaid, plead to them, and each of them, Not Guilty and put her Self upon Triall by God, and her Country.

A Jury being called Edward fflint fforeman and a͞cordingly sworne, no excep͞con being made by the Prisoner, the said Indictements, and each of them, being read, together with Evidences, and Examinations, and the Prisoners deffence being heard; the Jury went out to agree on their verdict, who returning, did then, and there, in open Court deliver the Same, That the said Marcy Wardwell, was Not Guilty of the ffellony by witchcraft, for which shee stood Indicted, in, and, by the said Indictements, and each of them.

The Court Ordered Marcy Wardwell, to be discharged, paying her fees

Records of the Superior Court of Judicature (1692/3), pp. 16–18, Massachusetts Supreme Judicial Court, Judicial Archives, Massachusetts State Archives. Boston, MA.

Wednesday, January 11, 1693

Grand Juries of Sarah Cole (of Lynn) & Mary Black

Trial of Elizabeth Johnson Jr.

Mary Black Cleared by Proclamation

783. Deposition of John Brown v. Sarah Cole (of Lynn)

[Hand 1] The Deposition of Jnᵒ Browne aged about twenty five yeares: This Deponant Testifieth & Saith that about the latter end of August Last 1692 being at the house of Jnᵒ Cole: Coming out of sᵈ house ^{Sarah Cole} hearing her husband talking with mee, she Broke out into these expressions, that all Church members were Devills & that her husband was going to bee a Devill too hee was then going to Joine with the Church; whervpon I sᵈ Browne Replyed to her she had often expressed her selfe very Badly & that if she did not suddenly amend & leave of such expressions against Church members, their was them that would take notice of it & she must answer for such speeches whervpon she was silent & looked stedfastly vpon mee & I was taken Ile [Hand 2] ^{in about a week} [Hand 1] presently as my evidence doth Declare

Owned before the Grand iury ~~upon the oath~~ by Jnᵒ Browne Jenᵉ 11ᵗʰ 1692/⟨3⟩ vpon the oath hee had taken

January 11, 1693   Jn° Cole Testifieth to the abovs^d ~~Attests~~ vpon the oath hee had taken.

[Hand 3] January 11th 1693

[Hand 1] Attests Robert Payne fforeman:

[Reverse] [Hand 2] the s^d J[Lost] [= John] Browne further sai⟨th⟩

That vpon the said John Browne being desired to adjust sum Damages Don by said Sarah Coles hogs had Don to Abraham Welman that is as he believes ~~about~~ about a fortnight aft^ε he haueing been ⟨I⟩ll as afores^d he desired an Indian puding to be made wch was don and ye flower and suet white and good when put into the pott but when Came out was red like a blud puding wch he belieues was don by Sarah Cole who had thretened him for medling wth the d⟨es⟩iding the damage saying he had better not to haue don⟨e⟩

[Hand 4] Jn° Brown Ju^ε

Notes: This and the following depositions against Sarah Cole of Lynn sworn before a grand jury on January 11, 1693, present a problem, since the only surviving indictment against her is dated January 31, 1693, at a court in Charlestown, in Middlesex County. See No. 826. Unless standard procedure was violated, there would have been an indictment on January 11 when these depositions were sworn before the grand jury. However, none survives. One possibility is that an indictment for January 11, returned with an ignoramus, is missing, and that the grand jury in a different county took up the case again later on other grounds. ◊ Hand 4 = Anthony Checkley

Suffolk Court Files, vol. 32, docket 2712, p. 49, Massachusetts Supreme Judicial Court, Judicial Archives, Massachusetts State Archives. Boston, MA.

784. Deposition of Abraham Wellman v. Sarah Cole (of Lynn)

[Hand 1] The Deposition of Abraham Welman ["W" written over "C"] Aged about 49 yeares: This Depo{na⟨n⟩t} Testifieth & saith, that I had a Cow which some told mee Sarah Cole Wife of Jn° Cole had a great desire to have & the s^d Cow was taken with such ffits though before she was ~~very~~ ^{as} Gentle a Cow as I would Desire to set paill vnder after this time when she see any person coming ~~to her~~ to milk her, she would run & let none come near her for about a week, when s^d Cole was brought vpon her examination that night & next morning, wee sent on of our children to milk s^d Cow, but she was wild as before, but after s^d Sarah Cole was sent from her own house to Cambridge when she was gone as wee thought to Reddin or ther about I sent one of my Children to milk her the Cow stood still & gave down her milk & did from that day till this ⟨d⟩ time

Abraham ["r" written over "b"] Welman owned the abovs^d before the Grand iury vpon the oath hee had taken

Jen^ε 11th 1692/3

[Hand 2] January 11th 1693 [Hand 1] Attests

Robert Payne foreman

[Reverse] [Hand 3] Abrā Wellman

Notes: Hand 3 = Anthony Checkley

Suffolk Court Files, vol. 32, docket 2712, p. 49, Massachusetts Supreme Judicial Court, Judicial Archives, Massachusetts State Archives. Boston, MA.

785. Deposition of Isaac Wellman v. Sarah Cole (of Lynn)

[Hand 1] The Deposition of Isaac Welman Aged forty five yeares, this Deponant Testifieth & Saith, that I have often heard the Wife of Jnº Cole of Linn, wish harm to her Husband, & one time being both at my house, having some words, sᵈ sarah Cole wished her Husband might Dye if ever hee came within Daniell Eattens Doore any more

Isaac Welman owned the abovsᵈ before the Grand iury
Jenᵉ 11ᵗʰ 1692/3 vpon the oath hee had taken
Robert Payne
foreman:

[Reverse] [Hand 2] Isā: Wellman

Notes: Hand 2 = Anthony Checkley

Suffolk Court Files, vol. 32, docket 2712, p. 49, Massachusetts Supreme Judicial Court, Judicial Archives, Massachusetts State Archives. Boston, MA.

Cleared by Proclamation: Examination of Mary Black
2ⁿᵈ of 2 dates. See No. 84 on April 22, 1692

786. Court Record of the Trial of Elizabeth Johnson Jr.

[Hand 1] {11ᵗʰ d⁽ᵉ⁾} Elisabeth Johnson Junioᵉ of Andover, in the County of Essex, Single Woman, being indicted by the Jurors for our Soveraigne Lord and Lady the King and Queen, upon their Oathes, by two Severall Indictements, That is to Say, 1ˢᵗ
For that shee the Said Elisabeth Johnson Junior of Andover Single Woman, about three yeares since, wickedly, ffelloniously, and malitiously, a Covenant with the Devill did make, and was baptized by the Devill, and Renounced her former Christian Baptisme, and God, and Christ, by which wicked, and Diabolicall Covenant, with the Devill, in manner, and forme aforesaid shee the said Elisabeth Johnson is become a detestable witch, against the Peace of Our Soveraigne Lord and Lady, the King and Queen their Crowne, and Dignity, and the Lawes in that case made, and Provided.
2ᵈˡʸ For that ^{shee} the said Elisabeth Johnson Junior of Andover in the County of Essex, Single woman on, or about the Elleventh Day of August, last ~~past~~ in this present Year 1692 aforesaid, and divers other dayes, and times, as well before, as after, certaine detestable Arts, called witchcrafts, and Sorceries, wickedly, malitiously, and ffelloniously, hath used, practiced, and Exercised, at, and in the Towne of Salem, in the County of Essex aforesaid, upon, and against, One Ann Putnam, of Salem, in the County of Essex, by which wicked Arts, the said Ann Putnam, the Day, and Year aforesaid, and divers other dayes, and times, as well before, as after, is Tortured, afflicted, tormented, consumed, Pined and wasted, against the Peace, of our Soveraigne Lord and Lady, the King and Queen, their Crowne, and Dignity, and the Law{e}s in that case made, & Provided.

Upon the aforesaid Indictments, and each of them, the said Elisabeth Johnson Junio$^{\varepsilon}$, was then, and there, before the Justices of our Lord and Lady the King and Queen aforesaid, arraigned, and upon her arraignment, did then, and there, the day, and Year abovesaid, plead to them, and each of them, Not Guilty, & put her self upon triall, by God, and her Country.

A Jury being called, Eliazer Gyles fforeman, and ācordingly sworne, no exception being made, by the Prisoner, the said Indictments, and each of them, being read, together with Evidences, and Examinations, and the Prisoners defence, being heard; the Jury went out to agree on their verdict, who returning, did then, and there, in Open Court, deliver their verdict, that the said Elisabeth Johnson Junior, was Guilty of covenanting with the Devill, for which shee stood indicted, in the first Indictment, as allso Guilty of the ffellony, by witchcraft, for which shee stood Indicted, in the Second Indictment.

The Court Ordered the Keeper of the Goale to take care of the prisoner ācording to law.

Jury Sworn
Eliazer Gyles
John Hall
Joseph Litle
John Abby
John Witt
Seth Story
John Ordway
John Emery
John Pickard
Benayah Tidcomb
Nathan^l Emerson
Edmund Gale

Notes: Although found guilty, Elizabeth Johnson Jr. received a reprieve from Governor Phips. See No. 836.

Records of the Superior Court of Judicature (1692/3), pp. 18–19, Massachusetts Supreme Judicial Court, Judicial Archives, Massachusetts State Archives. Boston, MA.

Thursday, January 12, 1693

Grand Juries of Sarah Bridges, Mary English, Philip English, & Thomas Farrar Sr.

Trials of Mary Bridges Sr., Mary Post, Hannah Post, Sarah Bridges, & Mary Osgood

Thomas Farrar Sr. Cleared by Proclamation

787. Indictment of Sarah Bridges, for Covenanting†

[Hand 1] Province of y^e Mattathusets Bay in New Eng^d Essex sc.

Anno $\overline{RRs}$ & Reginæ Gulielmi & Mariæ Nunc Angliæ &c quarto.Annoqʒ Domini. 1692.

The Jurors for Our Soueraign Lord & Lady y^e King & Queen doe p$^\varepsilon$sent That Sarah Bridges of Andover Singlewoman Sometime in y^e yeare of Our Lord ~~169(2)~~ One Thousand Six hundred Ninety One at Andover afores^d in y^e County aforesaid Wickedly feloniously and Malitiously a Couenant with y^e Evill Spirit y^e Deuill did Make & Signed to his Booke by Making A Red Marke Renouncing God and Christ & Gaue her Soul & body to ye Deuil and was Baptized by him by which Diabolicall Couenant ye Said ~~B~~ Sarah Bridges is become

a detestable Witch Contrary to yᵉ peace of Our Soueraign Lord & Lady yᵉ King & Queen &   January 12, 1693
yᵉ Laws in that Case made & provided
Witness.
her Owne Confession acknowledged before Authority

[Reverse] Sarah Bridges Indictmᵗ Couᵋ wᵗʰ yᵉ Deuill
Vide Confession
[Hand 2] Billa vera
Robert: Payne foreman:
[Hand 3] Ponet Se
[Hand 4?] Not Guilty
19

Notes: Hand 1 = Stephen Sewall; Hand 4 = Anthony Checkley

Massachusetts Archives Collection, vol. 135, no. 40. Massachusetts State Archives. Boston, MA.

788. Indictment of Sarah Bridges, for Afflicting Martha Sprague†

[Hand 1] Province of yᵉ   Anno R̄R̄s & Reginæ Gulielmi & Mariæ Nunc Angliæ
Mattachusets bay in New   &c. quarto Annoqȝ Domini One Thousand Six hundred
England Essex sc.   Ninety Two

The Jurors for Our Soueraign Lord & Lady yᵉ King & Queen pᵋsent That Sarah Bridges of
Andover in yᵉ County of Essex Singlewoman On ye 25ᵗʰ day of August in yᵉ yeare aforesᵈ in
yᵉ County aforesᵈ and diuers other Dayes and Times as well before as after Certain
detestable arts Caled Witchcrafts Wickedly Malitiously & feloniously hath vsed practiced &
Excercised at & in yᵉ Towne of Salem in yᵉ County aforesᵈ vpon & against One Martha
Sprague alias Tyler of Boxford in yᵉ County aforesᵈ by which Said Wicked Acts yᵉ Said
Martha Sprague alias Tyler ye day aforesᵈ & yeare aforesᵈ & diuers other Dayes & Times as
well before as after was & is Tortured aflicted pined Consumed & Tormented against ye
peace of Our Soueraign Lord & Lady yᵉ King & Queen thier Crowne & dignity & The
Lawes in that Case Made & prouided
Witness her owne Confession
Rose ffoster.

[Reverse] Sarah Bridges Aflicᵋ Martha Sprague
[Hand 2] Billa vera
Robert Payne foreman
[Hand 1?] Not Guilty

Notes: Hand 1 = Stephen Sewall

Massachusetts Archives Collection, vol. 135, no. 36. Massachusetts State Archives. Boston, MA.

January 12, 1693

789. Indictment of Mary English, for Afflicting Elizabeth Hubbard (Returned Ignoramus)†

[Hand 1] Essex in the Prouince of the Massachusetts Bay in New England ss//

Anno $\overline{RR}^s$ & Reginæ Gulielmi & Mariæ Angliæ &c^a Quarto Annoqȝ Domini 1692//

The Jurors for our Sou^ε Lord and Lady the King & Queen doe ꝑsent That ~~you~~ [Hand 2] **Mary English wife of Phillip English of Salem** [Hand 1] In the County of Essex [Hand 2] afors^d m^{ε}chant vpon the Twenty Second day of Aprill [Hand 1] In the Yeare aforesaid & diuers other days and times as well before as after Certaine detestable Arts Called Witchcraft & Sorceries Wickedly Mallitiously and felloniously hath used practised and Exercised At and [Hand 2] in the Towne of Salem in the County of Essex [Hand 1] Aforesaid in upon & against one [Hand 2] **Elizabeth Hobert of Salem** [Hand 1] Aforesaid [Hand 2] **Single Woman** [Hand 1] by which said Wicked Acts the said [Hand 2] **Eliz^a Hobert the day & yeare** [Hand 1] Aforesaid and diuers other days and times both before and after was and is Tortured Aflicted Consumed Pined Wasted and Tormented, & also for sundry other Acts of Witchcraft by the said [Hand 2] **Mary English** [Hand 1] Comitted and done before and Since that time against the Peace of our Sou^ε Lord and Lady the King and Queen theire Crowne & Dignity and the forme of the Stattute In that case made and Prouided,

[Reverse] [Hand 2] Ind: agst Mary English for bewitching Eliz^a Hobert
[Hand 3] Ignoramus
Robert: Payne foreman:

Notes: Hand 2 = Anthony Checkley

UNCAT MS, Vault 764, Series I, Beinecke Rare Book and Manuscript Library, Yale University, New Haven, CT.

790. Indictment of Philip English, for Afflicting Elizabeth Booth (Returned Ignoramus)†

[Hand 1] Essex in the Prouince of the Massachusett⟨s⟩ Bay in New England Ss//

Anno $\overline{RR}^s$ & Reginæ Gulielmi & Mariæ Angli⟨æ⟩ &c Quarto Annoqȝ Do$\overline{m}$ 1692

The Jurors for our Sou^ε Lord and Lady the King and Queen doe ꝑsent That [Hand 2] **Phillip English of Salem** [Hand 1] In the County of Essex [Hand 2] **merchant, vpon the Thirty first day of May** [Hand 1] In the Yeare aforesaid and diuers other days and times as well before as after Certaine detestable Arts called Witchcraft and Sorceries Wickedly Mallitiously and felloniously hath vsed ["v" written over "u"] practised and Exercised At and [Hand 2] in the Towne of Salem in the County of Essex [Hand 1] Aforesaid in upon and against one [Hand 2] **Elizabeth Booth of Salem** [Hand 1] aforesaid [Hand 2] **Single Woman** [Hand 1] by which said Wicked Acts the said [Hand 2] **Eliz^a Booth the day & yeare** [Hand 1] aforesaid and diuers other days and times ^{both} before and after was and is Tortured Aflicted Consumed Pined Wasted and Tormented, ~~and also for Sundry other Acts of Witchcraft by ye said~~ [Hand 2] ~~**Phillip English**~~ [Hand 1] ~~Comitted and done before and Since that time~~ Against ["A" written over "a"] the Peace of our Sou^ε Lord and Lady the

King and Queen theire Crowne and Dignity and the [Hand 2] ^{law} [Hand 1] ~~forme of the Stattute~~ In that case made and Prouided.

[Reverse] [Hand 2] Indic^t agst Phillip English for bewitching Eliz^a Booth
[Hand 3] Ignoramus
Robert: Payne foreman.

Notes: Hand 2 = Anthony Checkley

Thomas Madigan Collection, Manuscript & Archives, New York Public Library. New York, NY.

January 12, 1693

791. Indictment of Philip English, for Afflicting Mary Walcott (Returned Ignoramus)†

[Hand 1] Essex in the Prouince of the Massachusetts Bay in New England. ss//

Anno $\overline{RR}$^s & Reginæ Gulielmi & Mariæ Angliæ &^c Quarto: Annoqʒ Domini 1692.

The Jurors for o^ε Sou^ε Lord and Lady the King and Queen doe present that [Hand 2] **Phillip English of Salem** [Hand 1] In the County of Essex [Hand 2] **m^εchant vpon the Thirty first day of May** [Hand 1] In the year aforesaid and diuers other dayes and times as well before as after Certaine Detestable arts Called Witchcraft and forceries [= sorceries] Wickedly Mallistiously and felloniou⟨s⟩ly hath vsed practised and Exercised at and [Hand 2] **in the Towne of Salem in the County of Essex** [Hand 1] aforesaid in vpon and against one [Hand 2] **Mary Wallcott of Salem** [Hand 1] aforesaid [Hand 2] **Single Woman** [Hand 1] by Said wicked Acts the Said [Hand 2] **Mary Wallcott ye Day & yea^ε** [Hand 1] aforesaid and diuers other dayes and Times both before and after was and is Tortured afflicted Consumed Pined wasted & Tormented ~~and also for Sundry other Acts of witchcrafts by the said~~ [Hand 2] ~~**Phillip English**~~ [Hand 1] ~~Comitted and done before and Since that Time~~, against the Peace of o^ε Sou^ε Lord and Lady the King and Queen theire Crowne and dignity and the [Hand 2] ^{laws} [Hand 1] ~~forme of the~~ [Hand 2] {laws} [Hand 1] ~~Stattute~~ in that Case made and Prouided.

[Reverse] [Hand 2] Indictm^t agst Phillip English for bewitching Mary Wallcott
[Hand 3] Ignoramus
Robert: Payne foreman:

Notes: Hand 2 = Anthony Checkley; Hand 3 = Simon Willard

Thomas Madigan Collection, Manuscript & Archives, New York Public Library. New York, NY.

Sworn Before the Grand Jury: Testimony of William Beale v. Philip English
2nd of 2 dates. See No. 449 on Aug. 2, 1692

January 12, 1693

792. Deposition of Mercy Lewis v. Philip English, Mary English, Lydia Dustin, Elizabeth Johnson Jr., & Thomas Farrar Sr.

[Hand 1] 1692/3
Jan.12.
The Deposition of Mercy Lewis Aged ~~Eig~~ This Deponant Testifieth & Saith that Last night Philip English & his wife ^{came to mee} also ["also" written over "&"] Goodwife Dassten Eliz Johnson & old pharoh of Linn: s^d Mrs English vrged mee to set my hand to a Booke & told mee she would Aflict mee Dreadfully & kill mee if I did not, s^d also if I would but touch the Booke I should bee well, or else I should never, ⟨?⟩ s^d Mrs English s^d she might bring the Book now she thought ever one of them would bee Cleared, & now at this present time before the Grand iury s^d Philip English, his wife, & old pharoh, come into the Roome ⟨&⟩ or their shape & Stroke mee on the Brest.: & almost Choaked mee & s^d they ["they" written over "she"] would strangle mee if they Could

owned before the Gran iury vpon the
Oath she had taken Jen^ε 12th 1692/3
Attests Robert: Payne
Foreman:

Notes: The deposition appears to be directed primarily at the Englishes.

Salem Selections, Massachusetts Box, Essex Co., Manuscripts & Archives, New York Public Library. New York, NY.

793. Indictment of Thomas Farrar Sr., for Afflicting Ann Putnam Jr. (Returned Ignoramus)†

[Hand 1] Essex in the Prouince of the Massachusets Bay of New England } Anno $\overline{RR}$^s & Regina Gulielmi & Maria Angliæ &c Quarto Annoq҃ Domini: 1692

The Juriors for our Soueraigne Lord & Lady the King and Queen doe present that [Hand 2] **Thomas Pharoh** [ ] **of Linn** [Hand 1] In the County of Essex. [Hand 2] **husbandman y^e 18th of May** [Hand 1] In the yeare aforsaid and diuers other Dayes and Times as well before as after Certaine detestable Arts called witchcraft and Sorceries wickedly malitiously & feloniously hath vsed practised and Exersised at and in the Towne of [Hand 2] **Salem** [Hand 1] in the County of Essex aforsaid in and upon and against one [Hand 2] **Ann Putman of Salem Singlewoman** [Hand 1] by which Said wicked acts the Said [Hand 2] **Ann Putnam** [Hand 1] The day and yeare aforsaid and diuers other dayes & Times both before and after was and is tourtered afflicted Consumed wasted Pined and Tormented against the peace of our Soueraigne Lord & Lady the King & Queen their Crowne & Dignity and the law in that Case made & prouided
[Hand 2] Witnesses Ann Putnam
Elizabeth Hubbard.
Sarah Vibber

[Reverse] Thomas Pharoh Aflic^ε Ann Putnam
[Hand 3] Ignoramus

Robert Payne fo⟨re⟩man: January 12, 1693
[Hand 4] Cleared by proclamation paying fees

Notes: Hand 2 = Stephen Sewall

Suffolk Court Files, vol. 31, docket 2667, p. 149, Massachusetts Supreme Judicial Court, Judicial Archives, Massachusetts State Archives. Boston, MA.

794. Recognizance for Mary Bridges Jr. by John Bridges & John Osgood Sr.
See also: May 10, 1693.

[Hand 1] Memorandun
That on the Twelfth Day of January 1692 In the fourth year of the Reigne of o^ε Soveraigne
Lord and Lady William and Mary by the Grace of God ∧{of England &c} King and Queen
Defenders of the ffaith &c Personally appeared before William Stoughton Esq^ε Chief
Justice of their Maj^{ties} Province of the Massachusets Bay in New England Jno Bridges of
Andover in the County of Essex Blacksmith And Jno Osgood of the same Towne
Husbandman And acknowledged them selues to be Joyntly and severally Indebted unto o^ε
Said Soveraigne Lord and Lady and the Surviver of them Their Heires and Successors in the
su͞me of One hundred pounds to be leuied on their or either of their Lands and Tenem^{ts}
Goods and Chatles for the use of ~~the~~ our said Soverainge Lord and Lady the King and
Queen or Survivor of them ~~th~~ On Condition that Mary Bridges haueing Stood Comitted for
Suspition of Witchcraft shall make her personall appearance Before the Justices of o^ε s^d Lord
and Lady the King and Queen at the next Court of Assizes and Gen^{ll} Goal Delivery ∧{to be}
held for the County of Essex Then & there to answer to all such matters and things as shall
in their Maj^{ties} Behalfe be aledged against her and to doe and receiue that wch by the said
Court shall be then and there injoyned her and thence not to depart without lycence
                                        attest
                                                    Jon^a Elatson Cler^ε

[Reverse] [Hand 2] Recognizance of
John Bridges
        &   ⎫   for Mary Bridges
John Osgood   ⎬
may: 10^d Apears   ⎭

Notes: Mary Bridges Jr. had been free on a previous recognizance (see No. 695), and this recognizance suggests that rather than try her on January 12 she was released pending further disposition of her case. She was about thirteen years old. Her mother, Mary Bridges Sr., was tried and found not guilty on this day. See No. 796. Mary Bridges Jr. was found not guilty, May 10, 1693. See No. 849. ◊ Hand 1 = Jonathan Elatson

Massachusetts Archives Collection, vol. 135, no. 103. Massachusetts State Archives. Boston, MA.

January 12, 1693   **795. Recognizance for Eunice Frye by John Osgood Sr. & James Frye**
See also: May 10, 1693.

[Hand 1] Memorandum
That on y^e Twelfth day of Jan^ery 1692 in the fourth year of the Reigne of our Sovereigne
Lord & Lady William & Mary by the Grace of God of England &c King & Queen
Defenders of the faith &c Personally appeared before William Stoughton Esqr cheife Justice
of their Maj^ies Province of the Massachusets bay in New England John Osgood of Andiver
in the County of Essex Husbandman and ~~John~~ {James} Fry of the same Towne and
acknowledged themselves to be joyntly & Severally indebted unto our s̄d Sovereigne Lord &
Lady & the Surviver of them their Heires & Successors in the Sum of One Hundred Pounds
to be levied on their or either of their lands and Tennem^ts goods & Chattles for the use of
our s̄d Sovereigne Lord & Lady the King & Queen or Surviver of them On Condition that
Eunice Fry the wife of Jno Fry of Andivor haveing stood committed for suspition of
Witchcraft shall make her personall appearance before the Justices of our s̄d Lord & Lady
the King & Queen at the next Court of Assizes & Generall Goal Delivery to be holden for
the County of Essex then & there to answer to all such matters and things as shall in their
Maj^ies behalfe be alledged against her and to doe & receive that which by the s̄d Court shall
be then & there injoyned her & thence not to departe without licence.

                                                    attest
                                                                    Jon^a Elatson Cler̄

[Reverse] [Hand 2] John Osgood
              &   ⎫
James ffry   ⎬   for Eunice ffry the wife of John ffry of Andover
Apeared may the 10th 1692   ⎭

Notes: As in all the cases tried in May, Frye was not convicted. See No. 848.

Massachusetts Archives Collection, vol. 135, no. 102. Massachusetts State Archives. Boston, MA.

796. Court Record of the Trial of Mary Bridges Sr.

[Hand 1] {12^th d^⟨e⟩} Mary Bridges wife of John Bridges, of Andover in the County of Essex
Blaksmith, being Indi⟨c⟩ted, by the Jurors for our Soveraigne Lord and Lady the King, and
Queen, upon their Oathes, by two severall Indictments; That is to say 1st
For that shee the said Mary Bridges, wife of J⟨ohn⟩ Bridges, of Andover, in the County of
Ess⟨ex⟩, Blaksmith, Sometime in the Year 1691, malitiously, wickedly, and ffelloniously,
with the Devill, a Covenant did make, and Signed the Devills booke, and promised, and
Covenanted, to worship him, and Severall times, hath worshipped the Devill, and
ffrequented, witch meetings, by which Diabolicall Covenant, made by the said Mary
Bridges, with the Devill, shee the said Mary Bridges, is become a wicked, and detestable
witch, contrary to the Peace, of our Soveraigne Lord and Lady the King and Queen, their
Crowne, and Dignity, and the Lawes, in that case made, and Provided.
2dly For that shee, the Mary Bridges, wife of John Bridges, of Andover, in the County of
Essex, Blaksmith, on, or about, the 28th day of July last, in the year 1692 aforesaid, and
divers other dayes, and times, as well before, as after; certaine, detestable arts, called witch

crafts, and Sorceries, wickedly, malitiously, and felloniously, hath used, practized, and
Exercised, at, and in the town of Andover, in the County of Essex aforesaid, upon, and
against, One Timothy Swan, of Andover, by which Said wicked Arts, the said Timothy
Swan aforesaid, the Day, and Year aforesaid, and Severall other dayes, and times, as well
before, as after, was, and is, Tortured, afflicted, tormented, consumed, pined, and wasted,
contrary to the Peace, of our Soveraigne Lord and Lady the King and Queen, their Crowne,
and dignity, and the Lawes in that case made, and Provided.

January 12, 1693

Upon the aforesaid Indictments, and each of them, the {s^d}
Mary Bridges, was then, and there, before the Justices, of Our
Lord, and Lady the King & Queen aforesaid, arraigned, & upon
her arraignmen⟨t⟩ did then, & there, the day, & Year aforesaid,
plead to them, and each of them, Not Guilty, and put her selfe
upon Triall by God, and her Country.
A Jury being called Benayah Tidcomb fforeman and a̅cordingly
sworne, no exception being made, by the Prisoner, the said
Indictments, and each of them being read, together with
Evidences, and Examinations, and the Prisoners defence, being
heard; the Jury went out, to agree on their verdict, who returning,
did then, and there, in open Court, deliver the⟨ir⟩ verdict, that
the Said Mary Bridges, was Not Guilty of the ffellony, by
witchcraft, for which she stood Indicted, in, and by, the Said
Indictm^{ts}, and each of them.
The Court Ordered the said Mary Bridges, to be
discharged, paying her ffees

Jury Sworn
⟨Ben⟩ayah Tidcomb
⟨E⟩liazer Gyles
⟨J⟩ohn ⟨W⟩itt
Joseph Litle
John Prickard
Edmund Gale⟨?⟩
John Emery
John Ordway
John Abby
Seth Story
John Hall
Nathaniell Emerson

Records of the Superior Court of Judicature (1692/3), pp. 19–21, Massachusetts Supreme Judicial Court, Judicial Archives, Massachusetts State Archives. Boston, MA.

797. Court Record of the Trial of Mary Post

[Hand 1] Mary Post of Rowley, in the County of Essex, Single woman, being Indicted, by
the Jurors, fo⟨r⟩ our Soveraigne Lord and Lady, the King and Queen, upon their Oathes, by
two severall Indictments, That is to say; 1st
For that shee the Said Mary Post, of Rowley, in the County of Essex, Single woman, about
three yeares agoe, In the Towne of Rowley aforesaid, wickedly, malitiously, and ffelloniously,
a Covenan⟨t⟩ with the Devill, did make, and Signed the devil⟨l⟩s Booke, and was baptized, by
the Devill, and renoun⟨ced⟩ her former Christian Baptisme, by which Diabolicall Covenant,
with the Devill made, she the Said Mary Post, is become a detestable witch, contrary to the
Peace, of Our Soveraigne Lord and Lady, the King, and Queen, their Crowne, and dign⟨i⟩ty,
and the Lawes, in that case made, & Provided
2dly For that sh⟨ee⟩ the Said Mary Post, of Rowley, Single woman, Some time, in the month
of July las⟨t⟩ in the yeare 1692 aforesaid, and divers other dayes, an⟨d⟩ times, as well before, as
after, certain detestable Art⟨s⟩ called witchcrafts, and Sorceries, wickedly, malitious⟨ly⟩ and
ffelloniously, hath used; practized; and Exercised, at and in the Towne of Andover, in the
County of Esse⟨x⟩ aforesaid, upon, and against, One Timothy Sw⟨an⟩ of Andover aforesaid,
by which Said wicked Arts, the Said Timothy Swan, the day and Year aforesaid and divers

other dayes, and times, as well before, as after, was, and is, t⟨or⟩tured, afflicted, tormented, consumed, Pined, and wasted, against the Peace of Our Soveraigne Lord and Lady; the King and Queen, their C⟨ro⟩wne, and Dignity, and against the Lawes, in that case made, and Provided.

Upon the aforesaid Indictements, and each of them the Said Mary Post, was then, and there, before the Justices, of our Lord and Lady, the King, and Queen aforesaid, arraigned, and upon her arraignment, did then, and there, the day, and Year, aforesd plead to them, and each of them, Not Guilty, and put her Self, upon triall by God, and her Country.

A Jury being called Benayah Tidcomb fforeman, and a̅cordingly sworne, no Exeption being made, by the Prisoner, the said Indictments, and each of them, being read, together with Evidences, and Examinations, and the Prisoners defence, being heard; the Jury went out, to agree on their verdict, who returning, did then, and there, in open Court, deliver their verdict, that the Said Mary Post was Guilty of Covenanting with the Devill, for which shee stood Indicted, in the first Indictment, as also Guilty of the ffellony by witchcraft, for which shee stood Indicted, in the Second Indictement.

The Court Ordered, the Keeper of the Goale, to take care of the Prisoner a̅cording to Law.

Jury Sworn
Benayah Tidcomb
John Witt
Joseph Litle
John Pickard
Edmund Gale
John Emerson
John Ordway
John Abby
Seth Story
John Hall
Nathan[l] Emerson
Eleazer Gyles

Notes: Although found guilty, Mary Post received a reprieve from Governor Phips. See No. 836.

Records of the Superior Court of Judicature (1692/3), pp. 19–21, Massachusetts Supreme Judicial Court, Judicial Archives, Massachusetts State Archives. Boston, MA.

798. Court Record of the Trial of Hannah Post

[Hand 1] Hanna̅h Post, of Boxford, in the County of Essex, being Indicted, by the Jurors, for our Soveraigne Lord, and Lady the King and Queen, ~~by~~ upon their Oathes, by two Severall Indictments; That is to Say; 1st
For that shee the ⟨Sai⟩d h⟨anna⟩h [1 word illegible] [*SWP* = Post], of Box⟨f⟩[Lost] [*SWP* = Boxford in] the County of Essex aforesaid, some time in the m[Lost] [= month] of July, or August last, in the Year 1692, aforesaid, [Lost] [*SWP* = at] the towne of Boxford, in the County of Essex afo⟨re⟩said, ⟨w⟩ickedly, malitiously, and ffelloniously, a ⟨Co⟩venant, with the Devill, did make, and Signed [Lost] [*SWP* = the] Devills booke, with her blood, and was baptized by t⟨he⟩ devill, by ⟨w⟩hich wicked diaboliacll Covenant, with the Devill made, shee the Said hannah Pos⟨t⟩ is become, a detestable witch, against the Pea⟨ce⟩ of our Soveraigne Lord, and Lady, the King and Queen, their Crowne, and Dignity, and the lawes, in that case, made, and Provided. 2dly For that she the Said hannah Post, of Boxf⟨ord⟩ Single woman, in, and upon the 23d Day of August last in the Year of our Lord 1692, and divers othe⟨r⟩ dayes, and times, as well before, as after, certain detestable Arts, called witchcrafts, and Sorceries, wickedly, malitiously, and ffelloniously, hath used, practized, and Exercised, at, and in the towne of Boxford, in the County of Essex aforesaid, upo⟨n⟩ and

against, One Martha Sprague, of Boxford, aforesaid, now wife of [ ] by which Said wicked   January 12, 1693
arts, the Said Martha Spragu⟨e⟩ alias ~~Tyler~~ Martha Tyler, was, and is tortured, afflicted,
consumed, wasted, pined, and tormented against the Peace, of Our Soveraigne Lord and
Lady, the King and Queen, their Crowne, and dignity, and the Lawes, in that case made,
and Provided.

<u>Jury Sworn</u>	Upon the aforesaid Indictments, and Each of them the said hannah Post, was then, and there, before the Justices, of our Lord and Lady,
Benayah Tidcomb	the King and Queen aforesaid; arraigned, and upon her
John Witt	arraignm⟨ent⟩ did then, and there, the day, and Year aforesaid, plead
Joseph Litle	to them, and each of them, Not Guilty a⟨nd⟩ put her Self upon triall
John Pickard	by God, and her c⟨ou⟩nt⟨ry⟩.
Edmund Gale	A Jury being called Benayah Tidcomb fforeman and A̅cordingly
John Emerson	Sworne, no, Exception, being made by the Prisoner, the Said
John Ordway	Indictments, and each of them being read, together with Evidences,
John Abby	and examinations, and the Prisoners defence, being heard; the Jury
Seth Story	went out to agree on their verdict, who returning, did then, And
John Hall	there, the day, and year abovesaid, in open Court deliver their
Nathanl Emerson	verdict, that the Said Hannah Post was Not Guilty of the ffellony by
Eleazer Gyles	witchcraft, in, and by the Said Indictments, and each of them

The Court Ordered, Hannah Post aforesaid; to be
discharged, paying her fees.

Records of the Superior Court of Judicature (1692/3), pp. 19–21, Massachusetts Supreme Judicial Court, Judicial Archives, Massachusetts State Archives. Boston, MA.

799. Court Record of the Trial of Sarah Bridges

[Hand 1] Sarah Bridges of Andover, in the County of Essex, Single woman, being Indicted
by the Jurors for oᵉ Souveraigne Lord and Lady, the King and Queen, upon their Oathes, by
two severall Indictements; That is to Say; 1ˢᵗ
For that shee the Said Sarah Bridges, of Andover, Singlewoman, sometime in the Year of
our Lord, 1691, at Andover aforesaid, in the County aforesai⟨d⟩, wickedly ffelloniously, and
malitiously, a Covenant, with the Evill Spirit the Devill did make, and Signed to his booke,
by making a red mark, renouncing God, and Christ, and gave her soule, and body, to the
Devill, and was baptize⟨d⟩ by him, by which diabolicall Covenant, the Said Sarah Bridges, is
become a detestable witch, contrary to the peace, of our ~~Lord~~ Soveraigne Lord and Lady, the
King and Queen, their Crowne, and dignity, and the Lawes, in that case made, and Provided
[1 word illegible] [*SWP* = 2'dly] F⟨o⟩r that shee the Said [1 word illegible] [*SWP* = Sarah]
Bridges, ⟨of⟩ [1 word illegible] [*SWP* = Andover] in the County of Essex, Singlewoman, on
the [2 words illegible] [*SWP* = 25'th Day] of August, in the year of our Lord 1692, in t⟨he⟩
[1 word illegible]ty [*SWP* = County] afo⟨re⟩said, and divers other dayes, & times, as [1 word
illegible] [*SWP* = well] before, as after, cert⟨ai⟩n detestab⟨le⟩ arts, called wi⟨tch⟩crafts,
~~and Sorceries~~ wickedly malitiously [1 word illegible] [*SWP* = and] ffelloniously, hath ["hath
"written over "had"] ⟨us⟩ed, practised, and Exercis⟨ed⟩, at, and in the towne of Salem, in the
Coun⟨ty⟩ af⟨ore⟩said, upon ⟨and⟩ against, one ["one" written over "and"] Martha Sp⟨ra⟩gue
⟨alia⟩s Tyler, of Boxford in the County aforesaid, by which Said wicked arts, the Sa⟨id⟩

January 12, 1693

Martha Sprague alias Tyler, the day and [1 word illegible] [*SWP* = year] afor⟨e⟩said, and diverse other dayes, and times, as well before, as after, was, and is tortured, affl⟨i⟩cted pined, consumed, and tormented, against the peace of our Soveraigne Lord and Lady, the King and Queen, their Crowne, and dignity, and the Lawes, in that case made, and Provided.

Jury Sworn

Benayah Tidcomb
John Witt
Joseph Litle
John Pickard
Ed⟨m⟩und Gale
John Emerson
John Ordway
John Abby
Seth Story
John Hall
Nathan[l] Emerson
Eliaz⟨a⟩r Gyles

Upon the aforesaid Indictments, and each of th⟨em⟩ the Said Sarah Bridges, was then, and there, before the Justices of our Lord and Lady, the King and Quee⟨n⟩ aforesaid, arraigned, and upon her arraignment, s⟨hee⟩ did then, and there, the day, and Year abovesaid, plead to them, and each of them Not Guilty, and put her Self upon triall by God, and her Country.

A Jury being called Benayah Tidcomb – fforeman, and a̅cordingly Sworne, no exeption, being made by [1 word illegible] [*SWP* = the] Prisoner, the Said Indictments, and each of them, being read, together with Evidences, and Examinac̅⟨ons⟩, and the Prisoners defence being heard; the Jury went out, to agree on their verdict; who returning did then, and there, in open Court deliver their verdi⟨ct⟩, that the Said Sarah Bridges was not Guilty, of [1 word illegible] [*SWP* = the] fellony, by witchcraft, for which shee Stood Indi⟨cted⟩, in, and by the Said Indictments, and each of them.

The Court Ordered Sara⟨h⟩ Bridges aforesaid, to be dis⟨char⟩ged, paying her ffees.

Records of the Superior Court of Judicature (1692/3), pp. 24–25, Massachusetts Supreme Judicial Court, Judicial Archives, Massachusetts State Archives. Boston, MA.

800. Court Record of the Trial of Mary Osgood

[Hand 1] Mary Osgood wife of Cap⟨n⟩ John Osgood of Andover, in the County of Essex, being Indicted by the Jurors, for our soveraigne Lord and Lady, the King and Queen, upon their Oathes, by two severall Indictments, For that is to say 1st

For that shee, the Said Mary Osgood, wife of Cap[n] John Osgood, of Andover, in the County of Essex, about Ell⟨even⟩ Yeares agoe, in the Towne of Andover aforesaid, wic⟨ke⟩dly, malitiously, and ffelloniously, a Co⟨ve⟩nant with the Devill did make, and Signed the Devills Booke and took the Devill to be her God, and Consented to serve him and worship him; and was baptized by the Devill, and renounced her former Christian baptism, and promised to be the Devills, both body, and Soule, for Ever, and to serve him, by which diabolicall Covenant, by her made, with the Divell, shee, the said Mary Osgood, is become a detestable witch, against the Peace, of our Soveraign Lord and Lady, the King and Queen their Crowne, and Dignity, and the Lawes, in that case made, and Provided.

2[dly] For that shee, the Said Mary Osgood, wife of Cap[n] John Osgood, of Andover, in the County of Essex aforesaid, sometime about the month of August, or September last, in the Yeare of our Lord 1692, and divers other dayes and times, as well before, as after, Certain detestable arts, called witchcrafts, and sorceries, wickedly, malitiously, and ffelloniously, hath used, practized, and Exercised, at, and in, the town of Boxford, in the County of Essex aforesaid, upon, and against, One Martha Sprague, alias Tyler, by which wicked arts, the Said Martha Sprague, alias Tyler, the day, and year aforesaid, and diverse other dayes, and times, as well before, as after, is Tortured, afflicted, torment⟨ed⟩, ⟨con⟩sumed, Pined, and

January 13, 1693

wasted, [1 word illegible] [*SWP* = ag'st] the P⟨eace⟩ of our soveraigne Lord and Lady, the Ki[Lost] [= King] and Queen, their Crowne, and Dignity, and [Lost] [= the] Lawes, in that case made, and Provided.

<u>Jury Sworn</u>	upon the aforesaid Indictments, and each of the⟨m⟩, the said Mary Osgood, ~~wife~~ was then, and there, before the J⟨u⟩sti⟨ce⟩s, of our Lord
Nathaniel Howard	and Lady, the King and Que⟨en⟩ aforesaid, arraigned, and upon her
James ffreind	arraignment, sh⟨ee⟩ did then, and there, the day and Year abovesaid,
Samuel Morgan	plead to them, and each of them Not Guilty, and put her Selfe
John Kent	up⟨on⟩ Triall, by G⟨o⟩d, and her Country.
Richard Gross	A Jury being called Nathaniel Howard fforeman, and A̅cordingly
John Plats	Sworne, no Excep̅c̅o̅n̅ being made, by the Prisoner, the Said
John Lamson	Indictments, and each of the⟨m⟩ being read read, together with
Edward fflint	Evidences, and Examinations, and the Prisoners defence being
William Curtis	heard; the Jury went out to agree on their verdict, wh⟨o⟩ returning,
Josiah Gage	did then, and there, in open Court, deliver th⟨er⟩e verdict, that the
J [ ] Neal	Said Mary Osgood, was Not Guilty of the ffellony of witchcraft,
ffrancis Ellis	f⟨or⟩ which shee stood Indicted in, and by the Said Indictments,
	⟨a⟩nd each of them.

The Court Ordered, ~~the~~ Mary Osgood aforesaid, to be discharged, paying her ffees.

Records of the Superior Court of Judicature (1692/3), pp. 26–27, Massachusetts Supreme Judicial Court, Judicial Archives, Massachusetts State Archives. Boston, MA.

Friday, January 13, 1693

Grand Juries of Mary Barker, William Barker Jr., William Barker Sr., Hannah Bromage, Richard Carrier, Sarah Cloyce, Edward Farrington, Elizabeth Hart, Stephen Johnson, & Mary Lacey Jr.

Trial of Mary Lacey Jr.

801. Indictment of Mary Barker, for Afflicting Rose Foster†

See also: May 10, 1693.

[Hand 1] Essex in the Prouince of the Massachusetts Bay in New England ss/	Anno R̅R̅ˢ & Reginæ Gulielmi & Mariæ Angliæ &cᵃ Quarto Annoqȝ Domini 1692//

The Jurors for our Souᵉ Lord and Lady the King & Queen doe ꝑsent That [Hand 2] **Mary Barker of Anduor** [Hand 1] In the County of Essex [Hand 2] **On or about the 29ᵗʰ day of August last** ~~1692~~ [Hand 1] In the Yeare aforesaid and diuers other days and times as well before as after Certaine detestable Arts Called Witchcraft and Sorceries Wickedly Mallitiously and felloniously hath used practised and Exercised At and [Hand 2] **in the Towne of Andiuoᵉ in the County of Essex** [Hand 1] aforesaid in upon and against one

January 13, 1693   [Hand 2] **Rose ffoster of** [   ] [Hand 1] aforesaid [   ] by which said Wicked Acts the said [Hand 2] **Rose ffoster the day & yeare** [Hand 1] aforesaid & diuer⟨s⟩ other days and times both before and after was and is Tortured Aflicted Consumed Pined Wasted and Tormented, ~~and also for Sundry other Acts of Witchcraft by the said~~ [   ] ~~Comitted and done before and Since that time~~ Against ["A" written over "a"] the Peace of our Sou͛ Lord and Lady the King and Queen theire Crowne and Dignity and the forme of the Stattute In that case made & Prouided.

[Reverse] [Hand 2] Mary Barker: bewitching Rose ffoster
[Hand 3] Billa uera
foreman:
[Hand 2?] ponet se
[Hand 4] Not Guilty

Notes: The indictment was probably prepared in January 1693, but the case did not come to trial until May 10, 1693. See No. 850. ◊ Hand 2 = Anthony Checkley

Suffolk Court Files, vol. 32, docket 2678, p. 9, Massachusetts Supreme Judicial Court, Judicial Archives, Massachusetts State Archives. Boston, MA.

802. Indictment of Mary Barker, for Afflicting Abigail Martin†

See also: May 10, 1693.

[Hand 1] Essex in New England   } Annoq̃ RRˢ & Reginæ Gulielmi & Mariæ Angliæ &c
ss/   } quarto Anno Domini 1692//

The Juriors for our Soueraigne Lord & Lady the King & Queen doe present That [Hand 2] **Mary Barker of Andiuor in the County of Essex aforesaid** [ ] **On or about the 29ᵗʰ Day of August last In the yeare 1692 aforsaid** [Hand 1] and diuers other days and times both before and after, Certaine detestable Arts called Witchcraft & Sorceries Wickedly felloniously & Mallitiously hath used practised and Exercised in & upon the Body of [Hand 2] **Abigaill Martin of Andiuor** ⟨?⟩ [Hand 1] at and within the Township of [Hand 2] **Andiuor** [Hand 1] aforesaid, by which said Wicked Acts the said [Hand 2] **Abigaill Martin** [Hand 1] the day [Hand 2] **aforsaid** [Hand 1] in the yeare aforesaid And at diuers other days and times as well before as After was and is Tortured aflicted and Tormented. [Hand 2] ⟨A⟩nd ⟨Injurd⟩ ["⟨A⟩nd ⟨Injurd⟩" written over "and thereby"] [Hand 1] consumed pined and wasted, Against yᵉ peace of our Soueraigne Lord and Lady King and Queen theire Crowne and dignity and the Statute of the first of King James ~~in~~ the first in that Case made and prouided

[Reverse] [Hand 2] Mary Barker for bewitching Abigaill Martin
[Hand 3] Billa uera
Robert Payne foreman:
[Hand 2?] ponet se
[Hand 4] Not Guilty

Notes: The true bill was returned in January 1693, but Mary Barker was not tried until May 10, 1693. See No. 850. ◊ Hand 2 = Anthony Checkley

Suffolk Court Files, vol. 32, docket 2670, p. 10, Massachusetts Supreme Judicial Court, Judicial Archives, Massachusetts State   January 13, 1693
Archives. Boston, MA.

803. Indictment of William Barker Jr., for Covenanting†

See also: May 10, 1693.

[Hand 1] Prouince of the Massachusetts Bay in New England Essex ss } Anº R̄R̄s & Reginæ Gulielmi & Mariæ Angliæ &c Quarto Anoqʒ Dom̄ 1692

The Juᵉors for oᵉ Souᵉ lord & Lady the King & Queen pᵉsent That William Barker Junioᵉ of Anduoᵉ in the County of Essex aforsaid Sometime in the moneth of August last in the yeare 1692 aforsd Att or in the Towneship of Andivoᵉ in the County of Essex aforsd Wickedly mallitiously & ffelloniously A Couenant with⟨ʔ⟩ the Deuill did make & Signed the Deuills Booke and by the Deuill was Baptized & before him Renounced his formᵉ Baptizme & promised to be the Deuills for euer & euer By which wicked & Diabollicall Couenant the Said William Barker is become A Detestable Witch Against the peace of oᵉ Souᵉ lord & Lady the King & Queen their Crowne & dignity And the laws in that Case made & prouided.

[Reverse] William Barker Junᵉ for Couenanting wᵗʰ yᵉ Deuill
[Hand 2] Billa vera
Robert. Payne foreman:
[Hand 1?] ponet Se
~~fled~~
[Hand 3] Not Guilty
Court at Ipwich
Ipswich 2ᵈ Tuesday May 1693

Notes: This indictment originated in January 1693 when Robert Payne was grand jury foreman. William Barker Jr. appeared in court May 9 to face two indictments, but the case was not tried till the following day. See No. 851. The "2" on the verso means the second Tuesday, which was May 9, 1693. ◊ Hand 1 = Anthony Checkley

Suffolk Court Files, vol. 32, docket 2761, p. 102, Massachusetts Supreme Judicial Court, Judicial Archives, Massachusetts State Archives. Boston, MA.

804. Indictment of William Barker Jr., for Afflicting Martha Sprague†

See also: May 10, 1693.

[Hand 1] Province of yᵉ Massathutetts Bay in New England Essex } Anno RRs & Reginæ Gulielmi & Mariæ. Angliæ &ᶜ Quarto Annoqʒ Dom̄: 1692

The Juroᵉ for our Sovereigne Lord & Lady the King & Queen Presents That [Hand 2] **William Barker Junioᵉ of Andiuoᵉ in the County of Essex aforesaid Sometime in the moneth of August last in the Yeare 1692 aforesaid** [Hand 1] And Divers other Dayes & times as well before as after Certaine Destestable Arts called Witchcrafts & Sorceries: Wickedly Mallishiously & ffelloniously hath vsed Practised & Exercised at &: in the Towne

January 13, 1693 of [Hand 2] **Salem** [Hand 1] in the County of Essex aforesaid upon and against one [Hand 2] **Martha Sprague Allias Martha Tyler** [Hand 1] by which Wicked Artes the Said [Hand 2] **Martha Sprague Alli** [= alias] **Tyler** [Hand 1] the Day and Year aforesaid and Divers other Dayes & times as well before as after was & is Tourtered Afflicted Tormented Pined & wasted against yᵉ Peace of our Sovereigne Lord & Lady the King & Queen their Crowne & Dignity and the Lawes in that Case made & Provided./

[Reverse] [Hand 2] William Barker Junioᵋ for bewitching Martha Sprague
[Hand 3] Billa vera
Robert: Payne foreman:
[Hand 2?] ponet Se
[Hand 4] Not Guilty

Notes: Hand 2 = Anthony Checkley

Suffolk Court Files, vol. 32, docket 2761, p. 103, Massachusetts Supreme Judicial Court, Judicial Archives, Massachusetts State Archives. Boston, MA.

805. Indictment of William Barker Sr., for Covenanting‡

[Hand 1] Prouince of the Massachusetts Bay Essex In New England ss } Anno R̄R̄s & Reginæ Gulielmi & Mariæ Angliæ &c Quaᵋto Anoqȝ Dom̄ 1692

The Juroᵋs for our Souᵋ lord & lady the King & Queen pᵋsent That William Barker ^{senior} of Andiu⟨o⟩ᵋ In the County of Essex afor̄sd Husbandman About Three years past in the Towneship of Andiuoᵋ afor̄sd Wickedly mallitiously & ffelloniously A Couenant with the Deuill did make, And did Signe the Deuills Booke with Blood, & gaue himselfe Soule & body to the Devill, By which Wicked & diabollicall Couenant with the Devill made in maner & forme Aforesaid The Said William Barker is become A A detestable Witch Against the peace of oᵋ Soveᵋ lord & Lady the King & Queen their Crowne & dignity & the laws in that Case made & prouided.

[Reverse] William Barker Senioᵋ for Covenanting with the Deuill
[Hand 2] Billa vera
Robert: Payne foreman

Notes: William Barker Sr. had fled, but in accordance with English law, proceedings against him continued, and an indictment was brought against him. Seven people fall into the category of individuals who had indictments against them in January 1693 but where no evidence for more specific dating survives. These include William Barker Sr., Hannah Bromage, Richard Carrier, Sarah Cloyce, Edward Farrington, Elizabeth Hart, Stephen Johnson, and Mary Lacey Jr. These eight cases are dated at the end of the January sitting of the grand jury for Essex County that met in Salem. The true dates are not known, except that they were in January 1693. ◊ Hand 1 = Anthony Checkley

Massachusetts Archives Collection, vol. 135, no. 38. Massachusetts State Archives. Boston, MA.

806. Indictment of William Barker Sr., for Afflicting Abigail Martin‡

January 13, 1693

[Hand 1] Province of y^e Massathutetts Bay in New England Essex } Anno RRs & Reginæ Gulielmi & Mariæ Angliæ &^{c} Quarto: Annoq3 D$\overline{m}$: 1692

The Juro$^\varepsilon$ for our Sov$^\varepsilon$ Lord and Lady the King & Queen Presents That [Hand 2] **William Barker Seino$^\varepsilon$ of Adiuor in the County of Essex aforesaid Husband$\overline{m}$ Sometime in August last 1692 afors^d** [Hand 1] And Divers other Dayes & times as well before as after Certaine Detestable Arts called Witchcrafts & Sorceryes Wickedly Mallishiously & ffeloniously hath vsed Practised & Excercised at and in the Towne of [Hand 2] **Andiuor** [Hand 1] in the County of Essex afore$\overline{s}^d$ vpon & against one [Hand 2] **Abagaiele Martin of Andivo$^\varepsilon$ Single Woman** [Hand 1] By which Wicked Arts the said [Hand 2] **Abagaill Martin** [Hand 1] the Day and Year afor$\overline{es}^d$ and Divers other Dayes and Times as well before as after, was and is Tortured Afflicted. Tormented Consumed Pined & wasted ag^t the Peace of our Sov$^\varepsilon$ Lord & Lady the King and Queen their Crowne and Dignity & the Lawes in y^t case made & Provided:
[Hand 3] Wittneses: Rose ffoster
Matha Tyler

[Reverse] [Hand 2] William Barker Seino$^\varepsilon$ for afflicting Abigaill Martin
[Hand 4] Billa vera
Robert Payne foreman:
[Hand 2?] fled
[Hand 5] ffled Persons ffled

Notes: Hand 2 = Anthony Checkley

Massachusetts Archives Collection, vol. 135, no. 37. Massachusetts State Archives. Boston, MA.

807. Indictment of Hannah Bromage, for Afflicting Mary Walcott (Returned Ignoramus)‡

[Hand 1] Province of y^e Massathutetts Bay in New England Essex } Anno RRs & Reginæ Gulielmi & Mariæ Angliæ &^{c} Quarto Annoq3 D$\overline{m}$ 1692

The Juro$^\varepsilon$ for our Sov$^\varepsilon$ Lord & Lady the King & Queen Presents That [Hand 2] **Hannah Bromage of Hauerill wife of [   ] Bromage of Hauerill in y^e Count of Essex {aforsd} vpon the Thirtieth day of July last in the Yeare 1692 aforesaid** [Hand 1] And Divers other Dayes & Times as well before as After Certaine Detestable Arts called Witchcrafts & Sorceries: Wickedly Mallishiously & ffelloniously hath vsed Practised and Excercised at ^{&} in the Towne of [Hand 2] **Salem** [Hand 1] in the County of Essex Aforesaid upon and against one [Hand 2] **Mary Wallcott of Salem aforesaid Single Woman** [Hand 1] By which Wicked Arts the said [Hand 2] **Hannah Bromage** [Hand 1] The Day and Year afore$\overline{s}$d and Divers other Dayes and times as well before as after / was and is Tortured Afflicted Tormented ["ment" written over "tur"] Consumed Pined & wasted ag^t y^e Peace of our Sov$^\varepsilon$ Lord & lady the King and Queen their Crowne & Dignity and the Lawes in that Case made and Provided

January 13, 1693   [Reverse] [Hand 3?] Ignoramus
Robert Payne foreman:

Notes: The surviving manuscript is pasted into the book of the Suffolk records. *SWP*, I, p. 144, transcribes a reverse as reading "Ignoramus Robert Payne foreman:." Ink bleedthrough indicates that Payne's name is on the reverse, but does not reveal the word "Ignoramus." Whether *SWP* is accurate or not cannot be confirmed. Whether the ignoramus is there or not, that was the probable decision of the grand jury, since no trial record on Bromage is extant. ◊ Hand 2 = Anthony Checkley

Suffolk Court Files, vol. 32, docket 2674, p. 5, Massachusetts Supreme Judicial Court, Judicial Archives, Massachusetts State Archives. Boston, MA.

808. Indictment of Richard Carrier, for Afflicting Timothy Swan‡

[Hand 1] Province of the Massatutchetts Bay in New England Essex } Anno RRs & Reginæ Gulielmi & Mariæ Angliæ &^{c} Quarto Annoqʒ D$\overline{m}$: 1692

The Juro$^\varepsilon$ for our Sov$^\varepsilon$ Lord & Lady the King and Queens Presents That [Hand 2] **Richard Carier of Anduor in the County of Essex Son of Andrew Carier of Andiuo$^\varepsilon$ aforesaid Husbandman Sometime in the moneth of June in the Yeare 1692 aforesaid** [Hand 1] And Divers other Dayes & times as well before as after Certaine Destestable Arts called Witchcrafts & Sorceries Wickedly Mallishiously & ffelloniously hath vsed Practised and Excercised at & in the Towne of [Hand 2] **Andiuo$^\varepsilon$** [Hand 1] in y^e County of Essex afore$\overline{s}$^{d} vpon & against one [Hand 2] **Timothy Swan of Andiuo$^\varepsilon$ aforesaid** [Hand 1] by which wicked Arts y^e said [Hand 2] **Timothy Swann** [Hand 1] the Day and year afore$\overline{s}$^{d} and Divers other Dayes and times as well before as after, was and is Tortured Afflicted Tormented Consumed Pined and wasted against the Peace of our Sovereigne Lord and Lady the King & Queen their Crowne & Dignity. and the Lawes in that Case made and Provided

[Reverse] [Hand 2] Richard Carryer for Afflicting Timothy Swan
[Hand 3] Billa vera
Robert. Payne foreman:

Notes: In spite of the true bill, no trial record in Richard Carrier's case is extant. It may be that he fled, but no notation confirms this. ◊ Hand 2 = Anthony Checkley

Massachusetts Archives Collection, vol. 135, no. 30. Massachusetts State Archives. Boston, MA.

809. Indictment of Sarah Cloyce, for Afflicting Rebecca Towne (Returned Ignoramus)‡

[Hand 1] Essex in y^e Prouince of y^e Massachusetts Bay in New England } Anno $\overline{RR}$^{s} & Reginæ Gulielmi & Mariæ Angliæ &c Quarto Annoqʒ Domini 1692.

ss

The Juriors for our Soue^ε Lord and Lady the King and Queen doe present That [Hand 2]   January 13, 1693
Sarah Cloyce Wife of Peter Cloyce of Salem [Hand 1] In the County of Essex [Hand 2]
Husbandman In & vpon the ninth day of this Inst September [Hand 1] In the yeare
aforesaid and diuers other days and times as well before as after Certaine detestable Arts
called Witchcraft and Sorceries Wickedly Mallitiously and felloniously hath used practised
and Exercised At and [Hand 2] **in the Towne of Salem in the County of Essex** [Hand 1]
Aforesaid in upon and against one [Hand 2] **Rebeckah Towne of Topsfeild in the County of
Essex** [Hand 1] Aforesaid [Hand 2] **Single Woman** [Hand 1] by which said Wicked Acts
the said [Hand 2] **Rebeckah Towne the day & yeare** [Hand 1] Aforesaid and diuers Other
days and times both before and after was and is Tortured Aflicted Consumed Pined Wasted
and Tormented, and also for sundry other acts of Witchcraft by the said [Hand 2] **Sarah
Cloyce** [Hand 1] Comitted and done before and Since that time against the peace of our
Sou^ε Lord and Lady the King & Queen theire Crowne and dignity and the forme [Hand 2]
Of ["Of" written over "in"] [Hand 1] the Stattute [   ] In that case made and Prouided,

[Reverse] [Hand 2] Indictm^t ags^t Sarah Cloyce for bewitching: Rebecka Towne
[Hand 3] Ignoramus
Robert: Payne Foreman

Notes: In a document dated September 5, 1692, witnesses were called to appear on September 6 in response to indictments
against Mary Esty, Sarah Cloyce, Giles Cory, and Martha Cory. See No. 549. The other three were executed. This
indictment, referring to Sarah Cloyce afflicting Rebecca Towne on September 9, links to those September events,
although it does not explain why Sarah Cloyce escaped the fate of her sisters, Rebecca Nurse and Mary Esty. ◊ Hand 2
= Anthony Checkley

*Suffolk Court Files, vol. 32, docket 2677, p. 8, Massachusetts Supreme Judicial Court, Judicial Archives, Massachusetts State
Archives. Boston, MA.*

810. Indictment of Sarah Cloyce, for Afflicting Mary Walcott (Returned Ignoramus)‡

[Hand 1] Essex in the Prouince   Anno $\overline{RR}$^{s} & Reginæ Gulielmi & Mariæ Angliæ &c
of the Massachusetts Bay in New   }   Quarto Annoq Domini 1692//
England
ss/

The Juriors for our Sou^ε Lord and Lady the King and Queen doe present That [Hand 2]
Sarah Cloyce Wife of Peter Cloyce of Salem ~~in~~ [Hand 1] In the County of Essex [Hand 2]
In or vpon the Eleventh day of Aprill [Hand 1] In the yeare aforesaid and diuers other days
and times as well before as after Certaine detestable Arts called Witchcrafts and Sorceries
Wickedly Mallitiously and felloniously hath used practised and Exercised At and [Hand 2]
in the Towne of Salem aforesaid in the County of Essex [Hand 1] Aforesaid in and upon &
against one [Hand 2] **Mary Walcott of Salem** [Hand 1] Aforesaid [Hand 2] **Single Woman**
[Hand 1] by which said Wicked Acts the said [Hand 2] **Mary Walcott the day & yeare**
[Hand 1] Aforesaid and diuers other days and times both before and after was and is
Tortured Aflicted Consumed Wasted Pined and Tormented, and also for Sundry other Acts
of Witchcraft by the said [Hand 2] **Sarah Cloyce** [Hand 1] Comitted and done before and

January 13, 1693

Since that time against the peace of our Sou^e Lord and Lady the King and Queen theire Crowne and dignity and the forme in the Stattute In that case made and Prouided.

[Reverse] [Hand 2] Indictm^t Ags^t Sarah Cloyce for bewitching: Mary Walcott
[Hand 3] Ignoramus
Robert: Payne foreman

Notes: Hand 2 = Anthony Checkley

Suffolk Court Files, vol. 32, docket 2677a, p. 7, Massachusetts Supreme Judicial Court, Judicial Archives, Massachusetts State Archives. Boston, MA.

811. Indictment of Sarah Cloyce, for Afflicting Abigail Williams (Returned Ignoramus)‡

[Hand 1] Essex in the Prouince of the Massachusetts Bay in New England   }   Anno $\overline{RR}$^s & Reginæ Gulielmi & Mariae Angliæ &c Quarto Annoqʒ Domini 1692

ss

The Juriors for our Soueraigne lord & lady the King and Queen doe present That [Hand 2] **Sarah Cloyce Wife of Peter Cloyce of Salem** [Hand 1] in the County of Essex [Hand 2] **Husbandman vpon or about the 11**th **day of Aprill** [Hand 1] In the yeare aforesaid and diuers other days and times as well before as after Certaine detestable Arts called Witchcraft and Sorceries Wickedly Mallitiously and felloniously hath used practised and Exercised [Hand 2] **At** [Hand 1] and [Hand 2] **in the Towne of Salem in the County of Essex** [Hand 1] Aforesaid in upon and against one [Hand 2] **Abigail Williams of Salem** [Hand 1] Aforesaid [Hand 2] **Single Woman** [Hand 1] by which said Wicked Acts the said [Hand 2] **Abigaill Williams the day & yeare** ~~aforesaid~~ [Hand 1] Aforesaid and diuers other days and times both before and after was and is Tortured Aflicted Consumed Wasted Pined and Tormented. ~~and also for sundry other acts of Witchcraft by the said~~ [Hand 2] ~~**Sarah Cloyce**~~ [Hand 1] ~~Comitted and done before and Since that time~~ against the Peace of Our Sou^e Lord and Lady the King & Queen theire Crowne and dignity and the ~~forme Of~~ ["Of" written over "in"] ~~the Stattute~~ [Hand 2] {law} [Hand 1] In that case made and Prouided/

[Reverse] [Hand 2] Indictm̄ against Sarah Cloyce for bewitching Abigail Williams
[Hand 3] Ignoramus
Robert: Payne foreman

Notes: After June 30 Abigail Williams made no more appearances in the legal procedures, although her name continued to appear as in this document. ◊ Hand 2 = Anthony Checkley

Suffolk Court Files, vol. 32, docket 2677b, p. 8, Massachusetts Supreme Judicial Court, Judicial Archives, Massachusetts State Archives. Boston, MA.

812. Indictment of Edward Farrington, for Covenanting‡

January 13, 1693

| [Hand 1] Prouince of the Massachusetts Bay in New England Essex ss// | Anno R̄R̄s & Reginæ Gulielmi & Mariæ Angliæ &c Quarto Annoqȝ Dom̄ 1692 |

The Juᵉors for oᵉ Souᵉ Lord & lady the King & Queen Present That Edward ffarington of Andivoᵉ in the County of Essex aforsd About foure or fiue yeare Since, In the Towne of Anduoᵉ aforesaid Wickedly mallitiously & ffelloniously A Couenant with the Deuill did make & was Baptised by the Deuill & vnto him Renounced his first Baptizme & promised to be the Deuills both Soul & body for euer, And to Serue the deuill f(or)(f)euer & Signed the Deuills Booke: By which Diabollicall Couenant by him with the Deuill made In maner & forme aforesaid The Said Edward ffarington is become A detestable Witch Against the peace of oᵉ Soueraigne lord & lady the King & Queen their Crowne & Dignity & the laws in that Case made & prouided
Wittness his owne Confesion

[Reverse] Edward ffarington for Couenanting wᵗʰ yᵉ Deuill
[Hand 2] Billa vera
Robert. Payne foreman.
[Hand 1] fled

Notes: Farrington had fled and was apparently never brought to trial. The referenced confession has not been located. ◊
Hand 1 = Anthony Checkley

Massachusetts Archives Collection, vol. 135, no. 51. Massachusetts State Archives. Boston, MA.

813. Indictment of Edward Farrington, for Afflicting Mary Warren‡

| [Hand 1] Province of yᵉ Massathutetts Bay in New England Essex | Anno RRs & Reginæ Gulielmi & Mariæ. Angliæ &ᶜ Quarto Annoqȝ Dm̄ 1692 |

The Juroᵉ for our Sovereigne Lord & Lady the King & Queen Present That [Hand 2] **Edward ffarrington of Andiuoᵉ in the County of Essex aforsaid On the Seauenth day of September 1692 aforesaid** [Hand 1] And Divers other Dayes & times as well before as after Certaine Detestable arts called witchcrafts & Sorceries Wickedly ~~and~~ Mallishiously & ffelloniously hath vsed Practised & Exercised at & in yᵉ Towne of [Hand 2] **Salem** [Hand 1] in the County of Essex aforesd vpon and against one [Hand 2] **Mary Warren of Salem Single Woman** [Hand 1] By which wicked Arts the said [Hand 2] **Mary Warren** [Hand 1] the Day and year aforesᵈ and Divers other Dayes & times as well before as after was and is Tortured Afflicted ~~Pined~~ Tormented Consumed Pined & wasted Against the Peace of our Sovereigne Lord and Lady the King and Queen their Crowne and Dignity. and the Lawes in that case made and Provided:
[Hand 2] Wittness Martha Sprague
Ann Puttnam

January 13, 1693   [Reverse] Edward ffarington for Aflicting Mary Warren
                        [Hand 3] Billa vera
                        Robert: Payne foreman:

Notes: Hand 2 = Anthony Checkley

Massachusetts Archives Collection, vol. 135, no. 52. Massachusetts State Archives. Boston, MA.

814. Indictment of Elizabeth Hart, for Afflicting Mary Warren (Returned Ignoramus)‡

[Hand 1] Prouince of   } Anno $\overline{RR}$s & Reginæ Gulielmi & Mariæ Angliæ &c
the Massachusetts Bay In New   } qua$^\varepsilon$to Anoq₃ Do$\overline{m}$ 1692.
England Essex
ss

The Juro$^{\varepsilon s}$ for our Sou$^\varepsilon$ lord & lady the King & Queen p$^\varepsilon$sent That Elizabeth Hart of [   ]
~~Widow~~ vpon or about the 18th day of May In this pre$\overline{st}$ yeare 1692 And diuers other days &
times as well before as after Certaine detestable Arts Called witcchrafts & Sorceries
wickedly mallitiously & ffelloniously hath vsed practised & Exersised at & in the Towne of
Salem in the County of Essex aforesaid vpon & Against On [= one] Mary Warren Single
Woman [   ] By which wicked Arts the Said Mary Warren The day & yeare aforesaid &
diuers other days & times as well before as after was & is Tortured aflicted Tormented
Consumed Wasted & pined Contrary to y^e peace of o$^\varepsilon$ Sou$^\varepsilon$ lord & lady the King & Queen
their Crowne & dignity & the laws in that Case made & prouided
Wittness
Ann Putnam
Mercy Lewis

[Reverse] Eliz Hart.
[Hand 2] Ignoramus
Robert: Payne foreman

Notes: Hand 1 = Anthony Checkley

Suffolk Court Files, vol. 31, docket 2668, p. 149, Massachusetts Supreme Judicial Court, Judicial Archives, Massachusetts State Archives. Boston, MA.

815. Indictment of Stephen Johnson, for Covenanting‡

[Hand 1] Province of the   } Anno $\overline{RR}$ & Reginæ Gulielmi & Mariæ Angliæ &c
Massachusetts Bay in New   } Quarto Anoq₃ Do$\overline{m}$ ^{1692}
England Essex ss//

The Juro$^\varepsilon$s for o^r Sou$^\varepsilon$ lord & lady the King & Queen present That Stephen Johnson [   ]
Somtime In this Present yeare 1692 ⟨did⟩ Wickedly mallitiously & ffelonious with the Deuill

A Couenant did make, wherby he gaue himselfe both Soule & Body to the Diuel, And Signed the Deuills Booke with his Blood And By the Deuill was Baptized & vnto the Deuill Renounced his Christian Baptizme By which wicked & Diabolicall Couenant with the Deuill made The said Stephen Johnson is become A detestable witch Contrary to the peace of our Sou$^\varepsilon$ lord & lady the King & Queen their Crowne & Dignity & the Laws in that Case made & prouided

January 13, 1693

[Reverse] Stephen Johnson for Couenanting with thc Deuill
[Hand 2] 1692
[Hand 3] Billa uera
Robert: Payne foreman:

Notes: No record of a trial for Johnson survives. He was about 13 years old and had been freed on recognizance October 6, 1692. See No. 689. ◊ Hand 1 = Anthony Checkley

Massachusetts Archives Collection, vol. 135, no. 41. Massachusetts State Archives. Boston, MA.

816. Indictment of Stephen Johnson, for Afflicting Martha Sprague, Mary Lacey Jr. & Rose Foster‡

[Hand 1] Prouince of y^e Massachusets Bay In New England Essex ss// } Anno $\overline{RR}$s & Reginæ Gulielmiæ & Mariæ Angliæ &c Quarto Anoq$_\mathbb{Z}$ $\overline{Dom}$ 1692

The Juro$^\varepsilon$s for o$^\varepsilon$ Sou$^\varepsilon$ lord & lady the King & Queen Present That Stephen Johnson [   ] On or about the first Day of September last in the yeare aforesaid & diuers other days & times as well before as after Certaine detestable Arts Called Witchcrafts & Sorceries wickedly mallitiously & ffellonious[Lost] [= feloniously] hath vsed practised & Exersised, at & In the Towne of Salem In the County of [Lost]ssex [= Essex] aforesaid vpon & Against Martha Sprague Mary Lacey & Rose ffoster, By which Wicked Arts The Said Martha Sprague & Mary Lacey & Rose ffoster, The Day & yeare aforesaid And diuers oth$^\varepsilon$s days & times as well before as after was & is Tortured Afflicted Consumed Wasted Pined & Tormented, Against the peace of o$^\varepsilon$ Sou$^\varepsilon$ lord & lady y^e King & Queen Their Crowne & dignity & [Lost]he [= the] laws in that Case made & prouided

[Reverse] Step$\overline{h}$ Johnson for bewitching Martha Sprague Mary Lasey & Rose ffoster
[Hand 2] 92
[Hand 3] Billa uera
Robert: Payne foreman

Notes: Hand 1 = Anthony Checkley

Massachusetts Archives Collection, vol. 135, no. 42. Massachusetts State Archives. Boston, MA.

January 13, 1693

817. Indictment of Mary Lacey Jr., for Covenanting‡

Province of the Massachusetts Bay in New England Essex ss.	Anno R Rs & Reginae Gulielmi and Mariæ Anglice &c Quarto, Annoq. Dom. 1692

That Mary Lacey Jume [= junior] of Andivor Single Woman -

Sometime in the yeare 1692, At and In the Towne of Andivor in the County of Essex – Wickedly mallitiously and felloniously A Couenant with the Devill did make And Renounced her former Christian Baptisme And sett her hand to the Devil's Booke, whereby the said Mary Lacey is become a Wicked and detestable Witch Contrary to the Peace of our Sov. lord and Lady the King and Queen their Crowne and dignity and the laws in that Case made and provided.

Billa Vera	Witness her confession in the Booke of Examinations Robert Payne, Foreman.

Letter from T. B. Drew, Librarian of the Pilgrim Society, to Sarah Hunt, Secretary of the Danvers Historical Society, February 15, 1892. Danvers Archival Center, Danvers, MA.

818. Recognizance for William Barker Jr. & Mary Barker by John Barker & John Osgood Sr.

See also: May 10, 1693.

[Hand 1] Memorandum
That on the Thirteenth day of Jan^{ry} 1692 In the Fourth Year of the Reigne of our Sovereigne Lord and Lady William and Mary by the Grace of God of England &c King & Queen defenders of the faith &c Personally appeared before Wm Stoughton Esqr cheife Justice of their Maj^{ies} Province of the Massachusets bay in New England Jno Barker and Jno Osgood both of the Towne of Andiver in the County of Essex Husbandmen and acknowledged themselves to be Joyntly & Severally indebted unto our s͞d Sovereigne Lord & Lady and the Survivor of them their Heires & Successors in the Sum of one Hundred Pounds to be levied on their or either of their lands & Tenniments goods & chattles for the use of our s͞d Sovereigne Lord & Lady the King & Queen or Survivor of them on Condition that Wm Barker Junr & Mary Barker haveing stood Committed for Suspition of Witchcraft shall make their personall appearance before the Justices of our sd Lord & Lady the King & Queen at the next Court of Assizes and Generall Goale Delivery to be holden for the County of Essex then & their to answer to all such matters and things as shall in their Maj^{ies} behalfe be alledged against them and to doe & receive that which by the s͞d Court shall be then & there Injoyned them and thence not to departe without licence
[Hand 2] Attest.

Jon^a Elatson Cle͞r

[Reverse] Recognizance of   January 13, 1693

Jnᵒ B⟨ar⟩ker ⎫   for Wᵐ Barker Junᵉ
      &   ⎬   for   &
Jnᵒ Osgood ⎭   ~~Mary⟨T⟩yler~~
                                    Mary Barker

[Lost]y [= May] 10ᵗʰ Apeared

Notes: Both were cleared on May 10, 1693. William was about thirteen years old, and Mary about fourteen. ◊ Hand 2 = Jonathan Elatson

Massachusetts Archives Collection, vol. 135, no. 105. Massachusetts State Archives. Boston, MA.

819. Recognizance for Dorothy Faulkner & Abigail Faulkner Jr. by Francis Faulkner & Joseph Marble

See also: May 10, 1693.

[Hand 1] Memorandum

That on the Thirteenth day of Janᵉʸ 1692 in the fourth year of the Reigne of our Sovereigne Lord & Lady William & Mary by the Grace of God of England &c King & Queen Defenders of the faith &c Personally appeared before William Stoughton Esqᵉ cheife Justice of their Majⁱᵉˢ Province of the Massachusets bay in New England Francis Falkner Husbandman & Joseph Marble Mason both of Andiver in the County of Essex and acknowledged themselves to be joyntly & Severally Indebted unto our sd Sovereigne Lord & Lady & the Survivor of them their Heires & Successors in the Sum of One Hundred Pounds to be levied on their or either of their Lands and Tenniments, goods & Chattles for the use of our sd Sovereigne Lord & Lady the King & Queen or Survivor of them on Condition that Dorathy Forkner and Abigaile Forkner haveing stood committed for Suspition of Witchcraft shall make their ꝑsonall appearance before the Justices of our sd Sovereigne Lord & Lady the King & Queen at the next Court of Assizes and Generall Goal Delivery to be holden for the County of Essex then & there to answer to all such matters & things as shall in their Majⁱᵉˢ behalfe be alleadged against them and to do and receive that which by the sd̄ Court shall be then & there injoyned them & thence not to depart without licence

[Hand 2] Attest

Jonᵃ Elatson Cleꝛ̄

[Reverse] Recog:
ffrancis ffalkner
Joseph Marble
for
Dorothy ffalkner
&
Abigall ffaulkner

10 May
Apeard
Cleared by proclamation paying fees

January 13, 1693   Notes: Both were cleared on May 10. Dorothy was about thirteen years old, and Abigail about eight. ◊ Hand 2 = Jonathan
Elatson

Massachusetts Archives Collection, vol. 135, no. 104. Massachusetts State Archives. Boston, MA.

820. Recognizance for Martha Tyler & Johannah Tyler by Hopestill Tyler & John Bridges
See also: May 10, 1693.

[Hand 1] Memorandum
That on the Thirteenth day of Jan^{ey} 1692 in the Fourth year of the Reigne of our Sovereigne
Lord & Lady William & Mary by the Grace of God of England &c King & Queen
Defenders of the faith &c Personally appeared before Wm Stoughton Esq^e Cheife Justice of
their Maj^{ies} Province of the Massachusets bay in New England Hopstill Tyler & Jno Bridges
both of Andiver Blacksmiths in the County of Essex & acknowledged themselves to be
joyntly & severally indebted unto our sd Sovereigne Lord & Lady & the Survivor of them
their Heires & Successors in the Sum of one Hundred Pounds to be levied on their or either
of their Lands and Tenniments goods, & Chattles for the use of our sd: Soverigne Lord &
Lady the King & Queen or Survivor of them on Condition that Martha Tyler & ~~Abigale~~
{~~Abig~~} ^{Johana} Tyler haveing stood Committed for Suspition of Witchcraft shall make
their ꝑsonall appearance before the Justices of our sd Lord & Lady the King & Queen at the
next Court of Assizes & Generall Goale Delivery to be holden for ye County of Essex then
& there to answer to all Such matters & things as shall in their Maj^{ies} behalfe be alleadged
against them & to do & receive that which by the sd Court shall then & there Injoyned them
& thence not to departe without licence
[Hand 2] Attest^e

Jon^a Elatson Cler̄

[Reverse] Recog
Hopestill Tyler
      & }   Martha
Jno Bridges   ~~for~~ Tyler
            &
           ~~Abigall~~
           Johan^a Tyler

May 10 Appear

Notes: Both Martha and Johannah Tyler were cleared by proclamation on May 10, 1693. ◊ Hand 2 = Jonathan Elatson

Massachusetts Archives Collection, vol. 135, no. 107. Massachusetts State Archives. Boston, MA.

821. Recognizance for Sarah Wilson Jr., & Sarah Wilson Sr. by John Osgood Sr. & Joseph Wilson

See also: May 10, 1693.

[Hand 1] Memorandum

That on the Thirteenth day of January 1692 In the fourth year of the Reigne of our Sovereigne Lord & Lady William & Mary by the Grace of God of England &c: King & Queen defenders of the faith &c: Personally appeared before Wm Stoughton Esq^ε cheife Justice of their Maj^{ies} Province of the Massachusets bay in New England John Osgood of the Town of Andiver in the County of Essex husbandman & Joseph Wilson of y^e same Towne and acknowledged themselves to be Joyntly and Severally Indebted unto our s$\bar{d}$: Sovereigne Lord & Lady and the Surviver of them their Heires & Successors in the sum of One Hundred Pounds to be levied on their or either of their Lands and Tennements, goods and chattles for the use of our said Sovereigne Lord & Lady the King & Queen or Survivor of them On Condition that Sarah Wilson the wife of Joseph Wilson and Sarah her daughter haveing stood committed f̄or suspitian of Witchcraft shall make their Personall appearance before the Justices of our s̄d: Lord & Lady the King & Queen at the next Court of Assizes & Generall Goale Delivery to be holden for the County of Essex then and there to answer to all such matters & things as s̄hall in their Maj^{ies} behalfe be alledged against them and to doe & receive that which by the s̄d: Court shall be then & there injoyned them & thence not to depart wthout licence

[Hand 2] Attest

Jon^a Elatson Cler.

[Reverse] Recog⟨nizance of⟩
Jno Osgood
    &
Joseph Willson

Sarah Willson y^e wife of Joseph Willson and Sarah her daughter

may y^e 10th Appeard

Notes: Both were cleared on May 10, 1693. ◊ Hand 2 = Jonathan Elatson

Massachusetts Archives Collection, vol. 135, no. 106. Massachusetts State Archives. Boston, MA.

822. Court Record of the Trial of Mary Lacey Jr.

[Hand 1] {13th Janu^a} Mary Lacey Junio^ε of Andover in the County of Essex, being Indicted, by the Jurors, for o^ε soveraign Lord and Lady, the King and Queen, upon their Oathes, by two severall Indictments; For that is to say; 1st
For that shee, the Said Mary Lacey Junior of Andover, Singlewoman, Some time in the year 16[Lost] [= 1692] at, and in the towne of Andover, in the Count⟨y⟩ [1 word illegible] [*SWP* = of] Essex, wickedly, malitiously, and ffelloniou⟨sly⟩ w⟨i⟩th the Devill did make, ⟨and⟩

January 13, 1693

[2 words illegible] [*SWP* = renounced her] former Christian Baptisme, and Set her hand, to the Devils booke, whereby the Said Mary Lacey, is become, a wicked, and detestable witch, contrary to the Peace, of our Souveraigne Lord and Lady the King and Queen, their Crowne, and dignity, and the Lawes, in that case made, and Provided.

2dly For that shee, the Said Mary Lacey, of Andover, in the County of Essex, Single woman, on, or about, the 15th Day of July last, in the Year 1692, and divers other dayes, and times, as well before, as after, certaine detestable arts, called witchcrafts, and Sorceries, wickedly, malitiously, and ffelloniously, hath used, practized, and Exercised, at, and in the towne of Andover, in the County of Essex aforesaid, upon, And against One Timothy Swan, of Andover in the County of Essex, by which wicked arts, the Said Timothy Swan, the day, and year aforesaid, and divers other dayes, and times, as well before, as after was, and is, tortured afflicted, tormented; consumed, Pined, & wasted, against the Peace of our Soveraign Lord and Lady, the King and Queen, their Crown and Dignity, and the Lawes, in that case made, and Provided.

Jury Sworne
m^{r} Nathl Howard
James ffreind
Joseph Litle
Benayah Tidcomb
⟨Sam⟩^{l} Morgan
⟨J⟩ohn ⟨Pickard⟩
Edmund Gale
John Abby
Richard Gross
John Ordway
John Hall
Nathan^{l} Emerson

Upon the said Indictments, and each of them, the Said Mary Lacey, was then, and there, before the Justices, of our Lord and Lady, the King and Queen, arraigned, and upon her arraignment, shee did then, and there, the day, and Year abovesaid, plead to them, and each of them, Not Guilty and put her Self upon triall by God, and, her Countrey.

A Jury being called Nathaniell Howard – fforeman, and a͞cordingly Sworne, no Excep͞con being made, by the Prisoner, the said Indictments, and [Lost] [*SWP* = each] of them, being read, together with the Evidences, and Examinations, and the [1 word illegible] [*SWP* = Prisoners] [Lost]fence [= defence] being heard; the Jury went out to ag⟨ree⟩ [Lost] [*SWP* = on] their verdict, who returning, did then, and [Lost] [*SWP* = there], in open Court, deliver their verdict, that t⟨he⟩ Said Mary Lacy was Not Guilty of th⟨e⟩ ffellony by witch craft for which She S[Lost] [*SWP* = stood] Indicted, in, and by the said Indictments, and each of them.

The Court Ordered Ma[Lost] [= Mary] Lacey aforesaid, to be discharg⟨ed⟩ paying her fees.

Notes: Finding Mary Lacey Jr. not guilty is particularly significant for showing what had happened to the credibility of so central an accuser and confessor in the Andover phase. Equally significant is the fact that although her charges were no longer credited, no action was taken against her or others for false testimony. Her plea of not guilty conceded the falseness of her previous claims. One may speculate that she and others claimed that the Devil deluded them.

Records of the Superior Court of Judicature (1692/3), pp. 27–29, Massachusetts Supreme Judicial Court, Judicial Archives, Massachusetts State Archives. Boston, MA.

Saturday, January 14, 1693

823. Recognizance for Sarah Cole (of Salem) by Abraham Cole

See also: May 10, 1693.

[Hand 1] Memor^m

That on the fourteenth day of Janua^{ey} 1692 in the fourth year of the Reigne of our Soveraigne Lord & Lady William and Mary by the Grace of God of of England &c King and Queen Defenders of y^e faith &c Personally appeared before Jno Ha[   ] [= Hathorne] Esq^e one of their Maj^{ties} Justices for the County of Essex The⟨re⟩ Abraham Cole of Salem Taylor and acknowledged ⟨?⟩himselfe to be oweing and Indebted vnto our said Soveraigne Lord and Lady and the Survivor of them their Heires and Successors in the sume of fffifty pounds money to be Levied on his Lands and Tenements goods and Chattles for the use of our s^d Soveraigne Lord and Lady the King and Queen or the Survivor them [= of them] On Condition That Sarah Cole his wife shall shall personally appear before the ["the" written over "our"] Justices of our s^d Lord and Lady the King & Queen at the next Court of Assizes & Gen^{ll} Goall Delivery to be holden ⟨o⟩for the County of Essex and in the meantime to be of Good behaveour and then and there to answer to all Such matters and things as shall in their Maj^{ties} behaffe be alledged against her and to do and receiue that wch by the said Court Shall be by the said Court shall be then and there Injoyned her and thence not to depart without Lycence.

Attest

Jon^a Elatson Cler̄

[Reverse] Recognizance Abraham Coal of Salem for Sarah Coal his wife.
Appeared & Clear'd by proclamation

Notes: Although May seems the most likely date for Sarah Cole (of Salem) being cleared, an earlier date cannot be ruled out. For example, Jane Lilly was cleared by proclamation on February 3, 1693. See No. 827. However, the pattern of recognizances similar to this one does suggest May 10. ◊ Hand 1 = Jonathan Elatson

Massachusetts Archives Collection, vol. 135, no. 108. Massachusetts State Archives. Boston, MA.

Thursday, January 26, 1693

824. Crown's Reply to William Phips about Proceedings against Witches

[Hand 1] Touching proceedings agst witchcraft in New England.
Memd^m

That my Lord President be pleased to acquaint his Maj^{ty} in Councill with the account received from New England from Sr William Phips the Gov^e there touching Proceedings against Severall Persons for Witchcraft as appears by the Governors Letter concerning those Matters.

January 26, 1693

At the Court at Whitehall
the 26th of January 1692.
Present
The Kings most Excellent Maj^{ty} in Councill

Order upon Sr William Phips Letter about New England Witches

The R^t Honble the Lords of the Committee of Trade and Plantations having this day laid before his Maj^{ty} in Councill a Letter lately received from Sr William Phips Phips Govern^ε in cheif of the Massachusets Bay in New England, Setting forth that a most Horrible witchcraft or Possession of Devills had infested that Province and that divers Persons have been Convicted of witchcraft, some whereof had confest their guilt, But that others being of a known and good reputation these Proceedings had caused a great dissatisfaction among the Inhabitants, Whereupon he had put a Stop to the Same untill his Majesties Pleasure should be known concerning the same. His Majesty in Councill was thereupon pleased to Order the Right Honble the Earl of Nottingham His Majesties Princip^{ll} Secretary of State to prepare Letters for his Maj^{ts} Royall Signature to be sent to Sr William Phips Signifying his Maj^{ts} Approbation of his Proceedings in this behalf, and further to direct that in all Proceedings for the future against Persons accused for Witchcraft or being Possessed by the Devill the greatest Moderation and all due Circumspection be used so far as the same may be without Impediment to the Ordinary Course of Justice within the said Province/

To Sr Wm Phips ab^t proceedings agst witches.

Trusty and Welbeloved We Greet you well It having been Represented unto Us, That a most horrible withcraft or Possession of Devills hath infested Severall Townes in Our Province of the Massachusetts Massachusetts Bay under your Government, and that divers Persons have been convicted of Witchcraft, some whereof have Confest their guilt, but that others being of a known and good Reputation, these Proceedings had caused a great dissatisfaction among Our good Subjects for which reason you had put a Stop thereunto untill Our Pleasure should be known Concerning the same. We therefore approving of your care and Circumspection herein have thought fitt to Signify Our Will and Pleasure as We do hereby Will and require you to give all Necessary directions that in all Proceedings against Persons accused for Witchcraft or being Possessed by the Devill, the greatest Moderation and all due circumspection be used, so far as the same may be without Impediment to the Ordinary Course of Justice within Our said Province And so Wee bid you very heartily farewell. Given at Our Court at Whitehall the 15th day of Aprill 1693. In the fifth Year of Our Reign.

By her Majes^{ts} Command.

Colonial Office 5/905 62 05, pp. 417–18. National Archives, London, UK.

Tuesday, January 31, 1693

January 31, 1693

Grand Juries of Sarah Cole (of Lynn), Jane Lilly, Mary Taylor & Mary Toothaker

825. Superior Court of Judicature Record Book: Court of Assize and General Jail Delivery Held at Charlestown, Middlesex County

[Hand 1] Midlesex. ss.

At a Superiour Court of Judicature Court of Assize & Generall Goall delivery holden at Cha⟨r⟩les-Towne in the County Midles⟨e⟩x in the Province of the Massachusets Bay in New England on 31st day of January being the last Tuesday of sd Month ⟨A⟩nno Dom 1692/3 Annoqʒ $\overline{RR}$ & Reginæ Gulielmi et Mariæ Angliæ &c Quinto

Presens

William Stougton Esqᵉ Cheif Justice
Thomas Danforth Esqᵉ
John Richards Esqᵉ
Wait Winthrop Esqᵉ
Samuel Sewell Esqᵉ

Grad Jury

mr Symon Stone ffo⟨r⟩
Samuel Walker
John Pearce
Edward Johnson
John Spring
Thomas Prentice
Richd Martin
Edward Willson
Symon Davis
Humphray Barret
Nehamiah Hunt
Richd Norcross
John Moss
Henry Spring
John Sharp
Joh Sharp
John Jackson

Notes: For jury warrants see note, No. 730.

Records of the Superior Court of Judicature (1692/3), p. 31, Massachusetts Supreme Judicial Court, Judicial Archives, Massachusetts State Archives. Boston, MA.

826. Indictment of Sarah Cole (of Lynn), for Afflicting Mary Brown
See also: Feb. 1, 1693.

[Hand 1] Prouince of the Massachusetts Bay In New England ss//   At A Superior Court of Judicature held at Charlston for the County of Midlesex the 31th of January 1692/3 Annoqʒ $\overline{RR}$ˢ & Reginæ Gulielmi & Mariæ Angliæ &cᵃ Quarto The Jurors for our Soueraigne lord and lady the King and Queen Present That [Hand 2] **Sarah Cole Wife of John Cole of lynn in the County of Essex Coo**ₚ [Hand 1] On or about the [Hand 2] **twentysix**ᵗ [Hand 1] day of [Hand 2] **Sep**ᵗ [Hand 1] In the Yeare [Hand 2] **1692 aforesaid** [Hand 1] and diuers other days and times as well before as After, Certaine detestable Arts called Witchcrafts and Sorceries Wickedly Mallitiously and ffelloniously hath used practised and Exersi{s}ed at and in the Towne of [Hand 2] **Reding** [Hand 1] In the County of [Hand 2] **Midlesex** [Hand 1] Upon and against One [Hand 2] **Mary Browne of Redin In** ["In" written over "of"] **the County of Midlesex aforsd** [Hand 1] By which

Wicked Arts the said [Hand 2] **Mary Browne** [Hand 1] The day and Yeare aforesaid, and diuers other days and times as well befo⟨re⟩ As After was and is Tortured Tormented [Hand 2] ^{aflicted} [Hand 1] Consumed Pined & Wasted against the peace of Our Soueraigne Lord and Lady the King and Queen theire Crowne and Dignity and the Laws In that case made and Prouided,

[Hand 2] Wittness Mary Browne
Jnᵒ Browne Junᵉ
Elizᵃ Wellman
Jnᵒ Cole
Mary Eaton
Ben̄. Larobe

[Hand 3] Billa Vera
Atest Simon Stone foreman

[Reverse] [Hand 2] Sarah Cole for bewitching Mary Browne
[Hand 4] Ponᵗ se
not Guilty

Notes: Sarah Cole was found not guilty on February 1. Hand 2 = Anthony Checkley

Suffolk Court Files, vol. 32, docket 2712, p. 48, Massachusetts Supreme Judicial Court, Judicial Archives, Massachusetts State Archives. Boston, MA.

827. Indictment of Jane Lilly, for Afflicting Mary Marshall (Returned Ignoramus)

See also: Feb. 3, 1693.

[Hand 1] Prouince of the Massachusetts Bay in New England ss// } Att A Superior Court of Judicature held at Charlston for the County of Midlesex the 31ᵗʰ January 1692/3 Annoqȝ RRˢ & Reginæ Gulielmi & Mariæ Angliæ &⟨c⟩ {Quarto.}

The Jurors for Our Soueraigne Lord and Lady the King and Queen ꝑsent That [Hand 2] **Jane Lilly** [Hand 1] On or about the [   ] day of [   ] In the Yeare [   ] and diuers other days and times as well before as after Certaine detestable Arts. Called Witchcrafts and Sorceries Wickedly Mallitiously and felloniously hath used practised and Exercised at and In the Towne of [Hand 2] **Malden** ~~in~~ [Hand 1] In the County of [Hand 2] **Midlesex** [Hand 1] Upon and against One [Hand 2] **Mary Marshall Wife of Edward Marshall of Malden** ^{aforsᵈ} [Hand 1] By which Wicked Arts the said [Hand 2] **Mary Marshall** [Hand 1] The day and Yeare aforesaid & diuers other days and times as well before as After was Aflicted Tortured Tormented Consumed Pine⟨d⟩ Wasted, Against the Peace of Our Souᵉ Lord & Lady the King and Queen there crowne and Dignity & yᵉ Laws in yᵗ case made and Prouided,

[Reverse] [Hand 2] Jane Lilly for aflicting Mary Marshall
[Hand 3] ~~Billa Ver~~ Ignoᵉamus
[Hand 4] Atest Simon Stone foreman
[Hand 5] Cleard ꝑ ꝓclamacon 3: ffeb: 1692/3

Notes: A grand jury had heard evidence against Jane Lilly on January 5 (see No. 544), but no record of an indictment   January 31, 1693
then is extant. Why the matter was not pursued then is unknown. She was cleared by proclamation on February 3, 1693.
The canceled "Billa Ver" is written in the same hand that is found for the complete "Billa Vera" on Mary Toothaker's
indictment on January 31. See No. 829. ◊ Hand 2 = Anthony Checkley

*Suffolk Court Files, vol. 32, docket 2714, p. 52, Massachusetts Supreme Judicial Court, Judicial Archives, Massachusetts State
Archives. Boston, MA.*

828. Indictment of Mary Taylor, for Covenanting

See also: Feb. 1, 1693.

[Hand 1] Prouince of y^e   }   Att A Superio^ε Court of Judicature held at Charlston Jan^εy
Massachusetts Bay in New }   31th 1692 Annoqȝ $\overline{RR}$ & Reginæ & Gulielmi & Mariæ
England ss   }   Angliæ &c quarto
The Juro^εs for o^ε Sou^ε lord & lady the King & Queen p^εsent That Mary Taylor of Reding
Wife of Sebread Taylor of Reding aforsaid In ["In" written over "On"] or about the last
Winter in the yeare 1691 at & in the Towne of Reding in the County of Midlesex aforesaid
Wickedly mallitiou⟨sly⟩ & felloniously A Couenant with the Deuill did make, and made hir
marke vpon A Burch Ryne [= birch rind] to Confirme the Said Couenant & promised the
Deuill to Serue him & trust in him & to giue vp hir Soule & body to him, By which
diabollicall Couenant made with the Deuill in maner & forme aforsaid the Said Mary Taylor
is become a detestable witch Against the peace of o^ε Sou^ε Lord & Lady the King & Queen
their Crowne & dignity & the laws in that Case made & prouided

[Hand 2] Billa Vera
[Hand 3] Atest Simon Stone foreman

[Reverse] [Hand 1] Mary Taylor for Couenanting with y^e Deuill
[Hand 4] Po: se.
Non Cul͞l [= not guilty]

Notes: Mary Taylor was found not guilty on February 1. See No. 831. ◊ Hand 1 = Anthony Checkley

*Suffolk Court Files, vol. 32, docket 2710, p. 43, Massachusetts Supreme Judicial Court, Judicial Archives, Massachusetts State
Archives. Boston, MA.*

829. Indictment of Mary Toothaker, for Covenanting

See also: Feb. 1, 1693.

[Hand 1] Prouince of the   }   At A Superio^ε Court of Judicature held in Charlston for the
Massacusetts Bay in New }   County of Midlesex the 31: Jan^εy 1692/3 Annoqȝ $\overline{RR}$ &
England ss   }   Reginæ Gulielmiæ & Mariæ Angliæ &c Quarto
The Juro^εs for o^ε So͞uer lord & lady the King & Queen present That Mary Toothaker of
[Hand 2] Billrica [Hand 1] in th⟨e⟩ County of Midlsex Widow On or about [   ] at & In the
Towne of [Hand 1?] ^{Belerica} [Hand 1] in the County of Midlesex aforsaid Wickedly

felloniously And mallitiously A Couenant with the Deuill did make & for Confirmacon of the Said Couenant made A marke vpon A peece of Birch Ryne [= rind] which the Deuill brought to hir, & promised to Serue the Deuill, & to praise him with hir whole heart by which Diabollicall Couenant with the Deuill made in maner & forme aforsaid the Said Mary Toothaker is become A detestable Witch Against the peace of oᵉ Souᵉ lord & lady the King & Queen their Crowne & dignit⟨y⟩ & the laws in that Case made & prouided

[Hand 2] Billa Vera
[Hand 3] Atest Simon Stone foreman

[Reverse] [Hand 1] Mary ~~Tayke⟩r~~ {Toothaker} for Couenanting wᵗʰ yᵉ Deuill.
[Hand 4] Ponᵗ se:
[Hand 1] Non Cull [= not guilty]

Notes: The grand jury heard evidence against Mary Toothaker on January 6 (see No. 441), but no indictment for that date is extant. At her trial on February 1 she was found not guilty. See No. 830. ◊ Hand 1 = Anthony Checkley

Suffolk Court Files, vol. 32, docket 2713, p. 50, Massachusetts Supreme Judicial Court, Judicial Archives, Massachusetts State Archives. Boston, MA.

Wednesday, February 1, 1693

Trials of Sarah Cole (of Lynn), Lydia Dustin & Sarah Dustin, Mary Taylor, & Mary Toothaker.

Billa Vera: Indictment of Mary Toothaker, for Covenanting†
2ⁿᵈ of 2 dates. See No. 829 on Jan. 31, 1693

830. Court Record of the Trial of Mary Toothaker

[Hand 1] {Februᵃ 1ˢᵗ} All but yᵉ Ch⟨ei⟩f Justice present
Mary Toothaker of Billerica in the County of Midˣ Widow being Indicted by the Jurors for our Soveraigne Lord and Lady the King and Queen vpon their oaths by one Indictmᵗ That is to say For that Shee the sᵈ Mary Toothaker of Billerica in the County of Midlesex Widow on or about [   ] at ⟨&⟩ in the Towne of Billerica in the County of Midlesex aforesᵈ Wickedly feloneousely and malitiously a Covenant with the Devil⟨l⟩ did make and for Confirmation of the sᵈ Covenant, made a mark upon a peece of Birch Rinde wᶜʰ the Devill brought to her and Promised to serue the Devil⟨l⟩ and to praise him with her wholl heart by wᶜʰ diabo⟨l⟩icall Covenant with the Devill made in maner and forme aforesᵈ The sᵈ Mary Toothacker is becom a destable witch against the peace of our Soveraigne Lord and Lady the King and Queen their Crowne and dignity and the Lawes in that case made and provide⟨d⟩

<u>Jury of Tryall</u>
Samuel Green ffor⟨m⟩
Sam¹ Whitemore Senʳ
Sam¹ Thatcher
Jonathan ffuller
Sam¹ Hartwell
Stephen Willis
James Lowden
Benjᵃ Willington
William Hides
Joseph Willson
Thomas Welch Junᵉ
Vriah Clark.

Upon the aforesᵈ Indictment the sᵈ Mary Toothak⟨er⟩ was then   February 1, 1693
and there before the Justices of oᵉ Lord and Lady the King &
Queen aforesᵈ Arraigned and upon her arraignement did then
and there the day and year aforesaid plead Not Guilty and put
herself vpon Tryall by God and the Country A Jury being called
Samuel Green foreman And accordingly, Sworn no Exception
being made by the prisoner, The said Indictement Examinacōn
and Confession being read, and the prisoners defence being
heard, The Jury went out to agree on their verdict who
returning did then and there the day and year abouesᵈ in open
Court deliver their verdict that the said Mary Toothacker was
Not Guilty of the felony by Covenanting with the Devill in and
by the said Indictment

        The Court Ordered Mary Toothacker to be
        discharged paying her ffees

Records of the Superior Court of Judicature (1692/3), pp. 32–33, Massachusetts Supreme Judicial Court, Judicial Archives, Massachusetts State Archives. Boston, MA.

Billa Vera: Indictment of Mary Taylor, for Covenanting†
2ⁿᵈ of 2 dates. See No. 828 on Jan. 31, 1693

831. Court Record of the Trial of Mary Taylor

[Hand 1] Mary Taylor of Reding wife of Sebread Taylor of Reding aforesᵈ being Indicted by the Jurors for our Soveraigne Lord and Lady the King and Queen upon their oathes by one Indictment That is to say
For that the sᵈ Mary Taylor of Reding Wife of Seabread Taylor of Reding aforesaid in or about the last Winter in the Year 1691 at and in the Towne of Reding in the County of Midlesex aforesᵈ wickedly mallitiousely and feloneousely a Covenant with the Devill did make and made her mark vpon a peece of Birch Rinde to Confirme the said Covenant promising the Devill to serue him and to trust in him and to giue up her Soule and body to him by wᶜʰ Diabollicall Covenant made with the Devill in maner & forme aforesᵈ the sᵈ Mary Taylor is becom a detestable witch against the peace of our Soveraigne Lord & Lady the King and Queen their Crowne and dignity and the Lawes in that Case made and provided.

<u>Jury Swoar⟨n⟩</u>
Sam⟨u⟩el ⟨Hunting⟩
  ["Hunting" written
  over "Green"?]
  {f⟨orm⟩}
Samuel Whitmore
Nathaniel Bassam

Upon the aforesaid Indictment the said Mary Taylor was then and
there before the Justices of our Lord & Lady the King and Queen
aforesᵈ Arraigned & upon her arraignement did then and there
the day & year aforesᵈ plead Not Guilty and put herselfe upon
Tryall by God and the Country.
A Jury being Called Samue⟨ll⟩ Hunt⟨in⟩g foreman And
accordingly Sworne no Exception being made by the prisoner the
sᵈ Indictment Examination and Confession being read and the

February 1, 1693

Stephen Willis
Henry Green
James Lowden
Nathaniel Coolidge
Thomas Welch Jun⟨r⟩
Daniel Dean
Samuel Jenison
Joseph Willson
Josiah Convers

Prisoners defence being heard The Jury went out to agree upon th⟨eir⟩ verdict who returnin⟨g⟩ did then and there the day and year aboues^d in open Court deliver their verdict That the said Mary Taylor was not Guilty of the ffelony by Covenan⟨t⟩ing with the Devill in and by the said Indictment

The Court Ordered the said Mary Taylor ⟨b⟩e discharged paying ffees

Records of the Superior Court of Judicature (1692/3), pp. 33–34, Massachusetts Supreme Judicial Court, Judicial Archives, Massachusetts State Archives. Boston, MA.

Billa Vera: Indictment of Sarah Cole (of Lynn), for Afflicting Mary Brown†
2nd of 2 dates. See No. 826 on Jan. 31, 1693

832. Court Record of the Trial of Sarah Cole (of Lynn)

[Hand 1] Sarah Cole Wife of John Cole of Lynn in th⟨e⟩ County of Essex Cooper being Indicted by the Juror⟨s⟩ for our Soveraign⟨e⟩ Lord and Lady the King and Queen upon their Oathes by one Indictment That is to ⟨sa⟩y

For that Shee the said Sarah Cole wife of John Cole of Lynn in the County of Essex Cooper on or about the Twenty Sixth day of September in the Year of Our Lord 1692 and divers other dayes and times as well before as after Certaine detestable Arts called Witchrafts and Sorcerys Wickedly ["W" written over "C"] Mallitiously and ffeloneously hath used practised and Exersised at and in the Towne of Reding In the County of Midlesex Vpon and against one Mary Browne of Reding in the County of Midlesex afores^d by which Wicked Arts the s^d Mary Browne the day and year afores^d and divers other dayes and times as well before as after was and is Tortur⟨ed⟩ tormented afflicted Consumed pined & Wasted agains⟨t⟩ the peace of Our Soveraigne Lord & Lady the King and Queen their Crowne and Dignity & the Laws in that case made and provided.

Jury Sworne
Samuel Huting
James Thomson
John Clark
Danl D⟨ea⟩n
Nathaniel Bassam
Stephen ffrancis
Josiah Convers
Edward Jackson
Samuel Jenison
Nathan^l Coolidge
⟨J⟩oh⟨n⟩ Oldham

Upon the foresaid Indictment the said Sarah Cole was then and there before the Justices of Our Lord and Lady the King and Queen aforesaid Arrained and vpon her Arraignement did then and there the day and year aforesaid plead Not Guilty an⟨d⟩ put her selfe upon tryall by God and the Country

A Jury being Called Samuell Hunting foreman Accordingly Swoarn no Exception being made by the prisoner the said Indictment togeth⟨er⟩ with Evidences and Examination being read and the prisoners defence being heard the Jury went out to agree on their Verdict who returning did then and there in open Court deliver their Verdict That the said Sarah Cole was Not Guilty of the felony by Witchraft for wch Shee Stood Indicted ⟨i⟩n and by the said Indictment./

⟨H⟩enry Green

The Court Order the said Sa⟨ra⟩h Cole to be discharged paying her ffees.

Notes: Even though Sarah Cole was found not guilty, she remained in custody. She was apparently unable to pay her jail fees and remained in prison until March 23, 1693 (see No. 856).

Records of the Superior Court of Judicature (1692/3), pp. 34–35, Massachusetts Supreme Judicial Court, Judicial Archives, Massachusetts State Archives. Boston, MA.

833. Court Record of the Trial of Lydia Dustin

[Hand 1] Lidiah Dastin of Reding in the County of Midle⟨s⟩ex widow being Indicted by the Jurors ffor our Soveraigne Lord and Lady the King & Queen upon their oaths upon one Indictment. That is to say.

For that Shee the said Lydia Dastin of Reding in the County of Midlesex. widow on or about the second day of May in the year 1692 and divers other dayes and times as well before as after Certain detestable Arts called Witchrafts and sorceries wickedly mallitiousely and ffeloneously hath used practised and exercised at and in the Towne of Malden in the County of Midlesex aforesaid upon and against one Mary Marshall [   ] by which wicked arts the said Mary Marshall the day and year aforesaid & divers other dayes and times as well before as after was afflicted Tortured Tormented Consumed pined & Wasted Contrary to the peace of Our Soveraigne Lord and Lady the King and Queen their Crowne and dignity and the Lawes in that case made. and provided.

Jury Sworn
Mr Samuel Green
ffo:m
John ffrancis
Piam Blower
Thomas Pearce
Samuell Jones
Joseph Russell
Benja Symons
George Read
Jonathan Wyman
Abraham Temple
Samuell Hartwell
David Demmon

Upon the aforesaid Indictment the said Lidia Dastin was then and there before the Justices of our Lord and Lady the King & Queen aforesaid Arraigned and upon her Arraignemt did then and there the day and year aforesaid Plead Not Gu^{i}lty and put herselfe upon tryall by God and the Country.
A Jury being called Samuell Green foreman and accordingly Sworne no exception being made by the prisoner the said Indictment being read together with the E⟨vi⟩dences; and Examination and the prisoners defence being heard The Jury went out to agree on their verdict who returning did then and there in open Court deli⟨ver⟩ their verdict, That the said Lidia Dastin was Not Guilty of the ffellony by Witchcraft for wich she stood Indicted in and by the sd Indictmt

The Court Orderd the said Lydia Da⟨s⟩tin to be discharged paying her ffees

Notes: Even though Lydia Dustin was found not guilty, she remained in custody. The jail bills are incomplete, with a gap of a few days after the verdict when her wherabouts are unknown. She was apparently unable to pay her jail fees, and died in prison on March 10, 1693. See No. 856.

February 1, 1693   *Records of the Superior Court of Judicature (1692/3), p. 35, Massachusetts Supreme Judicial Court, Judicial Archives, Massachusetts State Archives. Boston, MA.*

834. Court Record of the Trial of Sarah Dustin

[Hand 1] Sarah Dastin of Reding in the County of Midlesex being Indicted by the Jurors for our Soveraigne Lord & Lady the King and Queen upon their Oathes by one Indictment. That is to say.

For that the said Sarah Dastin of Reding in the County of Midlesex single-woman on or about the month of May in the year 1692 And divers other dayes and times as well before as after certain detestable arts c⟨all⟩ed Witchcraft and sorceries wickedly mallitiously & ffeloneously hath used practised and Exercised at and in the Towne of Reding in the County of Midlesex aforesaid upon and against one Elizabeth Weston of Reding daughter of John Weston of Reding by which wicked Arts the said Elizabeth Weston the day and year aforesd and divers other dayes and times as well before as after was afflicted tortured tormented pined and wasted against ye pea⟨s⟩e of our Soveraigne Lord & Lady the King & Queen their Crowne and dignity and the Lawes in that case made and provided.

⟨J⟩ury Sworn.
⟨M⟩r Samuel Hunting
⟨S⟩amuel Whitmore
⟨N⟩athaniel Bassam
⟨S⟩tephen Willis
⟨H⟩enry Green
James Lowden
⟨N⟩athaniel Cooledge
Thomas Welch Junᵉ
Daniel Dean
Samuel Jenison
Joseph Willson
Josiah Convers

upon the aforesaid Indictment the said Sarah Dastin wa⟨s⟩ th⟨e⟩n and there before the Justices of ou [= our] Lord and Lady the Kin⟨g⟩ and Queen aforesaid Araigned & upon her Arraignement sh⟨e⟩ did then and there the day and year aforesaid plead to the sa⟨id⟩ Indictment Not Guilty and put herselfe upon Tryall by God and the Country A Jury being called Samuel Hunting fforeman and accordingly sworne no exception being made by the Prisoner The Indictment being read together with the evidences, And the prisoners defence being heard The Jury went out to agree upon their verdict who returning did then and there in open Court deliver their verdict That the said Sarah Dastin was not Guilty of the f⟨f⟩elony by witchcraft for which shee stood Indicted in and by the said Indictment.

The Court Ordered the said Sarah Dastin to be discharged paying her ffees.

Notes: Even though Sarah Dustin was found not guilty, she remained in custody. She was apparently unable to pay her jail fees, and remained in prison until March 23, 1693. See No. 856.

Records of the Superior Court of Judicature (1692/3), p. 36, Massachusetts Supreme Judicial Court, Judicial Archives, Massachusetts State Archives. Boston, MA.

Friday, February 3, 1693

Jane Lilly Cleared by Proclamation

Cleared by Proclamation: Indictment of Jane Lilly, for Afflicting Mary Marshall (Returned Ignoramus)
2nd of 2 dates. See No. 827 on Jan. 31, 1693

Thursday, February 16, 1693

835. Order for Paying Mary Gedney

[Hand 1] Upon Consideration of the Extraordinary Charge ariseing within ye County of Essex by the Special Court of Oyer and Terminer and Court of Assize and General Goal Delivery lately held within that County, and the long continuance of the Tryals there. Ordered

That Me Treasurer pay out of the publick Revenue unto Mes Mary Gedney Innholder in Salem, in part of her accompt for Entertainment of Jurors and Witnesses, the Summ of Forty pounds.

William Phips

Notes: This is probably for Gedney's expenses in 1692. On December 12, 1693 she was awarded what appears to be £70, presumably for her 1693 expenses. See No. 866. ◊ "Entertainment": 'maintenance, support, sustenance' (*OED* s.v. *entertainment* 3).

Colonial Office 5/785, p. 219. National Archives (Great Britain), London, UK.

Tuesday, February 21, 1693

836. Letter of William Phips to the Earl of Nottingham

[Hand 1] Boston In New England Feb^ey 21st 1692/3

S^r

By ye Cap^n of ye Samuel & henry, I gave an Account, that: att my arrivall here, I found ye Prisons full of People, comitted upon Suspicon of witchcraft, & that continuall complaints were made to me, that many persons, were grieveously tormented by witches, & that they cryed out upon Severall persons by name, as ye Cause of their torments. ye number of these complaints increasing every day, by advice of ye Liev^t Gov^er & ye Councell, I gave a Comission of oyer & terminer, to try the Suspected witches, & at that time, ye generality of ye people represented ye matter to me, as reall witchcraft, & gave strange instances of y^e

February 21, 1693

Same; The first in Com̄ission was yᵉ Lievᵗ Govᵉʳ & yᵉ rest were persons of yᵉ best prudence, & figure, that could then be pitched upon, & I depended upon yᵉ Court for a right method of proceeding, In cases of witchcraft, att that time, I went to com̄and the army, at yᵉ Eastern part of yᵉ Province, for yᵉ french and Indians, had made an attacque upon some of our Fronteer townes; I continued there for some time, but when I Returned, I found the people much disatisfied at the proceedings of yᵉ Court, for about Twenty persons were condemned, & executed, of which number, some were thought by many persons to be Innocent; the Court Still proceeded in yᵉ Same method of trying them, which was by the Evidence of yᵉ afflicted persons, who, when they were brought into yᵉ Court, assoon as yᵉ Suspected witches looked upon them, Instantly fell to yᵉ ground, in Strange agonies & grievous torments, but when touched by them, upon yᵉ arme, or some other part of their flesh, they Im̄ediately revived, & came to themselves ["v" written over "f"], upon which they made Oath, that the Prisoner at yᵉ bar did afflict them, & that they Saw their Shape, or Spectre come from their bodies, which put them to Such paines, & torments^: When I enquired into the matter, I was informed by the Judges, that they begun with this, but had humane testimony against Such as were condemned, & undoubted proofe, of their being witches; but at length I found, that yᵉ Devill did take upon him, yᵉ Shape of Innocent persons, & some were accused, of ⟨?⟩ whose Innocency I was well assured o̶f̶, & many considerable persons, of unblameable life, & conversation, were cryed out upon, as witches, & Wizards; The Deputy Govᵉʳ notwithstanding persisted vigorously in the Same method, to yᵉ great disatisfaction, & disturbance of yᵉ People, untill I put an end to yᵉ Court, & Stopped the proceedings, which I did, because I Saw many Innocent persons might otherwise perish, & att that time, I thought it my duty, to give an Account thereof, that their Maᵗⁱᵉˢ pleasure might be Signified, hoping that for yᵉ better ordering thereof, the Judges learned in the Law in England, might give Such direc̄ions [Hand 2] {& rules} [Hand 1] as have been practi⟨z⟩ed in England, for proceedings in so difficult, & nice a point: when I put an end to yᵉ Court, there were at least fifty persons in Prison, in great mis⟨ery⟩ by reason of the Extream cold, & their Poverty, most of them, having only Spectre Evidence, against them, & their Mittimisses being defective; I caused some to be let out upon Baile, & put yᵉ Judges upon considering of a way to reliei⟨f⟩e others, & prevent them from perishing in Prison, upon which some of them were convinced, & acknowledged, that their former proceedings were too violent, & not grounded upon a right foundation, but that if they might Sit againe, they would proceed after another [1 word overstruck] method; & whereas Mʳ Increase Mather & Severall other Divines, did give it as their Judgement; that yᵉ Devill might afflict in yᵉ Shape of an Innocent person, & that the look, & the touch of yᵉ suspected persons, was not sufficient proof against them; These thinges had not yᵉ Same Stress layd upon them as before; & upon this considerāion, I permitted a Spetiall Superior Court, to be held at Salem, in yᵉ County of Essex, on the third Day of January, yᵉ Lievᵗ Govᵉʳ being chief Judge, their method of proceeding being altered, all that were brought to tryall, to yᵉ number of fifety two were cleared, Saving three; & I was Informed, by the Kings Attorny Generall, that some of yᵉ cleared, & yᵉ Condemned, were under yᵉ same circumstances, or that there was yᵉ Same reason, to clear yᵉ Three condemned, as yᵉ rest ac̄ording to his Judgement; The Deputy Govᵉʳ Signed a warrant for their Speedy Execūcon & also of ffive others, who were condemned, at yᵉ former Court of oyer & terminer; but considering how yᵉ matter had been managed, I sent a reprieve, whereby yᵉ Execūcon was stopped, untill their Maᵗⁱᵉˢ pleasure be Signified, & declared; The Lievᵗ Govᵉʳ upon this occasion was inraged, & filled with passionate anger, & refu⟨sed⟩ to sit upon the   February 21, 1693

bench in a Superior Court, held at that time, at Charlestowne, & Indeed hath from yᵉ

beginning hurryed on these matters, wᵗʰ great precipitancy: & by his Warrant hath caused yᵉ

Estates, goods, & chattles of yᵉ executed, to be Seized, & disposed of without my

knowledge, or consent: The Stop put to the first method of proceedings ⌃{hath} dissipated

yᵉ black cloud, that threatned this Province with destruc̄c̄on, for whereas this delusion of yᵉ

Devill, did Spread, & its dismall effects, touched yᵉ ~~reputac̄on~~ lives, & estates of many of

their Maᵗⁱᵉˢ Subiects, & yᵉ reputāc̄on of some of yᵉ principall persons here, & indeed

unhappily clogged, & Interrupted their Maᵗⁱᵉˢ affaires, wᶜʰ has been a great vexation to me! I

have no new complaints, but peoples mindes before divided, & distracted, by different

opinions, concerning this matter, are now well

composed.

I am: ⟨&⟩ [= et cetera?]   Sʳ

                                     Yoᵋʳ most humble Servant,

                                     William Phips

[Reverse] [Hand 3] To The Honᵇˡᵉ william William Blathwayte Esquire att Whitehall

[Hand 4] Boston 21 ⟨f⟩[Lost] [= February]

nᵒ 1

From M⟨ʳ⟩ William ⟨Ph⟩[Lost] [= Phips]

abᵗ yᵉ proc⟨ee⟩di⟨n⟩g⟨s⟩ ag⟨ᵗ⟩ Witch⟨?⟩ [= witchcraft]

Receᵈ 24 May: 1⟨6⟩9⟨3⟩

⟨℞⟩ Capᵗ [1 word illegible]

The Court of Oyer & ter⟨?⟩ [= terminer] for tryall of Witchcraft d⟨?⟩ [= dissolved?]

another ⟨~~ɇ~~{c}⟩reated [= created] ⟨to sit⟩ – moderate in proceeding

3 Condemned for Witch⟨craft⟩ Warrᵗ Signed for Exe⟨cu?⟩ [= executing] them & 5 more

Condem⟨n⟩d formerly

They are repreved by yᵉ Go⟨ᵛ⟩ [= governor] till their Mᵗˢ Order

The Depᵗ Goᵛ [1–2 words illegible] d⟨i⟩d sig⟨ne⟩ Warrᵗˢ for Exe⟨cution⟩ ⟨?⟩ [= and?] seizes

& disposes of yᵉ Estates [Lost] [= of] the Condemned with⟨out⟩ Knowledge of the G⟨oᵛ⟩

[Hand 5] Entr. N: 8 [Several words illegible]

Notes: The minutes of the Governor's Council contradict the claim that Phips was away while the witchcraft cases were occurring. His comment on Increase Mather highlights the central theological issue of the trials. The three condemned people referenced by Phips were Elizabeth Johnson Jr., Mary Post, and Sarah Wardwell. Regarding the other five, both Rebecca Eames and Abigail Faulkner Sr. refer to reprieves by Phips (Nos. 888, 875), but it is not clear as to when these reprieves came. The other condemned survivors are Mary Bradbury, Dorcas Hoar, Abigail Hobbs, Elizabeth Procter, and Mary Lacey Sr. See particularly No. 930. Since Elizabeth Procter and Abigail Faulkner Sr. pled pregnancy, they seem to be tempting possibilities as the extra two not included in the group of five. However, Mary Bradbury had fled without returning until after the Phips pardon, and a reprieve for her while she was a fugitive would have been highly unusual. A definitive list of the five remains elusive. Note that Phips seems to imply that the seizures of estates by Stoughton may have been illegal. Sherrif George Corwin was doing the seizing, but this suggests that it was at Stoughton's direction. What happened with the things seized has never been established, and there is no evidence that anything taken, or of money made from it, went back to England where it would belong in cases of legal seizures. ◊ "assoon": 'as soon.' From the fifteenth to the eighteenth century, this adverbial phrase was often written as one word (see *OED*, s.v. *as soon, assoon* advb. phr.).

Letter of William Phips to the Earl of Nottingham, Feb. 21, 1693, Boston. The Colonial Williamsburg Foundation, John D. Rockefeller, Jr. Library, Williamsburg, VA.

Friday, March 10, 1693

Death of Lydia Dustin in Prison

Tuesday, April 25, 1693

John Alden Cleared by Proclamation

837. Superior Court of Judicature Record Book: Court of Assize and General Jail Delivery Held at Boston, Suffolk County

[Hand 1] Anno RR⁵ et Reginæ Gulielmi et Mariæ Qu⟨i⟩nto

Grand Jury Sworn
Capt. Timothy Clark ffor
⟨J⟩ames Barnes
James Pemberton
Giles Dyer
[Lost]seph [= Joseph]
   Townsend
⟨J⟩oseph Griggs
⟨E⟩dward Dor
⟨B⟩enjᵃ Tucker
Tymothy Tilestone
⟨Is⟩aac Jones Present

At ["At" written over "In"] a Superiour Court of Judicature
Court of Assize & Generall Goal Delivery held at Boston for
the County of Suffolk on the 25⟨th⟩ day of Aprill 1693
        Presens
   William Stoughton Esqᵋ Cheif Justice
   Thomas Danforth Esqᵋ
   John Richards Esqᵋ
   Samuel Sewell Esqᵋ

Notes: For jury warrants see note, No. 730.

Records of the Superior Court of Judicature (1692/3), p. 36, Massachusetts Supreme Judicial Court, Judicial Archives, Massachusetts State Archives. Boston, MA.

Cleared by Proclamation: Recognizance for John Alden by Nathaniel Williams & Samuel Checkley
2ⁿᵈ of 2 dates. See No. 744 on Dec. 31, 1692

838. Court Record of the Proclamation Clearing John Alden

[Hand 1] John Alden of Boston Marriner who Stood Recognized for his appearance at this Court upon Suspition of Witchraft being Called appeared and was discharged by proclamation

Records of the Superior Court of Judicature (1692/3), p. 52, Massachusetts Supreme Judicial Court, Judicial Archives, Massachusetts State Archives. Boston, MA.

839. Court Record of the Hearing of Mary Watkins

[Hand 1] Mary Watkins Single woman Being Accused of falce and Scandalous reports she had made and forged against her Dame [   ] Swift of [   ] as that she was a Witch and had murthered a Child The said Mary Watkins being brought to the Barr upon her Examination acknowledged they were falsce reports and that she had ronged her the Said Swift Whereupon the Court order'd the Sd Watkins to find Suretyes for her good behaviour and her Appearance at the next Court of assize And ["A" written over "h"] Generall Goal Delivery holden for the County of Suffolk and Stand Comitted untill the Same be performd

Notes: Mary Watkins, a servant of Swift, probably Sarah Swift of Milton, confessed on April 25, 1693, that she had falsely accused Swift of witchcraft and child murder. That the judiciary was now punishing people for such false accusations reveals a significant shift from its behavior in 1692 when incidents of known false claims occurred. The perpetrators in 1692 were permitted and even encouraged to continue their behavior. The case of Mary Watkins is almost certainly not connected to cases coming from the Court of Oyer and Terminer or with cases handled in 1693 related to uncompleted 1692 cases. It is included in this edition only to exemplify the return of the judiciary and the community to more traditional ways of dealing with witchcraft accusations.

Records of the Superior Court of Judicature (1692/3), p. 52, Massachusetts Supreme Judicial Court, Judicial Archives, Massachusetts State Archives. Boston, MA.

Wednesday, April 26, 1693

840. Letter of William Phips to George Corwin

[Hand 1] By his Excell^y Sr Wm Phips {Kn^t} Captai⟨n⟩ General & Governo^ε in chief of their Majesti⟨es⟩ Province of the Massachusets-Bay in New E⟨ng⟩[Lost] [= England]
To Capt George Corwi⟨n⟩ High Sheriff of y^⟨e⟩ County of Essex

Whereas Philip English late of Salem Merch^t did b⟨y⟩ his Peti$\overline{co}$n bearing [Lost]nto [= unto?] the second of March last past set forth that you th⟨e⟩ s^d George Corwin in the Month of August last did illegally seize into yo^ε hands the Goods Chattles Merchandi⟨ze⟩ belonging to t⟨he said Philip E⟩[Lost] [= English] and others, praying that you the ⟨s⟩^d G⟨eorg⟩e C⟨orwin might⟩ be ordered to appea⟨r⟩ before me and bring a true Invento⟨ry⟩ of the same Whereupon I then isssued out my Precept commanding you t⟨o⟩ appear before me on the sixth day of the s^d March and to bring with you a true Inventory of the same in eac⟨h⟩ perticular Specie in full Quantity and Quality To the [Lost]ch [= which] Precept you the s^d George Corwin did accordi⟨n⟩gly Appear and did on the [Lost] [= said?] day of the said Mo⟨n⟩th oblidge yo^ε Self by promi⟨se⟩ All the Goods Chattl[Lost] [= chattels] &c so seized from the s^d Philip English to restore them unto him the s^d Philip English or his order upon demand These are therefore in their Matie⟨s⟩ Name to will and re⟨q⟩uire you the s^d George Corwin upo⟨n⟩ sight hereof to deliv⟨e⟩r or cause to be delivered all & singu⟨la⟩[Lost] [= singularly?] the Goods Chattles r⟨ea⟩l & Personal Wares, Merchandize ketch Sloop or anyth⟨ing⟩ to them ⟨in a⟩ny ⟨wi⟩se ⟨a⟩pperta⟨ining⟩ or belonging with all ⟨th⟩e Produce Issues and Pro⟨f⟩fitts the⟨re⟩[Lost] [= therein?] by you received or in any wise from the s^d premisses

May 2, 1693   accruing or arising by you the s^d Ge⟨o⟩rge Corwin ~~seized~~ or yo^ε Order so seized taken or
received from t⟨h⟩e s^d Philip English o⟨r⟩ his Assignes (by vertue or pretence of an⟨y⟩ Order
or colour whatsoever) unto y^e said Philip English or his O⟨rde⟩r in their perticular Species in
full Quanti⟨ty⟩ and Quality And hereof fayle you not as you will Answer y^e contr⟨ary⟩ at yo^ε
Peril Given [Lost]⟨er⟩ [= under] ⟨m⟩y hand & Seale this 26th da⟨y⟩ of April Anno Dom̄
1693 Annoqȝ RR^[Lost] & R^⟨æ⟩ ⟨Guli⟩[Lost] [= Gulielmi & Mariæ] Quinto./

William Phips

[Reverse] [Hand 2] Govern^ε Phipps Prec̄p̄t for restoreing the goods seizd at Mr Englishes

Notes: Opinions have varied over the legality of Corwin's behavior. It is clear here that Governor Phips thought Corwin's
behavior inconsistent with the law.

UNCAT MS, Curwin Papers, American Antiquarian Society, Worcester, MA.

Tuesday, May 2, 1693

841. Account for Payment Submitted by John Arnold, Jailkeeper [?]

[Hand 1] <u>10</u>

<u>1691/2</u>	Brought from page 8 for Continuance D^r [= debtor]		218	13	8
March 9	To Keeping Henry Warren 18 Dayes		——	11	–
	To 2 Chaines for Sarah Good & Sarah Ozburne		——	14	–
14	To keeping Lewis Hutchins 8 Weekes		—1	——	–
April 5	To 2 Blankets for Sarah Good'^s Child ꝑ ord^ε of the				
<u>1692</u>	Governo^ε & Council		——	16	–
29	To 500 foot of Boards to mend the Goale and				
	Prison house	£1//10//–			
	4 Locks for the Goale	£–//8//–			
	2 C [= 200] of Nayles	£–//3//–			
	Repairing the Prison house	£2//8//–	—4	–9	–
May 10	To 3 large Locks for the Goal		——	–9	9
23	To Shackles for 10 prison^εs ꝑ his Excell^cis order		—2	–5	–
29	To 1 p^r [= pair] of Irons for Mary Cox		——	–7	–
	To Keeping Sundry Prison^εs Viz^t /.				
	Sarah Ozburne from the 7th of March				
	169½ the time of her Committment				
	to the 10th of May ∧{1692} when she Dyed				
	is 9 Weeks 2 Dayes – at 2/6 ꝑ Weeke	1//3//2½			
	Sarah Good from the 7th of March <u>1691/2</u>				
	to the 1° of June following 12 Weekes &				
	2 Dayes when d̄d̄ out – at 2/6 ꝑ	1//10//8½			

Rebeckah Nurse from ye 12th of April
   {1692} when rec^d into Custody to the 1° of
   June foll° when d̄d̄ out 7 Weeks 1 Day   –//17//6
John Willard from the 18th of May to the
   1° of June foll° 14 Dayes – at 2/6 ⍺ W   –//5//–
John Procter & Eliz^a his Wife from the
   12th April to the 1° of June is 7 Weeks
   one Day at 2/6 each ⍺ Weeke   1//15//8
Susannah Martin from the 2^d May
   to the 1° of June 4 Weeks 2 Dayes   –//10//8
Bridget Bishop a̅l̅s Oliver from the
   12th of May to the 1° of June 20
   Dayes – at 2/6 ⍺ Weeke   –//7//2
Alice Parker from the 12th May to
   the 1° of June 20 Dayes   –//7//2
Tituba an Indian Woman from the
   7th of March 1691/2 to the 1° of June
   12 Weekes 2 Dayes at 2/6   1//10//8   —8   –7 9
            //Carried to page 12   £237 13 2

12

1692   Brought from page 10 for Continuance of D^r   237 13 2

     To Keeping Sundry Prisoners as followeth Viz^t
+   Samuel Passanauton an Indian from the
     28th of April 1692 to the 27th of June   1//1//5
     8 Weeks 4 Dayes u̶n̶t̶o̶ at 2/6 ⍺ Weeke
     George Burroughs from the 9th of May
     to the 19th of June when d̄d̄ out is 5
     Weeks 6 Dayes – at 2/6   –//14//8
     George Jacobs from the 12th of May to
     the 19 June 5 Weeks 3 Dayes at 2/6   –//13//6
     Charles ffrancoy from ye 12th May to the
     27th of June 6 Weeks 4 Dayes at 2/6   –//16//5
     Roger Toothaker from the 18th May to
     the 17th June the time he Dyed 4 Weeks
     2 Dayes – at 2/6   –//10//8 —3 16 8
   To Keeping
     Martha Sparks from the 28th of Octob^ε
     1691 to the 8th of Decemb^r 1692
     58 Weekes – at 2/6 ⍺ W   7//5//–
     Martha Cory from the 12th of April 92
     to the 19th of June following is 9
     Weekes 5 Dayes – at 2/6   1//4//2
     Sarah Cloise from ye 12th of April to
     the 19th of June 9 W 5 Days at 2/6   1//4//2
     Jeane Duglas from the 22^d of April
     to the 6^t of Aug° is 15 Weekes one

May 2, 1693

Day – at 2/6 ⅌	1//17//6			

Lydia Dastein from the 2^d of May to
   the 19th June is 6 Weeks 6 Dayes at 2/6   –//17//–
Dorcas Hoare from D^o 2^d May to D^o 19th
   of June   –//17//–

+   ffrancis Lebarre & ffrancis Blang of
   Canada prison^{ᵉs} of Warre from the
   3^d of May unto the 25th of July
   11 Weeks 6 Dayes at 5/ each ⅌ Weeke   5//18//2
Sarah Dasten Bethia Carter &
Anne Seires from the 9th of May
   to the 19th of June is 5 Weekes &
   6 Dayes at 2/6 each ⅌ Weeke   2//3//10
Anne Pudeter Gyles Cory & Sarah Wild
   from the 12 May to D^o 19th June 5 Weeks
   3 Days at 2/6 each ⅌ Weeke   2//6//–   —23   12   10
                    //Carried to page 14   £265 –2   8

<u>14</u>
<u>1692</u>   Brought from page 12 for Continuance D^r   265   –2   8
To Keeping
   William Hobbs 30 Weekes 6 Dayes
      from the 12th of May 1692 to the 14th
      Decemb^ᵉ following at 2/6 ⅌ Week   3//17//⟨–⟩
   Elizabeth Hart from the 18th of May
      to the 7th of December – 29 Weeks
      at 2/6   3//12//6
   Mary Easty 3 Weeks 6 Dayes from the
      23^d May to the 19th of June at 2/6   –//9//6
   Sarah Basset from Ditto 23^d May to the
      3^d of Decemb^ᵉ following ~~at 2/6~~
      is 27 Weeks 5 Dayes – at 2/6 ⅌   3//9//2
   Susannah Roots 3 Weeks 6 Dayes from
      D^o 23^d May to the 19th June at 2/6   –//9//6
   Mary Derrick from D^o 23^d May to the
      11th of Septemb^ᵉ 15 Weeks 6 Dayes at 2/6   1//19//6
   Benj^a Proctor from D^o 23^d May to the
      30th of Novemb^ᵉ foll^o is 27 Weeks 2 Days   3//8//2
   Mary Cox 25 Weeks one Day from the
      30th of May to the 22^d Novemb^ᵉ at 2/6   3//2//10

+   7 prison^{ᵉs} ffrenchmen Viz^t Wm Bonny
   Anthony Sally, John ⟨T⟩haum Rheene=Pree,
   David Labatt, Christopher ffrancis
   & Anthony Vernon from the 29th of
   May to the 27 of June being 29 Dayes
   at 2/6 each ⅌ Weeke   3//10//–

May 2, 1693

Dorothy Good 34 Weekes 4 Dayes from
    the 12ᵗʰ of April to the 10ᵗʰ of Decembᵉ
    at 2/6 ℔ W   4//6//4
Sarah Rice from the 31ˢᵗ of May to the
    2ᵈ of Decembᵉ 27 Weeks 4 Dayes at 2/6   3//8//10
Thomas ffarrar 28 Weeks 2 Dayes from
    the 18ᵗʰ of May to the 2ᵈ Decembᵉ at 2/6   3//10//8
William Dutton from the 5ᵗʰ of July
    to the 17ᵗʰ Decembᵉ 23 Weeks 4 Dayes   2//18//10
Abigail Soames 32 Weeks one Day from
    the 23ᵈ May to the 3ᵈ of Janᵉʸ at 2/6   4//−//4
Sarah Murrel from the 2ᵈ May to the
    3ᵈ of Janᵉʸ 35 Weeks one Day at 2/6   4//7//10   —46   11   −

                     //Carried to page 16   £311   13   8

16

1692   <u>Brought from page 14 for Continuance Dʳ</u>   311   13   8

To Keeping
    Mary a Negro Woman 33 Weeks 5 Day{s}
        from the 12ᵗʰ of May 1692 to the 3ᵈ of
        Janᵉʸ following at 2/6 ℔ Weeke   4//4//2

+   John Morgan from the 31ˢᵗ of Janᵉʸ
        to the 8ᵗʰ of Febᵉʸ 9 Dayes 3/ ffees 5/   −//8//−   —4   12   2

    To mending the Stone Goale where
        ffleetwood & black Tom broke out   ——   10   −

+   To Keeping Sundry ffrench & Indian Prisonᵉˢ Vizᵗ
    One Indian Boy d̄d̄ ℔ ordᵉ to Capᵗ Richard
        Short being one of the fifteene prisoners
        brought from the Eastward Comitted the 24
        August 1692 & dd the 7ᵗʰ Sepᵗ following is
        14 Dayes at 2/6 ℔ Weeke   −//5//−
    One Indian Girle d̄d̄ To Sʳ Robinson one
        of the 15 Comitted Ditto Diem & d̄d̄ the
        12ᵗʰ of Sepᵗ is 19 Dayes − at 2/6 ℔ Weeke   −//6//8
    Francis Lateril frenchman from the
        4ᵗʰ of ffebᵉʸ 1692/3 to the 16ᵗʰ Dᵒ 12 Dayes at
        2/6 ℔ Week d̄d̄ ℔ ordᵉ to Mʳ Math̄ Cary   −//4//2
    John Brittoone from Dᵒ 4ᵗʰ Febᵉʸ to yᵉ
        11ᵗʰ of March 5 Weeks at 2/6 ℔ W
        d̄d̄ ℔ ordᵉ to Capᵗ Smithson   −//12//6
    Peter Alber & James Lafavory from
        Dᵒ 4ᵗʰ of Febᵉʸ to Dᵒ 11ᵗʰ March 5 Weeks
        at 2/6 each ℔ Week d̄d̄ ℔ order to
    Mʳ Mathew Cary   ⟨?⟩//⟨?5⟩//−
    Cockerandus an Indian one of the 15
        prisonᵉˢ, from the 24ᵗʰ of Augᵒ 1692 to the
        11ᵗʰ of March ^{⟨?⟩} 28 Weeks 3 Dayes at
        2/6 ℔ W d̄d̄ ℔ ordᵉ to Mʳ Math: Cary   3//11//−

May 2, 1693

Charles St Oben & Charles Lafloure & their family⟨e⟩s being 10 of the 15 prison^{εs} from D^o 24th of Aug^o 8 Weekes each 2/6 ℔ W	10//–//–	–16	–4	4
To Keeping Capt Richd Short from the 4th of Jan^{εy} 169^2/$_3$ three Weeks at 8/ ℔ Weeke		—1	–4	–
To 20 Cord of Wood Expended on Sundry ℔sons Committed for Witchcraft in the Winter 1692		—8	—	–
//Carried to page 18		£342	–4	2

18
1693

Brought from page 16 for Continuance of D^r		342	–4	2
+ To Keeping Elizabeth Emerson from the 3^d of May 1691 the time of her Commitm^t unto May the 2^d 1693 being 104 Weeks at 2/6 ℔ Weeke		–13	—	–
+ To Ditto of Grace a Negro Woman from Jan^{εy} 13th 1692 unto ^{D^o} May y^e 2^d 1693 is 15 Weeks 4 Days at 2/6		—1	18	10
To Keeping				
Mary Watkins from the 5th of Decemb^ε 1692 to to the 2^d of May following being 21 Weeks – at 2/6	2//12//6			
Susannah Davis from the 28th of Jan^{εy} 9^2/$_3$ {D̶o̶} D^o ["D^o" written over "y^e"] 2^d of May foll^o is 14 Weeks at 2/6	1//15//–			
Timothy Batt from the 8th of Feb^{εy} 92/3 to D^o 2^d of May is 12 Weeks at 2/6	1//10//–	—5	17	6
To Bedding Blankets & Clothes for sundry poore Prison^{εs} Committed for Witchcraft by Order of the Governm^t		–16	—	–
To my Sallery for one Yeare ^{&} Tenn months from the 27th of June 1691 unto May the 2^d ⟨1⟩693		–36	13	4
		£415	13	10

Notes: This account includes various entries unrelated to the Salem witch trials, but has valuable information pertaining to them as well. The account includes a number of items for which John Arnold received compensation on September 12, 1692. See No. 612. How this account was handled has not been determined, and it is assigned here in the chronology to the last dated entry in it. The "+" marks on the manuscript seem to identify non witchcraft cases, but the reliability of the marks, while dependable in some instances, is not always certain. A real possibility exists that they were inserted by a later archivist.

Judicial Volume 40 (1683–1724), pp. 10–18. Massachusetts State Archives. Boston, MA.

Tuesday, May 9, 1693

Grand Juries of Daniel Eames & Tituba

842. Superior Court of Judicature Record Book: Court of Assize and General Jail Delivery Held at Ipswich, Essex County

[Hand 1] At a Superiour Court of Judicature ⟨C⟩ourt of Assize & Generall Goal Delivery. ⟨h⟩olden at Ipswich the second Tuesday in ⟨M⟩ay 1693 for the County of Essex.

Present

Thomas Danforth Esq^ε
John Richards Esq^ε
Samuel Sewell Esq^ε

Grand Jury
M^ε Sam^{ll} Apleton ⟨ffo⟩
Richard Walker
William Andrews
Benj^a Marston
Benj^a Allen
John ffelton
William Haberfield
John Clifford
Thomas Hawkins
William Stone
Samuel Blanchar⟨d⟩
William Chandle
James Ordway
Benj^a Mors
Thomas Dorman
Abraham Hesleton
Caleb Bointon

Notes: For jury warrants see note, No. 730.

Records of the Superior Court of Judicature (1692/3), p. 53, Massachusetts Supreme Judicial Court, Judicial Archives, Massachusetts State Archives. Boston, MA.

843. Indictment of Daniel Eames, for Afflicting Mary Warren (Returned Ignoramus)‡

[Hand 1] Province of y^e } [Hand 2] Anno RRs & Reginæ Gulielmi & Mariæ Angliæ
Massathutetts Bay in New } &^{c} Quinto ["Quinto" written over "Quarto"] Annoqȝ D$\overline{m}$
England. Essex ss } 1693.["3" written over "2"]
The Juro^ε for our Sovereigne Lord & Lady the King and. Queen p^{ε}sents That [Hand 3] **Daniell Emms of [   ] in the County of Essex af~~ors~~d On or about the thirteenth day of August last in the Yeare 1692 af~~ors~~d** [Hand 2] and Divers other Dayes & times as well before as after Certaine Detestable Arts Called witchcrafts and Sorceries wickedly Mallishiously and ffelloniously hath vsed Practised and Excersised at and in the Towne of [Hand 3] **Salem** [Hand 2] in the County of Essex afor~~es~~d vpon and against one [Hand 3] **Mary**∧**{Warren}** ~~Walcott~~ **of Salem Single Woman** [Hand 2] by which wicked Arts the said

[Hand 3] **Mary Warren** [Hand 2] the Day and Year aforesaid and Divers other Dayes and times as well before as after, was and is Tortured Afflicted Tormented Consumed Pined and wasted. against yᵉ Peace of our Sovereigne Lord and Lady. the King and Queen their Crowne & Dignity and agᵗ the Lawes in that Case made and Provided/
[Hand 3] Wittness Mary Walcott
An Putnam

[Reverse] Daniel Emms for Aflicting Mary Warren
[Hand 4] Ignoramus
Abraham Haseltine foreman of yᵉ Grand Jury

Notes: This document is dated here May 9, but May 10 is also a possibility. ◊ Hand 2 = Anthony Checkley

UNCAT MS, *Miscellaneous Manuscripts (1692), Massachusetts Historical Society. Boston, MA.*

844. Indictment of Tituba, for Covenanting (Returned Ignoramus)

[Hand 1] Prouince of the }   At A Court of Assize & Generall Goale deliuery held in
Massachusetts Bay in New }   Ipswich for the County of Essex aforsaid the ninth day of
England Essex ss// }   May 1693. In the fifth yeare of their Majᵗˢ Reigne
The Juroᵋs for oᵋ Souᵋ Lord & lady the King & Queen pᵋsent That Tittapa an Indian Woman seruant to mᵋ samuel Parris of Salem Villag⟨e⟩ ∧{In the A⟨?⟩ County of Essex aforesaid} vpon or about the latter end of the yeare 1691 In the Towne of Salem Village ∧{aforsᵈ} wickedly mallitiously & felloniously A Couenant with the Deuill did make & Signed the Deuills Booke with A marke like A: C by which wicked Couenanting with yᵉ Deuill She the Said Tittapa is become A detestable Witch Against the peace of oᵋ Souēr lord & lady the King & Queen their Crowne & dignity & the laws in that Case made & prouided.

[Reverse] Indictmᵗ Agst Tittapa Indian seruant to mᵋ samˡ Parris
[Hand 2] Ignoramus
Abraham Haseltine foreman of the Grand Jury

Notes: The ignoramus on this indictment for Tituba completes the movement from acceptance of her witchcraft claims that were highly significant in the early stages of the witch trials, since she was the first to confess, to judicial rejection of those claims. ◊ Hand 1 = Anthony Checkley

Suffolk Court Files, vol. 32, docket 2760, p. 102, Massachusetts Supreme Judicial Court, Judicial Archives, Massachusetts State Archives. Boston, MA.

Wednesday, May 10, 1693

Grand Jury of Mary Bridges Jr.

Trials of Susannah Post, Eunice Frye, Mary Bridges Jr., Mary Barker & William Barker Jr.

Sarah Cole (of Salem)‡, Dorothy Faulkner, Abigail Faulkner Jr., Martha Tyler, Johannah Tyler, Sarah Wilson Jr., & Sarah Wilson Sr. Cleared by Proclamation

Appeared: Recognizance for William Barker Jr. & Mary Barker by John Barker & John Osgood Sr.
2nd of 2 dates. See No. 818 on Jan. 13, 1693

Appeared: Recognizance for Mary Bridges Jr. by John Bridges & John Osgood Sr.
2nd of 2 dates. See No. 794 on Jan. 12, 1693

Appeared: Recognizance for Sarah Cole (of Salem) by Abraham Cole‡
2nd of 2 dates. See No. 823 on Jan. 14, 1693

Appeared: Recognizance for Dorothy Faulkner & Abigail Faulkner Jr. by Francis Faulkner & Joseph Marble
2nd of 2 dates. See No. 819 on Jan. 13, 1693

Appeared: Recognizance for Eunice Frye by John Osgood Sr. & James Frye
2nd of 2 dates. See No. 795 on Jan. 12, 1693

Appeared: Recognizance for Martha Tyler & Johannah Tyler by Hopestill Tyler & John Bridges
2nd of 2 dates. See No. 820 on Jan. 13, 1693

Appeared: Recognizance for Sarah Wilson Jr., & Sarah Wilson Sr. by John Osgood Sr. & Joseph Wilson
2nd of 2 dates. See No. 821 on Jan. 13, 1693

845. Indictment of Mary Bridges Jr., for Covenanting†

[Hand 1] Prouince of the Massachusetts Bay In New England Essex ss } Anno $\overline{RR}$s & Reginæ Gulielmi & Mariæ Angliæ &c Quinto ["in" written over "ar"] Annoqʒ Dom 1693 ["3" written over "2"]

The Juro^{ε}s for o^{r} Sou^{ε} lord & Lady the King & Queen p^{ε}sent That Mary Bridges Junio^{ε} of Andiuo^{ε} In the County of Essex afo$\overline{rs}$d In or about the moneth of July last in the yeare 1692 afors^{d} in the Towne of Andiuo^{ε} in the County of Essex aforesaid Wickedly mallitiously & felloniously A Couenant with the Devill did make & Signed A pa₥ to the Deuill & [2 words overstruck] was Baptized by the Deuill By which Wicked Diabollicall Couenant with the Deuill made by the Said Mary Bridges Junio^{ε} ∧{shee} is become A detestable Witch Contrary to the peace of o^{ε} Sou^{ε} lord & Lady the King & Queen their Crowne & Dignity & the laws in that Case made & prouided
wittness hir owne Confession

[Reverse] Mary Bridges Junio^{ε} for Couenanting wth ye Devill
[Hand 2] Billa Verra

May 10, 1693   [Hand 3] Abraham Haseltine foreman of y^e granjurye
                      [Hand 4] not Guilty
                      Tryed

Notes: The date in the head of the indictment had been changed from "Quarto" to "Quinto" and "1692" to "1693," suggesting that an earlier hearing of Bridges's case may have been originally planned. ◊ Hand 1 = Anthony Checkley

Suffolk Court Files, vol. 32, docket 2729, p. 72, Massachusetts Supreme Judicial Court, Judicial Archives, Massachusetts State Archives. Boston, MA.

846. Indictment of Mary Bridges Jr., for Afflicting Rose Foster†

[Hand 1] Province of y^e Massathutets Bay in New England Essex } Anno RRs & Reginæ Gulielmi & Mariæ Angliæ &^c Quinto ["in" written over "ar"] Annoq̃ Dom̄ 1693 ["3" written over "2"]
The Juro^ɛ for our Sov^ɛ Lord and Lady the King & Queen p^ɛsents That [Hand 2] **Mary Bridges of Andiuo^ɛ Junio^ɛ On or about the Twenty fifth day of August last in the Yeare 1692 aforesaid** [Hand 1] And Divers other Dayes & times as well before as after Certaine Detestable Arts ⟨e⟩ called Witchcrafts and Sorceries wickedly Mallishiously and ffelloniously hath vsed Practised and Exercised at and in the Towne of [Hand 2] **Salem** [Hand 1] in the Cownty of Essex aforesaid vpon and against one [Hand 2] **Rose ffoster of Anduo^ɛ aforesaid Single Woman** [Hand 1] by which Wicked Arts the said [Hand 2] **Rose ffoster** [Hand 1] The Day and year aforesaid and Divers other Dayes and times as well before as after, was and is Tortured Afflicted Tormented Consumed. Pined and wasted against the Peace of our Sovereigne Lord and Lady the King and Queen their Crowne and Dignity, and ag^t the Lawes in that case made & Provided
[Hand 2] Wittness hir Confession
Martha Sprague All [= alias] Tyler & Rose ffoster hir selfe

[Reverse] Mary Bridges Junio^ɛ for Aflicting Rose ffoster
[Hand 3] Billa Verra
Abraham Haseltine foreman of y^e Grand Jury
[Hand 4] not Guilty
Tryed

Notes: See the note for No. 845 regarding the change made to the date. ◊ Hand 2 = Anthony Checkley

Suffolk Court Files, vol. 32, docket 2729, p. 72, Massachusetts Supreme Judicial Court, Judicial Archives, Massachusetts State Archives. Boston, MA.

Billa Vera: Indictment of Susannah Post, for Covenanting†
2nd of 2 dates. See No. 774 on Jan. 7, 1693

Billa Vera: Indictment of Susannah Post, for Afflicting Rose Foster†
2nd of 2 dates. See No. 775 on Jan. 7, 1693

847. Court Record of the Trial of Susannah Post‡

May 10, 1693

[Hand 1] Susanah Post of Andover in the County of Essex ["ss" written over earlier "x"] Single woeman being Indicted by the Jurors of our Soveraigne Lord & lady the King and Queen upon their oathes by Two Severall Indictments That is to Say 1st

For that she the Said Susannah Post of Andover Single woman about Three yeares Since in the Towne of Andover in the County of Essex aforesaid Wickedly malitiously & felloniously A Covenant with the Devill did make & Signed the Devills ["e" written over earlier "i"] booke & was Baptized by the Devill & promised to Serve the Devill By which diabolicall Covenanting with the Divill in manner and forme aforesaid by the Said S⟨u⟩sannah ["Sus" written over "H"] Post made the Said Susannah Post is become a Detestable witch against the peace of our Soveraigne Lord and Lady the King and Queen their Crowne dignity & the Laws in tha⟨t⟩ Case made & provided

2dly For that She the Said Susanah Post of Andover in the County of Essex Single woeman, on the 25th day of Augst in the yeare 1692 and divers other dayes and tymes as well before as after Certaine Detestable Artes Called Witch crafts & Sorceries wickedly Mallitiously and ffelloniously hath used practised at & in the towne of Salem in the County aforesaid upon and agst one Rose ffoster of Andover Single woeman By which wicked Arts the Said Rose Foster the day and yeare aforesd and divers other dayes and times as well as [2 words illegible] [*SWP* = after was] and is Tortured afflict⟨ed⟩ Tormented Consumed pined & wast⟨ed⟩ [1 word illegible] [*SWP* = agst] ⟨the⟩ [1 word illegible] [*SWP* = peace] of our Soveraigne Lord and Lady the King and Queen their ⟨C⟩rown⟨e⟩ and dignity and the law in Case made and provided.

[1 word illegible] [*SWP* = Upon] ⟨the⟩ aforesaid Indictments and each of them the said Susana [1 word illegible] [*SWP* = Post] was th⟨e⟩n and there before the Justices of our Lord and Lady the King ⟨a⟩nd Queen aforesaid arraigned ⟨&⟩ upon her [Lost]mt [*SWP* = arraignmt] She did then and [1 word illegible] [*SWP* = there] the day and [2 words illegible] [*SWP* = year abovesaid] pl⟨e⟩ad to them and each of them not Guilty and put [2 words illegible] [*SWP* = her Selfe] ⟨u⟩pon Try⟨a⟩ll by God and her Co⟨n⟩t⟨re⟩y

A Jury being call⟨ed⟩ Th⟨omas⟩ Burnham fforeman and accordingly ⟨S⟩worne noe exception being made by the pris⟨o⟩ner The Said Indi⟨c⟩tmts and each of them b⟨e⟩ing [1 word illegible] [*SWP* = read] together with Evidences, & Examinations ⟨a⟩nd the prisoners defence being ⟨he⟩ard, The j⟨u⟩ry went out to agree on their verdict who returning did then and there in open Court deliver That the Said Susannah Post was not Guilty of the fellony by witchcraft for wch she Stood indcted in and by the Sd Indictmts and each of them.

> The Court Order'd Susanah Post aforesaid To be
> Discharged Paying her ffees

Notes: Susannah Post was probably the first of the group tried and found not guilty on May 10.

Records of the Superior Court of Judicature (1692/3), pp. 56–57, Massachusetts Supreme Judicial Court, Judicial Archives, Massachusetts State Archives. Boston, MA.

May 10, 1693

848. Court Record of the Trial of Eunice Frye

[Hand 1] Eumice ffrie wife of John ffrie of Andov^ε in the County of Essex being Indicted by the Jurors of our Soveraigne Lord and Lady the King and Queen upon their oathes by T⟨?⟩ [*SWP* = Two] Severall Indictm^{ts} That is to Say 1st

For that she the Said Eumice ffrie the wife of John ffrie of Andov^ε in the County of Essex aforesaid about two yeares agoe in the towne of Andover afores^d Wickedly felloniously & Malitiously, A Covenant with the Devill did make, and Signed the Devills book and gave up her Selfe Soul and body to the Devil and by him was baptized and renounced her former baptizme & God & Jesus Christ By which wicked and Diabolicall Coven^t with the Devil made by her Eumice ffrie she is become a Damnable Witch against the peace of our Sover^ε Lord & Lady the King & Queen their Crowne &. dignity and the Laws in that case made and provided

2dly For that she the S^d Emice ffrie the wife of John ffrie of Andov^ε in the County of Essex On or about the begining of September last in the year 1692 aforesaid and Divers other dayes and times as well before and after Certaine Detestable arts called witch crafts and Sorceries wickedly Malitiously and ffelloniously hath used practised and Exercised at & in the Towne of Salem in the County of Essex afores^d upon and against one Martha Sprague Alias Marth⟨a⟩ Tyler by ∧{w^{ch}} wicked Arts the Said Martha Sprague alias Tyler the day and yeare afores^d & divers other dayes and tymes as well before as. after was & is Tortured afflicted Tormented Consumed pined and wasted against the peace of our Soveraign Lord & lady the King & Queen their Crowne and Dignity and against the Law⟨s⟩ in that case made and provided.

Upon the aforesaid Indictm^{ts} and each of them the Said Eumice ffrie was then and there before the justices of our Lord & Lady ⟨the⟩ King and Queen afores^d Arraigned and upon her Arraignm^t She did then and there the day and year abovesaid plead to them and each of them not Guilty and put her Selfe ⟨u⟩pon triall by God and her Countrey

A Jury being call⟨ed⟩ Tho: Burn⟨a⟩m foreman and accordingly Sworne no exception being made ⟨by⟩ the prisoner the Said Indictm^{ts} and each of them being ⟨read⟩ toge⟨ther⟩ ⟨w⟩ith Evidences & Examination⟨s⟩ and the prisoners defence being he⟨ar⟩d the jury went out to agree on their verdic⟨t⟩ who returning did then and there in open Court deliver their verdict. That the Said Eumice ffrie was not Guilty of the ffellony by Witchcraft for which she stood Indicted in & by the Said Indictm^{ts} and ∧{each} of them.

> The Court Orderd Emice ffrie aforesaid To be
> Discharged Paying her ffees.

Records of the Superior Court of Judicature (1692/3), pp. 57–58, Massachusetts Supreme Judicial Court, Judicial Archives, Massachusetts State Archives. Boston, MA.

849. Court Record of the Trial of Mary Bridges Jr.

[Hand 1] Mary Bridges Junior of Andover in the County of Essex Single woman being Indicted by the jurors of our Sov^{ε}n Lord and Lady The King and Queen upon their oathes by Two – Severall ["S" written over "I"] Indictments That is to Say 1st

For that the Said Mary Bridges ⌃{Jun^ε} of Andov^ε Single woeman In or about the moneth   May 10, 1693
of July last in the yeare <u>1692</u> afored in the Towne of Andov^ε in the County of Essex
afforesaid Wickedly malitious & felloniously A Covenant with the Devil did make and
Signed a pap to the Devil and was Baptized by the Devill, By which wicked Diabolical
Covenant with the Divell made by the Said Mary Bridges Jun^ε She is become A detestable
Witch Contrary to the peace of our Lord & lady the King & Queen their Crowne and
dignity and the lawes in that Case made and provided

2dly ffor that she the Said Mary Bridges Jun^ε of Andover in the County of Essex Single
woeman on or about the 25th day of August in the yeare 1692 aforesaid and divers other days
& times as well before as after Certaine detestable Arts called witch crafts and Sorceries
wickedly Maliciously and ffelloniously used Practiced & Exercis'd at and in the towne of
Salem in the County of Essex aforesaid upon and against one Rose ffoster of Andov^ε
aforesaid Single woman By which wicked arts the Said ⟨R⟩ose ffoster the day and year afores^d
and di⟨vers⟩ other dayes and t⟨ime⟩s ⟨a⟩s well before as after was and is Tortur'd afflicted
Tormented Cons⟨ume⟩d ⟨P⟩ined and wasted ag^t the peac⟨e⟩ of our Sovereigne Lord and Lady
the King and Queen their Crown & dignity & ag^t the laws in that case made & pro⟨vided⟩
⟨u⟩pon the aforesaid Indictm^{ts} and each of them the Said Mary Br⟨i⟩dges ⟨J⟩unior was then
and there before the justices of our Lord and Lady the King and Queen afforesaid Arraigned
& upon her Arraignment S⟨he⟩ did then and there ⟨the⟩ day and year aboves^d plead to them
and each of them not Guilty and put h⟨er⟩ Selfe upon tryall by God & her Country.

A Jury being Called Thomas Burnham foreman & Accordingly Sworne no exception being
made by the prisoner the s^d Indictm^{ts} & each of them being read together with Evidenc⟨es⟩
& Examinations and the prisoners defence being heard the jury went out to agree on their
verdict who returning did then and there in open Court deliver their verdict That the Said
Mary Bridges Jun^ε was not Guilty of the ffellony by Witch craft for wch She Stood Indicted
in & by the Said Indictments and each of them

> The Court Orderd Mary Bridges Junior to be
> discharged Paying her fees.

Records of the Superior Court of Judicature (1692/3), pp. 58–59, Massachusetts Supreme Judicial Court, Judicial Archives, Massachusetts State Archives. Boston, MA.

Billa Vera: Indictment of Mary Barker, for Afflicting Rose Foster†

2nd of 2 dates. See No. 801 on Jan. 13, 1693

Billa Vera: Indictment of Mary Barker, for Afflicting Abigail Martin†

2nd of 2 dates. See No. 802 on Jan. 13, 1693

850. Court Record of the Trial of Mary Barker

[Hand 1] Mary Barker of Andover in the County of Essex Single woman being Indicted by
the jurors of our Sovereigne Lord and Lady The King and Queen upon their oathes by two
Severall Indictments Thas [= That] is to Say 1st

For that the Said Mary Barker of Andov^ε Single woeman on or about the 29th day of Augs^t
last in the yeare 1692 afores^d and divers other dayes and times both before and after Certaine

detestable arts called Witchcraft and Sorceries wickedly and felloniously & Mallitiously ha⟨th⟩ used practise⟨d⟩ and Exercis'd in and upon the body of Abigail martin of Andivor at and within the Town ship of Andiv^ε afores^d by wch Said wicked acts the Said Abigail Martin the day aforesaid in the year afores^d And at divers other dayes & tymes as well before as after was and is Tortured aflicted and Tormented consumed pined and wasted against the peace of our Sovereigne Lord and Lady King and Queen their Crowne & dignity and the Statute of the first of King James the first in that case made and provided.

2^{d}ly For that she the Said Mary Barker of Andover Single woman on or about the 29th day of Augst last in the year aforesaid and divers other dayes and tymes as well before as after Certaine detestable arts Called Witchcraft and Sorceries Wickedly Malitiously & felloniously hath used practiced & Exercised at and in the Towne of Andover in the County of Essex aforesaid in and upon & against one Rose ffoster of Andover afores^d Single woeman. by which Said Wicked acts the Said Rose ffoster the day and yeare aforesaid & diuer⟨s⟩ oth⟨e⟩r dayes and tymes both before and after was and is Tortured afflicted Consumed pined Wast⟨e⟩d and Tormented ags^t the peace of our Sove^ε Lord and Lady the King & Queen their Crown and dignity and the forme of the Statute in that Case made & provided.

Vpon the afores^d Indictm^{ts} and each of them The Said Mary Barker was then and there before the Justices of ⟨ou⟩r Lord and lady the King and Queen aforesaid arraigned and upon her Arraingnment She did then and there the day and yeare abovesaid plead to them and each of them Not Guilty and put her Selfe upon Tryall by God and her Countrey

A Jury being Called Cap't Jn⟨o⟩ Putnam foreman & accordingly Sworne no Exception being made by the prisoner the Said Indictm^{ts} and each of them being read together with Evidences ["c" written over "d"] & examinations and the prisoners Defence being heard The jury went out to Agree on their verdict who returning did then and there in open Court deliver their verdict That the Said Mary Barker was not Guilty of the ffellony by Witchcraft for which she Stood indicted in and by the Said Indictments and each of them.

> The Court Orderd Mary Barker aforesaid to be Discharged. Paying her fees

Records of the Superior Court of Judicature (1692/3), pp. 59–60, Massachusetts Supreme Judicial Court, Judicial Archives, Massachusetts State Archives. Boston, MA.

Billa Vera: Indictment of William Barker Jr., for Covenanting†
2nd of 2 dates. See No. 803 on Jan. 13, 1693

Billa Vera: Indictment of William Barker Jr., for Afflicting Martha Sprague†
2nd of 2 dates. See No. 804 on Jan. 13, 1693

851. Court Record of the Trial of William Barker Jr.

[Hand 1] William Barker Jun^ε of And⟨o⟩ver in the County of Essex Being Indicted by the Jurors of o^ε Sovereigne Lord &. Lady the King and Queen upon their oaths by Two Severall Indictments That is to Say 1st

For that the Said William Barker ∧{Jun^ε} of Andover in the County of Essex Some time in the Month of August last in the yeare 1692 afores^d at or in the Township of Andover in the

County of Essex ["x" written over "s"] aforesd Wickedly Mallitiously & ffelloniously A Covenant with the Devill did make & Signed the Devills booke and by the Devill was Baptized & before him renounced his former Baptizme and promised to be the Devills for ever & ever, By which wicked and Diabolliacle Covenant the Said William Barker is become a detestable witch against the peace of o^ε Sov^ε Lord & lady the King and Queen their Crowne and Dignity And the laws in that Case Made and Provided

2^{d}ly ffor that he the Said William Barker Junior of Andover in the County of Essex aforesaid Sometyme in the moneth of August last ⟨i⟩n the yeare 1692 af⟨or⟩es^d And divers other dayes and times as well before as after Certaine detestable arts called Witchcraft and Sorceries Wickedly Malliciously and ffelloniously hath used P⟨r⟩actised and Exercised at and in the Towne of Salem in the County of Essex afforesaid upon and agst one Martha Sprague alias Martha Tyler, By wch wicked arts the said Martha Sprague alias Tyler the day and year afores^d and divers other d⟨a⟩yes and tymes as well before as after was and is Torture⟨d⟩ Affli⟨c⟩ted Tormented Pined & wasted agst the peace of o^ε Sov^ε Lord & Lady the King and Queen their Crown & Dignity & the laws in that Case Made and Provided.

upon the affores^d Indictments and each of them The Said William Barker Jun^ε was then and there before the justices of our Lord and Lady the King and Queen aforesaid Arraigned and upon his Arraignm^t he did then and there the day and yeare abovesaid plead to them and each of them not Guilty and put himselfe upon by God and his Countrey.

A Jury being Called Thomas Burnam fforeman & accordingly Sworne no Exception being made by the prisoner the Said Indictm^{ts} and each of them being read together with the Evidences and Examinations and the prisoners defence being heard The jury went out to agree on their verdict who returning did then and there in open Court deliver their verdict That he the Said William Barker was not Guilty of the fellony by Witchcraft for wch he Stood Indicted in and by the Said Indictm^{ts} and each of them

> The Court Orderd William Barker aforesaid to be Discharg'd Paying his fees

Records of the Superior Court of Judicature (1692/3), pp. 60–61, Massachusetts Supreme Judicial Court, Judicial Archives, Massachusetts State Archives. Boston, MA.

Thursday, May 11, 1693

William Hobbs Cleared by Proclamation

Cleared by Proclamation: Recognizance for William Hobbs by John Nichols & Joseph Town

2nd of 2 dates. See No. 720 on Dec. 14, 1692

Tuesday, June 13, 1693

852. Petition of Anthony Checkley

[Hand 1] To his Excelency Sr Wm Phips Knight Capt Generall & Gov$^\varepsilon$ in Cheife of their Maj^{ts} Province of the Massachusetts Bay in New England, ^{And vice Admirall of the Same} And To the Right hon$^\varepsilon$able Wm Stoughton Esqui$^\varepsilon$ Leif^t Gov$^\varepsilon$ of the Said Province, And the Rest of the hon$^\varepsilon$ble Councel, And the hon$^\varepsilon$ed Assembly Sitting in Boston June 1693

The petition of Anthony Checkley

Humbly Sheweth

That in the Yeare 1689 I was Chosen their Maj^{ts} Atturnie Generall by y^e Gou$^\varepsilon$ Councel & Asembly In which place I Continued, dureing that Gouerm^t, And his Excelency Sr Wm Phips After he had Receiued the Gou$^\varepsilon$ment, his Excelency & Councel was pleased to Chuse & Comitionate me to that place, both in the former Gouerment & in this I haue ^{had} much very dificall & troblesome Worke, In Indicting & Impleading A great number of people for ffellony by murther Piracy, Witchcraft Rape Burglary And theft & other Crimes, At Seuerall Courts in the Counties of Suffolke Essex & Midlesex, Seuerall haue bin Convict & Executed, Some tryed & Acquitt, And others their Bills Returned Igno$^\varepsilon$amus In this dificall Service for thir Maj^{ts} I haue borne my owne Expence (I haue not eate of the Kings bread Exept ^{at one Court} Some few meales at Salem) but the Charge of my Selfe & Horse And all helpe I haue paid my fees or allowance hath bin allmost nothing, for them that haue bin Executed Some That haue made escape & Some that haue died, haue had nothing, & for them that I was allowed any thing the fees was Soe low & the number of the ᵱsons able to pay Soe few, that I haue had Soe little that It would not bare my Expence, I haue Indicted neer fower Score ᵱsons that I never had any thing for my Comition allows me to take as large fees as any of their Maj^{ts} Atturny Generalls in their Maj^{ts} Planta͞cons in America, but how it Shall be had I am Ignorant There is neither fees nor Sallery Settled, whi(c)h is A great discouragm^t, I Am not desirous of great fees or A large Sallery Soe as to be Inriched by this place

But I humbly pray that I may haue Such A Compensation as may Suport me in the dilligent & faithfull discharge of my duty, If this honored Court will be pleased to Sett off my Rates, And allow me Some Satisfaction for the time past, And Sett me Rate free & At Resonable Sallery for the time to Come I Shall be thankfull

There is One thing more wherin I am vnder discouragm^t, I am Not Countenanced in the Execution of my of my Office in Severall matters which Conserne their Maj^{ts} Intrest & the publick good, As Impleading Ships & Goods, which are Informed Against for y^e Breach of Penall Stattutes, In these Cases I Canot be for the defend because I am y^e Kings Atturny I must not plead against the King, And I may not plead for the King nor for his Excelency the Gou$^\varepsilon$nor because the Informer Generall will not allow it, This may be Injurious to their Maj^{ts} & The Gou$^\varepsilon$ in Case & is Injurious ^{to me} I am forced to Stand like mum Chance & Can not be allowed to Speake or Act for their Maj^{ts} Intrest Allthough their Consernes be neuer Soe Ill managed I pray this Hono$^\varepsilon$ Court to Consider & Settle this matter.

There be Seuerall other matters which I humbly thinke the Atturny Generall ought to Intermedle in, As puting in Suite Bonds forficted to their Maj^{ts} And moueing for Execution to pass against forfiters ["s" written over "es"] of Recognizanses And many other matters which I had Rather receiue as the Comands of the Authority, Then Exert my power in the

July 14, 1693

Execution of I am willing to Serue their Maj^{ts} to my vtmost, But had rather be Called to my duty then to force myselfe vpon it,

> My humble Request to this Hono^ᴇd Court is That yo^u will please To Instruct me what my duty is, And Incourage me in the doeing of it The Incouragment which I pray for is That I may Receiue yo^ᴇ Comands with fauo^ᴇ & ffreindship, And haue Some Competent Satisfaction for the paines & troble I haue & Shall take & haue in the ꝑformance of my duty
> The granting of my Request will Oblige me to Serue their Maj^{ts} & this hono^ᴇd Court Cherfully & Thankfully And to be Yo^ᴇ Excelencies & Y^e honord Courts
> > Obliged humble Servant
> > Anthony Checkley

[Hand 2] Read. June. 13° 93.
and sent down.
[Hand 3] Read y^e first time

[Reverse] [Hand 1] Anthony Checkley{s} Petition
[5–6 words overstruck]
[Hand 2?] 28:9:1693.
60^{li} for Service to y^ᴇ Ma⟨i⟩[Lost] [= Majesties]

Notes: On October 28, 1692, after Checkley's role on the Court of Oyer and Terminer had ended, he was made Attorney General for the province. No reason has been established for his stated failure to receive compensation. ◊ "defend": 'defence' (*OED* s.v. *defend* n.). ◊ Hand 1 = Anthony Checkley

Massachusetts Archives Collection, vol. 40, no. 278. Massachusetts State Archives. Boston, MA.

Friday, July 14, 1693

853. Order for the Release of Mary Watkins

> [Hand 1] To mr. Caleb Ray Keeper of the Prison in Boston
> > Greeting.

Whereas Mary Watkins Singlewoman Was lately ^{remanded} ~~comitted~~ to Prison till she should find Sureties for the good Behaviour W^{ch} she hath not been able to procure, by reason of her deep poverty & want of Friends; And whereas the said Watkins is very infirm, and like to prove burdensom to the publick if longer continued in Custody. Therefore upon further consideration, these are to order you to discharge said Mary Watkins the Prison, she paying her Fees. Dated in Boston; July, 14. 1693. Aññoqʒ R̄R̄^s & Reginæ Gulielmi & Mariæ nunc Angliæ &c Quinto.

> > Wm Stoughton
> > Tho: Danforth
> > John Richards;//
> > Sam̄ Sewall. Wait. Winthrop

July 31, 1693   Notes: Hand 1 = Samuel Sewall.

Fogg Collection, vol. 8, no. 420, Maine Historical Society. Portland, ME.

Monday, July 31, 1693

854. Council Record Noting Arrival of Crown's Reply to William Phips

[Hand 1] At a Council held at his Ex^{cys} House in Boston upon Munday, July 31st 1693.

Present

His Ex^{cy} Sr William Phips K^{nt} &c^a

William Stoughton Esq^ε Lieu^t Gov^ε

Wait Winthrop.   John Richards

Samuel Sewall   Elisha Hutchinson.

John Foster. Esq^{εs} John Phillips. Esq^{εs}

John Walley   Peter Sergeant.

Isaac Addington Esq^ε

His Ex^{cy} likewise communicated to the Council a Letter he had received from the Queens Majesty by the Ships arrived yesterday from London relating unto the proceedings against Witchcraft approving his care and circumspection therein. Also signifying her Royal Will and Pleasure. and thereby willing and Requiring his Ex^{cy} to give all necessary directions that in all proceedings against p^{ε}sons accused for Witchcraft or being possessed by the Devil. the greatest moderation and all due circumspection be used so far as the same may be without impedim^t to the ordinary course of Justice within the Province. Given at the Court at White Hall the 15th of Aprill 1693 = W^{ch} was read at the Board.

Notes: The Crown approved of the way Phips had handled the witchcraft issue, although important parts of that approval probably came from the narrative Phips provided. See No. 836.

Colonial Office 5/785, p. 244. National Archives, London, UK.

Tuesday, December 12, 1693

855. Account for Payment Submitted by William Baker, Constable [?]

[Hand 1] June th [= the] 28: 92

Constaber Willam Bakers acount sarueing at the Cort at Salem

my salf and my Hors a weeak, Riding from Salem Betwixt Wenha⟨m⟩ and Ipswich to fech Sarah Dauis and Expencis of mony one shilling

Riding form [= from] Salam to Salabery as a marshalls deauibity [= deputy] to fech mistris
Bradbery June the 29//92 and mony Expencis 2 shillings

Dec. 12, 1693

July the 4 {92} for warning a jury of of wiming [= women] and Expencenc of mony 0ˢ 4ᵈ
August the 2:92 Goode Green Braking out of Prison and Expencis of finding Hur is one
shilling
august the 23//1692 Goode Green Braking out of Prison and Expenis of time finding hur
was one night and one {hal Hafe} day
August the 27 1692 I Imprest Simon Adams and His Hors to Cary John Jackso⟨n⟩ sener to
Salem and John osborn and His Hors to Cary John Jackson Juner to Salem and thomas
Norton and The widdow Dauis Hors to Cary John Howard to Salem and
Alaxainder Louell {I} Impreced to Cary old Cory to Salem and John Dennison Hors
saruing the 4 Cort at Salem my salf and my Hors one week

1
3
4
4
4
4
___
20.

1–0–0

[Reverse] [Hand 2] accots of ye County

Notes: The dating on this document and the following sequence of accounts is speculative. The fact that people presenting accounts are not on the payment list may mean that their requests were rejected, a not infrequent occurrence. Many appear to have been paid through money given to the sheriff. December 12, 1693, comes from the date of the Superior Court of Judicature addressing the issue of sums due. See No. 866.

Essex County Court Archives, vol. 2, no. 188, Massachusetts Supreme Judicial Court, Judicial Archives, on deposit James Duncan Phillips Library, Peabody Essex Museum, Salem, MA.

856. Account for Payment Submitted by Israel Cheever, Jailkeeper [?]

[Hand 1] An accᵗ of yᵉ time that the pᵉsons Comitted for Witchcraft unto yᵉ
Custody of Israel Chever Keeper of the Prison in Cambridge Continued in said
Prison

Lydia Dastin & Sarah Dastin were Comitted June 18ᵗʰ 1692 & by the sheriffe
were taken out yᵉ 3ᵈ of Januʳʸ following wᶜʰ is 28 weeks & 3 days & amounts to. . .07//02//00

Mary Colson Widow was Comitted Septʳ 5ᵗʰ 1692 & was by the sheriffe taken
out said 3ᵈ of Januʳʸ wᶜʰ is 17 weeks & one day 02//02//10

Elizabeth Colson Comitted Septʳ 14ᵗʰ 1692 was by yᵉ sheriffe taken out said
3ᵈ of Januʳʸ wᶜʰ is 15 weeks & six days amounting to 01//19//06

December 12, 1693

Sarah Cole Comitted Octob^r 3^d 1692 was by ye sheriffe taken out said 3^d of
Janu^{ry} wch is 12 weeks & 6 days amounting to 01//12//00

Lydia Dastin, Sarah Dastin, Elizabeth Colson,Sarah Cole, Mary Toothaker &
Mary Taylo^ε were by order of ye sheriffe Comitted Janu^{ry} 28th 1692/3 & taken
out by said sheriffe on ye 31st of ^{sd} Janu^{ry} wch is 3 days wch amounts to . . . 00//06//04

Lydia Dastin, Sarah Dastin, Elizabeth Colson, & Sarah Cole were by the
sheriffs warrant (after the tryall of said p^{ε}sons) Comitted ffebru^{ry} 11th 1692/3~
Elizabeth Colson went out of Prison ye 2^d of March following: Lydia Dastin
dyed ye 10th of said March Sarah Cole & Sarah Dastin went out of Prison y^e
23^d of said March the time of said persons Continuance in Prison from said
Comittm^t to their going out is as follows vizt. Sarah Cole & Sarah Dastin
5 weeks & 5 days wch amounts to 01//08//04

Lydia Dastin 4 weeks. amounts to 00//10//00

Elizabeth Colson two ^{weeks} & five days amounts to 00//06//08
                                                                          15//07//08

Notes: The people in prison after acquittal were presumably there because of their inability to pay jail fees.

Middlesex County Court Archives, Folio Collection 1698–164–4. Massachusetts State Archives. Boston, MA.

857. Account for Payment Submitted by William Dounton, Jailkeeper [?]

[Hand 1] to the anor [= honored] cort now Sitting in salem
the prison kppers acount consarning the wichcraft for diet
Impr{e}ms [= firstly] ~~for tetabe Indan A whole year and ⟨10⟩ month~~   ⟨?-?1-?⟩
{p^d 3^s} for S⟨r⟩ Sarah osborn on month   00-07-00
for sarah good 6 wecks and for hir child on month   01=01=03
for gils cory and his wiff 3 we⟨k⟩   00-11-03
will hobs 3 w   00-07-06
deleueranc hobs 12 munth   04-10-00
Abigal hobs 12 munth   04-10-00
⟨M⟩a⟨r⟩y waren 6 months diet   ⟨0?-?-?⟩
for Elesabeth scargen {6} monthe   3-00-00
and for her chilld 4 mounthe   1-00-00
for ⟨?⟩alles parker   01-00-00
for mary toheker 37^w dieat   03-07-00
~~for martha emerson 27 weeks~~   0⟨?⟩-0⟨?⟩-00
~~for Ruth willfo{o}rd 18 weak~~   02-07-00
henry salter 4 moun{th}ts   02-00-00
Rachel hatfel 10 weeks   01-05-00
the to gacksons 4 weeks each   01-00-00
John hollen 4 weeks   00-10-00
                                                                          24 09:00. ⟨?-?-?⟩

may it pleas this onered Court
this acount is only for dieat

your honers may Rememember that ther was 5 pound ayear seatlead [= settled] on the ~~the~~
prison keeper of sale⟨m⟩ of which I neuer Receued but twenty 3ˢ not this nin year

I desier the onered Cort would be plesed to conseder me with Rspect to go⟨o⟩d man wolen⟨s⟩
the⟨i⟩r Remains dew to me for him which hau nothing of his on to pay   03=00=00
                                              [Hand 2] as aboue   24-09[Lost] [= 24-09-00]
                                                  due   27[Lost] [= 27-09-00]

[Reverse] [Hand 3] Dountons accᵒ
Not allowᵈ

⟨Wᵐ⟩ Dounton Accᵒ

UNCAT MS, Miscellaneous Manuscripts (1692), Massachusetts Historical Society. Boston, MA.

858. Account for Payment Submitted by William Dounton, Jailkeeper, Copy [?]

[Hand 1] {Salem 1692}
The County of Essex is Dʳ [= debtor] To William Dounton Goale Keeper in Salem
Decemᵇʳ the. [   ] 1693.

To: Sarah Osburne 1 mᵒ dyet in prison. Except 3ˢ Recᵈ in part	0: 07. 00
To: Sarah Good 6 weekes and for her child Doriᵗ Good 1 mᵒ dyet	1: 01: 03
To: Giles Cory & his wifes dyet 3 weeks remaines due thereof	. 11. 03
To William Hobs 3 w. dyet	//. . 07: 06
To. Deliuᵉ Hobs 12 moneths dyet	//.4: 10. 00
To: Abigail Hobs 12 mᵒ dyet	//.4: 10. 00
To: Eliz Scargen 6 mᵒ Dyet and for her childˢ 4 mᵒ Dyet	// 4: 00: 00
To: Alce parker 8 weekes dyet	// 1: 00 00
To. Mary Toothaker 37 w dyet	// 3: 07. 00
To: Henᵉ Salter 16 w: dyet	// 2: 00: 00
To: Rachel Hafell. 10 w dyet	// 1: 05. 00
To: yᵉ two Jacksons 4 weeks dyet Each	// 1: 00: 00
To. Jnᵒ Hollen 4 w. dyet	// 0. 10. 00
To: Edwᵈ ["Edwᵈ" written over "Roger"] Wooland	// 3. 00: ⟨00⟩
	27: 09: 00

To: 9 yeares Salery at 5ˡ ℙ Anum agr⟨e⟩ed on & Setled. out of wᶜʰ I only
Recᵈ 23ˢ Rest due 43:17ˢ:00
William Dounton
Allowed Wᵐ Dounton for Salery since yᵉ Revolution or Sʳ Edm̄ ⎫
Andros Gouᵉ wᵗʰ wᵗ might be due before his sᵈ Gouernmᵗ; in full ⎬   12: 11: 00
                                                          ⎭   40: 00: 00

Alowed

Dec. 12, 1693   Notes: The copy includes information not found in the original. ◊ Hand 1 = John Hathorne ◊ Facsimile Plate 4.

Essex Institute Collection, no. 15, James Duncan Phillips Library, Peabody Essex Museum, Salem, MA.

859. Account for Payment Submitted by Thomas Fosse, Jailkeeper [?]

[Hand 1] The Acco^t of Thomas ffossey Prison Keeper of Ipswich

ffor Dyeting of Seuerall prisoners Comited by order of Authority & afterwards discharged by y^e Same as follows	l̄i s d
tt [= item] Dyetting of Rachell Clinton from y^e 11th of Aprill untill y^e 12th of Janu^{ε}y follow: in y^e year <u>1692</u>: }	4:10:3
tt ditto of y^e two Jacksons from y^e 27th of August untill y^e 12th of Janu^{ε}y in y^e Same year {4^l 10} }	[Lost] 10:=
tt Ditto of John Howard from y^e 27th of August untill y^e 12th of Decem^ε in y^e Same year }	2:00:=
{1693} tt Ditto of Tho: Dyer from y^e 27th of Aprill untill y^e 8th of Jully }	1:03:=
~~tt Tho: Battis his ffees~~	0:00:=
[Hand 2] Allow^d [Hand 1] 12^{li}: 3: 3^d Totall is	12:03:3

[Reverse] [Hand 3] Tho. Fosseys Acc^o [Hand 2] allow^d

Notes: The date "1693" appears in the left margin of the manuscript of Fosse's Account.

Essex County Court Archives, vol. 2, no. 186, Massachusetts Supreme Judicial Court, Judicial Archives, on deposit James Duncan Phillips Library, Peabody Essex Museum, Salem, MA.

860. Account for Payment Submitted by Joseph Fuller, Constable [?]

[Hand 1] Joseph fuller as cunstablle: for ye yere {1692} for seasing of	⟨s⟩ ⟨d⟩
Rachall Clenton & bring of har before: Justis ~~by:~~ According to warrant	0 – 1 – 0
for tending ye Court of oyer & tormener at Sallem ~~two: week~~ tenn: dayes	1 – 0 – 0
Cunstaball Choat ~~a~~ for seaseing of goody penne & Carreing of har to Sallem & bring of har back to Ipswich Goall from Sallem by uirtu of a mittemas: with one man to assist me }	s d 0 – 8 – 9
~~Cunst~~ for tending at ye Court of Oyer & turmener: – two weeks:	1 – 0 – 0
{1692} James fuller & nathanell fuller thre dayes: a pese: at Sallem being summaned to giue euedenc Against Rachell Clenton at ye Court of Oyer & Turminer	s 00 – 12 – 00

[Reverse] [Hand 2] acc^{ots} not allow^d

Essex County Court Archives, vol. 2, no. 132, Massachusetts Supreme Judicial Court, Judicial Archives, on deposit James Duncan Phillips Library, Peabody Essex Museum, Salem, MA.   Dec. 12, 1693

861. Account for Payment Submitted by Samuel Graves, Constable [?]

[Hand 1] A note of what. Samell Graues hath bin out about the witches
Inp: [= first] for Keeping Rachel Clinton in Ipswhich prisson two weekes and fees   0.10.0
2 Sarah Good with her Child 3 dayes   0.6.0
3 Six dayes his wife tended fiue dayes at Salem as wittnes 1 day to serch them   0.12.0
Samuell Graues was at the Charg for a hors. and man to bring his wife whome
from Salem then
[Hand 2] Ebin harris to: Sallem to: carry doun one woman: 3 – 0
:m^ɛ paine: carred goodwife Graues to Sallem one day: 3 – 0
ye widdow bellsher 5 dayes at Sallem to giue Euedenc   10 – 0
m^{ɛ}s dimand 5 dayes att Sallem To giue: Euedenc & har hosband to carry: har   4 – 0
a man to carry & fech widdow bellsher   4

[Reverse] Chargis for ye court of oyr & turmener

Essex County Court Archives, vol. 2, no. 187, Massachusetts Supreme Judicial Court, Judicial Archives, on deposit James Duncan Phillips Library, Peabody Essex Museum, Salem, MA.

862. Account for Payment Submitted by Nathaniel Ingersoll, Innkeeper‡

[Hand 1] March y^e 1st 1691/2

Vppon a meeteing of y^e Majestrates M^ɛ Jno Hathorne and Jonathan Corwin Esq^{ɛs} in an Inquirere after Witchcraft Expences upon y^e Countrys Acco^t for Majestrates Marshalls Constables & Assistance at my Howse Viz^t

	l̄i	s	d
Imp^ɛ [= first] To y^e Majestrate Dinner & Drink	//	//.8	//..
To y^e Marshalls 2 Constables & Assistanc & Vict⟨i⟩alls	//	// .3	//..
To 43^d Cakes 6 qts sider	//	//.2	//..
To 2 Constables att 2 qts of 3^d sider one Cake	//	//..	//.9
To Rum	//	//..	//.6
To Majestrates Horses	//	// ..	//.6
To y^e Marshall & Constable Herricks Horses	//	// ..	//.6
ye 3^d Instant ye Marshall Expences	//	// ..	//.6
ye Marshall & his Horse. 1 pott sider	//	// ..	//.6
Vpon Examination of Goodwife Corry			
To ye Marshall for Horse & Drink	//	// ..	//.6
To ye Majestrates Horses; Drink and Entertainement	//	// .4	//..
Vpon Examination of goodwife Nurse			
To ye Marshalls Horse standing, supper,			

December 12, 1693

Lodging one night and drink for his attendance . . . . //. . //.3 //.6
To Constable Herrick & Drink & Cake . . . . //. . //. . //.6
To yᵉ Majestrats' Drink & Entertainemᵗ and Horses wᵗʰ yᵉ Majestrats Horses . //. . //.5 //. .

Aprill 19 1692

A further Accont in Examinaᶜᵒⁿ of Witchcraft at Salem Villiage before yᵉ Worshipfull John Harthorn and Jonathan Corwin Esqᴱ & Assist: for the County of Essex./.

To yᵉ Majestrates Intertainemᵗ & Horses . . . . //. . // .6 //. .
The 22 ["The 22" written over "To yᵉ"] Majestrates Minesters & Attendane
        Diners . . . . //. . // 16 //. .
The ["The" written over "to"] 22 for 8 Horses Hey & Oates . . . . //. . // .4 //. .
{May 2ᵈ} ffor Majestrates Entertainemᵗ . . . . //. . // .4 //. .
           ffor Horses hey & Oates . . . . //. . // .2 //. .
           ffor yᵉ Marshell & Assistance Victualls and Drink . . . . //. . // .4 //. .
{ditto 3ᵈ} ffor Drink for yᵉ Gaurd upon yᵉ Committed persons one Night . //. . // .3 //. .
{ditto 3ᵈ} ffor Victualls & Drink yᵉ Next Morning for yᵉ Attendance Gaurd
           Committed woman to Boston Goal by order of Mittimus . . . . //. . // .3 //. .
{ditto 3} ffor oates for the Cart Horses & Marshalls Horse: . . . . //. . // .1 //. .
{May 9ᵗʰ} ffor Conveyance Mᴱ Burrows and other Prizoners ffor Victualls
           for the Majestrates & tendance & Horses & whole Charge at this
           Examinaᶜᵒⁿ is . . . . //. . // 16 //. .
{May 18} & 19 dayes for Victuall & drink for yᵉ Gaurd in watching John
           Willard Tho. ffarrier & others . . . . //. . // 16 //. .
           Carried over to the other side . . . . //.5 // .4 // .9

                                             l̄i s d
Brought over from yᵉ other side . . . . //. .5 // .4 // .9
To drink for yᵉ Majestrates & Victualls for Attendance & Horses Pastering //. . . // .5 //. .
May 20 To sider for Majestrates & Attendane . . . . //. . . // .5 //. .
21 To Victualls & Drink to Majestrates . . . . //. . . // .2 // .6
23ᵈ To Majestrats Horses Meat & Attendane . . . . //. . . // .3 //. .
24 To Attendane supper & drink next Morning . . . . //. . . // .5 // .6

May yᵉ 21 1692

Vpon the Examination of William Procter and severall
others to their Victualls Drink to yᵉ Majestrates & their
Attendane & Horse meat and victualls & drin⟨g⟩   }   //. .1 // 10 //. .
[= drink] to yᵉ Attendance of the Prisoners.

July 15 1692

Vpon an ["an" written over "yᵉ"] Examination to yᵉ
Majestrates Constables an [= and] others to Attend yᵉ   }   //. . . // 15//. .
Prisenᴱˢ Meat drink & Horse meat

                                           £ //. .8// 10 .9

[Reverse] [Hand 2] Nath: Ingersolls Acc°

Notes: This is dated to the payments ordered by the Superior Court of Judicature on December 12, 1693, where Ingersoll's account is listed. William Procter was examined on May 31 and not on May 21. See No. 866.

Essex County Court Archives, vol. 2, no. 131, Massachusetts Supreme Judicial Court, Judicial Archives, on deposit James Duncan Phillips Library, Peabody Essex Museum, Salem, MA.

863. Account for Payment Submitted by Thomas Manning, Blacksmith [?]

[Hand 1] ⟨?⟩ Thomas Manning his Acoumpe of work doun by him for y^e
County of in y^e yare 1692

	lb	s	d
Ito [= item] mending & pouting one [= putting on] Rachalls fetters	00 =	01 =	6
Ito John houward 1 pare of fetters	00 =	05 =	0
Ito John Jackshon Sener 1 pare of fetters	00 =	05 =	0
Ito John Jackshon Juner 1 pear of fetters	00 =	05 =	0
	00 =	15 =	0

[Hand 2] allow^d

[Reverse] Tho. Mannings Acc°

Essex County Court Archives, vol. 2, no. 130, Massachusetts Supreme Judicial Court, Judicial Archives, on deposit James Duncan Phillips Library, Peabody Essex Museum, Salem, MA.

864. Account for Payment Submitted by Abraham Perkins, Innkeeper [?]

[Hand 1] An Accomp^t of What was Taken vpon their majesties accomp^t in the yeare 1692
Im^pr [= first] by Geo: Herrick vnd^r sheriff for him selfe & prisoners viz

Jn° Jackson {sen^r} Jn° Jackson Junr Jn° Howard and Guard	00: 08: 00
To Entertainment for y^e Constables and their Prisoners from Hauerill	00: 06: 00
To Entertainement for y^e Constables and prisoners from Glossester	00: 04: 00
To Hauerill Constable another time	00: 02: 00
	0⟨1⟩: 00: 00

By Abraham Perkins
[Hand 2] allow^d

[Reverse] Ab. Perkins Acc°
allow^d

Notes: Hand 1 = George Herrick

Essex County Court Archives, vol. 2, no. 129, Massachusetts Supreme Judicial Court, Judicial Archives, on deposit James Duncan Phillips Library, Peabody Essex Museum, Salem, MA.

December 12, 1693 **865. Order of the Superior Court of Judicature Regarding Payment of Court Costs**

[Hand 1] At a Superiour Court of Judicature holden at Salem for the County of Essex the 12th December by Adjournem^t from the last Tuesday in November past
    Ordered
Whereas there hath arisen a great Charge in holding the severall Courts of Oyer and Terminer in the County of Essex in the year 1692 the payment of part of wch hath been ordered by the Governour & Councill out of the Publique Treasury and yet there remaines due to seuerall persons for their service and disbursem^{ts} One hundred and thirty pounds in money whose Acco^{ts} haue been Examined and allowed by this Court the discharge of wch properly belongs to said County This Court doth therefore Order the Clerk thereof to Signifie and make known the same unto their Maj^{ties} Justices of the peace in said County Who are directed at their next Generall Sessions of the p⟨e⟩ace to make an Assessment on the Inhabitants of said County proportionally for the payment of the said Summ And that by an Order they Cause the same to be paid to the County Trēar and that he pay the said sūm to the severall persons unto whom it is due According to the severall Acco^{ts} here with Transmitted

                    vera Copia Taken out of y^e Record of s^d Court Attest.
                    Jon̄^a Elatson Clēr

[Reverse] [Hand 2] Order of Super^ε Court

Notes: Hand 1 = Jonathan Elatson

Essex County Court Archives, vol. 2, no. 178, Massachusetts Supreme Judicial Court, Judicial Archives, on deposit James Duncan Phillips Library, Peabody Essex Museum, Salem, MA.

866. Superior Court of Judicature: Statement of Sums Due

[Hand 1] An account of what is due to the Severall persons hereafter Named from the publique for their respectiue disbursem^{ts} and seruices according to their acco^{ts} Gi⟨u⟩en in and & Examined by the Superiour Court holden at Salem by Adjournem^t December ye 12th 1693

viz:

Thomas Beadle C^r by his acc̄^o of disbursm^{ts}	£ 58:11:5	
D^r to what was p̄d by ye Sheriff	£ 17:17:6	
Due to ballance		£ 40:13:11
Samuel Beadle C^r by his acc̄^o	£ 21:00:00	
Dr to what p̄d by the Sheriff	£ 10:00:00	
		£ 11:00:00
Samuel Shattock C^r as ℔ his acc̄^o	£ 07:02:00	
D^r to whats p̄d by the Sheriff	£ 03:00:00	
		£ 04:02:00
John Cook C^r by his acc̄^o		£ 02:13:00

		December 29, 1693
Mary Gedey C^r by her acc^o	£ 70:00:00	
D^r by what's p̄d by the Trear & Sheriff	£ 55:13:00	
		£ 14:07:00
John Stacy C^r by his accō. of disbursem^{ts}		£ 04:00:00
Mr Thomas Newton for his seruice		£ 02:05:00
John Putman Constable 30^s & Jonathan Putman 30^s for their Extreordinary Seruice & Travell	}	£ 03:00:00
Joseph Neal for his service and Trauell		£ 02:00:00
Capt. Willard William Murry & Thomas Putnam for their seruice 5^l Each	}	£ 15:00:00
Nathaniel Ingorsoll his accō of disbursem^{ts}		£ 06:00:00
George Herrick for his Great seruice		£ 25:00:00
		£130:00:11

Allowed upon the accō aboue the severall Sūmes there amounting to the Summ of One hundred and thirty pounds Eleuen pence

Wm Stoughton

vera Copia

attest

Jon̄^a Elatson Clēr

[Reverse] [Hand 2] ord^r from ye Superiour Court

Notes: Thomas Putnam's receipt of money was for his services under the Court of Oyer and Terminer. Simon Willard and William Murray also received compensation. Murray and Willard worked primarily in recording examinations, although Willard also made many grand jury notations. Putnam's efforts were primarily in recording depositions, as well as other documents. ◊ Hand 1 = Jonathan Elatson; Hand 2 = Stephen Sewall

Essex County Court Archives, vol. 2, no. 179, Massachusetts Supreme Judicial Court, Judicial Archives, on deposit James Duncan Phillips Library, Peabody Essex Museum, Salem, MA.

Friday, December 29, 1693

867. Bill to Towns for Courts of Oyer & Terminer and Other Matters

[Hand 1] Att a Generall Sessions of the Peace holden att Salem Decemb^ε 26 1693./ Thursday 28th

Whereas there is transmitted to this Court Sundrey Acco^{ts} of Disburstments Arrisen in this County in holding the Severall Courts of Oyer and Terminer in the Year 1692: which Acco^{ts} have ben Adjusted Setled and Allowed by the Superiour Court holden att Salem by Adjournment the 12 day of December 1693: Amounting to 130^{li} which togather with Sever⟨all⟩ Summes more due from Said Countey to Severall ꝑsons for Killing Wolves and to the Geol Keep^{εs} for their Sallery and other Acco^{ts} for Repairing of Bridges, all which is Needfull to be discharged: ./.

December 29, 1693   Wherefore this Court doe order that a Rate be laid on this County forthwith for the raiseing
of the Severall Summes hereafter Mentioned on Each Towne in ye Same ꝓportionably
According to the Last Asseasem^t made by the Generall Court of this Province being in
ꝓportion to an Eight part thereof which is as followeth ./.

(Viz^t)	l̄i s d		l̄i s d
Salem	40–10–00	Ipswitch	51–19–00
Newbery	34–07–00	Salsbury	7–13–00
Rowley	12–15–00	Amsbury	5–01–00
Haverhill	10–15–00	Bradford	4–14–00
Andover	10–14–00	Boxford	5–11–00
Topsfeild	09–09–00	Marble head	24–03–00
Lynn	19–05–00	Wenham	8–08–00
Beverly	14–18–00	Gloster	8–11–00
		Manchest^ɛ	2–11–00

And that the Clarke of this Court Issue out Warrants to the Select Men of Each Towne
Respectively to Assess the Same proportionably on the Inhabitants thereof
~~Equivollent thereto unto the Treasurer,~~ And to cause the Same to be Collected and payed in
Money or Equivollent thereto unto the Treasurer of this County for the time being at or
before the first Day of: May next Ensueing the date hereof./

Att a Generall Sessions of the Peace holden att Salem Decem^bɛ 26th 1693:

A Copy of the Warrants Sent to the Severall Townes for the Raiseing the afores^d Rates./.
Essex ss
Whereas its Manifest to this Court that this County is Indebted to Severall Persons
Considerable Summs which ought of right to be discharged./.
Wherfore its ordered that a Rate be made and Layd on this County forthwith for the
Raiseing the Severall Summes One Each Towne in the Same proportionably According to
the Last Asssessem^t made by the Generall Court of this Province being in proportion to an
Eight part thereof and that the Clark of this Court Issue out Warrants to the Select Men of
Each Towne Accordinly
Wherofore to the Select Men of [   ] Greeting/
Pursuant to the above Order of Court you are in their Maj^ties Names Required to Assease the
Inhabitants of Your Towne Each one his due ⟨ꝑ⟩ Equall Proportion thereof being the Summe
of [   ] and Cause the Same to be Collected and paid in Money or Equivollant thereto unto
the Tresurer of this County for the time being at or before the first day of may Next
Ensueing ye date hereof According as the Law Dirrects in that case made and Provided./.
                                                    ꝑ order of Court Step: Sewall Clar̄s
                                                    Decemb^ɛ 29. 1693:/.

Townes Mentioned (Viz^t)

Wenham		Ipswitch		Rowley	
Newbery	}	Salsbury	}	Ambsbury	}
Haverill		Bradford			

Delivered the Warrant for Beverly to John Hill   March 26, 1694

for Salem to the Select Men   }   for Manchester to M$^\varepsilon$ West   }

Lin to Samuel Jonson   Marble head to John Stacey

Topsfield to Is: foster   Bradford to Abra: Reddington

Andavor to Sam^{ll} Huchins

Notes: No attempt has been made to calculate how much of this bill was due to costs of the special court that tried the witchcraft cases. There was more than one Court of Oyer and Terminer in 1692, another being established on October 22, 1692, in York County, according to the certified copy of the Governor's Council Executive Records for 1692, Vol. 2, p. 196. The document is carried here simply to give information on how such costs were billed.

Records of the Salem and Ipswich Court of General Sessions of the Peace (1692–1693), pp. 48–49. Massachusetts Supreme Judicial Court, Judicial Archives, on deposit James Duncan Phillips Library, Peabody Essex Museum, Salem, MA.

1694–1750

Monday, March 26, 1694

868. Account for Payment Submitted by William Starling, Constable

[Hand 1] hauerhill datt march 26: 1694

to the honouered corte of quarter sessetions to be houlden att Ipswich on the 22th of this instant the humble Requst of william Starlin constable for hauerhill in the yeere 1692 is that this honouered corte would be pleased to consider me and alow me for my charge expended for the contreys or county by comand of Authority to me giuen which chardg is as foloweth

on the 23 of july 1692 by warant fro⟨m⟩ bartholomw gidn John hathorn Jonathan Corwine John higgerson Esquiers for the sesuer [= seizure] of martha emerson I brought hur doun to Salam by the esistment of bartholomew heath mathew hereman which I did comand to assist me on the 29 of july by uartue [= virtue] of a warrant from the same hands as aboue: I brought doune to Salame goodwife brumidg and goodfife green and by order of Authority: went with them to Ipsiwich haueing to asste [= assist] me Josiah heath John giuel ~~Abraham~~ {Israel} hendrick which allso I did comand
on the 4th day of August by uartue of a warrant from cap^n bradstrit of Anduer to sese goodfiuef Clarck I allso went with hur to Salam being ~~ea~~ assisted by John Ayer and heluerd williams which I did comand to assist me
August the 18 by warrant by the same cap^n bradstree⟨t⟩ goodwife hucthins and Ruth wilford and caried them downe to Salam att two times haueing the first time for the first Josiah gags for my assistans and and peeter pato for the next time: and I was constrain⟨d⟩ to press horeses euery time and two men to wacth with one of them the Sabath day and night

March 27, 1694

expended of my own mony ~~on~~ in the performanc of the serues mad mention of one pound and eight shilings

Your saruant William Starlin⟨e⟩

[Reverse] [Hand 2]   s   d
3 day^s of 2 hand^s 12:00
3 day^s of 3 hand^s 18:00
3 day^s of 2 hand^s 12:00:
3 day^s of 2 hand^s 12:=
for horses   12:=
for 12 day^s Time of h⟨is⟩ own: ⎫
An^d his expencis   ⎬   1:10:00 ["10" written over "04"]
                                           ⎭
                                          ─────────────
                                               4:16=

[Hand 3] this acc^t allow^d For himselfe & others here⟨i⟩n Named.

[Hand 3?] Acco^{ts} Respited

Essex County Court Archives, vol. 2, no. 137, Massachusetts Supreme Judicial Court, Judicial Archives, on deposit James Duncan Phillips Library, Peabody Essex Museum, Salem, MA.

Tuesday, March 27, 1694

869. Account for Payment Submitted by Isaac Little & John Harris, Sheriff's Deputy

                                    [Hand 1] The County of Essex is D^r [= debtor] 1692:
~~Isack Littell Allee~~ for 18: pound of iran ∧{y^t was prest from ~~him~~} ~~of~~   s
Isack Littlle: Alle: for feetters: for y^e priseners: at a 4d a pound   0 – 6 – 0

An accoun^t from John Harris: sherefs: deputy of sondry: Charges: at y^e Corts of ir an
torminar: [= Oyer and Terminer] helld at Sallem in y^e yere <u>1692</u>:   £   s   d

Itt [= item] presing a hores: & man: to assist in Carriing of Sary: good: from   ⎫
    Ipswich goalle: to Sallem   ⎬   0 – 8 – 00
Itt: for going to Sallem to Carry: a Return: of y^e Juriars: of ipswich & Rowly
    & Attending y^t siting   0 – 4 – 6
{Itt for a man & horse: y^t was prest to Remoue Sary good & Chilld   0 – ⟨?⟩ – 0
    from ipswich to Sallem   0 – 7 – 6}
Itt: for presing of hores & man to gard me with: ye wife: of John willes: ⎫
    & ye widow pudeater from Ipswich to Sallem my: sellf: & gard   ⎬   0 – 9 – 6
Itt for tending ye Court at ye second siting   0 – 4 – 00

Itt: for prouiding a Jury: to make: search: upon Cori & his wife: & Clenton ~~Estty:~~ Easty: hore: Cloiss: & m^{rs} bradbury ~~ti~~   } 0 – 4 – 00

Itt: Tending ye Court on ajurnment August ye 2^d 1692 from Tuesday till Satterday   } – 04 – 00

Itt: for exspenc: & Time: to: git 3 paire of feetters made: for ye two Jacksons & John howard   } – 2 – 00

Itt: for ~~Carriing~~ Remoueing of howard ^{&} ye two: Jacksons & Joseph: Emmons: from Ipswich Goall to Sallem & thare: Tending ye Courts: pleasure ^{thre dayes:} till three of Them was sent back: to: ipswich Goall: by. me: which time: of: thre: dayes: ^{for my: sellfe:} & exspenc: for Thos y^t assisted me in y^t sarues   } 06 – 0
{for presing of men & horses for This designe: 0 – 02 – 0}

Itt for bringing of m^{rs} bradbury: from Sallem To: ipswich goall: & a man to assist me: } 0 – 4 – 0
                                                                                                    2 – 18 – 6

as attest John Harris deputy sheref:

[Hand 2] Att A Gen^{ll} Sessions of y^e peace holden at Ipswich March 27. 94
This account is allowed provided it be not Included in y^e High Sheriffs acc^o
attes^t St: Sewall Cler

[Reverse] Jno Harris Acc^o allow^d Condic͞onaly

Notes: Hand 2 = Stephen Sewall

Essex County Court Archives, vol. 2, no. 133, Massachusetts Supreme Judicial Court, Judicial Archives, on deposit James Duncan Phillips Library, Peabody Essex Museum, Salem, MA.

Wednesday, March 28, 1694

870. Account for Payment Submitted by Robert Lord, Blacksmith

[Hand 1] County Essix Dito ["i" written over "e"] July <u>92:</u>
Ittm ffor making fouer payer of Iron ffetters and tow payer of hand Cuffs and puting them on to y^e legs and hands of Goodwife Cloys estes Bromidg and Green all att one pound aleuen Shillings money   l͞i   s   d
                                                                                                    01=11=0
{mach 28th 94.} A making. a letter B att   <u>00=01=0</u>
                                                          [Hand 2] {1. 12. 0.}
[Hand 1] This work was done by order from athority Requiring me therevnto atest
                                                                    Rob^{tt} Lord smith
[Hand 2] deduct p^d by y^e Marshall 6^s rest is 26^{sh}
                                        allow^d

[Reverse] [Hand 3] Robart Lords aco^t for fetters & hancuffs

Essex County Court Archives, vol. 2, no. 180, Massachusetts Supreme Judicial Court, Judicial Archives, on deposit James Duncan Phillips Library, Peabody Essex Museum, Salem, MA.

Wednesday, May 27, 1696

871. Petition of Elizabeth Procter to Recover the Estate of John Procter

[Hand 1] To the Honourable Generall Court Asembled at Boston may twenty seuenth 1696 the Humble petetion of Elizabeth procter widow and Relect of John procter of Salem decesed Humbly sheweth

that in the yere of our lord 1692 when many persons in Salem and in other towns therabout were accused by som euill disposed or strangly Influenced persons; as being witches or for being guilty of acting witchcraft my s^d Husband John procter and my selfe were accused as such and we both; my s^d Husband and my selfe were soe farr proceded against that we were Condemned but in that sad time of darknes before my said husband was executed it is euident sombody had Contriued a will and brought it to him to signe wherin his wholl estat is dispose⟨d⟩ of not hauing Regard to a contract in wrighting mad with me before mariag with him; but soe it pleased god to order by his prouidenc that although the sentanc was executed on my dere husband yet through gods great goodnes to yowr petetioner I am yet aliue; sinc my husbands death the s^d will is proued and aproued by the Judg of probate and by that kind of desposall the wholl estat is disposed of; and although god hath Granted my life yet those that Claime my s^d husbands estate by that which thay Call a will will not suffer me to haue one peny of the Estat nither vpon the acount of my husbands Contract with me before mariage nor yet vpon the acount of the dowr which as I humbly coceiue [= conceive] doth belong or ought to belong to me by the law for thay say that I am dead in the law and ther⟨f⟩ore my humble Request and petetion to this Honoured Generall Court is that by an act of this honoured Court as god hath Contenewed my life and through gods goodnes without feare of being put to death vpon that sentanc yow would be pleased ⌃{to} put me Into a capacity to mak vse of the law to Recouer that which of Right by law I ought to haue for my nessesary suple [= supply] and support that as I yowr petetioner am one of his majestyes subjects I may haue the benifett of his laws soe Humbly prayeng that god would direct yowr honnours in all things to doe that which may be well pleasing to him I subscrib yowr honnours humble petetioner

Elizabeth procter
widow

[Hand 2] Read. 10th June. 1696. in Council

[Reverse] [Hand 1] Elizebeth procter her petetion
[Hand 3?] 1696

Notes: The story of John Procter's will and the disposition of Elizabeth Procter's claim remain open to further research.
Elizabeth Procter was "dead in the law" because of the attainder on her as a result of her conviction for witchcraft. The attainder was removed in 1703. See No. 877.

Massachusetts Archives Collection, vol. 135, no. 109. Massachusetts State Archives. Boston, MA.

Thursday, March 18, 1697

872. Petition of Timothy Phillips to Recover Expenses

[Hand 1] To the Honble William Stoughton Esqr Lieutenant Governour and Commander in chief in and over his Ma^tys Province of the Massachusetts Bay in New England and the Honble Council of the s^d Province {and Representatives of the Same convened in General Assembly}
The Petition of Timothy Phillips Sheriffe of the County of Middlesex
Humbly sheweth
     That your Petitioner and the Keeper of his Ma^tys Goale in Cambridge in the yeares 1692 & 1693. during the time of the great trouble by Witchcraft in the County afores^d were at great Cost and Charges out of their own Pockets in removing the Persons then in custody for Witchcraft. from place to place by writts of Habeas Corpus and in finding such persons with Provisions, besides the great trouble they were at, and time expended in that respect all which they did by order of the Superiour Court &c And have not yet received any Satisfaction for their time or money which they so expended and laid out as afores^d whereby they are in disburse on that Account between thirty and forty pounds, as yo^ε Petitioner can make appear Your Petition^r therefore humbly prayes this Honble Court ["Court" written over "Board"] to take the premisses into Consideration, and to grant an order for the payment of what your Petitioner and the s^d Prison Keeper have disbursed and expended as afores^d As also such Satisfaction as yo^ε honours shall think meet for their trouble and time imployed in the affair aforesaid
And your Pet^r as in duty bound shall ever pray &c
                              Tim° Phillips Sheriffe
March 18th 1696/7

Notes: Phillips made his original request January 3, 1693. See No. 751. Others also had long waits for compensation due to them. ◊ "disburse": in the phrase *to be in disburse* 'to be out of funds' (*OED* s.v. *disburse* n.).

Massachusetts Archives Collection, vol. 135, no. 110. Massachusetts State Archives. Boston, MA.

Wednesday, May 26, 1697

873. Response of the General Court to the Account Submitted by Timothy Phillips, Sheriff

[Hand 1] Province of the Massachusetts Bay
Anno $\overline{RR}^S$ Gulielmi Tertii Angliæ &c nono

At a Great and General Court or Assembly begun and held at Boston upon Wednesday the 26th of May 1697. and continued by several Prorogations unto Wednesday the 15th of December following. & then met

Upon reading the Petition and Accompt presented by Timothy Phillips Sheriff of the County of Middlesex amounting unto Forty two pounds, thirteen shillings and tenpence for Dyat [= diet] Expences and Fees for several Prisoners accused and tryed for Witchcraft within the s^d County in the year 1692

Voted That the Petitioner be allowed the Su$\overline{m}$ of Ten pounds out of the publick Treasury towards his s^d Accompt
And the Quarter Sessions of the Peace in s^d County o⟨f⟩ Middlesex are ordered and impowred to raise on s^d County the Remainder of s^d Accompt, and pay the Ballance thereof upon their adjustment

By Order of the Lieu^t
Gov$^\varepsilon$ Council and Assembly.

Is^a Addington. Sec$\overline{r}$y

Notes: Phillips had requested slightly over forty-two pounds. ◊ "Prorogations": 'extensions' (*OED* s.v. *prorogation*).

Middlesex County Court Archives, Folio Collection 1698–164–4. Massachusetts State Archives. Boston, MA.

Saturday, December 18, 1697

Payment Ordered: Account for Payment Submitted by Timothy Phillips, Sheriff
2nd of 2 dates. See No. 751 on Jan. 3, 1693

Friday, April 22, 1698

874. Account for Payment Submitted by Timothy Phillips, Sheriff

[Hand 1] Midd^x ss: 1698   At y^e Court ["Cou" written over "At"] of sessions held at
Ap$^{\varepsilon}$ill: 22d: Charlestoune by y^e speciall appointment of his Maj^{ties}
    Justices for s^d County
Jan$^{\varepsilon}$3^d 1692/3   The sheriiffs acco^t of Charges Expended upon p$^{\varepsilon}$sion$^{\varepsilon s}$ers
    [= prisoners] accused for wich Craft and tryd at
    Charlestoune {And for Diat to seuerall/}

	li s$^{(l)}$ d
By Carrying Elizab: Cols⟨on⟩ to Salem	1//00//00
To Carrying 6 p$^{\varepsilon}$ison$^{\varepsilon s}$ to Salem	4//05//00
To Expences on Prison$^{\varepsilon s}$ from Salem to Charlestoune.	2//00//00
To money for wood	0–9–00
To 8 p$^{\varepsilon}$sons Tryalls	0//16//00
To Transporting them to Cambridge	0//15//00
To 7 days p$^{\varepsilon}$suit by Hue and Cry	1//00//00
To y^e Prison keep$^{\varepsilon}$ for diat	15//00//00
To Henry Somers for diat	00//19//00
{Jn^o w⟨?⟩lde} To y^e Cryers ffees. in y^e Tryalls 8^s }	
To assisting in p$^{\varepsilon}$suit of y^e Hue and cryes 10^s }	0//18//00
Adjusted and allowed by y^e Justi⟨ce⟩s sitting in Court.	£27//02//00

Atts Sam^{ll} Phipps Cler. p̄a.

Notes: "Cler. p̄a.": Abbreviation for Latin *clericus pacis* 'clerk of the peace.' "Hue and cryes": 'outcry calling for the pursuit of a felon by a constable' (*OED* s.v. *hue and cry*).

Middlesex County Court Archives, Folio Collection 1698–164–4. Massachusetts State Archives. Boston, MA.

Thursday, June 13, 1700

875. Petition of Abigail Faulkner Sr.

[Hand 1] To the Hon$^{\varepsilon ble}$ the Greate and Generall Court of the province of y^e Massachusets Bay assembled att Boston.

    The petition of Abigall the wife of Francis ffaulkner of Andover in y^e County of Ess⟨x⟩ Humbly sheweth

That Whereas in y^e yeare 1692 when many were acused & Imprisoned att Salem as Witches and some Executed, my selfe was accused by ye afflicted who pretended to see me by theire spectrall sight (not with theire bodily Eyes) and that I afflicted them upon whose accusations (and theires only) I was Examined Imprisoned and brought to tryall these being all that gave

March 2, 1703

in anny Evidence against me upon oath yett y^e Jewry [= jury] (upon only theire Testimony) brought me in guilty, & the sentence of Death was passed upon me, But it pleased god to put it into y^e heart of his Ex^cy Sir Willm Phipps to grant me a repreve and att Length a pardon the Insufficiency of y^e proofe being in s^d pardon Exprest as the Inducement to the granting thereof soe that Through the greate goodness of God I am yett preserved

                                                                    Verte [= turn over]

[Reverse] The pardon haveing soe farr had its Efect as that I am as yett suffred to live, but this only as a Malefactor Convict upon record of y^e Most henious Crimes that mankind Can be supposed to be guilty off, which besides its utter Ruining and Defacing my Reputacion, will Certainly Expose my selfe to Iminent Danger by New accusations, which will thereby be y^e more redily believed will Remaine as a perpetuall brand of Infams [= infamy] upon my family And I Knowing my owne Inocency as to all such Crimes (as will att y^e last fully appeare) and being soe Defamed in my Reputation and my life Exposed besides the Odium Cast upon my Posterrity

                    Doe humbly pray that this high {&} hono^ble Court will please to
                    take my Case into serious Consideration and order the Defaceing of
                    y^e record against me soe that I and mine may be freed from y^e Evill
                    Consequents Thereof

                    And your Petion^r as in duty bound shall ever pray

[Hand 2] Boston Jun 13: 1700 y^e Court orderd y^e Reading of hir tryall

[Hand 3] [Lost]kner [= Faulkner] ⟨&c^a⟩ Pet^con
[Lost]⟨?⟩ly. [= July] 1703./.

Notes: The July 1703 date written later references the date when this and similar petitions were responded to by the House of Representatives. See No. 879. The court ordered reading of Faulkner's trial makes clear that a written record existed. It also strongly suggests that the reading was from a no longer extant Record Book of the trials held by the Court of Oyer and Terminer. See note 143 in the General Introduction for a nineteenth-century reference to a copy of it.

Massachusetts Archives Collection, vol. 135, nos. 113 & 114. Massachusetts State Archives. Boston, MA.

Tuesday, March 2, 1703

876. Petition of Francis Faulkner et al. to Clear the Records of Rebecca Nurse, Mary Esty, Abigail Faulkner Sr., Mary Parker, John Procter, Elizabeth Procter, Elizabeth How, Samuel Wardwell, & Sarah Wardwell

See also: March 18, 1703.

[Hand 1] To his Excellency the Governour, and Councill, and Representatives, now in Generall Court Assembled; {at Boston:}
The Petition of severall of the Inhabitants of Andover, Salem village & Topsfield, humbly
                                                                    sheweth;

That whereas in the year 1692 some of your Petitioners and the near Relations of others of   March 2, 1703
them, viz. Rebecca Nurse, Mary Estey, Abigail Faulkner, Mary Parker. ⁀{of Andover} John
Procter & Elizabeth his Wife: Elizabeth How. Samuel Wardwell & Sarah his Wife; were
accused of Witchraft by certain possessed persons, and thereupon were apprehended and
Imprisoned, and at a Court held at Salem were condemned upon the Evidence of the
aforesaid possessed persons; and sentence of Death hath been executed on them (except
Abigail Faulkner, Elizabeth Procter & Sarah Wardwell) of whose Innocency those that
knew them are well Satisfyed. And whereas the invalidity of the aforesaid Evidence and the
great wrong which (through Errors & mistakes in those tryalls) was then done, hath since
plainly appear'd, which we doubt not but this Hono$^\varepsilon$ed Court is sensible of:
Your Petitioners being dissatisfyed and grieved, that (besides what the aforesaid condemned
persons have Suffered in their persons and Estates) their Names are Exposed to Infamy and
reproach, while their Tryall & condemnation stands upon Publick Record. We therefore
humbly Pray this Hono$^\varepsilon$ed Court, that Something may be Publickly done to take off Infamy
from the Names and memory of those who have Suffered as aforesaid, that none of their
Surviving Relations, nor their Posterity may Suffer reproach upon that account. And yo$^\varepsilon$
Petition$^\varepsilon$s shall Ever pray &c.
Dated March 2^d 1702/3.

Francis Faulkner	Isaac Est⟨ɔ⟩{e}y
Abigail Faulkner	Samuel Nurse
Phebe Robinson.	john Tarbel.
Samuel Wardwel	John Nurse
Sarah Wardwel	Peter Cloys sen$^\varepsilon$
John Parker	Isaac Estey Jun$^\varepsilon$
Joseph Parker	{Sarah} Gill
Nathaniel Dane	Rebecca Preston
Francis Dane	Thorndick Procter
mary How	Benjamin Procter
Abigail How	

[Hand 2] In the House of Representatives March. 18th 1702. Read. & sent vp

[Reverse] [Hand 3] Pet^{con} of Fra. Faulkner &^{a} = Read.

Notes: All but four of the signatories are in the hand of the document recorder. Sarah Gill's last name is in this hand, but
her first name is not. Nathaniel Dane, Francis Dane, Mary How, and Abigail How are all in another hand.

Massachusetts Archives Collection, vol. 135, no. 121. Massachusetts State Archives. Boston, MA.

Thursday, March 18, 1703

Read in the House of Representatives: Petition of Francis Faulkner et al. to Clear the Records of Rebecca Nurse, Mary Esty, Abigail Faulkner Sr., Mary Parker, John Procter, Elizabeth Procter, Elizabeth How, Samuel Wardwell, & Sarah Wardwell
2nd of 2 dates. See No. 876 on March 2, 1703

Wednesday, May 26, 1703

877. An Act for the Reversing the Attainder of Abigail Faulkner Sr. et al.

WHEREAS Abigail Faulkner, wife of Francis Faulkner of Andover in the County of Essex, Sarah Wardel Wife of Samuel Wardel of the same place, Elizabeth Procter Wife of John Procter of Salem Village within the said County. In the Court of Oyer and Terminer and Goal Delivery holden at Salem within the said County of Essex in the year One Thousand Six hundred ninety two were arraigned convicted and attainted of Felony for practising Witchcraft, who have now humbly petitioned this Court, That the said Attainders may be set aside and made void. —Wherefore
be it Declared & Enacted by his Excellency the Governour Council and Representatives in General Court Assembled, and by the authority of the same,
That the said Several convictions, Judgements and Attainders of the said Abigail Faulkner, Sarah Wardel, Elizabeth Procter and every of them be, and are repealed, reversed, made and declared null and void to all intents, constructions and purposes whatsoever; as if no such convictions, Judgements or Attainders had ever been had or given. And that no corruption of blood, pains, penalties or Forfeitures of Goods or Chattels be by the said convictions and Attainders or any of them incurred, But that the said persons and every of them be and hereby are reinstated in their just Credit and reputation—
Any Law, usage or custom to the contrary notwithstanding [*Passed July 27.*

Notes: Enders A. Robinson has generously sent a copy of a manuscript from which he transcribed this document in his book, *The Devil Discovered*. However, the manuscript from which the copy has been made has not been located, and, in the absence of knowing its provenance, the publication in *Acts and Resolves* is used here on conservative grounds. Robinson's transcription is on pages xvi–xvii of his 2001 edition.

Acts and Resolves, Public and Private, of the Province of Massachusetts Bay, Private Acts. vol. 6, 1692–1780, no. 16 (Boston: Wright and Potter, 1896), p. 49.

Thursday, July 8, 1703

878. Petition of Ministers from Essex County

[Hand 1] To his Excellency the Governour, Council and Representatives of the Province of the Massachusets Bay, in Generall Court Assembled. June [   ] 1703. The Address of severall Ministers of the County of Essex.

Whereas in the year 1692 some of our neighbours of a good conversation, were apprehended and imprisoned upon Suspi⟨c⟩ion ["c" written over "t"?] of Witchcraft, upon the complaint of some young persons under Diabolicall molestations; and vpon their Tryall at the Court at Salem were condemned; great weight being layd vpon the Evidence of the Afflicted persons, their Accusers. Sentence of Death was Executed on severall of them, but ~~the rest~~ ∧{others} were Reprieved.

But ∧{since} it is apparent and hath been Acknowledged, that there were Errors and mistakes in the aforesaid Tryalls; and notwithstanding the care and consciencious [3rd "c" written over "t"] endeavour of the Honoᵉable Judges to do the thing that is right: yet there is great reason to fear that Innocent persons then sufferred, and that God may have a controversy with the land vpon that account.

We would therefore humbly propose to the consideration of this Honoᵉed Court, whether something may not, and ought not, to be ~~done~~ publickly done to clear the good name and reputation of some who have sufferred as aforesaid, against whom there was not as is {supposed} Sufficient evidence to prove the gvilt of such a Crime, and for whom there are ~~are~~ good grounds of Charity. Some of the condemned persons aforesaid, and others in behalf of their Relations who haue suffered, haue lately Petitioned this Honoured Court upon this Account. We pray that their case may be duely considered.

Thomas Barnard	Samuel Cheever
Joseph Green.	zech. Symmes
William H⟨u⟩bbard	Joseph Gerrish.
Benjamin Rolfe	John Rogers.
	Jabez ffitch.
	Jnᵒ Wise
	Joseph Capen
	Thomas Symmes

[Hand 2] July. 9ᵗʰ 1703 In Council Read and sent down./
[Hand 3] July 16ᵗʰ 1703. In the House of Representatiues Read.

[Hand 2?] Petition of sundry Ministers referring to persons condemnᵈ for Witchcraft. read. July. 8ᵗʰ 1703./

Notes: The signatures all appear in different hands and are probably authentic. John Higginson Sr. and Nicholas Noyes, ministers from Salem, are absent, but why is a matter for speculation.

Massachusetts Archives Collection, vol. 135, no. 124. Massachusetts State Archives. Boston, MA.

Tuesday, July 20, 1703

879. Order of the General Court Concerning a Bill of Attainder of Abigail Faulkner Sr. et al.

[Hand 1] In the House of Representatives.
July 20th 1703.

In Answer to the Petitions of Abigail ffaulkner, and Sundry of the Inhabitants of Andover, in the behalfe of Sundry persons in and late of s[d] Town, & elsewhere, who in the Year 1692 were Indicted, accused, and Condemned, & many of them Executed for the crime of Felony by ["by" written over "of"] witchcraft. And whereas it is Conceived by many worthy and pious Persons that the Evidence given against + {+ many of} the s[d] condemned Persons was weak and insufficient⟨?⟩ as to Taking away the lives of Sundry so condemned &c[a] Wherefore it is thought meet and it is hereby, Ordered, + That a Bill be drawn up for Preventing the like Procedure for the future, and that no Spectre Evidence may hereafter be accounted valid, or Sufficient to take away the life, or good name, of any Person or Persons within this Province, and that the Infamy, and Reproach, cast on the names and Posterity of the s[d] accused, and Condemned Persons may in Some measure be Rolled away
Sent up for Concurrence.

Jam[s] Converse Speaker

[Reverse] [Hand 2] Order for bringing in a bill to reverse the attainder of Abig[a] Faulkner &c[a] of witchcraft.

Notes: Such a bill was enacted on July 27, 1703. Included in it, in addition to Abigail Faulkner, were Sarah Wardwell and Elizabeth Procter. The process of reversing the attainder on Abigail Faulkner Sr. began with a bill on May 26, 1703. See No. 877.

Massachusetts Archives Collection, vol. 135, no. 123. Massachusetts State Archives. Boston, MA.

Wednesday, July 21, 1703

880. Memorandum for Bill to Acquit Abigail Faulkner Sr. et al.

[Hand 1] That a bill be br⟨o⟩ught in to acquit Mary falknar and the other present petiti⟨o⟩ners to acquit them severally of the penaltys to which they are lyable upon the said Convicti⟨o⟩n and Judge⟨m⟩ents on the said C⟨o⟩nts [= accounts?] and E⟨?⟩ Estat⟨e⟩s then in their Just Credit and reputation as if no such Judg⟨m⟩nt had been had,
[Hand 2] In Council
July .21th 1703. agreed to
die ꝑdict. agreed to.

Notes: The name "Mary" is apparently a clerical slip, written instead of the correct "Abigail." No Mary Faulkner appears   May 25, 1709
in the witchcraft cases.

Massachusetts Archives Collection, vol. 135, no. 122. Massachusetts State Archives. Boston, MA.

Wednesday, May 25, 1709

881. Petition of Philip English et al.

[Hand 1] To his Excelency the Gouenor and ye Honarable Counsell and Genarall Asembly for ye Province of ye Massatusetts Bay in New England Conuen^d at Boston 16⟨th⟩ [1 word overstruck] {May 25th} 1709
The Humble Adress and motion of Seuerall of ye Inhabitants of ye sd Prouince some of which had their near Relations Either Parents or others who suffered Death in ye Dark and Dollful times y^t past ouer this prouince in y^e Year 1692. under y^e suposition and in y^t Gloumy Day by some (thought proud) of Being Guilty of wichcraft wch we haue all y^e Reson in y^e world to hope and belieue they were Inocent off. and others of us y^t Either our selues or some of our Relations haue Been Imprison[Lost] [= imprisoned] impared and Blasted in our Reputations and Estates by Reson of y^e same. its not our Intent Neither Do we Reflect on y^e Judges or Jurors Concern^d in those Sorrowfull tryals whome we hope and ⟨Belieue⟩ Did y^t wch they thought was Right in y^t hour of Darkness. but y^t wch we moue and pray for is y^t You Would Pleas to pass some sutable Act as in Your Wisdom You may think meet and proper y^t shall (so far as may be) Restore ye Reputations to ye Posterity of ye suffurars and Remunerate them as to what they haue been Damnified in their Estates therby we Do not Without Remors and greif Recount these sorrowfull things But we Humbly Conceiue y^t we are Bound in Consience and Duty to god and to our selues Relatiues and posterity and Country Humbly to make this Motion praying God to Direct You in this and all Your Weighty Consultations.

We subscribe Your sorrowfull and Distrest Supliants//

philip English	John Ta{r}bell	Isaac Estey
I⟨?⟩sack Estey sen	John Park⟨a⟩r	Joseph esty
Beniamin Procter	Joseph Parker	Samuel nurs
John Procter	John: Johnson	Be{n}iamin Nurs
Thorndik Procter	Francis: Faulkner	John preston
George Jacobs		Samuel Nurs {j⟨n⟩}
William buckly		William Rusell
john nurs		francis Nurs
		Georg Nurs

[Reverse] [Hand 2] Original petion̄

Notes: This petition and No. 882 may have precipitated the action of the Massachusetts government in setting up a structure for hearing such petitions and responding to them. The records of these begin at No. 883, with the documents

May 25, 1709   dated September 1710. The authenticty of signatures has not been established, although some are in the same hand and not authentic.

Massachusetts Archives Collection, vol. 135, no. 125. Massachusetts State Archives. Boston, MA.

882. Petition of Isaac Esty Sr. et al. for Restitution for Mary Esty

[Hand 1] To his Exelency the Governour and ye Honourable Counsell and Generall Assembly for ye Province of ye Massatusetts Bay in New England [Hand 2] convened [Hand 1] at Boston May. 25 1709

The Humble Adress and motion of several of ye Inhabitants of ye s^d Provin⟨c⟩e some of which had their near Relations Either Parents or others who suffered Deat⟨he⟩ in ye Dark & Dolefull ⌃{times} y^t past over this province in ye year 1692. under ye Suposition (and in y^t Gloomy Day) by some thought proud of Being Guilty of Witch craft wch we have all ye Reason in ye world to hope & beleive they were Inocent of. and others of us y^t Either our selves or some of our Relations have been Imprisoned impar⟨e⟩d & Blasted in our Reputations and Estates by Reason of ye same its not [Hand 2?] ⌃{our} [Hand 1] Intent Neither doe we Reflect on ye Judges or Jurors Concer⟨n⟩^d in those Sorrowfull tryalls whome we hope did y^t w^ch ~~we move and~~ they Thought was Right in y^t hour of Darkness but [Hand 2?] ⌃{yt which} [Hand 1] we move & pray for is y^t you Would Please to pass some suitable Act [Hand 2?] as in [Hand 1] your Wisdome you may think meet & proper y^t shall so far as may be Restore ye Reputations to ye Posterity of ye Suffurrers & Remunerate them as to what they have been Damnifi⟨e⟩d in their Estates thereby: we do⟨e⟩ not without Remors & greif Recount these sorrowful things But we Humbly Conceive y^t we are Bound in Conscience and duty to god & to our selves Relatives & posterity & Country Humbly to Make this Motion praying God to Direct you in this & all Your Weighty Consultations

Wee subscribe Your sorrowful and Distresst Supliants

Isaac Esty

Jno Nurse

Joseph. parker

Thorndick Procte⟨r⟩

George Jacobs

[Hand 3] In ye Names & on Behalf of our Selves And several others

[Reverse] [Hand 4] petion

[Hand 5] May. 1709 – Pet^ion ab^t the Witchraft in 1692

[Hand 6] May 25 1709

Notes: All the "signatures" are by Hand 3.

Massachusetts Archives Collection, vol. 135, no. 126. Massachusetts State Archives. Boston, MA.

Friday, September 8, 1710

883. Petition of Isaac Esty Sr. for Restitution for Mary Esty

[Hand 1] Topsfield Septemb^ε 8th 1710

Isaac Esty Sen of Topsfield in ye County of Essex in N. E. Having been sorely exercisd through ye holy & awful providence of God ⟨d⟩epriving him of his beloved wife Mary Esty who sufferd death in ye year 1692 & under ye fearfull odium of one of ye wors⟨t⟩ of crimes y^t can be laid to ye charge of mankind, as if she had been guilty of witchcraft a piece of wickedness which I bel⟨i⟩eve she did hate with perfect hatred & by all y^t ever I could see by her never could see any thing by her y^t should give me any reason in ye lest to think her guilty of any thing of y^t nature but am firmly persuad⟨e⟩d y^t she was as innocent of it as any ⟨of those y^t some⟩ [1–2 words overstruck] to such a shameful death – Vpon Consideration of a Notification from ye Honored Generall Court des⟨i⟩ring my self & others undr like circumstances to give some account of what my Estate was damnify⟨d⟩ by reason of such a hell⟨i⟩sh molestation do hereb⟨y⟩ declare which may also be seen by comparing papers & records y^t my wife was near vpon 5 months imprisoned all which time I provided maintenance for her at my own cost & charge went constantly twice aweek to provi⟨d⟩e for her what she needed 3 weeks of this 5 months she was in prison at Boston & I was constrained to be at ye charge of transporting her to & fro. so y^t I can not but think my charge in time & mony might amount to 20 pounds besides my trouble & sorrow of heart in being deprived of her after such a manner which this world can never make me any compensation for.

Isaak Esty Se{⟨?g⟩}n^r
aged about 82 years

I order & appoint my son Jacob Esty to carry this to ye Honored Committ⟨ie⟩ {⟨&⟩}
Appointed by ye Honored Generall Court & are to meet at Salem
Sept 12 1710   Dated this ⟨8⟩th of Sep^t 1710

[Reverse] [Hand 2] Mary Easty {of Topsfield} Condem^d & Executed

Notes: In June 1710 the General Court authorized a committee to hear claims for compensation for people condemned during the witch trials of 1692 and 1693. The committee formally met in Salem on September 13, 1710, to receive petitions and to make recommendations to the General Assembly. The General Assembly reported its conclusions to Governor Dudley, and on December 17, 1711, he authorized payment, including specific sums in connection with names of people he listed. See No. 934. Since the one from Isaac Esty is the earliest dated one, it is the first of many included here, although the September 12 date on the document is an error as to when the committee would meet. Petitions to this committee that are undated have been placed in this edition on September 13, 1710, and are arranged alphabetically. The committee consisted of Stephen Sewall, formerly Clerk of the Court of Oyer and Terminer, as well as John Appleton, John Burrell, Nehemiah Jewett, and Thomas Noyes. Some of the people who had not been condemned petitioned anyway, out of either hope or misunderstanding. They received no compensation. ◊ Hand 2 = Stephen Sewall

Massachusetts Archives Collection, vol. 135, no. 130. Massachusetts State Archives. Boston, MA.

Saturday, September 9, 1710

884. Petition of Edward Bishop Jr. for Restitution for Himself & Sarah Bishop

[Hand 1] Rehobath Septem 9th – 1710

to the honerabell Jentelmen of the conmitey greating It hauing plesed the grate and Jenerall cort to apiont [= appoint] your honers a commitey to inquier who may be proper to be Justified in the bill Refering to the taking of the ⟨?⟩ attainder and what loss and damidg has bene sustained by reason of the tryalls which were {for} witch craft In the yere 1692 I with my wife were aprehended and examened and commited to Sallam prison and aftrewards cared [= carried] to boston prison and in my absanc the shrefe wente to̶o̶ my hous and a̶n̶d̶ tok away so mutch of my housall goods as afterwards I payed tene pounds for to haue It again six cows was caried away which I neuer had again four an⟨?⟩ [= and] [Lost]ey swine carid away which I neuer had again si⟨?⟩x an [= and] fortiey sheep of whitch I neuer had eney againe: the time that my sellf and wife were prisnors was thirtiey seuen wekes all which tim cost me ten shillings pu⟨r⟩ [= per] weeake for our bord besides other nesecri ⟨?⟩ chardges and proson feese whitch amounted to fiue pounds and I was cept from making eney Im̶p̶⟨?⟩proufment of my Estate to prouide for food for my famiely and had at that time twelue children the which I colld haue maintained out of the produce of my Esteat could I haue had the liburty to med the Improufment of It whitch grat damidg I leue to your honers to Judg:. the hole lose and damedg I comepute to be one hundr⟨?⟩d ["n" written over "i"] pounds money praying your honers I may be righted In neme and Esteat I Rest your honers humbl sarunt

Edward Bishop

[Reverse] [Hand 2] Edward Bishop & wife long Imprisoned not Condemnd

Notes: The Bishops had managed to escape, and it is unclear as to how much of what Sheriff George Corwin took was reasonable within the law as punishment for escaping. Calef strongly suggested that Corwin was going beyond a reasonable legal response. The case of the Bishops is puzzling in that no indictment or grand jury record for either survives as one would have expected, given that they were in prison from April 1692 (see No. 79) until early October 1692 (see No. 692). ◊ "housall": 'belonging to the house, domestic' (*OED* s.v. *housal* a.). ◊ Hand 2 = Stephen Sewall

Massachusetts Archives Collection, vol. 135, no. 132. Massachusetts State Archives. Boston, MA.

885. Petition of Mary How & Abigail How for Restitution for Elizabeth How

[Hand 1] Ipswich y^e 9 of Septemb⟨e⟩r 1710

Wheras y^e Honoured Generall court haue apointed a commity To consider what damieg persons haue sustained in there [Hand 2] {names &} [Hand 1] Estats in y^e yeare 1692 by there sufferings in y^t as was called witch craft y^e odom [= odium] whereof was as if thay ware y^e worst of mankind we mary {how} & Abegill How: we only siruiue in this familey: who doe Groundedly beleiue y^t our honoured mother [Hand 2] ^{Elizabeth How} [Hand 1] suffered as innosent of y^e crym charged with as any person in y^e world & as to y^e damieg done to our Estat we cannot giue a pertiquler acount but This we know y^t our Honoured

father went twise a wek yᵉ whole Tim of her Emprisonment to carey her maintains which
was procured with much difficulty & one of us went with him becaus he could not goe alone
for want of sight also one Jurny to boston for a Repleuey & for maintanance fiue shiling
money left with her yᵉ first coming down 20 shilings yᵉ secont time & forty shilings so yᵗ
som times mo som less ye neuer vnder fiue shillings per week which we know for charges for
her & nesseary charg for our selus [= selves] & horses can not be less then 20 pounds mony:
yet notwithstand so yᵗ yᵉ nam may be Repayard we are contented if your honours shall allow
vs ⟨fif⟩teen {twelue:} pounds yours to serue mary How & Abigell How

[Hand 2] This petition was ℘sented to sayd Comitte by Capᵗ Jnᵒ How & Abraham ["A"
written over "J"] How vncles to sᵈ Mary & Abigail ℘ Releif in yᵉ ℘mises & pray yᵉ sᵈ ℘sons
May be allowed yᵉ Sum.

[Reverse] [Hand 3] ⟨₂⟩ Elizᵃ How Condemnᵈ & Execut⟨e⟩d of Ipswich
[Hand 1] Mary & Abig⟨e⟩ll How

Notes: The family may have sought to free Elizabeth How on bail. ◊ "maintains": Probably an idiosyncratic spelling of
maintenance; the spelling may also echo the now obsolete noun *maintain* 'maintenance, support' (*OED* s.v. *maintain* n,
2). "Repleuey,": 'replevin,' "Baylement, Mainprise, or Repleuin, is the sauing, or deliuerie of a man, out of prison, before
that he hath satisfied the Law, sc. by finding suerties to answer, and be iustified by the Law. And to this purpose these
three termes (Baylment, Mainprise, and Repleuin) be indifferently vsed in our Statutes and bookes." Michael Dalton,
*The countrey iustice conteyning the practise of the iustices of the peace out of their sessions. Gathered for the better helpe of such
iustices of peace as haue not beene much conuersant in the studie of the lawes of this realme* (London: Adam Islip for the Societie
of Stationers, 1618), 269. See also *OED* s.v. *replevin* n, 1c: 'The bailing of, or bail for, a person.' Another possible
interpretation is 'a writ empowering a person to recover his goods by replevin, i.e. the restoration to, or recovery by, a
person of goods or chattels distrained or taken from him' (*OED* s.v. *replevy* n, 1; s.v. *replevin* n, 2). "ye": a misspelling or
alternative spelling of *yet*; or a spelling of *yea* 'truly, verily' (*OED* s.v. *yea* 2). ◊ Hand 3 = Stephen Sewall

Massachusetts Archives Collection, vol. 135, no. 131. Massachusetts State Archives. Boston, MA.

Monday, September 11, 1710

886. Petition of Jane True & Henry True for Restitution for Mary Bradbury

[Hand 1] Honred Gentle men We haue Receiued your Notification & send this to Signify
our Desiers that our good mother mᵉˢ Mary Bradburys name may be inserted in the bill
proposed for yᵉ takeing off the attaindᵉ &c, She throu ffaith obtained a good report among
all Christians for her Exemplary piety & vertue & was euer Lookt on as an Innosent in Her
Suffrings in that dark & gloomi day & we Doubt not but youl: se Cause as far as Can be in
this Method to recouer her reputation – She Indured aboute Six months Imprisonment
Which putt our Honred ffather & Sum̄ of vs her Children vpon very great Expence of which
we haue Indeed no purticuler accounte but are well assured by what we haue heard our father
Capᵗ Bradbury say of yᵉ money he Expended on that account or accasion & by our own
oberuation & Concerne in the Case as well as others of the family that it Could ^{not} be
Less then twenty pounds at the Lowest Calculation besids time & truble. – we doubt not but
Sum others might Suffer more in their Estates & it Semes very Just & reasonable that

September 11, 1710

restitution be in Sum measure made as far as the Case will b⟨e⟩are & therefore: we wold not discourage so Just & good a desine by any Excessiue Demands but rather Comply with any thing which your Honers shall think meet to allow therefore we not Expressly fix vpon any Sum but Leaue it to your honers fauerable Consideration only pray that we may haue that reasonalle Consideration & allowance which you make to others of Eaquall Surcomstances & which may be Consistant with & rather Incurrage then Discourage the gen^ll Desine now on foot our buisness is Shuch at home we Cant well attend your Honers at this Junture but hope our writting may as Efectiuely Answer the Ende being Confident that Such is your Justice & Cander that ⁀{You} will not Improue our Moderation in our Demands to our disaduantage we Subscribe – your most Humble Seruants & petisioners
Salisbury Sep^tε 11th = <u>1710</u>   Henry

                                                                                                        True
                                                              & Jane
                                                              Executor to y^e will
                                                              of m^rs Mary Bradbury

[Hand 2] Condemned for Witchcraft Sepr 1692.
not Executed: made her Escape.

[Reverse] Mary Bradbury Condemned not Executed

Notes: "reasonalle": 'rational, reasonable' (*OED* s.v. *reasonal*). ◊ Hand 2 = Stephen Sewall

Massachusetts Archives Collection, vol. 135, no. 135. Massachusetts State Archives. Boston, MA.

887. Petition of Ephraim Wilds for Restitution for Sarah Wilds

[Hand 1] Topsfelld Septem 11 – 1710 ["7" written over "6"]
To the honered Jentell men of the commitey greating: it hauing pleased the great and Jenaral cort to apiont [= appoint] your honars a comitte to inquier who may be proper to bee Justified in the bill refering to the taking ofe the attainder and what loss and damedg hes ⟨bee⟩ been sustained by reason of the tryalls which were for witchcraft in the yer 1692 under which soroful triall [Hand 2] {Sarah Wild} [Hand 1] my mother s⟨o⟩ffr⟨e⟩d: [Hand 2] {was Condemned & Executed} [Hand 1] my father being now dissesed and only my sellf left I here apere to giue in som short acount of the cost and damedg we sustained in them tims: my mother w⟨a⟩[Lost] [= was] carried to Salam prison sum time in Epral [= April] we ware at the cost of it and chardg of ceping har there a considrabl whille and afterwards shee was remoued to boston prison we wer⟨e⟩ at the cost of it and chardg of ceping hare ther for about tow months and then from boston shee was remoued back to Ipswech prison we ware at the cost of that and after a whill she was remoued to Salam again we ware at all the cost both of caring and prouiding for har maintance whill in all these prisons: besids ether ["t" written over "p"] my father or my self wen[Lost] [= went] once a wek to see how she deed and what she wanted and some tims twis a weke which was a grat cost and damedg to our estate my father would often say that the cost and damedg we sustained in our esteate was more th⟨e⟩n {wase} twenty pounds and I am in the mind he spok les then it was:. besids the los of so dere

a frind which cannot be mede up.: all which I leue to your honers considration: I remin your   Sept. 12, 1710
honers humbel sarua[Lost][= servant]

Ephraim Willdes

yet notwithstanding twas twenty pounds damedg to our Estate considring our nams may be
repaired I am willing to tak forten pounds

[Reverse] [Hand 3] ~~Ephraim Wilds~~ Sarah Wilds of Topsfield Condemned & Executed

Notes: Ironically, Ephraim Wilds, as Constable of Topsfield had brought in accused people, including Elizabeth How
(see No. 225), who like his mother was hanged on July 19, 1692. ◊ Hand 3 = Stephen Sewall

Massachusetts Archives Collection, vol. 135, no. 133. Massachusetts State Archives. Boston, MA.

Tuesday, September 12, 1710

888. Petition of Rebecca Eames for Restitution

[Hand 1] Boxford Septem 12 – 1710.
to the honred Jentlmen of the commitey greating It hauing pleased the grate and Jeneral cort
to apiont [= appoint] your honars a commity to inquire who may be propr to bee Justified in
the bill refering to the taking ofe the attainder and what loss and damedg has bene sustained
by reasen of the tryalls whitch wer for witchcraft In the yere 1692 Rebecka Emes releck [=
relict] of Roborth {Ems} lete of boxford dececed being aprehended for witchcraft In the yere
1692 sometime the begineng of ogust and sufered Imprisnment aboue seuen months and
condemned and afterwards repreued {by} gourner feps: I Rebeckan emes humbly pray and
desier that the attaintir may be tecken of and my neme may be restored again with the cost
and damedges Is sustain⟨e⟩d thereby to my husbands Esteat: paid in moniy to the prision
keepr and cort chardges four pounds Eaightten shillin⟨g⟩ for the repreue to the gourners
clark a⟨?⟩ ~~36ˢ~~ -1ˡᵉ-10ˢ-0ᵈ for prouisons and other nesecriy chardgs whils inprisened and upon
my tryall Expended by my husband for mee whils under those dollful surcomstances I think I
may sefly say amounted to ten poundes mor – 10-00-00 yete If the attaintur may be taken of
and my neme restored againe I am willing to take tene pounds all ~~and~~ witch I leue to your
honers consideration I remaine you⟨?⟩r humbell saru⟨a⟩nt

Rebeckah Emes

[Reverse] [Hand 2] Rebeccah Eames not Executed an Extraordinary Confessor

Notes: The "signature" of Rebecca Eames is in the hand of the person writing the document. Although not executed as
a result of a reprieve (see No. 836), she had been condemned. ◊ Hand 2 = Stephen Sewall

Massachusetts Archives Collection, vol. 135, no. 151. Massachusetts State Archives. Boston, MA.

Wednesday, September 13, 1710

889. Letter of Nehemiah Jewett to Stephen Sewell [?]

[Hand 1] Mr Sewall

S^r I thought good to returne you y^e Names of seuerall ꝑsons y^t were Condemned & Executed that not any ꝑson or relations appeared in y^e behalf of for y^e takeing of y^e Attainder or for other Expences. they I suppose were returned to y^e Genr^l Courts Consideration for to act about according to their best prudence.

> Bridget Bishop alias Oliuer:
> Susanna Martin. Alice parker
> An pudeter. Welmot Read
> Marget Scott.

S^r I am y$^\varepsilon$ Hon$^{\varepsilon s}$ to serue

Ne͞h. Jewet

[Reverse] [Hand 2] Mr J⟨ew⟩ets Note ab^o y^e ꝑsons condem[Lost] [= condemned] & not returnd to y^e Gener^{ll} Court

Notes: It seems likely that "Sewall" is Stephen and not Samuel, as a result of Stephen's role in the committee. This letter was presumably sent after the committee had met, but in the absence of dating evidence it is placed here with the committee activities of September 13.

Essex County Court Archives, vol. 2, no. 181, Massachusetts Supreme Judicial Court, Judicial Archives, on deposit James Duncan Phillips Library, Peabody Essex Museum, Salem, MA.

890. Petition of Ebenezer Barker for Restitution for Abigail Barker‡

[Hand 1] To the hono$^\varepsilon$able Comittee

An Account of what Ebenezer Barker of Andouer payd for his wife⟨?⟩ Abigail Barker who was accused of witchcraft and suffered Imprisonment 18 weeks at Salem in the year 1692 viz

To the keeper of the Goal	1 – 10 – 0
i͞t For Court charges	1 –7 – 4.
The su͞ms abovs^d he was forc'd to pay before his wife could be Released. Besides his maintaining his wife wholly in prison with provision and other necessaryes ⟨?⟩	2 – 10 – 0

p$^\varepsilon$ Ebenezer Barker.

Totall. 5^l – 7^s – 4^d

I desire Capt Barker to give in this account to the Hon$^\varepsilon$able Comittee

Eben. Barker

[Reverse] [Hand 2] Abigail Barker of Andover Imprisond not Condem⟨n⟩d   September 13, 1710

Notes: Hand 2 = Stephen Sewall

Massachusetts Archives Collection, vol. 135, no. 146. Massachusetts State Archives. Boston, MA.

891. Petition of John Barker for Restitution for Mary Barker‡

[Hand 1] An Account of what money was pay'd by John Barker of Andover, for his Daughter mary Barker who was accused of witchcraft, and Suffered Imprisonment in the year 1692; which he was forc'd to pay before Releasment could be obtain'd.
The time of her Imprisonment being six weeks.

	l̄	s	d
viz			
To the keeper of the Goal in Salem	00 –	17. –	6
it̄: To the sheriffe for the discharge of the prisoner vpon Bail and } for Bail Bond	00 –	6 –	0
it̄ To the clerk of the Court	01 –	17 –	4
for Provisions Expended in prison	0 –	15 –	0
℗ John Barker	3	15	10

[Reverse] John Barkers Account for his Daughter mary.
[Hand 2] Mary Barker Imprisond not Condem^d

Notes: Hand 2 = Stephen Sewall

Massachusetts Archives Collection, vol. 135, no. 139. Massachusetts State Archives. Boston, MA.

892. Petition of John Barker for Restitution for William Barker Jr.‡

[Hand 1] To the Honour⟨a⟩ble Committee
An Account of what was payd by John Barker of Andover for his kinsman William Barker Jun^ε of Andover who was accused of witchcraft and Suffered Imprisonm^t Six weeks at Salem; which he was forc't to pay before he could obtain a Release for his Kinsman
viz.

To the Keeper of the Goal at Salem	00 – 17 – 6
To Provisions ⟨⁑⟩ Expended in prison	00 – 15 – 0
it̄ To the sheriffe for Bail Bond	⟨0⟩0 – 6 – 0
it̄ To the Clerk of the Court	1 – 17 – 4.

p^ε John Barker

Totall 3^l : 15^s : 10^d

[Reverse] Jno Barkers Account of [1 word overstruck] Wm Barkers Jun^ε charges
[Hand 2] William Barker Inprisond not Condemnd ["e" written over "d"]

Sept. 13, 1710   Notes: Hand 2 = Stephen Sewall

Massachusetts Archives Collection, vol. 135, no. 149. Massachusetts State Archives. Boston, MA.

893. Petition of John Barker for Restitution for William Barker Sr.‡

[Hand 1] An Account of what was payd by John Barker of Andouer to the Deputy sheriff in leiu of cattel, which he had seis'd of the Estate of his Brother william Barker who was Imprisoned for witchcraft. &c in the year 1692
viz.

To the Deputy sheriffe	2 – 10 – 0
To the keeper of Salem Goal	1 – 1 – 0.

p$^\varepsilon$ John Barker

[Reverse] Jn° Barkers Estate of his Brother ~~m~~ williams Loss
[Hand 2] William Barker Imprisond not Condemnd Confessor

Notes: Hand 2 = Stephen Sewall

Massachusetts Archives Collection, vol. 135, no. 138. Massachusetts State Archives. Boston, MA.

894. Petition of Sarah (Bridges) Preston for Restitution‡

[Hand 1] To the Honourable Committee appointed by the Generall Court to Consider the Loss and dammage sustain'd by those who Suffered vpon the Account of the supposed witchcraft in the year 1692
An account of what was payd for Sarah Bridges, now the wife of Samuel Preston Jun$^\varepsilon$ of Andouer, who suffered Imprisonment Six weeks at Salem for the supposed witchcraft in the year 1692.

	$\bar{l}$	s	d
viz			
To the Keeper of the Goal	1 – 0 – 0		
$\bar{it}$ To Court charges vpon her Tryall	1 – 17 – 4		

$\bar{it}$ money and provisions Expended in Prison, & for A Bail bond, and expences in attending the Court a fortnight, which I judge could not be less then fiue and fourty shillings } 2 – 5 – 0.

If I may be allowed four pounds it Will be to my Satisfaction
I was not notify'd of the time when the Hono$^\varepsilon$able Committee met at Salem, therefore could not give this account then. I humbly pray this Honourabl⟨e⟩ Committee ~~that I~~ to consider my Loss and dammage. Sarah. Preston

[Reverse] [Hand 2] Sarah Preston

Massachusetts Archives Collection, vol. 135, no. 140. Massachusetts State Archives. Boston, MA.

895. Petition of William Buckley for Restitution for Sarah Buckley & Mary Whittredge

September 13, 1710

[Hand 1] To The Honourable Committee

The humble Representation of Willm Buckly of the Damage sustained by our family in the year 1692 &c.
1 My Honoured Mother Sarah Buckly & my sister Mary Witherige were both in prison from May ["M" written over "m"] until January following, dureing
2 which time we were at the whole charge of their Maintenance
3 And when they were cleared & came out of prison we were forced to pay [Hand 2] ^{for each of them} [Hand 1] five pounds to the officers – We shall leaue Your ["Y" written over "J"] honours and the honourable ["n" written over "a"] Gen^ll Court to judge and determine what our damage hath been by these sufferings – and so Rest
Your Honours humble serv^t

salem sept. 13. 1710.

Wm Buckly
in y^e name of ovr
family.

[Hand 2] If we may be allowed fifteen pounds it will be to our Satisfaction 15-00-00

[Reverse] [Hand 1] Wm Buckly.
[Hand 3] Sarah Buckl⟨e⟩y & Mary Witheridge Imprison^d &c not Condemned

Notes: Hand 3 = Stephen Sewall

Massachusetts Archives Collection, vol. 135, no. 160. Massachusetts State Archives. Boston, MA.

896. Petition of Charles Burroughs for Restitution for George Burroughs‡

[Hand 1] To the Honoured Comitte apoined by y^e Gennarell Court ["u" written over "r"] to Inquire into y^e Names of Such as may be Meet for takeing of ye atta⟨i⟩nder & for ye Makeing Some Restitucon & these Humbly & Sorroufully Shew that our Dear & Honou{d}rd father {M^r} George Burrough was aprehened In apriel – 1692 at wells & Imprisoned Seuerall Monthes in Bostone & Salem Goales and at last Condem{en}ed & Executed for whichcraft which we haue all ye reason in ye world to bleue he was innocent of by his Carefull Chatecizing ["iz" written over "h"] his Chilldren & upholding religon in his family and by his Solomn ["n" written over "e"] & Savory written In⟨s⟩tructions from prison we were Left a parsell of Small Chilldren of us helpless & a mother in Law with one Small Child of her owne to take care of whereby she was not So Capable to take care of us by all which our fathers Small Estate was most of it Lost & Expended and we Scattered we cannot tell Certanly what ye lose may be but ye Least we can Judge by best information was f⟨if⟩ty poundes besides ye damage that hath acrued to us many way{e}s thereby is Some hundreds of pounds wee Earnestly pray y^t ye attainder may be taken of & if you please y^e fifty pounds may be restored

Charles Burrough
Elder Son In y^e Name of the reast

September 13, 1710   [Reverse] [Hand 2] Mr George Burroughs Condemnd & Executed hauing been lately of
Wells in y^e Countey of York⟨e.⟩

Notes: "parsell": 'a group, flock' (*OED* s.v. *parcel* n, 6a.). ◊ Hand 2 = Stephen Sewall

Massachusetts Archives Collection, vol. 135, no. 136. Massachusetts State Archives. Boston, MA.

897. Petition of Thomas Carrier Sr. for Restitution for Martha Carrier

[Hand 1] To the Hono^εable Committe sitting at
Salem this 13 day of Sep^t 1710
These are to Inform your Honou^εs that my wife martha Carrier was condemned upon an
Accusation of witchcraft, and Suffered Death at Salem in the year 1692.
I payd to the Sherriff vpon his demand fifty Shillings.
I payd the prisonkeeper vpon his demand for prison fees, for my wife and four children. four
pounds Sixteen shillings
my humble request is that the Attainder may be taken off; and that I may be considered as to
the loss and dammage I Sustained in my estate.
Totall 7 – 6 – 0.

Thomas Carrier

I found my wife and children provision during their imprisonment

[Reverse] [Hand 2] Martha Carrier Condemnd & Executed
[Hand 3] 1710

Notes: Hand 2 = Stephen Sewall

Massachusetts Archives Collection, vol. 135, no. 163. Massachusetts State Archives. Boston, MA.

898. Petition of Sarah Cole for Restitution

[Hand 1] Salem Sep^t 13: 1710
Wh⟨ar⟩eas the Great & Generall Court has made Choyce of a Committe to he⟨are⟩ &
Receue the acc^{ots} of what Damag Seurall persons Sustained that w⟨a⟩re accues⟨e⟩d and
Imprison⟨e⟩d ffor witch Craft in the year⟨e⟩ 1692. & I the Subscrber being one. Doe pray
your honers to alow me a proportion with other vnder Like S⟨urc⟩umstanc⟨e⟩. The acc^{ot} is as
followeth Seuenteen week Imprisonment

	l⟨i⟩	s	d
paid the – Goaler – 40^s	02	– 0 – 0
writting bonds – 6^s	0	– 6 – 0
paid 18 for Court Charges	0	– 18 – 0
being Imprisoned ye second time writting of bonds 6^s	0	– 6 – 0
C⟨ar⟩ryed to Ipswig to be Clered ⟨&⟩ paid 20 and more	1	– 0 – 0
[Hand 2] I found my self provision during ⟨?⟩ my Imprisonment	2	– 0 – 0

[Hand 1?] £6•10•00

Sarah Cole

[Reverse] [Hand 3] Sarah Cole Long Imprisond not Condemnd   September 13, 1710

Notes: Whether this is Sarah Cole of Salem or Sarah Cole of Lynn cannot be established with certainty. The women were sisters-in-law. ◊ Hand 3 = Stephen Sewall

Massachusetts Archives Collection, vol. 135, no. 155. Massachusetts State Archives. Boston, MA.

899. Petition of John Moulton for Restitution for Martha Cory & Giles Cory

[Hand 1] To the Hon{r}able Commite Apointed by the Generall Court to make Enquire with Respect to the suferings in The yeer ~~19~~ 1692. &c
these are to giue you a short Acount of our sorrows {and suferings} which was in the yere 1692 some time in ma{r}ch our honerd {father} and mother Giles Corey & martha his wife ware acused {for} soposed wich Craft and imprisond and ware Remoued from on prison to another as from Salem to ipswitch & from ipswitch to boston and from {boston} to Salem againe and soe remained in Close imprisonment about four months we ware all the whole Charge of thar maintanance which was uery Chargable and soe much the more being soe farr a distance from us as also by Reason of soe many remoues in all which wee Could doe noe {less} then {less} Acompanie them. which further added both to our trouble and Charge and although that was very Great is the least of our greauence ar [= or] cause of Thease lines but that which breakes {our harts} and for which wee goe mourning still is that our father was put to soe Cruell and painfull a death as being prest to death our mother was put to death also though in another way.
And as wee Cannot sufficiantly Exspress our Griffe for the loss of our father and mother in such a way – soe we Cannot Compute our Exspences and Coast but shall Comite to your wisdome ~~to your wisdome~~ to judge {of} but after our fathers death the shi{r}fe thretend to sizes [= seize] our fathers Estate and for feare tharof wee Complied with him and paid him Eleauen pound six shillings in monie by all which wee haue bee grealy [= been greatly] damnified & impouer⟨shed⟩ by being Exsposed to sell Creaturs and other things for litle more then half the worth of them to get the monie to pay as afores^d and to maintaine our father & {mother} in prison
but that which is grieueous to us is that wee are not only impouereshed but also Reproached and soe may bee to all gen{e}ratians and that wrongfully tow [= too] unleess ⟨ss⟩ somthing {~~somth⟨?⟩~~} bee done for the remoueall thearof all which wee humbly Committe to the hon⟨a⟩ra⟨b⟩le Court Praying God to direct to that which may bee axceptable in his sight and for the good of this land
September the 13th 1710
                            Wee subscrib your humbl searuants in all Christian obediance.
[Hand 2] John Moulton who mared Elezebeth Cory daughtr {of the ab⟨us⟩s^d} in the behalf
    of the reast of that familie
[Hand 3] Wee Cannot Judge our necessary Expence to be less then Ten pounds

Giles Corey & Martha his wife Condemnd & Execut⟨i⟩d both of [Lost] [*SWP* = Salem]

Notes: This unusual petition declines to offer a financial amount because of the nature of the immeasurable loss. It also offers another example of seizure by Sheriff Corwin. ◊ Hand 3 = Stephen Sewall

Massachusetts Archives Collection, vol. 135, no. 161. Massachusetts State Archives. Boston, MA.

September 13, 1710   **900. Petition of Nathaniel Dane for Restitution for Deliverance Dane‡**

[Hand 1] An Account of the Expences of Nathaniel Dane of Andover for his wife
^{Deliverance} who was accused of witchcraft and Suffered Imprisonment 13 weeks in the
year 1692 And for his man Servant who ~~Su~~ was Imprisoned eight weeks vpon the same
account.

viz.

For Prison fees and money and provison necessarily Expended while they were in prison.	}	3 – 13 – 0
i̅t̅ money to the sheriffe & the Clerk and the keeper when my wife was discharged vpon Bail	}	1. – 0 – 0.

℘ Nathaniel Dane.

I desire m^r Barnard to give in this Acc^t to the Hon^{ε}abl comittee
N. D.

[Reverse] Nathan^{ll} Danes Account
[Hand 2] Deliueranc Dane Imprisond not Condemnd

Notes: Hand 2 = Stephen Sewall

Massachusetts Archives Collection, vol. 135, no. 147. Massachusetts State Archives. Boston, MA.

901. Petition of Mary DeRich for Restitution‡

[Hand 1] Mary Rich of Lynn widow in y^e year 1692 was Imprisoned & lost her bed & pot &
other household stuffe. in about halfe year

[Reverse] Mary Rich

Notes: Hand 1 = Stephen Sewall

*Essex County Court Archives, vol. 2, no. 177, Massachusetts Supreme Judicial Court, Judicial Archives, on deposit James Duncan
Phillips Library, Peabody Essex Museum, Salem, MA.*

902. Petition of Philip English for Restitution‡

[Hand 1] To the Honered Commitey Apointed by the Generall Court to Inquire in to the
names proper to be Insarted in the Bill for Tacking of the Attander and what damages thay
sustaned by thare prosecution these Are to signify that I Phillip English whas Imprisoned
togather with My whife in Salem Prison and then Carred to Boston Prison and thare Lay
Nine weeks from whance whe Made our Escape in which time besides our Charge in flying
had y^e Estate heareaftor Menchened Loast and Tacking [= taken] awhay

In the ware Hous att the Pint of Rocks   September 13, 1710

To 20 hogsheds of soatt [= salt?]	025//00//00
To 32^lt 2^qts 17^li of Spanish Iorn [= iron] bought of Capt John Brown	065//06//00
To 43 quntells of Rafedg [= refused] Cod fish	025//16//00
To 2 hogsheds of Melases	015//00//00
To 12 New axes	002//08//00
In the weare Hows behind Docktor Roundeys	133//10//00
To 500 butchells of Vorginiy whet	150//00//00
To 203 butchells of Engon [= Indian] Corn	027//00//00
To 3 pipes of whine	027//00//00
In the weare Hows in the Lane	137//12// 6
To 2 Bootts [= butts] of suger	024//00// 0
To 2 hogsheds of suger	024//00// 0
To 4 hogsheds of M⟨e⟩lases	030//00// 0
[Lost]ght [= wrought?] Iorn	100//00// 0
[Lost]⟨g⟩ key	036//00//[Lost]
[Lost] 18^li of New Cordeg	060//00[Lost]
[Lost] ⟨B⟩oo⟨tts⟩ of nialls [= nails?]	024//00[Lost]
To 1 shist [= chest] of Glass	003//00//[Lost]
In the weare Hows Next to Cartors on the wharlf	638//12//[Lost]
To 1 hogshead of Rum	012//00//[Lost]
To 8 bundells of Twine	014//00// 0
To 160 butchells of whet	040//00// 0
To 500 whate [= weight] of Rope	012//10// 0
To 5 Ketch Ankours whate 682^li	017//01// 0
To 2 shollops Ankours whate 64^li	001//12// 0
To 1 Bots Ankour whate 20^li	000//10// 0
One the wharlf	736//05// 6
To 58 thousands of Bords or more	145//00// 0
To 10 thousands of staues	012//10// 0
To 7 thousands of slitwoork or more	014//00// 0
Carred ower to the other side	907//15// 6
Brought Ouer from the Other side heare	907//15// 6
To 2000 of Clabbords	005//00// 0
To 28 thousands of shingells	008//00// 0
In My Dwelling Hous	920//15// 6
In a pine Chist 6 peses of Canton qt 31 anns [= ounce]	005//00// 0
To 5 duzen of wosted stockens	010//10// 0
To 40 yards of Broad Clath	025//00// 0
To 3 gross of Thimbells	001//10// 0
To 27 yards of Carsey	006//05// 0
To 14 yards of Ticking	002//02// 0
To 43 yards of hiy Brinns	006//09// 0
In another Chist	977//11// 6
To 2 half peses of fine Dowlis	015//00// 0
To 1 half pes of Luckrem	003//00// 0

September 13, 1710	To 8 peses of Kanton qt 40 anns	007//10// 0
	To 2 Duzen of fine woosted stockens	007//04// 0
	To 1 pess of sarge	003//10// 0
	Luse In the shop Chamber	1013//15// 6
	To 13½ yards of sarge	0002//14// 0
	To 11 yards of Broad Clath	0001//02// 0
	To 1 duzen of wimons shows	0002//08// 0
	To 3 Ramnants of fine hollond qt 45¾	0004//18// 0
	To 1 pess of San^t Johns, qt 92 anns	[Lost]
	To 24 yards of New England Canvis	[Lost]
	To 31 yards of Bast Nialls	[Lost]
	To 35 yards of hambrow dowlis	[Lost]
	To 90 yards of Brinns is 9^{li} 6^s 0	00⟨09⟩//0⟨6//0⟩
	To 28 yards of navalls	0004//04// 0
	To 74 yards of fagures	0007//08// 0
	To 20^{li} of Brown Thread	0003//00// 0
	To 2 small Caske of stell	0005//00//⟨0⟩
	To 1 thousand whate of frantch Lines at Lest	0075//00// 0
	To abought a thousand whate of Ladd	0014//00// 0
	To 7 gross of Cod Hucks [= hooks]	0010//00// 0
	To 1500 of Mackrell Hucks	0002//00// 0
	To 6 swine sold for	0002//00// 0
	To a Cow	0002//10// 0
	Carred Ouer to the othe side	1183//02/[Lost]

[Reverse] Brought our [= over] here from the other side

The foregoing is a true Account of what I had seized tacking away Lost and Embazeld whilst I was a prisoner in y^e Yeare 1692 & whilst on my flight for my Life besides a Considerable quantity of household goods & other things which I Cannot Exactly giue a pertickolar Acc^o off for all which I Neuer Resived any other or further satisfacon for them then sixty Pounds 3^s payd Me by ^{y^e} Administrators of George Corwine Late sherife deses'd and the Estate was so seisd & Tacking away Chiefly by the sherife and his vnder offisers not withstanding I had giuen fore thousand pound Bond with surety att Boston

Philip English

Notes: "lt": long ton, 2240 lbs. (*OED* s.v. *ton*[1] 4a). "quntells": quintal, 'a weight of one hundred pounds; a hundred-weight (112 lbs)' (*OED* s.v. *quintal, kintal, kentle*). Refused codfish: dried and salted codfish of the lowest grade. "shollops": shallops, 'large, heavy boats, fitted with one or more masts' (*OED* s.v *shallop* n, 1). "slitwoork": 'thin wooden boards laid on the outside of the bottom of a ship to protect it from the borings of marine animals' (*Webster's Third New International Dictionary of the English Language Unabridged* s.v. *slitwork*; *OED* s.v. *sheathing* vbl. n, 2). "Broad Clath": 'fine, plain-wove, dressed, double width, black cloth, used chiefly for men's garments' (*OED* s.v. *broadcloth, broad cloth*). "Carsey": kersey, 'a kind of coarse narrow cloth, woven from long wool and usually ribbed' (*OED* s.v. *kersey*). "hiy Brinns": the meaning is unclear, possibly 'strong linens of high quality', see Joseph Wright, ed., *The English Dialect Dictionary*, vol. 1 (London: Oxford University Press, 1923) s.v. *brin* sb[2]. "Dowlis": dowlas, 'a coarse kind of linen' (*OED* s.v. *dowlas* 1a). "Luckrem": lockram, 'a linen fabric of various qualities for wearing apparel and household use' (*OED* s.v. *lockram*[1] 1). "Kanton": 'The name of the city in southern China used attrib. to denote various manufactured articles' (*OED* s.v. *Canton* n[3]); perhaps silk or "Canton flannell", 'stout cotton fabric usu. softly napped on one side and twilled on the other' (see *Webster's* s.v. [1]*flannel* 1b2). "hambrow dowlis": Hamburg dowlas, 'a coarse linen cloth', see Brian Dietz, ed., *The Port and Trade of Early Elizabethan London: Documents* (London: London Record Society, 1972), Appendix II, s.v. *Hamburg cloth*.

"Sant Johns": the meaning is unclear, perhaps a commodity made in or associated with St. John's, Newfoundland, or St. John's, Antigua. "Bast Nialls": possibly noils made of bast, 'fibre obtained from plants and used for matting and cord' (*The Oxford Compact English Dictionary* s.v. *bast*; *OED* s.v. *bast* n[1] 1b); both bast-ropes and basts appear as commodities in sixteenth-century England, see Dietz, ed., *The Port*, 559, 563; noils, 'short fibers removed during the combing of textile fiber . . . and spun into yarn for cloth' (*Webster's* s.v. *noil*); in England, at least, noils were a regular trade commodity, see Wright, ed., *The English Dialect Dictionary*, vol. 5, s.v. *noil*. "navalls": the meaning of the word is unclear, but cf. George Francis Dow, ed., *Records and Files of the Quarterly Courts of Essex County*, vol. 2, p. 271 ("4 Bales nowells"), p. 272 ("30 3/4 nowells at 16d. 2li 1s"); possibly noils. "fagures": possibly "figures", figured cloths, 'fabrics adorned or ornamented with painted, stained, or printed patterns or designs' (see *OED* s.v. *figured* ppl. a, 4). "stell": perhaps "still-liquor", 'a coarse kind of spirit distilled from cider dregs' (see Wright, ed., *The English Dialect Dictionary*, vol. 5, s.v. *still*, sb[2]). "Ladd": the meaning of the word is unclear, possibly lead or lard. "Embazeld": 'carried off secretly (what belongs to another person) for one's own use' (*OED* s.v. *embezzle* v, 1).

Massachusetts Archives Collection, vol. 135, nos. 127, 128 & 129. Massachusetts State Archives. Boston, MA.

903. Petition of Philip English for Restitution‡

[Hand 1] To ye Comittee Appointed to Distribute ye money allowed to the Sufferers in 1692.

Gen^t
I request ye favour of you to represent it to ye Gen^ll Court what a great Sufferer I have been in my Estate by reason of ye Severe prosecution of me & my wife in that Dark time, It Cost me fifty pounds at Boston & we were forced to fly for our Lives at which time my Estate was Seised & Squandred away to a great Value & much of my provision used to Subsist ye numerous Company of prisoners – In ye whol⟨e⟩ I am Exceedingly Damnified ye most of my personal Estate to ye Value of many hundreds of poundes taken from me & Very Little of it Restored againe I pray to Consider my Extroardinary Sufferings

I am Gen^t yo^ε humble Serv^a

[Reverse] [Hand 2] Mr English To ye Comittie

Essex County Court Archives, vol. 2, no. 184, Massachusetts Supreme Judicial Court, Judicial Archives, on deposit James Duncan Phillips Library, Peabody Essex Museum, Salem, MA.

904. Petition of Abigail Faulkner Sr. for Restitution

[Hand 1] To the Honourable committee Sitting in Salem
Sept. 13. 1710
An Account of the Sufferings of Abigail Faulkner of Andover and of 2 of her children for Supposed witchcraft, and of the Damage she sustained thereby. in the year 1692.

1 I Suffer'd Imprisonment four moneths and my children were in prison about a moneth. And upon my Tryall I was condemned upon such evidence as is now generally thought to be insufficient as may be seen in the court Records ⟨£⟩of my tryal. I humbly pray that the Attaindre may be taken off, and that my name that has been wrong'd may be restored
2 ⟨2⟩ I was at the whole charge of provideing for myself and my children During the time of our Imprisonment

September 13, 1710

3 money payd the Sheriffe, Keeper, Kings
Attorney &c for prison fees, court charges,
⟨&⟩ for Bonds and for my Reprieue & pardon
$\Big\}$ 10 – 0 – 0

4 My ~~cha~~ Expences in providing for my self & children while we were in prison; time and expences in j⟨o⟩urneys and attending the Courts were consderable, which I leave {to} the honourable Committe & the Gen^ll Court to allow me what may be thought Reasonable, which will be to my Satisfaction [Hand 2] ⟨O⟩ If it be but 10^li

Abig⟨i⟩l Faulkner

[Reverse] [Hand 3] Abigail Faulkner of Andover Condemned not Executed

Notes: Hand 3 = Stephen Sewall

Massachusetts Archives Collection, vol. 135, no. 154. Massachusetts State Archives. Boston, MA.

905. Petition of Abraham Foster for Restitution for Ann Foster

[Hand 1] The Hono^r̃able Committee now
sitt⟨i⟩ng at Salem Sept 13. 1710
~~The~~ ⟨H⟩ Whereas my Mother Anne Foster of Andouer suffered Imprisonment 21 weeks and vpon her Tryall was condemned for Supposed witchcraft, vpon such evidence as is now Generally thought Insufficient And died in Prison. I being well perswaded of my mothers Innocency of the Crime for which she was condemned; Humbly desire that the Attaindre may be taken off

The Account of my charges and expences for my mother during her
Imprisonment is as followeth.
To money which I was forc'd to pay the Keeper before I could haue the dead body of my mother to bury to ~~bury her~~   2 – 10 – 0

money & provisions expended while she was in Prison   ⟨2⟩ 4
4 – 0 – 0.

p^r̃ Abraham Foster
the son of the Deceased

[Reverse] [Hand 2] Anne ffoster of Andouer Condemnd dyed in prison Confessor

Notes: Hand 2 = Stephen Sewall

Massachusetts Archives Collection, vol. 135, no. 159. Massachusetts State Archives. Boston, MA.

906. Petition of John Frye for Restitution for Eunice Frye‡

September 13, 1710

[Hand 1] To the Hone^εable Commi⟨tt⟩ee.

An Account of the Expences of John Fry late of Andover for his wife Eunice Fry who Suffered Imprisonment 15 weeks vpon an accusation of witchcraft, in the year 1692 viz

For Prison fees and money and provisions Expended in prison   3 – 0 – 0.

it̄ To the clerk for court charges   1 – 17 – 4.

Totall 4 – 17 – 4.   p^ε John Frie
Executo^ε to the Deceas'd

I desire Capt John Barker to give in this account to the Hono^εable Comittee
J: W

[Reverse] John Fry's Account
[Hand 2] Eunice Fry Imprisond not Condemnd

Notes: Hand 2 = Stephen Sewall

Massachusetts Archives Collection, vol. 135, no. 148. Massachusetts State Archives. Boston, MA.

907. Petition of William Good for Restitution for Sarah Good, Dorothy Good, & Infant

[Hand 1] To The Honourable Committee

The humble representation of Willm Good of the Damage sustained by him in the year 1692. by reason of the sufferings of his ["his" written over "my"] family upon the account of supposed Witchcraft.
{1} My wife Sarah Good was In prison about four months & then Executed.
{2} a sucking child dyed in prison before the mothers Execution.
{3} a child of 4 or 5 years old was in prison 7 or 8 months and being chain'd in the dungeon was so hardly used and terrifyed that she hath ever since been very chargeable haveing little or no reason to govern herself. – And I leave ^{it} unto the Honourable Court to Judge what damage I have sustained by such a destruction of my poor family – And so rest
your Honours humble servant
salem. sept. 13. 1710.   William Good

[Hand 2] 30^{li} proposed for to be allowed

[Reverse] [Hand 1] Wm Good
[Hand 3] Sarah Good of Salem Condemned and Executed

Notes: Hand 3 = Stephen Sewall

UNCAT MS, Witchcraft Collection, no. 4620, Division of Rare and Manuscript Collections, Cornell University Library.

908. Petition of Peter Green for Restitution for Mary Green

[Hand 1] September 1⟨3ᵗʰ⟩ 1710.
an akount of Peter Green of hauarell his caust [= cost] and charge a ⟨ring⟩ rising [= arising]
by reason of his wifeˢ being apprehended for wich craft in tha eayer [= the year] 92 which is
as foloeth for asisting tha constabell with my wife to Salam and from thenc to epswech

	0–12–0
for a iourny of myself and 1 ["1" written over "2"]	
man weth me to giue bond for my wife	01–4–0
and for riting tha bond	00–2–0
and for preson charges 19 we⟨ae⟩ks	0⟨2⟩–7–6
and upon hur triall	01–2–6
and for my iourne 4 days upon hur triall	00–16–⟨0⟩

and I would pray youer honners to conseder me as to hur impresement but that I desier to
leaue with youer h⟨o⟩nners to determen

[Reverse] [Hand 2] Petter Green

Massachusetts Archives Collection, vol. 135, no. 170. Massachusetts State Archives. Boston, MA.

909. Petition of Francis Johnson for Restitution for Sarah Hawkes

[Hand 1] To the Honoᵉable Comittee sitting in Salem
Sept 13. 1710
The Account of Sarah Hawks, now the wife of Francis Johnson of Andover, who sufferd
Imprisonment 5 moneths in the year 1692 for the Supposed witchcraft
viz
money payᵈ to the Sheriffe and to the Keeper, before she could obtain
   a discharge   2 – 14 – 0.

i̅t Her Expences for her Provisions while She was in Prison. which I desire
   may be allowed.   2 – 10 – 0.

pᵉ Francis Johnson
on behalf of his wife.

[Reverse] [Hand 2] Sarah Hawks Imprisond not Condemnd

Notes: Hand 2 = Stephen Sewall

Massachusetts Archives Collection, vol. 135, no. 166. Massachusetts State Archives. Boston, MA.

910. Petition of John King & Annis King for Restitution for Dorcas Hoar‡   September 13, 1710

[Hand 1] ⟨A⟩n Account of what John King and Annis his wife one of yᵉ Daughters of Dorcas Hoare late of Beverly Deceas'd. Disburs'd and expended on their aforesᵈ Mother ⟨du⟩ring yᵉ time of her imprisonmen[Lost] [= imprisonment] and Great Troubles in yᵉ year 1692.

	l̄l	s	d
Imprimis			
tt [= item] Subsistance for her 9. Months when She was in Salem prison	9=00=0		
tt a Journey to Boston and Money Carryed to her while in prison there	0=10=0		
tt my Journey to Boston to Carry ^{her} to Ipswich & Expence while there	0=15=0		
tt my wife's going two Journeys to Ipswich & Expence & attendance upon her	0=10=0		
tt two Journeys to Boston to procure a repreive	1=00=0		
tt a Journey to fetch her from Ipswich to Salem	0=05=0		
besides Considerable Cloathing & other things for her necessitys.	£ 12=00=0		

John King
her marke
Annis [   ] King

[Reverse] [Hand 2]

King	12	00	00
Reed	3	—	—
Green	1		
	16		

3 Children

Wᵐ Hoar. Chilldren 2 S⟨?⟩es	1.	11.	01
Mary Birtt:	–	15	6 ¼
Eliz Reed	3.	15.	6 ¼
Annis Kinge	12.	15	6 ¼
Jo⟨a⟩nnᵃ Green.	1.	15.	6 ¼
Tabath Slue 3 chilldr̄	0	15.	6 ¼
Charges 18ˢ	21	08:	5	["21 08: 5" written over "20 13: 3"]
		8.	0
	21:	1	3

Notes: Dorcas Hoar, having confessed shortly before her scheduled execution, received a repreive. See No. 676. The reference to two trips to Boston may mean that an unsuccessful attempt had been made prior to her confession.

Essex County Court Archives, vol. 2, no. 151, Massachusetts Supreme Judicial Court, Judicial Archives, on deposit James Duncan Phillips Library, Peabody Essex Museum, Salem, MA.

September 13, 1710

911. Petition of John King & Annis King for Restitution for Dorcas Hoar‡

[Hand 1] An account of what Dorkcas ["o written over "r"] Whore had Taken from her. ~~In~~
[Hand 2] {who was condemned for witchcraft in} [Hand 1] yᵉ year 1692:   l̄i

to 2 coues & one ox & mare	4=0=0
to 4 shotes [= sheets?] 10ˢ pr 2ˡⁱ to bed & curtains & beding 5ˡⁱ	7=0=0
to other house hold stuf 2ˡⁱ 11ˢ	2=11=0
to 11 months diet at 12ˢ pʳ month which they found while she was in prison	6=06=0
[Hand 2] To expences In carrying her from one prison to another and finding her wood and cloths	2—0—0.

Sū Totall 21–17–0

pᴱ John King [Hand 3] & marke X of Annis King daughter of yᵉ sᵈ Dorcas <u>Hoar</u>

[Reverse] Dorcas Hoar of Beuerly Condemned not Executed

Notes: Hand 3 = Stephen Sewall

Massachusetts Archives Collection, vol. 135, no. 134. Massachusetts State Archives. Boston, MA.

912. Petition of William Hobbs for Restitution for Abigail Hobbs

[Hand 1] Topfield 13 of September 1710

Whereas yᵉ great & Honoured court haue apoint⟨e⟩d a comity to consider what damieg persons sustained in there Estats in yᵉ Yeare 1692 by what thay svffered in that as was called witch craft yᵉ odom [= odium] wherof was as y⟨ᵉ⟩ worst of mankind: William hobs I ~~my wife & our daughter~~ ten month my charges And Exspences Amounted to twenty pounds money besids Los of time which my damieg I think can not be less then 40 pounds: Yet notwithstanding upon consideration yᵗ our names may be Repay⟨e⟩red againe I am willing to take ⟨1⟩0 ["1" written over "2"] pounds so leaueing it to your Honour[Lost?] [= honours'] consideration I Remain your vnworthy seruant William Hobs

[Reverse] [Hand 2] Abigail Hobbs Condemned not Executed of Topsfield Confessor [Hand 1?] Hobs

Notes: Hand 2 = Stephen Sewall

Massachusetts Archives Collection, vol. 135, no. 156. Massachusetts State Archives. Boston, MA.

913. Petition of George Jacobs Jr. for Restitution for George Jacobs Sr., Rebecca Jacobs, & Margaret Jacobs‡

[Hand 1] An acompt of what was seised and taken away from my fathers Estate Gorge Jacobs senʳ Late of Salem decd [= deceased] by shrif Corwin and his assistants in yᵉ yeare

1692 When my s^d father was Executed and I was forced to fly out of y^e Countr{e}y to my   September 13, 1710
great damige and destress of my fameley my wife and daughter Imprisoned viz my wife 11
months and my daughter seuen months in prison it Cost them twelue pounds money to y^e
oficers besides other Charges

fiue Cows faier Larg Cattle. 3^l por Cow	15–00–0
Eight Loads of English Hay taken out of ye Barn 35^s po^r Load	14–0–0
a parcel of appels y^t made 24 barils Cider to halues viz 12 barils Cider 8^s por bariel	4–16–0
60 bussells of Ind^n Corn 2^s–6^d po^r busel	7–10–0
a mare	2–0–0
2 good feather beds and furnituer Rugs blank⟨e⟩ts sheets boulsters and pilows	10.–0–0
2 brass Kittles Cost	6–0–0
money 12^s a Large goold thumb Ringg 20^s	1–12–0
fiue swine	3–15–0
a quatity of pwter which I Cannot Exactly Know ye worth po^rhaps	3–0–0
	67–13–0
besides abundance of small things meat in ye hous fowls Chaiers and other thing took Clear away	aboue 12–0–0
	79–13–0

G⟨e⟩org Jacob

[Hand 2] Sixty seuen pounds thirteen shillings my fathers Estate The Twelue pounds paid
for my wife & Children

[Reverse] Georg Jacobs sen^ε Condemnd & Executed.
George Jacobs ∧{Jun^ε} his acc°/
George Jacobs sen^r of Salem Condemned & Executed.//

Notes: What Sheriff Corwin did with his seizures remains unknown. ◊ "pwter": 'pewter ware' (*OED* s.v. *pewter* n, 3a.).
◊ Hand 2 = Stephen Sewall

Massachusetts Archives Collection, vol. 135, no. 144. Massachusetts State Archives. Boston, MA.

914. Petition of Francis Johnson for Restitution for Elizabeth Johnson Jr.

[Hand 1] To the Honourable Committee Sitting in Salem Sept 13. 1710
~~Whe~~ The Account of Francis Johnson of Andover

Whereas my Sister Elizabeth Johnson [Hand 2] {Jun^ε} [Hand 1] of Andov^ε, was
Imprisoned Six moneths for ye Supposed witchcraft, and vpon her Tryall ~~w~~ was condemned
by such Evidence as is now Generally thought to be Insufficient In the year 1692. She the
Said Elizabeth Johnson Humbly prayes that the Attainder may be taken off.

September 13, 1710

My Expences for maintaining my Sister with
provisions during her Imprisonment was   3 – 0 – 0.
Which I pray may be allowed.

p^ε Francis Johnson on behalf of his Sister

[Reverse] [Hand 2] Eliz^a Johnson {Junr} Imprisoned not Condemned
[Hand 3?] Confessor

Notes: The petition affirming that Elizabeth Johnson, Jr. was condemned is accurate. The notation of the recorder that she was "not condemned" is inaccurate. She received a reprieve from Governor Phips. ◊ Hand 2 = Stephen Sewall

Massachusetts Archives Collection, vol. 135, no. 162, p. 138. Massachusetts State Archives. Boston, MA.

915. Petition of Francis Johnson for Restitution for Elizabeth Johnson Sr.

[Hand 1] To The Honourable Committee Sitting in Salem Sept 13. 1710

The Account of Elizabeth Johnson Sen^ε of Andover, of her Imprisonment for the Supposed witchcraft in the year 1692.
viz
She was Imprisoned 5 moneths and found her self provision during that time: 2 – 10 – 0.

To money payd to the Keeper and the Sheriffe before she could obtain a Release   2 – 14 – 0
ī̄t To Charges for 2 of her children who were Imprisoned 5 weeks viz. Stephen ⎤
   & Abigaill vpon the account of y^e witchcraft   ⎦ 2 – 14.
p^ε Francis Johnson by order & on behalf of his mother

Totall. 7:18-0

[Reverse] [Hand 2] Expences
[Hand 3] Eliza. Johnson Imprisoned not Cond⟨e⟩mned/
[Hand 4?] Confessor

Notes: Hand 3 = Stephen Sewall

Massachusetts Archives Collection, vol. 135, no. 157. Massachusetts State Archives. Boston, MA.

916. Petition of John Johnson for Restitution for Rebecca Johnson & Rebecca Johnson Jr.‡

[Hand 1] To the Honou^εable Committee
An Account of what was pay'd & expended by Rebecca Johnson of Andover for herself and her Daughter Rebecca who were accused of witchcraft, and suffered Imprisonment at Salem thirten weeks in the year 1692

viz.   l̄   s   d   Sept. 13, 1710

money & provisions expended while they were in Goal   3 – 15 – 0

īt To the sheriffe for Bail Bonds for each of them   0 – 8 – 0.

īt To Court charges which she was forc'd to pay for her self }
& Daughter before they could obtain a Release   }
                                                                 1 – 17 – 4
                                                         Total 6 – 0 – 4

                                     pᵉ John: Johnson.
                         Son of the sᵈ Rebecca Jn°son
                           on ⟨ᵻ⟩ behalf of his mother

there were sundry other Expences that I was at but
shall be Satisfyd if this account may be allowed

[Reverse] [Hand 2] Rebecca Johnson of Andouer & daughter Imprisond

Notes: Little survives regarding Rebecca Johnson Jr. She is mentioned during the examination of her mother, Rebecca Johnson. See No. 562. ◊ Hand 2 = Stephen Sewall

Massachusetts Archives Collection, vol. 135, no. 142. Massachusetts State Archives. Boston, MA.

917. Petition of Lawrence Lacey for Restitution for Mary Lacey Jr.†

[Hand 1] To the Honᵉable Committee
An Account of money payd, expended or disburs't by Lawrence Lacy of Andouer for his
Daughter mary Lacy who was Accused of wictchcraft and Suffered Imprisonment in the year
1692, which he was forc'd to pay before a Release could be obtain'd.
The time of her Imprisonment was ten ~~moneths~~ weeks
viz.   l̄   s   d
                 To the keeper of the Goal at Salem   1 – 5 – 0

                 īt To the clerk of the Court   1 – 17 – 4.

                                         ℔ Lawrence Lacy.
I desire capt Barker to give in this account to the Honᵉable Comittee

[Reverse] Lawrence Lacy's account for his Daughter mary.
[Hand 2] Mary Lacey J⟨u⟩nr Confessor Imprisoned not Condemned

Notes: This undated petition presumably came at the same time as the dated one for Mary Lacy Jr.'s mother, No. 918, which explains the higher confidence level of the dating. ◊ Hand 2 = Stephen Sewall

Massachusetts Archives Collection, vol. 135, no. 137. Massachusetts State Archives. Boston, MA.

September 13, 1710   **918. Petition of Lawrence Lacey for Restitution for Mary Lacey Sr.**

[Hand 1] To The Hono$^\varepsilon$able Committee Sitting
at Salem Sept 13. 1710

The Account of Lawrence Lacy of Andou$^\varepsilon$
whereas my wife mary Lacy suffered Imprisonment above seven moneths and vpon her
Tryall was condemned for Supposed witchcraft, but Reprieved in {the year 1692} I humbly
pray that the Attainder may be taken off.

my Expences were
viz. To the keeper of the Goal   03 – 10 – 0
For Provisions Expended in Prison ~~Cour~~ and other charges during her }
     Imprisonment   5 – 0 – 0.
                                              Total 8 – 10 – 0

p$^\varepsilon$ Lawrence Lacy

I desire Capt Jno Barker to give in this account to
the Gent^n of the Comittee
Lawrence Lacy

[Reverse] [Hand 2] Mary Lacey Sen̄ Condemned not Executed

Notes: Hand 2 = Stephen Sewall

Massachusetts Archives Collection, vol. 135, no. 158. Massachusetts State Archives. Boston, MA.

919. Petition of John Marston for Restitution for Mary Marston‡

[Hand 1] To the Hono$^\varepsilon$able Committee
An Account of the Expences of John Marston of Andouer for his wife {mary –} who
Suffered Imprisonment vpon accusation of witchcraft, 20 weeks in the year 1692; which he
was forc'd to pay before his wife could be Releas'd
viz:
To the Prison keeper   1 – 7 – 0
īt For Court charges   1 – 7 – 4
Besides his maintaining his wife with provision during the time of her
     Imprisonment and for other expences   2 – 5 – 0

p$^\varepsilon$ John Marston

Totall 4^l 19^s 4^d

I desire capt Barker to give in this account to the
Hon$^\varepsilon$able Comittee

[Reverse] John Marstons Account
[Hand 2] Expences
[Hand 3] M⟨a⟩ry Marston Imprisond not Condemnd

Notes: Hand 3 = Stephen Sewall   September 13, 1710

Massachusetts Archives Collection, vol. 135, no. 143. Massachusetts State Archives. Boston, MA.

920. Petition of Mary Morey for Restitution for Sarah Morey‡

[Hand 1] To the honered Committy Now Setting apinted by The Ginerall Court
The Humbell pition of Mary Morey Widdow of Peter Morey of bavrly desest sen⟨ns⟩ our
Daftor Sarey Morey whas folsly accused & Imprisened for ye sin of whichcraft The Month
of May one Thousand six Hundred ninty Tew and remaned In prison, Teill Janvarey
following. our said daftor whas Treyed & Cleared by Law which Imprisonment whas Much
more To our Damage Then I Cann Think of Know or Cann speek but what fowlows Now
Is what I have pade out of My pocket for her Charges & our Expenes In Gurning [=
journeying] to Iscist [= assist] her

To 35 Wicks diet in prison att 3^s ℔	£ 05 // 05 = 0
To savarall Jorneys to Boston & to Salem	02 // 00 = 0
To The Keeper	05 // 00 // 0
	12 = 05 = 0

her
Mary X Morey
marke

[Reverse] [Hand 2] Mary Moreys acc°

Notes: Hand 2 = Stephen Sewall

Massachusetts Archives Collection, vol. 135, no. 150. Massachusetts State Archives. Boston, MA.

921. Petition of Samuel Nurse Jr. for Restitution for Rebecca Nurse

[Hand 1] To the Honourable Committee Appointed to make Enquiry [Hand 2] with
respect to y^r Sufferings in y^e Tryalls in ye year 1692///
[Hand 1] The humble Representation of sam^{ll} Nurse of the damage sustained by our family
in the year 1692. by reason of the Imprisonment condemnation and Execution of My
Honoured Mother Rebek⟨?⟩ah Nurse for supposed Witchcraft.
1. We were at the whole charge of provideing for her dureing her Imprisonm^t in Salem and
Boston for the space of almost four months.
2 And also we spent much time and made many Journys to Boston & salem & other places
in order to have vindicated her Innocency.
3 And altho̅ we produced plentifull testimony that my honoured and Dear Mother had led a
blameless life from her youth up – yet she was condemned and executed upon such Evidence
as is now Generally thought to be Insufficient, which may be seen in the court record of her
tryall.
4 and so her name and the name of her Posterity lyes under reproach the removeing of which
reproach is the principal thing wherein we desire restitution.
5 And as we know not how to express our loss of such a Mother in such a way; so we know
not how to compute our charge but shall leave {it} to the judgm^t of others, and shall not be

September 13, 1710

critical but ready to receive such a satisfaction as shall be by the Honourable Court judged sufficient – so Praying God to Guide unto such Methods as may be for his Glory and the good of this land – I rest

Your Honours In all christian obedience

sam^{ll} Nurse

salem septem. 13. 1710

In the name of my brethren.

[Hand 3] Altho fourty pounds would not repair my loss and dammage in my Estate, yet I shall be Satisfyd if may be allowed, five and twenty pounds. Provided the Attainder be taken off.

Notes: As with the Corey petition, No. 899, the Nurse petition declines to put a monetary value on the victim's death. The monetary sum is written in another hand at the end of the document. ◊ Hand 2 = Stephen Sewall

Massachusetts Archives Collection, vol. 135, no. 165. Massachusetts State Archives. Boston, MA.

922. Petition of Samuel Osgood for Restitution for Mary Osgood

[Hand 1] To the Honour⟨a⟩ble Committee Sitting at Salem
Sept 13. 1710

An Account of the Expences of Capt John osgood Late of Andover, for his wife mary Osgood who Suffered Imprisonment 15 weeks vpon accusation of witchcraft, in the year 1692 viz.

money and Provisions Expended in Prison & for Prison fees 3 – 10 – 0

it̄ For Court charges payd to the Clerk 1 – 17 – 4
[Hand 2] J Elatson [Hand 1] Totall 5 – 7 – 4.

There were other Expences which I do not charge.

p^ε samuel Osgood by order & on behalf of his mother

[Reverse] Mrs Osgoods account
[Hand 3] Mary Osgood wife of Capt Osgood late Andouer Decd [= deceased] Imprisond &c

Notes: Hand 3 = Stephen Sewall

Massachusetts Archives Collection, vol. 135, no. 152. Massachusetts State Archives. Boston, MA.

923. Petition of John Parker & Joseph Parker for Restitution for Mary Parker

[Hand 1] ~~In~~ To the Honourable Comittee sitting in
Salem Sept 13. 1710

The Representation of John Parker and Joseph Parker of Andover, of the Sufferings of their Hono^εed mother mary Parker Late of Andover deceas'd. And of the Loss and Damage they haue Sustained in their Estates thereby

Whereas our mother was Imprisoned, and vpon her Tryall was condemned for supposed   September 13, 1710
witchcraft (vpon such Evidence as is now Generally thought to be Insufficient,) and Suffered
the paines of Death at Salem in the year 1692. we being well sati⟨s⟩fy'd not only of her
Innocency of that Crime that she was Condemned for, but of her piety. humbly desire that
the Attaindre may be takeen off, ~~that the Reproch that th~~ that so [= so that] her name that
has Suffered may be restored.

   The Account of our charges and of the Loss and damage we haue Sustained in our
                                                                         Estate is as followeth:

To money pay'd the Sheriffe in lieu of Cattle and corn which he had Seis'd   2 – 15 – 0

To the Keeper & to the clerk of the Court   2 – 15 – 0

⟨2⟩ Our charges & Expences otherwayes for our mother we compute to   ⎫
    be besides our time which we desire nothing for   ⎬   4 – 16 – 0
                                                                             ⎭

We had a sister that suffered Imprisonment vpon the Same account, whose charges are
included in this Account.

Notwithstanding our Loss and damage hath been so great. If we may be allowed Eight
pounds we shall be Satisfy'd

                                               pᵉ John Parker
                                               Joseph Parker
                                               yᵉ sons of the Deceas'd

[Reverse] [Hand 2] Mary parker of Andouer Condemnd & Executed

Notes: On November 7, 1692, John and Joseph Parker had petitioned for restitution. See No. 705. This previously
unpublished document makes clear that their petition had not succeeded as they appealed again in 1710. The "sister" is
Sarah Parker. ◊ Hand 2 = Stephen Sewall

Massachusetts Archives Collection, vol. 135, no. 168. Massachusetts State Archives. Boston, MA.

924. Petition of Mary Post for Restitution

                [Hand 1] To the Honoᵉable Committee sitting at Salem
                            Sept 13 1710
An Account of what was payd by mary Post of Andover who suffered Imprisonment aboue
eight moneths, and was condemned upon her tryall for witchcraft at Salem in the year 1692
viz   l̄   s   d
To the Keeper of the Goal   4 – 7 – 6

ī̄t For Court charges to the sheriffe   1 – 17 – 4.
For provision I found my self in prison   2 – 10 – 0.
                                               ――――――――――
                                               8 : 14 : 10

September 13, 1710

The sums abovesᵈ she was forc'd to pay before she could obtain a Release
I humbly desire the Attainder may be taken off.

pᵉ mary Post.

my Loss and damage by my imprisonment was not
less than fourteen pound but I shall be satisfyd with.
8 – 14 – 0

I desire capᵗ Barker to give in this account to the Gentlemen of yᵉ Committee
mary Post

[Reverse] mary Posts Account
[Hand 2] Mary post Condemnd not Executed

Notes: Mary Post received a reprieve. See No. 836. ◊ Hand 2 = Stephen Sewall

Massachusetts Archives Collection, vol. 135, no. 153. Massachusetts State Archives. Boston, MA.

925. Petition of Mercy (Wardwell) Wright for Restitution‡

[Hand 1] An Account of what was pay'd by mercy wardwell, now the wife of John wright of Andover; who Suffer'd Imprisonment vpon accusation of witchcraft, above five moneths. in the year 1692
viz.

money to the Keeper of the prison	1 – 4 – 0.
it̄ For Court charges	01 – 10 – 0.
Besides her maintaining herself wᵗʰ provision all yᵉ time she was in prison	2 – 10 – 0.

pᵉ mercy Wright

Totall 5: 4 – 0

I desire Capᵗ Barker to give in this account to the C̶o̶ Honᵉable Comittee
M. W.

[Reverse] [Hand 2] Expences
[Hand 1] mercy wardwels Account
[Hand 3] Imprisond not Condemnd.

Notes: Hand 3 = Stephen Sewall

Massachusetts Archives Collection, vol. 135, no. 141. Massachusetts State Archives. Boston, MA.

926. Petition of Samuel Wardwell Jr. for Restitution for Sarah & Samuel Wardwell

September 13, 1710

[Hand 1] To the Honourable Committee Sitting in Salem
Sept 13. 1710.

An Account of what was seiz'd and taken away by the sheriffe or his deputy and assistants out of the estate of Samuel Wardwell late, of Andover Deceas'd who suffered the paines of Death, under condemnation, on the sorrowfull tryalls for witchcraft in the year 1692.
viz Seis'd and taken away

5 cowes at 2 ℔	10 – 00 – 00.
1 Heifer & a yearling	2 – 5 – 00.
1 Horse	3 – 0 – 0.
9 Hogs	7 – 0 – 0.
8 Loads of Hay	4 – 0 – 0.
A set of Carpenters Tools	1 – 10 – 0.
6 Acres of Corn vpon the ground	9 – 00 – 00
	£ 36 . 15 . 00

Sarah Wardwell the wife of Samuel Wardwell aforesaid was condemned vpon her Tryall ~~o~~for witchcraft, at Salem in the year 1692
I being well Satisfyed in the Innocency of my father and mother of the Crime for which they were condemned humby [= humbly] desire the attainder may be taken off.
p^ε Samuel Wardwell ^{Eldest} son of the Deceas'd

[Reverse] Samuel Wardwells Account [Hand 2] of Andouer
Condemned & Executed

Notes: Hand 2 = Stephen Sewall

Massachusetts Archives Collection, vol. 135, no. 164. Massachusetts State Archives. Boston, MA.

927. Petition of Margaret Towne for Restitution for John Willard

[Hand 1] Topsfield Septemb^ε 13th 1710

To y^e Honored Committee appointed by y^e Hon⟨o⟩red Generall Court (to make enquiry into ye dammage sustained by any persons in ye year 1692 by reason of ye great disturbance in our land from ye powers of darkness) ye Committee aforesaid being to meet at Salem Sept. ye 14.
Margarett Town of Topsfield in ye County of Essex in N. England, formerly Margarett Willard Relict of John Willard Late of Salem who suffered death in y^t hour of ye power of darkness as if he had been guilty of one of ye greatest of Crimes y^t ever any of ye Sons of Adan hav⟨e⟩ been left of God to fall into, Having been notified by order of ye Generall court to appear before your Honors to give an account as near as I can what dammage my self tog⟨e⟩ther with my aforesaid former Husband did Sustain in our Estate besides ye fearfull odium cast on him by imputing to him & causing him to suffr death for svch a piece of wickedness as I hav⟨e⟩ not ye l⟨ea⟩st reason in ye world to thinke he was guilty of I say besides y^{⟨e⟩} reproach & ye grief & sorrow I was exposed to by y^t means I do account our dammage as

September 13, 1710

to our outward estat⟨e⟩ to have been very Considerabl⟨e⟩ for by reason of my said former Husband being seized by order of yᵉ civil Authority & imprisoned all our Husbandry concerns were laid by for yᵗ summer we had not opportunity to plant or sow whereas we were wont to raise our own bread Corn, I Reckon (which your Honors may please more certainly to Inform your selves from yᵉ Records of those vnhappy times & things yᵗ happend) I say according to my best Remembran⟨c⟩ from yᵉ time of his first imprisonment to yᵉ time of his suffering was near vpon half a year all wh⟨i⟩ch time I was at yᵉ trouble & charge to provide for him in pr⟨i⟩son what he stood in need of out of our own Estate, my aforesaid Husband was 3 weeks a prisoner at Boston which occasioned me to be at yet more charge & troubl⟨e⟩ & altho I had after his sentence of death was past vpon him obtain a Replevin for him for a l⟨i⟩ttle time which not coming a⟨s⟩ was expected at yᵉ time appointed I was forced to hire a horse at Salem & go to Boston to see what was yᵉ reason of yᵗ fai⟨l⟩ure, I have nothing further to add but only to pray your Honors to guess at yᵉ dammage as well as you can by yᵉ Information I have here given & yᵗ God will direct you in & about what you are now concerned about & to take Leave to subscribe my self Your Honors Humbl &

sorrowfull servant
yᵉ marke of
Margarett X Town

[Hand 2] I Judge that my Loss and damage in my estate hath not been Less than thirty⟨?⟩ ["thirty" written over "twenty"?] pounds. But I shall be Satisfy⁴ If I may haue twenty pounds allowed me

[Reverse] [Hand 3] John Willard of Salem Condemnd & Executed

Notes: The reference to "Replevin" is intriguing but so far inconclusive. It appears as if at one point Margaret Towne may have had reason to believe that Willard would be spared execution. ◊ "yᵉ Sons of Adan": In the Douai-Rheims Bible of 1610, Ezra 8:6 mentions Abed "of the sons of Adan" among those who returned to Jerusalem from Babylonia (rendered as "sons of . . . Adin" in the Authorized Version). In the present instance, however, the name intended by the recorder is undoubtedly *Adam*. "Replevin": "Baylement, Mainprise, or Repleuin, is the sauing, or deliuerie of a man, out of prison, before that he hath satisfied the Law, *sc.* by finding suerties to answer, and be iustified by the Law. And to this purpose these three termes (Baylment, Mainprise, and Repleuin) be indifferently vsed in our Statutes and bookes." Michael Dalton, *The countrey iustice conteyning the practise of the iustices of the peace out of their sessions. Gathered for the better helpe of such iustices of peace as haue not beene much conuersant in the studie of the lawes of this realme* (London: Adam Islip for the Societie of Stationers, 1618), 269. In the *OED* this now obsolete sense of the word is recorded as 'The bailing of, or bail for, a person' (s.v. *replevin* n, 1c). Another possible interpretation is 'A writ empowering a person to recover his goods by replevin, i.e. the restoration to, or recovery by, a person of goods or chattels distrained or taken from him' (*OED* s.v. *replevin* n, 2). ◊ Hand 3 = Stephen Sewall

Massachusetts Archives Collection, vol. 135, no. 167. Massachusetts State Archives. Boston, MA.

928. Petition of Joseph Wilson for Restitution for Sarah Wilson Sr. & Sarah Wilson Jr.‡

[Hand 1] To the Honourable Committee.
An Account of what was payd by Joseph Wilson of Andouer for his wife ^{Sarah} and Daughter ^{Sarah} who suffered Imprisonment at Salem, vpon an Accusation of witchcraft in the year 1692. the one was Imprisoned fifteen weeks the other Six weeks viz

money and Provisions expended while they were in Prison	2 – 10 – 0	September 14, 1710
i̅t̅ For a̶ Bail Bonds, to the Clerk	0 – 8 – 0.	
i̅t̅ To the Deputy sheriffe for Court Charges	1 – 17 – 4	

p^ε Joseph willson

I desire cap^t Jn° Barker to give in this account to the Hono^εable Comitte

[Reverse] Joseph Wilsons account
[Hand 2] Sarah Willson sen^ε Sarah Willson Jun Imprisond not Condemned

Notes: Hand 2 = Stephen Sewall

Massachusetts Archives Collection, vol. 135, no. 145. Massachusetts State Archives. Boston, MA.

Thursday, September 14, 1710

929. Recommendation and Authorization for Compensation Claims and Amounts Allowed

See also: Oct. 26, 1711.

[Hand 1] To y^e Hon^εd Genr^{ll} Court Sitting.

We whose namss are subscribed, In Obedience to yo^ε Hon^εs Act at a Court held y^e vlt [= last] of May 1710: for ⟨?⟩our Inserting: y^e Names of y^e seuerall ꝑsons who were Condemned for witchcraft in y^e year 1692. & of y^e Damages they susteined by their prosecution: Being Mett at Salem y^e 13th Sep^t 1710. for y^e Ends aforesaid upon Examination of y^e Records of y^e seuerall ꝑsons Condemned: Humb⟨ly⟩ Offer to yo^ε Hon^εs the Names as Follow to be Inserted for y^e Reuersing of their Attaniders:

Executed	Elizabeth {T [= Topsfield]} How: Georg {S [= Salem]} Jacob. Mary {T} Easty. Mary {A [= Andover]} Parker. Mr George ["George" written over "Charles"?] {W [= Wells]} Burroughs: Giles {S} Core & ~~Martha Core~~ his wife. Rebeccah {S} Nurse. John {S} Willard. Sarah {S} Good. Martha {A} Carriar. Samuell {A} Wardell. John {S} Procter: Sarah {T} Wild
Condemned {⟨?⟩} & not Exe⟨cu⟩ted	Mary {S} Bradbury. Abigail {A} Falknor. Abigail {T} ~~F~~Hobs. Ann {A} Foster. Rebeccah {A [Hand 2] B: [= Boxford]} [Hand 1] Eams. Dorcas {B [= Beverly]} Hoar. Mary {A} Post Mary {A} Lacey.

And haueing heard y^e seuerall Demaunds of y^e Damages of y^e afores^d ꝑsons & those in their behalf, & upon Conferenc haue soe Moderated their Respectiue Demaunds y^t we doubt not but y^t they will be Readily Comply^d wth by yo^ε Hon^εs which Respectiue Demaunds are as follow. Elizabeth How 12^{li} Georg Jacob. 79^{li} Mary Easty. 20^{li} Mary Parker. 8^{li} m^r Georg

September 28, 1711

Burroughs. 50^{li} Giles Core. & Martha Core his wife 21^{li} Rebeccah Nurse 25^{li} John Willard. 20^{li} Sarah Good. 30^{li} Martha Carrier. 7^{li} 6^s Samuel Wardell & Sarah his wife 36^{li} 15^s John Procter. & [   ] Procter his wife 150^{li} Sarah Wild. 14^{li} m^{rs} Mary Bradbury. 20^{li} Abigail Falkner 20^{li} Abigail Hobs. 10^{li} Ann Foster. 6^{li} 10^s Rebecca Eams. 10^{li} Dorcas Hoar. 21^{li} 17^s Mary Post. 8^{li} 14^s Mary Lacey. 8^{li} 10^s the whole amounting vnto. 578^{li} 12^s
Salem. y^e 14th ["4" written over "5"] Sep^t 1710.

yo$^\varepsilon$ Hon$^\varepsilon$s most Humble Serv^{ts}
John Appleton
Thomas Noyes
John Burrill
Neh: Jewett

~~y^e Acco^t of yo$^\varepsilon$ seruants. Charges~~	$\overline{li}$
~~3 dayes a Peic ou$^\varepsilon$ selues & horses.~~	~~4.0.0~~
~~Entertainm^t at Salem m^r pratts.~~	~~1–3–0~~
~~Majo$^\varepsilon$ Sewals attendanc & sending~~	
~~Notifications to all Concerned~~	~~1–0–0~~
	~~6–3.⟨0⟩~~

[Hand 3] Octo$^{(r)}$ 23: 1711. Read & Accepted in the House of Representatives. sent up for Concurrence.
John Burrill speaker

[Hand 4] Oct^o 26° 1711. In Council Read and Concurr^d
Is^a Addington S⟨ecry⟩

[Reverse] [Hand 5] The Comittie Returne of the Names of persons attainted of Witch-craft and Damages Suffered.
accepted Octob^r 1711.

Notes: After the attainders had been lifted, the specific sums for compensation are listed. The list does not include the names of everybody who requested compensation and includes no name of any person not having been condemned. It applies only to those who had their attainders lifted. The document references May 1710 as the date authorizing the legislation. Elsewhere, June is indicated.

Massachusetts Archives Collection, vol. 135, no. 169. Massachusetts State Archives. Boston, MA.

Friday, September 28, 1711

930. Summary of the Amounts Requested by the Victims & Their Relatives†

[Hand 1] Mr Sewall, & Hon$^{\varepsilon d}$ freind
Sr Respects ꝑmised yo$^\varepsilon$s I receiued ꝑ yo$^\varepsilon$ son. bearing date y^e 2[Lost]$^{t⟨h⟩}$ [*SWP* = 27th] of this Instant moth & according to yo$^\varepsilon$ desire I haue drawne out y^e Names & sums (of y^e Respectiue sufferers) y^t y^e petition$^\varepsilon$s prayd for.

	li	s	d	
1st of those Executed.				September 28, 1711
Elizabeth How; Mary & Abigail her daughters prayd for.	12	0	0	
Georg Jacobs. Georg Jacobs his son prayd ꝑ:	79	0	0	
Sarah ["Sarah" written over "Ephraim"] Wild. Ephraim				
Wild her son prayd for	14	0	0	
Mary Easty. Isaack Easty her husband pr^d ꝑ	20	0	0	
Mary parker Joseph & Jno parker her sons pr^d ꝑ	08	0	0	
Mr Georg Burroughs. Charls Burroughs his son pr^d ꝑ	50	0	0	
Elizabeth Core. & Martha ye wife of Jno Molton he pr^d ꝑ	21	0	0	
Rebecca Nurse. Samuell Nurse her son pr^d ꝑ	25	0	0	
Jno Willard. Majeret Towne his relict pr^d ꝑ	20	0	0	
Sarah Good. William Good her husband pr^d ꝑ	30	0	0	
Martha Carried. Thomas Carriar her husband pr^d ꝑ	07	6	0	
Samuell Wardell. Executed & his wife Sarah Condemn^d				
Samuell Wardell their son. pr^d ꝑ.	36	15	0	
John procter. Jno & Thorndick his sons pr^d ꝑ	150	0	0	
ꝑsons Condemned & Not Executed				
Mrs Mary Bradbury Henry & Saml True her sons pr^d ꝑ	020	0	0	
Abigail Faulkner for her & her children pr^d ꝑ	020	0	0	
Abigail Hobs. William Hobs her Father pr^d ꝑ. 10$^£$	010	00	0	
Ann Foster. Abraham Foster her son pr^d ꝑ	006	10	[Lost] [= 0?]	
Rebeccah E{a}m{e}s prayes ꝑ	010	0	[Lost] [= 0]	
Dorcas King alius Whore pr^d ꝑ	021	1⟨7⟩	[Lost] [= 0]	
Mary post prayes ꝑ	008	14	0	
Mary Lacy. Lawrence her husband pr^d ꝑ	0:08	10	0	
Elizabeth procter & } I find their names amongst y^e aboue				
Elizabeth Johnson } Condemned ꝑsons & no sum put to them:				
ꝑsons Imprisoned & not Condemned petitioned for Allowances for their Imprisonm^t				
charges &c.				
Sarah Buckley ["c" written over "l" in Hand 2] & Mary	15	0	0	
Witredg for so much they pay^d				
John Johnson for Rebecca his wife & daughter	6	0	4	
Capt Osgoods wife Mary	5	7	4	
Sarah Cole for hers	6	10	0	
Edward Bishop petitions for	100	0	0	
Jno Barker ꝑ Mary ["Mary" written over "William"]	03	15	10	
Barkerr ∧{his daughter} expences he p^d for her ["her"				
written over "him"]				
Robt pease ꝑ his	13	3	0	
Nathl Dane – ꝑ his	4	13	0	
Jno Fry ꝑ his	4	17	4	
Joseph Wilson ꝑ his	4	15	4	
Jno Wright ꝑ his	0	4	0	
Mercy Woodell ye wife of Jno Wright for hers	5	4	0	
Jno Barker prayes for his Br^o Wm Barkers	3	11	0	
Lawrenc Lasy for his daughter Mary	3	0	4	

October 17, 1711	Jn° Marston ⅌ his wife		2	14	⟨?⟩
	Ebenezer Barker for his wife		5	7	4
	Francis Johnson for his wife then Sarah Hawks		5	4	0
	Francis Johnson for his mother		7	12	0
	& for his sister Elizabeth		3	00	⟨0⟩
		Totall	796	18	[Lost]

Ips. 28. 9. 1711
Sʳ yoᵉ Most humble: seruant
Neh: Jewet

besides Mʳ English his demaunds Left to yᵉ
Courts Consideration & deterimnation.

[Reverse] [Hand 3] accᵒ of yᵉ Comitte's return abᵗ yᵉ ⅌sons Suffering in yᵉ Witchcraft tim⟨es⟩

Notes: The requests made the previous year are summarized here presumably in anticipation of the government action soon to follow in October on these claims. ◊ Hand 3 = Stephen Sewall

Essex County Court Archives, vol. 2, no. 143, Massachusetts Supreme Judicial Court, Judicial Archives, on deposit James Duncan Phillips Library, Peabody Essex Museum, Salem, MA.

Wednesday, October 17, 1711

931. An Act to Reverse the Attainders of George Burroughs et al. for Witchcraft

[Hand 1] Province of the Massachusetts Bay.   Anno Regni Annæ Reginæ Decimo.

An Act to Reverse the Attainders of George
Burroughs and others for Witch-craft.

Forasmuch as in the year of our Lord One Thousand Six hundred Ninety two. Several Towns within this Province were Infested with a horrible Witchcraft or Possession of devils; And at a Special Court of Oyer and Terminer holden at Salem in the County of Essex in the same year 1692. George Burroughs of Wells, John Procter, George Jacobs, John Willard, Giles Core and [   ] his wife, Rebecca Nurse, and Sarah Good all of Salem aforesaid. Elizabeth How of Ipswich, Mary Eastey, Sarah Wild and Abigail Hobbs all of Topsfield, Samuel Wardell, Mary Parker, Martha Carrier, Abigail Falkner, Anne Foster, Rebecca Eames, Mary Post and Mary Lacey all of Andover, Mary Bradbury of Salisbury, and Dorcas Hoar of Beverly Were severally Indicted convicted and attainted of Witchcraft, and some of them put to death, others lying still under the like Sentance of the said Court, and liable to have Executed upon them.

The Influence and Energy of the Evil Spirits so great at that time acting in and upon those who were the principal Accusers and Witnesses proceeding so far as to cause a Prosecution to be had of persons of known and good Reputation; which caused a great Disatisfaction and a Stop to be put thereunto until their Majesty's pleasure should be known therein.

And upon a Representation thereof accordingly made Her late Majesty Queen Mary the   October 17, 1711
Second of blessed Memory by Her Royal Letter given at Her Court at Whitehall the
fifteenth of April 1693. was Graciously pleased to approve the care and Circumspection
therein; and to Will and require that in all proceedings ag^t persons Accused for Witchcraft,
or being possessed by the devil, the greatest Moderation and all due Circumspection be used,
So far as the same ^{may be} without Impediment to the Ordinary Course of Justice.
And

[Reverse] And Some of the principal Accusers and Witnesses in those dark and Severe
prosecutions have since discovered themselves to be persons of profligate and vicious
Conversation.

Upon the humble Petition and Suit of several of the s^d persons and of the Children of
others of them whose Parents were Executed.

Be it Declared and Enacted by his Excellency the Governo^ᵉ⟨s⟩ Council and
Representatives in General Court assembled and by the Authority of the same That the
several Convictions Judgement⟨s⟩ and Attainders against the said George Burroughs,
John Procter, George Jacob, John Willard, Giles Core and [   ] Core, Rebecc[Lost] [=
Rebeccah] Nurse, Sarah Good, Elisabeth How, Mary Easty, Sarah W[Lost] [= Wild]
Abigail Hobbs, Samuel Wardell, Mary Parker, Martha Carrier, Abigail Falkner,
Anne Foster, Rebecca Eame[Lost] [= Eames] Mary Post, Mary Lacey, Mary Bradbury and
Dorcas ⟨H⟩[Lost] [= Hoar] and every of them Be and hereby are Reversed made an⟨d⟩
[Lost] [SWP = declared] to be Null and void to all Intents, Constructions and purposes
wh[Lost]ever [= whatsoever?], as if no such Convictions, Judgments or Attainders had ever
[Lost] [SWP = been] had or given. And that no penalties or fforfeitures of Goods or
Chattels be by the said Judgments and Attainders or either of them had or Incurr'd.

Any Law Usage or Custom to the contrary notwithstanding
And that no Sheriffe, Constable Goaler or other Officer shall be Liable to any prosecution in
the Law for any thing they then Legally did in the Execution of their Respective Offices.

Made and Pass'd by the Great and General Court or Assembly of Her Majesty's
Province of the Massachusetts Bay in New England held at Boston the 17th day of
October. 1711.

Notes: Rebecca Eames of Boxford is here included in the Andover group. Of the twenty people executed for witchcraft in
1692, thirteen had their attainders reversed as the document indicates. Eight who were condemned but not executed also
had their attainders reversed on October 17, 1711. Those executed but not on this list were Bridget Bishop, Susannah
Martin, Alice Parker, Ann Pudeator, Margaret Scott, and Wilmot Redd. These were apparently excluded simply because
nobody applied on their behalf. Particularly significant in this document is the severe judgment on "Some of the principal
Accusers and Witnesses," strongly implying that however modern commentators may judge these accusers, they were
seen in 1711 as dishonest people, by implication engaged in fraud, their motives traced to the Devil. The blame is placed
on them, and the legal authorities are cleared of any blame, again no matter how later generations might assess them. The
title of the document carries the name of George Burroughs probably because of his prominence and his centrality to the
trials. Massachusetts in 1957 with Ann Pudeator, and 2001 with the others, formally acknowledged error in these cases –
the legal implications too murky for discussion here. Acting Governor Jane Swift chose Halloween as the day to make the
2001 pardons official, thus reflecting a cultural conflation of innocent individuals imprisoned, and in some cases executed,
with the celebratory festivities of a fantasy world inhabited by real witches, ghosts, and goblins. ◊ "attainted": 'subjected
to attainder, i.e. forfeiture of estate real and personal, corruption of blood, so that the condemned could neither inherit
nor transmit by descent, and generally, extinction of all civil rights and capacities' (OED s.v. attaint v, 6; s.v. attainder 1).

Essex County Court Archives, vol. 2, no. 136, Massachusetts Supreme Judicial Court, Judicial Archives, on deposit James Duncan
Phillips Library, Peabody Essex Museum, Salem, MA.

Friday, October 26, 1711

Passed by the Legislature: Recommendation and Authorization for Compensation Claims and Amounts Allowed

2nd *of 2 dates. See No. 929 on Sept. 14, 1710*

Tuesday, October 30, 1711

932. Expenses of General Court for Reversals of Attainders

[Hand 1] Province Mass^{ts} Bay D^r [= debtor] to sundry charges of the Comittee Appointed by the Generall Court in June 1710, to Inqvire what names were proper to be Inserted in the Bill for the Reversing of the Attainders of Persons condemn'd for Witchcraft. &c^a vizt
To 3 daies ~~entertainment of~~ themselves and horses, being four, ~~at Mr Prats, at Salem~~

	£	4	
To Entertainment at Mr Prats at Salem		1	3
To Maj^r Sewal's Attendence, & sending of Notifications, to all concerned		1	
	£	6	3

                                        [Hand 2] John Appleton
                                        in y^e behalfe of y^e Commit⟨e⟩e.
[Hand 3] In the House of Representatives Octo^r 27th 1711. Read & Resolved That the sum of six Pounds & three shillings be Allowed & Paid out of the publick Treasury to John Appleton Esq$^{\varepsilon}$ to Discharge the said acc^o sent up for Concurrence.
                                        John Burrill speaker
[Hand 4] Oct^o 30th 1711. In Council; Read and Concurrd.
                                        Is^a Addington Secry./.

[Reverse] Oct^o 1711. Resolve for paym^t of £6.3.0. to Jno Appelton Esq$^{\varepsilon}$ on behalfe of the Committee ab^t the Witchcraft.

Massachusetts Archives Collection, vol. 135, no. 171. Massachusetts State Archives. Boston, MA.

Monday, December 17, 1711

933. Request for Copy of Act for Restitution‡

[Hand 1] Whereas we the Subscribers are Informed that His Excellency the Governour Honourable Council, and Generall assembly of this Province have been pleased to hear Our Supplication and answer our Prayer in passing an act in favour of us respecting: our Reputations and Estates: Which we humbly and gratefully acknowledge.

And inasmuch as it would be Charge⟨a⟩ble and Troublesome for all or many of us to goe to   December 17, 1711
Boston on this affair: –Wherefore we have and do Authorize, and Request our Trusty Freind
the Worshipfull Stephen Sewall Esq^ε
To procure us a Coppy of the Said act, and to doe what may be further proper and necessary
for the reception of what is allowed us and to take and receive the Same for us and to
Transact any other Thing referring to the Premises on our Behalf: that may be requisite or
Convenient.
Essex December 1711

John Eames in behalf of his mother Rebecca
    Eames,
Abigail Faulkner
Samuel Preston on behalf of his wife Sarah
    Preston.
Samuel Osgood on behalf of his mother
    mary osgood
Nathaniel Dane
Joseph wilson
Samuel Wardwell
John Wright
Ebenezer Barker
Francis Johnson, on behalf of his mother,
    Brother & sister Elizabeth
Joseph Emerson on behalf of his wife
    martha Emerson of Hauerhill
Ephraim Willdes

Charles Burrough: eldes⟨t⟩ {Son}
John Barker
Lawrence Lacy
Abraham Foster
John Parker   ⎫   ye sons of mary
Joseph Parker ⎬   Parker deceased
John Marston
Thomas Carrier
John Frie.
Mary Post.
John: Johnson. in behalf of his mother
    Rebecca Johnson & his sister
William Barker sen^ε
ꝓ Gorge: Jacob on behalf of his father who
    sufferd
Thorndik Procter on behalf of his father.
    John Procter who suffered
Beniamin. Procter son of the {aboue⟨s^d⟩}

[Reverse] John. moulton on behalf of his wife
Elizabeth the daughter: of Giles Coree who suferd
Robert ~~pea~~ Pease on behalf of his wife
Annies King on behalf of heir mother
Doarcas hoare
willem town
Samuel nurs
Jacob estei
Edward Bishop

[Hand 2] ꝑsons Authorizing me to Transact the Matter about y^e money

Notes: The exact day in December cannot be verified, but it can be dated with reasonable confidence between December
17 and December 31. The "signatures" are generally not written by those "signing" the document. ◊ Hand 2 = Stephen
Sewall

*Essex County Court Archives, vol. 2, no. 139, Massachusetts Supreme Judicial Court, Judicial Archives, on deposit James Duncan
Phillips Library, Peabody Essex Museum, Salem, MA.*

December 17, 1711   **934. Order for Payment of Damages by Governor Joseph Dudley**

[Hand 1] By his Excellency The Gouerno$^\varepsilon$

Whereas y^e Generall Assembly in thier last Session accepted y^e report of thier comitte appointed to consider of y^e Damages Sustained by Sundry persons prosecuted for Witchcraft in y^e year 1692 vizt

	£ s d		£ s d
To Elizabeth How	12–0–0	John Procter {& wife}	150–0–0
George Jacobs	79–0–0	Sarah Wild	014–0–0
Mary Eastey	20–0–0	Mary Bradbury	20–0–0
Mary Parker	08–0–0	Abigail Faulkner	20–0–0
George Burroughs	50–0–0	Abigail Hobbs	10–0–0
Giles corey & wife	21–0–0	Anne Foster	6–10–0
Rebeccah Nurs⟨e⟩	25–0–0	Rebeccah {Eames}	10–0–0
John Willard	20–0–0	Dorc⟨e⟩s Hoar	21–17–0
Sarah Good	30–0–0	Mary Post	8–14–0
Martha Carrier	7–6–0	Mary Lacey	8–10–0
Samuel Wardwell {& wife}	36–15–0		269–11–00
	309–01–00		309–1–00
			578–12–00

The whole amounting vnto Five hundred Seventy Eight poundes & Twelue Shillings. I doe by & with the advice & consent of Her Maj^{ties} Council hereby order you to pay ye aboue Su͞m of fiue hundred Seuenty Eight poundes & Twelue Shillings to Stephen Sewall Esqr who together with ye Gentlemen of ye Comitte that Estimated and Reported ye Said Damages are desired & directed to distribute y^e Same in proportion as aboue to Such of y^e Said persons as are Liuing & to those that legaly represent them that are dead according as y^e law directs [Hand 2] & [Hand 1] for which this Shall be your Warrant/

To Mr Treasurer Taylor   Giuen vnder my hand at
By order of y^e Gouerno$^\varepsilon$ & Council   Boston the 17. Day of December 1711.
Is^a Addington Secr^{ty} J. Dudley

Copia vera

[Reverse] Copy of y^e allowance

Margaret Towne 1/3	6–12–8
margaret willard	3–4–6
Hanah Willard.	3–4–6
	13–1–8
	6–9–0
	19–10–8

Notes: The names on this list, including the absence of Martha Corey's first name, corresponds closely to the list of those who had their attainders lifted on October 17, 1711. See No. 931. Not on that list, but on this one are the wives of John Procter and Samuel Wardwell. Also, three names not indictated on the October 17 document are added on the reverse of this one. ◊ Hand 1 = Stephen Sewall

Essex County Court Archives, vol. 2, no. 138, Massachusetts Supreme Judicial Court, Judicial Archives, on deposit James Duncan Phillips Library, Peabody Essex Museum, Salem, MA.

Thursday, January 3, 1712

935. Division of Money in Burroughs Restitution

[Hand 1] Forasmuch as its made Manifest ~~to~~ that yᵉ Children of Mʳ George Burroughs
Dē̄ᶜᵉᵈ by his former wiues did ⟨in⟩ yᵉ time of his Imprisonment ⟨&⟩ adm⟨ini⟩ster vnto him
Necessary Things & were at considerable charge thereabout ⟨&⟩ for his I⟨n⟩terment & that
yᵉ widow had most or all of yᵉ personal Estate
In Consideraconₙ Whereof Wee yᵉ Subscribers a Comittee apoi⟨n⟩ted by yᵉ Gen⟨e⟩rall Court
& Consent agree & order that yᵉ Six pounds 6ᵈ Money yet remaing of yᵉ fifty pounds alowed
by yᵉ Gouerment shall be payd to yᵉ sᵈ Children in Equal Shares.
January 3ᵈ 1712

> John Appleton
> Thomas Noyes
> Stephen Sewall
> Neh. Jewett

[Reverse] Agreemᵗ [Lost] [= 6ˡⁱ] 6ᵈ yᵉ iij Burroughs
[Hand 2] G Borroughs

Notes: Hand 1 = Stephen Sewall

Essex County Court Archives, vol. 2, no. 158, Massachusetts Supreme Judicial Court, Judicial Archives, on deposit James Duncan Phillips Library, Peabody Essex Museum, Salem, MA.

Monday, January 7, 1712

936. Order of Thomas Carrier Sr. for Payment

[Hand 1] To the Gentlemen of the committee appointed by the Governoᵉ and Council to
distribute the money allowed by the Genˡˡ Court, to such as were Sufferers in the year 1692.
Please to pay and deliver unto Joseph Parker of Andover the sum̄ allowed vnto me, and his
Receipt Shall fully discharge you from the Same.

> Thomas Carrier.

Andouer
January 7. 1711/12

[Reverse] Tho. Carriers order [Hand 2] To Parker
[Hand 1] ~~To the Gentlemen of the committee appointed by the Genˡˡ Court~~

Notes: On January 7, 1712, instructions for payment of compensation due began to appear. These documents are "orders" on how the money is to be received. ◊ Hand 2 = Stephen Sewall

Essex County Court Archives, vol. 2, no. 155, Massachusetts Supreme Judicial Court, Judicial Archives, on deposit James Duncan Phillips Library, Peabody Essex Museum, Salem, MA.

January 7, 1712

937. Order of Rebecca Eames for Payment

[Hand 1] To the Gentlemen of the Committee appointed by the Governo$^\varepsilon$ and Council to distribute the money allowed by the Gen^{ll} Court to such as were sufferers in the year 1692 Please to pay and deliuer vnto my Son John Eames the Sum̄ allowed unto me and his receipt shall fully discharge you from the same.

January					[Hand 2] mark
7. 1711/12				rebackah X Ames
							har

[Reverse] [Hand 3] Reb Eames ord

Notes: Hand 3 = Stephen Sewall

Essex County Court Archives, vol. 2, no. 166, Massachusetts Supreme Judicial Court, Judicial Archives, on deposit James Duncan Phillips Library, Peabody Essex Museum, Salem, MA.

938. Order of Lawrence Lacey for Payment, Case of Mary Lacey Sr.

[Hand 1] To the Gentlemen of the Committee appointed by the Gouerno$^\varepsilon$ and Council to distribute the money allowed by the Gen^{ll} Court to such as were Sufferrers in the year 1692 Please to pay and deliver vnto Abraham Foster of Andouer the sum̄ allowed vnto me and his Receipt Shall fully discharge you from the Same

						[Hand 2] his mark
							X
Aadouer						larance lace
January
7: 1711/12

[Reverse] [Hand 3] Lawrence Laceys ⟨or⟩der

Essex County Court Archives, vol. 2, no. 182, Massachusetts Supreme Judicial Court, Judicial Archives, on deposit James Duncan Phillips Library, Peabody Essex Museum, Salem, MA.

939. Order of John Parker for Payment, Case of Mary Parker

[Hand 1] To the Gentlemen of the Committee appointed by the Governour and Council to distribute the money allowed by the Gen^{ll} Court to such as were Suffere⟨r⟩s in the year 1692. .
Please to pay and deliver unto my Brother Joseph Parker the Sum̄ allowed unto us, and his receipt Shall fully discharge you from the Same.

						John Parker.

Andouer January 7. 1711/12

[Reverse] [Hand 2] John Parkers Order

Notes: The hand of the signature matches the hand of the text.

Essex County Court Archives, vol. 2, no. 172, Massachusetts Supreme Judicial Court, Judicial Archives, on deposit James Duncan Phillips Library, Peabody Essex Museum, Salem, MA. January 7, 1712

940. Order of Mary Post for Payment

[Hand 1] To the Gentlemen of the Committee appointed by the Governour and Council to distribute the money allowed by the General Court to such as were Sufferers in the year 1692 Please to pay and deliver vnto Joseph Parker of Andouer the Sum allowed vnto me, and his Receipt Shall fully discharge you from the Same

[Hand 2] mark
mary X post
hur

[Hand 1] Andouer
January 7. 1711/12

[Reverse] [Hand 3] Mary posts order to parker

Essex County Court Archives, vol. 2, no. 173, Massachusetts Supreme Judicial Court, Judicial Archives, on deposit James Duncan Phillips Library, Peabody Essex Museum, Salem, MA.

941. Order of William Wardwell et al. for Payment, Cases of Samuel Wardwell & Sarah Wardwell

[Hand 1] To the Gentlemen⟨?⟩ of the Committee appointed by the Governour and Council to distribute the money allowed by the General Court to such as were sufferers in the year 1692.
Please to pay and deliver unto Samuel wardel our Eldest Brother the sum allowed unto us, and his Receipt Shall fully discharge you from the same.

William wardell
Eliakim wardel
John Right
Elisabeth wardell
Ezekiel Osgood
The children of Samuel wardel deceas'd.
~~william war~~

Andouer
January 7. 1711/12.

[Reverse] [Hand 2] Wardwells order

Notes: The "signatures" are written in the same hand, although not by the recorder of the document.

Essex County Court Archives, vol. 2, no. 165, Massachusetts Supreme Judicial Court, Judicial Archives, on deposit James Duncan Phillips Library, Peabody Essex Museum, Salem, MA.

Tuesday, January 15, 1712

942. Order of Mary Procter for Payment, Cases of John Procter & Elizabeth Procter

[Hand 1] To the Gentlemen of the Committee appointed by the Governour and Council to distribute the money allowed by the General Court, to Such as were Sufferers in the year 1692
Please to pay and deliver unto my Brother Thorndike Procter the Sum allowed unto me, and his Receipt Shall fully discharge you from the same.

mary Procter

January 15. 1711/12

[Reverse] [Hand 2] Mary Prockter

Notes: The hand of the signature matches the hand of the text.

Essex County Court Archives, vol. 2, no. 174, Massachusetts Supreme Judicial Court, Judicial Archives, on deposit James Duncan Phillips Library, Peabody Essex Museum, Salem, MA.

Wednesday, January 16, 1712

943. Order of Peter Thomas et al. for Payment, Case of George Burroughs

[Hand 1] Boston New England: Jan^r 16th 1711/12

Whereas we Are Inform'd The Generall Court hath Appointed a Committe To Disstribute To the Partys Concern'd: what the S^d Court have Allow'd To Make Repareation To The Sufferers In The Yere 1692: wherefor⟨e⟩ we desier And hereby Ord^e And Inpower Our Brother, Charls Burrough To Receive what is Allow'd To Each of us And his Receipt shall be A Suffcent Discharge

Peter Thomas   Rebekah Fowle
Jabez Fox
Jeremiah Burrough

[Reverse] [Hand 2] Jerem Burroghs & Sisters order
[Hand 3] J. & S. Borrough's order

Notes: Authenticity of signatures has not been established. ◊ Hand 2 = Stephen Sewall

Essex County Court Archives, vol. 2, no. 159, Massachusetts Supreme Judicial Court, Judicial Archives, on deposit James Duncan Phillips Library, Peabody Essex Museum, Salem, MA.

Monday, January 21, 1712

944. Petition of Nathaniel Dane et al. for Restitution

[Hand 1] Whereas severall of the neer Relations of us the Subscribers Suffered imprisonment at Salem in the year 1692. And we were put to great charges and Expence to provide for them while they were in Prison, and for Prison fees and court charges, which we were forc'd to pay before we could obtain their Release: An account of which we haue put in to the Gentlemen of the Committee, appointed by the Gen^ll Court: we do unanimously agree to make our Supplication to the Gen^ll Court to consider the Sufferings of our Relations, and the Dammage we then Sustained, and to allow us for it, according to the accounts ~~we~~ which we haue giuen to the committee aforesaid. And to that End we humbly request the worshipfull Stephen sewall Esq^ε to write a Petition for us to the General Court, at their next session:

Andouer
January 21. 1711/12

Nathaniel Dane
Joseph willson
Ebenezer Barker
ffrancis Johnson
John: Johnson.
~~John: John~~
John: wright
Samuel Osgood
Sara parker

[Reverse] [Hand 2] ⟨Sev⟩erall Andou⟨r⟩ [Lost] p[Lost]es [*SWP* = people's] prayer for [Lost]nce [= allowance]

Notes: Compensation remained for families of those condemned, not for those imprisoned or for related expenses. Sarah Parker is here seeking compensation for her own imprisonment, although her mother, Mary Parker, was executed. As with others who were not condemned, Sarah failed to receive anything. Authenticity of signatures has not been established, although some are written by the same hand.

Essex County Court Archives, vol. 2, no. 168, Massachusetts Supreme Judicial Court, Judicial Archives, on deposit James Duncan Phillips Library, Peabody Essex Museum, Salem, MA.

945. Order of William Good for Payment, Cases of Sarah Good and Dorothy Good

[Hand 1] To The Committee appointed by the Governour & Council for the distribution of the Money allowed by ye Generall Court to the sufferers in the year 1692.

Please to pay my part & proportion allowed me by the said Court unto Deacon Benjamin Putnam whom I have desired to pay my part or share of the necessary charge, And his receipt shall be your full discharge: from your servant

Wm Good X his mark.

salem: Vill: Janua: 21. 1711/12

January 22, 1712   *Essex County Court Archives, vol. 2, no. 142, Massachusetts Supreme Judicial Court, Judicial Archives, on deposit James Duncan Phillips Library, Peabody Essex Museum, Salem, MA.*

946. Order of Nathaniel Gowing for Payment, Cases of John Procter & Elizabeth Procter

[Hand 1] Whereas the Governour and Generall Court have been pleased to grant a Considerable Sum̄ towards Restitution to those who where Sufferers in yᵉ year 1692. & have appoin⟨t⟩ed a Com̄ittee to distribute yᵉ Same amongs't the [Lost]rsons [= persons] Concerned.

Wherefore inasmuch as I yᵉ Subscriber⟨s⟩ ^{Married} with Martha Procter one of yᵉ daughters of John Procter late of Salem decēd doe Request the Gentlemen̄ of yᵉ Committee to Deliver what part and proportion May belong to Me on behalfe of my Said wife, unto Capᵗ Ebenezar Bancroft of Lynn and his Receipt Shall be your full [Lost]scharge [= discharge]
from your Servᵗ

[Lost] ⟨J⟩anᵉʸ 21ˢᵗ 1711.

Nathanell Gowing

[Reverse] [Hand 2] [2–3 words illegible] ⟨accompte⟩

Essex County Court Archives, vol. 2, no. 145, Massachusetts Supreme Judicial Court, Judicial Archives, on deposit James Duncan Phillips Library, Peabody Essex Museum, Salem, MA.

Tuesday, January 22, 1712

947. Order of George Burroughs Jr. for Payment, Case of George Burroughs

[Hand 1] [Lost] [*SWP* = to] the Gentᵐ of the Com̄ittee: to Distribute the Mony
[Lost] [*SWP* = that] the Generˡˡ Court allowᵈ to yᵉ Famēelyes of tho⟨s⟩se
[Lost]at [= that] were Saffar⟨er⟩es in the tyme of yᵉ Witch Crafte
I Request that you woold. deliuer my ℔ᵗ of the mony
[Lost?]to [*SWP* = unto] Colᵒ John. Appleton: & his Recepᵗ shall bee
accepᵗᵈ pʳ George burrouhs
[Lost]⟨e⟩ [*SWP* = date] Jān 22. 1711

Essex County Court Archives, vol. 2, no. 157, Massachusetts Supreme Judicial Court, Judicial Archives, on deposit James Duncan Phillips Library, Peabody Essex Museum, Salem, MA.

948. Order of Mary How & Abigail How for Payment, Case of Elizabeth How

[Hand 1] Know all whom it doth or may Consarn That we mary and Abegill {How} both daughters of James. How Juner of Ipswich Late deceast: being informe That yᵉ honred Generall Court hath alowed som money for us in way of Restution for yᵉ damig we sustained

in ye yere [   ] 92 by that as was Called witch Craft. when our hono⟨u⟩red mother was   January 22, 1712
Executed

we pray your honours to send us y^e money alowed {us:} by our vncle Abraham How whom
we haue desiered & Employed to Recaue y^e same for us

dated in Ipswich 22 of January 1711 or 12

as witnes our hands

mark

mary X How

her

her

Abigill X How

mark

[Reverse] [Hand 2] Mary & Abigal Hows order

Notes: Hand 2 = Stephen Sewall

Essex County Court Archives, vol. 2, no. 156, Massachusetts Supreme Judicial Court, Judicial Archives, on deposit James Duncan Phillips Library, Peabody Essex Museum, Salem, MA.

949. Petition of Sarah Parker for Restitution

[Hand 1] To the Gentlemen of the Committee Sitting at Salem this 22 of January. 1711/1⟨2⟩

Whereas I the Subscriber Suffered imprisonment at Salem, 17 weeks in the year 1692, and was put to great charges and Expences before I could obtain a Release And not having an oppertunity to give your hono^Es an account of my Charges during my imprisenment, when others of my neighbours and fellow sufferers, put in their accounts: I haue thought meet to do it at this time, which is as followeth

　　　To the keeper of the Prison two pounds eight shillings and four pence
　　　For Court charges ~~one~~ Thirty shillings & four pence
　　　For necessary Expences while I attended the Court one pound four shillin⟨gs⟩
　　　For Provisions while I was in Prison four pounds five shillings

Sarah Parker:

⟨of⟩ Andover.

[Reverse] [Hand 2] Sarah Parker. acc° of Charges in prison &c

Notes: The history of Sarah Parker's case has been largely lost. The daughter of the executed Mary Parker, she was implicated in August during the Andover episode by Rebecca Eames and Susannah Post. See No. 511 & No. 519. Her name appears on the petition that includes, among others, that of Nathaniel Dane, asking for compensation. See No. 944. No extant document shows evidence of either an indictment or a trial in her case. Her continuing attempt to receive compensation for her imprisonment almost certainly failed. No record of such compensation is extant, the money being awarded only to families of the condemned, giving strong evidence that she was not condemned.

Essex County Court Archives, vol. 2, no. 175, Massachusetts Supreme Judicial Court, Judicial Archives, on deposit James Duncan Phillips Library, Peabody Essex Museum, Salem, MA.

Monday, February 18, 1712

950. Order of Joseph Procter & Abigail Procter for Payment, Cases of John & Elizabeth Procter‡

[Hand 1] Wheareas wee are Informed The Generall Couart hath apointed a Committe to distrubute to the pearties Consearnd what the s^d Court heath alowed To make Reparatian. to such as weare sufferers in the yeare 1692 – Whearfore wee doe desire And heareby order and Impower our brother Thorndik Procter to reciue what shall bee alowed To Each of us and to giue receit for the ~~sa~~ same – which shall fully dischargue you theareof

Joseph Procter
mark
the X of abigaill Procter

[Reverse] [Hand 2] ⟨J⟩oseph & Abigall Prockter

Notes: This is dated to the same date when the next order for payment, No. 951, from the Procter family was submitted. The money was paid on February 19.

Essex County Court Archives, vol. 2, no. 147, Massachusetts Supreme Judicial Court, Judicial Archives, on deposit James Duncan Phillips Library, Peabody Essex Museum, Salem, MA.

951. Order of Elizabeth Very for Payment, Cases of John Procter & Elizabeth Procter

[Hand 1] To the Gentelmen of the Comitee. appointed by the Gouerner and Councell to distribute the money allowed by the. General Court to such as weare sufferers in the year. 1692. ["6" written over "7"]
Please to pay and deliuer unto my Brother Thorndik Procter the sume allowed unto me and his Receipt shall fully discharge you ffrom the same

Elizabeth Very

Febuary 18th 1711/12

[Reverse] [Hand 2] Eliz Verrie

Essex County Court Archives, vol. 2, no. 144, Massachusetts Supreme Judicial Court, Judicial Archives, on deposit James Duncan Phillips Library, Peabody Essex Museum, Salem, MA.

Tuesday, February 19, 1712

952. Order of Abigail Hobbs for Payment

[Hand 1] Whereas ye Governour & Generall Court have been Pleased to grant a Considerable Sum̄ towards restitution to those who were Sufferers in ye year 1692 & have appointed a Committee to Distribute ye Same amongs't ye persons Con⟨c⟩ern'd.

Wherefore I yᵉ Subscriber (being then a Sufferer) doe request yᵉ Gentlemen of yᵉ Comittee   February 19, 1712
to Deli⟨v⟩er what Part and Proportion May belong to me unto My father William Hobbs, or
My brother William Hobbs, (both of Topsfeild) and either of their Receipts Shall be your
full discharge from your Servant.

[Hand 2] Thomas Tingley: benging [= being]: ~~present~~   the marke of
Jeremiah Ingraham: present   Abigiall X Hobbs
Fubuary yᵉ 19: 1711/12 ["11" written over "01"]

[Reverse] [Hand 3] ⟨Abigail Hobbs ₚ order To Wᵐ Hobbs who received her Share⟩

Notes: It is conspicuous, but not unique, that Abigail Hobbs received compensation in spite of her having been a confessor.
◊ Hand 3 = Stephen Sewall

Essex County Court Archives, vol. 2, no. 149, Massachusetts Supreme Judicial Court, Judicial Archives, on deposit James Duncan Phillips Library, Peabody Essex Museum, Salem, MA.

953. Petition of Elizabeth Johnson Jr. for Reversing Attainder and for Restitution

[Hand 1] To the Honourable the Gentlemen of the Committee Sitting in Salem Feb 19. 1711/12

Whereas the Honouble Generall Court hath Lately made an Act for the taking off the Attainder of those that were condemned for witchcraft. in the year 1692. I thought meet to Inform your Honours, that I was condemned by the Court at Salem. {in} January. in the year 1692. as will appear by the Records of the Tryalls at said Court, but my name is not inserted in said act. Being very desireous of the favour of that Act, am bold humbly to pray your Honours to represent my Case to the General Court at their next Session, that my name may be Inserted in that Act, if it may be, and that the Honourable Court would please to allow me Something in Consideration of my charges by reason of my Long Imprisonment, which will be ~~ae~~ thanfully [= thankfully] acknowledged as a great favour.

Andouer   by your Honours
Feb. 19. 1711/12   most humble servant
                                 Elizabeth ["z" written over "c"] Johnson junᵉ

[Reverse] [Hand 2] Eliz. Johnson Juʳ petition

Notes: Elizabeth Johnson Jr. had received a reprieve in 1693 as had Mary Post and Sarah Wardwell, both of whom had their attainders removed. No record of a reversal of Elizabeth Johnson Jr.'s attainder has been located, and why she was treated differently remains unknown. For the removal of Mary Post's attainder see No. 931. For Sarah Wardwell see No. 877. The 1692 date used by Elizabeth Johnson Jr. reflects old calendar usage.

Essex County Court Archives, vol. 2, no. 169, Massachusetts Supreme Judicial Court, Judicial Archives, on deposit James Duncan Phillips Library, Peabody Essex Museum, Salem, MA.

February 19, 1712

954. Order of John Nurse et al. for Payment, Case of Rebecca Nurse‡

[Hand 1] Wheareas wee are Informed the Generall Court hath apointed a Commite⟨e⟩ to ditribute to the parties Concearnd what the s^d Court hath alowed to make Rparatian [= reparation] to the sufferers in the yeare. 1692
Therefore wee doe desire and herby Impour our Brother Samuel Nurs to receiue what {is alowed} to us and to giue receipt for the same

John nurs
John tarbell
Rebaka preston
willem rusel
m⟨ar⟩tha boud⟨i⟩n
francis nurs

[Reverse] [Hand 2] Nurses's <u>order</u>

Notes: For whatever reason, this order is undated. Accordingly, it is placed just prior to the summary of receipts that follows. See No. 958. A dated order in connection with Rebecca Nurse also appears, and why there are two is puzzling. See No. 964. ◊ Hand 2 = Stephen Sewall

Essex County Court Archives, vol. 2, no. 148, Massachusetts Supreme Judicial Court, Judicial Archives, on deposit James Duncan Phillips Library, Peabody Essex Museum, Salem, MA.

955. Petition of Peter Osgood for Restitution for Mary Osgood

[Hand 1] To y^e honnorabl Camittee Salem febuary 19th 1711/12
{Jentlemen} In y^e Darke & sorrofull Tims in y^e yeare 1692 ["6" written over "7"]. when so maney persons of vndoubted Credett were accused of witchcrafte owe [= our] familie as well as others was vnder greatt truble & it Coste vs. vearey Considerabl in owre nessarey Expence for owe Honowred and tender Mother Duringe hir Imprismente Wherefore requeste of yowre honowrs to maneft [= manifest?] itt to y^e Memberrs of y^e Jennarall Cowrte. that wee might heave som⟨e⟩ reasonable allowance. for owe Ch⟨a⟩rge therein which will Euer oblidge yowrs: Searvent To pray

Peter osgood in y^e name of
y^e reaste of y^e familey..

Essex County Court Archives, vol. 2, no. 170, Massachusetts Supreme Judicial Court, Judicial Archives, on deposit James Duncan Phillips Library, Peabody Essex Museum, Salem, MA.

956. Petition of Benjamin Procter for Restitution

[Hand 1] Salem: ffeb^ε 19th 1711/12 To The Honour^a Committy

The petition: of Benjamin Procter: humbly sheweth: That
1 for as much as I your petitioner: was: Imprisoned: for several monthes In the time: they called wichcraft: and was by that a great sufferer

2 for: as much: as I was ye eldest son of my father: & worked hard with my father: till I was   February 19, 1712
about thirty years of age: and helped: bring up all my fathers children: by all his wives: one
after another

3: for as much as: after my fathers death: I your petitioner was at great: cost: and trouble: In
the disposition: of my s^d fathers: afairs as to: ye releiving: his s^d family: some of them: helples:
with answering debts ["b" written over "p"] charges: legasies &c

all which considered your petitioner: thinketh: he: deservs: a greater share of: this: that: y^e
country hath bin please: to alow us then: ye rest: of our family. {doe} which: I leave: to
consideration: of yor hon^rs and shall for ever remain your hon^rs most humble serv^t

                                                                    Benjamin Procter

[Reverse] [Hand 2] Benj^a Proctors Pet^o to Committee

Notes: As with other petitions seeking compensation for imprisonment, no record of such compensation survives. The
"signature" is in the same hand of the petition, that of Simon Willard. ◊ Hand 1 = Simon Willard

*Essex County Court Archives, vol. 2, no. 153, Massachusetts Supreme Judicial Court, Judicial Archives, on deposit James Duncan
Phillips Library, Peabody Essex Museum, Salem, MA.*

957. Petition of Samuel Wardwell Jr. for Reversing Attainder and for Restitution for Sarah Wardwell

[Hand 1] To the honourable, the Gentlemen of the Committee Sitting at Salem Feb. 19.
1711/12

Whereas my mother Sarah Wardel was condemned by the Court at Salem sometime in
January in the year 1692, as I Suppose will appear by the Records of the⟨s⟩ Tryalls at that
Court, but her name is not inserted in the late Act of the General Court, for the taking off
the Attainder of those that were condemned ~~for~~ in that year, my mother being since
deceased, I thought it my duty to Endeauour that her Name may have the benefit of that
Act. I therefore humbly pray your Honours to Represent this case to the Honourable Gen^ll
Court, that my mothers name may be inserted in the Said Act. And whereas in the Account
which I gave to your Hono^εs, when you met at Salem the Last winter, I mentioned only
what was Seized of my Fathers Estate by the Sherriffe, but gave no account of other charges
which did arise from the imprisonment of my Father and mother, they having provided for
their own subsistence while they were in Prison, and I Suppose ~~they~~ there was Something
considerable payd to the keeper of the prison, though I am not able now to giue a particular
account how much it was. If your Honours please to allow me something upon that account
It will be thankfully acknowledged by.

                                        your honou^εs
                                        most humble servant

Feb 19. 1711/12   Samuel wardel

[Reverse] War⟨d⟩well

Notes: Sarah Wardwell was one of three people convicted and condemned at the trials held in January 1693, but as with the
other two, Elizabeth Johnson Jr. and Mary Post, she received a reprieve. See No. 836. The Wardwell family's possessions

February 19, 1712   had been taken by Sheriff Corwin. See No. 926. Compensation was received for the executed Samuel Wardwell, but not for the condemned Sarah Wardwell.

Essex County Court Archives, vol. 2, no. 167, Massachusetts Supreme Judicial Court, Judicial Archives, on deposit James Duncan Phillips Library, Peabody Essex Museum, Salem, MA.

958. Summary of Receipts of the Relations & Sufferers

[Hand 1] Receipts of ye relac̅o̅n̅s &^c of ye Sufferers in ye year 1692
taken February 19: 1711/12

Mr Burroughs's family	widow
	Charles Burroughs
	George Burroughs
	Jeremiah Burroughs
	Rebecca Fowle alias Burrougs
	~~Eliz~~ Hanah Fox alias Burroughs
	Elizabeth Thomas
	Mary Burroughs.

Mrs Mary Bradburys progeny.	
	has left
Wymond Bradbury Dec^d	Wymond
	Anne
Judah Moodey Dc^d	Caleb Moodey
	Hana. Moodey
	Joshua Moody
	Samuel Moodey
	Mary Hale
	Jud⟨i⟩th Tapper
William Bradbury De^d	William Bradbury
	Thomas Bradbury
	Jacob Br⟨a⟩dbury
⟨Mary⟩ Stanian	
⟨Jane⟩ True	
⟨Eli⟩zabeth Buss Dec^d	John Buss
	Elizabeth Bus.

Families Intrested in ye allowance following/

Children of Elizabeth How	
viz.	
daughters.	Mary How
	Deborah How wife of Isa: How of Roxbury.
	Abigail How

Grandchildren	James How	being ye Children of her	February 19, 1712
	Martha How	only Son John How Dec^d	
	& Sarah How		

Dorcas Hoars family.	William Hoar Dec^d left 3 daughters	
	Mary Burt widow	
	Elizabeth Read wife of Christopher Read	4–0–0.
	Annis King wife of John King	12–0–0
	Johanna Green ~~wife of~~ widow	1–0–0
	Tabitha Slue Dec^d left Two children her Leonard & R⟨a⟩chel	

George Jacobs family.		
	George Jacobs only Son	46–0–0.
	Anne Andrews	23–0–0
	Margret Jacobs alias Foster	8–7–0
	for her goods taken away The Charge	1–13–0

Mary Easteys family.	
	x Isa Eastey
	Joseph ["Joseph" written over "Judah" or "Joshua"] Eastey
	x John Eastey
	x Ben. Eastey
	x Jacob Eastey
	x Joshua Eastey
	{p^d to Benj} Sarah Gill daughter
	x Hanah Abbot of Andover

Rebeccah Nurse family	
	John Nurse
	Sarah Bowden
	Rebeccah Preston
	Samul Nurse
	Francs Nurse
	Mary Tarbel
	Elizabeth Russel
	Benj. Nurse of fframingham

John Procters family	
	widow alias Richards.
	Benj. Procter.
	John Procter
	Eliz Verey
	Martha Join
	Mary Procter.
	Thorndick Procter
	William Procter
	Joseph Procter

February 19, 1712   Samul Procter
                                            Sarah Procter
                                            Eliz Procter.
                                            Abigail Procter

[Reverse] [Hand 2] Receipts [Hand 1?] Februrary 20. 1711/12

Notes: Hand 1 = Stephen Sewall

Essex County Court Archives, vol. 2, no. 141, Massachusetts Supreme Judicial Court, Judicial Archives, on deposit James Duncan Phillips Library, Peabody Essex Museum, Salem, MA.

959. Receipts for Sums Paid in Restitution

[Hand 1] Whereas His Excellency the Governour & Generall court haue been please[Lost] [= pleased] to grant to y^e persons who were Sufferers in y^e year 1692 Some considerable alowance towards restitucōn with respect to what they Suffered in thier Estates at that Sorrowfull time & haue alsoe appointed a Comitte viz John Applton Esqr Thomas Noyes Esqr John Burrel Esqr Nehemiah Jewett. & Stephen Sewall to distribute ye Same to & Amongst ye parties concern'd as in & by ye records & Court orders May. appear. Now Know yee that wee the Subscribers herevnto being Either ye proper parties or Such as represent ⟨them⟩ or ha⟨ue full power⟩ & Authority from them to Receiue thier parts & Shares doe Ac⟨k⟩nowledge to Haue Receiued of & from y^e s^d Comitte y^e Severall Sums Set against our respective Names in full of our parts & Shares of y^e money afores^d & Such of vs as haue orders from some of y^e parties concerned to receiue thier parts & shares doe avouch them to be real & good So that for whomsoeuer wee take vpons [= upon] vs to Receiue any Such ^{Sum} wee doe obleige oursel[Lost] [= ourselves] to Indemnify y^e Said Comitte to all Intents Construcōns & purposes wee Say Receiued this 19th Day of February anno Dom̄ 1711/12 & in y^e Tenth year of

Abram How For Mary & Abigail How	4–14–0.
Ephraim Rob⟨e⟩rdes for James Martha & Sarah How Children of John How marke of	4.14.–⟨0⟩
Abraham X foster for mother marke	6.10–0
Abraham X Foster for mary lacey by order	8–10–0.
S⟨a⟩muel wardel	36.15.0.
Benia putnam for Sarah Good marke of	30 – 0.0.
William X Towne for wife widow of Willard	6.12–8.
Isaac Estey	2–9–0.
John Estey	2–9–0.
William Cleves	11–0–0
John Ames ten pounds by ord^ε of his mother on file	10–0–0
Ephraim Wiles	14–0–0
Abigail Faulkner marke of	20–0–0

George X Jacobs   46–0–0.   February 19, 1712
    marke of
Anne X Andrews   23–0–0.
John foster   08–7–0.
Charge   01–13–0   79–0–0.
John King for himselfe & Sister Anne
     marke
Christopher X Read.
maried. Eliz. Hoar.
   marke
Joana X Green
{for selfe} Joseph Parker   8–0–0.
{for mary post} Joseph Parker   8–14–0.
{for M Carrier} Joseph Parker   7–6–0.

Receiued as on ye foregoing Side   £   s   d
Samuel Nurs for him Selfe & John Nurse & John Tarbell
Rebeccah Preston William Russel Martha Bowden & francis Nurse   21.14–0
     marke
Elizizabeth X Richards alias Procter
    marke
Benjam X Procter
⟨E⟩benezer Bancraft for Martha Procter
william Procter
John Procter
Thorndik Procter In behalf of my self and Joseph Procter and Abigill Procter and mary
Procter and my Sister Elizabeth Very
    marke
Sarah X Munion ⟨B⟩ alias Procter
     marke
Elizabeth X Pro⟨cter⟩
Charles Burrough for my self and for Jeremiah Burrough and
Rebekah Fowle. Hanah Fox & Elizabeth Thomas.//   4^£ 2^s 0^d Each of vs 20–10–0
John Appleton Rec^d for G^o Burrough ye Sume of ffore pounds & two shil͞l
       marke
23^d/   Abigail X Hoar
          marke   both 20^£ 4^s
        Rebeccah X Hoar
Fe⟨b⟩ 23 1711
     marke
    William X Hobbs   9–15–0
    for his Sister Abigail Hobbs   4–2
            {cha.   10}
          10–0–0
     marke
    Leonard X Slue for selfe & Sister Rachel   10–4^⟨s⟩
     marke
    Mary X Pittman alias Hoare

February 19, 1712   Rec̄ed as aforesᵈ   £ s d
                           for George Abbott & Hanah his wife daughter of Mary Easty   2–9–0
                           March 4 1711 by yʳ written order forty nine shillings John fa⟨rn⟩aum
                           ⟨M⟩arch 5 – Recēd for my Selfe forty ^{n}ine shillings   2–9–0
                                                                                                    Jacob esti

⟨Ma⟩rch 6. 1711.
Receiued for my selfe three pounds 4ˢ & 6ᵈ for my owne share.   marke
                                                                       Hanah X Willard

⟨March⟩ 6
Recᵈ for our daughter Margaret Willard b⟨ei⟩ng vnder Age
three pounds four shillings 6ᵈ   marke
                                              William X Town
                                                        marke
                                      Margaret X Towne wife of yᵉ sᵈ Wᵐ Town
⟨March⟩ 22 Recᵈ for my daughter Mary Burroughs four pounds 2ˢ in full for her share.
                                                             marke
                                              Mary X {Hall alias} Burroughs
March 22ᵈ 1711/12 Received for my Selfe Ten poundes //
                                                        Marke
                                              Mary X Hall alias Burroughs

Aprill 5: 1712 Recᵈd of Stephen Sewall as aforesᵈ 6–9–0
                                                        Marke
                                              John X Willard.
May 1. 1712. Recᵈ on behalfe of my wife Deborah How
                              Two pounds seuen shillings in full
                                                        Isaac How
Recēd for Benj. Nurse fifty four shillings & 6ᵈ
                                                        Samuel Nurs
Recēd for my Selfe yᵉ Subscriber & for my Broʳ in Law Peter Thomas {in} right of Elizabeth
his ⟨w⟩ife & my Sister Hanah ffox wife of mr Jabez ffox & Rebecca fowles four pounds Ten
shillings.
                                              George burrougs
Received for my Broʳ Jeremiah Burroughs & my Selfe [2–3 words illegible] [SWP = Two
pounds five] shillings. ⟨ṗ me⟩
                                              Charles Burrough
                      [Reverse] Newbury – May 22. 1712.
                      Recēd for & in behalfe of my wife Jane True & Mary Stanion &
                      daughters of Mary Bradbury & for John Buss & Elizᵗʰ Buss Children of
                      Elizabeth Buss. yᵉ Sum̄ of Nine poundes fifteen shillings. ṗ me
                                              Henry True

May 22ᵈ 1712   Recēd for my Brethren & Sisters being Six of vs i⟨n⟩ Number Children
                      of Judah Moodey one of yᵉ daughters of yᵉ aforesᵈ Mary Bradbury Dēcd
                      thre pounds fiue shill
                                              Caleb Moodey.

May 22ᵈ <u>1712</u>   Recd for my Sister Anne Allen & my Selfe Children of Wymond   February 23, 1712
                            Bradbury Decd three pounds fiue Shillings.
                                                    ꝑ me Wymond Bradbury

                            Reced for my Tw⟨o⟩ Brothers William Bradbury & Jacob Br⟨a⟩dbury {&
                            my selfe} Three pounds fiue shillings in full.
                                                    ꝑ me Thomas Bradbry

July. 27. 1712.   Recd on yᵉ accᵒ aforesᵈ Eleuen pounds fiue Shillings. for my part Recd
                            in full   marke
                                                    Samuel X Procter

Sepʳ 3ᵈ 1712   Receiued for my Brother Joshua & my selfe 4–18–0.
                            which I ingage to produce his recipt for & send to Sewall/
                                                    Banjamin Estie

Sepʳ 3ᵈ 1712   Reced for my Sister Sarah Gill forty [Lost] [*SWP* = nine] shillings
                            which I promise to send her recipt for
                                                    Banjamin Estie

Nouʳ 28. 1712   R⟨e⟩ced for Joseph Estie & by his written order Forty nine shillings
                                                    John Commings

Notes: The February 19 date simply indicates when the initial portion of this document was presented. Presumably, names appearing on the document acknowledge their payment on February 19. Other names appeared subsequently and are dated accordingly with the last entry as November 28, 1712. In several cases the "signatures" are in the same hand. Some others are probably authentic. ◊ "{in} right of": 'by justifiable claim of,' or by entitlement of (*OED* s.v. *right* n¹ 7a-b) ◊ Hand 1 = Stephen Sewall

Essex County Court Archives, vol. 2, no. 140, Massachusetts Supreme Judicial Court, Judicial Archives, on deposit James Duncan Phillips Library, Peabody Essex Museum, Salem, MA.

Saturday, February 23, 1712

960. Order of Rachel Slue for Payment

[Hand 1] Majᵋ Sewall please to pay to Leonard Slue the mony Comeing to yᵋ humble servᵗ
                                                    Rachell X Slue
Febʳ 23. 1711./1712 ["2" written over "1"].

[Reverse] [Hand 2] Rebeccah Slues ordʳ

Notes: Hand 2 = Stephen Sewall

Essex County Court Archives, vol. 2, no. 176, Massachusetts Supreme Judicial Court, Judicial Archives, on deposit James Duncan Phillips Library, Peabody Essex Museum, Salem, MA.

Tuesday, February 26, 1712

961. Order of George Abbott & Hannah Abbott for Payment, Case of Mary Esty

[Hand 1] Andouer feb y^e 26. 1711$\frac{12}{}$
honoured sir thes are to dezier you to deliuer to y^e bearer hereof [Hand 2] J⟨o⟩hn Farnum [Hand 1] the money y^t falleth to my share of what the cort alowed to the sufferers in 92 I being the daughter of Goodwife Estey of topsfeeld: and now wife to George Abbut in andou⟨o⟩re

George Abbut Hannah abbut

[Reverse] for the honoured maiger Suell in Salem
[Hand 2] Hanah Abbot alias Estey order to deliuer y^e money to Furnam

Notes: Hand 2 = Stephen Sewall

Essex County Court Archives, vol. 2, no. 152, Massachusetts Supreme Judicial Court, Judicial Archives, on deposit James Duncan Phillips Library, Peabody Essex Museum, Salem, MA.

Friday, March 14, 1712

962. Letter of Mary Burroughs, Case of George Burroughs

[Hand 1] Attelborow March the 14th 1711/12

Loving brother my Love Remembred vnto yov hoping that yov eare well as I am att this present: I make bold to wright a few Lins vnto yov desiring yov to be so kind vnto mee as to send me that which is my right and proper due from the Jenerall court I pray yov to send it by my mother which will take som care about it and Let me not be forgotten by yov who am yovr sister till deth

Mary Bvrrvs

[Reverse] [Hand 2] Mary Burroughs Order

Essex County Court Archives, vol. 2, no. 161, Massachusetts Supreme Judicial Court, Judicial Archives, on deposit James Duncan Phillips Library, Peabody Essex Museum, Salem, MA.

Monday, March 24, 1712

963. Order of John Stanyon & Mary Stanyon for Payment, Case of Mary Bradbury

[Hand 1] Hampton March-24th=1711=12

Maior Sewell S^r this is to desier you to diliuer to my Brother Henry True for my vse that part of money that y^e gen^{ll} Court haue allotted to my wife as one of Capt Bradburys Daught⟨o⟩rs & his receipt there of shall be your discharge from your frinds & Seruants

John stanyan
Mary Stanyan

[Reverse] [Hand 2] Stanyans order to Capt <u>True</u>
3-5-0
3-5-0
<u>3-5-0</u>
9-15

Notes: Both "signatures" are in the same hand.

Essex County Court Archives, vol. 2, no. 171, Massachusetts Supreme Judicial Court, Judicial Archives, on deposit James Duncan Phillips Library, Peabody Essex Museum, Salem, MA.

Thursday, May 8, 1712

964. Order of Benjamin Nurse for Payment, Case of Rebecca Nurse

[Hand 1] To ye Comittey appointed by ye Generall Court to distribute what was allow'd by ye s^d Court towards restitution to ye relations of those whoe Suffered in ye Sorrowfull times called y^e Witcchraft times./

pleas to pay & deliuer what ^{Share} & proportion belongs to me on that Score vnto my Brother Mr Samuel Nurse of Salem & his receipt Shall be a full & Sufficient discharge from

your friend &c. Beniamin Nurse

May 8th anno Do͞m 17<u>12</u>

Notes: Hand 1 = Stephen Sewall

Essex County Court Archives, vol. 2, no. 146, Massachusetts Supreme Judicial Court, Judicial Archives, on deposit James Duncan Phillips Library, Peabody Essex Museum, Salem, MA.

Saturday, November 1, 1712

965. Order of Joseph Esty for Payment, Case of Mary Esty

[Hand 1] To the much honrede mager Seuell pray S{e}r be pleased for to pay to the barer hear of John Cumins my part of the money that the generall court did geue to the sofferers in the ye{a}re 1692 and his recit shall be your descharg Sr I undourstand that you haue payed of all my brothars:. and so I would pray you for to pay the barer hearof so I rast your frind and saruent

Joseph Esti

from Dochestour nouembour
the 01 day 1712
as wetnes ~~our~~ my hand

[Reverse] This for John Comings In Topsfild

Essex County Court Archives, vol. 2, no. 154, Massachusetts Supreme Judicial Court, Judicial Archives, on deposit James Duncan Phillips Library, Peabody Essex Museum, Salem, MA.

Tuesday, December 16, 1712

966. Petition of the Children of George Burroughs

[Hand 1] Boston Decm^r 16<u>th</u> 1712

To The Honerable Gentlemen Appointed for A Committe Relateing To the affaire of Witchcraft In the yere 1692

Gentlemen

We The Subscribers And Chilldren of Mr Georg Burrough Late of wells, who Suffer'd Att Salem in the Trouble There

Humbly offer for your Honours Consideration A few Lines Relateing Our Case And Circumstances upon Acco^{tt} of Our Mother in Laws Conduct And Carriage Towards us. Affter Our Father was Apprehended And Taken Away Our Mother in Law Laide hands upon all she Could Secure (the Chilldren were Generally unable To shift for Themselus) And what she Could Lay hands on was her Own without Any Person but her Own Daught^ε to share with her, whom she Says Was To bring up but May it Plese your ^{Honours} To Consider there was Sea⟨v⟩en Chilldren More beside⟨s⟩ That ^{that were} To bring ^{up} the Eldest of which was but Sixteen years old att That Time.
but instead of shareing in what our father Left and she had Secur'd were Turn'd to shift for Our Selus ["us" written over "ues"] without Any Thing for So much as A Remembrance of

April 3, 1713

Our ffather. Tho Som of us Can Remember of Considerable in The House, besides his Liberary which she Sold: and Recd The Mony for: then Lett it out: att Intrest And was afftwards Recd by another Husband; And not One farthing bestowed upon Any Child but her Own: This being Matter of fact we Hu⟨m⟩bly Leave it with your Honours to Consider wheather of what The Honourble Generall Court Allow'd &c she have not allredy Recd To much And the Chilldren To Little

We Subscribe Our Selves your
Honours Humble Ser^tts

rebaker fowl   Charles Burrough

The Mark
     X
of Eli^z Thomas Jeremi Burrough hannah fox

[Reverse] [Hand 2] Petition of George Borroughs

Essex County Court Archives, vol. 2, no. 160, Massachusetts Supreme Judicial Court, Judicial Archives, on deposit James Duncan Phillips Library, Peabody Essex Museum, Salem, MA.

Friday, April 3, 1713

967. Letter of Rebecca Fowle, Case of George Burroughs

[Hand 1] Boston April⟨e⟩: ye 3:
Honnour⟨e⟩d Sir: the fauour which i would humbly ask of your honnour at this time is that you would please to let my brother George Burroughs haue what remains in your hands on the acount of my deceased but Honnoured father Mr: George Burroughs Sir my request is that it may be ⟨do⟩n with out delay for euery disscourse on this malloncely [= melancholy] subiect whi⟨ch⟩ doth but giue a fresh wound to my bleeding hart: but i desire to sit down in silence and remain: Sir your Honnours most obedein⟨t⟩ seruant.
                    Rebekah: Fowle:

[Reverse] [Hand 2] Reb⟨ec⟩ah Fowle

Essex County Court Archives, vol. 2, no. 163, Massachusetts Supreme Judicial Court, Judicial Archives, on deposit James Duncan Phillips Library, Peabody Essex Museum, Salem, MA.

Wednesday, April 8, 1713

968. Petition of the Children of George Burroughs for Restitution

[Hand 1] To the Gentlemen Appointed. A ⎱   Boston Apr^ll 8. <u>1713</u>
Comitte Relateing to the affairs of ⎰
Witchcraft &c   Gentlemen We the Subscribers &
Chilldren of M̅ᵉ Georg Burrough who suffered in the Late Troubles Att Salem. in the yere
1692. offer to your Consideration the Conduct of Our mother in Law, affter the Deth of our
ffather: she Made Sure of all that there was of household Goods &c togather with Our
ffathers Liberary which was off Som value, Said Liberary was Sold affterward & part of the
mony Came affterward into the hands of a Second husband, but Nothing thereof nor of the
household Goods &c Ever Came into our hands. we were Turn'd Out into a wide world to
shift for Our Selv's haveing nothing to trust unto but Divine Providence And the Generosity
of frinds (not On the Side of our mother in Law) & Som of us So young that we Can give no
Acco^tt of perticular Circomstances of the ffamily nor Capeable Any of us to Give A
perticuler Acco^tt of the wrong Don us Any ffurther then we are inform'd by Others, but Can
Assure you we Never had the value of Six penc[Lost?] [= pence] to Remember Our ffather
with when Dead And gon. And ["And" written over "let"?] we Cannot but observe to you
that what the Honerable Court Allow'd when Divided Among yᵉ Chilldren According to
the Direction of the Same A̅m̅o^ttd to but about four ["four" written over "fiue"] ^{four}
pounds apeice, which we think but A poor recompence (Setting asside the Deth of our
father) to make good Our Due proportion of his Substance which we were Deprived of by
means of his Deth, besides the Dificulties we were put unto & the Charge of bringing up. if
the Consideration of w^t we relate which is matter of fact well known to many besides our
selves, be⟨?⟩e motive sufficient to Enjage yo̅ᵉ Consideration of us in what you have stopt of
the Above mentioned Grant, of the Honerable Court: we desier you to deliver what you see
Cause to Allow us to Our brother [Reverse] Georg Burrough. if what we Offer be not
worthy of your Consideration or Argument Sufficient that we should have what Remains in
your hands, we Only desier the ffavour of A Speedy Answer; for the Sum as we are inform'd
is So Small that much Trouble in the buisness will Surmount it by ffarr should we be
Allowed it Att Last; So that An information of your resolves in the buisness will Prove more
of A ffavour then Tedious Delays should you Grant it Att Last. N̅ot ffurther Att pressent
but Remaine to Offer — We Remaine Gentlemen your humble S̅e̅r^ttes
                              Peter Thomas in behalf of my wife
                              [Hand 2] Jabez Fox in behalf of my wife

[Hand 3] Children of Mr Boroughs pet^n
[Hand 4] Children of Mr Burroughs

Notes: The reference to the possessions of Burroughs having been sold suggests that they were not taken by Sheriff
Corwin as happened in some of the other cases.

*Essex County Court Archives, vol. 2, no. 162, Massachusetts Supreme Judicial Court, Judicial Archives, on deposit James Duncan
Phillips Library, Peabody Essex Museum, Salem, MA.*

Monday, May 11, 1713

969. Order of Jeremiah Burroughs for Payment, Case of George Burroughs

[Hand 1] Salem may 11ᵗʰ 1713
Majeager Seuell Ser be pleased to let my brother Charles Burr⟨o⟩ug⟨h⟩ haue my part yᵗ was Leaft
So you will oblige your humble Serueant.
Jeremiah Burrough

[Reverse] [Hand 2] J. Borroughs <u>order</u>

Essex County Court Archives, vol. 2, no. 164, Massachusetts Supreme Judicial Court, Judicial Archives, on deposit James Duncan Phillips Library, Peabody Essex Museum, Salem, MA.

Wednesday, November 20, 1717

970. Order Appointing a Committee to Consider Philip English's Petition

A Petition of Philip English of Salem, Praying Consideration & Allowance for a great Part of his Estate taken from him (as was said) by lawful Authority in the late sorrowful time of the Witchcraft
In the House of Representatives; Read &
Ordered that Mʳ Speaker Burril, Mʳ Isaiah Tay & Jonathan Remington Esqʳ with such as the Honᵇˡᵉ Board shall appoint be a Committee to Consider of this Petition, & all the Papers relating thereto, & Report what they think proper to be done in Answer thereto to this Court at yʳ next Session:
Read & Concur'd; And the Honᵇˡᵉ Thomas Fitch & Elisha Cook Esqʳ are added to the Committee. [*Passed November 20.*

Notes: In the compensation for those condemned, Philip English did not receive any money, since he had not been condemned. He had fled the colony, had returned, and had his case heard probably on January 12, 1693, when ignoramuses were returned on two indictments. See No. 791 & No. 792. He went free, and having failed to get compensation when money was given for those condemned, he persisted independent of that legislative decision. On June 14, 1717, English petitioned for compensation, and this is the first of four records of responses culminating in compensation for him.

Acts and Resolves, Public and Private, of the Province of Massachusetts Bay, vol. 9, 1717–1718, chap. 126, (Boston: Wright and Potter, 1902), pp. 568–569.

Friday, February 7, 1718

971. Continuation of the Committee to Consider Claim by Philip English

Upon The Representation of the Committee upon Philip Englishes Petition, That by Reason of the Sickness of the said Philip English, which prevented his Meeting the said Committee at Boston, & other Accidents intervening, They could not come to any Determination nor give a Report on the said Affair this Session;

Ordered that the Committee be continued, And that they make Report as above at the Session of this Court in May next.   [*Passed February 7.*

Acts and Resolves, Public and Private, of the Province of Massachusetts Bay, vol. 9, 1717–1718, chap. 143, (Boston: Wright and Potter, 1902), p. 574.

Thursday, July 3, 1718

972. Order Continuing the Committee on Philip English's Petition

On The Petition of Philip English, As Enter'd June 14. 1717

Ordered that the Committee on this Petition be continued, And that they make Report to this Court at their Sessions in Autumn next.   [*Passed July 3.*

Acts and Resolves, Public and Private, of the Province of Massachusetts Bay, vol. 9, 1717–1718, chap. 49 (Boston: Wright and Potter, 1902), p. 607.

Monday, November 10, 1718

973. Final Action on Claim by Philip English

The Report of the Committee to consider the Petition of Philip English Enter'd June 14. 1717, & all the Papers relating thereto, & report what they think proper to be done in Answer thereto to this Court, is as follows; viz,

In Obedience to the Order within mentioned, Having had several Meetings on the Affair, At which the Petitioner & sundry of the Evidences have given their Attendance, & were heard & examined; & the Petition & the Papers relating thereto, with the Representation of the Damage & Loss, being duly considered; The Committee are humbly of Opinion, It is reasonable upon the whole, that the Petitioner be allowed & paid out of the publick Treasury Two hundred Pounds, in full Satisfaction for what he may have sustained & suffered as set forth in his Petition Accompts & Papers: Which is humbly submitted

Your Honors most obedient Servt Per Order of the Comm^tee

February 12, 1738

Tho. Fitch

Read & Accepted. [*Passed November 10.*]

Acts and Resolves, Public and Private, of the Province of Massachusetts Bay, vol. 9, 1718–1718, Chap. 82 (Boston: Wright and Potter, 1902), pp. 618–619.

Wednesday, July 1, 1724

974. Resolve Allowing £50 to Thomas Rich

Resolve Allowing £50 to Thos Rich.

A PETITION of Thomas Rich of Salem Shewing that his Mother, Martha Carey (who with her Husband & his Father in Law Gyles Carey Suffered death in the time of the Witchcraft) had in her hands Sixty pounds of personall Estate, left by his Father, which She Carefully Kept for the petitioner & which was lost by her Suffering, and therefore praying this Court to make Some allowance to him in Consideration thereof as they have done to others in the Like Circumstances,

Read [Accepted] &

Resolv'd That the Sum of Fifty pounds, be allowed & paid out of the publick Treasury, to the petitioner Thomas Rich in full Satisfaction for the Losses he might have Sustained, as at Large Sett forth, in his petition. [*Passed July 1.*]

Acts and Resolves, Public and Private, of the Province of Massachusetts Bay, vol. 10, 1720–1726, chap. 93 (Boston: Wright and Potter, 1902), p. 322.

Sunday, February 12, 1738

975. Deposition of Susannah Touzel, Regarding Philip English

SALEM Feb^r 12, 1738

Susanah Touzel [of ful Age Testyfyeth &] Saith that [in the year 1692] she was carried from Her Father Phillip Englishs House To Mr Arnolds the Goal Keeper and livd there wth my Father Phillip English & Wife while they continued there and when they left the Goal She was carried to Capt Jn° Aldens to Board and Continued there till the s^d Phillip English and Wife returned from N York to their own Dwelling in Salem and then they Sent for her home

SUSANNA TOUZEL

July 8, 1738

ESSEX ss. SALEM Feb: 12th 1738

Then Mrs Susañah Towzell (who by reason of Sickness & bodily Infirmity is incapable of Travelling to Court) made oath to the truth of the within Deposition She being carefully Examined & Cautioned to Declare the whole Truth, (The Adverse party whom this may Concern, living more than Twenty mile not being notifyed)

Jurat Coram

BENE LYNDE Junr *Just Pacs*

[*Endorsed*]

Susañah Towzells Deposition
Taken before Bene Lynde Jr

Publications of the Colonial Society of Massachusetts, vol. 10, Transactions 1904–1906, as taken from SCF, no. 48343 (Boston, Published by the Society, 1907), pp. 19–20.

Saturday, July 8, 1738

976. Deposition of Margaret Casnoe Regarding Philip English

Margaret Casnoe of Lawfull Age Testifieth & saith that in part of the Time when there was so much talk of the Witchcraft in this Country and severall persons suffered therefor being according to [the best of] this Deponents Rememberance about forty five years agone this Depont then being about Eighteen years of Age Livd with Mrs Margaret Pastre In the House & Family of Mr George Hollard in Boston and at that Time Mr Philip English of Salem and his wife being under Suspicion for the aforesaid Crime She was then taken up and put into Boston Goal & he the sd Mr Philip English came to Boston & Requested the aforesd [Mr] George Hollard to take him into his House who accordinly did & maintaind him there Secretly for some Time & the sd Hollards house being searched for the sd English he was hid behind a bag with Dirty Cloths by which means he Escaped then being taken and afterwards when he was put into prison for Witchcraft & his Estate and Effects thereupon Seizd sd Mr Hollard Supported Said Mr & his Wife in Goal & this Depont often & frequently carried victuals & provisions from sd Mr Hollards house & by his orders delivered the same to the sd English & his Wife in prison. And the sd Englishes Family wanting Subsitance when brought up to Boston his Effects being seizd this Depont well Remembers that Mrs Mary English Daughter to sd Philip English Livd at sd Mr George Hollards and was by him maintained & Supported for a Considerable Time (this Depont is not Certain how long) But sd Mr Hollard maintained & Supported the sd Mary English for a Considerable Time after the Rest of said English's family were gone from Thence

Sig

MARGARET X CASNOE

Boston July 8th 1738
Sworne to in Infr Court
Boston 18 July 1738

Att^r Ezek^L Goldthwait *Cler*.

A True Copy Exam^d

Per Ezek^L Goldthwait *Cler*

March 28, 1750

[*Endorsed*]

Casnoes Depocon̄

Publications of the Colonial Society of Massachusetts, vol. 10, Transactions 1904–1906, as taken from SCF, no. 47120:8 (Boston: Published by the Society, 1907), pp. 18–19.

Wednesday, March 28, 1750

977. Memorial and Petition by Thomas Newman et al. for George Burroughs

[Hand 1] To His Honour Spencer Phipps Esqr Lieutenant Governor and Commander in Chief in and Over his Majesty's Province of the Massachusetts Bay in New England, and to the Honourable the Council, and the Honourable the House of Representatives, in General Court Assembled.

> The Memorial of Thomas Newman, Abia Holbrook, and Elias Thomas, Agents for their Respective Relatives, the Surviving Children and Grandchildren of George Burroughs formerly of Falmoth in the County of York & Province aforesaid, Clerk, Deceased, As a Supplement to the Prayer of their Memorial & Petition humbly Presented to His Excellency Governor Shirley, and the Honourable His Majesty's Council, and this Honourable House of Representatives, on the Thirty first Day of May last.

Most humbly Suggesteth,

That their said Memorial and Petition setting forth the Awful and Miserable Condition of the Unhappy Children and Descendants of the Reverend Mr George Burroughs, who as therein set forth, had his Blood shed, and was one of the most deplorable Victims cut off in the fatal Catastrophe in the Year 1692. Was by the Honourable Court Referred to the Consideration of a Committee of both Houses in June last to Report what might be Proper for the Court to Act Thereupon, But so it seems it hath fell out that Honourable Mr Danforth Chairman of the said Committee hath not as yet called them together so much as once to Act thereon even to this Day, as some of the Honourable Committee themselves were pleased with real Concern to Signify ^{to} your said Petitioners,

Your Memorialists therefore most Humbly Supplicate (they having been put to great Expence already) That their said Memorial & Petition may be again brought Forward, Read and Acted upon before the final Rising of this Court, That so a Stop may be put to the Cry of the long oppressed Sufferers.

And Your Memorialists as in Duty Bound shall ever Pray &c
Thomas Newman
Abia Holbrook jun^r
Elias Thomas

Boston March 28, 1750.

[Reverse] The Memorial Petition of Thomas Newman, Abia Holbrook & Elias Thomas
[Hand 2] March 28. 1750
[Hand 3] Enterd
[Hand 4] In the House of Rep^ues March 28 1750 Read and Ordered that the Committee within refer'd to be directed to Sit fortuith Consider the Petition to them Committed and Report as soon as may be
Sent up for concurrence
Thos Hubbard Spk^r pro Tempore

Massachusetts Archives Collection, vol. 135, nos. 172 & 173. Massachusetts State Archives. Boston, MA.

Appendix: Documents Carried in *SWP* Not Considered as Related to 1692/93 Witchcraft Cases

978. Deposition of Elizabeth Fuller v. John Lee

[Hand 1] Thi⟨s⟩ deposition of Elizabeth fuller abought. 34 yeres testifieth that I herd John lee say in my herein [= hearing] in my house in a bosting way that [1st "t" written over "I"] hee had laid one of {mr} Clairke{s} hogs fast aslepe and this wos when {m^r} Clarke liued here

Notes: This document appeared in *SWP* (II, p. 535) with an April 11 date. At one point, the manuscript fragment had been placed by a modern archivist with two Procter documents dated April 11, No. 52 and No. 58. However, no known authority exists for this placement or dating. This document appears not to have been connected to the Salem witch trials. No record of any other appearance of Lee in connection with the episode has been found. A constable in Manchester named John Ley is found in the legal records, but there appears to be no connection to the document here. The document, as well as the following two documents in the Appendix, is placed in this edition for the convenience of anyone wishing to consider further a possible Salem witch trial connection.

Essex Institute Collection, no. 19, James Duncan Phillips Library, Peabody Essex Museum, Salem, MA.

979. Testimony of Elizabeth Nicholason v. Ann Dolliver

[Hand 1] Elizabeth the wife of Edmond Nicolasson will testify; that coming to the house of Samuell Dallabar; Peter Pitford and the wife of the said Dallabar were in discourse before the dore in the yard; and in theire discourse she heard Peter Pitford say: I meruaile how that old witch knowes every thing that is don in my house: Rebecca the wife of Samuell Dallabar replied oh Peter doe not say soe: for I beleiue she is no Witch; soe she came away and left Peter Pitford and the wife of Samuell Dallabar in discourse

Elizabeth Nicolasson

[Reverse] [Hand 2] Elizabeth Nicholson evidence.

Notes: This document appears in *SWP* (I, pp. 271–72). It has has not been included in the edition based on the research of Jedediah Drolet, a student of Mary Beth Norton at Cornell University. Drolet found that Peter Pitford died in 1659 without issue. He also pointed out that Rebecca Dolliver had been long dead in 1692. He concluded that the document probably referred to Jane James of Marblehead, accused of witchcraft by Peter Pitford in the 1650s. His argument for removing this document appears conclusive. The arrest warrant and examination that appear in the edition of a later Ann Dolliver correctly belong in the edition. The examination of Ann Dolliver does not appear in *SWP*. See No. 309.

Essex County Court Archives, vol. 2, no. 115, Massachusetts Supreme Judicial Court, Judicial Archives, on deposit James Duncan Phillips Library, Peabody Essex Museum, Salem, MA.

980. Deposition of Hannah Welch v. William Hobbs

[Hand 1] the depotion of han{n}ah welch the wife of Phelup we⟨l⟩[Lost] [= Welch] hannah walch eaged forty foer yers thus deponian t{e}stifieth and saith that I was with ~~with~~ m^r Salinston and capten eapes neer this land ~~w~~ now in contreeuarce and thay both of them

agreed that the fance shud stand as it was and that wee [2nd "e" written over "s"] ~~sud~~ shud
not transgrace of one side nor Jonathon hobs one the other side tel the line ⟨was⟩ run and the
agreement that thay agreed tow was that if eather hade transgresed shud make satesfaction to
the other: and the reason of thes agreement was becoas hobs and we was allways contanding

[Hand 2] Jurat   Att an Inferiour Court

[Reverse] [Hand 3] Hobbs Depo.

Notes: This document appears in *SWP* (II, p. 430). It is from a real estate case before the inferior court and unrelated to
the witch trials. ◊ Hand 2 = Jonathan Corwin

*Essex County Court Archives, vol. 2, no. 126, Massachusetts Supreme Judicial Court, Judicial Archives, on deposit James Duncan
Phillips Library, Peabody Essex Museum, Salem, MA.*

TIMELINE: COURT OF OYER & TERMINER AND
SUPERIOR COURT OF JUDICATURE

June 2, 1692   Grand Jury of Bridget Bishop

Trial of Bridget Bishop

June 3, 1692   Grand Juries of Rebecca Nurse & John Willard

June 10, 1692   Execution of Bridget Bishop

June 28, 1692   Grand Jury of Sarah Good

Trial of Sarah Good (Day 1)

June 29, 1692   Grand Juries of Elizabeth How (Day 1) & Susannah Martin

Trials of Sarah Good (Day 2), Susannah Martin, & Rebecca Nurse

June 30, 1692   Grand Juries of Elizabeth How (Day 2), Elizabeth Procter, John Procter, & Sarah Wilds

Trial of Elizabeth How

July 1, 1692   Grand Jury of Martha Carrier

July 2, 1692   Grand Jury of Dorcas Hoar

Trial of Sarah Wilds

July 19, 1692   Executions of Sarah Good, Elizabeth How, Susannah Martin, Rebecca Nurse, & Sarah Wilds

Aug. 3, 1692   Grand Juries of George Burroughs & Mary Esty

Trial of Martha Carrier

Aug. 4, 1692   Grand Juries of Martha Cory, Mary Esty, & George Jacobs Sr.

Trials of George Jacobs Sr. and John Willard

Aug. 5, 1692   Trials of George Burroughs, Elizabeth Procter, & John Procter

Aug. 19, 1692   Executions of George Burroughs, Martha Carrier, George Jacobs Sr., John Procter, & John Willard

Sept. 6, 1692   Grand Jury of Ann Pudeator (Day 1)

Trial of Dorcas Hoar

Sept. 7, 1692   Grand Juries of Alice Parker & Ann Pudeator (Day 2)

Trials of Alice Parker & Ann Pudeator

Sept. 8, 1692   Grand Jury of William Procter

Trial of Martha Cory

Sept. 9, 1692   Grand Juries of Mary Bradbury & Giles Cory

Trials of Mary Bradbury & Mary Esty

Sept. 10, 1692   Grand Juries of Abigail Hobbs & Rebecca Jacobs

Trial of Ann Pudeator (Day 2?)

Sept. 13, 1692   Grand Jury of Ann Foster

Sept. 14, 1692   Grand Juries of Sarah Buckley (Day 1), Margaret Jacobs, Mary Lacey Sr., Wilmot Redd, & Samuel Wardwell

Trials of Wilmot Redd & Samuel Wardwell

Sept. 15, 1692   Grand Juries of Sarah Buckley (Day 2), Rebecca Eames, Margaret Scott, Job Tookey, & Mary Whittredge

Sept. 16, 1692   Grand Jury of Mary Parker

Trials of Mary Parker & Margaret Scott

Sept. 17, 1692   Grand Jury of Abigail Faulkner Sr.

Trial of Abigail Faulkner Sr.

Sentenced to Death: Rebecca Eames, Abigail Faulkner Sr., Ann Foster, Abigail Hobbs, Mary Lacey Sr., Mary Parker, Wilmot Redd, Margaret Scott, & Samuel Wardwell

Sept. 19, 1692   Giles Cory Pressed to Death

Sept. 22, 1692   Executions of Martha Cory, Mary Esty, Alice Parker, Mary Parker, Ann Pudeator, Wilmot Redd, Margaret Scott, & Samuel Wardwell

Jan. 4, 1693   Trials of Sarah Buckley, Margaret Jacobs, Rebecca Jacobs, & Mary Whittredge

Grand Juries of Sarah Bassett & Sarah Bridges

Jan. 5, 1693   Grand Juries of Mary Colson, Elizabeth Johnson Jr., Jane Lilly, Margaret Prince, Henry Salter, & Hannah Tyler

Trials of Job Tookey & Hannah Tyler

Jan. 6, 1693   Grand Juries of Abigail Barker, Candy, Mary Marston, Abigail Soames, & Mary Toothaker

Trials of Candy, Mary Marston, Elizabeth Johnson Sr., & Abigail Barker

Jan. 7, 1693   Grand Juries of John Jackson Jr., John Jackson Sr., Rebecca Johnson, Susannah Post, & William Procter

Trial of Mary Tyler

Jan. 9, 1693   Rebecca Johnson Cleared by Proclamation

Jan. 10, 1693   Grand Juries of Mary Bridges Jr., Martha Emerson, & Mercy Wardwell

Trials of Sarah Wardwell, Sarah Hawkes, & Mercy Wardwell

Jan. 11, 1693   Grand Juries of Sarah Cole (of Lynn) & Mary Black

Trial of Elizabeth Johnson Jr.

Mary Black Cleared by Proclamation

Jan. 12, 1693   Grand Juries of Sarah Bridges, Mary English, Philip English, & Thomas Farrar Sr.

Trials of Mary Bridges Sr., Mary Post, Hannah Post, Sarah Bridges, & Mary Osgood

Thomas Farrar Sr. Cleared by Proclamation

Jan. 13, 1693   Grand Juries of Mary Barker, William Barker Jr., William Barker Sr., Hannah Bromage, Richard Carrier, Sarah Cloyce, Edward Farrington, Elizabeth Hart, Stephen Johnson, & Mary Lacey Jr.

Trial of Mary Lacey Jr.

Jan. 31, 1693   Grand Juries of Sarah Cole (of Lynn), Jane Lilly, Mary Taylor, & Mary Toothaker

Feb. 1, 1693   Trials of Sarah Cole (of Lynn), Lydia Dustin & Sarah Dustin, Mary Taylor, & Mary Toothaker

Feb. 3, 1693   Jane Lilly Cleared by Proclamation

April 25, 1693   John Alden Cleared by Proclamation

May 9, 1693   Grand Juries of Daniel Eames & Tituba

May 10, 1693   Grand Jury of Mary Bridges Jr.

Trials of Susannah Post, Eunice Frye, Mary Bridges Jr., Mary Barker, & William Barker Jr.

Sarah Cole (of Salem)‡, Dorothy Faulkner, Abigail Faulkner Jr., Martha Tyler, Johannah Tyler, Sarah Wilson Jr., & Sarah Wilson Sr. Cleared by Proclamation

May 11, 1693   William Hobbs Cleared by Proclamation

BIOGRAPHICAL NOTES

MARILYNNE K. ROACH

These notes identify, as far as possible, the individuals named in the Salem witch trial documents. Although all names are indexed elsewhere, individuals who could not be identified with reasonable certainty do not appear in this list. Also omitted are most jurors (unless mentioned for other reasons) and prisoners presumably jailed on charges unrelated to witchcraft. Likewise, uncertain or undiscovered details such as dates, locations, etc., are omitted. Entries are condensed using the abbreviations listed below and arranged as follows:

LAST NAME, FIRST NAME; occupation; dates of birth-death; parents of; date[s] of marriage[s] and name[s] of spouse[s] of; other kin; activity

For example:

STACY, WILLIAM; Salm; millwright; 1656–1694+; s Thomas & Susanna (Wooster) Stacy; m 1677 Priscilla Buckley; s-in-law Sarah Buckley; v Bridget Bishop

Since marriage changed women's surnames, former names appear in parentheses. For example:

Rebecca (Towne) Nurse was born Towne and married Francis Nurse.

Bridget (Playfer) (Wasselby) (Oliver) Bishop was born Playfer, married and was widowed from a Wasselby and an Oliver before marrying a Bishop.

Dates of birth and death are divided by a dash. "1630–" indicates only the birth date is known, while "–1698" indicates only the date of death is known. A + sign (1694+) shows the person was still alive in that year.

Dates are Old Style retaining the eleven-day difference except that the year is treated as if it began in January rather than the Old Style 25 March. i.e. February 1691/92 is here given as 1692.

"?" indicates speculation.

Locations are all in Massachusetts unless otherwise stated.

Trades are given when known although most men farmed, even those with other trades.

Judah, Israel and Ebenezer were sometimes women's names.

Names of suspects are in italics.

Names of suspects put to death are boldface.

Genealogical details are drawn primarily from the following sources:

Abbott, Charlotte Helen. "Early Records of the Families of Andover." Folders of typescripts in the Underhill Research Library, Andover Historical Society, Andover, Mass., also bound copies in the New England Historic Genealogical Society, Boston, Massachusetts.

Anderson, Robert Charles. *The Great Migration Begins: Immigrants to New England 1620–1633.* 3 vols. Boston: New England Historic Genealogical Society, 1995.

Anderson, Robert Charles; Sanborn, George F. Jr.; Sanborn, Melinde Lutz. *The Great Migration: Immigrants to New England 1634–1635.* 4 vols. of multi-volume set in progress. Boston: New England Historic Genealogical Society, 1999, 2001, 2003, 2005.

Babson, John J. *History of the Town of Gloucester, Cape Ann, Including the Town of Rockport.* Gloucester: Peter Smith, 1971, reprint of 1860 ed.

Davis, Walter Goodwin. *Massachusetts and Maine Families in the Ancestry of Walter Goodwin Davis (1885–1960): A Reprinting in Alphabetical Order by Surname of the Sixteen Multi-Ancestor Compendia.* 3 vols. Gary Boyd Roberts, ed. Baltimore: Genealogical Publishing Co., 1996. Also Family Tree Maker CD ROM #194 *Massachusetts and Maine Genealogies 1650's–1930's.* Brøderbund Software, Inc., 1998.

Hammatt, Abraham. *The Hammatt Papers: Early Inhabitants of Ipswich, Massachusetts 1633–1700.* Published by author in

7 parts, 1880–1899; one vol. edition indexed by Robert Barnes, Baltimore: Genealogical Publishing Co., 1980.

Hoyt, David W. *The Old Families of Salisbury and Amesbury, Massachusetts*. Somersworth, New Hampshire: New England History Press, 1981. One vol. reprint of original sections published 1897–1919.

Noyes, Sybil, Libby, Thornton Charles, and Davis, Walter Goodwin. *Genealogical Dictionary of Maine and New Hampshire*. Baltimore: Genealogical Publishing, Co. 1972. Original published in 5 parts, Portland, Maine, 1928–1939.

Perley, Sidney. *The History of Salem, Massachusetts*. 3 vols. Haverhill: Record Publishing Company, 1928.

Roach, Marilynne K. "Records of the Rev. Samuel Parris, Salem Village, Massachusetts, 1688–1698." *New England Historical Genealogical Register* 157(2003):6–30.

Savage, James. *A Genealogical Dictionary of the First Settlers of New England*. 4 vols. Reprint. Baltimore: Genealogical Publishing Co., 1965.

Schutz, John A. *Legislators of the Massachusetts General Court 1691–1780: a Biographical Dictionary*. Boston: Northeastern University Press, 1997.

Torrey, Clarence Almond. *New England Marriages prior to 1700*. edited by Elizabeth P. Bentley. Baltimore: Genealogical Publishing Co., 1985.

Trask, Richard. *"The Devil Hath Been Raised": a Documentary History of the Salem Village Witchcraft Outbreak of March, 1692*. Revised edition, Danvers, Mass: Yeoman Press, 1997.

ABBREVIATIONS

affl	afflicted
approx	approximate
b	born
bp	baptized
bef	before
bro	brother [of]
bur	buried
c	circa (about)
Capt	Captain
ch	church
Co	County
Col	Colonel
confess	confessed/confession
const	constable
d	died
dau	daughter [of]
Ens	Ensign

Exec	executed
f	father [of]
gr-dau	granddaughter [of]
gr-f	grandfather [of]
gr-mo	grandmother [of]
gr-s	grandson [of]
HC	Harvard College
legis	legislator
Lieut	Lieutenant
magist	magistrate
m	married
Maj	Major
merch	merchant
milit	military/militia
min	minister
mo	mother [of]
neph	nephew [of]
O&T	Court of Oyer and Terminer Massachusetts 1692 witch trials
perh	perhaps
petitn	petition
prob	probably
recant	recanted/recantation
Rep	Representative
s	son [of]
SCJ	Superior Court of Judicature, sat 1693
Serg	Sergeant
sis	sister [of]
Suff	Suffolk Co.
susp	suspect/suspected
unm	unmarried
unkn	unknown
v	versus (against)
wid	widow/widower
wit sum	witness summoned

Ames	Amesbury
And	Andover
Bev	Beverly
Bill	Billerica
Bost	Boston
Box	Boxford
Brad	Bradford
Camb	Cambridge
Chas	Charlestown
Chelm	Chelmsford
Conc	Concord
Dorch	Dorchester
Eng	England
Falm	Falmouth (Portland, Maine)
Glo	Gloucester
Hav	Haverhill
Ip	Ipswich
Lanc	Lancaster
Mald	Malden

Manch	Manchester
Mbl	Marblehead
Mass	Massachusetts
Med	Medford
NE	New England
Newb	Newbury
NH	New Hampshire
NY	New York
Read	Reading
Row	Rowley
Rox	Roxbury
Salis	Salisbury
Salm	Salem (town)
SV	Salem Village
Tops	Topsfield
Wat	Watertown
Wen	Wenham
Wey	Weymouth
Wob	Woburn

BIOGRAPHIES

A

ABBEY, MARY; SV; dau William Knowlton; m 1672 Samuel Abbey, 1699 Abraham Mitchell; sis Joseph & Thomas Knowlton; v Sarah Good

ABBEY, SAMUEL, also Abbe; SV; s John & Mary Abbey; m 1672 Mary (Knowlton) v Sarah Good

ABBOTT, ARTHUR; Ip; 1670–1729+; perh s Arthur Sr & Elizabeth (White) Abbott?; suspect, v Elizabeth Procter

ABBOTT, BENJAMIN; And; 1661–1703; s George Sr & Hannah (Chandler) Abbott; m 1685 Sarah Farnum; v Martha Carrier

ABBOTT, GEORGE; And; 1654–1724; s Capt George & Sarah (Farnum) Abbott; m 1689 Elizabeth Ballard, 1707 Hannah Easty

ABBOTT, HANNAH; And; dau Isaac & Mary (Towne) Easty; m 1707 George Abbott

ABBOTT, JOHN SR; And; selectman 1693; 1648–1721; s George & Hannah (Chandler) Abbott; m 1673 Sarah Barker; bro-in-law William Barker Sr; And petitn

ABBOTT, NEHEMIAH SR; Ip, Tops; c 1632–1706/07; s George Abbott Sr of Rowley; m 1659 Mary How; bro-in-law Elizabeth How; gr-uncle Nehemiah Abbott Jr; v Elizabeth How

ABBOTT, NEHEMIAH JR; Tops; weaver; s George & Elizabeth (Ballard) Abbott; gr-s George Abbot Sr of Rowley; gr-neph Nehemiah Abbott Sr; m 1691 Abigail Lovejoy; arrested, released

ABBOTT, SARAH; And; 1661–; dau Ralph & Elizabeth (Holt) Farnum; m 1688 Benjamin Abbott; v Martha Carrier

ABBOTT, WILLIAM; And; 1657–1713; s George Sr & Hannah (Chandler) Abbott; m 1682 Elizabeth Geary; And petitn

ABORN, SAMUEL SR; SV; c 1611–1700; m Catherine Smith; Rebecca Nurse petitn

ADAMS, SIMON; Ip; weaver; c 1654–1723; s William & Elizabeth (Stacy) Adams; m Hannah –; kin to Stacys; deputy

ADDINGTON, ISAAC; Bost; surgeon, legis, magist, deacon 1st Ch Bost; c 1644–c 1715; s Isaac & Anne (Leverett) Addington; m 1669 Elizabeth Bowen, 1713 Elizabeth (Morton) Wainright; observed Elizabeth Procter & Sarah Cloyce exams

AIRES, SAMUEL, also Ayers; Ip; –1697; m 1677 Abigail Fellows?; v Rachel Clinton

ALDEN, CAPT JOHN; Bost; merch, privateer; c 1626–1702; s John & Priscilla (Mullins) Alden; m 1659 Elizabeth (Phillips) Everell; arrested, escaped

ALLEN, ANDREW, also Allin; And; 1657–1690 small-pox; s Andrew & Faith (Ingalls) Allen; m 1682 Elizabeth Richards; bro Martha Carrier & Mary Toothaker, bro-in-law Phebe Chandler

ALLEN, ANN; 1666–1733; dau Wymond & Sarah (Pike) Bradbury; m c 1686 Jeremiah Allen; gr-dau Mary Bradbury

ALLEN, BENJAMIN; Salis; c 1650–1723; s Wm & Ann (Goodale) Allen; m 1686 Rachel Wheeler, 1695 Hopestill Leonard; Mary Bradbury petitn; 1693 jury

ALLEN, REV JAMES; Bost; min 1st Ch Bost; Oxford U; 1632–1710; m Hannah Dummer, Eliz (Houchin) Endicott, & Sarah (Hawkins) Breck

ALLIN, REV JAMES; Salis; min Salis 1687; HC 1679; 1657–1696; s Roger & Mary (Nash) Allin; m 1688 Elizabeth Cotton; for Mary Bradbury

ALLEN, JOHN; Salis; planter, mariner, vintner; s Wm & Ann Allen; m 1674 Mary (Pike) Andrews; Mary Bradbury petitn

ALLEN, MARY; Salis; 1647–1695; dau Robert & Sarah (Sanders) Pike; m 1668 Jedidiah Andrew, 1674 John Allen; Mary Bradbury petitn

ALLEN, RACHEL; Salis; –1694; dau Philip Squire?; m Henry Wheeler, Benjamin Allen, 1695 Hopestill Leonard; Mary Bradbury petitn

ALLEN, WILLIAM; Salis; 1650–1706; s William & Ann (Goodale) Allen; m 1674 Mary Harris; Mary Bradbury petitn

ALLEN, WILLIAM; SV; cooper; 1670–1747; s Samuel & Sarah Allen; m c 1695 Elizabeth Small, Sarah –; v Tituba, Sarah Good, Sarah Osburn

AMBROS, HENRY; Salis; weaver; 1649–; s Henry & Susanna Ambros Sr; m Susanna (–) Worcester; Mary Bradbury petitn

AMBROS, SUSANNA; Salis; m Timothy Worcester, Henry Ambros; Mary Bradbury petitn

ANDREW, DANIEL, SV; mason & merch; c 1644–1702; s Thomas & Rebecca (–) Andrews; m Sarah Porter; bro Sarah Jacobs; Rebecca Nurse petitn, accused, fled

ANDREWS, ANNA; Salm; –1712+; dau George Jacobs Sr; m John Andrews, sis George Jacobs Jr; v Sarah Churchill

ANDREWS, JOHN Sr, also Andras, Andros; Salis; planter, mariner, vintner; 1648–c 1697; s William & Alice Allen; m 1674 Mary –; bro Joseph Andrews of Glo; Procter petitn

ANDREWS, JOHN JR; Box; 1648–; s Robert & Grace Andrews; m c 1683 Sarah Dickinson; bro Joseph & Thomas Andrews, Mary Cummings & Elizabeth Symmonds; Procter petitn, v Sarah Wilds

ANDREWS, JOSEPH; Box; const 1692; 1657–; s Robert & Grace Andrews; m 1681 Sarah Perley, 1694 Mary Dickinson; bro John Jr & Thomas Andrews, Mary Cummings & Elizabeth Symmonds; Procter petitn, v Sarah Wilds

ANDREWS, JOSEPH; Glo; blacksmith; 1653–1724; s William & Alice Allen; m1680 Rachel (Griggs), 1684 Rose (Howard); bro John Andrews Sr

ANDREWS, MARY; Salis; m 1674 John Andrews Sr; Mary Bradbury petitn

ANDREWS, SARAH; Box; 1665–1694; dau Samuel & Ruth (Trumble) Perley; m1681 Joseph Andrews; niece Samuel, Thomas & Timothy Perley; v Elizabeth How

ANDREWS, SARAH; SV; bp 1649–1731; dau John & Mary? Porter; m Daniel Andrews

ANDREWS, THOMAS; Box; c 1640–; s Robert & Grace Andrews; m 1670 Martha (–) Antrum, 1681 Mary Belcher, & Rebecca (–); bro John Jr & Joseph Andrews, Mary Cummings & Elizabeth Symmonds; v Elizabeth How

ANDROS, SIR EDMUND; Royal Gov overthrown 1689; 1637–1714; s Amice & Elizabeth (Stone) Andros; m Mary Craven

APPLETON, JOHN; Ip; milit capt, legislature, magist; c 1652–1739; s Saml & Mary (Everard) Appleton; m 1651 Priscilla (Glover); bro Samuel & f Jose Appleton; reparation committee

APPLETON, SAMUEL; Ip; landowner, active in local & provincial govt, milit leader; c 1624–1696; s Saml & Mary (Everard) Appleton; m 1651 Hannah Paine, 1656 Mary Oliver; 1693 grand jury

ARNOLD, JOHN; Bost; –1725?; prison keeper & anchor smith; m Mary (–), &? Mercy (–) Fosdick; for Sarah Cloyce & Mary Esty

ARNOLD, MARY; Bost; m John Arnold; for Sarah Cloyce & Mary Esty

ARNOLD, WILLIAM, also Arnall; Read; c 1649–; deputy

ASLEBEE, JOHN; And; farmer, landowner, And selectman, later Rep; 1656–1728; bro Rebecca Johnson & Sarah Cole, bro-in-law Eunice Cole

ATKINSON, JOHN; Newb; hatter; c 1636–; s Theodore Atkinson; m c 1664 Sarah Mirick; v Susanna Martin

ATKINSON, NATHANIEL; Newb; s John & Sarah (Mirick) Atkinson; wit sum v Sarah Martin

ATKINSON, SARAH; Newb; dau – Mirick; m c 1664 John Atkinson; v Susanna Martin

AYER, JOHN; Hav; 1657–1743; m 1683 Hannah Travers; deputy

B

BABSON, EBENEZER; Glo; 1668– d by 1698?; s James & Eleanor Babson; v Margaret Prince & Elizabeth Dicer

BABSON, ELEANOR; Glo; c 1630–1714; dau – Hill; m 1647 James Babson; sis John & Zebulon Hill; v Margaret Prince, Elizabeth Dicer

BACON, DANIEL; Bev; s Daniel & Mary (Read) Bacon; m 1664 Susanna Spencer; v Job Tookey

BAGLEY, ORLANDO; Ames; const; 1658– d bef 1729; s Orlando & Sarah (Colby) Bagley; m 1681 Sarah Sargent (niece Mary Bradbury), 1704 Sarah Annis

BAILEY, ELIZABETH, also Bayley; SV; c 1665–1715+; dau John & Mary Wilkins; m Thomas Bailey; gr-dau Bray Wilkins; v John Willard

BAILEY, REV JAMES, also Bailey; Rox, formerly SV; min & physician; HC 1669; 1651–1707; s John & Eleanor (Emery) Bayley; m 1672 Mary Carr, Mary –; br James Bailey

BAILEY, REV JOHN; Bost; min 1st Ch Bost; 1644–1697; m Lydia –, Susannah Wilkins

BAILEY, JOSEPH; Newb; weaver; 1648–1723; s John & Eleanor (Emery) Bailey; m Priscilla Putnam; bro Rev James Bailey; v Procters

BAILEY, MARY; SV; 1652–1688; dau George & Elizabeth (Oliver) Carr; m 1672 Rev James Bailey; sis Ann Putnam Sr & Sarah Barker

BAILEY, PRISCILLA; Newb; –1704; dau John & Rebecca (Prince) Putnam; m Joseph Bailey

BAILEY, THOMAS; SV; –1714; m Elizabeth Wilkins; v John Willard

BAKER, CORNELL, also Cornelius; Bev; m 1658 Hannah Woodbury; v Sarah Bishop

BAKER, EBENEZER, see BARKER

BAKER, HANNAH; Bev; bp 1636–; dau John & Ann? Woodbury; m 1658 Cornelius Baker; sis-in-law John Hill; v Sarah Bishop

BAKER, JONATHAN; Bev; bp 1669–; Cornelius & Hannah (Woodbury) Baker; guarded Sarah Good

BAKER, WILLIAM; Ip; glover, Ip const 1692; c 1656–; s John & Katherine (Perkins) Baker; m 1686 Sarah Fitts, c 1713 Ann Burrill; v Rachel Clinton

BALCH, DAVID; Bev; 1671–1690; s Benjamin & Sarah (Gardner) Balch; d "bewitched" by Dorcas Hoar, Sarah Wilds, Sarah Bishop, Wilmot Redd

BALCH, ELIZABETH; Bev; 1654–; dau John & Elizabeth Woodbury; m Banjamin Balch Jr; sis Abigail Walden, sis-in-law David Balch; v Edward & Sarah Bishop

BALLARD, ELIZABETH; And; 1646–1692; dau Edward & Elizabeth (Adams) Phelps; m Joseph Ballard; aunt Sarah Phelps; d "bewitched"

BALLARD, JOHN; And; const; 1653–; s William & Grace Ballard; m 1681 Rebecca Hooper; bro-in-law Sarah Wardwell

BALLARD, JOSEPH; And; And const 1692; 1667–1722; s William & Grace Ballard, m Elizabeth Phelps, 1692 Rebecca Rea; bro William Ballard; v Samuel Wardwell

BALLARD, WILLIAM; And; s William & Grace Ballard; m 1682 Hannah Hooper; bro-in-law Sarah Wardwell; And petitns

BANCROFT, CAPT EBENEZER; Lynn; 1667–1717; s Thomas & Elizabeth (Metcalf) Bancroft; m 1692 Abigail Eaton

BARKER, ABIGAIL; And; 1656–; And; dau David Wheeler?; m 1686 Ebenezer Barker; sis-in-law William Barker Sr, aunt William Barker Jr, Mary Barker, Mary Marston; confess, recant

BARKER, EBENEZER; And; 1650–1746; s Richard & Joanna Barker; m 1686 Abigail Wheeler; And petitns

BARKER, JOHN SR; And; 1644–1732; s Richard & Joanna Barker; m 1670 Mary Stevens, 1717 Martha (–) Smith

BARKER, MARY; And; 1679–1752; And; dau John & Mary (Stephens) Barker; m 1799 William Barker Jr; niece William Barker Sr, Abigail Barker, cous William Barker Jr & Mary Marston; confess, tried, not guilty

BARKER, SARAH; Bost; 1654–; dau George & Mary Carr; m Thomas Barker; sis Ann Putnam Sr & Mary Bailey

BARKER, WILLIAM SR; And; 1646–1718; s Richard & Joanna Barker; m 1680 Hannah (Kimball); confess, accuser, escaped

BARKER, WILLIAM JR; And; 1677–1745; s William Sr & Mary (Dix) Barker; m 1700 Mary Barker; confess, tried, not guilty

BARNARD, ELIZABETH; And; 1671–1693; dau Theodore & Ann (Wood) Price; step-dau Dudley Bradstreet; m 1686 Rev Thomas Barnard; And petitn

BARNARD, REV THOMAS, also Bernard; And; min And; HC 1679; –1718; s Francis & Hannah (Marvin) Barnard; m 1686 Elizabeth Price, 1696 Abigail Ball, 1704 Lydia Goff; s-in-law Ann (Wood) (Price) Bradstreet; And petitn

BARNOTT, STEPHEN, also Barnard; And; c 1649–1722; s Robert & Joan Barnard; m Rebecca Hine; And petitn

BARRETT, THOMAS; Chelms; –1702; s Thomas & Margaret Barrett; m 1655 Frances Woolderson, 1695 Mary Dike; petitn for dau Martha Sparks

BARTON, JOHN; Salm; physician, surgeon, apothecary; –1694; s John Barton; m Lydia Roberts

BARTON, SAMUEL; SV; c 1664–1732; s Matthew & Martha Barton; m Hannah Bridges; s-in-law Sarah Cloyce; v Mercy Lewis

BASSETT, SARAH; Lynn; dau Richard Hood; m 1675 William Bassett Jr; sis-in-law Mary Derich, Elizabeth and John Procto; aunt Sarah Procter; arrested

BASSETT, WILLIAM; Lynn; bp 1624–1703; s Roger & Ann (Holland) Bassett; m c 1647 Sarah –; f Mary DeRich, Elizabeth Procter, f-in-law Sarah Bassett

BATCHELOR, JONATHAN; SV; 1678–1740; s John & Mary (Herrick) Batchelor, gr-s Zachariah Herrick; m 1702 Ruth Rayment; v Sarah Good

BEADLE, NATHANIEL SR; Salm; 1669–1717; s Samuel & Hannah (Lemon) Beadle; witt recog

BEADLE, SAMUEL; Salm; wood turner, tavern keeper; –1706; s Samuel & Susanna Beadle; m 1668 Hannah Lemon

BEADLE, THOMAS; Salm; mariner, tavern keeper (preliminary exams here); –1700; s Samuel & Susanna Beadle; m 1679 Elizabeth Drake

BEALE, GEORGE; Mbl; –1691; s George & Martha (Bradstreet) Beale

BEALE, JAMES; Mbl; –1691; s George & Martha (Bradstreet) Beale

BEALE, WILLIAM; Mbl; miller; c 1628–1694; m Martha Bradstreet, 1676 Elizabeth Jackson, 1684 Mary (–) Hart; v Phillip English

BECKETT, JOHN; Salm; shipwright; s John & Margaret Beckett; m Elizabeth Locker; wit sum v Ann Pudeator, Ann Parker

BELLSHER, –; Ip; "widow Bellsher" prob Mary Belcher; Ip; dau Edmund Lockwood; m 1652 Jeremy Belcher; wit sum

BEST, JOHN SR; Salm; carrier; c 1646–1711; m Susanna Durin; v Ann Pudeator

BEST, JOHN JR; Salm; 1671–1748+; s John Best Sr & Susanna Durin; m Edith Hull; v Ann Pudeator

BIBBER, JOHN; Salm; m Sarah; v Giles Cory

BIBBER, SARAH; Salm; c 1656–; m John Bibber; affl, v many

BISHOP, BRIDGET, "alias Bridget Oliver"; Salm; d 1692; dau – Playfer; m 1660 Samuel Wasselby, Thomas Oliver, Edward Bishop; tried, found guilty, hanged 10 June 1692

BISHOP, EDWARD SR; SV; c 1620–1705; f Edward Bishop Jr, f-in-law Sarah Bishop; (not m Bridget Bishop); Rebecca Nurse petitn

BISHOP, EDWARD JR; SV; farmer & unlicensed tavern keeper; 1648–1711; s Edward & Hannah (Moore) Bishop; m Sarah Wilds; s-in-law Sarah (Averill) Wilds; arrested, escaped

BISHOP, HANNAH; SV; Rebecca Nurse petitn

BISHOP, SARAH; SV; dau John & Priscilla (Gould) Wilds; m Edward Bishop Jr; step-dau Sarah (Averill) Wilds; arrested, escaped

BITTFORD, STEPHEN; Salm?; hired man; c 1669–; v Rebecca Nurse & Elizabeth Procter

BIXBY, HANNAH, also Bigsby; And; 1659–1730; dau Thomas & Hannah (Brewer) Chandler; m 1674 Daniel Bixby; aunt Sarah Phelps; affl

BIXBY, JOSEPH JR; Box; s Joseph & Sarah (Wyatt) Bixby; m 1682 Sarah Gould; summ witt v Sarah Wilds

BLACK, –,"Goody Black," prob Faith Black; Tops; dau Edmund and Elizabeth Bridges; m Daniel Black; sis-in-law Sarah Cloyce; named

BLACK, MARY; SV; "Lieutenant Nathaniel Putman's Negro"

BLANCHARD, SAMUEL; And; 1629–1707; s Thomas Blanchard; m 1654 Mary Sweetser, 1675 Hannah Doggett; And petit, 1693 jury

BLATHWAIT, WILLIAM; London; statesman; 1649?–1717; s William & Anne (Povey) Blathwait; m 1686 Mary Wynter

BLEZDEL, HENRY, also Blaisdell; Ames; tailor; c 1632– by 1707; s Ralph & Elizabeth? Blaisdell; m c 1656 Mary Haddon, aft 1690 Elizabeth –; bro-in-law Edmund Elliott, f-in-law Henry Starling

BLY, JOHN SR; Salm; brickmaker; c 1635–1709+; m 1663 Rebecca Gault; v Bridget Bishop

BLY, REBECCA; Salm; 1641–; dau William & Mary Gault; m 1663 John Bly; v Bridget Bishop

BLY, WILLIAM; Salm; s John & Rebecca Bly; v Bridget Bishop

BOND, WILLIAM; Wat; Speaker 1692; 1625–1695; s Thomas Bond; m 1650 Sarah Bisco, 1695 Elizabeth (Paynton?) Nevinson

BONFIELDS, GEORGE; Mbl; c 1635–; m Rebecca Bradstreet, 1690 Ann Freed

BOOTH, ALICE; Salm; 1678–; sis-in-law Elizabeth (Wilkins) Booth; dau George & Alice (Temple?) Booth ("widow Shafflin"); m 1700 Ebenezer Marsh; sis-in-law Elizabeth Booth; affl, v several

BOOTH, ELIZABETH; Salm; 1674–; dau George & Alice (Temple?) Booth ("widow Shafflin"); m 1695 Israel Shaw; sis-in-law Elizabeth (Wilkins) Booth; affl, v several

BOOTH, ELIZABETH; Salm; 1676–; dau Henry & Rebecca (Baxter) Wilkins; m 1692 George Booth, 1701 Edward Carrell; sis Rebecca & Daniel Wilkins; affl, v several

BOOTH, GEORGE; Salm; 1671–c 1696; s George & Alice (Temple?) Booth ("widow Shafflin"); m 1692 Elizabeth Wilkins; affl

BORMAN, THOMAS, also Boarman; Ip; c 1644–1719; s Thomas & Margaret Borman; m Elizabeth Perkins; v Rachel Clinton, 1693 grand jury

BOWDEN, SARAH; Lynn; 1651–1741+; dau Francis & Rebecca (Towne) Nurse; m 1669 Michael Bowden; for Rebecca Nurse

BRACKETT, ANTHONY CAPT; Falm; –1689; m Ann Mitton, 1679 Susanna Drake

BRADBURY, JACOB; Salis; 1677–1718; s William & Rebecca (Wheelwright) (Maverick) Bradbury; m 1698 Elizabeth Stockman; gr-s Mary Bradbury

BRADBURY, MARY; Sals; 1615–1700; dau John & Judith (Gater) Perkins; m bef 1637 Thomas Bradbury; mo-in-law Rev John Busse; tried, condemned, escaped

BRADBURY, THOMAS; Sals; planter; 1610–1695; s Wymond Bradbury; m bef 1637 Mary Perkins; Mary Bradbury petitn

BRADBURY, WILLIAM; Salis; 1649– d bef 1712; s Thomas & Mary (Perkins) Bradbury; m 1672 Rebecca (Wheelwright) Maverick

BRADBURY, WYMOND; Salis; 1669–1724; s Wymond & Sarah (Pike) Bradbury; m Maria Cotton

BRADFORD, RACHEL; Bev; 1659– d bef 1679; dau John & Rachel (Scruggs) Rayment; m 1676 William Bradford; v Mercy Lewis

BRADFORD, WILLIAM; Bev; fisherman; c 1639–1717; m 1678 Rachel Rayment; v Mercy Lewis

BRADSTREET, ANN; c 1648–; dau Richard & Ann (Priddeth) Wood; wid Theodore Price, m 1673 Dudley Bradstreet; mo-in-law Thomas Barnard; accused, fled

BRADSTREET, COL DUDLEY; And; land owner, magist; c 1649–1702; s Simon & Anne (Dudley) Bradstreet; m 1673 Ann (Wood) Price; accused, fled

BRADSTREET, SIMON; Bost; magist, land-owner; 1604–1697; s Rev Simon Bradstreet; m bef 1630 Anne Dudley, m 1676 Ann (Dowing) Gardner; f Dudley and John Bradstreet; bro-in-law Joseph Dudley; acting Massachusetts Gov until May 1692

BRAGG, HENRY, also Brag, Brogg; Salm; laborer; m 1677 Elizabeth Mackmallen; v Hannah Caroll, Sarah Cole (Salm)

BRAGG, WILLIAM; Salm; 1684–; s Henry & Elizabeth Bragg; affl

BRATTLE, THOMAS; Bost; merch, politician; 1658–1713; HC 1676; s Thomas & Elizabeth (Tyng) Brattle; criticized trials Oct 1692

BRAYBROOK, SAMUEL, also Bradbrook; SV; weaver; –1722; m Mary –; v Sarah Good, Mary Esty, etc

BRIDGES, JAMES; And; 1671–1734; s John & Sarah (How) Bridges; m 1692 Sarah Marston; step-s Mary Bridges

BRIDGES, JOHN; And; blacksmith; c 1648–; s Edmund Bridges; m 1666 Sarah How, 1678 Mary (Tyler) Post; f Sarah & Mary Bridges Jr, step-f Mary & Joanna Post; bro Faith Black; bro-in-law Sarah Cloyce & Elizabeth How; kin to Ann Pudeator; v Mary Tyler, posted bond for Tyler & Bridges children

BRIDGES, MARY SR; And; c 1644–; dau Job & Mary Tyler; m 1662 Richard Post, 1678 John Bridges; step-mo Sarah Bridges, mo Mary Bridges Jr, Mary, Susanna & Joanna Post; step-aunt Martha Sprague; confess, recant, tried, not guilty

BRIDGES, MARY JR; And; 1680–; dau John & Mary (Tyler) (Post) Bridges; confess

BRIDGES, SARAH; And; c1674–1723+; dau John & Sarah (How) Bridges; m 1694 Samuel Preston, 1722 William Price; half-sis Mary Bridges, step-sis Mary, Susanna & Hannah Post, niece James How Jr; confess

BRIDGHAM, JOHN; Ip; physician; HC 1669; 1645–1721; s Henry & Elizabeth Bridgham; wit sum v Rachel Clinton

BRITS/BRITZ, MARY; Salm; –1689; m 1664 Giles Cory

BROMAGE, HANNAH; Hav; d bet 1695–1701; m Abraham Tyler, Edward Bromage; arrested

BROWN, ABIGAIL; Salis; prob m c1641 Henry Brown; Mary Bradbury petitn

BROWN, ABRAHAM; Salis; 1650–1733; s Henry Sr & Abigail Brown; m 1675 Elizabeth Shepherd; Mary Bradbury petitn

BROWN, BENJAMIN; Salm; merch, town meeting moderator; c 1648–1708; s William & Sarah (Smith) Brown; m 1686 Mary Hicks

BROWN, ELIZABETH; Salis; dau –Murford; m c 1665 William Brown; "bewitched"

BROWN, ELIZABETH; Salis; bef 1655?–1733+; dau William Shepherd; m 1675 Abraham Brown; Mary Bradbury petitn

BROWN, HANNAH; Salis; 1648–1727; dau Samuel & Ann Fellowes; m 1666 Nathaniel Brown; mo Hannah Evans; Mary Bradbury petitn

BROWN, HENRY; Salis; prob c 1615–1701; shoemaker, farmer; m c 1641 Abigail –; Mary Bradbury petitn

BROWN, JOHN SR; Read; m 1659 Elizabeth Osgood, 1681 Sarah –; v Sarah Rice

BROWN, JOHN; Lynn?; c 1661–; s Nicholas Brown?; v Sarah Cole (Lynn)

BROWN, MARY; Read; c 1646–; dau Joseph & Ruth (Fraile) Fellows; m 1666 Josiah Brown (–1691); affl, v Sarah Cole (Lynn)

BROWN, NATHANIEL SR; Salis; 1642–1723; s Henry Sr & Abigail Brown; m 1666 Hannah Fellows; f Hannah Evans; Mary Bradbury petitn

BROWN, RICHARD; Newb; 1651–1716; s Richard & Elizabeth (Greenleaf) (Badger) Brown; m 1674 Mary Jaques; Mary Bradbury petitn, 1693 jury

BROWN, WILLIAM; Sals; planter; c 1622–1706; m Elizabeth Mumford; v Susanna Martin

BUBBEE, JOANE, also Boobyar; Mbl; d by 1697; dau Christopher & Mary (Bennett) Codner; m Joseph Boobyar; wit sum v Wilmot Redd

BUCK, EPHRAIM; Wob; const; 1676–; s Ephraim Buck; m 1671 Sarah Brooks

BUCKLEY, SARAH; SV; c 1637– d bef 1710; dau Thomas Smith; m c 1650 William Buckley; mo Mary Whittredge, Procter kin, mo-in-law William Stacy; arrested

BUCKLEY, WILLIAM, also Bulkley; SV; shoemaker; c 1630–1710; m Sarah Smith; father Mary Whittredge; for wife Sarah Buckley

BUCKSTONE, –, "Mrs Buckstone" see BUXTON, ELIZABETH

BUFFINGTON, THOMAS JR; Salm; 1672– bef 1705; s Thomas & Sarah (Southwick) Buffington; m 1699 Hannah Ross

BULLOCK, JOHN; Salm; vintner, innkeeper, brewer; 1654–1694; s Henry & Alice (Flint) Bullock; m Mary Maverick; v Alice Parker

BURBANK, JOHN; Row; –1709; s John & Ann Burbank; m 1663 Susanna Merrill

BURNHAM, JAMES; Ip; 1650–1729; s Thomas & Mary (Lawrence) Burnham; m Mary –; witt summ v Rachel Clinton

BURNHAM, JOHN SR; Ip; perh c 1620–1694; m Mary –; uncle of John Jr, Nathaniel & Thomas Burnham; Procter petitn

BURNHAM, JOHN JR; Ip; 1648?–1704?; s Thomas & Mary (Lawrence) Burnham; m 1669 Elizabeth Wells; Procter petitn

BURNHAM, NATHANIEL; Ip; 1662–; s Thomas & Mary (Lawrence) Burnham; wit sum v Rachel Clinton

BURNHAM, THOMAS; Ip; c 1644–1728; s Thomas & Mary (Lawrence) Burnham; m Lydia Pingrie, Esther Cogswell; v Rachel Clinton

BURRILL, JOHN; Lynn; land owner, legis; 1658–1721; s John & Lois (Ivory) Burrill; m 1680 Mary Stowers; 1711 reparations committee

BURROUGHS, CHARLES; 1680–; s Rev George & Sarah (Ruck) Burroughs; m 1706 Elizabeth Marston, 1712 Rebecca Townsend; bro Rebecca Fowle, Hannah Fox, Elizabeth Thomas

BURROUGHS, REV GEORGE, also Burrows, Burrough; Wells, Maine; min Wells; c 1650–1692; s Nathaniel & Rebecca (Stiles) Burrough; HC 1670; m c 1673 Hannah Fisher, c 1683 Sarah Ruck, Mary –; former min SV; tried, condemn, hanged 19 Aug 1692

BURROUGHS, GEORGE JR; bp 1681–; s Rev George & Sarah (Ruck) Burroughs; m 1713 Sarah Scales; bro Rebecca Fowle, Hannah Fox, and Elizabeth Thomas

BURROUGHS, HANNAH; SV; 1653–1681; dau Joshua & Mary (Aldis) Fisher; m c 1673 Rev George Burroughs

BURROUGHS, JEREMIAH; c 1682–1752; s Rev George & Sarah (Ruck) Burroughs; bro Rebecca Fowle, Hannah Fox, and Elizabeth Thomas

BURROUGHS, MARY; m Rev George Burroughs, 1693 Michael Homer, 1700 Christopher Hall Jr

BURROUGHS, MARY; c 1690–; dau Rev George & Mary Burroughs; m bef 1735 Joseph Tiffany; sis George Jr & Jeremiah Burroughs, Rebecca Fowle, Hannah Fox, Elizabeth Thomas

BURROUGHS, SARAH; dau John & Hannah (Spooner) Ruck; m Rev George Burroughs

BUSSE, ELIZABETH; Salis; 1651– d bef 1712; dau Thomas & Mary (Perkins) Bradbury; m 1673 Rev John Busse

BUSSE, ELIZABETH JR; dau Rev John & Elizabeth (Bradbury) Busse; gr-dau Mary Bradbury

BUSSE, REV JOHN, also Bussee, Burse; Bost/Eastward; preacher & physician; c 1640–1736; m 1673 Elizabeth Bradbury, Mary (Hill) (Valentine), Elizabeth –; named

BUSSE, JOHN; s Rev John & Elizabeth (Bradbury) Busse; gr-s Mary Bradbury

BUSSWELL, ANNA; Salis; dau – Ordway; m c1690 Isaac Busswell; Mary Bradbury petitn

BUSSWELL, ISAAC; Salis; 1657–1709; s Isaac & Mary (Esty) Busswell; m c 1690 Anna Ordway; Mary Bradbury petitn

BUTLER, WILLIAM; Ip; c 1653–1708+; m 1675 Sarah Cross; Procter petitn

BUTTON; "one Button a reputed witch", perh Elizabeth (Wheeler) (Dustin) Button; Hav; dau John Wheeler; wid Thomas Dustin

BUXTON, ELIZABETH; SV; 1660–; dau Joseph & Sarah (Ingersoll) (Haynes) Holton; m 1677 John Buxton; Procter petitn, Rebecca Nurse requests for search committee

BUXTON, JOHN; SV; c 1644–1715; s Anthony & Elizabeth Buxton; m 1668 Mary Small, 1677 Elizabeth Holton; v several

BYFIELD, NATHANIEL; Bost/ Bristol; legis, landowner; 1653–1733; s Richard & – (Juxon) Byfield; m 1675 Deborah Clark, 1718 Sarah Leverett; "much dissatisfied" Oct 1692

C

CALEF, ROBERT; Bost; clothier; bp 1648–1719; s Joseph Calef; m c 1670 Mary –; const 1692, later criticized trials, wrote *More Wonders of the Invisible World*

CALEY, JOHN, also Cauley?; Mbl; m 1685 Susanna Stacy; wit sum v Rachel Clenton but absent at sea

CANDY; Salm; "late of Barbadoes"; "Candy, a Negro woman"; confess, accused owner Margaret Hawkes

CAPEN, REV JOSEPH; Tops; min Tops; HC 1677; 1658–1725; s John & Mary (Bass) Capen; m Priscilla Appleton; volunteered to dep for Sarah Cloyce & Mary Esty, 1703 petitn

CARR, ELIZABETH: Salis; 1650–; dau Robert & Sarah (Sanders) Pike; m 1672 William Carr; Mary Bradbury petitn

CARR, GEORGE; Salis; c 1613–1682; m by 1642 Elizabeth –; f Mary Bailey, Sarah Barker, Ann Putnam Sr etc; suspected Mary Bradbury

CARR, JAMES; Salis; shipwright; 1650–1696+; s George & Elizabeth Carr; m 1677 Mary Sears; v Mary Bradbury

CARR, JOHN; Salis; 1656–1689; s George & Elizabeth Carr; uncle Ann Putnam Jr; "crazed or distempered," suspected Mary Bradbury

CARR, RICHARD; Salis; shipwright; 1659–1727; s George & Elizabeth Carr; m Dorothy –, 1702 Sarah Healey, 1727 Sarah Greely; v Mary Bradbury

CARR, WILLIAM; Salis; shipwright, land-surveyor for northern Essex Co; 1648–1715+; s George & Elizabeth Carr; m Elizabeth Pike; Mary Bradbury petitn

CARRIER, ANDREW; And/Bill; 1677–1749; s Thomas & Martha (Allen) Carrier: m 1705 Mary Adams; arrested, confess

CARRIER, MARTHA; And/Bill; c 1650–1692; dau Andrew & Faith (Ingalls) Carrier; m 1674 Thomas Carrier "alias Morgan"; mo Andrew, Richard, Sarah, & Thos Carrier Jr; tried, condemn, hanged 19 Aug 1692

CARRIER, RICHARD; And/Bill; 1674–1749; s Thomas & Martha (Allen) Carrier; m 1694 Elizabeth Sessions, 1707 Thankful Brown; confess

CARRIER, SARAH; And/Bill; 1684–1772; dau Thomas & Martha (Allen) Carrier; m 1707 John Chapman; confess

CARRIER, THOMAS SR; And/Bill; –1735; m 1674 Martha Allen

CARRIER, THOMAS JR; And/Bill; 1682–1740; s Thomas & Martha (Allen) Carrier; m 1705 Susannah Johns; confess

CARROLL, HANNAH; Sal; m Nathaniel Carroll; arrested

CARROLL, NATHANIEL; Salm; wheelwright; m Hannah –

CARTER, BETHIA SR; Wob; c. 1646–1706?; dau. John & Madeline Pearson; m Joseph Carter; arrested

CARTER, BETHIA JR; Wob; 1671-; dau Joseph & Bethia (Pearson) Carter; m. 1695 Roland Jones; arrested

CARTER, MARTHA; Salis; –1718; dau – Brown?; m John Carter; Mary Bradbury petit

CARY, ELIZABETH, also Carey; Chas; c 1655–1722; dau – Walker; m 1674 Nathaniel Cary; arrested, escaped

CARY, NATHANIEL; Chas; merch & mariner; 1645–; s Nathaniel & Eleanor Cary; m 1674 Elizabeth Walker; helped wife Elizabeth Cary escape

CASNOE, MARGARET, also Cazneau; Bost; 1671–1769; dau Jean Germaine; m Paix Cazneau

CHANDLER, BRIDGET; And; c 1650–1731; dau Thomas Henchman; m 1660 James Richards, 1679 William Chandler; mo Phebe Chandler, cousin Wyman; v Martha Carrier

CHANDLER, HANNAH; And; c 1630–1717; dau – Brewer; m Thomas Chandler: or 1650–1741 dau George & Hannah (Chandler) Abbott; m 1676 John Chandler; And petitn

CHANDLER, JOHN; And; c 1655–1721; s Thomas & Hannah (Brewer) Chandler; m 1676 Hannah Abbott

CHANDLER, PHOEBE; And; 1680–; dau William Sr & Bridget (Henchman) (Richards) Chandler; m 1708 Jonathan Tyler; affl, v Martha Carrier

CHANDLER, CAPT THOMAS SR; And; blacksmith; c 1627–1703; s William & Annis Chandler; m Hannah Brewer; bro William Chandler; f Hannah (Chandler) Bixby; v Samuel Wardwell

CHANDLER, THOMAS JR; And; 1664–1737; s Thomas Sr & Hannah (Brewer) Chandler; m Mary Peters; And petitns

CHANDLER, WILLIAM SR; And; brick maker, tavern keeper; c 1634–1698; s William & Annis Chandler; m 1658 Mary Dane, 1679 Bridget (Henchman) Richards; f Phebe Chandler; 1693 jury

CHANDLER, SGT WILLIAM JR; And; 1661–1727; s William & Mary (Dane) Chandler; m Sarah Buckminster; And petitn

CHAPMAN, MARY; 1648–1724; dau John & Mary Brewer; m 1666 Simon Chapman; for Elizabeth How

CHAPMAN, SIMON (or Symonds); Ip; carpenter; 1643–1735; s Edward & Mary (Symonds) Chapman; m 1666 Mary Brewer; for Elizabeth How

CHECKLEY, ANTHONY; Bost; c 1636–1708; merch, King's Attorney; s or neph John & Ann (Eyeres) Checkley?; m Hannah Wheelwright, 1678 Lydia (Scottow) Gibbs; King's Attorney 7 July 1692, Attorney General 28 Oct 1692

CHECKLEY, SAMUEL; Bost; 1653–1739; s William Checkley; m 1680 Mary Scottow; bond for John Alden

CHEEVER, EZEKIEL; SV; farmer & tailor; 1655–1731; s Ezekiel & Ellen (Lathrop) Cheever; m 1680 Abigail Lippingwell; half-bro Rev Samuel Cheever; recorder for 1 March exams, v Martha Cory, etc

CHEEVER, ISRAEL; Camb; bp 1662–; s Daniel & Esther Cheever; m 1690 Bridget Woodhead; Camb jailer

CHEEVER, REV SAMUEL; Mbl; min Mbl; HC 1659; 1639–1724; s Ezekiel & Mary Cheever; m 1671 Ruth Angier; half-bro Ezekiel Cheever; for Sarah Buckley, 1703 petitns

CHILDIN, JOANNA, also Chibbun; Salm; same as Susanna Shelden?; affl, accuser

CHINN, JOHN; Mbl; cooper; d bef 1712; s George & Elizabeth Chinn; m Rebecca Merritt; wit sum v Wilmot Redd

CHOAT, JOHN SR.; Ip; 1624–1695; m Ann –; witt summ v Rachel Clinton

CHOAT, JOHN; Ip; 1661–1733; s John & Ann Choat; m 1684 Elizabeth Graves, 1690 Elizabeth (–) Giddings, 1723 Sarah (–) Perkins, 1724 Prudence (–) Marshall; Ip const, Procter petitn

CHOAT, THOMAS; IP; s John & Ann Choat; m Mary –; Procter petitn

CHUBB, PRISCILLA; Tops?; c 1661–; v Abigail Hobbs

CHURCHILL, SARAH, also Churchwell; Salm; George Jacobs Sr's servant; 1667?–1731+; dau Arthur & Elinor (Bonython) Churchill; m 1709 Edward Andrews; affl, accused several, confess, recant

CLARK, DANIEL also Clarke; Tops; 1665–1749; s Daniel & Mary (Beane) Clark; m 1685 Damaris Dorman, Hannah (Young) Derby; wit sum v Sarah Cloyce, Mary Esty

CLARK, ELIZABETH; Newb; 1665–; dau Rev Peter & Jane (Batt) Toppan; m 1685 Nathaniel Clark Jr, James Wise; v Susanna Martin

CLARK, HUMPHRY; Tops; 1668– c 1693 or 1694; s Daniel & Mary (Beane) Clark; v Sarah Wildes

CLARK, MARY; Hav; dau John & Susanna Johns; m 1660 Ephraim Davis, Edward Clark; sis-in-law Elizabeth & Rebecca Johnson; arrested

CLARK, NATHANIEL JR; 1660–1690; s Nathaniel Sr & Elizabeth (Toppan) Clark; m Elizabeth Toppan; suspected Susanna Martin

CLARK, REV THOMAS, also Clarke; Chelm; min Chelm; HC 1670; 1653–1704; s Jonas & Elizabeth Clark; m Mary -, 1702 Elizabeth Whitney; cleared unnamed suspect

CLEEVES, WILLIAM; SV; fisherman, farmer; m Martha Edwards, 1683 Margaret Cory; s-in-law Giles Cory

CLINTON, LAWRENCE; Ip; c 1643–1704+; m 1665 Rachel Haffield, 1681 Mary Wooden bef 1681 divorce from Rachel, c 1691 Margaret (Painter) Morris

CLINTON, RACHEL, also Clenton, Klenton, Rachel Haffield or Haffeeld, Halfield, Hatfield; Ip; c 1629–c 1695; dau Richard & Martha (Mansfield) Haffield; m 1665 Lawrence Clinton, divorced 1681; arrested

CLOUGH, JOHN, also Cluff; Salis; 1649–1718; s John & Jane Clough; m 1674 Mercy Page; Mary Bradbury petitn

CLOUGH, MERCY; Salis; 1655–1719; dau John & Mary (Marsh) Page; m 1674 John Clough; Mary Bradbury petitn

CLOUGH, RUTH; Salis; 1670–; dau Cornelius & Sarah Conner; Mary Bradbury petitn

CLOUGH, THOMAS; Salis; 1651–1738+?; s John & Jane Clough; m 1687 Ruth Connor; Mary Bradbury petitn

CLOYCE, PETER; SV; 1640–1708; s John & Abigail Cloyce; m Hannah Littlefield, c 1680 Sarah (Towne) Bridges, c 1704 Susanna (Harrington) (Cutting) Beers; bro-in-law Rebecca Nurse & Mary Esty, uncle Mercy Lewis

CLOYCE, SARAH; SV; bp 1648- c 1703; dau William & Joanna (Blessing) Towne; m 1660 Edmund Bridges, c 1680 Peter Cloyce; sis Rebecca Nurse & Mary Esty, sis-in-law Faith Black & Mary Bridges

COBBETT, REV THOMAS; Ip; min Ip; Oxford; 1608–1685; m Elizabeth –

COGSWELL, JOHN SR; Ip; 1650–1724; s John & Elizabeth (Thompson) Cogswell; m 1684 Margaret Gifford; Procter petitn

COGSWELL, JOHN JR; Ip; 1665–1710; s William & Susanna (Hawkes) Cogswell; m bef 1693 Hannah Goodhue; Procter petitn

COGSWELL, JONATHAN; Ip; 1661–1717; s William & Susanna (Hawkes) Cogswell; m 1686 Elizabeth Wainwright; Procter petitn

COGSWELL, WILLIAM SR; Ip; 1619-c 1696; s John & Elizabeth (Thompson) Cogswell; gr- s John Cogswell Sr; m 1650 Susanna Hawkes; Procter petitn

COGSWELL, WILLIAM JR; Ip; 1659–1708; s William & Susanna (Hawkes) Cogswell; m 1685 Martha Emerson; s-in-law Rev John Emerson; Procter petitn

COIT, NATHANIEL, also Coyt; Glo; 1659–1743; s John & Mary (Stevens) Coit Jr; m 1687 Elizabeth Davis, 1702 Abigail (Sargent) Stevens, Hannah (Howard) Sargent; v Abigail Row, Margaret Prince, Rachel Vinson, Rebecca Dike & Esther Elwell

COLBY, SAMUEL; Ames; planter, innholder; s Anthony Colby; m Elizabeth Sargent; Mary Bradbury petitn

COLDUM, CLEMENT; Glo; 1622–1703; s Thomas Coldum; m Mary Pierce; v Elizabeth Hubbard

COLE, ABRAHAM; Salm; tailor; –1715; s Thomas & Ann Cole; m 1670 Sarah Davis; bro John Cole

COLE, JOHN; Lynn; 1640?-1703; cooper; s Thomas & Ann Cole; m1667 Mary Knight, c 1686 Sarah Aslebee; bro Abraham Cole; affl

COLE, SARAH; Lynn; 1658–1741; dau John & Rebecca (Ayer) Aslebee Sr; m –, John Cole; sis Rebecca Johnson; affl, accused sis-in-law Sarah Cole (Salm), accused, arrested

COLE, SARAH; Salm; 1651–1715+; dau George & Sarah Davis; m 1670 Abraham Cole; arrested

COLEMAN, SARAH; Row; 1670–1741; dau Tobias & Lydia (Jacks) Coleman; m 1696 Michael/Mighill Hopkins; affl, v Margaret Scott

COLLINS, BENJAMIN; Lynn; c 1650–1711; s Hnery & Ann (Riall) Collins; m 1673 Priscilla Kirtland, 1677 Elizabeth (Leach) Putnam; bro Hannah Ingersoll

COLLINS, HENRY, also Collings; Lynn; const; bp 1629–1722; s Henry & Ann (Riall) Collins; m c 1650 Mary Tolman; bro Hannah Ingersoll

COLSON, ELIZABETH, also Carlson; Read; 1676- c 1725; dau Adam & Mary (Dustin) Coleson; m c 1703 Adam Hart; fled, arrested

COLSON, MARY, also Carlson; Read; 1650–; dau Josiah & Lydia Dustin; m 1669 Adam Coleson, 1698 Cornelius Brown Jr; mo Elizabeth Coleson, sis Sarah Dustin; arrested

COMAN, RICHARD; Salm; tailor; c 1660–1716; m 1683 Martha (Gilbert) Rewe, 1693 Elizabeth (Dyne) McCallum; kinsman William Coman; v Bridget Bishop

COMAN, WILLIAM; Salm; m Mary Stacy, dau Thomas & Susanna Stacy; bro-in-law Richard & William Stacy, Elizabeth Woodwell, kinsman Richard Coman

CONANT, JOHN; Bev; const; 1652–1724; s Lot & Elizabeth (Walton) Conant; m 1678 Bethia Mansfield

CONANT, JOSHUA; Bev; sea captain; 1657–1700+; s Joshua & Sarah (Gardner) Conant; m 1670 Christian More, 1691 Sarah Newcomb

CONNER, ELIZABETH; dau John Purington; m 1691 John Conner; Mary Bradbury petitn

CONNER, JOHN; s Cornelius & Sarah Conner; m 1691 Elizabeth Purington; Mary Bradbury petitn

CONNER, SARAH; wid Cornelius Conner; mo Ruth Clough; Mary Bradbury petitn

COOK, – "widow Cook"; prob Judith Cook; Salm; –1689; dau – Birdsale; m 1639 Henry Cook

COOK, ELISHA; Bost; HC 1657; physician, politician; 1637–1715; s Richard & Elizabeth Cook; m 1668 Elizabeth Leverett

COOK, ELIZABETH; Salm; –1713; dau Anthony & Elizabeth Buxton; m 1664 Isaac Cook; Rebecca Nurse petitn

COOK, ISAAC; Salm; –1692; s Henry & Judith (Birdsale) Cook; m 1664 Elizabeth Buxton; Rebecca Nurse petitn

COOK, JOHN, also Cooke; Salm; 1647–1716; blacksmith; s Henry & Judith (Birdsale) Cook; m 1671 Mary Buxton; witch mark search committee

COOK, JOHN JR; Salm; 1674–1721; mariner; s Isaac & Elizabeth (Buxton) Cook; m 1701 Hannah Dean; v Bridget Bishop

COOKE, ELISHA; Bost; 1637–1715; HC 1657; physician, legis, land speculator; s Richard & Elizabeth Cooke; m c 1668 Elizabeth Leverett

CORE[Y], ELIZABETH see MOULTON

CORY, DELIVERANCE; Salm; 1658-; dau Giles & Margaret Cory; m 1683 Henry Crosby

CORY, GILES, also Corey, Coree, Koree, Kory, etc; Salm; 1621?–1692; m Margaret (–), 1664 Mary Brits/Britz, 1685 Martha (–) Rich; arrested, refused to co-operate, pressed to death 19 Sept 1692

CORY, MARTHA; Salm; –1692; m – Rich, 1685 Giles Cory; mo Thomas Rich; tried, condemn, hanged 22 Sept 1692

CORWIN, GEORGE, also Curwen, Curren; Salm; merch, Essex Co Sheriff; c 1666–1696; s John & Margaret (Winthrop) Corwin; m 1688 Susanna Gedney, bef 1693 Lydia Gedney; neph Jonathan Corwin; s-in-law Bartholomew Gedney

CORWIN, GEORGE; "Mr Curren's child" perh George Corwin; Salm; min Salm; HC 1701; 1683–1717; s Jonathan & Elizabeth (Sheaf) (Gibbs) Corwin; m 1711 Mehitable Parkman; affl?

CORWIN, JONATHAN; Salm; merch, magist, judge; 1640–1710; s George & Elizabeth (Herbert) (White) Corwin; m 1675 Elizabeth (Sheafe) Gibbs; O&T

COX, HANNAH; Bev; c 1662–; m Thomas Cox; v Dorcas Hoar

COX, MARY?; perh Mary (Mason) Cox; Salm; 1647–1712+; dau Elias and Jane (Conant) (Holgrave) Mason; m George Cox 1668: or their dau Mary Cox, b 1672; Bost jail, perh for witchcraft

COX, THOMAS; Bev; c 1664– by 1738; s John Cox; m Hannah –

COYT, NATHANIEL, see Coit, Nathaniel

CROSBY, ANTHONY; Row; physician; 1635–1673; s William & Anne (Wright) Crosby; m 1659 Prudence Wade; presum diagnosed James Carr as "behagged"

CROSBY, HENRY, also Crosley; Salm; m 1683 Deliverance Cory; v step-mo-in-law Martha Cory

CUMMINGS, ISAAC SR, also Comen, Commins, Commings; Ip; deacon; 1633–1721; s Isaac & Anne Cummings; m 1659 Mary Andrews; v Elizabeth How

CUMMINGS ISAAC JR; Ip; 1664–1746; s Isaac & Mary (Andrews) Cummings; m 1688 Alice Howlett, 1696 Frances Sherwen; v Elizabeth How

CUMMINGS, JOHN; Box; c 1630–1700; s Isaac & Anne Cummings; m Sarah Howlett

CUMMINGS, MARY; Ip; c 1640- bef 1712; dau Robert & Grace Andrews; m 1659 Isaac Cummings; sis John, Joseph & Thomas Andrews of Boxford, Elizabeth Symonds; v Elizabeth How

CURREN; "Mr Curren's child" see CORWIN, GEORGE

D

DALIBER, see DOLLIVER

DANE, DELIVERANCE; And; 1651–1735; dau Robert & Ann Haseltine; m 1672 Nathaniel Dane; dau-in-law Rev Francis Dane, sis-in-law Abigail Faulkner, aunt Dean Robinson; confess, recant

DANE, REV FRANCIS SR, also Dean; And; min And; King's College, Camb University 1633; bp 1615–1697; s John & Frances Dane; m bef 1645 Elizabeth Ingalls, 1677 Mary Thomas, 1690 Hannah (Chandler) Abbott; f Abigail Faulkner & Elizabeth Johnson Sr, f-in-law Deliverance Dane, uncle Martha Carrier & Elizabeth How, gr-f Abigail Jr & Dorothy Faulkner, Elizabeth Johnson Jr, Dean Robinson; named, Andover petitns

DANE, FRANCIS JR; And; 1656–1738; s Rev Francis & Elizabeth (Ingalls) Dane; m 1681 Hannah Poor; And petitn

DANE, HANNAH; And; c 1629–1711; dau William & Anna (Bayford) Chandler; m 1646 George Abbott Sr, m 1681 Rev Francis Dane; And petitn

DANE, NATHANIEL SR; And; c 1645–1725; s Rev Francis & Elizabeth (Ingalls) Dane; m 1672 Deliverance Haseltine

DANE, NATHANIEL JR; And; 1675–; s Nathaniel & Deliverance (Haseltine) Dane

DANFORTH, CAPT JONATHAN; Bill; bp 1628 or 1629–1712; s Nicholas & Elizabeth (Barber) Danforth; m 1654 Elizabeth Poulter, 1690 Esther (Champney) Converse; wit sum v Martha Carrier

DANFORTH, SAMUEL, "Mr Danforth"; Camb; 1696–1777; magist, legis, farmer, teacher, physician, alchemist; HC 1715; s Rev John & Elizabeth (Minot) Danforth; m 1726 Elizabeth Symmes

DANFORTH, THOMAS; Camb; land owner, politician; bp 1623–1699; s Nicholas & Elizabeth (Barber) Danforth; m 1644 Mary Withington; as Dept Gov observed exams Elizabeth Procter & Sarah Cloyce, condemned trials Oct 1692, SCJ

DANIEL, MARY; Row; c 1673–1727; m c 1710 Robert Greenough, 1719 Richard Style, 1725 Joshua Boynton; affl, v Margaret Scott

DARLING, JAMES; Salm; shoreman; c 1661-; s George & Katherine Darling; m 1683 Hannah (Lewis) Mains, 1712 Sarah (–) Procter; uncle Mercy Lewis; v Mary Esty

DAVIS, EPHRAIM; And; s Ephraim & Mary (Johnson) Davis; m Mary Ayers; And petitn

DAVIS, SARAH; Wen; wid John Davis; wit sum v Sarah Good

DAVIS, SUSANNA; Newb, "spinster"; petitn from Boston jail, charge unkn

DAY, PHEBE; Glo; 1653?-1723; dau John & Priscilla (Gould) Wilds; m 1679 Timothy Day; step-dau Sarah Wilds, sis Sarah Bishop & Ephraim Wilds, sis-in-law Mary Row; arrested

DAY, TIMOTHY; Glo; –1721+; s Anthony & Susanna (Machett) Day; m 1679 Phebe Wilds

DENNIS, LAWRENCE; Bev; –1700+; v Susannah Root

DENNISON, MAJ DANIEL; Ip; majist; 1612–1682; s William & Margaret (Chandler) (Monk) Denison; m 1632 Patience Dudley

DERICH, JOHN, also DeRich, Derrick, Dorich; Salm; servant; c 1674 or 1676 –; s Michael & Mary (Bassett) DeRich, neph Elizabeth Procter; m 1698 Martha Foster; affl, v Giles Cory, George Jacobs Sr, etc

DERICH, MARY, also DeRich, Derrick, Dorich; SV; c 1658-; dau William & Sarah? Bassett; m c 1676 Michael Derich; sis Elizabeth Procter, sis-in-law Sarah Bassett, mo John Derich; arrested

DERICH, MICHAEL; Salm; m 1676 Mary Bassett

DICER, ELIZABETH; Bost/Glo; –1704; dau – Austin; m 1664 William Dicer; arrested

DICER, WILLIAM; Bost; mariner; –1707; m 1664 Elizabeth Austin, 1706 Mary Blevet

DIKE, REBECCA; Glo; c 1640–1726; dau Samuel & Mary (Elwell) Dolliver; m 1667 Richard Dike; sis-in-law Ann Dolliver, aunt Mary Hill?; arrested

DIKE, RICHARD; Glo; c 1640–1729; m 1667 Rebecca Dolliver

DIX, JOHN; Read; c 1658–; s Ralph Dix?; m 1692 Lydia Burnap

DODD, JOANNA; Mbl; –1717; dau Thos Thomas & Sarah (Pitman) Dodd; affl

DODD, SARAH; Mbl; –1717; dau Thos & Joan Pitman; m Thomas Dodd; mo Joanna Dodd; v Wilmot Redd

DOGGET, WILLIAM; Mbl; d by 1695; m Rebecca Wormstall

DOLLIVER, ANN, also Anna, & Dalibar; Salm; c 1652–1739; dau Rev John & Sarah (Whitefield) Higginson; m 1682 William Dolliver; sis John Higginson Jr, sis-in-law Rebecca Dike; arrested

DOLLIVER, WILLIAM; Glo; 1656–1716?; s Samuel & Mary (Elwell) Dolliver; m 1682 Ann Higginson, deserted her

DOUNTON, WILLIAM, also Downton; Salm; carpenter & jail keeper; c 1630–1696; m Rebecca –, Joanna –

DOWING, MEHITABEL, also Downing; Ip; 1652-; dau Richard Braybrook & Alice Eliss; m 1669 John Dowing; step-dau Joan Penny; arrested

DOWNER, ROBERT; Sals; house carpenter; c 1650–1721; s Robert & Hannah (Vincent) Downer; m 1675 Sarah Eaton; v Susanna Martin

DOWNER, SARAH; Salis; 1654–1709+; dau John Eaton; m 1675 Robert Downer; Mary Bradbury petitn

DRAPER, JOSEPH; And; 1671-; s Adam & Rebecca (Braybrook) Draper; neph John Durant; confess

DUDLEY, JOSEPH; Rox; politician, landowner; HC 1665; 1645–1720; s Gov Thomas & Katherine (Dighton) (Hagborne) Dudley; m by 1670 Rebecca Tyng; half-bro-in-law Gov Simon Bradstreet; as Gov Mass signed 1711 Reversal of Attainder

DUNCAN, MARY; Glo; –1692; dau Daniel & Martha (Reade) (Symmonds) Epps; m Peter Duncan; mo Mary Sergeant, sis Daniel Epps of Salm.

DUNNELL, MICHAEL; Tops?; prob 1670–1761; s Michael & Mary Dunnell; guarded Sarah Good

DUNTON, JOHN; London; bookseller, publisher; 1659–1733; s Rev. John & Lydia (Carter) Dunton; m.1682 Elizabeth Annesley, 1697 Sarah Nichols

DURANT, JOHN, also Durrant; Bill; c 1645–1692; m 1670 Susanna Dutton, 1683 Ruth (–) Hooper; uncle Joseph Draper, kin to Sarah Wardwell; d in Camb jail 27 Oct 1692, presum arrested for witchcraft

DUSTIN, LYDIA, also Dastin, Dasting; Read; c 1613–1693; m Josiah Dustin; mo Sarah Dustin & Mary Coleson, gr-mo Elizabeth Coleson; arrested, tried, found not guilty, d Camb jail 10 March 1693 bef release

DUSTIN, SARAH; Read; 1653–; dau Josiah & Lydia Dustin; sis Mary Coleson, aunt Elizabeth Coleson; arrested, tried, not guilty

DUTCH, MARTHA; Salm; c 1656–; dau Robert & Mary Knight; m c 1672 Hezekiah Dutch, aft 1692 William Jewell; sis-in-law Esther Elwell; v Alice Parker

DUTCH, SUSANNA; Salm; bp 1650–1728+; dau Richard & Christian (Hunter) More; m c 1675 Samuel Dutch, c 1696 Richard Hutton, c 1714 John Knowlton; sis-in-law Joshua Conant, Elizabeth Elwell, kin to Hollingsworth; v Alice Parker, Ann Pudeator

E

EAMES, DANIEL, also Emms, Ames; Box; 1663–1694+; s Robert & Rebecca (Blake) Eames; m 1683 Lydia Wheeler; bro Hannah Foster, Tyler kin; arrested

EAMES, DOROTHY; Box; 1674–; dau Robert & Rebecca (Blake) Eames; m Samuel Swan

EAMES, JOHN; Box; 1670–; s Robert & Rebecca (Blake) Eames; m Priscilla Kimball

EAMES, REBECCA; Boxford; 1641–1721; dau George & Dorothy Blake; m c 1660 Robert Eames; mo Daniel Eames & Hannah Foster, gr-mo Rose Foster, Tyler kin; arrested, confess, recant

EAMES, ROBERT; Box; –1693; m c 1660 Rebecca Blake

EASTMAN, ANN; Salis; dau Edmund & Ann Pitts; m 1668 Samuel Joy, 1678 Benjamin Eastman; Mary Bradbury petitn

EASTMAN, BENJAMIN; Salis; tanner; 1653– c 1728; s Roger & Sarah Eastman; m 1678 Ann (Pitts) Joy, 1699 Naomi Flanders, 1719 Sarah (–) (Brown) Carter; Mary Bradbury petitn

EASTMAN, ELIZABETH; Salis; either c 1683–1734; dau Jonathan Hudson; m 1672 Nathaniel Eastman; or dau – Scriven; m 1680 Samuel Eastman; Mary Bradbury petitn

EASTMAN, JOHN; Salis; teacher, tailor, farmer; 1640–1720; s Roger & Sarah Eastman; m 1670 Mary Boynton; Mary Bradbury petitn

EASTMAN, MARY; Salis; 1648–1727; dau William & Elizabeth Boynton; m 1670 John Eastman; Mary Bradbury petitn

EASTMAN, NATHANIEL; Salis; cooper, farmer; 1643–1709; s Roger & Sarah Eastman; m 1672 Elizabeth Hudson; Mary Bradbury petitn

EASTMAN, ROGER; Salis; house carpenter, planter; c 1611–1694; m Sarah –; Mary Bradbury petitn

EASTMAN, SAMUEL; Salis; 1657–1725; s Roger & Sarah Eastman; m 1686 Elizabeth Scriven; Mary Bradbury petitn

EASTMAN, SARAH; Salis; c 1621–1697; dau – Smith; m Roger Eastman; Mary Bradbury petitn

EATON, DANIEL; Read; 1639–1708+; m by 1664 Mary Ingalls; neph Joshua Eaton; v Sarah Cole of Lynn

EATON, EPHRAIM; Salis; 1663–1723; s John & Martha (Rowlandson) Eaton; m 1689 Mary True; Mary Bradbury petitn

EATON, JOSEPH; Salis; 1661–; s John & Martha (Rowlandson) Eaton; m 1683 Mary French; const Salis; Mary Bradbury petitn

EATON, JOSHUA; Read; c 1653–1717; s Jonas & Grace Eaton; m 1678 Rebecca Kendall, 1690 Ruth –; uncle Daniel Eaton; v Mary Taylor

EATON, MARY; Salis; 1668–; dau Henry & Jane (Bradbury) True; m 1689 Ephraim Eaton; gr-dau Mary Bradbury; Mary Bradbury petitn

EATON, MARY SR; Lynn; dau Robert & Ann Ingalls; m by 1664 Daniel Eaton; v Sarah Cole (of Lynn)

EDWARDS, JOHN SR; Ip; c 1640–; m 1658 Mary Sams; v Rachel Clenton

EDWARDS, MARY; Ip; c 1640–; dau – Sams; m 1659 John Edwards Sr; v Rachel Clinton

ELATSON, JONATHAN; Bost; clerk SCJ; m – –, c 1695 Sarah? (Pemberton) (Purkis) Wessendank

ELLIOTT, ANDREW; Bev; –1704; m Mary Woodier, Mary Vivion; v Susannah Roots, jury 1692

ELLIOTT, DANIEL; SV?; c 1665–; m 1686 Hannah Cloyce; step-s-in-law Sarah Cloyce; v affl girls for Elizabeth Procter

ELLIOTT, EDMUND; Ames; c1629–1683; m–Blezdel?, Sarah Haddon; bro-in-law Henry Blezdel

ELWELL, ESTHER, also Hester; Glo; 1639–1721; dau Osman & Grace (Pratt) Dutch; m 1658 Samuel Elwell; arrested

ELWELL, SAMUEL; Glo; –1696; s Robert & Joan Elwell; m 1658 Esther Dutch

EMERSON, REV JOHN; Glo; min Glo; HC 1656; c 1625–1700; s Thomas & Elizabeth (Brewster) Emerson; m 1659 Ruth Symonds; uncle John Emerson Jr; wrote of Glo specters

EMERSON, JOHN JR; Chas; school teacher, preacher; HC 1675; 1654–1712; s Nathaniel & Sarah Emerson; m Sarah (Stowers) Carter; neph Rev John Emerson; v Mary Tyler to confess, petitn to delay Dorcas Hoar exec

EMERSON, JOSEPH; Hav; millwright, carpenter; 1669–1755; s Robert & Ann (Grant) Emerson; m 1690 Martha Toothaker, 1726 Hannah (Ross) Patten

EMERSON, MARTHA; Hav; 1668–1726; dau Roger & Mary (Allen) Toothaker; m 1690 Joseph Emerson; niece Martha Carrier, sis Allen & Mary Toothaker; practiced folk-magic, arrested, confess

EMONS, JOSEPH, also Emmons; Manch; cordwainer; 1651–1728+; s Thomas & Martha Emons; m 1694 Mary (Webster) Swain; accused

ENDICOTT, HANNAH; SV; bp 1663-; dau Nathaniel & Mary (Skelton) Felton; m c 1684 Samuel Endicott, 1697 Thorndike Procter; Procter petitn

ENDICOTT, SAMUEL; SV; mariner, yeoman; 1659–1692?; s Zerubabel & Mary (Smith) Endicott; bro Zerubabel Endicott Jr; Rebecca Nurse & Procter petitns, v Mary Bradbury

ENDICOTT, ZERUBABEL; Box; 1665–1706; s Zerubabel & Mary (Smith) Endicott; m 1689 Grace Symonds; bro Samuel Endicott; v Mary Bradbury

ENGLISH, MARY; Salm; c 1653–1698; dau William & Eleanor Hollingsworth; m 1675 Philip English; arrested, escaped

ENGLISH, PHILIP, also Phillipe L'Anglois; Salm; merch; bp 1651–1734; s Jean & – (DeCartaret?) L'Anglois; m 1675 Mary Hollingsworth, 1698 Sarah (–) Ingersoll; accused, fled, arrested, escaped

EPPS, CAPT DANIEL [SR]; Ip; magis 1692; c 1623–1693; m 1644 Elizabeth Symonds, 1685 Lucy (Woodbridge) Bradstreet; wit Arthur Abbott's statement re Elizabeth Procter

EPPS, DANIEL; Salm; school teacher, preacher; HC 1669; 1649–1722; s Daniel & Elizabeth (Symonds) Epps; m 1672 Martha Boardman, 1693 Hannah (–) Wainwright; petitn to delay Dorcas Hoar's exec

ESTY, BENJAMIN; Tops; bricklayer; 1669–1750; s Isaac & Mary (Towne) Esty; m 1702 Elizabeth Goodhue, 1716 Mary Holland

ESTY, ISAAC SR; Tops; c 1630-c 1712; s Jeffrey & Margaret (Pett/Pote) Esty; m Mary Towne

ESTY, ISAAC JR; Tops; c 1656–1714; s Isaac & Mary (Towne) Esty; m 1689 Abigail Kimball

ESTY, JACOB; Tops; 1675–1732; bricklayer; s Isaac & Mary (Towne) Esty; m 1710 Lydia Elliot

ESTY, JOHN; Tops; 1663–; m 1688 Mary Dorman, Hannah –

ESTY, JOSEPH; Tops; 1658–1739; s Isaac & Mary (Towne) Esty; m 1682 Jane Steward

ESTY, JOSHUA; Tops; 1678– d bef 1718; s Isaac & Mary (Towne) Esty; m Abigail –

ESTY, MARY, also Estey, Este, Estee, Easte, Easty; Tops; bp 1634–1692; dau William & Joanna (Blessing) Towne; m Isaac Esty Sr; sis Rebecca Nurse & Sarah Cloyce; arrested, jailed, released, arrested, tried, condemned, hanged 22 Sept 1692

EVANS, HANNAH; Salis; c 1665–1718; dau Nathaniel & Hannah (Fellows) Brown; m 1686 Thomas Evans; Mary Bradbury petitn

EVANS, THOMAS; Salis; c 1663- c 1718; s John Evans; m 1686 Hannah Brown; v George Burroughs

EVELETH, JOSEPH; Ip; bp 1643–1745; s Sylvester & Susan (Nuland) Eveleth; m 1668 Mary Bragg; jury 1692, Procter petitn

F

FAIRFIELD, WILLIAM; Wen; c 1662–1742; s Walter Fairfield; m c 1687 Esther Batchelder, 1723 Rebecca (Tarbox) Gott; const

FARNUM, JOHN; And; 1664–1729; s Ralph Sr & Elizabeth (Holt) Farnum; m 1684 Elizabeth Parker; s-in-law susp Mary (Ayers) Parker; wit sum v Martha Carrier, John Willard

FARNUM, RALPH SR, also Varnum; And; bp 1633–1692 or 93; s Ralph & Alice Farnum; m 1657 Elizabeth Holt; f Ralph Jr, John & Samuel Farnum; wit sum re Martha Carrier & John Willard

FARNUM, RALPH JR; And; 1662–1737; s Ralph Sr & Elizabeth (Holt) Farnum; m 1685 Sarah Sterling; wit sum v Martha Carrier & John Willard

FARNUM, SAMUEL; And; c 1665–1754, s Ralph Sr & Elizabeth (Holt) Farnum; m 1698 Hannah Holt; wit sum v Martha Carrier & John Willard

FARRAR, THOMAS; Lynn; 1617–1694; m Elizabeth –; arrested

FARRINGTON, EDWARD; And; farmer, cooper; 1662–1747; s John & Elizabeth (Knight) Farrington; step-s Mark Graves; m 1690 Martha Brown; confess, fled.

FAULKNER, ABIGAIL SR; And; 1652–1730; dau Rev Francis & Elizabeth (Ingalls) Dane; m 1675 Francis Faulkner; mo Abigail Jr & Dorothy Faulkner, sis Elizabeth Johnson Sr, sis-in-law Deliverance Dane, aunt Elizabeth Johnson Jr & Dean Robinson, cous Martha Carrier & Mary Toothaker; arrested, confess, tried, condemned, pregnancy postponed exec & so survived

FAULKNER, ABIGAIL JR; And; 1685–; dau Francis & Abigail (Dane) Faulkner; 1708 m? Thomas Lamson; sis Dorothy Faulkner; arrested, confess

FAULKNER, DOROTHY; And; 1680–; dau Francis & Abigail (Dane) Faulkner; m 1708 Samuel Nurse; sis Abigail Faulkner Jr; arrested, confess

FAULKNER, FRANCIS; And; c 1651–1732; m 1675 Abigail Dane

FELLOWS, ABIGAIL; Salis; dau Thomas & Eleanor Barnard; m 1681 Samuel Fellows Jr; Mary Bradbury petitn

FELLOWS, JOHN; Ip; 1668–1748; s Samuel Fellows; m 1692 Rachel Varney; Procter petitn

FELLOWS, SAMUEL SR, or Felloes; Salis; planter & weaver; c 1618–1698; m Ann –; f Hannah Brown; Mary Bradbury petitn

FELLOWS, SAMUEL JR; Salis; 1646– c 1730; s Samuel Sr & Ann Fellows; m 1681 Abigail Barnard; Mary Bradbury petitn

FELTON JOHN; Salm; c 1645–1718; s Nathaniel & Mary (Skelton) Felton Sr; m 1670 Mary Tompkins (d 1688); bro Nathaniel Felton Jr & Ruth Holton; Procter petitn, 1693 jury

FELTON, MARY; Salm; bp 1627–1701; dau Rev Samuel & Susanna (Travis) Skelton; m c 1646 Nathaniel Felton; Procter petitn

FELTON, NATHANIEL SR; Salm; c 1615–1705; s John & Ellen (Thrower?) Felton; m c 1646 Mary Skelton; f Nathaniel Jr & John Felton & Ruth (Felton) Holton; Procter petitn

FELTON, NATHANIEL JR; Salm; 1655–734; s Nathaniel & Mary (Skelton) Felton Sr; m Ann Horn; bro John Felton & Ruth Holton; Procter petitn

FERNEAUX, DAVID, also Fernax, Furnax; c 1669-; perh David Furness/Furnace; Mbl; m 1692 Sarah (Fluent) Brimblecom; v Sarah Procter

FISK, THOMAS, also Fiske; Wen; 1632–1707; m c 1649 Joanna White, 1695 Martha (Fiske) Fitch; foreman Rebecca Nurse jury 1692

FITCH, REV JABEZ; Ip; min Ip; HC 1693; 1672–1746; s Rev James & Priscilla (Mason) Fitch; m 1704 Elizabeth Appleton; 1703 petitn

FITCH, JOHN; Glo; c 1636–1715; m 1667 Mary (Stevens) Coit; v Abigail Row, Rebecca Dike & Esther Elwell

FITCH, MARY; Glo; –1692; dau William & Phillipa Stevens; m 1652 John Coit Jr, 1667 John Fitch; sis James Stevens, mo Nathaniel Coit; d "bewitched" by Abigail Row, Rebecca Dike & Esther Elwell 7 Nov 1692

FITCH, THOMAS; Bost; merch, legis; 1669–1736; s Thomas & Martha (Fiske) Fitch; m 1694 Abiel Danforth

FITTS, RICHARD; Ip; 1672–1745; s Abraham Fitts; m 1695 Sarah Thorne; wit sum v Rachel Clinton

FLETCHER, BENJAMIN; NY; Gov NY; 1640?–1703; s William & Abigail (Vincent) Fletcher; m Elizabeth Hodson; received fugitives

FLETCHER, ISRAEL; Sals; –1700; dau John & Mary Pike; m c 1644 Henry True Sr, c 1660 Joseph Fletcher; sis Robert Pike, mo Henry & Joseph True; Mary Bradbury petitn

FLETCHER, JOSEPH; Sals; c 1636–1700; m c 1660 Israel (Pike) True; Mary Bradbury petitn

FLINT, JOSEPH; SV; 1662–1710; s Thomas & Ann Flint; m 1685 Abigail Hayward; bro Thomas Flint; v George Jacobs Sr & Margaret Jacobs

FLINT, THOMAS; SV; farmer & carpenter; 1645–1721; s Thomas & Ann Flint; m1666 Hannah Moulton, 1674 Mary Dounton; bro Joseph Flint, s-in-law William Dounton; v Sarah Buckley & John Willard, on Daniel Wilkins coroner's jury, 1693 grand jury

FLOOD, JOHN, also Floyd; Rumney Marsh; c 1637–1701; m Sarah Doolittle; accused

FOSDICK, ELIZABETH; Mald/Chas; 1656–1716; dau – Thomas; m 1677 Robert Lisley (divorced 1679), m 1679 John Betts, m bet 1685–1687 John Fosdick; arrested

FOSSE, ELIZABETH; Ip; dau – Rayner; m 1685 Thomas Fosse; for Mary Esty

FOSSE, THOMAS, also Fossy, ffaccy; Ip; prison keeper; –1700; m 1685 Elizabeth Rayner; for Mary Esty

FOSTER, ABRAHAM; Ip; c 1622–1711; s Renald & Judith Foster; m Lydia Burbank;

FOSTER, ABRAHAM; And; 1648–1723; s Andrew Sr & Ann Foster; m 1681 Hester Foster; bro Andrew Foster; paid jailer for mother's body

FOSTER, ANDREW; And; c 1637–; s Andrew & Ann Foster; m 1662 Mary Russe; bro Abraham Foster; v Martha Carrier & Toothakers

FOSTER, ANN; And; –1692; dau – Alcock?; m c 1639 Andrew Foster Sr; mo & gr mo Mary Lacey Sr & Jr; arrested, confess, tried, condemned, ill, d in prison Dec 1692

FOSTER, EPHRAIM; And; blacksmith; 1657–; s Abraham & Lydia (Burbank) Foster; m c 1668 Hannah Eames, 1732 Mary (?) West; f Rose Foster; s-in-law Rebecca Eames; const 1692, v John Jackson Sr & Jr

FOSTER, HANNAH; And; 1661– by 1732; dau Robert & Rebecca (Blake) Eames; m c 1678 Ephraim Foster; mo Rose Foster, sis Daniel Eames; affl

FOSTER, ISAAC; Ip; bp 1656– c 1741; s Renald & Elizabeth (Dane) Foster; m Abigail; uncle Jacob Foster; Procter petitn

FOSTER, JACOB; Tops; 1662–; s Isaac & Mary (Jackson) Foster; m 1688 Sarah Wood, 1700 Mary Edwards; neph Elizabeth How & Isaac Foster; v Elizabeth How

FOSTER, JOHN; Bost; merch; 1648–c 1711; m c 1687 Lydia Turell, 1689 Abigail (Hawkins) (Moore) Kellond; 1692 Charter Council, O&T

FOSTER, LYDIA; Ip; dau Caleb & Martha Burbank; m Abraham Foster of Ip; mo Ephraim Foster; gr-mo Rose Foster; v Elizabeth How

FOSTER, REGINALD JR; And; c 1628–c 1707; s Reginald & Judith Foster; m Elizabeth Dane

FOSTER, ROSE; And; 1679–1693; dau Ephraim & Hannah (Eames) Foster; gr dau Rebecca Eames, niece Daniel Eames, gr-niece Elizabeth How & John Jackson; affl, accused many

FOWLE, REBECCA; Chas; bp 1674–; dau Rev George & Hannah (Fisher) Burroughs; m 1698 Isaac Fowle, 1716 Ebenezer Tolman; sis Charles, George Jr., Jeremiah, Sarah & Mary Burroughs, Hannah Fox, Elizabeth Thomas

FOWLER, JOSEPH; Wen; brick maker; c 1647–1718; s Joseph & Martha (Kimball) Fowler; m Elizabeth Hutton; v Sarah Bibber

FOX, HANNAH; 1680–; dau Rev George & Hannah (Fisher) Burrough; m 1705 Jabez Fox Jr; sis Charles, George Jr, Jeremiah, Sarah & Mary Burroughs, Rebecca Fowle, Elizabeth Thomas

FOX, JABEZ; Wob; min Wob; HC 1665; bp 1647–1703; s Thomas & Rebecca Fox; m Judith Reyner; step-bro Rebecca Jacobs

FOX, REBECCA; Camb; –1698; m Thomas Andrews, Nicholas Wyeth, 1685 Thomas Fox; mo Thomas Andrews & Rebecca Jacobs, step-mo Rev Jabez Fox; petitn for dau Rebecca Jacobs

FOXCROFT, FRANCIS SR; Bost; merch; c 1657–1727; s Daniel? Foxcroft; m 1682 Elizabeth Danforth

FRAIL, SAMUEL; Salm; wheelwright & yeoman; m 1678 Mary Carrell, 1684 Ann Upton; Procter petitn

FREEZE, JAMES; Salis; s James? Freeze; m Elizabeth –; suspects Susanna Martin

FRENCH, ABIGAIL; Sals; 1675–; dau John Jr & Mary (Noyse) French; m 1699 Henry True Jr (gr-s Mary Bradbury); Mary Bradbury petitn

FRENCH, ESTHER; Salis; m Samuel French; Mary Bradbury petitn

FRENCH, JOHN SR; Sals; tailor; s Joseph & Susanna French; m Mary Noyse; f Abigail French; Mary Bradbury petitn

FRENCH, JOSEPH; Sals; tailor; –1710; m Susanna; f John French Sr; Mary Bradbury petitn

FRENCH, MARY; Sals; dau Nicholas & Mary (Cutting) Noyse; m John French Sr; m Abigail French, sis Rev Nicholas Noyse; Mary Bradbury petitn

FRENCH, SAMUEL; Salis; –1692; s Edward & Ann French; m 1669 Abigail Brown, c 1681 Esther –; Mary Bradbury petitn

FROST, NICHOLAS; Piscataqua; d bef 1670; s Maj Charles & Mary (Bowles) Frost; accused

FRYE, EUNICE, also Fry, Frie; And; 1641–1708; dau Luke & Mary Potter; m 1660 John Fry; sis-in-law James Fry; arested, confess, recant, tried, not guilty

FRYE, JAMES, also Fry; And; c 1652- c 1734; s John & Ann Fry; m 1680 Lydia Osgood; employed Andrew Carrier, bond for sis-in-law Eunice Fry

FRYE, JOHN; And; –1696; deacon; s John & Ann Fry; m 1660 Eunice Potter

FRYE, SAMUEL; And; selectman; c 1649–1725; s John & Ann Fry; m 1671 Mary Aslebee

FULLER, ELIZABETH; Ip?; c 1658?–; v John Lee

FULLER, JAMES JR; Ip; 1673– c 1753; s James Sr & Mary (Ring) Fuller; m Phebe; bro Mary Fuller, cous Elizabeth Fuller

FULLER, JOSEPH; Ip; carpenter; 1658–1731; s John & Elizabeth (Emerson) Fuller; m 1685 Mary Wood or Haywoord; f Elizabeth Fuller; const 1692

FULLER, MARY SR; Ip; c 1641–1732; dau – Ring; m 1672 James Fuller Sr; mo Mary Jr & James Jr; v Rachel Clinton

FULLER, MARY JR; Ip; 1675–; dau James Sr & Mary (Ring) Fuller; affl, wit sum v Rachel Clinton

FULLER, NATHANIEL; Ip; –1719; s John & Elizabeth (Emerson) (Perrin) Fuller; m c 1708 Mary Jackson; wit sum v Rachel Clinton

FULLER, SAMUEL; Ip; 1661–1689 "suddenly"; s Thomas & Hannah Fuller

FULLER, THOMAS SR; SV; c 1618–1698; m Hannah; Daniel Wilkins' coroner's jury

FULLER, LIEUT THOMAS; SV; farmer, plow right; c 1644–; s Thomas & Elizabeth (Tidd) Fuller; m 1669 Ruth Richardson; Daniel Wilkins' coroner's jury

G

GAGE, MARY; Bev; c 1644–; dau – Grover; m 1666 Anthony Wood, m – Gage; mo Josiah Wood; v Dorcas Hoar

GAGE, SARAH; Bev; dau – –; m 1677? Thomas Gage; v Sarah Good

GAGE, THOMAS, also Gadge; Bev; blacksmith; 1656–1707; s Thomas Sr & Hannah (Knight) Gage; m 1677? Sarah –, 1695 Elizabeth (Northend) (Hobson) Mighill; v Roger Toothaker, Sarah Good

GALE, AMBROSE; Mbl; fisherman, planter, cooper, merch; –1708; m Deborah –; v Wilmot Redd

GALE, BENJAMIN; Mbl; cordwainer; c 1664–1714; s Ambrose & Deborah Gale; m Lydia –, aft 1699, Deliverance; bro Charity Pitman; wit sum v Wilmot Redd but too ill

GALE, – "Goody Gale"; Bev; prob Sarah Gale; dau Capt William & Anna Dixey; m by 1666 Edmund Gale

GARDNER, THOMAS JR; Salm; mariner; 1671–1696; s Thomas & Mary (Porter) Gardner; m 1695 Mary Higginson

GASKELL, EDWARD; Salm; 1667–; s Samuel & Provided (Southwick) Gaskell; m 1693 Hannah Endicott; Procter petitn

GASKELL, PROVIDED; also Gaskin, Gascoin; Salm; 1641–1725+; dau Laurence & Cassandra Southwick; m 1662 Samuel Gaskell; Procter petitn

GASKELL, SAMUEL; Salm; c 1639– c 1725; s Edward & Sarah Gaskell; m 1662 Provided Southwick; Procter petitn

GEDNEY, BARTHOLOMEW, also Gidney; Salm; bp 1640–1698; ship carpenter, justice, legis, milit leader, local magis; s John & Mary? Gedney; m 1662 Hannah Clarke, 1697 Anne (–) Stewart; O&T

GEDNEY, MARY; Salm; tavern keeper; 1648–1716; dau Edmund & Martha (Denham) Patteshal; m 1678 Eleazer Gedney (wid); sis-in-law Bartholomew Gedney & Susannah Gedney

GEDNEY, SUSANNA; Salm; bp 1643–1728; dau William & Katherine Clark; m 1659 John Gedney, Deliverance Parkman; owned Ship Tavern

GERRISH, BENJAMIN; Salm; merch; 1652–1713; s Capt William & Joanna (Goodale) (Oliver) Gerrish; m 1676 Hannah Ruck, 1685 Ann Paine, 1696 Elizabeth Turner; bro Rev Joseph Gerrish

GERRISH, REV JOSEPH; Wen; min Wen; HC 1669; 1650–1720; s Capt William & Joanna (Goodale) (Oliver) Gerrish; m Ann Waldron; brother Benjamin Gerrish, f-in-law Rev Joseph Green; signed Increase Mather's *Cases Conscience*, recorded Mary Herrick's recant, 1703 petitn

GETCHELL, ELIZABETH; Salis; 1662–1735; dau Robert & Joanna (Osgood) Jones; m 1679 Samuel Getchell; Mary Bradbury petitn

GIBSON, SAMUEL; Camb; s John & Rebecca Gibson; m 1668 Sarah Pemberton, 1679 Elizabeth (Remington) Stedman; deputy

GIDDING, SAMUEL; Ip; s George & Jane (Lawrence) Gidding; m 1671 Hannah Martin, Elizabeth –; Procter petitn

GIDNEY, – "widow Gidney," see GEDNEY, MARY

GILES, JOHN; Bev; 1645–; s Edward & Bridget (–) (Very) Giles; m? – –; 1679 Elizabeth (Galley) Trask; v Dorcas Hoar

GILL, SAMUEL; m 1678 Sarah Worth; Mary Bradbury petitn

GILL, SARAH; 1656–; dau Lionel & Susanna (Whipple) Worth; m 1678 Samuel Gill; Mary Bradbury petitn

GILL, SARAH; 1660–1749; dau Isaac & Mary (Towne) Esty; m Moses Gill

GILL, WILLIAM; Salm; weaver; m 1678 Hannah Meachum; male witch mark search committee

GLOVER, –; Bost; –1688; "widow Glover"; hanged as witch 16 November 1688.

GOLDTHWAIT, EZEKIEL; 1674–1761; s Samuel & Elizabeth (Cheever) Goldthwait; m 1696 Ellen Boyce

GOLTHITE, GOODY; Salm; wit sum v Giles Cory; prob Elizabeth (Cheever) Goldthwait; –1722+; m Samuel Goldthwait

GOOD, DOROTHY; SV; c 1687–1712+; dau William & Sarah (Soulart) (Poor) Good; confess, jailed

GOOD, SARAH; SV; c 1654–1692; dau John & Elizabeth Solart; m Daniel Poole, William Good, arrested, tried, condemned, hanged 19 July 1692

GOOD, WILLIAM; SV; weaver, laborer; m c 1683 Sarah (Soulart) Poor, 1693 Elizabeth Drinker?; f Dorothy Good; v Sarah Good

GOODALE, –, also Goodall; SV; "an ancient woman named Goodall"; affl; perh Elizabeth Goodale; bp 1643–1715+; dau Edward & Mary Beacham; m 1666 Zachariah Goodale; the older Margaret (Lazenby), wid Robert Goodale had d 1689

GOODALE, JACOB; SV; bp 1641–1676; s Robert & Katherine Goodale; "almost a natural fool"

GOODHUE, WILLIAM JR; Ip; 1645–1722; s William & Margery (Watson) Goodhue; m 1666 Hannah Dane; Procter petitn

GOULD, BENJAMIN; 1669–; s Thomas & Elizabeth Gould; v Corys, Procters

GOULD, JOHN; Tops; 1635–1710; s Zaccheus & Phebe Gould; m 1660 Sarah Baker; v Sarah Wilds

GOULD, SAMUEL; 1671–; s Thomas & Elizabeth Gould; v Bridget Bishop

GOULD, THOMAS SR, also Gold; Salm; 1630–1690; m Elizabeth –

GOULD, THOMAS JR; Salm; 1668–1732; s Thomas & Elizabeth Gould; m Abigail; v Giles Cory

GOWING, MARTHA; Salm; 1666–1712+; dau John & Elizabeth (Thorndike) Procter; m bef 1687 Nathaniel Gowing

GRAVES, –; "Goodwife Graves"; Ip; prob Grace Graves; 1635–; dau William & Anne Beamsley; m c 1656 Samuel Graves; mo-in-law John Choat; wit sum v Rachel Clinton

GRAVES, ELIZABETH; And; dau William & Elizabeth (–) (Ballard) Knight; m 1662 John Farrington, 1667, Mark Graves; mo Edward Farrington; wit sum v Martha Carrier & John Willard

GRAVES MARK; And; c 1620–; m c 1648 Amy –, 1667 Elizabeth (Knight) Farrington; wit sum v Martha Carrier & John Willard

GRAVES, JOANNA; Ip; dau – Pearce; m Samuel Graves; wit sum v Rachel Clinton

GRAVES, SAMUEL; Ip; hatter, feltmaker; 1658–1732; s Samuel & Grace (Beamley) Graves; m Joanna Pearce, Elizabeth –; const; wf witt v Rachel Clinton

GRAY, ROBERT; And; c 1634–1718; s Thomas Gray of Mbl?; m 1669 Hannah Holt

GREELEY, –; Salis; wife of Andrew Greeley; either Mary Greeley; –1703; dau Joseph & Hannah Moyce; m Andrew Greeley Sr; or Sarah Greeley; dau – Brown; m 1673 Andrew Greeley Jr; Mary Bradbury petitn

GREELEY, ANDREW; Salis; either Andrew Sr; shoemaker; c 1620–1697; m Mary Moyce; or their s Andrew Jr; 1646–; m 1673 Sarah Brown; Mary Bradbury petitn

GREELEY, PHILLIP; Salis; 1644–1718; s Andrew & Hannah (Moyce) Greeley Sr; m 1670 Sarah Isley; bro Andrew Greeley Jr, in-law Rachel Clinton; Mary Bradbury petitn

GREELY, SARAH; Salis; dau – Isley; m 1670 Phillip Greeley; Mary Bradbury petitn

GREEN, JOANNA; Bev?; dau William & Dorcas (Galley) Hoar; wid – Green

GREEN, REV JOSEPH; HC 1695; 1675–1715; s John & Ruth (Henderson?) Green; m 1699 Elizabeth Gerrish; min SV 1697–1715

GREEN, MARY; Hav; dau Henry & Mary Green; m 1678 Peter Green; sis-in-law John Shepard, Elizabeth Button kin; arrested, escaped twice, caught twice

GREENOUGH, ROBERT; Row; –1718; m Martha Epps?, 1688 Sarah (–) Mighill, c 1710 Mary Daniel; const

GREENSLIT, JAMES, also Greenslet, Greenslade, Greenslip etc; Salm; s Thomas & Ann Greenslit (ie Ann Pudeator); wit sum

GREENSLIT, JOHN; Salm; mariner, glover; d by 1693; s Thomas & Ann Greenslit (ie Ann Pudeator)

GREENSLIT, THOMAS; Salm; c 1652–; mariner; s Thomas & Ann Greenslit (ie Ann Pudeator); v George Burroughs

GREGORY, JONAS; Ip; 1641–; m 1670 Hannah Dow, 1672 Elizabeth Healy; wit sum v Rachel Clinton

GRIGGS, –; "Goody Griggs," Rachel Griggs; SV; 1628/9?–1718; dau – & Elizabeth (–) Hubbard; m c 1657 William Griggs; aunt Elizabeth Hubbard; named

GRIGGS, DR WILLIAM; SV; physician; d by 1698 "aged"; m – –, c 1657 Rachel Hubbard; uncle Elizabeth Hubbard; prob diagnosed "evil hand"

H

HACKETT, SARAH; Sals or Ames; perh 1647–1717, if dau Thomas & Eleanor Barnard, m Capt William Hackett: or their dau Sarah; (1668–1712+); Mary Bradbury petitn

HADLEY, DEBORAH; Row; c 1623–; m Thomas Skillings, 1668 George Hadley; for Elizabeth How

HAFFIELD, RACHEL see CLINTON

HAGGETT, MOSES; And; s Henry & Ann Haggett; m 1671 Joanna Johnson; bro Hannah Welch, bro-in-law Rebecca Johnson

HALE, REV JOHN; Bev: min Bev; HC 1657; 1636–1700; s Robert & Joanna Hale; m 1664 Rebecca Byley, 1684 Sarah Noyes, 1698 Elizabeth (Somerby) Clark; v Sarah Bishop & Dorcas Hoar, changed views, wrote *A Modest Enquiry Into the Nature Witchcraft*

HALE, MARY; Salis; 1678–1753; d Caleb & Judith (Bradbury) Moody; m 1699 Joseph Hale; Mary Bradbury petitn

HALE, REBECCA; Bev; 1666–1681; dau Rev John & Rebecca (Byley) Hale

HALE, SARAH; Bev; 1656–1695; dau Rev James & Sarah (Brown) Noyes; m 1685 Rev John Hale; cous Rev Nicholas Noyes; named

HALL, – "Goody Hall"; Groton; prob Sarah –, m by 1680 Christopher Hall; wit sum v John Willard

HARDY, THOMAS; Great Island, New Hampshire; –1700+; accused

HARRIS, EBENEZER; Ip; s Thomas & Martha (Lake) Harris; m 1690 Rebecca Clark; deputy

HART, ELIZABETH; Lynn; 1622–c 1700; dau Adam & Anne (Brown) (Hutchinson) Hawkes; m c 1650 Isaac Hart; kin to Sarah Wardwell & John Procter; arrested

HART, ISAAC; Lynn; c1614–1699; m c 1650 Elizabeth Hutchinson

HART, THOMAS; Lynn; bricklayer; c 1658–1731; s Isaac & Elizabeth Hart; petitn for mo Elizabeth Hart

HARWOOD, JOHN SR, also Harod, Herod, Hayward, Haywood, etc; Salm; bp 1632–1690; s Henry & Elizabeth? Harwood; m Emme –

HATFIELD, RACHEL see CLINTON

HATHORNE, JOHN; Salm; merch, magis; 1641–1717; s William & Ann Hathorne; m 1675 Ruth Gardner; O&T

HAWKES, MARGARET; Salm, "late of Barbadoes"; owned Candy; arrested

HAWKES, SARAH; And; 1671–1716; dau Adam & Sarah (Hooper) Hawkes; m 1693 Francis Johnson; step-dau Samuel Wardwell, half-sis Mercy Wardwell; accused, confess, tried, not guilty

HAWKINS, GAMALIEL; Mbl; ship master; d by 1692

HAYNES, THOMAS, also Haines; SV; maltster; bp 1651–; s James Haynes; m 1676 Sarah Ray; v William Hobbs, Daniel Wilkins' coroner's jury

HEASON, MARY; prob HAZEN; Box; dau Thomas? Howlett; m 1684 Thomas Hazen; wit sum v Elizabeth How

HEASON, THOMAS, prob HAZEN; Box; 1657–1725; s Edward & Hannah (Grant) Hazen; m 1684 Mary Howlett; wit sum v Elizabeth How

HEATH, BARTHOLOMEW; Hav; s Bartholomew & Hannah (Moyce) Heath; m 1691 Mary Bradley; deputy

HEATH, JOSIAH; Hav; 1674–1721; s Bartholomew Heath Sr?; m Mary Davison, Hannah Starling; deputy

HENLEY, ELIAS JR; Mbl; s Elias & Sarah Henley; m 1657 Sarah Thompson; summ as wit re Wilmot Redd, at sea

HERRICK, ELIZABETH; Bev; dau – Woodbury; m Joseph Herrick Jr; wit sum v Sarah Bishop

HERRICK, GEORGE; Salm; upholsterer; c 1658–1695; m Martha –; Marshall Essex Co 1692, under sheriff aft May, v Sarah Buckley & John Willard

HERRICK, HENRY; Bev; 1671–1747; s Zachariah & Mary (Dodge) Herrick; m 1694 Susannah Beadle; f Lydia Porter, s-in-law Samuel Beadle; v Sarah Good, jury 1692

HERRICK, JOHN; Bev; bp1650–1680; s Henry & Edith (Laskin) Herrick; m 1674 Mary Reddington; f Mary Herrick; s-in-law Mary (Gould) Reddinton; bro Zachariah Herrick; v Sarah Wilds

HERRICK, JOSEPH SR; SV; 1645–1718; s Henry & Edith (Laskin) Herrick; m 1667 Sarah Leach, c 1678 Mary Endicott, 1707 Mary (–) March; const 1692, v Sarah Good, Rebecca Nurse petitn, Daniel Wilkins' coroner's jury

HERRICK, JOSEPH JR; Bev; 1667–1749; s Joseph & Sarah (Leach) Herrick; m Elizabeth Woodbury; wit sum v Sarah Bishop

HERRICK, MARY; SV; 1668–; dau Zerubabel & Mary (Smith) Endicott; m c 1678 Joseph Herrick Sr; sis Samuel & Zerubabel Endicott; v Sarah Good

HERRICK, MARY; Wen; 1677–; dau John & Mary (Reddington) Herrick; affl

HERRICK, ZACHARIAH; Bev; house carpenter; bp 1636–1695; s Henry & Edith (Laskin); m 1653 Mary Dodge; f Henry Herrick, gr-f John Batchelor; v Sarah Good

HERRIMAN, MATTHEW, also Hereman; Hav; 1652–; s Leonard & Margaret Herriman; m 1673 Elizabeth Swan, 1700 Martha Page; bro-in-law Timothy Swan; v Martha Emerson

HEWS, BETTY, see HUGHES

HIGGINSON, REV JOHN; Salm; min Salm; 1616–1708; s Rev Francis & Anne (Herbet) Higginson; m by 1646 Sarah Whitfield, m aft 1676 Mary (Blakeman) Atwater; f Ann Dolliver; for Sarah Buckley, wrote introduction to John Hale's *Modest Enquiry*

HIGGINSON, JOHN JR; Salm; merch, legis, magist; 1646–1719; s Rev John & Sarah (Whitfield) Higginson; m 1672 Sarah Savage; bro Ann Dolliver

HIGGINSON, MARY; Salm; d 1709; dau Rev Adam & Jane Blakeman; m 1651 Joshua Atwater, m c 1676 Rev John Higginson; step-mo John Higginson Jr & Anne Dolliver; Rebecca Nurse requested her for search committee

HILL, ELIZABETH; Salm; dau – Dike?; m 1651 Zebulon Hill; female witch mark search committee

HILL, JOHN; Bev; cooper; m 1657 Abigail Woodbury; bro Zebulon Hill & Eleanor Babson, uncle Mary Hill

HILL, MARY; Salm; bp 1667; dau Zebulon & Elizabeth Hill; niece Eleanor Babson; m – Ashby?; affl

HILL, ZEBULON; Salm; d winter 1699/1700; m 1651 Elizabeth Dike?; bro John Hill & Eleanor Babson; male witch mark search committee, v Joan Penny

HINDERSON, –, "Goody Hinderson"; Salm; prob Ellen (Booth) (Bully) Hinderson/Henderson; 1634–1701+; dau Rev Robert & Deborah? Booth; m 1652 Nicholas Bully, 1664 John Henderson

HINE, WILLIAM; Salm or SV; male witch mark search committee; perh William Haines, m Sarah Ingersoll

HOAR, ABIGAIL; Bev?; restit, gr-dau Dorcas Hoar

HOAR, DORCAS, also Hoare; Bev; c 1635–c 1711?; dau John & Florence Galley; m c 1655 William Hoar; sis-in-law John Giles; arrested, tried, condemned, confess, temporarily reprieved & so lived

HOAR, ELIZABETH; Salm; dau William & Dorcas (Galley) Hoar; m 1682 Christopher Read

HOAR, JOANNA; Bev; dau William & Dorcas (Galley) Hoar; m – Green

HOBBS, ABIGAIL Tops; 1677–; dau William & Avis Hobbs; confess, v George Burroughs, etc

HOBBS, DELIVRANCE; Tops; m William Hobbs; step-mo Abigail Hobbs; affl, arrested, confess, accused several

HOBBS, JAMES; Ann Foster v Martha Carrier; his child said to be afflicted

HOBBS, WILLIAM; Tops; 1642?–; m. Avis –, Deliverance –; arrested

HOBBS, WILLIAM JR.; Tops; s William Hobbs; bro Abigail Hobbs

HOLBROOK, ABIAH JR; Bost; school master; 1718–1769; s Abiah & Mary (Needham) Holbrook; m 1746 Rebecca (Burroughs) Jarvis (gr-dau Rev George Burroughs)

HOLLARD, GEORGE; Bost; mariner; d c 1714; m Sarah; hid Philip English

HOLT, OLIVER; And; 1671–1747; s Henry & Sarah (Ballard) Holt; m 1698 Hannah Russell, 1716 Mary Hewes; And petitn

HOLT, SAMUEL SR; And; s Nicholas & Elizabeth (Short) Holt; m 1669 Sarah Allen; wit sum v sis-in-law Martha Carrier, And petitn

HOLTON, BENJAMIN, also Holten, Houlton, Houghton; SV; 1658–1689; s Joseph & Sarah (Ingersoll) (Haynes) Holton m Sarah –

HOLTON, JAMES; SV; 1665–1722; s Joseph & Sarah (Ingersoll) (Haynes) Holton; m Ruth Felton, 1706 Mary Linsey; Procter petitn, affl girls said Procters affl him

HOLTON, JOSEPH SR; SV; c 1621–1704; m Sarah (Ingersoll) Haynes; bro-in-law Nathaniel Ingersoll; Rebecca Nurse petitn, v Martha Carrier, etc

HOLTON, JOSEPH JR; SV; 1652–1732; s Joseph & Sarah (Ingersoll) (Haynes) Holton; m Hannah Eborne; Rebecca Nurse petitn

HOLTON, JOHN; SV; cooper & weaver; 1677–1721; s Joseph & Sarah (Ingersoll) (Haynes) Holton; m 1688 Mary Star; v Mercy Lewis for Elizabeth Procter

HOLTON, JOSEPH JR; 1652–1732; s Joseph & Sarah (Ingersoll) (Haynes) Holton; m Hannah Eborne; Rebecca Nurse petitn

HOLTON, RUTH; SV; bp 1648–; dau Nathaniel & Mary (Skelton) Felton; m James Holton; sis Nathaniel Jr & John Felton, sis-in-law Samuel Endicott; Procter petitn

HOLTON, SARAH; Salm; –1719; dau Richard & Ann/Agnes (Langley) Ingersoll; m 1644 William Haines, Joseph Holton Sr; mo Benjamin, Joseph Jr & James Holton, sis Nathaniel Ingersoll; Rebecca Nurse petitn

HOLTON, SARAH; SV; m Benjamin Holton, 1706 Benjamin Putnam; v Rebecca Nurse

HOOKE, ELIZABETH; Salis; –1717; dau – Dyer; m William Hooke; Mary Bradbury petitn

HOOKE, WILLIAM; Salis; merch; –1721; m 1717 Elizabeth Dyer; Mary Bradbury petitn

HOOPER, EDWARD; Bev; fisherman; c 1677– by 1708; s William & Elizabeth Hooper; m Elizabeth Haskins; v Dorcas Hoar

HOOPER, JOHN; Read; carpenter; 1670–1709; s William Hooper; m 1679 Sarah Harden; bro Sarah Wardwell, Thomas & William Hooper; And petitn

HOOPER THOMAS; Read; weaver; 1681–1708+; s William Hooper; m Elizabeth Richards; bro Sarah Wardwell, John & William Hooper; And petitn

HOOPER, WILLIAM; Read; 1658–1692; s William Hooper; m Susanna –; bro Sarah Wardwell, John & Thomas Hooper; 8 August 1692 death blamed on Jane Lilly, Mary Coleson, & Mary Taylor

HORTON, JOHN, also Houghton; Lanc; m 1672 Mary Farrar; bond for mo-in-law Ann (–) (Farrar) Sears

HOUGHTON, JOHN, see HOLTON

HOW, ABIGAIL; Ip; 1673–1753; dau James Jr & Elizabeth (Jackson) How

HOW, ABRAHAM; Tops; c 1649–1718; s James Sr & Elizabeth (Dane) How; m 1678 Sarah Peabody; bro James How Jr; v sis-in-law Elizabeth How

HOW, DEBORAH; Rox; dau James & Elizabeth (Jackson) How; m 1685 Isaac How

HOW, ELIZABETH; Ip; –1692; dau William & Joan Jackson; m 1658 James How Jr; sis John Jackson Sr; arrested, tried, condemned, hanged 19 July 1692

HOW, ISAAC; Rox; 1657–1718+; s Abraham How Jr; m 1685 Deborah How; s-in-law Elizabeth How

HOW, JAMES SR; Ip; weaver; –1702; m Elizabeth Dane; f James Jr & John How; for dau-in-law Elizabeth How

HOW, JAMES JR; Ip; weaver; c 1636- 1701; s James & Elizabeth (Dane) How; m 1658 Elizabeth Jackson; neph Rev Francis Dane; for wife Elizabeth How, named

HOW, CAPT JOHN; Tops; c 1637–1728; s James & Elizabeth (Dane) How; m by 1665 Mary (Cooper) Dorman, by 1678 Sarah Towne, c 1707 Sarah (–) Dennis; v sis-in-law Elizabeth How

HOW, MARK; Tops; 1666-d by 1692; s Capt John & Sarah (Towne) How

HOW, MARTHA; Ip & Hav; 1691–; dau John & Hannah (Brown) How; gr-dau Elizabeth How

HOW, MARY; Ip; 1664–1731; dau James Jr & Elizabeth (Jackson) How

HOW, SARAH; Ip & Hav; 1693–1715; dau John & Hannah (Brown) How; m 1712 Thomas Wood; gr-dau Elizabeth

HOW, SARAH; Tops; 1650–1732; dau Francis & Mary (Foster) Peabody; m 1678 Abraham How; wit sum v. sis–law Elizabeth How

HOWARD, JOHN; Row; hired man; arrested

HUBBARD, ELIZABETH, also Hubbert, Hubburt, etc; SV; 1675-; m 1711 John Bennett?; niece Rachel Griggs; affl, accused many

HUBBARD, MARTHA; Salis; 1646–1718; dau William & Anne (Goodale) Allen Salisbury; m by 1666 Richard Hubbard; Mary Bradbury petitn

HUBBARD, RICHARD; Salis; blacksmith; c 1630–1719; m by 1666 Martha Allen; Mary Bradbury petitn

HUBBARD, THOMAS; legis, money lender, Speaker of House; 1702–1773; m 1724 Mary Jackson

HUBBARD, REV WILLIAM; Ip; min Ip; HC 1642; c 1622–1704; s William Hubbard Sr; m c 1650 Mary Rogers, 1694 Mary (Giddings) Pierce; for Sarah Buckley, 1703 petitn

HUGHES, BETTY, also Hews; 1670–; Salm; dau James & Elizabeth Hughes; affl

HUGHES, JOHN; Bev?; hired man; v Sarah Good, Sarah Osburn, Tituba, & Bridget Bishop

HUNKINS, JOHN; Ip; perh 1660–1715; s John & Agnes Hunkins?; m Mary Leighton?; advises folk-magic

HUNNEWELL, RICHARD; York?, Maine; d by 1692; perh s Capt Richard & Elizabeth (Stover) Hunnewell?

HUNTING, CAPT SAMUEL; Chas; sea captain; c 1641–1701; s John Hunting; m 1694 Hannah Hackburn; magis & 1693 jury

HUTCHINS, FRANCES; Hav; –1694; m John Hutchins; arrested

HUTCHINS, SAMUEL; Hav; c 1645–1713; s John & Frances Hutchins; m 1662 Hannah Johnson; Rep in 1692, bond for mo's release

HUTCHINS, WILLIAM; Hav; c 1638–; son John & Frances Hutchins; m 1661 Sarah Hardy, 1685 Elizabeth (Eaton) Grath

HUTCHINSON, BENJAMIN; SV; −1733; s Joseph Hutchinson Sr; adopted s Nathaniel & Hannah (Collins) Ingersoll; m 1689 Jane Phillips, 1715 Abigail (−) Foster; v George Burroughs, Mary Esty, etc

HUTCHINSON, MAJ ELISHA; Bost; merch, milit; 1641–1717; s Edward & Katherine (Hanby) Hutchinson; m 1665 Hannah Hawkins, 1677 Elizabeth (Clark) Freke

HUTCHINSON, JANE; SV; c 1668–1711; dau Walter & Margaret Phillips; m 1689 Benjamin Hutchinson; affl

HUTCHINSON, JOHN; SV; bp 1666–1746; s Joseph Hutchinson Sr; m 1694 Mary Gould, 1710 Hannah Howard; v Bridget Bishop

HUTCHINSON, JOSEPH SR; SV; 1633–1716; s Richard & Alise (Bosworth) Hutchinson; m bef 1660?Bethia Gedney?, 1678 Lydia (Buxton) Small; f Benjamin & John Hutchinson; Rebecca Nurse petitn v. Sarah Good, Tituba, Sarah Osburn

HUTCHINSON, LYDIA; SV; −1708+; dau Anthony & Elizabeth Buxton; m 1672 Joseph Small, m 1678 Joseph Hutchinson Sr; Rebecca Nurse petitn

I

INDIAN, JOHN; SV; m Tituba; Samuel Parris' slave; affl, accused several

INDIAN, TITUBA see TITUBA

INGALLS −; "Mr Ingalls' child" perh Francis s Henry & Mary Ingalls; And; d 9 Dec 1690 smallpox

INGALLS, HENRY SR; And; 1627–1719; s Edmund & Ann Ingalls; m 1653 Mary Osgood, 1687 Sarah (Farnum) Abbott; And petitn

INGALLS, HENRY JR; And; 1656–1699; s Henry Sr & Mary (Osgood) Ingalls; m 1688 Abigail Emery; And petitn

INGALLS, JOHN; And; 1661–1743; s Henry Sr & Mary (Osgood) Ingalls; m 1696 Sarah Russell; And petitn

INGALLS, SAMUEL; And; 1654–1733; s Henry Sr & Mary (Osgood) Ingalls; m 1682 Sarah Hendrick; And petitn

INGALLS, SAMUEL; Lynn; 1650–1712; s Edmund & Ann (Tilbe) Ingalls; m Hannah Brewer; const Lynn 1692–93

INGERSOLL, HANNAH; SV; c 1635–1718; dau Henry & Ann (Riall) Collins; m Nathaniel Ingersoll; adopt Benjamin Hutchinson; sis Benjamin Collins, sis-in-law Thomas Farrar, for Rebecca Nurse

INGERSOLL, JOSEPH; Bost; 1646–1718; s George & Elizabeth Ingersoll; m Sarah Cave; neph Nathaniel Ingersoll, employed Judah White

INGERSOLL, NATHANIEL; SV; ordinary keeper; c 1633–1719; s Richard & Ann/Agnes (Langly) Ingersoll; m Hannah Collins; adopt Benjamin Hutchinson; v many, for Rebecca Nurse

INGERSOLL, SARAH; Salm; dau John & Sarah (Young) Marsh; m 1684 Capt Samuel Ingersoll, 1698 Philip English; niece-in-law Nathaniel Ingersoll; for Sarah Churchill

IRESON, BENJAMIN; Lynn; 1645–1705; s Edward & Alise Ireson; m 1680 Mary Leach

IRESON, MARY; Lynn; dau Richard & Sarah (Fuller) Leach; m 1680 Benjamin Ireson; arrested

J

JACKSON, GEORGE; Mbl; physician; m Mary (Aborn) (Concklin) (Nick) Star

JACKSON, JOHN SR; Row; farmer, hired hand; −1719?; s William & Joan Jackson; m 1669 Elizabeth Poor; bro Elizabeth How, f John Jackson Jr; arrested

JACKSON, JOHN JR; Row; hired hand; bp 1670−; s John Sr & Elizabeth (Poor) Jackson; neph Elizabeth How; arrested

JACOBS, GEORGE SR; Salm; 1609?–1692; perh s George & Priscilla Jacobs; m − −, Mary −; f George Jacobs Jr & Ann Andrews, gr-f Margaret Jacobs; arrested, tried, condemned, hanged 19 Aug 1692

JACOBS, GEORGE JR; SV; c 1649– c 1718; s George Jacobs Sr; m c 1674 Rebecca (Andrews) Frost; f Margaret Jacobs, bro-in-law Daniel Andrews; accused, fled

JACOBS, MARGARET; SV; 1675–1718+; dau George Jr & Rebecca (Andrews) (Frost) Jacobs; m 1699 John Foster; gr-dau George Jacobs Sr; affl, accused, confess, accused parents & g-f, recant

JACOBS, MARY; Salm; m George Jacobs Sr, 1693 John Wilds

JACOBS, MARY; Ip; d bef 1706; m Thomas Jacobs; v Sarah Bibber

JACOBS, REBECCA; SV; 1646–1718+; d Thomas & Rebecca Andrews; m 1666 John Frost, c 1674 George Jacobs Jr; arrested, confess, tried, not guilty

JACOBS, THOMAS; Ip; c 1641–1706+; s Richard & Martha (Appleton) Jacobs; m 1671 Sarah Browne, Mary (−); v Sarah Bibber, 1693 jury

JEWETT, JOSEPH; Row; carpenter, 1692 const; 1656–1694; s Joseph & Ann (−) (Allen) Jewett; m 1681 Ruth Wood; half-bro Nehemiah Jewett

JEWETT, NEHEMIAH; Ip; owned mill etc; 1643–1720; s Joseph & Mary (Mallinson) Jewett; m 1668 Exercise Pierce; half-bro Joseph Jewett; Rep 1689–1714, reparation committee

JOHNS, –, "Goodman Johns" see JONES

JOHNSON, ABIGAIL; And; 1682–; dau Stephen & Elizabeth (Dane) Johnson; m bef 1717 Joseph Black; sis Elizabeth Jr, Stephen, & Francis Johnson, gr-dau Rev Francis Dane, niece Rebecca Johnson & Deliverance Dane; arrested

JOHNSON, ELIZABETH SR; And; –1722; dau Rev Francis & Elizabeth (Ingalls) Dane; m 1661 Stephen Johnson; mo Abigail, Elizabeth Jr, & Francis Johnson, sis-in-law Rebecca Johnson & Deliverance Dane, Thomas & Mary Johnson; arrested, confess, tried, not guilty

JOHNSON, ELIZABETH JR; And; c 1670–1716+; dau Stephen & Elizabeth (Dane) Johnson; gr-dau Rev Francis Dane, sis Abigail, Stephen & Francis Johnson, niece Rebecca Johnson & Deliverance Dane; arrested, confess, accuser, tried, found guilty, reprieved

JOHNSON, FRANCIS; And; 1666–1738; s Stephen & Elizabeth (Dane) Johnson; m 1693 Sarah Hawkes, 1717 Hannah Clarke; gr-s Rev Francis Dane, bro Elizabeth Jr & Abigail Johnson, neph Rebecca Johnson & Deliverance Dane

JOHNSON, JOHN; And; 1667–1741; s Thomas & Mary (Holt) Johnson; And petitns

JOHNSON, JOHN; And; 1677–1761; s Timothy & Rebecca (Aslebee) Johnson; m 1710 Phebe Robinson, 1746 Frances (–) Pearson

JOHNSON, MARY; And; 1638–1702; dau Nicholas & Elizabeth Holt; m 1657 Thomas Johnson; And petitn

JOHNSON, REBECCA; And; 1652– d bet 1705 & 1721; dau John & Rebecca (Ayer) Aslebee; m 1674 Timothy Johnson sis John Aslebee & Sarah Cole of Lynn, sis-in-law Elizabeth Johnson, Thomas & Mary Johnson; arrested, confess

JOHNSON, STEPHEN; And; c 1679–; s Stephen & Elizabeth (Dane) Johnson; bro Elizabeth Jr, Abigail & Francis Johnson, gr-s Rev Francis Dane, neph Rebecca Johnson; arrested, confess

JOHNSON, THOMAS SR; And; 1634–1719; s John & Susanna (Kent) Johnson; m 1657 Mary Holt, 1703 Damaris Marshall; bro Timothy & Stephen Johnson; And petitn

JOHNSON, THOMAS JR; And; 1670–1733; s Thomas Sr & Mary (Holt) Johnson; m Hannah Stone; And prisoners petitn

JOIN, MARTHA see GOWING

JONES, HUGH; Salm; c 1630- c 1688; m 1660 Hannah Tompkins, 1672 Mary Foster

K

KENNEY, HENRY; SV; 1669–1724; s Henry & Ann Kenney; m 1691 Priscilla Lewis, 1714 Mary Curtis; v Martha Cory & Rebecca Nurse

KENT, CORNELIUS; Ip; m Mary –; v Rachel Clinton

KETTLE, JAMES; SV; potter; s John & Elizabeth Kettle?; m Elizabeth –; v Sarah Bishop

KEYSER, CAPT ELIZER, also Keaser, Kezer; Salm; tanner; c 1646–1721; s George & Elisa Keyser; m 1679 Mary Collins, Hannah (–) Ward; v George Burroughs, v Joseph Emmons

KEYSER, HANNAH; Salm; dau George & Elisa? Keyser; distracted

KIMBALL, JOHN; Ames; farmer, wheelwright; 1645- bef 1726; s Henry & Mary (Wyatt) Kimball; m 1665 Mary Jordan, 1713? Mary Pressy, 1715 Deborah (Weed) Bartlett; cous Samuel Kimball; wit sum v Susanna Martin

KIMBALL, MARY; Ames; d bef 1713; dau Francis & Jane Jordan; m 1665 John Kimball; wit sum v Susanna Martin

KING, ANN; Bev; dau John & Annis (Hoar) King; m Benjamin Parnal; gr-dau Dorcas Hoar

KING, ANNIS; Bev; –1712+; dau William & Dorcas (Galley) Hoar; m 1688 John King

KING, CAPT DANIEL; Salm; merch; c 1664–1708; s Daniel & Tabitha (Walker) King; m Mary Vaughan; for George Burroughs

KING, JOHN; Bev; 1662–1718; cooper, farmer; s John & Elizabeth (Goldthwait) King; m 1688 Annis Hoar

KING, JOHN; Bev; s John & Annis (Hoar) King; gr-s Dorcas Hoar

KING, SAMUEL; Salm; 1664-bef 1738; s John & Elizabeth (Goldthwait) King; m 1696 Elizabeth Marsh, Elizabeth Barton; v Job Tookey

KINGSBURY, JOSEPH; And; c 1656–1741; m 1669 Love Ayers

KNIGHT, JONATHAN; SV; c 1642–1683; s Jonathan & Ruth Knight; m 1665 Ruth –

KNIGHT, JOSEPH; Newb; 1652–1723; s John & Bathshua (Ingersoll) Knight; m 1677 Deborah Coffin

KNIGHT, MARGARET; Tops; bp 1649–1697+; dau Bray & Hannah (Way) Wilkins; m c 1688 Phillip Knight; v Abigail Hobbs, John Willard

KNIGHT, PHILIP; Tops; c 1646–1724+; s Jonathan & Ruth Knight; m c 1688 Margaret Wilkins; v John Willard

KNOWLTON, JOSEPH; Ip; shoemaker; 1650–; s William & Amy (Smith) Knowlton; m 1677 Mary Wilson; bro Mary Abbey, Thomas Knowlton; for Elizabeth How

KNOWLTON, MARY; Ip; 1657–; dau – Wilson; m 1677 Joseph Knowlton; for Elizabeth How

KNOWLTON, MARY; Ip; 1681–1719; dau Thomas & Hannah (Green) Wilson; m 1706 John Williams; v Rachel Clinton

KNOWLTON, THOMAS [JR]; Ip; shoemaker; c 1641–1715+; s William & Amy (Smith) Knowlton; m Hannah Green; bro Mary Abbey, Joseph Knowlton; v Rachel Clinton

KNOWLTON, THOMAS; Ip; 1670–1730; s Thomas & Hannah (Green) Knowlton; m Mary or Mercy –, 1694 Susannah –

KOREY see CORY

L

LACEY, LAWRENCE; And; c 1644–1729; m 1673 Mary Foster; s-in-law Ann Foster

LACEY, MARY SR; And; 1652–1707; dau Andrew & Ann Foster; m 1673 Lawrence Lacey; arrested, confess, accuser

LACEY, MARY JR; And; 1674–; dau Lawrence & Mary (Foster) Lacey; m 1704 Zerubbabel Kemp; arrested, confess, accuser

LANCASTER, JOSEPH SR; Ames; 1666–; s Joseph & Mary Lancaster; m 1687 Elizabeth Hoyt; const

LANE, JOHN; s John & Hannah (Abbott) Lane; wit sum v George Burroughs

LAWRENCE, – "Goodwife Lawrence," prob Mary Lawrence; Bost/Falm; –1705; dau John & Joanna Phillips; m by 1652 George Munjoy, bef 1681 Robert Lawrence, 1693 Stephen Cross; named

LAWRENCE, MARY; Falm; d bef 1692; dau Robert Lawrence

LAWRENCE, ROBERT; Falm; –1690; m bef 1684 Mary (Phillips) Munjoy

LAWSON, ANN; SV; –1687; dau Deodat & Jane Lawson

LAWSON, DEBORAH; Bost; m – Allen, 1690 Deodat Lawson

LAWSON, REV DEODAT; SV, Bost; min 1st Ch Bost, formerly SV; –1714+; s Rev Thomas Lawson; m Jane –, 1690 Deborah Allen

LAWSON, JANE; SV; –1687; m Deodat Lawson

LEACH, SARAH; SV; dau – & Ann (–) Fuller; m c 1645 Richard Leach; Rebecca Nurse petitn

LEWIS, MERCY; SV; servant; c 1675–; dau Philip Lewis; m bet 1695 & 1701 Thomas Allen; affl, accused many

LEY, JOHN, also Lee, Leigh; Manch; 1661–1744; m c 1690 Sarah Warren; const

LEYTON, – "Mr Leyton"; Lynn; prob Thomas Laughton; wine merchant, magis, town clerk; c 1612–1697; m Sarah –

LILLY, GEORGE, also Lylly, Lilly; Read; s George & Hannah (Smith) Lilly; m 1695 Elizabeth (Pratt) Hawkes; step s Jane Lilly

LILLY, JANE; Read; m 1667 George Lilly; arrested

LILLY, REUBEN; Read; 1669– bef 1699; s George & Jane Lilly; m Martha Gibson

LOADER, JOHN see LOUDER

LOCKER, CAPT GEORGE; Salm; const; m Lydia (Buffum) Hill; Procter petitn

LONG, ANNA; Salis; 1659–1704+; dau Joseph & Susanna French; m 1680 Richard Long, 1695 Thomas Mudgett; Mary Bradbury petitn

LONG, RICHARD; Salis; –1694; m 1680 Anna French; Mary Bradbury petitn

LORD, MARGARET; Bev; 1660–1682+; dau William & Jane Lord; Rev John Hale's maid

LOUDER, JOHN; Salm; tailor; c 1660–bef 1737; m 1687 Elizabeth Curtis; v Bridget Bishop, Job Tookey

LOVEKINE, THOMAS, also Lufkin; Glo; m Sarah –: or their s Thomas Lufkin Jr; m 1690 Mary Miles, 1692 Sarah Downing; Procter petitn

LOVELL, ALEXANDER; Ip; Elizabeth (Bachelor) Mascoll; deputy

LOVETT, BETHIA; Bev; c 1644–; dau Josiah & Susanna Roots; m John Lovett; v Dorcas Hoar

LOVETT, JOHN SR; Bev; c 1637–1727; s John & Mary Lovett; m Bethia Roots; s-in-law Susanna Roots; 1693 jury

LOVEJOY, JOHN; And; 1622–1690; m 1651 Mary Osgood, 1676 Hannah (–) Pritchard: or s John, 1655–1680; m 1687 Naomi Hoyt

LOVEJOY, NAOMI; And; 1655–c 1699; dau John & Frances Hoyt; m 1678 John Lovejoy, Richard Shattuck

LOW, THOMAS SR; Ip; 1632–1712; s Thomas & Susanna Low; m 1660 Martha Boreman, Mary Brown; Procter petitn

LYNDE, BENJAMIN SR; Salm; lawyer, legis, judge; HC 1686, Middle Temple 1692; 1666–1745; m 1699 Mary Browne

LYNDE, BENJAMIN JR; Salm; landowner, legis, judge; HC 1718; 1700–1781; s Benjamin & Mary (Brown) Lynde; m 1731 Mary (Bowles) Goodridge

M

MANNING, JACOB; Salm; 1660–1756; gunsmith; s Richard & Anstice (Calley) Manning; m 1683 Sarah Stone

MANNING, THOMAS; Ip; 1665–1737; gunsmith, blacksmith; s Richard & Anstice (Calley) Manning; m c 1681 Mary Gidding

MARBLE, JOSEPH SR; And; mason; m 1671 Mary Faulkner; And petitn, 1693 jury

MARSH, JOHN; Salm; 1665–1714+; s Zachariah & Mary (Silsbee) Marsh; m Alice –

MARSH, MARY; Salm; dau Henry & Dorothy Silsbee; m Zachariah Marsh; Procter petitn

MARSH, PRISCILLA; Salm; dau John & Margaret (Goodman) Tompkins; 1670 Samuel Marsh; Procter petitn

MARSH, SAMUEL; Salm; bp 1652– by 1708; s John & Susanna (Skelton) Marsh; m 1679 Priscilla Tompkins; Procter petitn

MARSH, ZACHARIAH; Salm; bp 1657– bp 1735; s John & Susanna (Skelton) Marsh; m Mary Silsbee; Procter petitn

MARSHALL, BENJAMIN; Ip; 1646–1715; s Edmund & Millicent Marshall; m Prudence Woodward; Procter petitn

MARSHALL, EDWARD; Read; –3 Aug 1692; m 1665 Mary Swain

MARSHALL, MARY; Read; c 1643–; dau Jeremiah & Mary Swain; m 1665 Edward Marshall; affl, v Jane Lilly, Mary Taylor, Sarah Rice, Lydia Dustin

MARSTON, JOHN SR; And; c 1664–1741; m 1689 Mary Osgood

MARSTON, MARY; And; 1665–; dau Christopher & Hannah (Belknap) Osgood; m 1689 John Marston; confess, tried, not guilty

MARTIN, ABIGAIL; And; 1676–; dau Samuel & Abigail (Norton) Martin; affl, v many

MARTIN, GEORGE; Ames; blacksmith; c 1618–1686; m c 1642 Hannah –, 1646 Susanna North

MARTIN, SAMUEL; And; 1645–1696+; s Solomon & Mary Martin; m 1676 Abigail Norton; v Elizabeth Johnson Sr, Abigail Johnson, And petitns

MARTIN, SUSANNAH; Ames; bp 1621–1692; dau Richard & Joan (Bartram) North; m 1646 George Martin; tried, hanged 19 July 1692

MASTON, JOHN; Bev; carpenter; c 1654–1716+; s Nathaniel & Ruth (Pickworth) Maston; m 1678 Elizabeth Ornes?; v Susannah Roots

MATHER, REV COTTON; Bost; HC 1678; min 2nd Church Bost; 1662–1728; s Rev Increase & Maria (Cotton) Mather; m 1686 Abigail Phillips, 1708 Elizabeth (Clark) Hubbard, 1715 Lydia (Lee) George; wrote *Wonders of the Invisible World*

MATHER, REV INCREASE; Bost; 1639–1723; HC 1658, Trinity 1658; min 2nd Church Bost; s Rev Richard & Katherine (Hoult) Mather; m 1667 Maria Cotton, 1715 Ann (Lake) Cotton; wrote *Cases of Conscience*

MAVERICK, REBECCA, "widow Maverick"; Salis; –1678; dau Rev John Wheelwright; m Samuel Maverick Jr, 1672 William Bradbury

MAXFIELD, ELIZABETH; Salis; –1704; dau – Hamons?; m 1679 John Maxfield; Mary Bradbury petitn

MAXFIELD, JOHN; Salis; –1703; m 1679 Elizabeth Hamons?; Mary Bradbury petitn

MILBORNE, REV WILLIAM; Bost; atty, Baptist min; c 1643–1694; s William & Abigail (Allen) Milborne; m Jane (–) Pierce, Susannah Turfrey; petitn v trials

MOODY, ANN; Bost; m Samuel Jacobs, Rev Joshua Moody; sis-in-law Thomas Jacobs of Ip; named

MOODY, CALEB; Salis; 1666–1710+; s Caleb & Judith (Bradbury) Moody; m 1696 Ruth Morse; gr-s Mary Bradbury, neph Rev Joshua Moody

MOODY, DANIEL; Salis; 1662–1718; s Caleb & Sarah (Pierce) Moody; m 1683 Elizabeth Somerby; Mary Bradbury petitn

MOODY, ELIZABETH; Salis; –1719+; dau – Somerby; m 1683 Daniel Moody; Mary Bradbury petitn

MOODY, HANNAH; Salis; 1699–1720+; dau Daniel & Elizabeth (Somerby) Moody; gr-gr-dau Mary Bradbury

MOODY, REV JOSHUA; Bost; HC 1653; c 1632–1697; s William & Sarah Moody; m Martha Collins, Ann (–) Jacobs; aided Philip & Mary English escape

MOODY, JOSHUA; Salis; 1686–1720+; s Daniel & Elizabeth (Somerby) Moody; m 1715 Elizabeth Allen; gr-gr-s Mary Bradbury

MOODY, JUDITH or Judah; Salis; 1638–1699 or 1700; dau Thomas & Mary (Perkins) Bradbury; m 1665 Caleb Moody Sr

MOODY, SAMUEL; Salis; 1689–1720+; s Daniel & Elizabeth (Somerby) Moody; gr-gr-s Mary Bradbury

MOREY, ISAAC, also Morrell, Morrill; Salis; blacksmith; 1646–1713; s Abraham & Sarah (Clement) Morey; m 1670 Phebe Gill; Mary Bradbury petitn

MOREY, JACOB; Salis; 1648–1718; s Abraham & Sarah (Clement) Morey; m 1674 Susanna Whittier; Mary Bradbury petitn

MOREY, MARY; Bev; –1714+; dau – Butler; m 1675 Peter Morey

MOREY, PETER; Bev; mariner; m 1675 Mary Butler

MOREY, PHOEBE; Salis; dau – Gill; m 1670 Isaac Morey; Mary Bradbury petitn

MOREY, ROBERT; SV; v Thomas Farrer

MOREY, SARAH; Bev; dau Peter & Mary (Butler) Morey; m 1698 John Ellenwood; arrested

MOREY, SUSANNAH; Salis; –1727; dau Thomas Whittier; m 1674 Jacob Morey; Mary Bradbury petitn

MORGAN, DEBORAH; Bev; c 1649–; dau John Hart; m Joseph Morgan; sis-in-law Edward Flint; v Dorcas Hoar

MORGAN, JOSEPH; Bev; bp 1666–; s Samuel & Elizabeth (Dixey) Morgan; v Dorcas Hoar

MORGAN, SAMUEL; Bev; bp 1657–1694+; s Robert & Margaret (Norman) Morgan; m 1658 Elizabeth Dixy; male witch mark search committee, 1693 jury

MORRILL, see MOREY

MORTON, REV CHARLES; Chas; 1627–1698; s Nicholas & Frances (Kestell) Morton; m 1644 Ann Cooper, Mary (Shelly) Harlow

MOULTON, JOHN; SV; 1654–1741; farmer, cordwainer; s Robert & Abigail (Goode) Moulton; m 1684 Elizabeth Cory; pro Cory

MOULTON, ROBERT SR; Salm; 1644–1720; s Robert & Abigail (Goode) Moulton; m 1672 Mary Cooke; v Susanna Shelden

MURRAY, WILLIAM; Salm; merch

N

NEAL, JEREMIAH; Salm; housewright; bp 1646–1722; s John & Mary (Lawes) Neal; m 1668 Sarah Hart, 1673 Mary Buffum; 1707 Dorothy Lord; v Ann Pudeator

NEAL, JOSEPH; Salm; joiner, const 1692; 1660–1718; s John & Mary (Lawes) Neal; m Judith Croade

NEAL, MARY; Salm; c 1648–1692; dau Robert & Tamsen Buffum; m 1673 Jeremiah Neal

NELSON, PHILLIP; Row; 1658–1721; s Capt Phillip & Sarah (Jewett) Nelson; m Sarah Hobson; v Martha Scott

NELSON, SARAH; Row; dau – Hobson; m Phillip Nelson; v Martha Scott

NEWMAN, THOMAS; Bost; merch; 1709–1754; s Thomas & Ann Newman; m 1732 Mary Thomas (gr-dau Rev George Burroughs)

NEWTON, THOMAS; Bost; barrister; 1669–1721; m Christian Phillips?; Mass Atty Gen 1692 until July, O&T York

NICHOLS, ELIZABETH; c 1680–; v Abigail Hobbs

NICHOLS, ISAAC; SV; 1673-bef 1692; s John & Lydia (Wilkins) Nichols

NICHOLS, JOHN; Tops; 1640–1700; s William Nichols; m c 1662 Lydia Wilkins

NICHOLS, LYDIA; Tops; bp 1664–1700+; dau Bray & Hannah (Way) Wilkins; m c 1662 John Nichols; v Abigail Hobbs, John Willard

NICHOLS, LYDIA; Tops; dau John & Lydia (Wilkins) Nichols; v Abigail Hobbs & John Willard

NICHOLS, THOMAS; Tops; 1670–1716+; s John & Lydia (Wilkins) Nichols; m 1694 Joanna Towne; v John Willard

NOTTINGHAM, EARL OF ie FINCH, DANIEL; London; Oxford 1662; Secretary of State; 1647–1730; s Heneage & Elizabeth (Harvey) Finch; m 1674 – Cheke, 1685 Anne Hatton

NOYES, REV NICHOLAS; Salm; min Salm; HC 1667; 1647–1717; s Nicholas & Mary (Cutting) Noyes; cousin Sarah Hale, Thomas Noyes; v many

NOYES, THOMAS; Bost; 1648–c 1730; s Rev James & Sarah (Brown) Noyes; m 1669 Martha Pierce, 1677 Elizabeth Greenleaf; bro Sarah Hale, cous Rev Nicholas Noyes; 1711 reparation committee

NURSE, BENJAMIN; SV; 1666–1748; s Francis & Rebecca (Towne) Nurse; m 1688 Tamsin Smith, 1714 Elizabeth (Sawtell) Morse; 1707 petitn

NURSE, FRANCIS SR: SV; 1618–1695; m 1644 Rebecca Towne

NURSE, FRANCIS JR; SV; 1661–1716; s Francis & Rebecca (Towne) Nurse; m c 1664 Sarah Craggen

NURSE, JOHN; SV; c 1645–1719; s Francis & Rebecca (Towne) Nurse; m 1671 Elizabeth Smith, 1677 Elizabeth Very

NURSE, MARY; SV; 1669–1716; dau John & Margaret (Buffum) Smith; m 1669 Samuel Nurse Sr

NURSE, REBECCA; SV; bp 1621–1692; dau William & Joanna (Blessing) Towne; m 1644 Francis Nurse; sis Mary Esty, Sarah Cloyce; tried, found guilty, hanged 19 July 1692

NURSE, SAMUEL SR; SV; 1649–1715; s Francis & Rebecca (Towne) Nurse; m 1669 Mary Smith; Rebecca Nurse petitn

NURSE, SAMUEL JR; SV; 1678–1740; s Samuel & Mary (Smith) Nurse; m 1708 Dorothy Faulkner

NURSE, SARAH; SV; 1664–1747; dau John & Sarah (Dawes) (McDonald) Craggen; m c 1684 Francis Nurse Jr; v Sarah Bibber

O

OLIVER, –, "Goodwife Oliver" see BISHOP, BRIDGET

OLIVER, THOMAS "Goodman Oliver"; Salm; – c 1679; m Mary –, 1666 Bridget (Plafer) Wasselbee

ORDWAY, SAMUEL; Ip; blacksmith; b bef 1653– d by 1694; m 1678 Sarah Ordway

OSBURN, ALEXANDER; ALSO OSBORN; SV; -c 1703; m –, Sarah (Warren?) Prince, Ruth (Cantlebury) (Small) Sibley

OSBURN, HANNAH; Salm; 164?–; dau Capt John Burton; m 1673 William Osburn; Rebecca Nurse petitn

OSBURN, SARAH; SV; –1692; dau – Warren?; m 1662 Robert Prince, Alexander Osburn; arrested, d 10 May 1692 in jail

OSBURN, WILLIAM; Salm; –1727+; m 1673 Hannah Burton; Rebecca Nurse petitn

OSGOOD, ABIGAIL; Salis; 1654–1715; dau Henry & Susanna Ambrose; m 1672 William Osgood; Mary Bradbury petitn

OSGOOD, CHRISTOPHER; And; millwright; c 1643–1723; s Christopher & Margery (Fowler) Osgood; m 1663 Hannah Belknap, 1680 Hannah Barker, Sarah –, Sarah Stevens?; And petitn

OSGOOD, CHRISTOPHER; And; 1675–1739; s Christopher & Hannah (Belknap) Osgood; 1711 Mary Keyes

OSGOOD, EZEKIEL; And; 1670–1741; s Christopher & Hannah (Belknap) Osgood; m 1710 Rebecca Wardwell

OSGOOD, HOOKER; And; saddler; 1668–1748; s Stephen & Mary (Hooker) Osgood; m 1692 Dorothy Wood?; And petitns

OSGOOD, CAPT JOHN; And; c 1630–1693; s John & Sarah Osgood; m 1653 Mary Clement; And petitn

OSGOOD, MARY; And; 1637–1695; dau Robert Clements; m 1653 John Osgood; arrest, confess

OSGOOD, PETER; Salm; tanner, farmer, const 1692; 1663–1753; s John & Mary (Clements) Osgood; m 1690 Martha Ayers

OSGOOD, SAMUEL; And; 1665–; s John & Mary (Clement) Osgood; m 1702 Hannah Dane

OSGOOD, STEPHEN; And; s John & Sarah Osgood; m 1663 Mary Hooker

OSGOOD TIMOTHY; And; 1659–; s John & Mary (Clement) Osgood

OSGOOD, WILLIAM; Salis; 1648–1729; s William & Elizabeth Osgood; m 1672 Abigail Ambrose; Mary Bradbury petitn

P

PAGE, JOSEPH; Salis; 1670–1722; s Onesiphorus & Mary (Hawksworth) Page; m 1691 Sarah Smith, aft 1691 Elizabeth –; Mary Bradbury petitn

PAGE, MARY; Salis; 1641–1695; dau Thomas & Mary Hawksworth; m 1664 Onesiphorus Page; Mary Bradbury petitn

PAGE, SGT ONESIPHORIS; Salis c 1641–1706; s John & Mary (Marsh) Page; m 1664 Mary Hawksworth, 1695 Sarah (Morey) Rowell; Mary Bradbury petitn

PAINE, ELIZABETH; Mald; 1639–1711; dau Edward & Elizabeth Carrington; m c 1657 Stephen Paine; step-aunt Martha Sprague; arrested

PAINE, ROBERT; Ip; farmer, clerk; HC 1656; c 1634–1704+; s Robert & Ann (Whiting) Paine; m 1666 Elizabeth Rainer; Jan 1693 Grand Jury foreman

PAINE, STEPHEN; Mald; c 1634–1693?; m c 1657 Elizabeth Carrington

PARKER, ALICE; Salm; –1692; m John Parker; arrested, tried, condemned, hanged 22 Sept 1692

PARKER, JOHN; And; 1653–1738; s Nathan & Mary (Ayers) Parker; m 1687 Hannah Brown; v Mary Taylor

PARKER, JOHN; Read; 1667–1741; m 1691 Elizabeth Goodwin; const

PARKER, JOHN; Salm; fisherman; m Alice –

PARKER, JOHN SR; SV; d by 1708; m 1673 Mary Cory; v f-in-law Giles Gorey

PARKER, JOSEPH; And; c 1669–1748; s Nathan & Mary (Ayers) Parker; m c 1700 Lydia Frye

PARKER, MARY; And; c 1631–1692; dau John & Hannah Ayer; m c 1652 Nathan Parker; arrest, tried, found guilty, hanged 22 Sept 1692

PARKER, MARY; Salm; d bef 1698; dau Giles & Margaret Cory; m 1673 John Parker

PARKER, SARAH; And; 1670–; dau Nathan & Mary (Ayer) Parker; arrest

PARKER, STEPHEN; And; 1651–1718; s Joseph & Mary (Stevens?) Parker; m 1680 Mary Marston, Susanna Hartshorne; neph Mary (Ayers) Parker; And petitns

PARRIS, ELIZABETH; SV; c 1648–1696; dau –, Eldridge; m c 1680 Samuel Parris

PARRIS, ELIZABETH, "Betty"; SV; 1682–1760; dau Rev Samuel & Elizabeth (Eldridge) Parris; m 1710 Benjamin Barron; affl, v Tituba, Sarah Good, Sarah Osburn

PARRIS, REV SAMUEL; SV; min SV; c 1653–1720; s Thomas & Ann Parris; m c 1680 Elizabeth Eldridge, c 1698 Dorothy Noyes; v many

PAROTT, SARAH; Salm?; perh dau – Crockett; m by 1675 John Parrett?; wit sum v Ann Pudeator & Alice Parker

PARTRIDGE, JOHN; Ports; Marshall of NH; s William & Mary (Brown) Partridge; m 1660 Mary Fernald

PATCH, RICHARD; Salm; 1648–; s John & Elizabeth (Brackenbury) Patch; m 1673 Mary Goldsmith, 1704 Hannah Eaton; v Sarah Good

PAYSON, REV EDWARD; Row; min Row; HC 1677; 1657–1732; s Edward & Mary (Eliot) Payson; m 1683 Elizabeth Phillips, 1726 Elizabeth (Whittingham) Appleton; s-in-law Rev Samuel Phillips; for Elizabeth How

PEASE, ROBERT; Salm; cowherd, weaver; 1628–1713+; s Robert & Mary Pease; m by 1660 Sarah –

PEASE, SARAH; Salm; –1713+; m by 1660 Robert Pease; arrest

PENNY, JOAN; Glo; m Richard Braybrook, 1682 Thomas Penny; step-mo Mehitabel Dowing; arrest

PENNY, THOMAS: Glo; tailor; d c 1692; m Ann –, 1668 Agnes (–) Clark, 1682 Joan (–) Braybrook

PERKINS, ABRAHAM; Ip; innholder, const 1692; 1640–1722; s John & Elizabeth Perkins; m 1661 Hannah (Bushnell) Beamsley; neph Mary Bradbury

PERKINS, ISAAC; Ip; 1650–1725; s John & Elizabeth Perkins; m 1669 Hannah Knight; neph Mary Bradbury; Procter petitn

PERKINS, JACOB JR; Ip; 1650–1725; s John & Judith (Gater) Perkins

PERKINS, MATTHEW; const Ip; c 1665–1755; s Jacob & Elizabeth Perkins; m – Burnham

PERKINS, NATHANIEL; Ip; Procter petitn

PERKINS, WILLIAM; Tops; –1695; s Thomas & Judith Perkins; wit sum v Sarah Wilds

PERKINS, ZACHEUS; Tops; c 1647–1730; s Thomas & Judith Perkins; m c 1704 Rebecca –; v Sarah Wilds

PERLEY, DEBORAH perh Dorothy; Ip; –1734+; m c 1680 Timothy Perley; v Elizabeth How

PERLEY, HANNAH; Ip; 1671– bef 1692; dau Samuel & Ruth (Trumbull) Perley; affl

PERLEY, JOHN; Ip; 1669–1723; s Samuel & Ruth (Trumbull) Perley; m 1698 Jane Dresser; v Elizabeth How

PERLEY, RUTH; Ip; dau John & Ellen Trumbull; m 1664 Samuel Perley; v Elizabeth How

PERLEY, SAMUEL; Ip; c 1640–1707+; s Allen & Susanna (Bokeson) Perley; m 1664 Ruth Trumbull; v Elizabeth How

PERLEY, TIMOTHY; Ip; c 1655–1719; s Allen & Susanna Perley; m c 1680 Deborah; v Elizabeth How

PETERS, ANDREW; And; c 1635–1713; m Mercy (Beamsley) Wilbourn; And petitn

PETERS, MARY; And; 1661–1733; dau John Edwards; m 1680 Andrew Peters Jr, widow; And petitn

PETERS, SAMUEL; And; c 1675–1736; s Andrew & Mercy (Beamsley) (Wilbourn) Peters; m 1696 Phebe Frye; And petitn

PETERS, WILLIAM; And; 1672–1696; s Andrew & Mercy (Beamsley) (Wilbourn) Peters; m 1694 Margaret Russe; And petitn

PHELPS, SAMUEL; And; 1651–; s Edward & Elizabeth (Adams) Phelps; m Sarah Chandler

PHELPS, SARAH; And; 1682–; dau Samuel & Sarah (Chandler) Phelps; m 1720? Samuel Fields?; affl, accused many

PHILLIPS, MAJ JOHN; Chas; 1633–1726; merch, legis; m 1655 Catherine Anderson, 1701 Sarah (Stedman) (Brackett) (Alcock) Graves; f-in-law Cotton Mather

PHILLIPS, MARGARET; SV; –1704+; m Walter Phillips; mo Jane Hutchinson; Rebecca Nurse petitn

PHILLIPS, REV SAMUEL; Row; min Row; HC 1650; 1625–1696; s Rev George Phillips; m Sarah Appleton; f-in-law Rev Edward Payson; for Elizabeth How

PHILLIPS, TABITHA; SV; –1704; dau Walter & Margaret Phillips; sis Jane Hutchinson; Rebecca Nurse petitn

PHILLIPS, TIMOTHY; Chas; s Henry Phillips; m 1681 Mary Smith; Sheriff Middlesex Co

PHILLIPS, WALTER; SV; innkeeper; –1704; m Margaret; f Jane Hutchinson; Rebecca Nurse petitn

PHIPS, SPENCER; Camb; HC 1703; 1685–1757; s David & Rebecca (Spencer) (Bully) Bennett; m 1707 Elizabeth Hutchinson; neph Mary Phips, adopted by Sir William Phips; Lt Gov 1732–57, acting Gov 1749–53

PHIPS, SIR WILLIAM; Bost; merch, shipwright, mariner, milit leader, Mass Gov 1692–1695; 1651–1695; s James & Mary Phips; m c 1674 Mary (Spencer) Hull; half-bro Phillip White

PICKERING, ALICE; Salm; –1713; dau Edward & Elizabeth (Hart) Flint; m Henry Bullock, 1657 Lt John Pickering; women's witch mark search committee

PICKMAN, LYDIA; Salm; dau Peter Palfrey; m Samuel Pickman; women's witch mark search committee

PICKWORTH, SAMUEL; Salm; s Samuel & Sarah (Marston) Pickworth; v Ann Pudeator

PICKWORTHY, ELIAS also Pickworth; c 1658–; m 1682 Anna Killegriff

PIERPOINT, REV JONATHAN; Read; min Read; HC 1685; 1665–1709; s Robert & Sarah Pierpont; m 1691 Elizabeth Angier

PIKE, REV JOHN; Newb & Portsm; min; HC 1675; 1653–1710; s Robert & Sarah (Sanders) Pike; m 1681 Sarah Moody; for Mary Bradbury

PIKE, MARTHA; Salis; –1713; dau – Moyce; m George Goldwyer, 1684 Robert Pike; Mary Bradbury petitn

PIKE, MOSES; Salis; 1658–1714+; s Robert & Sarah (Sanders) Pike; m Susanna –; v Susanna Martin

PIKE, ROBERT; Salis; c 1616–1706; s John Pike Sr; m 1641 Sarah Sanders, 1684 Martha (Moyce) Goldwyer; for Martha Bradbury

PITMAN, CHARITY; Mbl; 1664–; dau Ambrose & Deborah Gale; m John Pitman, 1697 Mark Haskell; sis Benjamin Gale; v Wilmot Redd

POOR, DANIEL; And; c 1624–1713; m 1650 Mary Farnum: or s Daniel; c 1656–1735; m Mehitable; And selectman, And petitn

POPE, BATHSHUA; SV; 1652–; dau Peter & Mary (Morey) Folger; m Joseph Pope; affl, v Rebecca Nurse, Martha Cory, etc

POPE, JOSEPH; SV; bp 1650–1712; s Joseph & Gertrude Pope; m Bathshua Folger; v John Procter

PORTER, BENJAMIN; SV; 1685–1691; s Israel & Elizabeth (Hathorne) Porter

PORTER, ELIZABETH; SV; 1649–1706+; dau William & Ann Hathorne; m 1672 Israel Porter; sis John Hathorne; for Rebecca Nurse & petitn

PORTER, CAPT ISRAEL; SV; bp 1644–1706; s John & Mary Porter; m 1672 Elizabeth Hathorne; for Rebecca Nurse & petitn

PORTER, JOHN; Wen; maltster, farmer; c 1658–1753; s Samuel & Hannah (Dodge) Porter; m Lydia Herrick; neph Israel Porter; v Sarah Bibber

PORTER, LYDIA; Wen; 1661– c 1738; dau Henry & Lydia (Woodbury) Herrick; m John Porter; v Sarah Bibber

POST, HANNAH; Box; 1666–; dau Richard & Mary (Tyler) Post; half-sis Mary Bridges, step-sis Sarah Bridges; arrest, confess, tried, not guilty

POST, MARY; Row; 1664–; dau Richard & Mary (Tyler) Post; arrest, confess, tried, found guilty, reprieve

POST, SUSANNAH; And; 1665–; dau Richard & Mary (Tyler) Post; arrest, confess, tried, not guilty

PRATT, JOHN; Salm; vintner, kept Ship Tavern; 1695–1727; –1730; m 1691 Margaret Maverick

PRESCOTT, PETER; SV; herdsman; m 1679 Elizabeth Reddington; v George Burroughs & John Willard

PRESSY, JOHN; Ames; planter; c 1639–1707; m 1663 Mary Gouge; v Susanna Martin

PRESSY, MARY; Ames; c 1646–; dau William & Ann Gouge; m John Pressy; v Susanna Martin

PRESTON, JOHN; And; s Roger & Martha Preston; m 1687 Sarah (Gerry) Holt; And petitns

PRESTON, REBECCA; And; 1647–1719; dau Francis & Rebecca (Towne) Nurse; m 1669 Thomas Preston; for Rebecca Nurse

PRESTON, SAMUEL JR; And; c 1651–; s Roger & Martha Preston; m 1672 Susanna Gullerson, 1713 Mary Blodgett; v Martha Carrier

PRESTON, SARAH see BRIDGES, SARAH

PRESTON, THOMAS; SV; 1643–1697; s Roger & Martha Preston; m 1669 Rebecca Nurse Jr; v Sarah Good, Sarah Osburn, Tituba

PRINCE, MARGARET; Glo; c 1630–1706; m 1650 Thomas Prince; arrested

PRINCE, THOMAS; Glo; 1650–1705; s Thomas & Margaret Prince; m Elizabeth Haraden

PROCTER, BENJAMIN; also Proctor; Salm; 1659– c 1717; s John & Martha Procter; m 1694 Mary (Buckley) Witteredge; step-s Elizabeth Procter; arrested

PROCTER, ELIZABETH; Salm; c 1647–1712+; dau William & Sarah Bassett; m 1674 John Procter, 1699 Daniel Richards; sis Mary DeRich, sis-in-law Sarah Bassett; arrested, tried, condemned, pregnancy postponed exec & so survived

PROCTER, JOHN; Salm; c 1632–1692; s John & Martha (Harper) Procter; m c 1652 Martha White or Jackson, 1662 Elizabeth Thorndike, 1674 Elizabeth Bassett; tried, found guilty, hanged 19 Aug 1692

PROCTER, JOHN; Salm; 1668–1749; s John & Elizabeth (Thorndike) Procter; m Mary

PROCTER, JOSEPH; Ip; –1705; s John & Martha (Harper) Procter; m c 1676 Martha Wainwright, c 1695–98 Sarah (–) Ingersoll; named, Procter petitn

PROCTER, SARAH; Salm; 1676–1712+; dau John & Elizabeth (Bassett) Procter; m 1700 Edward Manion; arrested

PROCTER, THORNDIKE; Salm; 1672–1758; s John & Elizabeth (Thorndike) Procter; m 1697 Hannah (Felton) Endicott, 1739 Sarah Allen

PROCTER, WILLIAM; Salm; 1675–1712+; s John & Elizabeth (Bassett) Procter; arrested

PUDEATOR, ANN; Salm; –1692; m Thomas Greenslade, Jacob Pudeator; mo James, John, & Thomas Greenslade; tried, condemn, hanged 22 Sept 1692

PUTNAM, ANN SR; SV; 1661–1699; dau George & Elizabeth (Oliver) Carr; m 1678 Thomas Putnam; affl, v Rebecca Nurse, John Willard, etc

PUTNAM, ANN JR; SV; 1679– c 1715; dau Thomas & Ann (Carr) Putnam; niece John Carr; affl, v many

PUTNAM, BENJAMIN; SV; 1664–; s Nathaniel & Elizabeth (Hutchinson) Putnam; m Sarah – or Hannah –, 1706 Sarah (–) Houlton; Rebecca Nurse petitn

PUTNAM, EDWARD; SV; 1654–1747; deac; s Thomas & Ann (Holyoke) Putnam; m 1681 Mary Hale; v several

PUTNAM, ELY; SV; perh Eleazer, 1665–1733+; s John & Rebecca (Prince) Putnam; m Hannah Boardman, 1700 Elizabeth Rolfe

PUTNAM, HANNAH; see ANN PUTNAM SR

PUTNAM, HANNAH; SV; 1658–1722+; dau Samuel & Elizabeth Cutler; m 1678 John Putnam Jr; Rebecca Nurse petitn

PUTNAM, CAPT JOHN SR; SV; 1627–1710; s John & Priscilla (Gould) Putnam; m 1652 Rebecca Prince; Rebecca Nurse petitn, v George Burroughs

PUTNAM, CAPT JOHN JR; const 1692; 1657–1722; s Nathaniel & Elizabeth (Hutchinson) Putnam; m 1678 Hannah Cutler; v Job Tookey, Mary Esty, George Burroughs

PUTNAM, JONATHAN; SV; 1659–1736; s John & Rebecca (Prince) Putnam; m Elizabeth Whipple, Lydia Whipple; v several, Rebecca Nurse petitn

PUTNAM, JOSEPH; SV; 1669–1725; s Thomas & Mary (–) (Veren) Putnam; m 1690 Elizabeth Porter; half-bro Thomas Putnam; Rebecca Nurse petitn

PUTNAM, LYDIA; SV; dau Anthony & Elizabeth Whipple; m Jonathan Putnam; Rebecca Nurse petitn

PUTNAM, NATHANIEL; SV; c 1619–1700; s John & Priscilla (Gould) Putnam; m 1652 Elizabeth Hutchinson; Rebecca Nurse petitn, v Sarah Buckley, Elizabeth Fosdick, Elizabeth Paine, John Willard, Daniel Wilkins' coroner's jury

PUTNAM, REBECCA; SV; dau – Prince; m 1652 John Putnam; Rebecca Nurse petitn, v George Burroughs

PUTNAM, SARAH; m Benjamin Putnam; Rebecca Nurse petitn

PUTNAM, SARAH; Salm; 1648?–; perh dau Thomas & Ann (Holyoke) Putnam Sr; sis Thomas Putnam; Rebecca Nurse petitn

PUTNAM, THOMAS; SV; 1652–1699; s Thomas & Ann (Holyoke) Putnam; m 1678 Ann Carr; v many

PUTNEY, JOHN JR, also Pudney; Salm; 1663–1713; s John & Judith (Cook) Pudney; m Mary Jones; v Job Tookey

R

RAYMENT, –; Bev; m Thomas Rayment; v Sarah Bishop

RAYMENT, THOMAS; SV; s John & Rachel (Scruggs) Rayment; neph William Rayment; m – –; v Sarah Bishop, etc

RAYMENT, WILLIAM SR; Bev; c 1637–1709; m Hannah Bishop, Ruth Hill; v Bridget Bishop

RAYMENT, WILLIAM JR; Bev; c 1666–1701; s William & Hannah (Bishop) Rayment; v Sarah Bishop, v Mercy Lewis & affl, for Elizabeth Procter

REA, DANIEL; SV; 1654–1715; s Joshua & Sarah (Waters) Rea; m1678 Hepzibah Peabody, 1709 Mary (Read) Tompkins; Daniel Wilkins' coronor's jury, v John Willard, Rebecca Nurse petitn

REA, HEPZIBAH; SV; dau – Peabody; m 1678 Daniel Rea; wit sum v Giles Cory, Rebecca Nurse petitn

REA, JEMIMA; SV; 1680–; dau Daniel & Hepzibah (Peabody) Rea; m Nicholas Howard; affl, v Goody Nurse, Cloyce & Black

REA, JOSHUA JR; SV; 1664–1710; s Joshua & Sarah (Waters) Rea; m 168? Elizabeth Leach; male witch mark search committee, Rebecca Nurse petitn

REA, JOSHUA SR; SV; c 1629–1710; s Daniel & Bethia Rea; m 1651 Sarah Waters; v John Willard, Rebecca Nurse petitn

REA, SAMUEL SR; SV–1718; m Mary –

REA, SARAH; SV; 1630–1700; dau Richard & Rejoice Waters; m 1651 Joshua Rea; Rebecca Nurse petitn

READE, PHILLIP; Conc; itinerant physician; c 1633–1696; m c 1669 Abigail Rice

REDD, SAMUEL; Mbl; "head fisherman"; m Wilmot –

REDD, WILMOT, also Reed, Read; Mbl; -1692; m Samuel Redd; tried, found guilty, hanged 22 Sept 1692

REDDINGTON, ABRAHAM; Box; bp 1617–1697; s Thomas & Hannah (Perry) Reddington; m 1643 Margaret –; wit sum v Sarah Wilds

REDDINGTON, JOHN; Tops; bp 1619–1690; s Thomas & Hannah (Perry) Reddington; m c 1648 Mary Gould, Sarah (–) Witt

REDDINGTON, MARGARET; Tops; c 1622–1694; m 1643 Abraham Reddington; v Mary Esty, Sarah Wilds

REDDINGTON, MARY; Tops; 1621–; dau Zaccheus & Phebe (Deacon) Gould; m 1648 John Reddington; gr-mo Mary Herrick [Jr]; v Sarah Wilds

REDDINGTON, SARAH; Tops; m John Witt, 167? John Reddington, 1691 Edward Bragg

REED, CHRISTOPHER; Bev; m Elizabeth Hour/Hoar?; v Dorcas Hoar

REMINGTON, JONATHAN; Camb; 1639–1700; s John Remmington?; m 1664 Martha Belcher

REMMINGTON, JONATHAN; Camb; tavernkeeper, lawyer, legis; 1677–1745; s Jonathan & Martha (Belcher) Remmington; m 1711 Lucy Bradstreet; reparation committee

RICE, SARAH; Read; –1698; dau – Clark?; m 1642 George Davis; m 1679? Nicholas Rice; arrested

RICH, THOMAS; –1723+; s – & Martha Rich; step-s Giles Cory

RICHARDS, JOHN; Bev; c 1646–; m 1674 Elizabeth Woodbury; v Dorcas Hoar

RICHARDS, JOHN; Dorch; merch, legis; –1694; m 1654 Elizabeth (Hawkins) (Long) Winthrop, 1692 Anne Winthrop; O&T, SCJ

RICHARDSON, NATHANIEL; Lancaster; 1673–; m 1694 Abigail Reed; v John Willard

RIGGS, THOMAS JR; const Glo; 1666–1756; s Thomas & Mary (Millett) Riggs; m 1687 Ann Wheeler, 1724 Elizabeth Wood, 1727 Ruth Dodge

RIGHT, JOHN see WRIGHT

RING, HANNAH; Salis; 1661–1736+; dau Thomas & Hannah (Jordan) (Francis) Fowler; m 1685 Jarvis Ring; Mary Bradbury petitn

RING, JARVIS; Salis; 1658–c 1728; s Robert & Elizabeth Ring; m 1685 Hannah Fowler; v Susanna Martin, Mary Bradbury petitn

RING, JOSEPH; Salis; 1664– bef 1704?; s Robert & Elizabeth Ring; v Susanna Martin, Thomas Hardy

RITE, ELIZABETH, see WRIGHT

ROBINSON, DEANE, also Dane; And; s Joseph & Phebe (Dane) Robinson; m 1694 Mary Chadwick; gr-s Rev Francis Dane; named

ROBINSON, JOSEPH; And; c 1645–1719; s – & Dorothy Robinson; m 1671 Phebe Dane; step-s Edmund Faulkner; And petitn

ROBINSON, PHEBE; And; dau Rev Francis & Elizabeth (Ingalls) Dane; m 1671 Joseph Robinson; And petitn

ROGERS, JOHN; Bill; 1641–1695; s John & Priscilla (Dawes) Rogers; m 1667 Mary Shedd, 1689 Abigail (Gould) Rogers; v Martha Carrier

ROGERS, REV JOHN; Ip; min Ip; HC 1684; 1666–1747; s John & Elizabeth (Denison) Rogers; m 1691 Martha Whittingham; 1703 petitn

ROGERS, MARTHA; Ip; dau John & Martha (Hubbard) Whittingham; m 1691 Rev. John Rogers

ROLFE, BENJAMIN; Hav; min Hav; HC 1684; 1662–1708; s Benjamin & Apphia Rolfe; m 1694 Mehitabel Atwater; 1703 petitn

ROOTS, SUSANNAH; Bev; wid Josiah Roots, mo Bethia Lovett; arrested

ROW, ABIGAIL, also Roe; Glo; 1677–; dau Hugh & Mary (Prince) Row; arrested

ROW, HUGH; Glo; s John & Bridget Row; m 1667 Rachel Langton (dau Rachel Vincent), 1674 Mary Prince

ROW, MARY; GLo; 1658–1723; dau Thomas & Margaret Prince; m 1674 Hugh Row; arrested

RUCK, ELIZABETH; Salm; bp 1643–1711+; dau Capt Walter & Elizabeth Price; m 1659 John Croade, 1672 John Ruck; wit sum v George Burroughs

RUCK, JOHN; Salm; c 1627–1697; s Thomas & Elizabeth Ruck; m c 1650 Hannah Spooner, 1661 Sarah Flint, 1672 Elizabeth (Price) Croade; f-in-law George Burroughs; v George Burroughs, grand jury foreman 1692

RUCK, SAMUEL; Salm; shipwright; 1676–1751+; s John & Elizabeth (Price) (Croade) Ruck; m 1699 Elizabeth Tawley, aft 1711 Sarah Cheever; wit sum v George Burroughs

RUCK, THOMAS Salm; 1658–1704?; s John & Hannah (Spooner) Ruck; m Damaris Buffum; v George Burroughs

RUSSELL, JAMES Chas; merch, brickyard; s Richard Russell; c 1664 Mable Haynes, 1677 Mary Holyoke, c 1679 Mary Walcott, 1684 Abigail (Corwin) Hathorne; 1692 Charter Council

RUSSELL, MARY; And; c 1642-; dau – Marshall; m Robert Russell; And petitn

RUSSELL, ROBERT; And; m Mary Marshall; And petitn

RUSSELL, WILLIAM; Read; farmer, fisherman; c 1647–1733; m 1678 Elizabeth Nurse; s-in-law Rebecca Nurse

S

SAFFORD, GOODY; Ip; c 1631–; dau – Baker; m 1660 Joseph Safford; distracted, v Bridget Bishop & Elizabeth How

SAFFORD, JOSEPH; Ip; c 1633–1701+; s Thomas & Elizabeth Safford; m 1660 Mary Baker; v Bridget Bishop, Elizabeth How

SALTENSTALL, NATHANIEL; Hav; landowner, milit; HC 1659; c 1639–1707; s Richard & Meriell (Gurdon) Saltonstall; m 1663 Elizabeth Ward; quit O&T, named

SALTER, HENRY; And; s Henry & Hannah Salter; m – –; arrested, confess

SARGENT, MARY; Glo; bp 1659–1725; dau Peter & Mary (Epps) Duncan; m 1678 William Sargent; affl

SARGENT, WILLIAM SR; Glo; mariner; m 1678 Mary Duncan

SAWDY, JOHN; And; c 1679–1702; s John & Elizabeth (Peters) Sawdy; step-kin Wright, Johnson; arrested

SCARGEN, ELIZABETH; jailed, reason unkn

SCOTT, MARGARET; Row; –1692; dau – Stevenson; m 1651 Benjamin Scott; tried, condemn, hanged 22 Sept 1692

SCOTTOW, CAPT JOSHUA; Bost; merch; c 1651–1698; m Lydia –

SEARGENT, see SARGENT

SEARGEANT, WILLIAM SR; Glo; mariner; m 1678 Mary Duncan

SEARS, ANN; Wob; dau –; m c 1640 Jacob Farrar, 1680 John Sears; arrested

SEARS, JOHN; Wob; –1697; m Susanna –, Esther Mason, 1680 Ann (–) Farrar

SEVERANCE, EPHRAIM, also Severans; Salis; s John & Abigail (Kimball) Severance; m 1682 Lydia Morey; Mary Bradbury petitn

SEVERANCE, LYDIA; Salis; 1661–; dau Abraham & Sarah (Clement) Morey; m 1682 Ephraim Severance; Mary Bradbury petitn

SEWALL, SAMUEL; Bost; merch, legis; 1652–1730; s Henry & Jane (Dummer) Sewall; m 1676 Hannah Hull, 1719 Abigail (Melzen) (Woodman) Tilley, 1722 Mary (Shrimpton) Gibbs; O&T, SCJ

SEWALL, STEPHEN; Salm; merch, clerk O&T court; 1657–1725; s Henry & Jane (Dummer) Sewall; m 1682 Margaret Mitchell

SHAFFLIN, ALICE, also Schafflin; "widow Shaflin"; Salm; –1714; dau – Temple; m George Booth, Michael Shaflin; mo Alice, Elizabeth, & George Booth

SHAFFLIN, MICHAEL; Salm; tailor; -1686; m Elizabeth –, Alice (Temple) Booth

SHATTUCK, SAMUEL; Salm; feltmaker, hatter; 1649–1702; s Samuel & Grace Shattuck; m 1676 Sarah Buckman; bro-in-law Abigail Soames; v Bridget Bishop, Alice Parker

SHATTUCK, SAMUEL [JR]; Salm; 1678–1695; s Samuel & Sarah (Buckman) Shattuck; "bewitched"

SHATTUCK, SARAH; Salm; dau – Buckman; m 1676 Samuel Shattuck; v Bridget Bishop

SHAW, DEBORAH; Salm; c 1652-; m William Shaw

SHAW, ELIZABETH; Salm; d by 1692; dau – Fraile; m 1668 William Shaw

SHAW, WILLIAM SR; Salm; c 1640–1726; m 1668 Elizabeth Fraile, Deborah –; v Sarah Good, Lydia Dustin

SHAW, WILLIAM JR; Salm; s William & Elizabeth (Fraile) Shaw; m 1683 Johanna Pudney

SHELDEN, EPHRAIM; Salm; c 1670–1694; s William & Rebecca (Scadlock) Shelden; m bef 1691 Jane? –; for Martha Cory

SHELDEN, SUSANNAH; see CHILDEN; Salm; c 1674–; dau William & Rebecca (Scadlock) Shelden; affl, accused many

SHEPHERD, –, "Mr Shepherd," perh Rev Jeremiah Shepherd; Lynn; min Lynn; HC 1664; 1648–1720; s Rev Thomas & Margaret (Boradil) Shepherd; m Mary Wainwright; bro-in-law Jonathan Cogswell, Joseph Procter; child affl?

SHEPHERD, ELIZABETH; Salm; d 1691 age 3; dau John & Rebecca (Putnam) (Fuller) Shepherd

SHEPHERD, JOHN; Row; tailor; –1726; m 1677 Rebecca (Putnam) Fuller, Hannah (Green) Acy, 1719 Rebecca Pryor; helped sis-in-law Mary Green escape twice

SHEPHERD, REBECCA; Salm; 1653–1689; dau John & Rebecca (Prince) Putnam; m 1672 John Fuller, 1677 John Shepherd

SHEPHERD, SARAH; Salis; 1655–1748; dau Roger & Sarah Eastman; m 1678 Joseph French, 1684 Solomon Shepherd; Mary Bradbury petitn

SHERRIN[G], JOHN, prob Sherwin; Ip; –1707+; m 1667 Frances Loomis, 1691 Mary Chandler; v Elizabeth How

SHILLTOW, ROBERT; Row; –1687; suspected Margaret Scott

SHORT, HENRY; Newb; 1652–1706; s Henry & Sarah (Glover) Short; m 1674 Sarah Whipple, 1692 Anne (Sewall) Longfellow; bro-in-law Samuel & Stephen Sewall; town clerk

SIBLEY, MARY; SV; dau – Woodrow?; m Samuel Sibley; suggests folk magic

SIBLEY, SAMUEL; SV; c 1657–; s John & Rachel (Leach) Sibley; m Mary Woodrow?; Rebecca Nurse petitn, v Sarah Good, John Procter

SLUE, LEONARD; Bev; m by 1678 Tabitha Hoar

SLUE, LEONARD; Bev; s Leonard & Tabitha (Hoar) Slue; gr-s Dorcas Hoar

SLUE, RACHEL; Bev; dau Leonard & Tabitha (Hoar) Slue; gr-dau Dorcas Hoar

SLUE, TABITHA; Bev; dau William & Dorcas (Galley) Hoar; m by 1678 Leonard Slue

SMALL, ANNE; Salm; c 1636–1688; m John Small

SMALL, HANNAH; Salm; bp 1657–1716+; dau John & Rachel (Leach) Sibley; m 1676 Stephen Small; v Giles Cory

SMALL, JOHN; Salm; –1688; m Anne

SMALL, STEPHEN; Salm; c 1656–1722; s John & Anne Small; m 1676 Hannah Sibley

SMITH, ELIZABETH; Salis; dau – –; m Richard Smith; Mary Bradbury petitn

SMITH, GEORGE; Salm; –1744; m Hannah Gaskill; Procter petitn

SMITH, JAMES; Mbl; sea capt, const; s James & Mary Smith; m bef 1660 –

SMITH, RICHARD; Salis; c 1640–1712 or 13; m 1666 Sarah Chandler, Elizabeth –; Mary Bradbury petitn, 1693 grand jury

SMITH, CAPT SAMUEL; "late of Boston"; mariner; d by 1692

SMITH, SAMUEL; Box; c 1667–; v Mary Esty

SMITH, THOMAS; Ip; tailor; ?166?–; s John & Elizabeth Smith?; v Rachel Clinton

SOAMES, ABIGAIL, also Somes; Salm; 1655-; dau Morris & Elizabeth (Kendall) Soames; arrested

SOAMES, ELIZABETH; Glo; –1697; dau John & Elizabeth Kendall; m 1647 Morris Soames

SOAMES, JOHN; Bost; cooper; 1648–1700; s Morris & Elizabeth (Kendall) Soames; m Hannah Shattuck; bro-in-law Samuel Shattuck

SOUTHWICK, JOSIAH, also Southerek; Salm; 1632–1692; s Lawrence & Casandra Southwick; m 1653 Mary Boyce; bro Provided Gaskell

SPARK, JOHN; Ip; –1704?; innkeeper; m 1661 Mary Sennet

SPARKS, HENRY; Chelm; m 1676 Martha Barrett

SPARKS, MARTHA; Chelm; 1656–; dau Thomas & Frances (Woolderson) Barrett; m 1676 Henry Sparks; arrested 1691

SPRAGUE, MARTHA; And; 1676-; dau Phineas & Sarah (Hasey) Sprague; m 1701 Richard Friend; step-dau Moses Tyler, step-niece Elizabeth Paine; affl, accused many

STACY, JOHN; carpenter; s Thomas & Susanna (Wooster) Stacy; v Job Tookey

STACY, PRISCILLA; Salm; d c 1690; dau William & Priscilla (Buckley) Stacy; gr-dau Sarah Buckley

STACY, WILLIAM; Salm; millwright; 1656–1694+; s Thomas & Susanna (Wooster) Stacy; m 1677 Priscilla Buckley; s-in-law Sarah Buckley; v Bridget Bishop

STANYON, JOHN; Hampton Falls, NH; 1643–1718; s Anthony & Ann (–) (Partridge) Stanyon; m 1663 Mary Bradbury Jr

STANYON, MARY; Hampton Falls, NH; 1643–; dau Thomas & Mary (Perkins) Bradbury; m 1663 John Stanyon

STARLING, WILLIAM; Hav const; m Elizabeth –, 1676 Mary (Blaisdell) Stowers, 1683 Ann (Nichols) Neal; s-in-law Henry Blezdel/Blaisdel

STERNES, ISAAC; Salm; 1658–1692; m Hannah Beckett

STEVENS, BENJAMIN; And; magis; 1656–1730; s John & Hannah (Barnard) Stevens; m 1715 Susanna (Symes) Chickering; accused

STEVENS, DOROTHY; Salis; 1673–1716?; d Richard & Martha (Allen) Hubbard; m John Stevens; Mary Bradbury petitn

STEVENS, ELIZABETH; And; dau George & Hannah (Chandler) Abbott; m 1692 Nathaniel Stevens; And petitn

STEVENS, EPHRAIM; And; c 1648–1719; s John & Elizabeth Stevens; m 1680 Sarah Abbott; And petitn

STEVENS, HANNAH; Salis; dau – Barnard; m John Stevens, wid; Mary Bradbury petitn

STEVENS, LT JAMES; Glo; ship carpenter; c 1630–1697; s William & Philippa? Stevens; m1656 Susanna Eveleth; bro Mary Fitch; v Rebecca Dike, Esther Elwell, Abigail Row

STEVENS, JOANNA; Salis; dau – Thorne; m 1670 John Stevens; Mary Bradbury petitn

STEVENS, JOHN; And; 1663–1728; s John & Hannah (Barnard) Stevens; m 1689 Ruth Poor

STEVENS, JOHN; Salis; 1670–; s John & Joanna (Thorne) Stevens; m Dorothy Hubbard; Mary Bradbury petitn

STEVENS, JOSEPH; And; 1654–; s John & Hannah (Barnard) Stevens; m c 1679 Mary Ingalls, 1700 Elizabeth Brown; And petitn

STEVENS, MEHITABEL; Salis; dau – Colcord; m 1677 Nathaniel Stevens; Mary Bradbury petitn

STEVENS, NATHANIEL; Salis; 1645–; s John & Katherine Stevens; m 1677 Mehitabel Colcord; Mary Bradbury petitn

STEVENS, WILLIAM; Glo; c 1654–1701; s James & Susanna (Eveleth) Stevens; m 1682 Abigail Sargent; neph Mary Fitch; v Esther Elwell, 1693 grand jury

STONE, JOHN; And; m c 1668 Mary Ross

STOREY, WILLIAM; Ip; s William Storey; m 1671 Susanna Fuller; Procter petitn

STORY, WILLIAM; Ip; carpenter; –1693+; or his s William; m 1671 Susanna Fuller; Procter petitn

STOUGHTON, WILLIAM; Dorch;; HC 1650, Oxford 1652; landowner, legis; c 1631–1701; s Israel & Elizabeth (Knight) Stoughton; Lt Gov 1692 etc, Chief Justice O&T, SCJ

SWAIN, MAJ JEREMIAH; Read; 1643–1710; s Jeremiah & Mary Swain; m Mary Smith; bro Mary Marshall; v Mary Taylor

SWAN, JOHN; And; 1668–1742; s Robert & Elizabeth Swan; m 1699 Susanna (–) Wood; v Mary Clark

SWAN, ROBERT; And; c 1626–1697; s Richard & Ann Swan; m Elizabeth Acey, 1690 Hannah (Acey) Ross; v Mary Clark

SWAN, TIMOTHY; And; 1663–1693; s Robert & Elizabeth (Acey) Swan

SWIFT, SARAH, Milton; –1718; dau – Clapp; m Thomas Swift; accused by maid Mary Watkins

SWINNERTON, ESTHER; SV; –c 1720; dau – Baker; m 1673 Job Swinnerton; Rebecca Nurse petitn

SWINNERTON, JOB; SV; c 1630–1700; s Job & Elizabeth? Swinnerton; m 1658 Ruth Symonds, 1673 Esther Baker; Rebecca Nurse petitn, 1693 grand jury

SYMMES, REV THOMAS; Box; min Box; HC 1698; 1678–1725; s Zachariah & Susanna (Graves) Symmes; 1703 petitn

SYMMES, REV ZECHARIAH; Brad; min Brad; HC 1657; 1638–1708; s Zachariah & Sarah Symmes; m 1669 Susanna Graves, 1683 Mehitabel Dalton; 1703 petitn

SYM[M]ONDS, ELIZABETH; Box; c 1640–1722; dau Robert & Grace Andrews; m Samuel Symmonds; sis John, Joseph & Thomas Andrews of Boxford & Mary Cummings; v Sarah Wildes

T

TARBELL, JOHN; SV; 1654–1715; s Thomas & Mary Tarbell; m 1678 Mary Nurse; Rebecca Nurse petitn

TARBELL, MARY; SV; 1659–1749; dau Francis & Rebecca (Towne) Nurse; m 1678 John Tarbell; for Rebecca Nurse

TARR, RICHARD; Glo; 1660?–1732; m 1680 Elizabeth –

TAY, ISIAH; Bost; merch, ship owner, distiller; c 1650–1730; s William & Grace (Newell) Tay; m Elizabeth –, 1719 Mary (–) Watkins

TAYLOR, MARY; Read; c 1652–; dau Richard & Elizabeth Harrington; m 1671 Seabred Taylor; arrest, confess, tried, not guilty

TAYLOR, SEABRED; Read; 1643–; d Thomas & Elizabeth Taylor?; m 1671 Mary Harrington

THATCHER, MARGARET; Bost; bp 1625–1694; dau Henry Gibbs; m 1642 Jacob Sheafe, 1664 Rev Thomas Thatcher; accused

THOMAS, ELIAS; Bost; 1710–; s Peter & Elizabeth (Burroughs) Thomas; m Hannah Mackmillon; gr-s Rev George Burroughs

THOMAS, ELIZABETH; bp 1682– d bef 1719; dau Rev George & Hannah (Fisher) Burroughs; m 1704 Peter Thomas; sis Charles, George Jr, Jeremiah, Sarah & Mary Burroughs, Rebecca Fowle, Hannah Fox

THOMAS, PETER; 1682–; s George & Rebecca (Maverick) Thomas; m 1704 Elizabeth Burroughs, 1719 Mary Roby

THOMAS, WARNEY, see VARNEY, THOMAS

THOMPSON, ALEXANDER JR; Ip; s Alexander & Deliverance (Haggett) Thompson; witt summ v Rachel Clinton

THOMPSON, WILLIAM; Ip; c 1647–; m 1673 Mary Grave; Procter petitn

TITUBA, also Tituba Indian; SV; Samuel Parris' slave; arrested, confess, v Sarah Good & Sarah Osburn

TOMPKINS, JOHN; Salm; c 1645–1706; s John & Margaret (Goodman) Tompkins; m 1672 Rebecca Knight, 1693 Mary Reed; deputy

TOMSON, JOHN; Salis; –1717; m Elizabeth Brewer, 1707 Mary (–) Ash; Mary Bradbury petitn

TONGUE, MARY; Salis; dau – Payn; m 1688 Steven Tongue; Mary Bradbury petitn

TONGUE, STEVEN; Salis; c 1640–; m 1688 Mary Payn; Mary Bradbury petitn

TOOKEY, JOB; Bev; mariner; c 1665–; s Rev Job & Ann Tookey; arrested

TOOTHAKER, ALLEN; Bill; 1670–1692+; s Roger & Mary (Allen) Toothaker; bro Martha Emerson & Margaret Toothaker; v aunt Martha Carrier

TOOTHAKER, MARGARET; Bill; 1683–1695?; dau Roger & Mary (Allen) Toothaker; sis Martha Emerson & Allen Toothaker

TOOTHAKER, MARTHA, see EMERSON, MARTHA

TOOTHAKER, MARY; Bill; dau Andrew & Faith (Ingalls) Allen; m 1665 Roger Toothaker; sis Martha Carrier, mo Martha Emerson, Allen & Margaret Toothaker; arrested, confess, tried, not guilty

TOOTHAKER, ROGER; Salm/Bill; folk healer, witch-finder; c 1634–1692; s Roger & Margaret Toothaker; m 1665 Mary Allen; f Martha Emerson, Allen & Mary Toothaker; arrested

TORREY, REV SAMUEL; Wey; min Wey; c 1632–1707; s William Torrey; m 1651 Mary Rawson, 1695 Mary (–) Symmes

TOUZEL, SUSANNAH; Salm; 1686– by 1722; dau Philip English; m 1700 John Touzel

TOWNE, SGT EDMUND; Tops; bp 1628–1678; s William & Joanna (Blessing) Towne; m c 1652 Mary Browning

TOWNE, ELIZABETH; Tops; 1669–; dau Edmund & Mary (Browning) Towne; m 1694 Thomas Wilkins; wit sum re Sarah Cloyce

TOWNE, MARGARET see WILLARD, MARGARET

TOWNE, MARY; Tops; d c 1717; dau Thomas & Mary Browning; m c 1652 Edmund Towne; sis-in-law Rebecca Nurse, Mary Esty, Sarah Cloyce; wit sum re Sarah Cloyce

TOWNE, REBECCA; Tops; 1668–; dau Edmund & Mary (Browning) Towne; m c 1693 Phillip Knight, 1701 Joseph Hutchinson; wit sum v aunt Sarah Cloyce

TOWNE, SAMUEL; Tops; 1673–1714; s Edmund & Mary (Browning) Towne; m 1696 Elizabeth Knight; wit sum

TOWNE, WILLIAM; Tops; 1659–1720+; s Edmund & Mary (Browning) Towne; m Eliza –, 1694 Margaret (Wilkins) Willard

TOWNSEND, PENN; Bost; wine merch, legis; 1651–1727; s William & Hannah Townsend; m c 1673 Sarah Addington, c 1693 Mary (Leverett) Dudley, 1709 Hannah (Porter) Jaffrey

TRASK, CHRISTIAN; SV; 1661–1689; dau Humphrey & Elizabeth Woodbury; m John Trask; suicide

TRASK, JOHN; SV; m 1663 Abigail Parkman, Christian Woodbury; v Sarah Bishop

TRASK, SARAH; c 1673–; dau William & Ann (Putnam) Trask; niece Thomas Putnam; v Mary Esty, John Willard, Mary Whittredge

TRUE, HENRY; Salis; house carpenter; 1645–1723+; s Henry & Israel (Pike) True; m 1668 Jane Bradbury; Mary Bradbury petitn

TRUE, JOSEPH; Salis; house carpenter; 1652–1718; s Henry & Israel (Pike) True; m 1675 Ruth Whittier; Mary Bradbury petitn

TRUE, RUTH; Salis; 1651–; dau Thomas & Ruth Whittier; m 1675 Joseph True; sis Nathaniel Whittier; Mary Bradbury petitn

TRUMBULL, JOSEPH; Salm; s John & Ellen Trubbull?; m Hannah Smith?; witt re Susanna Shelden

TUCKER, BENONY; Salis; 1662–1735+; s Morris & Elizabeth (Stevens) Tucker; m c 1685 Ebenezer Nichols; Mary Bradbury petitn

TUCKER, EBENEZER; Salis; dau – Nichols; m c 1685 Benony Tucker; Mary Bradbury petitn

TUCKER, ELIZABETH; Salis; dau – Gill; m 1663 Morris Tucker; Mary Bradbury petitn

TUCKER, MORRIS; Salis; cooper; m 1661 Elizabeth Stevens, 1663 Elizabeth Gill; Mary Bradbury petitn

TUFTS, CAPT PETER; Mald; c 1617–1700; s Peter & Mary (Pierce) Tufts; m 1670 Elizabeth Lynde, Mary Cotton, Prudence (Putnam) Wyman; v Elizabeth Fosdick, Elizabeth Paine

TURNER, JOHN; Salm; merch, sea capt; 1671–1742; s John & Elizabeth (Roberts) Turner; m 1701 Mary Kitchen

TYLER, HANNAH; And; c 1679–; dau Hopestill & Mary (Lovett) Tyler; arrest, tried, not guilty

TYLER, HOPESTILL; And; blacksmith; c 1645–1734; s Job & Mary Tyler; m 1668 Mary Lovett

TYLER, JOHANNA; And; 1681-bef 1728; dau Hopestill & Mary (Lovett) Tyler; arrested, tried, not guilty

TYLER, JOSEPH; Box; 1671–1699; s Moses & Prudence (Blake) Tyler; m Martha –; step-bro Martha Sprague; v John Jackson Sr & Jr, John Howard

TYLER, MARTHA; And; 1676–; dau Hopestill & Mary (Lovett) Tyler; arrested, confess

TYLER, MARY; And; c 1652–1703+; dau Richard & Joanna (Blott) Lovett; m 1668 Hopestill Tyler; arrested, confess, tried, not guilty

TYLER, MOSES; Box; c 1641–1727; s Job & Mary Tyler; m 1666 Prudence Blake, Sarah (Hasey) Sprague; v Elizabeth Johnson Sr & Abigail Johnson

U

USHER, HEZEKIAH; Bost; 1639–1697; s Hezekiah & Frances Usher; m 1676 Bridget (Lisle) Hoar; arrested, escaped

V

VARNEY, THOMAS; Ip; 1640–1692; s William & Bridget (Deverill) Varney; m Abigail Procter; bro Rachel Vincent, bro-in-law John Procter; Procter petitn

VARNUM, SAMUEL see FARNUM

VERY, ELIZABETH; Salm; c 1663–1736; dau John & Elizabeth (Thorndike) Procter; m 1681 Thomas Very

VIBBER, SARAH see BIBBER

VINCENT, SARAH, also Vinson; Glo; c 1631–1707; dau William & Bridget (–) (Parsons) Varney; m Thomas Cook, 1652 Joseph Langton, 1661 William Vincent

W

WADE, COL THOMAS; Ip; magis; c 1656–1696; s Jonathan & Susannah? Wade; m 1670 Elizabeth Cogswell

WALCOTT, JOHN; SV; carpenter, farmer; 1666–c 1737; s Jonathan & Mary (Sibley) Walcott; m Mary –, 1717 Elizabeth Perkins; v Martha Carrier etc

WALCOTT, CAPT JONATHAN SR; SV c 1639–1699; m 1664 Mary Sibley, 1685 Deliverance Putnam; Daniel Wilkins' coroner's jury, v several

WALCOTT, JONATHAN JR; SV; 1670–1745; s Jonathan & Mary (Sibley) Walcott; m Priscilla Bayley; v Sarah Procter

WALCOTT, MARY; SV; 1675–1730+; dau Jonathan & Mary (Sibley) Walcott; m 1696 Isaac Farrar; affl, v many

WALDEN, ABIGAIL; Bev; 1660–; dau John & Elizabeth Woodbury; m Nathaniel Waldon; sis Elizabeth Balch; v Edward & Sarah Bishop

WARDWELL, ELIAKIM, also Wardell; And; 1687–1753; s Samuel & Sarah (Hooper) (Hawkes) Wardwell; m by 1710 Ruth Braydon

WARDWELL, ELIZABETH; And; 168?–1712+; dau Samuel & Sarah (Hooper) (Hawkes) Wardwell

WARDWELL, MERCY; And; 1673–1754; dau Samuel & Sarah (Hooper) (Hawkes) Wardwell; m 1697 John Wright; arrested, confess

WARDWELL, REBECCA; And; 1691–1757; dau Samuel & Sarah (Hooper) (Hawkes) Wardwell; m 1710 Ezekiel Osgood

WARDWELL, SAMUEL; And; 1643–1692; s Thomas & Elizabeth (Woodruff) Wardwell; m 1670? –, 1673 Sarah (Hooper) Hawkes; arrested, confess, tried, recant, hanged 22 Sept 1692

WARDWELL, SAMUEL JR; And; 1677–1755; s Samuel & Sarah (Hooper) (Hawkes) Wardwell; m 1716 Return Ellenwood

WARDWELL, SARAH; And; c 1650–c 1711; dau William & Elizabeth (Marshall) Hooper; m 1670 Adam Hawkes, 1673 Samuel Wardwell; arrested, confess, tried, not guilty

WARDWELL, WILLIAM; And; 1679–1751; s Samuel & Sarah (Hooper) (Hawkes) Wardwell; m 1706 Dorothy White

WARNER, DANIEL SR; Ip; perh 1671-; s Daniel & Faith (Brown) Warner; for Elizabeth How

WARNER, SARAH; Ip; dau John & Eleanor (Clark) Dane; m 1668 Daniel Warner; for Elizabeth How

WARREN, ELIZABETH; sis Mary Warren

WARREN, MARY; Salm; servant; c 1672-; affl, recant, affl, accused, arrested, confess, v many

WATERS, JOHN SR; Salm; bp 1640-; s Richard & Rejoice Waters; m 1663 Sarah Thompkins; wit sum re George Jacobs Sr

WATKINS, MARY; Milton; dau Thomas & Margaret Watkins; servant; affl, v Sarah Swift, confess, tried, not guilty

WATSON, JOHN; Salis; –1710; m 1688 Ruth Griffin; Mary Bradbury petitn

WATSON, RUTH; Salis; –1710+; dau – Griffin; m 1688 John Watson; Mary Bradbury petitn

WAY, AARON; SV; 1674–; s Aaron & Joan (Sumner) Way; m Mary –; neph Bray Wilkins, Richard Way; v Rebecca Nurse

WAY, RICHARD; Bost; bp 1624–1697; m Hester Jones, Bethiha (Mayhew) Harlock, Katherine –, 1689 Hannah (Townsend) (Hull) (Allen) Knight; bro-in-law Bray Wilkins

WAY, WILLIAM; SV; s Aaron & Joan (Somers) Way; m Persis –; Daniel Wilkins coroner jury

WEBBER, MARY; Chas?; c 1639- by 1716; dau John & Mary Parker; m Thomas Webber; v George Burroughs

WEBBER, SAMUEL; Glo/Wells; millwright; s Thomas & Mary (Parker) Webber; m Deborah Littlefield; v George Burroughs

WELCH, PHILIP; Tops; c 1648–; m 1666 Ann Haggett

WELD, EDWARD; Salm; physician; 1666–1702?; s Daniel & Bethia (Mitchelson) Weld; m 1699 Mary (Higginson) Gardner; future s-in-law Capt John Higginson [Jr]; male witch mark search committee

WELLMAN, ABRAHAM; Lynn; c 1643–c 1717; s Thomas & Elizabeth Wellman; m 1668 Elizabeth Cogswell; v Sarah Cole (Lynn)

WELLMAN, ELIZABETH; Lynn; 1648–1736; dau John Cogswell; m 1668 Abraham Wellman; v Sarah Cole (Lynn)

WELLMAN, ISAAC; Lynn; c 1647–1724; s Thomas & Elizabeth (Cogswell) Wellman; m 1679 Hannah Adams; v Sarah Cole (Lynn)

WELLS, REV THOMAS "Mr Wells"; Ames; min Ames; 1647–1734; s Thomas & Abigail (Warner) Wells; m c 1670 Mary Perkins

WHEAT, – "Goody Wheat"; Groton; prob Elizabeth Wheat; dau – Mansfield; m 1675 Joshua Wheat; wit sum v John Willard

WHEELWRIGHT, – "Mr Wheelwright" Rev John Wheelwright; m 1621 Marie Storre, Mary Hutchinson; f "wid Maverick"

WEST, THOMAS; Salm; –1701+; m 1658 Phebe Waters, 1674 Mary Tenne, male witch mark search committee

WESTGATE, JOHN; Salm; mariner; c 1652-; v Alice Parker

WESTON, ELIZABETH; Read; dau John Weston; v Sarah Dustin

WESTON, JOHN; Read; c 1631?–1723; m 1653 Sarah Fitch, 1681 Mary Bryant

WHIPPLE, JOSEPH; SV; c 1666–; s John Whipple; m 1691 Sarah Hutchinson; v Elizabeth Fosdick, Elizabeth Paine

WHITE, JUDAH; Bost; servant, "a Jersey maid"; named

WHITE, PHILIP; Bev; c 1662–; s John & Mary (–) (Phips) White; m –; half-bro Gov William Phips; his child said to be affl

WHITTIER, MARY; Sals; dau John Osgood; m 1685 Nathaniel Whittier; Mary Bradbury petitn, v Susanna Martin

WHITTIER, NATHANIEL; Salis; 1658–; s Thomas & Ruth Whittier; m 1685 Mary Osgood, 1710 Mary (–) Ring; bro Ruth True; Mary Bradbury petitn

WHITTREDGE, MARY, also Witheridge; SV; 1652–1725; dau William & Sarah (Smith) Buckley; m 1684 Sylvester Whittredge, 1694 Benjamin Procter; arrested, tried, not guilty

WIGGLESWORTH, REV MICHAEL; Mald; min Mald; HC 1651; 1631–1705; s Edward & Esther (Reyner) Wigglesworth; m 1655 Mary Reyner, 1679 Martha Mudge, 1691 Sybil (Sparhawk) Avery

WILDS, EPHRAIM; const Tops; 1666–1725; s John & Sarah (Averill) Wilds; m 1690 Mary Howle; for mo Sarah Wilds

WILDS, JOHN; Tops; c 1620–1705; m Priscilla Gould, 1663 Sarah Averill, 1693 Mary (–) Jacobs

WILDS, SARAH; Tops; –1692; dau William & Sarah Averill; m 1663 John Wilds; tried, condemned, hanged 19 July 1692

WILFORD RUTH; Hav; wid Gilbert Wilford; arrested

WILKINS, BENJAMIN; SV; c 1656–1715; s Bray & Hannah (Way) Wilkins; m 1667 Priscilla Baxter; v John Willard, Sarah Buckley

WILKINS, BRAY; SV; c 1611–1702; m Hannah Way; v gr-s-in-law John Willard

WILKINS, DANIEL; SV; c 1675–1692; s Henry & Rebecca (Baxter) Wilkins; affl, v uncle John Willard

WILKINS, HENRY SR; SV; c 1651–1737; s Bray & Hannah (Way) Wilkins; m c 1672 Rebecca Baxter, 1691 Ruth (Fuller) Wheeler; v John Willard

WILKINS, JOHN; SV; c 1666–1718+; s John & Mary Wilkins; m c 1676 Lydia –, 1688 Betty Southwick; v John Willard

WILKINS, LYDIA; SV; –1689; m c 1676 John Wilkins

WILKINS, REBECCA; SV; c 1673–by 1737; dau Henry & Rebecca (Baxter) Wilkins; m 1695 Philip Mackentire; gr-dau Bray Wilkins; v uncle John Wilkins

WILKINS, SAMUEL; SV; c 1656–1715; s Bray & Hannah (Way) Wilkins; m 1677 Priscilla Baxter; v John Willard

WILKINSON, –; Mald; "wife of John Wilkinson of Malden," named, perh Abigail (Gowing) Wilkinson?

WILLARD, HANNAH; SV; bp 1616–1702+; dau Henry & Elizabeth (Batchelor) Way; m Bray Wilkins; sis Richard Way, aunt Aaron Way

WILLARD, JOHN; SV; –1692; m c 1687 Margaret Wilkins; gr-s-in-law Bray Wilkins; arrested, tried; condemned, hanged 19 Aug 1692

WILLARD, MARGARET; SV; c 1668–1751; dau Thomas & Hannah (Nichols) Wilkins; m 1687 John Willard, 1694 William Towne

WILLARD, REV SAMUEL; Bost; HC 1651; 1640–1707; s Maj Simon & Mary (Sharp) Willard; m 1664 Abigail Sherman, 1679 Eunice Tyng; criticized trials, aided escapes, named

WILLARD, SIMON; Salm; 1649–1731; weaver, clothier; s Maj Simon Willard; m 1679 Martha Jacobs, 1722 Priscilla Buttolph; bro Rev Samuel Willard; v John Emons, George Burroughs

WILLIAMS, ABIGAIL; SV; c 1681–; niece Samuel Parris; affl, accused many

WILLIAMS, NATHANIEL; Bost; dry goods shopkeeper; s Nathaniel & Mary Williams; m Lydia –, Mary (Oliver) Shrimpoton, 1700 Sarah Crisp

WILSON, JOSEPH; And; –1718; s William & Patience Wilson; m 1670 Mary Lovejoy, 1678 Sarah Lord; And petitns, 1693 jury

WILSON, SARAH SR; And; c 1643–1722; dau Robert & Mary Lord; m 1678 Joseph Wilson; arrested, confess

WILSON, SARAH JR; And; arrested, confess

WINSLEY, EPHRAIM; Salis; 1641–1709; s Samuel & Elizabeth Winsley; m 1668 Mary Greeley; Mary Bradbury petitn

WINSLEY, MARY; Salis; 1649–1697; dau Andrew & Mary (Moyce) Greeley; m 1668 Ephraim Winsley; Mary Bradbury petitn

WINTHROP, MAJ GEN WAIT-STILL, Bost; physician, legis; s John & Elizabeth (Read) Winthrop; m Mary Browne, 1707 Katherine (Brattle) Eyre; O&T, SCJ

WISE, REV JOHN; Ip; min Chebbaco; HC 1673; 1652–1725; s Joseph & Mary (Thompson) Wise; m 1678 Abigail Gardner; Procter petit, 1703 petitn

WOOD, JOSIAH; Bev; 1666–1683; s Anthony & Mary (Grover) Wood, see GRANT, MARY

WOODBURY, ABIGAIL see WALDEN

WOODBURY, ANDREW; perh Bev; d by 1685; s William & Elizabeth? Woodbury;

WOODWELL, ELIZABETH; Salm; 1659-; dau Simon & Sarah Stacy; m John Woodwell; sis William Stacy: or perh their dau?; v Giles Cory, George Burroughs

WORMALL, WILLIAM; v George Burroughs; prob WILLIAM WORMWOOD

WORMWOOD, JACOB; Mbl; perh s William Wormwood; m Margaret Reynolds?; wit sum v Wilmot Redd

WORMWOOD, CAPT WILLIAM; York; –1724?; perh s William; m Mary (–)Wormwood?; v George Burroughs

WRIGHT, ELIZABETH; And; 1662–; dau Andrew & Mary (Beamsley) (Williams) Peters; m 1678 John Sawdy Sr, 1684 Walter Wright; mo John Sawdy [Jr]; And petitn

WRIGHT, JOHN; And; 1675–1752; s Walter & Susanna (Johnson) Wright; m 1697 Mercy Wardwell

WRIGHT, WALTER; And; weaver; m Susanna Johnson, Elizabeth (Peters) Sawdy; step-f John Sawdy; And petitns, bail for several

WYCOMB, FRANCES; Row; 1675–1750; dau Daniel & Mary (Smith) Wycomb; m 1694 Samuel Johnson; affl, v Martha Scott

WYCOMB, CAPT DANIEL; Row; carpenter; 1635–1700; m 1658 Mary Smith, 1691 Lydia (Bailey) Platts; v Margaret Scott

WORKS CITED

Abbott, Orville Lawrence. "Verbal Endings in Seventeenth-Century American English." *American Speech* 33 (1958): 185–94.

The Acts and Resolves, Public and Private, of the Province of the Massachusetts Bay. 21 vols. Boston: Wright & Potter, 1869–1922.

Ady, Thomas. *A Candle in the Dark.* London, 1656. [Wing (2nd ed.) / A674.]

Alexander, Henry. "The Language of the Salem Witchcraft Trials." *American Speech* 3 (1928): 390–400.

Algeo, John, ed. *The Cambridge History of the English Language.* Vol. 6, *English in North America.* Cambridge: Cambridge University Press, 2001.

Algeo, John. "External History." In *The Cambridge History of the English Language.* Vol. 6, *English in North America*, edited by John Algeo, 1–58. Cambridge: Cambridge University Press, 2001.

Ankarloo, Bengt. "Sweden: The Mass Burnings (1668–1676)." In *Early Modern European Witchcraft: Centres and Peripheries*, edited by Bengt Ankarloo and Gustav Henningsen, 285–317. Oxford: Oxford University Press, 1993.

Archer, Dawn. "Can Innocent People Be Guilty? A Sociopragmatic Analysis of Examination Transcripts from the Salem Witchcraft Trials." *Journal of Historical Pragmatics* 3 (2002): 1–30.

Archer, Dawn. *Questions and Answers in the English Courtroom (1640–1760): A Sociopragmatic Analysis.* Amsterdam: John Benjamins, 2005.

Bailey, Sarah Loring. *Historical Sketches of Andover, Comprising the Present Towns of North Andover and Andover, Essex County, Massachusetts.* Boston: Houghton, Mifflin and Company, 1880.

Baker, Emerson W., and John G. Reid. *The New England Knight: Sir William Phips, 1651–1695.* Toronto: University of Toronto Press, 1998.

Baker, J. H. *An Introduction to English Legal History.* London: Butterworths, 1990.

Barber, Charles. *Early Modern English.* Edinburgh: Edinburgh University Press, 1997 [1976].

Baxter, Richard. *The Certainty of the Worlds of Spirits.* London, 1691. [Wing / B1215.]

Bernard, Richard. *A Gvide to Grand-Ivry Men.* London, 1627. [STC (2nd ed.) / 1943.]

BLD = Garner, Bryan A., ed. *Black's Law Dictionary.* 7th ed. St. Paul, MN: West Group, 1999.

The Book of the General Lawes and Libertyes Concerning the Inhabitants of the Massachusets. Cambridge, MA, 1648. [Wing / M987.]

Boyer, Paul, and Stephen Nissenbaum, eds. *Salem-Village Witchcraft: A Documentary Record of Local Conflict in Colonial New England.* Belmont, CA: Wadsworth Publishing Company, 1972.

Boyer, Paul, and Stephen Nissenbaum. *Salem Possessed: The Social Origins of Witchcraft.* Cambridge, MA: Harvard University Press, 1974.

Boyer, Paul, and Stephen Nissenbaum, eds. *The Salem Witchcraft Papers: Verbatim Transcripts of the Legal Documents of the Salem Witchcraft Outbreak of 1692.* 3 vols. New York: Da Capo Press, 1977.

Boyer, Paul, and Stephen Nissenbaum. "Salem Possessed in Retrospect." *The William and Mary Quarterly*, 3rd ser., 65 (2008): 503–534.

Brattle, Thomas. "Copy of a MS. Letter . . . Written by Thomas Brattle, F.R.S. and Communicated to the Society by Thomas Brattle, Esq. of Cambridge." *Collections of the Massachusetts Historical Society*, 61–80. Boston, 1798.

Breslaw, Elaine G. *Tituba, Reluctant Witch of Salem: Devilish Indians and Puritan Fantasies.* New York: New York University Press, 1996.

Brown, David C. "The Forfeitures at Salem, 1692." *The William and Mary Quarterly*, 3rd ser., 50 (1991): 85–111.

Brown, William. *The Clerk's Tutor in Chancery.* London, 1688. [Wing / B5079.]

Burr, George Lincoln. *Narratives of the Witchcraft Cases 1648–1706.* New York: Charles Scribner's Sons, 1914.

Calef, Robert. *More Wonders of the Invisible World, or, the Wonders of the Invisible World Display'd in Five Parts.* London, 1700. [Wing / C288.]

Caporeal, Linnda. "Ergotism: The Satan Loosed in Salem?" *Science* 192 (1976): 21–26.

Chapin, Bradley. *Criminal Justice in Colonial America, 1606–1660.* Athens: University of Georgia Press, 1983.

Chever, George F. "Philip English." *Historical Collections of the Essex Institute* 2 (1860): 21–32, 133–44, 185–204, 237–48, 261–72; 3 (1861): 17–28, 67–79, 111–20.

Cockburn, James Swanston. *A History of English Assizes 1558–1714*. Cambridge: Cambridge University Press, 1972.

Cooper, James F. Jr., and Kenneth P. Minkema, eds. *The Sermon Notebook of Samuel Parris 1689–1694*. Boston: The Colonial Society of Massachusetts, 1993.

Craker, Wendel D. "Spectral Evidence, Non-Spectral Acts of Witchcraft, and Confession at Salem in 1692." *The Historical Journal* 40 (1997): 331–58.

Cressy, David. *Literacy and the Social Order: Reading and Writing in Tudor and Stuart England*. Cambridge: Cambridge University Press, 1980.

Cusack, Bridget, ed. *Everyday English 1500–1700: A Reader*. Edinburgh: Edinburgh University Press, 1998.

Dalton, Michael. *The Covntrey Ivstice*. London, 1618. [STC (2nd ed.) / 6206.]

Dalton, Michael. *The Country Justice*. London, 1690. [Wing / D149.]

Davidson, Adele. "'Some by Stenography?' Stationers, Shorthand, and the Early Shakespearean Quartos." *Papers of the Bibliographical Society of America* 90 (1996): 417–49.

Dawson, Giles E., and Laetitia Kennedy-Skipton. *Elizabethan Handwriting 1500–1650: A Guide to the Reading of Documents and Manuscripts*. London: Faber and Faber, 1968.

Dekeyser, Xavier. "Relativizers in Early Modern English: A Dynamic Quantitative Study." In *Historical Syntax*, edited by Jacek Fisiak, 61–87. Berlin: Mouton de Gruyter, 1984.

Demos, John. *Entertaining Satan*. Oxford: Oxford University Press, 1982.

Denison, David. "Some Recent Changes in the English Verb." In *English Diachronic Syntax: Proceedings of the Vth National Congress of the History of the English Language*, edited by Maurizio Gotti, 15–33. Milan: Guerini, 1993.

A Dictionary of American English on Historical Principles. 4 vols. Chicago, IL: The University of Chicago Press, 1938–44.

Dietz, Brian, ed. *The Port and Trade of Early Elizabethan London: Documents*. London: London Record Society, 1972.

van Dijk, Teun A., ed. *Discourse Studies: A Multidisciplinary Introduction*. 2 vols. (1: *Discourse as Structure and Process*; 2: *Discourse as Social Interaction*). London: Sage Publications, 1995.

Dobson, E. J. *English Pronunciation 1500–1700*. 2 vols. Oxford: Clarendon Press, 1957.

Doty, Kathleen, and Risto Hiltunen. "'I Will Tell. I Will Tell': Confessional Patterns in the Salem Witchcraft Trials, 1692." *Journal of Historical Pragmatics* 3 (2002): 299–335.

Dow, George Francis, ed. *Records and Files of the Quarterly Courts of Essex County, Massachusetts*. 8 vols. Salem, MA: Essex Institute, 1911–21.

Ellegård, Alvar. *The Auxiliary 'Do': The Establishment and Regulation of Its Use in English*. Stockholm: Almqvist and Wiksell, 1953.

Elsness, Johan. "On the Progression of the Progressive in Early Modern English." *ICAME Journal* 18 (1994): 5–25.

Fidell, Thomas. *A Perfect Guide for a Studious Young Lawyer*. London, 1658. [Wing (2nd ed.) / F850.]

Fries, Charles C. "Shakespearian Punctuation." In *Studies in Shakespeare, Milton and Donne, by Members of the English Department of the University of Michigan*, 67–86. New York: Haskell House, 1964.

Gage, Thomas. *The History of Rowley*. Boston: Ferdinand Andrews, 1840.

Gaule, John. *Select Cases of Conscience Touching Witches and Witchcrafts*. London, 1646. [Wing (2nd ed.) / G379.]

Gibson, Marion, ed. *Witchcraft and Society in England and America, 1550–1750*. Ithaca, NY: Cornell University Press, 2003.

Glanvil, Joseph. *Saducismus Triumphatus: Or, Full and Plain Evidence Concerning Witches and Apparitions*. London, 1681. [Wing / G822.]

Godbeer, Richard. *The Devil's Dominion: Magic and Religion in Early New England*. Cambridge: Cambridge University Press, 1992.

Godbeer, Richard. *Escaping Salem: The Other Witch Hunt of 1692*. New York: Oxford University Press, 2005.

Gragg, Larry. *A Quest for Security: The Life of Samuel Parris, 1653–1720*. New York: Greenwood Press, 1990.

Gragg, Larry. *The Salem Witch Crisis*. New York: Praeger, 1992.

Grund, Peter, Merja Kytö, and Matti Rissanen. "Editing the Salem Witchcraft Records: An Exploration of a Linguistic Treasury." *American Speech* 79 (2004): 146–66.

Grund, Peter. "From Tongue to Text: The Transmission of the Salem Examination Witchcraft Records," *American Speech* 82 (2007): 119–50.

Grund, Peter. "The Anatomy of Correction: Additions, Cancellations, and Changes in the Documents of the Salem Witchcraft Trials." *Studia Neophilologica* 79 (2007): 3–24.

Haefeli, Evan. "Dutch New York and the Salem Witch Trials: Some New Evidence." *Proceedings of the American Antiquarian Society* 110 (2003): 277–308.

Hale, John. *A Modest Enquiry into the Nature of Witchcraft*. Boston, 1702.

Hall, David D. *Worlds of Wonder, Days of Judgment*. Cambridge, MA: Harvard University Press, 1989.

Hall, David D., ed. *Witch-Hunting in Seventeenth-Century New England: A Documentary History: 1638–1692*. Boston: Northeastern University Press, 1991.

Hand, G. J., and D. J. Bentley, eds. *The English Legal System*. London: Butterworths, 1977.

Hansen, Chadwick. *Witchcraft at Salem*. New York: George Braziller, 1969.

Hector, L. C. *The Handwriting of English Documents*. 2nd. ed. Dorking: Kohler and Coombes, 1980 [1966].

Hickey, Raymond, ed. *Legacies of Colonial English. Studies in Transported Dialects*. Cambridge: Cambridge University Press, 2004.

Hiltunen, Risto. *Chapters on Legal English*. Annales Academiæ Scientiarum Fennicæ, Ser. B, 251. Helsinki: Suomalainen Tiedeakatemia, 1990.

Hiltunen, Risto. "'Tell Me, Be You a Witch?' Questions in the Salem Witchcraft Trials of 1692." *International Journal for the Semiotics of Law* 9 (1996): 17–37.

Hiltunen, Risto. "Salem, 1692: A Case of Courtroom Discourse in a Historical Perspective." In *Approaches to Style and Discourse in English*, edited by Risto Hiltunen and Shinichiro Watanabe, 3–21. Osaka: Osaka University Press, 2004.

Hiltunen, Risto, and Matti Peikola. "Trial Discourse and Manuscript Context: Scribal Profiles in the Salem Witchcraft Records." *Journal of Historical Pragmatics* 8 (2007): 43–68.

Hoffer, Peter Charles. *Law and People in Colonial America*. Baltimore, MD: The Johns Hopkins University Press, 1992.

Hoffer, Peter Charles. *The Devil's Disciples: Makers of the Salem Witchcraft Trials*. Baltimore, MD: The Johns Hopkins University Press, 1996.

Hufford, David J. *The Terror That Comes in the Night*. Philadelphia: University of Pennsylvania Press, 1982.

Hundt, Marianne. "The Passival and the Progressive Passive: A Case Study of Layering in the English Aspect and Voice Systems." In *Corpus Approaches to Grammaticalization in English*, edited by Hans Lindquist and Christian Mair, 79–120. Amsterdam: John Benjamins, 2004.

Hutchinson, Thomas. *The History of the Colony and Province of Massachusetts-Bay*. 3 vols. Edited by Lawrence Shaw Mayo. Cambridge, MA: Harvard University Press, 1936.

Jaworski, Adam, and Nikolas Coupland, eds. *The Discourse Reader*. London: Routledge, 1999.

Jobe, Thomas Harmon. "The Devil in Restoration Science: The Glanvil-Webster Witchcraft Debate." *Isis* 72 (1981): 343–56.

Kahlas-Tarkka, Leena, and Matti Rissanen. "The Sullen and the Talkative: Discourse Strategies in the Salem Examinations." *Journal of Historical Pragmatics* 8 (2007): 1–24.

Karlsen, Carol F. *The Devil in the Shape of a Woman*. New York: W. W. Norton, 1987.

Kassin, Saul M., and Katherine L. Kiechel. "The Social Psychology of False Confessions: Compliance, Internalization, and Confabulation." *Psychological Science* 7 (1996): 125–28.

Konig, David Thomas. *Law and Society in Puritan Massachusetts: Essex County, 1629–1692*. Chapel Hill: University of North Carolina Press, 1979.

Kramer, Heinrich, and James Sprenger. *Malleus Maleficarum*. ca. 1486. Edited by Montague Summers. London: John Rodker, 1928.

Kulikoff, Allan. "The Transition to Capitalism in Rural America." *The William and Mary Quarterly*, 3rd ser., 46 (1989): 120–44.

Kytö, Merja. *Variation and Diachrony, with Early American English in Focus. Studies on CAN/MAY and SHALL/WILL*. University of Bamberg Studies in English Linguistics 28. Frankfurt am Main: Peter Lang, 1991.

Kytö, Merja. "Third-Person Present Singular Verb Inflection in Early British and American English." *Language Variation and Change* 5 (1993): 113–39.

Kytö, Merja. "'Therfor Speke Playnly to the Poynt': Punctuation in Robert Keayne's Notes of Church Meetings from Early Boston, New England." In *Language History and Linguistic Modelling. A Festschrift for Jacek Fisiak on his 60th Birthday*, edited by Raymond Hickey and Stanisław Puppel, 323–42. Berlin: Mouton de Gruyter, 1997.

Kytö, Merja. "The Emergence of American English: Evidence from Seventeenth-Century Records in New England." In *Legacies of Colonial English. Studies in Transported Dialects*, edited by Raymond Hickey, 121–57. Cambridge: Cambridge University Press, 2004.

Lass, Roger, ed. *The Cambridge History of the English Language*. Vol. 3, *1476–1776*. Cambridge: Cambridge University Press, 1999.

Lass, Roger. "Phonology and Morphology." In *The Cambridge History of the English Language*. Vol. 3, *1476–1776*, edited by Roger Lass, 56–186. Cambridge: Cambridge University Press, 1999.

Latner, Richard. "'Here Are No Newters': Witchcraft and Religious Discord in Salem Village and Andover." *The New England Quarterly* 79 (2006): 92–122.

Latner, Richard. "Salem Witchcraft, Factionalism, and Social Change Reconsidered: Were Salem's Witch Hunters Modernization's Failures?" *The William and Mary Quarterly*, 3rd ser., 65 (2008): 503–534.

Lawson, Deodat. *A Brief and True Narrative of Some Remarkable Passages Relating to Sundry Persons Afflicted by Witchcraft, at Salem Village: Which Happened from the Nineteenth of March, to the Fifth of April, 1692*. Boston, 1692. [Wing / L702.]

Lawson, Deodat. *Christ's Fidelity the Only Shield Against Satan's Malignity*. 2nd ed. London, 1704.

Levack, Brian P. *The Witch-Hunt in Early Modern Europe*. 3rd ed. Harlow, England; New York: Longman/Pearson, 2006.

Levinson, Stephen C. *Pragmatics*. Cambridge: Cambridge University Press, 1983.

Marckwardt, Albert H. *American English*. New York: Oxford University Press, 1958.

Massachusetts Acts and Resolves, 1851. Boston, 1851.

Mather, Cotton. *Memorable Providences, Relating to Witchcrafts and Possessions*. Boston, 1689. [Wing / M1123.]

Mather, Cotton. *The Wonders of the Invisible World: Being an Account of the Tryals of Several Witches, Lately Executed in New-England*. London, 1693. [Wing / M1174.]

Mather, Increase. *An Essay for the Recording of Illustrious Providences*. Boston, 1684. [Wing / M1206.]

Mather, Increase. *Cases of Conscience Concerning Evil Spirits Personating Men; Witchcrafts, Infallible Proofs of Guilt in Such as Are Accused with That Crime*. London, 1693. [Wing (2nd ed.)/ F2546.]

Matthews, William. "The Vulgar Speech of London in the XV–XVII Centuries." *Notes and Queries* 173 (1937): 2–5, 21–24, 40–42, 56–60, 77–79, 92–96, 112–15, 130–33, 149–51, 167–70, 186–88, 204–6, 218–21, 241–43.

McCarl, Mary Rhinelander. "Spreading the News of Satan's Malignity in Salem: Benjamin Harris, Printer and Publisher of the Witchcraft Narrative." In *Perspectives on Witchcraft: Rethinking the Seventeenth-Century New England Experience*. Essex Institute Historical Collections 129, no. 1, 39–61. Salem, MA: Essex Institute, 1993.

McDavid, Jr., Raven I. *Varieties of American English. Essays by Raven I. McDavid, Jr. Selected and Introduced by Anwar S. Dil.* Stanford, CA: Stanford University Press, 1980.

McNally, Richard J., and Susan A. Clancy. "Sleep Paralysis, Sexual Abuse, and Space Alien Abduction." *Transcultural Psychiatry* 42 (2005):113–22.

Mellinkoff, David. *The Language of the Law.* Boston: Little, Brown, and Company, 1963.

Monaghan, E. Jennifer, and E. Wendy Saul. "The Reader, the Scribe, the Thinker: A Critical Look at the History of American Reading and Writing Instruction." In *The Formation of School Subjects: The Struggle for Creating an American Institution*, edited by Thomas S. Popkewitz, 85–122. New York: The Falmer Press, 1987.

Monaghan, E. Jennifer. "Literacy Instruction and Gender in Colonial New England." In *Reading in America: Literature & Social History*, edited by Cathy N. Davidson, 53–80. Baltimore, MD: The Johns Hopkins University Press, 1989.

Monter, E. William. "Scandinavian Witchcraft in Anglo-American Perspective." In *Early Modern European Witchcraft: Centres and Peripheries*, edited by Bengt Ankarloo and Gustav Henningsen, 425–34. Oxford: Oxford University Press, 1993.

Murrin, John M. "Coming to Terms with the Salem Witch Trials." In *The Enduring Fascination with Salem Witchcraft*, 309–47. Worcester, MA: American Antiquarian Society, 2003.

Mustanoja, Tauno F. *A Middle English Syntax. Part I. Parts of Speech.* Helsinki: Société Néophilologique, 1960.

Nathan, Debbie, and Michael Snedeker. *Satan's Silence: Ritual Abuse and the Making of a Modern Witch Hunt.* New York: Basic Books, 1995.

Nevala, Minna. *Address in Early English Correspondence. Its Forms and Socio-Pragmatic Functions.* Mémoires de la Société Néophilologique de Helsinki 64. Helsinki: Société Néophilologique, 2004.

Nevalainen, Terttu. "Social Mobility and the Decline of Multiple Negation in Early Modern English." In *Advances in English Historical Linguistics (1996)*, edited by Jacek Fisiak and Marcin Krygier, 263–91. Berlin: Mouton de Gruyter, 1998.

Nevalainen, Terttu. *An Introduction to Early Modern English.* Edinburgh: Edinburgh University Press, 2006.

Nevalainen, Terttu, and Helena Raumolin-Brunberg. *Historical Sociolinguistics: Language Change in Tudor and Stuart England.* London: Longman, 2003.

Norton, Mary Beth. "Communications." *The William and Mary Quarterly*, 3rd ser., 48 (1991): 639–45.

Norton, Mary Beth. *In the Devil's Snare: The Salem Witchcraft Crisis of 1692.* New York: Alfred A. Knopf, 2002.

Nurmi, Arja. *A Social History of Periphrastic DO.* Mémoires de la Société Néophilologique de Helsinki 56. Helsinki: Société Néophilologique, 1999.

OED = *The Oxford English Dictionary.* http://www.oed.com/ (As accessed in 2006.)

Oldireva Gustafsson, Larisa. *Preterite and Past Participle Forms in English 1680–1790: Standardisation Processes in Public and Private Writing.* Studia Anglistica Upsaliensia 120. Uppsala: Acta Universitatis Upsaliensis, 2002.

Ong, Walter J. "Historical Backgrounds of Elizabethan and Jacobean Punctuation Theory." *Publications of the Modern Language Association of America* 59 (1944): 349–60.

Orbeck, Anders. *Early New England Pronunciation as Reflected in Some Seventeenth Century Town Records of Eastern Massachusetts.* Ann Arbor, MI: Gi Wahr, 1927.

Osselton, N. E. "Spelling-Book Rules and the Capitalization of Nouns in the Seventeenth and Eighteenth Centuries." In *Historical and Editorial Studies in Medieval and Early Modern English*, edited by Mary-Jo Arn and Hanneke Wirtjes, 49–61. Groningen: Wolters-Noordhoff, 1985.

Parkes, M. B. *English Cursive Book Hands 1250–1500.* 2nd ed. London: Scolar Press, 1979.

Parkes, M. B. *Pause and Effect. An Introduction to the History of Punctuation in the West.* Aldershot, Hants: Scolar Press, 1992.

Partridge, Eric, and John W. Clark. *British and American English since 1900.* London: Andrew Dakers, 1951.

Perkins, William. *A Discourse of the Damned Art of Witchcraft.* Cambridge, 1608. [STC (2nd ed.) / 19697.]

Perlmann, Joel, and Dennis Shirley. "When Did New England Women Acquire Literacy?" *The William and Mary Quarterly*, 3rd ser., 48 (1991): 50–67.

Petti, Anthony G. *English Literary Hands from Chaucer to Dryden.* London: Edward Arnold, 1977.

Poole, William Frederick. "The Witchcraft Delusion of 1692. By Gov. Thomas Hutchinson, from an Unpublished Manuscript . . . in the Massachusetts Archives." *New England Historical and Genealogical Register* 24 (1870): 381–414.

Powers, Edwin. *Crime and Punishment in Early Massachusetts 1620–1692: A Documentary History.* Boston: Beacon Press, 1966.

The Practick Part of the Office of a Justice of the Peace. London, 1681. [Wing / P3147.]

Preston, Jean F., and Laetitia Yeandle. *English Handwriting 1400–1650: An Introductory Manual.* Binghamton, NY: Medieval & Renaissance Texts & Studies, 1992.

Rantoul, Robert S. *William Phineas Upham: A Memorial.* Boston: The Society, 1910.

Ray, Benjamin C. "The Geography of Witchcraft Accusations in 1692 Salem Village." *The William and Mary Quarterly*, 3rd ser., 65 (2008): 449–478.

Records of the Court of Assistants of the Colony of Massachusetts Bay, 1630–1692. 3 vols. Boston: County of Suffolk, 1901–28.

Reis, Elizabeth. *Damned Women: Sinners and Witches in Puritan New England.* Ithaca, NY: Cornell University Press, 1997.

Rissanen, Matti. "The Choice of Relative Pronouns in Seventeenth-Century American English." In *Historical Syntax*, edited by Jacek Fisiak, 417–35. Berlin: Mouton de Gruyter, 1984.

Rissanen, Matti. "Periphrastic 'Do' in Affirmative Statements in Early American English." *Journal of English Linguistics* 18 (1985): 163–83.

Rissanen, Matti. "Spoken Language and the History of *Do*-Periphrasis." In *Historical English Syntax*, edited by Dieter Kastovsky, 321–42. Berlin: Mouton de Gruyter, 1991.

Rissanen, Matti. "'Candy No Witch, Barbados': Salem Witchcraft Trials as Evidence of Early American English." In *Language in Time and Space. Studies in Honour of Wolfgang Viereck on the Occasion of his 60th Birthday*, edited by Heinrich Ramisch and Kenneth Wynne, 183–93. Stuttgart: Franz Steiner Verlag, 1997.

Rissanen, Matti. "Salem Witchcraft Papers as Evidence of Early American English." *English Linguistics* 20 (2003): 84–114.

Roach, Marilynne K. "Records of the Rev. Samuel Parris Salem Village, Massachusetts, 1688–1696." *New England Historical and Genealogical Register* 157 (2003): 6–30.

Robbins, Rossell Hope. *The Encyclopedia of Witchcraft & Demonology*. New York: Bonanza Books, 1981.

Robbins, Stephen L. "Samuel Willard and the Spectres of God's Wrathful Lion." *The New England Quarterly* 60 (1987): 596–603.

Robinson, Enders A. *The Devil Discovered: Salem Witchcraft 1692*. Prospect Heights, IL: Waveland Press, 1991.

Rosenthal, Bernard. *Salem Story: Reading the Witch Trials of 1692*. Cambridge: Cambridge University Press, 1993.

Rosenthal, Bernard. "Tituba's Story." *The New England Quarterly* 71 (1998): 190–203.

Rosenthal, Bernard. "Tituba." In "Witchcraft," ed. Elizabeth Reis, special issue, *OAH Magazine of History* 17, no. 1 (2003): 48–50.

Ryan, Mary. *Womanhood in America: From Colonial Times to the Present*. New York: New Viewpoints, 1975.

Salmon, Vivian. "Early Seventeenth-Century Punctuation as a Guide to Sentence Structure." *Review of English Studies N. S.* 13 (1962): 347–60.

Salmon, Vivian. "Orthography and Punctuation." In *The Cambridge History of the English Language*. Vol. 3, *1476–1776*, edited by Roger Lass, 13–55. Cambridge: Cambridge University Press, 1999.

Scragg, D. G. *A History of English Spelling*. Manchester: Manchester University Press, 1974.

Several Acts and Laws Passed by the Great and General Court or Assembly of Their Majesties Province of the Massachusetts-Bay, in New England Convened and Held at Boston, the Eighth Day of June 1692. Boston, 1692. [Wing (2nd ed.) / M1016.]

Sewall, Samuel. *The Diary of Samuel Sewall, 1674–1729*. Edited by M. Halsey Thomas. 2 vols. New York: Farrar, Straus and Giroux, 1973.

Silverman, Kenneth, comp. *Selected Letters of Cotton Mather*. Baton Rouge: Louisiana State University Press, 1971.

Spanos, Nicholas P., and Jack Gottlieb. "Ergotism and the Salem Village Witch Trials." *Science* 194 (1976): 1390–94.

Stone, Lincoln R. "An Account of the Trial of George Jacobs for Witchcraft." *Historical Collections of the Essex Institute* 2 (1860): 49–57.

Strang, Barbara. "Some Aspects of the History of the *Be + ing* Construction." In *Language Form and Linguistic Variation.*

Papers Dedicated to Angus McIntosh, edited by John Anderson, 427–74. Amsterdam: John Benjamins, 1982.

SWP = Boyer, Paul, and Stephen Nissenbaum, eds. *The Salem Witchcraft Papers. Verbatim Transcripts of the Legal Documents of the Salem Witchcraft Outbreak of 1692*. 3 vols. New York: Da Capo Press, 1977.

Tannenbaum, Samuel A. *The Handwriting of the Renaissance*. New York: Columbia University Press, 1930.

Tanselle, G. Thomas. "The Editing of Historical Documents." *Studies in Bibliography* 31 (1978): 1–56.

Tanselle, G. Thomas. "Literary Editing." In *Literary and Historical Editing*, edited by George L. Vogt and John Bush Jones, 35–56. Lawrence: University of Kansas Libraries, 1981.

Thornton, Tamara Plakins. *Handwriting in America: A Cultural History*. New Haven, CT: Yale University Press, 1996.

Trask, Richard B. *The Devil Hath Been Raised: A Documentary History of the Salem Village Witchcraft Outbreak of March 1692; Together with a Collection of Newly Located and Gathered Witchcraft Documents*. Danvers, MA: Yeoman Press, 1997.

Trudgill, Peter. *On Dialect. Social and Geographical Perspectives*. Oxford: Basil Blackwell, 1983.

A Tryal of Witches, at the Assizes Held at Bury St. Edmonds for the County of Suffolk; on the Tenth Day of March, 1664. Before Sir Matthew Hale K^t Then Lord Chief Baron of His Majesties Court of Exchequer. London, 1682. [Wing / T2240.]

Upham, Charles W. *Salem Witchcraft; With an Account of Salem Village, and a History of Opinions on Witchcraft and Kindred Subjects*. 2 vols. Boston: Wiggin & Lunt, 1867.

Venezky, Richard L. "Spelling." In *The Cambridge History of the English Language*. Vol. 6, *English in North America*, edited by John Algeo, 340–57. Cambridge: Cambridge University Press, 2001.

Viereck, Wolfgang. "On the Origins and Development of American English." In *Papers from the 6th International Conference on Historical Linguistics*, edited by Jacek Fisiak, 561–69. Amsterdam and Poznań: Benjamins and Adam Mickiewicz University Press, 1985.

Vital Records of Andover, Massachusetts, to the End of the Year 1849. Topsfield, MA: Topsfield Historical Society, 1912.

Walker, Terry. Thou *and* You *in Early Modern English Dialogues: Trials, Depositions, and Drama Comedy*. Pragmatics and Beyond New Series 158. Amsterdam: John Benjamins, 2007.

Waters, Thomas Franklin. *Ipswich in the Massachusetts Bay Colony*. Ipswich: Ipswich Historical Society, 1905.

Webster, John. *The Displaying of Supposed Witchcraft*. London, 1677. [Wing / W1230.]

Webster's Third New International Dictionary of the English Language Unabridged. Springfield, MA: Merriam-Webster, 1993.

Weekley, Ernest. *The English Language, with a Chapter on the History of American English by Professor John W. Clark*. London: André Deutsch, 1952 [1928].

Weisman, Richard. *Witchcraft, Magic, and Religion in 17th-Century Massachusetts*. Amherst: University of Massachusetts Press, 1984.

Wells, J. C. *Longman Pronunciation Dictionary*. London: Longman, 1990.

Willard, Samuel. *Some Miscellany Observations on Our Present
Debates Respecting Witchcrafts, in a Dialogue Between S. & B.*
Philadelphia, 1692.

Woodward, W. Elliot. *Records of Salem Witchcraft, Copied From
the Original Documents.* 2 vols. Roxbury, MA, 1864–65.

Wright, Joseph, ed. *The English Dialect Dictionary.* 6 vols. London: Oxford University Press, 1923.

Wyld, Henry Cecil. *A History of Modern Colloquial English.* 3rd
ed. Oxford: Basil Blackwell, 1936.

Yeandle, Laetitia. "The Evolution of Handwriting in the
English-Speaking Colonies of America." *The American
Archivist* 43 (1980): 294–311.

INDEXES: INTRODUCTION

The edition includes two indexes to aid the reader: an index of Names Included in Document Titles (title index) and a Concordance of Names found in the documents (concordance). The titles of documents include the type of document, the names of the accused, and the names of any accusers or supporters. The title index lists all these names with the number of the document and what type of document each is; page numbers are not given in this index. The names of people who were accused are in bold. The reader interested in a particular case can follow it by going to the related documents.

Thus, for example, a person interested in the case of Sarah Good would simply go through the documents listed under her name, identifying them by number in chronological order. This index would include documents such as the warrant for her arrest, the examination, indictments against her, grand jury evidence, and such. However, there are documents associated with each case that are no longer extant; gaps in varying degrees will reflect this. Also, some cases will have documents associated with them that other cases do not, because these documents, as in the case of petitions of support, occurred on a limited basis.

The second index, the concordance, with page numbers, carries references to people named in the title index as well as almost all the names of people referenced in the documents. Names in the appendix are not indexed, nor are names of people unambiguously unconnected to witchcraft cases. However, in some instances a name that appears to be unrelated to a witchcraft case is included because the evidence to exclude it is insufficient to do so with certainty.

Given the radical inconsistency in the spellings of names at the time, decisions on what spelling of names to be used have been complex and at times necessarily arbitrary. These decisions have been made through some combination of usage frequency and genealogical publications. The use of "Jr." and "Sr." has been kept to a minimum and only used where differentiation was necessary or where reference to a person almost always carried one or the other. The reader who is searching for a name but not finding it should also check carefully Marilynne K. Roach's Biographical Notes for the main entry and for alternate spellings. Both indexes have been checked against these biographical entries; still, the reader should find that using these indexes with the biographical section can be helpful.

In some instances a parenthetical entry has been added in the concordance to identify a deceased child, an unnamed servant, a slave, or any individual associated with a named person. Marital status has been used parenthetically to differentiate two people with the same name, as occurs with Elizabeth Booth.

All "Elizabeth Booth" entries in the title index are to Elizabeth Booth, single-woman, except those for Document 656, where "Elizabeth Booth" is the married woman. Sometimes identifications in the concordance are uncertain, or only a last name is known, and a question mark so indicates.

One person "missing" from both indexes is "Dorcas Good," the daughter of Sarah Good, whose name is very familiar to followers of the Salem witch trial episode. Since it is clear that the name "Dorcas" was a misidentification made at the time, the daughter of Sarah Good is indexed by her actual name, "Dorothy." At times the reader will see a name in the index and not find it on the page cited. This will occur when a person is referenced on the page but not by name, as, for example, "his wife." By checking the Biographical Notes, the reader can find further information on the person cited. Attempts have been made to index every person, including some who were deceased at the time, although sufficient ambiguity exists in some cases so that the goal of complete identification may not have been achieved. It is also possible that "phantom" names may appear. That is, a person with variant name spellings, particularly where there has been inconsistent use of Jr. and Sr., may have been misidentified as two people or (rarely, if at all) as three. Or, conversely, two people may inadvertently have been indexed as one. Such occurrences, if any, are likely to be minimal, but the reader should be alert to their possibility.

The index of Names Included in Document Titles was generated by Margo Burns; the Concordance of Names was constructed by Bernard Rosenthal. Marilynne K. Roach offered valuable help with indexing issues. All associate editors have assisted in checking for errors, although they are not responsible for any errors that may appear.

(evidence), 383 (evidence), 384 (evidence), 385 (evidence), 386 (evidence), 494 (evidence), 495 (petition), 496 (petition), 497 (evidence), 498 (evidence), 499 (evidence), 500 (evidence), 502 (evidence), 708 (evidence), 871 (petition), 876 (petition), 942 (order for payment), 946 (order for payment), 950 (order for payment), 951 (order for payment)

Procter, John, 47 (council record), 55 (evidence), 56 (evidence), 57 (evidence), 58 (evidence), 59 (evidence), 60 (evidence), 61 (evidence), 66 (evidence), 101 (evidence), 194 (evidence), 209 (evidence), 217 (mittimus), 246 (evidence), 253 (letter & mittimus), 255 (evidence), 272 (physical examination), 384 (evidence), 387 (indictment), 388 (indictment), 389 (indictment), 390 (evidence), 391 (evidence), 433 (petition), 494 (evidence), 495 (petition), 496 (petition), 501 (evidence), 502 (evidence), 871 (petition), 876 (petition), 942 (order for payment), 946 (order for payment), 950 (order for payment), 951 (order for payment)

Procter, Joseph, 950 (order for payment)

Procter, Mary, 942 (order for payment)

Procter, Sarah, 194 (evidence), 195 (complaint), 202 (evidence), 209 (evidence), 210 (evidence), 211 (evidence), 212 (evidence), 213 (evidence), 502 (evidence)

Procter, William, 221 (complaint), 226 (arrest warrant), 581 (indictment), 582 (indictment), 583 (evidence), 663 (examination), 776 (indictment)

Pudeator, Ann, 143 (arrest warrant), 146 (mittimus), 255 (evidence), 258 (evidence), 399 (examination), 458 (evidence), 550 (summons), 555 (evidence), 568 (indictment), 569 (evidence), 570 (evidence), 610 (evidence), 655 (petition)

Putnam, Ann Jr., 9 (evidence), 11 (evidence), 13 (evidence), 26 (evidence), 30 (evidence), 53 (evidence), 59 (evidence), 73 (evidence), 92 (evidence), 110 (evidence), 125 (evidence), 136 (evidence), 157 (evidence), 158 (evidence), 170 (evidence), 185 (evidence), 206 (evidence), 249 (evidence), 276 (indictment), 285 (indictment & memorandum), 291 (evidence), 297 (indictment), 303 (complaint), 306 (evidence), 332 (indictment), 404 (evidence), 455 (indictment), 457 (evidence), 555 (evidence), 567 (evidence), 570

(evidence), 580 (evidence), 588 (evidence), 594 (evidence), 618 (indictment), 640 (evidence), 646 (evidence), 669 (evidence), 763 (indictment), 793 (indictment)

Putnam, Ann Sr., 30 (evidence), 267 (evidence), 269 (evidence)

Putnam, Edward, 18 (evidence), 21 (evidence), 32 (evidence), 54 (evidence), 103 (evidence), 124 (evidence), 125 (evidence), 127 (evidence), 177 (evidence), 303 (complaint), 363 (evidence), 601 (evidence)

Putnam, Hannah, 362 (evidence)

Putnam, John Jr., 60 (evidence), 137 (evidence), 182 (evidence), 187 (complaint), 192 (evidence), 195 (complaint), 211 (evidence), 362 (evidence), 395 (complaint)

Putnam, John Sr., 126 (evidence), 360 (evidence), 372 (evidence)

Putnam, Jonathan, 191 (evidence)

Putnam, Joseph, 5 (examination)

Putnam, Nathaniel Sr., 373 (evidence)

Putnam, Nathaniel, 229 (complaint)

Putnam, Rebecca, 126 (evidence), 372 (evidence)

Putnam, Thomas, 8 (evidence), 20 (evidence), 52 (evidence), 54 (evidence), 57 (evidence), 60 (evidence), 82 (letter), 91 (evidence), 96 (complaint), 103 (evidence), 109 (evidence), 111 (evidence), 124 (evidence), 125 (evidence), 127 (evidence), 137 (evidence), 151 (complaint), 157 (evidence), 176 (evidence), 177 (evidence), 195 (complaint), 212 (evidence), 224 (complaint), 361 (evidence), 363 (evidence), 395 (complaint), 457 (evidence), 467 (evidence), 553 (evidence), 673 (letter)

Putney, John Jr., 307 (evidence)

Ray, Samuel, 719 (recognizance)

Rayment, Thomas, 198 (complaint), 303 (complaint)

Rayment, William Jr., 369 (evidence), 497 (evidence), 498 (evidence)

Redd, Wilmot, 219 (evidence), 221 (complaint), 227 (arrest warrant), 247 (examination), 248 (evidence), 249 (evidence), 250 (evidence), 251 (evidence), 614 (summons), 623 (indictment), 624 (indictment), 625 (evidence), 629 (evidence)

Reddington, Margaret, 87 (evidence)

Rice, Nicholas, 698 (petition)

Rice, Sarah, 219 (evidence), 221 (complaint), 228 (arrest warrant), 252 (mittimus), 698 (petition)

Rich, Thomas, 974 (petition)

Richards, John, 208 (evidence)

Richardson, Nathaniel, 302 (evidence)

Ring, Jarvis, 148 (evidence), 149 (evidence)

Ring, Joseph, 149 (evidence)

Rogers, John, 448 (evidence)

Roots, Susannah, 195 (complaint), 196 (arrest warrant), 214 (evidence)

Row, Abigail, 702 (petition), 704 (arrest warrant), 707 (evidence)

Ruck, Thomas, 493 (evidence), 636 (evidence)

Safford, Joseph, 243 (evidence)

Salter, Henry, 563 (examination), 758 (indictment)

Sanders, James, 723 (recognizance)

Sawdy, John, 691 (recognizance)

Scott, Margaret, 471 (evidence), 641 (indictment), 642 (indictment), 643 (evidence), 644 (evidence), 645 (evidence), 646 (evidence), 647 (evidence), 648 (evidence)

Sears, Ann, 119 (arrest warrant), 710 (recognizance)

Sewall, Samuel, 673 (letter)

Sewall, Stephen, 264 (oath of office), 285 (indictment & memorandum), 435 (legislation), 889 (letter)

Shattuck, Samuel, 279 (evidence), 575 (evidence)

Shattuck, Sarah, 279 (evidence)

Shaw, Deborah, 333 (evidence)

Shaw, William, 333 (evidence)

Shelden, Ephraim, 48 (evidence)

Shelden, Susannah, 128 (evidence), 163 (evidence), 164 (evidence), 178 (evidence), 179 (evidence), 202 (evidence), 238 (evidence), 283 (evidence), 298 (indictment), 306 (evidence), 338 (evidence), 370 (evidence), 472 (evidence), 650 (indictment)

Shepherd, John, 678 (court record)

Sibley, Samuel, 354 (evidence), 501 (evidence)

Slue, Rachel, 960 (order for payment)

Small, Hannah, 551 (evidence)

Smith, Samuel, 88 (evidence)

Soames, Abigail, 147 (arrest warrant), 150 (examination), 255 (evidence), 765 (indictment), 766 (evidence)

Sparks, Martha, 703 (petition), 713 (recognizance)

Sprague, Martha, 627 (indictment), 628 (evidence), 661 (indictment), 665 (indictment), 666 (evidence & court record), 670 (evidence), 788 (indictment), 804 (indictment), 816 (indictment)

CONCORDANCE OF NAMES

Abbey, John, 744, 745, 746, 755, 757, 768, 769, 772, 779, 780, 781, 782, 798
Abbey, Mary, 424
Abbey, Samuel, 311, 402, 423, 587, 623
Abbott, Arthur, 324, 702
Abbott, Benjamin, 406, 494, 509, 510, 513, 541, 543, 544, 574
Abbott, George, 740, 908, 910
Abbott, Hannah, 905, 908, 910
Abbott, Hannah (Esty), 910
Abbott, John, 674, 676
Abbott, John Sr., 740
Abbott, Nehemiah Jr., 200, 287, 290
Abbott, Nehemiah Sr., 437
Abbott, Sarah, 406, 494, 509, 510
Abbott, William, 691, 740
Aborn, Samuel Sr., 349
Adams, Martha, 588, 599
Addington, Isaac, 347, 348, 716, 719, 741, 830, 846, 886, 890, 892
Aires, Peter, 723
Aires, Samuel, 166
Alden, John, 323, 324, 333, 334, 347, 348, 506, 733, 812, 917
Allen, Andrew, 467, 475
Allen, Andrew (Child), 475
Allen, Ann, 909
Allen, Benjamin, 484, 819
Allen, James, 486, 604
Allen, John, 392, 393, 403, 404, 425, 475, 484
Allen, Mary, 436, 484
Allen, Rachel Sr., 484
Allen, William, 141, 407, 417, 484
Ambros, Henry, 484
Ambros, Susanna, 484
Andrew, Daniel, 162, 270, 271, 277, 283, 309, 349, 549, 625
Andrews, Anna, 355, 905, 907
Andrews, Hannah, 358
Andrews, James, 199
Andrews, John, 418, 448, 449, 450, 458, 459, 461, 535
Andrews, Joseph, 351, 418, 419, 420, 448, 449, 450, 458, 459, 461, 535, 536, 587

Andrews, Mary, 203, 436
Andrews, Sarah, 349, 351, 358, 418, 419
Andrews, Thomas, 405, 451, 535
Andrews, William, 535, 819
Andros, Edmund, 505, 833
Appleton, John, 855, 886, 890, 893, 898, 906, 907
Appleton, Samuel, 171, 702, 819
Arnold, John, 154, 347, 624, 631, 632, 814, 818
Arnold, Mary, 624
Arnold, William, 277, 586, 626
Aslebee, John, 674, 676, 691, 740
Atkinson, John, 403, 425
Atkinson, Nathaniel, 403
Atkinson, Sarah, 403, 426
Austen, Leonard, 317
Ayer, John, 841

Babage?, 359
Babson, Ebenezer, 579, 747
Babson, Eleanor, 579, 583
Bacon, Daniel, 389, 749
Bagly, Orlando, 224
Bailey (Sister, Ann Putnam Sr.), 359
Bailey, Elizabeth, 525
Bailey, John, 486
Bailey, Joseph, 532
Bailey, Priscilla, 533
Bailey, Thomas, 526
Baker (Sister, Ann Putnam Sr.), 359
Baker, Cornell, 301
Baker, Ebenezer, 608
Baker, Hannah, 301
Baker, Jonathan, 411
Baker, William, 168, 204, 724, 830
Balch, Benjamin, 299
Balch, Benjamin, Sr., 592
Balch, David, 592
Balch, Elizabeth, 299
Ballard, Elizabeth, 468, 469, 470, 472, 473, 474, 478, 480, 544, 639, 644
Ballard, John, 325, 406, 468, 471, 475, 489, 495, 559, 644, 676

Ballard, Joseph, 469, 470, 475, 544, 639, 644, 737
Ballard, William, 740
Bancroft, Ebenezer, 898
Bare, John, 518
Barker (Captain), 860, 878
Barker (Maid), 576
Barker, Abigail, 608, 737, 738, 739, 740, 751, 752, 757, 758, 860, 861, 888
Barker, Ebenezer, 688, 691, 707, 751, 757, 758, 860, 888, 891, 897
Barker, John, 550, 684, 740, 794, 821, 861, 862, 882, 885, 887, 891–897
Barker, John (Captain), 871, 877, 878
Barker, Mary, 550, 558, 559, 560, 561, 565, 566, 567, 664, 688, 783, 784, 794, 795, 820, 821, 825, 826, 861
Barker, Mary Jr., 734, 887
Barker, Mary Sr., 693, 887
Barker, William Jr., 571, 572, 573, 575, 646, 663, 783, 785, 786, 794, 795, 820, 821, 826, 827, 861
Barker, William Jr.?, 578
Barker, William Sr., 550, 558, 560, 561, 562, 563, 564, 565, 567, 568, 581, 786, 787, 862, 887, 891
Barnard, Elizabeth, 740
Barnard, Mr. (Maid), 597
Barnard, Thomas, 396, 597, 661, 691, 738, 740, 851
Barnes, James, 812
Barnet, Stephen, 691
Barrett, Humphrey, 801
Barrett, Thomas, 698, 706, 707
Barsham, Nathaniel, 805, 806, 808
Bartlett, Richard Sr., 730
Barton, John, 362, 363
Barton, Samuel, 537
Bassett, Sarah, 203, 304, 305, 319, 737, 741, 816
Bassett, William, 304, 307, 737
Batchelor, Jonathan, 424
Bates?, 679
Batt, Timothy, 818
Batten, William, 409, 412, 424

Procter, Samuel, 906, 909

Procter, Sarah, 255, 304, 305, 309, 315, 316, 317, 319, 523, 539, 906

Procter, Sarah (Munion), 907

Procter, Thorndike, 849, 853, 854, 887, 891, 896, 900, 905, 907

Procter, William, 323, 324, 327, 333, 339, 348, 486, 607, 610, 611, 612, 664, 665, 758, 762, 763, 836, 837, 905, 907

Pudeator, Ann, 260, 261, 262, 263, 264, 319, 350, 353, 354, 454, 455, 506, 588, 589, 591, 592, 597, 602, 603, 625, 630, 646, 647, 658, 659, 674, 816, 842, 860, 889

Putnam, Ann Jr., 125, 126, 129, 130, 134, 137, 138, 139, 140, 141, 142, 148, 149, 150, 151, 152, 153, 154, 156, 157, 160, 161, 162, 165, 167, 170, 171, 172, 174, 176, 177, 178, 179, 180, 182, 183, 184, 185, 186, 191, 192, 193, 194, 195, 198, 200, 205, 208, 209, 211, 213, 217, 218, 219, 221, 222, 223, 224, 225, 227, 228, 230, 232, 233, 234, 235, 236, 238, 239, 241, 242, 243, 245, 246, 248, 252, 253, 255, 262, 264, 270, 272, 274, 275, 282, 283, 284, 285, 286, 287, 289, 290, 291, 292, 294, 296, 297, 298, 304, 305, 306, 312, 313, 314, 316, 320, 321, 322, 323, 324, 333, 335, 336, 337, 338, 339, 340, 342, 344, 345, 346, 353, 354, 359, 361, 364, 365, 366, 367, 374, 375, 376, 377, 378, 379, 380, 381, 382, 383, 384, 385, 386, 388, 394, 397, 402, 407, 408, 409, 412, 416, 417, 418, 419, 420, 422, 427, 429, 430, 437, 440, 441, 444, 445, 446, 447, 448, 450, 451, 452, 453, 454, 455, 456, 457, 458, 465, 489, 490, 496, 501, 502, 503, 504, 505, 506, 507, 508, 509, 512, 514, 515, 519, 520, 521, 522, 523, 525, 527, 530, 531, 533, 539, 540, 541, 542, 544, 545, 546, 558, 587, 591, 596, 600, 601, 602, 603, 610, 613, 614, 615, 616, 617, 618, 619, 623, 628, 629, 630, 635, 636, 641, 648, 650, 653, 657, 664, 665, 668, 669, 670, 737, 744, 745, 749, 752, 754, 762, 771, 776, 791, 792, 820

Putnam, Ann Sr., 142, 148, 154, 156, 157, 159, 160, 161, 165, 359, 360, 378, 381, 383, 384, 537

Putnam, Benjamin, 206, 242, 349, 518, 897, 906

Putnam, Edward, 125, 126, 142, 143, 149, 150, 151, 152, 153, 154, 157, 163, 177, 178, 189, 227, 234, 244, 245, 246, 247, 278, 282, 292, 293, 340, 386, 430, 431, 437, 447, 505, 506, 519, 520, 527, 531, 533, 587, 596, 612, 623, 624

Putnam, Elizabeth, 430

Putnam, Ely, 207

Putnam, Hannah, 430

Putnam, John Jr., 180, 182, 239, 246, 251, 255, 256, 273, 274, 278, 281, 282, 295, 298, 302, 304, 306, 308, 309, 313, 316, 327, 354, 403, 430, 451, 512, 513, 525, 531, 538, 623, 728, 839

Putnam, John Jr. (Child), 359

Putnam, John Jr.?, 295, 305, 312

Putnam, John Sr., 246, 282, 349, 429, 435, 728, 826

Putnam, Jonathan, 153, 154, 183, 271, 282, 302, 349, 354, 429, 587, 728, 839

Putnam, Joseph, 131, 132, 133, 349

Putnam, Lydia, 349

Putnam, Nathaniel, 200, 207, 264, 278, 282, 319, 329, 354, 357, 380

Putnam, Nathaniel Sr., 435

Putnam, Rebecca, 246, 247, 349, 435, 518

Putnam, Sarah, 297, 349

Putnam, Sarah (Deceased infant), 360

Putnam, Thomas, 125, 126, 129, 130, 134, 137, 138, 139, 140, 142, 148, 149, 150, 151, 152, 154, 156, 160, 162, 165, 167, 170, 171, 175, 176, 177, 178, 179, 180, 181, 189, 193, 194, 195, 200, 204, 210, 217, 218, 219, 220, 221, 222, 223, 224, 227, 232, 233, 234, 235, 236, 238, 239, 240, 242, 243, 244, 245, 246, 247, 248, 254, 255, 256, 270, 274, 275, 279, 282, 284, 285, 286, 291, 292, 293, 295, 296, 297, 303, 304, 305, 306, 312, 313, 314, 316, 320, 325, 326, 337, 338, 345, 346, 347, 359, 364, 365, 366, 367, 373, 378, 379, 385, 391, 403, 411, 412, 413, 426, 427, 428, 429, 430, 431, 441, 442, 444, 447, 450, 451, 457, 458, 461, 501, 505, 506, 507, 512, 513, 517, 518, 525, 527, 529, 531, 533, 537, 538, 589, 590, 596, 606, 610, 614, 615, 616, 617, 618, 619, 621, 622, 628, 629, 648, 652, 654, 657, 660, 668, 669, 670, 671, 839

Putnam, Thomas?, 217

Putney, John Jr., 389, 749

Rabson, Joseph, 309

Ray, Caleb, 829

Ray, Joshua, 727

Ray, Samuel, 711

Rayment, Thomas, 301, 307, 386

Rayment, Thomas (His wife), 301

Rayment, William Jr., 301, 434, 536, 537

Rayment, William Jr.? Sr.?, 570

Rayment, William Sr., 301

Rea, Daniel, 278, 349

Rea, Hepzibah, 183, 349

Rea, Jemima, 416

Rea, Joshua, 349, 363, 728

Rea, Joshua Sr., 288, 291

Rea, Sarah, 349

Read, Christopher, 905

Read, Elizabeth, 905

Read, George, 807

Read, Richard, 736

Redd, Samuel, 323, 327, 344

Redd, Wilmot, 227, 321, 323, 324, 327, 333, 344, 345, 346, 348, 633, 636, 640, 641, 643, 644, 664, 674, 860, 889

Redd, Wilmot (m. Mercy Lewis), 328

Reddington, Abraham, 462, 590

Reddington, Goody, 461

Reddington, John, 463

Reddington, Margaret, 210, 590

Reddington, Mary, 460, 463

Reddington, Sarah, 463

Rednap, Benjamin, 736

Reed, Christopher, 272, 907

Reed, Elizabeth, 873

Reed, Elizabeth?, 272

Remington, Jonathan, 915

Rice, Nicholas, 323, 328, 347, 692, 693

Rice, Sarah, 321, 323, 324, 328, 333, 347, 348, 582, 692, 693, 817

Rich, Thomas, 917

Richards, John, 315, 322, 487, 596, 720, 733, 736, 801, 812, 819, 829, 830

Richardson, Mary, 609

Richardson, Nathaniel, 386

Riggs, Thomas, 723

Ring, Hannah, 484

Ring, Jarvis, 265, 266, 403, 404, 426, 427, 484

Ring, Joseph, 266, 267, 403, 404, 427

Ring, Thomas, 586

Roberts, Ephraim?, 906

Robinson, Deane, 546

Robinson, John, 359

Robinson, Joseph, 740

Robinson, Phebe, 740, 849

Rogers, John, 166, 363, 406, 495, 498, 851

Rogers, Martha, 166

Rogers, Sarah, 203

Rolfe, Benjamin, 851

Roots, Susannah, 304, 305, 307, 317, 319, 595, 816

Roulston, John, 396

Row, Abigail, 699, 700, 701

Row, Hugh, 699

Row, Mary, 697

Ruck, Elizabeth, 529

Ruck, John, 241, 364, 365, 366, 367, 375, 376, 377, 381, 382, 384, 385, 497, 529

Ruck, Samuel, 529

Ruck, Sarah (m. George Burroughs), 199, 246

Ruck, Thomas, 529, 531, 647

Russell, Elizabeth, 905

Russell, James, 171, 487, 704, 706, 707, 709, 710, 712, 740

Russell, Joseph, 807

Printed in the USA
CPSIA information can be obtained
at www.ICGtesting.com
CBHW082111180824
13139CB00029B/324